Association for Computing Machinery

SIGCHI
special interest group computer human interaction

TEI '11

Fifth International Conference on
Tangible, Embedded and Embodied Interaction

January 23 - 26, 2011
Madeira, Portugal

Proceedings of the Fifth International Conference on **Tangible Embedded and Embodied Interaction**

Association for
Computing Machinery

Advancing Computing as a Science & Profession

The Association for Computing Machinery
2 Penn Plaza, Suite 701
New York, New York 10121-0701

ISBN: 978-1-4503-0628-7

Additional copies may be ordered prepaid from:

ACM Order Department
PO Box 11405
New York, NY 10286-1405

Phone: 1-800-342-6626 (USA and Canada)
+1-212-626-0500 (all other countries)
Fax: +1-212-944-1318
E-mail: acmhelp@acm.org

ACM Order Number: 609118

Printed in the USA

Foreword and Chairs' Welcome: TEI in its Fifth Year

The curves crossed several years ago: the number of CPUs embedded in things outpaced CPUs in "computers". Quickly we're growing accustomed to cities, rooms, furniture, clothing, appliances, and all manner of ordinary places and objects "enhanced" with computational behavior. Weiser's *Computer for the 21st Century* anticipated this trend, now variously called pervasive, ambient, invisible, and ubiquitous computing. As computation seeps seamlessly into everyday things, interaction moves on from point-and-click and entangles our bodies as well as our minds. The TEI community investigates interaction where physical and computational things can no longer be simply separated.

The 2011 ACM SIGCHI conference on Tangible, Embedded and Embodied Interaction marks five years of sharing interdisciplinary work on embedding computing technologies in physical objects and places. The first TEI conference was hosted by Louisiana State University in Baton Rouge (2007); subsequent annual TEI conferences were at the B-IT Center in Bonn (2008), Microsoft Research, Cambridge, UK (2009), and the MIT Media Lab (Cambridge, MA, 2010). The conference is young but no longer in its infancy. It's now concerned not only with "things that think" (to borrow a phrase from MIT) but with the *thoughtful* design of thinking things.

The diverse TEI community includes systems researchers, HCI researchers, interaction and industrial designers, and artists. Each constituency brings key knowledge, skills, and core values. Systems researchers build innovative hardware and software that explores, investigates, or demonstrates new ways of interacting with things. HCI researchers study interactions people have with these systems, bringing expertise in behavioral sciences and empirical study. Designers shape the interaction itself. And artists, free from pragmatic constraints of purpose, investigate the boundaries of the possible.

The TEI 2011 tracks include Papers—a blind reviewed track with 2, 4, and 8 page papers; Art Explorations—a juried track of innovative tangible interactive art and performance pieces; Workshops—mini-symposia on a theme or topic; Studios—hands-on explorations of a technology or technique. The Graduate Student Consortium invites emerging researchers, designers, and artists to exchange ideas with one another and with more seasoned members of the TEI community. Finally, new this year, the Design Challenge invites a student competition of designs demonstrated at the conference.

Three program chairs worked with six associate program chairs to shepherd reviews. Each paper received at least three reviews, one of which—usually a meta-review—was prepared by a member of the program committee. Based on these, program chairs selected papers for presentation at the conference. TEI's review process differs slightly from other ACM SIGCHI conferences: In addition to selecting which papers will be presented at the conference (and included in the Proceedings), the program chairs determine the presentation format. Some work is presented as a short or long talk; other work as an interactive demonstration or poster. All papers receive the same review process according to the same criteria, independent of eventual presentation format.

We received 203 paper submissions and accepted fewer than 32%. In detail: We accepted 11 papers for fifteen-minute talk + demo presentations, 7 for fifteen-minute talk presentations, 8 for five-minute talk + demo presentations, 12 for five-minute talk presentations, 19 for demo presentations, and 8 papers for poster presentations. In total we accepted 65 papers: 23 eight-page papers, 34 four-page papers, and 8 two-page papers.

You can see even from the titles of the papers, art pieces, studios, and workshops the diversity of interests that engage the TEI community. They range from toolkits to tabletops, from music to making, from programming to pillows. What brings it all together is a commitment to the synthesis of technology, physicality, design, and people.

Mark D. Gross, TEI '11 Conference Co-chair *(Carnegie Mellon University)*

Nuno Jardim Nunes, TEI '11 Conference Co-chair *(Universidade da Madeira)*

Ellen Yi-Luen Do, TEI '11 Program Co-chair *(Georgia Institute of Technology)*

Stephen Brewster, TEI '11 Program Co-chair *(University of Glasgow)*

Ian Oakley, TEI '11 Program Co-chair *(Universidade da Madeira)*

Table of Contents

Session 4: Learning

Session 5: Games and Narrative

Session 6: Design

Session 7: Applications

Session 8: Sensing and Interaction

Session 9: Audio, Music, Art and Playful Tangible Interactives

Studios and Workshops

Session: Art Explorations

Session: Graduate Student Consortium

TEI 2011 Conference Organisation

Conference Chairs: Mark D. Gross *(Carnegie Mellon University / Modular Robotics)*
Nuno Jardim Nunes *(University of Madeira)*

Program Co-Chairs: Ellen Yi-Luen Do *(Georgia Tech)*
Stephen Brewster *(University of Glasgow)*
Ian Oakley *(University of Madeira)*

Associate Chairs: Florian "Floyd" Mueller *(University of Melbourne / Stanford University)*
Sile O'Modhrain *(Queen's University Belfast)*
Alissa Antle *(Simon Fraser University)*
Ylva Fernaeus *(Stockholm University / KTH)*
Kristof Van Laerhoven *(Technische Universität Darmstadt)*
Paul Marshall *(The Open University)*

Treasurer: Sile O'Modhrain *(Queen's University Belfast)*

Demos Co-Chairs: Florian "Floyd" Mueller *(University of Melbourne / Stanford University)*
Vassilis Kostakos *(University of Madeira)*

Studio and Workshop Co-Chairs: Pedro Branco *(University of Minho)*
Jos van Leeuwen *(University of Madeira)*

Arts Track Chairs: Valentina Nisi *(University of Madeira)*
Ivan Poupyrev *(Disney Research Pittsburgh)*

Design Challenge Chair: Leah Buechley *(MIT Media Lab)*

Graduate Student Consortium Chairs: Jussi Ängeslevä *(Berlin University of the Arts / Art+Com)*
Ali Mazalek *(Georgia Tech)*

Sponsorship Chair: Nuno Correia *(New University of Lisbon)*

Publicity Co-Chairs: Enrico Costanza *(University of Southampton)*
Carson Reynolds *(University of Tokyo)*
Amanda Williams *(Concordia University)*
Daniela Rosner *(University of California, Berkeley)*

Web Chair: Ray Yun *(Carnegie Mellon University)*

Graphics and Web Design: Monchu Chen *(University of Madeira)*
Mayur Karnik *(University of Madeira)*
Rebeca Sa *(University of Madeira)*
Ko-Hsun Huang *(University of Madeira)*
Selected banner images courtesy of António Gomes

Steering Committee:

Mike Fraser *(University of Bristol)*
Hans Gellersen *(University of Lancaster)*
Eva Hornecker *(University of Strathclyde)*
Elise van den Hoven *(TU/e)*
Caroline Hummels *(TU/e)*
Hiroshi Ishii *(MIT Media Lab)*
Shahram Izadi *(Microsoft Research)*
Rob Jacob *(Tufts University)*
Ali Mazalek *(Georgia Tech)*
Albrecht Schmidt *(University Duisburg-Essen)*
Brygg Ullmer *(Louisiana State University)*
Nicolas Villar *(Microsoft Research)*
Ron Wakkary *(Simon Fraser University)*
Jamie Zigelbaum *(Zigelbaum + Coelho)*

Student Volunteers Chair:

Denzil Ferreira *(Carnegie Mellon University & University of Madeira)*

Program Committee:

Dzmitry Aliakseyeu *(Philips Research Europe)*
Kristina Andersen *(STEIM)*
Steffi Beckhaus *(University of Hamburg)*
Mark Billinghurst *(HIT Lab NZ)*
Leah Buechley *(MIT Media Lab)*
Marcelo Coelho *(Zigelbaum + Coelho)*
Darren Edge *(Microsoft Research Asia)*
Michael Eisenberg *(University of Colorado, Boulder)*
Morten Fjeld *(Chalmers University of Technology)*
Mike Fraser *(University of Bristol)*
Christian Geiger *(Duesseldorf University)*
Jonna Häkkilä *(Nokia Research)*
Paul Holleis *(DoCoMo Euro Labs)*
Kristina Höök *(Stockholm University)*
Mike Horn *(Northwestern University)*
Eva Hornecker *(University of Strathclyde)*
Jörn Hurtienne *(University of Cambridge)*
Giulio Jacucci *(Helsinki Institute for Information Technology)*
Sergi Jordà *(Universitat Pompeu Fabra)*
Martin Kaltenbrunner *(University of Art and Industrial Design Linz)*
Andruid Kerne *(Texas A&M University)*
Travis Kirton *(The Banff Centre)*
Peter Krogh *(Aarhus School of Architecture)*
Andrew Kun *(University of New Hampshire)*
Astrid Twenebowa Larssen *(Ashesi University College)*
Youn-Kyung Lim *(KAIST)*
Fred Martin *(University of Massachusetts Lowell)*
Masood Masoodian *(University of Waikato)*
David Merrill *(Sifteo)*
Miguel Nacenta *(University of Saskatchewan)*
Joe Paradiso *(MIT Media Lab)*

Program Committee (continued):

Thomas Pederson *(IT University of Copenhagen)*
Aaron Quigley *(University of St. Andrews)*
Hayes Raffle *(Nokia Research)*
Claudia Rébola *(Georgia Institute of Technology)*
Chris Schmandt *(MIT Media Lab)*
Albrecht Schmidt *(University of Duisburg-Essen)*
Orit Shaer *(Wellesley College)*
Ehud Sharlin *(University of Calgary)*
Jennifer Sheridan *(London Knowledge Lab)*
Beat Signer *(Vrije Universiteit Brussel)*
Itiro Siio *(Ochanomizu University)*
Andrew Smith *(Meraka Institute)*
Tomas Sokoler *(IT University of Copenhagen)*
Karen Tanenbaum *(Simon Fraser University)*
Nicolas Villar *(Microsoft Research)*
Andy Wilson *(Microsoft Research)*
Jamie Zigelbaum *(Zigelbaum + Coelho)*

TEI'11 Additional Reviewers

Edith Ackermann
Stefan Agamanolis
Teemu Ahmaniemi
Tristan Al-Haddad
Jussi Ängeslevä
Trent Apted
Carmelo Ardito
Amirhosein Azarbakht
Jonathan Bachrach
Naveen Bagalkot
Brian Bailey
Tico Ballagas
Jeffrey Bardzell
Olivier Bau
Tilde Bekker
Hrvoje Benko
Mike Bennett
Peter Bennett
Andrea Bianchi
Mark Bilandzic
Solomon Bisker
Alan Blackwell
Tina Blaine
Loes Bogers
Pedro Branco
Eva Brandt
Eoin Brazil
Johanna Brewer
Gregor Broll
Quincy Brown
Miguel Bruns Alonso
Winslow Burleson
Daniela Busse
Alex Butler
Eduardo Calvillo Gamez
Xiang Cao
Ole Caprani
Kirsten Cater
Daniel Cermak-Sassenrath
Ken Tin-Kai Chen
Keith Cheverst
Sonia Chiasson
Georgios Christou
Luigina Ciolfi
Jill Coffin
Nuno Correia
Enrico Costanza
Andrew Crossan
R. Jordan Crouser
Andreas Danser
Gauthier David
Charlie DeTar
Travis Deyle
Pierre Dillenbourg
Carl Disalvo
Tanja Doering
Gershon Dublon
Emmanuel Dubois
Bruno Dumas
Alan Dunning
Florian Echtler
Niklas Elmqvist
Nwanua Elumeze
Cumhur Erkut
Parisa Eslambolchilar
Georg Essl
Daniel Fallman
Chloe Fan
Elisabetta Farella
Mark Feldmeier
Frank Feltham
Daniel Fetzner
Sean Follmer
Marcus Foth
Dustin Freeman
Hugo Fuks
Cavan Fyans
Daniel Gallardo
Maribeth Gandy
Franca Garzotto
Lalya Gaye
Sven Gehring
Alicia Gibb
Steve Gill
Nick Gillian
Audrey Girouard
Nan-Wei Gong
Daniel Gooch
Elizabeth Goodman
Eric Gradman
Raphael Grasset
Keith Evan Green
Catherine Grevet
Mona Leigh Guha
Cheng Guo
Michael Gurevich
Sean Gustafson
Cordy Hall
Michael Haller
Tracy Hammond
Mark Hancock
John Paulin Hansen
John Harris
Chris Harrison
Bjoern Hartmann
Sebastian Heinz
Fabian Hemmert
Uta Hinrichs
Steve Hodges
Lars-Erik Holmquist
Jon Hook
Kevin Huang
Scott Hudson
Caroline Hummels
Seth Hunter
Katherine Isbister
Hiroshi Ishii
Suguru Ishizaki
Johann Habakuk Israel
Lars-Erik Janlert
Gabe Johnson
Rose Johnson
Lynette Jones
Staas de Jong
Martin Jonsson
David Joyner
Carles F. Julià
Heekyoung Jung
Karrie Karahalios
Matt Karau
Jarmo Kauko
Chris Kiefer
Daesung Kim
Hyungsin Kim
Kiyoshi Kiyokawa
Scott Klemmer
Florian Klompmaker
Sietske Klooster
André Knörig
Minoru Kobayashi
A. Kocaballi
Christian Baki Koehler
Boriana Koleva
Vassilis Kostakos
Matthias Kranz
Stacey Kuznetsov
Jean-Baptiste Labrune
Robin Laney
Celine Latulipe
Manfred Lau
Hyun Jean Lee
Jinha Lee
Sanghoon Lee
Sang-Su Lee
Karin Leichtenstern
Daniel Leithinger
Zeina Atrash Leong
Wu-Hsi Li
Natan Linder
Lian Loke
Martin Ludvigsen
Matthias Löwe
Jani Mäntyjärvi
Jörg Müller
Lindsay Macdonald
Javier Marco
Georgios Marentakis
Thomas Markussen
Nicolai Marquardt
Mark Marshall
Anijo Mathew
Takashi Matsumoto
Rene Mayrhofer
Chris Mcadam
Scott McCrickard
Marilyn McGee-Lennon
Zeljko Medenica
Richard Medland
David Mellis
Mónica Mendes
Helena Mentis
Dylan Menzies
Florian Michahelles
Droumeva Milena
Amon Millner
Jonathan Moeller
Jin Moen
Aurélie Mossé

Camille Moussette
Ingrid Mulder
Sean Munson
Lia Napolitano
Chris Nash
Elena Nazzi
Carman Neustaedter
David Nguyen
Valentina Nisi
Moira C. Norrie
Ross O'Neill
Adrian Ocneanu
Patrick Olivier
Izabel Olson
Nuno Otero
Grace Ngai
Volker Paelke
Narcís Parés
Laurel Pardue
Andrea Grimes Parker
Daniel Patel
Shwetak Patel
Gareth Paterson
Eric Paulos
Firaz Peer
Hannah Perner-Wilson
Bastian Pfleging
Tommaso Piazza
James Pierce
Thomas Pietrzak
Beryl Plimmer
Sara Price
Iulian Radu
Nicolas Rasamimanana
Umer Rashid
Matthias Rath
P.L. Patrick Rau
Janet Read
Stuart Reeves
Carson Reynolds
Julie Rico
Laurel Riek
Michal Rinott
Bernard Robben
David Robert
Andre Rocha
Jennifer Rode
Yvonne Rogers
Michael Rohs
Eric Rosenbaum
Daniela Rosner
Maria Roussou
Enrico Rukzio
Kathy Ryall
Daniel Saakes
Sajid Sadi
Alireza Sahami Shirazi
Daisuke Sakamoto
Pedro Sanches
Javier Sanchez
Rajesh Sankaran
Ari-Heikki Sarjanoja
Greg Saul
Thecla Schiphorst
Ralf Schmidt
Michael Schmitz
Martin Schrittenloher
Franziska Schroeder
Eric Schweikardt
Minneman Scott
Metin Sezgin
David Shamma
Michael Shiloh
Beat Signer
Jay Silver
Stephen Sinclair
Erin Solovey
Christoph Stahl
Danae Stanton Fraser
Paul Stapleton
Jack Stenner
Martin Strohbach
Sri Subramanian
Nicole Sultanum
Petra Sundström
Dipak Surie
Dag Svanaes
Axel Sylvester
Aurelien Tabard
Anthony Tang
Tony Sheng-Kai Tang
Orkan Telhan
Lucia Terrenghi
Jakob Tholander
Cornelius Toole
Zachary O. Dugas Toups
Brygg Ullmer
Selene Uras
Anna Vallgarda
Evelien van de Garde-Perik
Elise van den Hoven
Janet van der Linden
Anne Van Devender
Jos van Leeuwen
Vero Van den Abeele
Yolanda Vazquez-Alvarez
Frederic Vernier
Antti Virolainen
Thomas Visser
Sebastian von Mammen
Felix von Reischach
Akira Wakita
Bruce Walker
Nicholas Ward
Andrew Webb
Katharina Weber
Tamar Weiss
Michael Philetus Weller
Daniel Wessolek
Reto Wettach
Adam Whiton
Alexander Wiethoff
Daniel Wigdor
Danielle Wilde
Amanda Williams
John Williamson
Karl D.D. Willis
Raphael Wimmer
Ryan Wistort
Dan Witzner Hansen
Andy Wu
Kuan-ju Wu
Peta Wyeth
Cheng Xu
Yan Xu
Zhiquan Yeo
Ji-Dong Yim
Salu Ylirisku
Jim Young
John Zimmerman

Art Explorations Jury

Arianna Bassoli
Johanna Brewer
Carla Diana
Haakon Faste
Giovanni Innella
Jen Lewin Musk
Rudolfo Quitas

GSC Reviewers

Junia Coutinho Anacleto
Alissa Antle
Jonathan Bachrach
Mark Billinghurst
Alan Blackwell
Alvaro Cassinelli
Sheep Dalton
Gauthier David
Ellen Yi-Luen Do
Ylva Fernaeus
Gunnar Green
Mark D. Gross
Simon Holland
Mike Horn
Eva Hornecker
Caroline Hummels
Sadhna Jain
Matt Karau
Hyun Jean Lee
Christopher Lindinger
Lian Loke
Dylan Menzies
Scott Minneman
Grace Ngai
Markku Nousiainen
Sile O'Modhrain
Ian Oakley
Alex Olwal
Dennis Paul
Sara Price
Claudia Rébola
Yvonne Rogers
Ozge Samanci
Thecla Schiphorst
Andreas Schlegel
Albrecht Schmidt
Franziska Schroeder
Orit Shaer
Jack Stenner
Brygg Ullmer

TEI 2011 Sponsor & Supporters

SPONSOR:

SIGCHI
special interest group computer human interaction

SUPPORTERS:

STRATASYS®

NOKIA

NSF

Human-Computer Interaction Institute

Microsoft® Research

YDREAMS

LilyPad Arduino

Near Interaction®

sata The Atlantic and You

seeed studio

PHILIPS

hml human media lab

Disney Research

M-ITI Madeira Interactive Technologies Institute

PATINA
Personal Architectonics Through INteractions with Artefacts

User-Interfaces Based on the Water-Hammer Effect: Water-Hammer Piano as an Interactive Percussion Surface

Steve Mann, Ryan Janzen, Jason Huang, Matthew Kelly,* Lei Jimmy Ba, Alexander Chen
University of Toronto
email: hydraulophone at gmail dot com

ABSTRACT

Water hammer, a well known phenomenon occurring in water pipes and plumbing fixtures, is generally considered destructive and undesirable. We propose the use of water hammer for a musical instrument akin to hammered percussion instruments like hammered dulcimer, piano, *etc.*.

In one embodiment, the instrument comprises an array of mouths each for being struck with the open palm or fingers, each mouth connected to a separate hydraulic resonator. In another embodiment, we use a basin or pool of water as a multitouch user-interface where sounds made by water are acoustically sensed by an array of hydrophones (underwater listening devices).

Using water itself as a touch surface creates a fun and playful user interface medium that captures the fluidity of the water's ebb and flow.

Author Keywords

Absement, Filterbanks, Hydrophone, Hydraulophone, Hyperacoustic, Musical Instrument, Natural pitch notation, Nessie(TM), Nessonance, Nessonator(TM), Presement, Sensory Table, Shifterbanks, Tangible User Interface, Water Drum, Water Hammer, Water Table, WaterDrum, WaterHammer-Drum, WaterTouch(TM), Waterplay

ACM Classification Keywords

H.5.2 Info. systems: Interfaces—*Haptic I/O; Auditory feedback; Input devices; User-centered design*; J.2 Computer apps.: Physical sciences & engineering; J.5 Computer apps.: Arts & humanities—*Music*

General Terms

Design, Experimentation, Human Factors, Theory

INTRODUCTION

Background and related work

Water has a history of use in human computer interaction [18], public sculpture [16], and water therapy [15].

*Thanks to the Human Media Lab at Queen's University.

TEI'11, January 22–26, 2011, Funchal, Portugal.

Water is a natural "element" (element as in Earth, Water, Air, Fire), that can form a natural and fluid tangible interface.

Water has also been used in hydraulophones [13], which use pressurized jets of water as a tactile user-interface. In some sense, the hydraulophone may be regarded as an ORGANic user-interface [19]. Tangible user interfaces have proven themselves in many types of human-computer interaction. Ishii's bottles [6], and the Music Cube [1] form notable examples of tangible interfaces applied to the domain of music.

THE WATER HAMMER PIANO

Musical instruments are generally classified according to the manner in which the initial sound production occurs[8][17].

Previously known acoustic musical instruments make their initial sound from vibrations in solid (strings and percussion) or gas (woodwinds and brass).

Plumbing fixtures such as toilets, faucets, showers, and the like, often make strange noises, and sometimes even make sounds that are almost musical (or at least oscillatory). With the advent of sensor-operated electronic plumbing fixtures, such phenomenona are more prevalent than ever!

We're all familiar with the clanging sounds made by pipes when a solenoid actuated valve abruptly turns off the water to an automatic faucet when the user's hands are taken away, or the thump of an automatic flush urinal or toilet.

In many situations, these sounds originate, at least in part, by matter in its *liquid* state.

Ordinarily water hammer is very destructive, and plumbers go to great lengths to silence bathroom fixtures. There is a large aftermarket for products such as water hammer arresters or water hammer suppressors, as well as delayed valves, and the like. These products aim to suppress vibrations, resonances, and sounds made by pipes and plumbing fixtures.

But what if we could use this violent water-hammer phenomenon creatively to make a new musical instrument? We have made a variety of musical instruments that produce sound from matter in its liquid state. For example, Fig 1 shows two embodiments of the waterhammer piano.

The instrument is made from a dozen Type 316 stainless steel pipes each having extremely thick walls. Whereas most water pipes are Schedule 10, or at most Schedule 40, we

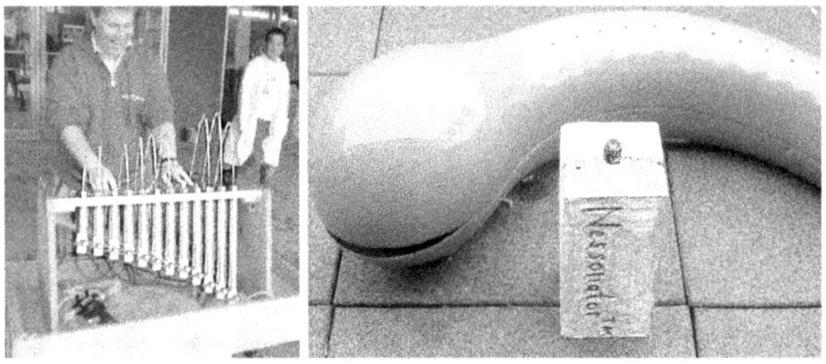

Figure 1. (left) Whereas a traditional piano uses hammers to strike strings, the water hammer piano creates sound by acoustic disturbances that originate as water hammer in any of its 12 pipes (a separate pipe for each note of the musical scale). The instrument is played by suddenly stopping the flow of water, resulting in a hammering effect similar to that observed in solenoid operated valves (e.g. automatic sensor operated faucets). Hydraulic resonance occurs at various notes due to the varying lengths of the pipes. (right) a single-note "Nessonator^{TM}" comprises a Bordeaux wine bottle encased in concrete (foreground). In the background is a 12-jet hydraulophone named "Nessie". The word "Nessonator" is a portmanteau formed from the words "Nessie" and "resonator".

made our water-hammer instrument from pipes having a wall thickness of Schedule 160, the highest wall thickness standardly available.

Water emerges through the opening of each of the 12 pipes. The instrument is played by striking the ends of the pipes (where the water emerges) with rubber mallets, or, simply, by blocking the water jets with the fingers, in an abrupt fashion. This sudden increase in water pressure produces a violently forceful acoustic impulse, which resonates within the pipe, as a water column.

This instrument has a range from 3A to 4E, as expressed in hydraulophone pitch notation, also called natural pitch notation. The lowest note of a hydraulophone, like the piano, is an "A".

Frequencies and natural pitch notation

We propose Natural Pitch Notation (NPN) to overcome the following 5 problems with previously proposed notation [20] (IPN, International Pitch Notation) [1] :

- **IPN reverses significant digits**, e.g. middle C is denoted C4 where the least significant digit "C" (the one that increments faster) is to the left while the most significant digit, "4", is on the right;
- **leftmost digit starts counting from three:** in counting, the "carry" occurs on the third letter (i.e. "C"), not the first letter (i.e. "A") of the alphabet.
- **reference frequency is non-integer:** "A440" is the standardized reference frequency, and every A from 55 CPS and up is an integer frequency. But IPN is C-centric, so every time the octave counter increments, it does so at a non-integer frequency.
- **leading zeros appear in the middle,** e.g. the note after B09 = B9 is C10; the new "1" digit jumps into the middle of the digit sequence, even though the "1" is now the most significant digit;
- **least significant symbol in the middle:** the sharp (♮) or flat (♭) is the least significant parameter, but improperly appears between the digits, e.g. between the "B" and the "4" of B♭4.

[1] There is confusion as to the terminology; e.g. International Pitch Notation (IPN); so-called "scientific" pitch notation; "scientific pitch", which is also a term for a special version of middle C at exactly 256 CPS, which itself is inconsistent with the widely recognized ISO 16 standard A pitch at exactly 440 CPS.

For example, in the existing IPN system, a frequency of 8.176 cycles per second is denoted "C-1". The negative sign appears between the two digits, rather than to the left, as should be the case.

Natural pitch notation, though, works like the odometer on a car: the rightmost digit or symbol moves fastest. Also the letters occur in their *natural* order, starting with the first letter of the alphabet. We use the word "natural" here as a double entendre, because it also refers to the *natural minor* scale, rather than the major scale that goes from "C" to "c". One reason this notation is natural for hydraulophones is that all hydraulophones are manufactured on a minor scale.

Moreover, the "tens" (i.e. the numbers with the rightmost digit being lowest), fall on integer frequencies once we get to 55 CPS and above:

Note	Freq/CPS				
-1A	6.875	4A	220	9A	7040
0A	13.75	5A	440	10A	14080
1A	27.5	6A	880	11A	28160
2A	55	7A	1760	...	...

Thus, for example, the first 12 white keys of the piano (which are exactly 2 octaves down from the 12 jets of the hydraulophone) are: **1A, 1B, 1C, 1D, 1E, 1F, 1G, 2A, 2B, 2C, 2D, 2E**. Sharps and flats now properly appear at the end. For example, -2B♭ is 3.642 CPS. Likewise, saying B♮ is like placing a zero after the decimal point, analogous to saying "2.0"; i.e. writing "2.0" is more specific and implies more precision than "2". In summary, the minus sign is on the left side, followed by the most significant digit, then the least significant digit, and finally the sharp, flat or natural sign.

Water-Hammer Piano Construction

To cause the water in each pipe to resonate at the desired frequencies, several types of resonators can be used. Fig 1(right) shows a single-note from a set of 12 "Nessonator^{TM}" hydraulic resonators. Each note is made from an appropriately modified (cut down to a selected length or the like) Bordeaux wine bottle encased in concrete. The concrete protects the bottle from being broken by hydraulic waterhammer forces, and also ensures the sound is influenced purely by vibrations of water and not of the solid container.

Another embodiment of the waterhammer piano is shown in Fig 2. In this embodiment there are 12 rigid toilet tubes each connected to an elastic hose of equal length, initially (until tuning begins). The hoses were connected to a manifold to supply water into all of them. One prototype embodiment of this was later built into a Spaberry hot tub.

In some embodiments, one or more hydrophones (underwater microphones) listen to the sound made by the vibrating water. The outputs of the hydrophones are electrically amplified, and sometimes various auditory effects processors are used, or other processors are used to generate other multimedia effects, not necessarily limited to auditory effects.

Figure 2. An early embodiment of the waterhammer piano comprised of rigid pipes connected to elastic thick-walled rubber hoses. The instrument was fine-tuned by trimming away the rigid pipes, or the rubber hoses, to raise or lower the resonant frequency of each note to the correct pitch.

In another embodiment of the invention, a user-interface comprises a dozen or so 3 inch pipes (approx. 76cm in nominal diameter), of various lengths, each connected to an identical rubber elastic medium, each of which has a filling nipple. The pipes are supplied by a gentle stream of water that maintains a meniscus that is concave downwards. The instrument is played by slapping the meniscus with the palm of the hand. The resulting shockwaves, water-hammer, or the like, sets a column of water into transient disturbance such that it settles into an oscillatory motion that decays exponentially, like that of a struck string on a piano. Oscillations occur due to the interaction between the inertia of water in the pipe, and the elasticity of the end cap on the bottom of each pipe (i.e. like a mass-spring oscillation).

We can relate a mass-spring resonator to a capacitor-inductor (C-L) resonator, using the force-current analogy. We define a quantity analogous to capacitance as follows:

$$C = \rho l / A \qquad (1)$$

where ρ is the density of the fluid, typically in units of kg/m^3, and l is the length of the pipe leading from the elastic hose to the user-interface port, and A is the cross sectional area of the pipe and its user-interface port.

Capacitance, C, of Equation 1 is in units of

$$\frac{\frac{kg}{m^3}m}{m^2} = kg/m^4. \qquad (2)$$

The eLastic hose or buLb of the bottle forms the spring part of the mass-spring arrangement that gives hydraulic resonance ("Nessonance"). The eLastic part is denoted by the letter "L" and is analogous to inductance. For example, a volume of water in the buLb of the bottle has eLasticity:

$$L = V\beta = V/K, \qquad (3)$$

where β is the compressibility given by $\beta = -\frac{1}{V}dV/dp$, whose reciprocal is the incompressibility, K, given by $K = -Vdp/dV$.

Inductance L is in units of:

$$\frac{m^3}{\frac{kg}{ms^2}} = \frac{m^4 s^2}{kg}. \qquad (4)$$

The resonant frequency of each note is given by:

$$f = \frac{1}{2\pi\sqrt{LC}}. \qquad (5)$$

In the case of the concrete-clad Bordeaux wine bottle, this is approximately:

$$f = \frac{c}{2\pi}\sqrt{\frac{A}{Vl}}, \qquad (6)$$

where c is the speed of sound in the water, $c = \sqrt{\frac{K}{\rho}}$, A is the area of the user-interface or neck, l is the length of the neck, and V is the volume of the bulb.

WATER HAMMER WITHOUT PIPES: 3-DIMENSIONAL VOLUMETRIC INTERACTIVE SURFACE

We desired a more volumetric medium of interaction than our 1-dimensional pipe interface of Fig 1 (rightmost) (actually 0-dimensional since the ability to expressively control the hand's linear position is lost in order to abruptly move toward the end of the pipe).

A 3-dimensional body of water can be touched, hit, and swirled side-to-side in a variety of ways. We thus took the waterhammer effect and made use of it in a tangible 3D interface inspired by a very old method of interaction.

The Baka People and *Liquindi*

Ancient traditions of the African rainforest, particularly of the Baka people, have used water as a tangible interface. The Baka have a practice known as *liquindi*, or water-drumming, whereby women and children use their hands to slap, beat and strike the water surface in various ways to produce complex rhythms as a group [14].

Typically the sound is produced by a person standing in water, hitting the surface of the water with her hands cupped to trap air in the palm when the surface is slapped.

The resulting sound cannot be produced with water alone, since it requires a solid-water or air-water boundary to sustain the sudden impact. As a result, the sound is not purely hydraulophonic [12].

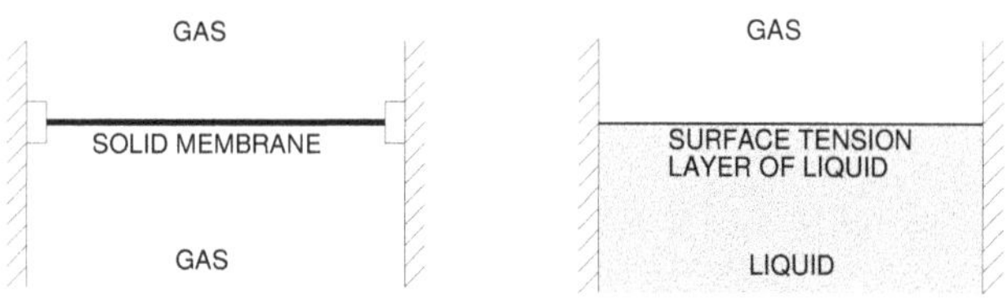

Figure 3. (left) Membranophones are solid percussion instruments, with a 2D membrane under tension. Examples include tabla, timpani, and snare drum. (right) Now the membrane is created by surface tension, becoming a percussion surface between water and air. In this case, the membrane itself (surface tension layer) no longer plays its exclusive role in determining the type of vibration, but instead becomes part of the surrounding media in doing so.

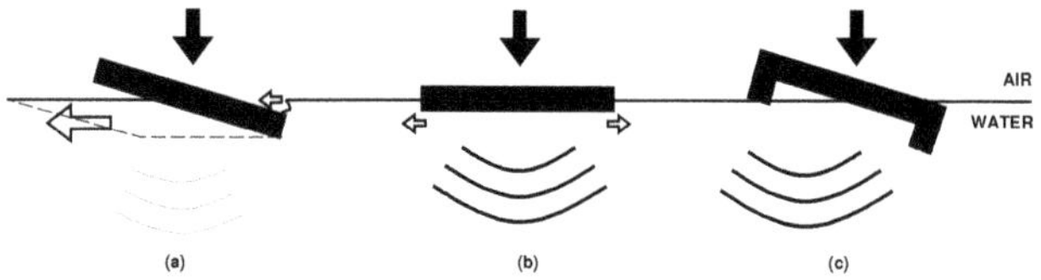

Figure 4. Simplified explanation of hand impact on a water surface: (a) Weak sound from off-angle impact, due to transverse water escape. (b) Co-planar impact produces a stronger acoustic wave. Less water escapes on impact, creating a better acoustic coupling and higher-pressure acoustic pulse. (c) Cupping the hand traps air which allows an uneven surface (or hand) to be impacted more uniformly, producing more sound than in (a).

3D Percussion with Amplification, Electronic Processing

Our work strives to reverse the trend toward electronic MIDI triggering drums by, instead, using sound that is produced acoustically, and merely passing these sounds through various continuously-responding filters (i.e. not merely triggering sound events). The result is an expressivity that comes from interacting with a tangible, richly tactile medium on the surface (e.g. slapping) as well as volumetrically (e.g. moving the hands through the water to create a more continuous sound). We use sound itself that is directly created in a physical medium, so that by swishing, splashing, *etc.* in the water, those complex sounds are not lost in the final sound. In this way, our instrument is a physiphone[11]. In particular, rather than merely triggering samples to be played back as discrete events, the ebb and flow of the water, no matter how subtle, is always present. The hydraulophone is another musical instrument—an underwater version of a pipe organ—that uses the highly expressive qualities of interacting directly with water [13]. As with the hydraulophone, our WaterDrum surface makes sound with musical notes or other sounds that have no beginning or ending, but ebb and flow for all time as long as the instrument is operating.

Touching the Surface-Tension Layer

Water makes an interesting tangible surface because it affords additional expressive capabilities not found in solid interfaces. Turbulence carries a rich set of information from the exact way it was instigated (and can even reveal a unique signature about the conditions around it, such as temperature [7])).

In this work we convert the solid boundary of a membranophone to a liquid surface tension boundary. See Fig. 3.

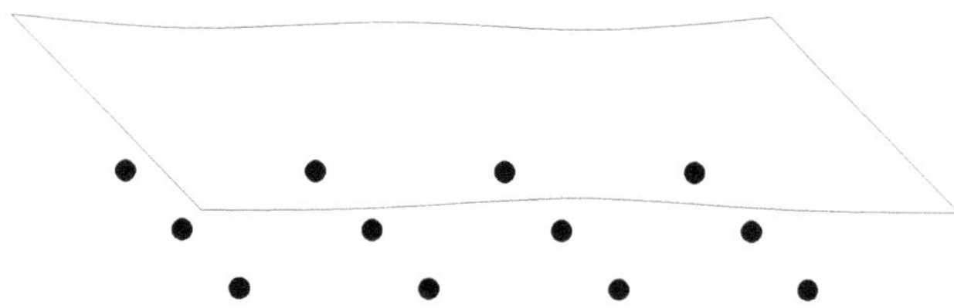

Figure 5. Pattern for 8 to 12 hydrophones under the water surface.

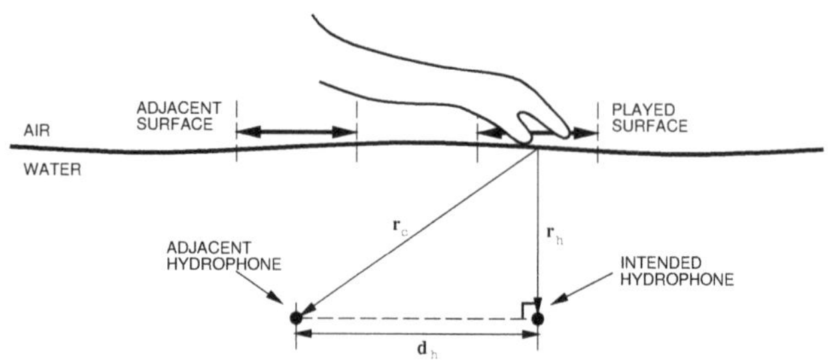

Figure 6. Reducing crosstalk between different playing areas of the waterdrum.

On this surface, a type of water hammer effect can be created once again (in addition to the other more gentle, expressive types of interaction). A sudden impact against the water boundary creates a high pressure pulse since the body of water cannot change its velocity instantaneously. A similar effect can occur with electricity flowing through an inductor. In each case, water current (equivalent to electrical current, *i.e.* motion of electrons) cannot change instantaneously, leading to a large surge in pressure (equivalently, a surge in voltage). If the hand impact Mach number were above 1, there would be shock wave generated in the water. Even in the case of a normal acoustic wave, the power of the pulse can be quite damaging, as is often seen in industrial accidents caused by the water-hammer effect.

In our case, we use hydrophones (underwater microphones) to pick up the sound of the pressure surge as it transforms to an acoustic wave and propagates through the water.

HYDROPHONES ARRANGED UNDER THE WATER DRUMMING SURFACE: THEORY

Hand impacting water directly

To properly set up the waterdrum to achieve its sound consistently, we considered near-field acoustic effects from the impact zone.

Let us consider the effects along a centre axis extending underwater below the hand, considering one frequency component of the impact spectrum. If the hand moved in a pure sinusoidal pattern, wave fronts originating from the centre of the hand (the direct wave) and the edge of the hand (the edge wave) lead to interference patterns as in Fig 7—a series of maxima and minima in front of the hand. Fortunately, at a certain distance away from the hand, the wave becomes more consistent, attenuating monotonically. This point occurs at the last maximum, which is positioned at a depth of:

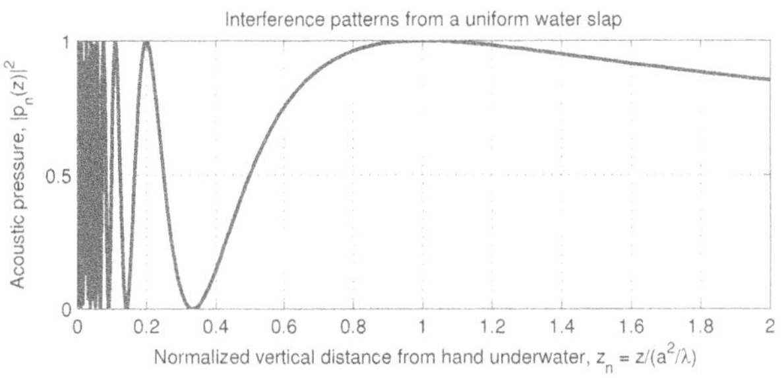

Figure 7. Sound radiation interference pattern from an ideal uniform water slap (covering radius a), as heard from various depths under the point of impact at the water surface. Past the right side of the graph, the sound level forever continues to monotonically decay to zero. Each wavelength λ out of the total frequency spectrum has its own scaled version of this interference pattern.

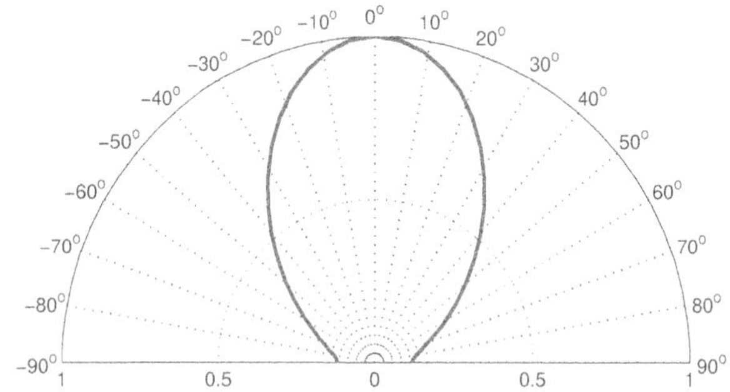

Figure 8. Sound radiation from an ideal uniform water slap, as heard from various angles under the point of impact at the water surface. This is a graph of angular directivity, illustrating how the intensity decreases compared to its maximum. The sound is strongest along the centre axis directly under the hand ($\theta = 0°$). The shape of the curve varies according to frequency.

$$z = \frac{a^2}{\lambda} = \frac{a^2 f}{c} \quad (7)$$

For example, taking $c = 1500$m/s in water, with the hand's maximum clean contact dimension as 0.08m, and stipulating that we want the system to detect impact frequencies up to 8kHz, produces a last maximum at z=0.034m. Thus, to avoid near-field effects, we preferred to position the hydrophones at approximately 5cm below the drumming water surface.

Note that diversity in the hand impact apodization (from a moving and uneven water surface) aided in making the wave fronts heard clearly at the hydrophones.

Hand impacting water with an air pocket

As the hand cannot form a perfectly flat surface, coplanar with the water surface, water can escape from under part of the hand without producing a wave front.

Cupping the hand as done by the Baka tradition helps to solve this problem. Cupping traps an air pocket inside the palm (Fig. 4c), and can help produce a strong wave front by synchronizing a pressure impulse across an irregular hand-water or air-water interface.

One consequence is that the frequency spectrum is generally lower with cupping (Fig. 4c) than with a direct flat impact (Fig. 4a) because the air pocket softens the impact and reduces the acceleration (and thus frequency) of the pulsing motion in the water.

Avoiding cross-talk between waterdrum areas

We experimented with having multiple sensitive areas on the same water surface, each with a separate hydrophone. Acoustic waves inevitably interfere with neighbour hydrophones to some extent; however, they will be attenuated if the areas are spaced far enough apart. If we want crosstalk to be C_{dB} decibels weaker than the desired drumming signals, we can carefully choose the hydrophone separation d_h as shown in Fig. 6. Approximating a spherical wave whose $\frac{1}{r}$ decay[2] dominates over lossy attenuation near the source, then the hydrophone separation is:

$$d_h = \sqrt{r_c^2 - r_h^2} = r_h\sqrt{\left(\frac{r_c}{r_h}\right)^2 - 1} \simeq r_h\sqrt{10^{\frac{C_{dB}}{10}} - 1} \quad (8)$$

where r_c is the nearest crosstalk distance and r_h is the direct distance to the hydrophone for the local drum region being played. Choosing a crosstalk attenuation of -12dB and a depth of $r_h = 5$cm as before, gives a hydrophone separation of at least 19cm. We built one prototype with 20cm spacing to experiment with very fast, intricate water drumming enabled by the close spacing of the drum regions.

The actual amount of crosstalk will be equal to or better than this first-order approximation because diffraction effects create the strongest sound at an angle directly under the hand (main lobe) and a weaker acoustic field at increasing angles from this centre axis (side lobes). The exact field profile can be found from Rayleigh's integral, Huygens principle[2][3][9], Rayleigh-Sommerfeld theory[2][3][5][9], the Kirchhoff formulation[2][3][5][9], and the angular spectrum model of plane waves[4][9]. A simple example is to model the hand as a perfectly round disk, in which case the angular directivity would be:

$$D(\theta) = \frac{2J_1(ka\sin\theta)}{ka\sin\theta} \quad \text{with } k = \frac{2\pi}{\lambda} \quad (9)$$

where J_1 is a Bessel function of the first kind. A maximum occurs directly under the hand ($\theta = 0°$), as shown in Fig 8.

WATER AS A 3D EXPRESSIVE TACTILE MEDIUM

Water makes additional expressivity possible which is not found on a solid drumming surface. Beyond just drumming, a user can touch, splash, swirl, and stir the water in various ways.

For this reason, we made the original physical sound have a strong role in the final output sound, rather than simply causing drum samples to be triggered. As a result, the user can expressively play the instrument.

Spraying a jet of water into the drum areas gave the effect of "bowing" the drum as one would bow a violin, except with an infinitely long bow.

[2]In acoustics, field quantities obey a $\frac{1}{r}$ law for a spherical wave, whereas power intensity decays as $\frac{1}{r^2}$.

FILTERBANKS TO TRANSFORM ONE PERCUSSIVE SOUND INTO ANOTHER

An array of filterbank effects processors were designed, consisting of various bandpass filters, convolutions, *etc.*, created for each drum region on the water surface. Each region was processed separately to create a multitouch surface.

Implementation of WaterDrum kit

To acheive unique, compelling output from our system we adopted technology that would allow us to rapidly prototype new signal processing methods and sounds. With twelve hydrophone outputs from the WaterDrum kit, connecting them directly to a single PC for processing was not a flexible option. Instead, we ported the leads from the hydrophones directly to a audio mixer board for preamplification before the signals were processed. This allowed us to process on multiple disparate PCs in a dynamic configuration. After processing on the PCs, the signal was sent back to the mixer for amplification and output (through speakers).

To achieve a natural and metaphor free experience to the users of the WaterDrum kit, we chose to retain the texture of the input signals. By doing so, we would capture the natural sound of the water-hammer effect in the output signal. One method included an array of high-Q bandpass filters, one for each input signal, with various tuned frequencies. This allowed some of the original signal to pass through while allowing the user to expressively play the water surface as if it were tuned like a xylophone or timpani.

The second method of signal processing that captured the expressive texture of the input signal was realtime convolution. By interfacing an M-Audio Delta 1010 input/output device to a PC, we then processed the signal within Puredata-extended. By using the *partconv* external in Puredata, we were able to convolve samples of percussion (and other) instruments with the water hammer input signals. In this way, the acoustic sound is continuously filtered according to an individual filtering process for each hydrophone.

Do filterbanks turn an acoustic instrument into an electronic instrument?

Our water-hammer piano uses filterbanks that post-process acoustically generated sounds from hydrophones.

It is an example of a hyperacoustic instrument or physiphone[11]. Physiphones typically use one of:

- geophones, contact "microphones", or the like (sound pickups for solids);
- hydrophones, or underwater "microphones" (sound pickups for liquids); or
- microphones (sound pickups for gases).

Such a "hyper-acoustic" instrument makes it possible to bring subsonic and ultrasonic acoustic vibrations into the audible spectrum and add to the richly physical experience of playing a real acoustic instrument.

Unlike a hyperinstrument[10] in which position sensors, or the like, add synthetic sounds to an acoustic instrument, hyperacoustic instruments use the original sound as their primary computer input, with other sensors affecting the processing of this sound.

We also constructed some variations of these instruments using mechanical resonators, as well as analog electric resonators (such as a computer-controlled Cry Baby (TM) Wah Wah pedal), to convince even a skeptic of the acoustic nature of the instrument (e.g. using computer vision sensing body motion to position the setting of an analog guitar pedal connected to a vacuum tube amplifier).

However, regardless of whether these post-processing effects are mechanical, analog, or digital, the instrument, in whole, remains a non-electrophone, since the initial sound production comes from three dimensional physical matter in the real world, also giving a fundamentally tactile and "real" playing experience.

We believe, therefore, that hyperacoustic instruments are not members of the Hornbostel Sachs 5th Radiophonic / Electrophone category [17] any more so than is an electric guitar with effects pedals, or a Steinway grand piano that's been electrically amplified.

WaterDrum as a hyperacoustic musical instrument

Inherent in the WaterDrum system is the complex response produced by intricate interaction with fluid dynamics.

Many of these dynamic disturbances are below the range of human hearing, but are nevertheless acoustic in nature, at least insofar as they are the natural sounds of water. Although the total sound is audible, a great deal of the frequency spectrum extends below the range of human hearing. We chose to embrace these sounds by capturing them, and shifting their frequencies up to desired notes on a musical scale. In this way, our WaterDrum system, when used as a musical instrument, is a hyperacoustic instrument.

To make this hyperacoustic instrument as expressive as possible, we wished to bring subsonic and ultrasonic sounds into the audible range by way of signal processing of the acoustically-generated signals. In a way similar to (but not the same as), superheterodyne radio reception, signals can be downshifted and upshifted by means of using an oscillator in the process of frequency-shifting and various forms of selective sound filtration. However, unlike what happens in a superheterodyne receiver, we prefer to scale frequencies logarithmically rather than linearly, in order to better match the frequency distribution of human perception. [12]

This digital signal processing is, in a general sense, a filtering operation, which may be highly nonlinear in certain situations.

In the WaterDrums, we have shifted ultra-low frequencies (of which a musician gains very detailed control [7]) into the audible range by means of a frequency-shifter imple-

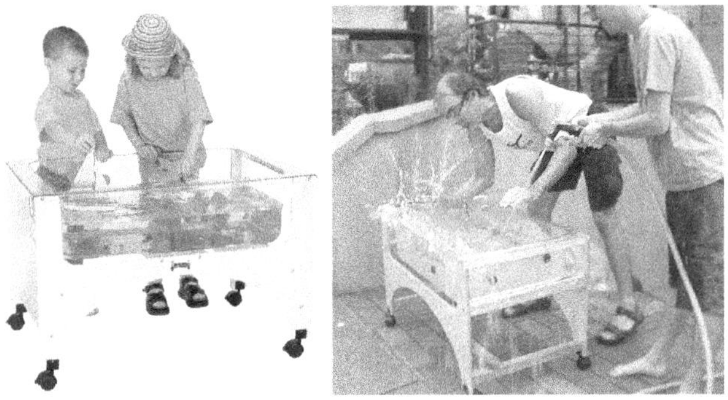

Figure 10. (left) Sensory Tables such as this product manufactured by Jonti-Craft are used in the classrooms at many child care centres. A basin is built into a table on wheels. There is a drain to empty the water into a bucket at the end of each play session. There are no sensors in a Sensory Table, but if we equip the table with sensing apparatus, it can be easily be made into a computational multimedia interface. (right) WaterDrum being played by two people at once: slapping the water surface with hands, and spraying a jet of water into different 3D drum regions to create a more smooth and continuous sound. The slapping is analogous to plucking a guitar, and the spraying is more like the bow of a violin.

mented on a computer having a broadband analog to digital converter, i.e. an A to D converter that responds all the way down to 0Hz (DC), and up to about 40kHz.

What we have done is brought the subsonic (as well as ultrasonic) frequencies into the audible range, as is commonly done with electric hydraulophones [12] (underwater pipe organs).

WATERDRUM FOR PUBLIC PERFORMANCES

We arranged 8 to 12 hydrophones (underwater listening devices) in an array underwater to create a multitouch haptic surface, located near the water surface, as shown in Figs 5, 9.

The hydrophone mounting frame was designed so it could be submerged in any body of water, just under the surface. For portable use on land, we used a product called a "Sensory Table" manufactured by Jonti-Craft. Sensory Tables are commonly used in child care centres such as nursery schools and day cares. The product consists of a transparent acrylic tub with a stand on wheels, as shown in Fig. 10 (leftmost). It can be filled with sand or water, to allow children to experience a variety of sensory input as they touch the and or water. Sensory Tables are also sometimes known as "Water Tables" or "Sand Tables" depending on the material they are filled with.

The name "Sensory Table" arises because the sand or water are used to stimulate the senses, not because the table has any sensors in it. But we can easily add sensing apparatus, to make the Sensory Table into a human-computer interface.

The instrument, seen in Fig. 10 (rightmost), was used in a variety of public performances.

For more information, pictures, and video, see http://glogger.mobi/s/waterhammer

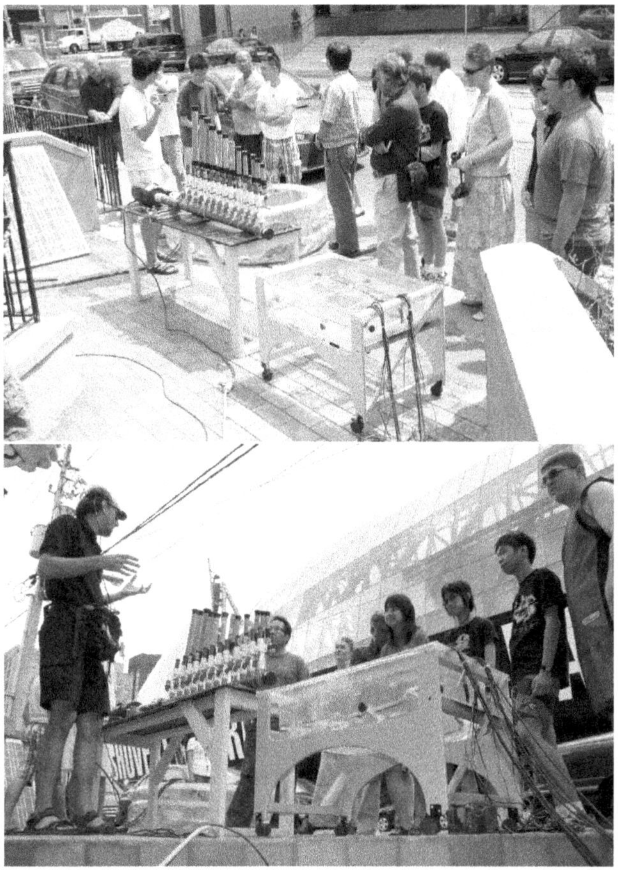

Figure 11. Various public performances, lectures, workshops, *etc.*, were based around the WaterHammer Piano and WaterHammer drum percussion surface.

Performances, lectures, and workshops

Over the Summer of 2010, we used this new interactive water surface in a wide variety of performances, lectures, and workshops. For example, we used it in a series of performances, ranging from a performance for the National Capital Commission in the nation's capital, to performances at various schools and street fairs.

In one of our workshops, the Department Head of the school commented: "That was the best field trip we had...".

One theme we taught was renewable energy and sustainable development, to raise awareness of natural resources, water, and energy. See Fig 11.

CONCLUSIONS

We successfully implemented and demonstrated a "WaterDrum" kit, water-hammer piano, etc., a user-interface based on a Sensory Table (Water Table). The apparatus was equipped with hydrophones that resulted in a water-based touch surface and volume. As a result, the user could provide expressive input by interacting with the natural physicality of the water, producing water waves, ripples, bubbles, and similar phenomena, all of which affect the resulting sound.

Figure 9. LEFTMOST: WaterDrum surface, with array of 8 to 12 hydrophones arranged underwater (in this figure, 8 hydrophones are shown, for a single octave compass); CENTER: Interactive art installation; four participants engaged in the experience; RIGHTMOST: Street performance, playing some jazz and classical reperetoire.

We also did a series of public performances and workshops for various schools and other organizations, and found that the our new user-interface had a positive effect on people from many diverse backgrounds and age groups.

ACKNOWLEDGEMENTS

Our thanks to Dr. Roel Vertegaal, founder of the Human Media Media Lab at Queen's University, to the NCC (National Capital Commission), Ottawa, Canada, and to Jonti-Craft, Inc. Wabasso, MN, for their assistance.

REFERENCES

1. M. B. Alonso and D. V. Keyson. *MusicCube: making digital music tangible*. ACM CHI, 2005.
2. E. B. Baker. *The Mathematical Theory of Huygens Principle*. Oxford Univ. Press, London, 2 edition, 1950.
3. C. Bouwkamp. Diffraction theory. *Rep. Prog. Phys.*, 17:35–100, 1954.
4. P. Clemmow. *The Plane Wave Spectrum Representation of Electromagnetic Fields*. Pergammon Press, London, 1966.
5. J. W. Goodman. *Introduction to Fourier Optics*. McGraw-Hill, New York, 1968.
6. H. Ishii. Bottles: A transparent interface as a tribute to mark weiser. *IEICE Trans. on Info. and Systems*, pages Vol. E87–D, No. 6, pp. 1299–1311, June 2004.
7. R. Janzen and S. Mann. Arrays of water jets as user interfaces: Detection and estimation of flow by listening to turbulence signatures using hydrophones. In *Proceedings of the 15th annual ACM international conference on Multimedia, September 24-29, Augsburg, Germany*, pages 505–8, 2007.
8. M. J. Kartomi. *On Concepts and Classifications of Musical Instruments*. Chicago Studies in Ethnomusicology (CSE). University of Chicago Press, 1990.
9. E. W. M. Born. *Principles of Optics*. Cambridge University Press, Cambridge, 6 edition, 1997.
10. T. Machover. Hyperinstruments: A composer's approach to the evolution of intelligent musical instruments. In W. Freeman, editor, *Cyberarts*. Spartan Books, San Francisco, 1991.
11. S. Mann. Physiphones... In *Proc. New Interfaces for Musical Expression*, 2007.
12. S. Mann, R. Janzen, R. Lo, and C. Aimone. Inventing new instruments based on a computational "hack" to make a badly tuned or unpitched instrument play in perfect harmony. In *Proc. International Computer Music Conference, ICMC '07, August 27-31, Copenhagen, Denmark*, volume 1, pages 105–112, 2007.
13. S. Mann, R. Janzen, and M. Post. Hydraulophone design considerations: Absement, displacement, and velocity-sensitive music keyboard in which each key is a water jet. In *Proceedings of the 14th annual ACM international conference on Mu ltimedia, October 23-27, Santa Barbara, USA.*, pages 519–528, 2006.
14. V. D. Mark Ellingham, Orla Duane, editor. *World Music: The Rough Guide (Africa, Europe and the Middle East)*. London: Rough Guides, Ltd., dist. by Penguin, 1999.
15. D. K. R. D. B. NK. Effects of a water-based program on women 65 years and over: a randomised controlled trial. *Australian Journal of Physiotherapy*, 52(2):102–8, 2005.
16. P. Richards. *The Wave Organ*. Exploratorium, http://www.exploratorium.edu/visit/wave_organ.html, Accessed 2005-8.
17. C. Sachs. *The History of Musical Instruments*. Norton, New York, 1940.
18. K. van Mensvoort. *Datafountain: Money translated to water*. Online documentation by the inventor, http://www.koert.com/work/datafountain/, 2005.
19. R. Vertegaal and I. Poupyrev. Organic user interfaces. *Communications of the ACM*, 51:26–30, 2008.
20. R. W. Young. Terminology for logarithmic frequency units. *J. Acoust. Soc. Am.*, 11(1):134–139, July 1939.

Modular Musical Objects Towards Embodied Control Of Digital Music

Nicolas Rasamimanana
Frederic Bevilacqua
Norbert Schnell
Fabrice Guedy
Emmanuel Flety
Come Maestracci
Bruno Zamborlin
IRCAM - CNRS STMS
Real Time Musical Interactions
1 place Igor Stavinsky, 75004 Paris France
Nicolas.Rasamimanana@ircam.fr

Jean-Louis Frechin
Uros Petrevski
NoDesign
12, passage Turquetil, 75011 Paris France
studio@nodesign.net

ABSTRACT
We present an ensemble of tangible objects and software modules designed for musical interaction and performance. The tangible interfaces form an ensemble of connected objects communicating wirelessly. A central concept is to let users determine the final musical function of the objects, favoring customization, assembling, repurposing. This might imply assembling the wireless interfaces with existing everyday objects or musical instruments. Moreover, gesture analysis and recognition modules allow the users to define their own action/motion for the control of sound parameters. Various sound engines and interaction scenarios were built and experimented. Some examples that were developed in a music pedagogy context are described.

Author Keywords
Music, Gesture, Interface, Gesture Recognition, Audio Processing, Design, Interaction

ACM Classification Keywords
H.5.2 Information interfaces and presentation (e.g., HCI): Miscellaneous.

General Terms
Algorithms, Design, Experimentation, Performance

INTRODUCTION
The expressive control of digital sound and audio processing has been the focus of important research over the last decade. In this perspective, gestural and tangible interfaces actually are promising approaches to control abstract, disembodied digital sounds. Such interfaces indeed afford the use of physical movements over digital sounds, and can therefore be used to create an embodied music experience. This approach has been recognized to recreate essential links akin to a musician with his/her instrument [9, 21, 6]. Thanks to the increasing availability of gesture sensing systems, innovative digital musical instruments emerged recently from the computer music community [14], opening several novel approaches for musical expression using digital sounds [7].

Using gesture input and tangible interfaces brings up important design and usage issues. In [22], authors posited that gestural controllers were in most cases designed to fit idiosyncratic needs, and as a consequence were inextricably bound to their creators. As a matter of fact, musical interfaces are often considered as part of an artistic endeavor, and not always meant to be embraced by a large community of users. Even if some counterexamples can be found [22, 10], no clear methodologies or approaches to design and evaluate musical interfaces has clearly emerged yet, which generally makes this research community not integrated in the mainstream of the HCI field.

As a design approach, low-level hardware components such as Arduino [23] have been largely embraced by the computer community, showing clearly that subcomponents, if generic enough, can be widely adopted as a means to build complex systems. This can be paralleled to software environments such as Max/MSP [11] or Pd [17], that are based on building complex applications from relatively simple modular components. In this paper, we describe a project on tangible music interfaces, based on a similar bottom-up approach. Our goal is to provide users with both hardware and software components, considered as building blocks to create various types of embodied music experiences. We aim at giving users opportunities to incorporate objects, gestures and sound materials of their choice in the interaction. We are particularly interested in scenarios where objects and gestures are taken or inspired from other (non-musical) applications, in order to provide some grounds to facilitate gesture control. From a general perspective, this can be compared to the use of natural user interfaces discussed recently by [1].

TEI'11, January 22–26, 2011, Funchal, Portugal.

The paper is structured as follows. We first present our general design approach. Second, we describe hardware and software components. Finally, we describe some examples that were experimented in a music school.

DESIGN STRATEGY

One can oppose two different strategies in designing complex systems: *top-down* and *bottom-up* approaches. The first one consists in creating objects[1] that are fully completed and developed with specific functionalities and uses. As such, objects can hardly be modified and users need to "adapt" to the preconceived functionnalities through learning [12]. On the contrary, in a *bottom-up* design strategy, users can actively create the final working system using simple elements. As such, this approach favors customization, assembling, repurposing. Typically, this approach encompasses do-it-yourself (DIY) such as proposed by Arduino.

As illustrated in Figure 1, we propose a bottom-up approach (points 2, 3, and 4 in Figure 1) we call *user-completed systems* [16], opposed to fully finished interfaces and applications with fixed, predefined usages. Major possibilities include:

- assemble existing basic modules
- "parasite/hack" existing interfaces or musical instruments
- invent new interfaces/usages

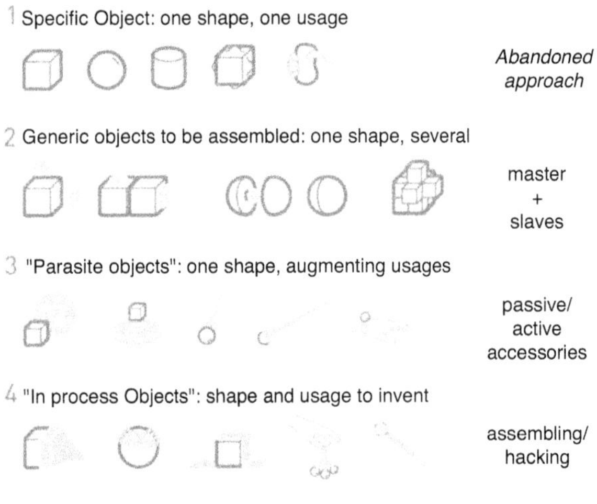

Figure 1. Design approaches

In this project, our goal is to develop hardware and software modules that are intermediate between low-level DIY systems like Arduino or Max/MSP and high level musical system or instruments. Therefore we propose basic elements that require no electronic or programming expertise (without precluding expert users to add new elements). We also propose scenarios or "recipes" to combine elements to create musical interfaces. Similar intermediate level and modular approaches can be found in systems such as the Re-acTable [8], BlockJam [15], or the Siftables [13]. However, unlike these examples, we encourage the possibility of hacking and repurposing other objects. Users can hence borrow performing concepts from other disciplines, in visual art (e.g. painting), game (e.g board games) and even sports (e.g ball games). Moreover, using dedicated gesture analysis and recognition software modules, users can propose and incorporate particular motion and actions in the interaction (see the section on software modules).

[1] here the term object must be understood in a broad sense as anything that is produced, a physical object or a software

Hardware Modules

We developed a modular set of objects, called MO, that can be assembled to create tangible sound interfaces. The platform is based on a central wireless module shown in Figure 2. This module, that can be easily held in one hand, contains 6 DOF inertial sensors (accelerometers and gyroscopes), two buttons and LEDs displays and a rechargeable battery. The wireless is based on the IEEE 802.15.4, generally called "Zigbee". We use a Jennic OEM JN-5139.

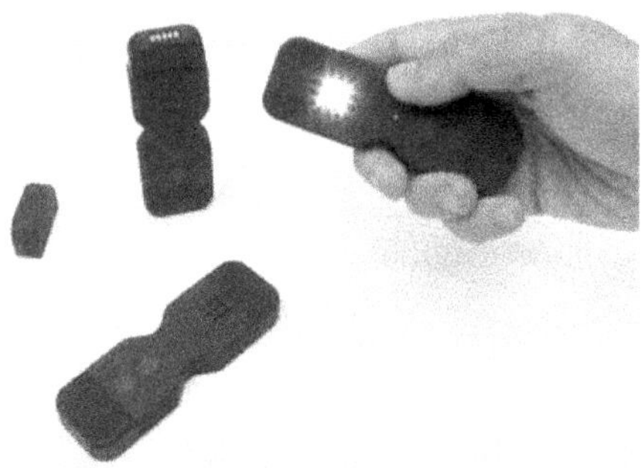

Figure 2. MO principal module

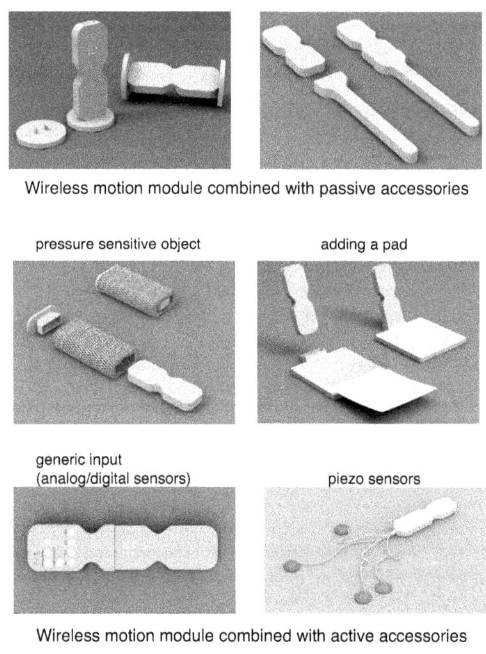

Figure 3. MO accessories (simulation)

Alone, this module allows for motion interactions. Hand gesture can directly be used. But, as already mentioned, we want to stress that its usages can be varied using either passive or active accessories. In particular, active accessories can be directly assembled at each extremity of the modules, using a I2C bus. A first set of accessories is in development (see Figure 3):

- Piezos sensors, e.g. to create a touch sensitive surface
- A pressure sensitive cover, e.g. to make a motion sensible graspable object.
- Generic analog and digital inputs to add any other sensors
- An additional 6 DOF inertial sensors, connected through a cable, e.g. to get relative motion between the module and the accessories

We plan to progressively add new components. Thanks to the "generic input" accessory, any new sensors can already easily be incorporated.

Software Modules

Similarly to the hardware developments, we conceived modular software components for both gesture/motion analysis and audio processing/synthesis. The elements are programmed in Max/MSP, which facilitates rapid prototyping.

One of the key components of the gesture analysis consists in a gesture recognition and synchronization engine called "gf" (standing for gesture follower) [2]. This component allows the user to simply record gestures that are then recognized by the system. The main algorithm is based on Hidden Markov Models, but using a non-classical implementation to take into accounts the two following specific constraints. First, a single example can be used for the training, which allows users to easily choose or adapt gesture to their capabilities. Second, the system can perform early-recognition of gestures and as a consequence can continuously synchronize gestures to audio processing. Specifically, the recognition system is designed to accommodate interaction paradigms using both discrete triggering and continuous control.

For audio processing, we integrate a set of synthesis and sound transformation modules [18, 20, 19] that enables to interactively work on recorded sounds. For example, we use various granular and phase vocoder techniques to specifically alter sound characteristics while preserving others (temporally stretching sounds without changing pitch or vice-versa).

EXAMPLE USES

In this section, we present different works integrating the presented hardware and software components. These works were made and used by music teachers and students with the help of our research team. The interaction systems were elaborated in a context of music creation and music pedagogy throughout the year, and were presented during the end-of-year student concert. These experiments were designed within a larger pedagogical context, which description is beyond the scope of this paper.

MO Ball in Collaborative Mode

In this case, the music interaction was based on a ball game, augmented with our wireless module (see Figure 4). It consisted in a percussive sound being played each times the ball is thrown and caught. We experimented with string pizzicati triggered one by one, respecting the score of an actual musical piece. The music performance was thus bound to the continuous and regular ball passing. This collaborative musical game could be played in pairs or with large groups. While everybody can easily play such a game, yet, it requires interesting group interaction, eye-contact, and collective concentration to perform the music. As a matter of fact, ballistic movements (as found when throwing ball) have always been a salient metaphor in music [4]. This indeed encompasses important musical notions such as up-beats, down-beats, phrasing and pulsation. Note that the use of balls as musical interfaces were previously experimented by other authors [5, 3].

Figure 4. MO Ball setup

MO Ball with Continous Control

Contrary to the previous mode where discrete events were triggered, this mode of MO Ball focuses on the control of continuous digital sounds. Users hold the ball and can define their own gestures, which are then used to directly act on the pacing on the sound: sounds are stretched when slowing down and sounds are shortened when speeding up. This mode enables the use of any continuous gestures to lead music, using metaphors ranging from conducting to dance. Users can re-perform music piece using their own gestures and interfaces.

Figure 5. MO ball with continuous control. The recognition system along with the sound engine allows the user to gesturally select and control continuously parameters of the sound. For example, sound can be stretched according to the pace of the gestures

MO Chess

In a particular music context, the teacher and students proposed to use a chess game as an interaction metaphor. The game was found to resonate with musical concepts about opposition and dialogue (e.g. canons or duets). A chess table was then augmented with a piezo sensor to register when a piece was put on the table. Players has also attached a MO module to their wrists to track the hand motion above the table. All the sensors were used to control the tempo of a musical piece. Using this setup, performance of a music duet was possible, where each player controls a different music line.

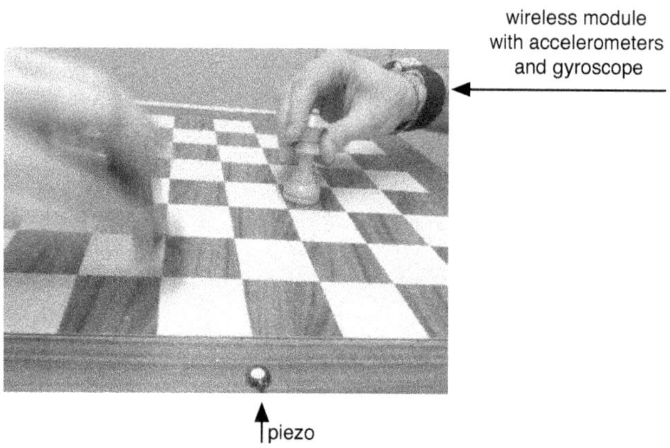

Figure 6. Sound control using a chess board game

CONCLUSION

We presented a modular set of tangible interfaces for sound control, emphasizing gesture and action. Our design strategy was to propose a bottom-up approach: assembling modules, augmenting existing objects and hacking in order to let emerge novel usages with basic interfaces. Moreover, the tangible interfaces are used in conjunction with gesture recognition modules, which invite users to define their own control gestures. Several sound modules were also implemented, based on recorded sound that remained opened to the users. Finally, we presented preliminary works achieved in a music school, which demonstrated promising potential of this approach for music creation and pedagogy. We are currently pursuing the work in this context, developing several other scenarios and applications.

ACKNOWLEDGMENTS

We acknowledge support of ANR and CapDigital (Interlude project ANR-08-CORD-010), and la Région Ile de France. We also thank the whole Interlude consortium and students of l'Atelier des Feuillantines. The second generation of MO prototypes were finalized by DaFact (www.dafact.com).

REFERENCES

1. B. Buxton. Interview on Channel 9. CES 2010. http://channel9.msdn.com/posts/larrylarsen/ces-2010-nui-with-bill-buxton/.

2. F. Bevilacqua, B. Zamborlin, A. Sypniewski, N. Schnell, F. Guedy, and N. Rasamimanana. Continuous realtime gesture following and recognition. In *LNCS*. Springer Verlag, 2009.

3. T. Blaine and T. Perkis. The jam-o-drum interactive music system: A study in interaction design. In *DIS*, 2000.

4. E. Dalcroze. *Rhythm, music and education*. Library Reprints (January 2001), 1921.

5. EZ3kiel. Musical ball. http://www.dailymotion.com/video/x4rub7_ez3kiel-ballon-musical-live-la-ciga_music.

6. R. Godøy and M. Leman, editors. *Musical Gestures: Sound, Movement and Meaning*. Routledge, 2009.

7. International Conference on New Interfaces for Musical Expressions. http://www.nime.org.

8. S. Jordà, G. Geiger, M. Alonso, and M. Kaltenbrunnera. The reactable: Exploring the synergy between live music performance and tabletop tangible interfaces. In *TEI*, 2007.

9. M. Leman. *Embodied music cognition and mediation technology*. The MIT Press, Cambridge, Massassuchetts, 2007.

10. J. Malloch, D. Birnbaum, E. Sinyor, and M. Wanderley. Towards a new conceptual framework for digital musical instruments. In *DAFx*, 2006.

11. Max/MSP. http://www.cycling74.com.

12. J. McGrenere, R. Baecker, and K. Booth. An evaluation of a multiple interface design solution for bloated software. In *Proceedings of CHI*, 2002.

13. D. Merrill, J. Kalanithi, and P. Maes. Siftables: Towards sensor network user interfaces. In *TEI*, 2007.

14. E. Miranda and M. Wanderley. *New Digital Musical Instruments: Control and Interaction beyond the Keyboard*. A-R, 2006.

15. H. Newton-Dunn, H. Nakano, and J. Gibson. Block jam: A tangible interface for interactive music. *Journal of New Music Research*, 32(4):383–393, 2003.

16. NoDesign. http://www.nodesignlab.net/.

17. Pure Data. http://puredata.info/.

18. N. Schnell, R. Borghesi, D. Schwarz, F. Bevilacqua, and R. Muller. Ftm - complex data structures for max. In *ICMC*, 2005.

19. N. Schnell, A. Röbel, D. Schwarz, G. Peeters, and R. Borghesi. Mubu and friends: Assembling tools for content based real-time interactive audio processing in max/msp. In *ICMC*, Montreal, Août 2009.

20. N. Schnell and D. Schwarz. Gabor, multi-representation real-time analysis/synthesis. In *DAFx*, 2005.

21. M. Wanderley and M. Battier, editors. *Trends in Gestural Control of Music*. Ircam, 2000.

22. M. Wanderley and N. Orio. Evaluation of input devices for musical expression: Borrowing tools from hci. *Computer Music Journal*, 26(3):62–76, 2002.

23. N. Zambetti. http://www.arduino.cc/.

MirrorFugue: Communicating Hand Gesture in Remote Piano Collaboration

Xiao Xiao and Hiroshi Ishii
MIT Media Laboratory
Tangible Media Group
75 Amherst Street, Cambridge, MA 02142
{x_x, ishii}@media.mit.edu

ABSTRACT
Playing a musical instrument involves a complex set of continuous gestures, both to play the notes and to convey expression. To learn an instrument, a student must learn not only the music itself but also how to perform these bodily gestures. We present MirrorFugue, a set of three interfaces on a piano keyboard designed to visualize hand gesture of a remote collaborator. Based their spatial configurations, we call our interfaces *Shadow*, *Reflection*, and *Organ*. We describe the configurations and detail studies of our designs on synchronous, remote collaboration, focusing specifically on remote lessons for beginners. Based on our evaluations, we conclude that displaying the to-scale hand gestures of a teacher at the locus of interaction can improve remote piano learning for novices.

Author Keywords
Gesture Interfaces, Computer Supported Learning, Computer Supported Collaborative Work, Music Learning Interfaces, Tangible User Interfaces

ACM Classification Keywords
H.5.3 Group and Organization Interfaces

General Terms
Design, Experimentation

INTRODUCTION
The creation of music is inextricably tied to the physical gestures of a performer on an instrument. Performance gestures include both the technique to play the notes and the movements imbuing expression to the sound [17]. These gestures play an integral role in music learning [7]. Learning by watching and imitating is crucial for students to acquire new techniques. Additionally, watching music being performed helps students process what they hear.

The physicality of sound creation limits musical collaboration in space. Though advancements in musical tele-presence networks enable remote performances, rehearsals, and lessons, music network systems have historically focused on achieving the highest fidelity reproduction of acoustic sound.

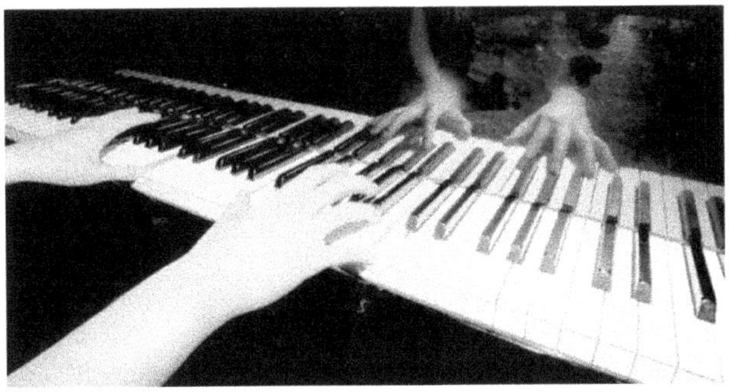

Figure 1: Photographic mockup of Reflection mode

This paper examines ways of communicating hand gesture in remote collaboration interfaces on the piano, focusing specifically on how these interfaces can aid remote lessons. We outline related work in remote music networks, remote collaborative workspaces, and music learning interfaces. We then describe three MirrorFugue interfaces, which take inspiration from research on bodily presence in remote collaborative workspaces. We detail evaluations of our systems and discuss their results.

RELATED WORK

Remote Music Systems
Many projects have aimed to bridge the gap of distance in collaborative music by connecting remote players in a shared virtual space. Until recently, the latency of transferring high volumes of data over the Internet has influenced these systems' designs [1]. Several groups have focused on creating sound-only environments. TransMIDI [4] and the piano master classes of Young and Fujinaga [20] employed MIDI data instead of audio. Transjam [2] enabled musical applications that did not require playing "in-time".

Attempts at remote musical collaboration with traditional instruments have included video as well audio. Zimmermann's Distributed Immersive Performance project [21], designed to investigate distance playing of classical piano duos, showed over the shoulder video of the remote

TEI'11, January 22–26, 2011, Funchal, Portugal.

partner on screens in front of the players. The MusicPath system [13] for remote piano learning displayed an over the shoulder view of the student on a projection screen in front the teacher. Both Distributed Immersive Performance and MusicPath displayed the body-level but not hand-level gestures of the performer. For Distributed Immersive Performance, expressive body gestures helped players synchronize musically. Gestures conveyed in MusicPath allowed a teacher to comment on the full-body elements of technique (such how to use shoulders and upper arm) useful for more advanced students.

The Distributed Musical Rehearsals project [8] installed teleconferencing environments in studios incorporating high definition video and 3d surround sound to create the impression that the musicians in Geneva and the conductor in Bonn were rehearsing in the same room. Both the conductor and the musicians' full body-gestures were visible to the other side.

Interfaces for remote music collaboration have largely been disembodied. Those that did communicate gesture have not explored spatial arrangements to tightly integrate the presence of the remote collaborator into physical space. They have focused on body-level gestures and not the detailed gestures to play specific instruments.

Remote Collaborative Workspaces

Interfaces for telepresence and shared workspaces often employed optical metaphors to portray the body of a remote collaborator in a meaningful manner. VideoPlace [9], DoubleDigital Desk [18], VideoWhiteboard [16], and Shadow Communications [10] used shadows or silhouettes to present remote parties. Interfaces like HyperMirror [12] used the metaphor of a mirror to display all remote parties in a common virtual space.

Remote collaborative workspaces have borrowed interpersonal spatial relationships from collocated interactions to make sense of the connection between disparate locations. Some interfaces, such as TeamWorkStation [6], VideoDraw [15], and Double DigitalDesk presented the shared space as if the collaborators were working side by side, looking over the same area. Others, like as ClearBoard [5] and VideoWhiteboard, presented the shared space as if the collaborators were working across from each other. Both simulated common workspace configurations in collocated collaboration.

Different interfaces showed varying degrees of a remote collaborator's body, depending on the task and space for which the systems were designed. TeamWorkStation, VideoDraw, and Double DigitalDesk focused on actions over a shared workspace and only showed the hands and forearm of a remote collaborator. Interfaces like ClearBoard and HyperMirror, which tried to simulate face to face communication showed the entire upper body of the collaborator. Some interfaces, like VideoPlace and Shadow Communications tried to convey an abstract sense of full body presence by displaying life-sized silhouettes.

Unlike interfaces for remote music collaboration, remote collaborative workspace projects have developed a nuanced vocabulary to communicate the gesture of remote partners using optical metaphors of shadows and mirrors and spatial metaphors of face to face and side by side discourse. Whether the interface supported sharing of hand, arm, or full-body gesture depended on the task.

Music Learning Interfaces

Learning to play a musical instrument involves not only gaining proficiency in playing the correct notes but also developing expressivity on the instrument. Several commercial piano keyboards include built-in interfaces for note learning. Yamaha [19] and Casio [3] both manufacture keyboards with keys that light up from underneath, and the MOOG Piano Bar [11] uses LED's in front of the keys to indicate the notes of a piece. The Yamaha Disklavier actuates the keys themselves. All of these systems cue what keys to play but do not show any relationship between keys and hand gestures. MusicPath, which displays the body-level gestures of a remote student, obscures much hand-level gestures due to the angle of its video.

Learning interfaces for instruments with more continuous performance gestures focus on fine-tuning these bodily movements. A notable example is i-Maestro [14], which uses motion capture and playback to help violinists visualize and reflect on their playing.

DESIGN

In music, a *fugue* is a contrapuntal composition in two or more voices; a *mirror fugue* is a set of two fugues where each is the mirror image of the other. We designed MirrorFugue to enable musicians from separate spaces to play together through a metaphorical mirror space that transmits gestures associated with making the music.

We chose the piano as the basis of our interfaces because of its popularity among musicians and because of the clear relationship between a performer's hand gestures and notes played. Playing the piano well involves not only hand movements but also movements of the wrist, arms, shoulders, and even feet. We focus on remote lesson interfaces for beginners, who are most concerned with learning how to use the hands.

We designed three remote lesson interfaces: Shadow, Reflection, and Organ. We first outline the design space and then describe the three interfaces.

Design Space

We considered three factors borrowed from remote collaborate workspaces when designing our systems: interpersonal space, placement of remote space, and orientation of remote space.

Shadow

Interpersonal Space	Side by Side	Face to Face
Placement of Remote Space	Overlay	Aligned and Offset
Orientation of Remote Space	90 Degrees	180 Degrees

Reflection

Interpersonal Space	Side by Side	Face to Face
Placement of Remote Space	Overlay	Aligned and Offset
Orientation of Remote Space	90 Degrees	180 Degrees

Organ

Interpersonal Space	Side by Side	Face to Face
Placement of Remote Space	Overlay	Aligned and Offset
Orientation of Remote Space	90 Degrees	180 Degrees

Table 1: Comparison of design choices

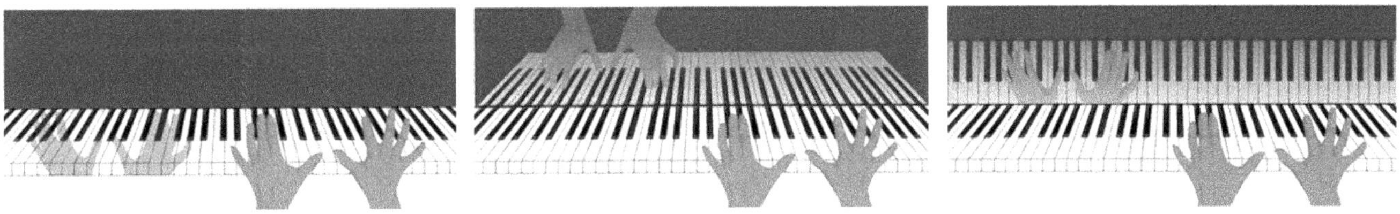

Figure 2: The Shadow, Reflection, and Organ configurations

Interpersonal Space

Two remote users can be presented as if working side by side (like TeamWorkStation) or working face to face (like ClearBoard).

Placement of Remote Space

The remote workspace can be overlayed directly on the physical workspace (like Double DigitalDesk) or located in a separate space. When located in a separate space, the remote workspace can be scaled and aligned or not spatially related at all to the physical workspace (like MusicPath).

Orientation of Remote Space

A scaled and aligned remote space can be oriented vertically or horizontally, placed at 90 degrees or 180 degrees to the physical workspace.

Interface Configurations

Shadow

Like Double DigitalDesk, this system uses shadows of hands projected directly onto the keyboard to convey the partner's presence. In our implementation, we project a video of the partner's hands instead of a strict silhouette.

The orientation of the projected video gives the impression that the remote partner is sitting next to the user. The projected keyboard from the remote video lines up exactly with the physical keyboard, and users can tell from the projected video which keys on the partner's side are pressed down. While this interface shows the remote partner's hands directly at the locus of interaction, it has the disadvantage that the shadow is not distinguishable when the two players' hands are at corresponding locations on the keyboard

Reflection

This system is inspired by the reflective surface on a lacquered piano where the keyboard and a player's hands are mirrored. Instead of showing the actual reflection of the present instrument, this system displays the reflection of the remote partner's hands. We prototyped Reflection by building a vertical back-projection surface directly in front of the keys onto which we projected the mirrored top-down video of another keyboard, distorting the image to simulate the perspective as seen from the player's point of view and making sure to line up the reflected keys with the physical keys. The implied interpersonal space is that of two players sitting across from each other. The remote keyboard is aligned and offset and is perceived to be displayed at 180 degrees in relation to the physical keyboard. In actuality, the remote keyboard is displayed on a vertical surface

Organ

Like Reflection, this configuration also uses the vertical display surface in front of the keys. Unlike Reflection, it displays an unaltered top-down image of the remote keyboard, with the bottom of the keys in the projection lined up with the physical keys. Like Shadow, the orientation of the projected video gives the impression that the remote partner is sitting next to the user. We call this configuration Organ because the position of the projected and physical keyboards is reminiscent of the two offset keyboards on an organ. The remote keyboard is shown at 90 degrees to the physical for better visibility to the player.

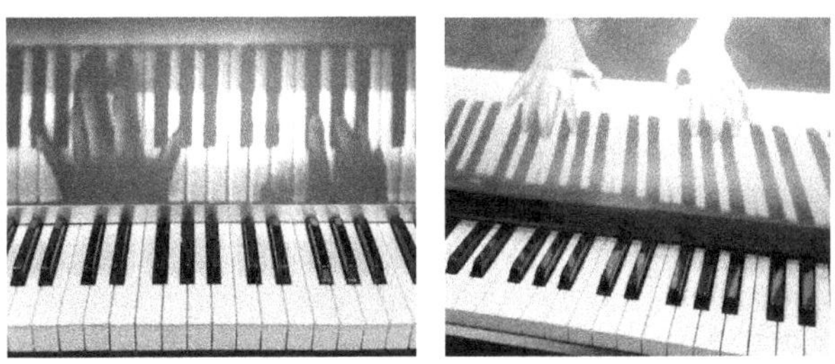

Figure 3: Prototypes of Organ and Reflection modes

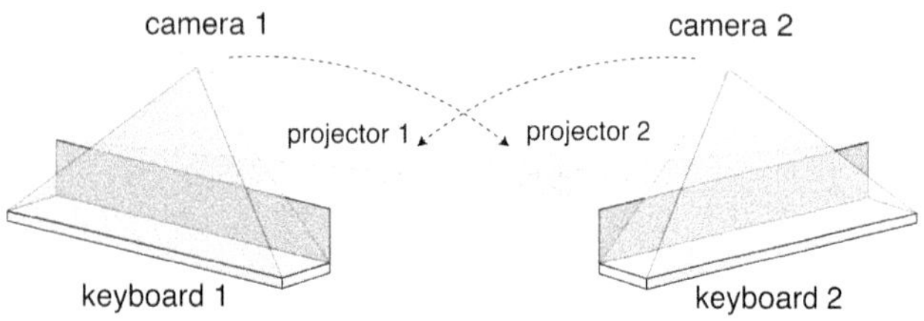

Figure 4: System Diagram

IMPLEMENTATION

We prototyped all three configurations with MIDI keyboards, wide-angle cameras, and projectors, using the MAX/MSP/Jitter platform to manage video and sound. We tested the remote communication by transferring 640x480 video at 30 frame per second over gigabit ethernet between two locations in the same building and were able to do so without noticible latency.

For our user studies, we placed two piano keyboards in the same room arranged to simulate a remote situation where two people cannot see each other but can hear each other and what is being played.

If our interfaces were deployed in actual remote locations, latency of video transfer over the Internet should not be a problem as long as the video is synced with the sound because student and teacher generally take turns playing during a lesson.

USER STUDIES

We conducted a pilot study to determine whether seeing the hands of a remote pianist helps musicians think about music, to identify the pros and cons of each configuration, and to establish which, if any, stands out over the others. We then conducted an informal user study to measure the effectiveness of the winning system from the pilot study against two other systems in the context of remote learning for novices.

Pilot Study

Method

Five amateur pianists (4 men, 1 woman, aged 20-35) participated in our initial study. The skill levels of these users ranged from beginner to advanced, with a variety of backgrounds from completely self-taught to trained in the classical and jazz styles. For this study, we presented the participants with a keyboard in each of our three configurations in random order. The investigator (first author of this paper), who is an advanced level amateur pianist, was situated at the corresponding keyboard, which was not displaying the hands of the study participant. For each configuration, the investigator played some chord progressions for five minutes and asked the user to improvise a melody over the chords. After all three improvisation sessions, the investigator debriefed with each participant in an informal interview.

Results

All but one of the users indicated that seeing the partner's hands helped them with "listening and synthesizing sound" and to "better anticipate what is coming next by seeing where the hands are heading". The one user who disagreed, an advanced pianist trained in classical and jazz, indicated that for him and other advanced musicians, improvising together involves a highly trained ear and does not require the extra help of seeing hands. These results seem to suggest that seeing a partner's hands could help beginner and intermediate pianists who are learning to play together with others.

Of the three setups, the Organ configuration was most preferred among almost all participants. All of the participants said that the Organ interface allowed them to clearly see what the remote partner is playing and that the location of the image is not distracting. Some participants remarked that the implied spatial arrangement "feels almost like having someone sitting next to you playing with you", which made having the displayed video feel "non-invasive". Because of the implied spatial arrangement, participants expressed that the system does not require the addition of eye contact to make sense because "when someone is sitting next to you playing, you don't often look at them". All the participants agreed that the Organ setup is best for remote learning ("because the student can see and follow exactly what the teacher is doing") and for watching a recording ("because it's in the same space as the keyboard but you can also easily join in").

All except for one user (self-taught classical pianist) liked Shadow the least, pointing out that players must be playing at least an octave apart for one's hands to not obscure the shadow hands. Some called the setup "distracting and chaotic". The one user who preferred Shadow (self-taught classical pianist) expressed that he liked seeing the remote partner's hands in the same place as his own.

Several users found the Reflection interface confusing, citing the "extra cognitive load of having to flip the image in one's head to make sense of it". One user (intermediate classically trained pianist) mentioned that the Reflection interface almost begs for more of the partner's body to be shown "to make sense of the spatial configuration of someone sitting across from you".

LEARNING STUDY

We designed an informal study to evaluate the Organ interface in the context of remote learning for novices. We chose this scenario because we envision that our system can be especially beneficial for potential students of piano who do not have regular access to a teacher and those who start learning piano through watching recordings. We asked the following research quetions:

- Is seeing the hands of an instructor more helpful than seeing abstract indicators of notes for novice students learning a piece?

- Is having visual aid at the locus of interaction of the piano keyboard preferable to visual aid on a separate screen?

Method

To answer these questions, we recruited 10 absolute novices in piano (7 men, 3 women, aged 19-33) and taught them three simple melodic sequences on Organ and two other interfaces, each designed to answer one of our questions. One involved projecting a small colored dot in front of the key corresponding to one played at a second keyboard. Similar to the Moog Piano Bar, which includes an LED in front of every key to help pianists visualize a piece, this setup indicates what is being played using abstract symbols. The other interface displays the same image as the one shown in Organ on a 24-inch monitor situated behind the keyboard where it is easily glance-able by the user. This simulates the configuration of when users try to learn a new piano piece by watching a video of a performance—where the visual aid is not spatially related to the piano keyboard.

We asked each user to first try to play something on the keyboard, to verify that they are indeed absolute beginners, and then to learn a randomly selected melody ("Twinkle Twinkle Little Star", "Row, Row, Row Your Boat", "Frère Jacques", or "I'm a Little Teapot") on each of the interfaces selected in random order. For each song, we began by having the instructor play the melody once through and then taught the piece in 3-5 note segments until the student can play the entire piece once without mistakes. All of the melodies contained between 16-21 notes, and repeats were eliminated from those whose original versions contained them. At the end of the study, we asked participants what they thought of each interface and to rank them by usefulness. We also videotaped each learning session to determine how long it took for users to learn each melody.

Qualitative Results

Most users found Organ the most helpful in learning (7 out of the 10 ranked it first, 1 ranked it a close second). Users said that Organ mode was "very easy to follow", "very direct", and "easy to get the hand position and finger use correct". One user described how on Organ, he noticed the teacher using different fingering from his for a part he was having trouble with and changed the fingering to the teacher's, which made playing much easier. Other users described how Organ mode was "good at allowing students to anticipate the next position of the teacher's hand".

	Screen	Dots	Organ
First	1	2	7
Second	4	5	1
Third	5	3	2

Table 2: Rankings of learning interfaces among users

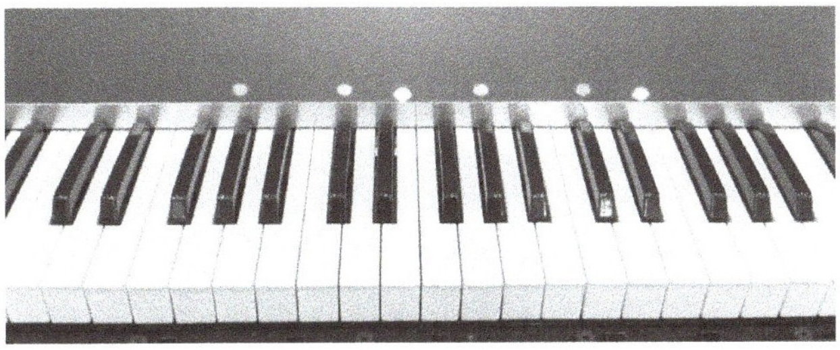

Figure 5: Dots indicating what keys are pressed at the corresponding keyboard

Two users found the abstract Dots the easiest to learn from because of the "very little visual processing involved" and because it "puts music into easy to understand patterns". However, one of these users suggested that the Dots "may be the easiest for following notes but may not be so good for the long term because it does not teach correct hand usage".

Only one user preferred the Screen setup because she felt like she learned the fastest on it. However, this user actualy took three more minutes (7 minutes 9 seconds) to learn the melody using Screen than on the other two interfaces (Dots: 4 minutes 54 seconds, Organ: 4 minutes 41 seconds).

5 out of 10 users ranked Screen as last place because of the "lack of reference frame between the image and physical keyboard" so that "it was difficult to tell where the teacher's hand was". "The difference of scale and the lack of correlation between the image and the physical" also contributed to the "increased visual processing load", making it the most difficult to learn from.

Dots was the worst for 3 users because "it made individual notes more individual" and "made learning into a game of follow the dots", which "made it difficult to remember sequences". Some users also felt that while the dots were the easiest for determining what notes the teacher was playing, "dots detached the lesson from actual musicality".

Two users found it "difficult to determine which keys were being pressed" in Organ mode and listed it as least favorite. These two users both found it easier to tell which keys were pressed in Screen mode than Organ mode even though both displayed the same image, suggesting that their difficulties could be attributed to the fact that the resolution of the video was perhaps too low to be projected on such a large surface. In fact, one of the user who preferred the Organ setup suggested that we should "increase the resolution of the video so that the projection in Organ mode is more clear".

Quantitative

Since we conducted an informal study, our quantitative results are not statistically significant but do suggest interesting hypotheses that can be tested in future studies. On average, users took about 1 minute 30 seconds longer to learn a melody using Screen mode than both Dots and Organ mode, which had very close average learning times. Participants learned melodies with better hand and finger

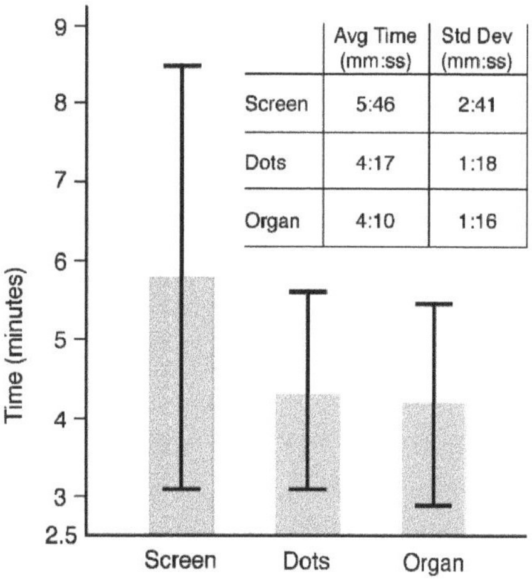

Table 3: Users took about 1 minute 30 seconds longer when learning melodies on Screen mode compared to both Dots and Organ modes.

usage for both Screen mode and Organ mode over Dots mode. Using both Screen and Organ mode, all participants played with correct hand position, and all but one (for Organ mode) and two (for Screen mode) employed correct finger usage. Using Dots mode, seven users played with only one or two fingers in Dots mode, two used the whole hand but made up very awkward finger crossings, and one asked the instructor what fingers to use for each key.

DISCUSSION

Study Reflections

Through the pilot study, we discovered that users seem to prefer the Organ configuration (side-to-side interpersonal space, aligned and offset image displayed at 90 degrees). In the learning study, we verified that displaying video of hands playing the piano at the locus of interaction of the keyboard seem to be the most helpful for novices learning from a non-physically present teacher.

Despite displaying hand gestures of the teacher, Screen mode seemed to be the most confusing for students while learning melodies. The difficulty of Screen mode can be attributed to two factors: the lack of relationship and the difference in scale between the physical and remote spaces. While the difference in scale likely contributed to the problem, most of the users commented on the lack of reference frame in Screen mode, which suggests that having no alignment between the two keyboards made it difficult for students to figure out where to play.

While Dot and Organ had almost the same average learning time, users learned to play with better technique on Organ when the performance gestures of the teacher were clearly visible. Almost all of the students used only one or two fingers to play in Dots mode. In contrast, almost all of the students used all the correct fingering when using Organ. Organ also has the advantage that students can anticipate when the teacher's hand is moving to another position by watching the motions.

While Organ mode was necessary for users to maintain correct hand and finger usage, Dots had the advantage that it involved the least amount of visual processing for users to determine what note to play. The fact that, on average, users took almost exactly the same amount of time to learn melodies on Dots mode and Organ mode could suggest that it took longer for them to process what notes they are supposed to play in Organ mode. On the other hand, users could figure out instantly what notes to play in Dot mode but forget them more easily when dots are not present.

For teaching novices on remote learning interfaces, it seems to be important to show both what notes to play and the gestures associated with playing them.

SCENARIOS

Our evaluations focused on synchronous playing by two remote users. In the interviews following the pilot study, we hinted at other scenarios our systems can be used for. We discuss these in more detail.

The Shadow, Reflection, and Organ systems could be beneficial when used in asynchronous playing scenarios. In this case, asynchronous playing involves a user playing with a pre-recorded sound and video of hands. Asynchronous scenarios can be separated into one-user and two-user modes. A single users can record oneself as part of practice. Users can record one hand of a difficult piece and play the other hand along with the first hand to get a sense of what the whole piece sounds like. They can also record a section of a piece, such as a particular chord progression or rhythmic sequence, play it on loop on our device, and play along with the recording to practice improvisation and coordination. When more than one user is involved, one user can record a piece or a segment of a piece for another user, who can then listen and watch the recording, learn to play using it, or play along with it.

Although all of these usage cases are currently possible using a sound-only recorder, displaying hands at the keyboard along with playing sound can be beneficial for two reasons. First, as found in our evaluations, watching hands play as a supplement to hearing music can help users process and learn music better. Second, being able to see and hear a composite piece can be more fun for users and encourage them to play more.

Our systems can also be useful for collocated applications, such as rehearsals, improvisational jam sessions, and group lessons. In group rehearsals and jam sessions, our systems can give novice users a head start in learning to play with others by providing them with an extra means of coordination and anticipation with others. In group lessons, where one teacher teaches a room of several students each on their own keyboard, our systems can serve as a means to help the teacher better monitor the playing of each student.

Our designs, especially Mirror and Organ modes, can also support usage cases with more than two users displayed at a time in the form of semi-transparent overlays, a technique pioneered by interfaces such as TeamWorkStation. This way, users can visualize multiple people playing in the same space and can also play along with the group.

FUTURE WORK

In the future, we plan to investigate how our configurations perform in more scenarios, to incorporate other sensory modes in interfaces for remote piano learning, and to design interfaces that share gestures of more than just the hands.

To continue evaluation of our system, we would like to test the effectiveness of combining Dots mode with Organ mode in a learning scenario. In addition, we plan to design studies to explore how our configurations can help with single user practicing and with lessons for more advanced pianists.

As advanced piano technique involves gestures of the wrists, arms, shoulders, and feet, we plan on designing remote communication interfaces that make visible gestures of more of the body. We are also interested in exploring ways to integrate eye contact for coordination of remote playing.

CONCLUSION

We designed and prototyped three interface configurations to display to-scale hand-level perforance gestures of piano playing at the locus of interaction of the piano keyboard, which we collectively call MirrorFugue. The three spatial metaphors—Shadow, Reflection, and Organ—were inspired by research in collaborative workspaces. We compared our designs in a pilot study and concluded that the Organ configuration was the most helpful for users to better process music when playing. Our results from a second user study seem to verify that showing hands at the keyboard can help novices learn to play simple melodies more quickly and more effectively. Finally, we discussed several different scenarios for which our designs can be used that we plan to evaluate in the future.

ACKNOWLEDGMENTS

We are grateful for the support of the Tangible Media Group and the Things that Think Consortium at the MIT Media Lab. Thanks especially to Leonardo Bonanni and Cati Vaucelle for their invaluable advice. We would like to extend a special thanks to Avid for its general donations that made this project possible.

REFERENCES

1. Barbosa A. 2003. Displaced soundscapes: a survey of network systems for music and sonic-art creation. *Leonardo Music Journal*, Volume 13, Issue 1, 53-59.
2. Burk, P. L. 2000. Jammin' on the web: a new client/server architecture for multi-user performance. *Proceedings of the 2000 International Computer Music Conference*. San Francisco, California: International Computer Music Association, 117-120.
3. Casio. http://www.casio.com/
4. Gang, D., Chockler, G. V., Anker, T., and Kremer, A. 1997. TransMIDI: a system for midi sessions over the network using transis. In *Proceedings of the 1999 International Computer Music Conference*. San Francisco, California: International Computer Music Association, 283-286.
5. Ishii, H. and Kobayashi, M. 1992. ClearBoard: a seamless medium for shared drawing and conversation with eye contact. In *Proceedings of the SIGCHI Conference on Human Factors in Computing Systems* (Monterey CA, May 1992). P. Bauersfeld, J. Bennett, and G. Lynch, Eds. CHI '92. ACM, New York, NY, 525-532.
6. Ishii, H. 1990. TeamWorkStation: towards a seamless shared workspace. In *Proceedings of the 1990 ACM Conference on Computer-Supported Cooperative Work* (Los Angeles CA, October 1990). CSCW '90. ACM, New York, NY, 13-26.
7. Klemmer, S. R., Hartmann, B., and Takayama, L. 2006. How bodies matter: five themes for interaction design. In *Proceedings of the 6th Conference on Designing interactive Systems* (University Park PA, June 2006). DIS '06. ACM, New York, NY, 140-149.
8. Konstantas, D. 1997. Distributed musical rehearsal. In *Proceedings of the 1997 International Computer Music Conference*. San Francisco, California: International Computer Music Association, 279-282.
9. Krueger, M. W., Gionfriddo, T., and Hinrichsen, K. 1985. VIDEOPLACE—an artificial reality. In *Proceedings of the SIGCHI Conference on Human Factors in Computing Systems* (San Francisco, CA). CHI '85. ACM, New York, NY, 35-40.
10. Miwa, Y. and Ishibiki, C. 2004. Shadow communication: system for embodied interaction with remote partners. In *Proceedings of the 2004 ACM Conference on Computer Supported Cooperative Work* (Chicago IL, November 2004). CSCW '04. ACM, New York, NY, 467-476.
11. Moog Piano Bar. http://www.moogmusic.com/.
12. Morikawa, O. and Maesako, T. 1997. HyperMirror: a video-mediated communication system. In *CHI '97 Extended Abstracts on Human Factors in Computing Systems: Looking To the Future* (Atlanta GA, March 1997). CHI '97. ACM, New York, NY, 317-318.
13. MusicPath: Networking People and Music. http://musicpath.acadiau.ca/.
14. Ng, K. 2008. Interactive feedbacks with visualisation and sonification for technology-enhanced learning for music performance. In *Proceedings of the 26th Annual ACM international Conference on Design of*

Communication (Lisbon, Portugal, September 22 - 24, 2008). SIGDOC '08. ACM, New York, NY, 281-282.

15. Tang, J. C. and Minneman, S. L. 1990. VideoDraw: a video interface for collaborative drawing. In *Proceedings of the SIGCHI Conference on Human Factors in Computing Systems: Empowering People* (Seattle WA, April 1990). J. C. Chew and J. Whiteside, Eds. CHI '90. ACM, New York, NY, 313-320.

16. Tang, J. C. and Minneman, S. 1991. VideoWhiteboard: video shadows to support remote collaboration. In *Proceedings of the SIGCHI Conference on Human Factors in Computing Systems: Reaching Through Technology* (New Orleans LA, April 1991). S. P. Robertson, G. M. Olson, and J. S. Olson, Eds. CHI '91. ACM, New York, NY, 315-322.

17. Wanderly, M. 2001. Performer-instrument interaction: applications to gestural control of sound synthesis. PhD Thesis, University Paris VI.

18. Wellner, P. and Newman, W. 1992. A desk supporting computer-based interaction with paper documents. In *Proceedings CHI 92 Conference,* 587-592.

19. Yamaha. http://music.yamaha.com/.

20. Young, J. and Fujinaga, I. 1999. Piano master classes via the Internet. *In Proceedings of the 1999 International Computer Music Conference*. San Francisco, California: International Computer Music Association, pp. 135-137.

21. Zimmermann, R., Chew, E., Ay, S. A., and Pawar, M. 2008. Distributed musical performances: Architecture and stream management. *ACM Trans. Multimedia Comput. Commun. Appl.* 4, 2 (May. 2008), 1-23.

Multisensor Broadband High Dynamic Range Sensing... for a Highly Expressive Step-based Musical Instrument

Steve Mann, Ryan Janzen, Tom Hobson
University of Toronto*
Department of Electrical and Computer Engineering
email: hydraulophone at gmail dot com

ABSTRACT

We propose the use of multiple sensors of different sensitivity that simultaneously sense the same signal. Outputs of these sensors are then combined in a way that allows the simultaneous sensing of large-signal and small-signal phenomena. This sensing methodology is applied to the andantephone, a musical instrument that allows a player to physically step through the notes of a song as if they were walking along the song's timeline. When you stop walking the music stops. If you walk faster the music plays faster. A new, more expressive design of andantephone was created using a wideband complementary set of geophones to detect seismic waves transmitted from human footsteps. Each tile in the andantephone has one or more high-frequency piezoelectric geophones that respond to small-signals, as well as one or more low-frequency carbon geophones that respond to large-signals. These sensors are subsequently connected to a real-time frequency-shifting system that shifts each geophone's output to the correct musical pitch or chord for a particular note in a song. The proposed HDR sensing principle may be applied to many different sensing scenarios.

Author Keywords

High Dynamic Range (HDR), dynamage range, high spectral range, large bandwidth interface, ORGANic User Interface, haptics, step-based interaction, footsteps, musical sculpture, music education, comparametric equations

ACM Classification Keywords

H.5.2 User Interfaces; H.5.5 Sound and Music Computing

General Terms

Design, Experimentation, Human Factors, Measurement, Theory

*We thank Sofsurfaces and London Mat for providing materials for this project.

TEI'11, January 22–26, 2011, Funchal, Portugal.

INTRODUCTION

This paper presents two new results: (1) a High Dynamic Range (HDR) sensor for sensing touch, vibration, pressure, force, sound, or seismic waves; and (2) the use of HDR sensing in sensing vibrations in solid matter with a specific application to a new musical instrument called the andantephone.

HDR sensing

Many situations arise in physics, engineering, the natural sciences, and the arts, in which it is desirable to sense, measure, or quantify a natural physical quantity that has a very large dynamic range. Human sensory perception often covers a tremendous dynamic range, whereas sensing, measurement, analysis, and recording apparatus often has limited dynamic range.

In image processing, previous work has dealt with situations in which a sensor has much greater possible dynamic range than the capture or recording media [4][7]. For example, a camera, when taken together with its shutter mechanism, forms a sensor that can span a dynamic range in the millions, whereas if we consider the image plane to be the sensed medium (exposures), the CCD array itself is of limited dymamic range. See Fig. 1. This work is based on a mathematical framework called Comparametric Equations [2].

In the foregoing, it is assumed that some of the sensors may saturate and thus *temporarily* produce unfaithful readings or recordings, but that this unfaithfulness is only temporary.

The dynamic range is the range between weakest and strongest signal that can be sensed faithfully. It is useful to define something called the "**dynamage range**", the range between the weakest signal that can be sensed faithfully, and the strongest signal that will not permanently damage the sensor.

In this paper assume that we are operating somewhere between the dynamic range and the dynamage range.

Andantephone

The application domain we chose for our HDR sensing is a newly invented musical instrument called the andantephone. This instrument presents unique dynamic range challenges because it is played by jumping or stomping on it, or by very lightly brushing the foot or skin or socks against the sensor tiles. Thus it has to sense very subtle light touches as well as kicking, stomping, and sometimes being driven over by a car, bus, or heavy truck.

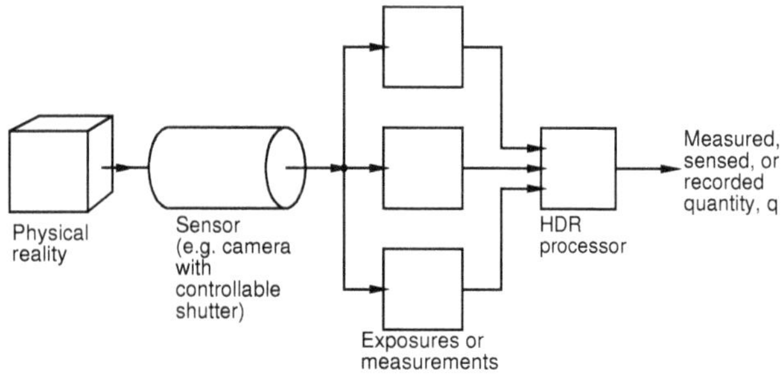

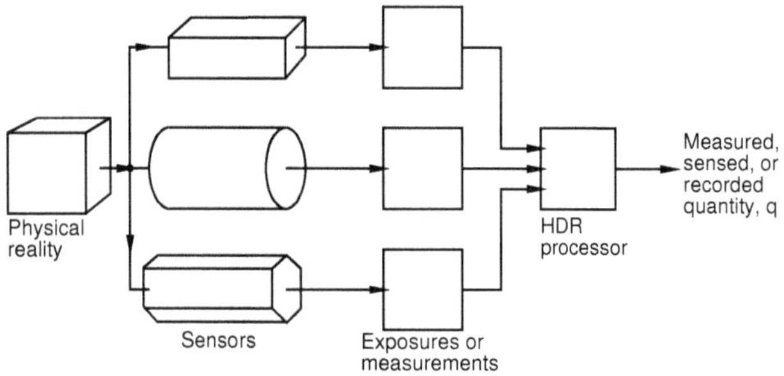

Figure 1. Topmost: Typical HDR sensing captures a plurality of differently sensitive readings, such as, for example, three different exposures, from the same sensing device. These exposures are then combined to produce a single audio, video, or other multimedia file or measurement or recording, having an extended dynamic range. Bottommost: In this paper we propose the use of a plurality of vastly different sensors each having different sensitivity. These might, for example, comprise a carbon microphone (e.g. FSR), a dynamic microphone, and a contact microphone (e.g. geophone), each of which has a different sensitivity to the physical reality being sensed.

The andantephone is a recently-invented musical instrument, played by simply walking on it [3]. A piece of music is played by walking along a series of tiles, which step through chords and melody of a song. A player can physically step through the notes of a song as if they were walking along the song's timeline.

Andante, in musical terminology, refers to a tempo that is "at a walking pace". Combining the Italian "andante" with the Greek word "phone" (meaning "sound", a commonly used suffix for musical instruments), results in "andantephone".

With an andantephone, the melodic line fluidly follows the rhythm paced out by the player. The player's footsteps continuously set the tempo as they speed up and slow down.

Previous andantephones (without any HDR or wide-spectrum capabilities) were featured in contemporary music compositions and performances, using layering of chords based on real-time matrix multiplication between a composition matrix and a vector of tile signals [1].

An andantephone is also suited to the demonstration of the simplest principles of music — basic rhythm, tempo, and dynamics — as it transforms a natural physical motion, walking, into a musical act. It is useful as both a educational and compositional instrument.

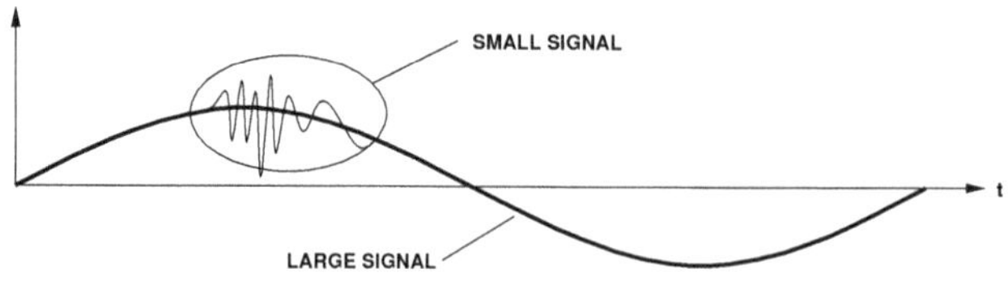

Figure 2. A low-amplitude, high-frequency *small-signal* superimposed on a high-amplitude, low-frequency *large-signal.*

Other recent work has involved a haptic floor surface [6]. In some sense, the andantephone may be regarded as an ORGANic user interface [5].

WIDE SPECTRUM SENSING

The wide spectrum andantephone incorporates two complementary breeds of sensors that both measure the same or similar physical signal, to provide dynamic expression. We combine a force-sensing resistor with a piezoelectric transducer as follows:

- For low frequencies and especially DC (0 Hz), force-sensitive resistors (FSRs) are attached to the bottom of rubber playground safety tiles. These sensors are capable of providing information about large, gradual changes in pressure, as well as capturing constant pressure (DC). This is useful for producing an organ-like playing experience where sounds can be manipulated fluidly and sustained for as long as desired.
- For high frequencies, piezoelectric transducers are used. These sense sudden changes in pressure. They are used to express quick, subtle dynamics such as vibrato. Additionally, due to their brief, finite response time, they allow for the creation of guitar or piano-like sounds that are characterized by a rapidly decaying envelope. Players need only tap a tile briefly to excite the piezoelectric sensors connected to it.

The result is an instrument that has the quick attack of a piano or guitar, combined with the ability to sustain notes like a violin or piano. For example, to play a sustained, dynamic note with vibrato and volume modulation, players can stand on a tile and shift their weight.

The concept of separating small-signal analysis and large-signal analysis is well-known in electrical engineering. For example, in the design of transistor circuits, we often separately analyze the nonlinear effects of DC bias voltages, and small AC signals that operate in an approximately linear regime. The smaller fluctuating AC signals hover around the DC operating point, becoming amplified in an approximately linear way.

What we present in this paper is the reverse of this concept, i.e. we use separate sensors to measure essentially the same signal (in our case a seismic wave, sound traveling through solid matter, or the like) in different ways.

Figure 3. The progression of the sensor layout on a single andantephone tile. A rubber tile, shown leftmost, was fitted with two carbon sensors and one piezo sensor. The current prototype (rightmost) has four force-sensing resistors, and one piezo sensor as illustrated in Fig. 4.

Figure 4. Mapping of sensors to underside of tile. The blue squares represents FSRs and the green circle a piezoelectric geophone.

Our general philosophy of HDR sensing, in its most general form, allows for a plurality of transducers, each processed using a plurality of processing channels. Whereas we might typically process the AC transducer at higher gain for small signal analysis, and the DC transducer output at lower gain for large-signal analysis, we can, more generally, if desired, process each transducer through various processing channels.

The following table shows four possible combinations of signal processing channels (most commonly used channels indicated by a check mark):

	Small signal	Large signal
AC	Small AC ✓	Large AC
DC	Small DC	Large DC ✓

In our andantephone, the large-signal DC operating point is determined by the player's overall mass and slowly varying footstep action. The small-signal AC information comes from the player's smaller, more nuanced movements.

Used in combination, these two types of sensor significantly increase the andantephone's spectral range such that it extends right down to and including zero frequency, and up to and including ultrasonic frequencies. Such broadband sensory information is then mapped to audible frequencies in a creative way, giving rise to what we call a "hyperacoustic instrument".

In doing so, the hyperacoustic instrument provides players, performers, and learners with additional expressivity.

AC processing was done in real-time by a bandpass filter. It was implemented on an ARM Cortex M3 processor to provide quick, sharp response, like a piano or guitar. The low-frequency (DC) output of each FSR was processed by a simple frequency shifter implemented using an embedded microcontroller.

Sensor Arrangement

Fig. 3 shows one of our prototypes of the HDR sensing tile.

In this specific embodiment, there are four FSRs and one piezoelectric transducer per tile (Fig. 4). The FSRs are positioned at the vertices of a square surrounding the centre of the tile and the piezoelectric sensor at the very centre, equidistant from the corners. We initially tried using each sensor as a separate pixel on the tile, but it was decided that having an equal effect across the tile surface was sufficient in favour of using each separate tile as one pixel. Indeed, to further attach sensors to every support post in one tile, 64 inputs are required of the frequency shifter. Instead, the output of all of the sensors are combined into one pixel, and can thus achieve a high dynamic and spectral range of expression on a one note per tile basis. This implementation is in keeping with the simple, step-based nature of the andantephone. Note that there is an implicit tradeoff between spatial resolution and tonal resolution (i.e. spatial domain and dynamic domain) that we have chosen to operate to the advantage of dynamic range.

Four FSRs connected in parallel were used in order to obtain a very simple form of signal-averaging, as one FSR on its own tends to quickly saturate and thus has limited dynamic range. Only one high-frequency piezoelectric sensor was necessary for each tile. The tiles, while bouncy, are stiff enough to indicate that high frequencies propagate more thoroughly than low frequencies. With this in mind and knowing that the piezoelectric sensor is attached directly to the underside of the tile (unlike the FSRs, which lie under the support posts), we determined that a single high-frequency transducer was sufficient, whereas, due to spatial variation in pressure (e.g. if a person stands on one side or the other) we needed four FSRs.

Furthermore, one can employ an understanding of seismic waves to justify this conclusion. High frequency waves produced from tapping or rapidly vibrating the surface of the tile can be propagated by surface waves such as Rayleigh waves. As these waves are more or less constrained to the surface of their medium, these waves experience less attenuation than those confined to the interior (which seismologists would call P-waves). As a result, these high-frequency waves can travel farther along the surface of the tile. On the other hand, compressional P-waves in this instance are the low frequency deflections of the tile caused by the nearly constant — or very gradual — application of a player's weight. These compressional disturbances cannot distribute as far across the tile surface.

As a result, we empirically found that, in order to sufficiently pick up low-frequency waves from the tile, four low-frequency transducers were needed, while only one high-frequency transducer at the centre of the tile was sufficient.

RUBBER TILES AS EXPRESSIVE SURFACES

In the implementation presented, the andantephone is made up of a series of rubber playground tiles laid out on the ground or floor and individually fastened to a set of complementary (large and small signal) geophonic sensors. The tiles themselves are specifically manufactured for deployment in playgrounds as shock-absorbent safety flooring. As a result, they are bouncy, which provides a pleasant and playful physical response. The robust, flexible material of the tiles allows players to shift and move their weight expressively to create various types of attacks, vibrato, etc..

TILE INSTALLATION & CONFIGURATION

Unlike previous implementations, this andantephone has been built into playground safety tiles, and realizing the inherently child-friendly nature of andantephones in general, it makes sense that it would be integrated into a playground environment. Playgrounds are communal spaces in which children can interact with the andantephone and from it learn to understand and enjoy playing music and controlling sound. The tiles themselves are made to absorb impact and so have a fair amount of bounce to them, adding a further aspect of play to the instrument's operation.

As well, the tiles are physically separate from one another, and each is connected to a remote central device. This individuality allows them to be physically rearranged into a variety of patterns. Simple symmetrical patterns lend themselves well to playing and understanding simple musical concepts. For instance, to play a song in 4/4 time, andantephone tiles could be set up in a square with a side length of four tiles (Fig. 5). This would demonstrate interactively the idea of dividing music into measures and beats, not to mention a general high-level conception of fractions and rational numbers. More whimsical arrangements, like a meandering pathway, are also possible.

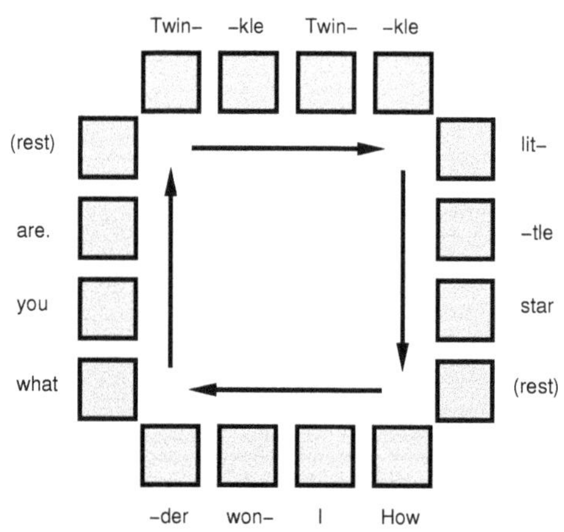

Figure 5. A typical arrangement for a simple song in 4/4 time. 16 sensors positioned in a square, one measure per side. *Twinkle, Twinkle, Little Star*, for example, can be mapped to this.

CONCLUSIONS

A high-dynamic range (HDR) sensing system was proposed using multiple sensors of differing sensitivity to measure the same quantity. It can be used for a variety of modalities including audio and video, and was used in this work to process geophonic vibrations from footsteps, in an andantephone. A new, more expressive design of andantephone was created, using a wideband complementary set of geophones to detect seismic waves transmitted from human footsteps.

A high-dynamic range (HDR) sensor was realized by using multiple sensors of differing sensitivity to measure the same quantity. A combination of high-frequency piezoelectric geophones and low-frequency carbon geophones allowed for wide spectral range of expression. These sensors were subsequently connected to a real-time frequency-shifting system that shifted each geophone's output to the correct musical pitch or chord for each particular note in various pieces of music which were programmed into an embedded microcontroller.

For videos and more information on andantephones, visit: http://www.wearcam.org/andantephone

REFERENCES

1. R. Janzen and S. Mann. *Stray:* a new multimedia music composition using the andantephone. In *Proc. ACM Multimedia, October 25-29, 2010, Firenze, Italy*, pages 683–6, 2010.

2. S. Mann. Comparametric equations with practical applications in quantigraphic image processing. *IEEE Trans. Image Proc.*, 9(8):1389–1406, August 2000. ISSN 1057-7149.

3. S. Mann. The andantephone: A musical instrument that you play by simply walking. In *Proc. ACM Multimedia, October 23-27, Santa Barbara, USA*, pages 181–4, 2006.

4. S. Mann and R. Picard. Being 'undigital' with digital cameras: Extending dynamic range by combining differently exposed pictures. In *Proc. IS&T's 48th annual conference*, pages 422–428, Washington, D.C., May 7–11 1995. Also appears, M.I.T. M.L. T.R. 323, 1994, http://wearcam.org/ist95.htm.

5. R. Vertegaal and I. Poupyrev. Organic user interfaces. *Communications of the ACM*, 51:26–30, 2008.

6. Y. Visell, A. Law, J. Ip, R. Rajalingham, S. Smith, and J. Cooperstock. Interaction capture in immersive virtual environments via an intelligent floor surface. *IEEE Virtual Reality*, 0:311–312, 2010.

7. Z. Zhu, S. Rahardja, Z. Li, and P. Franti. Detecting and composing near-identical hdr images without exposure information. In *Proc. ICIP*, pages 3337–3340, 2010.

Responsible Storytelling: Communicating Research in Video Demos

Madeleine Clare Elish
Columbia University, Department of Anthropology
New York, NY USA
mce2102@columbia.edu

ABSTRACT
This paper examines the under-explored role of video demos as a consequential form of communicating tangible computing research. Examining the production of video demos, in particular two videos from MIT's Media Lab, I explore the ethical complications of producing demo videos by bringing to the surface the tensions inherent in video representations of research, as understood from a social studies of technology perspective. In doing so, this paper hopes to generate discussion about the challenges and responsibilities of creating accurate and compelling narratives around technology research.

Author Keywords
Communication, demonstrations (demos), ethics, materiality, social studies of technology, storytelling, video.

ACM Classification Keywords
H5.m. Information interfaces and presentation (e.g., HCI): Miscellaneous.

General Terms
Theory.

INTRODUCTION
At stake in tangible user interfaces is the very materiality of the world and the human body. We want users to experience a bridge between atoms and bits. How, then, can such radical and physical interactions be communicated beyond the physical environment of the lab? Video demonstrations (demos) have emerged as a useful and wide-reaching vehicle of communication. They allow researchers to account for the "practice turn," demonstrating an action centric perspective on interaction. [1] Yet, unlike live demos, or the research papers that may accompany development, video demos often emerge as de-contextualized possibilities. That is, the incremental work that went into research is elided, and the technologies developed often are presented without clear explanation as to how and under what constraints they function.

TEI'11, January 22–26, 2011, Funchal, Portugal.

The goal of a demo video is two-fold: to communicate research as well as to excite an audience about the potential of this research. On the one hand, we have fact, work based in research. On the other hand, we have a mode of storytelling and the rhetoric of a better future. We want an audience to see what we have done, and we also want an audience to imagine what could be done. Straddling the present and the future, the edited image and the physical reality, video demos involve a complicated act of demonstration and reception that is far from transparent.

This paper contributes to the TEI discussion by critically examining positive and negative potentials of video demos, as well as contributing to an under-developed discussion about the ethical responsibilities in evaluating and communicating ongoing technological research.

This conceptual exploration is grounded in the analysis of two well-known video demos released from MIT's Media Lab in recent years. Based in this analysis, a series of consequential factors are articulated that may be useful to researchers as they produce video demos.

The Demo as a Medium of Research
Since the Enlightenment and the dawn of Modern science, witnessing a successful experiment has been the foundation for the validation and progression of the sciences. Shapin and Schaffer's research points to the fact that the physical presence of an audience was quintessential to the acceptance of scientific research beginning in the 17th century. [2] Along the history of Modern science, such witnessing has moved to the form of written papers and the reproducibility of an experiment. The work of Latour and Woolgar, among others, has demonstrated that representations of scientific research and what constitutes proof of innovation are still very much influenced by historical and social factors. [3]

Meanwhile, the witnessed demo of technology has emerged as a major genre of communicating technology. Consider, for instance, the "Mother of all Demos," Engelbart's famous demonstration of his oNLine System (NLS) in 1968, a demo, produced by Stewart Brand, which is generally understood to have changed the terrain of personal computing. Although Engelbart had been working for years at SRI, and previous prototypes of a mouse existed elsewhere, this demo stands as a pivotal moment in the history of computing, having brought to public attention a new mode of interacting with a computer. This was a moment when research moved beyond the lab to a general public, a moment when conceptions of the possible world radically changed.

Turning to the present moment, it is important to consider that unlike software running on a GUI, the very materiality and relationship of the object or system to the human body is fundamental to TUIs. Video, as a time-based visual media, provides a way to communicate the dimensions of TUIs. Still, this communication is deeply mediated. In the layers of mediation, complications emerge. We must take account of the ethical and social implications of how innovation is being communicated to colleagues and a general public.

Demoing at the MIT Media Lab

The MIT Media Lab is famous for its mantra of "demo or die." Frequently corporate sponsors and school groups come through on tours and are given live demos. In live demos, information about a project is communicated in a number of ways. Visitors to the lab witness a physical form and functionality. They also hear the researchers talk, contextualizing what the project does and what research is in process. Some systems may not be working during a visit. Some may malfunction. There can be no do-overs. The visitors may ask questions or touch the object or interface. In addition, visitors see and get a sense of the lab as a workspace, bumping into students or researchers on their way into the lab or seeing desks covered with papers and empty coffee cups.

However, communicating the ongoing work of research requires moving beyond the walls of the lab. Whether at academic conferences or to inform a broader public, video demonstrations have become an important medium of communication in technology and design research. Yet, video representations compound the act of mediating knowledge. [4] We lose an immediate sense of witnessing, as well as important insight into the physical or intellectual environment of research. We also expect demos to perform a kind of storytelling, to exist as a narrative and to excite an audience or funder about the potential of research in progress.

Thus, live and video demos offer two modes of communicating research, each with their own complications. We may refine the category of demos once again, within the set of demo videos, by pointing out differences in production. Live demos may be video-recorded. In this case, they distance the viewer but provide other viewers' responses and questions as a kind of proxy. There may also be demos in the form of videos that are in fact animations, 3-D computer simulated action, in which direct reference to the physical world and existing physical forms is elided. Thirdly, there may be demonstrations produced explicitly for a camera recording. They may be rigorous documentation, demonstrating how a fully functional project works, or they may be more of a concept video, where the emphasis is placed on the possibilities of a technology rather than the current state of functionality. In this paper, I am concerned with this latter mode of representation and the unique considerations and practices that inform this kind of production.

CASE STUDY: MIT MEDIA LAB'S NEXI VIDEOS

In this brief case study, I examine two of the most viewed videos created by the Personal Robots Group about the lab's mobile, dexterous, social (MDS) robot, also known as Nexi. This study is based on research I conducted over the course of a few weeks in 2010, during which I interviewed researchers and observed various live demos in the lab.

Within the Personal Robots Group, video demos are understood to fall within two genres, delineated by their intended audience. In one kind of video, termed "research videos," a robot is staged to perform a specific and typically innovative set of functionalities to be shown to colleagues or others in a professional setting, such as an academic conference or grant report meeting. The production of these videos tends to be prompted by exterior deadlines that do not necessarily coincide with milestones in research. A researcher spoke of numerous times in which he and the other researchers stayed up late into the night, finishing a program or fixing the robot, sometimes recording the robot only hours before the video needed to be shown. In "research videos," the goal is to demonstrate in order to prove a functionality of the robot.

"Official videos," the other genre, are more elaborate videos intended for a general audience and produced by a Media Lab videographer. In these videos the goal is to demonstrate in order to "inspire" and communicate the broader goals of the robot. The aim is to make a viewer eager and excited, as well as to create a compelling story and captivating image of what Nexi can be. The two genres demonstrate the constant negotiation between visually proving research and visually communicating research.

However, a series of events in 2008 brought the clear boundary between these two kinds of video into question. One "research video" was emailed to colleagues, but then was leaked to blogs and YouTube. [5] In response, the Personal Robots Group created an "official video," intended to ameliorate the issues created by the leaked video. [6] The most pressing concern about the leaked video was the lack of an explanation stating how the robot was functioning and what specific technologies were employed. Nowhere in the video was it explained how the robot was moving and talking. The "official video" has a disclaimer that reads, "Early demonstration of expressive performance using animation playback." In the other video, there is no such disclaimer, and the researchers feared that people would mistake the performance for AI. In non-research terms, one researcher described the distinction as one between robots and "real robots" in the minds of the general public that was imagined to see this video.

It was understood by the researchers at the lab that the leaked "research video" would have been adequately explained in its intended venue at the conference, as in-person narration does during live demos. However, with this leaked "research video" the claims of innovation the video was making were not clearly defined. In the case of the general public, viewers only had recourse to what they could discern visually – leaving the rest up to the imagination, a popular imagination which generally fears robots – and this was worrisome. Consider three comments that were among the first to be posted on YouTube: "LOL emotions...... that's crazy" and "im so afraid, this thing is awesome. but if i had one at home, id be building bunkers to hide from it in my room :]" and "OH, COME ON PEOPLE! Am I the only one who saw I Robot & learned something? RUN FOR YOUR LIIIIIIFE!!!" The researchers clearly could not adequately direct how people would interpret the video.

Conflicting Objectives

Researchers must consider different audiences and take account of the different contexts in which audiences will view a demo. They must also negotiate between the desire to demonstrate functionality, celebrating incremental achievements and the desire to inspire and prove an over-arching validity and worth of social robots. This negotiation has been eased by creating different videos for different contexts. However, the instance of leaked videos brings these conflicting desires to the forefront and perhaps necessitates a reconsideration of how demo videos are produced and circulated by researchers.

DISCUSSION

Drawing from this case study and other examples below, a series of important factors emerge when considering video demos as a medium of communicating research.

Specialist vs. Non-specialist Audiences

The work of communicating research and innovation must proceed along multiple paths. The kinds of information necessary to be communicated to colleagues and specialists will most likely differ from information communicated to a general audience. Yet, as the previous case demonstrates, such differentiation in intended audiences does not reflect the reality of the contemporary media landscape.

Even as we take account of the different kinds of information different audiences desire, we must also keep aware of precisely what information a video demo offers, especially when a video is intended for a public audience as a means of communicating innovation.

One relatively famous video to emerge from the Media Lab is Pranav Mistry's original Sixth Sense video demo. [7] This project was met with great excitement and mass media coverage, eventually leading to multiple TED talks (and more video demos.) Mistry's video is a complicated act of communication because, like the "official" Nexi video, Mistry is conveying an inspiring story about future technological possibilities rather than rigorous documentation of advancement in technology. In some senses, the video demo is misleading; the demo is performed in highly constrained scenarios, and with the help of editing, the technology is made to seem more seamless than its actual current state. A discussion of the project on the TED website indicates the range of interpretations by the general public. One commenter stated, "Thank you to show us the amazing possibility of our world tomorrow. Keep it up!," demonstrating that the viewer understood this as an act of storytelling, a proof of technological possibility. Yet, another commenter asked, "guys can i buy this and how much does it cost?" [8] My point here is not to find fault with Mistry's video demo, but rather, to point out the elisions made possible by video demos and the compelling narratives of the future which can both assist a project in reaching widespread recognition and public attention while also raising the question of ethically responsible communication of research. This video, as well as the Nexi "official video," serve to highlight the balancing act that must be achieved in demo videos. They must demonstrate and educate while also providing a compelling and inspiring narrative about the future.

Aesthetics

The possibilities and extent of communicating research to a variety of audiences has greatly expanded. Digital video production tools are accessible, and videos are easily shared over the internet. Video, a visual and time based medium, provides an excellent mode in which to convey TUIs. As discussed in the introduction, video can provide a sense of full-body interaction even if physical presence is not possible. Yet the adoption of video is not merely one of increased access. Video also comes with an established set of aesthetic conventions and attitudes, its own system of visual rhetoric. Especially in light of the examples presented above, it is important to note the pervading sense that documentary video is an index of reality. Many demo videos, especially "research videos," tend to have an *in media res* feeling. As such, they have a kind of "home video" aesthetic which is linked with an increased belief in the fidelity of what is being represented. This aesthetic can be a powerful form of visual rhetoric, and thus can highlight or misconstrue the reality of a technology.

Viral Media

Maintaining control of media after it has left the producer's hands and computer is difficult, if not impossible. As one of the researchers at the Personal Robots Group stated, "This was our YouTube wake-up call." Researchers should proceed assuming that any video produced may make its way to the web and general public consumption.

In addition, demo videos may quickly spread through a variety of websites without the researcher's knowledge. Consequently, the surrounding context for the video is unknown; providing adequate information within the video itself, with explanatory text, is all the more important.

Indeed, the researchers' responsibility also includes the recollection that researchers have response-abilities. For instance, if a journalist mis-represents a concept design as a ready-for-market product, the researcher can follow up with the journalist and attempt to rectify this presentation.

Institutional Affiliation

It is also important to note the role that institutions play in influencing reception of information. The association of an institution with a research project helps validate that research, especially in the minds of non-specialists. Therefore, producers of demo videos must be aware of how their research is branded with an institution. For instance, all official videos from the Media Lab are branded with the Lab's logo and a common opening sequence. In less formal videos, titles often indicate from which lab this research emerged and who is responsible. Even casual branding is a strategy; in Mistry's original Sixth Sense video, he wears an MIT T-shirt in many scenes.

New Media Literacies

Still, the responsibility of communicating information in video demos cannot be left to researchers alone. Alongside the development of technical research within tangible computing, a push must be made to increase public understandings of tangible computing. In a recent research report, Henry Jenkins and colleagues have proposed a set of new media literacy skills that middle and high school curriculums are advised to address. [10] To act as responsible citizens in an increasingly digital world, it is necessary to acquire a fundamental skill set in evaluating the information and technologies that surround us.

Of course, not everyone will be an advanced programmer or engineer. Still, an attention to educating and informing non-specialist audiences about how technologies work should not be left behind as we look to the future.

Methods of Evaluation

At this moment, the content within video demos of TUIs appears to be guided by a loose set of self-imposed standards that have emerged from within the tangible computing field. For instance, we would expect a video not to lie about technological achievements and to indicate an institutional affiliation.

Especially because TEI stands at an interdisciplinary intersection of computer science, art and design, it seems all the more exigent to begin a serious discussion about the role of video demos within ongoing research. Video is an excellent medium to communicate the very materiality and physical possibilities of TUIs. Yet, video representation is not a simple and transparent medium. What best practices should be employed in the production of video demos? How might such standards positively affect the way researchers evaluate their colleagues' work from afar, as well as public understandings of TUIs and technology in general?

Concluding Remarks

The previous discussion points to the necessity of thoroughly evaluating how video demos communicate the ongoing work of technological research and the subsequent mediation of information and diffusion along media networks. The issues involved in this communication have not been discussed in the depth they deserve over the course of this paper. Still, this paper aims to incite discussion and action by the TEI community. The potential consequences for public understandings of technological research and innovation must be further evaluated, as well as our own ethical responsibilities as researchers.

There is no easy formula for producing a video demo. Nor is the matter one of distinguishing right and wrong. Rather, with this analysis, I hope to enrich the discussion of how to be responsible technology researchers as well as responsible media makers.

ACKNOWLEDGMENTS

I thank the MIT Media Lab, and in particular the researchers in the Personal Robots Group for their time and assistance during this research. I also thank Lucy Suchman for her guidance during the initial stages of this project.

REFERENCES

1. Fernaeus, F., Tholander, J., and Jonsson, M. Towards a New set of Ideals: Consequences of the Practice Turn in Tangible Interaction. Proc TEI 2008, ACM Press (2008), 223–230.
2. Shapin, S. & Schaffer, S. *Leviathan and the Air-Pump: Hobbes, Boyle and the Experimental Life.* Princeton University Press, Princeton, NJ, 1985.
3. Latour, B. & Woolgar, S. *Laboratory Life: The Construction of Scientific Facts.* Princeton University Press, Princeton, NJ, 1986.
4. Collins, H.M. Public Experiments and Displays of Virtuosity: The Core-Set Revisited. *Social Studies of Science* 18, 4 (1985), 725-48.
5. MIT's Nexi MDS Robot: First Test of Expression [Video]. http://www.youtube.com/watch?v=XrmrU7P-ysA.
6. Official MDS Robot Video - First Test of Expressive Ability [Video]. http://www.youtube.com/watch?v=aQS2zxmrrA.
7. WUW/sixthsense a wearable gestural interface [video]. http://www.youtube.com/watch?v=ZfV4R4x2SK0.
8. An interview with Pranav Mistry, the genius behind Sixth Sense, TED Blog. http://blog.ted.com/2009/03/11/sixth_sense_pranav/

"It's just a toolbar!" Using Tangibles to Help Children Manage Conflict Around a Multi-Touch Tabletop

Izabel C. Olson **Zeina Atrash Leong** **Uri Wilensky** **Michael S. Horn**

Northwestern University
Learning Sciences
Computer Science
2120 Campus Drive
Evanston, Illinois 60208 USA
{izabel, zeinaatrash2012} @u.northwestern.edu, { uri, michael-horn, } @northwestern.edu

ABSTRACT

In this paper we present a case study of children's collaborative behavior around a multi-touch tabletop interface. The study includes data from four sessions with four children over a period of three weeks. The children in our study exhibited a diverse set of collaborative behaviors including territorial control of screen real estate, conflict over interface elements, and turn taking behavior, all of which seemed related to specific aspects of the interface design. Most notably, we observed conflict relating to a graphical toolbar that the children could drag around the screen. After observing this conflict, we redesigned the interface so that children were forced to use a tangible object (a wooden block) to make the toolbar appear on the screen. This tangible object seemed to help the children resolve their conflict and to promote spontaneous turn taking behavior. This paper is an effort to understand why the graphical toolbar alone seemed to spur conflict and why the introduction of a tangible object seemed to help children resolve the conflict on their own.

Author Keywords

Children, multi-touch tabletops, collaboration, tangible interaction, learning

ACM Classification Keywords

H5.m. Information interfaces and presentation: User Interfaces – *Interaction styles; Input Devices and strategies.*

INTRODUCTION

Multi-touch tabletop technology offers a dynamic and appealing medium for designers to create collaborative learning experiences for children. However, the nature of children's collaboration around tabletop devices remains largely unexplored. In particular, subtle interface design decisions seem to have a large impact on children's interactions with each other as well as with the tabletop interface itself.

In this paper, we present a case study examining the behavior of a group of four elementary school children interacting with a scientific modeling application on both a multi-touch tabletop and a desktop computer. The study includes data from four sessions over a period of three weeks. We selected this group of children for our case study because they exhibited a diverse set of collaborative behaviors including territorial control of screen real estate, open conflict over interface elements, and turn taking behavior, all of which seemed dependent on specific aspects of the interface design that changed over the course of four sessions.

Most notably, we observed unexpected conflict relating to a graphical toolbar that the children could drag around the screen (Figure 2). After observing this conflict, we redesigned the interface so that children were forced to use a physical block (Figure 3) to make the toolbar appear on the screen. This tangible token seemed to help the children resolve their conflict and to promote spontaneous turn taking behavior. This paper is an effort to understand why the graphical toolbar seemed to spur conflict and why the introduction of a simple tangible object seemed to help children resolve that conflict on their own.

This case study is part of a larger design research study with the goal of adapting the NetLogo modeling environment [16] for elementary school students through the use of multi-touch tabletop devices. Our goal is to support collaborative exploration of scientific models on a tabletop surface. NetLogo is an agent-based modeling language that enables students and professionals alike to model complex systems and emergent phenomena [16]. One advantage of agent-based models is that they are accessible to learners without the need for great mathematical sophistication. Many important physical, biological, and social phenomena can be modeled and

TEI'11, January 22–26, 2011, Funchal, Portugal.

understood through simple computational rules that describe the behavior of agents in a complex system [17].

BACKGROUND

Research has long suggested that work in small groups can result in productive learning experiences for children (e.g. [9, 14]). Studies have further explored the role of computers in small group work [2,3,6,10,11,12]. For example, Inkpen, Booth, Gribble, Klawe and Upitis found that children who collaborated around a single computer display to solve puzzles showed improvements in achievement and attitude over peers who worked alone [6]. The effect of computer collaboration on achievement was especially heightened within groups of girls.

Multi-touch tabletops provide a large horizontal display around which children can interact simultaneously—in many ways similar to that of everyday interaction that happens around non-computer tabletops (for example children playing cards or board games). Tabletop workspaces (interactive or not) provide a high degree of peripheral awareness of others and their actions in the workspace [15], and researchers have begun to investigate the potential of multi-touch tabletops to support both co-located collaboration and learning [1-4, 6, 7, 10-13].

Many interactive tabletops are implemented using computer vision technology (e.g. Microsoft Surface), which makes it possible to interact with the computer using tangible objects as well as touch input. For example, Antle, Droumeva, and Ha [1] have conducted research involving pairs of children solving jigsaw puzzles in three different conditions: with a desktop computer and mouse, with a standard cardboard puzzle, and with a digital tabletop and tangible puzzle pieces. Their results suggest that the direct physical manipulation of objects with the tangible puzzle leads to faster and easier problem solving involving less trial and error.

When children collaborate on multi-touch tabletops they negotiate meaning in a variety of ways. Often children will use physical behaviors such as blocking, "undoing", and grabbing to negotiate and collaborate [2]. Fleck, Rogers, Yuill, Marshall, Carr, Rick and Bonnett argue that these behaviors, in tandem with verbal discussion, can lead to effective collaboration in a tabletop environment [2].

In our research we have observed that children's existing repertoire of social protocols are not always sufficient to prevent conflict around interactive tabletops. Morris, Ryall, Shen, Forlines, and Vernier identified three conflict types emerging around tabletop interactions: global, whole-element, and sub-element [8]. Whole-element conflicts involve access to a single interface element such as the toolbar that is the focus of this study. Morris et al. suggest several coordination policies for resolving whole-element disputes on tabletop interfaces. Some of these policies relevant to our study include offering private or duplicate interface elements and creating personalized views for individual collaborators. In this paper, we consider an additional coordination strategy—the use of a tangible object to access a single, shared interface element.

A core concern of our research is the *fluidity of sharing* around our tabletop environment. According to Hornecker, Marshall, and Rogers, fluidity of sharing refers to the ease with which collaborators "can switch roles or interleave their actions" [5]. Fluidity of sharing can be compromised when users have a difficult time managing the tabletop real estate (territories). Research suggests that territories serve to coordinate tabletop interactions, and collaborators make use of three types of territories to help coordinate their interactions within the shared tabletop workspace: personal, group, and storage territories [13].

Another factor that affects collaboration is *orientation* [7]. Orientation on an interactive tabletop is the ability to move and reposition an item on the work surface. According to Kruger, Carpendale, Scott, and Greenberg, orientation serves functions of comprehension, communication, and coordination [7]. Orientation is important for negotiation in a tabletop environment as it communicates ownership and is used as a way to establish personal and group spaces.

Collaboration is also affected by group and table size. Ryall, Forlines, Shen, and Morris found that the size of a group greatly affected the way in which a physical shared resource was positioned [12]. While groups of two were able to orient a resource to a point of view that would satisfy both, groups of four had a harder time orienting resources and collaborating on a tabletop. Larger groups assign a person whose responsibility it was to manipulate the shared resource.

Figure 1. Our tabletop NetLogo interface

TABLETOP INTERFACE DESIGN

This case study involves a multi-touch tabletop interface that we designed for children to explore and create NetLogo models (Figure 1). We implemented the application on a Microsoft Surface, a commercially available interactive tabletop from Microsoft that allows multiple users to manipulate digital content using touch input. The Microsoft

Surface is a 30-inch horizontal display in a tabletop form factor, 22 inches high, 21 inches deep, and 42 inches wide.

During this study children interacted with two models from the NetLogo models library. The first model, *Wolf Sheep Predation*, explores the stability of predator-prey ecosystems. The second model, *Virus*, simulates the transmission and perpetuation of a virus in a population.

Figure 2. Graphical toolbar widget

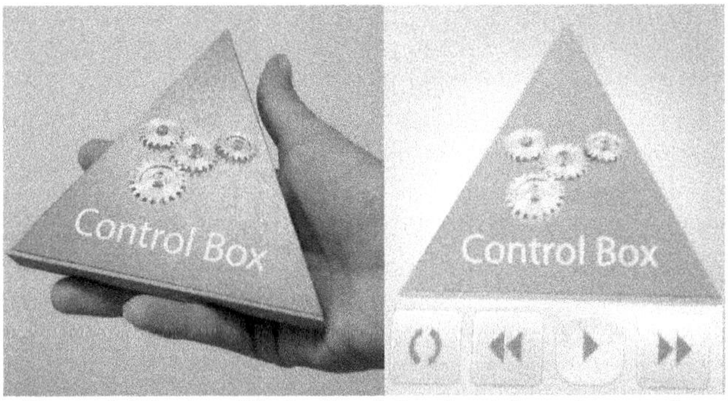

Figure 3. The tangible toolbar token is a triangular wooden block that children must place on the screen to make the toolbar widget appear (right).

Currently the interface consists of three components. The first is a window that displays a visual representation of the simulation. Children can drag this window around the screen and resize it using a pinch gesture. Initially positioned underneath with simulation window is a collection of sliders that children use to adjust a model's input parameters. Finally, a toolbar widget containing a collection of buttons to control the simulation is provided. The interface also incorporates a collection of tangible blocks that serve as entry points into NetLogo programming activities. For example, children can place a Create Turtle block on the table (Figure 1) to add agents to a model and a Forward block asks the existing turtles to move forward on the screen.

Control Toolbar

Children control NetLogo simulations using a toolbar widget (Figure 2). Pressing the play button on the toolbar starts a model simulation, which can then be controlled using fast-forward, rewind, pause, and reset buttons. In our initial design, we placed the control toolbar near one corner of the tabletop and allowed it to be dragged around the screen using a single finger. In the first session of the case study the children never repositioned the toolbar, apparently assuming it was fixed in place. In the third session, the children realized that the toolbar could be moved around the screen, which in turn created disputes over where the toolbar should be placed, and who controlled it. As a result, between the third and fourth sessions, we redesigned the interface to include a tangible toolbar token, a triangle shaped wooden block shown in Figure 3. In this iteration of the interface, children were required to place the physical block on the tabletop to make the toolbar widget appear on the screen. The toolbar widget always appeared alongside the physical token and moved with it on the screen.

METHOD

Participants

For this case study we observed a group of four children, three girls (ages 8, 9, and 11) and one boy (age 10) recruited from a suburban private school in the United States Midwest. As compensation for participating in the study children received a $5 gift card to an ice cream shop.

Procedure

The children participated in a series of three workshops over a period of three weeks. Each workshop lasted three hours. During the workshops children collaborated around a desktop computer, a multi-touch tabletop, and a physical board game. We prompted the children with challenges such as: "work together to find settings that will create a sustainable ecosystem." All workshop sessions were video recorded.

Case Study Sessions

From the three workshops with the children we selected four interaction sessions to highlight in this case study. These sessions consisted of the children working together with minimal adult interaction to explore a NetLogo model.

Session 1: Tabletop with Fixed Toolbar

In the first session the children worked on the tabletop to explore the wolf-sheep predation model. We asked the children to try to create stable populations of wolves and sheep. In this session the children apparently believed that the graphical toolbar was fixed in place—they never moved it from its default location on one corner of the tabletop. During this session one girl who was closest to the toolbar dominated its use. The other children would frequently reach across the table to press one of the buttons. This session lasted 21 minutes, 4 seconds.

Session 2: Desktop Computer with Single Mouse

In the second session the children worked with the same NetLogo model using a desktop computer and a mouse rather than the tabletop. In this session children passed the mouse from person to person, sharing control. This session lasted 15 minutes, 11 seconds.

Code	Description
Reach Over	Reaching over the workspace to try to use the control (successfully or not). 
Blocking	Preventing another child from using the control using one's body, arm, or a finger.
Possible Blocking	Positioning body to establish territory. However, due to lack of verbal or intentional cues the intention to block is uncertain.
Verbal Complaint	Expressing dissatisfaction over how the control is being use or how another child is acting with respect to the control (e.g. "I want to use it now!").
Grabbing	Physically taking the control away from another child. This includes dragging the toolbar on the screen or taking a physical input device (mouse or tangible block). 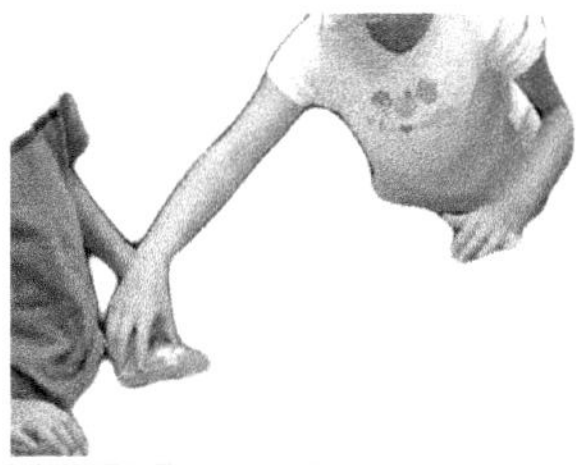
Passing Control	Passing the control to another child.
Tucking Away	Holding a physical control to prevent others from taking it. 
Asking for Control	Asking to use or hold the control (e.g. "Can I try it?")

Table 1. Coding scheme

Session 3: Tabletop with Floating Toolbar

The following week, we presented a virus model to the children and asked them to make the spread of disease faster, slower, extinct, and perpetual in the model. In this scenario, children noticed that the toolbar could be dragged around the screen. This realization seemed to spark an argument over control of the toolbar. This session lasted 18 minutes, 7 seconds.

Session 4: Tabletop with Tangible Control Bar

In an effort to control the argument, we introduced a tangible object in the following week. To make the toolbar appear the children had to first place the tangible object on the screen. In this session the children were able to develop a turn-taking protocol that appeared similar to what we observed in the second session with the computer mouse. This session lasted 5 minutes, 24 seconds.

Coding

We coded the video with a scheme based on [2] and shown in Table 1. The coding scheme was modified to accommodate particular interactions we were interested in, such as reaching across the table to take control of the interface element. The coding scheme provides a descriptive account of the interactions observed around the element of control in each interface. In the first and third sessions the element of control was a toolbar widget (Figure 1). In the second session the element of control was a mouse. And, in the fourth scenario the element of control was a tangible control box (Figure 2). The frequency of each code was found by counting the number of instances over the duration of the session.

Conversation topics were also coded. Students' conversations included two primary topics: *science-talk* and *control-related* conflict. *Science talk* is any stretch of time in which at least one child is discussing the workings of the model. This includes conjecture, discussion, and predictions about the model, as well as observation of individual agents in the model. For example, as one model converges with too many sheep:

A: Overpopulation
J: Not enough wolves. Then the animal who eat wolves dies too... It's a clog in the circle of life.
A: Chain reaction.... Oh, that is a lot of dying at once.
N: What about the animals that eat wolves? They can start eating sheep instead.

Control-related conflict was coded as any verbal comment or physical behavior that was related to the ownership or use of the model controller. For example:

A: [Reaches over] [Grabs control]
J: [Verbal Complaint] Stop!
T: [Verbal Complaint] J. said I could have a turn!
J: No, I didn't!
T: [Asks for control] May I please?
J: It's just a toolbar!
N: [Reach over]
T: Then why do you want it?
A: Yeah?

J: Because it belongs here
A: It doesn't have to; it doesn't have to... Look [Reach over] [Grabbing control]
N: [Verbal Complaint] Alex! Stop!
A: It can move! Doesn't HAVE to be there...

In some cases the situations overlapped; for example, two students discussed the model as the other two were engaged in control-related conflict. We calculated the total amount of time for each category by adding the duration of each segment per session. We then divided these sums by total session duration.

We also report the frequency of interruptions in science talk due to control-related conflict. For example, we coded this exchange as an interruption in science talk:

A: It's lasted pretty long
N: Yeah. That was pretty sustainable, right?
A: [Reaches over and takes the toolbar]
A: Miiiine.
N: They won't all die if you have it down here
J: [Takes the toolbar back from A]
A: MIIINE! [reaches over to grab the toolbar]
J: STOP!

RESULTS

Flow of Interactions

We calculated instances per minute of each behavior type in each session (Figure 4a-c). The results suggest that children adopted distinct collaboration styles in each session. The interactions in the first and third sessions were initially similar. The differences emerged in the 9th minute of the third session (Figure 4c) when children discovered that the toolbar widget could be moved around the screen, and an open conflict emerged. This transcript covers the start of the argument:

A: [Reaches over; realizes the toolbar moves]
A: [Reaches over; tries to take toolbar]
N: Wait, wait, wait—we need this at 6.
T: They will all die if you have it down here.
A: [Drags control away] Mine! Mine now.
J: [Reach over and drags control away]
A: [Reaches over]
J: [Blocks A with hand]
A: [Gasps] Mine!
A: [Reaches over again]
J: [Blocks again]

In the first tabletop scenario, when children did not know that the toolbar could be moved, they reached across the table to press buttons an average of 2.27 times per minute (SD = 1.95). Whereas, in the third scenario, when children found out the toolbar could be moved, they reached over to use it 3.1 times per minute (SD=3.43). The higher amount of reaching over, as well as higher standard deviation, probably reflects the dispute over toolbar control, which escalated at the ninth minute.

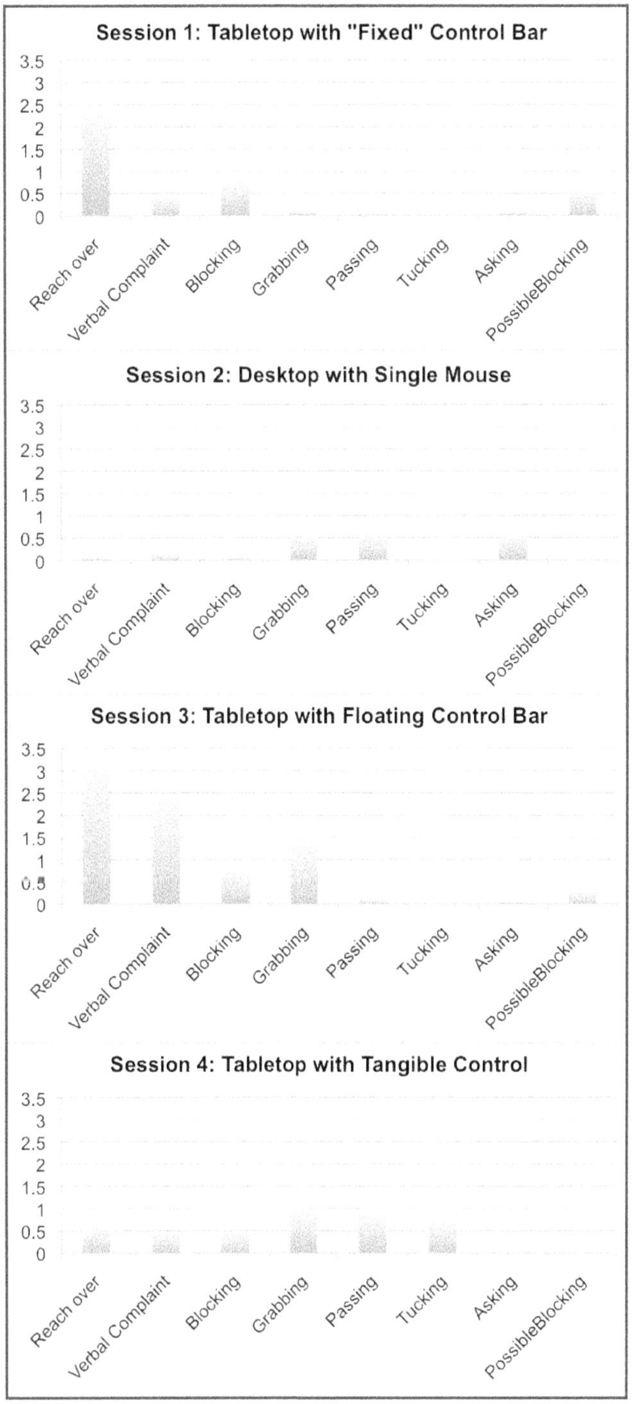

Figure 4. Average instances of behavior codes per session: (a) tabletop with "fixed" toolbar widget; (b) desktop computer with a single mouse; (c) tabletop with "floating" toolbar widget; and (d) tabletop with tangible control box.

The open conflict in the third session also brought about a higher amount of verbal complaining. In the third session the children complained 2.3 times per minute (SD= 4.31) compared to 0.41 times per minute (SD = 0.67) in the first scenario. The action of grabbing the control in the two sessions was also different. While in the first session there was a small amount of grabbing (0.09 grabs per minute; SD

= 0.43), in the third session the number went up to 1.35 grabs per minute (SD = 2.56).

Once the tangible object was introduced (session 4, Figure 4d), the flow of interactions changed substantially. Compared to the third session children passed the control more (0.86 times per minute, SD = 0.9), reached over less (0.57 times per minute, SD = 1.13), and blocked less (0.43 times per minute, SD = 0.79). The children also displayed a new behavior, that of taking the tangible object off of the table and tucking it away under their arms to prevent others from taking it (0.71 times per minute, SD = 0.76). The fourth session seems to more closely resemble the second session in which the children used a desktop computer with a single mouse. In the second session the most prevalent actions were grabbing, passing, and asking. Children grabbed the control 0.56 times per minute (SD=0.51), passed the control 0.56 times per minute (SD=0.72), and asked for the control 0.56 per minute (SD=0.72). We attribute the prevalence of these actions to the turn-taking behavior children spontaneously adopted in the mouse session.

Session	%Science talk	%Arguing and complaining	Interruptions / minute
1	100	1.64	0.429
2	91.38	4.49	0.198
3	72.72	16.63	0.828
4	80.64	4.12	0.556

Table 2. Percentage of science talk and arguing & complaining in each session. The final column shows the frequency with which science talk was interrupted due to arguing and complaining. Note: at times the children argued while simultaneously discussing the NetLogo model. Thus, percentages do not necessarily add up to 100.

Science Talk and Argument Sequences

We also analyzed the total amount of time spent in science talk during each session compared to the amount of time spent arguing or complaining over control of the toolbar. In the first session, when the children assumed that the toolbar was fixed in place, argument sequences were rare at less than 2 percent of the student work time; this session also included the largest percentage of science talk time. When the children moved to a desktop display with a mouse controller, the percent of time spent on science talk decreased by almost 10%; in addition the proportion of conflict increased to approximately 4.5%. The tabletop display with the tangible control showed similar results with further dip in science talk, to 80%. The most prominent results appeared in the third session when the children realized that the toolbar could be moved. During this session students' science talk dropped to nearly 70%, while their conflict level rose to over 16%. Table 2 presents the results of science talk, control-related conflict, and frequency of complaint-lead interruptions. In comparison to the tabletop with a fixed control bar (session 1), the rate of complaint-lead interruptions nearly doubled with the floating control bar (session 3). The lowest rate of conflict related interruptions occurred with the desktop display (session 2).

DISCUSSION

The children seemed to have a clash of expectations regarding appropriate social protocols in the tabletop sessions. Because tabletop interaction was new to these children, we speculate that they were unsure what set of social scripts or norms applied. Some of the children assumed turn taking scripts, asking to participate, passing the control, and complaining when those scripts were not applied. Others assumed territories and fought for having sole control of the tabletop.

In the first session with the "fixed" toolbar, the children established clear territories, and they struggled to position themselves in places where they had easy access to the control. We felt that the ongoing conflict compromised the fluidity of sharing because one child monopolized the territory where the interface element was located. Once the children noticed the toolbar could be moved, the struggle for territory control escalated into an open conflict—the frequency of reaching over and grabbing increased and verbal complaints interrupted the children's scientific conversations.

Morris et al. suggest several coordination strategies for conflict resolution including the use of duplicate control boxes at different points on the table [8]. Although, we didn't evaluate this option with our interface, we feel that it has potential downsides for the types of activities we hope to support. Duplicate control boxes might reduce a child's ability to observe the models and their awareness of complex structures. Duplicate controls could cause arguments and confusion as children press different controls at different times, as well as provoke a race for who will press the control first, detracting from the attention to the model. Using a fixed control bar works well, except that it implies an assigned "boss". As children had difficulty assigning roles themselves, this concept also caused some conflict. Ultimately, using a tangible object to access the control bar might be a good option for designing collaborative tabletop interfaces for children as it recalls familiar protocols children are accustomed to.

When we introduced the tangible control in session 4, there were less territorial disputes, and arguments. This is because the tangible control affords removal from the table, separating control of the interface element from the tabletop territories. It introduced a familiar idea into an unfamiliar interactive setting, and, allowed children to recall turn-taking scripts: a "passing the baton" protocol. Thus, we speculate that the tangible object acted as a catalyst for more fluid sharing. In the end of the fourth session, we asked children why they stopped fighting over the control. Their responses included:

> A: Because people were just like dragging it... like I was about to click it and they'd drag it towards them, and

stuff, but like this... If you are holding on to the control box, no one can drag it.

T: And, you can also take turns too.

LIMITATIONS & FUTURE WORK

There are limitations to this research that should be considered in the application of results to future designs. First, the study analyzed data from one case study, with a small number of children over a period of three weeks. It is possible that the children could have established similar turn taking protocols on their own, independent of our design change. It is also reasonable to assume a novelty effects (especially in the early tabletop sessions) that might have begun to wear off near the end of the three-week period. Likewise, fatigue and boredom could have played a role in the later sessions. We also did not try a tabletop interface design that offered the children multiple toolbars to share on the screen as suggested by Morris et al. (2004) [8]. As discussed above, we feel that this particular design decision would not be ideal for this type of collaborative learning; however, this is only based on our design intuition.

In the future we would like to explore different forms of coordination strategies and examine the resulting effects on collaboration with a larger, more diverse group of children. We also expect to perform a conversational analysis of children's scientific talk around the tabletop interface with a focus on the ways in which the threads of social negotiation and scientific talk intertwine.

CONCLUSION

Interactive tabletops are an increasingly popular tool for the design of learning experiences. In this paper we present a case study of four children interacting with four variations of the same interface. These interfaces included: (1) a multi touch tabletop interface with a fixed toolbar widget, (2) a desktop computer with a single mouse, (3) a tabletop interface with a floating toolbar widget, and (4) a tabletop interface with a toolbar widget accessed by a tangible object. We present evidence that the use of the tangible object in the fourth session was successful as a prompt for children to share control of the interface. In contrast, the floating toolbar widget in the third session seemed to spur conflict and interfere with the children's scientific discussion. We argue that through the use of the tangible object children were able to invoke familiar turn taking protocol—the mouse served a similar function in the desktop session. The use of the floating toolbar widget, on the other hand, resulted in conflicting expectations of appropriate social behavior on the part of the children.

ACKNOWLEDGMENTS

We would like to thank the Center for Connected Learning and Computer-Based Modeling at Northwestern University. We are also indebted to the children that volunteered to take part in this research and to Ana Duarte, and Gabriel Olson for all the support in this research study.

REFERENCES

1. Antle, A. N., Droumeva, M., & Ha, D., Hands on what?: comparing children's mouse-based and tangible-based interaction. In *Interaction Design and Children 2009*, ACM Press (2009), 80-88.
2. Fleck, R., Rogers, Y., Yuill, N., Marshall, P., Carr, A., Rick, J., & Bonnett, V. Actions speak loudly with words: unpacking collaboration around the table. In *Interactive Tabletops and Surfaces*, ACM Press (2009), 189-196
3. Harris, A., Rick, J., Bonnett, V.J., Yuill, N., Fleck, R., Marshall, P., and Rogers, Y. Around the table: Are multiple-touch surfaces better than single-touch for children's collaborative interactions. In *CSCL 2009*, ACM Press (2009), 335-344.
4. Hornecker, E. "I don't understand it either, but it is cool" – Visitor interactions with a multi-touch table in a museum. *In IEEE Tabletop 2008*, ACM Press (2008).
5. Hornecker, E., Marshall, P., & Rogers, Y. From entry to access: How shareability comes about. In *Designing Pleasurable Products and Interfaces*, ACM Pres (2007), 328-342.
6. Inkpen, K., Booth, K.S., Gribble, S.D., and Klawe, M. & Upitis, R. Playing together beats playing apart, especially for girls. In *Computer Support for Collaborative Learning*, ACM Press (1995), 177-181.
7. Kruger, R., Carpendale, M.S.T., Scott, S.D., & Greenberg, S. How People Use Orientation on Tables: Comprehension, Coordination and Communication. In *Conference on Supporting Group Work*, ACM Press (2003), 369-378.
8. Morris, M.R., Ryall, K., Shen, C., Forlines, C., & Vernier, F. Beyond "social protocols": multi-user coordination policies for co-located groupware. In *Computer Supported Cooperative Work 2004*, ACM Press (2004), 262-265.
9. Philips, S.U. Participant structures and communicative competence: Warm springs children in community and classroom. In C.B. Cazden, V. P. John & D.H. Hymes (Eds.), *Functions of language in the classroom*, Teachers College Press (1972), 370-394.
10. Piper, A.M., O'Brien, E., Morris, M.R., and Winograd, T. SIDES: a cooperative tabletop computer game for social skills development. In *Computer Supported Cooperative Work, 2006*, ACM Press (2006), 1-10.
11. Rick, J., Harris, A., Marshall, P., Fleck, R., Yuill, N., and Rogers, Y. Children designing together on a multi- touch tabletop: An analysis of spatial orientation and user interactions. In *Interaction Design and Children 2009*, ACM Press (2009), 106-114.
12. Ryall, K., Forlines, C., Shen, C., & Morris, M.R., Exploring the effects of group size and table size on interactions with tabletop shared-display groupware. In

Computer Supported Cooperative Work 2004, ACM Press (2004), 284-293.

13. Scott, S.D., Carpendale, M.S.T., & Inkpen, K.M., Territoriality in collaborative tabletop workspaces. In *Computer Supported Cooperative Work 2004*, ACM Press (2004), 294-303.

14. Sharan, S., Ackerman, Z., & Hertz-Lazarowitz, R., (1979). Academic Achievement of Elementary School Children in Small-Group versus Whole-Class Instruction. The Journal of Experimental Education, 48(2), 125-129.

15. Tang, J.C. (1991). Findings from observational studies of collaborative work. *International Journal of Man-Machine Studies*, 34, 143-160.

16. Wilensky, U. (1999). NetLogo [computer software]. Evanston, IL: Center for Connected Learning and Computer Based Modeling, Northwestern University. http://ccl.northwestern.edu/netlogo.

17. Wilensky, U., & Reisman, K. (2006). Thinking like a wolf, a sheep or a firefly: Learning biology through constructing and testing computational theories. Cognition and Instruction, 24(2), 171-209.

Tangible Navigation and Object Manipulation in Virtual Environments

Andy Wu[1], Derek Reilly[2], Anthony Tang[1], Ali Mazalek[1]

GVU Center[1]
Georgia Institute of Technology
85 5th St. NW, Atlanta, GA 30318, USA
{ andywu, tonyt, mazalek }@gatech.edu

OCAD University[2]
100 McCaul St.,
Toronto Ontario, M5T 1W1, Canada
dreilly@faculty.ocad.ca

ABSTRACT

In this paper, we introduce approaches to navigating and manipulating objects in a Collaborative Virtual Environment (CVE) that engage tangible objects and an interactive table interface. We also identify three design concerns that are common to physical-virtual connectivity for interaction with CVE systems. At last, we propose solutions to these issues within the context of CVEs.

Author Keywords

Tangible User Interface, TUI, HCI, Tabletop, 3D interaction, virtual world.

ACM Classification Keywords

H5.m. Information interfaces and presentation (e.g., HCI): Miscellaneous.

General Terms

Design

INTRODUCTION

Collaborative virtual environments (CVEs) were designed with the promise of supporting collaboration in a virtual, three-dimensional world: participants would be able to navigate through the world, and interact with virtual objects just as they would in the real world. CVEs have seen adoption in primarily two areas: gaming (e.g. first-person shooters, and massively multi-player online role playing games—MMORPGs), and in massively multi-user virtual worlds that are primarily social/recreational (e.g. SecondLife). While there has been interest in using CVEs for other purposes (meetings and collaborative work, for example), adoption remains low.

One of the core obstacles to more widespread adoption of CVEs is the absence of easy-to-use interaction mechanisms: first, to navigate through the virtual world, and second, to manipulate the virtual objects.

TEI'11, January 22–26, 2011, Funchal, Portugal.

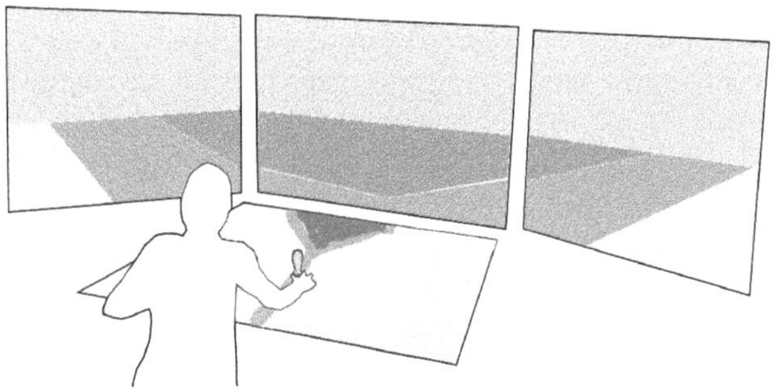

Figure 1. The user operates a grey tangible avatar on the tabletop that navigates through the virtual world. The coordinated view of the world on the upright displays shows that the avatar is at the fork in the road.

While most CVEs adopt a conventional keyboard+mouse scheme that works well for planar navigation, designers have been hard-pressed to find comparably easy-to-use mechanisms for full six-degree-of-freedom navigation (x, y, z position, and yaw, pitch, roll).

CVE systems typically only provide very crude methods of interacting with and manipulating objects in the virtual world: very often a large subset of objects cannot be moved, and those that can may only be moved along each plane (independently) in the virtual world. Changing the orientation of these objects (yaw, pitch, roll) is even more challenging. In general, this problem has been considered as a mismatch between the perceptual structure of the interaction task and the control space of the input device (i.e. that the desired degrees of freedom does not match the interaction device's available degrees of freedom) [12].

To support navigation, many CVE interfaces provide small inset maps. Because these maps are simplified, they may not provide enough detail to make navigation decisions relevant to collaboration: where a certain document is located, who is around, etc.

Top-down perspectives are common when configuring virtual environments, and anytime multiple virtual objects need to be arranged. A tangible+tabletop configuration offers interesting interactive possibilities for configuring virtual environments [20], both before and during collaboration.

In this work, we present approaches for navigating through and manipulating objects in a virtual world that employ tangible objects and a tabletop interface. As illustrated in Figure 1, tangible objects (tracked via a combination of cameras mounted above and under the table surface) are paired with objects in the virtual world: manipulating the tangible results in a corresponding action in the virtual world. The primary benefit of this mapping is that it allows users to fluidly manipulate virtual objects with a full six-degrees-of-freedom afforded by the physical object in the real world. Another benefit of this approach is that the tabletop provides a concrete perceptual frame of reference, absolutely positioning actions according to the view on the table. Thus, our tabletop interface provides a more concrete form of direct interaction when compared to typical 3D mouse/input devices, which only provide an indirect, relative form of interaction. Further, by devoting the tabletop display to presenting a live, interactive and view-controllable overview of the virtual environment, we provide a much richer information and interaction resource than the typical inset map.

While this approach has been foreshadowed and realized in prior research (e.g. [3]), the problems of the approach have rarely been addressed. From the context of supporting multi-user interaction in a CVE, we articulate three problems that arise from this approach: (1) potential for inconsistency between physical object and virtual object; (2) managing physical and digital constraints, and (3) controlling granularity. We illustrate several solutions that address and mitigate these problems within the context of CVEs, and begin the process of articulating a more general solution space.

This work makes three main contributions: first, we provide a system that supports navigation (and object manipulation) in a CVE using tangible objects; second, we articulate three problems that are common to systems that provide tangible control of virtual objects, and finally, we propose solutions to these problems within the context of CVEs.

RELATED WORK

Our general approach applies Tangible User Interfaces (TUIs) as a way to better connect users with virtual worlds by creating physical controls for digital information. By coupling digital information with everyday objects, people can apply the skills and practices used in their daily life when interacting with virtual worlds [5, 11, 23].

Some of the earliest work using tangible interfaces for 3D information focused on using physical objects to aid in the creation of 3D digital geometry [6, 7]. Triangles [9] is a canonical example in this space: users manipulate digital information using a physical construction kit. By tiling objects in the physical world, users could construct both 2D and 3D constructions in the physical world. This topography would be reflected through a connected computer, and updated in real-time based on the manipulation of the physical pieces.

Tangible Surrogates for Virtual Objects

The general approach of linking physical objects with objects in a virtual world has been explored in a variety of ways. Buxton [2] provides a sketch of a system where tangible props can be physically manipulated and placed on a stage. These props are linked to a 3D visualization of a car (in a virtual world). Gillet et al. [8] apply this approach to the domain of molecular visualization, using a 3D printer to create a set of molecules as props. The generated visualizations are then applied to an Augmented Reality (AR) scene with the virtual molecule. We call this approach for manipulating virtual objects *tangible handles* (phidgets in [11]), where physical objects represent a virtual object. Kruszyński et al. further extend this approach by allowing users to employ a physical stylus as a probe to explore both the tangible prop (in their case a coral structure) and the digital visualization of the prop [15].

Using a similar approach, Metoyer et al. developed a tangible tabletop system to coach the movements of animated football characters at a high-level [18]. Their system employs a miniature football field with small tangible players on the tabletop. Users control the movements of the tangible characters during the simulation of moves in a football game. Their work focuses on building timing of players' routes through the virtual world (i.e. the football field) in relation to one another. The system makes use of a projected tabletop as a concrete positional frame of reference, in a manner similar to our own use of the tabletop display.

Other approaches have provided fine-grained, articulated control of a virtual object and scene. In TUI3D, Mazalek et al. instrument a marionette puppet to control a virtual character [16] as a means to address the production and performative challenges involved in creating machinima (employing real-time 3D CGI for performance).

Tabletops in Collaborative Virtual Environments

The potential benefits of tabletop interfaces for collocated collaboration have been articulated and explored elsewhere [21]. A tabletop plus vertical display configuration promises some of the benefits of face-to-face interaction when working with remote collaborators. This has been explored using video streams by Tang and Minneman [22], Yarosh et al. [24] and others, and also for collaboration using a CVE by Hansson et al. [10] and Regenbrecht et al. [19]. By default, CVEs support group configurations in which all collaborators are remote. Tabletop CVE interfaces may also facilitate mixed-presence configurations, where some collaborators are collocated and share a single tabletop interface.

Navigating Virtual Worlds

Navigation is a fundamental activity in interactive virtual environments. Several researchers have explored how virtual worlds can be navigated using tangible approaches.

Kim et al. developed a TUI system for Cave Automatic Virtual Environment (CAVE) applications [14]. Their system used an AR technology and a regular tabletop surface for space navigation in a virtual environment (VE). They attached fiducial markers on physical objects that serve different purposes, e.g. proxies of virtual objects, controls of navigation in VE, paddles for simulating mouse clicks. Their AR navigation tool is very similar to a joystick, which controls the speed of the virtual object while our tangibles control the location of the object (or avatar). We build on this work by allowing the user to dynamically change the zoom level to gain more precise maneuverability and manipulation of virtual objects.

Finger Walking in Place is a planar navigational technique for virtual environments (presented on an upright display) using a tabletop surface [13]. A user employs finger gestures that are then mapped to moving commands like forward, backward and rotation in a walking area on the tabletop.

Bowman et al. [1] conducted a series of quantitative studies comparing several types of 3D navigation techniques. They discovered that "pointing" techniques are faster relative to "gaze-directed" steering techniques. Pointing techniques also have the advantage of decoupling 'look direction' and direction of movement. Our tangible+tabletop configuration permits a similar kind of decoupling of attention/gaze from movement.

Everyday Navigation in 3D Worlds
The problem of navigating 3D worlds was first appreciated in popular culture with the rise of first person shooter (FPS) games. Early control schemes in planar FPSs mapped to forward/backward and horizontal rotation movement. Within a short period of time, many of these users began using the mouse for rotation combined with left/right keyboard keys for strafing—a combination that is difficult for novices to learn, but has become the de facto method for navigating in FPS and MMORPGs.

At the same time, there have been many commercial attempts to bring more "natural" and "easy to use" interaction mechanisms for 3D environments. Such devices (e.g. 3D mice) have not achieved much popularity beyond computer-aided design applications.

APPROACH
To provide a system that supports navigation and object manipulation in a CVE, we believe building tangible controls integrated with a top-down view helps users to understand the 3D virtual world and provides more natural interactions (see Figure 2).

An interactive table has a large surface that is natural for a group of people to work together around, and is an ideal platform for 2D planar navigation in virtual space without requiring frequent context switching. Our interactive tabletop display combining TUI with AR techniques expands the physical working space from the 2D tabletop to include 3D space above the table surface.

Prototyping Tabletop Interfaces with TwinSpace
Our tabletop CVE interfaces were built using the TwinSpace architecture [4] for collaborative cross-reality. TwinSpace was originally designed to couple activities in a virtual world with activities in a physical space in order to support mixed-presence (collocated and remote) collaborative work. TwinSpace uses Open Wonderland as an MMO collaborative virtual world platform and the EventHeap service to communicate across diverse devices and services in the physical and virtual.

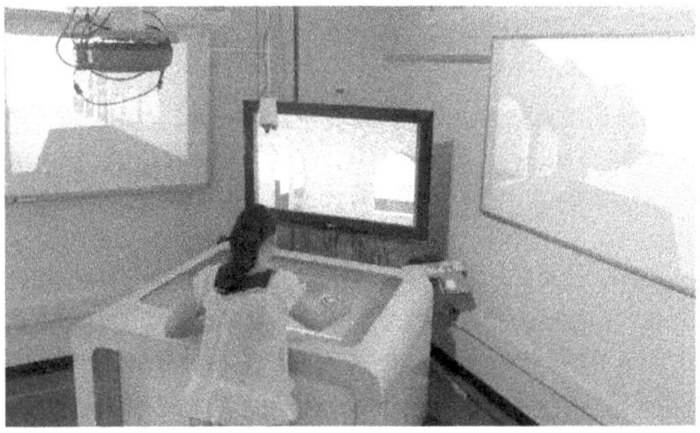

Figure 2. The user navigates through, and interacts with objects in the virtual world using the tangibles on the tabletop. A coordinated view of the world (as would be seen by the avatar—also a tangible) is presented on the upright displays.

A range of tabletop technologies has been integrated into TwinSpace-based projects so far. One uses a top down IR camera and IR pens to interact with digital content projected on the tabletop from a top-down projector. Another is the Tangible Tracking Table (TTT) [17], an interactive tabletop display that tracks multiple objects and finger touches on its surface. The TTT has been used in a number of ways as a virtual world interface: to permit camera control, object manipulation and virtual world navigation. Top-down, 3D fiducial tracking has also been used on different projects with a horizontal LCD display, the TTT, the IR pen table, and on a static horizontal surface. We base our assessment of the design challenges of tabletop CVE interfaces (and our proposed solutions) on the collected experience of design and evaluation across these multiple projects.

Most of these projects involved some form of tangible+tabletop interaction. These interactions fall under two broad categories: virtual object manipulation, and avatar navigation. Our experiences with each are discussed below.

Object Manipulation with Tangible Props
A user is configuring a room for a 3D online gallery. She walks to an interactive table, which presents a floor map of the virtual gallery. Each category of virtual object in the gallery (e.g. tables, seating, 3D artwork, 2D artwork) has its own physical prop. Specific virtual objects (e.g. a specific piece of 3D artwork) are added to a default location in the gallery by selection using the table's touch-based menu controls. After adding a specific 3D artwork

she then picks up the physical prop representing a 3D work, hovers over the newly instantiated object until it becomes active, and positions the prop on the tabletop where she wishes the specific art piece to be located. She releases the virtual object by hiding the fiducial on the prop. She finishes her job after placing all pieces on the tabletop to their positions.

The first environment built using TwinSpace was a physical collaborative team room. One of the key elements of this space is a tangible+tabletop interface. Using a tabletop interface with physical objects was an effective way to manipulate objects on a plane in the 3D virtual world. As we move the physical objects, the corresponding virtual objects change simultaneously. This simple interaction was found to be helpful in several applications: deploying furniture in a room, collaborative discussion over slides, moving groceries in a virtual supermarket, and positioning portals in a game space. In a traditional Wonderland client, a user has to select an object, launch the edit window and control the coordinate values using keyboard and mouse, providing high accuracy but more difficult manipulation.

The 2D object manipulation technique works well for objects that lay on a flat surface (such as furniture and some documents) or reside on the same plane. In several of our prototypes we considered extending the interaction to include 3D positioning. This can be achieved by extending the interaction space to include the region above the table (i.e. by lifting the tangibles above the table surface), and/or by allowing the view on the table to zoom or change vertical position or orientation. The first technique has been explored for adding and removing documents from a shared workspace, and for controlling a peripheral camera view of the tabletop region. We are exploring the latter technique in our game prototype. A combination of these techniques has been explored for navigation control, discussed next.

Navigation using tangible avatars

A visitor comes to our interactive table to explore our 3D virtual campus. On the table, there is an action figure, which serves as a tangible avatar. The tangible avatar controls a virtual avatar in the virtual world. Behind the interactive table stand three large vertical displays. The three vertical displays present the virtual avatar's perspective. As he glides and rotates the action figure on the tabletop, the vertical displays respond by showing the avatar's updated perspective. .

In addition to using an interactive tabletop display as a main working and viewing area, we use it as an interface to control avatars in the 3D virtual world. Most 3D computer games use keyboards, mice, joysticks or keypads to navigate the 3D virtual world. Usually, these games use first person views or third person perspective views for users to see the 3D world. Our interactive tabletop provides a top-down view of the virtual world. To move an avatar in the 3D world, instead of using a traditional controller, we use a tangible avatar (an action figure) to move the avatar in the virtual world. When a user moves the action figure forward, the avatar in the virtual world moves forward; when the action figure rotates, the avatar rotates in the same way. Figure 3 shows the actions performed on a tangible object on the tabletop – moving and rotating.

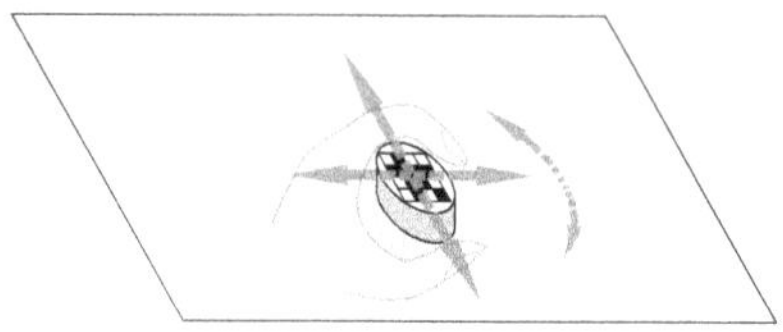

Figure 3. A tangible avatar can be moved and rotated on the tabletop.

However, moving an object on a tabletop (a two dimensional movement) does not provide a 3D navigation experience, unless elevation changes occur automatically, e.g. as a result of walking on stairs. The TwinSpace framework permits the simultaneous updating of views on multiple displays. In our prototypes we have used this to couple top-down and first-person views. The configuration in this section uses three vertical displays to provide a wide egocentric view of the 3D space (see Figures 1, 2). A user stands in front of the TTT and moves the action figure on the tabletop to navigate the 3D world. The interactive tabletop has become a TUI that provides visual feedback and direct manipulation of a physical avatar.

Changing level of details and navigating with a physical tangible object

A tabletop display shows only part of the virtual campus. When the visitor wants to see the whole virtual world, he has two options. He can use the tangible avatar and hand gestures one the tabletop to explore the map, or he can lift the tangible avatar. As the tangible avatar moves further away from the table surface, a larger unseen region of the map is revealed. Therefore, he can pickup the action figure, navigate the campus from different levels in the air, and place it at a different place.

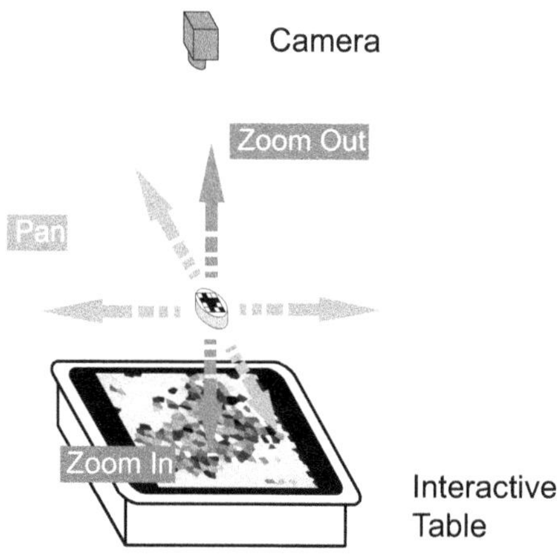

Figure 4. 3D navigation on GoogleMap.

Navigation with an object on an interactive tabletop gives direct visual and proprioceptive feedback of the location of an action figure. In 3D environments that only allow ground navigation, this implementation may be sufficient. However, many 3D games permit navigation in the vertical direction, and content-centric CVEs often exploit the vertical dimension. Therefore, we extended our tabletop interface to permit 3D navigation.

Our concept is to navigate the ground using the tangible tabletop interface, and navigate the 3D space when a user lifts the object in the air (see Figure 4). To implement this, we attached a second camera on top of the interactive tabletop to detect the 3D position of objects on the tabletop. We use NyARToolkit to detect a fiducial marker attached to the tangible object, and translate the physical location and orientation of the object into a 3D virtual world transformation matrix. This matrix is sent out through the TwinSpace infrastructure to update the virtual avatar's location and the views on the vertical displays.

We tested a number of related interaction concepts using Google Maps. In this case, when we raise the object, the map zooms out; when we put the object down, the map zooms in. We can also move the object in the horizontal to pan the map at any specific level.

LINKING PHYSICAL & VIRTUAL OBJECTS: DESIGN CHALLENGES

In designing these interactions, we encountered several design challenges that would likely also be encountered when linking virtual entities with tangible objects in other contexts. These are: potential inconsistency between tangible object state/location with virtual object state/location; potential mismatch between physical/virtual constraints, and the need for managing granularity of control.

Physical/Virtual Object Inconsistency

When the physical object is the sole input mechanism for manipulating the virtual object, then position and state information is unlikely to be a problem. There are two cases when inconsistency can become a problem: first, when there is another method to manipulate the state/location of the object (common in a CVE, where another user can change the location of an object), and second, if the state/location is represented via a *relationship*, and that relationship can be changed by another method. We return to this latter case more explicitly later when we describe how granularity of control is achieved.

Physical/Virtual Constraints

An inherent problem in linking physical and virtual objects is that our interactions with these objects in their different manifestations are subject to different constraints. For example, in the physical world, we might place a letter-sized digital document on a meeting table and pass it around to share it; in the virtual world, we might dispense with a meeting table altogether, and scale the document so that the content is legible from a distance.

Virtual objects have artificial constraints in the virtual world. For example, using arrow keys to move an avatar allows only linear movement, the boundary of the 3D virtual world restricts the objects to move further, and the physics in the virtual environment limit the way objects move.

Similarly, physical objects in the real world have intrinsic constraints (their weight, size, shape). An interactive tabletop provides a physical affordance (the tabletop surface) to support objects moving on its surface, but it constrains the object's freedom of movement in the vertical axis (and certainly, we cannot leave an object in midair!). There are also technical constraints in the physical world. For example, the view field of the lens of our tracking cameras create an invisible boundary for these physical objects and the discriminability of the optical sensor limits the minimum size of the marker on an object, and hence the size of the object itself.

Another constraint is the difficulty of manipulating physical objects from a virtual environment. For example, while we can manipulate the location of a virtual object when its physical surrogate is moved in the real world, when a user moves a digital document in the virtual world, the physical document does not move.

Since the constraints in these two worlds are different, we have to adopt transformations or mappings to manage them. In some cases, these mappings are straightforward (e.g. to solve the constraints of size mismatch between the tabletop and the virtual world is to scale the image of virtual world down to the size of the tabletop); however, in many cases, the "correct" mapping is a matter of interpretation.

Managing Granularity of Control

One constraint we employ in our tabletop+tangible prototype is the physical frame of the tabletop. As stated earlier, it provides a concrete frame of reference for users' interactions: their interactions on this frame of reference are thus absolute rather than relative.

Yet, if the user moves the tangible object 1" on the tabletop, how much should that move in the virtual world? How much of the world should the user see on the tabletop? Likely, the answer depends on the context: sometimes, it may be desirable for fine-grained control and positioning, while in other cases, the user may need to move long distances across the world. How can the user change this granularity of control dynamically?

Mental models of panning issues

In demos to visitors of our research center, we found differing expectations of how panning should work. There are two types panning on a map. When a user moves an object from location A to location B on the tabletop, this has two interpretations. In Figure 5 (a), a tangible object is about to slide to the right. Figure 5 (b) shows the navigation method that is commonly used for Google Map navigation on the iPhone. Figure 5 (c) shows the navigation method we are used to when we navigate a physical paper map or slide a scroll bar in a GUI. These two navigation strategies correspond with different mental models of navigation:

users either employed a "subject-centric" (5b), or an "object-centric" (5c) perspective.

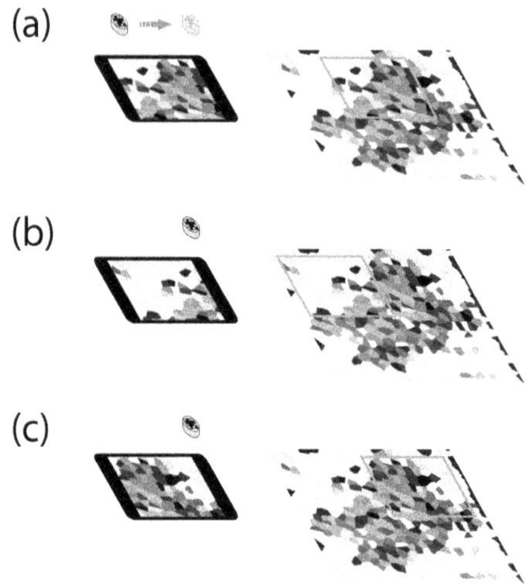

Figure 5. The movement of a tangible object and the two possible navigations on an interactive tabletop display.

ADDRESSING THE CHALLENGES FOR CVES

In this section, we outline how we addressed the design challenges identified in the previous section in our prototypes. We believe our approaches have wide applicability for object manipulation and avatar navigation in CVEs.

Inconsistency: Notify, Copy, Lock Virtual

We encounter the inconsistency problem in a cross-reality environment when a user manipulates an object in the CVE that is associated with a tangible handle. For example, a user may move or rotate a virtual document. We designed two solutions to this problem: notify and copy

Notify (a.k.a. Halo). In this design solution, we simply notify the users of the inconsistent state using a halo or colored aura drawn around both the virtual object (in the virtual world) and on the tabletop around the physical object. This halo also shows the link between the two objects to allow users to resolve the inconsistency by (for example) moving the one of the objects to the other object.

Copy. Creating a duplicate of the inconsistent object can satisfy every individual trying to control it. This is useful when several groups of people from different locations want to read one document.

Lock Virtual. A third possible solution that we did not implement was simply to lock virtual objects that have been associated with a tangible handle. In such a solution, users in the CVE simply are not allowed to manipulate the properties/state of such virtual objects.

Physical and Virtual Constraints: Clutch, Proxy, Elastic Link

Clutch. Permitting vertical movement by raising or lowering a tangible object partially overcomes the physical constraint of the 2D tabletop surface for 3D navigation. However it is difficult to move an object horizontally in mid air for extended periods, and impossible to leave it there. Whether the tangible controls the elevation of the tabletop view or the 3D position of an object relative to that view, we require a mechanism for turning elevation control on or off. A clutch can be implemented on the tangible (e.g. through a fiducial-based control) or on the tabletop interface.

Proxy. We have prototyped applications in which each virtual object in the virtual world has a physical representative in the real world, however this is problematic when there are many manipulable objects, or when the set of objects can change dynamically. In such cases a fixed set of tangible proxies can be assigned to virtual objects dynamically. Proxies are representative of the virtual object, rather than a physical counterpart to it. Proxies require a mechanism for attaching and removing their association with specific virtual objects.

Elastic Link. When there are three or more tangible objects on the tabletop, the objects and their underlying digital representation have become difficult to manage. Our tentative solution is not to create digital avatars right under the associated physical objects. Instead, displaying the digital object next to the physical object with a visual link between them. One reason for an elastic link is so the physical object will not block dynamic digital information and permit interactions beyond movement in space (as is the case with editable documents, for example. Another reason is when the map zooms, or pans, digital objects can move accordingly, and a call-out would appear that visually links the physical location of the tangible object with its virtual object's location.

Granularity: Coupled and Decoupled Zooming

The 3D tangible object manipulation method mentioned before provides zooming naturally. One can see the detail by moving the tangible object toward the tabletop and see the whole map by moving the object away from the tabletop. This is known as a coupled method that links zooming with the tangible.

Another navigation method is to use a tangible object with hand gestures when the tangible object is placed on the tabletop—where zooming is decoupled from the tangible object itself. In our design, moving a tangible object on the tabletop means panning the map, while rotating this object means changing the orientation of the avatar. What if we want to rotate the map or zooming into an area and keep the action figure on the tabletop? There are many reasons to do this. First, raising an avatar up and down can cause fatigue to users. Second, in 3D worlds where most activities occur on the ground, users may want to quickly zoom into the object. If we can achieve this with tangible objects staying on the table, this can save users effort.

The new system provides interactions using tangible object and finger gestures. In Figure 6, the tangible object is held still. (a) and (b) use one finger to rotate and zoom the map. These two interactions can be performed together, so a user can draw to rotate and zoom the map at the same time. (c) uses two fingers to pan the map. As a result, a user can manipulate her avatar on a 2D plane by moving or rotating the physical object. She can zoom out to have an overview of the map with one figure gesture. She can also rotate the map to have a front view of the avatar's face. If she does not want to change the granularity, she can use two fingers to pan the map as well.

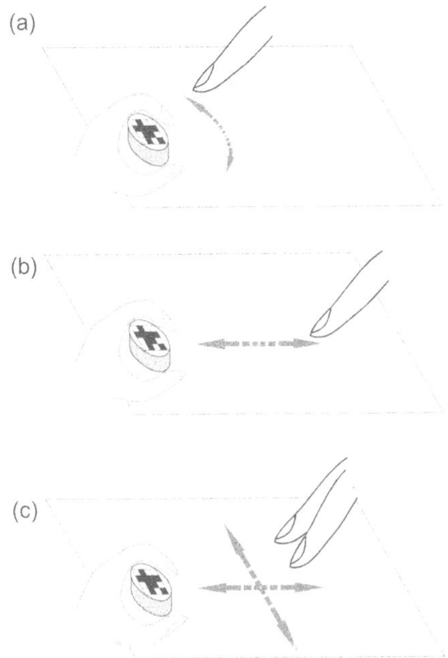

Figure 6. Tangible interaction with finger gestures: (a) gesture for rotating; (b) gesture for zooming; (c) gesture for panning.

Our 3D GoogleMap navigation concept began from this observation that one usually has to zoom out before panning. Therefore, creating a system that performed this transformation automatically was our goal. The 3D GoogleMap navigation was based on this scenario:

A map navigator stands at our table. His current location on the map is at Atlanta. He wants to move the center of the map to New York. When he raises the physical object from Atlanta, the map starts to zoom out. At some point, he is able to see New York at the edge of the map. He moves the object toward New York on the map. Slowly has New York moved toward the object. Finally, he places the object on top on New York City on the map.

Figure 7. The concept of navigation using a tangible object. The destination is out of current tabletop's view, which is bounded with red lines.

In other words, a user simply pickups the tangible prop, and put it onto a destination location as shown in Figure 7. Figure 8 illustrates the decomposed actions in four steps.

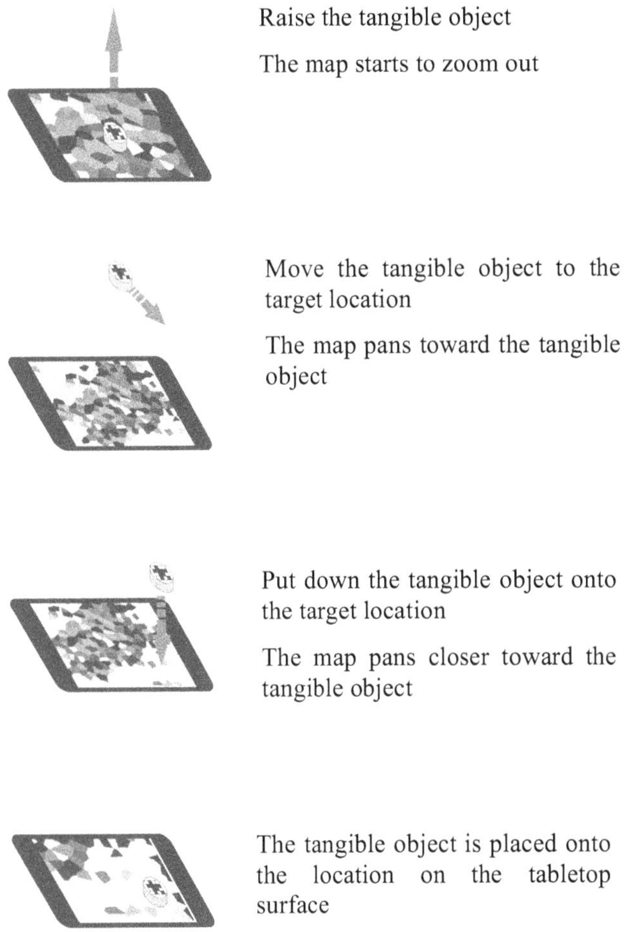

Figure 8. Moving a tangible object from one location to another.

To achieve this, the panning mechanism we chose was the one illustrated in Figure 5 (c). When the scenario described above happens, the navigator has to move the tangible object to the target location. However, this target location keeps moving toward the object's projected location. This navigation requires some practice to master. Yet the distance between the tangible object and the target location is provided visually and their relative movement is predictable.

CONCLUSION

We have presented results from our prototyping efforts involving object manipulation and avatar navigation in collaborative virtual worlds using tangible+tabletop interfaces. In particular, we present two new types of CVE navigation methods; one combines a tangible with finger gestures and the other builds on the action of relocating an object on a table. We summarized three issues that are common to using tangibles for object manipulation and navigation in CVEs and finally, we proposed solutions to these problems within the context of CVEs.

One possible extension to this work is to apply the Google Maps 3D navigation concept inside 3D games. So that the zoom level of the radar map reflects the avatar's vertical position. We can also adjust the three vertical displays' views from fixed-angle views to the view from the virtual avatar's eye to provide more degrees of freedom in navigation. We can achieve this by making an avatar's head a trackable camera using a fiducial marker.

Finally, we would like to get more control of a virtual avatar using TUIs. The future tangible avatar should not be just a physical model, but a figure with flexible joints that can perform more complex tasks.

ACKNOWLEDGEMENTS
We thank Andy Echenique, Jonathan Massey, Shashank Chamoli, Szu-Chia Lu and the Synaesthetic Media Lab for helping shape our ideas. This work is supported by NSF-IIS grant #0705569 and a research collaboration grant from Steelcase Inc.

REFERENCES

1. Bowman, D. A., Koller, D. and Hodges, L. F., Travel in Immersive Virtual Environments: An Evaluation of Viewpoint Motion Control Techniques, *Proc. VRAIS '97*, IEEE Computer Society (1997), 45-52.
2. Buxton, B., A Props-Based UI for Automotive Visualization on Large Format Powerwalls. Alias|Wavefront Research, 1999.
3. Buxton, W., Fitzmaurice, G., Balakrishnan, R. and Kurtenbach, G. Large Displays in Automotive Design. *IEEE Comput. Graph. Appl.*, 20, 4 (2000), 68-75.
4. Reilly, D., Voida, S., McKeon, M., Dantec, D. L., Bunde-Pedersen, J., Forslund, C., Verma, P., Edwards, W. K., Mynatt, E. D., Mazalek, A., Want, R., Space Matters: Physical-Digital and Physical-Virtual Codesign in inSpace, *IEEE Pervasive Computing vol. 9 no. 3*, (2010), 54-63.
5. Fitzmaurice, G. W., Ishii, H. and Buxton, W. A. S., Bricks: laying the foundations for graspable user interfaces, *Proc. CHI 95'*, ACM (1995), 442-449.
6. Frazer, J. H. *Three-Dimensional Data Input Devices*. National Academy of Sciences, 1982.
7. Frazer, J. H., Use of Simplified Three-Dimensional Computer Input Devices to Encourage Public Participation in Design, *Proc. of CAD '82*, (1982), 143-151.
8. Gillet, A., Sanner, M., Stoffler, D., Goodsell, D. and Olson, A., Augmented Reality with Tangible Auto-Fabricated Models for Molecular Biology Applications, *Proc. Vis. '04*, IEEE Computer Society (2004), 235-242.
9. Gorbet, M. G., Orth, M. and Ishii, H., Triangles: tangible interface for manipulation and exploration of digital information topography, *Proc CHI 98'*, ACM (1998), 49-56.
10. Hansson, P. R., Wallberg, A. and Simsarian, K., Techniques for "natural" interaction in multi-user CAVE-like environments, *ECSCW Poster*, (1997).
11. Ishii, H. and Ullmer, B., Tangible bits: towards seamless interfaces between people, bits and atoms, *Proc CHI 97'*, ACM (1997), 234-241.
12. Jacob, R. J. K. and Sibert, L. E., The perceptual structure of multidimensional input device selection, *Proc. CHI 92'*, ACM (1992), 211-218.
13. Kim, J.-S., Gračanin, D., Matković, K. and Quek, F., Finger Walking in Place (FWIP): A Traveling Technique in Virtual Environments, *Proc. ISSG 08'*, Springer-Verlag (2008), 58-69.
14. Kim, J.-S., Graˇcanin, D., Singh, H. L., Matkovi´c, K. and Juric, J., A Tangible User Interface System for CAVE Applicat, *Proc VR 06'*, IEEE Computer Society (2006), 261-264.
15. Kruszyński, K. J. and Liere, R. v. Tangible props for scientific visualization: concept, requirements, application. *Virtual Real.*, 13, 4 (2009), 235-244.
16. Mazalek, A. and Nitsche, M., Tangible interfaces for real-time 3D virtual environments, *Proc. ACE 07'*, ACM (2007), 155-162.
17. Mazalek, A., Winegarden, C., Al-Haddad, T., Robinson, S. J. and Wu, C.-S., Architales: physical/digital co-design of an interactive story table, *Proc. TEI 09'*, ACM (2009), 241-248.
18. Metoyer, R. A., Xu, L. and Srinivasan, M., A Tangible Interface for High-Level Direction of Multiple Animated Characters, *Proc. Graphics Interface 03'*, (2003), 167-176.
19. Regenbrecht, H., Haller, M., Hauber, J. and Billinghurst, M. Carpeno: interfacing remote collaborative virtual environments with table-top interaction. *Virtual Real.*, 10, 2 (2006), 95-107.
20. Rekimoto, J. and Saitoh, M., Augmented surfaces: a spatially continuous work space for hybrid computing environments, *Proc. CHI 99'*, ACM (1999), 378-385.
21. Stacey, D. S. *Guest Editors' Introduction: Interacting with Digital Tabletops*. 2006.
22. Tang, J. C. and Minneman, S. L. Videodraw: a video interface for collaborative drawing. *ACM Trans. Inf. Syst.*, 9, 2 (1991), 170-184.
23. Ullmer, B. and Ishii, H. Emerging frameworks for tangible user interfaces. *IBM Syst. J.*, 39, 3-4 (2000), 915-931.
24. Yarosh, S., Cuzzort, S., Müller, H. and Abowd, G. D., Developing a media space for remote synchronous parent-child interaction, *Proc. IDC 2009*, ACM (2009), 97-105.

iNkDraw: Physical Ink-Based Interface for Capturing and Manipulating Drawings on Digital Display

Kayato Sekiya
NEC Corporation
1-10 Nisshin-cho, Fuchu-shi, Tokyo
183-8501, Japan
kayato@bk.jp.nec.com

Shinpei Chihara
NEC Corporation
1753 Shimonumabe, Nakahara-ku, Kawasaki
211-8666, Japan
s-chihara@bk.jp.nec.com

ABSTRACT
This paper introduces a new drawing interface named iNkDraw for capturing ink marks on a digital display drawn using physical ink such as dry erase markers. By using ink-based FTIR, the interface directly detects the ink location on the drawing surface, thus any ink-oriented interactions are intrinsically supported – e.g. controlling the thickness and faintness of lines by varying pen/brush movement, erasing the drawings by wiping the ink off with a cloth or even with a finger. Furthermore, iNkDraw can distinguish between drawing and touch, which allows users to digitally manipulate the captured drawings using pointers and menus. Several applications using the interface have been implemented. Limitations on using physical ink as an interfacing medium are also discussed.

Author Keywords
Physical ink, tangible user interface, frustrated total internal reflection, interactive whiteboard, visual thinking.

ACM Classification Keywords
H5.2. Information interfaces and presentation (e.g., HCI): User Interfaces: Input devices and strategies.

General Terms
Design, Human Factors

INTRODUCTION
Freehand sketches are frequently used in creative meetings in order to quickly externalize and explore alternative design ideas [1]. Despite the various digital tools available for this purpose, physical ink-based tools such as whiteboards or flipcharts and ink markers have been the tool of choice mainly because of their ease of use and rapidity [2]. Firstly, people usually learn how to draw and erase on whiteboard-like tools very early in life, thus most people can use them without any difficulty. People are also well-acquainted with using physical tools like brushes to create expressive strokes of lines with various thickness and faintness, fluidly. Secondly, on physical ink-based tools, there is almost no lag between the input (hand movement) and the visual output (the drawing), which allows users to draw very quickly and more accurately [3]. Also, there is no required booting before one can start using the tool.

TEI'11, January 22–26, 2011, Funchal, Portugal.

Figure 1. iNkDraw interface prototype.

However, also because of their physical nature, it is not easy when using ink-based tools to store/retrieve past drawings, make multiple copies of them, to share them with your colleagues in remote sites over a network connection, etc., which are features readily available in most digital drawing systems. In our research, we have aimed to create an input interface that maintains the ease of use and the rapidity of the physical ink-based tools while providing digital features like store/retrieve and communication over a network, in a unified manner.

This paper introduces a new input interface named iNkDraw that employs ink-based FTIR (Frustrated Total Internal Reflection) for capturing drawing on a digital display drawn using physical ink. The interface uses camera-based sensing to directly detect the ink location on the drawing surface in real time thus any operations applied to the ink is faithfully reflected on its digital counterpart. Expressive lines of various thickness and faintness can easily be inputted by simple movement of pens or brushes while drawn objects may be erased by wiping the ink off with a cloth or even with a finger. Since it uses active sensing in the infrared (IR) spectrum, ink images can be isolated from their surrounding objects such as images on digital display with high contrast. Further, since immediate visual feedback is afforded by the physical ink itself, any delay in the digitizing process is unlikely to hinder user pen movement. Moreover, in addition to its capturing capabilities, iNkDraw distinguishes between drawing and touch, which allows users to digitally manipulate the captured drawings using pointers and menus.

RELATED WORK

Commercial digital whiteboards such as SmartBoard [http://smarttech.com] mimics pen-like input by combining pen position tracking sensors with digitally rendered ink on projectors. In these systems, there is a noticeable delay between the hand gesture and the visual feedback which could be disturbing in quick sketching applications. Also, much of the expressiveness available in ink-based tools is lost. FluidPaint [4] by Vandoren et al uses a real wet brush in FTIR setup to accurately detect the contact profile of the brush tip and reproduces the expressiveness of brush painting in digital form. However, since the system still detects the location of the drawing tool and not the drawing itself, many of the affordances of physical ink such as the ability to wipe off or smudge with your finger, is not available. Several researches have taken the approach to use real ink with camera-based sensing to maintain the affordance of physical ink. ZombieBoard [5] by Saund et al combines an ordinary whiteboard with a tilt/pan camera and mosaicking technique to digitally capture drawings and to store/print captured images using diagrammatic commands. Later in the Magic Table [2], Bérard has added displaying and pointing capabilities to ZombieBoard using a projector and an extra camera for tracking tagged objects. These systems can only capture static images of the drawings which limits their applications. Distinguishing between drawn objects and digitally displayed objects is also an issue. ClearBoard [6] by Ishii et al and VideoDraw [7] by Tang et al uses a camera with a polarizer film to capture ink marks and user body images apart from the displayed images, in real time. However, their configuration is unable to record ink images and user body images separately. Moreover, since the camera detects light component which originates from the ambient lighting then is reflected by the ink, fluorescent ink markers are needed to obtain sufficient contrast.

HARDWARE SETUP

Figure 2 shows the schematic overview of iNkDraw interface. The interface consists of an acrylic panel with polished edges, which acts as the drawing surface, a group of IR light emitting diodes (LEDs), an IR camera and a liquid crystal display (LCD). The LEDs inject IR light into the acrylic panel via its polished edges, which propagates through it by means of total internal reflection. Total internal reflection creates what is called "evanescent wave" – a thin layer of light field covering the reflecting surface with an intensity that decays exponentially with distance from the boundary. When the user draws on the acrylic panel using physical ink, the ink particles come in contact with the evanescent wave causing light to scatter out into the surrounding environment. The image of the scattered light is captured on the IR camera mounted above the drawing surface. The left image in Figure 3 shows an example of the captured ink image, wherein the ink marks appear brighter compared to their surrounding area. The captured image is in turn displayed on the LCD after image distortion removal and color enhancements (right image in Figure 3). The displayed image on the LCD illuminates the physical ink from behind which serves as a subtle feedback of the digitizing functionality in action (Figure 4). The captured images are also used to extract touch events and their coordinates which are used for supporting pointing-based interactions. In principle, the interface operates very similarly to Han's FTIR touch panel [8] or Vandoren's FluidPaint [4] except physical ink is used as the frustrating medium and remains on the panel during the lifetime of the drawings in tangible and manipulative form [9].

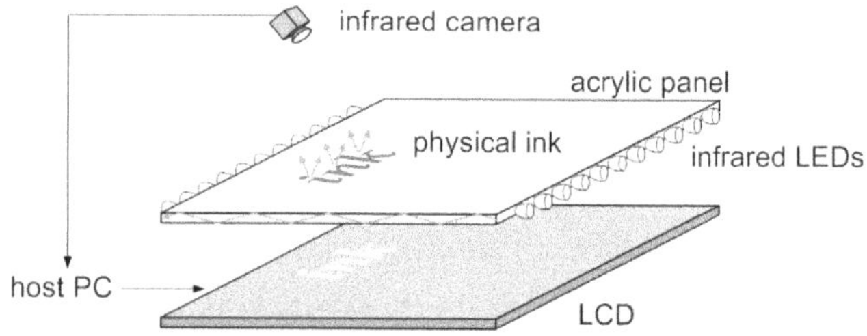

Figure 2. Schematic overview of iNkDraw interface.

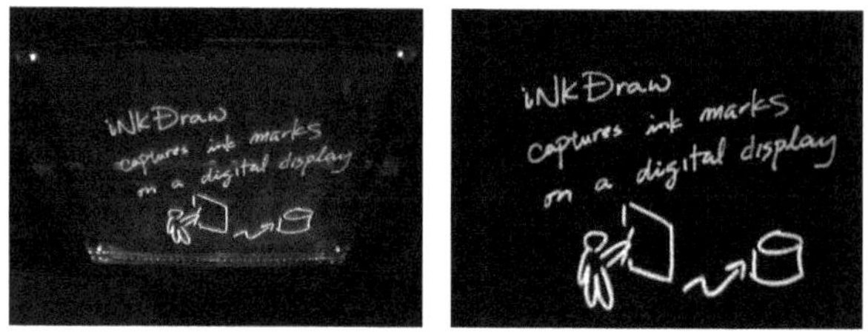

Figure 3. Captured ink image (left: raw image from camera; right: processed image displayed on LCD).

INTERACTIONS

Drawing and Erasing

Users can draw and erase on iNkDraw as on any other ink-based tool such as a whiteboard. As a user draws for example using a dry erase marker or wipes off ink with a cloth or with a finger, these operations applied to the ink are faithfully reflected on its digitally captured counterpart. There is a slight delay between the input gesture (e.g. marker movement) and the digital rendering on the display but this would not hinder user performance as immediate visual feedback is afforded by the physical ink itself. The captured image can also be displayed on a remote display in real time.

Figure 4. Physical ink on drawing surface and digital rendering of the captured ink image in close-up.

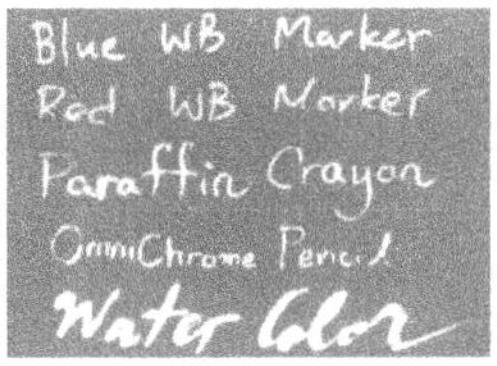

Figure 5. Various types of physical ink on iNkDraw.

Supported ink types

Dry erase markers (both fluorescent and non-fluorescent) of various colors and brands have been tested (Figure 5). Although the interface showed some brand and color preferences (black markers are the hardest to detect), almost all the markers scattered enough IR light to be detectable in our prototype. Watercolors are also a good medium. They can be used with tools like brushes, or on fingers for finger painting. Besides liquid ink, solid materials like crayons have also been verified to work. Paraffin wax-based crayons and OmniChrome pencils (plastic pencils designed for drawing on glass) were advantageous because they could be wiped off relatively easily.

Manipulating Captured Drawings

iNkDraw distinguishes between drawing and touch using simple time domain filtering on consecutive image frames. Using this touch recognition mechanism, a menu subsystem was implemented for accessing the applications' digital capabilities in a unified manner. The menu subsystem can be invoked by touching the bottom part of the drawing surface with a finger (Figure 6). This would cause a menu bar to appear. It is a hierarchical menu which can be drilled down to invoke a command. In command mode, command dependent operations can be implemented such as selecting an area on the drawing surface using multi-finger touch.

APPLICATIONS

Three applications were implemented on iNkDraw interface to illustrate its unique capabilities: QuickSketch, CollabDraw and iNkArt.

QuickSketch

QuickSketch is a digital whiteboard application which allows you to quickly draw and crop sketched ideas (Figure 7). After drawing, arbitrary areas on the drawing surface can be selected and saved using the menu subsystem. Users can retrieve and draw directly over their past sketches to add new ideas. The new sketch with added ideas can be saved with or without the retrieved sketch in the background for further iterative refinement. The user can also choose to upload the sketch to an Internet server to make the sketches accessible from other devices like cell phones. System can also load digitally rendered images such as CAD data or animations as background images.

Figure 6. Touch-based menu subsystem.

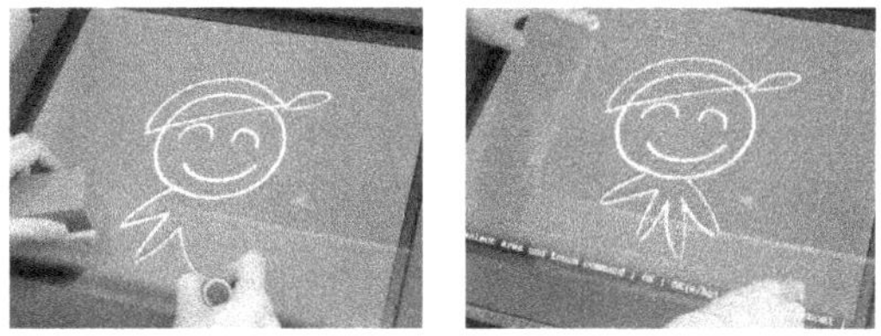

Figure 7. QuickSketch (left: drawing over retrieved image (in red); right: selecting area to save using touch).

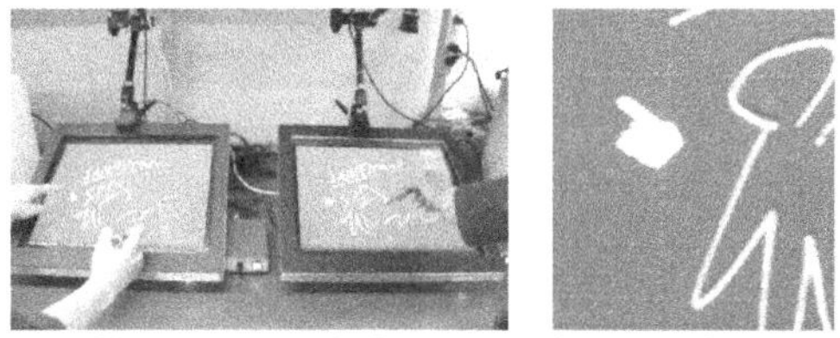

Figure 8. CollabDraw (left: system in use; right: pointer displayed by touch).

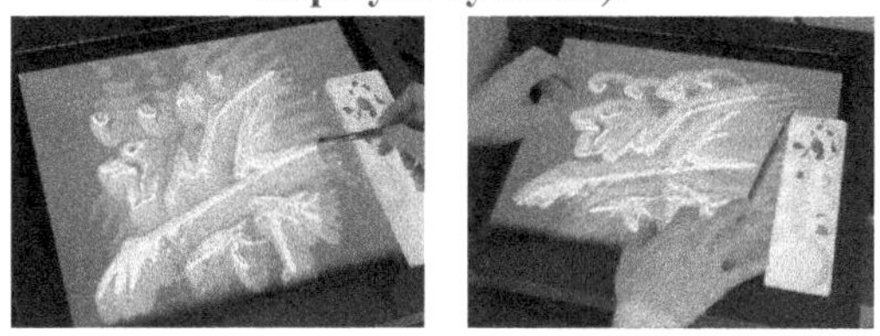

Figure 9. iNkArt (left: painting with brush; right: painting with fingers).

CollabDraw

CollabDraw is a collaborative drawing application which uses two sets of iNkDraw interface to allow a pair of remote users to draw over each other's drawings (Figure 8). Touching on the drawing surface brings up an arrow pointer on the displays that fades away with time which allows users to make references to a particular point on the drawing. Current implementation uses two iNkDraw interfaces on a single PC in dual display mode and provides no voice channel. However, the system can easily be extended to work on computers connected via a network.

iNkArt

iNkArt is a painting application that can be used for artistic expressions (Figure 9). Water colors on brushes or fingers can be used to draw or finger paint ink patterns in different thickness and faintness. Since the intensity of the scattered light depends on the amount of ink that is deposited on the drawing surface, users have more direct and intuitive control over their digital drawing. Digital effects can then be added to the captured images for further aesthetics. For example in Figure 7, as user draws, history of captured images drifts away from the physical ink location spirally as if blown by wind.

IMPLEMENTATION DETAILS

Implementation details are provided below for easier replication of the interface. A 4mm-thick acrylic panel with anti-abrasion coating was injected with 870nm IR light using LEDs placed 1.1cm apart on its longer sides. Anti-abrasion coated panel was selected for its superior performance in ink detachability. An IEEE1394b monochrome camera with 3.5mm focal-length lens and a Kodak/Wratten 87 range IR-pass filter was used for ink image capture. The camera was placed above the drawing surface at approximately 45-degree angle to the surface normal to reduce occlusion by user's hands. The camera captured VGA images at 60 frames per second. The radial distortion and perspective distortion were removed from the captured images on a Windows PC using OpenCV and Intel Integrated Performance Primitives libraries. Graphics rendering was done by OpenGL. Touch was detected using simple time domain filtering on consecutive image frames. Current system only detects finger down events. Alternate frame image subtraction in combination with LED gating (turning on/off in sync with the camera shutter) was used to remove IR noise emitted mainly from fluorescent lamps in the surrounding environment. The LCD was a 19-inch SXGA (1280x1024) panel with a 176-degree viewing angle in both horizontal and vertical directions.

DISCUSSIONS

Because iNkDraw uses ink as an interfacing medium, it has some limitations that arise from its physical nature. The most prominent limitation is that past drawings that are retrieved from storage can no longer be edited using the same interaction method as when it was originally created – by manipulating the physical ink. To overcome this limitation, one would need electrically controllable ink that can be re-deposited on the drawing surface. One interesting approach may be to combine printing technologies like inkjet printers or plotters to restore digitally stored drawings.

Color support is also an issue since iNkDraw uses light in the IR spectrum to detect ink locations. By using an IR camera to detect ink locations and an extra color camera to detect color (an AND operation between the two images), combined with some color saturation control, we have been able to distinguish between a few colors which probably is sufficient for simple whiteboard applications. However, accurate full-color reproduction is still under study.

Camera positioned in front of the LCD inevitably cases some occlusion, though the camera has been placed at an angle to minimize the problem. We have chosen the LCD for our first prototype because of its small form factor but a rear-projected display may also be an attractive alternative. Not only can it alleviate the occlusion problem, it will add a useful feature of allowing the user to draw on it without the power turned on. One can start drawing without the power on and later may decide to use its digital capabilities and turn on the system. On normal LCDs, it is harder to make out the ink when they are turned off.

There is also noticeable parallax. However, a simple pilot study has shown that users were not disturbed by this phenomenon. This may be because the visual feedback is afforded by the physical ink and the digital copy is acting as a supplemental illumination or a "digital shadow". Nevertheless, the parallax may be reduced by using a thinner waveguide, possibly a film on a reinforcing material.

Image resolution is limited by the camera resolution plus the blurring caused by the multipath reflection between the top and bottom surfaces of the acrylic panel and the LCD surface. The multipath component may be reduced by using a thinner waveguide and/or by placing an IR-cut filter over the LCD.

CONCLUSION

iNkDraw allows for digitally capturing and manipulation of ink marks on a digital display drawn using various kinds of physical ink via ink-based FTIR. While maintaining the ease of use and the rapidity of the physical ink-based tools, digital capabilities like store/retrieve and communication over a network can be provided through touch-based interactions. We are currently planning to build a larger prototype for extensive in-field evaluations.

ACKNOWLEDGMENTS

The authors would like to thank Prof. Hiroshi Ishii at the MIT Media Lab for his inspiring comments and discussions.

REFERENCES

1. Newman, M.W., Landay, J.A. Sitemaps, Storyboards, and Specifications: A Sketch of Web Site Design Practice. *Proc. DIS '00*, 263-274, 2000
2. Bérard, F. The Magic Table: Computer-Vision Based Augmentation of a Whiteboard for Creative Meetings. *ICCV Workshop on Projector-Camera Systems*, 2003
3. MacKenzie, I.S., Ware, C. Lag as a determinant of human performance in interactive systems. *Proc. INTERACT/CHI '93*, 488-493, 1993
4. Vandoren, P., Claesen, L., Laerhoven, T.V., Taelman, J., Raymaekers, C., Flerackers, E., Reeth, F.V. FluidPaint: an interactive digital painting system using real wet brushes, *Proc. Tabletop '09*, 53-56, 2009
5. Saund, E. Bringing the marks on a whiteboard to electronic life. *Proc. CoBuild '99*, 1999
6. Ishii, H., Kobayashi, M. ClearBoard: a seamless medium for shared drawing and conversation with eye contact. *Proc. CHI '92*, 525-532, 1992
7. Tang, J.C. Minneman, S.L. VideoDraw: a video interface for collaborative drawing. *Proc. CHI '90*, 313-320, 1990
8. Han, J.Y. Low-Cost Multi-Touch Sensing through Frustrated Total Internal Reflection, *Proc. UIST '05*, 115-118, 2005
9. Ishii, H. Tangible bits: beyond pixels. *Proc. TEI '08*, xv-xxv, 2008

Midas: A Declarative Multi-Touch Interaction Framework

Christophe Scholliers[1], Lode Hoste[2], Beat Signer[2] and Wolfgang De Meuter[1]
[1]Software Languages Lab
[2]Web & Information Systems Engineering Lab
Vrije Universiteit Brussel
Pleinlaan 2, 1050 Brussels, Belgium
{cfscholl,lhoste,bsigner,wdmeuter}@vub.ac.be

ABSTRACT
Over the past few years, multi-touch user interfaces emerged from research prototypes into mass market products. This evolution has been mainly driven by innovative devices such as Apple's iPhone or Microsoft's Surface tabletop computer. Unfortunately, there seems to be a lack of software engineering abstractions in existing multi-touch development frameworks. Many multi-touch applications are based on hard-coded procedural low level event processing. This leads to proprietary solutions with a lack of gesture extensibility and cross-application reusability. We present Midas, a declarative model for the definition and detection of multi-touch gestures where gestures are expressed via logical rules over a set of input facts. We highlight how our rule-based language approach leads to improvements in gesture extensibility and reusability. Last but not least, we introduce JMidas, an instantiation of Midas for the Java programming language and describe how JMidas has been applied to implement a number of innovative multi-touch gestures.

Author Keywords
multi-touch interaction, gesture framework, rule language, declarative programming

ACM Classification Keywords
D.2.11 Software Engineering: Software Architectures; H.5.2 Information Interfaces and Presentation: User Interfaces

General Terms
Algorithms, Languages

INTRODUCTION
More than 20 years after the original discussion of touch-screen based interfaces for human-computer interaction [9] and the realisation of the first multi-touch screen at Bell Labs in 1984, multi-touch interfaces have emerged from research prototypes into mass market products. Commercial solutions, including Apple's iPhone or Microsoft's Surface tabletop computer, introduced multi-touch user interfaces to a broader audience. Various manufacturers currently follow these early adopters by offering multi-touch screen-based user interfaces for their latest mobile devices. There is not only an increased use of multi-touch gestures on touch sensitive screens but also based on other input devices such as laptop touchpads. Some multi-touch input solutions are even offered as separate products like in the case of Apple's Magic Trackpad[1]. Furthermore, large multi-touch surfaces, as seen in Single Display Groupware (SDG) solutions [14], provide new forms of copresent interactions.

While multi-touch interfaces offer significant potential for an enhanced user experience, the application developer has to deal with an increased complexity in realising these new types of user interfaces. A major challenge is the recognition of different multi-touch gestures based on continuous input data streams. The intrinsic concurrent behaviour of multi-touch gestures and the scattered information from multiple gestures within a single input stream results in a complex detection process. Even the recognition of simple multi-touch gestures demands for a significant amount of work when using traditional programming languages. Furthermore, the reasoning over gestures from multiple users significantly increases the complexity. Therefore, we need a clear separation of concerns between the multi-touch application developer and the designer of new multi-touch gestures to be used within these applications. The gesture designer must be supported by a set of software engineering abstractions that go beyond simple low level input device event handling.

In software engineering, a problem can be divided into its *accidental* and *essential complexity* [1]. Accidental complexity relates to the difficulties a programmer faces due to the choice of software engineering tools. It can be reduced by selecting or developing better tools. On the other hand, essential complexity is caused by the characteristics of the problem to be solved and cannot be reduced. While the accidental complexity of today's mainstream applications is addressed by the use of high-level programming languages such as Java or C#, we have not witnessed the same software engineering support for the development of multi-touch applications. In this paper, we present novel declarative programming language constructs in order to tackle the accidental complexity of developing multi-touch gestures and to enable a developer to focus on the essential complexity.

TEI'11, January 22–26, 2011, Funchal, Portugal.

[1]`http://www.apple.com/magictrackpad/`

We start with a discussion of related work and present the required software engineering abstractions for multi-touch frameworks. We then introduce Midas, our three-layered multi-touch architecture. After describing the implementation of JMidas, a Midas instantiation for the Java programming language, we outline a set of multi-touch application prototypes that have been realised based on JMidas. A critical discussion of the presented approach and future work is followed by some general conclusions.

RELATED WORK

Recently, different multi-touch toolkits and frameworks have been developed in order to help programmers with the detection of gestures from a continuous stream of events produced by multi-touch hardware [7]. The frameworks that we are going to discuss in this section provide some basic software abstractions for recognising a fixed set of traditional multi-touch gestures, but most of them do not support the definition of new application-specific multi-touch gestures.

The *Sparsh UI* framework [11] is an open source multi-touch library that supports a set of built-in gestures including *hold*, *drag*, *multi point drag*, *zoom*, *rotate*, *spin* (two fingers hold and one drags) as well as *double tap*. The implementation of gestures based on hard-coded mathematical expressions limits the reusability of existing gestures. The framework only provides limited support to reason about the history of events. Sparsh UI provides historical data for each finger on the touch-sensitive surface by keeping track of events. As soon as a finger is lifted from the surface, the history related to the specific finger is deleted. This makes it difficult to implement multi-stroke gestures but on the other hand avoids any garbage collection issues. Furthermore, Sparsh UI does not deal with the resolution of conflicting gestures. Overall, Sparsh UI is one of the more complete multi-touch frameworks providing some basic software abstractions but offers limited support for multi-stroke and multi-user gestures.

Multi-touch for Java (*MT4j*)[2] is an open source Java framework for the rapid development of visually rich applications currently supporting *tap*, *drag*, *rotate* as well as *zoom* gestures. The architecture and implementation of MT4j is similar to Sparsh UI with two major differences: MT4j offers the functionality to define priorities among gestures but on the other hand it does not provide historical data. Whenever an event is retrieved via the TUIO protocol [6], multiple subscribed gesture implementations, called processors, try to lock the event for further processing. The idea of the priority mechanism is to assign a numeric value to each gesture. Gesture processors with a lower priority are blocked until processors with a higher priority have tried (and failed) to consume the event. With such an instantaneous priority mechanism, a processor has to decide immediately whether an individual event should be consumed or released. However, many gestures can only be detected after keeping track of multiple events, which limits the usability of the priority mechanism. Finally, the reuse of gesture detection functionality is lacking from the architectural design.

[2]`http://mt4j.org`

Grafiti [10] is a gesture recognition management framework for interactive tabletop interfaces providing similar abstractions as Sparsh UI. It is written in C# and subscribes to a TUIO input stream for any communication with different hardware devices. An automated mapping of multiple lists to multiple fingers is also not available and there are no constructs to deal with multiple users. Therefore, permutations of multi-touch input have to be performed manually which is computationally intensive and any reusability for composite gestures is lacking. Furthermore, the static time and space values are limiting the dynamic environment of multi-touch devices. The framework allows gestures to be registered and unregistered at runtime. In Grafiti, conflict resolution is based on instantaneous reasoning and there is no notion of uncertainty. The offered priority mechanism is similar to the one in MT4j where events are consumed by gestures and are no longer available for gestures with a lower priority.

The *libTISCH* [2] multi-touch library currently offers a set of fixed gestures including *drag*, *tap*, *zoom* and *rotate*. The framework maintains the state and history of events that are performed within a widget. This allows the developer to reason about event lists instead of individual events. However, multi-stroke gestures are not supported and an automatic mapping of lists to fingers is not available. Incoming events are linked to the topmost component based on their x and y coordinates. Local gesture detection is associated with a single widget element for the total duration of a gesture. A system-wide gesture detection is further supported via global gestures. Global gestures are acceptable when working on small screens like a phone screen, but these approaches cease to work when multiple users are performing collaborative gestures. The combination of local and global gestures is not supported and gestures outside the boundaries of a widget require complex ad-hoc program code.

Commercial user interface frameworks are also introducing multi-touch software abstractions. The Qt[3] cross-platform library provides gestures such as *drag*, *zoom*, *swipe* (in four directions), *tap* as well as *tap-and-hold*. To add new gestures, one has to create a new class and inherit from the `QGestureRecognizer` class. Incoming events are then fed to that class one by one as if it would have been directly attached to the hardware API. Also the *Microsoft .NET Framework*[4] offers multi-touch support since version 4.0. A simple event handler is provided together with traditional gestures such as *tap*, *drag*, *zoom* and *rotate*. In addition, Microsoft implemented a *two-finger tap*, a *press-and-hold* and a *two-finger scroll*. However, there is no support for implementing more complex customised gestures.

Gestures can also be recognised by comparing specific features of a given input to the features of previously recorded gesture samples. These so-called template-based matching solutions make use of different matching algorithms including Rubine [12], Dynamic Time Warping (DTW), neural networks or hidden Markov models. Most template-based

[3]`http://qt.nokia.com/`

[4]`http://msdn.microsoft.com/en-us/library/dd940543(VS.85).aspx`

gesture recognition solutions perform an offline gesture detection which means that the effect of the user input will only be visible after the complete gesture has been performed. Therefore, template-based approaches are not suitable for a number of multi-touch gestures (e.g. pinching). Some gesture recognition frameworks, such as iGesture [13], support template-based algorithms as well as algorithms relying on a declarative gesture description. However, these solutions currently offer no or only limited support for the continuous online processing of multi-touch gestures.

While the presented frameworks and toolkits provide specific multi-touch gesture recognition functionality that can be used by an application developer, most of them show a lack of flexibility from a software engineering point of view. In the following, we introduce the necessary software engineering abstractions that are going to be addressed by our Midas multi-touch interaction framework.

Modularisation Many existing multi-touch approaches do not modularise the implementation of gestures. Therefore, the implementation of an additional gesture requires a deep knowledge about already implemented gestures. This is a clear violation of the separation of concerns principle, one of the main principles in software engineering which dictates that different modules of code should have as little overlapping functionality as possible.

Composition It should be possible to easily compose gestures in order to define more complex gestures. For example, a *scroll* gesture could be implemented by composing two *move up* gestures.

Event Categorisation When detecting gestures, one of the problems is to categorise the events (e.g. events from a specific finger within the last 500 milliseconds). This event categorisation is usually a cumbersome and error-prone task, especially when timing is involved. Therefore, event categorisation should be offered to the programmer as a service by the underling system.

GUI-Event Correlation While the previous requirement advocates the preprocessing of events, this requirement ensures the correlation between events and GUI elements. In most of today's multi-touch frameworks, all events are transferred to the application from a single entry point. The decision about which events correlate to which GUI elements is left to the application developer or enforced by the framework. However, the reasoning about events correlating to specific graphical components should be straightforward.

Temporal and Spatial Operators Extracting meaningful information from a stream of events produced by the multi-touch hardware often involves the use of temporal and spatial operators. Therefore, the underlying framework should offer a set of temporal and spatial operators in order to keep programs concise and understandable. In current multi-touch frameworks, there is no or limited support for such operators which often leads to complex program code.

MIDAS ARCHITECTURE

The processing of input event streams in human-computer interaction is a complex task that many frameworks address by using event handlers. However, the use of event handlers has proven to violate a range of software engineering principles including composability, scalability and separation of concerns [8]. We propose a rule-based approach with spatio-temporal operators in order to minimise the accidental complexity in dealing with multi-touch interactions.

The Midas architecture consists of the three layers shown in Figure 1. The *infrastructure layer* contains the hardware bridge and translator components. Information from an input device is extracted by the hardware bridge and transferred to the translator. In order to support different devices, concrete Midas instances can have multiple hardware bridges. The translator component processes the raw input data and produces logical facts which are propagated to the fact base in the Midas *core layer*. The inference engine evaluates these facts against a set of rules.

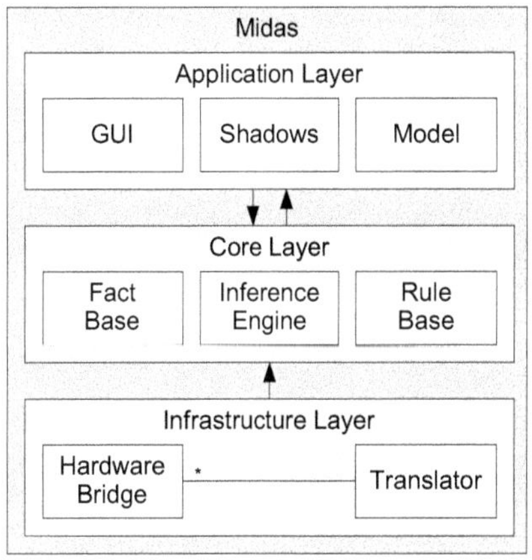

Figure 1. Midas architecture

The rules are defined in the Midas *application layer* but stored in the rule base. When a rule is triggered, it can invoke some application logic and/or generate new facts. Furthermore, GUI elements are accessible from within the reasoning engine via a special shadowing construct.

Infrastructure Layer

The implementation of the infrastructure layer takes care of all the details to address the hardware and transforming the low level input data into logical facts. A fact has a type and a number of attributes. The core fact that every Midas implementation has to support is shown in Listing 1.

Listing 1. Core fact

```
(Cursor (id ?id) (x ?x) (y ?y) (x-speed ?xs)
        (y-speed ?ys) (time ?t) (state ?s))
```

This core fact has the type `Cursor` and represents a single cursor (e.g. a moving finger) from the input device. The attributes `id`, `x`, `y`, `x-speed`, `y-speed` and `time` represent the id, position, movement and time the cursor moved. The attribute `state` indicates how the cursor has changed and can be assigned the values `APPEAR`, `MOVE` or `DISAPPEAR`.

Core Layer

The Midas core layer consists of an inference engine in combination with a fact base and a rule base that is going to be described in the following.

Rules

We use rules as an expressive and powerful mechanism to implement gesture recognition. Listing 2 outlines the implementation of a simple rule that prints the location of all cursors. The part that a rule should match in order to be triggered is called its prerequisites (before the $\Rightarrow$), while the actions to be performed if a rule is triggered are called its consequences.

Listing 2. Example rule

```
1 (defrule PrintCursor
2    (Cursor (x ?x) (y ?y))
3  =>
4   (printout t ''A cursor is moving at: '' ?x '','' ?y))
```

The first line shows the definition of a rule with the name `printCursor`. This rule specifies the matching of all facts of type `Cursor` as indicated on the second line. Upon a match of a concrete fact, the values of the two `x` and `y` attributes will be bound to the variables `?x` and `?y`. Subsequently, the rule will trigger its actions (after the $\Rightarrow$) and print the text "A cursor is moving at:" followed by the `x` and `y` coordinates.

Temporal Operators

As timing is very important in the context of gesture recognition, all facts are automatically annotated with timing information. This information can be easily accessed by using the dot operation and selecting the time attribute. Midas defines a set of temporal operators to check the relationship between the timing attribute of different facts. The temporal operators and their definitions are shown in Table 1.

Operator	Args	Definition
tEqual	f1,f2	$\lvert f1.time - f2.time \rvert < \varepsilon_t$
tMeets	f1,f2	$f1.time - f2.time = \varepsilon_{tmin}$
tBefore	f1,f2	$f1.time < f2.time$
tAfter	f1,f2	$f1.time > f2.time$
tContains	f1,f2,f3	$f2.time < f1.time < f3.time$

Table 1. Temporal operators

Note that the `tEqual` operator is not defined as the absolute equality but rather as being within a very small time interval ε_t. This fuzziness has been introduced since input device events seldom occur at exactly the same time. Similar ε_{tmin}, the smallest possible time interval, is used to expresses that `f1` happened *instantaneously* after `f2`.

Spatial Operators

In addition to temporal operators, Midas offers the definition of spatial constraints over matching facts as shown in Table 2. These spatial operators expect that the facts they receive have an `x` and `y` attribute.

Operator	Args	Definition
sDistance	f1,f2	$euclidianDistance(f1, f2)$
sNear	f1,f2	$sDistance(f1, f2) < \varepsilon_s$
sNearLeftOf	f1,f2	$\varepsilon_s > (f2.x - f1.x) > 0$
sNearRightOf	f1,f2	$\varepsilon_s > (f1.x - f2.x) > 0$
sInside	f1,f2	$\beta(f1, f2)$

Table 2. Spatial operators

Again, we have a small distance value ε_s to specify that two facts are very close to each other. This distance is set as a global variable and adjustable by the developer. Since the input device coordinates are already transformed by the infrastructure layer, the value of ε_s is independent of a specific input device. For `sInside`, the fact `f2` is expected to have a `width` and `height` attribute. The β function checks whether the `x` and `y` coordinates of `f1` are within the bounding box $(f2.x, f2.y)(f2.x + f2.width, f2.y + f2.height)$. Note that we also support user-defined operators.

List Operators

The implementation of gestures often requires the reasoning over a set of events in combination with temporal and spatial constraints. Therefore, in Midas we have introduced the `ListOf` operator that enables the reasoning over a set of events within a specific time frame. An example of this construct is shown in Listing 3. The prerequisite will match a set of `Cursor` events that have the same finger id and occurred within 500 milliseconds. Finally, the matching sets are limited to those sets that contain at least 5 `Cursors`. Note that due to the declarative approach the developer does no longer have to keep track of the state of the cursors in the system and manually group them according to their id.

Listing 3. ListOf construct

```
?myList <- (ListOf (Cursor (same: id)
                   (within: 500)
                   (min: 5))
```

A list matched by the `ListOf` operator is guaranteed to be time ordered. This is required for the multi-touch interaction domain as one wants to reason about a specific motion along the time axis. By default, rule languages do not imply a deterministic ordering but allow arbitrary pattern matching to cover all possible combinations. The spatial operators from the previous sections are also defined over lists. For example, `sAllNearBottomOf` expects two lists `l1` and `l2` and the operator will return true only if all the elements of the first list are below all elements of the second list.

Movement Operators

The result of the `ListOf` construct is a list which can be used in combination with movement operators. A movement operator verifies that a certain property holds for an entire list. For example, the *movingUp* operation is defined as follows:

$$movingUp(list) \iff \forall i, j : i < j \wedge list[i].y > list[j].y$$

In a similar way, we have defined the *movingDown*, *movingLeft* and *movingRight* operators.

Application Layer

The application layer consists of a regular program which is augmented with a set of rules in order to describe the gestures. A large part of this program however will deal with the GUI and some gestures will only make sense if they are performed on specific GUI objects. As argued in the introduction, the reasoning over GUI objects in combination with the gestures should be straightforward. Therefore, in a Midas system the GUI objects are reified as so-called *shadow facts* in the reasoning engine's working memory. This implies that the mere existence of the GUI objects automatically give rise to the associated fact.

The fields of a GUI object are automatically transformed into attributes of the shadow fact and can be accessed like any other fact fields. However, a shadow fact differs from regular facts in the sense that the values of its attributes are transparently kept synchronised with the values of the object it represents. This allows us to reason about application level entities inside the rule language (i.e. graphical objects). Moreover, from within the reasoning engine the methods of the object can be called in the consequence block of a rule. This is done by accessing the predefined `Instance` field of a shadow fact followed by the name and arguments of the method to be invoked. Listing 4 shows an example of calling the `setColor` method with the argument `"BLUE"` on a circle GUI element.

Listing 4. Method call on a shadow fact instance

```
(?circle.Instance.setColor "BLUE")
```

Finally, the attributes of a shadow fact can be changed by using the *modify* construct. When the modify construct is applied to a shadow fact, the changes are automatically reflected in the shadowed object.

Priorities

When designing gestures, parts of certain gestures might overlap. For example, the gesture for a single click overlaps with the gesture for a double click. If the priority of the single click would be higher than the double click gesture, a user would never be able to perform a double click since the double click would always be recognised as two single click gestures. Therefore, it is important to ensure that the developer has means to define priorities between different gestures. In Midas, gestures with a higher priority will always be matched before gestures with a lower priority. An example of how to use priorities in rules is given in Figure 5. The use of priorities allows the programmer to tackle problems with overlapping gestures. The priority concept further increases modularisation since normally there is no intrusive code needed in order to separate overlapping gestures.

Listing 5. Priorities

```
(defrule PrioritisedRule
  (declare (salience 100))
  <prerequisites>
  =>
  <consequence> )
```

'Flick Left' Gesture Example

After introducing the core concepts of the Midas model, we can now explain how these concepts can be combined in order to specify simple gestures. The *Flick Left* gesture example that we are going to use has been implemented in numerous frameworks and interfaces for photo viewing applications. In those applications, users can move from one photo to the next one by flicking their finger over the photo in a horizontal motion to the left. In the following, we show how the *Flick Left* gesture can be implemented in a compact way based on Midas .

One of the descriptions of the facts representing a *Flick Left* gesture is as follows: *"an ordered list of cursor events from the same finger within a small time interval where all the events are accelerated to the left"*. The implementation of new gestures in Midas mainly consists of translating such descriptions into rules as shown in Listing 6.

Listing 6. Single finger 'Flick Left' gesture

```
(defrule FlickLeft
  ?eventList[] <-
        (ListOf (Cursor (same: id) (within: 500) (min: 5)))
  (movingLeft ?eventList)
  =>
  (assert (FlickLeft (events ?eventList))))
```

The prerequisites of the rule specify that there should be a list with events generated by the same finger by making use of the `ListOf` construct. It further defines that all these events should be generated within a time frame of 500 milliseconds and that the list must contain at least 5 elements.

Gesture Composition

We have shown that set operators enable the declarative categorisation of events. The Midas framework supports temporal, spatial and motion operators to declaratively specify different gestures. Furthermore, priorities increase the modularisation and shadow facts enable the programmer to reason about their graphical objects in a declarative way.

In the Midas framework, it is common to develop complex gestures by combining multiple basic gestures as there is no difference in reasoning over simple or derived facts. This reusability and composition of gestures is achieved by asserting gesture-specific facts on gesture detection. The reuse and composition of gestures is illustrated in Listing 7, where a *Double Flick Left* composite gesture is implemented by specifying that there should be two *Flick Left* gestures at approximately the same time.

Listing 7. 'Double Flick Left' gesture

```
(defrule DoubleFlickLeft
   ?upLeftFlick <- (FlickLeft)
   ?downLeftFlick <- (FlickLeft)
   (sAllNearBottomOf ?downLeftFlick.events
                     ?upLeftFlick.events)
   (tAllEqual ?upLeftFlick ?downLeftFlick)
  =>
   (assert (DoubleFlickLeft)))
```

The implementation of this new composite gesture in traditional programming languages would require the use of additional timers and threads. By adopting a rule-based approach, one clearly benefits from the fact that we only have to provide a description of the gestures but we do not have to be concerned on how to derive the gesture.

JMIDAS PROTOTYPE IMPLEMENTATION

We have implemented a concrete JMidas prototype of the Midas architecture and embedded it in the Java programming language. This enables programmers to define their rules in separate files and to load them from within Java. It also implies that developers can make use of Java objects from within their rules in order to adapt the GUI. We first describe which devices are currently supported by JMidas and then outline how to program these devices based on JMidas.

Input Devices

In order to support a large amount of different multi-touch devices, we have decided to implement an abstraction layer currently supported by many multi-touch devices. Two important existing abstraction layers providing a common and portable API for input device handling are the TUIO [6] and the TISCH protocol [2]. We chose TUIO as one of the input layers in the JMidas prototype implementation because of its features in terms of portability and performance. This implies that any input device supporting the TUIO protocol can automatically be used in combination with JMidas.

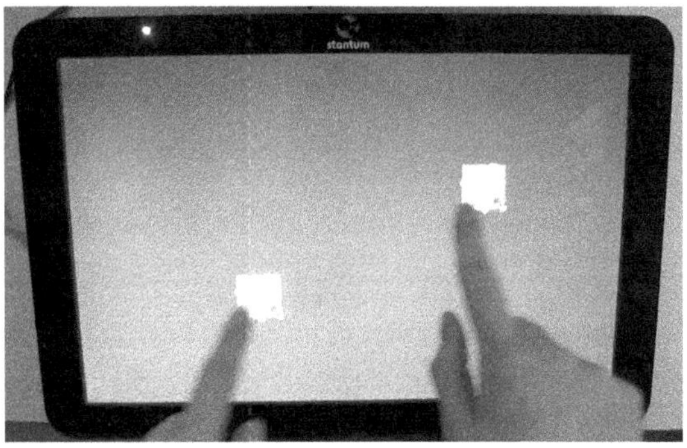

Figure 2. JMidas application on a Stantum SMK 15.4

A first multi-touch device that has been used in combination with the JMidas framework is the Stantum SMK 15.4[5] shown in Figure 2, a 15.4 inch multi-touch display that can deal with more than ten simultaneous touch points. Unfortunately, the Stantum SMK 15.4 does not offer any TUIO support and we had to implement our own cross-platform TUIO bridge that runs on Linux, Windows and Mac OS X.

Note that the Midas framework is not limited to multi-touch devices. A radically different type of input device supported by the JMidas framework are the Sun SPOTs[6] shown in Figure 3. A Sun SPOT is a small wireless sensor device that embeds an accelerometer to measure its orientation or motion.

[5] `http://www.stantum.com`

[6] `http://sunspotworld.com`

Figure 3. JMidas Sun SPOT integration

Previous experiments with the Sun SPOT device have shown that gestural movements can be successfully recognised by using a Dynamic Time Warp (DTW) template algorithm [5]. However, it was rather difficult to express concurrent gestural movements of multiple Sun SPOTs based on traditional programming languages due to similar reasons as described for the multi-touch domain. These difficulties can be overcome by using the temporal operators offered by JMidas and a developer can reason about 3D hand movements tracked by Sun SPOTs. The JMidas Sun SPOT support is still experimental but we managed to feed the reasoning engine with simple facts for individual Sun SPOTs and the recognition results for composite gestures look promising.

Initialisation

The setup of the JMidas engine is a two step process to be executed in the application layer as shown in Listing 8. First, a new JMidas engine is initialised (line 1) which corresponds to setting up the Midas core layer introduced earlier in Figure 1. The second step consist of connecting one or multiple input sources from the infrastructure layer (lines 2–8). This step also specifies a resolution for the display via the `RES_X` and `RES_Y` arguments. After this initialisation phase, the engine can be started and fed with rules. In Listing 8 this is highlighted by calling the `start` method and loading the rules from a file called `rules.md` (lines 9–10).

Listing 8. JMidas engine initialisation

```
1  JMidasEngine engine = new JMidasEngine();
2  TuioListener listener =
3      new TuioToFactListener(engine, RES_X, RES_Y);
4  TuioClient client = new TuioClient();
5  client.addTuioListener(listener);
6  SunSpotListener spListener = new SunSpotListener(engine);
7  SunSpotClient spClient = new SunSpotClient();
8  spClient.addSunSpotListner(spListener);
9  engine.start();
10 engine.loadFile(``rules.md'');
```

In JMidas, we use Java annotations to reify objects as logical facts. When a class is annotated as `Shadowed`, the JMidas framework automatically reifies the instances as logical facts with the classname as type and the attributes corresponding to the fields of the object. The field annotation `Ignore` is used to exclude specific fields from being automatically reified as attributes of the logical fact.

An example of how to use the Java annotation mechanism is given in Listing 9. Since the `Circle` object is annotated as `Shadowed`, its instances will be reified by JMidas as logical facts. The `Circle` class has the three fields `x`, `y` and `z`, whereas the last field has been annotated as `Ignore`. This implies that the `z` field will not be reified as an attribute of the logical fact. From within the logical rules, the programmer can match objects of type `Circle` by using the following expression: `(Circle (x ?x) (y ?y))`.

Listing 9. Shadowing GUI elements

```
public @Shadowed class Circle {
    int x;
    int y;
    @Ignore
    int z;
    Circle(int id, int x, int y) { ... }
}
```

Reasoning Engine

JMidas incorporates an event-driven reasoning engine based on the Rete [3] algorithm. The core reasoning engine used in JMidas is the Jess [4] rule engine for Java which had to be slightly adapted for our purpose. The Jess reasoning engine has no built in support for temporal, spatial or motion operations. Moreover, we have extended the engine to deal with ordered list operations. Other reasoning engines could have led to the same result but we opted for the Jess reasoning engine due to its performance and the fact that it already offers basic support for shadow facts. However, we felt that in the context of our work this integration was not convenient enough and added several annotations to ensure that the synchronisation between facts and classes is handled by the framework.

Implemented Gestures

JMidas implements all of the traditional gestures such as *drag*, *tap*, *double tap*, *stretch* and *rotate*. In addition to these standard gestures, we have validated our approach by implementing a set of complex gestures shown in Figure 4. According to the Natural User Interface Group, (NUI group)[7], these complex gestures possibly offer a more ergonomic and natural way to interact with multi-touch input devices.

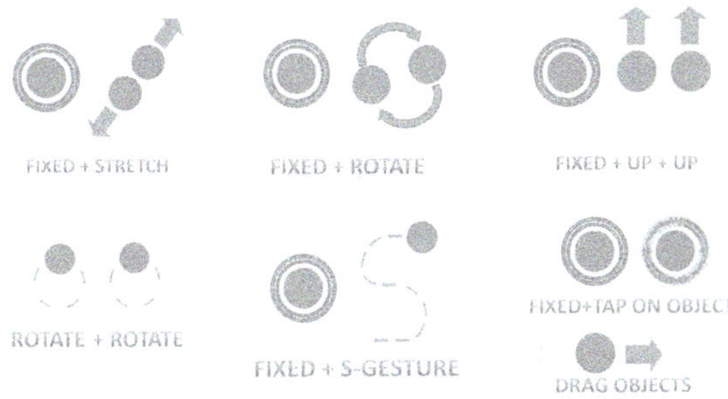

Figure 4. Complex gestures implemented in JMidas

Note that we have not empirically evaluated the claims of the NUI group since the focus of our work is to prevent the programmer from dealing with the *accidental complexity* while *implementing* multi-touch applications. To the best of our knowledge, our complex gestures shown in Figure 4 are currently not implemented by any other existing multi-touch framework.

[7]http://nuigroup.com

DISCUSSION AND FUTURE WORK

The implementation of gesture-based interaction based on low-level programming constructs complicates the introduction of new gestures and limits the reuse of common interaction patterns across different applications. Current multi-touch interfaces adopt an event-driven programming model resulting in complex detection code that is hard to maintain and extend. In an event-driven application, the control flow is driven by events and not by the lexical scope of the program code, making it difficult to understand these programs. The developer has to manually store and combine events generated by several event handlers. In Midas, a programmer only has to provide a declarative description of a gesture and the underlying framework takes care of how to match gestures against events.

Current state-of-the-art multi-touch toolkits provide limited software abstractions to categorise events according to specific criteria. Often they only offer information that there is an event with an identifier and a position or provide a list of events forming part of a single stroke. However, for the implementation of many multi-stroke gestures, it is crucial to categorise these events. The manual event classification complicates the event handling code significantly. With the presented Midas `ListOf` operator, we can easily extract lists of events with certain properties (e.g. events with the same id or events within a given time frame).

With existing approaches, it is difficult to maintain temporal invariants. For example, when implementing the click and double click gestures, the gesture developer has to use a timer which takes care of triggering the click gesture after a period of time if no successive events triggered the double click gesture. This results in code that is distributed over multiple event handlers and, again, significantly complicates any event handling. We have introduced declarative temporal and spatial operators to deal with this complexity. In contrast to most existing solutions, Midas further supports the flexible composition of new complex gestures by simply using other gestures as rule prerequisites.

Our Midas frameworks addresses the issues of modularisation (M), composition (C), event categorisation (EC), GUI-event correlation (G) as well as the temporal and spatial operators (TS) mentioned in the related work section. Table 3 summarises these software engineering abstractions and compares Midas with the support of these requirements in current state-of-the-art multi-touch toolkits. This comparison with related work shows that, in contrast to Midas, none of the existing multi-touch solutions addresses all the required software engineering abstractions.

As we have explained earlier, there might be conflicts between different gestures in which case priorities have to be

	M	C	EC	G	TS
Sparsh-UI	+/-	+/-	+/-	+/-	-
MT4j	+/-	-	-	+/-	-
Grafiti	+/-	+/-	+/-	+/-	-
libTISCH	+/-	-	+/-	+	-
Qt4	+/-	+/-	-	+/-	-
.NET	-	-	-	-	-
Templates	+	-	-	-	-
Midas	+	+	+	+	+

Table 3. Comparison with existing multi-touch toolkits

defined to resolve these conflicts. In current approaches, this conflict resolution code is scattered over the code of multiple gestures. This implies that the addition of a new gesture requires a deep knowledge of existing gestures and results in a limited extensibility of existing multi-touch frameworks [7]. In contrast, our Midas framework offers a built-in priority mechanism and frees the developer from having to manually implement this functionality.

In the future, we plan to develop an advanced priority mechanism that can be adapted dynamically. We are currently also investigating the JMidas integration of several new input devices, including Siftables[8] and a voice recognition system. Even though these devices significantly differ from multi-touch surfaces, we believe that the core idea of applying a reasoning engine and tightly embedding it in a host language can simplify any gesture recognition development.

CONCLUSION

We have presented Midas, a multi-touch gesture interaction framework that introduces a software engineering methodology for the implementation of gestures. While existing multi-touch frameworks support application developers by providing a set of predefined gestures (e.g. pinch or rotate), our Midas framework also enables the implementation of new and composed multi-touch gestures. The JMidas prototype highlights how a declarative rule-based language description of gestures in combination with a host language increases the extensibility and reusability of multi-touch gestures. The presented approach has been validated by implementing a number of standard multi-touch gestures as well as a set of more complex gestures that are currently not supported by any other toolkit. While the essential complexity in dealing with advanced multi-touch interfaces cannot be reduced, we offer the appropriate concepts to limit the accidental complexity. We feel confident that our approach will support the HCI community in implementing and investigating innovative multi-touch gestures that go beyond the current state-of-the-art.

REFERENCES

1. F. P. Brooks, Jr. No Silver Bullet: Essence and Accidents of Software Engineering. *IEEE Computer*, 20(4):10–19, April 1987.
2. F. Echtler and G. Klinker. A Multitouch Software Architecture. In *Proc. of NordiCHI 2008, 5th Nordic Conference on Human-Computer Interaction*, pages 463–466, Lund, Sweden, 2008.
3. C. L. Forgy. RRete: A Fast Algorithm for the Many Pattern/Many Object Pattern Match Problem. *Artificial Intelligence*, 19(1):17–37, 1982.
4. E. Friedman-Hill. *Jess in Action: Java Rule-Based Systems*. Manning Publications, July 2003.
5. L. Hoste. Experiments with the SunSPOT Accelerometer. Project report, Vrije Universiteit Brussel, 2009.
6. M. Kaltenbrunner, T. Bovermann, R. Bencina, and E. Costanza. TUIO: A Protocol for Table-Top Tangible User Interfaces. In *Proc. of GW 2005, 6th Intl. Workshop on Gesture in Human-Computer Interaction and Simulation*, Ile de Berder, France, May 2005.
7. D. Kammer, M. Keck, G. Freitag, and M. Wacker. Taxonomy and Overview of Multi-touch Frameworks: Architecture, Scope and Features. In *Proc. of Workshop on Engineering Patterns for Multi-Touch Interfaces*, Berlin, Germany, June 2010.
8. I. Maier, T. Rompf, and M. Odersky. Deprecating the Observer Pattern. Technical Report EPFL-REPORT-148043, Ecole Polytechnique Fédérale de Lausanne, Lausanne, Switzerland, 2010.
9. L. H. Nakatani and J. A. Rohrlich. Soft Machines: A Philosophy of User-Computer Interface Design. In *Proc. of CHI '83, ACM Conference on Human Factors in Computing Systems*, pages 19–23, Boston, USA, December 1983.
10. A. D. Nardi. Grafiti: Gesture Recognition mAnagement Framework for Interactive Tabletop Interfaces. Master's thesis, University of Pisa, 2008.
11. P. Ramanahally, S. Gilbert, T. Niedzielski, D. Velázquez, and C. Anagnost. Sparsh UI: A Multi-Touch Framework for Collaboration and Modular Gesture Recognition. In *Proc. of WINVR 2009, Conference on Innovative Virtual Reality*, pages 1–6, Chalon-sur-Saône, France, February 2009.
12. D. Rubine. Specifying Gestures by Example. In *Proc. of ACM SIGGRAPH '91, 18th Intl. Conference on Computer Graphics and Interactive Techniques*, pages 329–337, Las Vegas, USA, August 1991.
13. B. Signer, U. Kurmann, and M. C. Norrie. iGesture: A General Gesture Recognition Framework. In *Proc. of ICDAR 2007, 9th Intl. Conference on Document Analysis and Recognition*, pages 954–958, Curitiba, Brazil, September 2007.
14. J. Stewart, B. B. Bederson, and A. Druin. Single Display Groupware: A Model for Co-present Collaboration. In *Proc. of CHI '99, ACM Conference on Human Factors in Computing Systems*, pages 286–293, Pittsburgh, USA, May 1999.

[8] `http://sifteo.com`

PaperView: Augmenting Physical Surfaces with Location-Aware Digital Information

Dimitris Grammenos[a], Damien Michel[a], Xenophon Zabulis[a], Antonis A. Argyros[a,b]
[a] Institute of Computer Science –FORTH, Heraklion, Crete, Greece
[b] Department of Computer Science, University of Crete, Heraklion, Crete, Greece
{gramenos, michel, zabulis, argyros}@ics.forth.gr

ABSTRACT
A frequent need of museums is to provide visitors with context-sensitive information about exhibits in the form of maps, or scale models. This paper suggests an augmented-reality approach for supplementing physical surfaces with digital information, through the use of pieces of plain paper that act as personal, location-aware, interactive screens. The technologies employed are presented, along with the interactive behavior of the system, which was instantiated and tested in the form of two prototype setups: a wooden table covered with a printed map and a glass case containing a scale model. The paper also discusses key issues stemming from experience and observations in the course of qualitative evaluation sessions.

Author Keywords
Interactive museum exhibits; interaction design; magic lens

ACM Classification Keywords
H5.2. User Interfaces; I.4 IMAGE PROCESSING AND COMPUTER VISION; I.4.9 Applications

General Terms
Design, Experimentation

INTRODUCTION
In the past few years, a number of museums worldwide started exploring new ways for integrating novel interactive exhibits in their spaces, moving beyond the typical "multimedia information kiosk" paradigm of the past (e.g., [5, 6, 8, 10, 13]). The basic goal of this approach is to substitute sheer didactic information provision with captivating experiences that utilize a combination of active user participation through natural interactions and dynamic media in order to support constructive and engaging edutainment (i.e., entertainment designed to educate).

Maps and scale models constitute two types of exhibits that are frequently met in museums. A related need is to provide their visitors with location-related information about such exhibits. Typically, this is achieved by: (a) overlaying information on the exhibits and (b) putting up support material in nearby walls. In the first case, one problem is the limited available space and another one the fact that the actual exhibit content becomes visually cluttered. In the second case, a key drawback is that visitors have to look back and forth between the exhibit and the information and mentally correlate the two. An unsolvable problem shared by both approaches is multilingualism, since each language requires additional space. In this context, this paper suggests PaperView, an augmented-reality approach for supplementing physical surfaces with digital information through the use of pieces of plain paper that act as personal, location-aware, interactive screens.

TEI'11, January 22–26, 2011, Funchal, Portugal.

RELATED WORK
A number of interactive exhibits have been deployed in museums worldwide. The "Re-Tracing the Past" exhibition [5] of the Hunt Museum in Limerick, Ireland comprised two room-sized spaces and the "Fire and the Mountain" [6] exhibition at the Civic Museum of Como, Italy, comprised four hybrid exhibits. The Austrian Technical Museum in Vienna opened a digitally augmented exhibition [8] and ARoS, an art museum in Denmark, employed four interactive exhibits [10]. The Ragghianti Foundation in Milan, Italy also held an exhibition entitled "Puccini Set Designer" [13] that used new technologies.

PaperView implements a "magic-lens"-type augmented-reality approach, building upon the paradigm originally suggested by Wellner [15] for DigitalDesk. In this direction, Reitmayr et al. [11] augmented paper maps using a PDA and a rectangular piece of cardboard with a black border to browse images. A limitation of their implementation was that only a single PDA and one cardboard could be tracked. Following a different line of thinking, Bimber et al. [1] presented an approach for digitally augmenting pictorial artwork, also supporting user interaction through a secondary screen and a mouse. Holman et al. [7], project a windowing environment on physical paper to simulate the use of digital paper displays. The pieces of paper and the user fingers are augmented with IR markers in order to be tracked. The Magic Lenses framework [4] employs a handheld mirror-like prop with an attached magnetic tracking sensor and a "selection icon" with a secondary display to augment a 3D image projected on a workbench. In order to tack this icon, a surface coated with the retro-reflective material is used, along with an IR camera and IR illumination. Izadi et al. [9] present a rear-projection surface that can project a second image through it onto a sheet of projection film placed on it, acting as a magic lens. In order to be tracked, the magic lens is augmented with either passive or active tags.

THE PAPERVIEW SYSTEM

PaperView is a tabletop augmented reality system that builds upon Wellner's [15] DigitalDesk concept in combination with Reitmayr et al. [11] augmentation of maps using real world objects, but taken further, since multi-user interaction, finger-based input and concurrent tracking of diverse border colors are supported. In contrast to PaperWindows [7] and SecondLight [9] no IR markers are used to augment the paper or the users' fingers (something that would not be practical in a museum setting). Also, unlike Magic Lenses [4], no magnetic tracker, or special coating of the table surface are used. PaperView employs a projector and rectangular pieces of plain white paper upon which visual information and interactive controls are presented, digitally augmenting physical surfaces with context-sensitive data. Two alternative prototype setups were developed; a large wooden table covered with a printed map and a glass case containing a scale model. The key difference between the two is that the latter can easily be installed with practically no construction requirements or physical interventions.

Technical Overview

The system comprises the surface to be augmented, a projector, an RGB camera, a PC and speakers. Additionally, rectangular pieces of plain white cardboard of various sizes are used (20x20 to 30x30cm^2). Cardboard pieces are surrounded by a colored frame (1-2cm). A computer vision system is used to track the position and pose of the paper surfaces, as well as the activation of any related interactive areas by the users' fingers. This information is passed through a custom middleware layer to an application developed in Actionscript 3.0 using Adobe Flash, which implements the system's user interface.

Each cardboard appears in the camera field of view as a quadrilateral. Upon setup, the projector-camera system is spatially calibrated. The camera is set to adjust gain automatically, so as to adapt to scene illumination. The first goal of the vision system is to detect the quadrilaterals corresponding to the cardboards (see Fig. 1). This detection is based on the knowledge of the color of the border of each cardboard. A color similarity metric [12] is applied to each pixel, estimating its similarity to a reference color and resulting in a binary image B. A small colored palette in a predefined location of the scene provides the reference colors of the cardboards, invariantly to changes of global scene illumination (i.e. due to light coming in from the windows). The silhouettes of the contours appearing in image B are traced and fitted with straight lines. A check is performed regarding whether the arrangement of the resulting segments conforms to the hypothesis of two nested quadrilaterals. This prevents from ambiguities that may arise due to the presence of similarly colored objects. The detection of the quadrilaterals is tolerant to occlusions that might arise due to, e.g., users' hands.

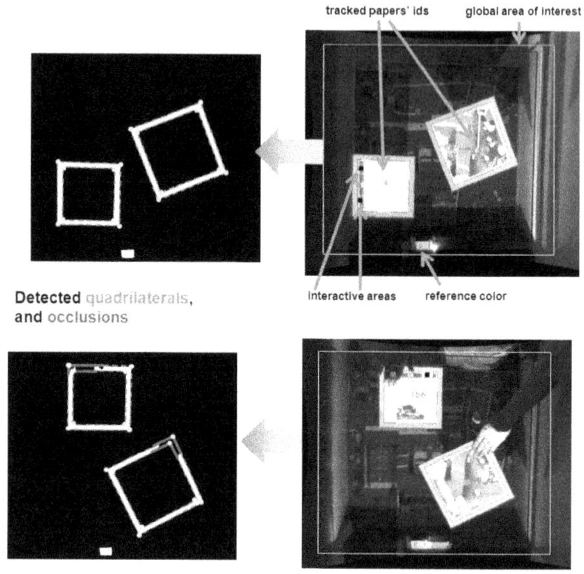

Figure 1. Computer vision system: (top-right) camera image; (top-left) color similarity image B; (bottom, right/left) images of quadrilaterals partially occluded by hands.

The system estimates the transformation that maps the detected quadrilateral(s) to rectangular regions, using a homography. The corners of the quadrilateral are estimated as the points of intersection of consecutive straight lines. The four corners are used to estimate this homography, and through the induced transformation the projected images appear undistorted on the slanted cardboard. The identity of each cardboard is maintained over time, based on polygon intersection tests across subsequent frames. The trajectories of the polygon corners are tracked using Kalman filtering modeling location and velocity, as in [14], to increase robustness and suppress jitter. The 3D location and pose of the cardboard is estimated given the size of its edges in the image and its size, during setup, by placing the cardboard in a frontoparallel posture on the surface of the table. By comparing the apparent sizes to its initial size, the slant and distance of the cardboard are estimated. Additionally, interactive areas are implemented as follows. Using the homography computed for each cardboard, various rectangular areas (dynamically defined by the application) are continuously checked for differences using a background subtraction method. The image projections of these areas are tested for the occurrence of skin-colored blobs, using the method in [1]. At the same time the neighboring area of the nested quadrilateral is checked for occlusions (such as the one shown at the bottom row of Fig.

1). Combining these two cues provides a detection event that is triggered when a user's finger continuously occurs above the interactive area.

Setup A: PaperView Table

The system (Fig. 2 and 3a) comprises a wooden table ($1.8x1m^2$), the surface of which is covered by a printed map of Macedonia, Greece, which does not contain any text or other kind of data. Underneath the table there are two wireless speakers and high above it, inside a false ceiling, there are an HD video projector, an IR camera and an RGB camera. Next to the table lies a 56'' HD TV screen, bearing a shelf with a stack of rectangular framed pieces of white cardboard. The frame color is used as a means for implicit language selection. Multiple users can concurrently use the table. Initially, the projector overlays on the map the location (as red spots) and names of ancient Greek cities with archeological interest (in English and Greek). If a visitor places a cardboard on the table surface, an image is projected on it, showing a satellite view of the respective printed map area ("map mode"). Furthermore, a circled crosshair is projected on the paper's centre along with a virtual red string connecting the paper with the closest site of interest. If a site's name intersects with a paper, then it is rotated so that it is aligned with the paper's orientation.

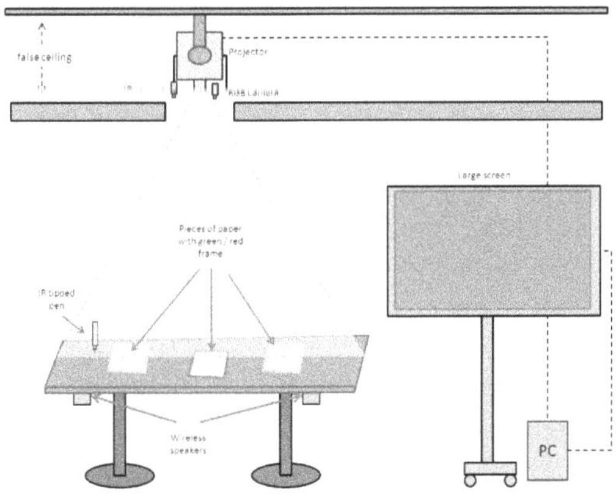

Figure 2. PaperView Table schematic installation layout

If the visitor moves the paper so that the site of interest lies within the boundaries of the crosshair, a multimedia slideshow starts ("info mode"). The slideshow comprises a series of pages, each of which may contain any combination of texts, images, and videos. When a cardboard piece is lying on the table, a toolbar is projected at its lower bottom area, containing an indication of the current page and the total number of pages (e.g., 4/23), and buttons for moving to the next/previous page. The user can interact with these "soft" buttons using his/her fingers (see Fig. 3b). If the paper is taken off the table's surface, the buttons disappear and the user can move to the next/previous page, by tilting the paper right or left, respectively. In this case, the projection is appropriately distorted (Fig. 4 - left), so that the visual content registers correctly on the paper surface. In order to avoid accidental browsing actions, page change does not happen instantly. Instead, an arrow-shaped progress bar is presented on the paper (Fig. 4 - right) and takes about 1 second to fill. In order to visually link information presented on a cardboard piece to the site it refers to, a red connecting string is used. If the cardboard is moved beyond a minimum distance, the string "breaks" and the paper's surface returns back to "map mode". The nearby TV screen presents a Google Maps view of the geographical area covered by the printed map, in order to help visitors correlate the areas presented on it to their location in the real world. Visitors can use the pen on the table surface to navigate in Google Maps. If the user selects a point of interest, related multimedia information is presented. Additionally, if the user keeps the pen at the same position for more than 1 second, a virtual remote control appears, through which she can zoom in/out in Google Maps and select alternative map views.

Figure 3. (a) Two users concurrently interacting with the map in different languages; (b) pressing the soft buttons

Figure 4. (left) lifting the paper above the table surface; (right) tilting the paper to browse content.

Setup B: PaperView Glass Case

The main goal of this setup was to create a self-contained "add-on" system, requiring minimal interventions to the installation space (see Fig. 5). In order to accommodate the space limitations, an ultra short throw projector was used, and the camera was equipped with a wide angle lens. For our prototype an exact replica of a museum glass case ($0.83x0.83m^2$) was constructed, inside of which a 1-to-1 scale printout of the original scale model (an ancient farmhouse of the 4th century BC) was placed. The system behaves similarly to the table setup, with just the following differences: (a) due to the glass case, no information is projected outside the tracked papers; (b) papers cannot be used when higher than a few centimeters above the surface, since the projector's beam is located very close and to the side of it – thus, the paper titling function is not supported; and (c) no secondary display, nor an IR pen are used.

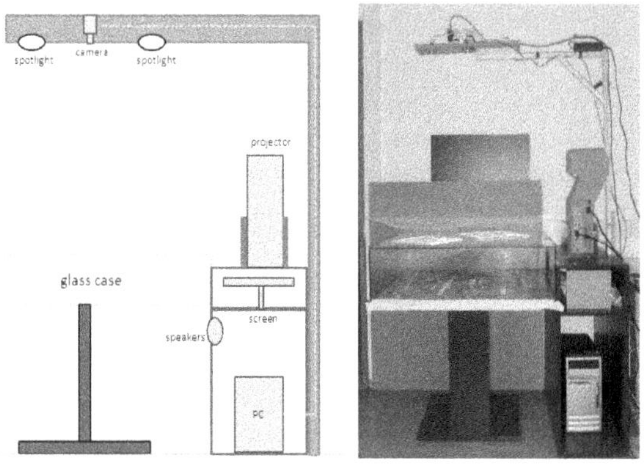

Figure 5. PaperView Glass Case schematic installation: (left) layout and (right)prototype system

DISCUSSION

Prior to installation in a real setting, both prototypes were tested and evaluated in an in-house space simulating a museum space, using a combination of the "observer participant" and "participant observer" approach [3]. During a 6-month period, more than 100 persons of various ages and backgrounds have interacted with the systems and their opinion ranged from positive to enthusiastic. The fact that interaction was supported through plain pieces of paper made a big impression, since the papers had a nice and soft feeling, and provided predictable, straightforward, interactions. Language selection is a challenging task for interactive exhibits, and is rarely addressed by previous efforts. Initially, PaperView users had to select their language from a dialogue on the cardboard, the first time it was detected. Thus, when the cardboard was taken outside the camera's viewport, the selection had to be repeated. During the evaluation sessions, this was spotted as a key usability problem. As a result, the "language selection through frame color" approach was devised, resulting in much simpler and smoother interaction.

Updated versions of both presented systems are now installed at the Archaeological Museum of Thessaloniki, Greece, as part of a permanent exhibition of interactive systems (for more information visit www.makedonopixels.org, exhibits "Multimodal Diverse travel" and "One day in a farmstead"). In order to accommodate the museum's requirements some modifications were made; e.g., the PaperView Table uses a short-throw projector, a much larger table and does not include the secondary screen. Additionally, based on *in situ* observations, additional software changes were made in order to improve the usability of the systems; e.g., to disambiguate the orientation of the projection on the cardboard, one of the colored edges is painted with a different color. Regarding usability improvements, the crosshair was replaced by a magnifying glass, the size of which changes depending on its distance from a site of interest (SOI), three different colours (green, orange and red) and sizes were used for visualizing the connecting string and when its connection to a SOI would "break", and animations were introduced to provide feedback when entering and leaving a SOI.

ACKNOWLEDGMENTS

This work has been supported by the FORTH-ICS internal RTD Programme "Ambient Intelligence and Smart Environments". Authors express their gratitude to M. Sifakis for the archaeological content of the prototype systems and to A. Katzourakis for the graphical designs.

REFERENCES

1. Argyros, A.A., Lourakis, M.I.A. 2006. Vision-based Interpretation of Hand Gestures for Remote Control of a Computer Mouse, in Proc. of the HCI'06 workshop, 40-51.
2. Bimber, O., Coriand, F., Kleppe, A., Bruns, E., Zollmann, S., and Langlotz, T. 2006. Superimposing pictorial artwork with projected imagery. In ACM SIGGRAPH 2006 Courses, 16-26.
3. Blomberg, J., Giacomi, J., Mosher, A. and Swenton-Wall, P. 1993. Ethnographic Field Methods and Their Relation to Design. In: Participatory design, LEA, 123-155
4. Brown, D., L. and Hua, H. 2006. Magic Lenses for Augmented Virtual Environments. IEEE Comput. Graph. Appl. 26, 4 (July 2006), 64-73.
5. Ferris, K., Bannon, L., Ciolfi, L., Gallagher, P., Hall, T. & Lennon, M. 2004. Shaping experiences in the hunt museum: a design case study. In Proc. of DIS '04, 205-214.
6. Garzotto, F. and Rizzo, F. 2007. Interaction paradigms in technology-enhanced social spaces: a case study in museums. In Proceedings of DPPI '07, 343-356.
7. Holman, D., Vertegaal, R., Altosaar, M., Troje, N., and Johns, D. 2005. Paper windows: interaction techniques for digital paper. In Proc. of CHI '05, 591-599.
8. Hornecker, E. and Stifter, M. 2006. Learning from interactive museum installations about interaction design for public settings. In Proceedings of OZCHI '06, 135-142.
9. Izadi, S., Hodges, S., Taylor, S., Rosenfeld, D., Villar, N., Butler, A., and Westhues, J. 2008. Going beyond the display: a surface technology with an electronically switchable diffuser. In Proc. of UIST '08, 269-278.
10. Kortbek, K. J. and Grønbæk, K. 2008. Interactive spatial multimedia for communication of art in the physical museum space. In Proceeding of MM '08, 609-618.
11. Reitmayr, G., Eade, E., and Drummond, T. 2005. Localisation and Interaction for Augmented Maps. In Proc. of 4th IEEE/ACM int/nal Symposium on Mixed and Augmented Reality, 120-129.
12. Smith, J. R. and Chang, S. 1996. VisualSEEk: a fully automated content-based image query system. In Proc. of ACM Multimedia '96, 87-98
13. Sparacino, F. 2004. Scenographies of the past and museums of the future: from the wunderkammer to body-driven interactive narrative spaces. Proc. of MM '04, 72-79.
14. Trucco , E., Verri, A. 1998. Introductory Techniques for 3-D Computer Vision, Prentice Hall, 201.
15. Wellner, P. 1993. Interacting with paper on the DigitalDesk. Commun. ACM 36, 7 (Jul. 1993), 87-96.

Handcrafting Textile Interfaces from A Kit-of-No-Parts

Hannah Perner-Wilson, Leah Buechley
MIT Media Lab
High-Low Tech
77 Mass. Ave, Cambridge MA 02139
plusea, leah@mit.edu

Mika Satomi
University of Art and Industrial Design Linz
Interface Cultures
Kollegiumsgasse 2, 4010 Linz, Austria
mika.satomi@ufg.ac.at

ABSTRACT

This paper explores the idea of handcrafted electronics. We introduce a kit-of-no-parts approach to building electronics from a diverse palette of craft materials, which we argue is more personal, understandable and accessible than the construction of technology from a kit of pre-determined components. We illustrate our approach by describing the design, construction, and dissemination of a collection of textile sensors, and detailing a website and a series of workshops through which we share our approach.

Author Keywords

Craft materials, construction kits, textiles, e-textiles, DIY, design methodology, sensors, personalization, documentation, workshops, kit-of-no-parts

ACM Classification Keywords

H.5.2 [Information Interfaces and Presentation]: User Interfaces; K.3.0 [Computers and Education]: General; C.3 [Special Purpose and Application-Based Systems]—microprocessor/ microcomputer applications, real-time and embedded systems.

General Terms

Theory

INTRODUCTION

The materials, tools and approaches we use to design, prototype and build technology greatly influence how we think about technology and the look and feel of the technology itself.

Construction kits make building technology easier. As systems of modular parts they lower the entry bar to science, engineering and technology disciplines. Their modularity allows for them to be assembled and almost as easily disassembled in order to iterate through a series of designs. But this modularity comes at the cost of constraint. The parts of a construction kit function inside modular systems and the designs realized with these kits are limited. They constrain what we build and how we think.

Craft on the other hand is associated with building as a form of personal expression. Craft materials are more often praised for their aesthetic, decorative and material qualities, than their ability to convey technological concepts. When we craft we draw from a wide palette of raw materials that allows for design explorations that construction kits of pre-manufactured parts cannot offer.

This paper proposes a new approach, where electronics are crafted from raw materials, from a *kit-of-no-parts*. Building electronics from craft materials provides novel pathways for understanding because it requires that the builder understand and work with the electrical, material, and aesthetic properties of raw materials. Understanding electronics at this level enables us to build electronics from a greater range of materials than are included in traditional electronics kits. Craft materials also enable us to personalize our technology in new ways—allowing for electronics that are fuzzy, stretchy, and colorful for example. We believe that incorporating new materials in electronics will help us broaden our approach to technology design and, more specifically, diversify the computer interfaces we build.

The following three themes summarize the benefits and affordances of handcrafting technology and helping others do the same:

(1) Personalization: leveraging the open palette craft materials to create unique and personal artifacts.

(2) Transparency: designing artifacts whose function can be determined from their form.

(3) Skills transfer: using craft materials to connect existing knowledge and skills to technology creation and customization.

The research described in this paper focuses on the application of craft techniques and the inclusion of craft materials and tools to create interface technology in the form of textile sensors. The aesthetic, expressive and cultural qualities of textiles play significant rolls in the process of combining textiles and electronics [5-7, 10-12]. They inform the process and are communicated through the results.

TEI'11, January 22–26, 2011, Funchal, Portugal.

In the remainder of the paper we explain the design and construction of our textile sensors, introduce a website that we created to document and disseminate our work, and describe the series of workshops through which we engage with the community and propagate our approach to crafting interfaces. We conclude with the results of a post workshop questionnaire and reflect on how a kit-of-no-parts supports our design approach.

TEXTILE SENSORS

The expressive diversity of the materials we choose to employ in our designs stand in contrast to those of popular construction kits. The following textile sensors are constructed from a selection of electrically conductive fabrics, threads and yarns using sewing needles, pompom makers, crochet hooks and spool knitting machines.

In line with our approach to designing technology to be more understandable we chose to display functionality and integrate it in the aesthetics as much as possible so that the function of the sensors can be deduced from their form.

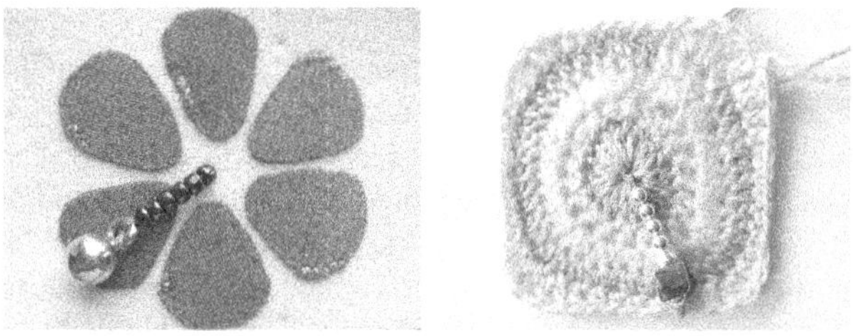

Figure 1) Tilt sensor (left) and crochet potentiometer (right).

The *fabric tilt sensor* shown in Figure 1 (left) is comprised of a free-swinging metal bead strung on a piece of conductive thread. The bead is surrounded by six petal shaped pieces of conductive fabric. Depending on the direction of inclination the metal bead will make electrical contact with different petals, enabling differentiation of six different positions of tilt. By replacing the discrete conductive petals with a resistive track, this sensor becomes a *crochet potentiometer*, like the one shown in Figure 1 (right).

Figure 2) Front (left) and back (right) of stroke sensor.

The *stitched stroke sensor* [Fig. 2] is made by stitching conductive threads through a base material to create a fur-like structure. On the back of the base material these threads are interconnected and belong to one of two contacts. When the hairs connected to one contact touch the hairs connected to the other contact the otherwise open switch is closed. By replacing the conductive thread with a more resistive thread, the stroke sensor responds to intensity of stroke.

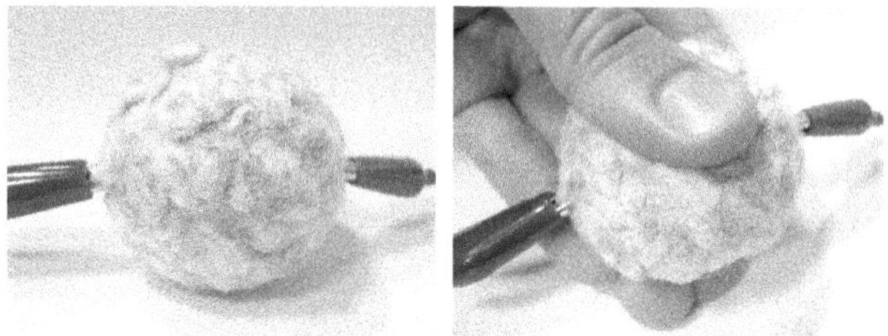

Figures 3) Felted pompom pressure sensor with alligator clips connected to either side.

The *felt pressure sensor* is constructed by making a pompom from a blend of regular and resistive yarn and then felting it by running it through the washing machine [Fig. 3]. Felting the pompom gives it a unique squishy feel that makes it appealing to squeeze. When squeezed, the conductive fibers throughout the pompom make better electrical connections, lowering the resistance between any two points on the pompom's surface.

The *knit stretch sensor* is a stretchy tube knit from the same resistive yarn as the pompom. When the yarn is stretched the twist of the yarn pressures the short conductive fibers together, improving the electrical contact between them and reducing resistance. Using a knitting machine to knit the yarn into a tubular structure creates a naturally stretchy knit structure. The bottom figures in Figure 4 show a close-up of this knit structure in its relaxed and stretched states.

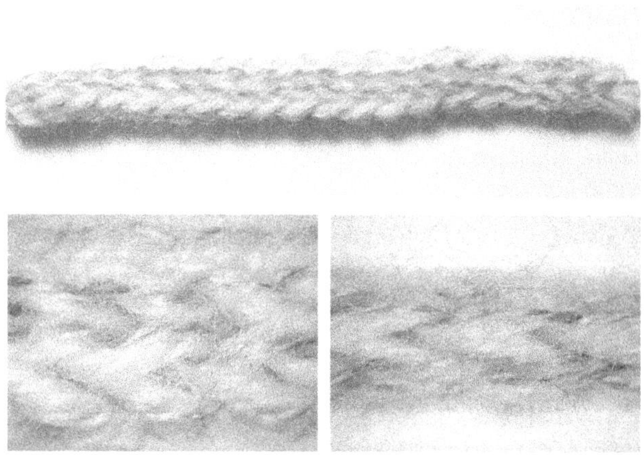

Figure 4) Tubular knit stretch sensor (top), close-up views of relaxed (bottom left) and stretched (bottom right) states.

A complete overview of these sensors as well as details on their construction can be found on our website [9] in the *Sensors* category.

WEBSITE

In order to share our sensor designs we began giving workshops and documenting and publishing how-to instructions, accompanied by photos and videos, online. In the summer of 2009 we launched a public website titled *How To Get What You Want* [9] where we continue to gather this documentation and present it in an organized structure. Access to information and resources are key aspects to our kit-of-no-parts approach and the website acts as a valuable reference library. Figure 5 shows a screenshot of the website.

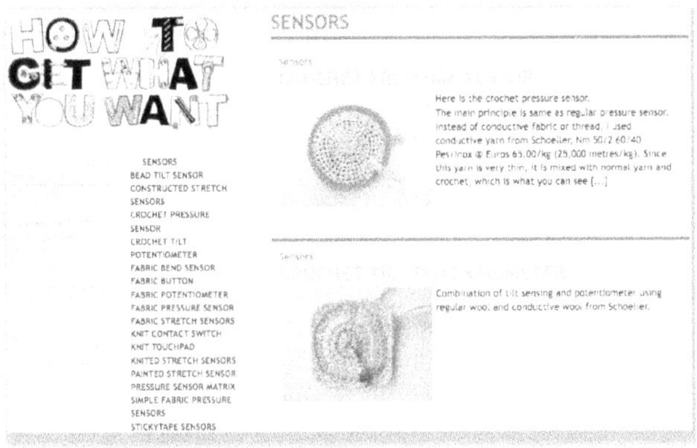

Figure 5) Screenshot of website.

The website is organized in categories which include *Example Projects*, *Solutions* (such as *Circuits*, *Connections* and *Sensors*), *Materials*, *Tools* and *Techniques*. The *Connections* category for example documents a variety of ways in which hard and soft conductive materials can be connected in permanent and non-permanent (pluggable) ways. The *Traces* category details different techniques for creating both stretchy and non-stretchy fabric trances. The *Sensors* category documents all of our sensors. Each sensor post includes step-by-step instructions, printable templates and links to retailers where users can purchase the materials and tools we used to make them. The *Conductive Materials* category contains information on all the conductive materials we have been able to get our hands on, with an emphasis on those that are soft, flexible and sewable.

WORKSHOPS

While the website has become a continuous platform for documenting and publishing our work, we initially started sharing our work through workshops [Fig. 6]. Since 2008 we have held close to 20 workshops in almost as many countries that involved between 5 and 20 participants and lasted anywhere from a few hours to a few days.

The aim of each of these workshops is to introduce participants to the prospect of personalizing interface technology through handcrafting textile sensors. We pursue the goal by engaging them in hands-on material explorations that require them to acquire and exercise both craft and engineering skills. As workshop facilitators we see our role in conveying the underlying ideas of material experimentation and in supporting participants to conceive of and realize their own designs. Rather than try to teach participants how to recreate what we previously designed, we try to convey a style of working that emphasizes curiosity, creative use of materials, diligence in testing and patience in debugging.

Figure 6) Snapshot of a workshop environment.

Our workshops were inspired by the approach of several others, most notably the Scrapyard Challenge workshops [4] in which participants construct interactive projects from cast-off materials and junk. The LilyPad workshops [5] introduced teenagers to a toolkit with which they constructed e-textile designs while learning programming and electronics skills. The TeeBoard [3], Eduwear [1] and i*CATch [2] workshops and construction kits stand in contrast to our approach of emphasizing handcrafting. Each of these projects take a construction kit approach to teaching electronics and programming to children using textiles.

Workshop Structure

We start each workshop by introducing the materials and tools that have become part of our repertoire and will be available for use throughout the workshop. We introduce a selection of our sensor designs, as well as the materials and tools we use to construct them. We have found it useful to follow this introduction with a hands-on activity in which participants select a sensor from our collection and try to recreate it. Although we like to stress personalization in every activity it often proves too challenging to introduce it in this very first activity and so simply re-creating a design is a good place to start. For workshops that last longer than three hours, we continue by introducing a topic that helps participants shape their individual designs. Themes have included *Wearable Sound Experiment*, *Piano T-Shirt* and *Bend, sew, touch, feel, read.* In the Piano T-Shirt workshop for example we provided cheap toy pianos and t-shirts. The pianos were gutted for their circuitry and components, and the piano keys were replaced with textile sensors. The sensors and the circuitry were mounted on t-shirts and other personal clothing items to make them wearable. Figure 8 (right) shows an example of a participant integrating textile sensors and circuitry to match the design of her t-shirt.

After participants have formulated an initial design sketch they present this to each other in order to collect feedback. This session also enables everyone to get an idea of what other participants are working on. After this first presentation of their idea, we help individual participants plan how they will realize their design. Part of our task here is to help participants develop designs that can be accomplished within the timeframe of the workshop. The rest of the workshop is spent building the designs. Although not everyone achieves the result they aimed for, it is rare that participants leave the workshop without some kind of functioning artifact. We wrap up the workshop with a quick show and tell where participants present their projects, explain their designs and convey their construction experience.

Throughout the workshops we make use of our website, pointing participants to detailed information that is published there. It has proven to be a valuable resource for participants during the workshop as well as a source for them to refer to for information after the workshop.

Participant Creations

To convey the nature of the workshop experiences, we now discuss several projects that were realized during the sessions. The projects we discuss are particularly nice examples of how craft materials, and textiles in particular, facilitate personalization.

The Human Violin is a performance piece realized by a group of seven participants. They designed and created a set of three costumes that allowed the performers to explore the connections between their bodies [Fig. 7]. Two of the costumes had a series of embroidered resistive stripes on them that wrapped around the limbs and torsos. The third costume had conductive patches adhered to it that acted as conductive sliders. All three performers were blindfolded during the performance so that the sensors replaced their senses. When the sliders came in contact with the resistive tracks pre-recorded sounds would play faster or slower, depending on the position along the resistive track, giving the blindfolded performers an idea of what body parts were touching. Their aim was to end the performance in a certain configuration that they had to achieve without being able to see one another.

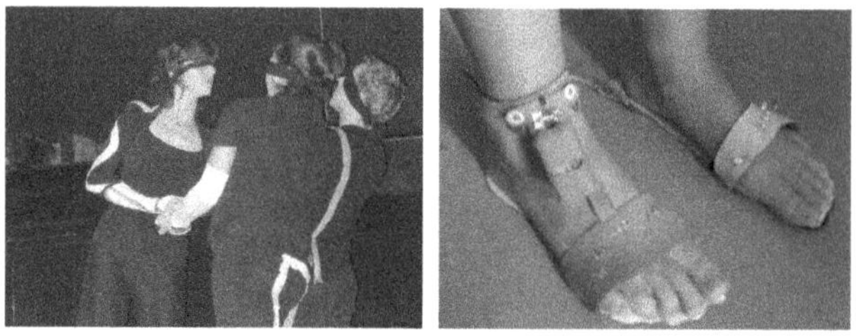

Figure 7) Participant projects: The Human Violin (left), pressure sensitive toe sandals (right).

In a workshop *Bend, Sew, Feel, Read, Touch* two participants collaborated to make a pair of sandals with five pressure sensors embedded in the soles under the toes of each foot in [Fig. 7]. Five separate LEDs were mounted on the sandal's front strap to indicate through brightness how hard each toe was pressing so that the wearer could practice pressuring each toe individually. Note the battery pouch on the top strap of the participant's right foot has been integrated in the their sandal design.

In a workshop where we provided toy pianos and t-shirts one participant brought her own top and integrated the circuit layout in the design that was printed on the fabric [Fig. 8]. In another sound toy hacking workshop one participant embedded the sound circuits from two different greeting cards in a fur shawl [Fig. 8]. She stitched conductive threads into the shawl that acted as a directional stroke sensor. Depending on which way the shawl is stroked it triggers one of two different sounds.

Figure 8) Participant projects: Fur shawl with integrated stroke sensors (left), personal Piano T-Shirt (right).

The example shown in Figure 9 on the left is a particularly beautiful version of our tilt sensor in which the participant replaced the metal bead with a conductive pompom that she made from conductive fabric. The sensor was decoratively mounted on a handbag where it causes LED lights to twinkle as the handbag swings.

Figures 9) Participant projects: Conductive fabric pompom on purse (left), Knit glove stretch sensor (right).

The last example shows the knit stretch sensor fully integrated in the fingers of a glove [Fig. 9], which a participant knit overnight from one workshop day to the next. The bending of different fingers trigger different musical sounds. The glove is part of a full body "one-man-band" suit that allows the wearer to trigger a whole range of instrument sounds though body movements.

Questionnaire Results

The aim of the questionnaire was to gather feedback regarding whether or not we are able to successfully convey our kit-of-no-parts approach in the workshops that we give. In particular, we were interested in the following questions: Were participants able to construct personally meaningful artifacts from the materials and tools we introduced? Did the materials and tools we introduced make the technology more understandable? Were participants able to leverage an existing skill in order to learn something new?

The questionnaire was sent out to 104 participants who had previously participated in one of our workshops that had taken place over the last 3 years and lasted six hours or more. We received 30 replies of which 12 were male and 18 were female, ranging from 20 – 57 years of age.

How did the use of craft materials have an impact on the personalization of the resulting artifacts?

We asked participants what had become of the artifact they had created during the workshop and were pleasantly surprised that 12 participants reported active use of their artifact beyond the workshop context. This included having displayed their artifact publically, given it as a gift or using it as a demonstration to help explain e-textiles to others. Further 9 participants mentioned that they have it stored away as a memory of the workshop. Only one participant noted that they had cannibalized it for parts. Further 2 participants left the field blank. Practically all participants kept their final projects, making a strong statement for the permanence of crafted objects.

Did the craft material approach taken in the workshops make technology more understandable?

When asked what had happened since the workshop. 50% or more responded positively to having started another e-textile project, feeling knowledgeable on an e-textiles subject and staying in contact with other workshop participants. When asked what skills and knowledge learnt in the workshop were most useful and how these had had impacted their future practice the written replies were diverse, but one notable statement "I feel like I can understand 'how'" supports the conclusion that the workshop gave some participants enough insight to feel knowledgeable on the subject matter and capable of understanding technology situated in a craft practice.

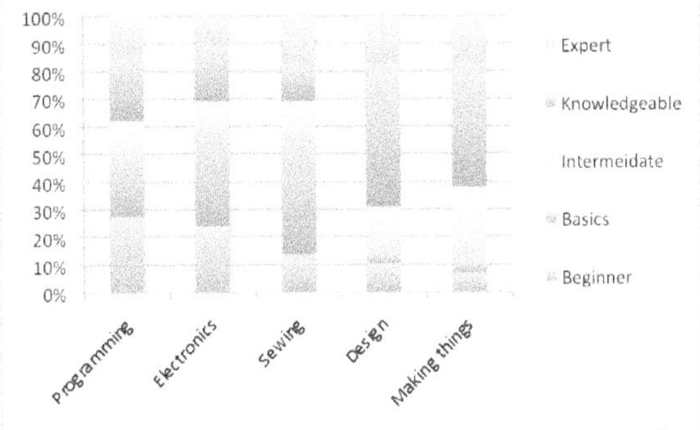

Figure 10) Graph showing how workshop participants rated their skills.

Were participants able to leverage an existing skill in order to engage in new activities?

The graph in Figure 10 displays how participants rated their skills from total beginner to expert in the areas of programming, electronics, sewing, design and making things. Participants rated themselves across the board with a tendency toward more *design* and *making things* skills. From the individual responses it is interesting to note that participants rated themselves *knowledgeable* or *expert* in at least one skill and total *beginner* or *basic skills* in another skill. This means that not only is the participant pool diverse in their skill-sets, but individuals come to the workshops feeling proficient in at least one skill and at an entry level in another. The downside of this is that not a single participant rated themselves to be below (nor above) *intermediate* in all skills and that the interdisciplinarity of the e-textiles field possibly closes it off to complete novices.

While these results convey that participants come to the workshop considering themselves *knowledgeable* or *expert* in at least one domain, it does not answer the question whether they were able to leverage these existing skills in order to learn new ones. The following responses, displayed in Figure 11, try to answer this question. Two thirds of participants replied that they had helped another participant during the workshop and all but two participants replied yes to the direct question of whether they were able to apply an existing skill during the workshop. 80% or more replied yes to having challenged themselves, having engaged in new activities as well as having gotten excited about the new possibilities they encountered during the workshop. While these replies are not definite indicators, they at least support the idea that participants did not stick to their own domains and raise the possibility that having an existing skill helped them explore a new domain.

How did participants experience the kit-of-no-parts approach taken in the workshops?

The following quotes were chosen to underline the influence that the kit-of-no-parts approach had on participant's experiences.

"Find unconventional solution for technical problems and simplify things. Hand's on working. Fast prototyping. Sharing knowledge among workshop participants."

"With e-textile/crafting work, the results are immediate and tangible. This shortens the design iteration cycle considerably and makes prototyping much more engaging than working with tools on a computer screen."

"I was surprised about the aesthetics and simplicity of solutions presented and found during the workshop. I was amazed about the seriousness and purposiveness the tutors and people in the DIY environment worked on the subject. I learned that excellence is not a question of resources and that it is important to share resources."

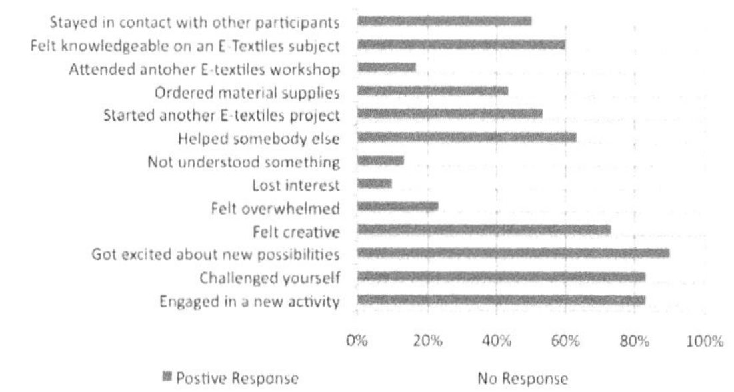

Figure 11) Graph showing replies that participants responded to with a positive response.

A KIT-OF-NO-PARTS

This section we evaluate how well the kit-of-no-parts approach that we detailed in the introduction is supported by our results as well as how it differentiates itself from building within a system of parts.

1) Personalize

When describing LilyPad Arduino projects Buechley [5,7] makes the observation that the e-textile projects that people realize with the LilyPad toolkit look nothing like traditional technology. We would like to expand on this statement and say that the projects that people realize in our workshops are not only unique, unusual and diverse but, as review of the images in the last section attest, they are also nothing like commercially available interfaces. Handcrafting technology not only fosters the realization of personal artifacts, it also enables people to build novel designs that represent the intimate process of their making.

2) Understand Technology

The design of our textile sensors and other solutions documented in our online database are informed by a desire for them to be as legible and reproducible as possible. Technology constructed through crafting tends to be less hidden than technology that is machined. The scale and methods of craft production naturally afford visibility and in our designs we take extra care to showcase functional elements instead of hiding them beneath others. By examining our designs you should be able to draw information regarding their function directly from them. This is a conscious decision that we make because we believe that if technology is more apparent, then more people will be able to understand it and in turn craft their own interfaces. In upcoming workshops we hope to be able to examine these issues in more depth by surveying participants about their technological understanding and its relationship to both the functional transparency of designs and the practice of craft.

3) Leverage Existing Skills

We have documented that our workshops attract a diverse audience. In any given workshop we usually have at least one electrical engineer and one sewing expert. This diversity has become a key aspect to how we are able to run our workshops, since participants are able to help each other, bringing their own knowledge into the workshop as a valuable resource for others.

In Pianos Not Stereos [8] Resnick et al. list two general principals for the kinds of "*doing*" that are most assistive to learning. To involve familiarity so that previous knowledge can be leveraged and for this to happen in a natural way. Without intention or planning we see these principals occurring naturally within our workshops where participants are faced with a multitude of challenges that include designing artifacts, constructing sensors, laying out circuits, programming microcontrollers and working with textiles. Participants will draw upon their existing skills and help others where they can. At the end of the day every participant has managed to navigate and work through the full set of challenges and as a result has built a unique artifact that is not only a result of personalization, but of the learning and making process that occurred.

CONCLUSIONS

We have described how craft materials support a more understandable approach to creating technology and that the results of this process can be more transparent and expressive. Participants in our workshops were able to conceive of and realize original interface designs from the palette of conductive fabrics and craft materials we provided. We believe that our approach to crafting technology, and electronics in particular, can be applied to build a richer and more diverse set of human-computer interfaces and that the examples presented here give preliminary but exciting windows into what a diversified and personalized landscape of interfaces might look like.

The research presented in this paper focused on blending electronics with traditional textile crafts, but we believe the approach could be expanded to many other domains. By applying the kit-of-no-parts approach to other material and craft disciplines we believe we could provide different and equally interesting opportunities for engineers and craftspeople to leverage their existing skills to master new domains and build new technologies.

ACKNOWLEDGEMENTS

We would like to thank all the workshop participants and organizers and the Distance Lab. This research was funded in part by the MIT Media Lab consortium and NSF grants # 0855773 and 0940520.

REFERENCES

1. Katterfeldt, E., Dittert, N. and Schelhowe, H. "EduWear: smart textiles as ways of relating computing technology to everyday life," in *Proceedings of the 8th International Conference on Interaction Design and Children* (Como, Italy: ACM, 2009), 9-17.
2. Ngai, G. et al., "i*CATch: a scalable plug-n-play wearable computing framework for novices and children," in *Proceedings of the 28th international conference on Human factors in computing systems* (Atlanta, Georgia, USA: ACM, 2010), 443-452.
3. Ngai, G. et al., "The TeeBoard: an education-friendly construction platform for e-textiles and wearable computing," in *Proceedings of the 27th international conference on Human factors in computing systems* (Boston, MA, USA: ACM, 2009), 249-258.
4. Moriwaki, K. and Brucker-Cohen, J. "Lessons from the scrapyard: creative uses of found materials within a workshop setting," *AI Soc*. 20, no. 4 (2006): 506-525.
5. Buechley et al., "The LilyPad Arduino: using computational textiles to investigate engagement, aesthetics, and diversity in computer science education," in *Proceeding of the twenty-sixth annual SIGCHI conference on Human factors in computing systems* (Florence, Italy: ACM, 2008), 423-432.
6. Buechley, L. & Eisenberg, M., 2009. Fabric PCBs, electronic sequins, and socket buttons: techniques for e-textile craft. Personal Ubiquitous Comput., 13(2), pp.133-150.
7. Buechley, L. & Hill, B.M., 2010. LilyPad in the wild: how hardware's long tail is supporting new engineering and design communities. In Proceedings of the 8th ACM Conference on Designing Interactive Systems. Aarhus, Denmark: ACM, pp. 199-207.
8. Resnick, M., Bruckman, W. and Martin, F. "Pianos not stereos: creating computational construction kits," *interactions* 3, no. 5 (1996): 40-50.
9. www.howtogetwhatyouwant.at
10. Vallgårda, A. and Redström, J. "Computational composites," in *Proceedings of the SIGCHI conference on Human factors in computing systems - CHI '07* (presented at the the SIGCHI conference, San Jose, California, USA, 2007), 513.
11. Post, R. et al., "E-broidery: Design and fabrication of textile-based computing," *IBM Systems Journal* 39, no. 3 (2000): 840-860.
12. Berzowska, J., & Bromley, M. (2007). Soft Computation Through Conductive Textiles. Proceedings of the International Foundation of Fashion Technology Institutes Conference, Toronto, Canada, April 12 - 14.

Interactive Fabrication: New Interfaces for Digital Fabrication

Karl D.D. Willis **Cheng Xu** **Kuan-Ju Wu** **Golan Levin** **Mark D Gross**

Carnegie Mellon University
5000 Forbes Avenue, Pittsburgh, PA
kddw@cmu.edu chengxu@cmu.edu kuanjuw@cmu.edu golan@andrew.cmu.edu mdgross@cmu.edu

ABSTRACT

We present a series of prototype devices that use real-time input to fabricate physical form: *Interactive Fabrication*. Our work maps out the problem space of real-time control for digital fabrication devices, and examines where alternative interfaces for digital fabrication are relevant. We conclude by reflecting upon the potential of interactive fabrication and outline a number of considerations for future research in this area.

Author Keywords

Interactive, fabrication, digital, prototyping, embodied, interface, real-time, tangible, interaction, creativity, design.

ACM Classification Keywords

H5.m. Information interfaces and presentation (e.g., HCI): Miscellaneous.

General Terms

Design, Experimentation, Human Factors, Theory.

INTRODUCTION

The once costly and exclusive domain of digital fabrication is already reaching wider audiences under the banners of 'desktop manufacturing' and 'personal fabrication' [3]. Computer output is moving beyond the two-dimensional display and into the world of three-dimensional physical objects. It is clear that most current interfaces catering to digital fabrication remain focused within the graphical user interface (GUI) paradigm. Figure 1 illustrates how the current digital fabrication process closely follows the desktop publishing metaphor: A design is created using a GUI interface, saved to file, fed to an output device, and finally manifested in physical form. This process is overly complex, requiring numerous disparate steps to go from design idea to physical prototype. It is far removed from traditional craft where the artist or designer interacts directly with the material using tools such as brushes or chisels to paint or sculpt. Generative, code-driven, and algorithmic approaches to fabrication are an important area of creative exploration, but are not always applicable for general design scenarios. Empowering users with purpose-built tools for digital fabrication opens up a range of new creative possibilities.

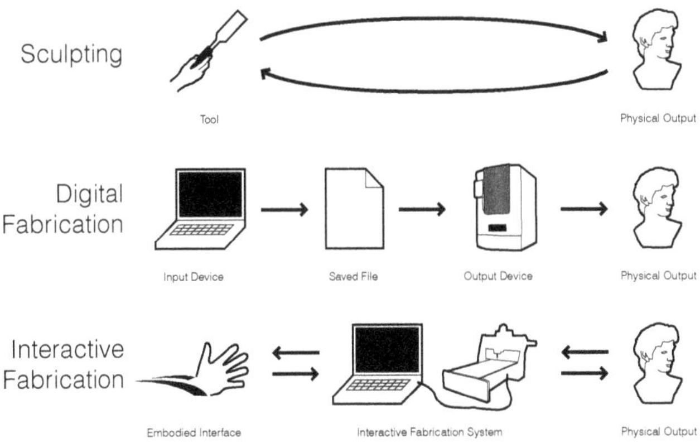

Figure 1. *Interactive Fabrication* contrasts with existing approaches by allowing real-time input to digital fabrication.

We present a series of prototype devices that take real-time input to fabricate physical form: *Interactive Fabrication*[1]. We do not suggest that these tools are a ready replacement for the current digital fabrication process; rather our work seeks to map out the problem space and understand where alternative interfaces are relevant. We conclude the paper by contextualizing our work within the broader framework of *Direct Manipulation* [8] and outline a number of considerations for researchers looking to explore this space.

MOTIVATION

Despite recent advances in digital tools there remains a considerable divide between the *designer* and the *constructor* of artifacts. We believe bringing physical input and output closer together can aid in recapturing the creative process seen in earlier forms of direct making. This has the benefit of establishing a closer relationship with materials and allows designers to better understand their properties and nuances.

TEI'11, January 22–26, 2011, Funchal, Portugal.

[1] http://www.interactivefabrication.com

Key to bringing together physical input and output are interfaces that support embodied real-time interaction and fabrication. By situating the interface with the fabrication device the user can view the material directly to understand the spatial relationships and structure of the form. Real-time feedback from the fabrication process can then directly inform the design. We envision this direct form of interaction will foster experimentation, improvisation, and an exploration of the medium's capacity [6].

RELATED WORK

Research in the separate fields of non-GUI interfaces and digital fabrication is currently flourishing. Despite the work done in each field, few projects cross the divide between embodied input and embodied output. A noteworthy early example of a computational interface bridging between physical input and physical output is Frazer's *Flexible Intelligent Modeling System*, developed in 1980 [1]. The system is intended to support the architectural design process and consists of sensor embedded blocks able to determine their configuration and output a 2D representation to a plotter. While there has been considerable research on tangible modeling systems as input devices, research crossing over into tangible output has to date been limited. The automated construction of architectural designs as physical models has been explored by Howe [7]. He outlines a number of principles aimed at allowing scale models to be constructed using a robotic arm and interlocking components. Gramazio and Kohler [4] have made extensive use of robotic arms as a fabrication technology to design prototype architectural structures and manufacture large scale building facades.

In the field of industrial design, the *Sketch Furniture* system uses a professional motion-capture system to create 3D geometry from sketches in physical space [2]. This geometry is then processed into a mesh that can be fabricated at full scale using a 3D printer. *Spatial Sketch* takes a similar approach with a 3D sketch interface that outputs patterns of slice forms for construction using a laser cutter and planar materials [9]. While these works bridge between embodied input and embodied output, the process suffers from a level of indirection: fabrication only begins once the design has been completed. Our interest lies in exploring direct real-time control of fabrication devices to integrate design and fabrication into a single process.

INTERACTIVE FABRICATION

We have developed several prototype devices that use real-time sensor input to directly affect fabricated output.

Shaper

Shaper is a prototype device that uses a three-axis computer numerical control (CNC) machine to interactively dispense expanding polyurethane foam material (Figure 2). The user controls the device via a translucent touch screen to create physical artifacts with sketch-like gestures. *Shaper* challenges the conventional process of digital fabrication by

Figure 2. *Shaper*, a prototype device for interactive fabrication (left) using expanding polyurethane foam (right).

allowing direct interactive control. The translucent touch surface is situated above the fabrication area, so that users can directly see the physical output. The gesture interface is projected onto the rear of the touch surface and a depth map is stored to allow multiple layers to be built up into three-dimensional form. The software detects when sketch lines intersect and raises the dispenser head to the appropriate height; material can then be built up layer by layer. The polyurethane foam dries into a lightweight and smooth material. Figure 2 illustrates the type of physical 'pixels' that can be created with expanding foam. We chose expanding polyurethane foam to enable quick fabrication. Unlike other additive 3D printing processes, foam quickly expands to a substantial volume.

A number of factors contribute to the fidelity and controllability of the fabricated foam design: the speed at which the machine moves, the amount of pressure inside the canister, the nozzle shape, and the dispensing surface. By observing and interacting with the material, designers can better understand how the material behaves and 'talks back' during the creation process. Despite the speed at which the foam could be dispensed, the speed of the CNC machine proved to be a bottleneck. The speed of user interaction was far beyond the response speed of the machine, meaning commands had to be placed in a queue for delayed execution. Future work on the project will involve developing the software interface further and trialing alternative materials. For example, using subtractive fabrication techniques opens up a variety of different materials that can be interactively milled by the user.

Speaker

Speaker interactively sculpts wire forms based on sound input. The user stands in front of the device and speaks into a small microphone. An Arduino micro-controller embedded in the device then begins to calculate a simplified contour from the sound wave. Two motors are used to push and bend the metal wire into a shape. Sounds are thus physically 'encoded' into the wire, creating a tangible manifestation of an intangible sound (Figure 3). The device explores the immediacy of the fabrication

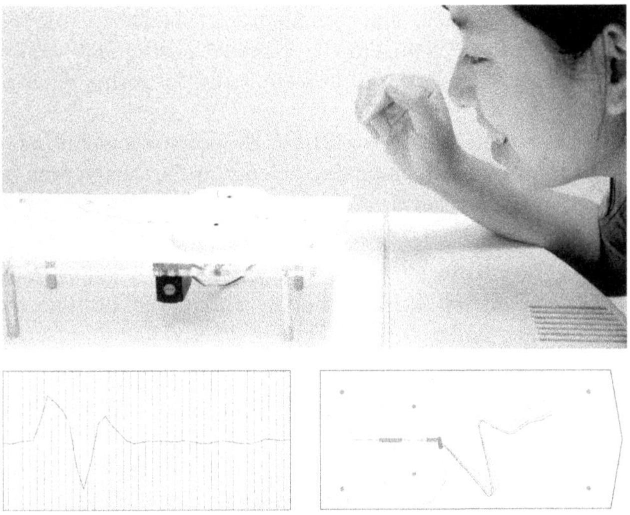

Figure 3. ***Speaker*** **sculpts wire forms from user sounds (top). Wire is bent to form a simplified sound wave (bottom).**

process by linking an ephemeral passage of sound to a physical entity. It furthermore acts as a means for the spoken word to be transcribed into an artifact of meaning. Figure 4 shows a pair of earrings constructed with the words 'I love you'.

Due to the physical actuation involved in shaping the wire, we found latency was again an issue. We experimented with two modes of interaction. In 'echo mode' the device echoes user input immediately, sculpting the wire with the minimum amount of latency possible. In 'replay mode', the device records a few seconds of speech, then immediately starts bending a section of wire. We observed that the latter mode would almost draw users into a conversation with the machine, transforming the waiting time into a playful experience. In future work we would like to explore how other qualities of sound can inform the shape. For example, a higher pitch can be mapped to sharper turns, while a lower pitch can appear smoother. This can give the voice of a child a very different visual style than that of an adult.

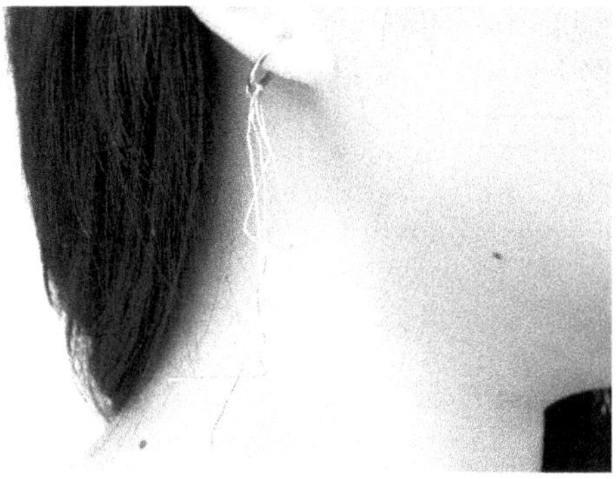

Figure 4. Earrings shaped with the words 'I love you'.

Cutter

Cutter is a tangible interface for generating three-dimensional digital models by hand crafting polystyrene foam. The user pulls, pushes, and rotates a custom hotwire cutter to sculpt, cut, and shape foam cubes. The position of the cutting path is processed in real-time by a computer to visualize the cutting process and generate a 3D model. *Cutter* aims to provide an intuitive way to explore physical form by combining traditional craft with digital fabrication.

Cutter consists of a hotwire cutter, a holder, and a visualization program. When the hotwire cutter comes into contact with the foam it cuts a path that is processed by the computer into a 3D model. The cutter is constructed using thin wire heated by electrical resistance, a linear potentiometer to measure the distance the cutter has been pushed or pulled, and a rotary potentiometer to record the tilt angle (Figure 5). The foam holder can be set in a stationary position or rotated via stepper-motor to allow more intricate and unpredictable forms. A real-time visualization shows the cube position, orientation, and cutting path on screen (Figure 6). Geometry is reconstructed based on sensor data and can be saved as an STL mesh file for immediate reproduction with a 3D printer or edited and revised using 3D modeling software.

The polystyrene foam material was chosen because of its

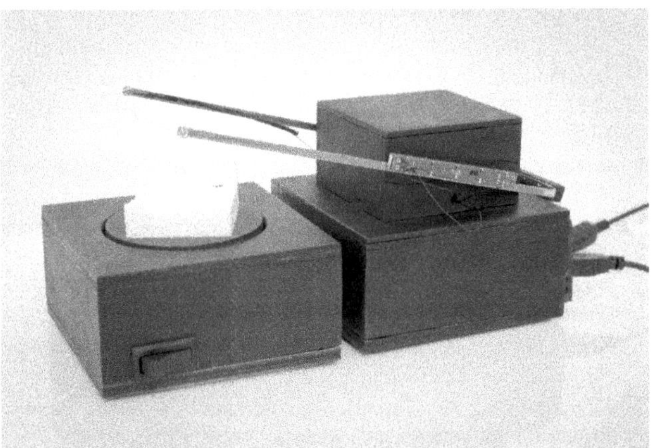

Figure 5. ***Cutter*** **is a tangible interface for generating three-dimensional digital models by hand crafting polystyrene foam.**

Figure 6. Potentiometers are used to sense the cutting path and visualize the shape of the material on screen.

malleability and the speed at which it can be molded. Due to the nature of the material, the foam can melt when overexposed to heat from the hotwire and cause unpredictable melting patterns. *Cutter* enables designers to play with the material and the randomness and unpredictability it brings. By enabling the physical process to be recorded and transferred into the digital realm, designers can gain from the immediacy of the physical and the flexibility of the digital. The next steps for the project are to replace the potentiometers with actuators that can control the physical position of the hotwire cutter. This enables the device to sense, record, and replay path movement. It opens up possibilities for editing cutting gestures to fabricate a remixed or refined physical object.

DISCUSSION

Shneiderman's concept of *Direct Manipulation* focuses on how screen-based interfaces can benefit from a 'what-you-see-is-what-you-get' approach [8]. Interactive fabrication systems that directly manipulate and produce physical form share many of the same aims.

Continuous representation of the object of interest. Our interactive fabrication prototypes avoid a 'representation' of the object of interest, but instead allow the user to look directly at the fabricated form. Additional information can be added to augment the user's view, but the main area of interest remains the fabricated form itself.

Physical actions. With each of our prototypes the user interacts through an embodied interface where their physical actions are sensed and interpreted in real-time. Physical action again determines the embodied output in the form of digital fabrication.

Rapid, incremental, reversible operations. Optimizing the speed and response time of our prototypes has been a major challenge. Due to the amount of actuation required and the speed of user interaction we have been unable to produce satisfactory fabrication speeds. Our approach has been to incrementally buffer user input and create a delayed response. This approach works well for short segments of interaction, as in the case of *Speaker*, but begins to break down when continuous interaction is required, such as with *Shaper*. The ability to reverse a physical action requires considerably more technological complexity. However, gestures that make up the final form can be digitally stored to allow the user to revisit a design, remove unwanted gestures, and fabricate the form again.

Layered or spiral approach to learning. We strived to create an interface like the pen or piano that is *instantly knowable* and *indefinitely masterable* [5]. We found the directness of interactive fabrication lent itself to accessible interfaces and the complexity and variety of materials provided a considerable range for expression.

Encountering *Direct Manipulation* interfaces in the physical world introduces a number of new considerations for research in this space.

Unexpected Results. The direct nature of interactive control introduces the potential for unexpected results that cannot easily be reversed. In the early stages of the design process it may be desirable to experiment with form, or have a roughly produced early prototype. However when crafting a final form factor, maintaining fidelity to the design idea is of upmost importance.

Waste. Unexpected results leads on to the issue of increased waste. Subtractive fabrication processes already suffer from large amounts of waste material. This could become an even greater problem for fabrication devices that function in real-time and do not require rigorous training to operate.

Disconnect between physical and digital. We have found that there are numerous subtleties to fabrication materials that complicate the process of digital representation. Regardless of how good a simulation can perform, there are numerous sources of variability in materials that can quickly make a digital representation unstable.

CONCLUSION

Although there are numerous advantages to the current GUI approach towards digital fabrication, by more closely linking *input* to *output* we can allow designers to benefit from computer controlled machinery and at the same time re-establish a relationship with the physical fabrication process. The prototypes presented in this paper have only scratched the surface of a much larger area of exploration. Interactive fabrication will not be appropriate for all circumstances, but we foresee a range of new creative possibilities for early stage prototyping, experimental form, improvisational fabrication, and many others. With the rapid growth of digital fabrication upon us, now is an ideal time for reimagining how we create physical form.

ACKNOWLEDGMENTS

We thank the Fine Foundation and The Carnegie Mellon School of Art for funding support, and Scott Hudson for assistance with equipment.

REFERENCES

1. Frazer, J. *An Evolutionary Architecture.* Architectural Association, 1995.
2. FRONT Sketch Furniture. 2006, http://www.designfront.org.
3. Gershenfeld, N.A. *Fab: The Coming Revolution on your Desktop - From Personal Computers to Personal Fabrication.* Basic Books, New York, 2005.
4. Gramazio, F. and Kohler, M. *Digital Materiality in Architecture.* Lars Müller Publishers, Baden, 2008.
5. Levin, G. Painterly Interfaces for Audiovisual Performance *Media Arts and Sciences* MIT, Boston, MA, 2000.
6. McCullough, M. *Abstracting Craft: The Practiced Digital Hand.* MIT Press, Cambridge, MA, 1998.
7. Scott Howe, A. Designing for Automated Construction. *Automation in Construction 9*, 3 (2000), 259-276.
8. Shneiderman, B. Direct Manipulation: A Step Beyond Programming Languages. *Computer 16*, 8 (1983), 57-69.
9. Willis, K.D.D., Lin, J., Mitani, J. and Igarashi, T., Spatial Sketch: Bridging Between Movement & Fabrication. In Proc. *TEI '10*, ACM (2010), 5-12.

SketchChair: An All-in-one Chair Design System for End Users

Greg Saul
JST ERATO IGARASHI
Design Interface Project
GregSaul@gmail.com

Manfred Lau
JST ERATO IGARASHI
Design Interface Project
manfred.lau@gmail.com

Jun Mitani
University of Tsukuba / JST ERATO
mitani@cs.tsukuba.ac.jp

Takeo Igarashi
The University of Tokyo / JST ERATO
takeo@acm.org

ABSTRACT
SketchChair is an application that allows novice users to control the entire process of designing and building their own chairs. Chairs are designed using a simple 2D sketch-based interface and design validation tools, and are then fabricated from sheet materials, cut by a laser cutter or CNC milling machine. This paper presents the concepts and details of *SketchChair*, and both miniature and full-sized chairs are designed using the application. We conclude with results and insights from a workshop in which novice users designed their own model chairs.

Author Keywords
User-generated Design, Rapid Prototyping, User Interface, Sketch-based modeling, Fabrication, Customization.

ACM Classification Keywords
I.3.5 [Computer Graphics]: Computational Geometry and Object Modeling; H.1.2 User/Machine Systems; J.6 Computer-aided engineering (computer aided design).

General Terms
Design, Experimentation.

INTRODUCTION
Recently, there have been significant advances in digital manufacturing technologies. Tools, such as 3D printers, laser cutters, and computer-controlled milling machines, have become cheaper and more accessible to consumers. These 'desktop manufacturing' or 'personal fabrication' [5] processes are providing the means for people who might normally be consumers to become creators. Just as desktop printers and desktop publishing software have enabled users to design and produce their own printed material, desktop manufacturing allows people to create their own products at home, quickly and precisely.

However, CAD (computer aided design) systems that enable novice users to design their own products have lagged behind. In many instances, inexperienced users are faced with complex programs intended for experts, such as SolidWorks [3] and AutoCAD [1]. Moreover, these tools are usually only part of the design process. Before a functional product can be developed, other steps may need to be performed outside the CAD system (e.g., sketching, prototyping, testing).

TEI'11, January 22–26, 2011, Funchal, Portugal.

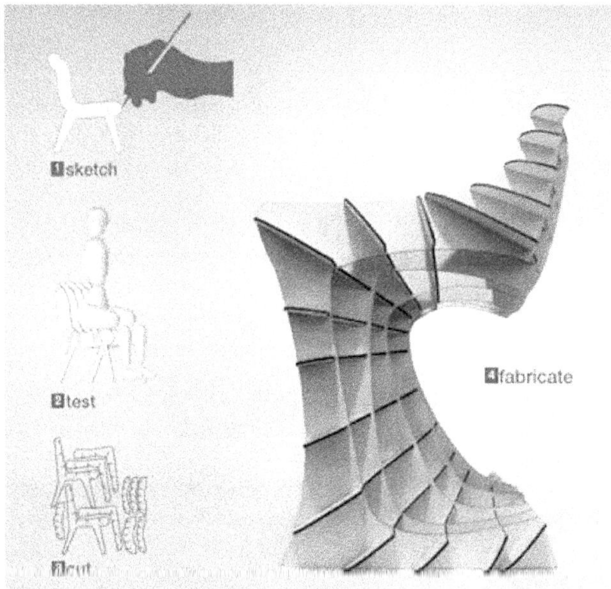

Figure 1. Process diagram for designing a chair using our system.

There are generally constraints on creating functional 3D products within a given fabrication process. For example, a laser cutter can only construct objects from planar materials. Most CAD systems do not permit users to incorporate constraints of specific fabrication processes into a design. Instead, they produce generic 3D models, leaving it to the user to translate the designs into patterns that can be used to create actual products.

If a product is designed poorly, it may not function correctly. For example, a chair designed in a CAD system may be unbalanced and fall over when it is actually constructed. Most CAD systems do not provide the average user with a way of assessing such potential problems.

All of these obstacles ultimately make it difficult for ordinary users to avail themselves of simple CNC manufacturing techniques and become creators.

We introduce a system that brings us one step closer to realizing the goal of personal fabrication. Our system is appropriate for the design and fabrication of furniture. In this paper, we focus on the design and fabrication of chairs, because there is a strong relationship between the user and the desired form of a chair. The advantage of our *SketchChair* software is that it allows even a novice user to control the entire process of creating an actual chair. This process includes concept development, refinement, testing, and fabrication. The system uses a simple 2D sketch interface that can easily be learned by novice users, but also includes more powerful tools for experienced users to fine-tune their designs. We provide several tools that enable users to sketch and refine chair designs. We also provide tools for testing the ergonomics of a design, including a physical simulation of a seated human figure that can be sized to match the height of the intended user. With the aid of these tools, users can refine their designs until the desired results are achieved. Our system then automatically generates 2D profiles of the individual pieces required to construct the chair. We use a laser cutter to produce the pieces, and assemble them to create the actual chair.

We provide examples of both scaled and full-sized chairs created with our system. The scaled models were made of paper or plywood, while the full-sized ones were constructed from plywood. The time required for sketching the chairs was 1-10 min. It took 10 min to cut and assemble the scaled chairs, and 90 min to cut and assemble the full-sized chairs. We also present results and insights obtained from a workshop in which novice users designed and constructed their own scaled chairs, including what worked and what could be improved.

BACKGROUND

An example of the benefits of custom design is furnished by the pianist Glenn Gould. When Gould was quite young, his father modified a folding chair for him, allowing him to sit at his piano at just the right height without obstructing his elbows while he played. Gould used this chair at virtually every concert for the rest of his career [2].

Digital fabrication processes that facilitate the production of custom one-off designs are becoming more commonplace. Various manufacturing cycles are being altered by digital fabrication, which has dramatically lowered the cost of producing certain products by eliminating the need for specialized machines and molds. Services such as Ponoko [13] take advantage of this by allowing people to upload designs for their own laser-cut products, which are then sold online and produced on demand.

The popularity of DIY communities that share plans and designs for projects, such as instructables.com [7] and makezine.com [10], has been growing steadily as more people find the right tools and resources to build things.

Several researchers have recently introduced systems for personal fabrication [9]. Plushie [11] is an interactive system for designing plush toys. It provides an interface and a set of tools for plush toy design. The algorithm automatically computes a 2D cloth pattern that corresponds to the user input. Spatial Sketch [17] allows the user to sketch immersively in a 3D real-world space. The 3D user sketch is converted to a set of planar slices, from which a real object can then be fabricated using a laser cutter. Our work also brings us a step closer to the larger goal of personal fabrication, in the specific case of chair design using a 2D sketch interface.

There are many systems [6, 18] for creating 3D models from 2D user sketches. These systems make it easy for novice users to create 3D models with a familiar 2D screen interface. Another approach allows users to sketch directly in 3D space. The Sketch Furniture [4] system enables rapid prototyping of 3D shapes resembling furniture. The Surface Drawing [14] system facilitates the creation of 3D surfaces and shapes that are appropriate for artistic expression. Our system provides a 2D sketch-based interface for creating 3D chairs. The user controls the entire process, from initial concept design to the eventual production of an actual chair.

OVERVIEW

The *SketchChair* system is a custom computational design environment written in Java™, enabling a user to design chairs via a 2D sketch interface (Fig. 2). A chair can be custom-tailored to the user's size (ergonomics). The system also permits users to design different styles of chairs (stools, office chairs, *etc.*). To create a chair, the user sketches the profiles with a mouse or a tablet PC. The system then extrudes these profiles to produce a frame made from interlocking planes. Legs are added by sketching their profiles with a leg tool. The resulting chair design is then tested in a physical simulation. A virtual figure representing the user is placed on the chair, in an appropriate posture, to check the ergonomics of the chair and to verify that the final design is stable enough to stand.

The profiles and slots to be fitted together are automatically generated by the system. These can be cut using a laser cutter, a CNC milling machine, or by hand. The user can then construct the chair.

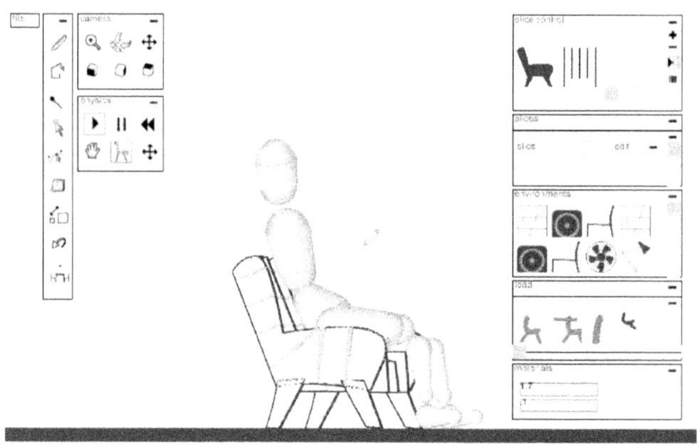

Figure 2. Screen shot of our system.

Figure 3. Sketching a path, editing, elongating, and retracting.

USER INTERFACE

In this section, we describe the *SketchChair* design tools.

Draw Tool

The draw tool allows users to quickly and intuitively sketch and edit appropriate curves for a seating contour (Fig. 3). The user selects a slice plane and draws the contour as if using a paintbrush or pen. The system automatically computes the offset outline. Any shape drawn on a plane is automatically merged with overlapping shapes.

All strokes drawn with the pen tool can be subsequently edited by dragging the stroke's path. If a middle point is selected and dragged, the surrounding points will be moved to maintain a smooth path. New points are added to lengthen a stroke when necessary. A stroke can be shortened by dragging an end point back toward the preceding points, and elongated by dragging an end point away from the preceding points.

Leg Tool

The leg tool allows legs to be added to a chair. The user clicks and drags a stroke to add a leg (Fig. 5). A supporting plane traversing the form is automatically added to the leg to strengthen it. The user is then able to edit the outline of the leg to ensure that it will rest flat against the floor.

Layers Panel

The layer panel allows the user to select and edit different slice planes. By editing slice planes separately, the user is able to create chairs with curved contours along the z-axis. For example, a chair can be given a curved bucket seat by moving profiles in the middle of the seat downwards. Curved slice planes in the z-direction are then automatically generated across the seat.

By editing 2D planes separately, users can design a wide range of chairs (Fig. 4). The system automatically creates cross-sections of the chair, and also checks for collisions between planes and removes invalid planes. Thus an interface is provided in which anything that can be drawn can be produced.

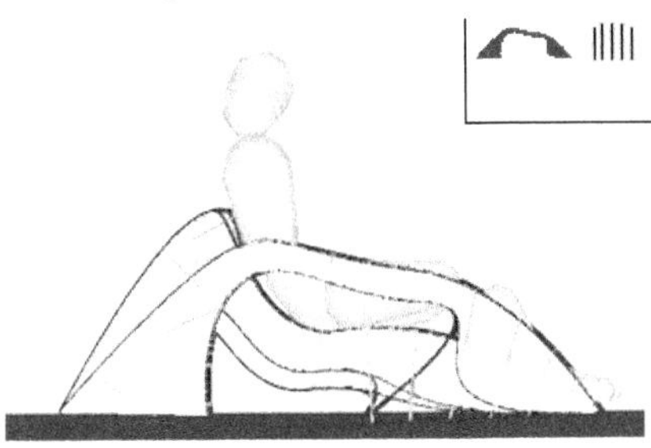

Figure 4. Slice control panel for selecting different slice planes in a chair.

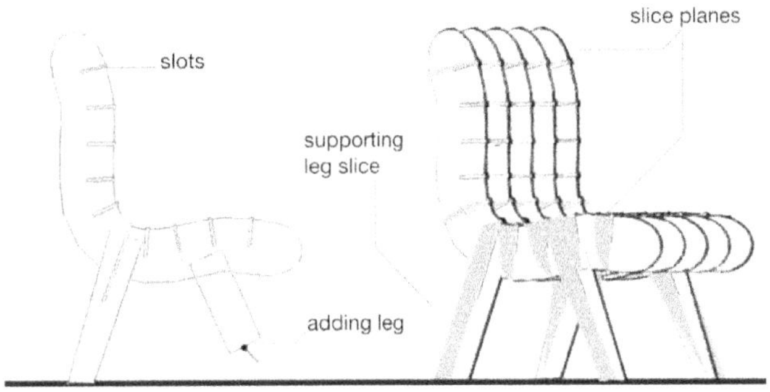

Figure 5. A leg being added to a chair.

Path Tool

The path tool allows the user to create far more varied chairs by drawing paths in a manner similar to many illustration programs. The user first draws a polyline via successive clicks. The shape of this line can be modified, and finely controlled curves can be created by adding Bezier points to the path. This tool allows the user to precisely specify the shape of a path with only a few control points.

Measure Tool

This tool allows the user to measure any part of the chair by clicking and dragging a selection box over the area. Dimensions are shown on the sides of the selection box. This is important for verifying the real dimensions of a chair or part of a chair, because it is easy to misjudge these in a virtual interface.

DESIGN AID TOOLS

To assist users in creating their own chairs, some design aid tools are also built into the editing environment.

Exploring Design Variations with Showroom and Hibernation

Experienced designers often start the design process with a sketch. Sketching provides a quick way of exploring many different ideas. CAD modeling is often not appropriate at this stage, because it is often slow and constrained, and the results are stored as a file on the user's computer, making it hard to compare designs visually.

Some novice users may prefer not to begin the design process with a hand-drawn sketch, and may have difficulty translating such a sketch into a 3D design in a CAD system. We address this issue by providing a simple sketch interface that allows a user to quickly sketch different chairs and then test them. Designs that are saved appear next to previously saved chairs in a showroom panel. The chairs in the showroom can be compared visually and loaded into the program for refinement.

When a new chair is created in the design environment, any existing chairs are 'hibernated,' and an image of each hibernated chair appears in its place. Right clicking on the image of a chair will load the corresponding design, replacing the image. In this way, the user can quickly explore many different possibilities before deciding on a particular design.

Ergonomics

When designing a chair (especially for a specific person), it is important to make sure that the chair fits the user's body. A chair should hold its occupant in a comfortable pose, with the feet typically resting on the floor. When designing products in a virtual environment, it is easy to lose track of scale and design products that are too small or too large. Prior to any actual production, professionals generally make a full-sized cardboard mockup of a product to verify that the proportions are correct. However, constructing a full-sized prototype chair can be difficult for novices, so our system provides a virtual human figure that can be resized to match any specified height (Fig. 6, 7). The figure can be virtually seated on a chair, thus making it possible to directly assess whether the chair will be suitable for the intended user. If the chair does not fit the user, it can be edited with the virtual figure sitting on it to provide reference.

The system supports users of different ages. In the design environment, a user's age and height can be specified. The virtual figure is then resized to match this height, and its proportions are changed to fit a user of the given age (for example, the heads of babies and children are larger in proportion to the rest of their bodies than those of adults [16]).

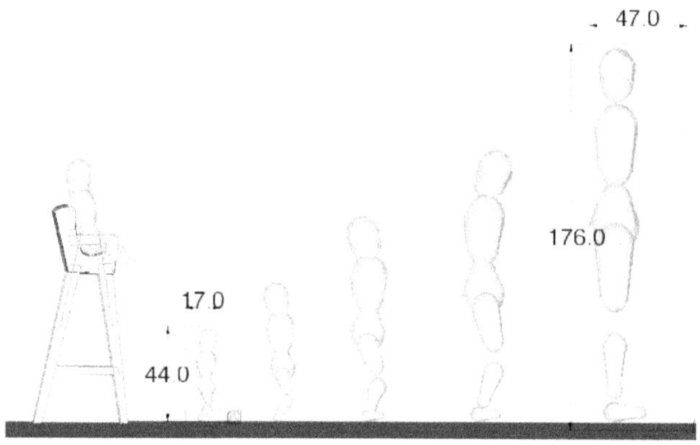

Figure 6. Resizing the figure, right. Highchair for a baby, left.

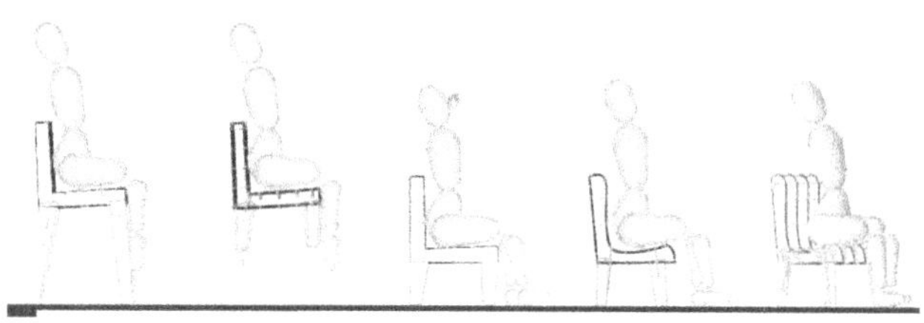

Figure 7. Using the virtual figure to adjust a chair so that the figure's feet rest on the floor.

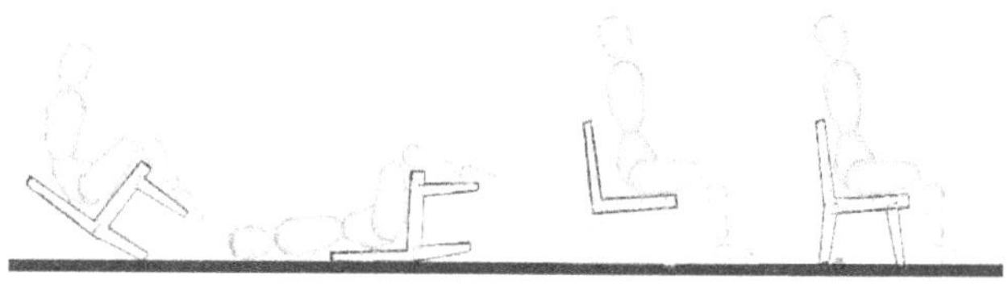

Figure 8. Testing and correcting an unbalanced chair.

Simulation

The rigid-body physics simulation jBullet [8] is included in the design environment. It enables the user to test the effect of gravity on a chair and occupant before actually producing the chair. Simulation in the design environment allows a user to quickly correct mistakes that might cause a chair to fail (for example, an unbalanced chair, as shown in Fig. 8). Simulation makes it possible to work with the constraints of designing an actual chair, instead of discovering them at a later stage. This reduces the time required to design a viable chair, and helps the user understand the limitations of chair design.

The physics of the chair is controlled with the play, pause, and rewind buttons. It is important to note that a chair or figure can be created or edited with the simulator running, and any changes made to the chair will be updated in the simulator without restarting.

Reference Geometry

When buying a piece of furniture, we generally consider whether it is compatible with other furniture in the home (e.g., a new chair for the dining table or a chair to sit on while playing the piano). One of the advantages of custom furniture is that it can be designed for compatibility with other furniture in the home. To facilitate this, our system provides a series of reference images that can be dragged into the design environment and resized to approximate the furniture in a user's home. Users can also load their own custom reference images into the program (for example, a photo of a table to which a new chair is to be matched).

Images or sketches of other chairs can be used as reference images to help the user design similar chairs. Photos taken by the user can be input to the program by adding them to the

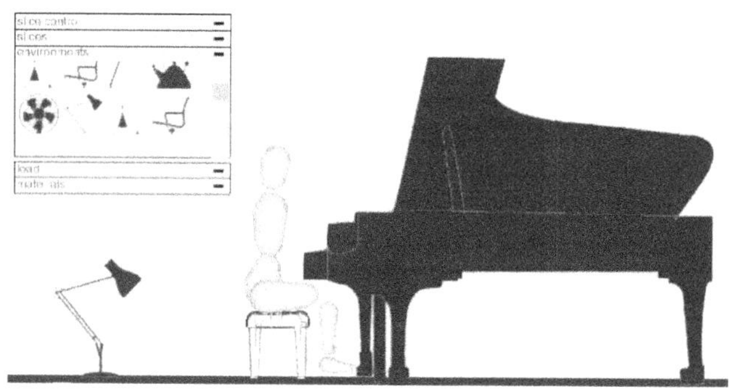

Figure 9. Reference geometry used to help design a chair.

environment directory. This makes it possible to design a chair that matches the style of other furniture found in the user's home (Fig. 9).

FABRICATION

Production is considered in the interface; that is, the system allows the user to work within the construction constraints. *SketchChair* will only create designs that can be fabricated from flat components.

Material usage and cost are calculated in the design interface in real time. This can be used to price chairs, and also to produce chairs that use material more efficiently.

Designing for flat materials offers a number of advantages. Products can be packed flat for cost-effective shipping. They can also be made from a range of materials, using a variety of production equipment, including laser cutters, CNC mills, and hand saws.

Designs can also readily be constructed on different scales, using materials, such as paper and cardboard, and this makes the system appropriate for prototyping designs, as well as for creating scale models that can be used as toys. The capacity to print directly to a paper cutter is included the *SketchChair* system. This means that designs can be created in the sketch interface, printed to a paper cutter, and fabricated for further testing within 10 min (Fig. 10).

To produce laser-cut profiles that are larger than the cutting bed of a laser cutter, we manually cut each oversized profile into smaller pieces. These pieces can then be tightly packed onto a sheet of material for further cutting. Once cut, the pieces are fit back together and glued in layers to provide strength at the joints. This approach allows chairs of any size to be manufactured using the smaller, more common CNC machines.

CONSTRUCTION DETAILS

Cover

Chairs designed with *SketchChairs* can be upholstered with layers of felt and palm fiber matting. This provides a soft seating platform, and also distributes the user's weight across the laser-cut slats. It is more comfortable for the user, and prevents too much stress from being placed on any one part of the frame.

The layer of fiber is lashed to the frame with a soft cotton lace similar to a shoelace (Fig. 11). This lace also holds the frame together and provides strength. It can be untied and unthreaded by the user, allowing the frame to be disassembled for storage or transport.

Frame braces

Optional aluminum corner braces can be added to the frame for additional strength. These are small sections of square extruded aluminum, about 50 mm long, with four slots cut into them. The *SketchChair* program generates extra slots at the junctions of each chair frame, permitting these braces to be inserted into the frame. This holds the frame together and supports the joints, preventing the chair from collapsing.

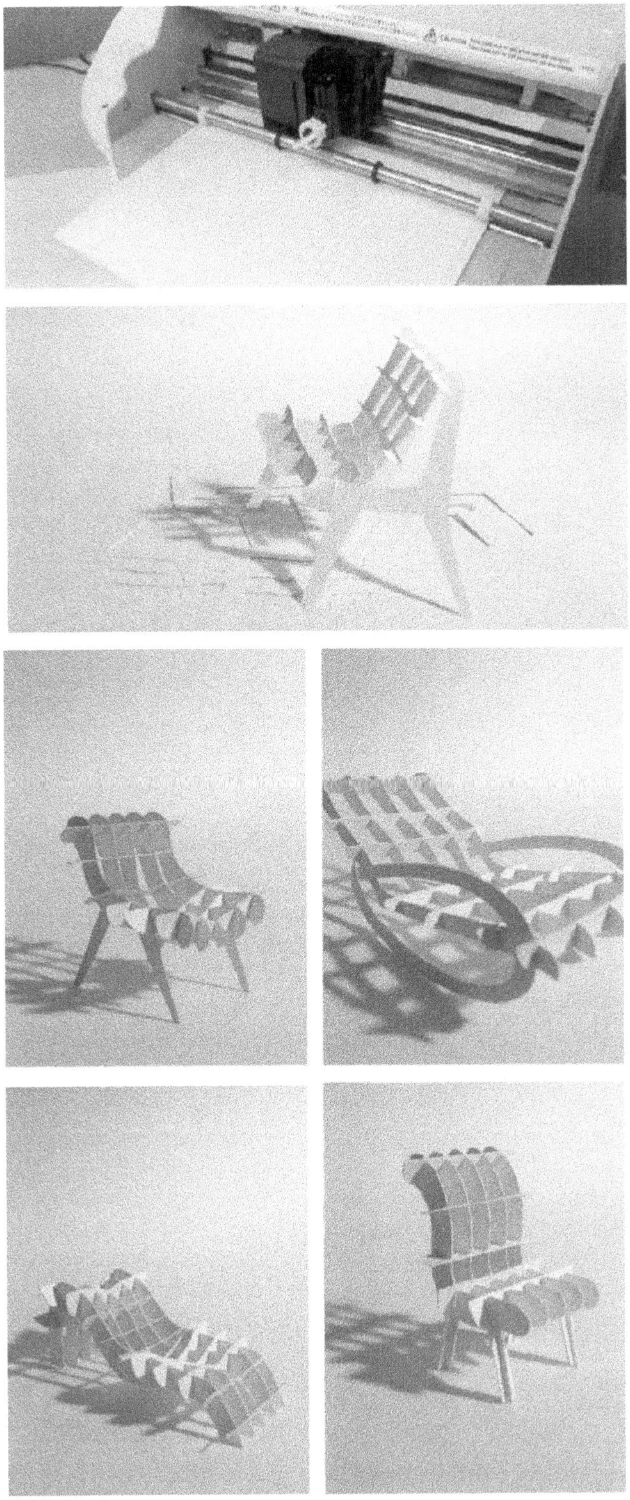

Figure 10. Paper chairs created using the system and cut with a cutter plotter (each chair is about 70 mm in height).

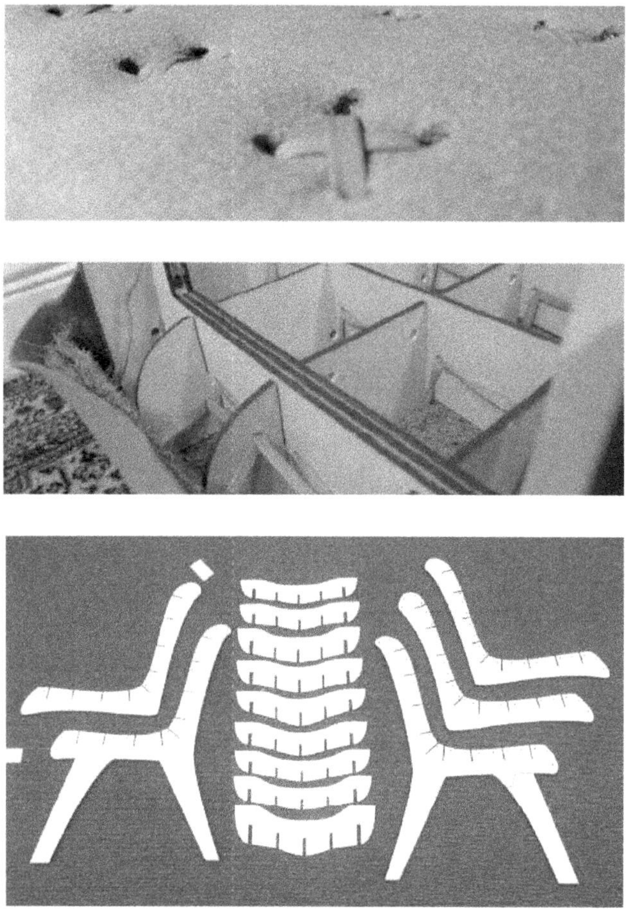

Figure 11. (Top) Felt cover and palm matting tied to a frame with cotton laces. (Bottom) Laser-cut plywood profiles for a finished chair.

RESULTS

Workshop

We organized a workshop in which seven participants, from 12 to 53 years old, were invited to design and build scale models using *SketchChairs*. During a short presentation, the participants were first introduced to the idea of designing furniture, and then to the features of the program. They were then given 30 min to practice with the software. During the practice session, the participants were given a range of images of different chair designs, and asked to reproduce similar designs using the *SketchChair* system. After the practice session, participants were asked to design a chair. Each chose a design and saved the cutting profiles for the design. The designs were then cut, and the participants constructed their chairs from the cut profiles. Finally, the participants were asked to fill out a short survey on their experience with the system and the idea of designing their own products.

All participants successfully produced miniature chairs, and all reported enjoying the experience of designing their own chairs. The concept of designing one's own furniture was well received, and all but one participant expressed a preference for their own designs over the chairs sold in stores. Furthermore, participants stated that they would place more value on chairs they had built themselves, and would consider them less disposable. One participant even articulated a wish to pass such a chair down to his/her children, to keep it in the family. This seems to indicate that products designed by the user have the potential to be more sustainable than their mass-produced equivalents, because people may be inclined to retain them for longer periods.

It was observed that a majority of the participants preferred to use the draw tool and the leg tool to design their chairs, reporting that these tools were more intuitive. Users who were more experienced with CAD systems enjoyed the control that the path tool gave them. Most users preferred to work only with one layer, and did not use the layers panel to alter their chairs in the z-direction. Three participants declared that they would like the option to "start with a template chair designed by a designer" and then "modify that one."

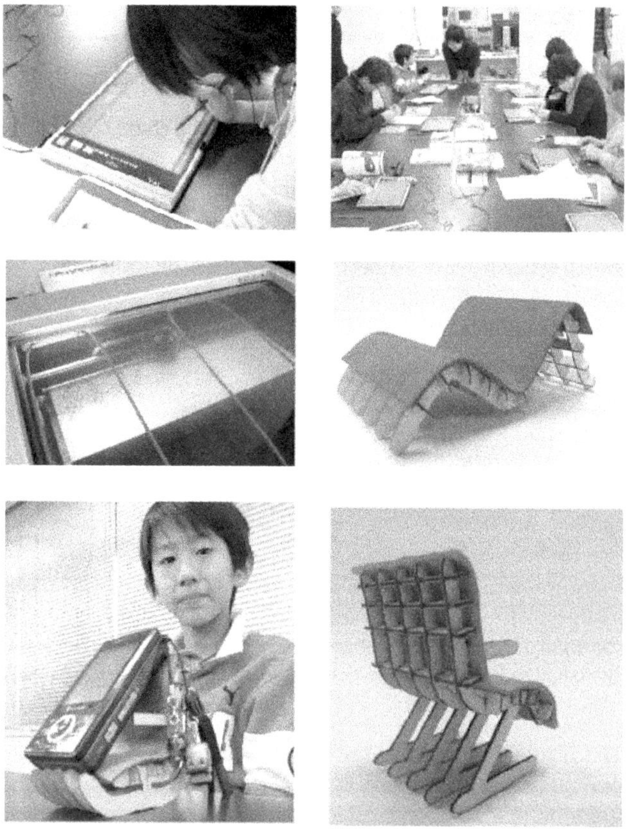

Figure 12. Scale chairs designed by users during the workshop.

Full-sized Chairs

Figures 1 and 13 show full-sized chairs designed using the system. They were designed in 20-min modeling sessions, cut with a laser cutter (taking 60 min), and produced with materials bought from a local hardware store.

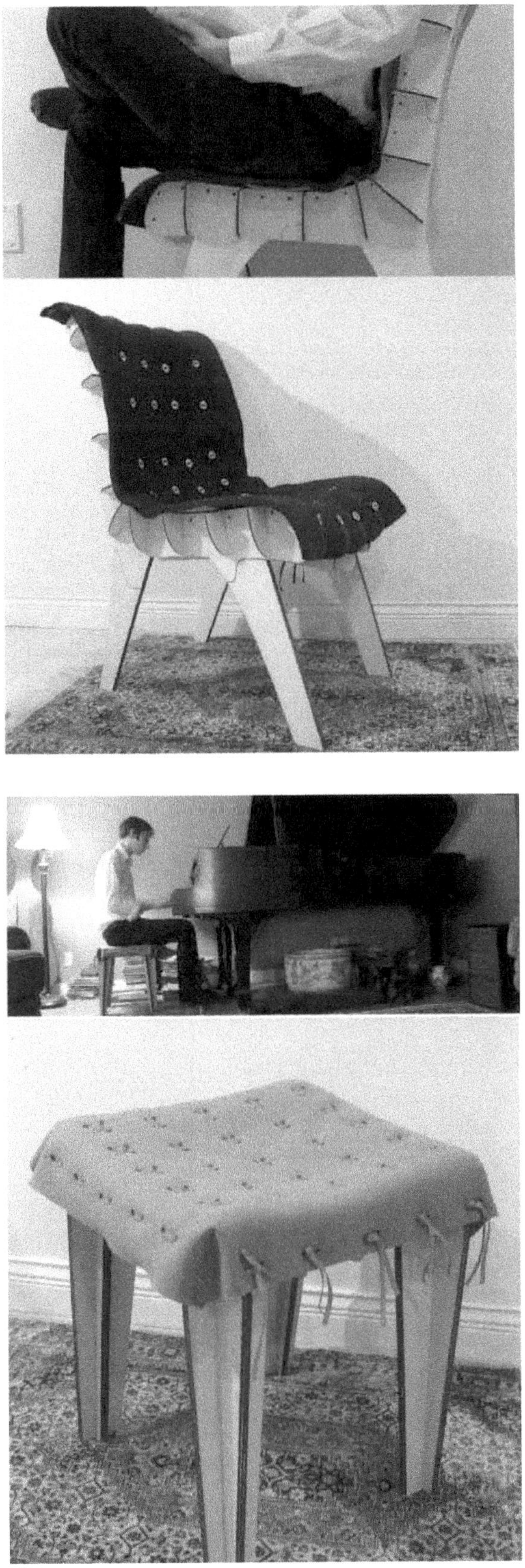

Figure 13. Finished chairs designed using the SketchChair system.

8. DISCUSSION AND FUTURE WORK

We introduced a chair design software as an example of a system that enables users to design their own products. It allows users to move successfully through the entire process of designing and fabricating a full-sized chair. The simple interface permits the user to sketch different concepts quickly and compare them visually. Designs can then be tested in a physical simulation to verify that they are balanced and will not fall over. A virtual human figure, scaled to match the size of the user, is placed on the chair to test the ergonomics and ensure a correct fit. Reference images can be added to the design environment to determine whether a newly designed chair will be compatible with existing furniture. Design patterns are produced by the system, and can be fabricated via rapid manufacturing techniques (e.g., with a laser cutter or by hand).

In the future, we plan to add the following features to the system: a strength of materials simulation to ensure that designs are strong enough to be used as chairs, automatic division of profiles to fit them onto smaller sheets (this is currently done manually), automatic measurement of the ergonomics of a chair, based on the seating of a virtual figure, and the pressure applied at different parts of the figure's body. Development of a plug-in version for a generic 3D CAD software will also be important for further development and dissemination.

REFERENCES

1. Autodesk. *AutoCAD*. 2010. http://www.autodesk.com/autocad
2. Bazzana,K., *Wondrous Strange: The Life and Art of Glenn Gould*. Oxford University press 2004.
3. Dassault Systèmes SolidWorks Corp, 2010. *SolidWorks 2010*. http://www.solidworks.com
4. FRONT Sketch Furniture. 2006, http://designfront.org/category.php?id=81&product=93.
5. Gershenfeld, N.A. *Fab: The Coming Revolution on your Desktop - From Personal Computers to Personal Fabrication*. Basic Books, New York, 2005.
6. Igarashi, T., Matsuoka ,S., and Tanaka, H. Teddy: a sketching interface for 3d freeform design. In *Proc. ACM SIGGRAPH 99*, 409–416, 1999.
7. Instructables, 2010, http://www.instructables.com/.
8. jBullet, 2010, http://jbullet.advel.cz/.
9. Landay, J., Design Tools for the Rest of Us. *Communications of the ACM*, Vol. 52, No. 12, 2009.
10. Makezine, 2010, http://makezine.com/.
11. Mori , Y., and Igarashi, T. Plushie: An Interactive Design System for Plush Toys. *ACM Transactions on Graphics (Proc. SIGGRAPH 2007)*, Vol. 26, No. 3, Article No. 45, 2007.

12. Panero, J., and Zelnick, M. *Human Dimension and Interior Space: A Source Book of Design Reference Standards*, Watson-Guptill, 1979.

13. Ponoko, 2010, http://ponoko.com/

14. Schkolne, S., Pruett, M., and Schroder, P. Surface Drawing: Creating Organic 3D Shapes with the Hand and Tangible Tools. In *Proc. CHI 2001*, 261-268, 2001.

15. Svenstedt,C F., http://www.carlfredriksvenstedt.com/infinity/project.html

16. Tilley, A R. *The Measure of Man and Woman: Human Factors in Design*, Henry Dreyfuss Associates, 2001.

17. Willis, K., Lin., J. Mitani, J., and Igarashi., T. Spatial Sketch: Bridging Between Movement & Fabrication. In *Proc. TEI 2010*, 5-12, 2010.

18. Zelenik, R., Herndon, K., and Hughes, J. Sketch: An Interface for Sketching 3D Scenes. In *Proc. SIGGRAPH 96*, 163–170, 1996.

Fab FM: the Design, Making, and Modification of an Open-Source Electronic Product

David A. Mellis
MIT Media Lab
75 Amherst St.
Cambridge, MA 02142 USA
mellis@media.mit.edu

Dana Gordon
MIT CAVS
265 Massachusetts Ave.
Cambridge, MA 02139 USA
d_gordon@mit.edu

Leah Buechley
MIT Media Lab
75 Amherst St.
Cambridge, MA 02142 USA
leah@media.mit.edu

ABSTRACT
This paper explores the ways in which digital fabrication allows for the small-scale manufacture and individual customization of consumer electronic products. We present Fab FM, an open-source FM radio that integrates an electronic circuit board, laser-cut wood, and fabric. We describe a workshop in which participants designed and built their own Fab FM variants, modifying the form, materials, and behavior of the radio. Drawing from this experience, we discuss three themes: the issues involved in working across design domains, the ways in which design can serve as source code, and the difference between open-source and hackable. We present potential business models for Fab FM, and discuss the possibilities that digital fabrication offers for a more diverse landscape of high-tech products.

Author Keywords
Digital fabrication, open-source hardware, consumer electronics, mass customization, DIY, design.

ACM Classification Keywords
J.6 Computer-Aided Engineering.

General Terms
Design, Economics.

INTRODUCTION
The spread of digital fabrication (machines that can produce objects directly from digital design files) is making manufacturing accessible to a growing audience [2]. Products can be designed with commonly-used drawing software or low-cost CAD programs. Services like Ponoko [9] (for laser cut products), Shapeways [13] (for 3d-printed objects), and BatchPCB [4] (for circuit boards) allow individuals to order one or more physical objects from these digital files, and provide marketplaces where others can order additional copies of the designs. The proliferation of fab labs [7] and other digital fabrication facilities allow their members to produce objects on demand and to rapidly iterate through multiple versions of a design. Low-cost rapid prototyping and CNC machines (e.g. [8] and [11]) make it increasingly feasible for individuals to establish their own digital fabrication capability. It's now possible for anyone to design a product, prototype it, and then manufacture arbitrary additional copies with the same files and processes.

This growing availability of the software to design objects and the machines to produce them makes it increasingly relevant to share designs with others. Many people publish their files online using sites like Thingiverse [14], which collect files for a variety of fabrication machines. This activity has accompanied the development of the concept of open-source hardware, paralleling that of open-source software. It shares the beliefs that users of a product should be able to study its design, make modifications to it, and share the design and modifications with others (i.e. the four fundamental freedoms listed by the Free Software Foundation). Although complicated by the fact that additional resources are required to create a physical object from its design, open-source hardware is gaining in prevalence, with examples like the Arduino microcontroller development platform [3] and the Bug Labs modular hardware platform [5].

Some companies (e.g. Adafruit Industries [1] and Evil Mad Scientist Laboratories [6]) have begun to apply digital fabrication and open-source hardware to consumer electronic products. These companies produce kits which combine electronics and laser-cut or other structural parts. These are then assembled by customers into complete electronic products. The economics of digital fabrication allow for relatively small production runs (in the hundreds or thousands). This type of production occupies a space somewhere between traditional manufacturing (with its large capital expenditures and up-front tooling costs) and handmade goods (which must be individually crafted by their maker). It makes viable products which would be too expensive to make individually but that lack the market size needed for mass manufacture.

Several research projects have used digital fabrication as a tool for making prototypes of construction kits (e.g. [10], [16]). Plywood Punk [12] provides an interesting example of a product that integrates electronics with laser-cut

TEI'11, January 22–26, 2011, Funchal, Portugal.

wooden parts. Spatial Sketch [15] shows the potential of digital fabrication for the customization of products.

Fab FM is an open-source FM radio, our case study in the use of digital fabrication for the manufacture of an electronic product. Through it, we hope to understand whether such processes can yield devices which are functional, desirable, and economically viable. We are also investigating the potential that digital fabrication offers for modifying or customizing the design of the product and the alternative business and distribution models that it allows.

This paper starts by describing the components and construction of the Fab FM. It then discusses a workshop in which participants built their own versions of the radio, showing some of the possibilities for customization allowed by this type of production process. It highlights three larger themes emerging from the workshop. Then, it describes some of the possible business models for further manufacturing and distribution of the radio. Finally, it reflects on the larger implications for digital fabrication and open-source hardware.

DESIGN

In designing Fab FM, we drew on the materials and forms of classic radios while taking advantage of the production processes allowed by digital fabrication. The electronics and casing were designed in parallel to ensure simplicity of construction and ease of assembly. This was complicated by the necessity of using separate software design tools for the electronics and the structure, but eased by the rapid testing and iteration allowed by digital fabrication.

At the heart of the radio is a digital FM receiver controlled by a microcontroller, whose output is sent through an amplification circuit to the speaker. The structure of the radio is provided by a laser-cut plywood frame, with a front and back face held together by press-fit horizontal struts. This technique allows the faces to take on any shape, and we choose a curve to highlight this flexibility. The electronic circuit board rests on a cut-out in the frame. Carefully positioned holes in the front face help to support the knobs, which are soldered to the PCB. The speaker is secured in a circular cut-out by fabric glued to the plywood. The frame is then wrapped with another piece of fabric, paper, or other soft material. Laser-cut veneer or other material is attached to the front and back faces.

In its current form, Fab FM isenvisioned as a kit of parts to be assembled by the user. These include the PCB, electronic components, laser cut plywood and veneer, and possibly the fabric. Within this format, however, we see several possibilities for variation. The separation of the structure and skin in the design of the radio allows users to select their own soft materials, giving the object a personal significance. With a little extra work, the front and back veneer faces could be replaced with another material, hand cut to the appropriate shape. The laser cut pieces were designed in Adobe Illustrator and Inkscape, making them

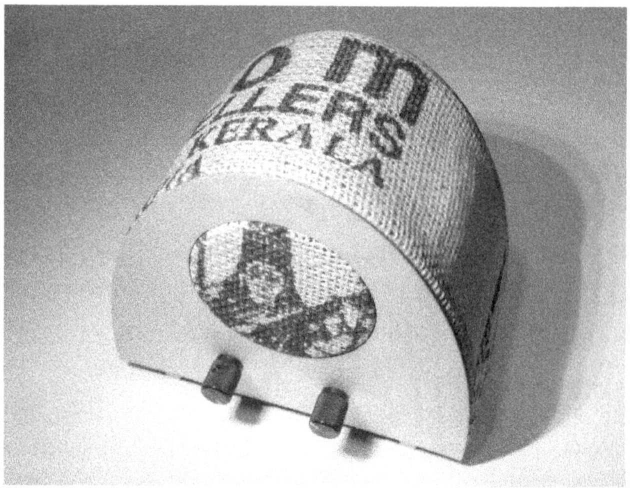

Figure 1. An assembled Fab FM.

straightforward to modify for the many users of these popular software packages. Modified forms could then be produced by the manufacturer of the Fab FM kit, by an individual with access to a laser cutter, or through a service like Ponoko. The design of the electronic circuit board can be edited with the freeware version of Eagle, a CAD package popular with hobbyists. Modified circuits could then be etched, milled on a CNC machine, or ordered from a service like BatchPCB. The radio's firmware can be compiled with the open-source GCC and uploaded via a programming socket on the circuit board.

WORKSHOP AND VARIATIONS

To explore the possibilities for customization of Fab FM, we held a one-day workshop in which participants were asked to design and construct their own variations on the radio. We invited people we thought likely to be especially creative in the modifications; eleven attended (seven men and four women). The workshop was held in the authors' lab space, which offered access to soldering irons, a laser cutter, and miscellaneous supplies. Each participant was provided with a kit containing the Fab FM circuit board and electronic components; the other materials needed to construct the standard design (e.g. plywood and fabric) were on hand. The workshop began with an introduction to the kit and the sharing of participants' ideas for their radios. Most of the day was spent designing and building Fab FM variants, which were presented and documented at the end of the workshop.

Participants quickly identified ideas for modifications to the design of the radio, including:

- harvesting energy from vibrations caused by sound waves hitting the speaker,
- speaking aloud the frequency of stations as the radio was tuned,
- analyzing the received audio signal in order to tune to a station with particular musical qualities,

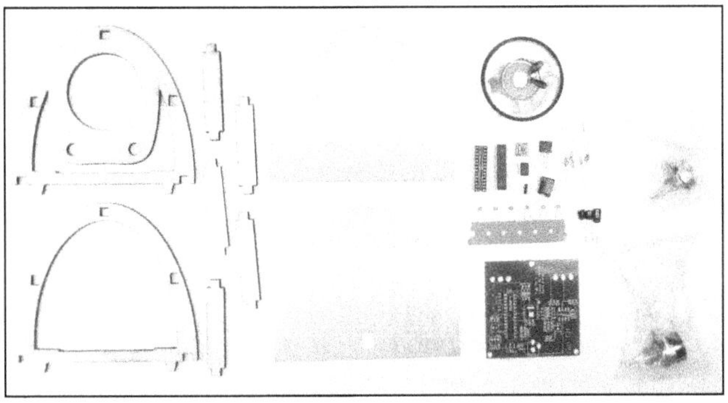

Figure 2. The Fab FM kit.

- constructing the speaker from laser-cut plywood, a magnet, and an electromagnet,
- a miniature version of the radio that also functions as a nightlight,
- using fabric matching a friend's newly handmade curtains, and
- tuning only to the one or two stations listened to by the intended user.

Although it was a struggle to both customize and build a radio within the day, many participants finished with a solid basis for their own Fab FM variation. Three participants created aesthetic variations on the case: one using curved transparent acrylic to reveal the electronics inside, one miniature version, and one square-shaped design with laser-etched text. Two participants constructed a prototype of the plywood speaker. One participant customized the Fab FM for a particular user, his girlfriend, using a fabric matching her curtains and modifying the radio's software to tune to her two favorite stations. Two other participants also modified the interface to the radio: one replaced the tuning knob with buttons for seeking up and down, while another evenly distributed the available stations across the range of the knob's movement. One participant tweaked the amplifier circuit to find the maximum volume possible without distortion. Another modified the design of the PCB in order to mill it on a CNC machine of his own design and construction.

Overall, we saw three main dimensions of customization: shape / form, materials, and behavior / functionality. These modifications seem to reflect participants' skills and interests as well as the relative accessibility of various fabrication processes. Given the availability of a laser cutter, participants were able to design, prototype, and construct modifications to the shape of the radio with little assistance. Changes to the materials and appearance were similarly straightforward. Modifying the behavior of the radio, however, was more difficult. Participants were able to customize the physical interface (i.e. knobs and buttons) more-or-less on their own, but the corresponding changes to the code required either a strong background in programming or close assistance.

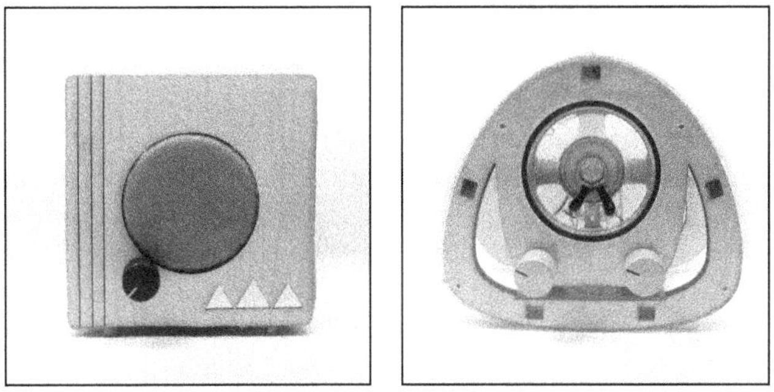

Figure 3. Fab FM variants made by workshop participants.

DISCUSSION

Several interesting themes emerged from the workshops. These are discussed below.

Working Across Multiple Design Domains

The workshop illustrated some of the issues involved in designing across multiple domains (code, circuit, and physical structure). First, it showed the value of a standard kit or pre-existing design as a default for people who only want to customize one aspect of a product. Second, it highlighted the significance of those elements of the design that must correspond between domains (e.g. the distance between the radio's knobs, or the microcontroller pin chosen to read from the tuning knob). It also showed the relative ease with which the design can be changed provided those correspondences are respected. This suggests possibilities for design tools that help people design across multiple domains or work within a particular one while maintaining compatibility with another.

Design as Source Code

Because the case is fabricated directly from a digital file, the modified radios are not simply one-of-a-kind, handmade objects. In creating their individual radios, the workshop participants frequently generated new digital files that could be replicated by others, making them designs in their own right. This is the essence of open-source as applied to hardware: a process in which new versions of a design can easily be shared, studied, produced, and further modified or combined. It stands in contrast to both craft processes, in which modifications likely don't exist in a digital form that can be easily replicated, and mass manufacture, in which tooling costs often make it infeasible to produce custom variations on a design.

Open-Source vs. Hackable

In addition to investigating the possibilities allowed by the open-sourcing of the designs for hardware, the workshop revealed other ways in which the Fab FM design could be made hackable. For example, participants seemed reluctant to add components to the circuit, despite having the necessary documentation and, in some cases, a clear idea for additional electronic functionality. The breaking out of additional microcontroller pins and the audio signals, along with a prototyping area on the PCB, might encourage modification to the circuit. Documentation embedded directly within the CAD files for the case would have helped people understand which parts they could modify and which dimensions were determined by other constrains (e.g. the circuit board or the material thickness). Source code written using the Arduino libraries and conventions (instead of standard AVR C) would have been accessible to more of the participants. In general, it seems that while making a design open-source gives people the formal permission to modify it, it may be other qualities that actually encourage them to do so.

BUSINESS MODELS

One goal of Fab FM is to explore the economics and feasibility of various potential production processes and scales. Table 1 presents the overall costs of components and materials for one, ten, and one hundred copies of the Fab FM. Presentations by Adafruit Industries and others suggest that the typical retail price for such products is around twice the component cost. This ratio suggests a selling price of around $80, comparable to that charged for similar kits from Adafruit and Evil Mad Scientist Laboratories. The success of those products suggest that this is a viable product, at least for the specific audience of DIY enthusiasts. Total investment in prototypes and the kits used in the workshop was less than $1000. The development was carried out by two individuals over the course of a few weeks. It has yielded a design and production process that should be able to scale to 100s or possibly 1000s of kits. In these ways, we feel it provides an interesting model for the development and distribution of other open-source electronic products.

We envision a number of possible alternative production and distribution models for Fab FM. It could be sold with a pre-populated circuit board, allowing it to be constructed by those interested only in the craft aspects. We (or others) could provide a service which would assemble a finished Fab FM from materials supplied by the customer, yielding a personalized object from a standard manufacturing process. Variations on the radio could be sold as their own kits for people who prefer those designs. Finally, an individual could create their own radio directly from the design files, using services like BatchPCB and Ponoko.

CONCLUSION AND FUTURE DIRECTIONS

Fab FM illustrates some of the possibilities for the digital fabrication of consumer electronic products. It shows how careful design can create an object which is attractive, easily prototyped and manufactured in small quantities, and amenable to modification. The workshop demonstrates that, given the opportunity, people are interested and able to customize electronic products in multiple ways, including form, materials, and functionality. The potential business models suggest that digital fabrication is a viable approach to the manufacture of electronic products, one which allows for an increased diversity of processes and objects.

Quantity	**x1**	**x10**	**x100**
Components	$38	$35	$29
PCB	$33	$6	$5
Materials	$12	$5	$5
Total	**$83**	**$46**	**$39**

Table 1. Cost of the parts for Fab FM in various quantities.

The domain of digitally fabricated electronic products seems rich with possibilities. In the future, we hope to explore both the market potential of the Fab FM as well as the possibility for the design and manufacturing of other similar products. We also see opportunities to create tools that help people design across multiple domains (e.g. electronics, structure, and code). We view Fab FM as an initial exploration in an exciting space.

ACKNOWLEDGMENTS

Thanks to Neil Gershenfeld and the workshop participants.

REFERENCES

1. Adafruit Industries. http://www.adafruit.com/
2. Anderson, C. In the Next Industrial Revolution, Atoms Are the New Bits. *Wired Magazine*, Feb 2010.
3. Arduino. http://www.arduino.cc/
4. BatchPCB. http://batchpcb.com/
5. Bug Labs. http://www.buglabs.net/
6. Evil Mad Scientist Laboratories. http://www.evilmadscientist.com/
7. Gershenfeld, N. *Fab: the Coming Revolution on Your Desktop--From Personal Computers to Personal Fabrication*. Basic Books, 2007.
8. MakerBot. http://www.makerbot.com/
9. Ponoko. http://www.ponoko.com/
10. Raffle, H. S., Parkes, A. J., and Ishii, H. Topobo: a constructive assembly system with kinetic memory. In *Proc. CHI 2004*, ACM Press (2004), 647-654.
11. RepRap. http://reprap.org/
12. Schmitt, P. and Seitinger, S. Plywood punk: a holistic approach to designing animated artifacts. *In Proc. TEI 2009*, ACM Press (2009), 123-126.
13. Shapeways. http://www.shapeways.com/
14. Thingiverse. http://www.thingiverse.com/
15. Willis, K. D., Lin, J., Mitani, J., and Igarashi, T. Spatial sketch: bridging between movement & fabrication. In *Proc. TEI 2010*, ACM Press (2010), 5-12.
16. Wu, K. and Gross, M. D. TOPAOKO: interactive construction kit. In *CHI EA 2010*, ACM Press (2010), 3619-362

MoSo Tangibles: Evaluating Embodied Learning

Saskia Bakker[1], Elise van den Hoven[1], and Alissa N. Antle[2]

[1]Department of Industrial Design
Eindhoven University of Technology
Eindhoven, the Netherlands
{s.bakker, e.v.d.hoven}@tue.nl

[2]School of Interactive Arts and Technology
Simon Fraser University
Surrey, B.C., Canada
aantle@sfu.ca

ABSTRACT

Using tangible interaction in interactive educational systems can benefit learning. This can be supported by relying on experientially originating schemata in the interaction design of learning systems. This paper presents the design and evaluation of MoSo Tangibles, a set of interactive, physical artifacts with which children manipulate the pitch, volume and tempo of ongoing tones, in order to structure their understanding of these abstract sound concepts in terms of multiple different concrete body-based concepts. The results indicate that MoSo provided children with a physical handle to reason about the targeted abstract concepts.

Author Keywords

Tangible and embodied interaction, design research, embodied schemata, metaphors, learning systems, children.

ACM Classification Keywords

H.5.2 Information Interfaces and Presentation (e.g., HCI): User Interfaces – *evaluation/methodology, interaction styles, user-centered design.* K.3.0 Computers and Education: General.

General Terms

Design

INTRODUCTION

For ages, physical activity and manipulating physical objects have played an important role in learning and development. Building on this, many studies in the area of tangible and embodied interaction [8, 26] have focused on developing physical interactive learning systems [10, 22]. Such studies discuss several potential benefits of these interaction styles for learning, such as promoting self-reflection [28], engagement [2] and self-directed activity [18].

In previous work on interactive learning systems [4, 5], we have developed and studied mappings between input actions and output changes that are based on so-called *embodied metaphors*, unconscious knowledge originating in body movement that can be applied automatically. A study with the interactive Sound Maker environment [3], designed to support children when learning about abstract sound concepts such as pitch and volume, indicated that systems with embodied metaphor based interaction models may support children in structuring their understanding of these abstract concepts. Furthermore, the study revealed that children may rely on multiple different embodied metaphors in their understanding of abstract (sound) concepts. This was verified in a further study, which indicated that seven to nine year old children can use different embodied metaphors in their reasoning about abstract sound concepts [5]. For example, they may understand soft and loud volume in terms of slow and fast movements, but also in terms of small and big movement.

Knowing that children can structure their understanding of abstract sound concepts in different ways, implementing more than one embodied metaphor in an interactive system could potentially benefit learning. This would enable children to explore multiple movements to reason about one concept, which could support developing a more comprehensive understanding of the learned concepts and potentially result in understandings that are more easily transferable to other domains. This also corresponds to a frequently used approach of using multiple representations when teaching complex scientific concepts [25]. The research presented in this paper aims at exploring if and why interactive systems that incorporate multiple embodied metaphors in their interaction models can support children's conceptual learning in abstract domains.

We present a user study in which 39 seven to nine year old children used a specifically designed tangible learning system, named Moving Sounds (MoSo) Tangibles that implements three different embodied metaphor based interaction models for learning about single sound concepts. The aim of this study was to compare learning effects of a system with multiple mappings, to learning effects of a similar system with one mapping. First we will look into the theoretical background and related work.

THEORETICAL BACKGROUND

Embodied Metaphors

In previous work, we have seen that learning of abstract concepts may be supported by interactive systems that rely on so-called embodied metaphors. This is grounded in

TEI'11, January 22–26, 2011, Funchal, Portugal.

theory suggesting that recurrent patterns of bodily experiences form the foundation of abstract thinking and reasoning [20]. These recurrent patterns emerging from bodily experiences are commonly called image schemata or embodied schemata [15]. For example, the IN-OUT schema is formed as a result of several experiences related to in and out: we put food into our mouth, go out of a room and poor milk out of a bottle. Numerous experiences we have from the day we are born contribute to the schema IN-OUT, which consists of two basic components: a container and a movement in or out of it (see Figure 1).

People apply these embodied schemata unconsciously to reason about abstract concepts. For example, when we say "I am backing out of the agreement", we view the concept 'agreement' as a container and ourselves as an entity that is in or out of this container. In other words, we understand one concept (the agreement) in terms of another concept (container). This form of projecting the structure of an experientially originating schema onto a conceptual domain is what is meant by metaphor [17]. When schemata find their origin in bodily experiences, we call them *embodied schemata* and their metaphorical extensions *embodied metaphors*.

Learning Theories

Manipulating physical objects plays an important role in children's education. Think of an abacus and simple building blocks that have helped us understand abstract concepts related to physics and mathematics. Several psychologists have studied benefits of such approaches for cognitive development. Bruner [7] has for example shown that physical objects play a major role in bridging the abstract and the concrete. Vygotsky and Galperin [19] even state that higher psychological functions such as logical thinking can only be developed through physical acts such as manipulating physical artifacts. For example when playing with an abacus, a child will first start sliding the beads, after which he or she will see the beads being regrouped. This combination of physical experience (sliding) and reflection (noticing the regrouped beads) lays at the basis of learning and knowledge acquisition (gaining a symbolic understanding of the concept 'addition') [1].

Although many studies are known on the manipulation of physical objects in mathematics education, body movement also plays a major role in learning about abstract concepts related to musical sound [14, 16], which is the area for which our MoSo Tangibles system is designed. Jensenius [14] uses the term 'embodied music cognition' when stating that children unconsciously apply embodied metaphors when learning new abstract musical concepts such as pitch or volume. For example, children can understand the concept pitch (low versus high) in terms of concrete, movement related concepts (for example up versus down or slow versus fast). Music teachers use various such movement related metaphors when teaching abstract sound concepts [14, 16], for example by encouraging children to move slowly when music with low pitch is played, and fast when high music is heard.

RELATED WORK

Several examples of tangible interaction for learning and education are known, most of which focus on learning in abstract problem domains. Zuckerman et al. [28] discuss SystemBlocks and FlowBlocks as examples of 'Montessori-inspired Manipulatives'; technology enhanced building blocks designed for learning about abstract mathematical principles. Smith [24] presents a tangible programming system for young children; simple cubes that can be arranged to construct a basic program directing a toy car. Girouard et al. [10] present SmartBlocks, a tangible interface with which children can explore the volume and surface area of 3D objects. Tangible and embodied interaction is also applied in the area of music education. For example "Marble Track Audio Manipulator" [6], with which children can create musical compositions, and BodyBeats [27], a whole body interactive system that supports children in recognizing patterns in sound.

Furthermore, the approach of designing interactive systems that rely on metaphorical mappings between input action and output change is promoted by several others. Hurtienne et al. [13] present a useful database of image schemata usable in interaction design. Fels et al. [9] use metaphor in their interface design for musical expression. The earlier mentioned Sound Maker interactive environment [3] used

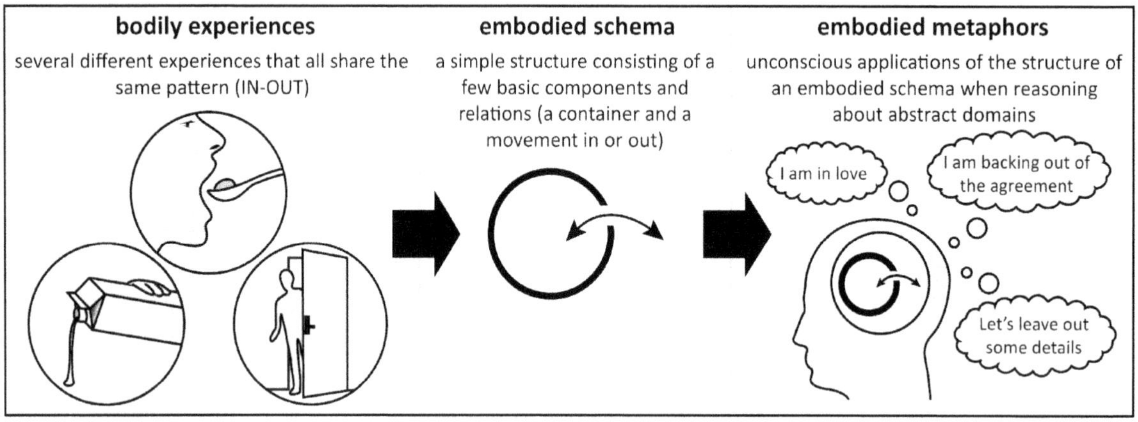

Figure 1. The relation between bodily experiences, embodied schemata and embodied metaphors.

embodied metaphor based interaction models to support children's learning of abstract sound concepts.

MOSO TANGIBLES DESIGN

The aim of the research described in this paper is to study learning effects of interactive tangible systems that rely on embodied metaphor based interaction models. Since our previous research [5] has shown that children may have multiple ways to structure their understanding of single abstract sound concepts, we expect that implementing multiple different mappings (each based on a bodily originating schema) can benefit the child's understanding of the targeted abstract concept. In order to evaluate this, we have developed an interactive learning environment, called Moving Sounds (MoSo) Tangibles, which implements multiple mappings to learn about single abstract concepts.

Building on previous work [3], MoSo focuses on teaching the abstract sound concepts pitch, volume and tempo. In consultation with two music teachers, we found that becoming acquainted with these concepts is the first step in music education. From the age of five, children are explained about the concepts in terms of body movement. For example, the teacher plays a simple melody slowly and children are taught to react to this with slow movements. After that, the melody is played fast and children make fast movements. This way children can start understanding the abstract concept tempo in terms of familiar movement related concepts (slow and fast). Such exercises provide them with a preliminary understanding of pitch, volume and tempo. A next step in this understanding would be to have the music react to the child's movement. This would enable free exploration of the concepts and will add to the child's ability to reason about changes in the concept parameters. According to the music teachers, children are ready for this step from the age of seven, when they have a preliminary understanding of the involved concepts. Our target group therefore consists of seven to nine year old children.

Moving Sounds (MoSo) Tangibles enables children to manipulate the pitch, volume or tempo of ongoing piano tones, by moving dedicated tangible artifacts. Each sound concept can be manipulated in three different ways (each based on a movement related schema), through three different tangible artifacts. This supports children in structuring their understanding of each concept in terms of three different embodied metaphors. We chose to use tangible interaction in this design rather than whole body interaction (which was implement in our Sound Maker environment [3]), as this allows a clear distinction between the different mappings, each in a separate tangible artifact.

MoSo was developed through an extensive iterative design process, described in [4]. In the first iteration, the embodied metaphors that underlie how children reason about the selected abstract sound concepts were identified through enactment studies with 65 children [5]. As a result of this study, we found for example that children structured their understandings of the concept volume by making movements related to the embodied schemata SMALL-BIG, QUIET-WILD, SLOW-FAST and LOW-HIGH. In the second iteration [4], low-fidelity prototypes designed based on the elicited embodied metaphors were evaluated with 50 children, which enabled assessing the implementation of embodied metaphors in terms of affordances.

Following from the above described iterations, we selected the embodied schemata NEAR-FAR, LOW-HIGH and SLOW-FAST to base our artifacts for manipulating pitch on. For volume, we selected QUIET-WILD, SMALL-BIG and SLOW-FAST. When enacting changing tempo, we found that all children based their movements on the schema SLOW-FAST, likely because the dynamics of action and sound are isomorphic (fast movements is directly related to fast sound). To enable children to structure their understanding of tempo in different ways, we subdivided the schema SLOW-FAST in SLOW-FAST succession (when a movement is *repeated* slowly and fast, e.g. clapping slowly or fast) and SLOW-FAST speed (when the *actual speed* of the movement differs, e.g. rotating your arms slowly and fast).

Resulting from the second design iteration, we designed three different tangible artifacts for each individual sound concept, based on the above mentioned schemata. These designs were developed into working prototypes of MoSo Tangibles. Figure 2 gives an overview of MoSo Tangibles, the embodied schemata they are based on, the mappings we used and the names we will use in this paper to refer to each separate artifact. As seen in Figure 2, the 'rotator' is used for all three concepts. Earlier iterations [4] revealed that a rotating movement seemed the clearest and most sensible way to map the schema SLOW-FAST speed to sound changes. Since this schema was applicable to all three concepts we decided to use the same artifact three times.

Each MoSo Tangible contains basic sensor technology to measure the intended movements. The sensor data is wirelessly transmitted to a computer which runs a dedicated program that determines the appropriate pitch, volume or tempo and produces piano tones accordingly.

USER EVALUATION

Based on previous work [5], we have found that children have multiple ways of structuring their understanding of abstract (sound) concepts. In line with approaches to teaching complex scientific concepts [25], we expect that the process of learning about abstract sound concepts may benefit from interactive systems that enable children to explore the targeted concepts through multiple different (embodied metaphor based) interactions. To evaluate this, we have set up a user study with MoSo Tangibles.

Participants and Conditions

For this user study, we recruited 39 participants (age seven to nine, 25 girls and 14 boys). Each participant interacted with MoSo in an individual session of about 20 minutes.

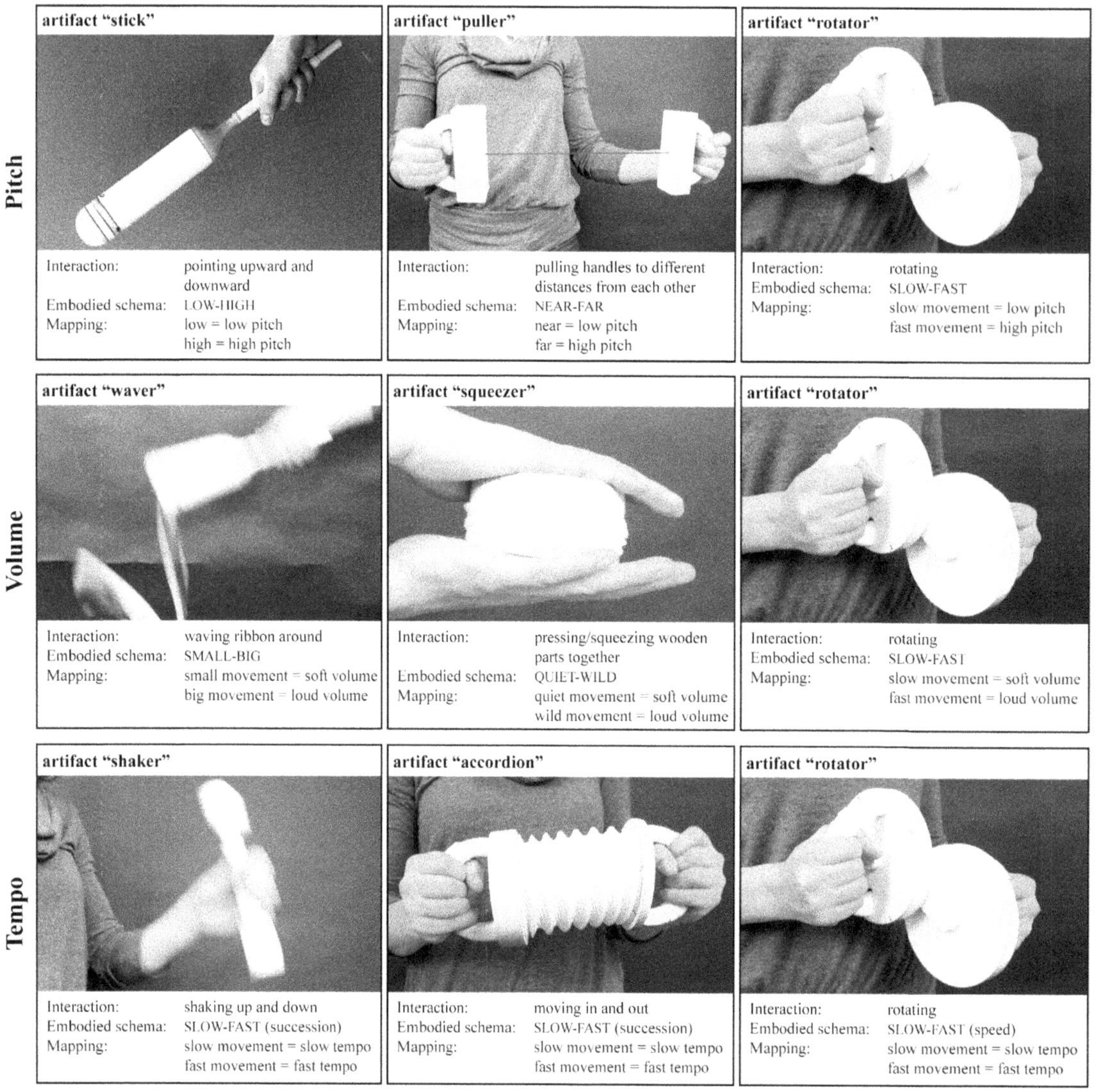

Figure 2. The tangible artifacts designed for manipulating pitch (top three), volume (middle three) and tempo (bottom three), and a description of the intended interactions, implemented embodied schemata and mappings.

These sessions were divided into three parts of equal length: one to learn about pitch, one to learn about volume and one to learn about tempo. The participants were divided over two conditions. Children in the *one-artifact-condition* learned about the sound concepts with one MoSo Tangible per concept: either stick, puller or rotator for pitch, either waver, squeezer or rotator for volume and either shaker, accordion or rotator for tempo. To keep it clear, no children in the *one-artifact-condition* were given the rotator to manipulate more than one concept. The children in the *three-artifact-condition* were given all three artifacts to explore each concept; puller, stick *and* rotator for pitch, etc.

The MoSo Tangibles system consists of three interactive artifacts for each of the concepts pitch, volume and tempo. All these tangibles implement an experimentally elicited embodied metaphor in their interaction models. As none of these metaphors can be considered stronger or weaker than others, we equally divided the artifacts over the *one-artifact-condition* sessions (for example one third of the children used the puller for pitch, one third used the stick and one third used the rotator). As the *one-artifact-condition* can therefore be regarded as three separate conditions, we assigned 27 children to the *one-artifact-condition* and 12 to the *three-artifact-condition*.

Pilot study

The procedure of this user study was verified in a pilot study with eight children of seven to eight years old. This led to a refinement in the instructions given to the children.

Procedure

In the individual sessions held in this user study, each child interacted with MoSo in three separate parts; one for pitch, one for volume and one for tempo. Each of these parts consisted of an exploration phase and three reproduction tasks. In the exploration phase, each child had three minutes to explore the working of one (*one-artifact-condition*) or three (*three-artifact-condition*) MoSo Tangibles to manipulate either pitch, volume or tempo. The children were not given any explanation about how to move the artifacts or which musical parameter to manipulate. The children were only told that the music would change as they moved the artifact(s).

After having explored the working of one (*one-artifact-condition*) or three (*three-artifact-condition*) tangibles, the child used (one of) the explored artifact(s) to perform three reproduction tasks with. In these tasks, which each lasted one minute, an example sound was played (e.g. low to high pitch) and the child was asked to reproduce this sound with the artifact. The children in the *one-artifact-condition* used the same tangible for all three tasks, while the children in the *three-artifact-condition* were given a different tangible for each task. After performing the reproduction tasks, the children in the *three-artifact-condition* were shortly asked which of the three artifacts they thought fit the sound change best. This was repeated for all three sound concepts (pitch, volume and tempo).

The order in which the children learned about pitch, volume and tempo was counterbalanced over the different individual sessions. This also holds for the order in which the children explored the different MoSo Tangibles in the *three-artifact-condition*. The individual sessions were performed in a room in which only one child and the experimenter were present. These sessions were captured on video to enable video analysis.

Formally Assessing Learning

In recent years, many studies on tangible interaction for learning have been published (e.g. [12, 28]). Evaluations of such systems often focus on user experience. However, hardly any studies aim at finding empirical evidence for an actual learning benefit of tangible systems (an exception is [21]). Although user experience may influence learning, we were interested in finding empirically grounded evidence for a learning effect of MoSo. Our user study therefore partly consisted of a quantitative analysis to evaluate if children in the *three-artifact-condition* would gain a better understanding of the sound concepts as a result of the exercises with MoSo, compared to the *one-artifact-condition*. Consultation with two music teachers revealed that no tool to measure understanding of pitch, volume or tempo exists. Therefore, the music teachers worked with us to develop a 'sound knowledge test' that assesses the children's understanding of these concepts. As the children may not yet be able to verbalize their understanding of sound concepts, the test consisted of multiple choice questions. For each question, an example sound was played in which one sound concept changed (e.g. low to high pitch), followed by three alternative sounds (e.g. one in which pitch changed, one in which volume changed and one in which tempo changed). The children were asked which alternative sounded most like the example. This test was iterated once by pilot testing it with 50 children.

Each child took the sound knowledge test three times: once before the experiment, once directly after interacting with MoSo Tangibles and once six weeks after the study. To assess the reliability of the knowledge test, we calculated the correlation between the results for each of the three times the test was administered. The results did not confirm the test's reliability ($n = 39$; $\rho = 0.2198$; $p>0.10$). Although the correlation between the results of the three tests is not an ideal measure for assessing the test's reliability, it is the only measure we have available. We did not administer the test more often or with other children. Therefore we cannot use the knowledge test results to draw conclusions regarding learning benefits of tangible systems. As a result, we have used video analysis results of the study to assess learning effects. Nonetheless, we feel that it is important to mention our attempt, as it may inform other studies in the field of tangible and embodied interaction for learning.

RESULTS

Video Analysis

To better understand the learning effects experienced by the children in the two conditions, we analyzed the videos of the user study. In the analysis, we identified and recorded the expressions children used when explaining about pitch, volume and tempo, as well as the expressions participants made when listening to sound samples. Though unsolicited, each child made such expressions. These expressions can indicate the children's understanding of the abstract concepts. In total, we captured 457 expressions (295 from the 27 children in the *one-artifact-condition* and 162 from the 12 children in the *three-artifact-condition*).

The expressions we found were either verbal (e.g. imitating sounds or using words such as slow and fast) or non-verbal (movements or gestures) and were categorized via open coding. As each expression related to one of the MoSo Tangibles, we were able to count the number of expressions in each category, related to each artifact. See Figure 3 for an overview of the relative number of expressions made about the concepts pitch, volume and tempo.

As depicted in Figure 3, in approximately 80% to 90% of the cases, children used words (verbal expressions) to explain about the concepts pitch, volume and tempo. 10% to 20% of the explanations were provided in movements. These expressions all related to artifacts the children had just used (e.g. when a child had just used the shaker to manipulate tempo, he would say "the music went like this" and move his hands as if he was moving the shaker).

The children in both conditions mainly used words related to soft and loud to explain about volume. For tempo, the children mainly used words related to slow and fast, however, we also saw quite a number of verbal expressions related to soft and loud. This is due to the fact that the user study was performed in Dutch. Different from English, the Dutch words for soft and loud (*zacht* and *hard*) can also be used to indicate speed. Compared to tempo and volume, the children less frequently used the 'correct' words to explain pitch (low and high). Instead, they resorted to other expressions such as the words slow and fast, or movements related to the artifacts they had just used.

When we compare the *one-artifact-condition* to the *three-artifact-condition*, we do not see clear differences for any of the concepts pitch, volume or tempo.

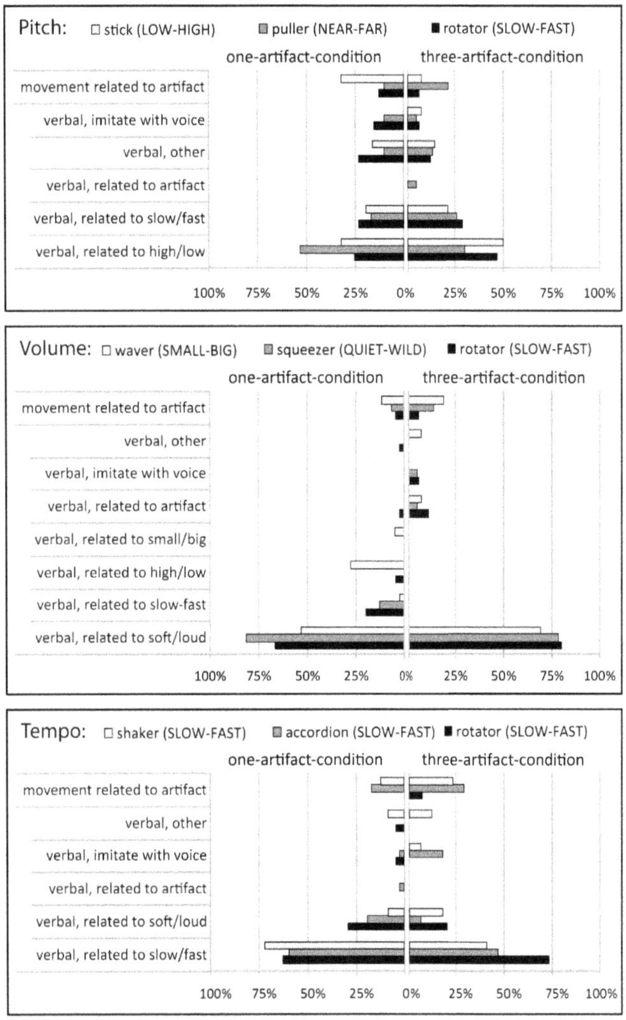

Figure 3. For pitch (top), volume (middle) and tempo (bottom), in the *one-artifact-condition* and the *three-artifact-condition*: the relative number of expressions found in each category, for each tangible (e.g. for pitch, in the *one-artifact-condition*, approximately 32% of all expressions related to the stick were non-verbal expressions).

From the video, we also analyzed the extent to which children were able to successfully reproduce sound samples using the MoSo Tangibles. As a result, we found that all children in both conditions were able to correctly reproduce the sounds within the given one minute for each task. Approximately 75% of the reproduction tasks were performed without any interference of the researcher, while the researcher needed to provide some additional explanation in approximately 25% of all reproductions. However, this was limited to giving hints such as "do you remember what you heard in the example?" or "how did you previously move the artifact?". The children were never explained how to move the artifacts to reach sound changes. The number of times such hints were needed did not differ significantly between the two conditions.

Interviews

In the *three-artifact condition*, each child interacted with three different MoSo Tangibles to learn about one single sound concept. After manipulating each sound concept, the children in this condition were asked which of three artifacts they thought fit the sound change best (i.e. which interaction model made most sense to them). The results of these interviews show an approximately equal division of the children's choices over the different artifacts. For example for pitch, three children chose the rotator, four children selected the puller and five children thought that the stick fit the pitch changes best.

DISCUSSION

The study described in this paper evaluated the learning experiences of children when interacting with MoSo Tangibles, which aims at learning about the abstract sound concepts pitch, volume and tempo. In this section we will discuss insights we gained through this research.

Using Multiple Metaphorical Mappings

The aim of the study presented in this paper was to evaluate whether interactive learning systems that enable children to reason about abstract concepts through multiple different embodied metaphors would lead to different learning experiences compared to systems that implement only one metaphor. When comparing the video analysis results between the *one-artifact-condition* and the *three-artifact-condition* however, we see no clear differences between the two. We have therefore not found evidence to prove that learning can be supported by enabling children to structure their understanding of abstract concept through multiple different movements. However, this also shows that being subjected to multiple different interactions did not confuse the children or hinder their learning experiences.

The fact that no difference was found between the two conditions may be a result of the short time of approximately six minutes that each child had to learn about pitch, volume and tempo with MoSo. It may have been unrealistic to expect strong differences in learning results in such a short period. Further research with longer term experiments would therefore be needed to validate the approach of implementing multiple metaphorical interactions in tangible learning environments for children.

Embodied Metaphor Based Tangibles and Learning

As discussed above, no clear advantage was found for using *multiple* different metaphorical mappings over a *single* mapping. In this section, we discuss learning benefits of embodied metaphor based mappings in MoSo, without comparing the two conditions. A video analysis of the children's interactions with MoSo was conducted to assess their learning experiences. As a result, we saw that the children mostly used verbal expressions to explain about pitch, volume and tempo, though movements or gestures were used in approximately 10% to 20% of the cases.

When looking at the verbal expressions children used to explain about the sound concepts, we see that for volume and tempo, children used the 'right' words in approximately 60% of all cases. For pitch, this percentage was lower, approximately 35%. Clearly, not all children were able to use the correct words to explain about the abstract concepts. In other words, not all children could verbally express their conceptual understanding of pitch, volume or tempo. When we look at the reproduction tasks however, we see that all participants were able to use the MoSo Tangibles to reproduce changes in pitch, volume and tempo. This indicates that the children could perceptually recognize the changes in sound concepts and use movement to reproduce them, regardless of the fact that some of these children were not able to verbalize their understanding of these concepts. This indicates that those children were able to reason about pitch, volume and tempo, be it using movement rather than words. This implies that when children do not yet have a conceptual understanding of a concept which they can verbalize, embodied metaphor based learning systems can serve as a handle to reason about such concepts.

Despite the small percentage of non-verbal expressions, we looked at these in more detail, as being able to gesture or move as a demonstration of knowledge is often seen as a good precursor to conceptual understanding [11]. Furthermore, gesturing can support children's verbalization, which is also referred to as 'embodied thinking' [23]. Although children may use different kinds of movements to structure their understanding of sound concepts (also see [5]), all movements that we have seen in our study related to artifacts that the children had just interacted with. This is partly expected as the participants had just been 'taught' to use that particular movement. However, the fact that no single other movement was found, even not in the *three-artifact-condition* where children explored multiple different movements, may indicate that tangible interactions based on embodied metaphors could guide children in using particular movements to structure their understanding of abstract (sound) concepts.

MoSo Tangibles Design

The user study presented in this paper used the specifically designed MoSo Tangibles learning system. The MoSo Tangibles each implemented a different embodied schema to map input movement to output sound change. As discussed before, all 39 participants in our user evaluation were able to successfully interact with MoSo tangibles, regardless of which of the artifacts they used. This shows that the design of the interactive artifacts was not stronger or weaker for particular tangible artifacts compared to others. This is further reflected in the results of the interviews taken in the *three-artifact-condition*, demonstrating that the children's preferences were equally divided over all the designs.

The result that our participants were able to find out how to interact with MoSo within the set timeframe of three minutes of exploration is also interesting when compared to our previous work. In our previously performed Sound Maker study [3], in which children manipulated pitch, volume and tempo of sound through whole body interaction, we saw that some children were not able discover the mapping of the system within the set timeframe, even though these mappings were also designed according to embodied metaphors. Tangible interaction can offer clearer affordances than whole body interactive environments, which has evidently enabled the participants to quickly find out how to operate the tangibles. This shows that tangible interaction is a suitable interaction style for embodied metaphor based systems.

Language and Cultural Differences

Embodied metaphor theory finds its basis in cognitive linguistics (see [15, 17]). Although it is important to understand that it is not just a linguistic mechanism as metaphorical thinking is fundamental to human thought, the link to language is important. We experienced this in our user study. We performed our study in the Netherlands, and the researchers communicated with the participants in Dutch. The Dutch words for soft and loud can also be used referring to slow and fast speed. As a result, many children used 'soft' and 'loud' to explain about tempo, or 'slow' and 'fast' to explain about volume. Furthermore, as a result of an iterative design process [4], we implemented the schema SLOW-FAST in one of our mappings for volume in MoSo Tangibles. As these words are differently used in English, one may question if iterations done with children whose first language is English would have lead to the same results. We extracted embodied metaphors from movements [5], which we believe to be cross cultural. However, evaluating this may indicate the potential influence of language on the identified embodied metaphors, and thus the way we reason about abstract concepts.

CONCLUSIONS

In this paper, we have presented the design and evaluation of MoSo tangibles, an interactive learning system that enables children of seven to nine years old to learn about the abstract sound concepts pitch, volume and tempo, through multiple different embodied metaphor based interactions. A user evaluation of this interactive system among 39 children in the target age group has shown that all children were able to successfully interact with the tangibles when reproducing examples sounds. As not all children were able to verbally express their understanding of the targeted abstract concepts, this indicates that embodied metaphor based learning systems can serve as a physical handle to reason about such concepts.

Our study contributes to the growing body of empirical work exploring how conceptual metaphor theory can be used to inform the design of abstract domain applications on tangible, embodied and embedded platforms.

REFERENCES

1. Ackermann, E.K. Perspective-Taking and object Construction: Two Keys to Learning. In *Constuctionism in Practice: Designing, Thinking, and Learning in a Digital World*. Lawrence Erlbaum Associates, Mahwah, NJ, USA, 1996, 25-37.
2. Antle, A.N. The CTI framework: informing the design of tangible systems for children. In *Proc. TEI 2007*, ACM Press (2007), 195-202.
3. Antle, A.N., Droumeva, M., and Corness, G. Playing with the sound maker: do embodied metaphors help children learn? In *Proc. IDC 2008*, ACM Press (2008), 178-185.
4. Bakker, S., Antle, A.N., and Hoven, E. van den. Embodied Metaphors in Tangible Interaction Design. *Personal and Ubiquitous Computing, special issue on Tangibles and Children*. In press.
5. Bakker, S., Antle, A.N., and Hoven, E. van den. Identifying embodied metaphors in children's sound-action mappings. In *Proc. IDC 2009*, ACM Press (2009), 140-149.
6. Bean, A., Siddiqi, S., Chowdhury, A., Whited, B., Shaer, O. and Jacob, R.J.K. Marble track audio manipulator (MTAM): a tangible user interface for audio composition. In *Proc. TEI 2008*, ACM Press (2008), 27-30.
7. Bruner, J.S. *Studies in Cognitive Growth, A collaboration at the Center for Cognitive Studies*. John Wiley & Sons, Inc., New York, NY, USA, 1966.
8. Dourish, P. *Where the action is: the foundations of embodied interaction*. MIT Press, Cambridge, MA, USA, 2001.
9. Fels, S., Gadd, A. and Mulder, A. Mapping transparency through metaphor: towards more expressive musical instruments. *Organised Sound 7*, 2 (2002), 109-126.
10. Girouard, A., Solovey, E.T., Hirshfield, L.M., Ecott, S., Shaer, O. and Jacob, R.J.K. Smart Blocks: a tangible mathematical manipulative. In *Proc. TEI 2007*, ACM Press (2007), 183-186.
11. Goldin-Meadow, S. *Hearing Gesture: How Our Hands Help Us Think*. Harvard University Press, Cambridge, MA, USA, 2003.
12. Hashagen, A., Büching, C. and Schelhowe, H. Learning abstract concepts through bodily engagement: a comparative, qualitative study. In *Proc. IDC 2009*, ACM Press (2009), 234-237.
13. Hurtienne, J., Weber, K. and Blessing, L. Prior Experience and Intuitive Use: Image Schemas in User Centred Design. *Designing Inclusive Futures*. 2008, 107-116.
14. Jensenius, A.R. Action - Sound; Developing Methods and Tools to Study Music-Related Body Movement. PhD thesis, University of Oslo, 2007.
15. Johnson, M. *The Body in the Mind: The Bodily Basis of Meaning, Imagination, and Reason*. Chicago Press, Chicago, IL, USA, 1987.
16. Juntunen, M. and Hyvönen, L. Embodiment in musical knowing: how body movement facilitates learning within Dalcroze Eurhythmics. *British Journal of Music Education 21*, 2 (2004), 199-214.
17. Lakoff, G. and Johnson, M. *Metaphors we live by*. University of Chicago Press, Chicago, IL, USA, 1980.
18. O'Malley, C. and Stanton Fraser, D. Literature Review in Learning with Tangible Technologies. 2004. http://www.futurelab.org.uk/resources/documents/.
19. Parreren, C.F.V. and Carpay, J.A.M. *Sovjetpsychologen aan het woord*. Wolters-Noordhoff, Groningen, The Netherlands, 1972.
20. Piaget, J. The *origins of intelligence in children*. International Universities Press, New York, USA, 1952.
21. Price, S., Falcão, T.P., Sheridan, J.G. and Roussos, G. The effect of representation location on interaction in a tangible learning environment. In *Proc. TEI 2008*, ACM Press (2008), 85-92.
22. Price, S., Sheridan, J.G., Falcao, T.P. and Roussos, G. Towards a framework for investigating tangible environments for learning. *International Journal of Arts and Technology 1*, 3/4 (2008), 351 - 368.
23. Rimé, B. and Schiaratura, L. Gesture and Speech. In *Fundamentals of nonverbal behavior*. Cambridge University Press, New York, NY, USA, 1991, 239-281.
24. Smith, A.C. Simple tangible language elements for young children. In *Proc. IDC 2009*, ACM (2009), 288-289.
25. Thompson, K. The value of multiple representations for learning about complex systems. In *Proc. ICLS 2008, volume 2*, (2008), 398-406.
26. Ullmer, B. and Ishii, H. Emerging frameworks for tangible user interfaces. *IBM Systems Journal 39*, 3-4 (2000), 915-931.
27. Zigelbaum, J., Millner, A., Desai, B. and Ishii, H. BodyBeats: whole-body, musical interfaces for children. *Ext. Abstracts CHI 2006*, ACM Press (2006), 1595-1600.
28. Zuckerman, O., Arida, S. and Resnick, M. Extending tangible interfaces for education: digital montessori-inspired manipulatives. In *Proc. CHI 2005*, ACM Press (2005), 859-868.

Futura: Design for Collaborative Learning and Game Play on a Multi-touch Digital Tabletop

Alissa N. Antle, Allen Bevans, Josh Tanenbaum, Katie Seaborn, Sijie Wang
School of Interactive Arts and Technology
Simon Fraser University
Surrey, B.C., Canada
{aantle; alb19; joshuat; kseaborn; swa50}@sfu.ca

ABSTRACT

This paper introduces a collaborative learning game called Futura: The Sustainable Futures Game, which is implemented on a custom multi-touch digital tabletop platform. The goal of the game is to work with other players to support a growing population as time passes while minimizing negative impact on the environment. The design-oriented research goal of the project is to explore the novel design space of collaborative, multi-touch tabletop games for learning. Our focus is on identifying and understanding key design factors of importance in creating opportunities for learning. We use four theoretical perspectives as lenses through which we conceptualize our design intentions and inform our analysis. These perspectives are: experiential learning, constructivist learning, collaborative learning, and game theory. In this paper we discuss design features that enable collaborative learning, present the results from two observational studies, and compare our findings to other guidelines in order to contribute to the growing body of empirically derived design guidelines for tangible, embodied and embedded interaction.

Author Keywords

Interactive surfaces, tabletop games, multi-touch interaction, collaboration, educational games, simulation games, design evaluation, design rationale.

ACM Classification Keywords

H5.2. Information interfaces and presentation: User interfaces. K.3.m Computers and education: Miscellaneous.

General Terms

Design

INTRODUCTION

With the commercialization of the Smart Table and Microsoft Surface, digital tabletops are now being placed in informal (e.g. museums) and formal spaces (e.g. schools). Digital tabletops offer unique opportunities to facilitate collaborative learning interactions in such spaces. Simultaneously, research in the discipline of game studies has lead to increased interest in games for learning and education in both public spaces and more formal settings [9]. Educational games, if done well, promise to couple the intrinsic appeal of strategic play with a learning process. The potential to use the affordances of tabletop displays and multi-touch surfaces to support collaborative games for learning is compelling. Recent research publications in tangible, embodied and embedded interaction provides conceptual and empirical guidance for design to support collaboration (e.g. [6, 12]). Similarly, research in gaming has begun to explore new game platforms such as tabletops and whole body interaction (see [11] for a review). However, there has been little empirical work that explores the design space of multi-touch tabletop games for learning.

We had the opportunity to showcase a game for learning about sustainable development, called "Futura: The Sustainable Futures Game", at a 2010 Winter Olympics Celebration Site (Vancouver, Canada). The three pillars for the Olympics were Sport, Culture and the Environment. People often have misconceptions about what is involved to create a sustainable environment. Sustainable development planning is a complex problem. Choices and decisions often have lasting and unforeseen effects on the environment and the way people live and work. Sometimes, meeting the needs of both humans and the environment is not possible. The learning outcomes for Futura are not related to the learning of specific concepts (e.g. about ecology or urban planning) but instead our goal is to give players a chance to experience the tradeoffs and complexity involved in planning for a sustainable future. In doing so, Futura supports players to become more aware of the contradictory demands of maintaining environmental health and supporting population growth in an urban environment.

Our main research question is: What design factors are important to enable the kinds of interactions that support collaborative learning in a multitouch tabletop environment? We address this question using a design-based research approach which includes a design case methodology. The design case is comprised of theoretical underpinnings which inform our design choices; a detailed description of our custom tabletop and Futura learning game; a design analysis and rationale; and a summary of two observational evaluations. Our design rational uses theoretical concepts to argue for the importance of specific design features that support the kinds of interactions that provide opportunities for learning. The use of both theory and empirical data provides rigor to our design based research. We also compare and contrast our design choices with guidance from other researchers in order to contribute to a growing body of knowledge concerning collaborative learning in tangible, embodied and embedded interactive environments as conceptualized broadly by Hornecker and Burr [6].

THEORETICAL FOUNDATIONS

In this section, we present the four theoretical perspectives that inform our design-based research in collaborative learning through multi-touch tabletop games. In the Related Work section, which is located near the end of this paper, we compare our work with other design oriented studies of collaborative learning through tangible, embodied and embedded interaction.

Experiential Learning (Learning by Doing)

Learning is a process that leads to change in behavior or change in ways of thinking [9]. The theory and value of experiential learning is often attributed to Dewey. It was later popularized in the North American education system by Kolb. Experiential learning is the process of learning, or meaning making, based on a person's direct experience with some event or element of the world [8]. This approach to learning is often contrasted with rote learning and with didactic learning. However, experiential learning may be misconstrued since people may learn things other than what was intended from their experiences. For example, a student may learn from attending didactic physics lectures that they dislike physics, rather than learning that they dislike didactic lectures.

To support learning of intended outcomes from experience, a learning environment must provide the following four elements: concrete experience, support for reflection on that experience, support for formation of abstract concepts based on that reflection, and the opportunity to test or try out the new concepts through concrete experience [10].

Constructivist Learning

Many researchers are familiar with Piaget's stages of cognitive development. However, it is the stage independent aspects of Piaget's theory that are foundational to theories of constructivist learning. Forman and Pufall [4] provide an excellent overview of Piaget's influence on constructivist learning. Briefly, Piaget's theory of how learning occurs can be summarized with three concepts: epistemic conflict, self-reflection, and self-regulation. Epistemic conflict occurs when our ideas about the world are challenged by new perceptions from or about the world. Self-reflection is our deliberate and conscious attempt to understand a given situation through reflection. Self-regulation is our deliberate and conscious process of structuring, planning, reflecting and acting in order to resolve epistemic conflict and achieve what Piaget calls "equilibrium". It follows that a successful learning environment must provide physical and/or social opportunities for learners to experience epistemic conflict and resolve this conflict through support for self-reflection and self-regulation.

Collaborative Learning

Piaget's theory of cognitive development has been criticized for largely ignoring the social aspects of learning. When designing games for learning in public spaces, social interaction is likely and desirable. Therefore, collaborative learning theory brings important perspectives to social aspects of learning and must be considered in our work. In the computer supported collaborative learning (CSCL) literature, collaboration has been defined as "a process by which individuals negotiate and share meanings" and "a coordinated, synchronous activity that is the result of a continued attempt to construct and maintain a shared conception of a problem" [14]. This differs from cooperative activities in which learners may coordinate their efforts, but the work performed is primarily individual [2].

CSCL theories outline three important elements required to support collaborative learning: objects of negotiation, referential anchors and support for meta-cognition. Objects of negotiation are shared external representations which can be modified by individuals or a group during the learning process [16]. Referential anchors are context-specific objects, utterances or gestures that support learners coming to common ground or understandings [1]. In a CSCL environment, referential anchors may be explicitly included through the use of digital representations. For example, the game status screens in collaborative digital games, which shows both individual and team progress, may serve as referential anchors. It grounds the players' communication in shared understandings of what has been achieved in the game, and what remains to be completed. Metacognitive processes that require support during group learning include monitoring, evaluating, and regulating individual and group understandings as they develop [3].

Game Theory: Microworlds, Simulations and Games

Educational technology and games researchers often distinguish between microworlds, simulations and games. Rieber [13] provides an excellent overview which we summarize here. *Microworlds* are a simple but complete model of a domain or system which enables a person to "live" in that domain for some period of time. Microworlds are accessible to novice users but support advanced exploration. In order to be accessible a learner must know immediately what to do within a microworld. For example, a natural microworld is a sand box. A child, with a bucket and shovel, can explore density and volume. It is often assumed or expected that learners can and will self-regulate their learning in a microworlds. This may occur when learners are motivated, take responsibility for goal setting and planning, and actively structure the learning to suit their own style. While self-regulated learning is effective, it is difficult to know how to design an artificial microworld to support self-regulated learning.

A *simulation* is a high fidelity model of some domain; and as such it may not be suitable or accessible to novice users [13]. An advantage of simulations for learning is that they provide direct access to subject matter or content which might not be readily accessible in the real world. A key assumption behind simulations is that users will "learn by doing".

Digital games have recently been used for instruction. Kirriemuir and McFarlane provide an excellent overview which we draw on here [9]. Digital games provide visual digital information to one or more players, take input from players, process that input according to a set of programmed game rules, and change the digital information displayed back to players. A defining characteristic of a game is the set of game rules. Developers of educational games have hoped to harness the motivational power of games to provide motivation for learning.

FUTURA: THE SUSTAINABLE FUTURES GAME

In this section we outline our design goals for Futura, and describe the system implementation, game overview, and user interface. We follow this section with a design analysis of Futura through the lenses of learning and game theories.

Figure 1. Futura interactive multi-touch tabletop

Design Goals

Futura was created in order to explore the novel design space of collaborative, multi-touch tabletop games for learning in public venues. We require players to be able to read simple texts and so the target audience was seven years old and above.

The main learning goal was to support people to improve their understanding the complexity of sustainable development. This goal applies to both children, who may know little about sustainable development, and to adults, who may be well read on the topic. We are interested in helping players improve their understanding of the importance and difficulty of achieving sustainable development through active participation in a simulated land use activity. We are not trying to teach concepts related to sustainable development. Our focus is on participation and simulation, which is in line with recent trends in research on pro-environmental behavior that suggests that providing people with information about issues of public concern is not sufficient to change their behaviors. Rather, people need to participate through various mechanisms in order to shift their awareness or understanding of the importance of change which in turn may lead them to engage in desired behavioral change [15].

Our secondary design goals were to create a tabletop game for a 2010 Winter Olympics Celebration Site that encouraged people to walk up and play together, and to create a game that was accessible to a wide range of ages.

System Implementation

Futura is run on a custom digital multi-touch tabletop (Figure 1). Our system is housed in a modified IKEA wood and metal table with telescopic legs and a custom metal undercarriage which supports the camera, PC and projector hardware. The surface of the table's wood frame supports an Endlighten™ acrylic surface. Our sensing system relies on a diffused surface illumination (DSI) technique with four infrared strips, one on each side of the rectangular surface. We capture touches with a single web camera with an infrared filter on a wide angle lens embedded in a custom mount. The camera can cover an active sensing area of 85 by 68 cm. The camera is connected to a PC (Intel Core2 Duo 2.66 GHz processor) with a firewire cable and provides 30 frames per second (fps) data capture. We process camera data using Community Core Vision, an open source finger tacking software. The game application is written using an existing C# multi-touch library called "Breezy" that takes TUIO input and provides multi-touch user interface components. A single short-throw projector provides 1024 by 768 resolution on the output surface of 103 by 68 cm. We use a velum mat, attached below the Endlighten™ acrylic, for the projection surface, leaving the top surface of the acrylic exposed, which results in better touch tracking.

Game Overview

Futura is a game in which players directly participate in a fictitious, yet realistic, land use planning process. Futura is a simulation that takes place in a microworld river basin derived from a map of the Fraser River basin surrounding

Vancouver, Canada (see Figure 2). Land use planning is a challenge that needs to be solved by many people working together. In Futura, players take on the role of important decision makers, responsible for providing people with food, shelter, and energy for the region. Each player must meet the growing population's need for their resources (food, shelter and energy). Each player is responsible for his or her own individual play, but all the players must work together in order to succeed, much like real-life decision makers.

Players of Futura have to learn how to meet the needs of an ever increasing population in the game world without endangering the health of the environment. They do this by dragging and dropping tokens representing facilities such as: energy facilities (e.g. solar energy), shelter (e.g. single dwelling, townhomes), and food production facilities (e.g. high productivity livestock, organic produce), onto the map. However, they can only place facility tokens if they have enough money which accumulates as time passes.

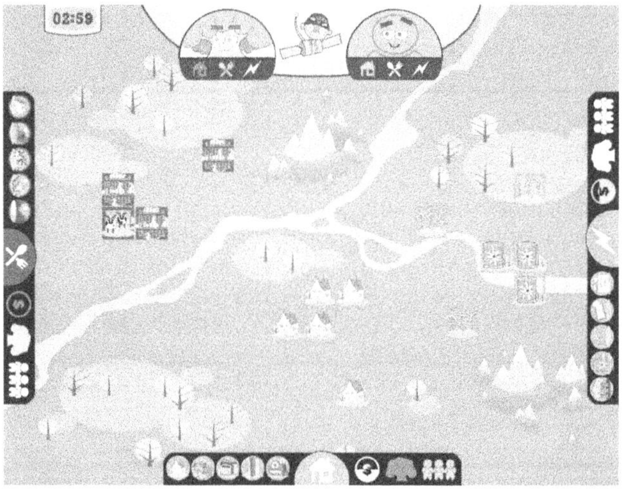

Figure 2. Futura user interface

Multi-touch interaction enables the kind of fast paced activity required to provide for the growing population while time quickly passes. Players can also touch facility tokens in their toolbar to learn more about them through displayed information cards. They can drag facility tokens onto the map to "build" them. If they are not careful, the choices they make can have serious consequences. The short duration of the game compels players to act while giving them opportunities to see how their decisions affect the world over time.

The individual scores of the players are combined into a single global impact score for the environment and the population, which are displayed in the global display and reflected in the map colour. Players win the game if they can meet the needs of both people and the environment. A video is available under "Videos" at http://www.antle.iat.sfu.ca/Futura/.

User Interface

The main interface is an interactive map which is augmented with three player toolbars and a global information display about the state of the world (Figure 2). The player toolbars are located on three sides of the interface (see Figure 2, left, bottom and right). There is a toolbar for each of three resources: food, shelter, and energy. Each toolbar contains facility tokens for its resource type (left side of toolbar), and information displays for money, environmental impact, population status (right side). For example, the energy toolbar has facility tokens for fossil fuel, bio-diesel, wind energy, solar energy and a clean energy research centre. The global information display is located at the top of the map (Figure 2). On the left side is a tree character which shows the state of the environment (Figure 3). On the right side is the population character which shows how well the growing population's needs are being met. The rest of the interface contains the microworld map and facilities that have been placed on the map through player actions during the game. The map changes its background colour from green to brown if the environment deteriorates, providing ambient feedback (Figure 4). The mood of the audio track also changes to reflect the world state.

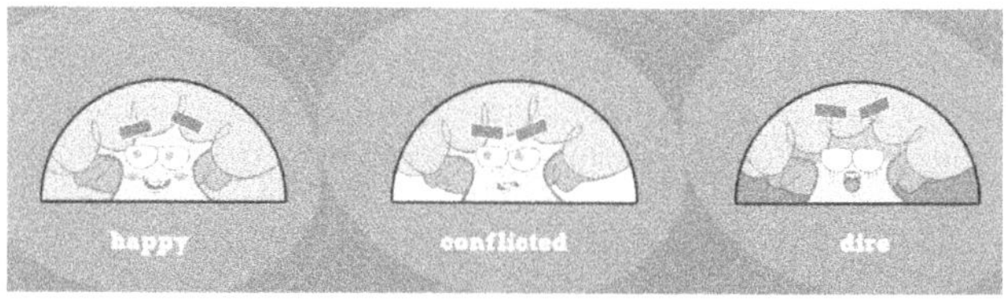

Figure 3. Global environment character: 3 states

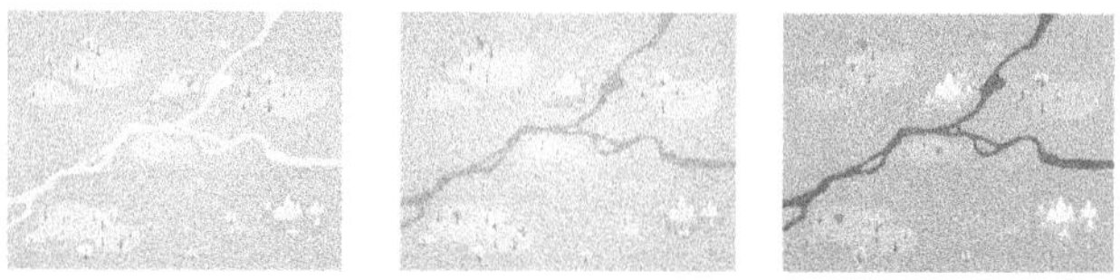

Figure 4. Ambient world state feedback

Figure 5. World events: mudslide (top), species saved (bottom)

During game play, world events pause the game and depict either a positive or negative world state (Figure 5). The game concludes with a final screen showing the state of the environment and population, and providing hints for future play. The satellite icon (top, Figure 2) can be used to access the game control menu that includes pause and, restart function, and an instructions/help feature.

DESIGN ANALYSIS AND RATIONALE

We now analyze Futura through the lenses of learning and game theories focusing on how specific design choices and features enable interactions which we have identified from theory as beneficial for learning.

Ludic Challenge, Motivation and Self-Regulated Learning

Each Futura game is very short; only three minutes long. In three minutes about one hundred years pass in the microworld. Multi-touch interaction combined with a persistent style game provides ludic challenge, which in turn fosters motivation to win the game. The game is challenging. It is difficult to win the first time. All of these factors work together to create a game that is exciting, engaging and supports repeat play which provides opportunities for learning. The repetitive and goal directed nature of the game combined with ludic challenge provide motivation and mechanisms for *self regulation* of *metacognitive processes* related to thinking, feeling, behavior, and attention which facilitate learning from play.

Learning through Experience: Win or Lose

Futura is designed to facilitate players to *directly experience* the complexity and difficulty of balancing environmental and human needs in sustainable development. The tabletop size and form enable a multiplayer game which blends features of digital games, simulations and microworlds, as suggested by Rieber [13]. Losing the game advances the learning outcomes since players directly experience the difficulty of balancing environment and population. This is true even if players only play once. Players win once they begin to understand the complexity of the problem and develop strategies to address it. This design strategy is in line with experiential learning in which players learn from a concrete experience, and then test out their ideas through their continued experience of playing the game. The result is a multiplayer, simulated microworld game that resembles stakeholder driven urban planning and enables opportunities for experiential learning whether players win or lose.

Balancing Individual and Group Play

Sustainable land use planning is a problem that needs to be solved by many people working together. An early design decision was that players would take on the role of important decision makers, responsible for providing people with food, shelter, and energy for the entire region. The tabletop form supports each player to literally take a "side". Each player is responsible for his or her own individual play, but all the players must work together in order to succeed, much like real-life decision makers. The size of the table and interface design precludes one player from taking over the game. It is physically not possible to reach all the toolbars from one position. These choices, enabled by the tabletop form and interface design, provide opportunities to learn through a *collaborative process*.

Reflection and Action in Knowledge Construction

Futura's challenge level was designed so that most groups of players would lose the first few times they played. From a constructivist perspective, we intentionally use game challenge to introduce *epistemic conflict*. From this starting point, we designed the game rules so that in order to get better at playing, players must also get better at thinking about the challenges of sustainable development. To facilitate this kind of thinking, there are various design features that explicitly support opportunities for *reflection* and *self-regulation*. These occur both during continuous action and in discrete pauses or breaks in game play.

The changing map colour provides ambient feedback continuously during play. There are also discrete opportunities for reflection. For example, players may pause the game at any time with the satellite button. The world events (e.g. mud slide) also pause the game, providing both a *reason* and the *time* to reflect. The end of game summaries provide feedback about how well the group did and provide some advice on how to do better in the future. These design features provided players with opportunities to break from the fast-paced action enabled by multi-touch interaction and reflect on their decisions and choices as they actively construct knowledge.

Learning from Others

The interface allows all the players to see how and what their co-players are doing. Each player's toolbar contains resources that any player can drag and drop onto the map. Successful collaboration relies on toolbars as *objects of negotiation*. The three sided interface design ensures that each player can see what the others are doing, and can help others by reaching over to another's toolbar. This provides opportunities for each player to learn from and help others, and in doing so, help the group succeed.

Providing Common Ground

Winning the game requires coordination among a potentially diverse group of players, from young children to the elderly. The overall game state is reflected in the changing map colour (green to brown), which should be easily understandable by novice players. The global information display at the top of the table is more complex and supports more advanced players. In both cases, the feedback serves as *referential anchors* because it changes as the game proceeds and provides common ground for shared understandings. This multi-layer feedback design enables players of all abilities to understand what is happening and what is needed and thus supports collaborative meaning making across a broad group of users.

OBSERVATIONAL STUDIES

Study Design

We had two opportunities to conduct observational design studies of Futura in informal settings. The aim of both studies was to observe Futura in use and collect data in order to explore how our design decisions impacted interactions which in turn create, shape or constrain opportunities for learning.

Futura was presented at the 2010 Winter Olympics. In this field study, we observed hundreds of users of all ages and nationalities using Futura. People queued to play and were given a brief introduction to the game by a volunteer using an instruction screen. Players often formed impromptu groups with friends or family. They were allowed to play as many times as they liked, depending on how long the queue was. We also presented Futura at a Simon Fraser University Open House. We have no numeric demographic data for the Open House participants because we focused only on informal observations. We collected field notes that included descriptions of behaviors and quotes from players. We analyzed our observational data using open coding to search for repeated patterns of verbalizations and interactions. The final themes we present were identified independently by two more of our researchers.

Study Results

We will focus on those results that help us identify and understand how design features enable attitudes and interactions that support opportunities for learning.

General Attitude to Futura

In terms of broad attitudes, many participants expressed enthusiasm about playing Futura. They liked crowding around the tabletop form, and enjoyed the retro-style cartoon graphics. One player said that Futura "… was easy to play but hard to win."

Learning about the Complexity of Sustainable Development

Most participants who talked about what they learned commented that keeping the planet healthy was difficult. Some participants verbally noticed the relationship between facility costs and environmental impact (e.g. cleaner energy facilities cost more). We did not hear participants verbalize that they learned any new specific knowledge from the game or information cards. However, it was not our goal to "teach" specific things related to sustainability concepts, but rather to enable a shift in awareness about the complexity of the issue. Our observations show support for the achievement of this goal.

Fun, Serious Play and Narrative

Players' affective responses while playing Futura varied tremendously. Children and teenagers seemed to express a sense of having fun more that adults. An older child commented that it was "Challenging … which made it really fun to play". Conversely, many adults seemed intimidated by their first round of play. They would generally play more "seriously" if they played subsequent rounds. A noticeable exception was adult women who were playing with (their) children. These women seemed to have more fun than adults in groups without children.

Many players created meaningful narrative around game events. For example, when the world map would change colour (usually for the worse), players would comment about their population dying, or water becoming scarce in their world.

Working Together

During the first play, much game-related talking between players was related to interface instructions. For example, "We need more farms" or "Press harder" or "Try this [token]". The most consistent form of coordination was during facility placement. Many players also talked to each other about where to put certain facilities on the map or where to place new facilities in relation to tokens that had already been placed. This is interesting since the game does not yet incorporate spatial location data into the simulation model.

In groups composed of parents and children, resources were often shared and discussed by two or more players. Parents would often reach over and point out, or physically drag out, a resource for their child. Some parents triggered information cards for their child's facilities while explaining why they should or should not use that facility at a particular time in game play. Other group configurations also helped each other. In a group with all teenagers, one player commented that they learned from working with other players … "That if you work together, it's easy to help." Another said, "You get much more help so you can achieve better goals and you can explain each others' ideas to get the world a better place."

Players who played the game more than once often began to talk to each other about how the environment and population were doing, and would work out strategies to keep the global indicators green (i.e. healthy). In situations with more than three players, there was often some discussion among players on the same team about which tokens to place next to win the game. In groups that played more than once, they often switched roles. "I want to be energy this time."

Understanding Multitouch Interaction

Since the touch-and-drag actions to place facility tokens and touch-and-hold actions to trigger information cards were usually explained to players before they started, most players did not seem to have difficulty understanding how to interact with the table. We observed many players, usually children or teens, simply walk up and touch the table. If the main start screen was active, then a player would often simply touch the large start button to begin the game. Once the game started, they often touched different areas of the interface before they discovered that the toolbars had facilities tokens that could be moved onto the map. Once they were shown or discovered how to move tokens onto the map, they progressed quickly.

Multitouch Tracking Issues

We observed some touch tracking issues which interfered with players' ability to smoothly interact with the game. For example, we noticed a "small finger problem" with some children who then resorted to using their fists. We also found the tracking system did not perform well on the Olympics site when the sun was high overhead, despite the tent covering the tabletop. To ensure optimal tracking, we limited the play hours to 4 pm and later when the sun was low in the sky. Some players who had issues with the system not registering their touch often tried touching harder or dragging more slowly and deliberately. Most did not give-up. However, we observed that tracking problems shifted players' focus from what was happening in the game, to the immediate task of trying to get a facility token onto the map, or trigger an information card.

Understanding the Interface

Players readily understood that their role required them to use their toolbar to place facilities and quickly realized that the facilities tokens could be moved onto the map. Players often tried to drag the money or population or environment indicator icons from the toolbars onto the map. A few players wondered aloud about what the global indicators meant, and what they were supposed to do in response. Few of the players understood the relationship between the individual toolbar indicators and the related individual status indicators on the global display (Figure 3). However, most were able to understand the local toolbar indicators, and the global environment and population indicators that reflected the cumulative game state.

Some players began to question and think about why the map was turning from green to brown and the global environment tree indictor to red. One said, "Look, the tree is turning red! Look the world is turning brown. What's happening?" While many players were able to determine what was happening and how to rectify the situation, some did not (e.g. "It was fun and I got to learn. But confusing!")

The world event screens (Figure 5) seemed to be easily understood. However many players expected these events to alter the game world (e.g. the mudslide event should results in players losing money). Players rarely expressed confusion with the end state screens. We observed that some players read the explanatory text aloud, especially if they were with a larger group of friends or family. Some players discussed which tokens or team members were responsible for the game end state. Others showed evidence of using the feedback to determine how they could improve their play for the next round.

Repeat Play

Just under half of the subjects played the game more than once. This was affected by how long the queue was and group configurations. At the Olympics site, we observed that many of the repeat players were pre-teens or teenagers. Groups of teenage event volunteers would often play multiple times during breaks, attempting to win the game or loose spectacularly.

We observed a temporal pattern when groups played repeatedly. Players often started out very focused on their own toolbar and played independently. After they lost, they began to give more attention to what other players were doing. After several plays, many groups shifted to not only be aware of others' actions but explicitly work out strategies together. For example, a group placed a few high yield facilities from each resource type early in the game and then countered the negative environmental impact by placing as many clean facilities as each of their money reserves would allow. This shift from an individual to group focus most often lead to winning strategies.

COMPARING TO RELATED WORK

Hornecker and Buur [5] introduce guidelines associated with supporting embodied facilitation. Embodied facilitation refers to how physical spaces and structures determine, constrain and direct user interactions which in turn shape how users collaborate. Embodied constraints restrict what people can do and make some behaviors more probable than others. In the Futura design, the assignment of toolbars to three sides of the table encouraged individual player roles but did not stop one player from reaching over to help or take control from another, both of which may contribute to the need for negotiation and subsequent coordinated action. Multiplayer game play was facilitated by the spatial structure of the tabletop and interface design rather than the traditional game design approaches of using turn taking or identification of tokens with specific users. This approach also eliminated the need to track individual players, which is difficult in a walk-up-and-play environment. The design was flexible: it encouraged intended role play without eliminating other ways to play. Thus we neither explicitly support nor constrain sharing of resources but rather designed to afford individual actions as part of group play and leave opportunities for emergent forms of group interaction.

Price et al. discuss opportunities for reflection and action during a study of students exploring optics with a tabletop TUI activity [12]. They suggest that the combination of visual feedback on the tabletop with both discrete actions (e.g. placing TUI objects on the surface) and continuous actions (e.g. dragging and dropping) enable acting and opportunities to reflect on the consequences of that action. In their system, reflection and action are intertwined. In Futura we provided opportunities for reflection *during* continuous action in a similar manner. We also provided opportunities for reflection *apart* from action such as the world events that pause the game and provide a reason to reflect and discuss what was happening in the game. Reflection *during* action was largely an individual activity since a player's attention was likely on their actions and thinking about the results of these actions. Reflection *apart* from action was a collaborative activity. In this way, the

Futura design supports both individual and social knowledge construction. We present our design as an alternative approach that can facilitate the kinds of interactions that support the interweaving of reflection and action.

Hornecker et al. also introduce the theme of designing to support lightweight interactions [7]. They suggest avoiding sequential interactions or predetermined territories because they may interfere with fluent interactions. Territoriality is of particular interest since we neither fully promoted nor inhibited a shared environment but supported flexibility of interaction. Because Futura required collaboration to win, negative interference between players was discouraged by the adverse affects it had on group outcomes. We suggest that the use of sharable individual and group territories balances structure and flexibility which supports emergent learning opportunities for a broad audience. We suggest this approach as an alternative to light weight interactions.

CONCLUSIONS

We presented the results of our design-based research which explored the novel design space of collaborative, multi-touch, tabletop games for learning. Using theoretical concepts and observational findings, we identified several key design features. These include using multi-touch interaction on a large surface to create a real-time simulation game world; using the spatial structure of the tabletop to support players to take roles ("take sides") but not allow a single player to take over the game; using discrete world events to pause fast-paced multi-touch interaction in order to facilitate reflection and self-regulation; and using spatially separate but sharable individual territories and resources to facilitate negotiation and learning from others. Our study results indicated that Futura was effective and enjoyable for well over half the general public who walked up to play. We suggest that our design can serve as an exemplar of design features which enable collaborative learning through game play on a digital tabletop.

ACKNOWLEDGMENTS

This research was supported by funds from the GRAND NCE (Graphics, Animation, and New Media Network Centre of Excellence).

REFERENCES

1. Clark, H.H. and Brennan, S.E. Grounding in communication. In Resnick, L.B., Levine, J.M. and Teasley, S.D. (eds.) *Perspectives on Socially Shared Cognition*, American Psychological Association, Washington, DC, 1991, 127-149.
2. Dillenbourg, P. What do you mean by "collaborative learning"? In Dillenbourg, P. (ed.) *Collaborative Learning: Cognitive and Computational Approaches*, Elsevier Science, New York, 1999, 1-16.
3. Duffy, T.M., Dueber, B. and Hawley, C.L. Critical thinking in a distributed environment: A pedagogical base for the design of conferencing systems. In Bonk, C.J. and King, K.S. (eds.) *Electronic Collaborators: Learner-centered Technologies for Literacy, Apprenticeship, and Discourse*, Lawrence Erlbaum Associates, Mahwah, NJ, 1998, 51-78.
4. Forman, G. and Pufall, P. (eds.) *Constructivism in the Computer Age*. Lawrence Erlbaum Associates, Hillsdale, NJ, USA, 1988.
5. Hornecker, E. A design theme for tangible interaction: Embodied facilitation. In *Proc. ECSCW 2005*, Springer, (2005), 23-44.
6. Hornecker, E. and Buur, J. Getting a grip on tangible interaction: A framework on physical space and social interaction. In *Proc. CHI 2006*, ACM Press, (2006), 437-446.
7. Hornecker, E., Marshall, P., Dalton, S. and Rogers, Y. Collaboration and interference: Awareness with mice or touch input. In *Proc. CSCW 2008*, ACM Press, (2008), 167-176.
8. Imai, Y. Walter Benjamin and John Dewey: The Structure of Difference Between Their Thoughts on Education. *Journal of Philosophy of Education 37,* 1, (2003), 109-125.
9. Kirriemuir, J. and McFarlane, A. Literature Review in Games and Learning, Futurelab Series, 2004, 1 - 35.
10. Kolb, D. *Experiential Learning: Experience as the Source of Learning and Development.* Prentice-Hall, Englewood Cliffs, NJ, USA, 1984.
11. Magerkurth, C., Cheok, A., Mandryk, R. and Nilsen, T. Pervasive games: bringing computer entertainment back to the real world. *Computers in Entertainment 3*, 3, (2005), 1-19.
12. Price, S., Falcao, T.P., Sheridan, J.G. and Roussos, G. The effect of representation location on interaction in a tangible learning environment. In *Proc. TEI 2009*, ACM Press, (2009), 85-92.
13. Rieber, L.P. Seriously considering play: Designing interactive learning environments based on the blending of microworlds, simulations, and games. *Educational Technology Research and Development 44*, 2, (1996), 43 - 58.
14. Roschelle, J. and Teasley, S. The construction of shared knowledge in collaborative problem solving. In O'Malley, C. (ed.) *Computer-Supported Collaborative Learning,* Springer Verlag, Berlin, Germany, 1995, 69-197.
15. Stirling, A. Analysis, participation and power: Justification and closure in participatory multi-criteria analysis. *Land Use Policy 23*, (2006), 95-107.
16. Suthers, D. and Hundhausen, C. An empirical study of the effects of representational guidance on collaborative learning. *Journal of the Learning Sciences 12*, 2, (2003), 183-219.

Math Propulsion: Engaging Math Learners Through Embodied Performance & Visualization

Jason Mickelson & Wendy Ju
California College of the Arts
1111 8th Street, San Francisco, CA 94107
{jmickelson, wju}@cca.edu

ABSTRACT
This paper describes a series of interaction design sketches we created to supplement mathematics curricula. These sketches were deployed in a variety of secondary school math classrooms in the San Francisco Bay Area. The activities purposefully use visualization and embodiment to engage students with the math concepts of geometric transformations and symmetrical patterning. These experiments exemplify how applying embodiment and visualization to traditionally impersonal and abstract subjects like math can make the learning experience more fun and active for students and offer new pedagogical strategies for teachers.

Author Keywords
Embodied, cognition, visualization, mathematics, education

ACM Classification Keywords
H5.m. Information interfaces and presentation (e.g., HCI): Miscellaneous.

General Terms
Design, Experimentation

INTRODUCTION
Mathematics is commonly vilified as the most difficult subject in primary and secondary school curriculum; the educational research literature documents the prevalence of "math anxiety" [1, 11] and "math avoidance" [26] behaviors, with anxiety levels peaking in grades 9 and 10 when students are studying geometry and algebra [16]. This aversion to mathematics is deeply troubling, not only because mathematics capability is the cornerstone to careers in science and technology, but also because we believe, as mathematician and teacher Paul Lockhart states so well, "that there is nothing as dreamy and poetic, nothing as radical, subversive, and psychedelic, as mathematics." [15]

TEI'11, January 22–26, 2011, Funchal, Portugal.

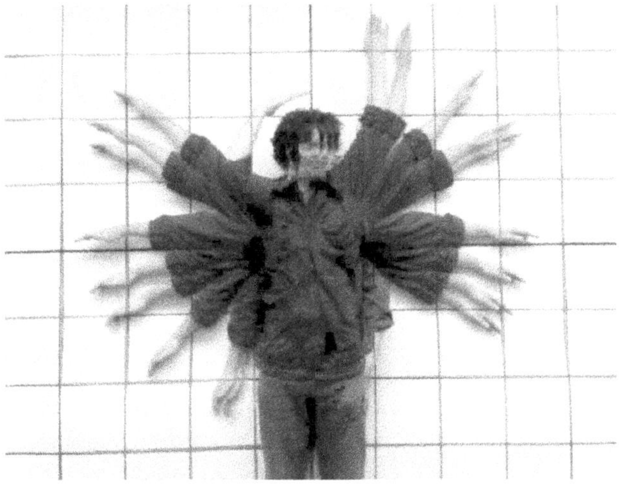

Figure 1. Superimposing video frames enables students to explore geometric rotations - by making "math angels"

MATH PROPULSION
In this paper, we describe a series of experiments we conducted employing embodied performance and visualization that emphasizes conceptual exploration, collaboration, and creativity over "getting the right answer." These formative experiments share the theme of "Math Propulsion" because they engage students with math using bodily action. This strategy is grounded in the thesis that embodied interactions [6, 8, 14]—those that are tangible, social and also corporal—would increase students' engagement with and understanding of the subject of math.

We expect the use of embodied performance and visualization to contribute to mathematics education in several ways:

1. Physical engagement helps to entail mental engagement as students reason about how their actions are influencing the visual feedback they are receiving.
2. Social engagement and negotiation of joint actions enables students to apply mathematical vocabulary and concepts to an immediate situation, and to engage in criticism and appraisal of mathematical issues.
3. Direct physical control over mathematical variables, coupled with real-time feedback, gives students a chance to discover for themselves how different factors relate to one another; for instance, they can see how

movement of vertices on a polygon affects the area and symmetry of the shape.

4. Mathematics can be seen in a personal and situated context, where the numbers, shapes or equations are part of the immediate world rather than something from a hypothetical and isolated one.

5. Mathematics can be presented as a subject for open-ended inquiry and invention rather than a series of prescribed exercises.

BACKGROUND

This work is motivated by substantial bodies of prior work in education pedagogy, digital learning tools, embodied cognition, and the visual and performing arts. This narrative overview highlights some of our key inspirations and influences.

The Need for New Tools in Mathematics Education

The National Council of Teachers of Mathematics (NCTM) has long promoted the following steps to promote wider interest and acceptance of math [16]: Accommodating for different learning styles; emphasizing the importance of original, quality thinking rather than rote manipulation of formulas; letting students have some input into their own evaluations; designing positive experiences in math classes; and allowing for different social approaches to learning mathematics

These recommendations are based on years of research showing that traditional mathematics education poorly adapts to different learning styles and also fails to address students' spatial, kinesthetic, interpersonal and intrapersonal intelligences [11]. As Lockhart points out,

> The only people who understand what is going on are the ones most often blamed and least often heard: the students. They say, "math class is stupid and boring," and they are right.

One of the chief problems is that math teachers are given high level directives to transform mathematics education, but not a lot of specific tools that exemplify these new ways of thinking. Dunn and Dunn's recommendations to help accommodate students' learning strengths [9], for example, asks teachers to consider how learners are affected by (1) immediate environment (sound, light, temperature, and design); (2) own emotionality (motivation, persistence, responsibility, and need for structure or flexibility); (3) sociological needs (self, pair, peers, team, adult, or varied); and (4) physical needs (perceptual strengths, intake, time, and mobility). This is almost antithetical to the traditional mathematics curriculum we all experienced, which is based on behaviorist rote learning, where students are given problem sets, are proscribed solution techniques, and are expected to repeat practice problems until mastery is achieved.

The consequences of this impoverishment in our educational curriculum are dire. The phenomena of math anxiety [1] and math avoidance [26] has been passed down through generations, and there is a cultural assumption that there are "math people" and "non-math people, "as if there could be some sort of genetic or anatomic disposition that makes one person more capable of understanding and executing mathematics than another.

Constructionism & Mathematics

Constructionist Seymour Papert was intimately concerned with trying to reform the problems of mathematics education [18]. Most math curricula are repurposed from traditional exercises to pursue correct answers to planned problems using narrow methods consistent with only a logical-mathematical intelligence. In the scheme of rigorous and overpopulated classrooms, educators have bandwidth for little else. This perpetuates a "relative poverty of culture in providing the materials to make the concept simple or concrete" [19]. Even more importantly, it prohibits any student investigation into exploring math data in ways that would be more relevant to personal understanding.

Papert's LOGO was originally targeted at the subject of math. Its creators argued that programming facilitated the acquisition of rigorous thinking and expression, gave students specific insights into how numbers, variable and functions work, motivated heuristics for problem solving, and helped students to analyze larger problems into smaller ones, among other things [10]. While many of the Digital Manipulatives [21] inspired by the LOGO/Lego research have extended LOGO's reach in teaching important and complex concepts such as emergent behaviors, dynamic systems, and programming paradigms, few of these projects in making programmable bricks, blocks, balls, beads and badges have addressed LOGO's original target subjects of geometry and algebra.

Art & Dance in Mathematics

Our work was inspired by Schaffer and Stern's *Math Dance*, a workbook with activities for interpreting beginning geometry concepts through performing choreography with gesture and movement and exploring the architecture of bodies in space (see Figure 2, next page) [23]. Similarly, instructors like Alexis Dekel of Pittsfield High School in Pittsfield, Massachusetts collaborated with a dance instructor and calculus students to create a Math Dance Team that concentrated on improvisation to create group choreography of advanced math concepts. Instead of a literal translation of a figure or equation, Pittsfield's Math Dance Team [7] embraces personal interpretations of how a math concept might look or feel in the body and communicates that understanding through movement that informs the choreography of the group; a unique interpretation of how embodied cognition can form mathematical understanding [14]. Our design sketches extend the movement lessons of Schaffer, Stern and Dekel by explicitly incorporating real-time visual feedback about position and movement through simultaneous camera capture and screen display. This allows the embodied activity to be studied further for its underlying math relationships while promoting students to be original and artistic to create visual designs. Interactive video installations like Ed Tannenbaum's *Recollections* series [25] allow participants to "paint" the screen with stacked layers of silhouettes made with body movement. Visualization tools such as the *Synchronous Objects* project from William Forsythe and Ohio State University's Advanced Computing Center for the Arts and Design [17], turned complicated dances into data in order to create virtual objects. Video filters and data visualization reveal relationships between dancers, objects, and the patterns they sculpt in space. Development of visualization and modeling tools that convert complicated gesture and movement into data are available for study [12, 17, 26]. The objects created from these systems, both virtual and fabricated, exploit the creative tendencies of bodies in motion while revealing some obstacles of transitioning between 3D and 2D space.

Methodology

This work employs design experimentation as a strategy for formative research. Our focus at this stage is to broaden the design space of possible mathematics curricula through speculative designs; formal evaluations of specific techniques will be conducted at a later point once the most promising designs have been identified and integrated into a more structured and controlled curriculum.

Our goal was to encourage mathematical exploration and discussion through rapid deployment of "interaction sketches" [4]. Each design is only a starting point with which to engage students and instructors, allowing them to construct their own words and actions in context of a creative activity. These activities uncover unique observations and insights within the group, and create connections about what changes and reactions each strategy might bring to future math curriculum. From the design evaluation standpoint, we studied the deployments through direct observation, video documentation and surveys when possible, and review of the creations/ compositions students made using our interaction sketches.

Technology

Our technology choices were largely driven by a desire to maximize the future deployability and access of our designed tools. All of the experiments described in this paper were created and tested on a laptop computer using the Processing programming environment [20]. We employed libraries such as JMyron (an open-source computer-vision library which enables Processing towards motion detection, color tracking, and blob recognition) and TUIO (an application protocol interface to enable the recognition and tracking of fiducial markers) [3]. Occasionally, the use of separate USB web cameras and bluetooth keyboards were used to enable greater flexibility in spatial configuration of the designed activities. We also experimented with using a grid background in several of the experiments. All of these materials and tools are commercially available and inexpensive or free.

While we experimented in the lab with using wall projection and multi-camera set-ups, all of our sketch deployments used the laptop/web camera setup to maximize flexibility and minimize set-up time. These constraints also worked to maximize the future deployability of the designs we developed, as instructor preparation time is as limited as access to computers and peripheral technologies in many educational environments.

Participants

We solicited local mathematics teachers to volunteer one class period to try out each of our experiments. In total, we worked with one grade six class, one grade seven class, five high-school geometry or geometry/algebra classes, and one group of 12 teachers as part of a workshop at the San Francisco Exploratorium Learning Museum. In an effort to try out these sketches in many environments during a short deployment phase, we only made one visit per classroom. Hence, there was little opportunity for close collaboration or follow-up exercises with teachers.

Topics of Instruction

Our tool was targeted at the topics of geometry and algebra, specifically transformations of figures which are addressed at numerous points in elementary and high

Figure 2. Adapting Schaeffer and Stern's *Math Dance* exercises to improvise choreography for geometric symmetries. The combination of dancers, camera, space, and virtual screen geometry keys opportunities for visualizing embodied experiences.

school education, but handled as a specific focus in grades 8-10 in the California Public School System [2, 5, 24].

To develop understanding of transformations, the concepts the students and instructors are working on are: figure, preimage, image, variables, formulas, vectors, functions, equations, symmetry, isometries, area, vertices, planes, angles, rotation, reflection, translation, dilation, tessellation, approximation, models, similarity, congruence, patterns, sequences, series, and rules.

In the course of learning these concepts, students are expected to develop skills to do the following: design and conduct experiments to verify or disprove predictions; understand and make inferences based on the analysis of experimental results; recognize, create, extend, and generalize patterns, and understand, develop; and express rules describing patterns; use reading, listening, and observation skills to access and extract mathematical information from multiple, self-selected sources such as pictures, diagrams, physical models, oral narratives, and symbolic representations.

DESIGN EXPERIMENTS

The following are descriptions of the different interaction design sketches we made to test with students:

Patterned Poses

In Patterned Poses (Figure 3), captured frames from Math Angels (see this page, right column) were used as the root node to construct abstract patterns that enriched the visual exploration with elements like scale, color, and angles of rotation. This extended the discussion of transformations by starting with translations and reflective symmetry and visualizing effects from dilation and rotation. The Math Angels "shape" was turned into a silhouette to be repeated in different ways. The use of the body as a root form helped to personalize and make relevant the otherwise abstract forms; students were able to readily identify the original form and even whose body was imaged. One student survey response said, "Today was a '4' because we have found a new way of using geometry and art combined."

These example compositions are made using Illustrator scripts. A new digital prototype would use image processing software to create and isolate the silhouette. To create the desired aesthetic pattern, students could tune variables like scale, color, and angles of rotation, etc. via a screen interface. Most importantly, however, students can tune the overall shapes in their wallpaper visual by re-calibrating their body and repeating the capture process. The visual output simultaneously serves as a visual reference point to explain the finished transformations and an artistic exhibition of math relationships.

Math Angels

Inspired by the visual tools like Glowdoodle [22] and the construction of snow angels, Math Angels is an investigative tool using pixel recognition code to create multiple renderings of kinesthetic activities on a light-colored background surface. Students see a superimposition of the current feed of a web camera and previously-captured images; they can add the current frame to the stored stack by hitting a key on a USB keyboard (see Figure 1). By setting the alpha value of all the light colored pixels in the frame to zero, we create compositions that merge successive moments in time onto one screen image.

Math curriculum references transformations as an event that happens to a point, line, or shape on a plane, changing position, size, or orientation. By using the body as the "object" to be transformed, students have the opportunity to use layered screen captures to investigate what a transformation looks like during and after they try it kinesthetically. Two different versions placed the web camera pointed at a wall or directly overhead. This design factor encouraged students to attempt transformations by jumping in mid-air or by using more of their body without being limited by gravity. We constructed a grid of black lines on white vinyl to be in camera view. This dressing helped draw the best possible contrast for the alpha-value of pixels. It also helped students position themselves in space and served as a valuable visual marker for a math activity. During different tests we changed the orientation

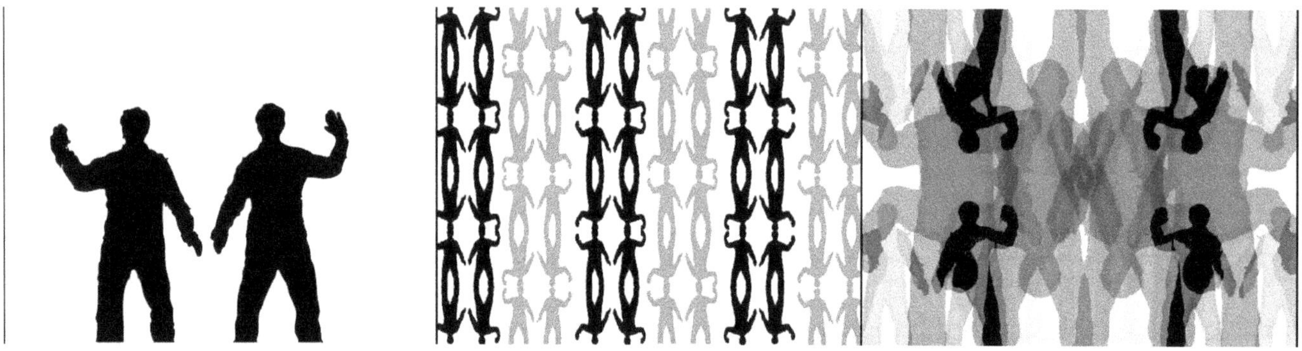

Figure 3. Using the silhouette images captured from video, Pattern Poses provides an artifact of embodied symmetry that becomes personal and artistic through tuning variables (color, scale, angles, tessellation patterns) in order to extend the dialogue about transformations further.

Figure 4. A group of sixth grade students create "Blob Shapes" on screen, using, flashlights and "blob detection" software to construct and manipulate the shapes, exploring congruency and symmetry using screen feedback and social interaction.

of the laptop screen to accommodate the performer or the audience.

Students were engaged to create examples of symmetry by themselves or by collaborating with others. The audience was also involved by directing the performers or suggesting new types of transforming movements. Teachers mostly observed students, managed audience members, and sometimes participated in creating different symmetries with students. Often times students completed a transformation like a translation or reflection and then added new layers of poses that created visual story elements instead of a specific math topic. 15 year old Gonzalo told us, "I never thought about geometry like this way."

Blob Shapes

Using Processing code and the JMyron external library, we track points of light and use them as vertices to construct simple polygons (triangles and quadrilaterals). This sketch was called Blob Shapes (Figure 4). Students position lights (we used handheld flashlights, headlamps and LED pucks) to different points on their body, or distribute lights amongst different players. Each light acts as vertex of the shape; when the player moves through the camera's field of vision virtual lines are drawn between the vertices to create the polygon. The shape of the polygon (its dimensions, perimeter, area) change along with the movement of the student's body (and the movement of the blobs). Students use the shape on the screen to inform their movements in order to achieve a desired transformation.

We used the grid background to better enable students to position their lights symmetrically. The screen display included numerical data about the length of each side of the polygon and the overall perimeter. The physical grid helped students make sense of the numbers on the virtual display. Additionally, the fill color (red) of the polygon on the screen increased opacity with an increase in the overall size of the polygon. This feedback was meant to help students maintain congruent shapes but also to observe how their body adjusted in response to screen output and vice-versa. Overall, this sketch was helpful in theorizing how body parts (especially the head, joints, and extremities) can be translated into vertices of polygons to reveal the geometry of the body. The animation of the shapes on screen also did much to help visualize the transitions that shapes make between transformations, similar to geometry software applications like Key Curriculum's Geometer's Sketchpad [12] but quite different from static renderings in math curriculum texts.

Video Kaleidoscope

Using a web camera and some customization of basic Processing code, we created different models of repeating video displays called Video Kaleidoscopes (Figure 5, next page). Some math textbooks use kaleidoscopic imagery and tessellation as visual examples[2, 24]. However, very few of the exercises lead students to create these patterns to form understanding of different symmetries. This sketch provided a way for teachers and students to discuss what they see on the page by participating directly in creating visual patterns that adhere to the same math rules.

Using a laptop with built-in camera, students take turns moving to affect the screen display. In several deployments we were able to project the screen display on an opposite wall for the entire class to view. Activating a button on a Bluetooth keypad saved the screen display as a static frame to be viewed later for reference. The video engaged participants to constantly try new orientations and combinations of position, depth, and movement. Students quickly brought in physical materials and hand-drawn designs from previous activities to augment the composition, creating new visual effects with shadows, reflection, and texture. While students did not immediately pick up on the mathematical aspects of this exercise, instructors were able to reference the Video Kaleidoscopes to discuss symmetry in further classroom discussion, and they could cite shared experiences, saying things like "remember when you walked from right to left and the pattern expanded outward." We received feedback that the expressive and artistic nature of this sketch helped different students engage: "we didn't write all the time and we had fun by learning as well."

REFLECTION

While we learned many things through our successive deployments, we wish to highlight the following lessons:

Figure 5. Video Kaleidoscopes display updating tessellation (left), rotations (center) and reflections (right) that motivate movement in front of the camera; curiosity about how repeating images interact evolves into a structure for embodied geometry challenges.

Introducing New Tools

While we wanted to motivate self-directed and open-ended student inquiry, we found that students would not engage with our tools without well-structured introductions. Although each student session was limited to less than an hour, we found it worthwhile to explain and demonstrate how the tools worked, how they could control them, and what the results would be. For future development, these demonstrations should be performed by teachers themselves. We designed one written activity that mimicked the visual and content styles of a classroom lesson plan. This handout helped teachers make connections back to their curriculum while giving students an optional nudge but not constraining their creativity.

Early on we had questions whether we were working towards particular curriculum design or tools for specific learning concepts. In our workshop with math teachers at the Exploratorium, we got feedback that the latter was the best way to support and encourage the former; it was hard for teachers to generate these types of tools on their own even if they liked the ideas they embodied. Having the tools readily available (for free, they emphasized) would make it easier for them to rethink their curriculum to accommodate more visual and kinesthetic learning. We agree that this framework respects various teaching styles where technology tools are flexible enough to accommodate classroom diversity.

Social Engagement

While our one-laptop-per-classroom setup was driven largely by economic considerations and the ability to setup/takedown quickly, we found that students sharing the capture tools motivated social engagement in many surprising and wonderful ways.

First, the sketches were treated as a performance activity. Just as video played on a screen or a guest speaker creating an experiment at the front of class demands attention, the sketches performed by one or a handful of students reinforced an actor/audience dynamic in the classroom. So, even with an expected amount of class commotion, the sketches kept the overall attention level high throughout the test visits. Some eager teachers who tried the sketches were indeed modeling creative behavior in a math activity for their students to follow.

Secondly, in spite of clear roles between performer and audience, students in the audience interacted with the sketch by offering advice or new ideas to the performer, supplying positive feedback to success as well as articulating critical responses to the quality of a performer's transformation. In this way the entire class behaved collaboratively, brainstorming new ways to use the tools. Figure 6 (next page) is just one example how students used the Math Angels program to build moral narratives (such as the gunfight with innocent bystanders on top of the framework of creating reflective symmetry), invent special effects (such as capturing successive frames mid-jump to create an illusion of floating while showing off rotational symmetry around a cardboard tube "axis") and experiment with layering and depth (by standing closer to the camera to create a "friendship collage" while exhibiting a dilation transformation).

Third, the verbal and kinesthetic communication about where to stand, how to pose, how to hold things, and what was being controlled extended the vocabulary used to describe the mathematical relationships in the sketches. For instance, references to "raise your arm a little more" to adjust vertices, "move back one step" explains action on the x-axis, and "face front…now turn around" portrays a specific rotation on the body's axis. Students used expressions like: "Make a class star!," "I can hang it from my head and make a pentagon," and "You can try to put someone inside of a shape."

Abstraction

Our experiments with abstracting the screen images (for example, in Patterned Poses) was an attempt to make the tools more artistic while simultaneously engaging with math. We could challenge students to think about shapes in a less structured way by abstracting where the initial forms came from through silhouetting.

Although our experiments are far from conclusive with regard to abstraction, we underestimated how much the students *enjoyed* being able to see their friends faces and forms on the images we captured. They were constantly

Figure 6. Students using "Math Angels" sketches to construct narratives with reflections(left), generate special effects with rotations and translations (center), and to explore identity and social engagement using dilation (right).

looking for recognizable aspects and were very concerned about who the images "belonged to." At the same time, it's important to note that such a literal capture of body likeness was distressing for some students who were engaged as audience but were adamant about not performing. It was an important reminder of the influence of camera/screen technology and the psychology of self image in young adults.

In our session with math teachers at the Exploratorium we found that the teachers preferred when the sketches included numbers on the interface; it made them feel more confident the activities were appropriate for a math class. Their suggestions were often tied to specific lessons or topics that they covered, such as grid relationships and graphing functions. We were heartened to find that many of the sketches could be adapted to a wide variety of lesson plans. But we also wonder whether the specific adaptations should be made by instructor rather than be built into the tools themselves.

Narrative

We were pleasantly surprised by the way that the performative aspects of our tool led directly to storytelling, an uncommon outcome in mathematics curriculum. The examples in Figure 6 all had strong story-telling elements that also revealed surprising moral components. In one Math Angels composition, students processed the concept of reflective symmetry in their performance through both their characters' *personality* as well as *body position*. Compositions made with Video Kaleidoscope became a lot more interesting to students when one of them posed a challenge–for example, to try to create a triangle using the six-sided reflection tool. By combining the faculties of the body with the creative mind to investigate math, students have more leverage to use intuition and self-expression to create personal agency and compelling stories as references for understanding concepts.

FUTURE WORK

This series of interaction design sketches illustrates and tests our basic ideas about combining kinesthetic, visual, social, expressive and mathematic learning. It is necessary to explore more intuitive screen and wireless controller interface as well as possibilities for projecting digital displays onto physical spaces (wall, floors) to facilitate embodied thinking into kinesthetic action more immediately. Teachers at the Exploratorium effectively used masking techniques with white paper to affect alpha values on Math Angels screens, a type of "visual hack" that has huge potential for manipulating patterns.

Additionally, it would be beneficial to build in screen prompts to encourage participation through basic "training" exercises. Formal evaluations with specific math classes over the course of a school year to understand the longer-term effects of these designs and better adapt these tools so they can be readily integrated by mathematics instructors teaching in varied contexts and stages of curriculum development. In this way, it's essential to formulate a model of assessment that supports math comprehension but does not discount or undervalue the creative aspects of these interactions.

CONCLUSION

In Math Propulsion, we present a different vision of how computation can be used to engage math learners with spatial relationships of geometry. Instead of using the computer's language to interact with numbers, students translate body movement into the flexible virtual worlds of math data through a performance with interactive elements in the classroom environment. In this sense, students develop math knowledge in real life as well as on screen. This more personal exploration of math and movement becomes a learning model for students in other aspects of their world.

We think that our tool embodies valuable techniques that researchers recommend to combat the perceived difficulty and irrelevance of math. We hope that widespread dissemination of tools such as ours might inspire math instructors to think about how they, too, could engage different learning styles and intelligences, and motivate students to be creative, take risks, and engage in social discussion around mathematical concepts.

One of our key motivations was to use kinesthetic action as a way to make the abstract concrete through the embodied mind. But our experiments showed us something more. In the end, the most effective simulations will not just supply a more concrete way of exploring abstract math. The interactions should be expressive, beautiful, and elicit a "it was fun" reaction, which we heard often in classrooms. In this sense, this inquiry will contribute to the growing definition of successful interaction design, where designs encourage self-expression and creativity, not just utility and efficiency. If a combination of curriculum and technology reveal new avenues for kinesthetic learning as effective problem-solving strategies, creativity and intuition will gain currency in the world of education and industry.

ACKNOWLEDGMENTS

We would like to thank Brenda Laurel, Paul Montgomery, Matthew Canton and the Graduate Program of Design at the California College of the Arts; Sebastian Martin at the Exploratorium; Math teachers and students at MetWest High School and Lighthouse Charter School in Oakland, CA and Lipman Middle School in Brisbane, CA.

REFERENCES

1. Ashcraft, M.H. Math Anxiety: Personal, Educational, and Cognitive Consequences. *Directions in Psychological Science*, 11, (2002), 181-185.
2. Bass, L, Charles, R, Johnson, A. Kennedy, D. *Prentice Hall Mathematics: Geometry*. Pearson Education, Inc., 2004.
3. Bencina, R., Kaltenbrunner, M., and Jorda, S. Improved Topological Fiducial Tracking in the Reactivision System. IEEE Conference on Computer Vision and Pattern Recognition, Workshop (2005), 99.
4. Buxton, B. *Sketching User Experiences: Getting the Design Right and the Right Design*. Morgan Kaufmann Pub, 2007.
5. California Board of Education, *Mathematical Frameworks for California Public Schools; Kindergarden through Grade Twelve*. Calfornia Department of Education Press, Sacramento, 2006.
6. Clements, D. and Battista, M.T. Geometry and Spatial Reasoning, in *Handbook of Research on Mathematics Teaching and Learning,* Grouws, D.A., ed. New York: Simon & Schuster Macmillan, (1992), 420-464.
7. Dekel, Alexis, producer. Pittsfield High School Math Dance at Mass MoCA." Pittsfield ETV. May 16, 2008. http://www.pittsfieldtv.net/Cablecast/Public/Show.aspx?ChannelID=2&ShowID=8888
8. Dourish, P. *Where the Action Is: The Foundations of Embodied Interaction*. The MIT Press, 2004.
9. Dunn, R. and Dunn, K. *Teaching Students Through Their Individual Learning Styles: A Practical Approach*. Reston Pub. Co., 1978.
10. Feurzeig, W., Papert, S., Bloom, M., Grant, R., Solomon C. Programming Languages as a Conceptual Framework for Teaching Mathematics. *ACM SIGCUE Outlook* 4(2), (1970), 13-17.
11. Gardner, H. and Hatch, T. Educational Implications of the Theory of Multiple Intelligences. *Educational Researcher,* 18, 8 (1989), 4.
12. The Geometer's Sketchpad. Key Curriculum Press. http://www.keypress.com/x24070.xml/
13. Hembree, R. The Nature, Effects, and Relief of Mathematics Anxiety. *Journal for Research in Mathematics Education*, 21, (1990), 33-46.
14. Lakoff, G. and Nunez, R., *Where Mathematics Comes From: How the Embodied Mind Brings Mathematic Into Being*. Basic Books, 2000.
15. Lockhart, P. A Mathematician's Lament. Devlin's Angle. March 2008. http://www.maa.org/devlin/LockhartsLament.pdf/.
16. National Council of Teachers of Mathematics (NCTM), *Curriculum and Evaluation Standards for School Mathematics*, Reston, VA: NCTM, 1989.
17. Palazzi, M., Shaw, N.Z., Forsythe, W., et al. Synchronous Objects for One Flat Thing, Reproduced. *ACM SIGGRAPH 2009 Art Gallery*, ACM (2009), 1.
18. Papert, S. Teaching Children to be Mathematicians Versus Teaching about Mathematics. *International Journal of Mathematical Education in Science and Technology* 3, 3 (1972), 249-262.
19. Papert, S. and Harel, I. Situating Constructionism. *Constructionism*, (1991), 1-11.
20. Reas, C. and Fry, B. Processing: a Learning Environment For Creating Interactive Web Graphics. *Proc. ACM SIGGRAPH 2003,* ACM Press (2003), 1.
21. Resnick, M., Martin, F., Berg, R., et al. Digital Manipulatives: New Toys to Think With. *Proc. SIGCHI conference on Human Factors in Computing Systems*, ACM Press (1998), 281-287.
22. Rosenbaum, E. Glowdoodle: A Medium for Expressive Inquiry. *Proc. ACM Conference on Creativity and cognition*, ACM Press (2009), 469-470.
23. Schaffer, K., Stern, E., Kim, S. *Math Dance: with Dr. Schaffer and Mr. Stern*. Schaffer, Stern, Kim, 2001.
24. Serra, Michael. *Discovering Geometry: An Investigative Approach, third ed*. Key Curriculum Press, 2003.
25. Tannenbaum, E. Recollections. 1981-present. http://www.et-arts.com/reco.htm/.
26. Turner, J.C., Midgley, C., Meyer, D.K., et al. The Classroom Environment and Students' Reports of Avoidance Strategies in Mathematics: A Multimethod Study. *Journal of Educational Psychology* 94, 1 (2002), 88-106.
27. Willis, K., Lin J.,Mitani, J., Igarishi, T. Spatial Sketch: Bridging Between Movement & Fabrication. *Proc. TEI'10*. ACM Press 2010, 5-12.

Supporting Embodied Exploration of Physical Concepts in Mixed Digital and Physical Interactive Settings

Zeynep Ahmet, Martin Jonsson, Saiful Islam Sumon, Lars Erik Holmquist
Dept. of Communication, Media and IT
Södertörn University
14189 Huddinge
zeynep@tii.se, martin.jonsson@sh.se, saiful.islam.sumon@sh.se, larserik.holmquist@sh.se

ABSTRACT
In this paper findings are presented from a study on how sensor equipped computer game technologies can be used to create tools for educational settings to learn about for example concepts in physics. In a workshop focusing on the concept of gravity, a group of children interacted with an environment consisting of both physical and digital interactive components. We discuss how the mixed digital and physical setting affects the children's coordination and collaboration and their strategies to solve the given assignment. Findings suggest that the embodied nature of the technology create new opportunities for collaboration and that the alignment of the physical and digital parts of the interactive setting is important in order to create a seamless experience that takes advantage of the properties of the respective media.

Author Keywords
Tangible interaction, Embodied learning, Sensor based interaction.

ACM Classification Keywords
H5.m. Information interfaces and presentation (e.g., HCI): Miscellaneous. .

INTRODUCTION
In a recently initiated project, the aim is to investigate how familiar technology can be incorporated in the everyday school environment to support children's learning and creativity when practically exploring various school subjects. One of the goals for the first year of the project has been to introduce science education to learners through the use of specific technology: computer and video games. A great number of educational and edutainment projects have already used video games to teach topics such as physics, math, language arts, etc., using traditional game or computer controls. Recently, however, commercial games have shifted to incorporate gestures and body motion, as exemplified by a variety of games where the player is required to actually perform real-world physical movements to control the game. This includes an array of dancing games, where the player follow a sequence of instructions by dancing on a sensor mat (e.g. *Dance Dance Revolution*); sports games, where the player performs movements mimicking those required in real games of bowling, boxing, tennis, etc. (e.g. *Wii Sports*); and music games, where the player acts out pieces of music by playing on replicas of real instruments (e.g. *Guitar Hero, Rock Band*). This new focus on physicality in video games has had several benefits, both by making the games more socially engaging for a co-located group of players, and by introducing a degree of physicality to an activity that was previously considered unhealthy and inactive. There is even a popular exercise program, *Wii Fit,* which includes a special sensor board to track the player's movements.

In this project, we are using the popular *Wii game controller,* aka *Wii Remote*, manufactured by Nintendo. This piece of commercial hardware has the advantages of being cheap, easy to modify and write software for, and in particular, it includes a very advanced and robust motion sensor (the technical term is accelerometer). However, rather than using the Wiimote as a direct controller for the player's on-screen avatar, as in most popular games, we want to apply the technology to let students explore phenomena related to physics and natural sciences. Thus, by leveraging the sensory capabilities of game controllers that youths already enjoy outside of school, we can introduce physical exploration as a means to engage in learning about phenomena from natural science. Key concepts of physics – work, energy, force, potential energy, kinetic energy, momentum – may be introduced as aspects of the interactive setting that students are exploring. The students will get real-time feedback about how different actions taken with the Wii controller affect various physical measurements. In addition, we can help familiarize students with the practice of scientific experimentation by enabling the use of Wii controllers in students' open-ended exercises.

THEORETICAL AND PEDAGOGICAL BACKGROUND
The importance of physical aspects of interaction is being increasingly acknowledged within the HCI community. This is most evident in notions of embodied interaction and situated conduct in the works of Dourish [1] and Heath and Luff [2]. Issues of physicality, materiality, embodiment,

TEI'11, January 22–26, 2011, Funchal, Portugal.

and social space are also central in research on pervasive computing and tangible interfaces, in which the particular physical manifestation of a computational artifact and its consequences for people's interaction with and through the artifact is commonly brought to discussion [3, 4]. Recent research along these lines suggests a shift away from an information-centric to an action-centric perspective on interaction [5, 6]. These developments indicate how complex cognitive processes are deeply intertwined with and dependent upon our physical bodies and our relations to the material and physical properties of our social world. Thus, new interactive technologies that support mobile, bodily, and social activities beyond the desktop setting enable a shift both in the development of new forms of user interactions, as well as new tools to be used in learning activities.

Learning and tangible artifacts

The theoretical backdrop of our project is in line with the current trend towards conceptualizing cognition and learning as embodied and situated phenomena. This perspective posits that our thinking and knowledge acquisition is intrinsically intertwined and dependent upon the people and artifacts around us and how they mediate the physical world [7, 8]. These perspectives are also central to the research fields of Computer Supported Collaborative Learning (CSCL), which focuses on the role of designed artifacts in people's joint meaning-making [9], and secondly, in current work in CSCW and Ubiquitous Computing that attempts to more closely integrate physical and social reality in interaction with software [1]. From our point of view, CSCL research is not only the study of how people interact and learn with designed artifacts, but also the study and design of the situations in which efficient learning is taking place. Learning situated outside a dedicated learning environment such as the school is often referred to as informal learning. Learning then arises from the activities and interests of individuals or groups and may not even be recognized as learning [10]. Until now, research has paid only limited attention to the artifacts used in informal learning and play situations such as after school centers and homes, nor has much effort been put into the design of such artifacts. An emerging body of research is concerned with educational research as a process of design. Central to this kind of work is that it has transformative agendas, e.g. developing technologies and activities in support of renewed educational situations. Similarly, in research about Interaction Design and Children, an important element has been to design new educational technologies together with children in school settings and to study how children use these technologies for their own learning [11]. This work has lead to the development of e.g. story telling tools, digital libraries, and game programming environments.

Approaches to the design of interactive computer based educational material that explicitly takes the embodied and enactive perspectives on thinking and action into consideration are few. One example of such a representation is tangibles, which lets physical, as well as virtual objects, be a part of the computational system. Tangible approaches to interactive learning may make abstract concepts more concrete and easier to manipulate. It is also argued that since tangible objects simultaneously work as input and output devices, they provide a tighter connection between control and the representation of the underlying computation [12]. In the proposed project we take informal learning situations and the artifacts commonly used in those as the starting point for the design of novel technologies for in-school learning.

Bodily engaging technologies

Our choice of video game controllers as an entry point was made to explicitly address how technologies commonly used in everyday play and leisure practices can be incorporated into educational settings. These technologies are pervasive: for instance, over a quarter (29%) of US children have played with console games before the age of 6 [13]. By integrating elements of video game technologies into our educational curricula, we believe that we can enhance students' interest in their educational activities, materials, and technologies, and, conversely, make them consider the underlying scientific principles that they've learned about whenever they use these video game controllers.

We selected the Nintendo Wii game controller as a platform for our project both because it is very popular with a wide age range of children and because the controller features numerous sensors and actuators that make physics experimentation possible. A main feature of the Wii Remote, or Wiimote, is its motion sensing capability, which allows the user to interact with and manipulate items on screen via movement and pointing through the use of accelerometer and optical sensor technology. This allows the user to make physical actions and gestures with the controller for gameplay, rather than traditional button pushing. Such actions include swinging the controller, making slicing motions, steering, balancing, thrusting, and pointing. [14]. The Wiimote uses the Bluetooth protocol to communicate wirelessly with the Wii game station, which makes it easy to adapt the Wiimote to use with any PC with Bluetooth capability, without any hacking or modification of the Wiimote or the PC—an important factor to adoption and accessibility of our project. In addition, the Wiimote has been designed to interface with additional devices (e.g. the Wii Nunchucks) and also to be housed in a variety of shells (e.g. steering wheels, guitars, tennis rackets) that afford different kinds of motions and gameplay—this will make it easier both to augment the Wiimotes and to incorporate the Wiimote into student-designed experimental apparatuses.

There is currently a wide array of projects investigating the use of the Wii technology in pedagogical settings;

developing the motor skills of preschoolers [15], supporting disabled students in education [16], teaching musical rhythm [17], and, of course, promoting physical activity [18]. Walsh, in a study on the use of Wii technology in educational settings [19], argues that the technology can be useful for example by supporting groups of students with learning disabilities or with a "bodily-kinesthetic" approach to learning. Price et al. [20] also studied the Wii technology in a pedagogical setting and points out that although the technology seemed to facilitate co-located collaboration, the physical distance between point of interaction and visual feedback created issues with respect to representations and coupling.

SUPPORTING KINESTHETIC LEARNING

The findings in this paper are initial results from a close collaboration with a newly started elementary school in the Stockholm region. This ongoing collaboration started in large parts due to their pedagogical planning, their continuous use of technology in the classrooms and their extensive work with learning styles. The school incorporate the research grounded theories originally presented by Dunn & Dunn [21-23] as The Learning Styles Model, which was later on adopted by a Swedish researcher and tested in Swedish school environments [24]. The Learning Styles Model presents over 20 factors that influence the learning process of learners when learning new subject matters. These factors emphasizes the environment (sound, light, temperature, design), emotional (motivations, persistence, structure, responsibility), sociological preferences (learning alone, in pair, group work, team work and in variations) and physiological characteristics (visual, auditory, tactile, kinesthetic, energy levels and mobility needs).

The model cover seven types of learning styles, of which the school have adopted four, namely auditive, visual, tactile and kinesthetic. The general idea is that different persons have different preferences with respect to how they engage in pedagogical activities. A person can thus be described as "auditive", meaning that he or she prefer learning situations where one listen to instructions and information and can also more easily remember things they hear. Similarly, a person can be a "visual" learner, meaning that he or she learn best by looking, drawing and making up pictures in their minds and remember things by connecting information with pictures or using mind maps. Someone being "tactile" would prefer learning situations where you work with your hands, for example by using various tools such as crayons, clay, calculators and scales for manipulating and creating information. Finally a person characterized as primarily "kinesthetic" learn best by incorporating their entire body in the learning process. These persons often have problems sitting still in one place and might prefer dramatizing and learning by doing or acting out. The acknowledgement of the importance of the tactile and kinesthetic dimensions in the learning style model fits well with recent research on tangible user interfaces as described above.

A five weeks field trial was undertaken to understand how the teachers at the school plan and perform its pedagogical planning, how and which subjects are taught, the methods used by the teachers to teach the children and how their work with learning styles is incorporated in their teaching. The field trial showed how the different learning styles were supported by the variations of assignments and individual and teamwork tasks they were given. Children learning best with techniques for auditive and visual styles were greatly helped, as much of the instructions and presentations were done orally and with the use of Smartboards in the classrooms. There were several tools and materials for children needing tactile learning support, as well as several of the subjects including experimentation and paper and clay modeling to simulate different topics they were working on. While the three aforementioned learning styles were easy for the teachers to incorporate in their classroom settings, supporting kinesthetic learning was more challenging. The children would do theater performances of classical children stories or stories related to their subject to perform for their classmates, or assignments where they had to go outside to solve or work in pairs and visualize concepts through whole body movements. However, in comparison to the other three learning styles, this learning style was supported the least. It was also this learning style we decided together with the teachers to focus the project on, as a way of supporting both the children and the teachers in their everyday learning environment. Since science is a subject still not included in the curriculum, we observed a possibility to introduce the subject to the young students and talk about abstract concepts they hadn't discussed yet.

USING WII MOTES TO LEARN ABOUT GRAVITY

The workshop presented in this paper was an experimental study examining how video game technology can be used as a tool for science experiments in elementary school classes. The theme of the workshop was physics and the chosen subject for the day was gravity. Six groups of children with three children in each group (a total of 18 children) took part in the workshop. Each group assignment lasted approximately 20 minutes.

A prototype system was developed consisting of both physical and digital interactive components. The digital representative was a prototype system consisting of a 3D-environment where the users can throw a ball on a wall of boxes by doing a throw-motion with their arm using a Wii Mote (see Figure 1). When the thrown ball hits the wall of boxes the boxes will fall over and tumble to the ground. On the left side of the interface is a scale showing the controlling the gravity in the 3D environment. Next to the scale is a number of planets positioned along the scale according to their respective gravitational force. Depending on where the slider on the scale to the left is placed, the boxes fall according to the set gravitation. At the bottom left is a colored bar that display the force that is applied to the Wii Mote when throwing the ball. In the study setting the application was shown on a large projection screen.

Figure 1. The digital application with the ruler to set the gravity to the left and the ball and boxes in the middle. The bar at the lower left shows the applied force to the ball when throwing it using the will-controller

To complement the digital interface, there was an setup of a physical counterpart. The physical counterpart consisted of a set of boxes similar in shape to the boxes in the prototype system. The boxes were placed on a table situated next to the projected screen. A tennis ball was placed next to the boxes, to be used by the children to throw at and knock down the boxes.

By using a mixed digital and physical setting to explore the concept of gravity, the aim was to investigate how the children would discuss about and around gravity and how they would go about to solve their assignment. As the Nintendo Wii game console is, by our groups of children, associated with games and fun, we were also interesting in understanding just how much the Wii Motes as a piece of game technology would affect their focus and interest on the assignment.

Study setup

The study was performed in a room were only one group at the time was present. Each session began with a short introduction to the concept of gravity, the digital and physical setup, the technology and their assignment. The experiment was explained to the children as a collaborative assignment to solve the question of where on the scale on the graphical user interface the slider should be placed for the gravitational force to be equal to the gravity on Earth. Then of course, Earth was not present among the planets next to the scale. The children were encouraged to examine the gravitational force on earth by mixing between the physical and digital setup. They were also encouraged to take into account the colored bar at the bottom of the graphical user interface, and what that would mean for their results. The entire setting and an example of the interaction is depicted in the series of pictures in Figure 2.

They were then left to experiment freely with the demo and the physical setup as they liked for approximately 10-20 minutes depending on if the group felt they were finished and had an answer to the assignment. Each experiment session followed with a short semi-structured interview with a set of questions about the experiment and the concept of gravity.

Five out of six sessions were documented using a video camera, as was the short semi-structured interviews that followed, during which the children would at times continue hypothesize, experiment and show their conclusions. The sixth group was not included in filming or data analysis by request of the parents to one of the children in that group. After each session, the children were told to keep the experiment a secret from the other class mates so that they would get a fresh chance at their task.

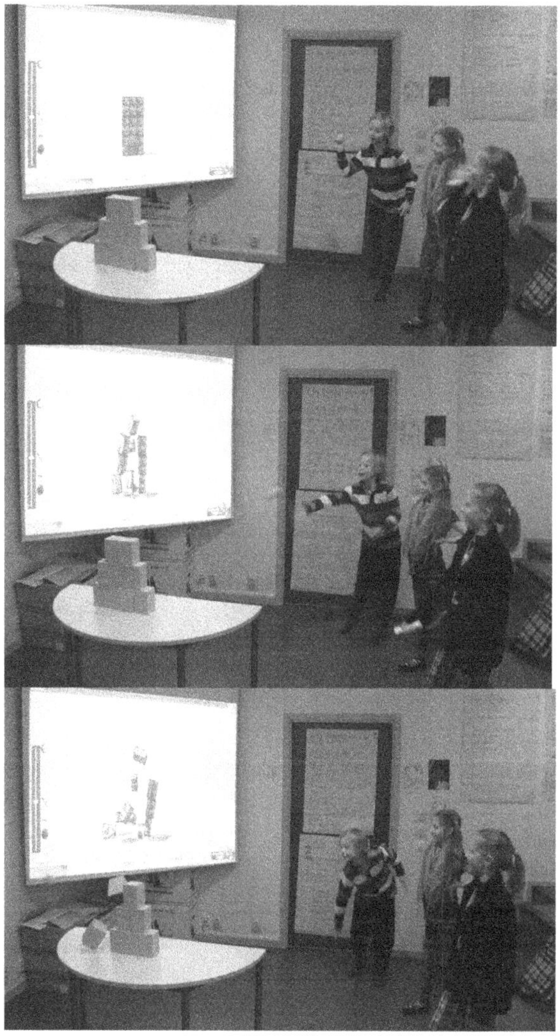

Figure 2. A series of pictures showing a simultaneous interaction with the physical and digital parts of the interactive setting

RESULTS

The video from the five sessions was analyzed looking specifically at:

- The characteristics of the activity (focus on the assignment or the technology through play or problem solving)
- The interplay between the digital and the physical setup (the interaction with the digital/physical setup)
- Collaboration and group dynamics (group collaboration, roles and turn taking).
- Forming conclusions (how the groups arrive at and formulate answers to the given assignment)

Characteristics of the activities

After the introduction to the experiment, all groups began the experiment with an initial 'exploratory mode' where they tested the demo and the physical setup in a rather playful manner, with an exception for the first group. The children in the first group were modest in their testing and discussions throughout their session and seemed very shy when asked any questions. This, we believe, was the result of the presence of the organizers and one of their teacher. As a result, the remaining groups were left alone to experiment freely. For the rest of the groups, the exploratory state included tests of how the extreme points of gravity would effect the boxes in the demo, they would take turns in hitting the physical boxes with the tennis ball to see how many boxes they would hit, and would frequently comment on their own or their friends results and laugh. They would also comment on different positions on the scale for the gravitational force, encourage their friends by saying *"Try that one* [position], *that one was fun!"* or *"Nah, this one is boring, you try another one"*. During this state, and occasionally throughout the game, the children would make up their own game with the demo by i.e. competing on who could hit the most boxes, or who could hit the boxes with enough force to make them fall off the end of the digital platform.

After a while of free exploration of the system, most groups would get back to the assignment and try out different amounts of gravitational force in the demo and how it more or less differed to how the physical boxes fell when throwing a ball at them. This occurred sooner for two of the groups, while the other two had an extended exploratory phase. Even though both the digital and physical setups were available at the same time, most focus would be given to the screen based part of the system. The children would observe over and over again how the boxes fell when swinging the Wii Mote, compared to their own previous testing with the physical setup. They would then report to their class mates if they felt the set gravity was accurate or not, using terms such as *"too much", "too little", "feels good", "doesn't feel good", "not quite right"* or *"I think it's somewhere here"*.

Group three and five began with the experiment after a short while of exploring the setups. These groups would still enjoy playing with the physical and digital setup, but would work together to find an efficient solution to come up with an answer to the task. While they were trying to reach and individual answer, they would discuss their impressions of their finding openly and accept or discard an idea depending on if the demonstrated ideas were accepted by everyone in the group. Often the children in these groups would try to come up with a hypothesis in pairs and simulate it to see if they were accurate or not. While these two groups were quick to start with the experiment, group two and four continued a rather playful style of experimenting. These two groups would, in comparison to the other two, not engage too much in a collective attempt to draw any conclusions, but would discuss briefly between themselves about their own impressions and continue a playful style of testing. The discussions amongst the two groups regarding the experiment would be so briefly, that it was almost difficult to discern any discussions taking place at all to reach an answer. In other words, in comparison to the other two groups, they were operating a more individualistic style of experimentation. This was evident by their discussions at the end of the experiment when one of the organizers asked if they had reached an answer. The children would then talk between themselves about which level of gravitational force they had observed as being the accurate one, test their ideas in order to demonstrate and then give an answer they would all more or less agree on.

Interplay between the digital and physical

During the exploration mode, all groups would try out the digital and physical setup, mostly with little thought of their assignment. But when focus shifted from play to problem solving, the children started to create their own solutions to find the right answer, even several to find the most efficient method for problem solving. The exception was the first group, where the children were quite modest in testing the physical setup at all. Including the introduction, this group only tried the physical setup twice, and the demo once each. This was as previously mentioned a result of the presence of too many bystanders. The rest of the groups soon introduced their own solutions to solving the task. In the second group, the children would try to synchronize themselves in order to observe a similarity between the setups. The child holding the Wii Mote and the child holding the physical tennis ball would count down and try to throw the balls on their respective physical/digital boxes, in order to observe how similar or different the boxes would fall. In the third group, the children considered the formation of the physical boxes to have an impact on their testing. As a result, they tried to "match" the physical and digital setup by placing the physical boxes in a 3 by 3 formation as shown in the demo interface, instead of the pyramid formation arranged by the organizers.

Figure 3. Upper picture showing the initial setting for all groups. Lower picture showing how one group changed the physical setup to make it easier to synchronize the physical and digital actions

The fourth group didn't change anything on the physical setup, but instead focused on keeping the pyramid formation on the boxes before testing their ideas. This group also took more time to explore the demo and playing with the physical setup. The children in the fifth group re-arranged their setting the most in order to solve the task. They re-arranged the physical boxes to a 3 by 3 formation to match the demo interface. After a while, one of the children asked for one of the organizers to help them move the table which the boxes were placed on, right under the screen for the demo (at the beginning of all sessions, the table was placed on the side to make room for the children to test the demo). After a while they would take turns on swinging the Wii Mote with a certain amount of force, and try to mimic the same amount of force when throwing the physical tennis ball on the boxes and estimate how similar the boxes fell in both setups at the set gravity.

Collaboration and group dynamics

There was one significant factor that influenced the children's focus on the assignment, which was the presence or absence of a group leader. In the first group there were barely any discussions among the children resulting in a more or less estimation from their part on the answer to the task. In group two and four, none of the children took on the role as leader. In group two, in comparison to group four, the children were keen on trying out new ideas for solving the task, and the turn taking between who would try out what and discussions in the group were on a calm and joyful level. In group four, the atmosphere was hectic and loud. Even though the turn taking was done frequently, it was merely done whenever the next in line was loud enough to ask for his/her turn. In comparison to group three and five, these two groups were the ones that had a longer exploration phase. With the absence of a leader, coordinating the group, the activities in the groups during the experimenting was unstructured but playful with reflections more towards the end of their session. In group three and five, there was one apparent leader in each group that would structure the activities in their respective groups and introduce changes if the current method for solving the task was unsatisfactory. In group three i.e. the group leader would observe the classmates, and whenever they seemed to play with the setups, he would remind them that they're supposed to solve a task.

C1 - Try again, but higher up [on the gravity scale], ok. There [pointing on the screen], try there.

C2 trying out the suggested level of gravitational force, whereby she tries out and hits a few of the boxes

C3 - Right [C2]. Here, let me try!

C1 – But comp[are]... [breathes out]. We're not doing this because it's fun. [Pause]. We're not doing it to have fun.

C3 - [Swinging the Wii Mote] Hm, perhaps a bit too much gravity

(Discussion in group 3, C1-C3 meaning child 1 to 3)

In group five, the one of the kids would instead interrupt the classmates by giving suggestions on what to try next, or she would just take the Wii Mote or the tennis ball to try out an hypothesis, interrupting the play. Even though the class mates didn't appreciate it every time, they would ease up when it was their turn to test and comment on the hypothesis.

Even though these self-appointed group leaders would take charge every now and then to re-focus the group, the exchange in who got to do what was done in a rather democratic way and without much argument. Everyone would get their turn in testing both setups and give suggestions for the correct answer.

Forming conclusions

After each experiment was done, one of the researchers would conduct a short semi-structured interview, asking questions about what the group had done, if they believed they had an answer to the task and what they had observed while working with the task. While the responses from the first group were modest, the other four groups were keen on discussing and testing their suggestions over and over. The testing and interaction with the system during the semi-structured interview were in general the result of uncertainty regarding their answer. None of the groups presented a single answer at the first question. They would most often give several suggestions and motivate them through different perspectives. In group two, the children were motivating their suggestions by pointing to and discussing the *incorrect* suggestions. They were i.e. absolutely certain that the accurate amount of gravitational force was *not* at the same position as Saturn but close enough. They kept demonstrating the positions on the scale closest to Saturn and kept experimenting until they reached an answer. In group three, the children proposed several positions on the scale, because they had varied ideas on how close each position was to the physical counterpart. When they finally had decided, they motivated the choice by stating why they shouldn't choose any position underneath or above their suggestion. They would also explain by demonstration why certain events occurred in the demo.

C1 demonstrating their answer by showing the position on the scale they've agreed on and testing the demo once again. The ball slightly hits the boxes

C1 - [Laughter] Not enough

R - You mean you hit the ball too loose?

C1 - Yeah

C2 - But if you look, she hit the ball upwards, and the more you lessen the gravity, the more the ball fly upwards. It's the gravity

(Discussion in group 3)

In group four and five, the children had multiple suggestions as well. In group four, the children would i.e. refer to the planets for comparison, stating "it should be more that what is for the moon". In group five, the children would instead solely focus on finding a match between the physical and digital setups.

In all, the children used the exclusion method to reach an answer, while motivating their choices by pointing to either why the nearby positions would be wrong, or how well their chosen position matched reality.

C1 - Can I try this position near Saturn?

C1 received the Wii Mote from C2, starts to test the demo, receives the tennis ball from C3 and test the physical setting. She continues with the demo again

C1 - Yes, around there

C3 - Mm. And it's close to this one [*points to a nearby position to the previous one*]

C1 - Yeah, it's this one

R - It looks the same then

C1 - Yeah, it should be

(Discussion in group 5)

During the semi-structured interview, the children would also take the opportunity to ask questions to the team member about the positions of the planets and if there were actual planets with very little gravity. One of the children even asked why the moon was placed where it was. When the team member explained that it was the simulated gravitational force for the moon shown at that position, she seemed to have just realized why the boxes would take more time to fall.

DISCUSSION AND CONCLUSIONS

From the findings resulting from the workshop with our young participants, we have described a staged setting that not only allows for direct interaction and manipulation with physical and digital material, but also a setting in which experimentation can occur in an open and playful manner. Creating an interactive setting that comprises both experimentation in the physical world as well as experimentation in a simulated world, makes it possible to utilize the different properties of these two worlds. While the physical setup allows for rich sensory experiences and realistic experiments, the digital setting allows for explorations that go beyond what is possible to in the real world. By complementing the simulation with a physical setting that partially overlaps the exploration it also helps to make the simulated experiments more realistic. As have been shown in the study, the children put some effort in aligning the physical world with the digital dito, e.g. by making sure that the boxes were arranged in similar ways in the two settings, and also by rearranging the furniture to minimize the gap between the two experiences. It is thus important to realize that the non-computational parts of an interactive setting can play a crucial role in the interaction. This has been acknowledged in previous studies, e.g. by [6] where the notion of "offline interaction" has been used to describe actions that are not directed towards the interactive system but rather towards other participants or non-computational objects in the setting.

The system setup also seemed to encourage collaboration, for example by making it possible for the kids to work simultaneously on the task at hand and to coordinate actions directed towards the digital system with actions on the physical setup. Finally, all the kids in the study expressed that the exercise was fun. Compared to several other educational settings, there were no right or wrong ways to approach the task. Instead, the system became an instrument for the children to freely explore the concept of gravitational force and what this means when we i.e. are discussing the difference between taking a walk on earth compared to a walk on the moon. For young students just learning about the concepts of physics, a tool for spurring experimentations and discussions would provide ideas and material enough for whole class discussions or debates led by the teacher.

REFERENCES

1. Dourish, P. *Where the Action Is: the foundations of Embodied Interaction*. Massachusetts Institute of Technology, Cambridge, 2001.
2. Heath, C. and Luff, P. *Technology in action*. Cambridge Univ Pr, 2000.
3. Hornecker, E. and Buur, J. *Getting a Grip on Tangible Interaction: A Framework on Physical Space and Social Interaction*. ACM Press, 2006.
4. Klemmer, S. R., Hartmann, B. and Takayama, L. *How bodies matter: five themes for interaction design*. ACM Press, 2006.
5. Fernaeus, Y., Tholander, J. and Jonsson, M. Beyond representations: towards an action-centric perspective on tangible interaction. *International Journal of Arts and Technology*, 1, 3 2008), 249-267.
6. Fernaeus, Y., Tholander, J. and Jonsson, M. Towards a new set of ideals: consequences of the practice turn in tangible interaction. In *Proceedings of the The 2nd international conference on Tangible and embedded interaction* (Bonn, Germany, 2008). ACM
7. Lakoff, G. and Johnson, M. *Philosophy in the Flesh: The Embodied Mind and Its Challenge to Western Thought*. Basic Books, New York, 1999.
8. Säljö, R. *Lärande i praktiken - ett sociokulturellt perspektiv*. Bokförlaget Prisma, 2000.
9. Koschmann, T., Hall, R. and Miyake, N. *CSCL. Carrying Forward the Conversation*. Lawrence Erlbaum Associates, 2001.
10. McGivney, V. *Informal Learning in the Community: A Trigger for Change and Development*. National Institute for Adult Continuing Education, 21 De Montfort Street, Leicester, LE1 7GE, United Kingdom 1999.
11. Druin, A. *The Design of Children's Technology*. Morgan Kaufmann Publishers, 1999.
12. Ullmer, B. and Ishii, H. *Emerging Frameworks for Tangible User Interfaces*. Addison-Wesley, City, 2001.
13. Rideout, V. and Hamel, E. *The media family: Electronic media in the lives of infants, toddlers, preschoolers and their parents*. Menlo Park, CA: The Henry J. Kaiser Foundation 2006.
14. Morgan, M., Butler, M. and Power, M. *Evaluating ICT in education: A comparison of the affordances of the iPod, DS and Wii*, ICT: Providing choices for learners and learning. Proceedings ascilite Singapore 2007.
15. Bryant, J., Akerman, A. and Drell, J. Wee Wii: Preschoolers and Motion-Based Game Play. In *Proceedings of the Annual meeting of the International Communication Association* (Montreal, Quebec, Canada, 2008)
16. Pearson, E. and Bailey, C. Evaluating the potential of the Nintendo Wii to support disabled students in education. *ICT: Providing choices for learning: Proceedings ascilite Singapore 2007*2007).
17. De Bruyn, L., Leman, M. and Moelants, D. Quantifying Children's Embodiment of Musical Rhythm in Individual and Group Settings. In *Proceedings of the The 10 International Conference on Music Perception and Cognition (ICMPC10)* (Sapporo, Japan., 2008)].
18. Graves, L., Stratton, G., Ridgers, N. D. and Cable, N. T. Comparison of energy expenditure in adolescents when playing new generation and sedentary computer games: cross sectional study. *British Medical Journal BMJ*, 2007;335: (22 December)2007), 1282-1284.
19. Walsh, G. Wii can do it: using co-design for creating an instructional game. In *Proceedings of the Proceedings of the 27th international conference extended abstracts on Human factors in computing systems* (Boston, MA, USA, 2009). ACM
20. Price, S., Sheridan, J. G. and Falc, T. P. Action and representation in tangible systems: implications for design of learning interactions. In *Proceedings of the Proceedings of the fourth international conference on Tangible, embedded, and embodied interaction* (Cambridge, Massachusetts, USA, 2010). ACM, [insert City of Publication],[insert 2010 of Publication].
21. Dunn, R. and Dunn, K. *Teaching elementary students through their individual learning styles*. Allyn & Bacon Inc, Boston, 1992.
22. Dunn, R. and Dunn, K. *Teaching secondary students through their individual learning styles: Practical approaches for grades 7-12*. Allyn & Bacon Inc, Boston, 1993.
23. Dunn, R. and DeBello, T. *Improved test scores, attitudes and behaviors in America's schools: Supervisors success stories*. Praeger, Westport, 1999.
24. Boström, L. and Engblom, K. *Från undervisning till lärande*. Brain Books, 1998.

Digital Games for Physical Therapy: Fulfilling the Need for Calibration and Adaptation

Luc Geurts[1,3], Vero Vanden Abeele[1,2], Jelle Husson[1], Frederik Windey[1], Maarten Van Overveldt[1], Jan-Henk Annema[2], Stef Desmet[1]

[1]e-Media Lab, Group T – Leuven Engineering College, (Association K.U.Leuven)
A.Vesaliusstraat 13, 3000 Leuven, Belgium
{luc.geurts;vero.vanden.abeele;jelle.husson;frederik.windey;
maarten.van.overveldt;stef.desmet}@groept.be
[2]CUO, IBBT/K.U.Leuven – Parkstraat 45, 3000 Leuven, Belgium
janhenk.annema@soc.kuleuven.be
[3]ESAT, K.U.Leuven – Kasteelpark Arenberg 10, 3001 Heverlee, Belgium

ABSTRACT
With the advent of computer games involving the movement of the player's whole body or body parts, an opportunity arises to develop games for people with motor disabilities. In this paper we present four minigames developed for people suffering from spasticity and loss of motor control. We thereby focus on the input devices, sensor signal processing and mapping of players' actions on events in the game. In order to adapt the game to the player's motor skills and goals, specific attention should be paid to calibration procedures and adjustable parameters. We illustrate how this can be done and simultaneously, we demonstrate the feasibility for the development of digital games for physical therapy with currently available commercial input devices.

Author Keywords
Games for physical therapy, Mapping of sensor data to game events

ACM Classification Keywords
H.5.2 [Information Interfaces and Presentation]: User Interfaces---input devices and strategies

General Terms
Algorithms, Design

INTRODUCTION
In the past decade, there has been an apparent shift in the way computer games are controlled: from classic game controllers with joysticks and buttons to controllers including sensors like accelerometers, gyro sensors, webcams, IR cameras, microphones and touch screens. Instead of fine motor control skills with hands and fingers, players need to move their arms, legs, head, or their whole body in order to play a game. Well-known commercial examples are Nintendo's Wii remote, Sony's EyeToy, and Microsoft's Kinect. Many games have been successfully developed for the consumer market, in other words, for normal people looking for fun, active entertainment. However, this evolution has also opened opportunities for developing games for people with motor disabilities. Tiresome exercises that are often needed to recover from injury or to (partly) overcome the limitations of motor disorders, can now be incorporated in computer games, thereby offering a more motivating environment.

TEI'11, January 22–26, 2011, Funchal, Portugal.

Target group: spasticity
This paper presents the development of four minigames that were especially designed for people with motor disabilities, and more specifically spasticity. Spasticity is a motor disorder defined by involuntary muscle contractions, due to lesions in the central nervous system, that regulates and coordinates muscle tone [14]. It is a symptom of a number of conditions such as cerebral palsy, Multiple Sclerosis (MS), spinal cord injury and acquired brain injuries including stroke. Spasticity can result in uncoordinated gait, stiff body posture and shortening of range of limb movement.

Games for physical therapy
The first line treatment for these types of motor disorders is physical therapy, focusing on stretching and strengthening of muscles. These exercises have the ultimate goal of maintaining and/or increasing the range of motion, preventing deformities and contractures, increasing muscle strength and enhancing coordination of movements, in order to maximize comfort and optimize mobility of the patient.

As with any therapy, success depends for a large part upon the dedication of the patient and his/her motivation to actively partake in the physical exercises. These factors determine the quality of the exercises and augment the quantity of physical therapy. Although patients often look forward to spending time with the therapist [2], the actual motivation for executing repetitive, tiresome, and boring exercises is not always present. Therefore, combining these physical exercises with the immediate and intrinsic motivation associated with a game [15] can be beneficial.

In this paper, we report on the development of four such minigames that can be used during therapy sessions. These games aim to extend the player's range of motion, and to increase their ability to make controlled movements. Additionally, we focus on how to ensure that proper calibration and adaptation accommodates a wide variety of players. When designed properly, these computer games will result in the improvement of the quality of life of the players.

Related work

During the past few years, games for physical therapy have gained increasing success, perhaps inspired by the Wii console, its Wii remote and its balance board. Indeed, the current commercial sensors and input devices, open source software libraries and development kits, have lowered the threshold for designing physical games. Nevertheless, designing games that map the 'physical exercise' to a 'fun goal' is not a straightforward matter. Several research projects have taken a similar endeavor of designing physical games.

Burke et al. [5] developed several games with webcams and Wii remotes for people recovering from stroke, and illustrated the importance of meaningful play and challenge. Decker et al. [8] proposed a game with the Wii remote as pointing device for wrist rehabilitation. Other researchers developed games for therapeutic purposes with other input devices, such as haptic gloves [12,13], robotic devices [7] and pen-like haptic devices [4].

Perhaps, most relevant to our work is that of Alankus et al. [1] who developed minigames for stroke rehabilitation, for use at home. As input devices they used standard Wii remotes and webcams. Their games show some similarities with the games presented in this paper. One of their conclusions was the need for the games to be adaptable to the player's abilities and goals. This paper specifically addresses the issue of adaptability and illustrates how this can be implemented.

With this research project, we aim to build on the lessons learned from previous research projects and contribute to the growing body of knowledge of game design for physical therapy. More specifically, we developed games to treat spasticity, for use in therapy sessions. In this paper we focus on the design and implementation of the actual interaction. We describe how the sensor data are *calibrated* and mapped to events in the game. Additionally, a detailed description is given of how we ensured that the therapist can *adapt* the parameters of these mapping algorithms, in order to fit the game to the player's abilities and the therapist's goals. However, we will start by summarizing our design method and motivating why calibration and adaptability are key factors of games for physical therapy.

DESIGN METHOD

In order to design and develop the games, we relied on a participatory design method over a period of 18 months, involving three physical therapists and four occupational therapists from four different institutions: two schools for special education, one clinic for Multiple Sclerosis patients, and one centre that organizes leisure activities for people with mental and physical impairments. User tests were performed in the institutions, with therapists and their clients. In total 21 persons from the target group participated in the design and evaluation process: thirteen children between 9 and 13 years old, three younger adults of 16, 25 and 37, and five older adults between 50 en 69. The etiology of the children and the younger adults varied substantially, but all suffered from limited motor control, caused by disorders such as cerebral palsy, spinal cord injury, or hereditary muscle deterioration ailments. The older adults were all Multiple Sclerosis patients.

1. Workshops

At the start of the design process, we organized workshops with therapists and their clients during which we played commercially available games. Among the games that were tested were Wii Sports, Mario Kart, Sonic and Mario at the Olympics, Dancing Stage: hottest party, Wii Fit and Rockband on Nintendo's Wii console, and the standard EyeToy games on the PS2 console. During these workshops we discussed the appropriateness of games and the observed player motions for physical therapy.

During the next stage, we discussed with therapists which movements they would like to train using games. The goal was to translate these movements to game actions, in such a way that correct movements are rewarded in the game. Rather than adapting existing games we chose to create new games, partly through brain storm sessions with patients and therapists. We decided to design and develop four different minigames that train on different muscle groups and typical patterns for spasticity.

2. Low-fidelity prototypes

For each minigame, first a low-fidelity (lo-fi) prototype was developed and tested. The focus of such a lo-fi prototype is on the monitoring of the players movements and the mapping to game events, such as the actions performed by a game character. Appropriate sensors were chosen and calibration procedures and signal processing algorithms were developed and tested. Graphics were kept simple (see Figure 4 and Figure 6) and no cognitive challenges were included. With the low-fidelity prototypes we checked whether the games evoked correct movements. Many parameters of these prototypes were adjustable, and the purpose was to find out which parameters are the most relevant, and what their range should be.

3. High-fidelity prototypes

The high-fidelity (hi-fi) prototypes contain fully worked out graphics and additional cognitive challenges (see Figure 1 and Figure 5). As this paper focuses on the interaction between player and game, which was user tested with the lo-fi prototypes, we will not further detail the high-fidelity prototypes. However, as two games are already developed as hi-fi prototypes, relevant results will show up in this paper.

RESULTS – GAME REQUIREMENTS

From the first workshops, we found that existing commercial games are not suitable for therapy sessions, which is in line with other studies [9,10]. In general, these games are designed for 'normal' people not suffering from motor disabilities. Both gross and fine motor skills are needed to play these games successfully. Most of the players from our target group lack the skills to even finish the basic levels. The required speed and accuracy of execution is often too demanding. A related study emphasized the need for designing for slow fun for this target group suffering from spasticity [17].

We found that not only the difference in motor skills between normal players and the target group is substantial, but also the variation of the motor skills within the target group should be taken into account. Even intra-individual differences can be immense, e.g., patients with Multiple Sclerosis can suffer from relapses where performance temporarily deteriorates and necessary adjustments should be made easily. Therefore, each game should be adaptable to the current potential of the player and to the goals defined by the therapist. This was also concluded in the study of Alankus et al. [1].

Calibration

In order to optimize the 'fit' of the game to the patient, and taking differences in morphology of patients into account, a thorough but quick calibration procedure is indispensible [2]. Its main purpose is to measure the abilities of the player, such as the furthest desired positions of the limbs that are played with. Typically, the therapist asks or helps the player to take a certain pose, and the corresponding sensor values are measured. In addition, reference positions are taken and 'recorded' by the sensors. The calibration also ensures that player and sensors are positioned right such that all relevant player's actions can be monitored.

Adaptability

Additionally, game mechanics such as speed and accuracy should be easily adjustable and designed to accommodate for a wide range of skills. Each game algorithm is controllable by several parameters that can be adjusted by therapists. These parameters can be related to the mapping of user actions to game events, such as the sensitivity of the game character's motions to the player's motions, or are unrelated to this mapping, such as the allowed time to complete a task. Correct settings of these parameters will elicit a (motivating) flow experience in the game, forcing the player to perform at the edge of his/her potential, while successful play is still possible.

Game	Physical exercise	Sensors
Catching Dishes	Stretching and bending of the arms	Webcam
Collecting Eggs	Maintaining balance standing on one leg	Wii remote & MotionPlus
Preparing Recipes	Controlled head movements	Wii remote (IR camera)
Flying Dragons	Transfer of weight and balancing when seated	Balance board

Table 1. The four minigames with corresponding physical exercises and used sensor technologies.

Equipment and Development Tools

In order to promote the actual use of the game in a therapeutic context in a later stage, additional requirements are imposed. The equipment should be relatively inexpensive, easy to acquire, accurate and reliable. Therefore we opted for a standard laptop (Dell Latitude E6500) running Windows 7 as 'game console'. Software is developed using Unity's game engine in conjunction with MS Visual Studio. We chose commercially available input devices, such as the game controllers of Nintendo's Wii console, and a webcam. The Nintendo controllers include the Wii remote, from which we use the accelerometer data and the data from the infrared camera, the Wii MotionPlus, measuring angular rate around three axes, and the Balance Board, measuring force with four strain gauges. To communicate with the these controllers, the WiimoteLib library is used [16]. For the camera, we chose the built-in webcam of the laptop. We developed a plug-in for Unity, using OpenCV, to read out the camera's data.

RESULTS – THE FOUR MINIGAMES

Table 1 gives an overview of the four minigames, indicating the physical exercises and the sensor technologies that are used. In the next subsections we will describe the four minigames with focus on the analysis of the sensor data, the calibration procedure, the mapping to game events, the algorithm parameters that can be adjusted by the therapist and the observations from the user tests.

Minigame 1: Catching Dishes

Description

The first minigame (see Figure 1) requires players to stretch their arms in order to catch flying dishes at the edge of the screen and put them on a pile in the middle. The physical exercise focuses on the extension of the elbow and exo-rotation of the shoulder. Each dish is thrown quickly by a character in the center of the screen and then remains at its end position during an adjustable time. This way the player

Figure 1 The minigame 'Catching Dishes' is controlled by the player's hand covered by a colored cloth. The player sees and controls a virtual hand on the screen (top left) to catch a dish (right to the virtual hand).

has enough time to reach for the dish, so a slow motion will suffice. Once a dish is caught, the player has to move his/her hand to the middle, in order to release to dish. This way the repetitive movement of bending and stretching the arm is continuously encouraged.

Analysis of sensor data

The webcam in front of the player is used to track the position of his/her hand. The player wears a colored cloth on his/her hand, to allow the software to track its position. The color tracking algorithm is based on the CAMSHIFT algorithm, for which an implementation exists in OpenCV [3,11]. We developed a plug-in for Unity, using OpenCV, that returns the <x,y> coordinates of the center of the colored cloth for each frame that is generated.

Calibration

During calibration, the camera data are directly shown on the screen (see Figure 2). First, the therapist adjusts the position of the camera and the player, ensuring that the player is always in view of the camera, also when his/her arm is stretched fully upwards or sidewards. Secondly, the color of the colored cloth is analyzed by the CAMSHIFT algorithm. Next, the therapist drags a green circle, using the mouse, to the position of the player's shoulder (Figure 2). Finally, the player is asked to stretch his/her arm to the side

Figure 2 Calibration screen of Catching Dishes. The green circle has to be dragged to the shoulder position. The green circle with the hand indicates how far the arm can be stretched.

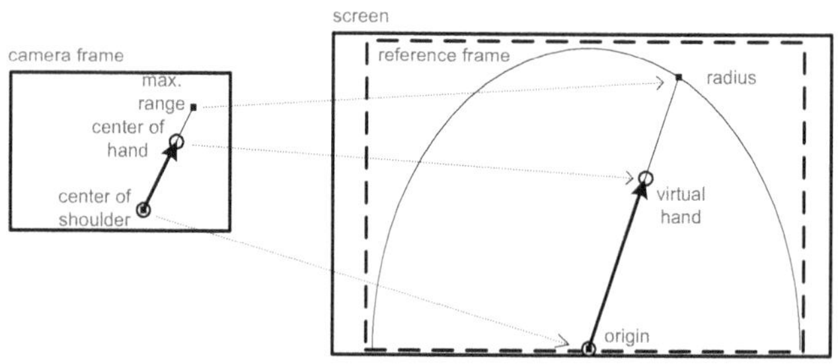

Figure 3 Mapping of the camera data (position of shoulder, hand and maximum range) to the position of the virtual hand on the screen.

as far as possible. The distance between the measured position of the hand and the shoulder defines a radius corresponding to the range in which the player's hand can move.

Mapping to game events

During the game, the position of the player's hand is continuously measured, and it defines the end point of a vector with its origin at the position of the shoulder (see Figure 3). For the mapping of the virtual hand on the screen, a reference frame with the same aspect ratio as the camera is used that covers as much of the viewable screen as possible. Within this reference frame, a half ellipse is defined that maximally fills this reference frame. Dishes will always appear at the edge of this ellipse. Now, the origin of the aforementioned vector is mapped to the bottom center point of the reference frame. The direction of the vector is preserved, and its length is scaled such that the maximum range, as measured during calibration, corresponds to the radius of the ellipse at that angle. The motivation for this scaling of the camera data is that the whole screen is used, even if the player has only a limited range to stretch his/her arm. Intermediate user tests revealed that a player has a tendency to stretch an arm further, if a dish appears closer to the border of the screen.

Adjustable parameters

A dish is caught when there is a collision between the virtual hand and a zone around the dish. The zone around the dish is a sphere in 3D space which radius can be set by the therapist (see the green circle around the plate in Figure 1). This way the accuracy of the desired position of the hand can be adjusted to the player's abilities. A second parameter is the time the player has to catch the dish. During this time interval the dish will remain at its end position. On a separate screen the therapist can also select in which zones the dishes will appear.

Observations

User tests on the lo-fi prototype and the hi-fi prototype revealed that the software was able to accurately track the hand, even if the player moved rather fast. However, care should be taken that the player's arm is never outside the camera's view as this disrupts the tracking. Therefore, in the final version a loss of view will be indicated by a warning on the screen, and the request to point with the hand to the camera.

The difficulty is set by defining the radius of sphere around the dish that has to be entered by the virtual hand, and the time interval the dish can be caught. For any player, adjustments could be made such that the game was playable, i.e. that the players could catch at least some of the dishes. The therapists also confirmed that this is an appropriate way to adapt the game to the player.

Minigame 2: Collecting Eggs

Description

This minigame requires players to remain in balance standing on one leg in order to collect eggs by jumping from mountain top to mountain top (Figure 4). The game character will start a jump once the inclination of the player's thigh is above an adjustable threshold, and it will keep on flying as long as this threshold is exceeded. Once the inclination is below this threshold the character will land automatically on the nearest mountain top. The player collects eggs by landing on each mountain top supporting an egg.

Analysis of sensor data

A Wii remote with the MotionPlus extension is connected to the thigh of the leg to be lifted. In order to measure the inclination, only the accelerometer data of the Wii remote are used. The gyro sensor data of the MotionPlus are used to detect the direction in which the knee was moved during lifting: to the right, to the left, or forward, allowing the player to change direction (only in the hi-fi prototype).

Calibration

In order to calibrate the system, the player is first asked to stand on both legs. The inclination of the Wii remote is then measured, and will be used as the reference position. In this way, the Wii remote's y-axis – the axis along the length of the device – does not need to be aligned with the gravity vector at that position. Next, the therapist will ask the player to lift his/her leg to a desired position, and the inclination will be measured again. The threshold value that will be used during game play is an adjustable percentage of the difference between the measured value at the lifted position and the reference position.

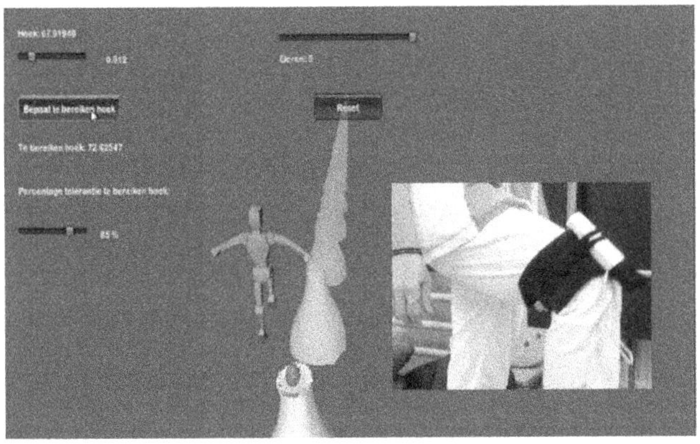

Figure 4 The minigame Collecting Eggs is played with a Wii remote on the upper leg. When lifted high enough, the game character will jump from mountain top to mountain top.

Mapping to game events

As mentioned above, this threshold should be exceeded to start a jump and keep on flying. In order to enrich the interaction, the angle of the inclination is also mapped to three other game events. First, the speed of the character will increase with higher angles. Consequently, there is the reward of faster play if the thigh is lifted higher. Second, the height of flying is proportional to the angle. Third, the arms of the character are more spread with a higher angle. Although these three additional mappings do not result in a higher game score, they improve the player's impression to have full control.

Adjustable parameters

Besides setting the threshold, the therapist can also adjust the difficulty level by changing the distance between mountain tops supporting eggs. Increasing this distance means that the player has to stay in balance for a longer time, making the game more difficult.

Observations

The physical exercise of standing on one leg (outside a game environment) is rather boring. With this minigame, it was apparent though how long the players could persevere playing the lo-fi prototype. This confirms the added value of a game in a therapeutic setting. Most participants could play the game, even with more difficult parameter settings. For one player the game was not suitable: he could lift his foot only a few centimeters from the floor, making it difficult to discriminate between a lifted leg and a supporting leg.

The therapists suggested possible extensions of the minigame. By attaching Wii remotes on lower leg and foot, a so called *triple flex* – a stretching of foot, knee and hip – could be monitored.

Minigame 3: Preparing Recipes

Description

This minigame requires players to sit still and move their head in order to select ingredients from the left and right side of the screen and throw them in the cooking pot in the middle (see Figure 5). The physical exercise focuses on a rotation of the head in a horizontal plane and/or bending forward of the neck. It is crucial that the head moves slowly and accurately in order to control the ingredient's position.

Analysis of sensor data

A Wii remote is connected to a hat worn by the patient. The infrared camera is used as a pointing device, just as in the standard Wii games. The LED-bar is positioned right above or below the screen. The coordinates of the LEDs in the

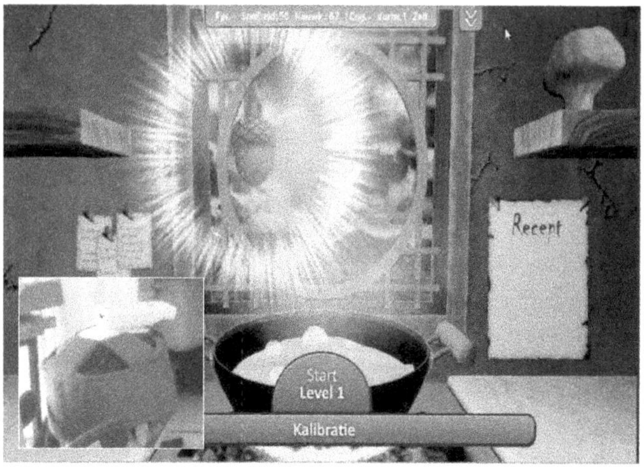

Figure 5 Preparing Recipes is played with the Wii remote on the head. The player controls the magic selection circle to catch ingredients and put them in the cooking pot.

camera frame determine the point on the screen the Wii remote is pointing at.

Calibration

For this game, the therapist only needs to ensure that the player and the hat are positioned right so that any position on the screen can be pointed at by moving the head.

Mapping to game events

Through the Wii remote, the player controls a 'magic' selection circle on the screen. When an ingredient is 'caught' by the circle, it will move along with the circle, as long as this movement is not too fast. The greatest challenge for this game was to find a way to force the player to move slowly. If the player moves too quickly or shaky, e.g. due to a spasm, the ingredient should drop and be caught again. This was solved by calculating for each new frame the new position of the ingredient according to the formula:

$$pos_{new} = pos_{old} + (pos_{target} - pos_{old}) * drag$$

in which pos_{new} is the new position of the ingredient, pos_{old} the previous position, pos_{target} the target position which equals the center position of the selection circle, and *drag* is an adjustable parameter. If the new position is not within the selection circle, the ingredient will drop.

Adjustable parameters

The *drag* factor, a scalar, plays a crucial role in the adjustment to the patient's skills. If this factor is 1, the ingredient is always at the center of the selection circle, at whatever speed this circle is moving. A small value increases the likelihood that the ingredient will fall out the circle in the new frame. So, at small *drag* values the player has to move very slowly. The second adjustable parameter is the size of the circle. A smaller size means that more accurate and controlled movements are necessary.

Figure 6 Flying Dragons: By shifting weight on the Balance Board, the player controls the dragon that has to fly through the rings.

Observations

The participants of the user tests were all dyskinetic cerebral palsy patients, since this game was specifically designed for this subgroup. Keeping their head in a stable position in the middle is very challenging for most of them. Occasionally, the therapist aided the player in maintaining a correct posture, e.g. by stretching the neck. In order to keep the game playable, the drag factor needed to be maximized, and a large radius of the selection circle was needed. However, therapists were very pleased observing that the players kept their head in a middle position during the game, which is already a successful result. Since these types of movements are trainable, the therapists believe that smaller parameter values could be used after sufficient practice time.

Minigame 4: Flying dragons

Description

This minigame requires players to change their balance in a seated position in order to fly on a dragon through the rings on the screen (see Figure 6). The physical exercise relies on a transfer of weight and balancing of the center of gravity, thereby strengthening muscles of the back and abdomen. The game character sits on a dragon and the player steers to left or right by changing his/her balance to left or right, and steers up and down by changing his/her balance forward or backward. The dragon's speed is adjustable, but remains constant during the game.

Analysis of sensor data

As input device the Wii Balance Board is chosen, which measures force in four positions using strain gauges. The WiimoteLib library returns the center of gravity of the forces on the balance board.

Calibration

Prior to playing the game, the player is asked to sit as closely as possible in an upright position in the middle of the balance board. The measured center of gravity will be used as the reference position during the game.

Mapping to game events

The deviations from the reference position in left/right direction (*dev.x*) and in forward/backward direction (*dev.y*) are mapped linearly to the rotational speeds (*yaw* and *pitch*) of the dragon in the 3D world, according the formulae:

$$yaw = dev.x * sensitivity$$
$$pitch = dev.y * sensitivity$$

Adjustable parameters

The *sensitivity* factor determines the difficulty level. As revealed by the formulae, a high accuracy is needed for precise control when this factor is high. The radius of the rings can also be adjusted by the therapist, increasing the necessary accuracy. The last factor that can be adjusted by the therapist is the dragon's speed. The therapists thus has three parameters to make adjustments to the player's skills and goals.

Observations

The therapists confirmed that playing the game was a good exercise, since the muscles have to remain tense during a certain time. Holding this tension is a challenge for most people from our target group, and the longer it has to be done, the more fatiguing it is. The slow action also gives enough time to react to the game events. Adjustments could be made for any player to make the game playable. The therapists also suggested to enable simplifications, such as the ability to only steer left/right or up/down.

DISCUSSION AND FUTURE WORK

Input devices

In order to promote the use of these physical minigames by therapists, we opted for commercially available input devices, such as the Wii controllers and a standard webcam. The user tests revealed that the reliability and the accuracy of these devices are sufficient for our applications. Obviously, the limitations of these devices were taken into account when designing the games. The most important limitations were the difficulty of measuring rotations in a horizontal plane with accelerometers and gyro sensors, and the limited viewing angle of the Wii remote's IR camera (for the Preparing Recipes game specifically). It is likely that more advanced input devices, such as a 3D camera, will enable a more detailed registration of the player's movement. However, the current high cost of hardware and middleware would impede widespread use.

Adaptability

The report of Alankus et al. [1] included several suggestions to improve the quality of digital games for people with motor disabilities, such as the importance of calibration and the importance of direct and natural mapping. The authors also included that it should be ensured that the full range of motions is used and that therapists are needed to determine the difficulty. We believe that these 'guidelines' are taken into account in our games. Through testing the lo-fi prototypes, the calibration procedure was optimized. The tests also revealed which parameters should be adjustable by the therapists and what range should be targeted at. Often initial settings still resulted in a too difficult game, again illustrating the importance of adaptability and of user testing.

A drawback of adaptability and calibration is that it takes time before an exercise can start. Since therapy sessions last typically around 30 minutes, including transportation to and from the therapy room, these adjustments should only take a few minutes. In case of our minigames, this requirement was always met. Calibrating and defining the parameters only takes 2 or 3 minutes.

Further steps

The next step is the development of four high-end minigames, including fully worked out graphics and menus, and cognitive challenges. Depending on the game, this challenge relies on e.g. visual discrimination, visual memory, spatial perception and mental rotation skills. Allowing the therapist to set these physical and cognitive challenges individually, allows for balancing a wide range of physical impairments and mental disabilities, ensuring everyone can experience flow and have fun [6]. The games will also be extended with an on-line database that logs all activities and performance of the users. The high-end games will be used during one year in all interested institutions, by the therapists during their therapy sessions. These ultimate user tests will allow a thorough assessment both by players and therapists and a thorough evaluation of the users' experience.

CONCLUSION

We presented four minigames designed and developed especially for people with motor disabilities, and illustrated the feasibility of using commercially available input devices as game controllers. User tests revealed that a reliable and natural mapping can be obtained. It is important however that the game parameters can be adjusted to the player's skills and development goals. For each minigame we illustrated how proper calibration and proper adjustment of the mapping of user actions into game events help to achieve this goal. We hope that this paper can inspire and help other developers to develop novel computer games for people with motor disabilities.

ACKNOWLEDGMENTS

This work is part of the Theraplay project, a TETRA funded research project by IWT –Flanders (80135). We like to thank all participating therapists and children of Dominiek Savio, MS Centrum, Windekind, and 't Balanske for their cooperation.

REFERENCES

1. Alankus, G., Lazar, A., May, M., and Kelleher, C. Towards customizable games for stroke rehabilitation. *Proceedings of the 28th international conference on Human factors in computing systems*, ACM (2010), 2113-2122.
2. Annema, J., Verstraete, M., Vanden Abeele, V., Desmet, S., and Geerts, D. Video games in therapy: a therapist's perspective. *Proceedings of the 3rd International Conference on Fun and Games*, ACM Press (2010).
3. Bradski, G. Computer Vision Face Tracking For Use in a Perceptual User Interface. *Intel Technology Journal*, Q2 (1998).
4. Broeren, J., Bjorkdahl, A., Claesson, L., et al. Virtual rehabilitation after stroke. *Studies in Health Technology and Informatics 136*, (2008), 77-82.
5. Burke, J.W., McNeill, M., Charles, D., Morrow, P., Crosbie, J., and McDonough, S. Serious Games for Upper Limb Rehabilitation Following Stroke. *Proceedings of the 2009 Conference in Games and Virtual Worlds for Serious Applications*, IEEE Computer Society (2009), 103-110.
6. Chen, J. Flow in games (and everything else). *Commun. ACM 50*, 4 (2007), 31-34.
7. Colombo, R., Pisano, F., Mazzone, A., et al. Design strategies to improve patient motivation during robot-aided rehabilitation. *Journal of NeuroEngineering and Rehabilitation 4*, , 3-3.
8. Decker, J., Li, H., Losowyj, D., and Prakash, V. *Wiihabilitation: Rehabilitation of Wrist Flexion and Extension Using a Wiimote-Based Game System.* Rutgers University, 2009.
9. Deutsch, J.E., Borbely, M., Filler, J., Huhn, K., and Guarrera-Bowlby, P. Use of a low-cost, commercially available gaming console (Wii) for rehabilitation of an adolescent with cerebral palsy. *Physical Therapy 88*, 10 (2008), 1196-1207.
10. Flynn, S., Palma, P., and Bender, A. Feasibility of using the Sony PlayStation 2 gaming platform for an individual poststroke: a case report. *Journal of Neurologic Physical Therapy: JNPT 31*, 4 (2007), 180-189.
11. Hewitt, R. Seeing With OpenCV, Part 3: Follow that Face! *SERVO Magazine*, 2007, 36-40.
12. Huber, M., Rabin, B., Docan, C., et al. PlayStation 3-based tele-rehabilitation for children with hemiplegia. *Virtual Rehabilitation, 2008*, (2008), 105-112.
13. Jack, D., Boian, R., Merians, A.S., et al. Virtual reality-enhanced stroke rehabilitation. *IEEE Transactions on Neural Systems and Rehabilitation Engineering: A Publication of the IEEE Engineering in Medicine and Biology Society 9*, 3 (2001), 308-318.
14. Lance, J. What is spasticity? *Spasticity: Disordered Motor Control. Chicago Yearbook Medical Publishers*, (1980).
15. Malone, T.W. and Lepper, M.R. Making learning fun: A taxonomy of intrinsic motivations for learning. *Aptitude, learning, and instruction 3*, (1987), 223-253.
16. Peak, B. WiimoteLib. http://www.brianpeek.com/blog/pages/wiimotelib.aspx
17. Vanden Abeele, V., Geurts, L., Husson, J., et al. Designing Slow Fun! Physical Therapy Games to Remedy the Negative Consequences of Spasticity. *Proceedings of the 3rd International Conference on Fun and Games*, ACM Press (2010).

Exploring Mixed Reality Robot Gaming

David Robert
MIT Media Laboratory
20 Ames Street, E15-468, Cambridge, MA
lifeform@media.mit.edu

Ryan Wistort, Jesse Gray, Cynthia Breazeal
MIT Media Laboratory
20 Ames Street, E15-468, Cambridge, MA
{rwistort, jg, cynthiab} @media.mit.edu

ABSTRACT
We describe an interactive, mixed reality (MR) robot gaming platform in which the user controls a tangible, physically embodied character. Miso, an expressive tele-operated robot plays with its virtual peers by passing a graphical object back and forth seamlessly through an integrated physical and virtual environment. Special emphasis is placed on the importance of maintaining perceptual continuity by closely coupling the simulated world's physical laws to our material reality. We present our implemented MR robot gaming environment and describe the design of an interreality portal at the boundary of the physical and virtual realities.

Author Keywords
Robot gaming, Blended Reality, interreality portals

ACM Classification Keywords
H5.m. Information interfaces and presentation (e.g., HCI): Miscellaneous. I.2.9. Robotics

General Terms
Design.

INTRODUCTION
Mixed Reality (MR) encompasses and merges both real and virtual worlds to produce new environments where physical and digital objects coexist and interact in real-time. Exploring the critical design parameters of creating a simple robot video game that effectively extends MR and spans the continuum from the fully physical to the fully virtual can yield insights for designers of novel gaming platforms. As blending reality becomes more commonplace for recreational, educational and other endeavors this paper focuses on methods for maintaining cognitive continuity throughout the user interface. If done effectively, the MR boundary window becomes transparent to the user.

TEI'11, January 22–26, 2011, Funchal, Portugal.

RELATED WORK
Recently, several projects combining Mixed Reality and robots have been described in the literature. In *Physical Interfaces for Tabletop Games* Leitner and Haller describe a collaborative tabletop, mixed-reality game.[5] Their system uses a small robot that can be moved with augmented fiducial markers across the table's surface area. Similarly, Calife et al explore the influence of virtual objects on real objects.[1] Our approach shares many similarities with these projects but extends the game play context onto a larger space on the floor.

Justine Casell's shared reality concept introduced a novel interface in which objects are passed from the human user to a conversational agent in the virtual world.[3] Our work focuses on a similar type of transfer between the physical and digital but places emphasis on the kinetic continuity of objects transiting over the interreality boundary. Gintautas and Hubler present experimental data detailing the transition from an uncorrelated dual reality state to a mixed reality state system by adjusting simulation parameters of the virtual world to match those of the real world.[3] Our project aims to establish a simple superphysics model that models a singular, fused game play context across the interreality boundary.

THE SYSTEM
Input
The user operates a wireless joystick traditionally used as a game controller. Incoming button presses and joystick movements are parsed by a computer running the robot control subsystem. The simple, open loop control system translates the user's input into serial commands output to the robot's motor controllers thus actuating movement. To ensure the robot is untethered and free to move within the play space, it's connected to the simulation framework by an RF serial link facilitated by Xbee radio transceivers. In tandem, a 3D motion capture system localized the robot and updates both the graphics engine and the simulation software with live 3D coordinates using a custom inter-application communication protocol, IRCP (inter-robot-communication-protocol).

Robot
Miso [Fig.1], a small, socially-expressive and tele-operated mobile robot represents the game player's tangible character and engages in cooperative play with its' on-screen counterparts. Using two servo-controller motors, the

robot can translate and rotate simultaneously in response to the user's joystick commands. Miso is a third-generation robot created as an exploration into realizing animated characters embedded in the physical world.

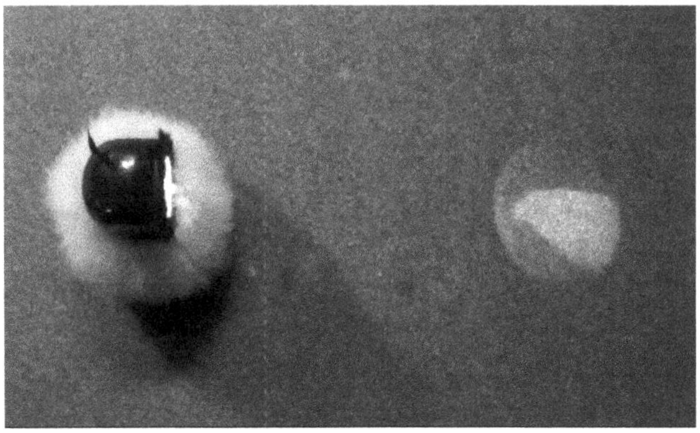

Figure 1. Miso robot, the game player

Hybrid Spaces

A rectangular, physical floor space measuring approximately ten feet long by five feet wide serves as a hybrid tangible augmented reality game play space and human-robot interaction area. An affixed and carefully aligned ceiling mounted projector covers the carpeted floor area with sparse, real-time 3D graphics output from Touch, the integrated graphics engine.[6] At the far end of this space a plasma screen computer monitor measuring approximately five feet wide by three feet tall is floor-mounted perpendicular to the ground. The width of the projected area matches the width of the precisely aligned computer monitor fluidly negotiating the boundary between the physical (floor space) and the virtual (on-screen graphics). Small reflective dots placed on the robot are used in conjunction with the motion capture system to localize and track the robot's movement through the Augmented Reality(AR) physical play space.

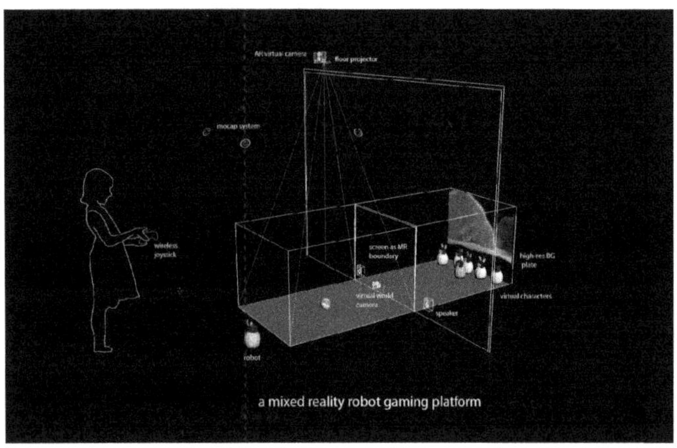

Figure 2. Play context modeled as singular, fused reality

C6 Mixed Reality Simulation Framework

C6, our research group's Java code base provides the framework that computes the mixed reality environment and integrates all subsystems. C6 handles live user input, the robot controller and motion capture sensor data dispatching signals to the designated subsystems. A fused representation of both the physical and virtual spaces is synthesized in the software and mathematically normalized as a single geometric bounding box. A superphysics model is generate in order to coordinate and pair the physics of the real with its simplified virtual counterpart.[3] This approach minimizes perceptual discontinuities as graphic objects transit between realities. C6 communicates with Touch over IRCP providing the graphics engine with user-input events and live robot location coordinates informed by real-time, filtered motion capture data. Additionally, C6 preview renders debugging information to assist the mixed reality robot game architects in calibrating the various systems involved.

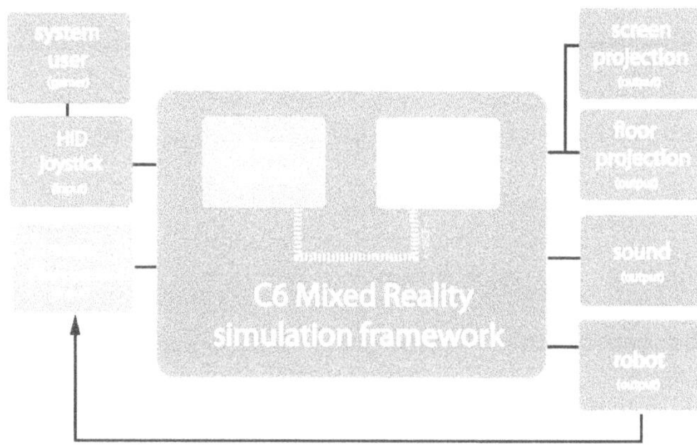

Figure 3. System framework

Graphics and Content

Linked to the C6 simulation framework via a C++ authored custom IRCP to Touch interoperability executable, the graphics engine simultaneously renders two live 1280 by 720p HD streams connected to the floor-mounted screen and ceiling-mounted projector. Rendering is done on the GPU and optimized for real-user and robot interaction.

The floor-mounted screen placed at the far end of the physical play space depicts a nocturnal scene populated by several procedurally animated characters playing with a ball that is passed through the screen. These characters' respective geometries are based on the physical robot's virtual 3D model. Additionally, the virtual characters' behavior and movements mimic (and are constrained to) the robot's own expressive, signature squash and stretch animations. The virtual characters' animations are parametrically varied per instance in both duration and sequence resulting in a more natural and unpredictable feel.

The characters are set in a grassy, fantasy environment that appears to have depth and detail beyond the capabilities of current real-time rendering. This is achieved by compositing the characters on top of a pre-rendered background plate. Created through a lengthy pre-production process, the background (see Figure 2) is the result of a 420 frame high-resolution simulation of 2 million blades of grass grown on various 3D surfaces and blown by artificial wind. The lighting in the background scene matches both the lighting of the characters as well as the ambient light conditions of the physical play space the user and robot are interacting in. This technique extends the notion of the aforementioned superphysics system and underlines the importance of matching the rendered world's lighting to the real world's lighting as coherently as possible within a certain tolerance. By smartly combining high-resolution background assets with the real-time, interactive characters in the foreground we were able to render a compelling and visually rich virtual world scene.

The camera is locked down and positioned to view the world from the diminutive perspective of the two-foot tall physical robot. Consequently, the virtual scene (when rendered from this angle) correctly lines up the ground plane of the virtual world with the ground plane of the real world. The virtual/real ground plane alignment plays an integral role in establishing a transparent, interreality boundary giving the illusion that the floor is a window. It effectively extends the physical play space on to the screen. In turn, the on-screen virtual world's ground is thus extended off the screen into material reality.

To take advantage of this affordance the ceiling-mounted projector is oriented downwards at the floor play space and projects graphic assets as they travel on and off the screen. For our game, Touch renders a 3D ball from a top view through a camera matched to the real world position of the projector. The resulting projection augments physical reality with a virtual ball that appears to travel along the length of the physical play space.

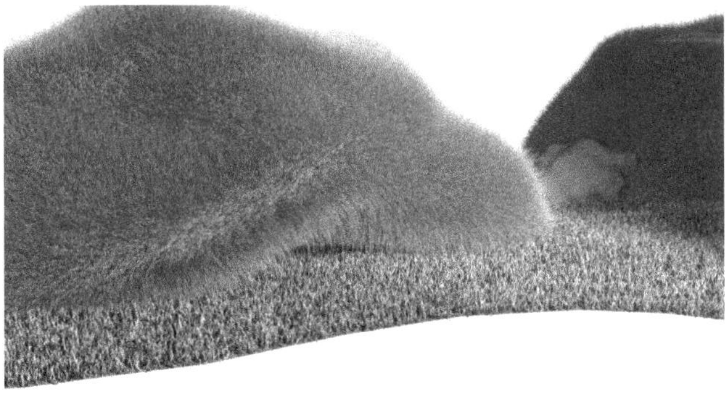

Figure 4. High-resolution background plate

Sound

Two mid-sized speakers are hidden out of view and placed behind the screen at the far end of the physical play space. Field recordings of a quiet summer night in the country provide some ambiance and create a sense of space. Game event sound effects are triggered by default. Additionally, an optional sound effect can be toggled on to highlight the moment a graphics asset moves off the screen into the augmented reality in the physical play space. The robot's motors also produce sound as long as they're activated.

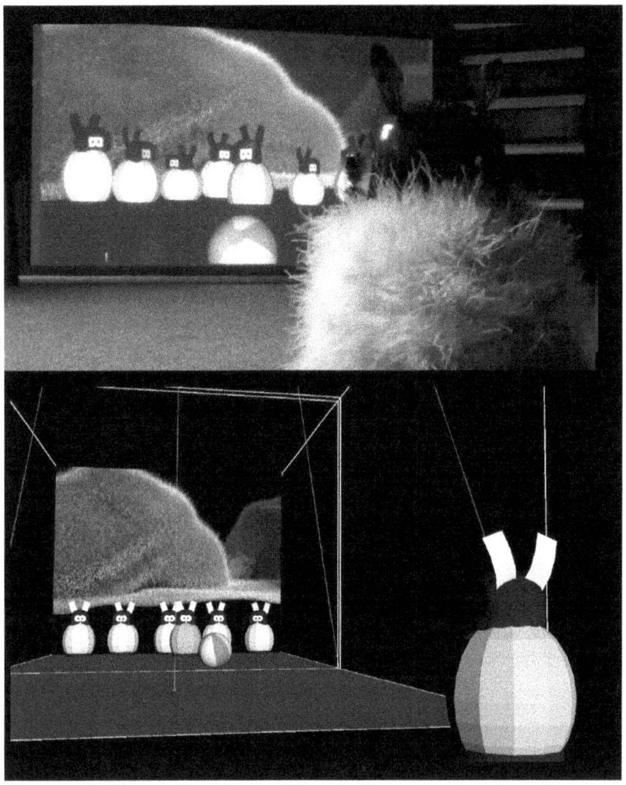

Figure 5. User view(top), Simulation view(bottom)

PLAYING THE GAME

The ball is the focus of the cooperative game play. The virtual characters invite the user to play a simple, Pong-like game. The robot, controlled by the player, orients itself to face the virtual characters. With the robot positioned at the near end of the physical play space, the session begins with the virtual ball projected in front of the robot. Once the initial kick-off is triggered by C6 the ball begins to move away from the robot towards the screen and the game begins. As the ball crosses the interreality boundary it appears in the virtual world and the on-screen characters always kick it back out towards the physical space and the robot. The user then proceeds to use the joystick to drive the robot to intercept the ball, now projected onto the physical play space. If the robot gamer successfully returns the ball the game continues. Otherwise, the game starts anew. The game's difficulty level is adjusted through the expansion or contraction of the margin of error by scaling the definition of the ball-robot intersection in the C6 simulation framework. Our goal as game designers is to enable the user to project herself into the robot's perceptual frame of reference. The mixed reality robot game would thus become akin to a first-person video game with the player embodied in the robot and embedded in the blended reality.

DISCUSSION

The co-presence of Miso, the physically embodied robot character, with the game's user creates a unique tangible interface and adds a point of access to the fantasy world.

An important consideration in designing a fluid interaction that maintains the user's perceptual continuity throughout the game's duration is the creation of a superphysics that coherently models the mixed reality environment. Although no formal evaluation was conducted, altering the gravity and speed parameters of the virtual model seemed to fracture the continuity across the MR boundary as the ball inexplicably sped up once on-screen.

FUTURE WORK

Currently, our system employs an AR projection technique to display a graphical asset in both spaces. We would like to explore methods for designing characters that inhabit both real and virtual spaces. To this effect, we plan to create a "robot-hutch", a physical portal device placed at the boundary of the virtual and material realities that aids in transporting the character on and off the screen. As the character enters the physical hutch, its presence is detected and the door shuts behind it and reopens in the virtual world representation of the portal to continue its adventures on screen. In order to preserve the illusion of life during the character's on-screen time, the physical robot should be hidden from view instead of remaining motionless at the boundary line in material reality.

CONCLUSION

Although still in its initial, exploratory phase mixed reality robot gaming holds a tremendous amount of potential for new ways to entertain, learn and communicate. To build these new gaming platforms we should make sure systems designed can fluidly extend virtual and eventually real objects on and off the screen. Beyond a simple game feature, the importance of blending the realities together augments the play context and may aid in bringing the game's fantasy world off the screen and our world on to it.

ACKNOWLEDGMENTS

We would like to thank Jason Alonso, Roman Zadov and Matt Berlin for their invaluable help.

REFERENCES

1. Calife, D., Bernardes, J. L., and Tori, R. 2009. Robot Arena: An augmented reality platform for game development. Comput. Entertain. 7, 1 (Feb. 2009), 1-26.
2. Cassell, J et al., *Shared Reality: Physical Collaboration with a Virtual Peer.* In *Proc. CHI 2000,* ACM Press (2000), pp. 259-260.
3. Gintautas, V., Hubler, A.W., *Experimental evidence for mixed reality states in an interreality system.* In *Physical Review –Series E,* American Physical Society (2007), Vol. 75,5, part 2, pp. 57-61.
4. Leitner, J., Haller, M., Yun, K., Woo, W., Sugimoto, M., Inami, M., Cheok, A., and Been-Lirn, H. D. 2009. *Physical interfaces for tabletop games.* Comput. Entertain. 7, 4 (Dec. 2009), 1-21.
5. Milgram, P. and Kishino, F., *A Taxonomy of Mixed Reality Visual Displays,* IEICE Transactions on Informationn Systems e77-D, Vol 12, 1994, pp. 1321-1329.
6. Touch. http://derivative.ca

I'm in the Game: Embodied Puppet Interface Improves Avatar Control

Ali Mazalek[1], Sanjay Chandrasekharan[2], Michael Nitsche[1], Tim Welsh[3], Paul Clifton[1], Andrew Quitmeyer[1], Firaz Peer[1], Friedrich Kirschner[1], Dilip Athreya[4]

Digital Media Program[1]
School of Interactive Computing[2]
Georgia Institute of Technology
Atlanta, GA, USA

Faculty of Physical Education & Health[3]
University of Toronto
Ontario, Canada

Department of Psychology[4]
University of Cincinnati
Cincinnati, OH, USA

mazalek@gatech.edu, sanjayan@cc.gatech.edu, michael.nitsche@gatech.edu, t.welsh@utoronto.ca, paulgclifton@gmail.com, andrew.quitmeyer@gmail.com, firaz.peer@gmail.com, friedrich@zeitbrand.net, athreydn@mail.uc.edu

ABSTRACT

We have developed an embodied puppet interface that translates a player's body movements to a virtual character, thus enabling the player to have a fine grained and personalized control of the avatar. To test the efficacy and short-term effects of this control interface, we developed a two-part experiment, where the performance of users controlling an avatar using the puppet interface was compared with users controlling the avatar using two other interfaces (Xbox controller, keyboard). Part 1 examined aiming movement accuracy in a virtual contact game. Part 2 examined changes of mental rotation abilities in users after playing the virtual contact game. Results from Part 1 revealed that the puppet interface group performed significantly better in aiming accuracy and response time, compared to the Xbox and keyboard groups. Data from Part 2 revealed that the puppet group tended to have greater improvement in mental rotation accuracy as well. Overall, these results suggest that the embodied mapping between a player and avatar, provided by the puppet interface, leads to important performance advantages.

Author Keywords

Puppet, tangible user interface, embodied interface, virtual character, video game, common coding, body memory, creativity.

ACM Classification Keywords

H.5.2 [Information Interfaces and Presentation]: User Interfaces---*input devices and strategies, interaction styles*; J.4 [Social and Behavioral Sciences]: *Psychology*; J.5 [Arts and Humanities]: *Performing arts*. K.8 [Personal Computing]: *Games*.

General Terms

Design, experimentation.

TEI'11, January 22–26, 2011, Funchal, Portugal.

INTRODUCTION

When players move through a virtual environment, they need a means to project their intentions and expressions into the virtual space, such as a control device or interface. Most current game systems make use of a number of generic controllers for this purpose, such as keyboards, mice, joysticks and gamepads. These input devices are generally 2D positioning devices, or arrays of buttons that provide low-bandwidth single-channel streams of information. Complex characters, however, have many degrees of freedom to control, which is not easily done with input devices that provide two degrees of freedom at most. As a result, there is significant abstraction between the movement of the control device and the movement of the virtual object that is being controlled. Jacob and Sibert describe this problem as a mismatch between the perceptual structures of the manipulator and the perceptual structures of the manipulation task [11]. They have shown that for tasks that require manipulating several integrally related quantities (e.g. a 3D position), a device that naturally generates the same number of integrally related values as required by the task (e.g. a Polhemus tracker) is better than a 2D positioning device (e.g. a mouse). A high level of abstraction limits the player's ability to precisely control their character across all its degrees of freedom, and also restricts their freedom to generate a variety of different movements and expressions in the virtual space. For example, in many video games 'walking forward' in virtual space is accessed by pressing the 'w' key on a standard keyboard. This single response coding for a complex movement pattern restricts the degrees of control to the extreme, as the player is not able to easily access a range of different walking expressions for their virtual character.

Given the limited form factor of existing control interfaces, application designers and researchers have been exploring new ways to better integrate the physical and digital spaces in which we exist. These efforts have resulted in emerging areas of human-computer interaction research, such as tangible, gestural and embodied interaction. These approaches leverage the capabilities of the human hands and body, enabling users to control virtual characters and objects in ways that build on or even simulate real-world interactions. These new forms of interaction are gaining popularity in the gaming world, such as the Nintendo Wii Remote, the Sony Playstation Move, and Microsoft's Kinect for the Xbox 360. These interfaces offer a much more direct sensori-motor mapping to the virtual space than conventional mouse or keyboard-based interfaces. With the growing relevance of consumer level control devices of this kind, it has become increasingly important for HCI designers to consider fundamental aspects of the interaction between perceptual, cognitive and motor processes [22]. One model that has great potential in this context is common coding theory.

Common coding (ideomotor) theory [9, 18, 19] posits a common neural representation connecting perception, execution and imagination of movements. This creates a tight coupling between action plans and their associated effects, and allows for fluid, automatic and bidirectional connections between the planning, perception, imagination and execution of action. This model provides an interesting design framework to derive new interaction formats [3, 16], and has the potential to help us better understand the role played by the motor system in our interactions with computational media. One of the most interesting experimental results from common coding research is the consistent ability of people to recognize their own movements shown in the abstract (such as a person's writing movement displayed by the movement of a point-light). People also tend to coordinate better with their own actions [13]. In an effort to exploit this 'own-movement' effect for the development of new media, we designed a full-body control interface (puppet) for video games that maps a player's own body movements onto a virtual avatar using a puppet (see Figure 1). The puppet provides a fine-grained connection between self movements (action planning and execution) and virtual avatar movements (perception/imagination of action effects). The common neural coding between perception of movements and imagination/execution of movements suggests that this connection, provided by the embodied interface, could eventually be used to transfer novel movements executed by the on-screen character back to the player.

Unlike the Wii, which tracks the position and movement of a single point/joint using heavily simplified mappings with its Wii Remote, the puppet can transfer a player's whole body movements to their virtual avatar with many degrees of freedom. And unlike the Kinect, which exploits camera-based motion capture, the puppet does not constrain the player's interaction to a fixed area defined by the visual field and the tracking abilities of the camera. In comparison to professional motion capture systems, the puppeteering approach is low-cost and portable. It can also open up a space for expressive exaggeration, since puppets can be made to perform actions unachievable with the human body alone. The abstraction of a puppeteering device can thus allow players to execute actions in virtual space that are impossible in real space, while their body movements still map directly onto the virtual avatar. Such an exaggeration is often part of video games, where players might control non-human avatars or perform specialized actions. In addition, the puppets have been used to raise engagement of new audiences in digital media. For example, primitive puppets have been used as digital storytelling devices for young audiences that are not computer-literate [14].

Figure 1. Full-body puppet interface.

Our earlier experiments have shown that the puppet interface supports players' recognition of their own movements in a 3D virtual character. The puppet approach is thus effective in personalizing an avatar by transferring a player's own movements to the virtual character [17]. Building on this work, the present paper reports the results of a study that examined the use of the puppet interface in comparison to standard video game control interfaces (keyboard and Xbox game controller). We looked at: (1) whether the puppet interface facilitated player performance by providing more accurate responses when controlling their avatar, and (2) whether perceiving a 'personalized' avatar executing novel body movements lead to improved cognitive performance of the user. The study made use of a custom-designed game in which the player had to make their avatar complete a series of aiming movements to touch virtual objects in 3D space, while at the same time having to constantly recalibrate their own body space in relation to the orientation of the avatar in the virtual world.

The following section summarizes the background for our project. We then provide a brief overview of the design of our puppet interface and the 3D virtual environment it manipulates. Next we describe the design of the experiments, and present the results. We conclude with future directions and implications of this work.

RELATED WORK

A number of efforts have centered on new physical interfaces for character control and animation. For example, the Monkey input device was an 18" tall monkey skeleton equipped with sensors at its joints in order to provide 32 degrees of freedom from head to toe for real-time character manipulation [5]. While its many degrees of freedom allowed a range of expressions to be translated into the virtual space, smooth whole-body real-time manipulation was in fact difficult to achieve and the device was thus better suited for capturing static poses (e.g. as in stop-motion animation). Johnson et al.'s work on "sympathetic interfaces" used a plush toy (a stuffed chicken) to manipulate and control an interactive story character in a 3D virtual world [12]. The device captured a limited range of movements (wing movements, neck rotation, and pitch/roll) and did not map the user's own full-body movements to the virtual space. Similarly, equipped with a variety of sensors in its hands, feet and eye, the ActiMates Barney plush doll acted as a play partner for children, either in a freestanding mode or wirelessly linked to a PC or TV [1]. Additionally, our own past and ongoing research has used paper hand puppets tracked by computer vision [10] and tangible marionettes equipped with accelerometers to control characters in the Unreal game engine [15].

Related approaches are already in use in professional production companies, which have increasingly turned to various forms of puppetry and body or motion tracking in order to inject life into 3D character animation. Putting a performer in direct control of a character like in puppetry, or capturing body motion for real-time or post-processed application to an animated character, can translate the nuances of natural motion to computer characters, which can greatly increase their expressive potential. For example, The Character Shop's trademark Waldo devices are telemetric input devices for controlling puppets (such as Jim Henson's Muppets) and animatronics that are designed to fit a puppeteer or performer's body. Waldos allow puppeteers or performers to control multiple axes of movement on a virtual character at once, and are a great improvement over older lever-based systems that required a team of operators to control all the different parts of a single puppet. The Character Shop's control interfaces evolved into real-time digital controllers of varying granularity: the characters in the PBS series *Sid the Science Kid* are controlled in real-time, each by two puppeteers with different systems [8].

A comparable approach is also used by Animazoo in their Gypsy 7 exo-skeletal motion capture technology. A big limitation of motion capture puppetry is that it typically requires significant cleanup of sensor data during the post processing stage. Further, the high price-point of both camera and exo-skeleton-based systems targets professional motion capture applications and precludes their use in the consumer space. As a result, it is not feasible to make use of these systems as control devices for everyday game players.

In the home entertainment domain, standard game controllers remain the dominant paradigm, with the exception of the newer interfaces (Nintendo Wii Remote, Sony Move, and Microsoft Kinect).

To our knowledge, none of the work on tangible interfaces for virtual character control is based on ideomotor theory. The rich experimental techniques from this literature (such as self-recognition, and better coordination with self-movements) have thus not been used to examine how such interfaces improve the user experience, or change the user's cognitive abilities. Most of these systems focus on fidelity of motion capture, and not on control of a character by a user. They therefore do not examine how the user's experience of control can be pushed further, and in what situations the feeling of control breaks down. As such, we believe our interface provides a valuable interdisciplinary approach towards the design of control systems that can help enhance the user's expression and problem-solving.

SYSTEM OVERVIEW

As described in [17], our puppet interface is designed to support the player's self-identification with the virtual avatar through faithful transfer of own body movements to the avatar, while still providing the abstraction of a control device between one's own movement and that of the virtual avatar. The system consists of two main components: the puppet control interface and the 3D engine, described in the following sections. The 3D engine enables us to implement and deploy small "games" that provide the player with tasks to solve in the virtual world. We describe the virtual contact game developed for our experiments.

Puppet Interface

The puppet is a hybrid full-body puppet that is strapped to the player's body, and controlled by the player's arms, legs and body. This approach provides a high level of articulation and expressiveness in movement without requiring the skill of a professional puppeteer. And in contrast to motion capture systems, the puppet interface is both low-cost and portable.

The puppet consists of 10 joints at the knees, hips, waist, shoulders, elbows and neck, allowing us to capture a range of movement data (see Figure 2). Its feet attach to the player's knees, its head attaches to their neck, and its midsection attaches to their waist. The player uses their hands to control the hands of the puppet. This configuration allows the puppet to be easily controlled by both the hand and full-body movements of the player, and allows the puppet to faithfully transfer the player's own movements to their virtual avatar. While not implemented in the current version, the full-body puppet form factor could also enable us to incorporate vibrotactile feedback into the puppet device. This would allow the virtual avatar's movements to feed back into the physical device and stimulate player movements.

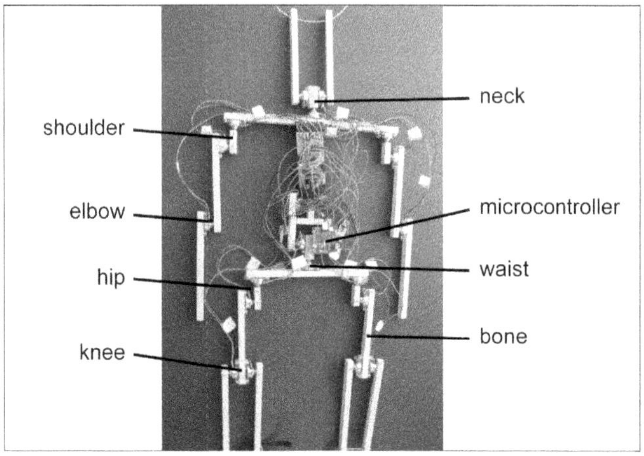

Figure 2. Puppet interface with 10 joints across the knees hips, waist, shoulders, elbows and neck.

The puppet is built out of wooden "bone" pieces connected across the 10 joints using potentiometers, allowing the movement of the joints to be measured. Joints such as the shoulders and hips, which rotate in two directions, contain two potentiometers oriented at 90 degrees in order to sense the rotation in each direction independently. The potentiometers are connected via a multiplexer to an Arduino Pro microcontroller attached to the chest of the puppet. The microcontroller sends the movement data to a host computer via a Bluetooth connection, where a software application written in Processing normalizes the values and sends them to the rendering engine via the OSC (OpenSound Control) protocol.

3D Engine

The 3D renderer allows the physical puppet interface to steer a virtual puppet in real-time (see Figure 3). It is based on the Moviesandbox (MSB) application, an open-source, OpenGL-based, machinima tool written in C++ (www.moviesandbox.net). The renderer uses XML files to store the scenes and settings for the characters allowing for very flexible usage.

The 3D renderer receives the OSC messages sent by the Processing application, and maps them onto the virtual avatar. Based on the settings for the joint rotations in the currently loaded XML character file, positions of the bones are set relative to one another using forward kinematics. In addition to character control, the application currently supports camera placement, panning and tilting. The 3D renderer also includes advanced import functions for standard 3D modeling files and has basic animation recording options. Both are valuable for experimenting with different virtual puppets and comparing the animations our puppeteers create with them.

The system provides us with a basic but highly flexible virtual puppetry engine that mimics the functionality of video game systems – in fact, its first installment used Epic's *Unreal* game engine as renderer, but to provide better flexibility and access to the animations we moved to an Open GL approach. This allowed us to better adjust the necessary control mechanisms to the interfaces we were designing.

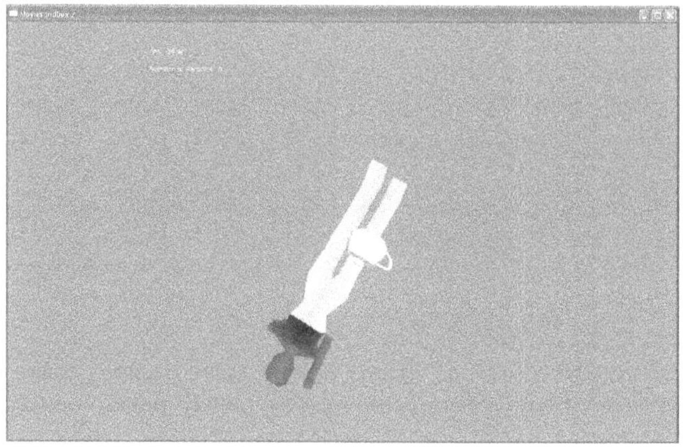

Figure 3. 3D renderer with avatar in the teapot game.

Virtual Contact Game

The first game developed in our 3D engine was designed to investigate two research questions. First, we wanted to examine how the puppet performed as a control interface, in relation to standard interfaces such as joysticks and keyboards. Secondly, we wanted to examine how novel movements executed by a virtual avatar might contribute to the player's cognition, specifically mental rotation. To examine the first question, we needed a 'neutral' task, different from standard tasks seen in games, because if game-related tasks are used, expert game players would perform at high levels, and possibly skew the data towards standard interfaces. Further, the puppet interface affords novel forms of interactions within video games, and we therefore wanted to develop a task not commonly seen in standard video game interactions. To examine the second question, we needed a task where the user perceived movements not commonly executed in the real world, so that we could examine the effects these movements had on the player's ability to imagine related movements, in isolation from any previous motor training.

Based on these experimental constraints, we developed a game where players saw virtual objects (teapots) appear in proximity to their 3D avatar, and they had to move their body and the puppet interface to make the virtual avatar touch these objects (see Figure 4). The teapots appeared randomly at different points near the avatar, and the player had to move her hands or feet to make the avatar touch the teapot. To investigate the effect of perceived novel movements on mental rotation abilities, we added a special camera behavior to this game task. The camera slowly rotated around the avatar in an unpredictable manner, making the avatar float in space in different orientations (see Figure 3). This apparent movement of the avatar forced the player to constantly reconsider the position and orientation of the virtual avatar in relation to their own body, the interface strapped to their body, and also the virtual teapots they have to touch. Once touched, each teapot disappeared and a new one appeared in a different location. The player's goal was to touch as many teapots as possible in the time provided (13 minutes). The number of teapots touched and the time at which each teapot was touched were tracked by the system.

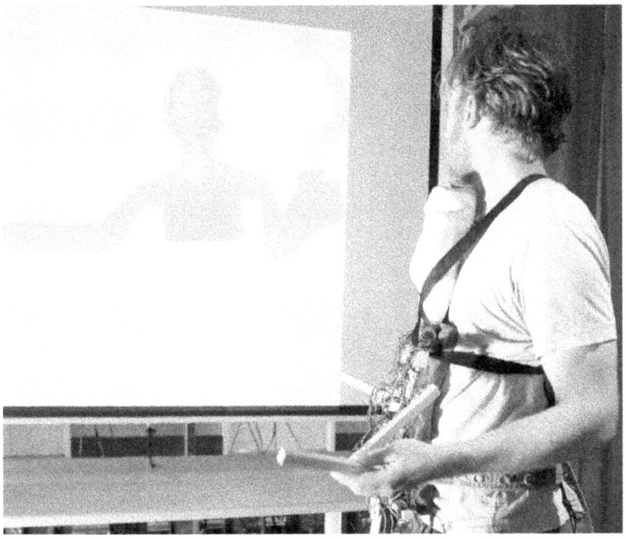

Figure 4. Playing the virtual contact game with the full-body puppet controller.

EXPERIMENT DESIGN

Previous experiments have shown that our puppet interface is effective in personalizing an avatar by transferring a player's own movements to the virtual character [17]. Building on this work, we presently report a study that examined the performance of the puppet interface in comparison to standard video game control interfaces. Specifically, we looked at: (1) whether the puppet interface facilitates player performance by providing more accurate responses when controlling their virtual avatar, and (2) whether perceiving a 'personalized' video game character executing novel body movements leads to improved cognitive performance in the player. The study involved 30 participants playing the virtual contact game and completing mental rotation tests. The participants were pseudo-randomly assigned (our only constraint was having equal n across the conditions) to one of three interface conditions: puppet, Xbox controller, and keyboard. There were thus 10 participants per interface condition, of which 50% were female (i.e. 5 per condition, or 15 overall).

The two components of the study (teapot touching and mental rotation) were conducted within a single session. The participant was first asked to complete two sessions of a standard mental rotation test. After this, the participant was asked to play the virtual contact game using one of the three control interfaces. After they had played the game for 13 minutes, participants completed another two sessions of the mental rotation task. The mapping between the character's body and the Xbox/keyboard interfaces were as follows.

	Arm/leg toggle	Shoulder/hip movement	Knee/elbow bending
Keyboard	F (left) H (right)	W,A,S,D (left) I,J,K,L (right)	Q,E (left) U,O (right)
Xbox	Click joysticks (left/right)	Move joysticks (left/right)	Triggers (left/right)

PART 1 RESULTS

To determine if the puppet device has performance advantages over the more conventional devices (Aim 1), we analyzed the mean number of successful teapot contacts using a one-way between-subjects ANOVA (alpha set at 0.05). Post-hoc analysis of the significant effect (F=5.87; p<.01) using paired one-tailed t-tests (p<.05) revealed significant advantages for the puppet and Xbox controllers over the keyboard. Performance advantages of the puppet over the Xbox controller, although numerically large, only tended toward statistical reliability (p<.13; see Figure 6). Despite the absence of a statistically reliable difference, effect size calculations of the differences between puppet and Xbox controllers were in the medium range (Cohen's d=.52) suggesting important functional and practical differences in performance.

	Puppet	Xbox	Keyboard
Contacts	123.9	90.6	41.1
Std. Dev.	74.1	50.74	28.33

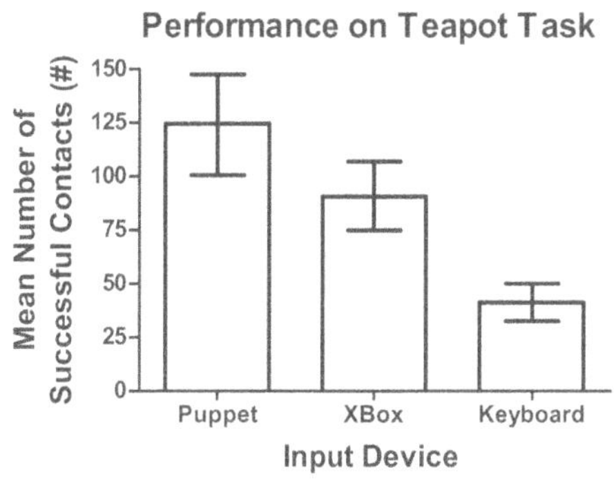

Figure 6. The average number of teapots touched across the three conditions (puppet, Xbox and keyboard).

MENTAL ROTATION TASK

Playing video games has been shown to have cognitive effects, such as improvement in attention, spatial ability and mental rotation [6, 7]. Manipulating virtual objects has been reported to improve subsequent mental rotation and recognition of such objects [21]. Games have also been shown to help overcome cognitive limitations, such as fear of flying [20] and post-traumatic stress disorder in the wake of the 9/11 attacks [4]. Based on these previous findings, we wanted to examine whether interacting with an avatar that encodes the player's own body movements using an embodied interface leads to improvement in imagined movements, primarily mental rotation, compared to interactions based on standard control interfaces, which do not as faithfully transfer the player's own body movements to the avatar. Such a transfer would be predicted by common coding theory, as a common neural representation underlies perceived and imagined movements. To examine this prediction, we had players complete a mental rotation task before and after interacting with the avatar, and we then compared the accuracy and the time taken for their responses. This analysis was done for the three interface conditions. The task is described below.

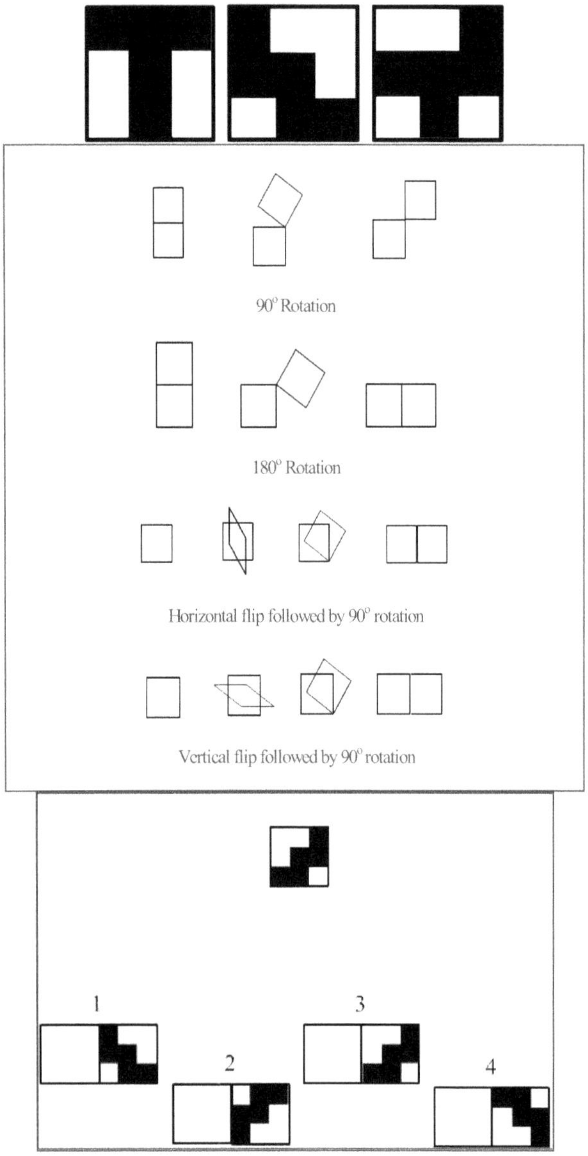

Figure 5. The top panel shows the patterns used, the middle panel shows the rotation operations used, and the last panel shows a screenshot of the decision task. For each trial, a video of one of the operations was displayed first, and then the decision screen. One of the bottom figures shows the top pattern rotated in the sequence displayed in the video. The task is to pick this option.

Stimuli: A set of three small 2D patterns within a white square (frame) were prepared on a 3x3 matrix with only five cells being filled, as illustrated in panel 1 (top) of Figure 5. The visual angle was 1.5° x 1.5°. With each of these patterns, three more patterns were generated by rotating the original three patterns by 90°, 180° or 270°. Any one of the possible four orientations of a particular stimulus pattern was randomly used as a stimulus in a particular trial.

There were eight rotational operations (4 x left/right directions; see Figure 5, panel 2). There were two levels of complexity (low or high). Low complexity operations were rotations of 90° (right and left) and 180° (right and left). High complexity operations were vertical and horizontal flips followed by a rotation of 90° (left or right). The rotational task was given a reference by providing an empty-blank white square (frame). To demonstrate the operations, video clips were created using Flash. Each rotation in the low complexity condition took twenty seconds of display time. In the high complexity condition, each flip operation took twenty seconds in addition to each rotation operation, which also took twenty seconds to complete. There was a two second gap between flip and rotation. The end position (frame) after the rotational operation, stayed for five seconds.

Procedure: The experiment consisted of twenty-four trials (8 operations x 3 patterns), presented randomly. Each trial had two phases. In the first phase, a rotation was demonstrated using a video clip. Participants were asked to remember the rotation they saw, apply the same operation on the pattern coming up in the second phase and select the answer that best fitted the mentally rotated pattern.

The second phase started after 2 seconds, during which the screen was blank. This phase presented a pattern to be mentally rotated, along with four possible answers (as shown in Figure 5, panel 3), which remained on screen until participants produced a response, by typing 1, 2, 3 or 4 using the keyboard. This response initiated the next trial, which started after two seconds. Participants responded to 48 trials (two 24-trial blocks) before and after the virtual contact game. The program that controlled stimuli presentation and data collection was designed using ExperimentBuilder software.

PART 2 RESULTS

The low complexity trials were not included in the analysis, as previous work [2] showed that participants typically reach a ceiling of perfect performance on this simpler task. The influence of the different task conditions on the mental rotation task was assessed by submitting accuracy and response time on the mental rotation tasks to a 3 (Group: puppet, Xbox, keyboard) by 2 (Test: pre, post) mixed ANOVA. The main effect for Test (F=11.27, p<.01) revealed that, as a whole, participants improved in accuracy in the mental rotation task following the experience with the teapot game. Specific planned comparisons of the accuracy of the different groups in the pre- and post-tests using paired t-tests revealed that this increase in accuracy was driven by the performance of the puppet group. That is, of all three groups, the puppet group demonstrated the largest improvement and was the only group to demonstrate a statistically reliable improvement in performance ($p<.05$). Improvements in the Xbox ($p>.07$) and keyboard ($p>.20$) were not significant. Further, effect size for the improvement following the puppet controller was in the medium range (d=.61), but were in the small range following the Xbox (d=.28) and keyboard (d=.46).

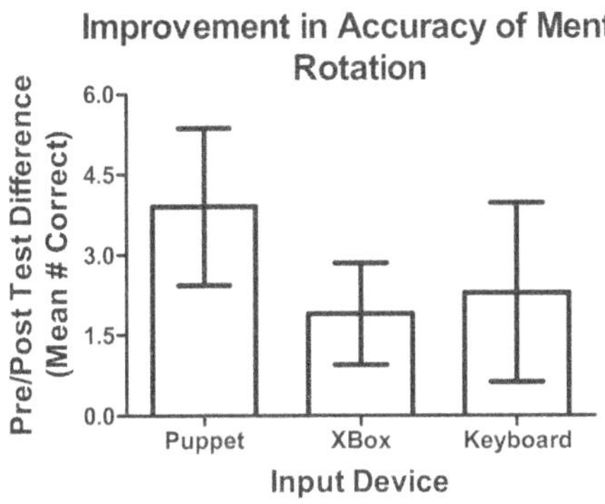

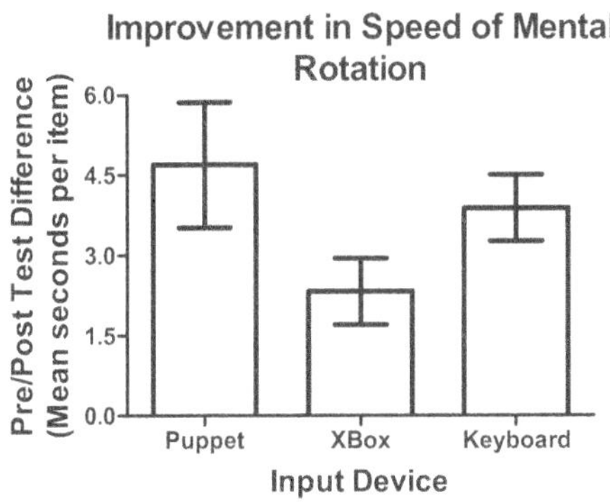

Figure 7. Mean accuracy and speed improvement in the mental rotation task across the three conditions (puppet, Xbox and keyboard).

The absence of similar between-group differences in response time suggests that these improvements were not the results of a speed-accuracy trade-off in which the puppet group performed more accurately because they took more time to complete the task in the post test. Thus, consistent with our hypothesis, it seems that the more consistent perceptual-motor mapping provided by the puppet interface had some facilitatory influence on the users' cognitive capabilities.

	Puppet Pre/Post		Xbox Pre/Post		Keyboard Pre/Post	
Accuracy	15.1	19.0	15.5	17.4	16.5	18.8
Std. Dev.	6.2	6.6	7.1	6.5	4.8	5.2
Time	11.9	7.2	9.43	7.1	14.38	10.5
Std. Dev.	3.7	2.7	3.7	3.5	7.3	7.8

DISCUSSION

Overall, the execution component of the study revealed that the embodied puppet interface improved performance in the virtual contact game, compared to Xbox and keyboard interfaces. This finding indicates the value of embodied interfaces for the development of more personalized and less restricted interaction with virtual worlds (such as video games). Additionally, almost all participants who used the puppet interface commented on its ease of use, and many found it to be a fun and novel way of interacting with the avatar. If interaction design seeks to move away from the currently dominant model of abstraction, then the puppet interface offers the necessary opportunities for participation and involvement.

Consistent with previous research [6, 7], the embodied interface, and the transfer of the player's own movements to the virtual character, showed improved accuracy in mental rotation. Further experiments are required to examine this effect more clearly, but the results demonstrate a positive effect of the puppet interface. One element that might influence the results here is the fact that the puppet interface, even though generally perceived as unobtrusive and engaging, presents a completely new interaction format to the test participants. None of the test participants was a trained puppeteer. In comparison, it can be assumed that the Xbox controller and the keyboard are much more familiar. It could, thus, be projected that the puppet interface would perform even better once users get used to it.

CONCLUSION AND FUTURE WORK

In our past work [16] we have shown the level of self-recognition supported by our embodied interface. The research presented in this paper shows the positive cognitive effects of this interface usage. We conclude that development of similar embodied interfaces could help unlock potential opportunities for game interface design. It is worth noting that while these interfaces use game-based technology, they are not limited to the entertainment sector. Instead, these designs might have applications in other fields, such as movement education and rehabilitation. The success of novel interfaces like the Wii in new areas, such as retirement homes, indicates that such systems can be developed as assistive technologies as well.

Some questions raised by our research remain unanswered and left to future work. One is the question of interface familiarity and different effects along different learning curves of novel interfaces. In order to explore the puppet interface's long-term impact on user performances, a comparative training study would be insightful. Findings of such a study could become relevant for the discussion of other novel interfaces (Xbox Kinect, Playstation Move). Will the level of virtual body control be consistently higher in these kinds of embodied interfaces? How will it develop as users adapt to the new device?

A more pressing question, however, is how we can utilize the connection between one's own movements and the virtual character movements that we have traced in our work. Our ultimate challenge is to see whether an embodied interface can help users learn new movements from a virtual character. We suggest using the self-recognition in a virtual avatar, and the cognitive effects discussed in this paper, to assist a user in this learning process. In our future work, we hope to explore the application of such a system to the medical domain. To this end, we are currently examining how the full-body puppet form factor can incorporate feedback (e.g. using vibrating motors at the joints). This would allow the movements of the avatar to feed back into the physical device and stimulate player movements. We believe this sort of enhancement would be useful for training or movement rehabilitation applications.

ACKNOWLEDGMENTS

We thank the Synaesthetic Media Lab, the Digital World & Image Group and the Cognitive & Motor Neuroscience Lab for helping shape our ideas. This work is supported by NSF-IIS grant #0757370 and NSF-REESE grant #0909971 (awarded to Nancy Nersessian and Wendy Newstetter).

REFERENCES

1. Alexander, K. and Strommen, E. (1998). Evolution of the Talking Dinosaur: The (Not So) Natural History of a New Interface for Children. In *CHI 98 Conference Summary on Human Factors in Computing Systems*, ACM, 7-8.
2. Chandrasekharan, S., Athreya, D., and Srinivasan, N. (2006). Twists and Oliver Twists in mental rotation: Complementary actions as orphan processes. In R. Sun & N. Miyake (Eds.), *Proc. 28th Annual Meeting of the Cognitive Science Society*, 1092-1097.
3. Chandrasekharan, S., Mazalek, A., Chen, Y., Nitsche, M., and Ranjan, A. (2010). Ideomotor Design: using common coding theory to derive novel video game interactions. In *Pragmatics & Cognition*, 18 (2), 313-339.
4. Difede, J. and Hoffman, H. (2002). Virtual Reality Exposure Therapy for World Trade Center Post-traumatic Stress Disorder: A Case Report. In *CyberPsychology and Behavior*, 5: 529-535.
5. Esposito, C. and Paley, W.B. (1995). Of mice and monkeys: A specialized input device for virtual body animation. In *Proc. Symposium on Interactive 3D Graphics*, 109-213.
6. Feng, J., Spence, I., and Pratt, J. (2007). Playing an action video game reduces gender differences in spatial cognition. In *Psychological Science*, 18: 850-855.
7. Green, S. and Bavelier, D. (2003). Action video game modifies visual selective attention. In *Nature*, 423: 534-537.
8. Henson, B. (2009). Keeping It Real. *American Theatre*, Sept 2009, 56-60.
9. Hommel, B., Müsseler, J., Aschersleben, G., and Prinz, W. (2001). The theory of event coding (TEC): A framework for perception and action planning. In *Behavioral and Brain Sciences*, 24: 849-878.
10. Hunt, D., Moore, J., West, A., and Nitsche, M. (2006). Puppet Show: Intuitive puppet interfaces for expressive character control. In *Medi@terra 2006, Gaming Realities: A Challenge for Digital Culture*, 159-167.
11. Jacob, R. and Sibert, L. (1992). The perceptual structure of multidimensional input device selection. In *Proc. Human Factors in Computing Systems*, ACM, 211-218.
12. Johnson, M.P., Wilson, A., Blumberg, B., Kline, C., and Bobick, A. (1999). "Sympathetic Interfaces: Using a Plush Toy to Direct Synthetic Characters." In *Proc. Human Factors in Computing Systems*, ACM, 152-158.
13. Knoblich, G. and Sebanz, N. (2006). The social nature of perception and action. In *Current Directions in Psychological Science*, 15, 99-104.
14. Mayora, O., Costa, C., and Papliatseyeu, A. (2009). iTheater Puppets Tangible Intearctions for Storytelling. In *Proc. Intelligent Technologies for Interactive Entertainment.* Springer, Berlin / Heidelberg, 110-118.
15. Mazalek, A. and Nitsche, M. (2007). Tangible interfaces for real-time 3D virtual environments. In *Proc. international Conference on Advances in Computer Entertainment Technology*, ACM, 155-162.
16. Mazalek, A., Chandrasekharan, S., Nitsche, M., Welsh, T. Thomas, G., Sanka, T., and Clifton, P. (2009). Giving your self to the game: transferring a player's own movements to avatars using tangible interfaces. In *Proc. Sandbox 2009: ACM SIGGRAPH Videogame Symposium*, ACM, 161-168.
17. Mazalek, A., Nitsche, M., Chandrasekharan, S., Welsh, T., Clifton, P., Quitmeyer, A., Peer, F., and Kirschner, F. (2010). Recognizing Self in Puppet Controlled Virtual Avatars. In *Proc. Fun and Games 2010*, ACM.
18. Prinz, W. (1992). Why don't we perceive our brain states? In *European Journal of Cognitive Psychology*, 4, 1–20.
19. Prinz, W. (2005). A common coding approach to imitation. In S. Hurley, N. Chater (Eds.), *Perspectives on imitation: From neuroscience to social science*, Vol. 1. Cambridge, MA: The MIT Press, 141-156.
20. Rothbaum, B., Anderson, P., Zimand, E., Hodges, L., Lang, D., and Wilson, J. (2006). Virtual Reality Exposure Therapy and Standard (in Vivo) Exposure Therapy in the Treatment of Fear of Flying. In *Behavior Therapy* 37: 80-90.
21. Wexler, M. and van Boxtel, J.J.A. (2005). Depth perception by the active observer. In *Trends in Cognitive Sciences*, 9: 431-438.
22. Welsh, T.N., Weeks, D.J., Chua, R., and Goodman, D. (2007). Perceptual-motor interaction: Some implications for human-computer interaction. In, A. Sears, J.A. Jacko (Eds.), *Human-Computer Interaction Handbook*, 2nd Ed., Lawrence Erlbaum, 27-41.

Experiencing the Reading Glove

Karen Tanenbaum, Joshua Tanenbaum, Alissa N. Antle,
Jim Bizzochi, Magy Seif el-Nasr, and Marek Hatala
School of Interactive Arts + Technology
Simon Fraser University
350 – 13450 102 Avenue
Surrey, BC V3T 0A3 Canada
{joshuat, ktanenba, aantle, jimbiz, magy, mhatala}@sfu.ca

ABSTRACT

In this paper we describe the Reading Glove, a wearable RFID reader for interacting with a tangible narrative. Based on interviews with study participants, we present a set of observed themes for understanding how the wearable and tangible aspects of the Reading Glove influence the user experience. We connect our observational themes to theoretical notions from interactive narrative and tangible interaction to create a set of design considerations such as *enacting a role*, *ownership and permission*, *multiplicity of interpretations* and *boundary objects*.

Author Keywords

Tangible user interfaces, wearable computing, interactive storytelling, design

ACM Classification Keywords

H.5.2 [Information Systems]: User Interfaces – input devices and strategies.

General Terms

Theory, Design

INTRODUCTION

Many tangible systems claim to have a particular benefit of making the narrative or other content more "real" or more "engaging" by virtue of the tangible nature of the experience, but this claim is often not persuasively demonstrated. In particular, the impact of tangible and wearable design elements on the user experience of an interactive narrative has not been comprehensively explored. In this paper, we discuss the Reading Glove, a wearable interface that allows the user to engage with physical objects that are part of an interactive narrative. In previous papers we have discussed the challenge of authoring the interactive narrative content [20] and our process of interaction design [19]. This paper presents the first study results on how using the Reading Glove impacts the experience of the story. Based on our study data, we develop a set of themes for understanding how the wearable and tangible aspects of the Reading Glove influence the user experience. We then identify areas of both challenge and opportunity in designing for tangible interactive narrative experiences.

TEI'11, January 22–26, 2011, Funchal, Portugal.

RELATED WORK

There have been several attempts to merge research in interactive narrative with research in tangible interaction. One popular approach has been to distribute narrative fragments across a series of tangible objects. Holmquist et al. describe an object-based tangible storytelling system in which readers used a barcode scanner to retrieve video clips in a narrative puzzle [9]. Mazalek et al. created a tangible narrative system called genieBottles in which readers open glass bottles to "release" trapped storytellers (genies) which reveal fragments of narrative information [15]. Mazalek et al. also designed graspable "pawns" for the Tangible Viewpoints project, which were used to access different character perspectives in a multi-viewpoint story [14]. Unfortunately, all three of these systems provide little to no data on how users of the system experienced the tangible interface or the story being presented. Most of the discussion of these systems is oriented towards the technical challenges of the interface and sensor design. Our focus with the Reading Glove is on user experience and the meaning of the story and the system as interpreted by the participants. While a number of interactive systems have used a combination of glove-based interfaces and RFID technology, none of them have dealt specifically with storytelling. Instead, research with glove-based interfaces tends to focus on gaming applications [11, 13] or assistive and enabling technology [12]. The exploration of how users experience a story told via a tangible and wearable interface has not been undertaken in any detail.

THEORY

To frame our work, we present some theoretical notions from interactive narrative and tangible interaction design.

Interactive Narrative

Hypertext

One of the earliest models of interactive narrative is the branching "choose your own adventure" structure, which matured into a new form of literature with the advent of hypertext fiction. In its most elemental form, hypertext consists of a system of narrative fragments, often referred to as *lexia*, interconnected by *hyperlinks*, which are navigated to form linear routes through much larger narrative spaces. Theorists and aficionados of hypertext positioned it as the next significant literary movement: one uniquely suited to the computational medium [5]. While the early promise of hypertext was never fulfilled, game narratives and interactive art pieces continue to investigate how to create engaging stories that can be encountered via a multiplicity of paths and support interactive exploration.

Narrative Parameters

These non-linear or open ended stories do not follow a classical narrative arc, however, and thus present unique challenges for both authoring the stories and ensuring that they make sense to readers encountering them in a variety of permutations. Bizzochi defines a set of parameters for evaluating narrative experiences aimed particularly at game narratives which are open ended in this way [2]. These elements are: 1) Storyworld: the environment within which the game unfolds; 2) Characters: the beings that populate this game world; 3) Emotions: both the emotions shown by the games characters and those elicited in the player; 4) Narrativized Interface: how the narrative sensibilities are instantiated in the appearance and the functionality of the interface design; 5) Micro-Narratives: the smaller moments of narrative flow and coherence that occur within a broader context of game play [2]. Central to Bizzocchi's framework is a move away from reliance on the notion of the "grand narrative arc" and a move toward understanding narrative as a multidimensional phenomenon. His concept of the narrativised interface is of particular relevance in the context of this paper [3].

Non-linear Narrative

Aarseth also looks at the ways in which traditional literary notions break down when confronted with nonlinear texts [1]. He makes a distinction between "text" and "script": a script is comprised of the "visible words and spaces" while a text also includes a "practice, a structure, or ritual of use." One consequence of this is that the experience of reading hypertext can be unsatisfying, as there is often a perception that the "real text" is somewhere just out of reach, and that all attempts to read the script as presented are inadequate experiences of the story. Aarseth describes this as a "metaphysical belief in a transcendental text" that is somehow outside the physical manifestation of a given story [1]. As we detail the design of the Reading Glove as a nonlinear narrative, we will return to this issue and consider how it might be overcome.

Hypermediacy and Transparent Immediacy

One of the most influential works in the study of new media forms was Bolter and Grusin's *Remediation,* which introduced the concepts of *transparent immediacy* and *hypermediacy* [4]. In their writing, interactions with mediated experiences exist in a state of immediacy (often associated with immersion), unless something happens to jolt the viewer into an awareness of the mediated nature of the experience, which they term hypermediacy. In most interactions, people oscillate between these two modes. This state of oscillation occurs at the point of intersection between the reader and the media artifact: the interface. Bizzocchi's notion of the narrative interface provides a useful way for thinking about that point of contact, by exploring how narrative sensibilities in the interface can reduce the disruption to transparent immediacy that occurs when a reader experiences hypermediacy.

Tangible Interaction

Boundary Objects

One of the unique affordances of a tangible storytelling system is its ability to leverage the tactile and associative properties of physical objects. There is a rich history of object use for narrative communication, elicitation and preservation. Historically, objects have allowed people to communicate across social, cultural, and linguistic divides. In sociology there is a notion of *boundary objects:* artifacts that exist between two different worldviews. Boundary objects are sites of negotiation between opposing perspectives, and allow members of different groups to translate between a familiar view and an alien one [17]. Cassell has developed a series of such boundary objects to support storytelling and story listening in children, including Storymat and SAM the CastleMate [6]. In our the Reading Glove system, we treat the objects as situated between the world of the fiction and the world of the reader. They are material manifestations of the fiction, and are a very literal example of a narrative interface.

Heidegger

In our previous work [19], we presented an extension of Heidegger's notions of ready-to-hand and present-at-hand as framed by Dourish [7]. Dourish interprets the notion of present-at-hand to refer to situations in which tools "breakdown", suddenly becoming the focus of our attention. He contrasts this against the notion of ready-to-hand, wherein tools disappear from our perceptions and serve as invisible extensions of ourselves. In some ways, Heidegger's notions are very similar to Bolter and Grusin's concepts of *transparent immediacy* and *hypermediacy* [4]: we see transparent immediacy as a form of being ready-to-hand while hypermediacy is akin to present-at-hand. While this oscillation between two binary levels of awareness is sufficient for understanding functional tools, and for understanding passively mediated interactions, we believe that this model misses a crucial aspect of lived experience that becomes particularly relevant when working with TUIs. We argue that this binary model ignores the critical role that semantic meaning and context play in our relationships with designed artifacts. Heidegger's two states represent functional extremes: either invisibly functioning or presently malfunctioning. We think that there is a third, related mode of interacting with objects that is differentiated along semantic lines instead of functional lines. We term this semantic engagement "present-at-mind" [19].

Present-at-mind may be used to describe any situation in which an awareness of the tool as a *locus of meaning* occurs; it encompasses the ways in which we slip between different associative awarenesses while interacting with an object or tool. This can be elucidated by extending the canonical example of someone using a hammer: I can use a hammer to drive nails and, as long as I do not slip or hit myself, it will remain invisibly ready-to-hand. However, should I slip and miss the nail or hit my thumb, "breakdown" occurs and the hammer becomes present-at-hand: an awkward tool which is not performing properly and thus becomes the object of the user's attention. But what if I become aware of the wear of the hammer's grip, which in turn puts me in mind of my father, to whom the hammer once belonged? What if this calls my attention to a place where he carved his initials in the handle? The hammer has not broken down as a functional tool, but is no longer an invisible extension of my hand. It has shifted into a state of being present-at-mind, due to a web of associative entanglements in which it exists, rather than to a breakdown of functionality. These entanglements are unique to this particular tool: a different hammer would not evoke the same reaction. In this case the hammer is not just a stand-in for any hammer or an extension of the body, but instead a specific hammer with a specific story: it is present-at-mind.

In TUI research, one of the canonical properties of tangibles is a meaningful coupling of physical and digital representations [21]. In this case, the binary notions of ready-to-hand and present-at-hand are insufficient because the operation of the tangible object as an interface device often involves paying attention specifically to the object. The incorporation of a third, semantic, vector allows this model to account for the relationship between physical and digital representations in a tangible interface. When the tangible object or interface is present-at-mind, it exists in the mind of the reader as a meaningful physical representation; however, as an interface device it remains ready-to-hand as a functional physical stand-in for its associated digital representations. The notion of present-at-mind provides us with a powerful frame for designing and understanding semantic interactions in tangible systems.

The Turn to Practice

A number of frameworks for tangible interaction exist which might be brought to bear on a system like the Reading Glove. For this study, we turn to the recent work of Fernaeus et al. They describe the "practice turn" in design [8], which they situate as arising out of Suchman's critical take on HCI and AI from the 1980s [18] and currently exemplified in the work of Dourish on embodied interaction [7]. The turn to practice is characterized by bringing the embodied, social, contingent and subjective aspects of human interaction to the fore, while de-emphasizing the objective and dualistic approach that formerly dominated HCI as a field of study. Fernaeus et al. lay out a set of four design ideals that highlight the conceptual shifts inherent in the practice turn, relating them specifically to designing for tangible interaction [8]. The first shift is from information centric to *action centric* interpretations of interaction. Instead of understanding the physical artifacts of TUIs as simply information-laden data representations or input/output devices, this ideal suggests that they be viewed as being resources for action within a shared space of physical activity. The second shift is from properties-of-systems to *interaction-in-context*. This suggests that tangible systems can be best understood as part of a larger setting of action and use, rather than as a separate and self-contained system. The third shift is from individual to *shareable use*, highlighting the collaborative and social functions of tangible systems. Finally, they discuss the shift from focusing on objective to *subjective interpretations*. This shift requires the designer to imagine the perspective of the user of the system and how they might appropriate and adopt the technology in ways not originally planned. Fernaeus et al. suggest that one consequence of the turn to practice is to focus design and evaluation efforts on understanding "how users make meaning through interaction, and what aspects they orient themselves towards and use in their specific interactional practices" [8]. This perspective is one we adopt in this paper, as we use our study participant's words and observed actions to explicate the personal meanings and orientations they constructed while using the Reading Glove.

SYSTEM

The Reading Glove is a wearable RFID glove that engages readers in an audio-based interactive narrative by allowing them to "extract memories" from tagged physical objects.

Figure 1. The components of the glove: Arduino Lilypads, XBee radio & RFID reader

The Glove and Objects

The interface consists of a fingerless fabric glove containing an Arduino Lilypad microcontroller, an Innovations ID-12 RFID reader, and an Xbee Series 2 wireless radio [Figure 1, left]. Interactors pick up objects associated with the story, each of which has been tagged with an RFID chip [Figure 1, right]. When the RFID reader in the palm of the glove detects a tag, the tag ID is sent wirelessly to a laptop running MaxMSP. This triggers the audio playback of recorded story fragments associated with the object. Further details on the design of the technical and interactive elements of the Reading Glove can be found in our previous paper [19]. The glove interface was chosen to invoke the metaphor of "psychometry" or object-reading, the fictional power to invoke the memories and history of an object by touching it.

One of our central critiques of previous object-based narrative systems is a broad tendency toward using generic objects with few intrinsic narrative associations of their own. To address this, we resolved to write a narrative that grew out of a specific collection of meaningful objects. We started with the objects, selecting ones that invited touch and interaction, that fit together in terms of the time and place they came from, and that lent themselves to having a wide range of uses, associations, and past history. Once the objects were assembled, we generated themes and narrative uses for each of them, building these gradually into a story that was uniquely rooted in the specific items.

The Story

The Reading Glove's story is an espionage thriller about a spy who is forced to go on the run when his cover is blown. It includes several twists and surprises, and ends with him discovering – too late – that his own agency is involved in the plot to sell him out for political gain. The story is told in the first person, as if the narrator is relating events in his own past. Each tagged object is associated with two story fragments, ranging in length from 17 to 42 seconds. The total story takes 8 minutes and 50 seconds if played straight through, although when the story is encountered via the system, it is played in a random order and at least some of fragments are likely to be played multiple times. Further details on the design of the narrative content can be found in our previous paper [20]. One of the design goals of a modular narrative like the Reading Glove is to overcome the hypertextual difficulties raised in our discussion of Aarseth above [1], that lead to a discontinuity between the experienced narrative and the "imagined real narrative". By making the interactions about "piecing together a puzzle" rather than about "choosing between alternatives" we bypass the challenge of a text with multiple contradictory possible paths. By providing the reader with an apprehensible set of narrative objects, we delimit the possible narrative space, and reduce the sense that there is "more story" waiting just out of reach.

Scenario of Use

A reader using our system is presented with a collection of artifacts arrayed on a table. The artifacts each have a tag attached to them, much like items in a museum or at an estate sale. The reader may pick up any of these objects, and explore its weight, its texture, its scent, and any mechanically interactive elements and moving parts that it might have [Figure 2]. Should the participant bring the palm of the glove close to the tag on the object, a chime will sound and a piece of narration will playback, in which the object is prominently featured. Navigating the narrative consists of selecting objects in order to experience their physical properties, and to reveal the pieces of narration associated with them.

Figure 2. A study participant interacting with the objects

Each object has two different pieces of narration associated with it, and is featured at two different points within the narrative timeline. The first time a reader selects an object, he is given the chronologically first piece of narration associated with it. Should he return to the object a second time, the later piece of narration will play, and a third interaction will re-play the first piece of narration. In this way, readers may return to any point in the narrative to hear it again. The one restriction on this is that no object may be "activated" twice in a row; a reader must select a new object before returning to the previous one.

USER STUDY

One of research goals of the Reading Glove prototype was to investigate the effect of a tangible and wearable interface on the experience of an interactive story. In particular, we wanted to explore the impact of the unique affordances of tangible interaction with narrative objects to support the process of narrative meaning making and present-at-mind experiences. Once the system was constructed, we ran a small user study to investigate how people experienced the interactive narrative and the novel interface. The results of this study will be used to iterate the design of the system to produce a new version and for further studies. Here we present the design insights yielded by this first study.

Methodology

We conducted a study with 10 participants recruited via email from the graduate and undergraduate population of our school. Each participant was given a short tutorial on how to use the glove to interact with a set of generic objects. After this introduction, they were presented with the story objects laid out on a table and told they could interact with them for as long as they liked. When the participants indicated that they were finished with the story, we conducted a short interview asked them to fill out a survey. Our questions focused on two basic areas: their understanding of the story and their experience of the glove and the system as a whole. In this paper, we look primarily at the interview responses as well as some anecdotal evidence from observing their interactions with the system. The interview data was analyzed qualitatively, with two of the researchers independently coding the interview transcripts for sections of interest. These codes were then arranged into a network of themes, highlighting areas where the researchers had produced similar codes and identified recurring patterns. Because of the non-linear path which readers would take through the story, and the complexity of the story itself, we did not think that all readers would emerge with a clear and accurate understanding of the story content. We hoped that they would come away with a basic grasp of the story, and have the experience of being immersed in the storyworld through the physicality of the objects and the interface.

Observed Themes

For each of the 5 themes identified in the data, we present representative quotes from the interviews and discuss the observations made. To preserve confidentiality, participants were assigned reference numbers instead of names.

Kickstarting Imagination

The first theme we identified was that participants reported that the presence of the physical objects helped to kickstart their imaginative immersion in the story. Participant 1 said "it was definitely a different experience with the gloves and the objects at hand, because I felt that it made it more immersive in a way. Yeah, you can definitely imagine the things happening." Participant 7 said "It's not like reading a book…it's set up for you, there's already a mood. Because when you read a book, you make up your own setting but in this case it was already set up." That same person later described the system as "having your thoughts be projected in reality…when you're reading a book it's like it's all in your head and the voices are all in your head and here it's like they're talking and you don't have to think about it." Similarly, participant 8 identified the visual properties of the objects as grounding the narrative in her imagination "I create scenarios…visual scenarios in my head when I'm reading so I have very specific ideas of what things look like. So what was different about this experience is that the prop cues made the creation of the visuals seem to occur more quickly without having to get into the narrative." The look and feel of the objects set the scene for encountering the story, helping ease them into the mood and setting of the narrative. This can be seen as a benefit, in that it bootstraps immersion into the storyworld. It can also provide a cautionary note, however, in that part of a reader's enjoyment of a story is in the use of their imagination. If the physical system over-determines the look and feel of a storytelling environment, the reader may find themselves less drawn into the story because there is less for them to contribute.

Engaging Multiple Senses

In addition to providing a kickstart to imagining the story, we found that the physically embodied nature of the experience provided multiple modalities for the participants to acquire specific additional information. In particular, the objects served as markers for the time period. Nothing in the text of the story identified the year or era that the narrative took place in. In the interview, we asked participants to estimate the time the story took place in, and the majority of them were able to accurately guess that it was intended to take place around the turn of the 20th century, or the year 1900. Five of seven transcribed interviewees specifically make reference to the objects when attempting to determine what the year was, remarking that their feeling of the time period came from the attributes of the physical objects.

Participant 8 talked about how she read additional information into the objects when making selections about what to interact with next. She said she focused "on context and what I thought the objects meant in terms of that context. So if the storyline mentioned he was going to be outside, or going to the wharf, I'd pick up the globe because I thought maybe it represented travel, or if he was going outside the top hat because you put on a hat when you leave." In both of these examples, the participants have used their physical experience of the objects to fill in gaps in knowledge about the story and to infer information about the narrative that is not provided within the "script" as read by the narrator. In Aarseth's terms, this is a part of the narrative "text", however it is a multimodal text that relies on the embodied situation of the participants for the creation of meaning.

Engaging with the Objects

One common claim for tangible interfaces is that they can provide scaffolding and structures for external cognition, by allowing users to offload information on to the physical arrangement of the tangible objects [10]. We found that very few of the participants made use of this feature of the objects. Our first participant, in fact, did not pick up any of the objects all, and instead just touched the glove to the tags as they lay on the table. From that point on, when we laid the objects out at the start of a session, we tucked each of the tags under or inside the objects so that they had to be picked up in order to access them with the reader in the glove. This achieved the goal of getting people to pick the objects up, but the physical engagement with the objects was still less than we expected. Most participants picked the objects up, activated the story fragment, and then set them back down in approximately the place where they had been before. Participant 8 said in the interview afterwards that she felt a hesitation about playing with the objects too much or moving them around. "For me, if objects aren't my own, I don't like rearranging them or moving them because it doesn't seem like mine." Several participants also made an analogy between this system and the experience of encountering objects in a museum. This may have influenced the desire of people to handle the objects, as museums tend to discourage this behaviour.

There was one extreme exception to this rule, however. One participant engaged fully with the physicality of the objects, beginning by putting on the top hat and the goggles and examining each of the objects in some detail [Figure 2, left]. Later, in the interview, participant 10 described this part of his interaction: "At the very beginning, as I was just picking up these fragments, what it was most enjoyable for me to do was to interact with the objects physically like putting on the hat, putting on the goggles because they're interesting objects in their own right. Figuring out how the coffee grinder works and just kind of letting things wash over." As his time with the system continued, he began to attempt to figure out the exact order that the story fragments should go in, by flipping back and forth rapidly between objects to hear them again and again. "It was cool, I feel like I went through these stage of first just enjoying these objects for their value, for their own physical value and just listening the narration and being like oh, it's a spy story, that's cool and then realizing I could actually put these together." As he began to figure out what objects came first, he sorted them into an ordered line [Figure 2, right]. In the interview afterwards, he recalls "I can't remember at what point I began to clue in that it would be possible to arrange things, touch things in an order to make things happen. But I did. And then I started trying to create a system for keeping track of that visually, you saw what that was like where I was trying to lay things out in a 2D grid".

Establishing Connection to the Character

Although people did not physically manipulate the objects as much as we had thought they would, one area where their response surprised us was in identifying with the main character of the tale. Participant 1 said "It's easier to relate to the main protagonist, in a way, when you have the objects at hand and you can… feel what he's going into in some ways." Similarly, participant 3 said "The person going to the place…he sees different objects and there is story behind it like what he thinks about it." The objects were seen as triggers for the story, not just for the participants, but for the character in the story, as if these were his objects and he was telling his story through them.

Participant 10, who rearranged the objects extensively, described this process as being motivated not just with attempting to understand the story but with connecting to the character. "You know, I really like the narrator, I really began to feel empathetic towards him. Me trying to arrange the sequence of events it's like me trying to remember what happened…And then the act of trying to put things together and then suddenly finding this continuity, it was like 'Aha! Yes, now that makes sense to me' and somehow it also felt like now it makes sense to the character too." Other participants formed a clear connection between specific objects and other minor characters in the story. One link that we explicitly designed into the story was that one of the villains was consistently identified as the "man in the goggles", and both of the story fragments associated with the goggles object talked about this man. In the interview, when participants were asked what they remembered about the goggles object, the majority of them were able to link the goggles to the villain character. We also asked about the vase and the camera objects, which were not directly linked to a recurring character but instead to crucial plot moments or items in the story. We found that in general, participants were less able to provide a coherent association with those objects than for the goggles. The linking of character and object appears to have been more salient and memorable than other associations.

Attracting and Distracting

The final theme we have identified relates to the intrinsic qualities of the objects themselves, which provided both an attractive gateway into the story and, occasionally, a distraction from the story. The participant who engaged most fully with the objects relates "Ok, the best part about using the glove was at the very beginning, when I felt like I could put on things. What I really wanted was to take the glove…take the hat and put it on…I wanted to interact not just like…because I had to be really deliberate. (slaps hand on the table, as if activating a tag) Whereas I really wanted to fondle this thing and look at this…it's those kinds of things. Because these things have affordances that are so rich and so inviting."

This rich invitation sometimes got in the way of experiencing the story, however. Participant 2 recalls: "When I interact with a book…all the distracting things about the book are on the outside, so I can't see them when I'm reading. Sometimes I got caught up in…particularly the rose, I just really liked the way that the brass felt and I kinda got distracted by that." This description of getting caught up in the physicality of the experience is an example of what happens when the phenomenon of hypermediacy interferes with a reader's ability to experience transparent immediacy. The same participant commented on this again when asked what she found confusing about the experience: "This isn't so much confusing, but I found when I picked up stuff I was like looking for the tag, I wasn't necessarily looking at the thing."

DISCUSSION

We can apply the lens of theory to our five observed themes in order to derive some more general design recommendations for tangible storytelling systems. This list is not intended to provide an exhaustive framework for TUI design, but to explore several important concepts for future TUI research into interactive storytelling via our analysis of user experiences with the Reading Glove.

Design themes

Enacting a Role

The first ideal listed by Fernaeus et al. is to shift from considering tangible interaction as an information-centric activity to an action-centric one. Several of the participants remarked on the fact that the act of wearing the glove and interacting with the objects led them to connect with or empathize with the main character. The actions that they took with the glove could be seen as the actions that the character in the story took, allowing the user to take on his role through physical actions. We found it interesting that participants reported a strong sense of character association and empathy through the use of the objects. We see this as a manifestation of Bizzocchi et al's notion of Narrativized

Interface, in that the logic of the interaction placed the interactors into a bodily situation that paralleled that of the character. We believe there is something qualitatively different about handling an object that a character is said to have touched and held that is not captured through reading about that object on a page, or seeing it on a screen, or even manipulating a virtual version of the object in a game. This can be seen as an extension of the "mixed-reality" type of narrativised interface [3]. As a result of this effect the interface became a site for the other significant aspects of Bizzocchi's framework: character, emotion, storyworld, and micro-narrative. This is a poetic that is unique to tangible systems, and it entails an understanding that designing an interaction is also about designing a role for the interactor to enact with that system.

Ownership and Permission

In their discussion of interaction-in-context, Fernaeus et al. talk about social and personal factors that can impact human activity, one of which is the notion of ownership and attachment. We saw this play out in implicit and explicit ways in our study, where most participants evinced a hesitation to pick up and move the objects around to any great degree. One participant specifically said afterwards that she did not feel a sense of ownership of the objects and thus did not want to rearrange them too much. This suggests that when presenting people with physical objects that are meant to be interacted with, they should be given explicit permission or at least encouragement to feel a sense of ownership of these objects. Our objects were not *obviously* interactive artifacts or toys and we believe that the lack of explicit signifiers of interactivity served to reinforce pre-existing cultural conceptions of property and ownership that our participants brought to the experience. While the tags on the objects served to indicate that each object had an interaction point, they also signified a certain "artifact" or "heirloom" quality that we believe reinforced this approach, as did the apparent age and fragility of some of the objects. Some of the hesitation we observed was also likely a result of the experimental context of the interaction: we avoided explicitly instructing the participants to handle the objects, to prevent influencing their behaviour, however this may have had the unintended consequence of not providing them with sufficient permission to interact naturally with the objects. The novelty of the interaction was also a factor. With any new media form, a certain amount of literacy is required in order to get the most out of an experience. None of our participants had any prior experience with a system like this, which shaped how they interacted with it. If there is one lesson to be learned from this experience, it is that object-based storytelling systems need to either explicitly or implicitly provide their interactors with permission to engage with the objects.

Multiplicity of Interpretations

Fernaeus et al.'s final ideal, on shifting from objective to subjective interpretations, connects to our observations of how people engage with the objects. Participant 10's playful interactions with the objects, such as wearing them or opening them up to look inside were not interactions that the system recognized in the sense of reacting to them, but they were also not disallowed by the system. The space was left open for participants to engage with the objects in whatever way was comfortable for them. Participant 8 also touched on this notion when discussing how she picked which object to touch next, i.e. she chose the globe after hearing a story fragment about taking a ship, because she thought the globe could represent travel. The semantic and aesthetic richness of the objects lent themselves well to this kind of personal, subjective meaning-making. Sengers and Gaver discuss the role of openness in design as potentially powerful tool exploring a range of interpretations, and the multiplicity of meanings created by the participants here demonstrates the value of this approach [16]. Here we also see evidence of our notion of present-at-mind interactions. It was clear that the objects were neither invisible interfaces to the narrative script, nor were they problematic hindrances to the function of reading. Instead, the participants treated the objects as an integral part of the text, to which they could bring their own sets of memories and associations. The objects were suspended between transparent immediacy and hypermediacy, and were able to serve as a point of imaginative departure for the interactors, and as a site for grounded knowledge about the story.

Boundary Objects

The final general theme that we have observed returns us to the notion of boundary objects. Interactive systems like the Reading Glove exist in a strange suspension between the (digital/virtual) world of the fiction, and the (physical) world of the reader. Objects in this system already invoke narratives, even without the explicitly narrative layer of the digital system to underlie them. A number of our participants commented that they were more interested in the objects than they were in the pre-recorded narration that we had associated with them. The intrinsic narrative texture that surrounds these objects was one of the central criteria for selecting them for inclusion in our story. Here again, we see the objects operating in the present-at-mind mode, by retaining meaningful associations from their own intrinsic physical properties, and conjoining them with the narrative meanings that we encoded within them.

Design Considerations

These four themes provide us with some useful criteria for the design of future tangible storytelling systems. Briefly summarized, we can recommend that designers:

- **Provide support for role-playing:** Narrative interfaces can provide opportunities for the interactor's embodiment to mirror that of the characters in the story, which in turn supports a richer association with character.
- **Give interactors permission to play:** The contextual framing of the interaction can unintentionally constrain the interactor's sense of freedom to engage.
- **Design for open interpretations:** Narrative engagement increases when interactors are free to make their own meanings within the system.

- **Use boundary objects to "suture" the gap between the conceptual world and the physical world:** Semantically rich interfaces which support a wide variety of interpretations and imaginings are able to act as intermediaries between the reader and the storyworld.

Much work remains to be done in order to further test these recommendations, and to uncover other poetics of tangible storytelling systems. This initial design exploration has provided us with insight about how users experience these systems, and about how to improve future design iterations.

CONCLUSION

In this paper we have analyzed the responses of study participants using the Reading Glove to experience an interactive narrative. We have used their reported experience to craft a set of design themes that articulate some of the benefits and challenges of merging tangible interaction with non-linear storytelling. We believe our themes of *enacting a role*, *ownership and permission*, *multiplicity of interpretations* and *boundary objects* have applicability outside of the system we have designed and can help guide design thinking about tangible and wearable interaction more broadly. We provide a set of recommendations for designers to consider when crafting tangible interactive narratives.

ACKNOWLEDGMENTS

This work is supported by the GRAND NCE.

REFERENCES

1. Aarseth, E. J. Nonlinearity and Literary Theory. N. Wardrip-Fruin and N. Montfort (ed.), *The New Media Reader*, 1994, 761-780.
2. Bizzocchi, J. Games and Narrative: An Analytical Framework. *Loading - the Journal of the Canadian Games Studies Association*, 1, 1, 2007, 10 pages.
3. Bizzocchi, J., Lin, B. and Tanenbaum, J. *Games, Narrative, and the Design of Interface*. forthcoming.
4. Bolter, J. D. and Grusin, R. *Immediacy, Hypermediacy, and Remediaton*. The MIT Press, Cambridge, Mass, USA, 1999.
5. Bolter, J. D. and Joyce, M. Hypertext and creative writing. In *Proceedings of the Proceedings of the ACM conference on Hypertext* (Chapel Hill, North Carolina, United States, 1987). ACM, 1987, 41-50.
6. Cassell, J. Towards a Model of Technology and Literacy Development: Story Listening Systems. *Journal of Applied Developmental Psychology*, 25, 1, 2004, 75-105.
7. Dourish, P. *Where the Action Is: The Foundations of Embodied Interaction*. MIT Press, Cambridge, 2001.
8. Fernaeus, Y., Tholander, J. and Jonsson, M. Towards a new set of ideals: consequences of the practice turn in tangible interaction. In *Proceedings of the Proceedings of the 2nd international conference on Tangible and embedded interaction* (Bonn, Germany, 2008). ACM, 2008, 223-230.
9. Holmquist, L. E., Helander, M. and Dixon, S. Every object tells a story: Physical interfaces for digital storytelling. In *Proceedings of the NordiCHI2000* (2000), 2000.
10. Kirsh, D. and Maglio, P. On Distinguishing Epistemic from Pragmatic Action. *Cognitive Science*, 18, 1994, 513-549.
11. Konkel, M., Leung, V., Ullmer, B. and Hu, C. Tagaboo: a collaborative children's game based upon wearable RFID technology. *Pers. Ubiq. Comput.*, 8, 5, 2004, 382-384.
12. Lustig, C., Novatchkov, H., Dunne, L., McHugh, M. and Coyle, L. Using Colocation to Support Human Memory. In *Proceedings of the Workshop on Supporting Human Memory with Interactive Systems, HCI Conference* (Lancaster, UK, 2007), 2007, 41-44.
13. Martins, T., Sommerer, C., Mignonneau, L. and Correia, N. Gauntlet: A Wearable Interface for Ubiquitous Gaming. In *Proceedings of the International Conference on Human-Computer Interaction with Mobile Devices and Services* (Amsterdam, The Netherlands, 2008). ACM Press, 2008, 367-370.
14. Mazalek, A., Davenport, G. and Ishii, H. Tangible viewpoints: A physical approach to multimedia stories. In *Proceedings of the Multimedia* (Juan-les-Pins, France, 2002). ACM Press, 2002.
15. Mazalek, A., Wood, A. and Ishii, H. genieBottles: An interactive narrative in bottles. In *Proceedings of the ACM SIGGRAPH Conference* (August 12-17, 2001). ACM Press, 2001.
16. Sengers, P. and Gaver, B. Staying Open to Interpretation: engaging multiple meanings in design and evaluation. In *Proceedings of the DIS* (University Park, Pennsylvania, June 26-28, 2006). ACM Press, 2006, 99-108.
17. Star, S. L. and Griesemer, J. R. Institutional ecology, 'translations' and boundary objects: Amateurs and professionals in Berkeley's museum of vertebrate zoology, 1907-39. *Social Studies of Science*, 19, 3, 1989, 387-420.
18. Suchman, L. A. *Plans and Situated Actions: The Problem of Human-Machine Communication*. Cambridge University Press, New York, 1987.
19. Tanenbaum, J., Tanenbaum, K. and Antle, A. The Reading Glove: Designing Interactions for Object-Based Tangible Storytelling. In *Proceedings of the Augmented Human* (Megeve, France, 2010). ACM Press, 2010, 132-140.
20. Tanenbaum, J., Tanenbaum, K., Seif El-Nasr, M. and Hatala, M. Authoring Tangible Interactive Narratives Using Cognitive Hyperlinks. In *Proceedings of the 3rd Workshop on Intelligent Narrative Technologies (INT3) at Foundations of Digital Games Conference (FDG)* (Monterey, CA, 2010). ACM Press, 2010, 8 pp. .
21. Ullmer, B. and Ishii, H. Emerging Frameworks for Tangible User Interfaces. J. M. Carrol (ed.), *Human-Computer Interaction in the New Millenium*, 2001, 579-601.

Rudiments 1, 2 & 3: Design Speculations on Autonomy

John Helmes[1], Alex S. Taylor[1], Xiang Cao[1], Kristina Höök[2], Peter Schmitt[3], Nicolas Villar[1]

[1]Microsoft Research
7 J J Thomson Avenue
Cambridge, CB3 0FB, UK
{jhelmes, ast, xiangc, nvillar}@microsft.com

[2]Mobile Life, Stockholm
University Forum 100
164 40 Kista, Sweden
kia@dsv.su.se

[3]MIT Media Laboratory
20 Ames Street
Cambridge, MA 02142, USA
peter@media.mit.edu

ABSTRACT

This work describes the design process and installation of three speculative, rudimentary machines, or *rudiments*. Through careful iterations in their design, the rudiments are intended to provoke curiosity and discussion around the possibility of autonomy in interactive systems. The design of the rudiments is described in detail, alongside the design decisions that were made to suggest a machine autonomy and to provoke discussion. Some preliminary reflections from installing the rudiments in two separate households are also reported. Widely divergent opinions of the rudiments from the two households are used to discuss a number of themes for thinking about autonomy and interactive systems design. Overall, the presented work adopts a perspective strongly oriented towards guiding future research, but, importantly, aims to do so by opening up and exposing the design possibilities rather than constraining them.

Author Keywords

Autonomy, social robots, speculative design.

Categories and Subject Descriptors

H5.m. Information interfaces and presentation (e.g., HCI): Miscellaneous.

General Terms

Design.

INTRODUCTION

In this paper, we describe our recent efforts to explore the role machine autonomy has in interactive systems design. The work we present builds on a small but growing body of research that has been investigating how innovations in areas like robotics and artificial intelligence might introduce new possibilities for designing interactive systems.

A central theme to our work has been to consider what the implications would be for interactive systems if we remained open to the way autonomy is exhibited. That is, our interests have not been limited to the kinds of autonomy we are familiar with—for example, the autonomy we would normally associate with human or animal behaviour. Instead, we've sought to investigate the possibilities for designing interactions with technologies that are autonomous in curious and perhaps very different ways.

TEI'11, January 22–26, 2011, Funchal, Portugal.

Naturally, an interest in autonomy and especially autonomous machines leads to a host of challenging philosophical and empirical problems. Can machines truly be autonomous? How, exactly, would a machine exhibit autonomy? What would the broader social consequences of a machine autonomy be? And so on. Rather than attempt to answer these arguably insoluble questions, however, our work pursues what might be thought of as a pragmatic, design-oriented approach. In practice, this has involved us designing three working concepts, or 'rudiments', intended to invite speculation and provoke discussion around the possibility of autonomy in machines. To obtain some initial insights, it has also involved us installing the rudiments in two households and interviewing the households' members.

Related Work

Research into social robotics and artificial agents has until relatively recently been a niche in computing. Various well-publicised projects from MIT's Media Lab have, for example, been hugely influential [3, 6], but they have also remained largely the preserve of blue-sky, laboratory research and rarely produced machines robust enough to be studied in unsupervised, social environments [14].

In recent years, however, there has been an increasing interest in building robots and agents, and, to a lesser extent, investigating their interactive characteristics in real-world settings. An indication of this is the growth of dedicated conferences such as Human-Robot Interaction (HRI) and Ro-Man, as well as a receptiveness to robotics in HCI. A cursory scan of the published work in these forums reveals much of it has focused on building systems that behave, in some fashion, like humans. For example, many systems address utilitarian concerns, enabling robots to accomplish tasks usually designated to humans. Zhao et al. [25] have designed a system using visual tags, or "Magic Cards", that designates housework tasks to robots. Other work has aimed to build robots that can interact in human-like ways, no matter how primitively. Again, the Media Lab has played a significant role in this with their 'social robotics' research [3, 4], as well work on conversational agents [16]. Elsewhere research has investigated human forms of communication with robots and agents, examining the impact of facial appearance [20], eye contact [13], emotional expression [11], etc.

It is along these lines that a small body of research has begun to part company, and where the presented work also provides a point of departure. A number of researchers have distinguished their work by adopting more exploratory approaches to studying autonomy and, in some cases, designing systems that challenge the prevailing interest in systems that recognise and simulate human behaviour [8, 9, 15, 19, 21]. Of these works, three related areas have been of particular relevance in shaping the work we present.

One important influence has been the rethinking of some of the fundamentals in artificial intelligence (AI). A stable of researchers associated with AI have, since the 1990s, challenged the notion that AI systems must have complete representations or models of the worlds they operate in (e.g. [1, 5, 12]). Broadly, they have questioned and in some cases entirely eschewed the need for fully-fledged, *a priori* models, suggesting, instead, that artificial agents might model their environments bottom-up—that is, they might initially have a limited set of representations that 'evolve', dynamically, as the agent operates in its environment.

These developments—although seen as somewhat inconsequential in mainstream AI today—have prompted some broad proposals in interactive systems design. Leahu et al. [14] have suggested, for example, that ubiquitous computing might learn something from AI's efforts to build dynamic systems, robust enough to operate in real-world environments. To grossly oversimplify their arguments (but hopefully capture their overall gist), they suggest that ubicomp might find solutions to building robust, scalable sensing and awareness systems by looking to AI and it efforts to work with partial or incomplete representations of the world. Leahu et al. claim it is when users engage with these partial, relatively simple systems that subtleties and sophistication of interaction can emerge. Taylor [23] has built on this position, specifically focusing on intelligence as an emergent phenomenon. He makes a case that the design of interactive systems might be broadened if HCI opened itself up to systems that exhibited partial and unfamiliar forms of intelligence that were open to interpretation.

A second influence for us and one that puts some of these broader ideas into practice revolves around two concepts, 'Expressive AI' and 'Alien Presence' [17, 21]. Mateas, Pousman and Romero have used these ideas to conceive of systems that expose their computational workings in strange and unfamiliar ways. In their words, they aspire to designing 'enchanting' systems that prompt curiosity and wonder. Their approach to using AI raises a particularly compelling proposition; instead of trying to achieve the illusive 'AI-complete' system that can accurately model all human behaviours and respond to them in humanly intelligible ways, they intentionally exploit the partial models that AI systems are able to construct. Their aim, they explain, is to create a "sense of the system as an independent, non-human subject, who has its own interpretation of the activity" (p 374, [21]). Hence their use of the word 'alien'.

Last but by no means least, a number of projects from Goldsmith University's Interaction Research Studio and especially their collaboration with members of Cornell University's Information Science Dept. [9] have played a significant role in our thinking. The Goldsmith's-Cornell project involved the use of sensors placed in a house to generate 'home health horoscopes': short printouts, worded like horoscopes, conveying "interpretations of domestic well being based on sensor data and simple pattern-recognition" (p 538, [9]). The research was especially concerned with the 'approximate' results achieved using sensing and inference systems. Yet, as with the alien presence work, the aim was to exploit the ambiguity resulting from the supposed limitations of the system and encourage interpretation on the part of users. This was born out in the deployment of the Home Health Horoscope; the household the system was customised for and deployed in speculated on its workings throughout the trial. Of particular relevance to the work that follows were the different ways the household members made sense of and judged how meaningful the system was for them. The research highlights the struggle and frustration that can arise from trying to make sense of a system that is ambiguous in its function. As we will see, this introduces a salient theme in our interviews.

Together, these three roughly circumscribed areas of research have helped to orient our investigations into autonomy. Crucially, however, our intention has not been to use them to narrow down the broad issues associated with machine autonomy. Instead, we have used this work alongside our designs to open up new possibilities. In this vein, we have also intentionally avoided defining autonomy in any strict sense. Our interests lay in how it is people get to grips with notions of autonomy in their own terms. What we wanted to avoid was any theorising on our part as to what constitutes autonomy, *per se*. Our sense was this would run counter to the efforts to provoke open discussion.

RUDIMENTARY DESIGN

Our use of design to provoke discussion draws heavily on a speculative design approach usually associated with the Design Interactions Dept. at the Royal College of Art [7] and popularised in HCI by the Goldsmith's Interaction Research Studio [10], amongst others [2, 15, 24]. Informed by these past examples, we chose to design three relatively simple working concepts, named rudiments 1, 2 & 3—the naming intended to reflect their novel but crude and basic behaviours.

We aimed to invite a level of curiosity in building the rudiments by experimenting with a combination of different materials, aesthetics and interactions. Also, we purposefully pursued an open-ended system design, using an ambiguity in the concepts to promote curiosity and discussion [7, 10, 22]. For instance, we chose to design behaviours into the rudiments that were of no obvious benefit, but could potentially be seen as responsive to and thus reflective of people's presence and activities.

To further encourage speculation around autonomy, different levels of sophistication were designed into each of the three rudiments. As a general rule, their behaviours and computational workings were designed to increase in sophistication from Rudiment 1 to 3. Thus, in their design, we tried to accentuate the differences in sophistication between the rudiments while expressing a common aesthetic so that they would be seen as a 'family'.

Rudiment #1: 'Wandering around'

Rudiment 1, the least sophisticated of the three machines, is made up of two modules connected via a flexible cable.

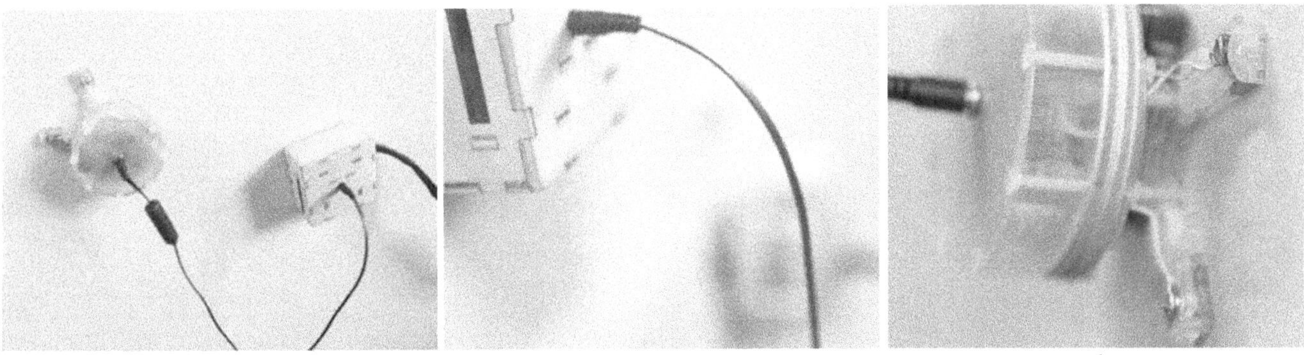

1a. 1b. 1c.

Figure 1. Rudiment 1 on vertical surface, with acrylic moving module connected to a wooden switchbox.

One of the modules quite literally wanders around a magnetic surface, e.g., a fridge door. Its round-shaped wood and acrylic case encapsulates its magnetic wheels and also a narrow-range IR sensor to detect nearby movement. Its speed and direction are randomly changed when the IR sensor is triggered. The second module, a switchbox (Fig. 1b), is magnetically affixed to the same surface as the moving module. It simultaneously provides power and sends signals to the moving module whenever its own wide-range IR sensor detects peripheral movement. On receiving a signal, the moving module is activated and moves for a random amount of time (limited by a set min and max). To prevent it from falling off a surface, two sensors protrude from the front of the moving module (Fig. 1c). Each sensor contains two switches, one to detect an obstacle and the other to detect when an edge is reached. If these sensors are triggered, the module backs up and changes its direction. Both modules contain Arduino micro-controller boards to control the sensors, actuation and communication.

Rudiment #2: 'Listening to the home soundscape'

Rudiment 2 consists of a plywood servomotor and base (Fig. 2a), and two acrylic microphone cases (Fig. 2c)—all three wirelessly connected using the Zigbee standard. The servomotor, with an articulated arm and pencil attached, is slotted into the middle of the wooden base (Fig. 2b). As well as its mechanical parts, the bespoke servomotor houses a customised Arduino micro-controller and an FIO board (see: funnel.cc/Hardware/FIO) with XBee module (the latter for wireless comms).

The two encased microphones function as a trigger for the servomotor and the arm/pencil attachment. The rotation and direction of the motor's arm are dictated by the level of sound input and which of the two microphones detects a louder sound. Also, the system's sensitivity is varied using a simple caching mechanism: sustained or particularly loud noises make it increasingly sensitive and consequently the motor arm's frequency and degree of rotation are increased. The intended effect is a machine that appears to draw in response to sounds but, to some degree, controls its own movements. The rudiment's output is drawn on removable paper sheets that in effect visually record a soundscape. Because they communicate with the motor wirelessly, the microphone modules can also be used to explore or further accentuate certain sounds. For example, placing the microphones relatively close to the base allows for experimentation with feedback of its own 'sketching sound'.

Rudiment #3: 'Dangling from a string'

Rudiment 3 consists of an acrylic cog system and casement suspended on a horizontally extended, toothed belt of adjustable length (Fig. 3c). Using suction cups, the flexible belt can be mounted on any smooth, vertical surface, e.g., a window. Under the cog system, the oval-shaped casement contains a video camera. Actuated by a DC motor, the cog system moves the casement left and right along the belt's entire length. The camera can also be rotated left or right by up to 70 degrees. These movements effectively change the viewing direction of the camera. In addition, the opaque casement can display eight different colours using three integrated LEDs (red, green, and blue).

The rudiment's movement and colour are controlled by an Arduino micro-controller, which in turn communicates with a small PC encased in a wooden box (Fig. 3c). The PC receives the video signal from the camera and triggers the rudiment's behaviour through a set of simple yet nondeterministic computer vision processes. The program, written in C++, searches for human faces in the video frame using an object detection algorithm based on the Haar classifier cascade [18]. Each time a face is detected, the rudiment will adjust itself by either moving along the belt or turning the camera (randomly choosing between the two actions), so that the face remains centred. As this happens continuously, the camera appears to follow any movement of a detected face. When more than two faces are detected, the rudiment randomly chooses one face to follow. In addition to faces, the rudiment also responds to gross motion in the camera view, momentarily turning towards it. Finally, it occasionally makes random movements, adding a degree of ambiguity to its behaviour.

The rudiment also turns one of its eight possible colours when a face is detected. The colour is chosen by comparing the detected face with eight face categories, each consisting of three sample faces. The category that contains the most similar face is chosen and the associated colour displayed. The face comparison is based on a straightforward pixel-level comparison, without leveraging any predefined knowledge of facial features. This results in a somewhat "machine-defined" similarity measure, which may or may not appear recognisable to users. With a small probability (0.05), the newly detected face may replace an old face

2a. **2b.** **2c.**

Figure 2. Rudiment 2 with wooden servomotor and drawing arm, and two acrylic microphone modules.

sample in the category. As such, the face categories gradually evolve as the rudiment is exposed to more faces. This simple machine learning technique allows the rudiment to adapt to the people who interact with it and present the same colour each time it recognises similar facial features.

INSTALLATIONS

As we've noted, the three rudiments were installed in two households (both in the South East region of the UK). Seb and Mari, a couple living in the first household, had the machines for four weeks. The second household, made up of Adrian and Anna, again a couple, had them for just under four weeks. From the outset, we made it clear in both households that the rudiments were designed to prompt speculation and that as researchers we were interested in the thoughts and discussions they provoked as opposed to any opinions of them as final products.

Both couples were able to choose where to install the rudiments, although, as we intended, their placement was restricted by their design. They were also asked to have the machines running as often as they wanted, but told to turn them off when they were away from home (to avoid any chance of the machines being damaged or damaging the properties). We received impromptu feedback during the installations, on the occasions we made short visits to tweak the machines, and via emails and phone conversations. Also, the couples were interviewed about their experiences with the rudiments when we removed them.

Seb and Mari had all three machines in their living room, an open plan, but crowded, home-work room populated with numerous musical instruments, computers and other electrical equipment, as well as the usual furniture. They reported having the machines turned on daily, and described extended periods in which they actively interacted with them, as well as letting them run in the background. Adrian and Anna initially had the machines in their kitchen/dining room, the space they spend most time in. Later, they moved Rudiment 2 to the sitting room, and experimented with different places for the microphones. Their reported use was less frequent than the first household, with the machines turned on for thirty minutes to an hour, for three or four days a week. However, from their interview, Adrian, in particular, seemed very familiar with each rudiment.

Perhaps the most striking result from the interviews was the contrasting views from the two households. In their interview, Seb and Mari were very positive about the rudiments. They enthusiastically described their interactions with them and openly discussed ideas around autonomy with little to no prompting from the interviewer. They appeared very willing to see the machines in poetic terms (for lack of a better phrase), treating them as curiosities with varying degrees of independence. Conversely, Adrian and Anna, although open to discussion, expressed a palpable dislike of the rudiments. In their interview, they alluded to them more than once as the cause of irritation because of their seemingly "pointless" actions. For the purposes of this initial investigation, we found this contrasting set of opinions to be especially valuable. It provided us with what felt like a dialogue between the two households, drawing attention to several provocative themes. In the remains of this section, we've chosen to present the materials relating to three of these themes because, although still preliminary, they have pointed us towards what seem to be some useful ways to begin thinking about autonomy and design.

It should be emphasised that this component of our work was not intended as a full deployment. That is, the installations were not treated as evaluations in any conventional sense, using formal methods for data collection and analysis. Rather, our hope was they'd offer an early resource to orient our future design work. The deliberations in the interviews were seen as a means to develop our own thinking about the relationship between autonomy and interaction design. This explorative, open-ended quality to our investigations will be evident below in our concern for not only the content, but also the form and structure of the interview discussions; we discovered there were insights to be found not only in what people thought about the rudiments but also how they discussed them (hence our use of relatively long excerpts from the transcripts). The preliminary nature of our results will also be clear from the topics we have omitted, not least, the commonly considered themes of anthropomorphism and zoomorphism—the popularity of these topics being one reason why we have, at this stage, chosen to focus elsewhere.

Function and Engagement

The most prominent discussion point for both households was around the utility or function of the rudiments. As we've discussed, we gave a good deal of thought to the form and aesthetic of each rudiment. By accentuating the cabling, electronics and mechanical movements, they were purposefully designed to echo machine-like qualities. At the same time, we contrasted this mechanical aesthetic with

3a. 3b. 3c.

Figure 3. Rudiment 3 attached to a window using suction cups, and wooden box containing micro-controller and computer.

varying degrees of independent behaviour, intentionally setting up the mechanistic against allusions to autonomy.

This juxtaposition was a source of discussion for Seb and Mari. In one interview excerpt, Seb expresses his thoughts about utility by comparing the machines with a dog:

Seb: I like the idea of not being a dog, but something new. Because these shapes are kind of new shapes.
Mari: You get bored, no? [Laughs] You want something new!
Seb: No, no, no. You already have a dog. Why would you do a dog as a robot? [...] Cause I mean I like the functional side, cause that guy draws, right? [points to #2] So the whole thing is revolving. [...] Their shape comes from a functional style. So the dog, it looks like a dog, cause at some point it has grown bigger teeth and a tail or, you know, and so on. So nature has this kind of reasoning. [...] Cause I mean I think you get into this discussion about improving or replacing, and these are not about improving or replacing. They're about something new.
Mari: You're right, yeah, about replacing...
Seb: Cause I think that's one of the bad kind of views on machineries or robots, because of this fear that they might replace us, but it's not about that.

Seb's meandering thoughts are indicative of the couple's struggle to make sense of the shapes and behaviours of the rudiments. At no point are they able to draw any strong conclusions, but clearly the rudiments prompt a dialogue about issues of form, movement and function. Seb contrasts the evolving appearance of the dog, with that of the machines. He implies that, unconstrained by any need for improvement or even replacement, the machines offer the opportunity for "something new".

Pursuing this idea of newness, Mari and Seb appear to construct a particular relationship between aesthetic and function. They make reference to the functional-looking aesthetic and movement of machines but, simultaneously, discuss how they have no prescribed function or at least none that is familiar:

Interviewer: What is it about them that allows you to treat...
Seb: I think it is the actions. That they do stuff.
Mari: Yeah, the movements, the designer one [points to #2 and starts to mimic its rotation] because he's doing so much movement and all the articulation. Actually he behaves like... he is drawing!
Interviewer: But how is that different to other things you have?
Seb: I think the biggest difference is, err, the fact that they don't do something for a reason, for our own good... [points to them] for themselves. They don't kind of... they're not useful. [...] It's not good or bad. It's how they are.

So in characterising the movements of Rudiment 2, Mari and Seb articulate a different kind of machine-like functionality, one that might not be "for our own good" or "about improving or replacing" what we do. Nevertheless, it is the responsive movements that appeal—the 'behaviours', the 'drawing!'

Less enamoured with the rudiments, Adrian and Anna find themselves frustrated by their unclear function. They want the machines to be more directly engaging and interactive:

Adrian: If something is going to be completely functionless it has to engage you at another level.
Anna: Yes, it's that interaction isn't it? It's just something that connects you with the thing.
Adrian: Whereas something that appears to have some irritations but is entirely pointless, it's just irritating [...] No, I mean coming to this one which we haven't really talked about [points to #3], that's getting to the point where it's starting to be a bit more interesting because, whether it's real or imagined, when it looked at me it went blue. Now whether it really recognises me or not I don't know. But it tended towards blueness with me... Which is kind of cute! You know it sees me and goes blue. It's like 'ah, hello." So there's a certain amount of something to do with recognition and, you know, it's getting towards interactivity.

Here, Adrian contrasts the "pointless" behaviours of the other two machines with Rudiment 3's intelligible interactions. The couple explain that their interest or engagement is a result of direct interaction. However, perhaps inadvertently, Adrian expresses a subtlety in this:

Adrian: ... whereas something which appears to have some irritations but is entirely pointless is just irritating [cat makes noise behind him] just like our cat [laughing].

With the help of a pet (again), Adrian mocks the value of having a cat—irritating because it is pointless. Clearly, however, he and Anna are fond of their cat.

Of course, it's of no coincidence that both couples make reference to pets in their interviews. The rudiments, even though intentionally designed not to resemble anything animal-like, provoke questions about machines that might be autonomous in pet-like ways. As with pets, we find debate around the value of machines that have no apparent function. Whatever one's personal inclination towards pets, these discussions point towards a possible way of thinking about the rudiments and, more generally, autonomy. We see a tension being worked out by the interviewees as they speak about the rudiments in terms of how engaging they are, and their functionality and independence (or autonomy). Moreover, we find the relationship between these qualities is constructed in a fluid, evolving fashion as the particular characteristics of the rudiments are reconciled.

For the purposes of this paper, the point we wish to draw out, then, is how notions of autonomy turned on the ways function and engagement were seen, understood and articulated. It is not that there was one definitive definition of autonomy that the couples were able to judge the rudiments by. Instead, they used the qualities of function and engagement to make sense of the machines and, in part at least, how they were or were not autonomous.

Temporality and Persistence

In the excerpts above, Adrian also explains his preference for Rudiment 3 in terms of its ability to recognise him. "Whether it's real or imagined", the machine's choice of colours suggests a recognition of sorts. It's this apparent persistence of behaviour that appeals to Adrian. A visible response by Rudiment 3 persists over time so that he is able to at least imagine a kind of relationship with the machine.

Mari expresses a similar interest in Rudiment 3, although she does so rather more enthusiastically by playfully mimicking how her friends have responded to its colours:

> **Mari**: Everyone is enjoying the colours, [points to #3] because maybe it was the shape of this one, cause it looks a little bit… the curves, and it looks like, I don't know, a character. And people are coming and we're telling them, now this one is going to show you a colour, and it's moving. And they're like, "oooh, ooh, hello! Oohooh, I'm here, what colour I have? Hmm? Show me."

Later, she and Seb explain their experimentation with Rudiment 3's colours:

> **Mari**: It was interesting to plug [it] in and plug [it] out [gestures pulling the power plug in and out], and leave it in a little bit to see how it was working and then when it started to move, to plug it out to see when it's stopping, and then to plug it in again.
> **Seb**: Yeah, actually I did try that, I was kind of curious whether my colour would be changed.
> **Mari**: And?
> **Seb**: And, errr, it wasn't
> **Mari**: Oh, but your colour was all the time blue? Or no… It was blue and violet.
> **Seb**: No it is blue and before it was green.

Mari and Seb are responding to Rudiment 3's adaptive system for categorising facial features. They describe their attempts to test the system's persistence over time and, in their banter with one another, demonstrate their grasp of the system's capacity to adapt to the faces it has seen. It is, then, the seeming persistence of Rudiment 3's recognition, a 'memory' of sorts, that appears to be a source of interest and engagement in both households. However, Mari and Seb, appear equally interested in different forms of persistence in the rudiments. For example, Mari also describes their experimentation with Rudiment 2:

> One day we played with the sounds, different sounds and also with the voice, big sounds, small sounds, and we wanted to see how it's moving. And it was really fun to develop movement and how he responds to different sounds.

Again, Mari expresses a curiosity in the machine's behaviours, yet this time the engagement isn't so much associated with a persistence of some observable response. Her interest is in the general rules or patterns of behaviour, and how these might persist across different encounters.

It's these different forms of persistence exhibited by the rudiments and the different kinds of interactions the rudiments afforded during the installations that raise some further ways to reflect on autonomy. In general, it's evident there is a temporal quality to the interactions the couples had with the machines. As we've seen above, in both households there was an interest in how the machine's behaviours changed or persisted over time and, in some cases, the couples experimented with this. In short, the sorts of things that persisted had some bearing on the relationships the couples had with the machines.

Although perhaps obvious, this insight allows us to see how particular forms of persistence might have been instrumental. If we consider the comments above, the machines appear to differ in terms of the qualities that persist. We see that sometimes it is the persistence of individual behaviours that provoke curiosity and, at others, it is an apparent set of rules. So with Rudiment 3, it was a consistency in response to individual faces that triggered interest, whereas with Rudiment 2 it was how its movements in response to sound were governed by perceptible and persistent rules.

Rudiment 3, however, adds a further aspect. In this case, the rules are open to relatively long cycles of change as new facial features are detected. In effect, while the rules persist over time, they do eventually change as the rudiment is exposed to new facial features. This is in notable contrast with Rudiment 1; although it has a random element built into it, for the most part both its individual behaviours and rules persist. On detecting motion it moves, and on detecting edges or obstacles it turns.

For the purposes of this research, what we find particularly interesting is how Rudiment 3 engaged the couples more and appeared more compelling (particularly for Adrian and Anna, even in light of their skepticism). We would need to investigate this further, but there seemed to be some correspondence with how the rudiment's rules persisted but also how this persistence was dictated by the machine's response to its surroundings. What seems key is that the change in rules could be associated with a recognisable input (i.e., detection of facial features) and that the changes were understood as part of a continuing sequence of intrinsic modifications in the system. In short, the system appeared to have stable states, where interactivity was consistent, interspersed with intelligible changes in rule-state and then behaviour.

Accountabilities

We've seen, so far, that the installations led to direct engagements with the rudiments and, in some instances, sustained interactions. Reflecting on the interviews further, we have also begun to wonder about other possible dimensions of interactivity. As well as prompts for interactivity at the human-machine level, we've started to think of the rudiments as triggers for particular patterns of talk between the couples and, at an even more abstract level, as active constituents of an overall character to the households.

A pattern to the discussions between the couples was especially pronounced with Rudiment 3, where exchanges revolved around recognition and the persistence of colours:

Anna: It didn't like me…
Adrian: No, it didn't really like you did it, for some reason… It wouldn't really kind of lock onto you in the way it did with me for some reason.
Anna: I think it's hair… [said with mocking sad face]
Adrian: Hair, because of the hair [also said with sad face]. [Pause] It seemed to prefer me with specs on… [Turn to interviewer]. Yeah, so it would be kind of random red and purples and then [for me] it tends to flash blue or go hard blue. It could be that I was imagining it.
Anna: No, it was going blue.
Adrian: Certainly more often than not.

Between Seb and Mari, these two-way exchanges developed into broader discussions. Below, for instance, Seb tries to develop his earlier thinking about usefulness:

Mari: You think of a person as useful?
Seb: I mean as a first thing? When you meet someone, you don't think "oh, this person might be useful". But when you look at an object that's what you do.
Mari: Ah right, differences between person and…
Seb: I mean that would be the difference between, I don't know, the camera that makes photos and the keyboard that…
Mari: But this one [#3] shows you colours and is moving.
Seb: Yeah, but it shows me *its* colours […] I mean I'm not controlling him, that's what I'm saying.
Mari: Umm, you can control…
Seb: … It's more like a discussion, not a control.

Of course, these exchanges and others like them took place during our interviews, so will have not surprisingly focused on the rudiments. However, what we believe we see is an inkling of the sort of talk that occurs between people who are trying to make sense of their relationships with an entity. In this case, the sophistication of the rudiments (or lack thereof) is of less importance. What we think we catch sight of is a way that something exhibiting a degree of autonomy, no matter how slight, might engage its audience beyond its immediate interactions. Not unlike a pet, one source of interest or even pleasure appears to be the mere speculation of what it might be doing or even 'thinking'.

Its continuing along these lines, that we see how the rudiments can be embedded in the ideas the couples had of their homes and how they are made sense of in ways that echo or characterise their households. For instance, the more utilitarian perspective voiced by Adrian and Anna appeared to reflect their overall relationship towards technology. We found Anna's thoughts particularly telling:

Anna: Maybe I don't have enough imagination. I can see… I can easily compromise with the noise [of #2] if I get benefit from it. So if it's something that entertains me or does something useful then, yeah, fine. But I just didn't find it very interac… I wasn't getting anything from it […]. Noise was definitely the problem.
Adrian: I seem to remember you saying "I'm going shopping now. Please make sure you turn that off by the time I come home." [Both laugh].
Interviewer: So in the beginning, the fact that you didn't switch them on, was because you thought they were fragile, or…
Anna: It was mostly Adrian who switched them on, and as I said, I didn't… I knew they were there, but I didn't, you know, I didn't miss them.

A feel for the home is thus captured in Adrian and Anna's discussions of the rudiments; a place is articulated in which intrusions, particularly of the pointless or noisy variety, are guarded against. By contrast, Seb and Mari seemed far more open to the rudiments' intrusions. Indeed, they expressed a willingness to be drawn into their behaviours:

Seb: Now of course they're three and you kind of… because they're in the same place we do feel in a unitary way about them. But it might help to put them all together so you can… So perhaps the drawing machine [point to #2] is at the end of the camera [points to #3] and the fridge stuff is also connected somehow it makes to the other people seeing them or interacting with them, it makes it more… it's like a narrative in the end cause you keep discovering things.

Thus we find the rudiments expose the appreciation for silence and control in one home, while in the other an openness to very present, almost visceral intrusions.

Although oversimplifying matters, what we feel these insights achieve are a sensitivity to autonomous machines and how they will likely have particular roles in shaping people's accountabilities. That is, people are likely to find themselves accountable in ways that go beyond the immediate interactions they have with the machines, and that reflect the machines' broader roles as autonomous 'social agents'. So for Anna, we see her having to account for her appearance and, indeed, powers of imagination as a result of her overall reaction to the rudiments. Likewise, the rudiments persuade Seb to rethink his relationship to objects.

Of course, many things in our homes take on this role—our choices of furnishings and general tastes say much about who we are (or wish to be). The interesting possibility with autonomous agents, however, is that as Seb struggles to articulate, they provide the possibility for playing a more active and dialectic role in that process. In some sense, one may become accountable to the objects as well as other people one lives with.

DISCUSSION AND CONCLUSIONS

In this paper, we've tried to give particular emphasis to the use of design as a speculative resource. Our hope has been to demonstrate a concern for the material and interactive qualities of machines and how such a concern can be used to open up new possibilities for further design-oriented, research investigations. In short, the decisions we made around form, interaction and the different levels of computation in the three presented rudiments were elaborated on to illustrate how design, in practice, can be used to provoke speculation. In this sense, we hope the work to have made a methodological contribution to the small but impactful speculative design movement in interactive systems design.

Beyond this, our design thinking and the interpretations of the early installations have been directed towards opening up compelling ways of imagining autonomy in interactive systems. Hopefully we've illustrated our experimentation with design as a means to explore alternative ideas of autonomy. Also, we hope to have shown that a lightweight approach to getting early feedback to speculative designs, and specifically to the three rudiments, provides some alternative ways for thinking about autonomy and design.

What we've aimed to capture in discussing the divergent opinions resulting from the installations are the fluid ways that people construct and articulate their interpretations of unfamiliar machines. We found, perhaps unsurprisingly, that opinions can vary widely around issues of utility, and the temporal character of what machines, as it were, 'remember'. However, also apparent were the internal tensions that can arise in people's own dialogue. We've seen how people can grapple with the role machines play by setting up various dichotomies associated with autonomy to make sense of the possibilities, and that these varied ideas of machine autonomy introduce some quite different ways of people accounting for themselves in their homes.

It's these dialogues and ideas, then, that we've found constructive and that we hope to use as guides in future designs. As opposed to narrowing down a design so that it conforms to familiar relationships between the different design elements, we hope they offer alternative trajectories along which an autonomous machine might be thought about. It's hoped such trajectories might provide us with a basis to ask, for instance, how we could re-design the rudiments to appeal to Adrian and Anna, but in ways that begin to suggest the uneasy or unfamiliar. Thus, our hope is they offer a starting point for us to go beyond the supposed prerequisite ideas of "improving or replacing" and of machines "for our own good", to a possibility of interactive machine's that might exhibit autonomy, but not as we know.

REFERENCES

1. Agre, P. *Computation and Human Experience.* Cambridge University Press, Cambridge, 1997.
2. Aipperspach, R., Hooker, B., & Woodruff, A. The heterogeneous home. In *Proc. UbiComp '08*, ACM (2008), 222-231.
3. Breazeal, C. Emotion and sociable humanoid robots. *Int'l Jn'l Hum. Comp. Std. 59*, 1-2 (2003), 119-155.
4. Brooks, A. G., Gray, J., Hoffman, G., Lockerd, A., Lee, H., & Breazeal, C. Robot's play: interactive games with sociable machines. *Computers in Entertainment. 2*, 3 (2004), 1-18.
5. Brooks, R. A. Intelligence without representation. *Artificial Intelligence. 47*, 1-3 (1991), 139-159.
6. Brooks, R. A., Breazeal, C., Marjanovi´c, M., Scassellati, B., & Williamson, M. M. The Cog Project: building a humanoid robot. In Nehaniv, C. (Ed.), *Computation for Metaphors, Analogy, and Agents.* Springer-Verlag, Heidelberg Berlin, 1999, 52-87.
7. Dunne, A. *Hertzian Tales: Electronic Products, Aesthetic Experience, and Critical Design.* MIT Press, 2006.
8. Forlizzi, J. & DiSalvo, C. Service robots in the domestic environment: a study of the Roomba vacuum in the home. In *Proc. HRI '06*, ACM (2006), 258-265.
9. Gaver, W., Sengers, P., Kerridge, T., Kaye, J., and Bowers, J. Enhancing ubiquitous computing with user interpretation: field testing the home health horoscope. In *Proc. CHI '07*, ACM (2007), 537-546.
10. Gaver, W., W., Beaver, J., & Benford, S. Ambiguity as a resource for design. In *Proc. CHI '03*, ACM (2003), 233-240.
11. Gockley, R., Forlizzi, J., & SimMaris, R. Interactions with a moody robot. In *Proc. HRI '06*, ACM (2006), 186-193.
12. Kaplan, F. & Oudeyer, P.-Y. Intrinsically Motivated Machines. In Lungarella, M., Iida, F., Bongard, J., & Pfeifer, R. (Eds.), *50 Years of AI.* Springer-Verlag, Berlin, 2007, 304–315.
13. Kuno, Y., Sakurai, A., Miyauchi, D., & Nakamura, A. Two-way eye contact between humans and robots. In *Proc. ICMI '04*, ACM (2004), 1-8.
14. Leahu, L., Sengers, P., & Mateas, M. Interactionist AI and the promise of ubicomp, or, how to put your box in the world without putting the world in your box. In *Proc. Ubicomp '08*, ACM (2008), 134-143.
15. Ljungblad, S. & Holmquist, L. E. Transfer Scenarios: Grounding innovation with marginal practices. In *Proc. CHI '07*, ACM (2007), 737-746.
16. Maes, P., Darrell, T., Blumberg, B., & Pentland, A. The ALIVE system: full-body interaction with autonomous agents. In *Proc. CA '95*, IEEE Comp. Soc. (1995), 11.
17. Mateas, M. Expressive AI: A hybrid art and science practice. *Leonardo. 34*, 2 (2001), 147-153.
18. OpenCV 2.0 C Reference. *http://opencv.willowgarage.com/documentation/object_detection.html.*
19. Park, J. & Kim, G. J. Robots with projectors: an alternative to anthropomorphic HRI. In *Proc. HRI '09*, ACM (2009), 221–222.
20. Powers, A. & Kiesler, S. The advisor robot: tracing people's mental model from a robot's physical attributes. In *Proc. HRI '06*, ACM (2006), 218-225.
21. Romero, M., Pousman, Z., & Mateas, M. Alien presence in the home: the design of Tableau Machine. *PUC. 12*, 5 (2008), 373-382.
22. Sengers, P. & Gaver, B. Staying open to interpretation: engaging multiple meanings in design and evaluation. In *Proc. DIS '06:* ACM (2006), 99–108.
23. Taylor, A. S. Machine intelligence. In *Proc. CHI '09*, ACM (2009), 2109-2118.
24. Taylor, A. S., Swan, L., & Durrant, A. Designing family photo displays. In *Proc. ECSCW '07*, Springer (2007), 79-98.
25. Zhao, S., Nakamura, K., Ishii, K., & Igarashi, T. Magic cards: a paper tag interface for implicit robot control. In *Proc. CHI '09*, ACM (2009), 173–182.

Material Probe: Exploring Materiality of Digital Artifacts

Heekyoung Jung
School of Informatics and Computing
(HCI Design) at Indiana University
jung5@indiana.edu

Erik Stolterman
School of Informatics and Computing
(HCI Design) at Indiana University
estolter@indiana.edu

ABSTRACT
We present an approach for exploring materiality of digital artifacts by suggesting a study method—*material probe*. The purpose with the method is to understand how people perceive material qualities of artifacts and to discuss how designers could intentionally and methodologically include such non-functional user desires related to material qualities in the design of digital artifacts. The study procedure and results from preliminary studies are described with their implications for future work.

Author Keywords
Materiality, material probe, digital artifacts, design method.

ACM Classification Keywords
H5.m. Information interfaces and presentation (e.g., HCI): Miscellaneous.

INTRODUCTION
As computational technology becomes more tangible, it pervades everyday life in various forms of objects such as interactive furniture, responsive architecture, or electronic clothing. No longer constrained to a particular type of digital devices, computers now tend to be considered as *a material for interaction design* [8, 12, 14, 15]. Accordingly, exploration of materiality of computational technology is in demand in terms of how to seamlessly combine physical and digital qualities in computational materials and how to create new aesthetic qualities (i.e., affective, embodied, experiential values) of digital artifacts in designing with those materials.

However, forms and material qualities of digital artifacts have been rarely considered compared to their functionality in interaction design and Human-Computer Interaction (HCI) research [8, 9]. With too much emphasis on intangible functionality, recently the design of digital artifacts has become minimal in physical aspects and their materiality seems like disappearing by merging physical and digital design elements as in touch screen devices. These new designs have brought significant functional benefits including intuitive interaction from direct manipulation and portability from compact design. But, the qualities of rich sensory feelings from physical materials and active user engagement with them have not been fully explored in interaction design. In this study, we attempt to explore materiality of digital artifacts by questioning how well material qualities of physical artifacts are adopted to digital artifacts. The exploration first needs to be based on the understanding of how materials and materiality have been considered in traditional design disciplines and in recent interaction design and research.

Materiality in Design
Traditionally materiality has been an essential element of design. Specifically, material selection—based on the understanding of physical properties of a variety of materials—is critical in forming aesthetic and functional qualities of an object, for instance, in architecture and product design [1, 11]. At the same time, unique symbolic meanings of a certain material—based on its social or economic values—are also something designers need to consider beyond functional qualities of a design—as in fashion design. Through the lens of materials, design can be considered as a process of creating meaning with proper materials based on exploratory practice with them. Moreover, materials are not just a given to be incorporated in designer's calculation, but are a part of design problems [4]. Invention of a new material sometimes brings design innovation and changes our experiences with objects, as seen in many examples such as plastics in modern design. The advent of new materials in the modern era often poses a new design problem—both in terms of operationalizing new manufacturing process for them and envisioning their social and cultural impact in use—rather than providing a simple solution for what design opportunity is considered.

Materiality of Digital Artifacts
Recently designers of digital artifacts are facing a particular challenge regarding design material due to its complex composition of physical and digital qualities. Especially with respect to the computational aspect of interaction design materials, Löwgren and Stolterman [12] described digital technology as *material without qualities,* indicating its unlimited yet undefined design potentials—both aesthetic and functional qualities that designers could realize with digital technology. In other words, the design

of digital artifacts is largely open, leaving designers with significant power to shape a future and also with corresponding responsibility.

There have been many technical attempts to fabricate new computational materials and to explore their applications from computer interfaces to interactive products—as in studies of transmaterial [3] and computational composite [15], to name a few. These technical explorations have brought an increasing attention to aesthetic forms and interactive behaviors of digital artifacts enabled by new computational materials—as in studies of organic user interfaces or kinetic user interfaces [9]. Based on these technical attempts, now physical and digital qualities of computational materials are not separately considered anymore, but tend to be explored more holistically with focus on aesthetic qualities of a design [14].

While technical and aesthetic potentials of computational materials are explored mainly in the context of research and development, there are also increasing attempts in art and design to expand design possibilities of digital artifacts by diversifying material selection. Similar with the approaches of fashion design, designers and artists apply authentic materials or visual patterns to decorate surfaces of digital devices. As seen from some examples of designer computer collections [5] or luxury mobile phones [16], unique material selection creates a greater emotional or expressive value within digital devices that cannot be replicated by other devices with similar functionality.

There are also experimental design projects that explore materiality of digital artifacts with new design processes. For example, Nokia personalization project manufactured mobile phones out of metal, wood, and rubber with a craft approach [13]. Designers from IDEO developed prototypes by applying physical materiality to new forms of interactive devices such as felt-covered printer or card-based music player [2]. These explorations illustrate that materiality can significantly affect how a digital device is designed and experienced beyond how it is looked or felt. At the same time, the design outcomes from these projects show promising potentials of an alternative design approach that is *inspired and driven by material explorations*, not necessarily following functional requirements.

Objectives: New Approaches for Materiality

Our study is motivated by increasing technical and aesthetic potentials of materiality of digital artifacts with questions of (1) how well material qualities of physical artifacts are adopted to digital artifacts, and (2) how to consider materiality in designing digital artifacts. Here, by digital artifact we mean existing as well as potential types of physical product that delivers digital contents through its interactive features. One of the assumptions of our approach is that materiality, as more than physical qualities of materials, can significantly affect how a digital artifact is designed and experienced. Since material selection in design is closely related to aesthetic intention of a design as well as its functional requirements, approaches for materiality require both methodological and intentional deliberation. Based on the understanding of approaches for materiality from traditional design disciplines and recent interaction design (as briefly described earlier), we attempt to investigate people's desire related to material qualities and to apply the insights to design of digital artifacts with our study of *material probe*.

OUR APPROACH: MATERIAL PROBE

We present our approach—*material probe*—that explores conceptual dimensions of materiality in interaction design. Inspired by the approach of cultural probe [7], we aim to understand how people perceive materiality qualities of artifacts and to discuss how designers could intentionally and methodologically include such non-functional user desires related to material qualities in the design of digital artifacts. Specifically, we examine materiality of artifacts by *comparing* and *contrasting* the material qualities of digital and physical artifacts. To do this, we consider artifacts as a whole, as a combination of individual design variables (i.e., shape, color, texture, historical/cultural reference) that are perceived, experienced, and interpreted holistically by a user. In this sense, artifacts are used in our study as catalysts to develop personal stories or preferences of materiality. This exploratory motivation is distinguished from other approaches that use artifacts to evaluate affective qualities of specific design variables as in [10].

Study Procedure

The study of material probe consists of three parts, where participants are asked 1) to talk about stories of physical artifacts based on their memories, 2) to play with material samples while speculating on their material preferences, and 3) to compare and contrast the material qualities of physical artifacts to their experience with digital artifacts.

1) Tell stories about material qualities

This part is to explore how people perceive, value, and articulate material qualities of objects from their memories. Followed are the questions that we asked:

- Do you have any object that you like/dislike because of its material qualities?
- Could you describe specific experiences or memories about that object and its materiality?

2) Play with material samples

In this part, a set of material samples is provided so that people develop conversation regarding material qualities of artifacts by playing with them. The samples include rubbery toy balls, plastics, wood, papers, fabric pieces, and so on by covering a certain range of different physical properties (i.e., soft, hard, shiny, warm). They are selected for an inspiring purpose instead of representing a broad range of design materials in general (Figure 1). In this part we asked:

Figure 1. Material Samples.

- From these material samples, could you select 2-3 ones that you like/dislike?
- Could you explain why you like/dislike them specifically in terms of their material qualities?

3) Compare and contrast to digital artifacts

This part is to investigate how people's desire related to material qualities are satisfied in design of digital devices. People were asked to compare and contrast their experience with digital artifacts to their preferences of material qualities discussed in previous parts. In this part we asked:

- Which digital device do you use most frequently? Please describe its features and context of use.
- Could you compare the experiential qualities of the digital device to the material qualities that you picked out as your favorable/unfavorable ones?
- Could you imagine how current digital devices would be transformed if your favorable material qualities would be incorporated into their forms?

Findings and Insights

We conducted 3 sessions of material probe studies with 15 participants, each lasting about an hour. 10 participants of two groups were graduate students who volunteered to the study in the HCI Design program at Indiana University, and 5 participants of one group were researchers who attended to the workshop on *artifacts in design* at CHI 2010. Followed are the main findings from each part of the study:

1) In the first part, participants described materiality mainly in terms of their tactile and visual perception. For example, as their favorite objects, they picked out microfiber t-shirt (because its soft texture invites touching), buttery turkey (because the feeling of organic skin makes cooking enjoyable), bubble wrap, cat (because of its silky fur), memory foam pillow (because of its squeezable and responsive shape), bear doll or blanket (because of the memory of childhood), herbal leaf (because it feels like a life that needs my care), sharp pen (that writes smooth), high-end digital camera (because of its mechanical shutter sound), desk made of stone (because of its masculine look and feel), etc. For unfavorable ones, they mentioned new towels or clothes (because of their hard and rigid textures), chalkboard (because its rough surface makes disturbing sound when scratched with nails), rubbery frame around sink at kitchen (because of its slimy, unhygienic look and feel), forks and knives (because of their metallic coldness and sound), etc. What was noticeable here is that people care about materiality in their experience with everyday artifacts and associate diverse meanings to their perception and appreciation of material qualities.

2) In the second part, playing with a set of material samples, participants talked about materiality more specifically in terms of economic values, design process, aesthetic qualities, and practical applications of certain samples. Many people picked out soft and rubbery pieces from toy balls, pieces of knits or papers with delicately crafted textures, soft cotton, and shiny and silky fabric pieces as their favorite ones. On the contrary, plastic or fake leather pieces were chosen as unfavorable because of their flat textures and cheap connotations. What was noticeable in this study is not which types of materials people liked or disliked in general, but that people are very *sensitive at perceiving subtle differences of material characteristics* and easily determine their preferences among them for a broad range of functional or aesthetic reasons.

3) In the last session, the focus shifted from physical artifacts to digital ones. At first, participants mentioned that they had never thought of digital artifacts having different forms or made of other materials than the current ones. However, by comparing and contrasting their experiences with physical and digital artifacts, they furthered conversations about their discontents and expectations in the use of digital devices. Some talked about how they care about the sound when typing a keyboard (as a feedback to the amount of their work), how they are worried about dropping their phones or making scratches on them, etc. Moreover, they suggested imaginative design concepts that merge physical material qualities to digital devices in a way to solve their problems—not just to decorate them with nice look and feel. The concepts include *a bouncy phone* that is made of soft, protective case and safe even when dropped, *a smelly phone* that generates sweat odors if used too much, *an encouraging keyboard* that gives pleasant sound and spring touch, etc.

Some general issues on forms and materials of digital artifacts were discussed as well. For example, it was mentioned that digital devices might display less social presentation in a sense that their forms do not have causal relations with their functions. Specifically, it is obvious to tell what a person is doing when s/he looks at a physical book, but not quite apparent when s/he looks at a laptop. In some contexts, such as during classes or lectures, this could be a problem if students use their laptops for other purposes (i.e., chatting, browsing websites) insisting that they are taking notes. Again, this reveals that materiality of digital artifacts is deeply related to other dimensions of user experience beyond look and feel of digital devices, and can significantly affect our social experience as well. At the same time, recent design efforts to simulate materiality of physical objects within digital devices were discussed—for example, by making wooden cover of mobile phones or by emulating mechanical shutter sound of digital cameras. The issues discussed in this study provide insightful design implications to be further investigated—not by informing how to satisfy people's subjective preferences to diverse material qualities, but by revealing that *people care about experiential qualities of materiality that might be lost or obtained in using digital devices.*

DISCUSSION AND IMPLICATIONS

In our preliminary study of material probe, it was clear that people do perceive the materiality of artifacts critically and that there is a gap between how they experience physical and digital artifacts in terms of their material qualities. Our approach here showed its potential in provoking interesting design concepts by adopting physical material qualities to interaction and functional aspects of digital devices beyond decorative purposes. The results imply that designers of digital artifacts need to consider materiality as playing a significant role in user experience [14].

Based on the specific findings and insights from the study, some tentative design implications can be suggested in terms of how to consider materiality in designing digital artifacts, namely *material simulation*, *material expression*, and *material exploration*. *Material simulation* is to emulate sensorial feelings of physical materiality within digital artifacts, as seen in graphical effects of turning pages in e-books or sound effects of shutter press in digital cameras. *Material expression* is to create more visible, physical forms of digital artifacts for expressing affordance or social presence of interaction. *Material exploration* is to create new types of forms or functions of digital artifacts by considering materiality at an early phase of design (instead of representing functional requirements or simulating physical materiality at a surface level). The concepts of rubbery phone or smelly phone discussed in the study can be examples of the approach of material exploration. We expect that these tentative implications can initiate further methodological explorations regarding how to consider materiality in designing digital artifacts.

We also saw some limitations of our approach; user responses tended to be influenced by the group discussions and the actual selection of the material samples prepared for the study. For instance, many participants commented that most of material samples reminded them of toys, which are fun to play but hard to apply for broader contexts or purposes of use. It was also mentioned that participants' responses regarding their material preferences maybe very spontaneous as well as subjective. This means that the study cannot be applied to make design decisions for material selection as a rigorous method. Instead, its contribution lies on initiating a conversation regarding material qualities of digital artifacts as a methodological attempt. In our future study, we plan to develop this exploratory study into a valid design method by complementing those limitations.

REFERENCES

1. Ashby, M. & Johnson, K. (2002). *Materials and design: The art and science of material selection in product design.* Oxford: Butterworth-Heinemann.
2. Bone, M. and Johnson, K. (2009). *I Miss My Pencil,* Chronicle Books. San Francisco, CA.
3. Brownell, B. (2006). *Transmaterial - A Catalogue of Materials that Redefine Our Physical Environment.* Princeton, Architectural Press, New York, NY.
4. Doordan, D. P. (2003). On materials. *Design Issues, 19*(4), pp. 3-8.
5. Eee PC Seashell Karim Rashid Collection by ASUS. Retrieved July 2, 2010, from http://mocoloco.com/archives/013438.php/
6. Furry Object 2.0: MAGNHILD DISINGTON. Retrieved July 2, 2010, from http://www.magnhilddisington.com/
7. Gaver, B., Dunne, T., Pacenti, E. (1999). Design: Cultural probes, *Interactions, 6* (1), p.21-29, ACM.
8. Hallnäs, L. & Redström, J. (2002). Abstract information appliances - methodological exercises in conceptual design of computational things. *In Proc of DIS,* ACM.
9. Holman, D. and Vertegaal, R. (2008). Organic user interfaces: designing computers in any way, shape, or form, *Communications, 51(6)*, p. 48 – 55. ACM.
10. Isbister, K., Höök, K., Sharp, M., Laaksolahti, J. (2006). The sensual evaluation instrument: developing an affective evaluation tool, *Conference on Human Factors in Computing Systems (SIGCHI),* ACM.
11. Kesteren, I. E. H., Stappers, P. J., Bruijn, J. C. M. (2007). Materials in products selection: tools for including user-interaction in materials selection, *International Journal of Design, 1* (3).
12. Löwgren, J., and Stolterman, E. (2004). *Thoughtful Interaction Design.* MIT Press.
13. Material explorations – Blog – BERG. Retrieved July 2, 2010 from http://berglondon.com/blog/2005/12/12/material-explorations/
14. Robles, E. & Wiberg, M. (2009). Texturing the "material turn" in interaction design. *Conference on Tangible, embedded, and embodied interaction (TEI),* ACM.
15. Vallgårda, A. and Redstrom, J. (2007). Computational composites. *Conference on Human Factors in Computing Systems (SIGCHI),* ACM.
16. Vertu | Pioneering Luxury Mobile Phones. Retrieved July 2, 2010, from http://vertu.com

Concepts for Life-Like Interactive Objects

Michael Schmitz
German Research Center for Artificial Intelligence
Stuhlsatzenhausweg 3, 66123 Saarbrücken, Germany
Michael.Schmitz@dfki.de

ABSTRACT
As part of our work on anthropomorphic and zoomorphic interfaces for physical, interactive objects we have conducted an exhaustive literature review spanning the disciplines of anthropomorphism, affective computing, tangible interaction and industrial design, aggregating relevant research to inform our efforts. In this paper we summarise the results by deriving concepts and design guidelines for the realisation of life-like, tangible objects, with which we also aim at fostering discussions and a scientific exchange in this highly interdisciplinary field.

Author Keywords
Life-Like User Interfaces, Anthropomorphism, Zoomorphism, Tangible User Interfaces, Smart Object Systems, Guidelines, Concepts

ACM Classification Keywords
H.5.2 Information Interfaces and Presentation: User Interfaces.

General Terms
Human Factors, Theory

INTRODUCTION
One technological trend is to augment everyday objects with sensing, computing and actuation power in order to provide new services beyond the objects' traditional purpose, indicating that such smart objects might become an integral part of our daily lives. To be able to interact with smart object systems users will obviously need novel and appropriate interfaces, which hold for multiple domains and do not require an intensive learning phase, considering that a user might often be exposed to smart objects that demand spontaneous usage of unfamiliar systems. Such situations will require that a user should be able to build up a mental model quickly, which particularly holds for novice users.

TEI'11, January 22–26, 2011, Funchal, Portugal.

The term *anthropomorphism* describes the tendency of people to think of objects as if they had human characteristics. Similarly, *animism* as defined by Piaget and other psychologists is the "attribution of life to the nonliving" [36]. Throughout this work, we use the terms animism and zoomorphism synonymously, whenever objects are associated with animalistic attributes that do not include human traits such as etiquette, gender specifics or emotions that go beyond primal desires. Furthermore, we use the term *life-likeliness* as an embracing concept for both anthropomorphism and animism/zoomorphism.

People often tend to treat objects similar to humans, according to findings of Reeves and Nass [37], which allows users to explain the behaviour of a system if they lack a good functional conceptual model. This is an important issue for the envisioned application scenarios, where users have to spontaneously deal with unfamiliar smart object environments. Other researchers conclude that for intuitive and efficient human-environment interaction with thousands of networked smart objects a "limited animistic design metaphor" might be appropriate [32]. Similarly, Mithen [27] pointed out that "the most powerful metaphors are those which cross domain boundaries, such as by associating a living entity with something that is inert or an idea with something that is tangible."

Anthropomorphic interfaces generally attempt to build on established human skills, learned in daily social encounters. The research domain of tangible user interfaces shares this goal, focusing on motor skills mainly related to physical manipulation of tangible objects. Both concepts complement each other, thus we attempt to exploit the naturalness of conversational and social interaction and the physicality of real world objects as the foundation for an interaction paradigm for smart objects. We believe that life-like behaviour in combination with a gesture interface will provide an intuitive user interface for quick and casual interaction in scenarios where learning time is not given or not appropriate. We also consider elderly and children as notably interesting user groups that have the potential to profit from such an interface paradigm. It is further important to identify the limitations of this approach: For instance, we do not expect to be able to handle complex and recurring tasks as efficiently as specialised user interfaces tailored for a specific application.

Singular instances of "tangible life-likeliness" have appeared in recent years, but merely constitute single explorations into the design space. For example, the Living Interfaces project

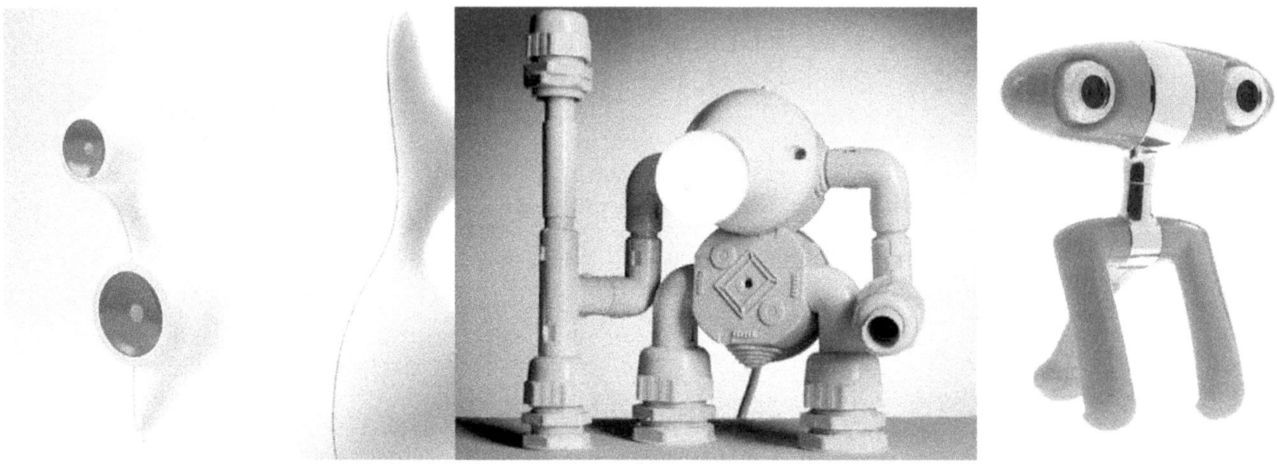

Figure 1. Anthropomorphic/Zoomorphic product design examples, resembling limbs and facial elements. (sources: http://www.madebymakers.dk, http://www.robolamps.eu, http://www.minoru3d.com)

of the Deutsche Telekom Laboratories explores in series of experiments and prototypes how reduced life-like movements can be beneficial for interaction with everyday objects. The idea of the Impatient Toaster [6] is to create sympathy and a closer relationship to a kitchen appliance by enabling the device to indicate needs by certain movement patterns. This means in particular that the toaster starts to shake nervously after a longer period of inactivity in order to remind the dweller of eating something. Once bread is inserted into the toaster and the start button is pressed, it calms down. Singular, subtle movements during the toasting period signalise activity. After the toasting phase the bread moves upwards such that it can be taken out, while the machine again moves excitedly until the toast bred is removed. Rubbing the toaster would also "calm" it down and stop any movements. Another example is the Proverbial Wallet, which utilises the haptic channel in different ways to reflect on account balance and previous transactions [22]. For example, one wallet type is called *peacock* and is able to grow and shrink, depending on account balance changes. The general idea here is to promote a sense of financial health and encourage the user to save money. The idea of the *mother bear* instance is similar: The item "protects" the money inside by making it difficult to open, when a certain threshold of a bank account is crossed.

In the remains of this paper we will discuss concepts and design guidelines on several levels as a starting point for a holistic approach of the realisation of tangible interfaces for life-like smart objects. We will start with summarising possibilities of triggering the anthropomorphic stance in users, followed by a discussion of industrial design issues. Furthermore, to support developers and designers of smart object systems, three classes of life-like smart objects will be proposed with their distinct properties. This includes suitable application scenarios and strategies of designing interaction concepts for each class. The last section concludes this paper with a brief summary and outlook on future work.

TRIGGERING THE ANTHROPOMORPHIC STANCE

Applying anthropomorphism or zoomorphism changes the way how users try to understand and make sense of a computer by projecting everyday expectations of human and animalistic life onto it. We believe that such an interaction paradigm has the potential to apply a strong *metaphor of verb*, which regards to the motion of an object or to the interaction in relation to the real-world action according to Fishkin's taxonomy on tangible user interfaces [11]. The anthropomorphic stance can be triggered by various means, which we will summarise and adapt for the domain of smart objects in this section.

Humans are inherently well-trained to perceive life, already from childhood on [39]. The device's **visual appearance** will often shape first impressions and can therefore play a considerable role in establishing first expectations. Organic shapes or those that resemble limbs, parts of the face and other body parts can be effective visual cues, which has also been applied by systems described in [20] [46] [5].

The mere **presence of voice** is another strong trigger for anthropomorphic perception [33], irrespective of contents and sounds. The effect can be intensified by increasing its naturalness as done by work such as [16] or [14]. Natural language interfaces in public settings - particularly when talking to objects - have to be considered with caution. Work by Wasinger et al. has revealed that users dislike to directly converse in natural language with a bar of soap but would be generally willing to talk to digital cameras, cars or personal computers [47]. Beside the fact that talking to objects obviously violates social conventions, the results of the study suggest that speech as a sophisticated interaction modality might only feel natural when applied to a physical object, if the object is perceived as an item with inherent complexity, such as electronic appliances or computer systems. One reason for this might be that it feels awkward for the user to build up a mental model, in which a very primitive object is capable of managing rather complex computational tasks such as speech processing. Instead, a more complex and compound artefact, the inner workings of which are not completely grasped by the user, might be more suitable for the attribution of such abilities. These findings might be taken as guidelines in the choice of application scenarios, suggesting to select objects, which do not appear to be obviously incapable of computational functions at all, such as the aforementioned bar of soap, stones, food etc.

Besides speech, the acoustic channel can be used to deliver alternative feedback that resembles **life-like, physiological sounds or haptics** instead of conventional sound feedback, for example pulse, breath, snore or cough, which is for instance applied in [17] and [46]. Furthermore, **pro-active and autonomous behaviour** can be a fundamental strategy in order to evoke anthropomorphic/zoomorphic interpretation [33]. This can already be instantiated with very simple means, for example by autonomous movement, which is the most basic distinction of living matter [48] and for instance applied in [6]. On a next level, **stereotypical behaviour**, which expresses e.g. shyness or curiosity, addresses more complex processes but adds essentially to anthropomorphic strategies [38] [46].

INDUSTRIAL DESIGN ISSUES

A product designers traditional task is to design the outer appearance of an object, generally aiming at a pleasant visual design and functionality. The latest generation of products, with embedded electronic components and richer functionality, extends the conventional scope to the design and the composition of interactivity [7]. In this section we will examine the consequences the particular characteristics of life-like smart object design have for industrial designers, starting with general considerations in the design process. We consider smart objects as objects that already exist in their original, analogue world with certain purposes and requirements that specify or constrain their general shape. Certainly, these traditional requirements still exist and constitute primary parameters. Integrating electronic components is a common part of the design phase in industrial design, such that the additional instrumentation of a smart object is not a completely new process. But, the more complex requirements of sensors and actuators and their interrelation with other design parameters including materials, shape and mechanics pose new challenges to the stages of both design and construction.

Within the visual scope for design, the outer appearance can have an important impact on the overall perception of an anthropomorphic smart object. The concept of the *metaphor of noun* regards the analogy of the shape, texture, look and sound of objects to their metaphorical counterpart [11]. A high analogy is therefore obviously advantageous and can be achieved on the visual channel by fostering a first primitive categorisation of living matter. We can facilitate an zoomorphic stance towards the object by applying an organic shape or by resembling configurations that look like faces and bodies (see examples in Figure 1). Also limbs or just facial elements have a particular salience to humans and help to express anthropomorphism [33]. The texture of living objects could for instance be imitated by soft and furry materials at the outmost layer. It is not necessary to overly exert anthropomorphic product design, small efforts can already lead to good results [37]. It has further been shown that the overall impression of appearance triggers certain feelings and action tendencies, and thus, a general stance towards an entity, which can be utilised in the design process as well. For instance, "cuteness" triggers feelings of "infantile helplessness" and a tendency to care for and protect. Accordingly, perception of "ugliness" and "beauty" activate an action tendency to avoid or to approach that particular face or body [45].

Since people tend to refuse to directly address simple objects in natural language interaction, applying more complex shapes might help to attain a less simple impression of the object on a visual level, and thus to create to a certain extent the general impression of a more complex device.

Affordances are also an important factor in the physical design of anthropomorphic smart objects and interrelate with what we call **anthropomorphic affordances**. This notion describes affordances that arise from an anthropomorphic stance and the impact on shape and its affordances. Furthermore, affordances can also be utilised to suggest interaction modalities: Body parts that are associated with senses could indicate that the object is capable of perceiving the corresponding modality (e.g. eyes suggest seeing and ears hearing, respectively). The resemblance of limbs, facial components or other body parts afford new interaction possibilities that are beyond the traditional affordance characteristics, which are mainly based on physical and mechanical laws. Common examples are the big belly of a chinese buddha that invites to rubbing, while a horizontally stretched arm might invite for shaking the hand. So, if the user has already taken up the anthropomorphic stance, a yet unexplored type of affordances comes into play that has to be considered by the product designer as well.

CLASSES OF LIFE-LIKE SMART OBJECTS

Aligned to Persson's analysis of multi-layered anthropomorphism [34] we propose three basic classes of anthropomorphic smart objects. This classification is based on the dimensions *Complexity* and *Duration* and maps the discrete classes to application scenarios that are categorised accordingly. Figure 2 visualises the relation of these object classes and indicates their relative position on the scales of complexity and duration. We complement the general design rules of this paper with more specific concepts about variations of tangible, life-like smart objects. For each class we start with a general description of their relevant characteristics, propose guidelines for their realisation and outline suitable application scenarios.

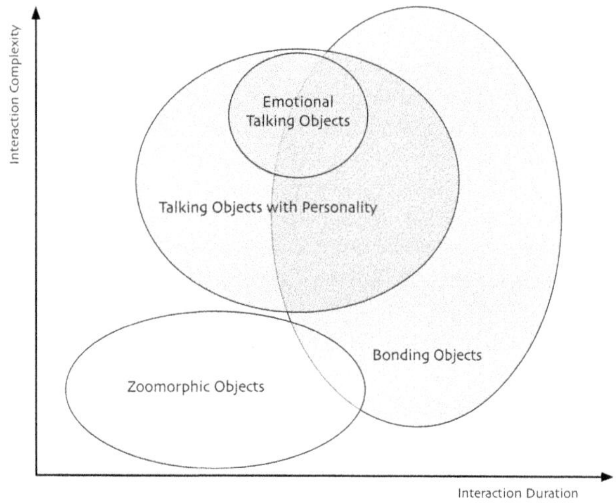

Figure 2. Classes of life-like smart objects

Zoomorphic Objects

Basic desires can easily be projected onto simple behaviour, exploiting expectations about such needs and desires. This includes actions that relate to life preservation, pain, hunger, desire for sleep, exhaustion, fear, excitement and similar conditions. This relates to the concept of *Primitive Psychology* and allows to predict and interpret simple animalistic behaviour immediately [34].

This class of objects can be realised by mapping important system states to suitable basic needs and implementing reactions to status changes by associated animalistic expressions. For example, an object that observes its state and attempts to preserve primary conditions (e.g. intactness, energy level, temperature) could render acoustic animalistic feedback if one the conditions is violated. For instance a sound of pain, when the object falls, is being squeezed or has detected damage by other means. Sounds of fatigue or exhaustion could be mapped to low energy status and inform the user proactively. If the temperature exceeds or falls below a threshold, the reaction could consist of moaning sounds or shivering. If the mapping is well-thought-out and the critical parameters of the object known by the user, an understanding of the anthropomorphic feedback will happen intuitively. If the user is then taking action to correct the issue (e.g. recharging the object or taking it to a cooler place), the corresponding feedback can again inform about the state change. The tangible component in this class of objects is important as well, as it fits to the immediacy of this anthropomorphic class. Touching the object can already trigger a response to let the user know that the object recognises and values that its issues are being addressed - this would not only provide intermediate feedback, but also intensify the anthropomorphic stance.

This type of zoomorphic smart objects can be applied to comparably simple artefacts, which employ functionality that can be modelled as action/reaction systems depending on given parameters. This also avoids the problem that people refuse to talk to simple objects [47] by providing simplified anthropomorphic means, and thus a potentially more appropriate mental model. An example for this class of smart object is the smart pizza packing [42], which observes its own state and checks whether, for instance, the cool-chain is interrupted. Other examples can be imagined in domestic environments, e.g. electronic home appliances. A coffee machine that appears sad, when it is supposed to prepare coffee but has to be refilled with water or coffee powder before. The alarm clock that wakes someone up in a good mood, getting nervous when not switched off by the user within a certain time, until it finally panics. A USB memory stick could be shaken to check the amount of stored data, the feedback would resemble nauseous sounds in different frequencies and speed to reflect the amount of space taken up by data with a low frequency of clunky, dull sounds correlating to a rather full state and high frequency of high, agile tones correlating to an empty state.

In all these examples zoomorphic feedback reflects different states of a system in a manner that can be intuitively understood. The user can quickly evaluate the situation and estimate whether it is for instance required to turn her or his attention to the system. If necessary, this sort of zoomorphic interaction paradigm can be extended by conventional means of displaying more detailed information. For instance, a temperature drop below a certain threshold might be followed by an inquiry about the exact temperature or for how long it has been under the threshold. A simple possibility, which also utilises the tangible channel, would be to place the object beside a screen that is able to retrieve and display this data.

Talking Objects with Personality

The next level of anthropomorphic smart objects crosses the zoomorphic domain and employs interaction with more human-like objects through natural language dialogues. Combining speech and tangible interaction will facilitate more complex systems than the previous class, but also requires a more complex design and implementation process. Applying a personality to an object does not only support the anthropomorphic aspect, but holds additional benefits in speech based interaction, if implemented with care:

Previous studies have shown that interacting with embodied conversational agents that have consistent personalities is not only more fun, but also lets users perceive such agents as more useful than agents without consistent personalities [30, 10]. Furthermore is has been shown that the speech of a consistent personality enables the listener to memorise spoken contents easier and moreover reduces the overall cognitive load [12, 30]. Similar findings have been made concerning human computer interaction employing speech synthesis: The computer was evaluated as more believable and the communication as more pleasant, whenever the synthesised voice characteristics fitted the speech output contents [31] and the perceived personality.

Personalities can be modelled by different means - for instance by sophisticated personality models as the five factor model [26] or simplified *traits* that summarise impressions about a person, such as shy, extrovert or aggressive. The chosen modelling method and level of detail depend on the application scenario and the intended effect on the user. One possibility is to align the personality to qualities of the object, e.g. a product in a shopping context, with its speech aligned to its brand image [41] [40]. Another possibility is to model it after the user's personality, as suggested by the *Similarity-Attraction-Principle*, which claims that people prefer personalities that are similar to their own [8]. Alternatively, theories from personality psychology propose the principle of *interpersonal complementarity* which specifies how a person's interpersonal behaviour evokes behaviour from an interactional partner [23]. In this notion, correspondence tends to occur on the so called *affiliation axis* (friendliness invites friendliness, and hostility invites hostility), while reciprocity tends to occur on the *power axis* (dominance invites submission and vice versa).

Social stereotypes, which are generated by mix of assumptions towards people, are an option as well, as outlined in [33]. Typical cases are occupancy roles (doctors, waiters, police) or family roles schemas, all applicable to situations when the role is a dominant factor in the user-object relationship. Such stereotypes are another way to leverage expectations on goals, beliefs, morals, and behaviour of entities and might simplify the process of modelling distinct personalities.

This class of anthropomorphic smart object interaction makes sense for more complex functions that can be effectively interfaced through speech as the main modality. It still allows for intuitive, occasional interaction, like product inquiries in a shopping context (e.g. [47]), exhibitions or providing instructions for programmable home appliances (e.g. video recorder).

Emotional Talking Objects

An extension of Talking Objects with Personality is the application of emotions and moods, in a more holistic manner than is the case with zoomorphic objects, which already reflect a sense of emotion by the notion of affective behaviour, but only in terms of basic desires. The primary purpose of this is that emotion helps to increase the believability of anthropomorphic interfaces. Artificial emotion can also provide feedback to the user, such as indicating the internal states, goals and (to some extent) intentions.

The intention here is to support a mental model that results from folk-psychological processes of explaining *"how perceptions, beliefs, goals, intentions and actions relate"* [33]. Main element for such a model is the *appraisal theory*, which formulates the idea that emotions are formed from our evaluations (appraisals) of events, which cause particular reactions in different people. The interdependencies between personality, moods and emotions are for instance modelled by ALMA [13]. Emotions can be displayed by different means, including facial expressions and body language of virtual characters (e.g. [1]) or also, more valuable for smart object scenarios, through speech as in [43].

With such a module that describes and manages the effects of personality and emotion on a time axis, we will be able to further create talking objects with a believable model of their behaviour for short- and midterm interaction processes.

Bonding Objects

The class of bonding objects builds on *Emotional Anthropomorphism* and basically comprises the social relation of the interactive device to the user. Both aforementioned classes of objects can be utilised as a base interaction paradigm in order to establish a relationship. The key aspect of this class is that relationship is a persistent and evolving construct that develops over time and spans multiple interaction sessions. Hong et al. have summarised in their overview paper "Advances in Tangible Interaction and Ubiquitous Virtual Reality" that criticism within the TUI community was formulated towards the fact that research activities focus on short-duration application while it appears worthwhile to to consider longer periods of interaction in the user's life [18]. It has also been stated in that paper that *"tangibles could open new avenues for bonding with products, allowing products to physically evolve over time"*. This is further supported by Hornecker, who referred to studies showing that bodily interaction and touch rouse emotions and enhance inner sympathy [19].

Only few studies on embodied agents have taken the endeavours to examine such long term effects on users. Bickmore and Picard have investigated long-term relationships in HCI within the FitTrack project and recapitulated strategies for social relationship management - mainly for reducing social distance - that could be employed by a computer [4], which we have adapted for anthropomorphic smart object scenarios:

Social Dialogue: A form of talk that is particularly lacking in task-oriented content, also called *small talk* or *phatic communication*. Such a social dialogue can be used to maintain relational nuances even when no explicit task is being performed [21].

Social Deixis: The encoding of relational status in language is a phenomenon called *social deixis* [25]. A familiar example is the form of address, greeting and parting routines that are used between people having different relationships, with titles ranging from professional forms ("Dr. Smith") to first names ("Joe") and greetings ranging from a simple "Hello" to the more formal "Good Morning". A further example is *politeness theory*, which describes different forms of indirectness for a request depending on the nature of the relationship between the requesting person and potential supporter and on how cumbersome the request is (e.g. the difference between asking your boss for $5 or a close friend). Thus, appropriate use of social deixis can help to affirm and maintain the status of an existing relationship, while using language features indicating a different form of relationship can signal a desire to change the relational status.

Empathy: Delineating the process of attending to, understanding, and responding to another person's expressions of emotion is not only important for intimate relationships but also cited as most important for building good working alliances between helpers and clients or physicians and patients. Klein et al. have shown that an empathetic and accurate computer can achieve significant behavioural effects on a user, similar to what could be expected from human empathy [24].

Self-Disclosure: Reciprocal self-disclosure increases trust, closeness and liking, which has been demonstrated in text-based human-computer interaction. Users are also more likely to buy a product from the computer if reciprocal, deepening self-disclosure is applied [28].

Continuity behaviour: Bridging the time people are apart can be facilitated by appropriate greetings and farewells and talk about the time in separation. Such behaviour is important to maintain a feeling of persistence in a relationship [15].

Humour: Computer systems that employ humour are rated as more likeable, competent and cooperative and thus form an important relationship management strategy (e.g. [29]).

Reeves and Nass have further demonstrated several relational effects, which result in a more sympathetic attitude towards the computer if it [37]:

- ...uses flattery, or praises rather than criticises users.
- ...praises other computers or criticises itself, instead of praising itself or criticising others.
- ...becomes more like the user over time or if it maintains a consistent level of similarity.
- ...*teams* with a user, which can be achieved by simply signifying that user and computer are a team - which will also increases the willingness for cooperation.

All of these strategies can be employed by conversational means (i.e. Talking Objects), while some can also be implemented in a more subtle manner by zoomorphic processes, e.g. expressing empathy towards the user. The application of such methods does at the same time address joy of use qualities that relate to the individuality of the interface, namely the key factors *personal experiences of use* and *individualisation*, and furthermore the desire for social interaction.

The domain of applications for bonding objects can be derived from the range of scenarios that relationships are generally good for, as provided by models of social psychology. These include emotional support (e.g. esteem, reassurance of worth, affection, attachment, intimacy), appraisal support (e.g. advice and guidance, information, feedback), instrumental support (e.g. material assistance), group belonging, opportunities to nurture, autonomy support, and social network support (e.g. providing introductions to other people) [3]. In particular, relationships can also play a role in **persuasive scenarios**. Perceived trustworthiness and overall charm of a source of persuasive information play an important role in the *Elaboration Likelihood Model of Persuasion* [35]. In this theory, if a decision is of low personal importance, then characteristics such as trustability and sympathy of the source of information have significant influence on the decision. Thus, bonding objects could be used in sales scenarios, which aim at building relationships with client users just as one could expect from a human sales person [2]. **Education scenarios** are another possible field of application. It has been shown that within elementary school, students feelings of relatedness towards both their teacher and classmates strongly influence their cognitive, behavioural, and emotional engagement in classroom activities [44]. Furthermore, there is evidence that relationships between students are important in peer learning situations, including peer tutoring and peer collaborative learning methodologies [9].

Summing up, qualities of relationship can have major impact on tasks in diverse areas, such as education, sales, or different types of service situations. Thus, employing bonding objects in such and similar contexts does not only have the potential to create more believable and enjoyable smart object interaction, but also for significantly improving user performance and results.

SUMMARY AND CONCLUSIONS

We have summarised and discussed a body of research that relates to the interface paradigm of life-like smart objects, crossing domains of anthropomorphism and affective computing as well as tangible user interfaces and industrial design. With this work we aim at informing future realisation efforts of anthropomorphism and zoomorphism in interactive devices with concepts and guidelines grounded in a thorough literature review. We furthermore intend to provide a starting point for continuing discussions in this interdisciplinary field, further refining the potentials and key aspects of this type of physical interface on various levels, which can help to align research agendas of active researchers. We are currently working on instances in all proposed classes and different application domains and attempt to identify additional benefits and drawbacks, from which we believe to have significant impact not only on this particular type of interfaces but also on related disciplines, such as anthropomorphic interfaces, tangible interaction, auditory interfaces, smart objects or robotics.

ACKNOWLEDGEMENTS

This research was partially funded by the German Federal Ministry of Education and Research under grant number 01 IA 08002 A. The responsibility for this publication lies with the author.

REFERENCES

1. E. André, M. Klesen, P. Gebhard, S. Allen, and T. Rist. Integrating models of personality and emotions into lifelike characters. *Affective interactions: Towards a New Generation of Computer Interfaces*, LNCS 1814:150–165, 2000.
2. K. Anselmi and J. Zemanek. Relationship selling: How personal characteristics of salespeople affect buyer

satisfaction. *Journal of Social Behavior and Personality*, 12:539–550, 1997.

3. E. Berscheid and H. Reis. Attraction and close relationships. *The handbook of social psychology*, 2:193–281, 1998.

4. T. W. Bickmore and R. W. Picard. Establishing and maintaining long-term human-computer relationships. *ACM Transactions on Computer-Human Interaction*, 12(2):293–327, 2005.

5. C. Breazeal, G. Hoffman, and A. Lockerd. Teaching and Working with Robots as a Collaboration. In *Proceedings of the Third International Joint Conference on Autonomous Agents and Multiagent Systems (AAMAS '04)*, pages 1030–1037. Los Alamitos, CA, USA: IEEE Computer Society Press, 2004.

6. E. Burneleit, F. Hemmert, and R. Wettach. Living interfaces: the impatient toaster. In *Proceedings of the 3rd International Conference on Tangible and Embedded Interaction (TEI'09)*, pages 21–22. New York, NY, USA: ACM, 2009.

7. A. Butz, M. Schmitz, A. Krüger, and H. Hullmann. Tangible UIs for Media Control: Probes into the Design Space. In *Proceedings of the SIGCHI Conference on Human Factors in Computing Systems (CHI'05)*, pages 957–971. New York, NY, USA: ACM, 2005.

8. D. Byrne and W. Griffitt. Similarity and awareness of similarity of personality characteristics determinants of attraction. *Journal of Experimental Research in Personality*, 3:179–186, 1969.

9. W. Damon and E. Phelps. *Peer relationships in child development*, chapter Strategic uses of peer learning in children's education, pages 135–157. Hoboken, NJ, USA: Wiley, 1989.

10. B. Duggan and M. Deegan. Considerations in the usage of text to speech (tts) in the creation of natural sounding voice enabled web systems. In *Proceedings of the 1st International Symposium on Information and communication technologies (ISICT '03)*, pages 433–438. Dublin, Ireland: Trinity College Dublin, 2003.

11. K. P. Fishkin. A taxonomy for and analysis of tangible interfaces. *Personal Ubiquitous Computing*, 8(5):347–358, 2004.

12. S. Fiske and S. Taylor. *Social cognition*. New York, NY, USA: McGraw-Hill, 1991.

13. P. Gebhard. ALMA: A Layered Model of Affect. In *Proceedings of the Fourth International Joint Conference on Autonomous Agents and Multiagent Systems*, pages 29–36. New York, NY, USA: ACM, 2005.

14. P. Gebhard, M. Schröder, M. Charfuelan, C. Endres, M. Kipp, S. Pammi, M. Rumpler, and O. Türk. IDEAS4Games: building expressive virtual characters for computer games. In *Proceedings of the 8th International Conference on Intelligent Virtual Agents (IVA 2008)*, pages 426–440. Berlin, Heidelberg, Germany: Springer, 2008.

15. J. Gilbertson, K. Dindia, and M. Allen. Relational continuity constructional units and the maintenance of relationships. *Journal of Social and Personal Relationships*, 15(6):774, 1998.

16. S. Göbel, O. Schneider, I. Iurgel, A. Feix, C. Knöpfle, and E. Rettig. Virtual Human: Storytelling and computer graphics for a virtual human platform. In *Proceedings of Technologies for Interactive Digital Storytelling and Entertainment 2004*, LNCS 3105, pages 79–88. Berlin, Heidelberg, Germany: Springer, 2004.

17. F. Hemmert and G. Joost. Ambient life: Calm and excited permanent tactile life-like actuation as a status display in mobile phones. In *Proceedings of the Conference on Design and Emotion*, Hong Kong, October 2008.

18. D. Hong, T. Höllerer, M. Haller, H. Takemura, A. D. Cheok, G. J. Kim, M. Billinghurst, W. Woo, E. Hornecker, R. J. K. Jacob, C. Hummels, B. Ullmer, A. Schmidt, E. van den Hoven, and A. Mazalek. Advances in tangible interaction and ubiquitous virtual reality. *IEEE Pervasive Computing*, 7(2):90–96, 2008.

19. E. Hornecker and F. Bruns. Interaktion im Sensoric Garden. In *Tagungsband der Mensch und Computer (MuC 2004)*, pages 65–74. Munich, Germany: Oldenbourg Verlag, 2004.

20. E. Horvitz, J. Breese, D. Heckerman, D. Hovel, and K. Rommelse. The Lumiere project: Bayesian user modeling for inferring the goals and needs of software users. In *Proceedings of the Fourteenth Conference on Uncertainty in Artificial Intelligence*, pages 256–265. San Francisco, CA, USA: Morgan Kaufmann, 1998.

21. R. Jakobson. Linguistics and poetics. *Style in language*, pages 350–377, 1960.

22. J. Kestner, D. Leithinger, J. Jung, and M. Petersen. Proverbial wallet: tangible interface for financial awareness. In *TEI '09: Proceedings of the 3rd International Conference on Tangible and Embedded Interaction*, pages 55–56. New York, NY, USA: ACM, 2009.

23. D. Kiesler. The 1982 Interpersonal Circle: A taxonomy for complementarity in human transactions. *Psychological Review*, 90(3):185–214, 1983.

24. J. Klein, Y. Moon, and R. Picard. This computer responds to user frustration: Theory, design, and results. *Interacting with Computers*, 14(2):119–140, 2002.

25. S. Levinson. *Pragmatics (Cambridge Textbooks in Linguistics)*. Cambridge, MA: Cambridge University Press, 1983.

26. R. McRae and O. John. An introduction to the five-factor model and its applications. *Journal of Personality*, 60:175–215, 1992.

27. S. Mithen. *The prehistory of the mind: a search for the origins of art, religion and science*. London, UK: Thames and Hudson, 1996.

28. Y. Moon. Intimate exchanges: Using computers to elicit self-disclosure from consumers. *Journal of Consumer Research*, 26(4):323–339, 2000.

29. J. Morkes, H. Kernal, and C. Nass. Effects of humor in task-oriented human-computer interaction and computer-mediated communication: A direct test of SRCT theory. *Human-Computer Interaction*, 14(4):395–435, 1999.

30. C. Nass, K. Isbister, and E.-J. Lee. Truth is beauty: researching embodied conversational agents. *Embodied Conversational Agents*, pages 374–402, 2000.

31. C. Nass and K. Lee. Does computer-synthesized speech manifest personality? Experimental tests of recognition, similarity-attraction, and consistency-attraction. *Journal of Experimental Psychology: Applied*, 7(3):171–181, 2001.

32. A. Nijholt, T. Rist, and K. Tuijnenbreijer. Lost in Ambient Intelligence? Panel Session. In *Proceedings of the SIGCHI Conference on Human Factors in Computing Systems (CHI'04)*, pages 1725–1726. New York, NY, USA: ACM, 2004.

33. P. Persson, J. Laaksoiahti, and P. Lönnqvist. Anthropomorphism - a multi-layered phenomenon. In K. Dautenhahn, editor, *Proceedings of AAAI Fall symposium, Socially Intelligent Agents: The Human in the Loop*, pages 131– 135. AAAI Press, 2000.

34. P. Persson, J. Laaksolahti, and P. Löonnqvist. *Socially Intelligent Agents*, chapter Understanding Social Intelligence, pages 21–28. Berlin, Heidelberg, Germany: Springer, 2002.

35. R. Petty and D. Wegener. Attitude change: Multiple roles for persuasion variables. *The Handbook of Social Psychology*, 1:323–390, 1998.

36. J. Piaget. *A Handbook of Child Psychology*, chapter Children's philosophies, pages 505–516. Worcester, MA, USA: Clark University Press, 2nd edition, 1933.

37. B. Reeves and C. Nass. *The media equation: How people treat computers, television, and new media like real people and places*. Cambridge, MA: Cambridge University Press, 1996.

38. S. Ruzanka, B.C., and D. Strakovsky. (in)security camera, 2003.

39. B. Scassellati. Discriminating Animate from Inanimate Visual Stimuli. In *Proceedings of the 17th International Joint Conference on Artificial Intelligence*, pages 1405–1410. San Francisco, CA, USA: Morgan Kaufmann, 2000.

40. M. Schmitz, J. Baus, and R. Dörr. The Digital Sommelier: Interacting with Intelligent Products. In C. Floerkemeier, M. Langheinrich, E. Fleisch, F. Mattern, and S. E. Sarma, editors, *Proceedings of the First International Conference on The Internet of Things (IOT 2008)*, LNCS 4952, pages 247–262. Berlin, Heidelberg, Germany: Springer, 2008.

41. M. Schmitz, A. Krüger, and S. Schmidt. Modelling Personality in Voices of Talking Products Through Prosodic Parameters. In *Proceedings of the 10th International Conference on Intelligent User Interfaces (IUI'07)*, pages 313–316. New York, NY, USA: ACM, 2007.

42. M. Schneider and A. Kröner. The Smart Pizza Packing: An Application of Object Memories. In *Proceedings of the International Conference on Intelligent Environments*, pages 1–8. Stevenage, UK: IET, 2008.

43. M. Schröder. Emotional Speech Synthesis: A Review. In *Proceedings of the European Conference on Speech Communication and Technology*, pages 561–564. Grenoble, France: International Speech Communication Association, 2001.

44. D. Stipek. *Handbook of Educational Psychology*, chapter Motivation and Instruction, pages 85–113. London, UK: Prentice Hall International, 1996.

45. E. Tan and B. Fasting. *Emotion and the structure of narrative film: Film as an emotion machine*. Hillsdale, NJ, USA: Lawrence Erlbaum Associates, 1996.

46. K. Wada and T. Shibata. Living with seal robots - its sociopsychological and physiological influences on the elderly at a care house. *IEEE Transactions on Robotics*, 23(5):972–980, 2007.

47. R. Wasinger and W. Wahlster. *True Visions: Tales on the Realization of Ambient Intelligence*, chapter The Anthropomorphized Product Shelf: Symmetric Multimodal Human-Environment Interaction, pages 291–306. Berlin, Heidelberg, Germany: Springer, 2005.

48. P. White. *The understanding of causation and the production of action: From infancy to adulthood*. London, UK: Psychology Press, 1995.

Designing from Everyday Experience

Jill Coffin
Department of Digital Media, Georgia Institute of Technology
Atlanta, Georgia, USA
jill@gatech.edu

ABSTRACT
The domain of tangible and embedded interaction (TEI) provides a valuable opportunity to explore design issues that are related to novel interactive high technologies embedded in our familiarity with the everyday world. In this paper, I present an example of a design conceptualization process that draws heavily on personal everyday experience. This activity would not be recognized as valid for research or practice within a rationalist framework, yet it results in concrete knowledge relevant to TEI. This knowledge relates to key aspects of TEI such as expanding the design domain of traditional practice, the integration of behaviour, mechanism and form, and multi-disciplinarity. The example also illustrates the hermeneutics of TEI design.

Author Keywords: Design, hermeneutics, validity.

ACM Classification Keywords: H5.m. Information interfaces and presentation (e.g., HCI): Miscellaneous.

General Terms: Design, theory.

INTRODUCTION
The domain of tangible and embedded interaction (TEI) provides a valuable opportunity to explore design issues that are related to novel interactive high technologies embedded in our familiarity with the everyday world. The conceptual coupling of TEI and everyday experience distinguishes these technologies from the idea of tangible technologies as simply off-the-desktop, physical interfaces. The centrality of everyday experience radicalizes these notions because it shifts the participation of the human in the technological space to the participation of the technology in the human space. Thus people interact with TEI technologies through their own tacit competencies. TEI's unique concept-ualization of high technology has enabled the community to expand the dialogue of design practice. See [1, 2, 3] for examples.

TEI conference papers present a refreshingly broad spectrum of methodologies including those from traditional human-computer interaction (HCI), traditional and experimental design, design theory, technological arts and music, and engineering. Each of these methodologies is implicitly accompanied by validation criteria. Almost all of the contributions include a designed prototype, yet very few describe details of that prototype's genesis. This could be because such descriptions are difficult to validate particularly in light of TEI's historical connection to HCI, which has a rationalist design tradition. To contradict this tendency, I present a trace of a design conceptualization process driven primarily by everyday personal experience. The purpose of this presentation is to instigate by giving an example of valid knowledge from processes that defy validation in the rationalist paradigm. The process I describe will likely be intuitively familiar to designers, yet these aspects of design are often black-boxed when it comes to formally reporting results, further contributing to illusions about valid design practice.

TEI'11, January 22–26, 2011, Funchal, Portugal.

THE DESIGN PROJECT
The designer remembers the charm bracelets her grandmother and other neighborhood women wore when she was a child. The charms were silhouettes of heads of little girls and boys. Each charm bore the name of a grandchild. As a child, the designer was fascinated with the charms and the idea that her grandmother carried her grandchildren with her everywhere she went. On the other hand, on closer look the charms were disappointingly generic cutouts.

Image © Ryan Benyi

When the designer was away from her own children, she wondered about having them closer through such a charm bracelet. What if instead of charms of impersonal silhouettes, this bracelet had charms that held their heartbeats, silently, so that when she touched each charm she could feel a heartbeat just as she did when she put her hand to one of their chests?

When the designer's children were newborns, she would soothe them at night by placing them to sleep prone on her chest or her husband's chest.

Sudden Infant Death Syndrome (SIDS, cot death, or crib death) is a concern of many parents of newborns. Public health initiatives and pediatricians strongly advise parents to keep their newborns sleeping on their backs for the first months of life in an effort to prevent SIDS [4].

When the designer expressed concern about her newborn child sleeping prone on a parent's chest, her pediatrician replied that there was nothing to fear because the gentle stimulation of the parent's rising chest and heartbeat would keep the infant from falling into sleep apnea [5].

The designer was given a hand-me-down infant seat that vibrates using electromotors. The crude vibration soothed her colicky infant and he stopped crying, though the motion seemed crude and jarring.

While tending houseplants, the designer imagines a large jade (rubber) plant with small devices embedded in some of its leaves. Visitors could pluck one of these leaves, hold it to their chest, record their heartbeat into it, and then put the leaf back on the plant. The leaf would throb with the heartbeat of the visitor. Other visitors could touch the heartbeats of the visitors before them. After a time, the jade plant would be throbbing with the heartbeats of many different visitors.

To actualize the heartbeat charms, the designer thinks about sound charms similar to the jade plant leaves, possibly using a material like that of the jade leaf as a diaphragm. From her training in polymer and textile engineering, she makes the association:

rubber (plant) → elastomer → polymer → fiber → textile.

Based on the association of heartbeat and textile, the designer decides to design an infant soothing and SIDS/ premature apnea therapy blanket. The blanket is meant to be an infant swaddler or other contact textile. The blanket will transmit a low frequency sound wave of a heartbeat recorded from a parent or other caregiver. This sound wave will manifest in the blanket as inaudible felt pressure.

The designer works to develop an engineering model of sound in a textile in order to find the mechanism that will make a blanket pulse with heartbeat. She follows a traditional engineering process, adapting calculations from the literature and devising lab experiments.

While walking with a friend and carrying a nearly empty cardboard coffee cup, the designer feels her friend's voice vibrating the walls of the cup as she is speaking. Having discovered the mechanism that will create the heartbeat in the blanket, the designer abandons the engineering model.

The experience with the coffee cup reveals that the low frequency heartbeat sound waves could be transmitted from a transducer such as a speaker or piezoelectric film through sealed air pockets. This mechanism would create the feeling of heartbeat pulses. A miniaturized grid of transducers would be cushioned by the air pockets within a quilted blanket. Thus the blanket would remain soft and flexible.

DISCUSSION

We can see a constellation of experiences, some conceptual, some perceptual, some from memory, participating in the outcome. Some are culturally shared, some are from domain knowledge, and some are idiosyncratic. Much HCI-related work explores meaning and experience on the part of people acting with technologies in the everyday world, yet the situatedness and experiences of the designer creating technologies for this everyday world remain under-explored. I suggest that this is because the rationalist legacy of traditional HCI does not recognize the validity of the designer's situated experiences. These experiences do not meet rationalist validity criteria such as objectivity, generalizability, and portability of process. Yet the social and cultural situatedness of the designer provides an important connection to the situatedness of the technologies she is designing. This relationship should not be bracketed out.

Expanding the design domain

In this example, we can see how the designer's inclusion of personal experiences into the design circle expands the design domain in meaningful ways. Familiarities from everyday life outside the conventional problem-solving domain of designing infant soothing and therapy devices, such as charm bracelets and coffee cups, become as relevant to the design as blankets, soothing chairs, sleeping practices, and public health advice. This domain expansion results in a solution that is different from current infant soothing technologies such as vibrating chairs and SIDS/ apnea therapies such as infant monitoring technologies. There is a direct relationship between the genesis of the design in the charm bracelet, the mechanism found in the coffee cup, and the overall design concept.

We can also see from this example how design from experience is highly interpretive, or hermeneutic. These experiences have meaning to the designer on her own terms, but they also have meaning in relation to the evolving design concept. In turn, they change and evolve the concept as it reflects meaning back on them. For example, the memory of the charm bracelet has meaning for the designer, but once she projects the idea of replacing the silhouettes with heartbeats, the memory of the charms is changed. The experiences with the sleeping infant were meaningful on their own, but unintelligible with respect to the design until a later connection was made between sound "charms" and textiles. Then these experiences were interpreted by the designer as meaningful to the design. They in turn guided the design toward SIDS/ apnea therapy which then became the primary design concept.

Design paradigms

Across disciplines we can find similar categories of frameworks. Positivist frameworks gain their validity from the community of scientific practice. They seek information through formal propositions, quantification of variables, hypothesis testing, and the drawing of inferences. The rationalist design paradigms of technical systems theory, Herbert Simon's theory of design, engineering design, and traditional HCI methodologies fall into this category. In this paradigm, design activity is understood as using well-defined, objective, generalizable, and portable procedures and principles to find optimized solutions to a design problem. This paradigm was dominant in Western design research during the 1970s and 1980s and is still the primary design paradigm for engineering and HCI.

Critical and reflective frameworks, such as Schön's reflection-in-action [6] and reflective HCI [7], show the restrictions of the normative paradigms and move forward from there. For example, Schön's reflection-in-action arose to describe aspects of practice concealed by the rationalist paradigm. Schön saw the rationalist paradigm as having no means to account for the tacit understandings and skill that are part of the professional practice of designers, as well as the uniqueness of each design situation. In *The Reflective Practitioner*, Schön describes design activity as tacit and experience-based. Because each design situation is unique, it makes no sense for the practitioner to apply standard theories or techniques. Professionals build up a repertoire of understandings, cases, theories, and actions to make sense and act within a design situation. He describes a cyclic process of design activity whereby the designer names relevant factors in the design situation, frames the problem using a repertoire of experience and theory, makes active design moves, and evaluates these moves. Instead of using a problem solving metaphor as does the rationalist paradigm, Schön describes design as a "reflective conversation with the situation."

In hermeneutic, interpretive, or phenomenological frameworks, phenomena are understood through the meaning-making activities of the people experiencing them. Hermeneutics traditionally refers to the interpretation of texts. The phenomenological philosophers Heidegger and Gadamer developed hermeneutics beyond textual interpretation to include the everyday interpretive meaning-making of our experience. The hermeneutic circle, as developed by Heidegger and Gadamer, describes how our interpretation of the world depends upon co-emergent, interdependent, partial understandings of parts and whole. We cannot understand the meaning of part of an event until we understand the whole, and we cannot understand the whole until we grasp the meaning of the parts. Another way to understand this circular relationship is to consider that we cannot understand the meaning of a concept until we understand its context, but the context is made up of the concepts that give it meaning. Any act of understanding consists of this circular interplay between inseparable parts and wholes. The hermeneutic circle is not a method, but is prior to logic and methods. It describes something integral to thoughts, perceptions, actions, and interpretations. It is inseparable from experience.

Design as a hermeneutic circle

Design theorists Snodgrass and Coyne describe design activity as a hermeneutic circle [8]. They quote Gadamer:

> A person who is trying to understand a text is always performing an act of projecting. He projects before himself a meaning for the text as a whole as soon as some initial meaning emerges in the text. Again, the latter emerges only because he is reading the text with particular expectations in regard to a certain meaning. The working out of this fore-project, which is constantly revised in terms of what emerges as he penetrates into the meaning, is understanding what is there [9].

Snodgrass and Coyne read the above quotation with "design" in mind as "text." They consider a design project as a project(ion) of experiences into the anticipated whole of the design. This gives us a portrait of the designer and the design process as embedded in the world of experience instead of preceding, detached, or over and above it as in other design paradigms. Snodgrass and Coyne thus extend Schön's metaphor of design as a reflective conversation to participation in a hermeneutic circle.

In our example, an idea is projected forward through the vision of the charms as heartbeats. The concept of the infant blanket was unintelligible at that time. Anticipation of the heartbeat charms refers other experiences toward it. These experiences change the whole, and the whole contextualizes them. As the whole of the design experience proceeds, the design is modified, clarified, and refined. Sometimes the design is completely reoriented, as in the case of the shift from charms toward infant blankets and the shift from the engineering model to the implications of the coffee cup experience.

Many of our familiarities, experiences, thoughts, associations, and daydreams remain in the background of our experience unless they are called out by some relevancy. This is also true for the designing process. Once these elements are part of the design, they form the background considerations that bring further things to light. Michael Polanyi, a scientist and philosopher of the phenomenology of tacit knowledge, describes our ability to bring background familiarities to the topic at hand:

> This power resides in the area which tends to function as a background because it extends indeterminately around the central object of our attention. Seen thus from the corner of our eyes, or remembered at the back of our mind, this area compellingly affects the way we see the object on which we are focusing. We may indeed go so far as to say that we are aware of this subsidiarily noticed

area mainly in the appearance of the object to which we are attending [10].

Some of this background will be culturally shared, some will be domain knowledge, and some will be idiosyncratic. A constellation of concepts and perceptions emerged from the background experiences of the designer in our example: the information about SIDS, the sensation of a child's heart beating through their chest, and the crudeness of the infant chair's electromotor vibration all are projected forward when called upon as part of the project of designing. As projections, they form the design concept. In return, the design concept contextualizes and focuses them. This contextualization also weeds out inappropriate contributions, while it incorporates and is transformed by appropriate ones.

Hermeneutic circle of behaviour, mechanism, and form

The idea of design as a hermeneutic circle can inform TEI in ways other than providing an understanding of overall process. In the example, a design concept could not be manifested without an understanding of how the heartbeat behaviour would be enacted through a mechanism within a soft, flexible, infant blanket form. The experience with the coffee cup revealed a way to incorporate the heartbeat behaviour while retaining the natural handle of the blanket. This everyday experience was more effective than the isolated engineering work being conducted to find a mechanism. To understand the design of behaviour, mechanism, and form as part of a hermeneutic circle recognizes their interdependence and co-evolution.

Multidisciplinary competencies

Both design and engineering competencies come into play in this example. Again, it is interesting to note the slippage of the conventional engineering competency. While the engineering model failed to be relevant in producing a mechanism, engineering knowledge of polymers and textiles conceptually sparked the idea of the heartbeat in textile form. Multidisciplinary work is often imagined categorically, as if the designer or design team atomistically programs the behaviour, engineers a mechanism, and finally designs an aesthetic form. This example illustrates how integrated multidisciplinary experience can cross categorical boundaries in helpful and unexpected ways.

CONCLUSION

The novel class of TEI technologies gives us the opportunity to carve new design paths with corresponding notions of value. The example presented here is not intended to be prescriptive, but to broaden the horizons of our understandings of practice and validity. An investigation of a design concept guided by personal everyday experience, typically considered too unreliable with respect to rationalist paradigms, is yet able to address key characteristics of TEI. From the example we can understand the following:

- Drawing upon familiarities from everyday life can beneficially expand the design domain beyond the conventional problem-solving domain.
- Treating behaviours, mechanisms, and forms as co-evolving and interdependent can benefit the design.
- Integrated multi-disciplinary competencies can contribute in cross-categorical ways.

These results speak to primary characteristics of TEI technologies, respectively their engagement in the everyday world, their integration of behaviour, mechanism, and form, and multidisciplinary, if not interdisciplinary, approaches. Finally, the example and discussion illustrate that we can use the hermeneutic circle to understand experiential design activity, as we in the TEI field participate in the larger hermeneutic circle of the overall TEI project(ion).

ACKNOWLEDGMENTS

The final version of this paper reflects the thoughtful and considerate comments of the TEI reviewers, Jay David Bolter, Ali Mazalek, and Carl DiSalvo. The technology described here as well as some others related to haptic sound are protected by US provisional patent 61/410,383.

REFERENCES

1. van den Hoven, E., Frens, J., Aliakseyeu, D., Martens, J-B., Overbeeke, K., and Peters, P. Design Research & Tangible Interaction. In *Proc. of the 1st Intl. Conference on Tangible and Embedded Interaction* (TEI '07). ACM Press. 2007.
2. Fernaeus, Y., Tholander, J., and Jonsson, M. Towards a new set of ideals: consequences of the practice turn in tangible interaction. In *Proc. of the 2nd Intl. Conference on Tangible and Embedded Interaction* (TEI '08). ACM Press. 2008.
3. Fernaeus, Y. and Jacobsson, M. Comics, robots, fashion and programming: outline the concept of actDresses. In *Proceedings of the 3rd International Conference on Tangible and Embedded Interaction* (TEI '09). ACM Press. 2009.
4. Markestad, T., Skadberg, B. Hordvik, E., Morild, I. and Irgens, L.M. Sleeping position and sudden infant death syndrome (SIDS): effect of an intervention program to avoid prone sleeping. In *Acta Paediatrica*, Vol. 84, No. 4. 1995. 375-378.
5. McNamara, F., Wulbrand, H., and Thach, B.T. Characteristics of the infant arousal response. In *Journal of Applied Physiology*, Vol. 85, Issue 6. December 1998. 2314-2321.
6. Schön, D. A. *The Reflective Practitioner: How Professionals Think in Action*. Basic Books. 1984.
7. Sengers, P., McCarthy, J., and Dourish, P. Reflective HCI: articulating an agenda for critical practice. In *CHI '06 Extended Abstracts on Human Factors in Computing Systems* (CHI '06). ACM Press. 2006.
8. Snodgrass, A. and Coyne, R. Is Designing Hermeneutical? In *Architectural Theory Review*, Vol. 1, No. 1. 1997.
9. Gadamer, H-G. *Truth and Method* (Second Edition). Sheed and Ward. 1989 [1960]. p. 36. Quoted in [8].
10. Polanyi, M. Experience and the Perception of Pattern. In *The Modeling of Mind*, K. M. Sayre and F.J. Crosson (eds.). Notre Dame University Press. 1963. p. 214.

A Sufism-Inspired Model for Embodied Interaction Design

Umut Burcu Tasa
Yıldız Technical University, Faculty of Art and Design, Istanbul, Turkey
umuttasa@gmail.com

Enis Âli Yurtsever
Yıldız Technical University, Faculty of Art and Design, Istanbul, Turkey
ea.yurtsever@gmail.com

ABSTRACT
This paper presents a concise overview of argumentations about the body and the concept of embodiment in the field of technology by also referencing to the similar debates in philosophy, critical theory and social studies. In view of the observation that advances in technology call for a re-definition of embodiment, and in many different fields of life embodied approaches are increasingly looked for, it briefly revisits Modernity's ideal of disembodiment, which for those of us who live in modern societies, still dominates our approach to life and our understanding of existence, and as a corollary, our daily interactions with technologies as well. Then drawing from Sufism, the mystical tradition of Islam, and from a phenomenological interpretation of its approach to human body, the authors finally propose a four-layer understanding of embodiment as a model to be implemented in embodied interaction design.

Author Keywords
Body and technology, embodied interaction design, Sufism.

ACM Classification Keywords
H5.m. [Information interfaces and presentation]: Miscellaneous; K4.m. [Computers and society]: Miscellaneous.

General Terms
Design; Theory.

INTRODUCTION
With the advent of ubiquitous and pervasive computing, gestural interfaces, wearables and alike, human body has increasingly become the fundamental element in the design of tools and devices that make use of information and communication technologies. It has been proposed by many that as the human technology interface gets more and more transparent; boundaries between the body and technology become less and less certain. While information and networking technologies become an indispensable part of our everyday lives, with their ever increasing proximity, they also turn into extensions of our bodies, which, in turn, develop synthetic senses of their own [6,8,14]. Such a convergence has rather been challenging to the concept of embodiment, putting the notion of skin as its demarcation in question, and demanding, therefore, a new definition [10].

The growing attention of researchers to the body and to the concept of embodiment in technology and design has, rather expectedly, followed a parallel path with the increasing interest for body studies in the field of social sciences. When we look at the academic literature of the last 30 years in both fields, we can observe an apparent shift from a disembodied approach to an embodied one. While it can be argued that now the body is no more an entity, which is mostly ignored or at times may even be despised, the notion of embodiment still remains controversial.

THE BODY CONTROVERSY
From Antiquity to Christianity, then to Enlightenment and Modernity, in Western lineage of thinking a disembodied approach to human existence has been persistent in one form or another. The body has been perpetually subjugated to the power of either mind or soul, and regarded as something to be transcended [15]. Even in the aesthetics of the Ancient Greek, where "body image" was at the forefront of any type of social conduct, the body was acknowledged so much as it represented a transcendent sacredness and supremacy which was beyond its material self [9]. Western tradition, as culminated in the mind-body duality of the Cartesian thought, accommodates an intellectual history of splits such as soul versus body, nature versus culture, subject versus object, real versus ideal etc., which can all be understood in terms of the externalization and objectification of the body.

Consequently, we see that the body has almost been absent in the mainstream philosophy and sociology throughout Modernity [11]. While the world as an external reality independent of our cognition and experience has been accepted as a "scientific fact" by analytic philosophy - which still represents the mainstream in the contemporary academia, classical sociology has adopted the Cartesian dichotomy at its very foundations, and established the mind as the key attribute that defines humans as social beings [7, 11]. Despite body's absence in the mainstream academic discourse, in social systems of Modernity, body has become the principal field of political and cultural activity. As we see in the case of nation states with their practices relating to gender, sports, warfare and other various fields of private and social life, power structures of the modern era have

TEI'11, January 22–26, 2011, Funchal, Portugal.

extensively used the body both as a medium and a tool to construct their control mechanisms [11].

While this is the picture of the mainstream, several alternative approaches to the body have also emerged. In philosophy, a tradition referred to as continental philosophy has developed outside the territory of analytic philosophy towards the end of 19th century. While analytic philosophy sought, for the sake of objectivity, to transcend from "human embodiment, cultural embeddedness, imaginative understanding and location within history and tradition", continental philosophers such as Heidegger and Husserl came up with novel arguments which discussed in detail how knowledge depended on being in a world that was inseparable from our bodies, our language, and our social history, i.e. from our embodiment [13]. Phenomenologist Merleau-Ponty suggested the body as a "point of view upon the world" without which thought, reason, and mentality could not exist. Embodiment in Merleau-Ponty's thought echoes a different sense of duality: it encompasses both the body as physical, biological and "outer" entity, which is the context of cognitive mechanisms, and also the body as an experiential, phenomenological and "inner" being. With its inner and outer aspects tightly interwoven, body is indeed an expressive space, and in Merleau-Ponty's words, "the very condition for the coming into being of a meaningful world" [7,13].

Phenomenology as an embodied approach to understand the human condition had lost most of its appeal since the rise of the postmodern thought. While "the body" issue has been embraced by a significant number of postmodern scholars, majority of their approaches was still incomplete and maintained the same fragmented perception of the West. The postmodern discourse, led by feminist scholars and thinkers like Foucault, exposed the power and political structures of Modernity over body, but it fell short of supplying a novel conceptual framework that would facilitate a holistic understanding of embodiment [11].

In postmodern thought, the body has often been referred to as a "project", an entity always in the process of becoming, and identified with attributes like flexibility, instability, transformativity, fluidity, etc. Its corporeality has been superseded by its socially constructed virtuality. Self care regimes such as dieting and bodybuilding, and medical procedures like sex reassignment (SRS) and plastic surgery, all serve for the transformation of the body not for the sake of the body itself, but as a display of constructed identities. However, defining the body solely as an identity construct, although it offers a new perspective to comprehend the postmodern human condition, is in fact nothing but reviving the same old externalization and objectification of the Cartesian dichotomy.

Nevertheless, during the last three decades of social and critical theories, prominently developed from the alternative approaches of thinkers like Husserl and Merleau-Ponty, a significant corpus of literature on body and embodiment has still emerged, mostly as an attempt to transcend the Cartesian dualism of Modernity and Postmodernity. Theorists such as Strathern even called embodiment as a new form of humanism, and Varela et al proposed a dialogue between Buddhist tradition and cognitive science to achieve a new embodied understanding [12, 13].

BODY AND DIGITAL TECHNOLOGIES

Modernity's vision of the rational mind reigning over the body, and therefore not being bound and limited by it has been rejuvenated with the advance of digital technologies and the consequent evolution of cyberculture. For the advocates of cyberspace, it initially seemed that the mind/body segregation of the West has just found the right "media" to reach its ultimate goal: the utopian dream of the pure mind achieving an unconditional freedom through disembodiment. While novel technologies like artificial intelligence (AI) and virtual reality (VR) were encouraging the dream of an ultimate disembodiment, robotics and cybernetics were cultivating the idea of the cyborg, the cyber- or post-body, which again represented the pure domination of mind over body, and its right to transform and replace it by and through any technology [15].

Despite the initial excitement over this new version of the disembodiment myth, as its Cartesian nature became more and more exposed, serious alternative approaches soon were proposed, which reasserted the body as the primary context that digital designers must take into account [1]. Embodied implementation of digital technologies was first seen in the VR works of artists like Gromala and Davies, who came up with innovative ideas such as using breath, balance and meditation as interaction elements.

Based on the recent findings of neuroscience, it is now being accepted that sensory and motor processes are fundamentally inseparable in a lived cognition. Cognition depends upon experience that comes from having a body with various sensorimotor capacities, and these sensorimotor capacities are themselves embedded in a more encompassing biological, psychological, and cultural context [7,13]. Consequently, in the field of HCI and interaction design, the idea of "embodied interaction design" is becoming increasingly popular, which posits interaction to be experienced as a participatory and holistic practice rather than designing technological artifacts as rational devices alien to human nature [2]. Design problems related to new areas like ubiquitous computing, social situation of interaction, and non-task-oriented computing all call for an alternative approach based on full embodiment as hinted by Harrison et al [4]. More recently, Suzan Kozel offered a phenomenological approach in our intimate interaction with technologies; and Schick and Malmborg proposed a distributed and shared embodiment through connected wearable and ubiquitous technologies [6, 10]. This entire shift has gone parallel with the emergence and development of ubiquitous, pervasive, sensory, and wearable technologies, and the rising importance of contextuality and gestural interfaces, all of which require the design procedures to be body-centered.

Although the ambition of many technologists to develop interfaces that could be matched to human sensory and cognitive capacities can be traced back to early 1950s, it is rather hard to conclude that embodied approaches in interaction design are well established and mainstream today [3]. Just at the turn of the new century, in his trumpet instrument comparison, Malina was warning the interaction designers that most wearables and hand held devices were still alien to the body and the mind [8]. Yet after a decade into the 21st Century, developments in biomedical and genetic engineering, and advances in emerging technologies like biomechatronics and neuroprosthetics turn the body increasingly into a phenomenon of options and choices. While this situation gives a fake feeling of "control" over our bodies, we are getting deprived of the fundamental guiding values of our lives. As Schilling puts it, "as science facilitates greater degrees of intervention into the body, it destabilizes our knowledge of what bodies are, and runs ahead of our ability to make moral judgments about how far science should be allowed to reconstruct the body" [11]. The more we are able to control and alter the limits of our corporeality, the greater is our uncertainty about what constitutes an individual's body, and what its "natural" essence actually is.

In order to contribute to the search for a new understanding of embodiment, we believe it is rather crucial to step outside of this conceptual bewilderment, and be alert for the ever persisting and insidious traps of Cartesian thinking. In this regard, we propose to defer our rational and analytical conventions for a while, and take a fresh look at the body concept in Sufi tradition.

SUFISM AND RE-EMBODIMENT

"... and W*e are closer to them than their jugular veins" (Qur'an, 50:16)*

Sufism is the mystical dimension of Islam. Similar to other esoteric and mystical traditions of the East and West, the quest for Unity, re-unity with God (*Tawhid*) is its ultimate purpose. This view of oneness, contrary to the Cartesian duality of the West, manifests itself in the unity of the mind, soul and body. While some of Sufist rituals and teachings may be misinterpreted as symbolisms of despise and destruction of the body, the actual target of disdain and destruction is not the material body but the ego, or the individual self, which is seen as responsible for the separation from Unity [15]. Sufism calls for abandoning the self, the individuation, and emancipation from the weaknesses of the ego, or the *nafs'*, the Sufi term that stands for these concepts.

Sufis see the human body, along with all the creation, as the manifestation of God's names and attributes. In Sufi rituals, the experiences are basically body-centric and somatic. Sufi fasting *oruç*, the embodied prayer *namaz*, dance rituals *tarab* and *sema*, the Sufi meditation *murakaba* and *zikr*, which is a ritual performed collectively through rhythmic body movements while repeating the verses from Qur'an, are all practices that require full body awareness to attain their true meanings.

One contemporary interpretation of Sufism's understanding of embodiment is given by Farid al-Zahi, the Moroccan scholar of Islamic studies. His phenomenological schema of embodiment in Sufism proposes four basic dimensions of bodily experience, which collectively define a singular body, as follows: (1) *Physical embodiment* (body matter); (2) *Social embodiment* (bodily movement); (3) *Biological embodiment* (biological dynamics); (4) *Spiritual embodiment* (interpretation of body's meaning) [12].

The very first aspect of Zahi's four-dimensional model is the "physical body" or body matter, which lies at the core of every bodily experience. Physical body is primordial to human existence; it is the substance around which life, motion, actions and consciousness are shaped. The second dimension, "social body", relates to the body's external appearance, where movement is the key. The body moves in ways regulated by traditions and existing norms and values; it works, communicates and socializes with other bodies, establishing an identity for itself within the society. While this second dimension defines body's outer reach, the third stands for its inner dynamics. It is the "biological body" with its life-support and cognitive mechanisms built around chemical and mechanical processes. And the last dimension represents the "spiritual body", a superstructure which acknowledges that human existence is dependent on body's materiality and sociality but is not limited by them. It attests to a holistic understanding of embodiment, which signifies humanity's interconnectedness with the rest of the existence [12].

A PROPOSED MODEL FOR EMBODIED INTERACTION

Each dimension presented by Zahi in his phenomenological schema, maintains a different point of view on the body. Only when all these distinct but entangled perspectives are considered together, we can talk about a holistic and complete understanding of embodiment. We propose that all of these embodiment dimensions should be taken into consideration as different conceptual phases in an embodied interaction design approach.

The pre-given physical body matter requires the material being of the body to be considered before anything else, which is already the case for almost all design approaches.

Then we have the social body, which is moving and acting, experiencing the outer world, communicating and interacting with other bodies and artifacts around itself. For this design phase we propose a phenomenological approach to human experience and interaction. The famous motto of the activity theorists "you are what you do" should be kept in mind while designing *what* the technological artifacts will *make* our bodies *do* [5]. Besides, this is the phase that would contribute to a networked and interconnected society through distributed, extended and shared bodies, as the body connects with technologies and to other bodies through those technologies.

At the third phase, the biological and cognitive dynamics of the body should be included into the design process utilizing findings of disciplines like ergonomics and cognitive science. At this stage the design should be compatible with those inner mechanisms of the body for it to remain healthy and content with itself.

The final phase, which probably corresponds to the most neglected aspect of embodiment in mainstream interaction design, is to reflect upon the spiritual dimension of the body. This layer tells us that the corporeal body is also the means to connect with ethereal realms of human existence. The rituals that Sufis practice to nourish the spiritual body establish for them a bond with the sacred and divine, or the oneness of being. For others, this layer can be perceived as a gateway to altered states of consciousness, or even artistic inspiration and creativity. It is no coincidence that the greatest Sufi mystics like Rumi and Yunus Emre or Lao Tszu, the spiritual leader of Taoism, were also great poets. In the final analysis, spirituality, more than anything else, represents that which is purely subjective and personal. However, it also mandates that subjectivity and individuality be transcended through an awareness of interconnectedness and unity with the whole. And embodiment, with its fourth layer of the spiritual body, is our means to attain such awareness. From a design point of view, therefore, we can conclude that addressing the spiritual layer of embodiment would practically mean, for one thing, not to concentrate only on satisfying the needs and expectations of *isolated individual users*, but, as a key ethical responsibility, embrace and cherish the interests and well being of the whole web of existence as well.

CONCLUSION

At this current state of the human condition, it really is undisputable that an embodied approach is urgent and necessary in all areas of life, from daily social practices to our interaction with technologies. What is in question today is how to define embodiment, and how to generate a relevant framework to guide the design process of human-technology interactions so that technology does not turn out to be something that alienates us to our bodies and to the nature of our existence. Our approach in this paper has been drawn from a phenomenological interpretation of Sufism's understanding of embodiment. The model, which we put forward based on this approach, and which is yet to be implemented and tested in concrete design projects, proposes that the body should be considered as a holistic entity consisting of material, social, biological and spiritual layers, and a truly embodied interaction design should duly address the needs of all layers again in a holistic manner. Although we have taken Sufism here as our point of reference, it should be noted that other ancient mystical teachings of the world attest to the same principles of interconnectedness and unity, and to the body's crucial role in being in touch with the rhythm of life. We believe that our ancient cultural heritage may still provide essential guidelines for science and technology to cultivate a new human condition of re-embodiment, interconnectivity, and re-unity, an advanced state of well being for all of us.

REFERENCES

1. Bolter, J.D. and Gromala. D. *Windows and Mirrors: Interaction Design, Digital Art, and the Myth of Transparency.* The MIT Press, Cambridge, MA, 2003.
2. Dourish, P. *Where the Action Is: Foundations of Embodied Interaction.* The MIT Press, Cambridge, MA, 2003.
3. Fisher, S.S. Virtual Interface Environments. In *Multimedia: From Wagner to Virtual Reality*, W. W. Norton & Company Press (2002), 257-267.
4. Harrison, S., Tatar, D. and Sengers, P. The Three Paradigms of HCI. In *Proc. CHI 2007*, ACM Press (2006).
5. Kaptelinin, V. and Nardi, B.A. *Acting with Technology: Activity Theory and Interaction Design.* The MIT Press, Cambridge, MA, 2009.
6. Kozel, S. *Closer: Performance, Technologies, Phenomenology.* The MIT Press, Cambridge, MA, 2007.
7. Lakoff, G. and Johnson, M. *Philosophy in the Flesh: The Embodied Mind and Its Challenge to Western Thought.* Basic Books, NY, 1999.
8. Malina, R. A Forty-Year Perspective on Aesthetic Computing in the Leonardo Journal. *Aesthetic Computing*, The MIT Press (2006), 43-52.
9. Sayın, Z. Doğu'da ve Batı'da bedenin temsilinde haysiyet ve zillet. *Defter 39*, 1 (2000), 159-211.
10. Schick, L. and Malmborg, L. Bodies, embodiment and ubiquitous computing. *Digital Creativity 21*, 1(2010), 63-69.
11. Shilling, C. *The body and social theory.* SAGE Publications, London, 2003.
12. Scott, K. *Sufis and Saints' Bodies: Mysticism, Corporeality, and Sacred Power in Islam.* The University of North Carolina Press, Chapel Hill, 2007.
13. Varela, F.J., Thompson, E.T. and Rosch, E. *The Embodied Mind: Cognitive Science and Human Experience.* The MIT Press, Cambridge, MA, 1992.
14. Weiser, M. The computer of the 21st century. *Scientific American September,* (1991), 94–100.
15. Yurtsever, Â. and Tasa, U.B. Redefining the body in cyberculture: Art's contribution to a new understanding of embodiment. In *The Real and The Virtual,* Inter-disciplinary Press (2009), 3-13.

Pediluma: Motivating Physical Activity Through Contextual Information and Social Influence

Brian Y. Lim Aubrey Shick Chris Harrison Scott Hudson
Human-Computer Interaction Institute
Carnegie Mellon University
5000 Forbes Ave., Pittsburgh, PA 15213, USA
{byl, ashick, chris.harrison, scott.hudson}@cs.cmu.edu

ABSTRACT

We present Pediluma, a shoe accessory that tracks and visualizes the wearer's physical activity by varying the intensity of a lighted enclosure. In particular, the more physically active the wearer is, the more the device glows. We hoped the desire to maintain a positive, "glowing" state would encourage users to engage in more physical activity. We describe our two-week, four-condition, 18-participant deployment and user study. Results indicate participants wearing our device were more physically active than participants in our three control groups (each isolating different design and experimental factors). We share the many lessons we learned from our iterative design, post-deployment data analysis and interviewers with participants.

Author Keywords

Wearable computing, persuasion, captology, smart clothes, visualization, ambient information, behavior change.

ACM Classification Keywords

H.5.2 [Information interfaces and presentation]: Graphical User Interfaces. C.5.3 [Microcomputers]: Portable devices.

General terms: Human Factors

INTRODUCTION

Motivating behavior change is a considerable challenge. People find comfort in familiar routines and attitudes, and naturally resist change, even if to their benefit. Computing technology is increasingly being applied in persuasive ways in order to promote behavioral change [10,20]. Previous efforts have primarily relied on two methods to motivate users: 1) displaying timely and relevant information, 2) and leveraging social influence.

One approach to promoting behavior change is to target the point-of-decision. This is the point when people consult their memories for relevant information, and attempt to make informed choices about how to proceed. Any pertinent information injected into the environment at this moment will be salient. This salience often makes the information highly influential. This strategy has been leveraged in numerous domains, including physical activity [2,31], diet [15], energy conservation [1,13], recycling [14], and water usage [5]. Furthermore, although some recommendations have universal applicability (e.g. consuming less sugary drinks), many systems tailor the information they present to a particular user. Doing so allows the information to be far more relevant, and ultimately more effective.

A second approach to promoting behavioral change is to use social influence. The desire to project a positive image to other people is often at the root of behavioral changes [7]. Technology can amplify this effect by enhancing the communication and interaction between users and the people they interact with. For example, social networking can be used to stimulate competition or facilitate support groups (see e.g., [1,20,32,36]), both of which motivate behavioral change. Additionally, public commitment has been shown to significantly improve the likelihood the associated behavior change will be achieved [17,23].

DEMONSTRATION DOMAIN: PHYSICAL ACTIVITY

We capitalize and extend on the aforementioned effects by designing a new persuasive technology to support behavior change, specifically in the physical health domain. Lack of physical activity is regarded as a "public health crisis," leading to a wide range of health problems, including coronary heart disease, type II diabetes, cancer of the colon, and many other ailments [22]. It has been shown that as little as 30 minutes of moderate physical activity four or more days a week can provide substantial health benefits [22,28]. In particular, walking can be easily incorporated into everyday life and sustained into old age [26], thus offering the best opportunity to impact personal health [21].

PEDILUMA

We developed Pediluma, a shoe accessory designed to encourage opportunistic physical activity (Figure 1). It features a light that brightens the more the wearer walks and slowly dims when the wearer remains stationary. This interaction was purposely simple so as to remain lightweight, both visually and cognitively. Even simple, personal pedometers have been shown to promote walking [6]. Pediluma takes this a step further, attempting to engage people around the wearer to elicit social effects. It should be noted that lights have been previously incorporated into shoes

TEI'11, January 22–26, 2011, Funchal, Portugal.

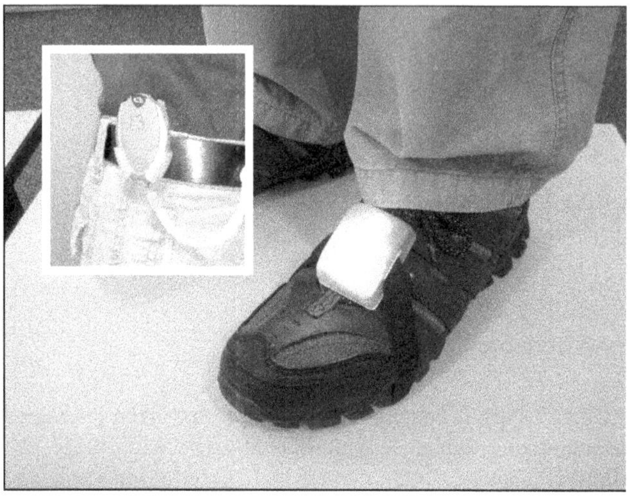

Figure 1. Pediluma strapped to a shoe and fully lit. Inset: The covered Omron HJ-112 pedometer that all participants would wear to log their step counts.

(e.g., UFOS [8], L.A. Lights [12]). However, this is the first time they have been used to display motivational information. We also draw upon decades of research into the larger field of wearable computers.

Design

Pediluma expresses *personal* information about the wearer's walking to motivate physical activity. Mounted on the top (as opposed to, e.g. the heel) of the shoe, Pediluma is visible to the wearer, serving as a *personal* display, and to other people, serving as a *public* display, alerting them to the wearer's recent physical activity. This, in turn, might promote discussion, encouragement, and/or other social pressures. Pediluma also acts as a *persistent* display that can continually remind users of their walking behavior. Located on the shoe, the information is *peripheral*, allowing users to engage in other tasks without excessive distraction or discomfort. Furthermore, the light only brightens when users are walking (i.e., making progress), coupling the visual response with their *present* activities. This brightening, which occurs during walking may serve as a *positive* reinforcement. Lastly, we hypothesize the desire to maintain a *positive* state could encourage the wearer to engage in more physical activity [30].

The decision to place Pediluma on the shoe was motivated by several factors. Foremost, this location provided the highest accuracy to sense walking [16]. Additionally, the weight and size of our prototype device, complete with sensors, microprocessor and batteries, was less obtrusive here, both to the wearer and onlookers. Moreover, feet are generally located in the periphery of one's vision during most physical activities, and often entirely hidden when working (e.g., in a seated position or tucked under a desk). Finally, unlike other articles of clothing, shoes have an obvious conceptual connection with walking and other physical activities, unlike, for example, the waist.

To refine the design and increase utility and appeal, we employed a user-centered strategy to design the hardware, software, housing and harness. The authors wore the earliest prototypes, allowing for major issues to be identified. This was followed by iterative pilot presentations of the device to potential users. Feedback collected during these sessions was used for further refinement. This process led to the creation of five distinct designs, each with a unique circuit board, lighting array, control logic, housing, and harnessing (Figure 2 illustrates three major revisions).

Early prototypes featured a longitudinal electroluminescent wire, which provided excellent visibility from all angles. However, the high power consumption would have limited battery life to three days. Focusing on improving battery life, they were substituted with low-power LEDs. The housing had to be adapted to diffuse the light from a point source. Durability was also crucial to successful deployment. To ensure proper operation and to test the robustness of the hardware and harnessing, the authors wore each version for several days. We learned of the need for a secure harness to prevent the devices from flying off the shoe from vigorous activity.

Implementation

The final prototype is small: measuring 4.5x6x3cm, weighs 50g with batteries, and boasts roughly 500 hours of run time on three AAA batteries (Figure 2, right). Substantial effort was invested in making the units energy efficient, small and robust – all units had to survive real world deployment without the ability to recharge or reset for more than a week (all units did). We now briefly discuss implementation specifics.

Various sensors were considered for step detection. Although many advanced pedometers use accelerometers, they were unnecessarily complex for our needs. Piezo films are

Figure 2. From left to right: 1) First prototype using an Arduino and electroluminescent wire. 2) Second prototype using "wings" for batteries to achieve a flatter profile. 3) Sketch of final design. 4) Photo of final PIC-based Pediluma platform.

simpler, but require calibration to reduce false positives to an acceptable level. A tilt switch proved to be a simple and robust solution. When oriented vertically, the sensor trips whenever an impact (acceleration) of 1g or greater occurs. In addition to capturing walking steps, this sensor also reliably captured motion in a variety of other contexts, including dancing and bicycling.

Our prototype uses light to convey the wearer's current and recent walking activity. If the wearer has remained stationary for a length of time, no light will be emitted. As the wearer begins to walk, the light will quickly brighten to indicate increasing levels of activity. When the wearer stops walking, the light will slowly decay in brightness until it returns to an inactive state. The growth and decay of brightness has been designed to change linearly with step accumulation and time, respectively. We utilized Stevens' power law [33] to linearize the perceptual brightness.

The rate of brightness change was calibrated such that walking was quickly rewarded to motivate even brief actions, while decay was calibrated to be slow to leave a lingering impact of recent walking activity. For a comfortable walking speed of 3mph, Pediluma would light up to maximum brightness in 5 minutes, and when stationary, it would take 15 minutes to decay fully. If the wearer walks for more than 5 minutes, internal points for walking effort were accumulated to a threshold such that the light would remain at maximum brightness for sometime before decaying.

Initial prototypes were developed on the Arduino platform [4]. Our final prototype utilizes a diminutive, down-clocked (for greater energy efficiency), PIC processor. The electronics were housed in a custom enclosure vacuum formed from frosted PETG plastic (Figure 2). Various shapes and sizes for the housing were tested — the final shape being a compromise between a stylized, aerodynamic look and volume minimization. The housing comprises two tightly fitting pieces that form a strong and tight seal. This is water resistant to protect from rain and sufficiently rigid to protect the electronics from shocks and drops.

Experiences with several mounting techniques (e.g., clips, Velcro, nylon) led to the use of rubberized straps to secure the device to the foot. We developed a double-looped design, with one strap going around the bottom of the foot and the other around the ankle. This harness is secure enough such that the user can engage in vigorous activity (e.g. running, jumping, and biking) without Pediluma shifting position or slipping off.

RELATED WORK

B.J. Fogg has established seven strategies of persuasive technology tools: *reduction*, simplification of a complex task; *tunneling*, expert guided persuasion; *tailoring*, presentation of personally relevant information; *suggestion*, point of need intervention with compelling suggestion; *self-monitoring*, automatically tracking desired behavior; *surveillance*, observing one's behavior publicly, and *conditioning*, or the reinforcement of desired behaviors [10]. Given the appropriate cultural background, these strategies for persuasion may be more effective than suggestion.

Kahled proposed that collectivist cultures are more receptive to suggestion while individualist cultures are not. This theory reasons that while collectivists are already used to "acting upon the suggestions of others," individualists focus on their personal values and priorities to determine their choice of action [18]. Considering this, collectivists in an established group may be more receptive to a suggestion in the context of other's perceptions and progress, where as individualists may be more responsive to the strategies of personal feedback established by Fogg [10]. In many ways, western culture can be classified as individualist, calling demand to the exploration and implementation of these persuasive tactics.

Persuasively influencing behavior [7,19] through point-of-decision displays and ambient visualizations has been explored in a variety of prior projects. Our work builds on this by exploring the highly personalized experience inherent in a wearable point-of-decision display with a personal and public ambient component.

Consolvo et al. developed Houston [9], a software application for the mobile phone that allows users to track and share their progress toward a physical activity goal. Two versions of the software were created: a personal version for reviewing personal history, and a sharing version, which allowed groups of people to view each other's progress and communicate. Results from a user study showed that participants using the sharing version were significantly more likely to meet their physical activity goals. The authors discuss numerous qualitative effects they observed, which they use to make a set of design requirements.

An extensive literature review by Andrew et al. [3] produced a comprehensive mapping of the design tactic space of persuasive technologies in the health domain. Their paper identifies three exemplary technologies: ViTo, a point of need system for monitoring and influencing TV watching [24], MPTrain, an augmented music system that detects heart-rate as the wearer is running and selects the next song by either higher or lower beats per minute in order to influence the target heart rate [27], and the Nike+iPod [25]. These systems are compared on both technological dimensions (subtleness, display, notification modality, context source, timeliness, and interactivity) and content dimensions (specificity, affect, adaptive affect, argumentation strategy, overtness, explicitness, and social components).

IMPACT is a system for monitoring personal health while providing the context for a specific activity [11]. The objective is to bridge the gap between perceived and actual behavior by informing wearers about which daily activities have the greatest impact on their health. With this knowledge, the user is able to make healthier activity decisions. Instead of providing the information in a reflective context, as IMPACT does, Pediluma displays impact of daily activities in real time.

Bridging the domains of health and conservation, Waterbot provides information at the point-of decision when people are using a sink [5]. Waterbot utilizes light and sound to indicate water usage for hygiene and water conservation. Through this lighting display, users gain information about the temperature of the water, the duration they have been washing, and a comparative indication of their water use in relation to the other members of the household. Although similar in some ways, Pediluma differs in its user-centric rather than household-centric focus and application to the physical activity domain. Also, Waterbot is a solitary experience, whereas Pediluma is designed for social settings.

USER STUDY

Eighteen participants were recruited using an email campaign (7 female, 11 male) for a two-week study, for which they received a small payment. The participants had a mean age of 30 (min=21, max=53) and represented a diverse range of physical fitness levels.

Following the methodology employed in [9], to better ensure our sample sufficiently represented the population at large, a preliminary survey was given that incorporated the *Sample Physical Activity Questionnaire to Determine Stage of Change* [34] to measure people's Transtheoretical Model (TTM) stage of behavioral change [29]. Our assessment indicated that participants were at a variety of motivation stages regarding their physical activity: 2 contemplation, 3 preparation, 1 action, 11 maintenance (of which 5 had no intention to change). Previous research efforts have tended to recruit only motivated participants. However, using participants with a strong predisposition to wanting to increase their physical activity introduces a significant experimental bias. Although harder to achieve motivational effects with potentially unmotivated participants, we believe this choice yielded a more real-world study outcome.

For a baseline, at the commencement of the study, all participants were asked to wear an Omron HJ-112 pedometer for one week (see Figure 1 inset). This served only as a sensor, recording participants' daily step counts. The pedometer's buttons and display were covered so participants could not tamper with their data. This also prevented wearers from viewing their step counts and setting personal goals — an effect we were not measuring. Participants were given no instructions other than to wear the pedometer whenever possible. At the conclusion of the first week, the experimenters met with each participant and recorded the step counts from the pedometers for the past seven days. Participants were not told what their step counts were. This initial period was used to establish each participant's base level of physical activity.

In the second week, participants continued to wear the covered pedometers. However, they were also randomly assigned to one of four conditions, balancing for their TTM motivation stages. For each TTM stage, participants were randomly assigned to each condition until the conditions were each populated with four participants. By week two, one participant dropped out, leaving 17 participants. The extra participant was assigned to the *Pediluma condition*.

The four conditions were as follows:

Control - Four participants continued to wear only the pedometers given to them in the first week. They were given no new instructions or devices to wear.

Pediluma - Five participants were given full-featured Pedilumas. Each featured a light that grew in intensity in response to a user's physical activity.

Random Light - Four participants were given devices that looked identical to the full-featured Pediluma. However, the lighting behavior was random and was not associated with the participants' physical activity. This condition was included to test whether the mere presence of a lighted, but non-informational shoe-mounted device would increase physical activity. The behavior of the lighting display was programmed to mimic a full-featured Pediluma, including frequency, duration and intensity.

No Light - Four participants were given devices that looked identical to the full-featured Pediluma, but did not utilize lights or sensors. This condition acted as an additional comparison, testing to see whether the mere presence of a shoe-mounted device would increase physical activity.

Participants were not given any new instructions or hints that the objective was to increase their physical activity. For the two conditions with lights, participants were simply told, "here is the device you are going to wear on your shoe. You will notice that it has a light that varies. The light is related to the unit's operation." For the non-lighted condition, only the first sentence was spoken. This was necessary to minimize any demand effects. At the conclusion of the second week, data from the pedometers was recorded. Similar to week one, participants were not told their step counts.

We aimed to investigate if participants in the *Pediluma condition* would benefit in several aspects when compared to the *Control condition*. We also hypothesized that the other two intermediate conditions (*No Light* and *Random Light*) would perform no worse than the *Control condition*.

Over the course of the two-week study, three surveys were administered — one in the beginning, middle, and end. The first survey measured participants' initial state, including their TTM motivation stage towards physical activity. This information was used to ensure a balanced distribution of participants in different stages into the four conditions introduced in week two. These questions were also included in the following two surveys to detect if there were any subsequent motivational changes, though no significant changes were detected. The second survey was administered at the conclusion of week one, but before participants were given the shoe-mounted devices that they would wear for the next week (all conditions except *Control*). This survey captured participants' experiences with the covered pedometers and posed several scale questions to measure their awareness and attitudes towards physical activity.

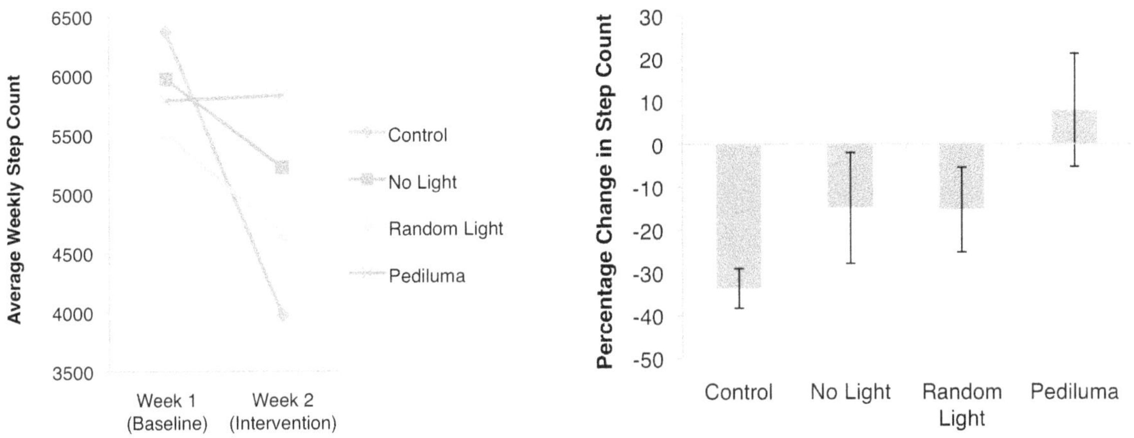

Figure 3. Left: Change in step count from first to second week. Notice that all conditions except Pediluma decreased. Right: Mean of percentage difference of each participant by group. The Control condition decreased the most, the No Light and Random Light conditions saw similar, although less dramatic decreases, while Pediluma condition step counts increased.

Additionally, a social confidence scale from the Jackson Personality Inventory (JPI, 1994) [34] was included to learn if the devices influenced peoples' behavior or attitudes. The concluding survey once again captured participant's awareness and attitudes towards physical activity for comparison.

At the conclusion of the study, questions were posed to gauge participants' experiences with the shoe-mounted devices: how much the devices were noticed, who noticed and remarked about them and how much, and whether participants found the devices useful and liked them. Additionally, participants were interviewed for approximately half an hour. This covered a variety of topics, mostly qualitative in nature, including how they felt about the device (if they wore one), if and how others reacted to it, and other body locations for the device that might be preferable to the shoe.

RESULTS

We collected two weeks (baseline and intervention) of pedometer readings, and three survey responses from each of the 17 participants. Due to a pedometer setup error, data from one participant in the *Pediluma condition* had to be discarded (leaving four participants' data in that condition). Anomalies in pedometer step count were noted and dropped when verified through interviews as abnormal behavior (e.g. some participants had days with particularly low count, due to forgetting to wear the pedometers; some pedometers recorded zero count on some days possibly due to resetting by accidentally pressing a covered button; one participant was sick for two days). Even though there were fluctuations in the TTM motivation stages through the repeated surveys, the changes were statistically insignificant and not unique to any condition. As such, there remained no significant imbalance in TTM motivation stages across the conditions. As an additional reliability check, social confidence scores were computed. This also revealed no significant differences amongst the conditions.

Of immediate note is that participants in all *non-Pediluma conditions* decreased in step count from week one to week two, while participants in the *Pediluma condition* did not (Figure 3). This is likely attributable to the Hawthorne and novelty effects wearing off, as well as varying environmental conditions that could have hindered walking. We found a significantly greater number of steps taken by those in the *Pediluma condition* when compared to the *Control condition* (M=7.9% vs. M=-33.7%, $t[6]=2.98$, $p<.05$). Although only a preliminary finding, it does suggest Pediluma has some motivational effect. Moreover, Figure 3 shows that the *No Light* and *Random Light conditions* slightly outperformed the *Control condition*, revealing the magnitude of the novelty effect of introducing a device in week two. However, this difference is not significant, indicating that novelty was not a major effect.

During the study, there were no significant changes in attitudes towards physical activity and health. This suggests that the change in walking behavior for *Pediluma condition* may had been a subconscious decision. Similarly, we did not detect significant differences in how participants perceived other people influencing their physical activity, or vice versa. However, our data suggest that wearers were reminded of the device by catching it in their peripheral vision, and through social interaction when other people noticed the devices.

As shown in Figure 4, participants in each condition noticed their shoe-mounted device at significantly different levels of frequency ($F[3,13]=14.7$, $p<.01$). As expected, participants in the *No Light condition* noticed their device fewer times a day when compared to the *light-enabled conditions* ($F[1,13]=7.48$, $p<.05$). Interestingly, participants in the *Random Light condition* noticed their device the most (although not significantly so). This could be due to illumination occurring at unexpected times, thus catching the wearer's attention. In the *Pediluma condition*, users are unlikely to be surprised because the light is coupled with their physical activity.

While Figure 4 illustrates how effective lighting is at providing wearers with a regular reminder of the device's presence, Figure 3 indicates that a random light (i.e., non-

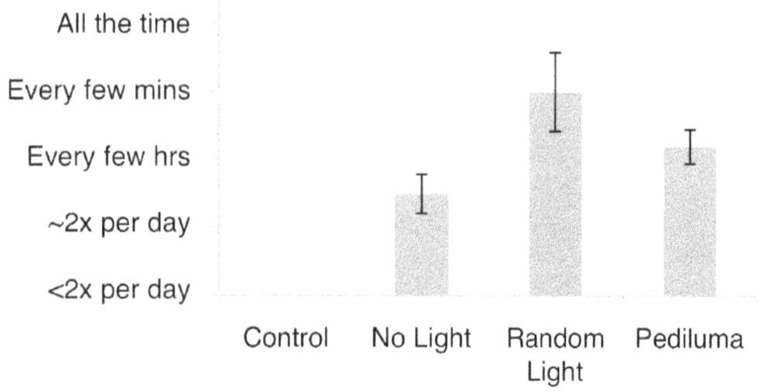

Figure 4. Participants in the *No Light condition* noticed the device less than *the light-enabled conditions*. The *Control condition* (no device) is the theoretical minimum.

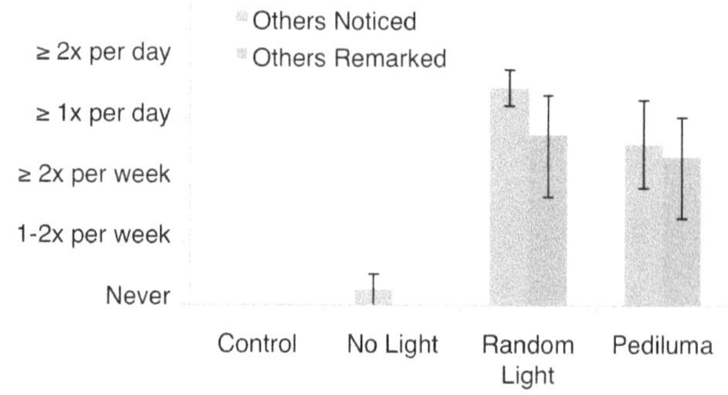

Figure 5. Participants in the *No Light condition* experienced almost no social interaction in contrast to the two *light-enabled conditions*.

contextual light) did not increase walking. We hypothesize this is due to people not associating the light with their walking, instead viewing it as an unrelated distraction, and thus not explicitly reminded about their physical activity. On the other hand, by leveraging a timely presentation of the light with positive reinforcement, the full-featured Pediluma allowed users to develop a comfortable mental model of how the device related to their walking. Through the change in display as the participant walks, the participant is made more conscious of his or her walking. This awareness of their walking allows them to make the conscious activity choice to walk rather than, for example, unconsciously choosing the habit of driving.

The public visibility of the shoe-mounted devices led to other people noticing and remarking to the participants. The frequency of such events was estimated from survey questions. Figure 5 indicates that participants wearing light-enabled devices (*Random Light* and *Pediluma conditions*) experienced significantly more social interaction than those wearing the unlit device (*No Light condition*), (Others noticed: $F[1,13]=25.7$, $p<.01$; Others remarked: $F[1,13]=19.9$, $p<.01$). Participants in the *No Light condition* reported almost no one noticing their devices and never talked to others about the item on their shoe. This difference in social interaction is correlated to how much participants noticed the devices they wore (Others noticed vs. Self notice: $r=.67$; Others remarked vs. Self-notice: $r=.49$). Both the wearer and others were able to notice the lighted devices significantly more than the unlit versions.

Figure 6 provides a breakdown of the types of people that noticed the devices. This data illustrates that participants tended to talk to people they are more comfortable with (family, friends, and colleagues) than a random stranger in public ($M=23.6$ vs. $M=5.4$).

DISCUSSION

Encouragingly, the initial results suggest that Pediluma induces wearers to increase their walking. We believe there are several factors that contributed to t

ahis successful outcome, which, overall, mirror the literature [7,19]. Foremost, wearing a *personal* information display of this nature provides a *persistent* reminder. Additionally, we believe the *positive* reinforcement provided by Pediluma was vital to remind and induce the wearer to walk both longer and more frequently. As we hoped, some participants enjoyed showing the lit device to others, and sought to maintain a positive state with sustained physical activity. Pediluma was somewhat successful in demonstrating the value of the *present* design property. Although the lighting display was received favorably, participants noted that it would have been more rewarding (and perhaps more effective) if the light remained on longer to acknowledge their walking effort (a careful balance to strike).

Bar a few unavoidable distractions, Pediluma generally allowed people to concentrate on their primary activity, remaining in the *periphery* of their vision. However, the devices did interfere with one participant's driving, drew unnecessary attention from security personnel, and was considered to be inappropriate in certain social or office settings. Potentially, many of these effects lie more in the particular implementation of Pediluma, a prototype, than Personal-Public Displays in general.

In regard to the *public* nature of the devices, we found that positive and direct encouragement did not occur, contrary

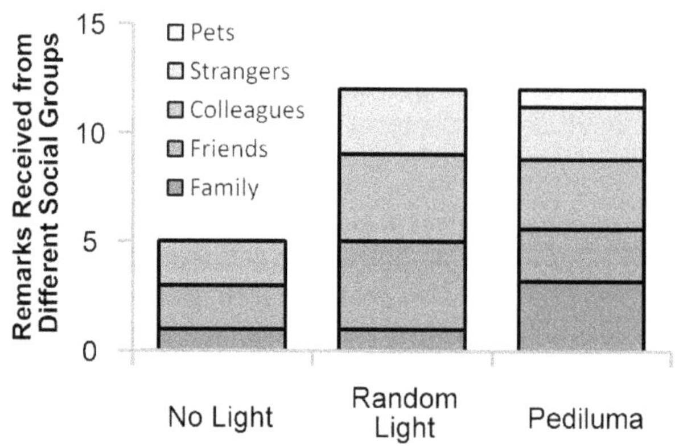

Figure 6. Types of people who remarked to participants as they wore their devices. Note that participants tended to socially engage with closer contacts. One participant favorably explained her cat noticed the light.

to our hypothesis. Instead, for some participants, Pediluma appeared to create a negative social pressure. Participants felt more self-aware, and sufficiently embarrassed to the extent of wanting to hide or take off the device. Though opposite to the effect we intended, this negative pressure may have provided an even more potent reminder to participants. We believe through careful design, the same benefits could be realized, but in a more palatable manner.

Although most of our participants were apprehensive of the devices, two of our participants (both in the *Pediluma condition*) did react positively. Both individuals felt that Pediluma provided an interesting social "ice-breaker" and allowed them to stand out in a crowd. They enjoyed talking about Pediluma and welcomed questions. People in this demographic, who enjoy sharing their state and the added attention that comes from it, may be stronger candidates for this type of social influence. Furthermore, several participants indicated that Pediluma would be more acceptable in certain settings, such as a gym. In these scenarios, where there is a pretext for use, it would be less socially awkward to wear a device like Pediluma. Participants also suggested more natural placements for the display, most notably the arm, which is more common for wearable devices and generally more socially acceptable.

DESIGN IMPLICATIONS

Through a combination of quantitative findings and qualitative feedback, we have compiled a list of design implications can be applied to our future research and aid in the creation of similar technologies.

Aesthetic to Others, Important to Self

While participants saw great value in the ability to monitor their progress in real time, they felt somewhat uncomfortable about sharing their personal information with the public. One participant remarked, "I would never purchase a device that would give my friends a reason to tell me I'm fat. I don't want to hear, hey, it looks like you haven't been walking today." This suggests that the display needs to be sufficiently ambiguous in order to provide adequate privacy; the device should appear decorative or meaningless to others. However, to leverage social effects, we believe it should be sufficiently unique and prominent to spur people to inquire. The wearer can then share the meaning to trusted friends and family if desired.

Adapting for Pace and Peripheral Vision

Although the pace at which the light brightened or dimmed in reaction to walking (or the lack thereof) is reasonable (5 and 15 minutes, respectively) when calibrated for a walking speed of 3 mph, it seems that participants did not appreciate the gradual changes in brightness, and only recognized whether it was either fully lit or off. One participant remarked that "it seemed like it really only had two states, walking or not walking, and I already knew when I was walking." This is probably because people tend to walk faster than 3mph, so the light would reach maximum brightness too soon. They would end up missing the intermediate steps in brightness and only see it in the two states. In addition to using variable luminance, the design could also be improved by employing multiple colors.

Appropriate Visual Attention

Few participants were comfortable with the additional attention they drew due to Pediluma. Many felt the light was too bright, and suggested a more subdued appearance. This was especially problematic at night when the light was visible for more than a city block. One participant felt unsafe and "like a target" walking through a parking garage late at night with the light on. Given their uncommon design and placement, the devices also posed security concerns with guards approaching two participants to enquire of them. Moreover, the lighting display used in Pediluma caused concern among participants that others perceived the device as "attention getting," "juvenile," or "unprofessional." Participants stated that they would feel more comfortable in public if the device did not appear to be so bright, (though only a problem at night). These factors led us to conclude that 1) the information display needs to sensitive to a variety of social and environmental conditions, and 2) be able to adjust the light magnitude to appropriate levels.

Sensitivity to Established Associations

Displays need to consider various pre-existing associations; color, shape, size, location and other factors may have unwanted connotations. For example, although many people associate green objects with concepts like progress, environmentalism, and life, some participants viewed the green LED light used in Pediluma as "creepy" and "weird."

Clear Mapping of Functionality to User

The display of the device must match the expectations and mental models of the user. Failure to do so may not simply lead to confusion or lack of attention, but distrust, anger, and ultimately discontinuation of use. Participants in the random light condition had a negative reaction to the light, describing it as "out of control," and remarking "it seemed like only lit up when I didn't want it to... like I was in a dark parking garage alone late at night," but not when they wanted. These experiences led to distrust in the device, and a wariness of its usefulness.

Blend Form With Wearer Lifestyle

The form must not interfere with personal habits and blend with the personal style and identity of the wearer. Ideally the wearable device should be of a size and weight that are virtually imperceptible, and not interfere with personal habits such as crossing legs or sitting styles. Even inadvertently causing a participant to cross their legs in a manner they are not accustomed to may cause annoyance and physical discomfort. Also the aesthetics of the device must not make the wearer feel strange or out-of-character.

Goal Setting

Several people wanted the ability to set goals, which if achieved, would reward them with a special display state, such as a change in color or light pattern. This begins to morph the experience into that of a game, with objectives and rewards - an approach that has been successful in the past. We avoided goal setting as that added a confound to our study. However, it could prove useful in future systems.

CONCLUSION

We presented a simple shoe-mounted device designed to motivate physical activity through positive reinforcement at the point-of-decision, and social influence through public exposure. The results from our preliminary two-week deployment indicate Pediluma has the potential to increase physical activity, awareness and social interaction. From post-hoc analysis, reflections and interviews, we learned that our Pediluma prototype could be improved in several ways. Chief among them is designing the device to be more appealing and socially acceptable. Overall, we believe our positive result with some users is not limited to Pediluma, but likely extends to a variety of domains and device types.

ACKNOWLEDGEMENTS

This work was supported in part by grant IIS-0713509 from the National Science Foundation and the Agency for Science Technology And Research, Singapore. We also thank Tom Bartindale for help with the accompanying video.

REFERENCES

1. Abrahamse, W., Steg L., Vlek, C., Rothengatter, T., A review of intervention studies aimed at household energy conservation. *Journal of Environmental Psych,* 25 (3). 2005, 273-291.
2. Andersen, R.E., Franckowiak, S.C., Snyder, J., Bartlett, S.J., Fontaine, K.R., Can inexpensive signs encourage the use of stairs? Results from a community intervention. *Annals of Internal Medicine*, 1998, 129:363–9.
3. Andrew, A., Borriello, G., Fogarty, J. Toward a Systematic Understanding of Suggestion Tactics in Persuasive Technologies. *Proc. Persuasive '07*, 259-270.
4. Arduino electronics prototyping platform. http://arduino.cc. Retrieved 15 July 2010.
5. Arroyo, E., Bonanni, L., and Selker, T., Waterbot: exploring feedback and persuasive techniques at the sink. *Proc. SIGCHI '05*, 631-639.
6. Bravata et al., Using Pedometers to Increase Physical Activity and Improve Health. *J. of the American Medical Association 2007, 298(19):2296-2304.*
7. Cialdini, R. *Influence: Science and Practice*. Allyn & Bacon, Boston, 2001.
8. Co, E., Pashenkov, N., UFOS. Demonstrated in Guerilla Studio Cyber Fashion Show. *SIGGRAPH '05*, http://psymbiote.org/cyfash/2005. Retrieved 28 Oct 2007.
9. Consolvo, S., Everitt, K., Smith, I., Landay, J.A., Design Requirements for Technologies that Encourage Physical Activity. *Proc. CHI '06*, 457-466.
10. Fogg, B.J., Persuasive computers: perspectives and research directions, *Proc CHI' 98,* 225-232.
11. Forlizzi, J., Li, I., and Dey, A. Ambient Interfaces that Motivate Changes in Human Behavior (Position Paper), *Proc. Workshop at Pervasive '07*, 6-8.
12. Fountain, H., Inside the Flashy Shoe That Encourages Children to Step on It. *New York Times,* p. 7. Retrieved December 7, 2007 from Lexis-Nexis Universe/General News database.
13. Gyllensward, M., Gustafsson, A., Bang, M., Visualizing Energy Consumption of Radiators. *LNCS Persuasive Technology,* Springer, Vol. 3962. 2006. 167-170.
14. Holstius, D. Kembel, J. Hurst, A. Wan, P.-H., Forlizzi, J., Infotropism: Living and Robotic Plants as Interactive Displays. *Proc. DIS '04*, 215-221.
15. Intille, S.S., Kukla, C., Farzanfar, R., Bakr, W., Just-in-time technology to encourage incremental, dietary behavior change. *Proc. AMIA '03,* 1434-7.
16. James, B. Sallis, F. Owen, N., *Physical Activity & Behavioral Medicine*. Sage Publications Inc., 1999.
17. Katzev, R. and Wong, T., Can commitment change behavior? A case study of environmental actions. *Journal of Social Behavior and Personality*. 1994.
18. Khaled, R., Barr, P., Noble, J., Biddle, R., and Fischer, R., Our Place or Mine?: Exploration into Collectivism-Focused Persuasive Technology Design. *Proc. Persuasive '06*. 72-83.
19. Thaler, R.H. and Sunstein, C.R. *Nudge: Improving Decisions About Health, Wealth, and Happiness*. Penguin, New York, NY, 2009.
20. King, P. and Tester, J., The landscape of persuasive technologies. *Communications of the ACM,* 42(5). 1999, 31-38.
21. Leslie, E. et al., East Queensland Quality of Life Study Regional Variations in Walking for Different Purposes: The South. *Environment and Behavior*, 39(4). 2007, 557-577.
22. Matthews et al., Physical Activity. *American Journal of Epidemiology*, (165). 2007. 1343-1350.
23. McKenzie-Mohr, D., Fostering sustainable behavior through community-based social marketing. *American Psychologist*, 55 (5). 2000. 531-537.
24. Nawyn, J., Intille, S. and Larson, K., Embedding Behavior Modification Strategies into a Consumer Electronic Device: A Case Study. *Proc. UbiComp* '06. 297-314.
25. Nike+iPod. http://apple.com/ipod/nike. Retrieved 26 Sep '07.
26. Ogilvie D, Foster CE, Rothnie H, Hamilton, V., Fitzsimons, C.F., and Mutrie, N., Interventions to promote walking: systematic review. *BMJ '07*, 334:1204-1213.
27. Oliver, N. and Flores-Mangas, F., MPTrain: a mobile, music and physiology-based personal trainer. *Proc. Mobile HCI '06*, 21-28.
28. Pate, R.R., Pratt, M., Blair, S.N., et al., Physical activity and public health: a recommendation from the Centers for Disease Control and Prevention and the American College of Sports Medicine. *JAMA,* 273. 1995. 402–407.
29. Prochaska, J.O. DiClemente, C.C. Norcross, J.C., In search of how people change: Applications to addictive behaviors. *Amer Psych*, 47(9). 1992. 1102-14.
30. Pryor, K. (1997). *Don't Shoot the Dog! The New Art of Teaching and Training. Revised Edition.* Bantam Books, 1999.
31. Singh, V. and Mathew, A. P., WalkMSU: an intervention to motivate physical activity in university students. *Extended Abstracts CHI '07*, 2657-2662.
32. SparkPeople. http://sparkpeople.com. Retrieved 26, Sep. 2007.
33. Stevens, S. S., On the psychophysical law. *Psych Review*, 1957, 64(3):153–181.
34. "The Items in the 15 Preliminary IPIP Scales Measuring Constructs Similar to Those in the Jackson Personality Inventory" http://ipip.ori.org/newJPI-RKey.htm. Retrieved 10 Dec 2007.
35. U.S. Department of Health & Human Services. A Guide for Community Action, Champaign, IL: Human Kinetics. 1999.
36. WalkingSpree. http://walkingspree.com. Retrieved 26, Sep. 2007.

A Mobile System for Industrial Maintenance Support based on Embodied Interaction

Jens Ziegler, Johannes Pfeffer, and Leon Urbas

Chair of Distributed Control Systems Engineering, Dresden University of Technology
01062 Dresden, Germany
{jens.ziegler, johannes.pfeffer, leon.urbas}@tu-dresden.de

ABSTRACT

This paper presents a mobile assistance system for service and maintenance personnel in industrial facilities. It provides an innovative interaction metaphor designed to fit domain specific working conditions. As a result of a strictly user-centered design process, the presented system follows the principles of *Embodied Interaction*. The system is evaluated using a sophisticated scenario in a typical industrial environment. The evaluation also includes a comparison with the conventional paper & pencil-based maintenance workflow. A detailed discussion addresses problems of mobile usability evaluation in industrial environments and provides appropriate solutions. The results presented in this paper demonstrate that the proposed system allows for effective and satisfactory service and maintenance. It contributes further insights for utilization and evaluation of embodied systems in industrial applications. Potential applications of this research include design guidelines for future interface configurations using embodied interactive devices.

Author Keywords

Mobile Maintenance, Usability Evaluation, Embodied Interaction, Process Industry, Fieldwork, Human Computer Interaction, HCI

ACM Classification Keywords

H.5.2 Information Interfaces and Presentation: User Interfaces—*Ergonomics; Input devices and strategies, Interaction Styles*

General Terms

Design, Experimentation, Human Factors

INTRODUCTION

Industrial facilities are of growing complexity and flexibility. The advancing integration of information and communication technologies into management, production and maintenance processes has significant impact on the service and maintenance personnel working in these facilities. As facilities become more and more autonomous, management and monitoring are centralized in large control centers, not necessarily located close to the facilities themselves [17]. Hence, there is an increasing demand for remote control and remote maintenance. Service and maintenance personnel has to face greater heterogeneity of the contextual constraints, increased diversity of tasks, greater responsibility and autonomy as well as higher demand for mobility and flexibility. This extended range of tasks leads to a growing demand for ubiquitous access to relevant information as well as guidance and decision support for successful task performance.

At present, however, service and maintenance personnel has only little or no access to data using digital support systems. The prevalent work equipment still relies on paper & pencil for information collection and radio or mobile phone for communication [12], [17]. Only few projects on computerized mobile assistance found their way from field studies to broader industrial application. As a result, today's industry suited devices are still based on the same interaction styles and input modalities as ten years ago. Even though it has has been repeatedly shown that conventional *WIMP (Windows, Icon, Menu, Pointer) Interaction* is unsuitable for mobile applications, e.g. in [4], [13] and [18], it is still the predominant interaction metaphor. Promising concepts like *Embodied* or *Tangible Interaction* [5], [9], only have little impact on current industrial applications. To a large part this is caused by the slow adaption of novel and unusual solutions in the industrial domain. Most fieldwork activities could be improved by computerized support – but do not necessarily require it [8]. Hence, industry tends to keep such activities unassisted as long as off-the-shelf solutions do not immediately lead to considerable improvements.

As a result, many innovative solutions that could have been valuable for fieldwork activities have been discarded, as poor user interfaces render them unusable in the relevant domain. Many systems operate perfectly under laboratory or office conditions, but are either not operable in industrial environments or not usable under industrial working conditions. Harsh environmental conditions like dirt, humidity, noise or bad lighting dramatically decrease reliability and detection rate of voice and gesture recognition systems. Stylus- or touch-based interaction is virtually impossible under working conditions that require one-handed or even free-handed

TEI'11, January 22–26, 2011, Funchal, Portugal.

operation in variable working posture wearing mandatory protective clothing including helmet and heavy gloves. The major drawback of most mobile systems is the increased physical workload. System properties such as weight, body placement, noise or heat-dissipation may cause diminution of performance as well as physical and psychological stress during long-term use [18]. Especially heavyweight hardware such as wearable computers and head-mounted displays are critical parts in mobile systems [11], [18]. System design, in particular the design of the user interface, and body placement may cause distraction or obstruction during typical activities. These shortcomings are well-known and have already been addressed extensively, e.g. in [13], [17] and [18]. A comprehensive analysis of the requirements for mobile systems in industrial environments can be found in [19].

To meet these challenges, development of mobile systems must become considerably more focused on usability and simplicity than on technical refinement [3]. The principles of *Embodied Interaction* may be helpful to overcome these challenges [2], [5], [6], [9], [16]. Several investigations in the industrial domain showed promising results, e.g. in [10], [14].

This paper presents a mobile system for industrial maintenance support based on *Embodied Interaction*. The system design is derived from a strictly user-centered development process and was evaluated in an industrial environment under domain-specific conditions. The evaluation scenario consists of representative tasks common for maintenance personnel. To give a reference for effectiveness and efficiency, a paper & pencil based work flow, which is still customary to the examined scenario, was also evaluated. The presented system avoids typical drawbacks that arise from media discontinuity between paper & pencil based and digital tool chains.

SYSTEM SETUP

Context of Use

Industrial process plants and production sites characterized by electrical, mechanical and hydraulic technical equipment, by pipe systems and large tanks and reactors are common working environments for service and maintenance personnel. Equipment may be accessible via stairs, bridges, gangways and sometimes only via ladders. The environmental conditions are characterized by dirt, humidity, noise and fluctuations in temperature and lighting conditions.

User Group

The challenges of computer-supported mobile working are common to a wide range of industrial fieldwork activities. This paper focuses on professional service and maintenance in industrial facilities. The main tasks in this domain include service, repair, replacement and improvement of technical equipment. These activities often require working on physical objects, sometimes in difficult working position. Safety regulations usually demand protective clothing including heavy gloves and helmet. Work at computers is usually only a secondary activity. Service and maintenance personnel usually have similar professional qualifications, and are usually fit and in good health. Due to a high level of technical education, field workers usually have a strong technical background.

Maintenance Support System

A maintenance support system (MSS) is an interactive handheld or body-worn system supporting maintenance personnel in their routine. It is comprised of a visual output and variable means for user input. The main purpose of a MSS is to provide workflow guidance and sophisticated information management. It provides information about the maintenance circuit, pending tasks and expected results. A MSS is occasionally or permanently connected and synchronized with a maintenance management system.

A requirements-analysis in cooperation with industrial partners has lead to the hierarchical task model shown in figure 1. The goal *perform maintenance circuit* is comprised of two operations and one sub-goal. The sub-goal *complete task* is comprised of six operations. The model only reflects the mobile part of the fieldwork. Additional parts like negotiating access to the plant control room, getting dressed or preparing equipment are not considered.

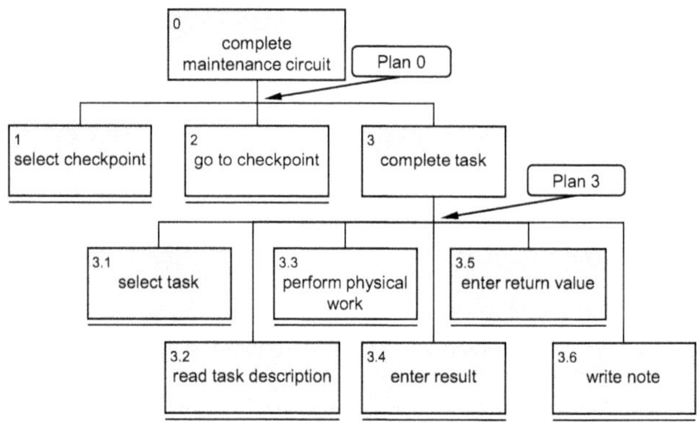

Figure 1. Hierarchical task model of a maintenance circuit

The task model consists of two plans. Both plans are shown in table 1. According to *plan 0* the user has to select a checkpoint and go there, and then has to complete all necessary tasks. *Plan 0* is performed repeatedly until all checkpoints have been completed. *Plan 3* describes the necessary workflow to complete a certain task. The user has to select a task and read the task description. Afterwards, the physical work has to be performend and, if available, the return values have to be recorded. It is possible to add a note at any time. The task model consists both of physical work (*go to checkpoint*, *perform task*) and interaction with the MSS (all others, marked with grey). As can been seen in table 1, the physical work and interaction with the MSS are closely coupled.

The data model shown in figure 2 has been applied to formally describe a task set. A maintenance circuit consists of one or more maintenance checkpoints (e.g. a device or an instrument). For each of these checkpoints one or more tasks need to be performed. Tasks and checkpoints are ordered

plan	description
Plan 0:	Do (1, 2) in any order, then 3; If checkpoint remaining repeat from 1; Else exit
Plan 3:	Do 3.6 at any time if necessary; Do 3.1 then 3.2 then 3.3 then 3.4; If return value exists do 3.5; Then exit

Table 1. Plans for the task model of a maintenance circuit

in a recommended sequence. Each task has a description and an expected result. The system therefore provides several predefined selectable items in a list (*Undone*, *Done* and additional task-specific result descriptions) from which the user can choose the appropriate result. Some tasks also require a return value (e.g. a temperature value) which can be entered into a provided input screen. If applicable, this screen provides meta information such as upper and lower limit, unit or expected data structure (e.g. time format) and a validity test for the entered data. In addition, the user can add a note for each task.

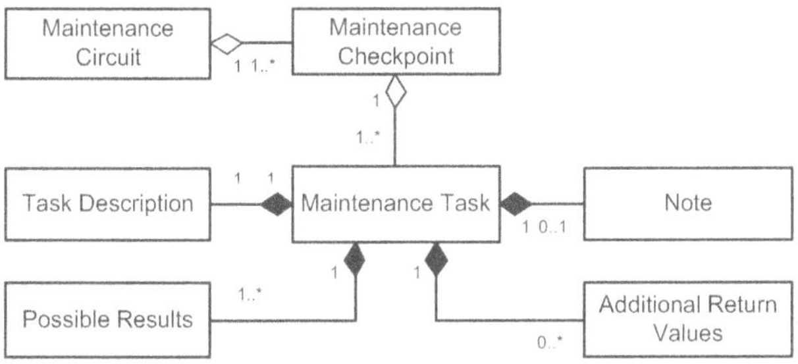

Figure 2. Data model of the Maintance Support System

User Interface Design

Main objective of the user interface design was to limit the number of control elements (e.g. buttons, slider) as well as the number of different interactions (e.g. scroll, flick, select) to create a simple but expressive design solution [3]. The user interface consists of a small display and a detached input device. As can be seen in figure 3, the display is fixed at the user's lower arm and the input device is attached at the hip. Both devices are connected wirelessly via *Bluetooth*. The presented setup allows for single-handed interaction and hands-free reading. It is easy to use in various working positions without significant obstruction. There is no need to stow the MSS when it is not in use. Both display and input device are small of size, light-weight and rugged.

The input device provides a rotary-pushbutton in conjunction with two separated pushbuttons. Being well-known from previous research, e.g. in [15] or [20], this interaction metaphor has proved to be suitable for navigation and selection tasks. The input device is designed for single-handed blind control, and is usable with protective clothing including heavy gloves.

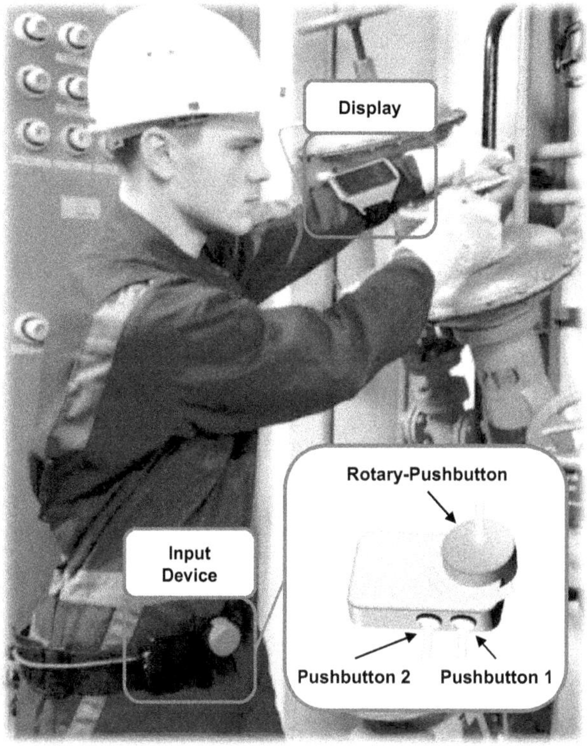

Figure 3. Spatial arrangement and input device description of the MSS

The input device is used for navigating the graphical user interface and for selecting and deselecting items from a list. The function assignment between input device and graphical user interface is summarized in table 2. Turning the rotary-pushbutton always scrolls the current list. Pushbutton 1 always selects an item, whereas pushbutton 2 always deselects an item. The user can adapt the function assignment to his or her needs by inverting the scrolling direction or swapping the function assignment of the pushbuttons.

Figure 4 shows the menu structure of the graphical user interface (the *note menu* has been left out for reasons of space). It consists of five menus: *main*, *checkpoint* and *task menu* are equally structured. Data is being presented in a grey list

control element	function assignment
turn rotary-pushbutton	scroll list
press rotary-pushbutton	enter *note menu* delete last character*
press pushbutton 1	enter next menu select item*
press pushbutton 2	leave current menu save and leave*

*(*input* and *note menu*)

Table 2. Function assignment between the input device and the graphical user interface

scrolling around a red-colored circle on the left side of the menu. This circle visually represents the also red-colored rotary-pushbutton of the input device. A scrollbar on the right shows the amount of items in the list. Icons in the corners of the list indicate the current status of the item (*Undone*, *Partly done*, *Done* or *Done with errors*) and the presence of a note. This presentation metaphor exactly matches the input metaphor of the rotary-pushbutton. When a task has been selected in the *task menu*, the red circle (see figure 4) moves towards the right side, the grey list dissapears and a data-specific input dialog is displayed. A list appears in the *result menu* and an entry form appears in the *input* and *note menu*. In the latter case, a keyboard appears on the right, again scrolling around the red-colored circle. In order to avoid confounding effects, the MSS does not provide input support like T9 or auto-completion. For each menu, items can be scrolled by turning the rotary-pushbutton. Pressing pushbutton 1 selects the currently highlighted item and triggers a navigation to the subordinate menu. The navigation path is given in figure 4. In the *input* and *note menu*, pressing pushbutton 1 saves the current input and triggers a navigation to the superordinate menu. Pressing pushbutton 2 always discards the selection or input and triggers a navigation to the superordinate menu. Pressing the rotary-pushbutton navigates to the *note menu*. The interaction metaphor is reduced to navigating and selecting data within a list. The design of the input device is directly reflected both in the visual appearance and in the functional behaviour of the graphical user interface.

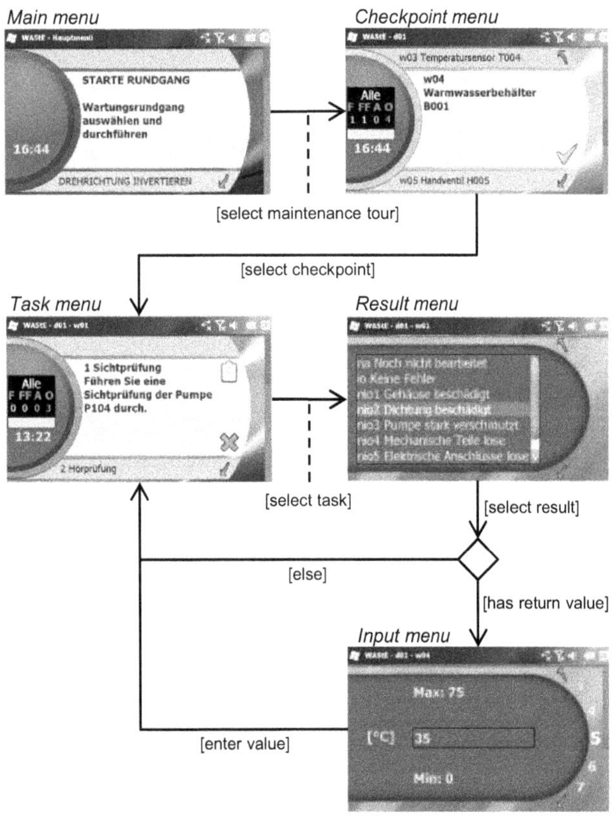

Figure 4. Menu structure of the MSS

METHOD

Experiment Design

The experiment was designed to measure three important characteristics of (industrial) usability in compliance with EN ISO 9241-110 [1]: effectiveness, efficiency and satisfaction. The characteristics were calculated through statistical analysis of the generated log files and the evaluation survey.

Dependent variables of the experiment are *effectiveness* determined by degree of task completion and correctness (in terms of complete text entries and correct values), *efficiency* determined by completion time for the overall maintenance circuit and for individual tasks, and *user satisfaction* derived from an *IsoMetrics* evaluation survey [7].

Setup

The experiment was performed in a test plant of reduced industrial scale. All checkpoints were located indoors under constant environmental conditions (room temperature, high humidity, constant noise, good lighting with fluorescent lamps).

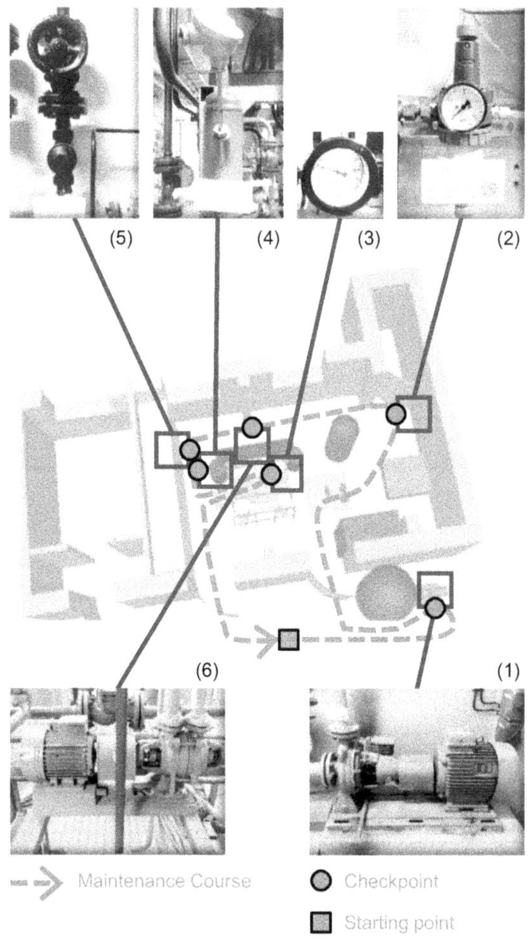

Figure 5. Overview of the maintenance circuit

The designed maintenance circuit consists of 6 checkpoints with 1 to 3 tasks each. The circuit is shown in figure 5 and a description is provided in table 8. Inspection tasks and values to be gathered were simulated by signs attached to the checkpoint devices. Operations, such as installation, removal, rotation or adjustment, have been carried out highly controlled.

Twenty-four students (all male) participated in the experiment for which they received no compensation. All students reported a strong or very strong technical background, all of them were engineering master students, and aged from 21 to 26. They were asked to use the mobile maintenance support system to complete the maintenance circuit described above. The students were required to wear an industry typical blue overall as protective garment and heavy gloves. The display was attached to their arm and the input device to a tool-belt (see figure 3).

Procedure

All subjects had to complete the full circuit 3 times (with varying values) to allow the learning curve to level (see figure 6). The checkpoints stayed the same in all runs, but results and numbers were altered. Thus the subjects were able to grow accustomed to the plant and to the usage of the mobile device avoiding introduction of habituation. On the device the checkpoints were presented in a fixed and reasonable order. The checkpoint numbers in table 8 don't necessarily correspond to this order.

The subjects were given a short introduction, shown all checkpoints and then given 5 minutes to study a quickstart guide. They were told to complete the circuit as quickly and accurately as possible, however, without a defined time limit. Between each run there was a short break. After all 3 runs the subjects had the chance to have a snack before they were asked to complete an evaluation survey. The whole procedure took around 1.5 hours per subject.

Learning curve

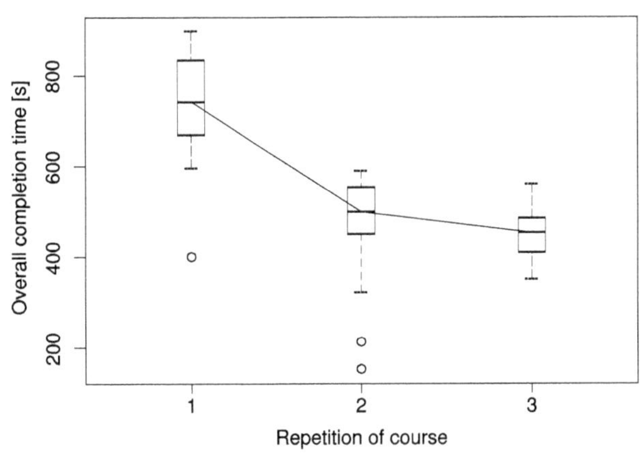

Figure 6. Line plot of the completion time CT_{MSS} for the 3 runs

To control the learning effect, all subjects were briefed thoroughly. They were given time to study the quickstart guide and get acquainted with the maintenance circuit. However, to further take the learning curve into account (figure 6), only the data of the third run was used for the analysis.

RESULTS

Pretest

Efficiency and effectiveness of the MSS were compared to the data of a similar experiment with identical checkpoints and tasks. This pretest was conducted at the same chair in May 2009 using paper & pencil in combination with a typical maintenance form instead of an electronic system. All results marked with an asterisk (*) have been calculated from the data of the paper & pencil pretest (P&P).

Analysis of effectiveness

Effectiveness, in the context of industrial usability, is defined as "the accuracy and completeness with which users achieve specified goals" (EN ISO 9241-11 [1]). To determine this characteristic, the subject's results, recorded by the maintenance support system, were compared to correct reference values. Free text entries were checked for completeness and plausibility.

The overall mean effectiveness, denoted as CT_{MSS} (maintenance support system) and $CT_{P\&P}$ (paper & pencil), has been calculated as follows:

$$CT_{\beta} = \sum_{i=1}^{n} \left(\frac{\sum \text{error-free tasks of subject } i}{\text{all tasks}} \right) \cdot \frac{1}{n} \quad (1)$$

Where β is the method (MSS or P&P) and n is the number of subjects.

	effectiveness	std. error
CT_{MSS}	100%	0
$CT_{P\&P}$*	98%	0.0084

Table 3. Effectiveness for the maintenance support system and the paper & pencil method

As can be seen in table 3, the effectiveness of the MSS is comparable to the effectiveness of the P&P method. After the first two runs, all subjects using the MSS have carried out the tasks completely error-free. The slightly lower P&P value results from the pretest (see discussion).

Analysis of efficiency

The resources expended, with which users reach the specified goals, lead to a characteristic efficiency of the system (EN ISO 9241-11 [1]). The resource that shall be taken into account here, is the time needed to complete a maintenance checkpoint.

$$T_{\beta,\gamma} = \sum_{i=1}^{n} \left(T_{\gamma,i} \right) \cdot \frac{1}{n} \quad (2)$$

Where γ refers to the checkpoint (1-6) and $T_{\gamma,i}$ is the task completion time per subject per checkpoint.

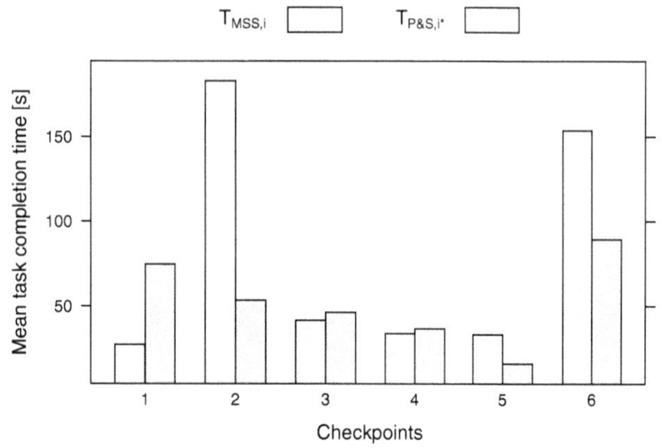

Figure 7. Bar chart of $T_{MSS,i}$ and $T_{P\&P,i}$ – MSS is more efficient at checkpoint 1 and 3 through 5 while P&P prevails at checkpoint 2 and 6

Figure 7 shows that the MSS is more efficient at checkpoint 1 and 3 through 5. These checkpoints include tasks such as checking and entering values – but no free text. At checkpoint 2 and 6, the subject was required to enter a free text describing an unexpected problem. Whenever a free text had to be entered, the efficiency of the P&P system was higher. Whenever only values and predefined items had to be selected, MSS was more efficient. On an $\alpha = 0.99$ confidence level, the attribute *free text* has a highly significant influence on efficiency (see table 4). Consequently, the tasks were grouped according to this differentiating attribute (see figure 8).

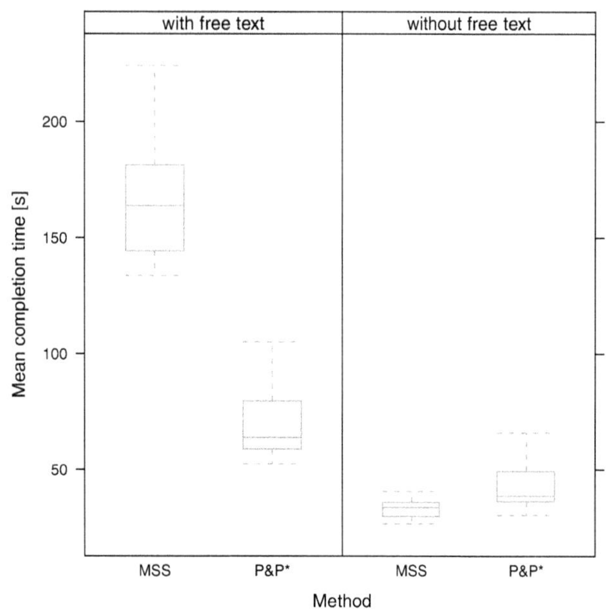

Figure 8. Box plot of the completion times with and without free text

It can be shown that P&P is significantly more efficient at checkpoints *with free text* while MSS is significantly more efficient at those *without* (see tables 5 and 6).

H_1	t-value	df	p-value
two-sided	10.4109	84	< 0.01

Table 4. T-test – influence of the attribute *free text* on efficiency

H_1	t-value	df	p-value
one-sided	13.8074	41	< 0.01

Table 5. T-test – checkpoints *with* free text entry

Analysis of user satisfaction

Satisfaction by the means of "freedom from discomfort and positive attitudes toward the use of the product" (EN ISO 9241-11 [1]) was assessed by an *IsoMetrics* survey [7]. The survey was taken electronically after the three maintenance runs. The collected answers refer to the seven dimensions of user satisfaction: suitability for the task, suitability for learning, suitability for individualisation, conformity with user expectations, self descriptiveness, controllability, and error tolerance.

The subjects benchmarked these dimensions in 75 questions on a scale from *1* (lowest rating) to *5* (highest rating). Questions that a subject judged to be not applicable were to be marked as *no opinion*. Because the scope of the *IsoMetrics* survey is not explicitly adapted to mobile single-purpose-applications, questions that were rejected by more than 20% of the subjects have been categorized as inapplicable and therefore excluded from the calculation. Results of the survey can be seen in table 7. All marks are comparatively high (see [7]) except for *suitability for individualisation* and *controllability*. The table also shows the original vs. the consolidated number of items for each survey dimension.

DISCUSSION

The evaluation of the MSS was conducted with a very homogenous group of students with high technical background. On the one hand, the actual target group (working in relevant positions within the industries) differs in terms of experience (generally higher) and familiarness to modern mobile devices (generally lower). On the other hand, experienced engineers have specific contextual expectations that may introduce a bias to their answers. Homogeneity of the subjects can reduce scattering and thus the beta error. In addition, the authors deem it important to take the coming demographic changes into account. Current maintenance engineers will eventually be replaced by the next generation, which is highly skilled in the usage of PDA-like devices. Therefore, students could even be considered more representative for future users. An evaluation with specifi-

H_1	t-value	df	p-value
one-sided	-4.5054	41	< 0.01

Table 6. T-test – checkpoints *without* free text entry

number	checkpoint	physical task	interaction with MSS
(1)	main pump	visual inspection acoustic inspection leak test	enter inspection result (select from list) enter inspection result (select from list) enter inspection result (select from list)
(2)	compressed air supply	get current pressure set new pressure recognize a leak	enter value (data input) get new pressure value take a note (text input)
(3)	temperature sensor	dismount sensor put sensor on a shelf	enter work result (select from list) enter work result (select from list)
(4)	warm water tank	get current temperature get nominal temperature	enter value (data input) enter value (data input)
(5)	heavy hand valve	open and close valve	enter work result (select from list)
(6)	auxiliary pump	visual inspection	enter inspection result (text input)

Table 8. Description of the maintenance circuit

Dimension	items	mean	std. err.
suitability f. the task	13/15	4.07	0.11
suitability f. learning	7/8	4.04	0.11
suitability f. individualisation	1/6	2.98	0.24
conformity w. user expect.	8/8	4.52	0.06
self descriptiveness	6/12	3.97	0.13
controllability	5/11	3.26	0.11
error tolerance	5/15	4.18	0.16
Overall satisfaction	45/75	3.86	

Table 7. User satisfaction on a scale from *1* to *5* (5 → highest rating)

cally maintenance-oriented engineers is being prepared as a follow-up study.

The effectiveness of the MSS comparable to the prevalent P&P method, and all subjects were able to perform all tasks completely and correctly. The 2% difference between P&P and MSS is due to incorrectly recorded values caused by spelling mistakes or hard-to-read handwriting.

As described above, there is a significant difference in efficiency between tasks that included longer text input, and those that did not. The efficiency of the MSS was significantly higher for tasks without text input. It can be concluded that for tasks without extensive text entry the use of a MSS is more efficient. Due to the reduced input space and the lack of input support, text input was time-consuming and decreased efficiency. This result, however, refers only to the user activity in the field and doesn't consider the media discontinuity of the P&P method. It excludes the time that is necessary to transfer manually written text to the management system. Automatic information transfer is likely to lead to substantial additional time-saving.

The measurement of user satisfaction is based on an *IsoMetrics* survey. Not all dimensions of this standardized tool are equally applicable to the presented MSS. This is due to the fact that user satisfaction wasn't evaluated with a full desktop-application but a single-purpose mobile application. Questions that were rejected (i.e. marked *no opinion*) by 20% or more of the subjects have been excluded from the calculation of user satisfaction. After consolidation, 45 of the original 75 items remained. This amount complies with the IsoMetrics recommendation for formative evaluations [7].

It is notable that all marks for the categories of satisfaction are quite high (see table 7), except the mark for *suitability for individualization* and *controllability*. Since the prototype was developed as a single-purpose-application, only minor individualization was allowed. However, it was possible to adapt the interface to left-handed users. The highest rating was achieved for *conformity with user expectations*, which suggests that a maintenance support system, as proposed in this paper, would be accepted well by a new generation of engineers. This conclusion is supported by the fact that the overall satisfaction with a mark of 3.86 is also far above the neutral value of 2.5.

The authors are aware that it is always delicate to compare methods based on disparate media as presented in this paper. Care was taken to ensure that there was no informational advantage in either of the groups (e.g. additional information on the paper forms). For the MSS, time was measured by analysis of the logfiles, for P&P a stop watch was utilized. Special care was taken to make measurements of time comparable: Time required for walking between the checkpoints was not measured, only time for actual occupation with the task was taken into account. The same scenario and task-model was used for both groups, ensuring comparability of measured characteristics.

The result of the empirical research suggests that the principles of *Embodied Interaction* can improve usability of mobile support systems, in particular for difficult working conditions in harsh environments.

CONCLUSION

The findings of this paper show that the presented mobile support system (MSS) can be competitive to prevalent paper & pencil solutions. The *Embodied Interaction* metaphor proved to be suitable for demanding and restrictive application domains. A mobile maintenance support system that features simplicity and reliability allows for effective and satisfactory maintenance. It does not necessarily reduce effectiveness or efficiency. Further research should study alternative input metaphors, in particular for more efficient text input. Multiple metaphors could be used in parallel to improve adaptability of the system to varying conditions. It is also conceivable to embed the mobile support system into clothing to improve handling and mounting.

ACKNOWLEDGEMENTS

The authors wish to thank Markus Graube and Jan Hegewald for their involvement in this project. Special thanks to Michael Pfab for conducting the paper & pencil pretest.

REFERENCES

1. *EN ISO 9241.11 - Ergonomics of Human System Interaction: Guidance on usability*. 1998.
2. A. N. Antle, G. Corness, and M. Droumeva. What the body knows: Exploring the benefits of embodied metaphors in hybrid physical digital environments. *Interact. Comput.*, 21:66–75, January 2009.
3. A. Chang, J. Gouldstone, J. Zigelbaum, and H. Ishii. Simplicity in interaction design. In *Proceedings of the 1st international conference on Tangible and embedded interaction*, TEI '07, pages 135–138, New York, NY, USA, 2007. ACM.
4. L. Chittaro. Visualizing information on mobile devices. *Computer*, 39(3):40–45, 2006.
5. P. Dourish. *Where the Action Is: The Foundations of Embodied Interaction (Bradford Books)*. The MIT Press, 2004.
6. Y. Fernaeus, J. Tholander, and M. Jonsson. Towards a new set of ideals: consequences of the practice turn in tangible interaction. In *Proceedings of the 2nd international conference on Tangible and embedded interaction*, TEI '08, pages 223–230, New York, NY, USA, 2008. ACM.
7. G. Gediga, K.-C. Hamborg, and I. Duentsch. The isometrics usability inventory - an operationalisation of ISO 9241-10 supporting summative and formative evaluation of software systems. 1999.
8. L. Gorlenko and R. Merrick. No wires attached: Usability challenges in the connected mobile world. *IBM Syst. J.*, 42(4):639–651, 2003.
9. E. Hornecker. A design theme for tangible interaction: embodied facilitation. In *Proceedings of the ninth conference on European Conference on Computer Supported Cooperative Work*, pages 23–43, New York, NY, USA, 2005. Springer-Verlag New York, Inc.
10. M. V. Jensen, J. Buur, and T. Djajadiningrat. Designing the user actions in tangible interaction. In *Proceedings of the 4th decennial conference on Critical computing: between sense and sensibility*, CC '05, pages 9–18, New York, NY, USA, 2005. ACM.
11. J. F. Knight and C. Baber. Effect of head-mounted displays on posture. *Human Factors*, 49(5):797–807, 2007.
12. A. S. Krausman and M. A. Nussbaum. Effects of wearing chemical protective clothing on text entry when using wearable input devices. *International Journal of Industrial Ergonomics*, 37(6):525–530, 2007.
13. S. Kristoffersen and F. Ljungberg. "making place" to make it work: empirical explorations of hci for mobile cscw. In *GROUP '99: Proceedings of the international ACM SIGGROUP conference on Supporting group work*, pages 276–285, New York, NY, USA, 1999. ACM.
14. L. Sitorus, S. S. Cao, and J. Buur. Tangible user interfaces for configuration practices. In *Proceedings of the 1st international conference on Tangible and embedded interaction*, TEI '07, pages 223–230, New York, NY, USA, 2007. ACM.
15. A. Smailagic, D. P. Siewiorek, R. Martin, and J. Stivoric. Very rapid prototyping of wearable computers: a case study of custom versus off-the-shelf design methodologies. In *DAC '97: Proceedings of the 34th annual Design Automation Conference*, pages 315–320, New York, NY, USA, 1997. ACM.
16. E. van den Hoven, J. Frens, D. Aliakseyeu, J.-B. Martens, K. Overbeeke, and P. Peters. Design research & tangible interaction. In *Proceedings of the 1st international conference on Tangible and embedded interaction*, TEI '07, pages 109–115, New York, NY, USA, 2007. ACM.
17. C. Wittenberg. User requirements for the use of mobile devices in the industrial automation. *Automatisierungstechnik at*, 52(3):136–146, 2004.
18. J. York and P. C. Pendharkar. Human-computer interaction issues for mobile computing in a variable work context. *International Journal of Human-Computer Studies*, 60(5-6):771–797, 2004. HCI Issues in Mobile Computing.
19. J. Ziegler and L. Urbas. Realization of tangible mobile human machine interfaces using wireless personal area networks. In *Communications in Computer and Information Science*, pages 37–48, New York, NY, USA, 2009. Springer.
20. J. E. Zucco, B. H. Thomas, and K. Grimmer. Evaluation of three wearable computer pointing devices for selection tasks. In *ISWC '05: Proceedings of the Ninth IEEE International Symposium on Wearable Computers*, pages 178–185, Washington, DC, USA, 2005. IEEE Computer Society.

Spinning in Control: Design Exploration of a Cross-Device Remote

Floris Kimman[1], Hans Weda[2], Elise van den Hoven[1], Tin de Zeeuw[2] and Steven Luitjens[2]

[1]Eindhoven University of Technology
Department of Industrial Design
Den Dolech 2, 5612 AZ
Eindhoven, the Netherlands
E.v.d.Hoven@tue.nl

[2]Philips Research
Human Interaction & Experiences
High Tech Campus 34, 5656 AE
Eindhoven, the Netherlands
Hans.Weda@philips.com
Steven.Luitjens@philips.com

ABSTRACT
You buy a new TV and get a new remote, you buy a DVD player and you get another remote, you buy a sound system and guess what… Almost every digital media product comes with its own designated remote control (RC). What would happen if one remote adapts to the owner's activities and is able to have cross-device control? In this paper we describe a design exploration conducted to create new ways to interact with digital media products. The main ingredients are: fit for a social setting, portable, and including physical interaction. The result is an exploration of a button less single-hand remote control concept.

Author Keywords
Remote control, cross-device interaction, physical interaction, interaction design

ACM Classification Keywords
H.5.2. Information interfaces and presentation: User Interfaces

General Terms
Design, Human Factors

INTRODUCTION
Since the appearance of the first commercial remote controls in the 1950's the number of remote controls per household has gradually increased. Nowadays there are remote controls for digital media devices such as TV's, sound systems, and DVD-players, but also for controlling environment conditions such as lighting and temperature. Each RC has its own set of dedicated buttons with a specific functionality, such as Volume UP/Down, channel choice, or lighting ON/OFF. Originally, these buttons were the result of what was technically possible at the time and since than it has been taken for granted as the way to interact with products. Advantages of these traditional types of RC are the functionality overview, the potential speed of interaction and the interaction from a distance.

The task of controlling all the individual devices with different traditional RC's can become very tedious as each product has its own designated RC and each activity requires a different set of devices. Clustering of relevant devices that relate to a certain activity is a typical solution to circumvent this problem [13, 14] and is task or experience based [12-14].

In this paper we present a design exploration on how to interact with digital media products in the context of the home. We focused our work on two aspects. In the first place is the fact that remote controls are public devices that often come with one appliance. But this appliance is often used by a complete household and at times even by visitors. How can the content of one RC fit the individual user's needs? Secondly it consists of taking the interface beyond the default button-based interaction and explores new interaction possibilities. For this we adopt ideas from physical interaction for their intuitive use that might work well for digital media product users [6]. What could the physical design of a remote look like?

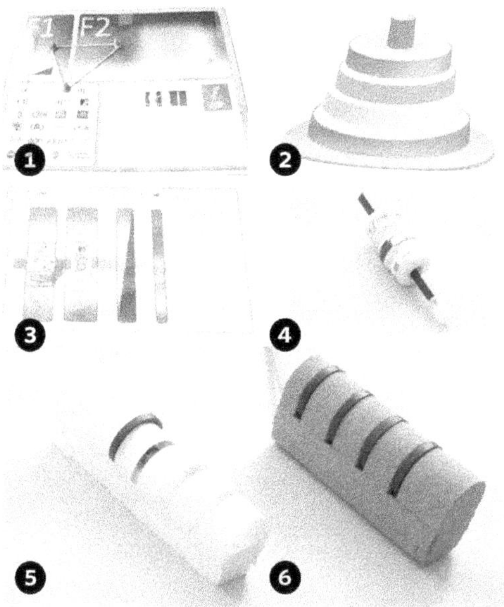

Figure 1: Concept stages, first top left to last bottom right

TEI'11, January 22–26, 2011, Funchal, Portugal.

Related Work

For our work we took a look at related work, including generic multifunctional RC's such as the Logitech harmony, and strong conceptual examples in the field of physical interaction. The first related conceptual example is the TUISTER [2]. This is a double-handed physical remote control. Here the user has to twist both ends of the remote to interact with a media product. Another interesting work is the Pipet [10], a concept that supports photo sharing by sucking up and shooting a photo from the remote to the display. A third example is the Peppermill [15] which is a two handed RC that uses a mechanical rotary system to harvest just enough power to execute the intended operation.

Several interesting concepts use inspiring types of interaction: Siftables [11] consist of several small blocks with displays that are able to interact with each other; CubeBrowser [17] makes use of the rotation of a cube to navigate through photos; Alarm Clock [16] allows the user to use his expression to set an alarm clock; Marble Answering Machine [1] translates messages into marbles that can be picked up and dropped into several action fields; and the Magical Interaction remote [4] a remote that allows interaction by simple gestures without touching the device. We have used this work as input into our design exploration.

METHODLOGY

For the process we have followed the Reflective Transformative Design Process (RTDP) [8] in combination with design research for physical interaction [7]. In the design process we put an emphasis on the creation process that allowed us to have three iterations that included a focus group, co-design and an expert review. And prototyping methods like paper prototyping, tinkering models and working prototypes.

The concept of personal RC's can best be explored in dynamic social environments with different digital product availability and use. Therefore we have chosen a family environment composed of adults from 35 to 55 and children who live at home.

CONCEPT DEVELOPMENT

Based on observations, focus groups and related work we were able to abstract our focal point in three axes: and define our design directions: first of all "*Generic – Specific/Personal*"-axis from general 'unisex' RCs to tailor-made RCs, it should be personal: the user should be able to adjust and engage with the RC on design, layout, functionality and workflow. Secondly an axis "*Traditional – Physical*" defining the amount of physical interaction used to control and creating a concept that goes beyond traditional buttons [3]. Lastly, the "*Immobile – Mobile*" axis defines the degree of portability of the remote, and depends on size, weight and functionality. Our RC should have a compact design and the functionality has to adapt to environment, increasing the mobility of the RC.

The first iteration concepts consist of rather basic tinkering materials, such as paper, rubber bands, and wooden sticks (Figure 1, number 1 to 3). In next iterations the concepts grow more mature, as do the construction material (Figure 1, number 4 to 6). The concepts can be categorized into three main types. The first type of concepts consists of tabletop concepts: an RC device on a centralized location, e.g. coffee table. The available functions are bound to the products available to that room. Interaction is located around a playing field, which could consist of a centrally localized device, or the combination of several artifacts. One example of such concept is the *Game board* (Figure 2, bottom left). It consists of a field where each subfield represents different functions. With pins and rubber bands the user can make networks, personal presets and keeping an overview of what others might be doing or using. In general tabletop concepts resulted in a good overview of functionality.

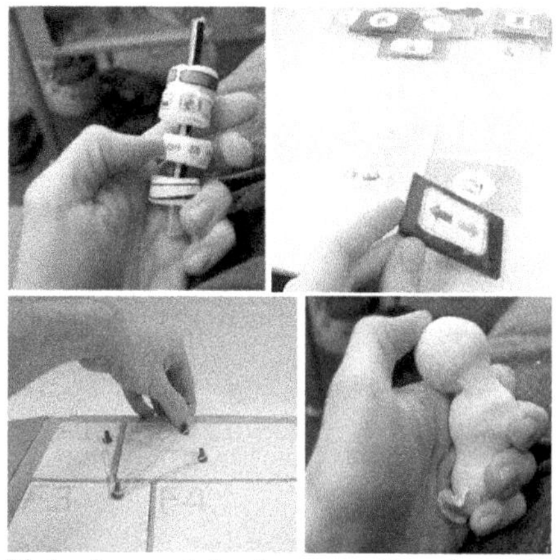

Figure 2. Tinkering models of concept directions. Top left to bottom right: Slider Stick, Puzzle Piece, Game Board and Ball

The *Puzzle piece-class* is the second main class, which is characterized by many separate interaction artifacts. These elements can be randomly placed and give their own context and meaning to the controlled products. An example is given by *Blocks* (Figure 2, top right): blocks that can be shuffled and stacked in a random order to activate products. Each product or function has its own dedicated block. For example: one for the TV (on/off), one to change channels up/down and one to change volume up/down. This class can be considered as a more mobile variation to the tabletop.

The last class is the Hand held-class, and consists of portable devices, similar format as traditional remotes. However, our concepts make use of physical interaction: browsing, navigating, and interacting on a more natural way by making use of people's manipulation skills and experience. The Ball (Figure 2, bottom right) is an example of the hand held class. Two spherical shapes are connected by a flexible material that can be pulled, twisted, turned, flicked to control objects. Each movement results in an interaction with the device. This allows many degrees of freedom in the movement, facilitating small hand and finger gestures. The *Slider stick* (Figure 2, top left) is another example: an object with rotating wheels that are used as dedicated knobs, for example one for the up/down of the volume, one for channels and one to browse through music libraries. The user is able to compose his own remote to what he wants and needs at that moment by selecting the related wheels to place on the stick.

User Involvement

A focus group was organized to extract the values of ideas and concepts. The group consisted of two female and two male participants in the age range of 24 to 50 years. All have experience with digital media products and were living together with their partner. From the focus group we have learnt that the available choices presented to the user should be limited. As a participant explained that too many choices generate noise that causes people to fall back to an obvious choice. This refers to in the aesthetics introduced "Less is more" or 80/20 rule [9]. In RC design this could be a cut in the total number of functions and result in the consumer using for example 15 of the 25 functions instead of 20 of the 75 functions. Another participant added that additional functionality does not directly result in an increased product experience.

Producers of electronic products have tried to simplify the interaction by means of generic presets e.g. pre-installed color and audio settings. From the focus group we learned that these presets typically do not fit individual wishes and therefore are seldom used. Additionally, the participants also mentioned the functionality of the RC as an important aspect; it should only provide the information and functionality that is currently relevant. For our exploration it was important to provide ease of use for novice users and feedback about performed actions to all users.

Expert Involvement

A group of experts was also asked to contribute with their knowledge and experience in the field of industrial design and physical interaction in an expert evaluation. This expert evaluation was conducted with 3 trained industrial designers that have experience and knowledge in the field of physical interaction.

A general, but important comment, regarding this RC design is to take the original function of the RC into account, which is to "not having to walk over" to the TV. The slogan Zenith Electronics used in the 1950's applies to this comment „Change the life of the lazy people for good". Considering this a tabletop system would have a lower chance of success, as the user would need to get up and out of his sitting position to alter settings, which is not the intended goal of a remote control.

Another element the experts found intriguing was a Lego like approach, having a remote control that each user can alter to his own needs. They indicated that this could be software or hardware based 'Lego'. However the remote should not contain more than three physical building blocks as more could negatively affect the usability of the design. More blocks allow more room for interpretation and thus more room for confusion. Additionally more elements require a higher cognitive load and more hands compared to the two handed TUISTER [2]. So a one-handed controllable remote would be preferred by the group of experts.

Furthermore the RC should allow for playful interaction that makes it nice to hold, fiddle around with, and become skilled in fast and easy navigation. Besides this it is worthwhile to understand unpredictable usage of a product. Two expert evaluation participants mentioned that they have an unusual and pointless habit of constantly removing and putting back the battery of the RC while watching TV. Taking these elements into account, we were able to evaluate the available concepts and use these guidelines for new and improved concepts.

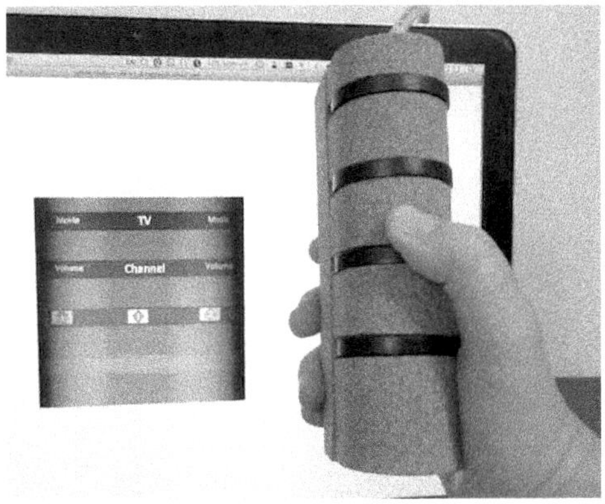

Figure 3. Spinning Remote demo, changing channels.

Final Design

The process described above has led to the *Spinning Remote* that is an individual remote control that allows for multi-product-control. The concept consists of four wheels that contain the functionality of the remote. Each wheel should be accompanied by a small display that generates a peripheral view and provides the user with functional feedback and feed forward. In the prototype (Figure 3) we decided, for practical reasons, to separate the input and the output (display) from each other. The peripheral view is displayed on a monitor and programmed in Flash while the input is controlled by a set of Phidgets [5] actuators.

The user controls the activity through a hierarchical menu structure (Figure 4). That provides him with the options that he needs, preventing from distraction and noise. The wheel is used to select a function; the subsequent wheels set the parameters. For example the first wheel is used to select the activity of watching movies, with all relevant products connected to it such as TV, sound system, lighting and media station. The second wheel is used to select the movie from a database, the third to start/pause playing, and the fourth for setting the volume. Obviously the function of the lower wheels depends on the selections made with the wheels above. For proper feedback to the user the wheels should be embedded with flexible screens that show the options available. The options should be presented such that the user always sees the previous and next item on the hierarchical wheels, creating a peripheral view (Figure 3). For an additional personal experience we decided to use an organic and soft material that should increase the experience of holding it (soft and smooth in the hand) and make it become part of the owner by the natural wear and tear from the cork material.

EVALUATION

The final concept was evaluated by consulting four experts from academia and the Consumer Electronics industry. The

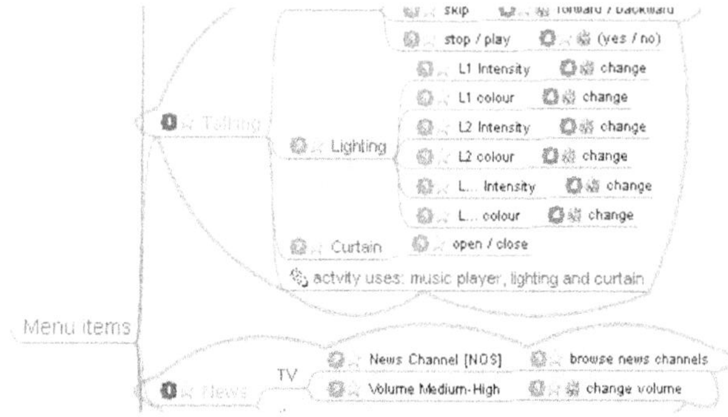

Figure 4. Element of hierarchical menu structure.

unconventional idea of using cork for the finishing of the RC was generally appreciated. Furthermore the interaction concept of the rotary wheels should be taken some steps further. First, the user needs a means to confirm a selection. This is important since otherwise the whole system changes on each move of a wheel. Confirmation can be implemented by means of clickable rotary wheels, similar to clickable mouse wheels. Second, the user can be supplied with a tangible feel of the amount of data that is available on the wheel. For example, 10 items would allow larger interval between rotation steps than 500 items would. This could be achieved by developing dynamically changing discreet rotation sensors. The feasibility of the hierarchical wheels has not fully been evaluated. The content and flow might need to be altered, depending on the outcome of further research with the working prototype.

DISCUSSION

From a design perspective the RC currently is fairly bulky, which could unpractical, but eventually it should allow the user to have a good grip and single handed control on the RC which is not possible with the TUISTER remote [2]. The extent to which the user is willing to use the Spinning Remote will depend largely on the final size and functionality of the device. With respect to the functionality of the design two additional aspects need to be further tested and considered. Firstly, the user may get disoriented, as the four wheels are identical in size and placement. Although the design has already offset the location on the wheel, this will still be a potential danger. Secondly, the tree structure of the operation flow could be too complicated. (Novice) users might get lost or experience a high mental load while navigating. On the other hand we do see a lot of potential for this type of RC as it allows us to browse through vast amounts of items (e.g. channels, songs, and photos) rapidly. And after a short learning curve users will be able to navigate without having to look at the remote.

CONCLUSION

In this paper we have described our exploration study to find cross-device remotes that employ physical interaction. The physical interaction is implemented by means of rotary wheels that provide a more natural interaction with content and functions. The personal appearance is realized by using the cork finishing that erodes through usage.

REFERENCES

1. Bishop, D. *Marble Answering Machine*. MA thesis (1992) Retrieved 2 Nov. 2010 from Royal College of Art: http://design.cca.edu/graduate/project/show/746.
2. Butz, A., M. Gross, and Krueger, A. Tuister: a Tangible UI for hierarchical structures. In *Proc. IUI 2004*, ACM (2004), 223-225.
3. Dourish, P. *Where the action is: the foundations of embodied interaction*. The MIT Press, 2004.
4. Gelder, J.v. *Magical Interaction*. (2007) Retrieved 2 Nov. 2010 from: http://www.jorisvangelder.com.
5. Greenberd, S. *Phidgets*. Phidgets Inc. (2001) Retrieved 2 Nov. 2010 from: http://www.phidgets.com.
6. Hornecker, E. and Buur, J. Getting a grip on tangible interaction: a framework on physical space and social interaction. In *Proc. CHI 2006*, ACM (2006), 437-446.
7. Hoven, E.v.d, Frens, J., Aliakseyeu, D., Martens, J-B., Overbeeke, K. and Peters, P. Design research & tangible interaction. In *Proc. TEI 2007*. ACM (2007), 109-116.
8. Hummels, C. and Frens, J. Designing for the unknown: A design process for the future generation of highly interactive systems and products. In *Proc. EPDE 08*, (2008), 4-5.
9. Koch, R., *The 80/20 principle: The secret of achieving more with less*. Random House Inc, 1999.
10. Meerbeek, B., Bingley, P., Rijnen, W. and Hoven, E.v.d.. Pipet: a design concept supporting photo sharing. In *Proc. NordiCHI2010*, ACM (2010).
11. Merrill, D., Kalanithi, J., and Maes. P. Siftables: towards sensor network user interfaces. In *Proc. TEI 2007*, ACM (2007), 75-78.
12. Ross, P. and Keyson, D. The case of sculpting atmospheres: towards design principles for expressive tangible interaction in control of ambient systems. In *Proc. PUC*, (2007) 69-79.
13. Sluis, R.v.d. and Diederiks, E. The experience of being connected. *Univers. Access Inf. Soc. 3*, 3 (2004), 239-251.
14. Vastenburg, M. *Please do not disturb: modeling user experience for considerate home products*. PhD Dissertation, Delft University of Technology (2007).
15. Villar, N. and Hodges, S. The peppermill: a human-powered user interface device. In *Proc. TEI'10*, ACM, (2010), 29-32.
16. Wensveen, S.A.G., Djajadiningrat, J.P. and Overbeeke, C.J. Interaction frogger: a design framework to couple action and function through feedback and feedforward. In *Proc. DIS 2004*, ACM, (2004), 177-184.
17. Zeller, L. and Scherffig, L. CubeBrowser: a cognitive adapter to explore media databases. In *Proc. CHI 2009*, ACM, (2009), 2619-2622.

The Lega: A Device for Leaving and Finding Tactile Traces

Jarmo Laaksolahti[1], Jakob Tholander[2], Marcus Lundén[1], Jordi Solsona Belenguer[3], Anna Karlsson[1], Tove Jaensson[4]

[1]Mobile Life@SICS	[2]Mobile Life@DSV	[3]Dept. Comm. Sys., KTH	[4]TeliaSonera
Box 1263,164 29 Kista	Forum 100,164 40 Kista	Electrum 229, 164 40 Kista	123 86 Farsta
jarmo,marcusl@sics.se anna@borisdesignstudio.com	jakobth@dsv.su.se	jordisb@kth.se	tove.jaensson@teliasonera.com

ABSTRACT

This paper describes experiences from development and deployment of the Lega, a hand held device for physical sharing of experiences during an art exhibition. Touching and moving the device in different ways creates a tactile trace that can be experienced by others through their own device. The system was successfully deployed at an art exhibition for two months where user studies were performed. Here we present some general observations regarding the systems performance and discuss issues that we encountered.

Author Keywords

Tactile interaction, gestural interaction, individual and social use

ACM Classification Keywords

H5.m. Information interfaces and presentation (e.g., HCI): Miscellaneous.

General Terms

Design

INTRODUCTION

This paper presents the Lega, a hand held device that lets visitors to an art hall share their experiences via physical traces that are created through bodily means of interaction. The Lega has an ovoid form that fits into the palm of your hand and has a soft surface that encourages tactile and gestural interaction. By touching and moving their device in various ways users create expressions of their experience that are left at their approximate location. There they can be discovered and experienced as vibration and light patterns by others in the group. Our intention was to create an experience reminiscent of someone drawing in your palm.

The design draws on experience oriented HCI research where there has been an increasing number of attempts to map out interaction qualities such as pliability [4] and suppleness [3] and the challenges related to designing for them. They all recognize the fact that experiences arise in use and depend on a combination of hardware, software and design elements. This holistic view makes the task of designing a system challenging as you constantly have to juggle several interdependent factors. Matters become even more complex when taking the view that representative use experiences are not likely to arise, and are therefore difficult to evaluate, until there is a sufficiently polished prototype available. When working with novel hardware and form factors this could in essence mean having to develop several more or less completed devices before design goals are reached.

There is a substantial body of work on the use of tactile information for non-visual information display [see e.g., 1] and input [see e.g., 5]. Our own work has been less focused on the use of tactile input/output for information transfer purposes but has rather focused on the experiential qualities afforded by tactile interaction. In that sense it bears greater resemblance to tactile messaging systems such as Share2Talk [2] which supports sharing of sensations between users.

While having a strong identity of its own, the Lega concept builds on experiences from *eMoto* [7] and *FriendSense* [6], two earlier prototypes developed within our group. In particular it shares the focus on communication and interaction within groups of friends, but also its focus on bodily interaction, with those earlier prototypes.

Here we discuss how hardware, software and infrastructure constraints together with ethnographic findings contributed in forming the design space out of which the Lega evolved.

DESIGNING THE LEGA

The Lega, named after the Swedish word for a place in the woods where you can see that an animal has slept, was developed in an iterative process that continued throughout the deployment at the art hall. Early users during the two months of the deployment at the art exhibition thus used a slightly different system compared to later users.

The annual Vårsalongen event at Liljevalchs exhibits professional and amateur art selected by a jury from anonymously submitted pieces. Each year around 250 pieces are exhibited for a period of two months. The event is visited by ~ 40.000 visitors each year and has a long-standing tradition of stirring up emotion and engagement from both visitors and media. The ethnographic study we made on-site during Vårsalongen 2009, as well as the art halls own statistics, showed that most visitors visit the

TEI'11, January 22–26, 2011, Funchal, Portugal.

exhibition in small groups of 2-5 people, with some larger organized tours taking place during evenings and weekends. For our purposes this was a perfect match between our interest in emotional and bodily communication of experiences among friends, and an emotionally evocative event visited mainly by small groups of friends.

The starting point for the design of the system was an ethnographically inspired study of art exhibition visitors and the way they experience and communicate about art through their bodily gestures. As an outcome of that study, we developed an approach to more explicitly taking bodily experiences as inspiration for design. In order to allow for creative linking between ethnographic findings of bodily practices and design, we developed a set of *body act* cards that were used in idea generation and prototyping. The cards are developed to carry experiential qualities from ethnography to design, providing details about movement, touch, gesture, spatiality and so forth, while still opening up for the creativity and interpretation necessary in productive design work.

Much of the design work was conducted within the premises of the art hall allowing ideas and concepts to be tried out in-situ. The design team, of about 15 people, consisted of interaction designers, industrial designers, hardware, sensor and software engineers, as well as HCI-specialists. In using the body cards in design we started out by giving the design team a presentation of the situations in the video material out of which they were derived and collaboratively analysed short snippets of video. This gave the team a first understanding of the setting and the phenomena of specific interest that had been identified. We presented the body cards and how these related to our studies. The design process consisted of a number of design exercises, lo-fi prototyping, and efforts to imagine the experience of users. The key inspiration for the idea that led up to the Lega was the *dancing eyes, fingers, and bodies* and *urge-to-touch* cards. The first card builds on observations of how visitors used the physical space to split up, re-gather, and invite each other to share experiences. The second card builds on observation on the substantial interactional work visitors did to experience the physical and material qualities of the art and the role this played in sharing, seeing, feeling, and imagining the art together with other visitors.

The design process itself started on site at Liljevalchs with a five day workshop that resulted in early implementations of several different concepts. Later several of those were merged to form the Lega concept. Over the course of the following months we involved art hall staff in testing and discussing prototypes as the concept was gradually refined. We also held weekly "build fests" for the design team where features and ideas that we had been working on during the week were tested and discussed, and where we decided what to focus on until the next build fest.

We also returned to Liljevalchs for testing prototypes with art hall staff on two occasions before the Vårsalongen event and received valuable feedback. Finally for three weeks before the event we gained free access to the art hall for testing and deploying the system while the exhibition was being set up.

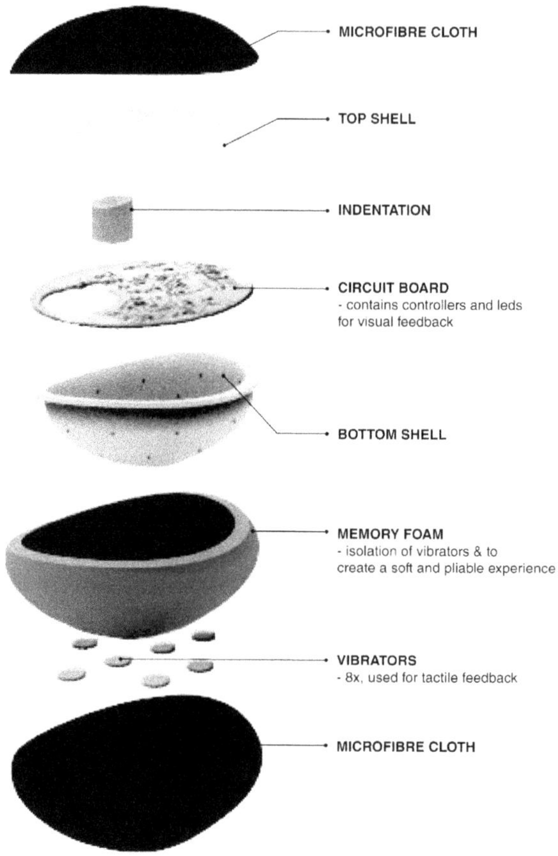

Figure 1. Exploded view of a Lega showing it's layers

Construction

Throughout the design process careful attention was paid to the visual and tactile qualities of the device. We wanted its shape and visual appearance to invite users to pick it up and touch it. The Lega has an ovoid shape that is designed to fit comfortably into a users palm. Users can carry it in one or both hands while walking through the exhibition or let it hang by its strap. The ovoid shape also makes the device orient itself naturally in a users palm although it is possible to hold it comfortably in a variety of ways (see Figure 2, top left).

The device consists of two pieces, a top and a bottom part. The bottom part is a four layer structure (see Figure 1) consisting of a hard inner shell made from plastic, housing and protecting most of the electronics, covered by two layers of 4mm memory foam, and topped with cloth. The foam layers make the surface soft and pliable so that users to some extent can "squeeze" the device, while the cloth layer affords a soft silky surface that invites tactile interaction.

In between the foam layers eight vibrators catering for tactile feedback are embedded (see Figure 2, bottom left and right). Vibrators can be turned on and off – and their intensity can be set – individually to create various patterns of vibration. Vibrators fill a second function as electrodes for the non-contact capacitive touch sensor circuit that provides the means for tactile input. In addition a thin metallic foil to improve the sensitivity of the touch sensor also covers each vibrator used in this capacity. The foil is thin enough to not interfere with the overall tactile quality of the device.

The top part houses a servo-powered button that is used to alter the depth of the indentation on top of the device. Through a simple modification we were able to read the state of the servo's internal potentiometer thereby enabling it to also function as a sensor, telling us when the button was pushed. A single layer of cloth to create a seamless appearance covers the whole top, including the button. In addition the thin cloth layer allows light from the multi colored LEDs inside the device to shine through.

Figure 2. An assembled Lega, the inner shell, vibrator placement, and touch sensor placement.

Infrastructure

Positioning in the system relied on an infrastructure consisting of small, networked, sensor nodes placed around the art hall (See Figure 3). Each node corresponded to a rough location that usually covered more than one art piece. At regular intervals each node would broadcast its ID using a low transmission power to limit the range of the signal. Measuring the signal strength of all ID transmissions that their Lega could pick up and choosing the strongest one would then determine a visitor's position in the art hall. When a visitor left a trace it was uploaded to the infrastructure node "closest" to their position where it could be picked up by others. The art hall consists of 12 rooms and a lobby that are used for exhibiting art works. Each room was covered by 2-3 beacons creating an equal amount of "places" in the room.

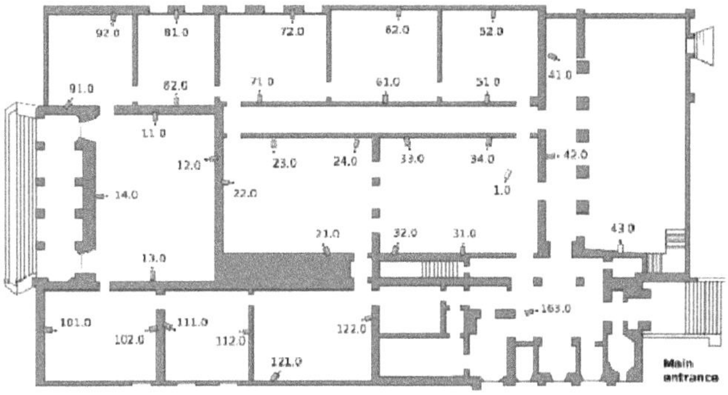

Figure 3. Deployment of infrastructure beacons at the exhibition.

Usage

Lega devices are used in groups of 2-5 people. Each person gets their own Lega and moves around the exhibition freely. To make it possible to identify the source of a trace each device is associated with a color that is shown when a trace is found. The Lega constantly records signals from touch sensors and accelerometers. When the indentation on top of the Lega is pressed a trace based on how the Lega has been moved and touched for the past five seconds is transmitted to the infrastructure. This causes the servo-powered button to move down increasing the depth of the indentation, symbolically creating a "lega". Once the trace has been transmitted to the infrastructure the button resumes its original position. By changing how they move and touch their device different expressions can be created. Currently traces are based on how energetic the movement of the Lega has been and the rate of change in touch sensor activation.

Figure 4. Lega devices being used at the art exhibition

When a trace is found by another user the button again moves down to indicate that there is a trace present. At the same time LED patterns light up to show which of the other users left the trace (see Figure 4). When found, traces are experienced as vibration patterns that attempt to capture the characteristics of actions taken to create a trace. Note that traces have no inherent meaning. They are ambiguous by design to allow for a wide range of interpretations. Instead users make sense of them based on their knowledge about the person that left them, e.g. their likes and dislikes and ways of expressing themselves.

DISCUSSION

Over the two months that the exhibition lasted we performed extensive user studies using a wide range of methods. Here we present early findings along two themes that were crucial for users experiences and future technical development: the individual experience of traces, and how positioning of traces in the art hall played out in the practical circumstances of daily visits.

Experiencing vibrations. Our intention with the Lega was to create an experience reminiscent of someone drawing in your palm using a grid of vibrators. While developing the Lega we made interaction tests that convinced us that this would be possible. However, as we later found out users sometimes had difficulty distinguishing between characteristics of patterns other than their intensity of vibration. Due to the construction of the device vibrations easily propagate through the hard inner shell like vibrations that travel through human bone [1]. This makes it difficult to distinguish exactly where vibrations are coming from. A solution to the problem is to take advantage of this "flaw" and make vibration patterns more distinct by basing them more on intensity and rhythm rather than individual vibrator activations. Another is to find a transducer technology more suited for the intended experience as suggested by reviewers of this paper.

Positioning and people. The positioning scheme that was used is quite coarse. Due to the nature of radio communication this would on occasion result in more distant nodes being selected as the closest one For our design an approximate location was sufficient but when a trace was, as happened sometimes, left in a different room it was of course confusing for users.

On the other hand something we believed could be an issue actually turned out to work in our favor. As the exhibition would at times be quite crowded we worried that transmissions from the infrastructure would be absorbed by the mass of visitors. However, in the end this turned out to be an advantage instead as it further localized the range of broadcasts thereby making positioning more consistent.

Another issue became apparent when group size became larger or when users were very active in leaving traces. In such situations the exhibition would be flooded with traces causing the Legas to constantly find traces and replay them. As an effect it diminished the sense users had of finding something valuable left behind for them. One workaround for this would be to instead let users scan for traces when they want them, or to notify them in some more unobtrusive way that there are traces to be experienced.

CONCLUDING REMARKS

In many respects the Lega design was successful. It successfully merged hardware, software and design elements to create a system that is evocative of the type of experiences that were sought. However, it also emphasized the need for thorough exploration of the qualities of the components that go into the design at an early stage in the design process. For instance, although the vibrator grid was tried out at an early stage, the way in which vibrations were experienced changed dramatically once it was mounted on the hard shell of the Lega device. The challenge in designing systems such as the Lega involves not only exploring experiences provided by different technologies, but also finding ways of keeping those experiences intact throughout the development process.

ACKNOWLEDGEMENTS

This work was funded by the Swedish Agency for Strategic Research (SSF) and the Mobile Life VINN Excellence Centre in Sweden. The system was deployed during two months at the annual Vårsalongen exhibit at Liljevalchs art hall operated by the Stockholm City Municipality.

REFERENCES

1. Brewster, S. and Brown, L.M., Tactons: structured tactile messages for non-visual information display. in *Proceedings of the fifth conference on Australasian user interface - Volume 28*, Australian Computer Society, Inc. (2004), 15-23.
2. Brown, L.M., Sellen, A., Krishna, R. and Harper, R., Exploring the potential of audio-tactile messaging for remote interpersonal communication. in *Proceedings of the 27th international conference on Human factors in computing systems*, ACM (2009), 1527-1530.
3. Isbister, K. and Höök, K., On being supple: in search of rigor without rigidity in meeting new design and evaluation challenges for HCI practitioners. in *Proceedings of the 27th international conference on Human factors in computing systems*, ACM (2009), 2233-2242.
4. Löwgren, J. Inspirational Patterns for Embodied Interaction. *Knowledge, Technology & Policy, 20* (3). 165-177.
5. Murray-Smith, R., Williamson, J., Hughes, S. and Quaade, T., Stane: synthesized surfaces for tactile input. in *Proceeding of the twenty-sixth annual SIGCHI conference on Human factors in computing systems*, ACM (2008), 1299-1302.
6. Sundström, P., Jaensson, T., Höök, K. and Pommeranz, A., Probing the potential of non-verbal group communication. in *Proceedings of the ACM 2009 international conference on Supporting group work*, ACM (2009), 351-360.
7. Sundström, P., Ståhl, A. and Höök, K. In situ informants exploring an emotional mobile messaging system in their everyday practice. *Int. J. Hum.-Comput. Stud., 65* (4). 388-403.

The Phone Lock: Audio and Haptic Shoulder-Surfing Resistant PIN Entry Methods for Mobile Devices

Andrea Bianchi
KAIST
Daejeon, Korea
andrea@kaist.ac.kr

Ian Oakley
Madeira-ITI
Funchal, Portugal
ian@uma.pt

Vassilis Kostakos
Madeira-ITI
Funchal, Portugal
vk@uma.pt

Dong Soo Kwon
KAIST
Daejeon, Korea
kwonds@kaist.ac.kr

ABSTRACT
Tangible user interfaces are portals to digital information. In the future, securing access to such material will be an important concern. This paper describes the design, implementation and evaluation of a PIN entry system based on audio or haptic cues that is suitable for integration into such physical systems. The current implementation links movements on a mobile phone touch screen with the display of non-visual cues; selection of a sequence of these cues composes a password. Studies reveal the validity of this approach in terms of task times and error rates that improve over prior art. In sum, this paper demonstrates the potential of non-visual PINs as a mechanism for securing access to a range of systems, ultimately incorporating mobile, ubiquitous or tangible interfaces.

Author Keywords
Security, Authentication, Mobile, PIN entry, Haptic, Audio.

ACM Classification Keywords
H.5.2 User Interfaces: Input devices and strategies.

General Terms
Design, Security.

INTRODUCTION
Security technologies underpin modern digital information systems. Clearly, the value of virtual data lies not only in the possibility to access it at anytime from anywhere, but also on the ability to securely restrict that access to particular individuals. This fact is illustrated by the ubiquity of personal passwords (or PINs), a security technique employed many times a day by millions of users (e.g. on bank ATMs and other public kiosks).

Although such techniques are simple and effective, they are susceptible to observation attacks in which viewing the PIN entry process results in uncovering the PIN contents. The difficulties that unintentional, non-malicious observations cause during secure data access in collaborative settings, such as group use of tabletop surfaces, has recently been highlighted [5]. Many other devices, such as mobile phones are subject to the same problems when used to perform secure transactions in public spaces. For example, a user initiating an online banking session via mobile phone in a crowded space will likely have the phone screen under the direct, but typically undesired or unintentional, visual observation of one or more other people.

This paper proposes a solution to this problem in the form of the design, implementation and evaluation of the Phone Lock, a PIN entry system based on audio or haptic cues. We argue that such non-visual PINs are less susceptible to observation attacks and that systems with this property are likely to grow in importance as authentication in tangible, ubiquitous, collaborative and public settings becomes more commonplace [4]. Furthermore, by considering and explicitly comparing the rich symbolic modality of audio with the less well understood haptic modality this paper aims to shed light on how haptic cues can be effectively designed to support authentication systems.

The remainder of this paper is structured as follows: previous mobile phone authentication techniques are introduced; the Phone Lock system and audio and tactile cues are presented; two short user studies and a security test are discussed; future avenues of research are highlighted.

RELATED WORK
Numerous researchers have explored techniques to make authentication on mobile devices less susceptible to observation attack. Typically these rely on the rich physical and multimodal cues that mobiles afford. For example, Vibrapass [3] uses tactile cues displayed on a user's mobile phone as a secondary channel to obfuscate a PIN entry that takes place on a public terminal. Mayrhofer [6] describes a system in which accelerometer data is used to pair two mobile devices - shaking them together results in similar sensor data and serves to secure the pairing. Awase-E [8] involves authenticating though a graphical password composed of a sequence of user-generated pictures. Although each of these methods uses interaction with a mobile phone to make authentication easier for users and safer against observation, none is entirely secure. The method proposed in this paper offers an improved resilience to observation and intersection (e.g. repeated observations) attack because relies on entirely non-visual cues (audio and haptic) as the means to represent PINs.

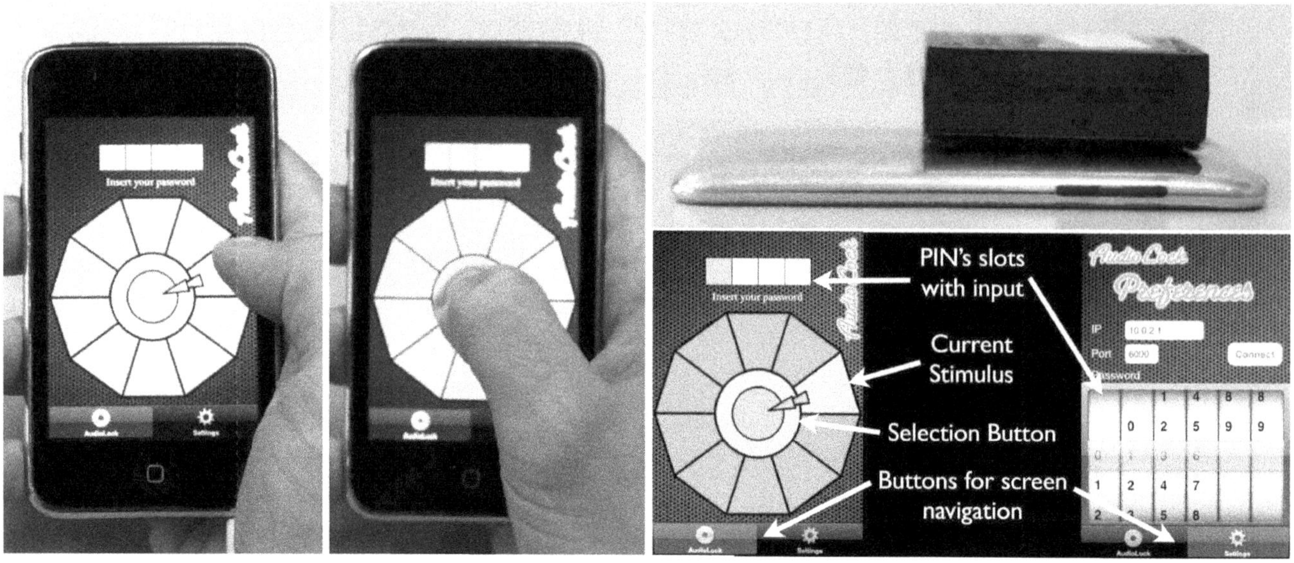

Figure 1. Virtual Wheel in use: navigation and selection (left). External motor attached to the device (top right) and screenshots of input and configurations screens with details about the GUI components (bottom right).

THE PHONE LOCK

System Description and Interaction

The Phone Lock is a PIN entry system for mobile phones that allows users to insert a PIN solely based on auditory or tactile stimuli. In the system, PIN items are drawn from a limited set of tactile or audio cues and PINs are composed of a sequence of these items. Both the size of the cue set and length of the PIN can be varied. Due to its lack of visual cues, the system is both an observation-resistant and an eye-free input technique.

The system displays a graphical wheel composed of a set of 10 equally sized, undifferentiated targets (Figure 1). Cues are mapped to particular targets and cue sets are required to possess a predetermined sequential order. This order is always maintained, although its orientation on the set of wheel targets is randomized for every digit of the PIN. In order to allow the sequences to wrap consistently around the wheel, cue sets must match or perfectly divide the number of targets in the wheel.

Cues are triggered by touching one of the on-screen targets. After experiencing a cue, users can move to another target via scrolling to an adjacent item or jumping to a more distant one. Alternatively, if they identify the item as the one they are seeking (e.g. the next PIN item), they simply select it by moving to the center of the wheel and releasing the screen. After an item has been selected in this way, it is recorded as a PIN item, the position of the cues is randomized and the system is ready to accept input relating to the following item. At any time during the interaction the user can erase the current PIN data by shaking the device.

Audio and Tactile Cues

Stimuli sets in the *Phone Lock* system must be clearly ordered. This was achieved for audio cues by the selection of generated computer speech expressing the digits 0-9 in English. The implementation of this feedback closely followed that described in Zhao et al.'s earPod [9]. The haptic stimuli were generated by variations of duration and beats to compose a scale with crescendo, a technique inspired by the work of Brown and Brewster [2]. They were composed of combinations of repetitions of beats (one, two or three) of different durations (40, 80 and 160 ms). The time between beat start points was always 160 ms, such that the final item in the sequence was a single sustained burst. A tenth tacton, featuring no vibration took the first place of this sequence.

Implementation

The *Phone Lock* is implemented for Apple's iPhone OS and intended for the physical form factor of the iPhone and iPod Touch devices. It relies on the touch screen for input, uses the devices' inbuilt capabilities for audio output (earphones are used to keep the audio authentication secure) and connects via Bluetooth to a SHAKE SK6 [7] device to generate tactile stimuli. The SHAKE is a matchbox-sized unit manually mounted on the back of the phone. Onboard processing allows it to natively support the generation of a rich set of tactile cues. Future versions of the system will provide haptic feedback directly on the mobile device via its internal pager motors.

The *Phone Lock*'s GUI has two screens, one to customize settings and the other to enter PINs. In the former, users can specify the current system PIN and length while in the latter they can insert their PINs and receive a visual confirmation of their progress and success or failure. This is shown as a series of initially white slots at the top of the device screen. Each represents a PIN item and is grayed out as items are entered. When the PIN is complete the set of slots turns green or red to indicate the correctness of the PIN as a whole. The lower part of the screen displays the decagonal wheel on which the users make input. The inner and outer diameters of the wheel are 2cm and 4.5cm respectively.

USABILITY EVALUATION

Experiment Setup

Two studies were conducted. The first was a short pilot to ascertain raw recognition rates for the tactile cues. The second evaluated user performance during PIN entry and took approximately 1 hour to complete. Four participants were recruited for the pilot, aged between 25 and 28. Three were female and one male. 12 participants age between 19 and 43 years old completed the full experiment. Five were female and seven male, and each was compensated with 10 Euro. In both studies, participants were a mix of university students, staff and employees of companies.

Pilot

The pilot study used the SHAKE SK6 hardware (connected via Bluetooth to a PC) to render the tactile stimuli. It was composed of a series of trials in which participants were exposed to a random tacton that they had to identify using a simple GUI showing a graphical representation of each of the ten cues. Each participant completed a practice stage composed of 30 trials (three of each cue) followed by an experimental stage of twice that length. Task completion time and errors (in the form of incorrect identification of tactons) were measured. The results showed a mean task completion time of 2.25 seconds and a mean error rate of 14% indicating the task could be accomplished relatively quickly, but was challenging. An analysis of results for each tacton indicated that those featuring the mid-length 80ms element were the most challenging to recognize.

Phone Lock Experiment

This experiment had two objectives. Firstly, it compared performance between the haptic and audio interfaces. Beyond a simple modality comparison, this also acted a comparison between performance with a highly familiar stimulus set (spoken numbers) and a novel one composed of vibro-tactile cues. Secondly, it explored two configurations of the PIN length and cue set size. This allowed exploration of the optimal arrangement of these parameters for each modality and facilitated comparison with previous research that has taken this approach [e.g. 1].

The study used a partially balanced repeated measures design with two binary independent variables: modality (audio and haptic) and two variations of PIN length and cue size (*4 PIN-10 cue* and *6 PIN-5 cue*). Modality was balanced among participants, while PIN length was balanced among each modality sub-group. The 4 PIN-10 cue configuration was chosen because 4-PIN systems are a standard in applications such as bank ATMs; 4 tokens selected from a set of 10 options leads to 10000 possible PINs. The 6 PIN-5 cue variation offers an increased level of security - a total of 15625 possible PINs and was chosen to offer a direct comparison with a previous system, the Haptic Wheel [1]. PINs were randomly generated and assigned to participants on notes showing numerical digits and icons representing the different audio and haptic cues.

Each participant completed four identical conditions composed of 10 practice followed by 10 experimental PIN entries. The measures were authentication time, error rate and reset (or self-cancelation) of a PIN entry. Participants continued with each condition until 10 successful PIN entries were made and data for authentication time was drawn only from successful trials. All interaction data was streamed from the mobile phone to a host PC. Prior to the experiment participants were given instructions on the system operation and a chance to test it out. They were also presented with tactile and audio stimuli used by the system in order to gain experience with them prior to the start of the study. In the audio modality participants used earphones to listen to the audio cues; in the haptic modality the SHAKE was attached to the back of the mobile device.

Results

Experimental data are shown in Figure 2. All variables were tested using two-way ANOVAs. The authentication speed showed a significant main effect of modality ($F(1,44) = 65.1$ $p<0.01$), while the effect of PIN length did not attain

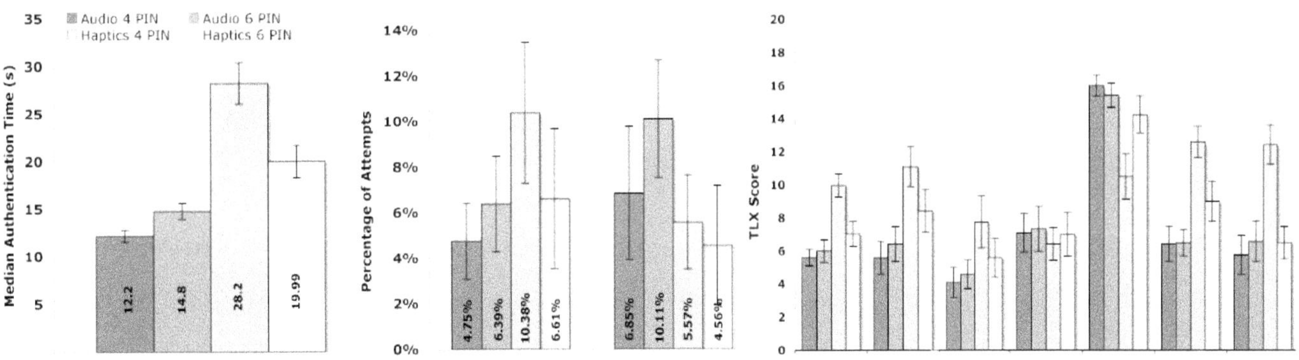

Figure 2. Mean authentication time (left); percentage of failed/reset authentications (center); NASA TLX (right). In each chart, columns from left to right show: Audio 4 PIN-10 cue; Audio 6 PIN-5 cue; Haptic 4 PIN-10 cue; Haptic 6 PIN-5 cue.

significance ($F(1,44) = 3.07$, $p=0.086$). The interaction between these two variables was significant ($F(1, 44) = 12.01$, $p<0.01$) indicating that users performed significantly faster with the smaller set of haptic cues and the larger set of audio cues. Authentication errors showed no significant differences in performance ($F(1, 44) < 1.7$, $p>0.18$ in all cases), while the workload measures revealed significant differences between the two modalities ($F(1,44) = 16.36$ $p<0.001$) but not between PIN lengths ($F(1,44) = 3.6$ $p=0.064$). A significant interaction mirroring the result from the temporal data was found ($F(1,44) = 6.16$ $p=0.016$).

Discussion

Perhaps unsurprisingly, the audio interface performed significantly faster than the haptic one: it used a familiar cue set composed of highly distinct items. This fact is clearly illustrated by the optimal performance seen in the audio 4 PIN-10 cue condition. However, in the haptic condition, users showed improved performance and workload with a reduced stimulus set of five tactons and a longer PIN entry. This highlights the fact that recognition among large sets of tactile cues is challenging.

However, beyond these broad trends, the results are encouraging. No significant differences were detected in the error rate among the conditions and the overall mean of 7% is low for an experimental setting. This suggests that, overall, users found the Phone Lock PIN entry process to be relatively easy to learn and use. This is held up by a comparison with the performance on PIN entry supported by tactile feedback in the literature [1], which reports authentication times up to 23.5 seconds and errors rates of up to 18%. Furthermore, the concept appears secure against prolonged observation attack – one way ANOVAs on the time spent recognizing each cue within each set showed no significant differences ($F(9,110) <1.27$, $p<0.29$ in all cases) except in the 4 PIN-10 cue haptic condition ($F(9,110) = 2.09$, $p=0.035$). These results suggest that, this one haptic condition aside, an attacker would not be able to reverse engineer a password from observing a user's dwell times on individual targets in the Phone Lock system. Security implications are discussed further in the following section.

THREAT MODEL AND SECURITY EVALUATION

The threat model in this work supposes an attacker capable of repeatedly observing a user authenticating at short range (i.e., from over the shoulder). Furthermore, it assumes they can also capture a close-up audiovisual recording of the interaction for analysis. To validate the security of the systems to observation, a short study was run on the 6 PIN-5 cue interfaces in both modalities. This took place in a quiet lab and involved a single user entering the same six digit PIN three times using both audio and haptic cues. This was observed from a position directly behind the shoulder (60 cm from the device and affording a clear view of its screen) both in person and with a camcorder with built-in microphone. The video and audio were analyzed in an attempt to deduce the PIN. It could not be recovered from either modality suggesting that both interfaces are secure; more rigorous testing is required to confirm this finding.

CONCLUSIONS AND FUTURE WORK

This paper introduced a novel observation-resistant authentication system that uses either audio or haptic cues to obfuscate a PIN entry process. Studies showed the feasibility of the concept in terms of task completion time, error rate and user acceptance. Future work should explore other combinations of PIN length and stimuli set size. We also believe the tactile PIN entry method has considerable potential in the context of securing tangible interfaces; in such systems, users may have to insert PINs into physical elements that have no graphical display. A haptic system to achieve this seems an elegant solution worthy of further investigation. In summary, the work presented in this paper makes steps towards the production of a rapid, easy to learn, reliable and secure non-visual authentication system; further work is required to fully realize this vision.

ACKNOWLEDGMENTS

This work was partially supported by the Portuguese Foundation for Science and Technology (FCT) grant CMU-PT/SE/0028/2008 (Web Security and Privacy).

REFERENCES

1. Bianchi, A., Oakley, I., Lee, J., Kwon, D. The haptic wheel: design & evaluation of a tactile password system. In CHI'10 EA, pp. 3625-3630.
2. Brewster, S. A. and Brown, L. M. 2004. Non-visual information display using tactons. In Procs of CHI '04 Extended Abstracts, pp.787-788.
3. De Luca, A., von Zezschwitz, E., and Hußmann, H. 2009. Vibrapass: secure authentication based on shared lies. In Procs. of CHI '09. ACM, NY, pp. 913-916.
4. Kainda, R., Flechais, I., and Roscoe, A. W. Two heads are better than one: security and usability of device associations in group scenarios. In Proceedings of SOUPS '10, vol. 485, pp. 1-13.
5. Kim, D., Dunphy, P., Briggs, P., Hook, J., Nicholson, J., Nicholson, J., Olivier, P. Multi-touch authentication on tabletops. In Proceedings of CHI 2010, pp. 1093-1102.
6. Mayrhofer, R., Gellersen., H., Shake well before use. In Proc. Pervasive 2007: 5th International Conference on Pervasive Computing. Springer, 2007.
7. SHAKE SK: http://code.google.com/p/shake-drivers
8. Takada, T., Koike, H., Awase-E: Image-based authentication for mobile phones using user's favorite images. In MHCI, LNCS 2795, pp. 347–351, 2003.
9. Zhao, S., Dragicevic, P., Chignell, M., Balakrishnan, R., and Baudisch, P. Earpod: eyes-free menu selection using touch input and reactive audio feedback. In Proceedings of CHI '07, pp. 1395-1404.

inTUIt – Simple Identification on Tangible User Interfaces

Alexander Wiethoff, Robert Kowalski, Andreas Butz
LMU University of Munich
Amalienstr. 17, 80333 Munich, Germany
{firstname.lastname}@ifi.lmu.de, kowalski@cip.ifi.lmu.de

ABSTRACT
In this paper we present *inTUIt*, an experience prototyping approach to investigate different simple identification techniques for tangible user interfaces (TUI) on digital surfaces. We have developed four different experience prototypes, proposing alternative approaches to the establishment of temporary ownership of digital content and TUIs in public environments.

Author Keywords
Identification, TUI, Prototyping.

ACM Classification Keywords
H5.2. Information interfaces and presentation (e.g., HCI): User Interfaces – Haptic I/O, Input devices and strategies

General Terms
Design, Experimentation.

INTRODUCTION

Tangible user interfaces (TUI), in combination with digital surfaces, have gained more awareness in the field of interaction design. They offer physical affordances connected to digital actions. Under the umbrella term "graspable interface", interesting projects have been developed in recent years [3,6]. However, as these deployed digital surfaces are intended to be used within collaborative scenarios by multiple users, a critical challenge is the establishment of user identity within the TUI context, which is a prerequisite to establish ownership between the personal digital content and the user. An example of such a collaborative use case was *Photohelix* [6], which controlled a photo-browsing application with a TUI object on a digital surface. A comparative study revealed that content in a large collection was accessed faster using a graspable interface. However, accessing personal content in the implemented prototype was only possible after a login process, in which the username was entered through a virtual keyboard. This was a time-consuming task and broke the tangible paradigm. The original vision behind *Photohelix* was that every user would carry his or her own TUI object, which would grant him or her access to the application and his or her personal content. Especially when dealing with content on digital surfaces that has already been declared as public by its producers (e.g., one's music listening history on the *last.fm* music service, or one's photo-stream from the picture sharing platform *flickr.com*), heavyweight identification mechanisms, such as entering passwords and usernames, can prove overprotective and too time-consuming to users. Another reason to improve the memorability of an identification mechanism is that users might forget their dedicated username because remembering passwords and usernames already overwhelms them when accessing their web applications and services, as discussed by Adams et al. [1]. We wanted to investigate alternative and more lightweight identification mechanisms that might be acceptable to users when accessing these types of data on a digital surface with a TUI. We selected a collaborative deejaying music application mockup as the contextual framework for our research. The application is designed for public access via a digital surface and is controlled using two TUIs simultaneously. In our envisioned scenario, multiple users continuously create and shuffle new playlists together based on their existing *last.fm* listening histories, as could happen, for example, at a party. To judge which identification method might be favored by the users for accessing their content, we have implemented four experience prototypes, equipped with different identification techniques such as gesture, rhythm, handwriting, and fingerprint scanning. These prototypes were compared against each other in a qualitative/quantitative user study and evaluated against one conventional authentication mechanism on a digital surface: A login field in combination with a virtual keyboard.

RELATED WORK

Many recently deployed TUI projects use digital surfaces and a graspable interface for interaction with audio content or processing [4,7,14]. Most of these projects, however, do not address identification mechanisms for accessing personal content. Stajano et al. [15] described security policy as an authentication method, which could be also applicable to a TUI, but might prove overprotective for accessing public data, as in our approach. Balfanz et al. [2] exemplified identification in ad-hoc wireless networks using a combination of mechanisms such as physical contact, infrared and speech recognition. Since our user

TEI'11, January 22–26, 2011, Funchal, Portugal.
Copyright 2011 ACM 978-1-4503-0478-8/11/01...$10.00.

research emphasized embodied interactions, we interpreted the idea of physical contact more literally, with physical actions. Claycomb et al. [5] proposed an approach where identification was established via image recognition on visual tags, which is more suitable for establishing a connection between two devices. Toye et al. [17] explored using smart phones as an identification mechanism. In contrast to their work, we decided not to require any additional infrastructure from the user, because not everyone possesses such a device and compatibility problems would aggravate real life deployment. Furthermore, a smart-phone as a tangible user interface does not offer the appropriate physical affordances to perform the digital actions we envisioned. Additional approaches include analysis of tapping patterns [11], Radio Frequency Identification (RFID) and its successor Near Field Communication (NFC) [12] and gestures such as pointing [16]. These served as an inspiration to select different techniques that we first presented in the user study and later implemented in our prototypes. Kumar et al. [8] described a study of individual pairing mechanisms and methods. While some of these methods are promising, they are also highly technological; our approach is more oriented towards embodied interactions, potentially providing a higher memorability as concluded by Wobbrock et al. [18]. In addition, Orr et al. demonstrated with their *Smart Floor* [10] that a physical, embodied approach can mitigate confounding issues, such as noise and varying light conditions, that plague other authentication mechanisms.

PROCESS AND PROTOTYPE

Following a user-centered design process [9] in the initial user research phase we interviewed eight different people, aged 23-28 years old, from various backgrounds. When presented with the possibility of identifying themselves using a TUI as an input method, the participants favored the ideas of using tapped signals or direct handwriting recognition, as compared to other suggested approaches.

Concepts of the Experience Prototypes

The prototypes we built offered five different identification techniques to the users. After a successful identification through the TUI, a digital surface would bring up their dedicated personal content, in our case a representation of their music collection categorized in different genres, arranged around the TUI. The implementations allowed the following identification forms. **Fingerprint scanning**: Identification was established when users swiped their finger over a scanner. To recognize their biometrics, a button had to be activated, which saved their fingerprint in the database (see Figure 1a). **Handwriting recognition**: Users identified themselves by metaphorically signing the TUI. To do this, users wrote their initials with their finger on an embedded touchscreen (see Figure 1b). **Spatial gestures**: Users defined a three-dimensional (6 DOF) gesture with the TUI and retrieved their personal content by repeating it (see Figure 1c). **Tapping signals**: Identification was established through a dedicated knocking pattern, e.g. a rhythm from a song. (see Figure 1d). **Virtual keyboard**: A virtual keyboard on the digital surface, in combination with a username login-field, served as a standard mechanism for identifying users.

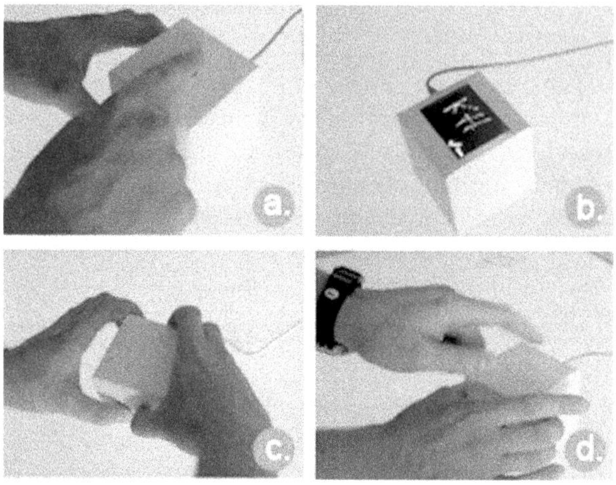

Figure 1. Different identification mechanisms embedded in TUIs : a.) Fingerprint scanning b.) Handwriting recognition c.) Spatial gestures and d.) Tapping signals

USER STUDY

As we intended only to measure the user's satisfaction in the different identification mechanisms, we explicitly left out design factors of the TUIs in order to avoid bias in our study. Thus, four simple geometrical forms of the same shape and size were created out of white cardboard and served as representations of the TUI (see Figure 1). The user study took part over two days with 13 participants, between 25-35 years, from various backgrounds. Each session lasted about 40 minutes and was recorded on video. Qualitative and quantitative data was collected using a questionnaire. The questionnaire focused on the evaluation of the different identification mechanisms via five-point Likert Scales ranging from "strongly agree" to "strongly disagree", as well as qualitative questions about willingness of use, identification alternatives and whether these techniques are perceived as an improvement in comparison with traditional mechanisms.

Results

Figure 2 shows the results for each individual identification method. **Fingerprint scanning:** Concerning the pleasantness of use, participants repeatedly stated that the fingerprint scanner requires a finger to slide in the direction opposite to the common one used on laptop computers. Regarding quickness of use, the extent of necessary learning on how to program the TUI, programming the TUI, identification via the TUI and the memorability of the method, the majorities "strongly agreed" that these tasks are easy. However, all participants indicated that they have strong privacy concerns because they do not know where the fingerprint is stored or who has access to it. **Handwriting recognition:** Here, the majority of the participants "strongly agreed" on the ease and quickness of use measures. However, the usage pleasure received a lower score, which, according to the feedback, was due to the small display size. As seen in Figure 2, the characteristics of "easy to learn", "easy to program" and "easy to ID", were "strongly agreed" with by most participants. In contrast, due to the limited number of permutations with two initials, users repeatedly mentioned security concerns with this kind of identification, even though they were reminded of the harmlessness of the content. **Spatial gestures:** The participants voted this TUI as the least popular one. This is reflected by the lowest scores for ease and pleasantness of use, "easy to learn", "easy to program" and "easy to ID". Remembering the identification patterns proved hugely problematic for the participants. Nevertheless, one participant mentioned that this problem would be reduced over time as soon as users performed the patterns a few times and their muscular memory automated the process. **Tapping signals:** In contrast to spatial gestures, rhythm tapping was the most popular identification method. This is facilitated by its high scores throughout all questions, apart from memorability, privacy and security. Considering the memorability, participants mentioned that it might be too difficult for unmusical persons to remember the pattern. Furthermore, the users had the impression that the knock pattern could easily be replicated by other persons, resulting in the low security score. **Virtual keyboard:** As expected, the virtual keyboard achieved high scores for ease of use, "easy to learn", "easy to program" and "easy to ID". From the qualitative feedback, this is due to the fact that all participants were already familiar with this kind of identification. However, the issue of keeping an additional password in mind was mentioned repeatedly and affects the score of "easy to remember".

For the evaluation of the user rankings we used the Copeland's method [13]. Regarding the popularity, tapping signals was the Condorcet winner. This was followed by fingerprint scanning, handwriting recognition and the virtual keyboard in second place with 2 wins and 2 losses each. The Condorcet loser is the spatial gestures technique. Concerning the ease of use, the resulting ranking is as follows: Fingerprint scanning, virtual keyboard, tapping signals, handwriting recognition and spatial gestures. For pleasure of use, the Condorcet winner and loser are the same as with the popularity ranking. In between, fingerprint scanning, handwriting recognition, and the virtual keyboard achieved positions two to four. The last comparative question dealt with perception, which method the participants perceived as the quickest to use. An interesting observation with this question is that the measured identification times do not coincide with the perceived usage speed. While the ranking identifies the fingerprint identification as the Condorcet winner, the time measurements for the user identification revealed the rhythm recognition as being over six seconds faster than the fingerprint on average. This seems to be due to the fact that the fingerprint reading trial often required two identification attempts because the finger had been scanned in the wrong direction at first. Also faster than the fingerprint was the handwriting recognition, with a three second advantage. Considering the slowest kinds of identification methods, the virtual login and the gesture recognition have been ranked forth and fifth and measured in reverse order with a two-second gap.

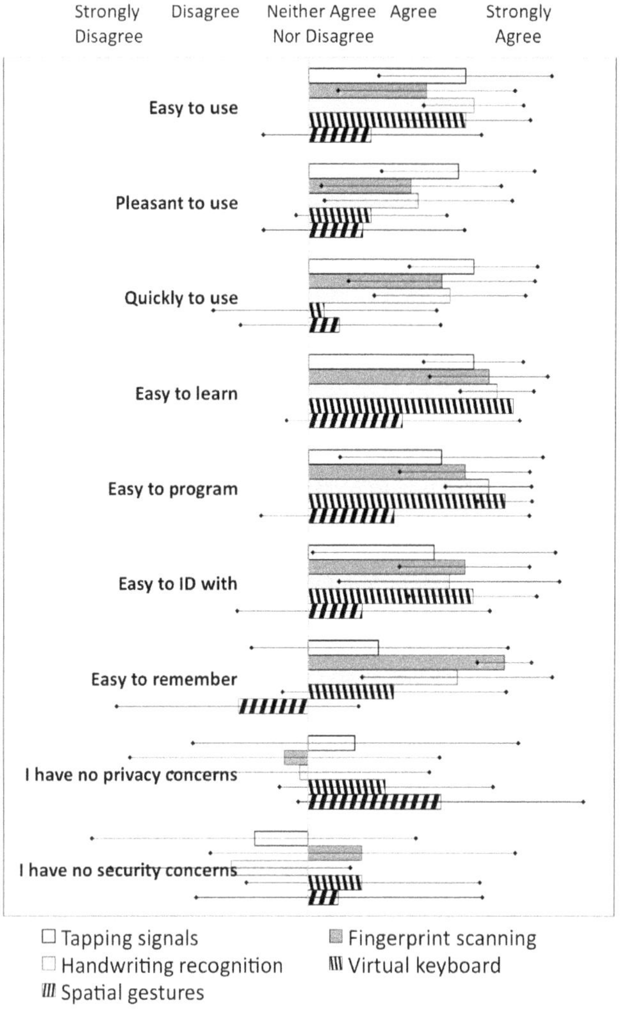

Figure 2. Overview of the ratings from the different experience prototypes

When asked about their willingness to use the TUIs, nine participants chose the fingerprint identification (four votes) as well as the rhythm recognition (five votes) over the other techniques, whereas three could not imagine using any of the presented methods. In considering further identification alternatives, voice- and facial recognition, as well as iris scans, and the drawing of line patterns, similar to the *HTC Sense®* UI, were mentioned. The final general question dealt with what the user's impression if these identification TUIs made the identification process less abstract. While five participants denied that it would have any impact, four stated that it does and might be especially true for persons with less technical aptitude.

DISCUSSION

Due to minor identification time measuring errors, the results for the measured usage speed were not 100% accurate, and therefore not extensively discussed. Initial trends are already visible from the evaluated data, which support our hypothesis that alternative techniques are generally preferred over traditional ones. However, this might be only the case if they are comparatively more fun to use and quicker to learn. Furthermore, the degree of memorability, together with security and privacy aspects, plays an important role. The performed user study did not cover long-term memorability. This is especially important with regards to gesture identification: with repeated physical actions, the identification process might be automated by the user and accelerated over time. Considering the security and privacy aspects, it should be noted from the users' feedback that the underlying public data scenario reduced the concerns of the participants. For private data, these concerns are likely to be much more serious.

CONCLUSION AND FUTURE WORK

In this paper we presented four different identification mechanisms embedded in TUIs and one conventional mechanism on a digital surface. These also included more conventional authentication mechanisms that had not been explored in conjunction with TUIs before, thereby proposing alternative approaches to the establishment of temporary ownership of digital content and TUIs in public environments. Therefore we propose simple identification mechanisms, as exemplified in this work, when dealing with non-sensitive data in combination with digital surfaces and TUIs, thus saving users' time in identifying themselves or accessing URLs. The results of our study show that the participants favor these rather opportunistic identification approaches in comparison with traditional techniques used in TUIs. Further investigation might improve the users' experience. In particular, privacy concerns have to be considered extensively with public content, as this was one aspect consistently mentioned by users in the study. Finally, since our implementations were mainly based on explicit interaction forms, it would be interesting to look at implicit identification techniques (e.g. grasp-sensing) as well, which might incorporate a higher degree of privacy.

REFERENCES

1. Adams, A., Sasse, M. Users Are Not the Enemy. In *Communications of the ACM.* 1999.
2. Balfanz, D., Smetters, D.K., Stewart, P., Wong, H.C. Talking To Strangers: Authentication in Ad-Hoc Wireless Networks. *Citeseer* 2003.
3. Baudisch, P., Becker, T., Rudeck, F. Lumino: tangible blocks for tabletop computers based on glass fiber bundles. In *Proc. CHI 2010*
4. Bischof, M., Conradi, B., Lachenmaier, P., Linde, K., Meier, M., Pötzl, P., Andre, E. XENAKIS - Combining tangible interaction with probability-based musical composition. In *Proc. TEI'08.*
5. Claycomb, W.R., Shin, D. Secure Real World Interaction Using Mobile Devices. In *Proc. PERMID* 2006.
6. Hilliges, O., Baur, D., Butz, A. Photohelix: Browsing, Sorting and Sharing Digital Photo Collections. In *Proc. Tabletop 2007*
7. Jordà, S., Fabra, P., Geiger, G., Alonso, M., Kaltenbrunner, M. The reacTable: Exploring the synergy between live music performance and tabletop tangible interfaces In *Proc. TEI'07*
8. Kumar, A., Saxena, N., Tsudik, G., Uzun, E. A comparative study of secure device pairing methods. In *Pervasive and Mobile Computing*. 2009.
9. Mao, B.J., Vredenburg, K., Smith, P.W., Carey, T. User-centered design practice. In *Communications of the ACM.* 48.
10. Orr, R.J., Abowd, G.D. The smart floor. In *Proc. EA. CHI '00*
11. Rekimoto, J., Ayatsuka, Y., Kohno, M. SyncTap: An Interaction Technique. In *Proc. Mobile HCI'03,*
12. Rukzio, E., Wetzstein, S., Schmidt, A. A Framework for Mobile Interactions with the Physical World. In *Proc. WPMC'05*
13. Saari, D., Merlin, V. The Copeland method. *Springer* 1996.
14. Schiettecatte, B., Vanderdonckt. J. AudioCubes: a distributed cube tangible interface based on interaction range for sound design. In *Proc. TEI '08.*
15. Stajano, F. The Resurrecting Duckling: Security Issues for Ad-hoc Wireless Networks. *CiteSeerX* 2000.
16. Swindells, C., Inkpen, K.M., Dill, J.C., Tory, M. That one there! Pointing to establish device identity. In *Proc. UIST '02.*
17. Toye, E., Sharp, R., Madhavapeddy, A., Scott, D. Using Smart Phones to Access Site-Specific Services. In *IEEE Pervasive Computing* 2005.
18. Wobbrock, J.O. TapSongs: tapping rhythm-based passwords on a single binary sensor. In *Proc.UIST '09*

Design and Evaluation of Techniques for Mobile Interaction with Dynamic NFC-Displays

Gregor Broll, Wolfgang Reithmeier, Paul Holleis, Matthias Wagner
DOCOMO Euro-Labs
Munich, Germany
{broll, reithmeier, holleis, wagner}@docomolab-euro.com

ABSTRACT

Near Field Communication (NFC) is a technology for mobile, touch-based interaction with tagged objects that can serve as physical user interfaces (UI). Dynamic NFC-displays use a grid of NFC-tags as a physical UI and combine it with a projected application UI to enable direct interactions between mobile devices and large screens. In this paper, we explore the design of interaction techniques for dynamic NFC-displays beyond the common touch-select interaction with single tags and evaluate them with an NFC-pinboard prototype. A user study confirms the general preference for the simple touch-select, but also shows that other techniques can provide alternatives, e.g. to implement interactions for which users want to feel more in control.

Author Keywords

Near Field Communication (NFC), physical user interfaces, dynamic NFC-displays, interaction techniques, gestures

ACM Classification Keywords

H.5.2 [Information Interfaces and Presentation]: User Interfaces – input devices and strategies, interaction styles

General Terms

Design, Human Factors

INTRODUCTION

Near Field Communication (NFC) is an emerging technology for mobile interaction with everyday objects [19]. It is a wireless technology for exchanging data over short distances, similar to Radio Frequency Identification (RFID) but targeted at mobile devices. NFC can store digital data on passive tags that can be attached to almost arbitrary objects. Users can retrieve data from a tag by touching it with a reading device, e.g. a mobile phone, or by holding them closely together. The simple, touch-like interaction between NFC-enabled mobile devices, tags, readers or smartcards can facilitate mobile interaction with tagged objects, associated digital information and services in different ways: NFC-tags can be used as physical hyperlinks [14] that reduce complex interactions to touching a single tag, e.g. to open a website in a mobile browser. Many applications already use mobile interaction with NFC for mobile payment, ticketing or information retrieval. Other applications map options and features to multiple tags on physical objects from where users can select them directly, instead of browsing nested menus on the small screens of mobile devices. That way, tagged objects can serve as physical user interfaces (UI) that adopt features of mobile UIs and thus complement them. Examples are posters for mobile ticketing [2], tagged maps [10] or control panels for multimedia players [13].

In the next step, dynamic NFC-displays [5] combine the physical interaction with tagged objects and the visual output-capabilities of large screens (Figure 1): They comprise a server that manages the logic of an application and projects its graphical UI onto a grid of NFC-tags that serves as the physical UI. Users can manipulate the content of the projected application UI by touching the tags of the physical UI with an NFC-enabled mobile phone. The phone returns the position of the tag in the grid to the server which updates the application UI according to the interaction.

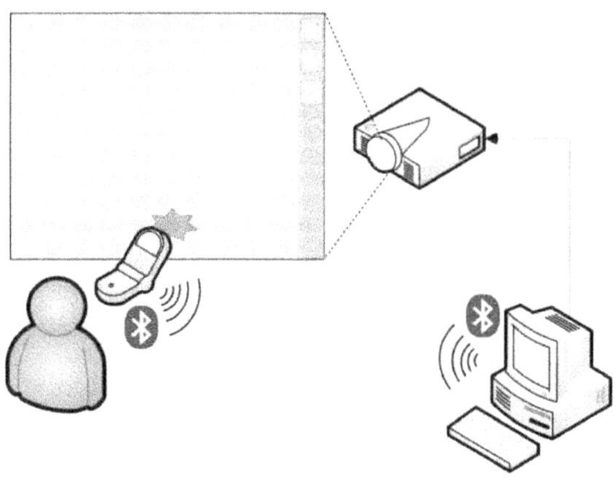

Figure 1. Basic setup of a dynamic NFC-display including the application server, the grid of NFC-tags and the mobile device

In this paper, we investigate interaction techniques for dynamic NFC-displays beyond the common touch-select interaction with single tags. The simplicity of this single-tag interaction is the greatest advantages of mobile interaction with NFC. But as NFC-based physical UIs evolve, their technical capabilities increase and enable new ways to interact with applications and their features. In the following sections, we build upon related work and the technology of dynamic NFC-displays to design interaction techniques such as click-select, double-touch, touch&hold or simple gestures. In order to demonstrate the technical feasibility of these techniques and to evaluate their usability, we have implemented and tested them with an NFC-pinboard prototype. A user study confirms the general preference for the simple touch-select, but also shows that other techniques can partially replace it, e.g. to implement actions for which users want to feel more in control.

RELATED WORK

Mobile interaction with NFC and RFID has considerably evolved since 1999, when Want et al. [18] tagged everyday objects such as books or business cards with RFID-tags to link them with electronic documents or email-addresses. Since then, NFC and RFID have been used for an increasing number of mobile applications, such as payment (e.g. i-mode FeliCa [7]), ticketing (e.g. Oyster Card [8]), access control, home care or entertainment [16]. In Ubicomp research, NFC and RFID are used to tag physical objects in order to identify them, to link them with digital resources and to facilitate the interaction with them [2, 12].

While most applications rely on simple interactions with single NFC-tags, others follow a multi-tag approach to facilitate mobile interactions. They map features to multiple tags on everyday objects, turning them into physical UIs that complement and extend mobile UIs. Examples include posters that comprise multiple tags to let users invoke Web Services for mobile ticketing [2]. Sanchez et al. [13] use a tagged panel to operate a multimedia player whose controls have been mapped to RFID-tags that users can select with their mobile devices. Reilly et al. [10] use RFID-tags on the back of maps to interact with points-of-interest (POI).

In the next step, physical UIs comprise a grid of NFC-tags to provide a completely interactive surface for the manipulation of dynamic application UIs. Opposite to static posters, these tags do not refer to specific items of information, e.g. POIs on a map, but merely indicate their position in the grid. That way, tags can be dynamically mapped to the UI elements of different applications. Vetter et al. [17] and Hardy et al. [5] have created and refined the first dynamic NFC-displays that use a grid of NFC-tags for the interaction with an application UI that is projected onto this interactive surface. Similarly, Ramírez-González et al. [9] have combined a grid of NFC-tags and a projected application UI to build an interactive NFC-panel. Seewoonauth et al. [15] use a grid of tags on the back of a laptop display to enable direct, touch-based interactions.

Dynamic NFC-displays are a prototyping technology that can be used to emulate touch-based interactions between mobile devices and large screens. Their technology allows more direct interactions between mobile devices and items on a screen than other approaches to mobile interaction with public displays that use different input features of mobile devices. *WebWall* [4] allows users to interact with different features of its virtual displays, e.g. by sending requests through an SMS-gateway. Ballagas et al. [1] present two techniques for mobile interaction with public displays: *Sweep* uses optical-flow recognition of phonecam images to recognize the movement of a mobile phone and to control a cursor on a display. With *Point & Shoot,* users take pictures of a grid of visual markers to identify and select objects on a display. Boring et al. [3] have compared the techniques *Scroll* (using input from keys or joysticks of mobile phones), *Tilt* (sensed by an accelerometer) and *Move* (using optical-flow image recognition) for controlling a cursor on a public display.

Our design of interaction techniques for dynamic NFC-displays builds upon different existing techniques for mobile interaction with NFC, desktop computing and pen-based interaction: Reilly et al. [10] have investigated *Click-select, Path-select, Multi-select, Lasso-select* and *Menu-select* for the interaction with POIs on tagged maps. The dynamic NFC-display of Vetter et al. [17] has supported *bounding box selection* and *path selection.* Hardy et al. [5] have added new interaction techniques for their *Touch & Interact*-approach: *Hovering* shows information about a tag on a mobile device when holding them close to each other. The selection of single/multiple tags is achieved by touching them and pressing/holding a key. *Polygon-select* requires users to hold a key and to touch multiple tags in order to outline an area and to select the tags within this area. *Pick-and-drop* emulates Rekimoto's *Pick-and-drop* [11] as it uses the mobile phone to pick up/drop items from/to a screen by touching NFC-tags.

Example interaction techniques from WIMP interfaces in desktop computing include *(double-)click, drag&drop,* context menus or the (de)selection of single and multiple items. Li et al. [6] describe techniques for mode switching in pen-based interaction that can be adopted for dynamic NFC-displays. Examples are pressing a button or the *Press and Hold* technique, which can be translated to touching a dedicated tag or touching a tag for a certain amount of time.

TECHNIQUES AND GESTURES FOR MOBILE INTERACTION WITH DYNAMIC NFC-DISPLAYS

Dynamic NFC-displays can be used for a wide range of applications at private (e.g. homes), semi-public (e.g. pubs, arcades) and public places (e.g. stations, malls), including information retrieval, interactive advertisements, maps or games. In these and other examples, NFC-enabled mobile phones serve as pointing devices for the interaction with the diverse content of dynamic NFC-displays, including text, pictures, links, maps or custom widgets. Their small, private screens can handle sensitive data, while the large NFC-displays can give a public overview of information. These aspects provide the background for the design of new interaction techniques for dynamic NFC-displays based on related work and the capabilities of their basic technologies.

Technical Capabilities of Mobile Interaction with NFC

The design, implementation and performance of interaction techniques for dynamic NFC-displays depend on the technical capabilities of reading devices, tags and physical UIs. The selection granularity of dynamic NFC-displays depends on the size of tags, target items and mobile devices. Small tags can increase the resolution of physical UIs and enable more precise interactions. On the other hand, mobile devices occlude tags and items during the interaction with them, making their selection the more difficult the smaller they are.

In addition to this "fat phone"-problem, NFC-enabled mobile phones that are currently available, e.g. the Nokia 6212, can only read one tag at a time. These devices cannot recognize multiple tags that they occlude during the interaction with one or several items. They also have problems to interact with areas where tags adjoin or overlap. Therefore, the size of tags and items should take the form factor of mobile devices into account.

NFC-enabled devices need a short, but considerable amount of time to read a tag – about 0.5 seconds with currently available devices like the Nokia 6212. This delay prohibits the continuous reading of tags, which is necessary for the recognition of continuous strokes, shapes or gestures. This constraint inevitably divides every multi-tag interaction into a series of discrete interactions with single tags.

Basic Interaction Techniques

These techniques can be used for simple interactions like the selection of items, triggering actions or activating links.

- **Touch-select** is the most basic interaction technique. Users touch a tag with a mobile device and remove it after the tag has been recognized. This atomic interaction can be diversified through the combination with input from keyboards, joysticks or sensors.
- **Click-select** is a touch-select followed by pressing a dedicated key on the mobile device to confirm the selection of a tag. This technique was adopted from [5] and [10] who use it as the default technique to select tags or items that are associated with them.
- **Touch&hold** requires users to touch a tag for a period of time that is longer than a regular touch-select, e.g. 2 seconds. This technique was adopted from Press and Hold [6], a technique for pen-based interaction.
- For **double-touch-(select)**, users have to touch the same tag twice in a row, similar to a double-click.

Advanced Interaction Techniques

Building upon these basic interaction techniques, we have developed some more advanced techniques to manipulate tags and items on dynamic NFC-displays.

Selection of multiple tags and items: The basic interaction techniques can be used to (de)select single or multiple tags or items directly (*multi-select*). Advanced techniques can adopt basic techniques for the indirect selection of multiple tags or items within an area that is outlined by selecting unoccupied tags.

- **Polygon-select** was adopted from [5] and can be used to outline areas of arbitrary shapes for the selection of tags and items as long as the first and the last tag that define the outline of an area are the same.
- For **bounding-box-select,** users have to touch two tags to define a rectangular shape and to select items within it. This technique was adopted from [17].

Drag&drop: Touch&drop was adopted from Pick-and-drop [5, 11] and uses touch-select or touch&hold to pick up and drop items with a mobile device. Larger items can also have a dedicated area, e.g. their upper-left corner, for picking them up with a simple touch-select.

Gestures: We have also sounded the capabilities of dynamic NFC-display to implement gestures or shape-based input. Due to the above-mentioned constraints of the basic technology, we have used discrete NFC-touch events to design gestures that are recognized by their shapes and offsets rather than by continuous reading of tags.

- **Offset gestures** are performed by touching two tags with a specific distance between them, e.g. from the top of an NFC-display to its bottom or from one side to the other (Figure 2a). These gestures have a tolerance level so that users do not have to find the exact offset between two tags. Figure 2a shows alternatives for the same offset gesture within this tolerance level.

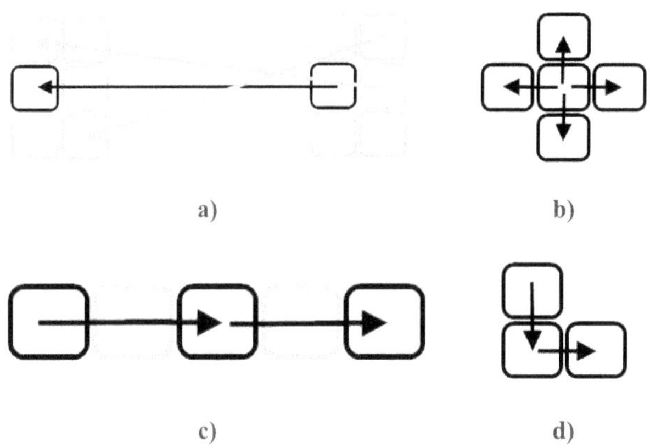

Figure 2. NFC-based gestures: offset gesture (a), one-stroke gestures (b, c) and offset-shape gesture (d)

- To perform **one-stroke gestures**, users have to touch a fixed number of tags in a fixed direction and with fixed offsets between them, including an offset of zero tags. Examples are gestures that start on one tag, e.g. a specific item, and touch one of the four adjacent tags, e.g. to perform an action on the item (Figure 2b). For another example, users have to touch three tags in a row with an offset of one tag (Figure 2c).

- **Offset-shape gestures** extend one-stroke gestures and allow different offsets between their tags. That way, gestures can adopt different shapes (Figure 2d).

THE NFC-PINBOARD

In order to be able to evaluate the interaction techniques and gestures that we designed for dynamic NFC-displays, we have developed a prototype of an NFC-pinboard. This section presents its features and explains how interaction techniques and gestures can be mapped to them.

Basic Features

The NFC-pinboard (Figure 3) provides a testbed for the implementation and evaluation of different interaction techniques and gestures for dynamic NFC-displays. It emulates the features of a regular pinboard and can serve as an information hub at semi-public or private places, e.g. companies or homes. Small communities like families can use it to post, view and share digital content from mobile devices like messages, pictures or bookmarks. The NFC-pinboard contains different items that can be manipulated by touching the tags of the physical UI. The prototype supports messages and pictures that can be organized in folders. Each item can be opened to expose its contents or closed to save space as an abstract icon. A toolbar contains additional options, e.g. to filter the items on the display.

Figure 3. The NFC-pinboard prototype

Application-dependent Interactions

This section gives an overview of the unique features of the NFC-pinboard and explains which of the previously presented interaction techniques could be used to implement them. Based on this overview, a user study will later investigate the applicability and acceptance of specific interaction techniques for specific application features in the next section.

- **Opening and closing items:** The basic interaction techniques can be used to open and close items. Alternatively, a one-stroke gesture from an item to the tag above it can open it (Figure 4a) and another gesture from the item´s top-right corner to its bottom-left corner can close it (Figure 4b).
- **Views:** The NFC-pinboard supports three views on its items: In the *overview*, all items are closed. In the *standard view*, items are either open or closed. The *exposé* presents all open items next to each other, similar to the homonymous Mac OS feature. Users can select any item to bring it to the foreground in the standard view. Users can switch between the views with options from the phone menu or the toolbar or by performing offset-gestures from one side of the NFC-display to the other.

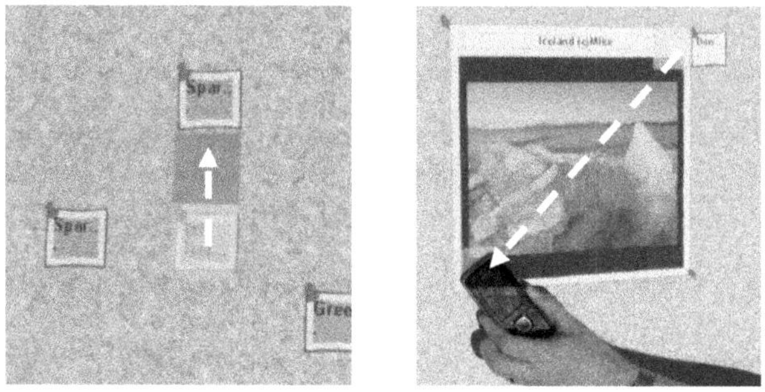

a) b)

Figure 4. Opening (a) and closing (b) items with gestures

- **Tooltip:** In order to get more information about closed items, users can apply a basic interaction technique to them (Figure 5a), similar to Hovering [5].
- **Downloading items:** Users can download items to their mobile devices with a basic interaction technique or a one-stroke gesture from the item to the tag beneath it (Figure 5b).
- **Uploading items:** Users can also create messages or pictures on their mobile devices and upload them to the NFC-pinboard by touching it. To upload an item as a closed icon, the target tag can be selected with a basic interaction technique. To upload an open item, users can define the target area with bounding-box-select.

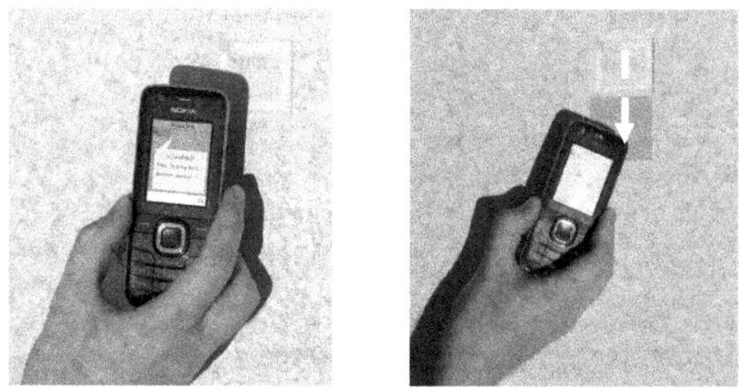

a) b)

Figure 5. Showing details about an item with the tooltip feature (a) and downloading an item (b) with a gesture

Application-independent Interactions

Apart from application-specific features, the prototype also supports interactions that are independent from the NFC-pinboard and can also be used by other applications.

- **Selection of single and multiple items:** The basic interaction techniques can be used to (de)select single and multiple items directly. For the indirect selection of items, the prototype supports polygon-select and bounding-box-select (Figure 6).

Figure 6. Selecting multiple items with bounding-box-select

- **Context Menu:** Each item has a context menu that can be opened with a basic interaction technique or a one-stroke gesture from the item to the next tag on its right (Figure 7a). The menu comprises options to delete an item, to download and to move it (Figure 7b).

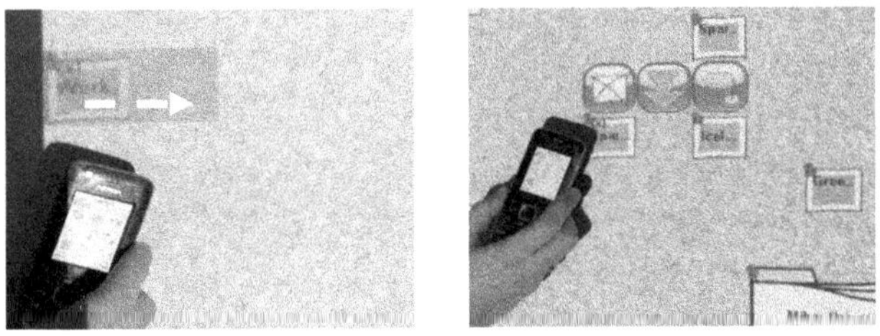

a) b)

Figure 7. Using a one-stroke gesture (a) to open the context menu of an item (b).

- **Drag&drop:** Users can move items around the display with touch&drop or an option from the context menu. Open items can also be picked up at their upper-left corner using touch-select (Figure 8).

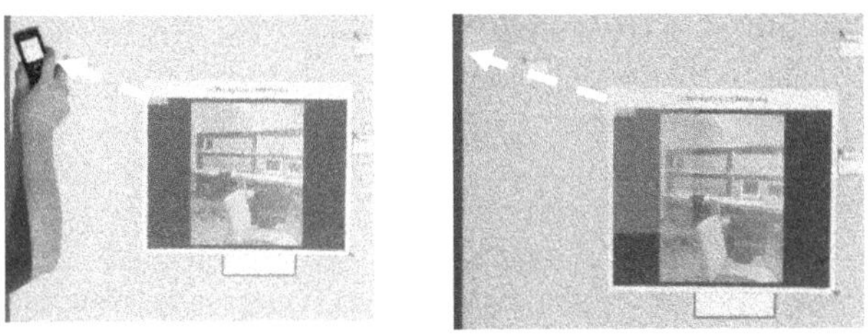

Figure 8. Moving an item by applying touch-select to its upper-left corner

Technical Setup and Implementation

The NFC-pinboard implements the conceptual hardware-setup of dynamic NFC-displays (see Figure 1). The physical UI of the prototype is a poster with a grid of 20 by 15 adjacent NFC-tags, based on the Philips MiFare Ultralight standard, providing an interactive area of 90 cm by 67.5 cm. The server application for the NFC-pinboard was implemented with Java SE and runs on a laptop. An LCD projector is used to project the application UI of the NFC-pinboard onto the physical UI.

The prototype is completed by a mobile Java ME application that runs on NFC-enabled mobile devices – in this case the Nokia 6212 mobile phone. Like other NFC-enabled mobile phones that are currently available, it only supports discrete interactions with multiple tags. Therefore, the prototype does not support continuous interactions between tags of the grid but only discrete interactions with single tags. Gestures or shape-based input like polygon-select or the offset-shape-gestures are carried out as a series of discrete single-tag interactions (see discussion above). Apart from that, the phone serves as a smart pointing device to manipulate the projected application UI, to read the tags on the physical UI, to communicate with the application server via Bluetooth and to provide visual and vibration feedback during the interaction.

USER STUDY AND EVALUATION

The NFC-pinboard and its implementation of the interaction techniques allowed us to investigate their mapping to application features and to evaluate their applicability, usability and acceptance among users.

Experimental Design and Tasks

The study was conducted with 11 subjects (10 male, 1 female) with an average age of 26.6 years (from 23 to 33) that were recruited from our lab and a university. All subjects had a background in computer science and thus rated their general technical experience and their experience with mobile device with high averages of 6.3 and 5.1 on a Likert-scale from 1 ("inexperienced") to 7 ("experienced").

During the study, each subject had to carry out 8 tasks with the features of the NFC-pinboard. The tasks were designed to evaluate the applicability of different interaction techniques for specific application features. Therefore, each subject had to carry out each task with several different techniques and gestures. All subjects carried out the tasks in the same order because some of them built upon each other. The different interaction techniques and gestures that were tested during a task were used in random order.

- **Tooltip:** The subjects had to use touch-select, double-touch, click-select, touch&hold and options from the toolbar and the phone menu to get details about items (see Figure 5a).
- **Opening and closing items:** The subjects had to open and close items with touch-select, double-touch, click-select, touch&hold and gestures (see Figure 4).
- **Switching views:** The subjects had to switch between the views of the NFC-pinboard using options from the toolbar and the phone menu and performing offset gestures from one side of the NFC-display to the other.
- **Uploading an item:** The subjects had to upload an item from their mobile devices to the NFC-display using touch-select, click-select, touch&hold, double-touch and bounding-box-select.

- **Context menu:** The subjects had to open the context menu of an item with touch-select, double-touch, click-select, touch&hold and a one-stroke gesture (see Figure 7a) and then select the delete-option with touch-select.
- **Downloading an item:** The subjects had to download an item to their mobile phones using touch-select, double-touch, click-select, touch&hold, options from the toolbar and the phone menu and a one-stroke gesture (see Figure 5b).
- **Drag&drop:** The subjects had to move items with the option from their context menus, touch&drop based on touch-select and touch&hold as well as touch-select with the dedicated upper-left corner of open items.
- **Selection of multiple items:** The subjects had to select multiple items directly and indirectly. The direct selection could be activated with an option from the toolbar or the phone menu and could be performed by selecting items with touch-select or touch&hold. The indirect selection was done by drawing a bounding-box around items using touch-select or touch&hold.

During the study, we collected qualitative and quantitative data to evaluate the different interaction techniques, their usability, their mapping to application features and the preferences of the subjects. The subjects were recorded on video for a post-hoc analysis of errors and attention shifts from mobile devices to the NFC-display or vice versa.

Results

User Preferences

After each task, the subjects had to fill out a questionnaire to assess which interaction technique or gesture they liked the best and the least for the tested feature of the NFC-pinboard. They also had to rate different properties of the gestures on a Likert-scale from 1 ("fully disagree") to 7 ("totally agree").

- **Tooltip:** Most subjects (7) preferred touch-select for this feature and regarded it as fast, simple and intuitive. Two subjects preferred the option from the toolbar and one subject voted for click-select and touch&hold each. The least preferred interaction techniques were click-select (4), the phone menu (3) and double-touch (3) because of their added complexity which did not fit the simplicity of the feature. Double-touch caused problems because of the delay between its two touches.
- **Opening and closing items:** For this feature, five subjects preferred touch-select because of its speed and simplicity. Two subjects preferred the one-stroke gestures and three subjects favored click-select because they felt more in control with it and appreciated the explicit triggering of actions. On the other hand, three subjects disliked click-select because of the added attention shift. Interestingly, two subjects rejected touch-select as too simple for this feature. Three subjects each did not like touch&hold and the gestures and thought that they were tedious and intricate. Consequently, the subjects rated the gestures as very easy to learn (mean = 6.5; standard deviation = 0.5) and easy to use (m = 5.9; sd = 0.7), but neither as very fast (m = 4.2; sd = 0.8) or effective (m = 4.5; sd = 1.8).
- **Switching views:** Eight subjects liked the toolbar and its options to switch between the views and regarded it as fast and easy to use. Three subjects preferred the phone to switch the views because it gave them a better overview of the NFC-display. Three subjects disliked the same technique because of the added attention shifts. Six subjects disliked the gestures from one side of the display to the other, which were difficult to carry out. Nevertheless, the gestures received good ratings for ease of learning (m = 5.9; sd = 1.2) and ease of use (m = 5.0; sd = 1.4), but not for speed (m = 3.7; sd = 1.0) and effectiveness (m = 3.9; sd = 1.7).
- **Uploading items:** For this feature, most subjects preferred touch-select (5) or bounding-box-select (4). The former was liked for its speed, simplicity and intuitiveness, the latter for the possibility to define the size of an open item. Click-select (7) and double-touch (3) were the least liked interaction techniques because of their added complexity compared to touch-select, respectively the additional touch-input (double-touch) and attention shifts (click-select).
- **Context menu:** For this feature, five subjects preferred the one-stroke gesture because it was easy to distinguish from other techniques. It was also very easy to learn (m = 6.6; sd = 0.5) and to use (m = 6.4; sd = 0.8), as well as fast (m = 5.8; sd = 1.0) and effective (m = 6.0; sd = 0.9). Three subjects liked touch&hold which seemed familiar from interactions with other applications. The remaining three subjects voted for touch-select because of its simplicity. On the other hand, three subjects each regarded touch&hold, double-touch and click-select as the least suitable technique for this feature. Compared to touch-select, touch&hold was too slow and not accurate enough. Double-touch was rejected because of the delay between the single touch-selects. Click-select was seen as uncomfortable.
- **Downloading items:** For this feature, five subjects preferred the one-stroke gesture, which was regarded as intuitive, very easy to learn (m = 6.5; sd = 0.5) and use (m = 6.3; sd = 0.8), fast (m = 5.9; sd = 0.7) and effective (m = 6.1; sd = 0.8). Three subjects liked the option from the context menu, which was familiar from PCs and not easy to be confused with other techniques. The context menu was disliked by three subjects because it was too slow. Touch&hold and touch-select were rejected by two subjects each. Touch&hold was regarded as too imprecise and touch-select could be

performed too easily and cause accidental and unwanted downloads.

- **Drag&drop:** Five subjects preferred touch&drop with touch-select to move items around the display. Four subjects preferred the interaction with the upper-left corner of items. Both techniques were regarded as intuitive, fast and easy to use. Two subjects preferred touch&drop with touch&hold as it gave them a better feeling of picking items up. The least preferred technique for drag&drop was the option from the context menu (6), which was too complicated, not intuitive and required too many steps. Three subjects disliked touch-select with the corner of the item because it could only be performed with open items. Two subjects disliked touch&drop with touch&hold because of its delay.
- **Selection of multiple items:** Seven subjects preferred the indirect selection of items with bounding-box-select using touch-select because it was simple, fast and familiar from similar desktop interactions. Two subjects liked the activation of multi-select from the toolbar because it allowed them to select single items with touch-select. Most subjects disliked the combination of touch&hold with the phone menu (6) or the toolbar (4). Switching to multi-select via the phone menu was regarded as very uncomfortable.

Errors and Attention Shifts

We complemented the qualitative evaluation of interaction techniques and gestures with quantitative data about errors and attention shifts for the most common interaction techniques. Touch&drop and the selection of multiple items were not included in this evaluation because they employ more specialized interaction techniques. A caveat for the interpretation of this data is the learning effects that result from the fixed order of the tasks. They were not randomized or counter-balanced because they partly built upon each other. The interaction techniques and gestures that were tested within a task were randomized.

Figure 9 shows the mean numbers of errors for the most common interaction techniques that were tested for the different application features. It shows the learning curve as the number of errors for most interaction techniques and the total number of errors for each feature decrease during the study. During the first task with the tooltip-feature, the subjects made quite a lot of errors with every interaction technique but quickly became better. Towards the end of the study, they had gotten used to most interaction techniques and made hardly any errors, which is shown by the results for the download-task. Figure 9 also indicates that apart from the combination of gestures and views, double-touch and click-select caused the most errors (0.35 and 0.24 on average), followed by touch&hold (0.20), touch-select (0.18), the toolbar (0.16) and the phone menu (0.12). These average values are only indicative, as the techniques were not equally tested across all features.

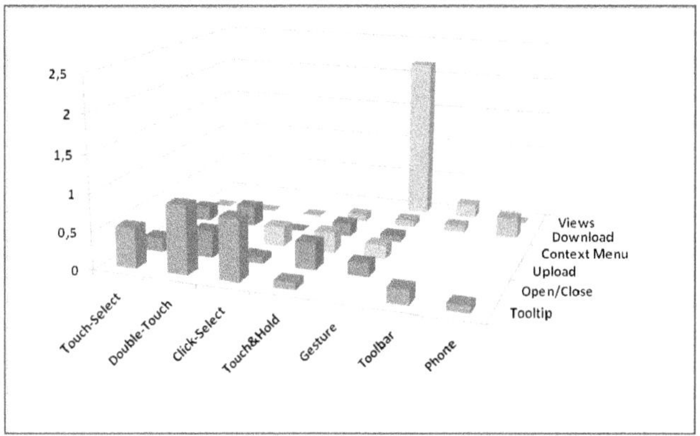

Figure 9. Overview of the mean numbers of errors for interaction techniques and application features

The mean numbers of attention shifts in Figure 10 do not show a consistent learning curve, because some features cause them almost automatically. For example, users often look from the NFC-display to their mobile devices when they perform a click-select, which often causes high numbers of attention shifts during different tasks. Together with the phone menu, click-select causes the highest total average of attention shifts (3.93 vs. 3.62). Touch-select, double-touch, touch&hold and the toolbar cause about the same total average of attention shifts (2.11, 2.20, 2.31, 2.25), outplayed by gestures which cause only 1.35 attention shifts on average.

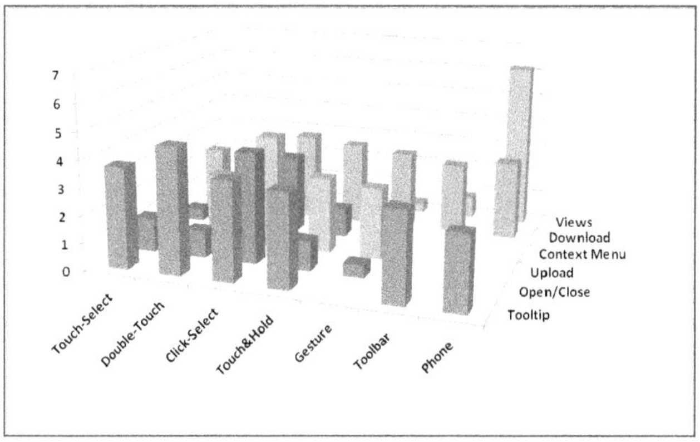

Figure 10. Overview of the mean numbers of attention shifts for interaction techniques and application features

SUMMARY AND CONCLUSION

In this paper, we have presented the design, application and evaluation of interaction techniques for dynamic NFC-displays. Based on the capabilities of this technology, we have partially adopted interaction techniques from related work and have created new techniques like touch&hold, double-touch or discrete gestures. We have implemented these techniques with an NFC-pinboard prototype in order to evaluate their mapping to specific application features in a comprehensive user study. Apart from their applicability for different application features, we have also investigated their usability, (dis)advantages and user acceptance.

Some results of the user study are not surprising: The evaluation of touch-select confirms the simplicity of touching a single tag as the greatest advantage of mobile interaction with NFC, making it the preferred technique for all kinds of interactions and application features. However, some results also indicate that touch-select might actually be too simple for interactions for which some users prefer a feeling of being in control, e.g. triggering or confirming important actions with the familiar press of a button or avoiding accidental actions.

Disregarding the general appreciation of touch-select, the more interesting results are provided by the evaluation of the other interaction techniques: Double-touch, touch&hold and click-select did not perform too well. Many subjects disliked the additional time and effort that was required by these techniques to touch another tag, to press a key or to shift one's attention on top of touch-select. However, the results indicate that this effort can be accepted for interactions for which touch-select is too simple and lightweight. Although these interaction techniques are not as simple, intuitive or popular as touch-select, they can be used to diversify this atomic interaction technique for applications that require different techniques to implement their different features.

Furthermore, the comparison of menus showed that the subjects prefer the simple interaction with the toolbar and dislike the interaction with the uncomfortable phone menu. While the context-menu was seen as an opportunity to avoid interference with other interactions, it also caused additional effort. The gestures were well-received and seen as alternatives for other techniques as long as they were easy to perform. The subjects preferred short gestures that were applied to items and disliked gestures that required them to interact across the whole display.

With our work on interaction techniques for dynamic NFC-displays, we also tried to push the limits of mobile interaction with NFC and what is possible with this technology. Current limitations and challenges for future work in this area include the interaction with smaller and with multiple tags, the continuous selection of tags to improve gestures and shape-based input or the combination of NFC and other technologies, e.g. sensor data.

Although dynamic NFC-displays are only a prototyping technology, they anticipate technologies for more direct and physical interactions between mobile devices and displays. Our work on interaction techniques for this technology can provide preliminary results to inform the design and development of future mobile interactions with NFC-based physical UIs. The results of our work show that dynamic NFC-displays have a potential for interaction techniques and even discrete gestures beyond touch-select.

REFERENCES

1. Ballagas, R., Rohs, M., and Sheridan, J. G. 2005. Sweep and point and shoot: phonecam-based interactions for large public displays. In: CHI '05 extended abstracts. 2005, ACM Press.
2. Broll, G., Rukzio, E., Paolucci, M., Wagner, M., Schmidt, A., and Hussmann, H. 2009. Perci: Pervasive Service Interaction with the Internet of Things. IEEE Internet Computing 13, 6 (Nov. 2009), 74-81.
3. Boring, S., Jurmu, M., and Butz, A. 2009. Scroll, tilt or move it: using mobile phones to continuously control pointers on large public displays. In Proc. of OZCHI '09, ACM, 161-168.
4. Ferscha, A. and Vogl, S. 2002. Pervasive Web Access via Public Communication Walls. In: Proc. of Pervasive 2002 F. Mattern and M. Naghshineh (Eds.). Lecture Notes In Computer Science. vol. 2414. Springer-Verlag, 84-97.
5. Hardy, R. and Rukzio, E. 2008. Touch & interact: touch-based interaction of mobile phones with displays. In Proc. of MobileHCI '08. ACM, 245-254.
6. Li, Y., Hinckley, K., Guan, Z., and Landay, J. A. 2005. Experimental analysis of mode switching techniques in pen-based user interfaces. In Proc. of CHI '05, ACM, 461-470.
7. NTT DOCOMO i-mode Felica, www.nttdocomo.co.jp/english/service/imode/make/content/felica/index.html
8. Oyster Card website: https://oyster.tfl.gov.uk/oyster/entry.do
9. Ramírez-González, G., Muñoz-Organero, M., Kloos, C. D., and Astaiza, Á. C. 2008. Exploring NFC interactive panel. In Proc. of Mobiquitous 2008. July 21 - 25, 2008.
10. Reilly, D., Welsman-Dinelle, M., Bate, C., and Inkpen, K. 2005. Just point and click?: using handhelds to interact with paper maps. In Proc. of MobileHCI '05, ACM, 239-242.
11. Rekimoto, J. 1997. Pick-and-drop: a direct manipulation technique for multiple computer environments. In Proc. of UIST '97. ACM, 31-39.
12. Riekki, J., Salminen, T., and Alakärppä, I. 2006. Requesting Pervasive Services by Touching RFID Tags. IEEE Pervasive Computing 5(1): 40-46.
13. Sánchez, I., Riekki, J., and Pyykknen, M. 2008. Touch & control: Interacting with services by touching RFID tags. In Proc. of IWRT 08, June 12-13 2008.
14. Schwieren, J. and Vossen, G. 2007. Implementing Physical Hyperlinks for Mobile Applications Using RFID Tags. In Proc. of IDEAS`07. IEEE Computer Society, 154-162.
15. Seewoonauth, K., Rukzio, E., Hardy, R., and Holleis, P. 2009. Touch & connect and touch & select: interacting with a computer by touching it with a mobile phone. In Proc. of MobileHCI '09. ACM, 1-9.
16. SmartTouch website. www.smarttouch.org
17. Vetter, J., Hamard, J., Paolucci, M., Rukzio, E., and Schmidt, A. 2007. Physical Mobile Interaction with Dynamic Physical Objects. Demo at MobileHCI´07, September 9, 2007.
18. Want, R., Fishkin, K. P., Gujar, A., and Harrison, B. L. 1999. Bridging physical and virtual worlds with electronic tags. In Proc. of CHI '99. ACM, 370-377.
19. Want, R. 2006. An Introduction to RFID Technology. IEEE Pervasive Computing 5, 1 (Jan. 2006), 25.

Sensing Through Structure: Designing Soft Silicone Sensors

Ronit Slyper
Carnegie Mellon University
Disney Research Pittsburgh
rys@cs.cmu.edu

Ivan Poupyrev
Disney Research Pittsburgh
ivan@disneyresearch.com

Jessica Hodgins
Carnegie Mellon University
Disney Research Pittsburgh
jkh@cs.cmu.edu

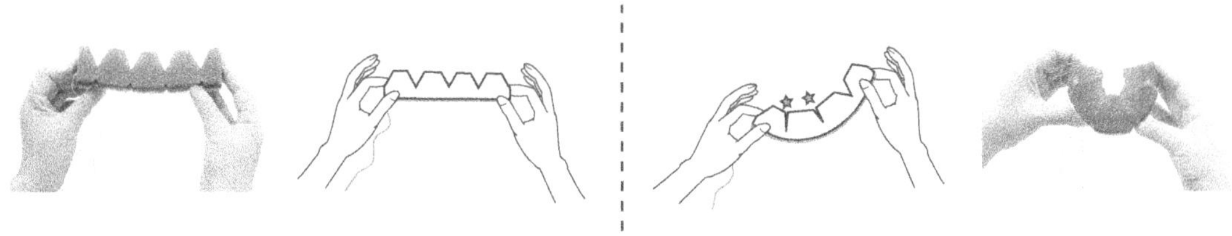

Figure 1. Sensing structures, such as our bend structure, above, physically remap a continuous deformation into a set of discrete displacements.

ABSTRACT

We present a method for designing and constructing rugged and soft multi-point sensors. Interactions applied to a soft material are reduced to structural units of deformation. These structures can then be embedded and instrumented anywhere inside a soft sensor. This simplification lets us design complex, durable sensors in easily manufacturable ways. In particular, we present a construction method of layering electronics between silicone pours to easily create sensors for arbitrary combinations of these deformations. We present several prototype sensors and discuss applications including toys, games, and therapy.

Author Keywords

Bend, sensors, games, controllers

ACM Classification Keywords

H5.2 Information interfaces and presentation: User Interfaces—*Input devices and strategies*

General Terms

Design, Human Factors, Measurement

INTRODUCTION

Objects in the physical world are being linked to the cyber world with increasing frequency, whether the objects manifest as input devices to computers, game controllers, or computer-augmented toys. As these computing devices become more prevalent and more personal, users are expecting them to have both a softer look and a softer feel. Boxy desktop computers now sit alongside soft Chumbys [3] and soon, flexible displays; hard actuated toys share aisle space with robotic plush animals; body-worn computing devices are moving from bulky calculator wrist watches to a range of soft e-textile materials; user input devices are pushing the bounds with attempts at soft input, from digital clay [19] to reactive fur [7]. Consequently there is a growing need for new design techniques that allow easy and natural integration of sensing into these emerging categories of soft computing devices.

Our approach to sensor design, "sensing through structure", exploits the deformability of the materials that are used to design these soft, flexible computing objects. We consider the character of the deformations induced by the user manipulating an object made of a flexible material such as silicone, and distill simple atomic structures that undergo consistent and easily measurable topological changes when such deformations are performed. Figure 1 illustrates one such atomic structure, used for capturing bend. We can calculate the approximate curvature of an object by using a set of simple binary switches embedded in the valleys of the structure: when the user bends the object, the valleys are closed and the switches are triggered. We can easily embed such structures into a wide variety of objects.

Sensing through structure is a simple, scalable approach to designing and integrating sensors into soft objects. A sensor can be easily designed to match its application: various basic structural units can be selected in any combination, captured with either digital or analogue sensors, and constructed with shapes customized to respond to specific ranges of motion.

Sensors built using this approach have a nice physicality. One can see – and feel – the structural units deforming, and

TEI'11, January 22–26, 2011, Funchal, Portugal.

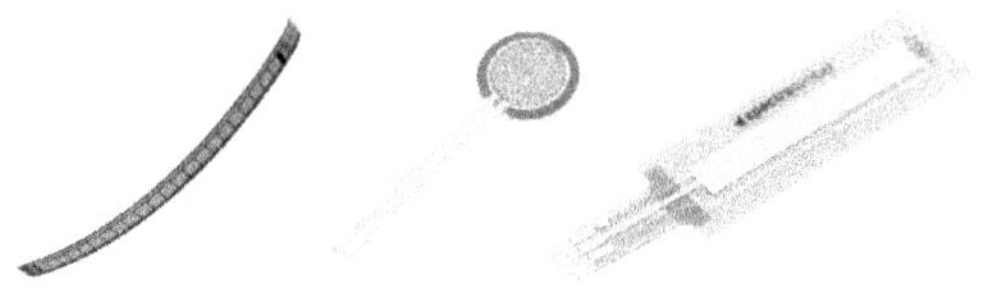

Figure 2. Common commercially available sensors – bend, pressure, and position. (images copyright Spectra Symbol and Interlink Electronics)

readily understand the inherent affordances and limitations of the sensor. The sensing structures can be designed to be clearly visible in the object where they are integrated, so the user can directly see the kinds of manipulation afforded by the object. Furthermore, the sensor's look and tactile feel can be controlled by selecting from a range of soft, pliable materials, and easily manufactured using methods we will describe in the paper.

In the next section, we describe related work. We then discuss the concept of sensing through structure, and sketch example structures. We detail the construction of several of our sensors and present applications. We conclude the paper with a discussion of future work.

RELATED WORK

While sensing through structure focuses on the topological properties of materials, sensors for most common motions – position, twist, bend, stretch, and pressure – rely on monitoring changes in the electrical properties of materials. For example, common bend, stretch, and pressure sensors are often built with a piezoresistive material; changing the length or cross-sectional area changes the resistance of the material. The off-the-shelf sensors shown in Figure 2 are built using this method. Another technique for sensing is electro-optical sensing. For example, Zimmerman [28] created an optical flex sensor that senses bending by measuring the amount of light able to pass through a flexible light guide. He placed a light source and photodiode on opposite sides of the light guide; when the guide was bent, the amount of light reaching the photodiode decreased. This technology was used in early data gloves. Measurand's ShapeTape [14] makes use of the same concept, building in multiple fiber optic sensors to measure bend and twist continuously along its length.

While these sensors work well with traditional hard devices and objects, embedding them in soft and malleable objects presents a number of difficulties. Most of today's sensors are either rigidly encapsulated in metal or hard plastic, or built on a thin plastic backing. These latter flexible sensors can bend and twist, but not shear and stretch. Hence they do not conform well to soft materials such as human skin, textiles, and foam. For example, if the bend sensor is placed at a human joint, e.g. in a data glove, it will shift and slide, interfering with natural motion. These sensors are also somewhat fragile and cannot be creased, which limits their applications and reliability. Most importantly, embedding hard sensors into soft objects alters the tactile, malleable properties of these objects, which is their key distinguishing characteristic from traditional hard devices. Our work introduces sensing solutions using a foam or silicone base, which avoids these problems.

The e-textile community has built flexible analogues of some of these sensors, using the same principles [2]. Sturdy fabric is used instead of a plastic base, and resistive foam or thread is used as the piezoresistive conductor; bend, pressure, and stretch sensors have been built this way [16]. For example, Shimojo et al. [21] created a pressure sensor grid from resistive foam and characterized its hysteresis. Our work provides a flexible and principled way to incorporate these materials.

An alternative approach to augmenting soft objects with sensing is to use external tracking, e.g. vision [6], magnetic sensing [5], or RFID [18]. Previous work has imbued silicone with structure to aid in tracking. GelForce [24] embedded markers in silicone to track its deformation using a camera-based system. Cameras also track silicone in ForceTile [12] using ID tags and PhotoelasticTouch [20] using polarization of light. While tracking generally requires less modification of the object being deformed (in particular, the object can be unpowered), it limits use of the object to specific locations. In the sensing through structure approach, all sensing is localized to the device itself, thus making it compact and portable.

Ideas of exploiting structural properties in sensor design can be found in the work of Mannsfeld et al. [13] and Papakostas [15]. In the former, the authors built an extremely sensitive pressure sensor by molding an elastomer with microstructural pyramidal holes in its surface; these holes squashed when pressed, changing capacitance. In the latter, Papakostas created a two-dimensional array of force-sensing elements on a polyester substrate with a spiral pattern cut around each element, restricting movement of the sensing elements to the perpendicular plane.

Unlike previous approaches, sensing through structure does not separate the *object* that the user deforms and the *sensors* used to measure it. Instead of adding sensing to pre-existing objects, we start by designing objects with their sensing capability in mind. In a broad sense, our approach can be described as "form equals function" [23][4], where the physical input, interactions, and device embodiment are designed in tandem, in harmony with its material construction. We present the details of this approach in the rest of the paper.

SENSING THROUGH STRUCTURE

Sensing through structure uses the physical changes in the topology of a deforming material to suggest structures for simple multi-location sensing. These atomic sensing structures make up a sensing vocabulary, to be used as building blocks when a sensor is designed.

Figure 3 gives some example structures. Diagrams *A* and *B* show bend structure configurations; *A*'s contacts trigger when bent a certain amount; *B*'s trigger as soon as they are bent. Diagram *C* contains contacts on both sides, which trigger in pairs when it is twisted, but only singly when it is bent,

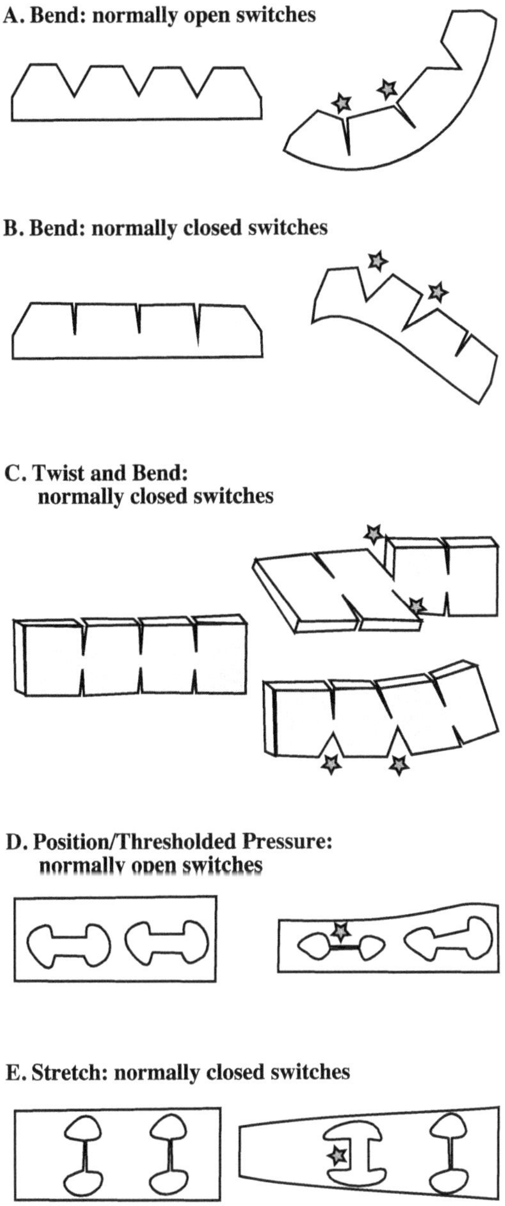

Figure 3. Examples of sensing through structure. The structure is in its default configuration in the left column. Stars are shown on the right where switch contacts are toggled when the structure is manipulated.

thus allowing us to measure both twist and bend with a single structure. Diagram *D* contains a structure for sensing pressure. As the material is compressed, the two sides of the switch meet; the width and shape of the switch allows the activation pressure to be customized. In diagram *E*, the switch is rotated to measure stretch. When the left side of the material is stretched, the left switch triggers as its contacts are pulled apart.

Other structures or combinations are possible. For example, the bend structure in *A* or B may be mirrored to measure two-directional bend, or combined with position or stretch structures.

Our approach simplifies the problem of complex multidimensional sensing, transforming it to the easier and cheaper problem of sensing a set of one-dimensional displacements. The nature of the sensors used for measuring the displacement is not essential; we can choose from a range of sensors, from simple contact switches to analogue capacitive proximity sensors, depending on the application.

The physical structure, also, is customizable to a range of applications. For example, the angle of the valleys in the bend structure should be chosen to measure an amount of bend appropriate to the particular application. Small and large angles could be alternated to trigger at two angles of bend. The shape of the cut in the pressure and stretch units should be altered to fit the dynamics of the base material; for example, we found that a double-convex cut worked best for silicone.

Finally, our structures are designed to naturally guide the user by providing clear physical affordances and constraints so that he can see and feel what can be done with the sensor.

DESIGNING SENSORS THROUGH STRUCTURE

In the following two sections, we describe the design of a bend sensor and a stretch/pressure sensor. To illustrate the generality of our approach, we build the bend sensor with bases of both silicone and foam, using fabric binary contact switches. We use a resistor network to minimize wiring. The stretch/pressure sensor we build out of silicone using analogue magnetic distance sensors whose values are transmitted over an I2C bus.

Multi-Location Bend Sensor

We built the bend sensor from the normally open bend structure in Figure 3A. We tested bases of both silicone and foam. The silicone is colorful and has a fun feel that demands to be touched and squished, and would work well in sensors that are handled directly by the user. The foam we used has easier overall compression, and thus is appropriate for applications such as stuffed-animal innards. We now describe the construction and wiring.

Construction

The silicone bend sensor was constructed from a stretchy silicone, Smooth-On Dragon Skin, with a hardness of Shore 10 and elongation break at 1000%. Stranded 32-gauge wire was connected to a copper polyester conductive fabric for the contact switches.

We laser-cut the mold layers from 4.6mm cast acrylic sheets. Figure 4 shows the molding process, with trace layers sandwiched between insulating layers.

In Step 1, the mold is set up for the outside insulating layer and the first trace layer. Trace layers create zigzag tunnels in which to place the wiring. In Step 2, these layers are poured.

In Step 3, the trace mold is removed and replaced with wiring and contact switches. We coil the wire before placing it in the tunnels so that it pushes against the tunnel walls. This friction lock anchors the wires and resistors while more

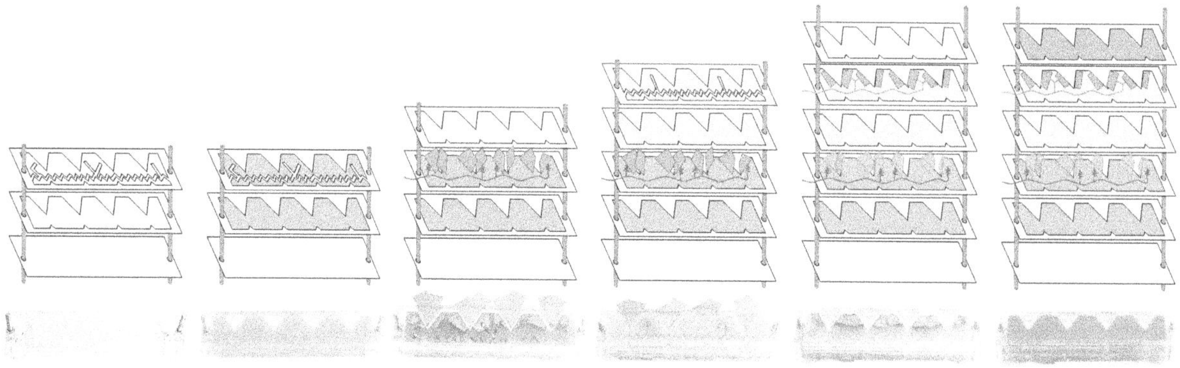

Figure 4. The silicone bend sensor was built with successive silicone pours from back to front, with alternating insulating layers and and trace layers. Wiring is shown with purple and orange lines; contact switches made from conductive fabric are orange polygons.

silicone is being poured on top, stopping the wires from floating. The traces also guide the wires into a zigzag pattern, giving them slack for bending. Wires in an early prototype without this feature promptly snapped at the solder joints.

In Step 4, an insulating layer and the second trace layer are poured. In Step 5, the contact switches are threaded through the mold and folded over on top. The unconnected half are connected to the signal tracing being laid.

Step 6 creates a top insulating layer which also anchors the contact switches in place. Opposite ends of the switches are thus embedded between layers of silicone, using the self-stick property of silicone to anchor them firmly without glues or mounting hardware. The conductive fabric we chose does not shred and is tarnish resistant, so this construction creates rugged switches that cannot peel off. Figure 5 shows the result.

An important strain-relief feature in our design are the small valleys across from the switch-containing valleys; these move the center of rotation away from the bottom of the sensor and towards the middle, in line with the wire. These valleys make the silicone easier to bend at these points, and reduce the amount the wire has to stretch when the sensor is bent backwards. Additionally, all solder joints are moved away from the centers of rotation.

The foam bend sensor was made out of a base of soft foam with a firmness of 5 psi and 25% deflection. Conductive fabric tape with conductive adhesive backing was placed along the valleys to create contact switches; conductive thread was attached to the underside of the tape and then wired through

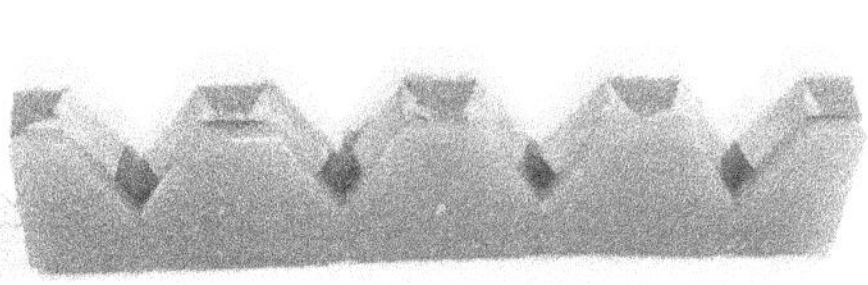

Figure 5. A completed silicone bend sensor.

Figure 6. ***Top*****, the foam sensor was built from back to front; shown is the ground plane wiring being laid on the first layer.** ***Bottom*****, the completed sensor.**

the sensor. We isolated the ground layer and the signal layer between slices of foam. The sensor is shown in Figure 6.

Electronics

The challenge in sensor construction with many points of contact is to minimize the wiring as much as possible. The naive approach (Figure 7A), connecting each switch to a single microcontroller input, does not scale. We solved the problem by using a binary-weighted resistor Digital-to-Analogue Converter (DAC) technique (Figure 7B). With this technique, only two wires come out of the sensor body. Binary-weighted DACs and a similar idea, R-2R ladders, have been around since at least the 1920s in communication systems [17]. They can be found in toys and midi keyboards.

Every switch is connected to its own resistor and acts as a single bit; the DAC combines the bits into a single analogue resistance. Each resistor is a power of two larger than the previous, and thus all combinations can be differentiated by a microcontroller reading this analogue value. We used resistor values of 470 ohms, 1K, 2.2K, and 4.7K.

Using the circuit described above, we can track the state of the switches using the following algorithm. Let the indicator variables $S_i \in \{0, 1\}$ represent the state of the N switches. Using the formula for sum of resistances in parallel, the re-

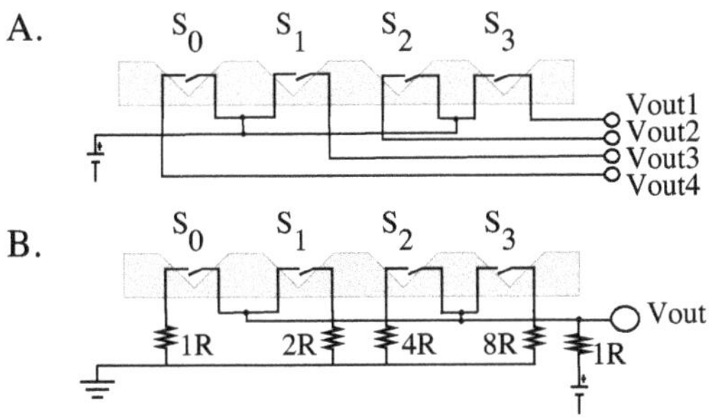

Figure 7. Two methods for wiring switches.

sistance of the sensor, R_{total}, takes the following form:

$$\frac{1}{R_{total}} = \frac{S_0}{2^0 R} + \frac{S_1}{2^1 R} + \frac{S_2}{2^2 R} + \frac{S_3}{2^3 R} + \ldots = \sum_{i=0}^{N-1} \frac{S_i}{2^i R}$$

Then the following loop would continuously sample $(S_0, S_1, \ldots, S_{N-1})$, the configuration of the sensor:

$R_{remaining} \leftarrow \frac{1}{R_{total}}$
for $i = 0$ to $N - 1$ **do**
  if $R_{remaining} \geq \frac{1}{2^i R}$ **then**
    $S_i \leftarrow 1$
    $R_{remaining} = R_{remaining} - \frac{1}{2^i R}$
  else
    $S_i \leftarrow 0$
  end if
end for

This method, however, is subject to error; small variations in resistance could result in the "$\geq$" incorrectly evaluating false, and a completely wrong answer being returned. In practice we found it safer to precalculate the 16 resistance values expected from all different combinations of switches, store these as integer values in the microcontroller's memory, and in real time find the closest.

Analogue Stretch/Pressure Sensor

The concept of sensing through structure encourages any sensing mechanism to be used to measure the deformation in a structural unit. Up until now we have been using only binary contact switches, appreciating the elegance of using a resistor DAC for the wiring. It is possible, however, to use analogue sensors. We built a prototype stretch/pressure sensor which uses magnetic distance sensors to monitor the width of four oval holes along its body.

Construction

For the silicone stretch/pressure sensor, we wired an SS49E magnetic hall sensor to each of the four ovals, and placed small rare earth magnets on the other sides. The setup with zigzag traces is shown on the right of Figure 8. Silicone was then poured over both the electronics and the magnets, encasing them completely.

The ovals allowed about 15mm of travel, a range trackable by the magnetic sensors. The sensor could thus monitor both stretch and pull, shown in Figure 9.

Figure 8. ***Left*, top and bottom views of our I2C-bus PCB. *Right*, a snapshot of the molding process with the PCB placed on the bottom layer of the analogue stretch/pressure sensor.**

Electronics

To minimize wiring, we switched to a bus-based system. We designed a PCB, shown in Figure 8, which takes four analogue inputs and transmits them on an I2C bus using a TI ADS1015 chip. The boards are designed to be chained together. The four bus wires connect to the top of the chip (left image) and come out the bottom (center image). An I2C address selector switch is located on the bottom of the board. Any analogue sensors can be connected to the connectors on the top of the board.

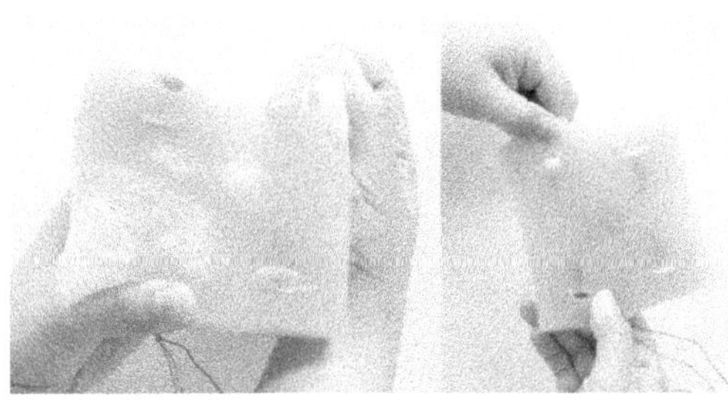

Figure 9. With analogue magnetic distance sensors, both stretch and pressure can be tracked.

APPLICATIONS

We evaluated the sensing through structure approach by building a computer game, two toys, and an interactive cellphone case. We present these designs, and discuss the potential applications of our approach in other areas.

Games

Sensing through structure can be used to design inexpensive interfaces to video games, in instances where they have the right tactile feel. Similar to the game BopIt! [9], one could combine a multitude of structures to create a highly customized user interface.

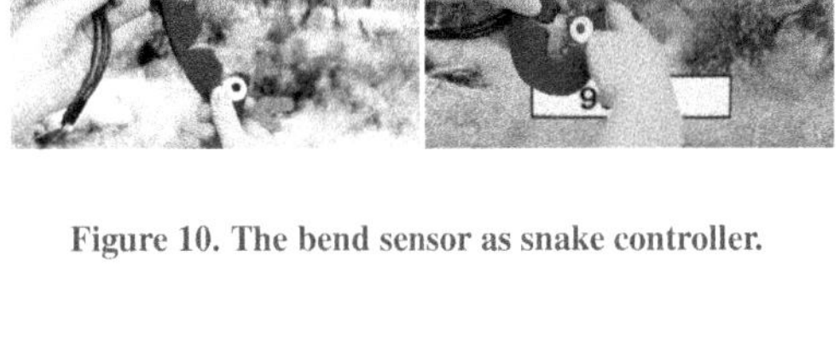

Figure 10. The bend sensor as snake controller.

As an example, we created a game based on the American folklore legend of the hoop snake. This snake would place its tongue in its mouth so it was shaped like a wagon wheel, then roll down hills chasing after its victims. In the game, moving the snake by undulating the snake sensor in an s-curve shows off our sensor's ability to recognize complex gestures using only binary sensing. The speed of undulation controls the speed of the snake onscreen. Folding the snake sensor into a hoop to roll the snake down hills demonstrates using our bend sensor as a configuration sensor. Figure 10 shows our game in action. We tried our game with both the foam and silicone bend sensor as the snake. An informal user study showed that the bend sensor was easily understood as a controller, and very entertaining.

Toys

An increasing connection is being made between toys and computers. A good example of this trend is the popular Webkinz [25], which shows how a commercial success can be created using even a nebulous connection between real and virtual toys. Research projects such as Huggable [22] and Swamped! [11], and commercial animatronics such as the Pleo [10], show how sensors can make a toy more interactive and compelling.

Figure 11. A bend-sensor rabbit earmuff.

Instrumenting dolls and stuffed animals with sensing skeletons is expensive and introduces hard elements into a soft toy. Our sensing structures, however, fit perfectly sewn into fabric doll clothes, and achieve a good price / performance point. A proof of concept is shown in Figure 11. The rabbit's earmuff contains our bend sensor, allowing the rabbit's virtual double to mimic ear poses.

We also designed a custom toy, which we call "Cat Stretch". The cat-shaped toy has embedded in it four of the normally closed stretch structures from Figure 3E, two along its body and one each along its ear and tail.

In contrast to the bend sensor, the cat stretch sensor was built from the inside out. Trace layers were poured around a central insulating layer and small slits made through the layers with a sharp knife. The contact switches were threaded through the slits and wiring laid around this core layer, as shown in Figure 12. As each outer insulating layer was poured, the cuts were continued with a sharp knife. Figure 13 shows the result. When the cat is stretched, the two sides of a given contact switch part, sending a unique resistance to the microcontroller.

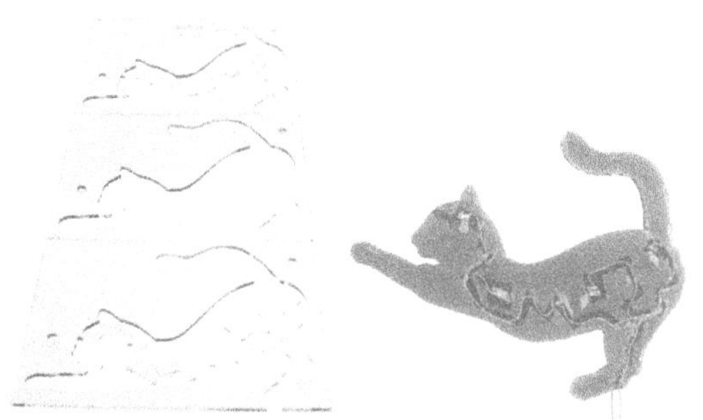

Figure 12. Middle mold layers and central core of the cat stretch sensor.

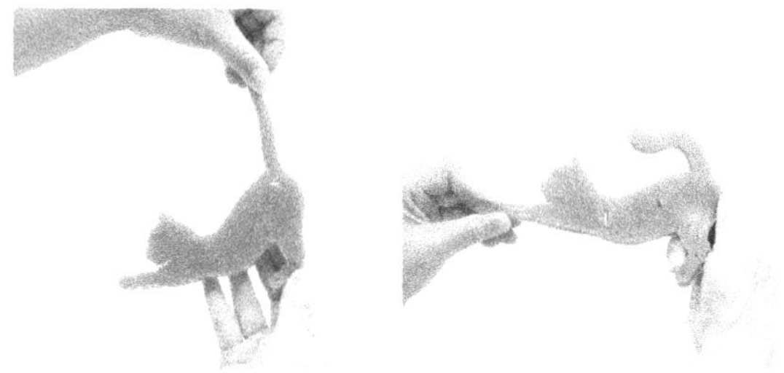

Figure 13. Cat Stretch: The cat has stretch switches around its body.

Our cat-shaped stretch sensor is a toy simple and cheap enough to be a giveaway, and could be used as a stress toy, or for computer-mediated play. Sensing through structure works well with Cat Stretch: instrumenting the silicone to get complete knowledge of the forces on it would be a difficult problem, but here a few switches are enough to roughly encode the state of the system given the affordances of cat stretching.

These two example toys, both using binary switches, are also well suited to the interactions between toys and children. Children often push toys to the extremes of their (joint) limits; cheap binary sensing is thus appropriate. Also, our sensors provide more control by having tactile, built-in limits, thus eliminating frustration from ambiguity in sensor use.

Personal Electronics Accessories

To demonstrate the "form equals function" approach of sensing through structure, we designed an iPhone® case whose physical affordances embody the intended interactions with the cellphone.

The interactive cellphone case was built out of silicone in the shape of a guinea pig, using the same methods and materials as the previous sensors. To interface with the phone, we took apart a pair of iPhone® earphones with remote, soldering wires directly to the contact pads of the remote's three buttons. These wires were then connected to the switches inside the case.

In the guinea pig case, a bend structure is located in each of the two sets of fur. The fur along the length of the phone demands to be stroked downward, as shown in Figure 14; doing so lowers the cellphone's volume. In contrast, stroking the upward-facing fur raises the phone's volume. A pressure

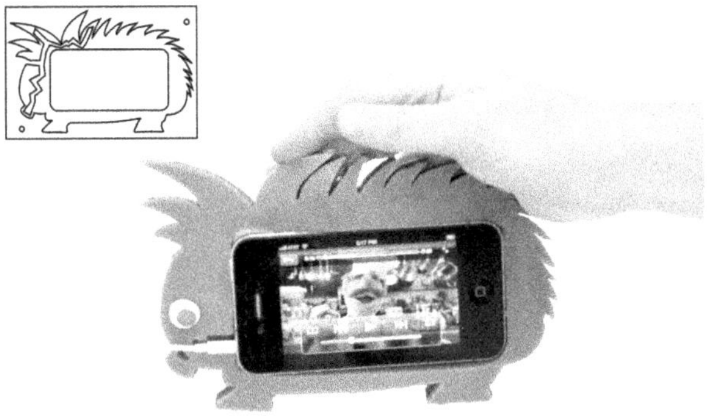

Figure 14. A user turning down the volume with the cellphone guinea pig case. The diagram of a mold slice shows the routing to the three switches.

structure is located in the guinea pig's button nose; pushing it controls play/pause.

Other Uses

Many other areas exist where sensing through structure can be effectively used. For example, sensors designed with our approach could be useful in wearable computing. Stretch and pressure formulations could measure movement of the torso. Our bend sensor nestles into the curve of a finger, and would work well in a data glove.

Computer modeling presents another possible application. An analogue version of the bend sensor could work well for curve editing. Alternatively, a squishable touchscreen made out of the stretch / pressure sensor could be used for 3D surface modeling. Because our sensors are cheap and quick to home-manufacture, custom versions could be created for control of individual animation riggings.

Our sensors have also generated interest from an autism therapist. She was excited by their potential ability to collect child play data while being non-threateningly soft and colorful. Play is used for both assessment and intervention in autism [27], but is hard to analyze [1]. Recent work by Westeyn et al. [26] instrumented several plastic toys with sensors, but found the form factors of the toys too general to elicit specific actions. Our sensors' distinctive affordances could encourage a child into a particular action. The bend sensor could test pose mimicry; the stretch sensor, strength. We hope to explore work in this area in the near future.

DISCUSSION

People found our sensors to be engaging and liked their softness. The silicone bend sensor was particularly successful – the colors drew the eye, and everyone who picked it up spent a minute or two just bending it into different configurations, testing its limits and enjoying its tactile sensation.

In general, our game controllers, toys, and cellphone case were easily understandable. The snake controller proved amusing and its gestures masterable. The cat toy looked fun, but its interactions were not as easily grasped by people; designing the outer insulating layer to reveal more of the switch contacts would make its affordances more apparent. People enjoyed the natural motion of stroking the interactive cellphone case. At its current scale the case could be part of a speaker stand; with miniaturization and covered magnetic switches it could be a practical cellphone case.

The exposed contacts in our sensors beg the question of whether our sensors will remain rugged over time. The fabric contacts we used are tarnish resistant, and the silicone durable. Accumulated dirt on the contacts, however, would increase the resistance of the material, breaking the resistor DAC calculations. A calibration routine where the user closes (or opens) each switch individually would give the computer enough data to recalculate the resistances. If the sensor is being used in an application which expects certain configurations, changes in resistance could be tracked over time transparently to the user. As long as the contacts degrade somewhat uniformly, maintaining an order of magnitude difference in resistance, the sensor will continue to work. Alternatively, the contacts could be protected by encasing the sensor in an outer layer of foam or stretchy fabric, possibly filling the holes in the structural units with a piezoresistive foam.

CONCLUSION

We have presented sensing through structure, an approach that uses the topological, rather than electrical, properties of objects and materials to design and construct sensing solutions for measuring motion. The approach is general: arbitrary combinations of sensing units can be constructed using our silicone method, and either analogue or binary measurements can be made. We have used only soft materials and low-cost manufacturing methods, which can be replicated by anyone interested in creating custom sensing interfaces.

Our sensors enable interactions ranging from dynamic, time-based gestures, to static poses and configurations. We have shown both types of input in the hoop snake game, and static poses in the toy proofs of concept. Dynamic gestures can be more complex with multi-location sensing. Onscreen visualizations can tween between configurations, covering for the lack of more expensive continuous sensing. In the static case, the conformability of the sensor lets the user hold it in a pose with a comfortable amount of tension. The sensor can also be designed, and the contacts placed, to capture poses with maximum robustness and efficiency.

Our approach emphasizes building multi-location sensors with discrete inputs. This approach works well for toys and games, where the physicality of the device can be more important than its accuracy. In our work, as switch contacts are made, the sensor provides tactile feedback, making gesturing more efficient. A traditional bend sensor, for example, reveals little about its limits.

In the future we would like to explore new applications of our sensors. We are particularly excited about applying our results to child therapy, customizing our sensors to children's needs. We would also like to exploit a particular facet of sensing through structure in games and toys: its transparency. Gross [8] argues against the increasing trend of technology-enhanced children's toys being "black boxes" whose interior functioning is hidden from the user. Our sensors, when made with clear silicone, completely reveal their inner workings. With unambiguous use and understandable construction, they present a viable alternative to the current trend.

REFERENCES

1. G. Baranek, C. Barnett, E. Adams, N. Wolcott, and E. Crais. Object play in infants with autism: methodological issues in retrospective video analysis. *American Journal of Occupational Therapy*, 1:20–30, 2005.
2. L. Buechley. A construction kit for electronic textiles. In *International Symposium on Wearable Computers*. IEEE, 2006.
3. Chumby Industries. www.chumby.com, 2010.
4. M. Coelho, I. Poupyrev, S. Sadi, R. Vertegaal, J. Berzowska, L. Buechley, P. Maes, and N. Oxman. Programming reality: from transitive materials to organic user interfaces. In *Conference on Human Factors in Computing Systems Extended Abstracts*, pages 4759–4762. ACM, 2009.
5. A. T. Corporation. www.ascension-tech.com, 2010.
6. M. Dontcheva, G. Yngve, and Z. Popovic. Layered acting for character animation. *ACM Transactions on Graphics*, 22(3), 2003.
7. M. Furukawa, Y. Uema, M. Sugimoto, and M. Inami. Fur interface with bristling effect induced by vibration. In *Augmented Human International Conference*, pages 1–6. ACM, 2010.
8. M. Gross and M. Eisenberg. Why toys shouldn't work "like magic": Children's technology and the values of construction and control. In *International Workshop on Digital Game and Intelligent Toy Enhanced Learning*, pages 25–32. IEEE, 2007.
9. Hasbro BopIt! www.playbopit.com, 2010.
10. Innvo Labs. www.pleoworld.com, 2010.
11. M. Johnson, A. Wilson, B. Blumberg, C. Kline, and A. Bobick. Sympathetic interfaces: Using a plush toy to direct synthetic characters. In *Conference on Human Factors in Computing Systems*. ACM, 1999.
12. Y. Kakehi, K. Jo, K. Sato, K. Minamizawa, H. Nii, N. Kawakami, T. Naemura, and S. Tachi. Forcetile: tabletop tangible interface with vision-based force distribution sensing. In *SIGGRAPH Emerging Tech Demos*. ACM, 2008.
13. S. Mannsfeld, B. Tee, R. Stoltenberg, C. Chen, S. Barman, B. Muir, A. Sokolov, C. Reese, and Z. Bao. Highly sensitive flexible pressure sensors with microstructured rubber dielectric layers. *Nature Materials*, 9:859–864, 2010.
14. Measurand. www.measurand.com, 2010.
15. T. V. Papakostas. Tactile sensor: Stretching the limits. In *International Conference on Intelligent Environments*, pages 472–476, 2007.
16. H. Perner-Wilson and L. Buechley. Making textile sensors from scratch. In *Conference on Tangible, Embedded, and Embodied Interaction*, pages 349–352. ACM, 2010.
17. P. M. Rainey, 1926. US Patent 1608527.
18. R. Raskar, P. Beardsley, J. van Baar, Y. Wang, P. Dietz, J. Lee, D. Leigh, and T. Willwacher. RFIG lamps: interacting with a self-describing world via photosensing wireless tags and projectors. *Transactions on Graphics*, pages 406–415, 2004.
19. M. Reed. Prototyping digital clay as an active material. In *International Conference on Tangible and Embedded Interaction*, pages 339–342. ACM, 2009.
20. T. Sato, H. Mamiya, H. Koike, and K. Fukuchi. Photoelastictouch: transparent rubbery tangible interface using an LCD and photoelasticity. In *Symposium on User Interface Science and Technology*, pages 43–50. ACM, 2009.
21. M. Shimojo, A. Namiki, M. Ishikawa, R. Makino, and K. Mabuchi. A tactile sensor sheet using pressure conductive rubber with electrical-wires stitched method. *Sensors Journal*, 4(5):589–596, 2004.
22. W. Stiehl, J. Lieberman, C. Breazeal, L. Basel, L. Lalla, and M. Wolf. Design of a therapeutic robotic companion for relational, affective touch. In *International Workshop on Robots and Human Interactive Communication*, pages 408–415. IEEE, 2005.
23. R. Vertegaal and I. Poupyrev. Organic user interfaces. *Communications of the ACM*, 51(6):26–30, 2008.
24. K. Vlack, T. Mizota, N. Kawakami, K. Kamiyama, H. Kajimoto, and S. Tachi. Gelforce: a vision-based traction field computer interface. In *Conference on Human Factors in Computing Systems*, pages 1154–1155. ACM, 2005.
25. webkinz. www.webkinz.com, 2010.
26. T. Westeyn, J. Kientz, T. Starner, and G. Abowd. Designing toys with automatic play characterization for supporting the assessment of a child's development. In *International Conference on Interaction Design and Children*, pages 89–92. ACM, 2008.
27. S. Wulff. The symbolic and object play of children with autism: A review. *Journal of Autism and Developmental Disorders*, 15(2), 1985.
28. T. Zimmerman, 1982. US Patent 4542291.

Grasp Sensing for Human-Computer Interaction

Raphael Wimmer
University of Munich
Amalienstr. 17, 80333 Munich, Germany
raphael.wimmer@ifi.lmu.de

ABSTRACT

The way we grasp an object depends on several factors, e.g. the intended goal or the hand's anatomy. Therefore, a grasp can convey meaningful information about its context. Inferring these factors from a grasp allows us to enhance interaction with grasp-sensitive objects. This paper highlights an grasp as an important source of meaningful context for human-computer interaction and gives an overview of prior work from other disciplines. This paper offers a basis and framework for further research and discussion by proposing a descriptive model of meaning in grasps The GRASP model combines five factors that determine how an object is grasped: goal, relationship between user and object, anatomy, setting, and properties of the object. The model is validated both from an epistemological perspective and by applying it to scenarios from related work.

ACM Classification Keywords

H.5.2 Information Interfaces and Presentation: User Interfaces;
H.1.2 User/Machine Systems: Human factors

General Terms

Human Factors, Theory

Author Keywords

grasp recognition, tangible user interface, grasp, meaning

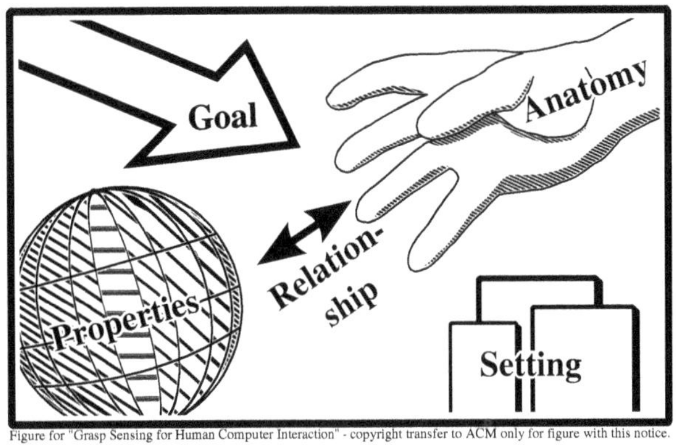

Figure 1. The way we grasp an object conveys meaningful information. Several factors determine a grasp. Our GRASP model groups them into five general factors: Goal of the grasp, Relationship between user and object (e.g. knowing that an object is very expensive), Anatomy of the user (including neuropsychological processes), Setting (i.e. environment in which the grasp takes place), and Properties of the object. Factors were chosen to represent orthogonal types of meaning

INTRODUCTION

During evolution, humans gained the unique ability to grasp tools and apply them skillfully. Nowadays, a multitude of versatile or specialized tools extend our manual abilities. Oftentimes, Human-Computer Interaction (HCI) also relies on our ability to grasp objects - be it a computer mouse, a tangible user interface, or a mobile phone. Given that we spend a reasonable amount of time grasping objects while using them, it seems straightforward to use the contact between device and hand for transmitting information to the user. *Haptic feedback* sends short cues to users via actuators that stimulate tactile receptors in the skin. Such cues and status information can also be represented as changes in weight distribution or shape [9, 10]. However, a grasp actually allows bi-directional data transfer. The way we grasp an object also conveys information about us, our goals, and other aspects. Inferring these aspects from the grasp can allow us to enhance interaction with graspable user interfaces. The way we grasp an object is determined in part by what we want to do with it. Knowing the intended goal of a grasp, a grasp-sensitive object could support this goal. For example, a mobile phone would infer from your grasp that you want to call someone - and would present the call list. A bottle might know that you want to drink from it, and open itself - because you grasped it near its center of gravity. And a power drill might refuse to power on because you are not holding it safely enough. With each grasp we convey information - and given that we grasp objects all the day, this is a lot of information we produce. Currently, almost all of this information is ignored, however. The aim of this paper is to raise awareness to grasping as an important source of meaningful context for human-computer interaction, give an overview of existing work from other disciplines, and provide a basis for further research by proposing a descriptive model of meaning in grasps (see Figure 1).

This paper is structured as follows: In the next section I give an overview of related work from robotics, medicine and neuropsychology. Then I discuss technical foundations of grasp sensing, presenting a three-stage process for capturing, identifying, and interpreting grasps. Afterwards, I present a descriptive model of the meaning of grasps and discuss its validity, applications, and limitations.

RELATED WORK

Human's ability to purposefully grasp arbitrary objects has been subject of intensive research in different disciplines. The biomechanical properties of the human hand are subject of medical research [20]. In neuropsychology, researchers investigate how grasps are planned and controlled [6]. In robotics, researchers investigate how robotic hands may reliably grasp arbitrary objects [25]. MacKenzie and Iberall [17] give a comprehensive but slightly dated overview of research in these fields.

Definitions

In this paper, a *grasp* is defined as a "firm hold or grip" [1]. Accordingly, *grasping* means performing a grasp.
Stable grasps can be divided into two different types [21]:
Force closure - whereby the object is held by opposing fingers exerting pressure against the object's surface.
Form closure - whereby the object is enclosed by the hand so that it cannot move even if no force is exerted by the fingers. Often the terms grasping and prehension are used interchangeably [17]. For others, prehension is the coordinated act of reaching for an object and grasping it [29]. Kang and Ikeuchi state that a grasping task is composed of pre-grasp phase, static grasp phase, and manipulation phase [13].

Classifications of Grasps

Several classifications of grasps have been proposed over time. Schlesinger [24] classified grasps based on the shapes of objects they were applied to. Napier [20] proposed a simple classification of grasps into power grips, which generally involve the palm, and precision grips, which only employ fingers and thumb. Cutkosky and Wright [7] use a tree hierarchy for classifying grasps, beginning with Napier's power and precision grasps. Kang and Ikeuchi [13] recognized that the aforementioned models lack a formal description of the grasps which makes them unsuitable for automated grasp recognition. They proposed the *contact web*, as a formal classification of grasps that is based on contact points between object and fingers. Feix at al. condensed 147 grasp descriptions found in a review of 17 publications into 33 unique grasps [8]. These were classified based on involved fingers, Napier's distinction, opposition type, and thumb position.

MEANING IN A GRASP

Existing classifications focus on defining groups of visually or functionally distinctive grasps. However, a multitude of factors contribute to a grasp which are not considered in these classifications.
Iberall and MacKenzie offer an abstract model of grasping [12, 17]. They describe grasping as a black box with a goal and an object as inputs and a specific grasp as output. Several additional constraints are given that affect the outcome, like the placement and orientation of the object. However, MacKenzie and Iberall do not explain the formal difference between inputs and constraints. These constraints are grouped by MacKenzie and Iberall [17] as follows:

- **High Level:** Social/Cultural, Motivational, Informational, Functional
- **Physical:** Object Properties, Biomechanical/Mechanical
- **Sensorimotor:** Neural, Perceptual, Anatomical/Physiological, Evolutionary/Developmental

However, for HCI the question is not how a grasp should look like for a certain combination of object and goal (humans are quite good at figuring it out themselves). Instead it would be useful to know what a grasp actually *means*. That is, what can a grasp tell us about the context it is happening in, and what can we do with this context intformation. For a certain grasp - which we can capture by different means - we want to know which factors contributed to it.

GRASP SENSING

This section explains why it is acceptable and helpful to only capture stable grasps, and defines three interpretative steps for grasp-sensing systems: capturing the grasp, identifying it, and interpreting it (Figure 2).

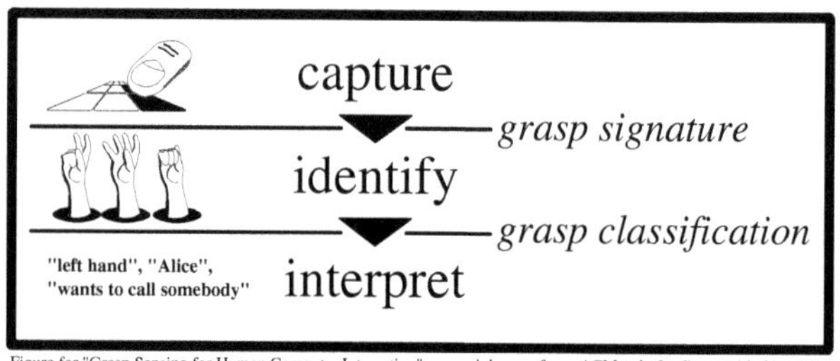

Figure 2. General workflow for grasp sensing: sensors capture a grasp signature which gets mapped to a specific group of grasps. Finally, interpreting the grasp generates meaningful context.

An important simplification

Grasping is a complex action. Depending on the point of view it also includes initial reaching movements and exploratory adjustments until we find a stable grasp. Sometimes, we move through a number of different grasps, even involving different hands - e.g. when picking up an object and putting it somewhere else. Complex hand movements are needed to transform one stable grasp into another. However, in the following I will use the term *grasp* to refer only to single, stable, static grasps, performed by a human hand. This has a formal and a technical reason:

- a series of grasps can be broken up into a number of stable grasps. The transitional hand movements between those stable grasps primarily depend on the previous and next grasp. Therefore, these transitions add only very little information about the meaning of a grasp [1]. Excluding those

[1] An exception would be a slippery object that is held in a form-closure grasp. The (stable) grasp does not need to adress the slippery surface. However, any transitional hand movement would need to take this into account.

transitions from our analysis removes much complexity while forfeiting only little information.

- the aforementioned complexity of transitional movements makes them hard to interpret using heuristics or machine-learning. Concentrating on stable grasps makes it much easier to extract meaningful patterns.

Step 1: Capturing Grasps

Grasps can be captured by either capturing the grasping hand or by equipping the object with a grasp-sensitive surface. Both approaches have unique advantages and disadvantages. For everyday use, objects with grasp-sensitive surfaces are probably more convenient and socially acceptable, however.

Instrumenting the User

For tracking fingers and hand, often an optical or magnetical tracking system is used. A marker or receiver needs to be attached to each finger. This method allows for a high-resolution capture of hand pose and position. It does not provide any information about contact forces between finger and object. Therefore it can not detect whether a finger is touching the object or not. Such tracking systems need to instrument the user. Additionally, capturing grasps works only within the tracking infrastructure. Therefore such systems are of limited use for real-world applications. However, they are very flexible and therefore well suited for laboratory studies. External tracking systems also provide a high-resolution ground truth for other technologies.

Instead of using markers for defining finger joints, some approaches use computer vision techniques for an image of the hand pose to a grasp [31]. Another approach that does not require a tracking infrastructure are data gloves. These are thin gloves - often with a mesh surface on the palmar side - that are equipped with strain sensors. These sensors allow capturing each finger joint's angle. From these, a hand pose can be derived [11]. These gloves are less obtrusive than tracking markers. However, they limit tactile perception. Force-sensing with gloves is difficult, as force sensors attached to the fingertips obviously result in greatly reduced tactile perception. An alternative way of determining grasp forces is to capture images of the finger nail and interpret changes in blood flow that can be observed there [19].

As the fingers are controlled by muscles in the forearm, some information about the hand pose can also be gained from measuring changes in these muscles or the wrist shape [22]. Another option is not to capture grasps but only detect which object is held. This can be done by attaching RFID tags to all objects and strapping an RFID reader to the user's wrist [4]. This method does not provide any information about the actual grasp, however.

Instrumenting the users allows for easily capturing grasps for a multitude of object shapes. The objects need not be modified. However, putting markers on hands would severly impede everyday manual tasks. Additionally, in most applications the object itself shall react to a grasp. Therefore, the grasp information would first need to be transferred to the object - either wirelessly or by electrical coupling [34]. This would require a standardized communications protocol for grasp information.

Grasp-sensitive Surfaces

Grasp information can also be captured by the grasped object itself. To this end, the object needs to be equipped with a *grasp-sensitive surface* that can capture the contact area between object and hand. Grasp-sensitive surfaces require more engineering effort than external tracking solutions and usually do not offer identification of single fingers or digits. Implementing a grasp-sensitive surface is more difficult than implementing a touch-screen for two reasons:

Shape Sensing. Instead of single or multiple touch points, a grasp-sensitive surfaces should capture multiple complex shapes and possibly additional information like pressure. Therefore, common commercial touchscreen technologies like (analog) resistive[16] or self-capacitance [3] touch sensing cannot be used. Digital resistive [23] or mutual-capacitance technologies are better suited for capturing contact areas shapes. Additionally, the driver software needs to be able to represent complex shapes.

Sensor Shape. The sensing surface is usually non-planar and continuously wrapped around the whole object. While it is possible to embed only a few sensors at strategic positions within the surface[5, 33], often large parts of the surface shall be made grasp-sensitive. This requires flexible or very small sensors. Additionally, a normal cartesian coordinate system - as used in displays and touch input - may not correctly represent the sensing surface. Possible alternatives are spherical coordinate systems[15] or a relative mapping[32].

In research prototypes a multitude of sensor technologies are used for making surfaces grasp-sensitive. Often researchers build their own capacitive sensors [14, 27, 33]. Other prototypes use resistive pressure sensors [15, 30], impendance sensors [18] or optical sensors [5, 32]. A comparison of the inherent properties of the different types of sensors can be found in [32].

Capturing a grasp results in a *grasp signature*, a digital representation of contact points or digit positions.

Step 2: Identifying Grasps

Once a grasp signature has been captured, the system needs to derive the grasp that caused this signature [13]. This is commonly done by mapping the signature to a certain category of grasps, either using heuristics or machine learning. The classification algorithm to be used depends both on the format of the sensor data and the type of information that is needed in the interpretation stage. Commonly used classifieres include support vector machines [14, 26], Bayesian classifiers [14, 26], and Hidden-Markov-Models [27]. Grasp categories can be defined formally, using e.g. one of the models described above. More often, grasp categories are defined by example. To this end, a machine-learning classifier is trained with grasp signatures of grasps the developer deems similar. Without a set of formally defined grasps, however, it is not possible to compare different classifiers and sensing technologies. In several cases, grasps with completely different signatures should actually be interpreted as the same grasp. For example, when grasping a uniform sphere, the grasp signature greatly depends on the rotation of the sphere. In these cases, an appropri-

ate mapping needs to be found that ignores certain features of a grasp. Wimmer et al. [33] recognize different types of left-handed and right-handed grasps using slightly modified heuristics for both. Kry et al. [15] use spherical harmonics for rotation-invariant grasp classifications.
Classifying a grasp signature results in a *grasp classification* - for example a list of grasps that might have generated the grasp signature.

Step 3: Interpreting Grasps

The final step in graps sensing is to determine what a captured and classified grasp actually means. What is to be considered meaningful depends on the application. For authentication purposes [30], it is relevant whether the grasp belongs to a certain category - whereby different categories represent different users. When using grasps to switch an object between different modes [27], the mapping from a certain grasp category to a mode provides meaning. However, existing grasp-sensitive systems capture only one meaningful aspect of a grasp (see below), ignoring the other aspects. While such systems attribute a certain meaning to a grasp, the actual meaning of a grasp is ultimately defined by the user. This leads to unexpected behavior if the system attributes a meaning to a grasp that the user did not intend. For example, a grasp-sensitive mobile phone might interpret a certain grasp as the intention to switch to camera mode [14]. However, the user might just hold the phone this way for a variety of other reasons - and would be annoyed if the phone suddenly changed into a different mode.

Insofar it seems advisable to try to capture as much information about the meaning of a grasp as possible. In the following section I look at meaningful factors that influence which grasp is chosen.

GRASP - A MODEL OF MEANING IN GRASPS

As stated above, a model of meaning within a grasp is needed. The model I present here is based on the model by MacKenzie and Iberall that is described in the second section. The new model considers the constraints and inputs they described and re-organizes them into *meaningful* factors. An important simplification is abstracting the user, hiding much of the neuropsychological and anatomical complexity. This probably does not remove meaningful information as most statements we might be able to make about such sub-factors will not help us in improving the user interface. Being aware of this abstraction allows us to replace it with a more fine-grained representation, if needed.

In the following I present GRASP, a model of human grasping that describes five meaningful factors. These factors all influence which grasp a user applies, and each of them represents a different group of meaningful information. Figure 3 illustrates these factors. All factors are independent of each other. The validity of this model is discussed in the next section.

Goal

A very important factor determining how to grasp a given object is the goal that is to be achieved by the grasp. Goals are all factors that cause a grasp to be initiated. Goals can be divided into sub-goals. As goals *are* essentially meaning, they are discussed here in more detail than the other factors. I propose grouping goals by two dimensions: *implicit* vs. *explicit* grasps and *primary* vs. *supportive grasps.* Table 1 shows examples for each combination of implicit/explicit and primary/supportive grasps.

	implicit	explicit
primary	user picks up mobile phone	user holds phone horizontally to invoke photo mode
supportive	user holds phone while typing on touchscreen with other hand	user holds phone, scrolling a map with the other hand, zooming by squeezing the phone

Table 1. Examples illustrating the distinction between implicit and explicit grasp interaction, respectively primary and supportive grasps.

Usually, a grasp is implicit, meaning that its goal is to manipulate an object. Implicit grasps are similar for grasp-sensitive and non-grasp-sensitive objects. Explicit grasps are conducted primarily in order to trigger a certain effect in a grasp-sensitive object. For example, a user might authenticate himself to the device using a certain grasp, or switch the mode of an object by holding it in a certain way. Likewise, there is a difference in the user's intention for primary and supportive grasps. A primary grasp is a grasp that is executed with the intention to manipulate the grasped object. For example, a primary grasp is used for moving a computer mouse. A supportive grasp serves to fixate or position an object in order to interact with it using e.g. the other hand or fingers that are not involved in grasping. For example, holding a mobile phone while typing a short message is a supportive grasp. These distinctions are not random but are needed to judge the amount of meaning gained from a grasp. An explicit grasp always conveys information about the user's intention. It can and should always be seen as meaningful. The user expects a reaction. An implicit grasp may convey some information about the user's intention. However, this intention is not necessarily aimed at interacting with the object. A user might just want to put away an object and would be annoyed if it reacts to the grasp. Therefore, determining whether a grasp is implicit or explicit is necessary for interpreting the grasp's meaning. Likewise, a supportive grasp conveys less meaning than a primary grasp as the main focus of the interaction lies not on the grasp but on the action that is supported by it. Additionally, a supportive grasp is restricted by the requirements of the main interaction and usually can not be modified as easily as a primary grasp. One might use this distinction to assign different meanings to a grasp. For example, when holding a mobile phone to the ear (primary grasp), different grasps can launch actions. When holding the phone while interacting with its touchscreen using the other hand, different supportive grasps might only switch between modes or adjust viewport properties.

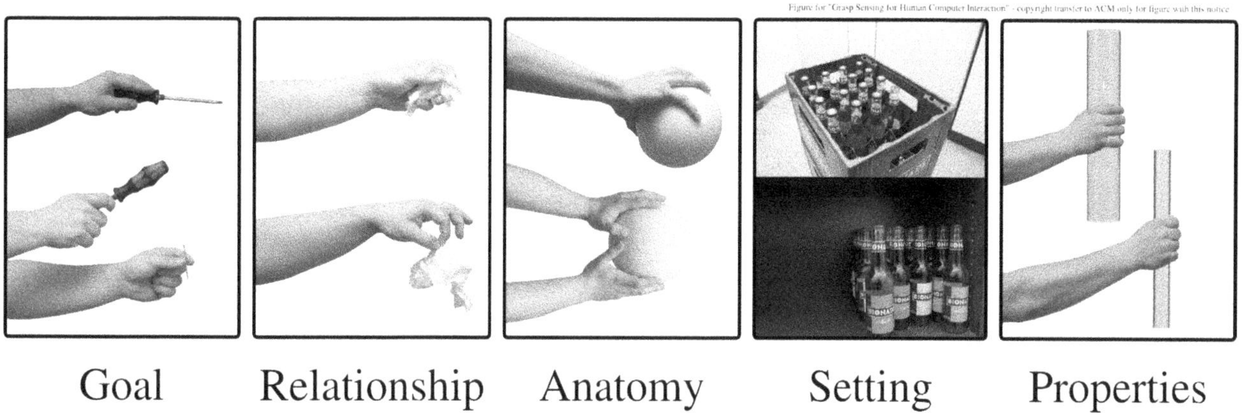

Figure 3. Examples for each of the meaningful factors that contribute to a grasp. A user might hold a screwdriver differently, depending on the *Goal* he wants to achieve with it. The mental *Relationship* to an object determines how we grasp it. In the illustrated case, a paper towel that belongs to oneself is held differently than one found on the floor. Depending on our *Anatomy* we need to apply different grasps to achieve the same effect. Due to different *Settings*, a bottle in a shelf has to be grasped differently than a bottle in a crate. The *Properties* of an object, for example its size, have a major influence on the grasp to be used.

Relationship

Feelings like disgust, fear, or anger can also influence the way we grasp. *Relationship* includes all non-physical factors that apply to a combination of user and object. The relationship between user and object can be different for every user-object combination. For example, many people seem to find a used paper towel disgusting. They would only pick it up with a pinching grasp, trying to avoid contact with anything attached to it. However, if the used paper towel belongs to oneself, one might just pick it up like any arbitrary piece of paper. Unlike anatomical properties, the relationship can also change over time, like when someone overcomes a fear of spiders and is able to touch one. How a feeling changes a grasp is also determined by the knowledge about an object. An angry person might unconsciously grasp the steering wheel more tightly but would not do the same with an egg. These effects are not solely properties of the grasping person or the object but depend on the combination of grasping person and grasped object. *Relationship* probably has little impact on most grasps. However, this factor has not been explored in detail so far.

Anatomy

Not every hand grasps the same way. Anatomy includes all factors that are inherent to the grasping person's body. Obviously, differences in palm size, finger length, or finger count result in slightly different grasps. Additionally, differences in sensorimotor control of grasps also causes different grasps. Differences in people's grasps might be used for automatically identifying the person grasping an object. A power tool might also detect insufficient grasp forces for a stable grasp and warn users that they have to hold it more tightly.

Setting

The environment within which a grasp takes place also affects its outcome. Setting includes all factors that pertain to the environment in which a grasp takes place, i.e. all physical factors that are independent of user and object. For example, the grasp used for pulling a bottle out of a crate differs from the one used for picking the bottle from a shelf. Additional environmental factors might include lighting conditions, space constraints, or temperature.

Properties

The properties of the object to be grasped naturally have a huge influence on the grasp to be used. Properties are all factors that are intrinsic to the object. This includes shape, size, surface texture, weight and weight distribution, or surface temperature.

VERIFYING GRASP

This section explains why GRASP is indeed a model, and that it fulfils formal requirements of a model. Finally, several examples highlight how GRASP can be applied.

Formal Validity

There are a variety of views what a model actually is. Bailer-Jones offers the definition[2]: "A model is an interpretative description of a phenomenon that facilitates access to that phenomenon.". GRASP is a model according to this definition as it describes a certain aspect (the meaning) of a phenomenon (a grasp). However, what are the criteria for a good model? I have chosen Vaandrager's definition of a good model [28]. While it pertains to models in computer system analysis, it is a concrete checklist that with plausible requirements. Vaandrager lists seven properties of a good model but notes that some of these contradict each other sometimes. These properties have been rephrased in the following to keep them succinct.

According to Vaandrager, a good model should:

...have a clearly defined object of modeling.
GRASP pertains to static human grasps.

...have a clearly specified purpose.
GRASP defines meaningful factors contributing to a grasp

...clearly show the links between model and empirical world.
each factor is clearly tied either to a clear concept (Goal, Relationship) or a physical object (Anatomy, Setting, Properties)

...be truthful, i.e. correctly represent relevant properties of the object of modelling.
As a model is a simplification of a complex matter, there is not only one correct model. Additionally, a model inherently oversimplifies certain aspects of a phenomenon. Therefore, a model can not be completely truthful (as acknowledged by Vaandrager). Additionally, meaning is a property that is attributed to a phenomen by humans. Therefore it is hard to tell if our distinction of meaningful factors in a grasp is correct. However, we can look at the meaning other researchers attribute to a grasp and see whether it matches to the factors we defined:

- Veldhuis et al.[30] solely try to derive the Anatomy of a user from a grasp.
- Taylor and Bove[27] solely try to derive an explicit Goal from a grasp.
- Kim et al.[14] solely try to derive an explicit Goal from a grasp.
- Wimmer and Boring[33] solely try to derive an implicit Goal from a grasp. In the two cases without a grasp, a Setting is guessed from the sensor data.
- SpherUID - a yet unpublished project - tries to determine the user's position in relation to the object (Setting) from a grasp.
- Kry et al.[15] solely tries to derive an explicit Goal from the grasp.

Therefore our model seems to correctly identify at least Goal, Anatomy, and Setting as meaningful factors of a grasp. I do not know of any application deriving Relationship or Properties from a grasp, however.

...be as simple as possible - but not too simple.
For GRASP this would mean that none of factors can be omitted. Otherwise, the model could be simplified. That is, for each factor at least one situation exists where the grasp is primarily determined by the factor. Examples of such situations are given in the descriptions of the factors. The requirement also indicates that none of the factors may be partially covered by another (i.e. they should be orthogonal). Otherwise the model would need to be more granular and therefore more complex. A *goal* can be defined without knowing any of the other factors. Therefore it may not contain sub-factors also found in the other factors. *Relationship* explicitly covers sub-factors that are independent of the user's and the object's physical properties. The Relationship also only pertains to a certain user-object combination and is therefore independent of goal and setting. *Anatomy*, *setting* and *properties* pertain to inherent properties of user, environment, and object. Each of them is a clearly defined physical object. Thus, they share no common sub-factors with each other or the other factors.

...be extensible and reusable.
GRASP is intended as a working draft. Therefore, it is also intended to be extended. For example, GRASP could be used as a basis for a predictive model. I discuss this idea in the Future Work section.

...allow interoperability with related models.
GRASP shares the the concepts of Goal and Properties with other models. Anatomy combines multiple factors from other models. Setting - while not explicitly named in the other models - seems to be compatible to them. Relationship is a newly introduced factor. It is not yet completely clear how it relates to other models.

Overall, using above criteria, GRASP seems to be a useful and robust model of meaning in grasps.

Practical Applications

In the following, the GRASP model is exemplarily applied to two different grasp-sensitive applications which have been proposed in related work. The goal is to identify which issues need to be considered when actually implementing such applications

Both Taylor and Bove [27] and Kim et al [14] propose to use grasp recognition for mode switching. For example, a mobile phone might switch between camera mode (two-handed grasp) and short-message typing mode (one-handed, thumb on keypad), depending on the way it is being held. The GRASP model can be used to highlight which factors of a grasp were investigated in the prototype, and which importance these factors have in real-life scenarios:
Goal: recognized: switch mode (implicit, might become explicit with regular use)
Relationship: ignored, in real-life scenarios probably mostly constant, as a mobile phone is a personal device
Anatomy: varied, in real-life scenarios probably *mostly* constant, as a mobile phone is a personal device
Setting: assumed constant (lab study), in real-life scenarios setting changes constantly
Properties: assumed constant, prototype does not change properties

GRASP also allows a structured analysis of the design space, revealing a number of challenges faced when implementing mode-switching functionality for mobile phones:

- Users might get accustomed to the mode-switching behavior. It should be checked - e.g. with a long-term study - whether this affects their use. Persons using such a phone for the first time might get irritated.
- The phone should achieve good grasp recognition accuracy for a single user but should not completely fail if another person uses it (both systems were trained using grasps from multiple persons).
- It should be tested how different settings affect recognition performance.
- It should be tested how well the system performs if the phone's weight distribution or shape change [10, 9].

Veldhuis et al [30] present a a prototype of a grasp-sensitive gun. It recognizes its user based on the pressure pattern of the grasp. Only authorized users shall be able to use the gun. Like before, GRASP can be used to investigate which meaningful factors of a grasp are considered by this prototype:
Goal: assumed constant, defined as 'fire gun" (implicit)), in real-life scenarios probably mostly constant
Relationship: ignored, in real-life scenarios probably mostly constant, as a gun is a personal device
Anatomy: recognized
Setting: controlled (*lab study*), will vary greatly in real-life scenarios
Properties: constant, *prototype does not change properties*

Similarly, a structured analysis of the design space reveals a number of challenges:

- Users might have different goals when grasping the gun, e.g. cleaning it. The system should not treat this as an unauthorized attempt to use the gun.
- A gun may be used in various different settings, e.g. while running, or in tight spaces. The system needs to correctly identify authorized users in all these conditions.
- Sweat or rain might make the gun's handle slippery, requiring the user to grasp differently.

In summary, the GRASP model proposed in this paper can be used for categorizing grasp-sensitive objects, exploring the design space of grasp-sensing applications, and analyzing challenges when implementing grasp-sensitive user interfaces.

Limitations

GRASP is a descriptive model of meaning in grasps. As such it is based on a subjective concept. Different persons and cultures might prefer other groupings. GRASP is also limited to meaningful interaction. Thus it is not necessarily suited for other domains. While I have tried to show that this model is formally valid and can be useful for reseachers and designers, ony time will tell whether this model is actually helpful. Finally, I am not yet certain whether Relationship really is an own factor. One might als group it with Anatomy into a Human factor. Some might argue that Relationship is a actually just a modifier to a Goal. In the end, it might depend on whether it is useful to define Relationship as an own factor.

CONCLUSION AND FUTURE WORK

In this paper I have argued that grasp sensing is an important source of meaningful information for human-computer interaction. I have given an overview of existing work from other disciplines and have shown that existing models are not sufficient for describing grasps in the context of human-computer interaction. Therefore, I propose a descriptive model of meaning in grasps. This model is supported by examples and an epistemological analysis. GRASP is intended as a working model. The main goal for GRASP is to serve as a vocabulary and basis for discussing meaning in grasps and grasp interaction utilizing this meaning. This model may also help in structuring research, e.g. by highlighting interesting areas of further research. It can also be used to determine which factors need to be controlled in a user study. An important long-term goal would be to automatically extract all factors contributing to a grasp from just the signature of the grasp. For this, a classifying model would be helpful, associating certain quantitative features of a grasp with the meaningful factors contributing to it.

REFERENCES

1. *The American Heritage Dictionary of the English Language, Fourth Edition*. Houghton Mifflin, 2009.
2. D. Bailer-Jones. *Scientific models in philosophy of science*. Univ of Pittsburgh Pr, 2009.
3. G. Barrett and R. Omote. Projected-Capacitive Touch Technology. *Information Display*, 26(3):16–21, 2010.
4. E. Berlin, J. Liu, K. van Laerhoven, and B. Schiele. Coming to grips with the objects we grasp: detecting interactions with efficient wrist-worn sensors. In *TEI '10: Proceedings of the fourth international conference on Tangible, embedded, and embodied interaction*, pages 57–64, New York, NY, USA, 2010. ACM.
5. A. Butler, S. Izadi, and S. Hodges. Sidesight: multi-"touch" interaction around small devices. In *Proceedings of UIST '08*, pages 201–204, New York, NY, USA, 2008. ACM.
6. U. Castiello. The neuroscience of grasping. *Nature Reviews Neuroscience*, 6(9):726–736, 2005.
7. M. Cutkosky. On grasp choice, grasp models, and the design of hands for manufacturing tasks. *IEEE Transactions on Robotics and Automation*, 5(3):269–279, 1989.
8. T. Feix, R. Pawlik, H.-B. Schmiedmayer, J. Romero, and D. Kragic. The generation of a comprehensive grasp taxonomy. Technical report, 2009.
9. F. Hemmert, S. Hamann, M. Löwe, A. Wohlauf, and G. Joost. Weight-Shifting Mobiles: One-Dimensional Gravitational Displays in Mobile Phones. *Adjunct Proceedings of UIST*, 9, 2009.
10. F. Hemmert, G. Joost, A. Knörig, and R. Wettach. Dynamic knobs: shape change as a means of interaction on a mobile phone. In *CHI'08 extended abstracts*, pages 2309–2314. ACM, 2008.
11. G. Heumer, H. Amor, M. Weber, and B. Jung. Grasp recognition with uncalibrated data gloves-A comparison of classification methods. In *IEEE Virtual Reality Conference, 2007. VR'07*, pages 19–26, 2007.
12. T. Iberall and C. MacKenzie. Opposition space and human prehension. In *Dextrous robot hands*, pages 32–54. Springer-Verlag New York, Inc., 1990.
13. S. Kang and K. Ikeuchi. Grasp recognition using the contact web. In *Proc. IEEE/RSJ Int. Conf. on Int. Robots and Sys., Raleigh, NC*, 1992.

14. K. Kim, W. Chang, S. Cho, J. Shim, H. Lee, J. Park, Y. Lee, and S. Kim. Hand Grip Pattern Recognition for Mobile User Interfaces. In *In Proc. AAAI '06*, volume 21, page 1789, 2006.

15. P. G. Kry and D. K. Pai. Grasp recognition and manipulation with the tango. In *International Symposium on Experimental Robotics*, volume 10. Springer, 2006.

16. J. Loviscach. Two-finger input with a standard touch screen. In *Proceedings of the 20th annual ACM symposium on User interface software and technology*, page 172. ACM, 2007.

17. C. MacKenzie and T. Iberall. *The grasping hand*. North Holland, 1994.

18. J. Mäntyjärvi, K. Nybergh, J. Himberg, and K. Hjelt. Touch Detection System for Mobile Terminals. In *Proceedings of MobileHCI '05*. Springer, 2004.

19. S. Mascaro and H. Asada. Measurement of finger posture and three-axis fingertip touch force using fingernail sensors. *IEEE Transactions on Robotics and Automation*, 20(1):26–35, 2004.

20. J. Napier. The prehensile movements of the human hand. *Journal of Bone & Joint Surgery, British Volume*, 38(4):902, 1956.

21. J. Ponce, S. Sullivan, A. Sudsang, J. Boissonnat, and J. Merlet. On computing four-finger equilibrium and force-closure grasps of polyhedral objects. *International Journal of Robotics Research*, 16(1):11–46, 1997.

22. J. Rekimoto. Gesturewrist and gesturepad: Unobtrusive wearable interaction devices, 2001.

23. I. Rosenberg and K. Perlin. The UnMousePad: an interpolating multi-touch force-sensing input pad. *ACM Transactions on Graphics (TOG)*, 28(3):65, 2009.

24. G. Schlesinger. Der Mechanische Aufbau der Kunstlichen Glieder. Ersatzglieder und Arbeitshilfen, part II, 1919.

25. K. Shimoga. Robot grasp synthesis algorithms: A survey. *The International Journal of Robotics Research*, 15(3):230, 1996.

26. B. T. Taylor and M. V. Bove. The bar of soap: a grasp recognition system implemented in a multi-functional handheld device. In *CHI '08: CHI '08 extended abstracts on Human factors in computing systems*, pages 3459–3464, New York, NY, USA, 2008. ACM.

27. B. T. Taylor and M. V. Bove. Graspables: grasp-recognition as a user interface. In *In Proc. CHI '09*, pages 917–926, New York, NY, USA, 2009. ACM.

28. F. Vaandrager. What is a good model? http://www.cs.ru.nl/ fvaan/PV/ what_is_a_good_model.html, 2010.

29. C. van de Kamp and F. Zaal. Prehension is really reaching and grasping. *Experimental Brain Research*, 182(1):27–34, 2007.

30. R. N. J. Veldhuis, A. M. Bazen, J. A. Kauffman, and P. H. Hartel. Biometric verification based on grip-pattern recognition. In E. J. Delp and P. W. Wong, editors, *Security, Steganography, and Watermarking of Multimedia Contents*, volume 5306 of *Proceedings of SPIE*, pages 634–641. SPIE, 2004.

31. R. Y. Wang and J. Popović. Real-time hand-tracking with a color glove. *ACM Transactions on Graphics*, 28(3), 2009.

32. R. Wimmer. FlyEye: Grasp-Sensitive Surfaces Using Optical Fiber. In *In Proc. TEI '10*, Jan. 2010.

33. R. Wimmer and S. Boring. HandSense - Discriminating Different Ways of Grasping and Holding a Tangible User Interface. In *In Proc. TEI '09*, February 2009.

34. T. Zimmerman. Personal Area Networks: Near-field intrabody communication. *IBM SYSTEMS JOURNAL*, 35(3&4):610, 1996.

Casier: Structures for Composing Tangibles and Complementary Interactors for Use Across Diverse Systems

Brygg Ullmer[1,2], Christian Dell[1,2], Claudia Gill[1], Cornelius Toole, Jr.[1,2], Cole Wiley[1,2], Zachary Dever[1,2], Landon Rogge[1,2], Rachel Bradford[2,5], Guillaume Riviere[2,6], Rajesh Sankaran[2,3], Kexi Liu[1,2], Chase Freeman[4], Alvin Wallace, Jr.[1,2], Michael DeLatin[2,3], Christian Washington[2,3], Alex Reeser[1,2], Christopher W. Branton[1,2], Rod Parker[4]

Louisiana State University (Dept. of Computer Science[1], Center for Computation and Technology (CCT)[2], Dept. of Electrical Engineering[3], Graphic Design Program[4]); Hillsdale College[5]; ESTIA[6]
ullmer@lsu.edu

ABSTRACT

Casiers are a class of tangible interface elements that structure the physical and functional composition of tangibles and complementary interactors (e.g., buttons and sliders). Casiers allow certain subsets of interactive functionality to be accessible across diverse interactive systems (with and without graphical mediation, employing varied sensing capabilities and supporting software). We illustrate examples of casiers in use, including iterations around a custom walk-up-and-use kiosk, as well as casiers operable across commercial platforms of widely varying cost and capability.

Author Keywords

core tangibles; cartouche tangibles; casier tangibles; tangible interfaces; reality-based interaction; slotted widgets

ACM Classification Keywords

H.5.2: User Interfaces (D.2.2, H.1.2, I.3.6)

General Terms

Design

INTRODUCTION

The tangible interaction community has grown rapidly for more than a decade. Some common research platforms have begun to gain broad traction (e.g., [4,5]). However, tangibles which serve common roles across multiple applications on a given platform – and especially which function across dissimilar platforms – are not yet widespread. Several papers have argued such developments could be an important foundation for broader adoption of tangible interfaces, framing these ideas in terms of *core* and *domain tangibles* [24,30].

The objective of core tangibles is to provide common, interoperable interface elements for physically embodying digital information and operations within and between a variety of interactive systems. Example systems include tangible user interfaces (TUIs), other reality-based interfaces (RBIs) [15], and traditional graphical user interfaces (GUIs) and their more recent variations (e.g., multitouch). Domain tangibles are more specific physical+digital elements, often both in form and function, which are frequently particular to specific application domains, datasets, etc.

Figure 1. Casier operating across different platforms: *(a) standalone tray from [20]; (b,c,d) casier on Apple iPad, Microsoft Surface, Wacom Bamboo Fun – systems marked by diverse sensing, display, and cost. This is prospectively compatible with many other interactive systems.*

One example of core tangibles, cartouches, has been discussed at some length [24]. Cartouches serve variously as physical containers, tools, and tokens for representing and engaging digital data and operations [13, 14, 31]. They are distinguished from other tangibles in several respects. Cartouches employ a regular constellation of physical footprints, supporting both mechanical interoperability and the composition of multiple cartouches. Other cartouche conventions include an identifying visual mark (the cartouche colorbar,

TEI'11, January 22–26, 2011, Funchal, Portugal.

with both humanly and computationally legible representational aspects); ensembles of visible and RFID tags; and metadata and protocols supporting interoperability.

To be meaningingfully employed, cartouche tangibles must be used in combination with other interface elements [24, 30]. For example, interoperability across diverse physical contexts raises the question of how cartouche-capable interaction locales can be identified by users. This includes interface loci supporting the use of cartouches in general, and also interface compatibility with specific subclasses of cartouches (e.g., operations, parameters, or data).

Another property of cartouches relates to expanded interaction "real estate" – the ability to represent interface content both on and off dynamic interactive display surfaces. Moreover, the design of cartouches is intended to support multi-cartouche composition (e.g., as illustrated by the multi-tile composition of DataTiles [19, 24]). Taken together, these suggest the potential desirability of migrating cartouches on and off different systems collectively as groups of elements.

In this paper, we extend and generalize "interaction trays" [24, 30] in a class of core tangibles and a conceptual approach we call *casiers*. We introduce several examples of casier tangibles which frame the manipulation of cartouches across several interaction platforms. We discuss implications for interaction real estate and composition. Finally, we consider implications for paths by which tangibles might find broader incorporation within our physical environments, and some of the design, technical, and community opportunities and needs that likely shape these prospects.

RELATED WORK

Casier tangibles build upon a long series of related work. Most directly and recently, they extend the interaction tray concept [30]. Building upon this and [24], we extend interaction trays with conventions for an open-ended constellation of form factors; tagging and interaction mechanisms supporting interoperability across different platforms; visual conventions that complement cartouche colorbars [24]; an improved conceptualization; and a broader set of examples.

The introduction of interaction trays briefly referenced Bricks, MagicBook, and DataTiles as related work [7, 12, 19]. In Bricks, the GraspDraw drawing system introduces a "physical tool tray" integrating two sets of digitally-bound receptacles [11,12]. These include a 2x3 array of circular "ink-well" compartments, each with a unique color binding; and a linear array of six rectangular compartments bound to "brick" function bindings (each labeled with both text and icons). Both sets of interactors operate by "dipping" the brick handle into the respective compartments.

The Bricks tool tray was located off the ActiveDesk display surface, thus providing extended interaction real estate. The tray also provided passive haptic feedback. Per [11], "the physical tool tray has advantages in that the user always knows what functions are available (predictableness), learns the approximate gesture to get to the tool, and can use the physical constraints of the tool compartments to make a coarse, imprecise, ballistic gesture to activate the tool."

The MagicBook system describes books containing a series of paper pages, with each page bearing a combination of printed text, imagery, and visual codes parsable with computer vision [7]. In text labeled "putting everything together" in the context of a tangible augmented reality interface, the authors describe using a "[magic]book as a menu object... one stack of tiles as *data tiles...* [and] *operator tiles...* used to perform basic operations on the data tiles" [8].

DataTiles is a system of transparent, RFID-tagged acrylic tiles used in conjunction with an illuminated surface that senses tile placement+ID as well as pen gesture [19]. The function of each DataTile is labeled on its rim. Many DataTiles also have "partial printing" – fixed information that is printed or etched onto the tile – and/or "grooved widgets" – passive haptic constraints which guide the motion of a stylus. On placement upon the display worksurface, DataTiles are back-illuminated with interactive text and graphics. This content responds to the composition of multiple tiles (a "physical language" expressed by juxtaposing application, parameter, container, and portal tiles); to stylus-based interaction within and between tiles; and to the software dynamics between the underlying constellation of DataTile applets.

As with these examples, we seek to leverage augmented interaction real estate (both in the presence and absence of augmenting dynamic graphical displays). We endeavor to engage and extend the kinds of passive haptic feedback within Bricks and DataTiles; the multi-page ensembles of interaction surfaces within MagicBook; and the open-ended composition and multi-device ecologies of DataTiles and TAR tiles [8]. We are particularly motivated by the ways DataTiles and TAR tiles span multiple interaction genres, and similarly seek to realize interfaces relevant to a range of reality-based interfaces [15] and modern graphical interface variations.

A number of other past systems are also relevant and inspirational to casier. The Slot Machine was built around a set of colored bars, each containing a series of slots within which cartouche-like action and data cards could be inserted [17]. Building upon Bricks, the metaDESK system used "phicons" (physical icons) with a physical tray, which was described as an analog of GUI menus [25]. The mediaBlocks and tangible query interface systems mapped sets of physical racks, pads, and slots to digital operations, which were used in conjunction with a set of media-tagged blocks and wheels [26, 27]. ToonTown, LogJam, and QBA also mapped physical racks to digital operations performed upon physical data-tokens [9, 10, 22]. Strata/ML, a predecessor to DataTiles, also used systems of RFID-tagged transparent tiles with partial printing and grooved widgets on an ensemble of back-illuminated, pen tracking worksurfaces [29].

Each of these systems employs mechanical constraints to channel and map digital semantics upon the manipulation of digitally-tagged tokens, per previous discussions of token-and-constraint and relational object semantics [21,28]. Generally, these constraints have been tightly integrated (both from electrical + mechanical fixturing and software integration perspectives) into existing ad-hoc interfaces.

CASIER

With casier, we seek to de-integrate and generalize the compositional use of tangibles with diverse interface platforms, allowing reuse and composition between multiple applications and systems. We begin by considering the casier name, then elaborate upon some of casiers' distinctions from prior work before continuing with specific examples.

Earlier work introduced interaction trays as a generalization of the tool tray term and concept introduced by Bricks [12, 30]. We regard this as a potentially enduring term, with a stronger case for continued use than the tangible menu term [30] (reconceived as "cartouche" in [24]). In parallel, we have interest in a term that, like "cartouche," has multiple complementary nuances; is applicable across diverse embodying physical scales and mediums; and invites generalizations and broader applications. We are also attracted to terms from languages other than English, partly motivated by efforts toward culturally-specific tangibles.

One candidate is the Japanese term 盤 (ばん, "ban," with an English pronunciation closer to "bon"). This term's ensemble of meanings includes a tray, bowl, phonograph record, grid, and board (as in board games) [1]. Among other attractions, many of these artifacts have proven fruitful points of departure for tangible interfaces. However, the typical English pronunciation of "ban" seems likely to yield confusion. The term we suggest, "casier" (pronounced "kah-zee-ay"), is a French word with meanings including pigeonhole or set of pigeonholes, filing cabinet, rack, compartment, and locker [2]. The term resonates with the earlier "cartouche" usage [24], and has been supported by French colleagues.

Operability across diverse interaction platforms

A primary function of casiers is to identify and structure the use of cartouches and other tangibles in combination with other interaction elements, in fashions operable across diverse interactive systems. This can take several forms. First, an individual casier can function without modification on different interactive systems. For example, the casier pictured in Figure 2 contains no internal electronics (beyond RFID tags), and currently functions on the Wacom Bamboo Fun, Apple iPad, and Microsoft Surface platforms. Casiers can also incorporate significant supporting electronics. For example, the "parameter tray" of [20, 30] is is implemented in [20] with active electronics, and here without; we seek to make both addressable by identical software [23].

Form factor conventions

In introducing core tangibles, several specific form factors for tangible menus (cartouches) and interaction trays (casiers) were described [30], with an assertion that these had implications for tangible interoperability and composition. The introduction of cartouches [24] extended this concept from three specific sizes to an open-ended constellation of physical sizes. This proposition partially mirrored the ISO B-series formats and common imperial-unit approximations (e.g., 2.5×3.5", 5×3.5", and 5×7"), but also supporting alternate

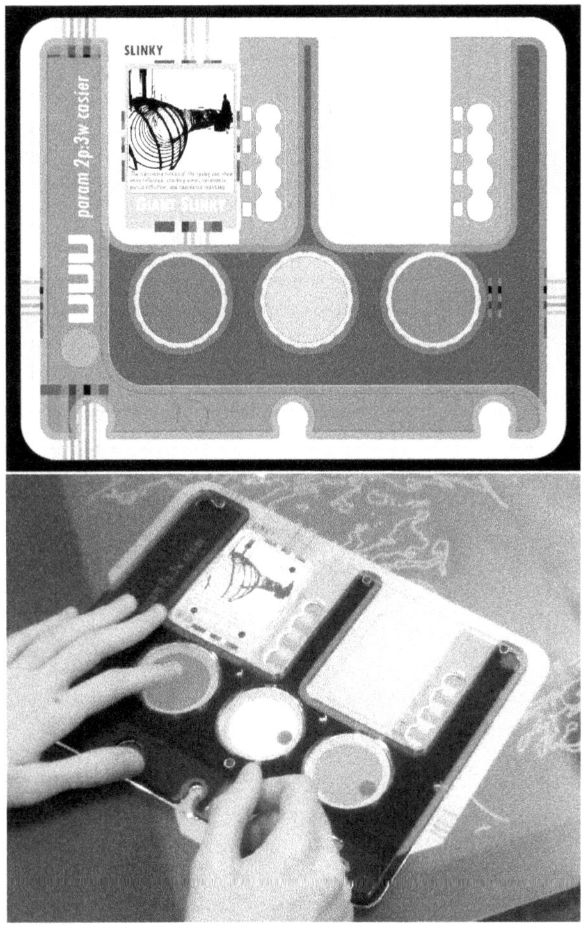

Figure 2. Views of new param casier. *This casier currently operates on Microsoft Surface, Apple iPad, and Wacom Bamboo Fun (multitouch+pen), and likely is compatible with numerous other platforms. a) View from design software. A graphical "halo" is visible surrounding all detected tangibles, with cartouche and casier colorbars graphically "extruded" as an indication the correct artifact is detected. b) View as placed upon Microsoft Surface. Three rotary "slotted widgets" are present. In Figure 1c, these are pictured with Surface-tagged wheels inserted. Here, they are pictured with touch interaction bounded by the passive haptic constraints. Two cartouche pads are present, each with four adjoining button/slider slotted widgets. The left pad is occupied by a cartouche. All interactors are placed so as to allow functionality on the sensing surfaces of both the iPad and Bamboo. RFID sensing by supporting electronics is being realized from underneath the Bamboo, and alongside the iPad. The three holes at the bottom of the casier facilitate storage within a traditional three-ring binder.*

aspect ratios. However, while trays with several different physical footprints were illustrated, only one tray form factor was proposed: letter (8.5×11") or ISO A4.

Just as the original "tangible menu" dimensions were found limiting, we have found need for larger and smaller trays than letter/A4, and also for different aspect ratios. In response, we propose conventions for varying casier footprints modeled after the system proposed for cartouches [24] (Table 1). As with cartouches, we envision a halving and doubling of form factors, this time referencing ISO/DIN A and the U.S. letter series. This yields many of the advantages for casier as described for cartouches – storage and organizing products, available media and printers, etc. There are also size complementarities between the ISO A and B series (and their imperial approximations) which support cartouche+casier composition.

y-in	y-cm		4	5	6	7	8	9	10
		x-in	1.4	2.8	5.5	11.0	22.0	44.0	88.0
		x-cm	3.5	7.0	14.0	27.9	55.9	111.8	223.5
1.1	2.7	E							
2.1	5.4	F		FF5:*B10*	*B9*				
4.3	10.8	G			FG6:A6	FG7:*A5*			
8.5	21.6	H				FH7:*A4*	*A3*		
17.0	43.2	I					FI8:*A2*	*A1*	
34.0	86.4	J						*A0*	
68.0	172.7	K							

Table 1. Dimensions of casier tangibles: *subset centering on FH7 (U.S. letter, 8.5"×11"). The corresponding metric format, EH7, is equivalent in size to ISO A4. ISO A-series format parallels are highlighted in light gray. (Cartouches were proposed with prefixes beginning C and D, for metric and imperial units, respectively [24]; we suggest E and F as prefixes for casier formats.) As with cartouches, these abbreviations are not envisioned for end-users, but rather for clarity in work by designers and developers.*

Visual conventions supporting legibility

One challenge with tangibles – especially those intended for walk-up-and-use contexts – relates to how users can distinguish between "ordinary objects" and those loaded with digital semantics. The prospect of ecologies of tangibles raises the question of which tangibles can be expected to interoperate, and which not. Once interaction begins, how can diverse systems consistently communicate with users that their physical interactions are being interpreted (and with what consequence)? These issues relate to the five questions for sensing systems posed by Bellotti et al. (esp. #2 and 4) [6].

One strategy introduced in [24] is a specific colorbar, with both human- and machine-legible aspects, which labels cartouches. We have attempted to carry forward this strategy in several ways. First, we also label casiers with these colorbars, thus identifying them as physical/digital artifacts (Figure 2a). Second, we have investigated several ways to embed "shadows" of these colorbars, as well as colored borders matching cartouche colors, within casiers on cartouche pads (e.g., Figure 4c). Third, we are beginning to employ digital shadows [14]/halos of cartouches and casiers on graphically-mediated surfaces as a feedback mechanism (Figure 2).

CASIER EXAMPLES AND DESIGN EVOLUTION

Building on the interaction trays of [30], we have conducted two extended design studies and deployments of casier. These are a walk-up-and-use tangibles-based interaction kiosk; and several FH7-format (US letter-sized, page-format) casiers initially designed for use across the Apple iPad, Wacom Bamboo, and Microsoft Surface platforms. These each illustrate the casier concept and our associated design evolutions.

Walk-up-and-use kiosk

Our first effort has been in the context of a walk-up-and-use use interaction kiosk designed for informal science education, with middle school students (age ~11-14) as the target audience. This effort is aligned with a regional science education center (operated within a national science facility) which conducts extensive outreach activities throughout the state. State education personnel expressed interest in extending the "hands-on" style of science exposure afforded by the science center exhibits, but in lower cost, computational variations potentially deployable in schools, libraries, and other public venues.

Figure 3. Mid-stage implemented kiosk + envisioned next-gen iteration. *In left (implemented) kiosk, a relatively long (32x7"), black casier with captive cartouches and a haptic navigation wheel is visible as manipulated by a student. In the right (envisioned) view, five casiers on two worksurface tiers are depicted. Four are for storage (potentially sensed and illuminated) of thick (here, 3.5x2.5x2.5") and thin DG6 (card) cartouches. The lower-center casier houses a composition of data, operation, and parameter cartouches on an iPad touch-display surface (see Figure 5 for inset).*

Several views of our developing kiosk are pictured in Figure 3, with inset views of our developing casier and cartouches in Figures 4 and 5. In an early kiosk prototype, we employed a small standalone casier, surrounded by a small ensemble of cartouches (Figure 4a). We quickly encountered concern from those familiar with informal science installations and middle schools that this style of approach might not fare well (at least unattended) in our target contexts. We were encouraged to develop a "hardened" approach geared toward an active audience inclined to "move whatever moves."

In our next kiosk generation, we attempted to follow this advice. We decided to engage with graphic design collaborators in most visual aspects of the kiosk, including the kiosk façade and cartouches (Figures 3a and 4b). This variation employed the same interactors as the first generation, but with recessed buttons and indicator LEDs that allowed captive cartouches to slide over the cartouche interaction area.

This installation included four cartouches, each associated with a subject area relating to space science. Each cartouche contained four subregions: details, video, explore, and quiz. These contained introductory images and navigable video, small games, and simple review quizzes associated with the given subject area. Interaction was expressed through placement of a chosen cartouche on the cartouche interaction pad; selecting a category of interaction with the selector buttons; and rotating and pushing the selection wheel. Feedback relating to this interaction was graphically mediated on the kiosk's left embedded screen; video, game, etc. content was primarily channeled to the right screen.

Our team had very limited previous experience in the targeted deployment context. Interaction was intentionally limited both to increase likelihood of the kiosk's physical sur-

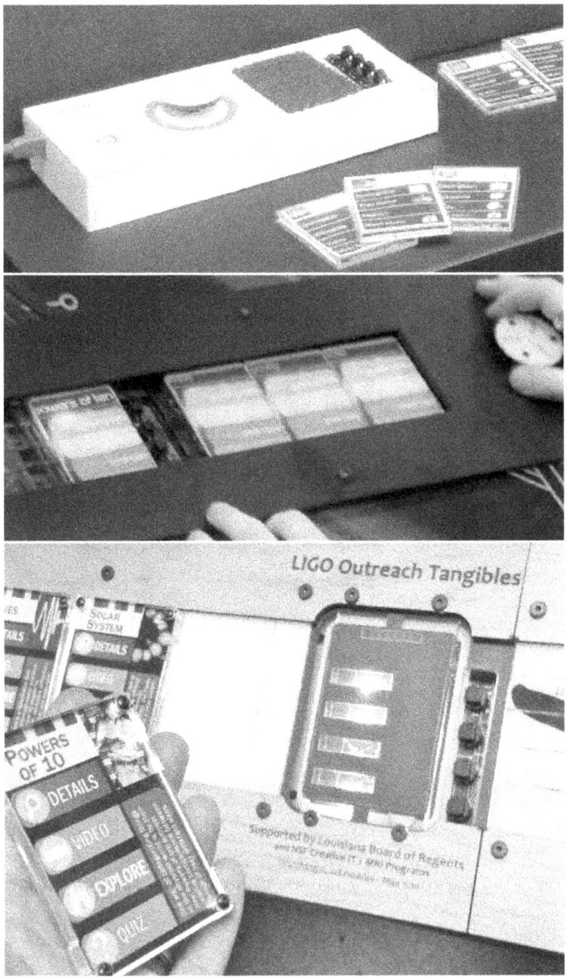

Figure 4. First three generations of kiosk casiers. *a) Standalone casier (4×10"), including embedded selection buttons and rotor. b) Embedded casier (32×7") with captive cartouches. c) Evolved casier and cartouches.*

vival, and to reflect the small initial corpus of accompanying digital content. We deployed this system in our collaborating science education center for several months.

Focusing here on lessons relating to the kiosk's casier and cartouches, one major finding related to interaction legibility for first-time unsupervised visitors. This was most users' first experience with cartouches (by this or any other name). For a number of visitors, it was not clear how to engage with the system. It was not obvious that the cartouches should be moved within their captive channel; that the adjacent recessed buttons should be pushed to trigger content; or how the physically-offset rotor played into the interaction.

We also felt there were challenges relating to the cartouche and casier visuals. The graphic designers had no prior experience with designing cartouches, and faced a very tight deadline (far earlier than anticipated). We expressed general interests to them, and shared a copy of [24]. In retrospect, [24] seems oriented to academics, and not (e.g.) practicing graphic designers. We also did not express a specific brief, identify design challenges to be resolved, or provide many exemplary reference examples. We implemented the casier, without sufficient attention to how it complemented cartouche visuals. We feel these decisions were problematic.

Consequently, we conducted a third design iteration on the kiosk's casier and cartouches (Figure 4c inset). In this, we:

- selected a border color for cartouches, and used this color to indicate cartouche interaction areas on the casier;
- included a thumbnail image on each cartouche and visual icons complementing each subfunction (video, quiz, etc.);
- faced the casier with a silhouette hand and short text highlighting the cartouche interaction buttons; and
- added back-illuminating LEDs to the cartouche pad, thus directly illuminating selected subfunctions on the cartouches.

We returned this third iteration to the field, and received more positive feedback from staff and visitors. Ultimately, the kiosk faced larger conceptual and content challenges. Simply adding tangibles, even with attention to design, was not enough to ensure a strong overall interaction experience.

Implications of early kiosk experiences for casiers

These first kiosk experiences raised many questions and possibilities for next-generation casier design. As one example, we followed the cartouche form factor conventions described in [24], but did not initially envision form factor conventions on the casier iterations of Figure 4.

After spending time with our second-generation kiosk, an education professor challenged us – "the laptop is tough competition; you need to go beyond what's already possible there!" This led us to feel our intentionally conservative initial design was in fact too conservative, with success likely depending upon high-risk entangling of physical and digital media.

To our surprise, embracing this challenge seems to have implications for casier form factor conventions. As we began to plan integration of robotic and multitouch interaction into the kiosk, each design alternative seemed to potentially transform the kiosk's physical structure.

From this and other experiences, we came to believe that one way to support frequent TUI iteration – both from physical design and field end-use perspectives – was to systematize the footprint and other aspects of casiers. This could allow their modular exchange and (potentially) ad-hoc composition. This might resemble the kinds of tangible composition realized with DataTiles [19] and envisioned for cartouches [24] (albeit perhaps at longer time-scales). This led us to propose Table 1, and to adopt a revised design approach for the remaining interfaces of this paper.

As another lesson, while the cartouche proposal explicitly sought operability in the absence of dynamic displays [24], at least as a bootstrapping process, learning to use a new medium requires considerable user education. Even highly successful interaction platforms like Apple's iPhone and iPad make use of explanatory animations and text labels for tasks as basic as unlocking the home screen. Thus, we have begun to re-embrace use of animated graphics with input-space proximal to output-space (at least for some system elements), even as many of our envisioned casier applications have no dynamic graphics capabilities.

Figure 5. Next-generation interaction kiosk casier (envisioned). *Inset view of Figure 3b, described briefly there. Several color- and text-labeled classes of cartouches (blue action, yellow subject, gray details) mate with both physical casier constraints and dynamic touchscreen graphics.*

Figure 6. Example of two FH7 (letter page) three-wheeled parameter casiers used on a Microsoft Surface.

Casiers for heterogeneous interaction platforms

After embracing the integration of richer sensing and display technologies with casiers and cartouches, we began to consider different interaction platforms for bearing out this functionality. We were also attracted to the prospect of casiers that could function across heterogeneous interaction platforms. An example envisioned casier employing such capabilities for our kiosk is illustrated in Figure 5.

We began work toward interoperable casiers with the Wacom Bamboo multitouch tablets. We noted the smallest family member – the Touch – physically fits within our second- and third-generation kiosk casier. From a sensing perspective, this raised the prospect for supporting some of the intertile physical gestures demonstrated by DataTiles [19] – potentially both with stylus and touch. With the more recent release of Apple's iPad and our laboratory's acquisition of a Microsoft Surface, the diverse capabilities and costs of these platforms nicely complemented the Bamboo. This lead us to co-design casiers toward all three platforms.

As a point of departure, we initially focused upon a casier reimplementing the three-wheeled, two-pad "parameter tray" of [30]. Figures 1, 2, and 6 illustrate an FH7-format (8.5"× 11") casier which functions in combination with both the Microsoft Surface, Apple iPad, and Wacom Bamboo Fun platforms. Each platform senses the casier, cartouches, and interaction with casier interactors in a different fashion[1].

Figure 6 provides a view of multiple casiers in operation. One casier is placed directly upon the Surface's sensing+display region. The casier and its three physical wheels are recognized and tracked with four separate visual Surface tags. On the right, the same casier is placed upon an augmented Apple iPad. The TouchOSC iPad app is used to sense touch-based wheel and button interaction. The casiers' wheels allow parametric interaction with a Deepwater Horizon visualization, complementing Surface-based spatial interations.

As pictured, the iPad-based casier sits upon the Surface, but is placed outside the Surface's sensing+display region. The Surface's active work area is relatively limited, and would quickly be obscured if many Surface-tracked casiers were simultaneously in operation. Using casiers as shown with the iPad both increases interaction real estate, and allows casiers to be used (literally and conceptually) on and off the Surface. Among other implications, this allows both colocated and distributed collaboration with more people than could fit around the Surface's physical perimeter.

We have also implemented other casiers on both the Surface and iPad. Figure 7 illustrates one simple casier (again, FH7/letter format) which contains four DG7 (5x3.5") cartouches. These are special cartouches which, like the earlier parameter casier, employ what we call "slotted widgets." Grooved widgets provided passive haptic guidance and constraint for the tip of a stylus [19,29]. Slotted widgets perform a similar function, but for (finger-based) touch (potentially as well as stylus, depending upon the sensing platform).

Like grooved widgets, slotted widgets allow users to manipulate "soft widgets" while attending visually to visual screen real estate, conversation partners, or other demands that require visual attention. Unlike grooved widgets, slotted widgets do not necessarily require a stylus, thus offering reduced "set-up/tear-down" time, at the cost of increased physical real estate and lower precision. Also, our examples of casiers on the Surface (Figure 2b + 6) illustrate a case where parameters can be manipulated either through slot-constrained touch contact with the Surface, or using a Surface-tracked knob as a physical proxy. We see this as another attractive, promising usage modality of slotted widgets.

IMPLEMENTATION

To realize our kiosk casier implementations (Figures 3a, 4), we used the blades and tiles hardware/software library [20]. This hardware performed well for us, especially after we replaced the inter-tile connector from the original USB con-

[1] As discussed in Implementation, we have verified RFID-based cartouche sensing on the iPad and Bamboo platforms, but not yet stably integrated software or hardware for this function.

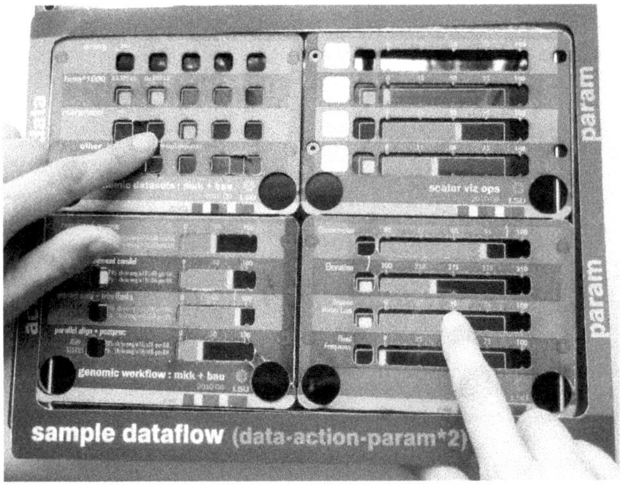

Figure 7. Ensemble of cartouches using slotted widgets on an iPad-backed casier. *Four DG7 cartouches describing different aspects of a scientific data flow are present within an FH7 casier on an iPad. Each cartouche – one data, one operation, and two parameter – makes different use of slotted widgets, illuminated and sensed by the iPad. Here, the iPad touchOSC app is the backing software.*

nectors to a dual-row rectangular header. (When early tiles were mechanically fixtured, the USB connectors were vulnerable to electrical noise.) The mechanical structure of Figure 3a was built around a Metro-like modular wireframe shelving system, with wooden substructure and a printed adhesive vinyl-coated Sintra (closed-cell PVC foamboard) façade. Graphics on the two VESA-mounted kiosk screens were generated with internally developed PyGame software, hosted by a low-end PC enclosed within the kiosk.

One of our group's broader goals is to help make tangibles more readily replicable and deployable beyond their home laboratory context. As our realization of casiers progressed, we felt our exclusive use of blades could impose impediments to replication by other groups. We were also interested in exploiting properties of several newly-developed commercial platforms, especially those easing the economical integration of dynamic mediating graphics.

We have designed a three-layer lasercut implementation of the three-wheeled parameter casier. We are releasing the mechanical aspects of the casier for open-source download, modification, and non-commercial use (cc-by-nc). For those with access to a laser cutter, the mechanical source files for the casier pictured in Figure 2 can be accessed at [3]. For others, this can be purchased from vendors listed at [3].

From a software perspective, our current casier implementation is ad-hoc. The Surface implementation is written in C# using WPF; the iPad, upon touchOSC (with remote parsing via Python in SimpleOSC); and on the Bamboo, via TUIO 1.1 and Python + pyTUIO. We are in the process of porting all code to a unified API provided by the tuikit middleware [23]. In the case of Surface, no supporting electronics are required – only placement of Surface visual tags to the underside of the casier and cartouches. As described in [24], we envision an ensemble of visual and electromagnetic tags allowing interoperability between different platforms.

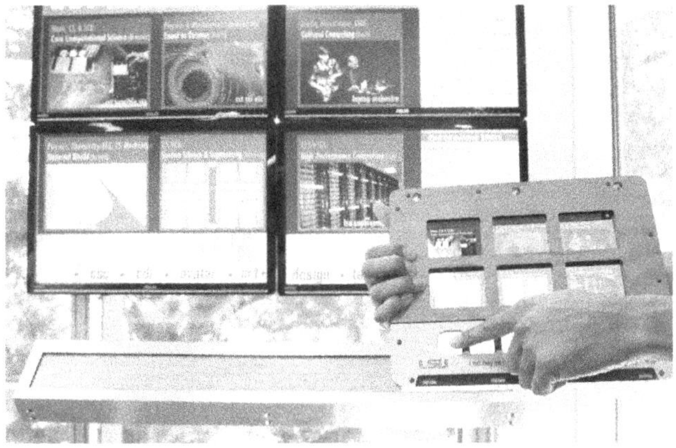

Figure 8. iPad-backed casier in use with a tiled display: *Six upper casier regions (illuminated and sensed by the integrated iPad tablet) are used to select presentation options upon the tiled display. A line of six lower casier regions allows selection of which screen is displayed (paralleling content on the tiled display's lower border). The tile display includes an integrated G8a-format (4.3"×33") casier, upon which cartouches expressing alternate screen content and behaviors can be placed.*

The Bamboo and iPad require custom electronics to sense both casiers and cartouches. The Bamboo chassis and internals contain relatively little metal. As a result, in all but the center of the tablet, 125 kHz RFID readers on the rear of the unit are able to read RFID tags present on or slightly above the Bamboo's surface. This includes RFID tags embedded within casiers, as well as more vertically-offset cartouches. The Bamboo's sensing antenna appears to prevent multiple RFID readers from *simultaneously* employing this technique on a given tablet. However, the time-multiplexing strategy employed by (e.g.) the RFID blade of [20] allows multi-point RFID reading without antenna interference.

The iPad's aluminum chassis electromagnetically obstructs the Bamboo through-tablet RFID sensing strategy. This leaves several alternatives. We have found that 125 kHz RFID reader antenna with roughly 2mm horizontal offset from the iPad chassis are able to function with proximal RFID tags. This is the approach we are currently employing. In addition, placing the RFID antennas on or under the iPad's surface glass (as in [19]), or using front- or rear-facing computer vision provide additional strategies. We have tested both of these Bamboo and iPad strategies in prototype form, and are now implementing stable integrated prototypes.

DISCUSSION AND FUTURE WORK

In the history of graphical user interfaces, "real estate" has been a persistent technical and conceptual theme and challenge. The advent first of tiled windows, then of overlapping windows, are seen as important enabling landmarks in GUI evolution [16]. We feel casiers also have implications for real estate within a variety of physically-situated interactive systems. Figure 6 illustrates a clear example where casiers realize an "overlapping windows" analogue. We have also discussed casiers both "on and off the surface," an extension that resonates with [18] and broader ubicomp efforts.

Our casier example of Figures 1 and 6 builds directly on the earlier "parameter interaction tray" examples of [20,30], while the examples of Figures 3b, 5, 7, and 8 illustrate novel casier designs. We have also begun developing casiers embodying interactive maps, timelines, system diagrams, and other examples ranging from the general to the specific. Most of these casiers employ slotted widgets. Some are relatively "flat;" others engage 2.5D and three-dimensional relief; and others intended for rendering in multiple physical mediums. Thus, while this paper has illustrated a few narrow examples, we see the casier concept as generalizing more broadly.

Figure 7 raises another important question. Here, the screen real estate of the underlying tablet is almost fully occluded by cartouches. Conversely, from a real estate perspective, one could advance an opposite design decision: occluding as little screen real estate with tangibles as possible, thus leveraging representational qualities and freeing screen real estate for alternate uses. In practice, we suspect both heuristics are valuable and complementary, with many tangibles migrating frequently between more and less heavily mediated spaces.

The future of physical and electronic books is today a heavily discussed topic. We see casier and cartouches as having resonances and implications for these conversations. We have designed most of our casiers to include three-ring binder holes. Using these, we have begun to use and store binders of multiple casiers – some empty, others containing cartouches – in ways comparable to physical books. Per [24], an interesting way of viewing cartouches and casiers is as legible, actionable physical embodiments of online content. Moreover, cartouches' and casiers' use of (often cryptographically-secure) RFID gives them powerful properties as license tokens. Borrowing both from the history of tool lending libraries and the future of personal fabrication, we see personal and organizational libraries of casiers, cartouches, and other tangibles as promising prospects for TEI and beyond.

ACKNOWLEDGEMENTS

This work has been supported in part by NSF MRI-0521559, IIS-0856065, EPSCoR RII-0704191, and La. BoR LEQSF (2008-09)-TOO-LIGO Outreach. Guillaume Ardaud and Courtney Barr made key contributions to the system pictured in Figure 8. Marcia Carter and members of the LOT Science Advisory Board provided key guidance for the evolution of the LIGO Outreach kiosk. Thanks also to Miriam Konkel, Werner Benger, Kazim Sekeroglu, Sanjay Kodiyalam, Amitava Jana, Stephen D. Beck, S.S. Iyengar, and Ed Seidel.

REFERENCES

1. `http://www.jisho.org/kanji/details/%E7%9B%A4`.
2. `http://dictionary.reverso.net/french-english/casier`.
3. `http://tangint.org/tangibles/casiers/core/FH7/param/edu.lsu/`.
4. Arduino homepage. `http://www.arduino.cc`.
5. Software implementing TUIO. `http://www.tuio.org/?software`.
6. V. Bellotti, M. Back, W. K. Edwards, R. E. Grinter, A. Henderson, and C. Lopes. Making sense of sensing systems: five questions for designers and researchers. In *Proc. of CHI'02*, pp. 415–422, 2002.
7. M. Billinghurst, H. Kato, and I. Poupyrev. The magicbook – moving seamlessly between reality and virtuality. *IEEE Computer Graphics and Applications*, 21(3):6–8, 2001.
8. M. Billinghurst, H. Kato, and I. Poupyrev. Tangible augmented reality. In *Proc. of SIGGRAPH Asia '08 (Courses)*, pp. 1–10, 2008.
9. A. Blackwell, M. Stringer, E. Toye, and J. Rode. Tangible interface for collaborative information retrieval. In *Proc. of CHI'04*, pp. 1473–1476, 2004.
10. J. Cohen, M. Withgott, and P. Piernot. Logjam: a tangible multi-person interface for video logging. In *Proc. of CHI'99*, pp. 128–135, 1999.
11. G. Fitzmaurice. *Graspable user interfaces*. PhD thesis, University of Toronto, 1996.
12. G. Fitzmaurice, H. Ishii, and W. Buxton. Bricks: laying the foundations for graspable user interfaces. In *Proc. of CHI '95*, pp. 442–449, 1995.
13. L. E. Holmquist, J. Redström, and P. Ljungstrand. Token-based access to digital information. In *Proc. of HUC'99*, pp. 234–245, 1999.
14. H. Ishii and B. Ullmer. Tangible bits: Towards seamless interfaces between people, bits and atoms. In *Proc. of CHI'97*, pp. 234–241, 1997.
15. R. Jacob, A. Girouard, L. Hirshfield, M. Horn, O. Shaer, E. Solovey, and J. Zigelbaum. Reality-based interaction: a framework for post-WIMP interfaces. In *Proc. of CHI'08*, 2008.
16. B. A. Myers. A brief history of human-computer interaction technology. *interactions*, 5(2):44–54, 1998.
17. R. Perlman. Using computer technology to provide a creative learning environment for preschool children. *MIT Lego Memo*, #24, 1976.
18. J. Rekimoto and M. Saitoh. Augmented surfaces: a spatially continuous work space for hybrid computing environments. In *Proc. of CHI '99*, pp. 378–385, 1999.
19. J. Rekimoto, B. Ullmer, and H. Oba. DataTiles: a modular platform for mixed physical and graphical interactions. In *Proc. of CHI '01*, pp. 269–276, 2001.
20. R. Sankaran, B. Ullmer, J. Ramanujam, K. Kallakuri, S. Jandhyala, C. Toole, and C. Laan. Decoupling interaction hardware design using libraries of reusable electronics. In *Proc. of TEI'09*, 2009.
21. O. Shaer, N. Leland, E. H. Calvillo-Gamez, and R. J. K. Jacob. The TAC paradigm: specifying tangible user interfaces. *Personal and Ubiquitous Computing*, 8(5):359–369, 2004.
22. A. Singer, D. Hindus, L. Stifelman, and S. White. Tangible progress: less is more in somewire audio spaces. In *Proc. of CHI '99*, pp. 104–111, 1999.
23. C. Toole, B. Ullmer, C. W. Branton, and C. D. Dell. Toward toolkit support for integration of distributed heterogeneous resources for tangible interaction. Submitted to Proc. of TEI'11 WIP.
24. B. Ullmer, Z. Dever, R. Sankaran, and et al. Cartouche: conventions for tangibles bridging diverse interactive systems. In *Proc. of TEI'10*, pp. 93–100, 2010.
25. B. Ullmer and H. Ishii. The metaDESK: models and prototypes for tangible user interfaces. In *Proc. of UIST'97*, pp. 223–232, 1997.
26. B. Ullmer, H. Ishii, and D. Glas. mediaBlocks: physical containers, transports, and controls for online media. In *Proc. of SIGGRAPH'98*, pp. 379–386, 1998.
27. B. Ullmer, H. Ishii, and R. Jacob. Tangible query interfaces: Physically constrained tokens for manipulating database queries. In *Proc. of INTERACT'03*, pp. 279–286, 2003.
28. B. Ullmer, H. Ishii, and R. Jacob. Token+constraint systems for tangible interaction with digital information. *ACM Transaction on Computer-Human Interaction (TOCHI)*, 12(1):81–118, 2005.
29. B. Ullmer, J. Patten, and H. Ishii. Strata: Physical representations for layered information structures. Submitted to Proc. of SIGGRAPH'00. `http://tangviz.cct.lsu.edu/papers/ullmer-siggraph00sub-strata.pdf`.
30. B. Ullmer, R. Sankaran, S. Jandhyala, B. Tregre, C. Toole, K. Kallakuri, C. Laan, M. Hess, F. Harhad, and U. Wiggins. Tangible menus and interaction trays: core tangibles for common physical/digital activities. In *Proc. of TEI'08*, pp. 209–212, 2008.
31. R. Want, K. P. Fishkin, A. Gujar, and B. L. Harrison. Bridging physical and virtual worlds with electronic tags. In *Proc. of CHI'99*, pp. 370–377, 1999.

Surging Verticality: An Experience of Balance

Lian Loke
Faculty of Engineering and Information Technology
University of Technology, Sydney
PO Box 123, Broadway, NSW, AUSTRALIA
lian.loke@uts.edu.au

George Poonkhin Khut
Faculty of Design, Architecture and Building
University of Technology, Sydney
PO Box 123, Broadway, NSW, AUSTRALIA
george@georgekhut.com

ABSTRACT
In our approach to body-focused interactive art, the tangible material with which we craft interactional aesthetic experiences is *body experience*. Touch and proprioception become primary materials for exploration and embedding in technology-mediated interactional situations. We applied the Feldenkrais Method of somatic bodywork in the development of a prototype interactive artwork, *Surging Verticality*, to pursue our understanding of how to craft audience experience, where the artwork offers a framework for critical reflection and self-enquiry. The Feldenkrais Method is based on an appreciation of musculo-skeletal organization as a fundamental component of our self-image and subjectivity. Our preliminary reflections on our experience of making, testing and evaluating body-focused interactions reveal the importance of the contract between artist and audience, the care, skill and sensitivity required by the artist and the receptivity of the audience.

Author Keywords
Aesthetics, balance, body experience, Feldenkrais, interactive art, movement, somatics.

ACM Classification Keywords
H5.m. Information interfaces and presentation (e.g., HCI): Miscellaneous.

General Terms
Human Factors.

INTRODUCTION
A significant strand of practice within interaction design research is body-focused interactive art and aesthetics. Body-focused interactive art can be applied as a framework for critical reflection and self-enquiry. The subjective experience and construction of self-image and embodiment becomes a central focus of exploration and is foregrounded in the aesthetic experience of the audience or participant interacting with such artworks.

TEI'11, January 22–26, 2011, Funchal, Portugal.

In our work, we go beyond body-based interactions of novelty and proposition, toward an appreciation of musculo-skeletal organization as a fundamental component of our self-image and subjectivity. Uncanny art experiences allow us to momentarily glimpse the role of bodily processes in the colouring of our experience and the sense of availability to the world around us.

In the context of tangible and embedded interaction, the tangible material around which we craft interactional aesthetic experiences is *body experience*. It is not object manipulation in the traditional sense of tangible interaction, but the manipulation of attention and sensation, grounded in the physical body. Touch and proprioception become primary materials for exploration and embedding in technology-mediated interactional situations.

While much has been said about the significance of body-focused practice, there is a need for research and documentation of the process by which these works are devised, presented and evaluated, especially with regards to the specifics of participant's felt experience. The crafting of body-focused interactive art experience, capable of facilitating 'improved' body-image/body-experience, is one area of our inquiry, with clear potential for applications that reach beyond 'pure aesthetics' into the domains of rehabilitation and physiotherapy.

We used Feldenkrais somatic bodywork and human-centred design methods to explore the crafting of body-focused interactive art experience, in the Thinking Through The Body art research project. The main focus of our work is on the creation of situations that reframe the audience's experience of themselves—with special attention to musculo-skeletal dimensions of our experience in moving and resting. Through the making, testing and evaluation of prototype body-focused interactive art experiences, we sought to refine our understandings of how we could make these kinds of artworks and what kinds of experiences were produced. In this paper, we present a preliminary sketch of our process and findings through the example of one of the interactive artworks, *Surging Verticality* developed in the project.

BACKGROUND
We briefly summarise the Thinking Through The Body research project, then position our research within related work on body-focused interactions in art and design, and

finally introduce the Feldenkrais Method of somatic bodywork.

Thinking Through The Body

Thinking Through The Body (TTTB) is a research project led by Dr George Khut and Dr Lizzie Muller, in collaboration with six practitioners, combining expertise in visual art, design, sound, performance and somatic bodywork. The aim of the project is to investigate the potential of touch, movement and body-focused interactions in art.

The project consisted of three residencies distributed over a year and culminated in an open studio day at Performance Space, Sydney, Australia called the Sensorium Gymnasium, attended by over 60 visitors. We presented a collection of interactive art experiences—devised as 'offerings' to an invited audience. The notion of creating experiences to share with others was central to our concept for the Sensorium Gymnasium event: building a situation that would allow our guests to experience some aspect of their embodiment anew.

Body-focused Interaction in Art and Design

The ability to work with the nuances of our bodily experience is an active area of design research. Researchers are inquiring into how to develop a design sensibility for working with movement and bodily experience, by drawing on first-person methodologies from dance and somatics (e.g., [3, 4, 5, 6]). In works like *Whisper* [6] and *BodyBug* [5], the aim is to reflect aspects of the kinaesthetic experience of movement in the actual interaction afforded by the system.

Works by artists such as James Turrell, Lygia Clarke, and more recently Carsten Höller and Olafur Eliasson reveal a line of practices stretching back to the late Sixties, that focus explicitly on the process and mechanisms of perception, highlighting the active, constructive nature of perception and subjective experience. Perception itself becomes the object of our attention in this type of work—we reflect on our own subjectivity and its embodiment through the experiential framework provided by the artwork [1].

Within this tradition and with the notable exception of Lygia Clarke, the sense of touch and movement has remained relatively underdeveloped; where touch or body movement is used it is rarely developed in any sustained and nuanced manner. Reflection on our experience in these artworks seldom moves beyond basic acknowledgement and novelty. In body-focused interactive art, as we practice it, the participant's embodiment is developed as the primary subject matter—in contrast to wearable or gesture based interfaces that direct our attention outward toward phenomena external to the body.

This inward shift in attention, from external to internal phenomena invites a corresponding shift in compositional emphasis from displays directed to exteroceptive sensory modalities (sounds and visuals) toward an increasing emphasis on interoceptive modalities (kinaesthesia, proprioception, balance, visceroception, etc.). Where exteroceptive sensations call attention of events in the world around us, interoceptive sensations focus our attention towards processes of being (standing, resting, breathing, etc.).

For artists, designers and researchers with a special interest in the phenomenology of embodiment and subjectivity, the possibility of an aesthetics of interoception holds a special appeal, but it also presents considerable challenges: there are few precedents for this type of experience in existing exhibition contexts.

Western somatic bodywork practices such as the Feldenkrais Method provide a conceptual and practical framework for evaluating the mechanics and poetics of the body as a living subjectivity: a way to evaluate what it means to be held, move or be moved in a certain way, and what this tells us (often unconsciously) about how we can move, rest, etc.

About Feldenkrais Somatic Bodywork

The Feldenkrais Method is a form of somatic education and physiotherapy devised by physicist and martial arts teacher Moshe Feldenkrais (1904-1984) [2]. The method contains two key approaches to physical therapy/education: Awareness Through Movement (ATM) and Functional Integration (described no further as we only used ATM). Both forms are presented as 'lessons'—the emphasis is on the development of movement awareness and skill, not the manipulation of passive flesh and bone. ATM lessons take place in groups, with the practitioner leading the class through a series of movements designed to develop sensitivity required for improved musculoskeletal coordination in everyday living.

In the Thinking Through The Body research project, we incorporated the Feldenkrais Method as a way of exploring, evaluating and evolving interaction concepts: to explore what is at stake (physically and psychologically) when for example we ask a person to reach forward on the balls of the feet; to risk the possibility of a momentary de-stabilisation; or to allow oneself to be moved by an external force.

SURGING VERTICALITY

The development of the prototype interactive artwork, *Surging Verticality* is now described. The concept for the interactive artwork is to experience an upward surge in the body through the simple act of rising to balance on the balls of the feet. As an experience, the interaction focused on the primary action of reaching up and out, feeling gravity through the skeleton, shifting through and across the body as the action unfolds. Sound was used to highlight the moment at which weight was shifted from the heels in standing, to the balls of the feet in full upward extension.

A prototype for the concept was developed through the integration of Feldenkrais ATM, a suspended cloth apparatus, the Nintendo Wii™ balance board and digitally generated sound using Max/MSP™ (see Figure 1).

Figure 1. Participant and aide in Surging Verticality

A critical element in this artwork was the decision to have a human 'aide' to guide the participant through the stages of engagement and interaction. It is by design not an autonomous artwork, but one that requires the participant to be inducted into interaction, with the assistance of the artist or their proxy. The implications of this for the participant experience are discussed later.

Two Stages of Interaction

The artwork is designed to be experienced in two distinct stages. The first stage involves the ritual of installing the person in the apparatus and preparing them for the second stage of interaction. The second stage shifts to the participant's direct interaction with the apparatus through physical movement. Each stage is described in more detail below.

Installing, Listening and Responding

The aide briefly explains the structure of the artwork and what the participant is expected to do. The aide then binds the cloth hanging from the pulley to the heels and ankles of the participant (shoes are first removed). The participant steps onto the balance board, facing the black curtain, and puts on a pair of headphones connected to a clip-on mpeg player. The assistant leaves the participant alone to listen to a 10-minute recording of a Feldenkrais ATM lesson, specifically written for this movement experience—exploring the movement of balancing on the balls of the feet.

The 'lesson' structures awareness of, and sensitivity to, the organization of the body and gaze in gravity through movement. The participant is instructed to bring their attention to sensations of weight (gravity) through various parts of the body, and to reflect on interactions between these different sensations as revealed through the various movements described in the lesson.

Pulling and Balancing

At the conclusion of the prerecorded ATM lesson, the participant signals to the aide, their readiness to begin the second stage of the experience. The aide gently, but firmly, pulls on the rope connected to the cloth bound to the participant's feet. This creates an upward tension on the cloth around their heels, an invitation to move up and outwards. As the participant begins to rise and shift their balance towards the front of the balance board, layers of birdsong recordings are 'released' by the computer to underscore this gesture of elevation and expansiveness. The aide maintains the tension on the rope until the participant decides to descend. As the participant begins to lower their heels down, the aide releases the tension on the rope accordingly. The cloth acts as a gentle trigger and support.

Audience Response

During the Sensorium Gymnasium, audience members were invited to participate in and explore any of the interactive artworks, or simply observe others interacting. The event was notable for the intensely focused quality of engagement that participants brought to their interactions, facilitated by the 'open studio/laboratory' nature of the event, the venue itself (a large, dedicated residency/rehearsal space), and the collective momentum of the six exhibits. For Surging Verticality, the participants were also invited to write down some comments on their experience of the artwork, directly after their encounter. Twenty people contributed written comments on their experience and one of the participants was interviewed after the event. A selection of participant quotes is found in Table 1.

Tracing the memory of the sensation and physical movement in space.
Body memory does not equal control.
Beautiful strangeness in the pull from the ankles—giving the impetus for being uplifted into the skies.
Freeing and landing like a bird …
The sound of birds enhanced the impression of height and aspiration.

Table 1. Participant comments on their experience of Surging Verticality

We only briefly discuss the themes identified in the audience responses, before moving on to a broader discussion of our experience in making this artwork.

- *Negotiating balance*: The negotiation of balance involved sensations or feelings of centering, shifting weight, being supported and lifted or fear of falling.

- *Moving from body memory*: The preparation for interaction through listening and moving to the ATM lesson, provided participants with a body memory and gave them physical strategies for balancing.
- *Unlike everyday experience of body*: The choice of binding the cloth to the ankles and heels resulted in people experiencing their body and its movement in unfamiliar ways, physically reorienting their perception of their own bodies.
- *Imagination intensifies experience*: The arousal of the imagination can intensify physical sensation and create poetic dimensions of experience, enabling participants to go beyond a simple movement exercise.

DISCUSSION

We briefly reflect on the bringing together of Feldenkrais somatic bodywork and interactive art, drawing particular attention to the common ground shared by the two practices and the challenges identified in our exploration of the two.

In developing an aesthetics of interoceptive engagement and reflection through body-focused interaction, our research has highlighted the importance of context and individual subjective orientation. Feldenkrais and human-centered design methodologies have both provided a framework for paying attention to the experience of interaction—to the specific details of an interactive experience that contribute to how we feel when we are moved or asked to move in a certain way, and culmination of these sensations into 'an experience' that we take away with us at the conclusion of our interaction.

Foremost amongst the factors that enabled audiences to engage with the work in the way that they did, was the sense of safety and permission we provided, as the interaction hosts and facilitators, and the highly focused contemplative environment of the open-studio exhibition setting. As in somatic bodywork—so in the work we presented at the Sensorium Gymnasium: what we are dealing with here is a collection of intelligent, moving and sensing subjects, not simply a set of bodies that we do things to. The sensitivity we were able to bring to the design of these interactions via the Feldenkrais work enabled us to establish a sense of trust and openness that was essential in order for audiences to feel safe to engage in this type of highly personal investigation.

Meeting audiences at this level, entails a contract between the artist/facilitator and audience: a degree of confidence, skill and sensitivity with respect to the use of touch and body manipulation on the part of the makers, and a sense of willingness and availability on the part of the audience, to enter into a sustained examination of their own body experience. This contract takes form in a ritual of engagement, from the moment the audience participant agrees to the contract, through the preparation and sensitizing of the mind-body and the trajectory of interaction, to concluding the experience, all of which must be given careful consideration.

Cultivating an appropriate state of attentiveness and receptivity to interior experience takes time, care and experience. This state of attentiveness on the part of the participant, presents an inner context that requires special attention by the artist/designer, if the interaction is to succeed. We can draw parallels with experiences of audiences in 'live art' and of people in clinical practice. The role of the artist goes beyond making, to an active, sensitive and skilful presence in the audience experience.

CONCLUSION

As a culture we provide very few opportunities to take our attention inwards, our subjectivity and movement habits are taken as given—despite much evidence to the contrary. These questions of subjectivity and embodiment go to the core of our practices as artists and designers working with body-focused interaction, and have a significant impact on the development of individual works. Further investigation of the challenges and issues arising in this area is required to advance our understandings and imaginings of body-focused interactive experiences and the role they can play in our lives.

ACKNOWLEDGMENTS

This project has been supported through the Australia Council, Inter-Arts Office's 'ArtLab 2008' initiative, and generously supported by Campbelltown Arts Centre, The Bundanon Trust, and Performance Space.

REFERENCES

1. Bishop, C. (2005) 'Chapter 2: Heightened Perception', in Installation Art, Tate Publishing, London, pp. 80.
2. Feldenkrais, M. *Awareness Through Movement.* HarperCollins, 1972.
3. Jensen, M. V. A physical approach to tangible interaction design. In *Proc. TEI01*, ACM (2007), 241-244.
4. Loke, L. and Robertson, T. Studies of dancers: Moving from experience to interaction design. *International Journal of Design 4*, 2 (2010), 39-54.
5. Moen, J. From hand-held to body-worn: Embodied experiences of the design and use of a wearable movement-based interaction concept. In *Proc. TEI01*, ACM (2007), 251-258.
6. Schiphorst, T. and Andersen, K. Between bodies: Using experience modeling to create gestural protocols for physiological data transfer. In *Proc. CHI 2004 Fringe*, ACM Press.

MagiMusic: Using Embedded Compass (Magnetic) Sensor for Touch-less Gesture Based Interaction with Digital Music Instruments in Mobile Devices

Hamed Ketabdar
Quality and Usability Lab,
TU Berlin, Deutsche Telekom
Laboratories, Ernst-Reuter-Platz
7, 10587 Berlin
hamed.ketabdar@telekom.de

Amirhossein Jahnbekam
Deutsche Telekom Laboratories,
Ernst-Reuter-Platz 7, 10587 Berlin
amirhossein.jahanbekam@telekom.de

Kamer Ali Yüksel
Computer Vision and Pattern
Analysis Laboratory
Sabanci University
Istanbul, Turkey
kamer@sabanciuniv.edu

Tobias Hirsch
TU Berlin,
10587 Berlin
tobias.hirsch@mailbox.tu-berlin.de

Amin Haji Abolhassani
Centre for Intelligent
Machines,
McGill University, Canada
amin@cim.mcgill.ca

ABSTRACT
Playing musical instruments such as chordophones, percussions and keyboard types accompany with harmonic interaction of player's hand with the instruments. In this work, we present a novel approach that enables the user to imitate the music playing gestures around mobile devices. In our approach, touch-less gestures, which change magnetic field around the device, are employed for interaction. The activity of playing an instrument can be transparently pursued by moving a tiny magnet in hand around new generation of mobile phones equipped with embedded digital compass (magnetic sensor). The phonation intentions of the user can be simulated on the mobile device by capturing the gestural pattern using magnetic sensor. The proposed method allows digital imitation of a broad number of instruments while still being able to sense musical hits and relative plectrum gestures. It provides a framework for extending interaction space with music applications beyond physical boundaries of small mobile devices, and to 3D space around the device. This can allow for a more natural, comfortable and flexible interaction. We present several mobile music applications developed based on the proposed method for Apple iPhone 3GS.

Author Keywords
Digital Music Instruments, Mobile Devices, Magnetic Field Sensor, 3D Magnetic Gestures, Around Device Interaction.

ACM Classification Keywords
H5.m. Information interfaces and presentation (e.g., HCI): Miscellaneous.

TEI'11, January 22–26, 2011, Funchal, Portugal.

Figure 1: Gestural interaction with music applications using 3D space around a mobile device based on magnetic field.

General Terms
Design, Experimentation.

INTRODUCTION
The technological advances in the digital devices have dramatically changed the concept of musical performance as well. Today's bands are effectively using instruments (e.g. keyboard) enhanced with embedded digital computers having a variety of software including effectors and equalizers. Nowadays, mobile devices also became popular digital instruments for musical performance [3, 7]. The touch-screen and accelerometer are mainly used for interaction in order to simulate traditional instruments [5, 6, 2].

In this work, we propose to use the magnetic field sensor (magnetometer) embedded in new mobile devices (such as Apple iPhone 3GS and Google Nexus), for interacting with music related applications on mobile devices. The embedded magnetometer provides a measure of magnetic field along X, Y, and Z directions. Moving a peripheral magnet in the device surroundings changes the magnetic pattern of the space around the device and causes continues deviations in the values of mentioned axes. Collecting values of magnetometer in temporal order forms a 3D vector set that can be used to represent various activities. In the same context, MagiTact [8], the use of magnetic field sensor for general-purpose interaction with mobile devices, has been recently proposed. In this method, the user takes a magnet that can be in shape of a rod, pen or ring; in his hand and draws coarse gestures in 3D space around the device. These gestures can be interpreted as interaction commands. As presented in this paper, a similar methodology can be applied for interaction with music performance applications on mobile devices (Fig. 1). This allows effective use of 3D space around the device for more flexible and natural gesture based interaction with music performance applications.

Using traditional instruments involves the harmonic motion of hands, which alters according to instrument type and shape. In our methodology, we establish a mapping between those motions of hand (or fingers), and movement of a magnet (taken in fingers) in the space around the device. Several audio characteristics such as frequency, equalization, filtering, etc. can be altered based on changes in magnetic field caused by the magnetic gestures. Position, movement, shape, and orientation of the magnet can be used as an input modality to alter parameters of the music being played or being adjusted. Similar designs of musical instruments based on electric field sensor (cathode relays) and IR proximity sensor [4, 10] was investigated for musical performance. Our interaction method is based on magnetic field which can capture the 3D motion in a more effective and detailed way. Since magnetic field can pass through different materials, the device does not need to be in line of sight for the interaction. As the magnetic sensor is a cheap, simple and small sensor, integrating it in mobile devices does not impose major change in hardware or physical specifications of devices. The magnetic sensor is already integrated in many modern mobile devices such as Apple iPhone 3GS, iPad, Google Nexus, etc.

Recently, the requirements for using mobile devices as digital instruments are defined by [3, 7]. In this context, there have been several attempts using touch-screen and/or accelerometer [5, 6] including a gesture-based DJ-effecting mobile game and collaborative composing approaches (e.g. flute using microphone and multi-touch). There has also been analysis of embedded sensors regarding musical performance [2, 3] where the sound generation using striking, shaking and sweeping types of natural gestures are experimented. However, playing musical instruments on the surface of a mobile device is not natural enough, and usually requires both user's hands on a single small screen of the mobile phone. In comparison with touch-screen or keypad input, our technique provides higher degree of flexibility for musical performance, because the interaction space is extended beyond the physical boundary of the device. When using accelerometer based interaction, the user has to repeatedly rotate the device to launch certain actions which makes the user loose direct sight to the screen [1]. In our proposed method, however, device orientation can be maintained and be adapted to user's natural behavior.

In the next section, we discuss in more details how the output of magnetic sensor influenced by movement of an external magnet can be used for interacting with music applications. We then present different prototype music applications that we have developed based on our interaction method.

METHODOLOGY

In this section, we propose different mappings of sound characteristics for sonification of the 3D vector data provided by the magnetometer. Besides the mappings, we explain how such digital instruments can be realized using gesture-based interaction. As shown in Fig. 2, the magnetic sensor provides a measure of magnetic field along X, Y, and Z directions. The mapping of sound characteristics to the 3D vector set provided by the magnetometer can be explored in two ways considering excitation type: sustained and impulsive. The sustained mappings are based on continuous energy transfer such as the 3D motion data that is captured using different type of sensors; whereas, the impulsive mappings are discontinuous and generally triggered using gestural interactions. In other words, there are two distinct methods that one can employ magnetic field to play a musical instrument. The first way is using direct sensor values where the projection of sensor value to X, Y and Z axes provides 3 different modalities which can be mapped to different sound parameters. In the second approach, a sequence of sensor values shapes a 3D gesture pattern. This pattern can be matched against a model to realize their corresponding gesture class as suggested in [8]. We present samples of both approaches in the next sections.

Depending on the application, sometimes a transformation of magnetic sensor output can be more useful than raw signals. The transformation can be time derivative or calculating norm of magnetic signals. Time derivative operation can be especially important when there is a need to remove effect of earth magnetic field on the sensor. In this case, time derivative operation acts as a high-pass filter and removes the effect of earth magnetic field. For instance, in a guitar application, a triggering like gesture in the air (by magnet) can be easily highlighted in time derivatives of magnetic sensor output.

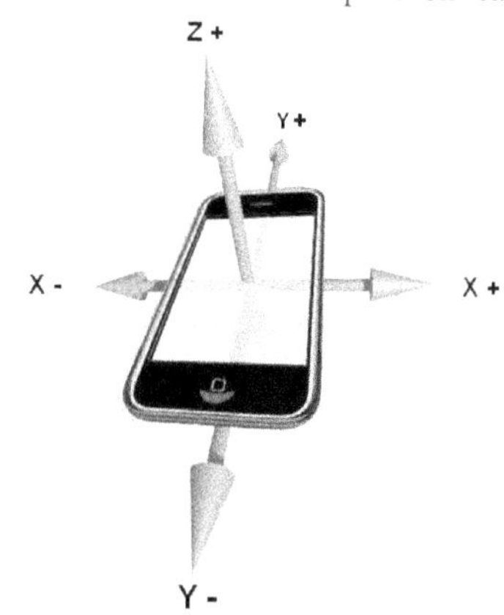

Figure 2. The magnetic sensor provides a measure of magnetic field along X, Y, and Z axis.

In the following sections, we present the mobile music applications we have implemented based on the magnetic field interaction. The applications are developed for Apple iPhone 3GS. In order to facilitate actual implementation of music applications in the first trial, magnetic signals captured by the mobile device (iPhone) are sent to a PC based SuperCollider (SC) [9] server. SuperCollider is a real-time audio synthesis and algorithmic composition environment. Sending data to the SC server is only to simplify sound synthesis part, and the magnetic interaction is fully implemented through the mobile device. Therefore, there are two components for each application: a client on iPhone 3GS, and a SuperCollider server on PC. The client sends the data related to magnetic field surrounding the mobile device to the server over wireless network. The SC server takes the data from one or multiple clients and synthesizes the parameterized sound.

IMPULSIVE INSTRUMENTS

As mentioned earlier, for simulation of impulsive instruments, we check for a certain gesture pattern in the data provided by the magnetic sensor. This data corresponds to a certain gesture which the user has performed using the magnet in hand.

Air Guitar

Guitar is a musical instrument belonging to chordophone family which has 6 attached strings. Playing a guitar is performed by 2 distinct actions: strumming and holding (locking). In a normal guitar, strumming comes along with periodically scratching of the instrument strings with right hand fingers. The left hand presses different pitches on different strings alongside the neck of the guitar to generate different tones. In touch-screen based guitar applications offered recently on mobile phones, one can pluck the simulated guitar by scratching the touch screen. The action of holding a note is also done on the same screen (3 different areas for each string). Such arrangement for playing guitar can be to some extent unnatural and inconvenient since it requires using both hands on small screen of the mobile device.

In our guitar application (*Air Guitar)*, we have replaced the touch screen based strumming action with a 3D gesture based action in the space around the device. We let the holding (locking) action to be remained on the touchpad. However, the strumming is implemented with magnetic interaction to imitate the natural action. For string triggering (strumming), values obtained by X-axis component of the magnetometer determine the string which should be triggered. The range of values is divided into 6 intervals each representing a particular string. The key factor to detect the triggering gesture (action) is a rapid change in the magnetic field sensed by the magnetic sensor, which corresponds to rapid movement of fingers with magnet in a gesture similar to strumming. This can be detected by comparing the variance of magnetic field (estimated over an interval/window) with respect to a pre-defined threshold. The rapid movement of fingers in the air (with magnet) creates a rapid temporal change in the magnetic field around the device, and makes the variance of sensed magnetic field exceed the threshold. To avoid stepping changes from one string interval to another, we have considered a gap between these intervals (X component values) in which no tone will be played. The combinations of pitches (selected by touch screen), and strings (6 string triggered in the air) results in 24 different states that are sent to the server for playing corresponding sound.

Drum-Kit

Drum is a cylindrical shape instrument from percussion family of musical instruments. Normally in percussion instruments, the head of cylinder is covered by some sort of elastic skin that one can hit by hands or by some special sticks. In playing a drum, two main factors are taken into account: the strength of the hit and the radius of hitting point to the center of surface. In our model, to simulate the hand gesture on the instrument, the Z component of the magnetic sensor output is mapped to the vertical movement of the hand towards the surface. The second time derivative of the Z component signal is interpreted as strength or energy of hitting. The more the strength (energy) of the signal is, the louder the generated sound will be. The X component of magnetic sensor output represents the radial distance to the center of the instrument, indicating the tone to be played. Having a magnet in hand, one can magically play a drum by hitting back and forth in the air towards the surface of the device, and right and left with respect to the center, to obtain different tones. The tone is played only if the strength (second derivative of Z component) exceeds a threshold. If the tone is played, the strength (loudness) of the tone would be proportional to the second derivative of the Z component. Using touch-less magnetic interaction in our Drum-kit for detecting the hit action can be superior to the use of touch screen, as strength of the hit can't be easily calculated in touch screen. In addition, in our Drum-Kit, we are using a hitting gesture similar to the real Drum, which can be more natural than hitting on a rigid screen surface.

Harmonics

Sound harmonics are integer multiplicands of a base sound frequency. In some instruments such as metallophones or xylophones, on any consecutive pitch of the instrument, an individual harmonic can be produced. In metallophone, different metal bars with different sizes are mounted to an oscillating frame. With a mallet, one can strike on different bars to generate different harmonics. To play one particular metallophone, 2 factors determine the type and quality of the output: The metal bar that is stricken and the strength of the strike. In our framework, the X value of the magnetic field (sensed by magnetic sensor) is dedicated to represent the bars on the instrument. We have split up the X-axis value range of magnetic sensor into 24 different intervals. Depending on the value of X component, the index of its corresponding interval (1:24) represents the bar which should be stricken on the simulated metallophone. The strength of the strike can be also obtained in the same way as Drum-Kit.

SUSTAINED INSTRUMENTS

For simulating sustained instruments, we use the output of magnetic sensor in raw, time derivative or normalized format directly for tuning certain parameters of the sound being generated. The output of magnetic sensor (when the magnet is not engaged in performing a gesture) can be a function of intensity, position, polarity and orientation of the magnet. This means that the sound parameters can be tuned based on position, polarity, orientation, etc. of the magnet in the hand of the performer.

Theremin

Theremin is a touch-less electronic instrument that is controlled by two different shape antennas. The task of one of antennas is to detect the distance of player's hands to the antenna, and the other one has to track the oscillations of the player's hands. The distance of players' hand to one antenna is used to change the frequency (pitch) of the sound and the distance of the other hand to the second antenna is used to adjust the amplitude (volume) of the sound. In order to simulate Theremin based on our framework, we have assigned the X-axis of the magnetic sensor to control the frequency of the sound. The Y-axis value is also used to control the volume of the sound. Forwarding these settings to the SC server, we can play the appropriate sound resembling the original Theremin.

Sound Modulation and Effecting

After creation of a certain type of sound, it is possible to modify its characteristics through a high number of parameters, including amplitude, resonance, pan and spread, velocity, attack/decay/sustain/release, legato and vibrato. Modifications on characteristics of an already created sound enable different expressions to be obtained. Different sound effects, thus, can be obtained by alterations and diversifications applied to signals. Sound effects can create dramatic changes on any possible parameter of sound and enable a number of opportunities for shifting musical components to various forms. Value of the magnetic signals registered by the magnetic sensor can be used as a basis for altering different sound parameters. As a sample for sound effecting, we briefly mention to a Disk Jockey (DJ) application developed based on the concept of magnetic interaction.

Disc Jockey

DJ (disc jockey) is title of a person who plays and synthesis different types of recorded music for audience. To simulate a DJ medium, we developed an application on a mobile device that enables the DJ to tune and combine music by means of magnetic field interaction. For a demonstration we have implemented two standard effects that a DJ can control: Crossfading and Scratching. Crossfading is the way to interlace two playing sounds. In a simpler sense, crossfading means to increase the power of one sound and decrease the power of the other. On a DJ desk, there is a fader slider that overlaps music with another. How smooth or fast two songs fade depends on the DJ's skills. If M is the first sound and N is the second sound and $C1$, $C2$ are their corresponding coefficients, the output sound can be defined as following:

$$\text{Sound} = (M * C1) + (M * C2), \qquad \text{where} \quad C1 + C2 = 1.$$

Scratching is a technique to play a part of previously recorded music back and forth. The effect of doing such action is hearing a cutting sound. Naturally, scratching is the act of moving, stopping and reversing a disk on a music turntable. In our work, we have assigned the X-axis values of the magnetic sensor to the crossfading action, and the Y-axis to the scratching action. $C1$ and $C2$ coefficients are calculated based on X component of magnetic sensor output, hence relative position of hand with magnet on the X axis. In this way, the DJ can obtain different mixtures of two sounds by moving his hand left and right with respect to the device. Scratching effect is produced when a sharp movement of the magnet in Y direction is detected. The tuning data obtained by mobile phone will be sent through wireless network to a SC server to synthesis the output sound based on the user settings. The advantage of such setting is that the DJ can keep his natural gesture to tune the sound output while he can freely move through the audience. DJ pooling can also be imagined when several mobile DJ terminals join to a central server.

CONCLUSION AND FUTURE WORK

In this paper, we have presented a new approach that mimics the music playing gestures on mobile device. We have proposed interaction with music and audio applications based on changing magnetic field around the mobile device using an external magnet. The change in magnetic field is sensed by internally embedded compass (magnetic) sensor on mobile device. We have presented several music applications that we developed based on the proposed method for mobile devices (Apple iPhone 3GS in our case). Our method provides the possibility of extending interaction space with mobile music applications beyond physical boundaries of the device and to 3D space around the device. This allows the user to interact naturally using gestures as he acts in normal life. Developing more sophisticated gesture recognition techniques can enhance interaction with music applications and reduce the chance of wrong actions. We are also interested to further investigate using multiple magnets (and possibly multiple magnetic sensors) for the interaction. As touch-less interaction with music applications is relatively a new concept in music production, one can also think of inventing totally new instruments using the presented method.

REFERENCES

1. R. Bencina, D. Wilde, and S. Langley. Gesture sound experiments: Process and mappings. In Proceedings of 8th International Conference on New interfaces for Musical Expression (NIME 08), pages 197–202.
2. G. Essl and M. Rohs. Interactivity for mobile music- making. Organised Sound, 14(02):197207, 2009.
3. G. Essl, G. Wang, and M. Rohs. Developments and challenges turning mobile phones into generic music performance platforms. In Proceedings of the Mobile Music Workshop, 2008.
4. I. Franco. The AirStick: a free-gesture controller using infrared sensing. Proc. New Interfaces For Musical Expression (NIME), pages 248–249, 2004.
5. G. Geiger. Using the touch screen as a controller for portable computer music instruments. In Proceedings of the 2006 conference on New interfaces for musical expression, page 64, 2006.
6. N. Gillian, S. O'Modhrain, and G. Essl. Scratch-Off: a gesture based mobile music game with tactile feedback.
7. A. R. Jensenius. Some challenges related to music and movement in mobile music technology. In 5th International Mobile Music Workshop, Vienna, Austria, 2008.
8. H. Ketabdar, K. A. Yüksel, and M. Roshandel. MagiTact: interaction with mobile devices based on compass (magnetic) sensor. In Proceeding of the 14th international conference on intelligent user interfaces, pages 413–414, Hong Kong, China, 2010, ACM.
9. J. McCartney. Rethinking the computer music language: SuperCollider. Computer Music Journal, 26(4):61–68, 2002.
10. L. S. Theremin and O. Petrishev. The design of a musical instrument based on cathode relays. Leonardo Music Journal, 6:49–50, 1996.

Leveraging Behavioral Models of Sounding Objects for Gesture-Controlled Sound Design

Kristian Gohlke, David Black
Hochschule Bremen
(University of Applied Sciences)
kgohlke@acm.org, dblack@mevis.fraunhofer.de

Jörn Loviscach
Fachhochschule Bielefeld
(University of Applied Sciences)
joern.loviscach@fh-bielefeld.de

ABSTRACT

Sound designers and Foley artists have long struggled to create expressive soundscapes using standard editing software, devoting much time for the calibration of multiple sound samples and parameter adjustments. We present an intuitive approach that exploits the capabilities of off-the-shelf motion-sensing input devices to enable quick and fluid interaction with sound to trigger and modulate digital sound generators based on adaptable behavioral models of familiar physical sounding objects. Rather than requiring profound technical knowledge of sound design, the system leverages the user's motor memory and motion skills to mimic generic and familiar interactions with everyday sounding objects. This allows the user to fully focus on the expressive act of sound creation while enjoying a fluent workflow and a satisfying user experience.

Author Keywords

Foley Art, Motion Gestures, Sound Effects, Audio Editing, HCI.

ACM Classification Keywords

H.5.2.: Information interfaces and presentation: User Interfaces – Input devices and strategies

INTRODUCTION

Professional Foley Artistry

Over the history of the profession, Foley artists – sound effect artists for movie, television, radio, and theater – have developed workflows that exploit the physical properties of various everyday sounding objects for creating a wide spectrum of sounds [18]. For instance, the sound of footsteps in snow may be reproduced by pressing a fist into a tray of corn starch, galloping horses may be mimicked by beating coconut shells on a hard surface, and crumpling aluminum foil may substitute for frying eggs. Foley artists use microphones to record these physical sounding objects, which are manipulated in many ways to produce the desired sound effect. To create the appropriate soundscape for a production, the sound is often recorded while the Foley artist watches movie or theater scenes to synchronize sound and motion. This workflow allows the Foley artist to instantly react to the images with fine expressiveness, as the artist directly interacts with a selection of tangible sound-producing artifacts. However, the approach is not without its drawbacks. The flexibility is highly dependent on the available "library" of these physical objects, many of which are bound to a narrow range of applications. A versatile collection of such objects can take up a considerable amount of space and thus often limits the artist to purposefully constructed studios. Once a specific sound has been recorded, expressive parameters are only digitally editable to a certain degree, and often, content must be re-recorded to achieve the desired results. Because of these factors, the classic Foley workflow has been restricted to the domain of specialists. The widespread availability of digital production tools has enticed a growing number of casual users to shoot, edit, and publish their own video content. Professional Foley gadgets and the appropriate recording environment are often not available in such contexts.

Digital Foley Work

Much Foley-style work has been transferred to the digital realm. Instead of recording physical sounding objects themselves, many sound designers now rely on large databases of sound recordings for their work. Finding and arranging these snippets on a timeline is a time-consuming process that often involves much manual setup: to achieve desired results, the user must locate a desired audio file, edit low-level audio parameters such as reverb decay times, filter frequencies, sample loop starting times, and start and end points. Values are entered into the digital audio workstation (DAW) with keyboard and mouse or manipulated on-screen by tweaking parameter envelope graphs.

TEI'11, January 22–26, 2011, Funchal, Portugal.

Although this approach can potentially yield a high amount of accuracy and in-depth control over the resultant sound, it also suffers from persistent difficulties. First, the approach requires a profound technical knowledge, as it adds an additional layer of abstraction that needs to be resolved by the user, leaving amateur users with little options other than basic sound sample placement and elementary parameter editing. Because sound parameters must be individually altered, much of the directness and expressiveness found in traditional Foley methods is lost. Second, manually inserting and editing samples is time consuming and demands repetitive on-screen interactions, as usually only one parameter is edited at a time. Third, non-realtime editing of sound events on a timeline limits the ability of the editor to react directly with the flow the motion picture, as precision placement and manipulation of events often requires stopping the playback to fine-tune the parameters. This limits the expressiveness available, particularly in the context of live media like theater or artistic performances.

Merging Foley Workflows

We present an approach that combines the salient elements from both the traditional Foley workflow and contemporary digital sound effect design to achieve a more satisfying user experience with enhanced expressiveness when working with digital sound generators. We propose a system that leverages the sensor capabilities of readily available motion input devices to activate and modulate digital sound generation. We introduce a toolset of basic behavioral models of physical sounding objects which couples the expressiveness and immediacy of the traditional Foley workflow with the accuracy and accessibility of current digital sound design methods. Thereby, the toolbox helps to resolve many of the individual limitations inherent in each of the two individual methods.

RELATED WORK

Levitin et al. [11] describe a systematic framework for controlling musical instruments by mapping gestures to sound. They detail the relevant features by which different sound events develop over time and how they may be controlled by physical interaction. Our work incorporates many of their findings to define a musical control space.

Research on virtual reality instruments has been conducted by Mäki-Patola et al. [12], who identify factors that are relevant for the playability of such new instruments and discuss the impact of these features on the learning curve. Paine et al. [16] attempt to develop mapping strategies for entirely new electronic instruments, using different types of physical input.

The standard input capabilities of laptop computers, such as the camera or built-in motion sensors, have been used in novel ways to control sound performances [9].

The modulated objects of Burtner [5] describe an attempt to link motion sensing controllers to many parameters of different sound generators. Thereby the system provides high-level control over a large set of low-level sound features.

VIRTUAL SOUND TOOLS

Our approach allows the user to control digital sound generators with a set of motion gestures that resemble interaction with physical sounding objects. The user is provided with gesture-controlled sound toolbox that exhibits a behavior which is largely similar to interacting with familiar physical sounding objects from the classic Foley toolbox while being flexible enough to create a wide spectrum of sounds. Familiar mind models allow for an intuitive interaction with the sound. As detailed in an earlier work [3], slight modifications to the expected behavior of such sound tools can be employed to provide the user with added expressiveness, for instance, by enabling control of various digital audio effects. By recombining the basic behavioral properties of different physical objects and mapping them to motion gestures, new sound tools with different characteristics can be created.

PROTOTYPE

Our system consists of a toolbox of plugins for use in common DAW software. The software includes two main components. The first component receives and processes motion data from commercial motion-sensing devices such as the Nintendo Wii Remote [10, 13], Sony Playstation Move controller [17], or any other device with sufficient inertial measurement capabilities. The second component consists of a set of templates that interpret the incoming motion data and maps them to sound parameters in a semantically meaningful way. The user can control many audio parameters simultaneously, which can also be recorded as MIDI note events and control-change values in the user's DAW. These note events and other control data may be played back to reproduce the original recorded sounds.

Behavioral models of physical sound producing objects

The heart of the system is a set of models that mimic the behavior of physical sounding objects. These models follow the design principles for computer music controllers as detailed by Cook [6]. The user handles the controller device as if it were the mimicked physical object. Other approaches attempt to create sound based on specific physical models [4, 7, 9, 14]. Deviating from this approach, our system is not centered on such highly precise physical models; we work with simplified pseudo-physical abstractions of such models which are focused on instantly covering a wide range of sounds. To illustrate these, which we have called *behavioral models*, we present a selection of the various included elements:

Shot Mode

This model uses a trigger button on the motion device to play a sound sample. An example of this use might be a gun duel in which two opponents are shooting different sounding guns: pointing the device to the left and triggering produces one opponent's gun sound, while pointing to the right produces the other gun sound. The sounds are automatically panned in the stereo field according to the orientation of the controller. The tilt-angle of the device controls the overall volume and several reverberation parameters to create a basic auditory impression of depth, thereby allowing the user to virtually place sounds in two dimensions. This mode can also be used to trigger and modify any other one-shot sample.

Strike Mode

In this behavioral mode, sound events are generated using a striking or whipping motion for which the instantaneous velocity of the device relates to the intensity of the resulting sound event. This mimics, for instance, the motion of hitting a drumhead, slapping a table, or cracking a whip. This model is especially useful for applications such as a series of footsteps or knocking on a door. Other scenarios that can be accommodated with this model include hitting drums, breaking glass, slamming doors, hammering nails, and crashing cars. Employing two motion controllers, sword fights or other fighting action could also be sonified.

Shake Mode

In this model, the aggregate motion of the device is mapped to the intensity and rate of repetition of sound events. This may be used to model such sounds as rush hour traffic, swarms of bees or birds, cheering audiences, steam engines, or a jar of coins being shaken.

Mechanical Control Mode

The system may also be used to activate and control continuous sounds. The motion device may model the function of an accelerator pedal – tilting the device forward modulates the sound of a car engine in a similar way as the driver's foot in a real car modulates the acceleration. Different sounds loaded into this model can be used to simulate different engine types. This mode is also suitable for controlling friction or stretching sounds such sawing wood or rubber being stretched.

Magic Wand Mode

The magic wand mode can be used to create trajectory-based sounds. The user accelerates and moves the device through the air at different speeds to control the volume and the intensity of the resulting sound. This mode allows the creation of sounds such as a passing airplane or car, a sword cutting through the air, or imaginary sounds such as light sabers or the jingling sound of a magic wand in a fairy tale.

Flow Mode

In this model, the tilt angle of the controller modulates the intensity of matter being poured from a container, the available sounds range from liquids of different viscosity to grit, such as rice, sand or gravel. The further the user tilts the device, the higher the flow of matter.

Hybrid Modes

By combining the existing behavioral models, new modes can be created. A combined model of the shake mode with the strike mode can, for instance be used to control the sound of events such as rolling thunderstorms which involve an initial strike followed by a variable length of a sustained trailing sound. The sound of a whip swooshing through the air followed by a cracking sound can be achieved by combining the magic wand mode with the knock mode. The recombination of different behavioral models with different sounds can be used to create sounds for a range of different scenarios.

Two-handed & collaborative interaction

Multiple controllers can be employed to simultaneously control different behavioral models. The user can, for instance, control the sound of a car engine with one controller the while adding the friction sound of tires skidding over the asphalt. Simultaneously, another user could add gunshot sounds and crashing car sounds, thus allowing the on-the-fly creation of an entire soundscape for an action movie scene.

INTEGRATION

The current prototype system receives data from a motion controller via Bluetooth and maps it to Open Sound Control (OSC) messages[1] The OSC messages are received by a plug-in in the targeted DAW software. In our setup, we used Ableton Live in conjunction with a Max for Live patch. In the DAW, control parameters and activation methods of standard factory-included sound generators such as samplers, synthesizers, and effects units are linked via MIDI messages and note events. These may be changed in real-time according to the processed motion data. The settings in both the FoleySonic plug-in patch and the individual DAW plugins may be further modified to fit a wide range of sounds. To facilitate entry into this method of Foley artistry, a set of basic "atomic" sound samples is included in the package. For more information, see [2].

CONCLUSION

Professional Foley artists, game sound designers, recording artists, and amateur video editors were asked to interact with the system and provide feedback both during use and in subsequent interviews. These observations indicated that the system was accepted as a viable means of creating expressive Foley soundtracks in a fast and intuitive process. Users reported that the system was particularly suitable for exploring the possibilities of the sounds and quickly recording ideas. Although users were drawn to the playful interaction, some expressed a desire for a higher degree of accuracy in the resultant sound. This indicates that providing a balance between the accurate control of sound and serendipitous and unexpected results should be a critical factor in the design of new behavioral models.

---

[1] http://opensoundcontrol.org/spec-1_0

Ongoing work is aimed at simplifying the process of creating custom behavioral models. Similar to the set of atomic sounds used in the included behavioral models, a set of low-level atomic gestures, based upon the approach presented by Ashbrook et al. [1] could be employed to easily construct user-defined virtual sound tools. In addition to the included set of behavioral models, an assisted mapping mode could further enable the user to associate elementary motion gestures with high-level sound control parameters, thereby allowing the user to define custom modes of interaction by capturing movements.

We have presented a system that provides a flexible and entertaining way to efficiently create Foley soundtracks by combining the interaction of the classic Foley workflow with the vast range of capabilities afforded by digital sound tools. It allows the user to explore many aspects of digital sound generators without being hampered by individually tweaking technical sound parameters. Along with its compatibility with industry-standard software, protocols, and controller devices, the system holds potential for becoming a useful addition to the Foley editor's toolbox.

REFERENCES

1. Ashbrook, D. and Starner, T. 2010. MAGIC: a motion gesture design tool. In Proc. Conference on Human Factors in Computing Systems. CHI (2010). pp. 2159–2168.
2. Black, D., Heise, S., Loviscach, J. Generic Sound Effects to Aid in Audio Retrieval. In Proc. 126th Convention of the Audio Engineering Society (2009), Paper 7795.
3. Black, D., Gohlke, K., Loviscach, J. FoleySonic: Placing Sounds on a Timeline Through Gestures. In Proc. 128th Convention of the Audio Engineering Society (2010), Paper 8004.
4. Böttcher, N., Gelineck, S., and Serafin, S. PHYSMISM: a control interface for creative exploration of physical models. In Proc. Conference on New interfaces For Musical Expression. NIME (2007). pp. 31–36.
5. Burtner, M. A theory of modulated objects for new shamanic controller design. In Proc. Conference on New interfaces For Musical Expression. NIME (2004). pp. 193–196.
6. Cook, P. Principles for designing computer music controllers. In Proc. Conference on New interfaces For Musical Expression, NIME (2001). pp.1–4.
7. Cook, P. Modeling Bill's Gait: Analysis and Parametric Synthesis of Walking Sounds. In Proc. 22nd I. Conf. on Virtual, Synthetic, and Entertainment Audio of the Audio Engineering Society (2002), Paper 222.
8. Fiebrink, R., Wang, G., and Cook, P. R. Don't forget the laptop: using native input capabilities for expressive musical control. In Proc. Conference on New interfaces For Musical Expression. NIME (2007). pp. 164–167.
9. Heise, S., and Loviscach, J., A Versatile Expressive Percussion Instrument with Game Technology, Proceedings of IEEE ICME (2008). pp. 393–396.
10. Lehrman, P. D. The Wii Remote as a Musical Instrument: Technology and Case Studies. In Proc. 127th Convention of the Audio Engineering Society (2009), Paper 7888.
11. Levitin D. J., McAdams, S., Adams, R.L. Control parameters for musical instruments: a foundation for new mappings of gesture to sound. Organised Sound 7(2). (2002) Cambridge University Press, UK. pp.171–189.
12. Mäki-Patola, T., Laitinen, J., Kanerva, A., and Takala, T. 2005. Experiments with virtual reality instruments. In Proc. Conference on New interfaces For Musical Expression. NIME (2005). pp. 11–16.
13. Nintendo Wii Motion Plus http://www.nintendo.com/wii/what/accessories/wiimotionplus (last accessed: July 29, 2010).
14. O'Modhrain, S., Essl, G., PebbleBox and CrumbleBag: Tactile Interfaces for Granular Synthesis. In Proc. Conference on New interfaces For Musical Expression. NIME (2004). pp. 74–79.
15. Paine, D. G. 2004. Gesture and musical interaction: interactive engagement through dynamic morphology. In Proc. Conference on New interfaces For Musical Expression. NIME (2004). pp. 80–86.
16. Paine, G., Stevenson, I., and Pearce, A. 2007. The Thummer Mapping Project (ThuMP). In Proc. Conference on New interfaces For Musical Expression. NIME (2007). pp. 70–77.
17. Sony PlayStation Move Controller http://us.playstation.com/ps3/accessories/scph-98060.html (last accessed: July 29, 2010).
18. Yewdall, D. L. Practical Art of Motion Picture Sounds. (2007). Focal Press, Burlington, MA, USA. pp. 403–439.

The Augmentalist: Enabling Musicians to Develop Augmented Musical Instruments

Dan Newton and Mark T. Marshall
Interaction and Graphics Group
University of Bristol
dn6326@bristol.ac.uk, mark@cs.bris.ac.uk

ABSTRACT

We present the Augmentalist: a system that allows a musician to augment their existing musical instrument using a variety of sensors. This system is focused on the musician and their musical aims, rather than the sensor technology being used. The overall goal is to create allow musicians to easily explore new musical performance techniques with augmented musical instruments. We present the design process and implementation of the system, an example of an instrument developed by one of the 10 participating musicians and a discussion of a number of issues raised by the project, including musicians as designers, the potential for exploration and mastery and the transferability of instruments between performers.

Author Keywords

Interaction, Music, Augmented Instruments, Tangible Interfaces, Embodied Interaction

ACM Classification Keywords

H.5.5 Information Interfaces and Presentation (e.g., HCI): Sound and Music Computing

General Terms

Design, Human Factors

INTRODUCTION

The simultaneous availability of inexpensive computing hardware, new sensors capable of measuring a variety of physical parameters, and software for real-time sound synthesis and manipulation has resulted in the development of new digital musical instruments. Increasing numbers of such instruments are being produced each year, with 266 new instruments presented in the first 8 years of the NIME conferences[6]. However, with a few notable exceptions such as the Reactable[1], these instruments tend only to be played by their designers, rather than being taken up by other musicians. Why then do these new instruments not appear on the (more mainstream) music scene?

TEI'11, January 22–26, 2011, Funchal, Portugal.

A number of possible reasons exist for this lack of uptake. Armstrong suggests one possibility: a disconnect between the performer, the instrument and the audience[2]. The interactions involved in controlling a digital musical instrument are not always obvious to the audience. Alongside this, the audience often have no experience of the instrument being played, and as such have no point of reference with regards to the performance.

An exception to this can be the type of digital musical instrument known as augmented or extended instruments[8]. Such instruments are created by embedding additional sensors on a traditional instrument and using them to allow the performer additional control over the sonic output of the instrument (e.g. [7], [9], [5]). These instruments can maintain some characteristics of the instrument with which the audience is familiar, allowing the audience to better relate to the performance.

Another possible issue is that of musicality. In the course of our research, we asked participating musicians to view a number of videos of digital musical instrument performances. Several musicians spoke of a lack of (perceived and/or traditional) musicality in the performances that would discourage them from playing such an instrument.

How then can we produce an instrument that offers a performance experience that is somewhat familiar to the audience, while also producing sounds that are "musical" enough to appeal to more traditional musicians and allow them to be incorporated into performances with other musicians and instruments? The work discussed in this paper attempts to deal with this issue by enabling musicians to create their own augmented instruments. This allows the performer to design the sound and interaction of their new digital musical instrument, which is based on their existing traditional musical instrument. During the entire design process, two core principles formed the basis for all of the decisions made: the system needs to be able to produce musically pleasing results and a musician must be able to tailor the system to their needs.

SYSTEM DESIGN

The design process for the Augmentalist took an iterative, user-centred approach. This involved numerous consultation, testing and design sessions with musicians. The overall goal of this process was to ensure that the system is designed in such a way as to be useful to the musicians themselves.

The consultation process began as soon as the project itself was conceived. It began with a series of short meetings with a number of different musicians. These meetings included sessions with single musicians and also with groups of musicians. The aim of these initial sessions was simply to gauge interest in the project itself and to attempt to determine what features of the system would be useful to a variety of musicians.

From these sessions, we arrived at a design that involved allowing the musicians to attach sensors the their instruments and then map the output from these sensors to MIDI signals to control parameters of audio software with which the musicians are familiar. Our job then is to provide a system that allows this mapping to take place in as simple a way as possible, so that the musician can concentrate on the effect they wish to create, rather than on the intricacies of reading, processing and translating sensor data. Figure 1 shows an example of an augmented instrument created using the system.

Figure 1. An example of an instrument augmented using the Augmentalist system. A slider, attached to the body of the guitar, allows the performer to modify effects with their strumming hand.

IMPLEMENTATION

Hardware

After experimenting with different available sensors and sensor systems, we decided to use Phidgets[4]. These sensors required no soldering or programming on behalf of the users. Thus they are ideal for a system designed for musicians due to their plug and play capabilities[1]. The choice of the Phidgets system also allows for a large range of sensors to be available to the user, with dozens of sensors currently available from the manufacturers that plug directly in to the interface with no electronic skills required to use them.

The sensors are connected via USB 2.0 to a computer. For our initial implementation we used a 2.53GHz MacBook Pro Running OS X 10.6 using a Stanton Scratch Amp firewire audio interface for audio input/output. This setup showed no perceptible latency for live performance.

Software

To convert the sensor data into MIDI signals we used the Max/MSP programming environment. This had the advantage of being easy to use, as well as being fully compatible with the Phidget sensors. It is also an environment with which some musicians are familiar. The interface in Max/MSP allows the user to choose which sensors to map to specific MIDI channels, as well as setting the desired input range from the sensor, output range for the MIDI channel and the mapping between them.

The software allows the user to select which sensor is mapped to to which MIDI signal using a simple graphical interface. The range of sensor values to be mapped can be selected by demonstration, with the performer moving the sensor through its desired range. The MIDI output range can also be limited to a specific range in the software. Finally, the user can specify the mapping function used to convert sensor data to MIDI data. This can be selected from a range of presets (linear increasing, logarithmic increasing, linear decreasing, etc.) or by drawing a mapping function in the interface.

The MIDI data from Max/MSP and the raw audio signal from the instrument are combined in the digital audio workstation Logic Pro 9. Here the MIDI signal can be linked to any control in the software, allowing the musicians to both manipulate the incoming audio and to add new synthesised sounds to this audio.

There are two levels of mapping in this set up. Firstly the gesture data from the sensor must be mapped to a control signal in the software. The sensor parameters are set up by the user within Max/MSP. Secondly the MIDI signal must be mapped to a parameter in Logic Pro, again by the user. Both levels of mapping are left to the musician, maintaining their control of the actions of the system.

THE AUGMENTALIST IN USE: AN EXAMPLE SETUP

Over the course of the development of this project we have constantly involved a number of musicians in the design, testing and development process. In total 10 musicians have spent over 60 hours using the system with more signed up for future development. The musicians involved have included guitarists, DJs, bassists, saxophonists and vocalists. In this section we discuss an example instrument developed by one of the musicians, as it provides an insight into the type of instruments being developed and the process used by the musicians in developing them.

For this example we have chosen an augmented guitar created by one of the guitarists that took part in the development process. This example has been chosen for a number of reasons. Firstly, the guitar is an instrument with which most people have some familiarity, which allows for an easier understanding of the final instrument, Secondly, the guitar has been the focus of some research in terms of sensing, augmentation and interface development (for examples, see [5], [3]). Finally, electric guitarists in particular commonly make use of sound processing and effects in the course of their performances and so are comfortable with how such effects can be used.

[1]Due to the modular nature of the system, other sensor interfaces could be used in place of the Phidgets.

After much experimentation, the guitarist arrived at a configuration using 3 sensors mapped to 3 specific effects in Logic Pro. Firstly, an accelerometer was mounted to the guitar neck. Used as a tilt sensor this allowed the angle between the guitar neck and the ground to be used as a control. Secondly, a slider was placed on the body of the guitar, below the pickups and parallel to the strings. This allowed the guitarist to control effects using fingers from their picking hand, without interfering with their playing. Finally, an infrared distance sensor was attached to the body of the guitar, in such a way that when the guitarist strummed the strings their hand would pass over the sensor. This sensor was configured as an on/off switch which triggered whenever the guitarist's hand passed over it.

The data from these sensors were then mapped to effects in Logic Pro. The guitarist first mapped the angle of the neck to the volume of a delay effect. The system was set up so that moving the neck up in respect to the body caused the volume of the delay effect to increase. The slider on the guitar body was then mapped to a distortion effect known as the BitCrusher. The guitarist was able to use the extra fingers of his picking hand to move the slider forwards and backwards whilst playing, changing the resolution of the BitCrusher effect and thus adding different harmonics to the sound. Finally the infrared detector was used as a switch to control the volume. By mapping the on signal of the switch to a drop in volume, a rhythmic effect was generated from the speed of the strumming hand.

DISCUSSION

Musicians as developers

The Augmentalist system was designed from the start to allow musicians to become the developers of their own augmented instruments. We believe that it is musicians who know the most about their instruments and about the sounds and music they wish to create and so it is the musician who should make the decisions on how the instrument should work.

Over the course of the development of this system so far, the participating musicians developed hundreds of different gesture to sound mappings. While this is a large number of different mappings, what is interesting is that the musicians themselves considered far more of these mappings to be successful than not. The system not only enabled them to develop new mappings, but resulted in mappings the musicians found to be interesting, useful and musical.

The use of the Augmentalist also resulted in some interesting discoveries. Most notable is the use of the infrared distance sensor as a switch to detect strumming by one guitarist. This provides a very simple and robust method of detecting strumming, and is one that we have been not previously seen in the literature on augmented instruments.

Secondly, we found that one of the musicians developed a mapping for their guitar that mirrored that presented in [5] and did so within the first 2 hours of using the system. This emphasises how quickly interesting and usable instruments can be developed by a musician when given access to such a system.

Focus on technology

Our initial idea of how musicians would develop their instruments was that they would focus on cause and effect. That is, that they would decide on a gesture to detect and a sonic output to control with that gesture, However, over the course of this work we found that many of the musicians instead focused on the technology. This meant that the started by examining the sensors that were available to them, what parameters these sensors could detect and where on the instrument they could be easily mounted. Only then would they think about the gestures that the sensors could be used for.

Such a focus on the technology is a somewhat interesting finding. We had expected that musicians would concentrate on the gesture and the sound, rather than the technology. It seems that the musicians consider the sensor technology to be the weakest link in the system and so allow themselves to be guided by the limitations of the sensors. While musicians' creativity can often thrive off such boundaries and limitations [10], if we wish to develop a system that truly focuses on the gestures and sounds then we must alter the users' perception of such limitations of the sensors.

Potential for exploration and mastery

Wessel and Wright state that a goal for designing new digital musical instruments should be for them to have a "low entry fee" together with "no ceiling on virtuosity" [11]. This means that such instruments should be simple to begin playing, but complex and engaging enough to offer the possibility of exploration and mastery.

One of the advantages of augmented instruments is that they are based around existing musical instruments. A guitarist will still be able to play an augmented guitar as though it is a regular guitar. This makes the instrument easy to begin using. The additional sensors then extend the performance possibilities of the instrument, thus allowing for more potential for creative exploration.

When speaking with the musicians who worked with the system, we found they commonly expressed the belief that they could gain full control of the instrument and make best use of the system given enough time. This shows that the Augmentalist offers potential for further exploration and creativity.

Transferability of developed instruments

We have already mentioned that one musician developed a mapping for their instrument that directly mirrored a system discussed on the literature. This indicates that there is some common pool of gestures that are suggested by the design of the instrument itself. As such, we would also expect that it is possible to transfer developed instruments between performers that play the same instrument.

To examine this we asked another guitarist to try and perform using the mappings developed by one of the guitarists working with our system. The new guitarist found it easy to begin performing using any of these mappings. In each case, it took only a few minutes of practice before they were able to utilise the gestures in performance. The guitarist also made a number of comments on how "easy" and "natural" the mappings were to use.

It is possible therefore to transfer mappings between performers of the same instrument. This means that the potential exists to share instrument designs and mappings across users. One possibility would be the creation of a community to promote such sharing between musicians interested in developing augmented instruments. We are now beginning to investigate this possibility.

Creativity and enjoyment

One of the main aims of this project was to produce a system that facilitated both creativity and enjoyment for the musicians using it. As has already been discussed, the musicians who used the system expressed the belief that the Augmentalist allows for new musical possibilities and offers much potential for further exploration and mastery. The question that then arises is: did the musicians enjoy using the system?

Throughout the development of the Augmentalist there were regular testing, development and performance sessions involving musicians. At the end of each session, we ask each musicians to fill out a short questionnaire, which involved rating the system on a 1-to-5 scale on a number of criteria. Perhaps the most interesting result of this was that every musician gave the system a maximum rating of 5 (Very High) for enjoyment at the end of every session.

While these ratings show that musicians definitely enjoyed working with the system, we think that the following quote, received from one participant several hours after a session, fully illustrates the level of enjoyment felt by those using the system:

> *"I haven't stopped smiling for ages, that was ****** awesome. When can I come back?"*

CONCLUSION

The main goal of the Augmentalist system was to enable musicians to begin experimenting with digital musical instruments through augmenting their existing musical instruments. Our belief was that by focusing on existing instruments and augmenting them with sensors, musicians could produce new instruments with extended interaction and performance possibilities. Such instruments would also have the advantage of reducing the performer-instrument and audience instrument disconnect that can be present with many new digital musical instruments.

The Augmentalist project has met all of our expectations. From working with musicians we have developed a system that they find easy to use, that offers new performance potential and that provides an enjoyable creative experience. The Augmentalist allows musicians to explore new musical techniques, while also allowing them to design and create their own instruments. This opens up new avenues for research into the longer term development of these instruments by musicians, the possibility of sharing and exchanging ideas and mappings for such instruments and the innovative performance and interaction techniques that musicians develop as part of this process.

REFERENCES

1. Reactable. http://www.reactable.com.
2. N. Armstrong. *An Enactive Approach to Digital Musical Instrument Design*. PhD thesis, Princeton University, Nov. 2006.
3. N. Bouillot, Z. Settel, J. R. Cooperstock, and M. Wozniewski. A mobile wireless augmented guitar. In *Proc. NIME 2007*, 2007.
4. S. Greenberg and C. Fitchett. Phidgets: easy development of physical interfaces through physical widgets. In *Proc. UIST 2001*, pages 209–218. ACM, 2001.
5. O. Lahdeoja, M. M. Wanderley, and J. Malloch. Instrument augmentation using ancillary gestures for subtle sonic effects. In *Proc. SMC 2009*, pages 327–330, 2009.
6. M. T. Marshall, M. Hartshorn, M. M. Wanderley, and D. J. Levitin. Sensor choice for parameter modulations in digital musical instruments: Empirical evidence from pitch modulation. *Journal of New Music Research*, 38(3):241–253, 2009.
7. M. T. Marshall, J. Malloch, and M. M. Wanderley. Non-conscious control of sound spatialization. In *Proc. ENACTIVE 2007*, pages 377–380, 2007.
8. E. R. Miranda and M. M. Wanderley. *New Digital Musical Instruments: Control and Interaction beyond the Keyboard.* A-R Editions, 2006.
9. C. Palacio-Quintin. The hyper-flute. In *Proc. NIME 2003*, pages 206–207, 2003.
10. A. Tanaka. Musical performance practice on sensor-based instruments. In M. M. Wanderley and M. Battier, editors, *Trends in Gestural Control of Music*, pages 389–405. IRCAM - Centre Pompidou, 2000.
11. D. Wessel and M. Wright. Problems and prospects for intimate musical control of computers. *Computer Music Journal*, 26(3):11–22, 2002.

Six-Forty by Four-Eighty: The Post-Industrial Design of Computational Materials

Marcelo Coelho
MIT Media Lab
75 Amherst St., Cambridge
marcelo@media.mit.edu

Jamie Zigelbaum
Zigelbaum + Coelho
359 Green St., Cambridge
jamie@zigelbaumcoelho.com

Joshua Kopin
Zigelbaum + Coelho
359 Green St., Cambridge
josh@zigelbaumcoelho.com

ABSTRACT

In this paper we describe the development of Six-Forty by Four-Eighty: an art and design installation composed of 220 interactive lighting tiles. We discuss previous work that addresses the physicality of computation, our design and fabrication processes, technical implementation, the development of a novel technique for data transmission through the body, the piece's exhibition context and public response. By describing the interrelationship between these elements we hope to shed light into the forging of a post-industrial design practice that straddles the art, design and technology trichotomy.

Author Keywords

Art, post-industrial design, materiality, pixel, interface design.

ACM Classification Keywords

H.5.2 User Interfaces — Theory and methods.

General Terms

Design.

INTRODUCTION

As computers progressively permeate our ecology of physical objects, the language of interaction once relegated to the world of GUIs now finds itself intertwined with the affordances of physical things. The result is the emergence of a new class of objects that are crafted with computational tools, carry within them embedded computers, and communicate and behave through the use of computational metaphors. This has fostered the development of an integrated and multidisciplinary design practice requiring a broad fluency across domains such as fine arts, industrial design, interface design, mechanical engineering, electrical engineering, and computer science. We have come to call this practice Post-Industrial Design.

TEI'11, January 22–26, 2011, Funchal, Portugal.

Figure 1. Six-Forty by Four-Eighty.

Six-Forty by Four-Eighty is an installation composed of 220 interactive lighting tiles and was presented at Design Miami/ Basel 2010 in conjunction with Art Basel in Basel, Switzerland. Through its form factor, interaction model and conceptual definitions, this work conveys to viewers a future in which computation will leave the confines of computer screens and spread itself onto the physical world.

At a conceptual level, Six-Forty by Four-Eighty uses the metaphor of the pixel as the ambassador for computation, and more specifically, references how our tacit understanding of what computers are (and can be) is mediated by the prevalence of addressable displays. The pixel-tiles in Six-Forty by Four-Eighty can be packed into a grid as one would traditionally expect and be controlled in unison at the aggregate level, but can also break away from this grid, making the interaction physical and bringing focus to the particulate level. As users start rearranging and sculpting with this luminous medium, a new interaction model opens up, where it is possible to touch a pixel-tile to change its color and, most interestingly, it becomes possible to physically 'copy-and-paste' color from two distinct pixel-tiles by using the user's body as the information conduit. In a future in which computation is to become highly tangible, our bodies will have to play an intrinsic role in our ecology of computational objects.

RELATED WORK

The drive to turn pixels and computers into tangible, graspable artifacts is far from new and has continuously pervaded the Human Computer Interaction consciousness, seeking new implementations and rationales as technological possibilities advance. In this section, we introduce a few noteworthy examples.

An early example of this motivation is John Frazer's *Universal Constructor*, which implements a working model of self-organizing interactive environment composed of stackable physical pixels [1]. In a similar vein is Kelly Heaton's *Physical Pixel Project*, which focuses on the convergence of physical sculpting and computer animation by developing light orbs and cubes that are networked and respond to touch [2]. More recently, Susanne Seitinger's *Urban Pixels* has brought these ideas to the scale of the city and implemented wireless, solar-powered lighting units that influence how we experience the city as a display [4].

In Six-Forty by Four-Eighty, we have chosen to focus on two fundamental aspects: (1) that physical pixels can concomitantly operate at global and local scales depending on the spatial proximity, perspective, and level of physical engagement of the user; and (2) that it is important for the user's body to play a role in how the computation metaphors cross differing levels of perspective and engagement.

In order to implement the physical 'copy-and-paste' capability, we built upon two different works, namely: the *Personal Area Network* project developed by Thomas Zimmerman, wherein handshakes are used to transmit data between two users [6]; and Jay Silver's *Drawdio*, in which people can draw resistive networks with a paintbrush, and by touching different parts of such a drawing one can modulate a sound output [5].

Finally, by straddling the art, design and technology domains, we have drawn inspiration from the work of visual artist and photographer Vik Muniz, who composes images from unorthodox materials. Muniz provides viewers with an experience wherein the work presents a subject when viewed from far away, but reverts to its materiality when viewed up close, interlacing a deeper connection between the represented subject and the medium chosen to represent it. [3]

DESIGN PRINCIPLES

The design principles behind Six-Forty by Four-Eighty were elicited from the necessity to create a piece that could straddle the art, design and technology trichotomy chasm, while communicating to our audience the latent possibilities of physical computing. It was important that the piece (1) conveyed a strong conceptual motivation captured in its form factor, aesthetics, and exhibition context; (2) supported a utilitarian functionality that could be easily communicated to visitors; and (3) that the technology implemented could reveal and support the conceptual and functional motivations.

Art

Conceptually, Six-Forty by Four-Eighty examines the materiality of computation and a future where computers will leave the confines of screens and keyboards to become an integral part of the physical world. Since pixels and their graphical user interfaces are the way that most people understand what computers are, we have chosen to render pixels as independent physical objects. This creates an experience where visitors can touch and metaphorically break computation into pieces, acting as co-creators able to re-sculpt the work, and provides a gateway to discuss the larger conceptual idea.

Design

Functionally, Six-Forty by Four-Eighty can also be deployed in the home, doubling as a modular, interactive lighting system that supports a high degree of customization. This functional design role portrays a scenario where lighting becomes a personal experience, which one can physically interact with to create different ambience, moods and living environments.

Figure 3. Pixel-tiles as a lighting system in the home.

Technology

Technically, it was important to back the conceptual and functional aspects of the piece with technology that brings people into the 'computing' experience and where their physical presence plays a role in the behavior and interaction of the pixel-tiles. To achieve this, we developed and implemented a novel technique where people's bodies are used as a conduit for serial data, literally acting as a wire to transfer information from one pixel-tile to another and allowing the human body to become an integral part of the computation and communication process. When touched with one hand for a short period of time, the pixel-tile starts pulsing – to indicate its transmission state – and starts transmitting its color through the person's hand. By keeping the first hand in place and touching other pixel-tiles, the color is transferred from one pixel-tile to another, creating a form of physical 'copy-and-paste'.

INTERACTION MODEL

Six-Forty by Four-Eighty's only form of output is the light produced by an RGB LED housed inside of the case, while user input happens through touch and an infrared remote control. This simple system allows people to interact with it in four different ways: (1) The pixel-tiles are magnetic and can be rearranged on a ferrous surface; (2) Touching a pixel-tile makes it cycle through a color palette; (3) Touching a pixel-tile and holding, while using your other hand to touch other pixel-tiles, 'copy-and-pastes' color from one pixel-tile to another; (4) The remote control allows users to control a pixel-tile's animation by changing the speed and sharpness in which they pulse a certain color. Additionally, it allows users to switch between a warm or a cool color palette.

In order to bring together these distinct interaction modalities into a cohesive interaction experience, the affordances are broken down into micro and macro behaviors and the light quality is designed under the constraints of a physical model, which furthers the understanding of these pixel-tiles as a physical material.

Micro Behavior: The Particulate Level

At the micro scale, the pixel-tiles are designed to be interacted with in exclusively physical ways. First, a person needs to be within arm's reach of the tiles, which facilitates a sense of becoming surrounded by the installation and losing the sense of scale and behavior of the sum arrangement. From this standpoint, the tiles can be grabbed and moved around into different arrangements, and by touching their screens it is possible to make their colors change. Finally, by sequentially touching two pixel-tiles at the same time, it is possible to physically 'copy-and-paste' their colors from one to another. At this micro scale, the pixel-tiles act as an interactive particulate and their behavior is highly supported by the physical model programmed into the light animation.

Macro Behavior: The Aggregate Level

When a user steps back from the micro level, taking a more distanced and macro perspective of the installation, the intimate physicality melts away. The three-dimensionality of the cases disappear into darkness and the viewer sees only floating squares of light animating in unison. The macro behavior requires users to control the installation as an aggregate through an infrared remote control. The pixel-tiles acting together foster the emergence of behaviors that cannot be perceived when one is standing up close. Additionally, the directionality of the IR beam preserves the sense of direct control but shifts its scope from operating onto a single pixel-tile to acting upon the computational substrate as a whole.

Physical Model

Conceptually, Six-Forty by Four-Eighty is about computation and physicality. Its form references the rectangular field of color most people associate with the pixel and its behavior evokes materiality. The outstanding material property constructed by the embedded firmware, in our case, was the color of the light emanating from the pixel-tile and the ways this color changed in response to touch. Because ordinary material properties tend to be instantaneously evident and consistent, care was taken to make the properties constructed by the computation similarly responsive and consistent. For example, clock rates were chosen to ensure the light did not flicker and that the system responded quickly to touch. The software was structured asynchronously to maintain responsiveness.

In addition, the constructed properties were designed to be as similar as possible to the properties of common materials. Specifically, when a touch is detected, the light's brightness changes according to an exponential decay model, which was based on the behavior of incandescent light bulbs and the human retina, but also simulates the experience of elastically deforming a soft object with applied pressure.

PROCESS AND TECHNOLOGY

Figure 4. Injection molded cases with diffuser-ITO composite.

Six-Forty by Four-Eighty is composed of 220 pixel-tiles, which are 3" x 3" x 1.5" boxes injection molded from ABS/Polycarbonate white polymer and covered by a special light diffuser and ITO (indium tin oxide) glass composite. Each pixel-tile is outfitted with a lithium polymer rechargeable battery, rare earth magnets so it can be attached to ferrous surfaces and a custom-designed circuit board responsible for its interactive behavior and functionality.The diffuser-ITO composite was created by layering flashed opal diffusive glass and Pilkington TEC 7 conductive glass (a glass infused with ITO while molten). The edges of the composite were covered with a conductive copper vinyl that was connected to our sensing and data transmission circuits.

Hardware

Six-Forty by Four-Eighty's technical innovation is the ability of a pixel-tile to transmit its color state to other tiles through the human body. To accomplish this, we use the diffuser-ITO composite as an electrode for capacitive touch sensing, data transmission (TX) and reception (RX), providing users with a minimal and simple interface that can handle multiple functionalities. An AVR microcontroller cycles between the three different modes alternating between sensing and data receiving when a touch is not being detected and sensing and transmission when touch is detected.

The most challenging aspect of this design was to ensure consistent UART data reception that was free of noise and unaffected by the circuit's large stray capacitance. This required the use of a two-step analog amplifier, buffering and a common ground between the pixel-tiles shared through a steel back plate and spring-loaded pin located at the bottom of all cases. The capacitive sensor was implemented through loading mode, where the charge and discharge frequency is controlled through firmware, allowing us to easily calibrate its sensitivity.

The aggregate interaction was implemented by using an infrared receiver at an interrupt port, which allowed people to control and modulate several pixel-tiles at a time.

INSTALLATION

Six-Forty by Four-Eighty was commissioned as a new work by Design Miami/ Basel to be featured at their yearly design fair in Basel, Switzerland. The attendance of this type of fair is comprised primarily of collectors, dealers, critics, artists and designers, who are not particularly familiar with technological artifacts that operate outside of the consumer electronics industry. Moreover, work shown in this environment is rarely meant to be touched or interacted with; on the contrary, touching is highly discouraged.

Figure 6. Six-Forty by Four-Eighty at Design Miami/ Basel.

The piece was installed in a dark room covered with black oxidized steel so that it was possible to attach the pixel-tiles anywhere. From our observations, visitors' initial impression was to approach the piece and observe it, completely unaware of its interactive possibilities. After observing others interact with the piece or being instructed to do so, a visceral connection with the tiles started to develop. First, visitors tried to grasp the full extent of its functionality, gaining control of its behavior and color, similar to how we observe and physically explore a new material we've never encountered before. After this exploration stage was overcome, then the piece became a tool for co-creation, and visitors used it to create their own designs and arrangements, continuously transitioning between the micro and macro interaction levels.

CONCLUSION AND FUTURE WORK

As with any design work, the possibilities for improvement and directions for future work are seemingly endless. At a first instance, the ability to locate the physical position of the pixel-tiles in space would allow for video display and a whole new range of interactions. Additionally, new materials and form factors (shape and size of the pixel-tiles) would open new interaction spaces and use scenarios.

ACKNOWLEDGMENTS

We would like to acknowledge Ambra Medda, Wava Carpenter and the Design Miami team for supporting this work. Many colleagues have helped with the design and realization of Six-Forty by Four-Eighty, specifically: Varun Perumal, Madeleine Claire Elish, Ryan Wistort, Jeff Lieberman, Mark Feldmeier, Jay Silver, Aaron Zinman, Jean-Baptiste Labrune, Natan Linder, David Merrill, Seth Hunter, Pol Pla, Nicholas Zigelbaum, Emma Lazrove, Silas Maniatis, Grace Escano, Alexander Dawson, Pat Lian, Dylan Rykerson, Juan Gorris and Catherine McMahon. Finally, we would like to acknowledge W Hotels for supporting the Designer of the Future Award and Professor Pattie Maes and the MIT Media Lab for providing the support, inspiration and infrastructure without which this work would not have been possible.

REFERENCES

1. Frazer, J. (1995) *An Evolutionary Architecture*. Architectural Association Publications.
2. Heaton, K. (2000). *Physical Pixel*. MIT Media Lab Thesis.
3. Muniz, V. (2005) *Reflex: A Vik Muniz Primer*. Aperture.
4. Seitinger, S., Perry, D. S., and Mitchell, W. J. (2009) *Urban pixels: painting the city with light*. In Proceedings of the 27th international Conference on Human Factors in Computing Systems. CHI '09. ACM, New York, NY, 839-848.
5. Silver, J. S. (2009) *Nature as interface: MacGyver'ing and Martha-Stewart'ing interactivity with trees, pencils, grandpa, even the kitchen sink*. In Proc. of the 7th ACM Conference on Creativity and Cognition. C&C '09. ACM, New York, NY, 483-484.
6. Zimmerman, Thomas. (1995) *Personal Area Networks (PAN): Near-Field Intra-Body Communication*. MIT Media Lab Thesis.

Plushbot: an Application for the Design of Programmable, Interactive Stuffed Toys

Yingdan Huang and Michael Eisenberg
Department of Computer Science
University of Colorado, Boulder CO USA
Yingdan.Huang@Colorado.EDU

ABSTRACT

In recent years, a burgeoning landscape of tangible, interactive toys has emerged–construction kits, robotic characters, and so on. At the same time, there has been relatively little development in software systems that permit users (including younger users) to design and create their own computationally-enhanced tangible figures. This paper presents *Plushbot*, a prototype system whose purpose is to allow people to create and customize programmable stuffed toys. Plushbot includes features specifically aimed at facilitating the incorporation of computational elements within stuffed fabric designs. Here we describe the current (still early) state of the system, show a completed project employing the system, and outline near- and medium-term directions for its continued development.

Author Keywords

Tangible interfaces, stuffed toys, Plushbot.

ACM Classification Keywords

H5.m. Information interfaces and presentation (e.g., HCI): Miscellaneous.

INTRODUCTION

The area of toy design has undoubtedly been a fertile one for research and development in tangible computer interfaces. Recent years have seen the development of all sorts of computationally-enhanced toys: responsive robotic figures such as Furby [cf. 5], powerful computational construction kits [cf. 7] such as Topobo [6] and Posey [8], educational devices such as "talking globes", and many more. In general, such artifacts have vastly expanded the range of interaction that youngsters are capable of having with tangible play materials.

At the same time, however, there has been relatively little software development allowing users (including young users) to create their own personalized, computationally-enhanced toys. In general, such toys tend to be pre-programmed (such as Furby); or, alternatively, when the child does the "programming" (as with construction kits) she employs the pre-designed pieces and materials supplied to her. Undoubtedly these models of play are pleasurable and creative; but the toys *themselves* are not objects of the child's creation.

This paper introduces a software system, *Plushbot*, whose purpose is to allow people to create their own interactive stuffed toys. In essence, Plushbot is a design application through which users can interactively place computational elements on the construction template for a plush toy; the system then assists the user in the actual physical creation of the toy itself. Plushbot is still, at present, in a very early stage; and there are numerous enhancements and likely directions for future development of the system, even in the near term. Nonetheless, the system–even in its current rather embryonic state–raises a variety of interesting questions for the larger project of permitting users to design and create their own interactive, programmable computational artifacts.

The remainder of this paper is organized as follows: in the second section, we describe the current Plushbot interface and show a working stuffed toy created with the system. The third section of the paper uses the current implementation of Plushbot as a springboard for a wider-ranging discussion of issues related to user-initiated design of computational toys. This final section also discusses some relevant related work, and sketches some of the planned future directions for enhancing and extending our current system.

TEI'11, January 22–26, 2011, Funchal, Portugal.

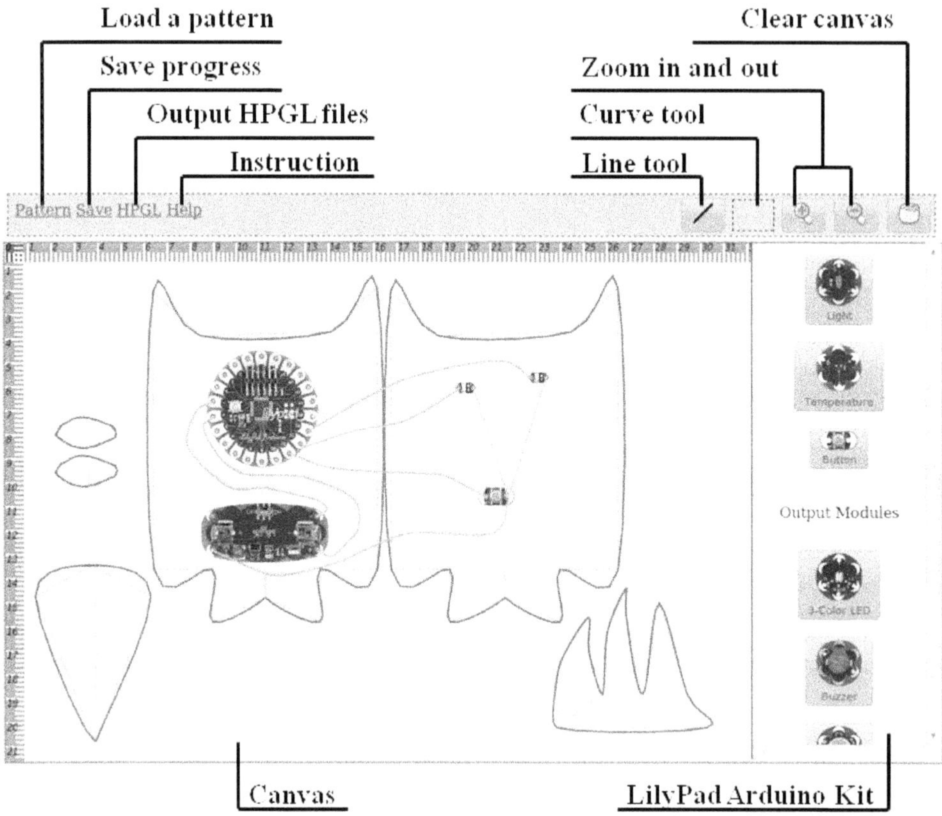

Figure 1. The Plushbot screen interface, in the context of a construction scenario. The main portion of the screen depicts the pieces of a sample construction (outlined in blue), extended by LilyPad Arduino components (selected from the menu of pieces at right), and linked by purple lines that denote the placement of conductive threads. The various features of the interface are described in the accompanying text.

PLUSHBOT: A DESCRIPTION AND SCENARIO

The easiest way to introduce Plushbot is through a construction scenario, as illustrated by Figure 1. Here, the user has begun by choosing a pattern for a plush toy to create (in this case, a cat). The various pieces for the toy are depicted on the screen in outline form; these outlines represent the fabric cutouts that will eventually be sewn together to create the final toy.

With the pieces visible on the screen, the user now selects icons for computational elements–processors, batteries, sensors, and actuators–and positions these on the outlines in drag-and-drop fashion. The computational icons themselves represent components from the popular LilyPad Arduino system [3], and are specifically designed for incorporation within textile-based craft projects. As positioned, the icons will be used to indicate where LilyPad components will eventually be sewn onto the fabric pieces. Briefly, for those unfamiliar with the LilyPad Arduino system: the components allow the eventual constructed plush toy to respond in programmed fashion to sensor inputs (e.g., ambient light levels, or a "squeeze" from the user at a particular spot) and to represent that response through a variety of actuators (e.g., flashing lights, speakers, motors). (See [2] for a discussion of e-textiles in the context of children's crafts.)

In short, then, the Plushbot user is not merely constructing a static toy, but is also constructing the design template for a potentially limitless range of distinct programmable artifacts. It should also be mentioned–as an aside–that to date, the vast majority of LilyPad projects focus on the creation of programmable wearables; as such, the use of the LilyPad within plush toys represents a (mild) stretch for the device and gives rise to several design issues to which we will return in the final section.

To continue with the scenario represented in Figure 1: the user now links the various LilyPad components using flexible line- and curve-drawing tools indicated at the top of the figure. The lines drawn in this case indicate to the user precisely where to sew conductive threads into the eventual fabric pieces; these threads effectively serve as the "electronic wire" for the computational elements of the construction.

Once the overall design of the plush toy is completed on the screen to the user's satisfaction, she now outputs the design of the toy in a format that can be directly sent to a laser cutter (this is indicated by the "output HPGL" icon shown in the figure). The output file created by Plushbot, once sent to a laser cutter, will cut out the various pieces in felt and etch (or engrave) markings on those pieces indicating where the LilyPad components should be placed, and where the conductive thread linking those components should be sewn.

Before proceeding any further, it should be noted that–simple as these capabilities are–the use of Plushbot to allow users to position computational components and their connections on fabric pieces on the screen represents a valuable type of assistance for LilyPad users, as any practitioner knows. In general, the most difficult step for the creation of an e-textile artifact (such as a LilyPad-enhanced garment) is in visualizing where components will be placed and how they will be connected by sewn threads. Not infrequently, the placement of conductive threads gives rise to errors in the operation of the eventual construction (inelegant paths, short circuits, and so forth). Thus, the Plushbot interface provides a valuable template for planning out e-textile design in a way that reflects actual practice among designers.

Once the felt pieces have been cut out and etched by the laser cutter, they constitute a customized template for sewing on the LilyPad components and conductive thread connections. The pieces are then sewn together at the boundaries (as in standard plush toy design) and filled with padding; the LilyPad program is downloaded to the sewn-on processor; and the result is an interactive plush toy. In the scenario shown here, the stuffed figure permits the user to light up the eyes by squeezing the toy in its "belly".

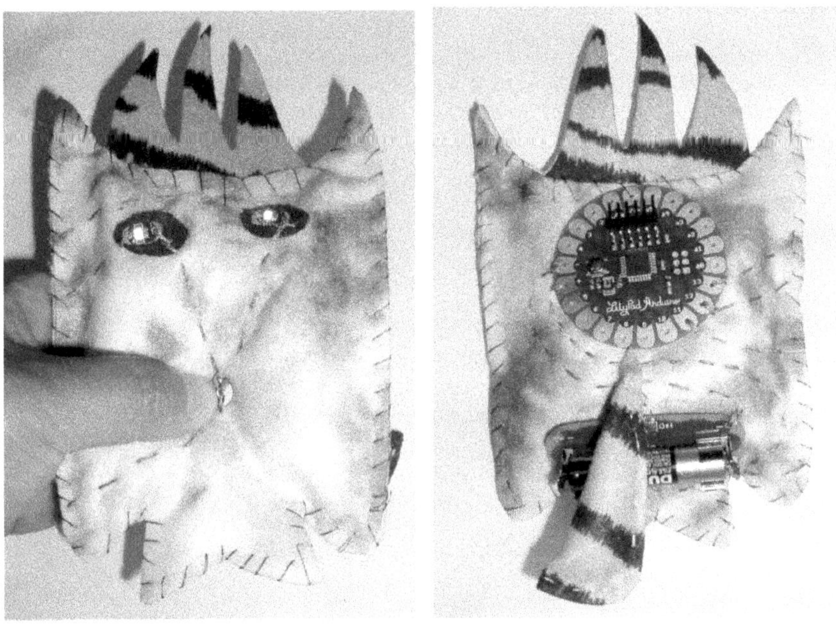

Figure 2. The finished plush toy created from the template shown in Figure 1. A touch sensor in the middle of the toy allows the user to give the character a gentle squeeze that causes the LEDs in the eyes to light up. At right, a back view of the toy shows the sewn-on microprocessor (at top) and battery component. Note also the conductive threads that are sewn into the processor and that lead to the various other computational/electronic elements of the toy. A video of the working toy can be found at: http://www.vimeo.com/13783319

REFLECTIONS ON PLUSHBOT: RELATED WORK AND POTENTIAL FUTURE DIRECTIONS

Plushbot is, as noted, a relatively early working prototype at this stage, and is not ready for widespread release; but even now, it raises a variety of interesting questions worth exploring.

First, it should be noted that in its current version, Plushbot does not include features for designing novel cutout forms for plush toys, in the manner of the recent (and beautiful) "Plushie" software system. [4] That is, Plushbot–at present–makes use of pre-existing fabric cutout templates (in the near future, our system will include a small library of such templates). Combining the features of Plushie with those of Plushbot would, arguably, result in a whole much greater than the sum of its parts: a system that could be used to create wholly original (in form), programmable, interactive toys.

Yet another likely addition–or augmentation–to Plushbot is a programming and simulation capacity. That is, the Plushbot user does not merely wish to place icons of LilyPad components on the cutout forms shown on the screen, but to write programs and simulate them; this would permit the user to envision how the eventual plush toy will look and behave before she goes to the trouble of sewing the object together. We plan to incorporate some programming/simulation component into Plushbot within the near future; very likely this will involve combining our application with a LilyPad simulation system currently under development elsewhere (as opposed to creating a complete system of this sort ourselves). In other words, Plushbot will be designed to combine with other applications rather than as an attempt at a "universal" standalone application.

The previous two paragraphs are suggestive of a larger important theme that is worth at least mentioning here, given the available space: namely, that Plushbot is deliberately designed with an eye toward its placement in a larger technological "ecosystem"–a system of possibly supportive design tools (such as Plushie), language systems, hardware components (the LilyPad), and fabrication devices (the laser cutter). This design philosophy is in contrast to a style of "standalone" software design that attempts to incorporate all functions and features within itself, and that assumes a minimum of external supportive hardware. Again, this is a principled decision, and reflects a view of multiple technologies–both software and hardware–as constituting a mutually supportive web of functions. This view is substantially inspired by the eloquent discussion of technological advancement in Arthur [1]. In this view, "pieces" of already-existing technology can be reconfigured, recombined, and extended to produce new functionality. Plushbot thus exists within–indeed, only makes sense within–a larger surrounding infrastructure of devices and tools.

At the same time, the Plushbot system–by focusing on the design of interactive plush toys in particular–raises design issues that are specific to its domain. Just to take a simple example: consider the sample toy shown in Figure 2. Here, the computational elements (prominently including processor and battery) have been placed on the exterior of the toy. In certain projects it might, of course, be desirable to place these components on the inside of the toy, within the padded region (e.g., to avoid incorporating these elements into the toy's character, or simply for aesthetic reasons). In such a case, however, it would still be advisable to allow the user to access the computational elements–say, to change a battery or reprogram the LilyPad. These considerations result, in turn, in slightly different constraints on plush toy design: namely, we might wish to create a toy that can be easily "opened up" for access to its interior (an atypical consideration for this type of toy, and one not usually encountered in the "wearables" projects that characterize most LilyPad tutorials).

It should thus be clear that the design of a tool such as Plushbot–a tool that permits users to create an identifiable (but still quite varied and rich) genre of tangible artifacts–raises a host of still relatively unexplored questions. These questions will be the focus of our near-term work on the system; and once the system is released for more widespread use, it will be possible to study and assess the way in which Plushbot is employed in combination with a continually burgeoning technological landscape.

ACKNOWLEDGMENTS

The work described in this paper has been funded in part by the National Science Foundation under grant CNS0940484. We wish to thank Leah Buechley, Mark Gross, and Nwanua Elumeze for helpful conversations.

REFERENCES

1. Arthur, W. B. [2009] *The Nature of Technology*. New York: Free Press.
2. Buechley, L.; Elumeze, N.; and Eisenberg, M. [2006] Electronic/Computational Textiles and Children's Crafts. *Proceedings of IDC 2006*, pp. 49-56.
3. LilyPad Arduino: http://www.arduino.cc/en/Main/ArduinoBoardLilyPad
4. Mori, Y. and Igarashi, T. [2007] Plushie: an interactive design system for plush toys. In *ACM SIGGRAPH 2007*.
5. Pesce, M. [2000] *The Playful World*. New York: Ballantine Books.
6. Raffle, H. S.; Parkes, A. J.; and Ishii, H. [2004] Topobo: a constructive assembly system with kinetic memory. *Proceedings of CHI '04*, pp. 647-654..
7. Schweikardt, E. and Gross, M. [2007]. A brief survey of distributed computational toys. In *Proceedings of DIGITEL 2007*, pp. 57-64.
8. Weller, M.; Do, E.; and Gross, M. [2008]. Posey: instrumenting a poseable hub and strut construction toy. In *Proceedings of TEI 2008*, pp. 39-46.

The RayMatic: A Thermostat with a Human Face

Ray Yun **Mark D. Gross**
Carnegie Mellon University
Computational Design Lab
5000 Forbes Avenue, Pittsburgh, PA 15213, USA
ryun@andrew.cmu.edu, mdgross@cmu.edu

ABSTRACT
This paper presents the concept and the design of an ambient display with an anthropomorphic interface to communicate environmental data. Numeric display and control, as in a thermostat, is replaced by a digital interactive portrait with the aim of making interaction engaging and undemanding.

Author Keywords
Tangible interface, facial expression, gesture, ambient display, user interface, ubiquitous computing, awareness

ACM Classification Keywords
H5.m. Information interfaces & presentation (e.g., HCI): Miscellaneous

General Terms
Design

AMBIENT DISPLAYS & ANTHROPOMORPHIC INTERACTION
The RayMatic, a thermostat with a human face, illustrates a class of anthropomorphic machines that use facial expressions to indicate the machine's internal state. We attempted to make a thermostat control more interesting, fun, and friendly than the typical numeric display.

Many meters such as thermometers, barometers, and air pollution meters display values as numbers, which users must read and interpret. When precise information is needed then numeric displays are important. However sometimes only approximate information is desired; then a numeric display needlessly demands attention.

Early human-computer communication employed command-based interfaces [1] but today human-to-human communication modalities are becoming increasingly common. Anthropomorphizing the interface adds human characteristics such as appearance, voice, gesture, affect, and so on. The human face is among the most compelling components and has played an important role in computer interfaces since the early days of HCI. Our RayMatic interface to a simple household appliance, the home heating/cooling system, demonstrates how such an interface can be engaging, amusing, and playful.

RayMatic has two principal characteristics: it is anthropomorphic and it is an ambient display. An anthropomorphic interface such as an interface agent, guide, or wizard interacts using voice, gesture and facial expression. Employing a face to represent an agent has been shown to increase engagement and motivation and makes a user pay more attention [2].

Ambient displays inform people without demanding attention. For example, the well-known Ambient Orb™ device (http://www.ambientdevices.com/cat/orb) is a frosted glass sphere containing a bicolor LED. Its hue depends on changes with information that the Orb receives, such as weather conditions or stock market performance. A user can track real time information merely by glancing at the color of the Orb.

THE RAYMATIC
The RayMatic is a thermostat in the form of an interactive wall-mounted photograph: It appears to be an ordinary picture frame on the wall (Figure 1a). It's mildly amusing—when you tap Ray in the face, his head pushes back and he turns away as though responding to your tapping. More seriously though, the RayMatic is actually part of the home heating and cooling (HVAC) system. If the room is too hot or too cold the image of Ray in the frame fans himself or shivers (Figure 2).

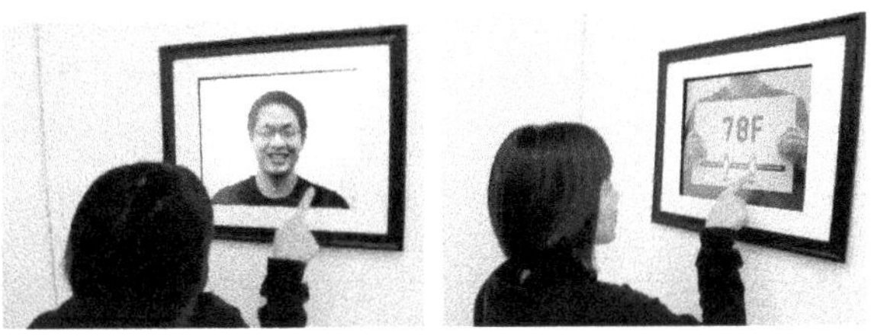

Figure 1. a) RayMatic is a playful interface to a home heating system. b) Adjusting the set-point on the RayMatic.

When the user taps Ray's shoulder area (Figure 1a), the device enters setting mode and allows the user to see numeric values and adjust their preferred range (Figure 1b). Figure 2 shows all states of the RayMatic.

The RayMatic prototype is implemented using Flash with Actionscript 3.0. I took videos of myself: smiling (good state), shivering and wearing a scarf (cold state), fanning myself (hot state), being pushed (touch state), and doing nothing (neutral state). When the system detects a change in temperature through a temperature sensor (LM35DZ) connected to an Arduino microcontroller board, it signals Flash via a socket (TinkerProxy). The Flash program uses this value as an input and plays a corresponding movie clip in the RayMatic frame. 3M™ MicroTouch™ M1700SS Display allows users to interact with the agent in the picture frame by touching.

Figure 2: RayMatic conveys messages through facial expression, corresponding to ambient conditions: (Clockwise) Doing nothing (default state), smiling (good state), being pushed (touch state), fanning himself (hot state), shivering and wearing a scarf (cold state), and setting mode.

DISCUSSION

Walker, Sproull, and Subramani [1] argue that people spend more time and respond better to face-based than text-based interfaces because psychologically, the presence of another person increases arousal and motivation. Nourbakhsh et al. [5] observe that it is increasingly common to use expressive faces for mobile robots to engage users and argue that this makes them more willing to interact with a robot. Our device takes advantage of facial expression and gesture but using them alone to represent a complex message has a limit. If we added voice to the RayMatic, it would have been straightforward to convey its message, but this would also make RayMatic more demanding. Instead, we wanted a quiet and subtle home agent in an ordinary picture frame.

To avoid confusion it is good that the facial expressions and gestures in the frame are expressive, realistic, and universal to avoid confusion. However, RayMatic can also be customized. Users make videos of their own gestures and with facial expressions, then, at the setting mode they assign each video clip to the appropriate state. Although we represent each state with movie clips, we could have used static images.

CONCLUSION AND FUTURE WORK

RayMatic is a touch-based interactive display that represents ambient information using human facial expressions and gestures. Designed for monitoring home energy usage and controlling home HVAC systems, RayMatic could serve other purposes, for example an air pollution monitor (Ray coughs or has trouble breathing), a noise meter (Ray covers his ears and frowns). Like the Ambient Orb, RayMatic can display other information such as weather, traffic [6], daylight [6], elders' health [3,4], or someone's emotional state as indicated in Facebook. In addition to this flexibility of input signals, RayMatic can be customized to indicate conditions with a wide variety of facial expression and gestures.

Figure 3: RayMatic could be added to personal objects such as a keychain, or a wallet to monitor important signs.

RayMatic is also not limited to the picture frame. Using a wireless protocol, RayMatic can be applied to personal objects such as a keychain, a necklace or a wallet (Figure 3) so that a user can monitor electricity usage, or a friend's emotional state with the object. The RayMatic points to a style of interaction with household appliances and devices that is simple, fun, and friendly.

REFERENCES

1. Walker J. H., Sproull L., Subramani R., Using a human face in an interface, *CHI 1994*, ACM Press (1994), 85-91
2. Zanbaka C. A., Ulinski A.C., Goolkasian P., Hodges, L.F. Social responses to virtual humans: implications for future interface design, *CHI 2007*
3. Mynatt E.D., Rowan J., Craighill S., Jacobs A., Digital family portraits: supporting peace of mind for extended family members, *CHI 2001*, ACM Press (2001), 333-340
4. Jiang S., Cao Y., Iyengar S., Kuryloski P., Jafari R., Xue Y., Bajcsy R., Wicker S., CareNet: an integrated wireless sensor networking environment for remote healthcare, *ICST 3rd international conference on Body area networks 2008*.
5. Nourbakhsh I., Bobenage J., Grange S., Lutz R., Meyer R., Soto A. An affective mobile educator with a full-time job. *Artificial Intelligence 114 (1–2) 1999*. 95–124.
6. Mankoff, J., Dey, A.K., Hsieh, G., Kientz, J., Lederer, S. and Ames, M., Peripheral and ambient displays: Heuristic evaluation of ambient displays, *CHI 2003*, ACM Press (2003), 169-176.

PotPet: Pet-like Flowerpot Robot

Ayumi Kawakami[1] kawakami.ayumi@is.ocha.ac.jp

Koji Tsukada[1,2] tsuka@acm.org

Keisuke Kambara[1] kambara@sappari.org

Itiro Siio[1] siio@acm.org

[1] Ochanomizu University, 2-1-1 Otsuka, Bunkyo-ku, Tokyo 112-8610, Japan

[2] PRESTO, Japan Science and Technology Agency, 4-1-8 Honcho Kawaguchi, Saitama 332-0012, Japan.

ABSTRACT

We propose a flowerpot-type robot called PotPet that helps users grow plants more effectively and enjoyably. PotPet acts autonomously like pets: it automatically moves to sunny places or approaches people when it requires water. Basically, PotPet consists of a "real" plant, several sensors to detect plant status, a robot with wheels for mobility, and a microcontroller to control the above devices. Here we explain the concepts and implementation of the PotPet.

Author Keywords

Plants, robot, sensor, pet

ACM Classification Keywords

H5.2 [Information interfaces and presentation]: User Interfaces.

General Terms

Design, Human Factors

INTRODUCTION

Many people grow plants at home, often placing flowerpots in their kitchens or living rooms and planting flowers or trees in their gardens. Thus, plants are a common hobby. However, many people often experience difficulties in keeping their plants healthy. For example, people sometimes kill plants by forgetting to water them. We consider this difficulty to result from the inability of plants to express their needs.

For this reason, we propose a flowerpot-type robot called PotPet that helps users grow plants effectively and enjoyably.

Figure 1. PotPets installed at Ocha House[1]

Figure 2. Basic behaviors of PotPet

POTPET

The main concepts underlying the development of the PotPet are as follows:

- Autonomous behavior that imitates that of pets to help grow plants effectively
- Immediate feedback to user actions for entertainment

To achieve the above concepts, we propose two functions: (1) detecting proper plant status and (2) presenting the status *via* physical movement.

Detecting proper plant status

To detect the proper plant status using sensors, we selected three fundamental conditions that significantly affect plant growth: the need for sunlight, water, and people.

First, while plants need an appropriate amount of sunlight, too strong sunlight may damage leaves and flowers. Second, serious problems often arise from under- or over-watering as people cannot accurately judge the plants needs at a glance. Third, we need to detect the presence of the people growing the plants to provide the proper feedback mentioned in the following section.

Presenting the status *via* physical movement

We decide to enable plants to physically move in their flowerpot to imitate the autonomous behavior of pets. Moreover, we propose immediate feedback to the action people in the vicinity *via* movement to make growing plants more enjoyable. Here, we explain basic behavior of the PotPet (Figure 2). First, the PotPet automatically moves to

[1] Ocha House: an experimental smart house for evaluating ubiquitous computing applications in Ochanomizu University.

sunny spots in search of sunlight. Second, the PotPet moves around a person to attract her/his attention when in need of water. Third, the PotPet turns round to express happiness when it is watered, either by a person or by rain.

IMPLEMENTATION

The PotPet basically consists of a driving component, a sensor component, a control component, and a flowerpot component, as shown in Figure 3. Next, we briefly explain each component.

Driving component

We developed the driving component based on the Wifibot[1], a commercial robot with 4 wheels and good mobility. We can control the Wifibot by sending several bytes of commands via the RS232 connection.

Sensor component

We attached four types of sensors in the sensor component: a humidity sensor to detect soil moisture level, a light sensor to detect sunlight, motion sensors to detect the presence of people, and ultrasonic sensors to detect distance to walls or objects.

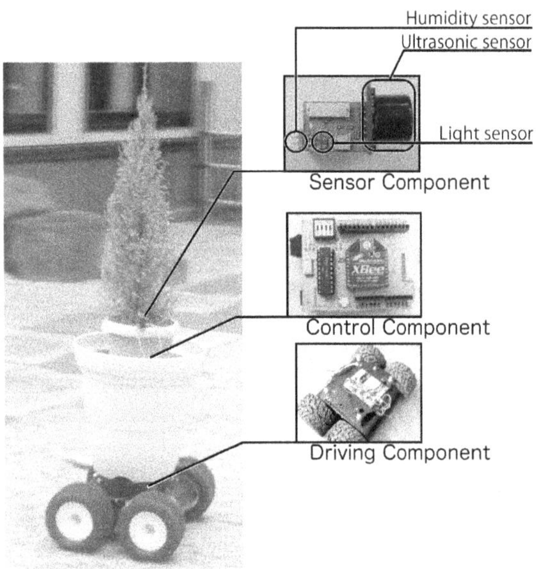

Figure 3. The PotPet prototype.

Control component

We developed the control component based on a microcontroller (Arduino Duemilanove) and a wireless communication device (XBee[2]). The control component collects output from the sensors, and controls the Wifibot based on several rules, as shown in Figure 2. Moreover, this component transmits the sensor data to the backend server at regular intervals for future expandability (Figure 4).

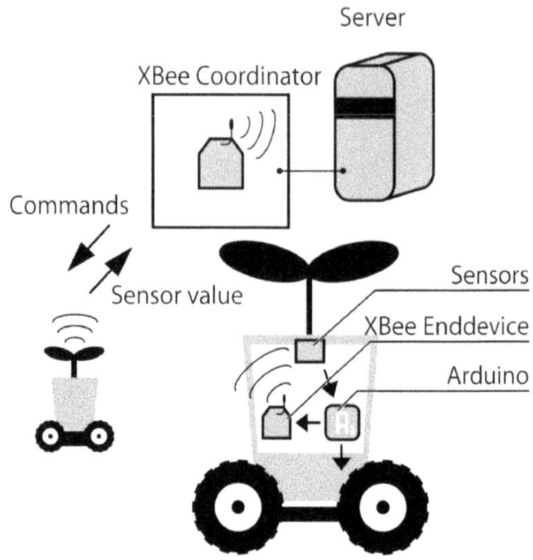

Figure 4. The system architecture of the PotPet.

Flowerpot component

The flowerpot component consists of a "real" plant in a flowerpot. Finally, we assembled the above 4 components: the sensor component, control component and flowerpot component were assembled in a larger flowerpot, which was then set on the driving component.

RELATED WORK

I/O Plants[1] is one trial that uses plants as interactive input/output devices by attaching actuators and sensors. DIGITAL POT[2] is a flowerpot with a display to indicate facial expressions according to the values from sensors attached to the plant. Social Trash Box[3] is a trash robot that moves autonomously in a public space. The robot is not able to collect litter, but encourages people to pick up litter by its interactive movement.

CONCLUSION

We proposed a flowerpot-type robot called PotPet that helps users grow plants effectively and enjoyably. We designed PotPet to act autonomously like a pet: it automatically moves to sunny places or approaches people when it requires water. We plan to extend the behavior of PotPet based on the types, sizes and growth phases of the "real" plants attached to it, and will install PotPet in a garden of an actual house and evaluate its effectiveness (Figure 1).

REFERENCES

1. Kuribayashi, S., Sakamoto, Y., and Tanaka, H. I/O Plant: A Tool Kit for Designing Augmented Human-Plant Interactions. CHI '07: Extended abstracts on Human factors in computing systems, ACM Press(2000), 2537-2542
2. Junyi Heo, DIGITAL POT, http://www.yankodesign.com/2008/05/28/plantstell-you-what-they-want/
3. Yoshiike, Y., Yamaji, Y., Miyake, T., Silva, P., and Okada, M. Sociable Trash Box. HRI '10: Proceeding of the 5th ACM/IEEE international conference on Human-robot interaction , ACM Press(2010), 197-198

---

[2] Wifibot: http://www.wifibot.com

[3] XBee: a small wireless module compatible with ZigBee.

Mechanix: An Interactive Display for Exploring Engineering Design through a Tangible Interface

Tiffany Tseng
Stanford University
Stanford, CA
tsengt@stanford.edu

Coram Bryant
Stanford University
Stanford, CA
cabryant@stanford.edu

Paulo Blikstein
Stanford University
Stanford, CA
paulob@stanford.edu

ABSTRACT
Mechanix is a low-cost, interactive system for children to design and explore mechanical systems using computer-vision-tracked, magnetic components. It employs a semi-transparent magnetic surface that supports the placement and tracking of magnetic simple machine pieces and acts as a projection screen. A back-mounted webcam captures the position of the pieces using visual tags, while a projector depicts virtual components in user-generated challenges and solutions. Designed as a museum exhibit and grounded in constructionist learning theory, Mechanix combines a virtual library of user-generated content with a tangible interface to enable asynchronous and synchronous interactions.

Author Keywords
Tangible interfaces, constructionism, simple machines

ACM Classification Keywords
H.5.2 Information Interfaces and Presentation: User Interfaces: K.3 Computers and Education

General Terms
Design.

INTRODUCTION
Discovering physics principles underlying simple machines helps children appreciate how things work, inspires them to engage in creative design, and encourages analytical thinking. We introduce Mechanix, an interactive display for engaging children in learning about mechanical systems through the use of tangible, simple machine components. These components are arranged on a vertical magnetic surface while a webcam behind the surface tracks the position and orientation of the pieces to provide feedback and record new designs. Designs are added to a library of user-generated challenges and solutions that may be projected onto the surface during subsequent use, enabling new users to learn from past examples.

The design of Mechanix emerged from a review of museum-based engineering installations, which revealed four opportunities for design: **(1) Lower cost**: Similar exhibits use large displays and expensive touch surfaces [4]; Mechanix uses a low-cost LED projector, webcam, and a magnetic mesh. **(2) Combining tangible and on-screen interaction**: Many installations rely solely on on-screen interaction [2] despite evidence that tangible interfaces offer a more engaging entry point for children to learn about engineering [3, 8]. Mechanix supports learning through tangible simple machine components and virtual projections of user solutions and formal tutorial content. **(3) Trackable, open-ended design challenges**: Existing methods for teaching about simple machines tend to rely on scripted curricula, which limit opportunities for children to create their own designs. Mechanix allows for free-form construction and, due to its built-in tracking system, scaffolds designs with recommendations to help learners. **(4) User-generated content to facilitate learning:** With traditional construction kits such as LEGOs, children often do not have immediate access to others' work and resort to using external references such as online forums. The Mechanix library of exemplars enables novices to view and test others' examples while constructing their own designs.

Figure 1. Middle school students using Mechanix.

LEARNING THEORY
Mechanix is informed by constructionist and social constructivist learning theories. Social constructivism [7] suggests that learning can be augmented via socially mediated scaffolding; interaction with a more experienced peer can help

realize the learner's full cognitive potential. Mechanix incorporates this principle in two ways: (1) By using a large visual display and multiple tangible parts, it invites simultaneous involvement among users of varying skill levels, and (2) it enables asynchronous access to user-generated challenges and solutions. Mechanix is also aligned with a main tenet of constructionism: learning happens best in a context where the learner is consciously engaged in constructing a public entity that can be discussed, examined, and admired [6]. As children gain familiarity with the tangible components, they combine and test them in an exercise of personal knowledge construction by generating unique solutions to the challenges. This public expression of ideas makes them concrete, which refines corresponding knowledge structures [1].

HARDWARE

The primary interface for Mechanix is a toolkit of tangible magnetic components arranged on a semi-transparent vertical display. The vertical surface is composed of projection material, a steel wire mesh, and acrylic backing. The wire mesh was designed to be fine enough to allow image detection but dense enough to enable a strong magnetic grip. All graphics are back-projected onto the display. The Mechanix toolkit consists of magnetic components and command pieces. Each component represents a particular type of simple machine, such as a wheel and axle or inclined plane. Command pieces are used to save and view challenges. Each magnetic piece has a fiduciary marker on the back, enabling a camera behind the screen to detect the location and orientation of each component. A Java-based system employing the reacTIVision library [5] processes the camera input to record simple machine configurations and respond to commands.

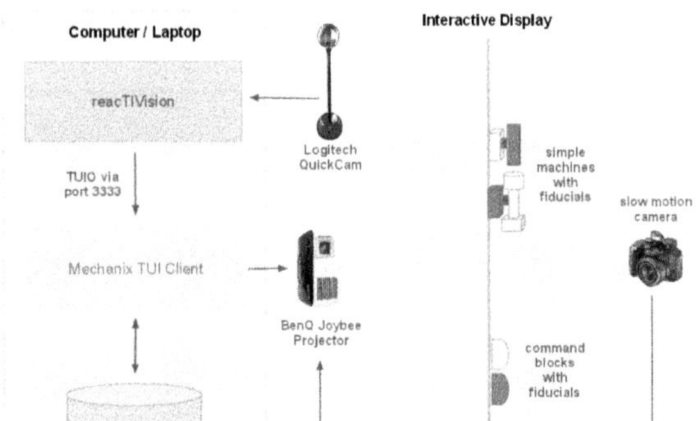

Figure 2. System overview.

INTERFACE DESIGN

When users approach the wall, they are invited to "Take a Challenge" by placing the corresponding command piece on the wall and rotating it to cycle through user-generated challenges containing mandatory start and end pieces. After selecting a challenge and lining up the initial physical components with their projected images, children freely arrange the remaining simple machine components to guide a physical ball from start to finish. When a successful design has been completed, the user is able to save the design to the library of exemplars. If a user needs help, she can access prior solutions from the library. The "View a Solution" piece may be rotated to cycle through all saved solutions, while "# of Pieces" can be rotated to slowly reveal the components in a solution. With this design, children are able to recreate and test others' solutions, enabling asynchronous social learning. Once a user has saved a design, she is invited to create challenges for others to solve.

CONCLUSIONS & FUTURE WORK

Mechanix presents an engaging experience for a variety of age groups. One recurring issue, made evident by our informal user studies, is that children would like to leave a personal touch on their design; a tagging system is being developed to enable children to express ownership in this way. New methods for users to interact with their designs after leaving the museum is another key element being explored. One proposed idea is to link a challenge with an email address so that a user can be notified when others have created solutions to their challenges. Finally, the Mechanix toolkit represents only one application that may be achieved by the described framework. Future work includes abstracting and defining the generic framework in order to develop novel interactive toolkits for learning topics ranging from musical composition to optics.

REFERENCES

1. Ackermann, E. Piaget's Constructivism, Papert's Constructionism: What's the Difference? http://learning.media.mit.edu/content/publications/EA.Piaget%20_%20Papert.pdf, 2001.
2. Allen, S. Designs for learning: Studying science museum exhibits that do more than entertain. *Science Education 88*, S1 (2004), S17–S33.
3. Horn, M., Solovey, E., Crouser, R., and Jacob, R. Comparing the use of tangible and graphical programming languages for informal science education. In *Proc. of CHI '09* (2009), ACM Press, pp. 975–984.
4. Hornecker, E. "I don't understand it either, but it is cool" - Visitor Interactions with a Multi-Touch Table in a Museum. In *IEEE Tabletop 2008* (2008).
5. Kaltenbrunner, M., and Benica, R. reacTIVision: A computer-vision framework for table-based tangible interaction. In *Proc. of TEI '07* (Baton Rouge, Lousiana, 2007).
6. Papert, S. Situating constructionism. In *Constructionism*, S. Papert and I. Harel, Eds. Cambridge, MA: MIT Press, 1991.
7. Vygotsky, L. *Mind in Society: The Development of Higher Psychological Processes*. Cambridge, MA: Harvard University Press, 1978.
8. Zuckerman, O., Arida, S., and Resnick, M. Extending Tangible Interfaces for Education: Digital Montessori-Inspired Manipulatives. In *Proc. of CHI '05* (2005), ACM Press.

MiniBUG: From Concept to Production in a Prototyping System

Alicia Gibb
R&D
Bug Labs
New York, USA
alicia@buglabs.net

Robert Faludi
Interactive Telecommunications Program (NYU)
New York, USA
rob@faludi.com

Dan Steingart
Department of Chemical Engineering (CCNY)
New York, USA
dan.steingart@gmail.com

ABSTRACT

Bug Labs [i] is an open source company attempting to democratize innovation through Linux-based prototyping devices. To scale our product line we recognized certain factors that needed to prioritized: functionality, connection, shape and size, and economics. While three of these factors were addressed by the original BUGbase, the original unit is relatively expensive. At a cost of roughly $800, the BUGbase is beyond the reach of many prototypers [ii]. MiniBUG is in development—a smaller unit with a streamlined feature set and sale price of less than $100. This work represents the critical assessment of the original unit and the resulting miniBUG unit. The research collected was used to reflect on the process of designing miniBUG while considering price point, flexibility, affordances in the functionality, and the usability of the complete system.

Author Keywords

Bug Labs, miniBUG, prototyping systems

ACM Classification Keywords

Hardware

General Terms

Design, Experimentation

INTRODUCTION

The miniBUG modular computing platform [iii] is in development at Bug Labs in conjunction with Robert Faludi of NYU's ITP program and Dan Steingart of the Department of Chemical Engineering at the City College of New York. MiniBUG is a prototyping platform meant to streamline the evolution of a proof-of-concept to a production device. The industry lacks an inclusive system that goes from prototype to pilot to production, though there are many choices for toolkits and microcontrollers with a prototyping focus [iv]. We will share the exploratory nature of developing the miniBUG system and explain the design flow of using the miniBUG to get from an initial prototype to a production level device. MiniBUG is being developed as part of the Test Kitchen [v], Bug Lab's open R&D lab, thus the process itself is open.

TEI'11, January 22–26, 2011, Funchal, Portugal.

THE PROCESS OF DEVELOPING MINIBUG

For several years we have observed [vi] the difficulty DIY physical computing prototypes face making it into a pilot or production phase, especially in academia. It is notoriously challenging for prototypes to reach a wide-scale distribution channel [vii]. The miniBUG system incorporates a process to accommodate the manufacturing and distribution of DIY and physical computing projects, giving developers the ability to turn prototype units into pilot or production units. Similar to the research-practice gap [viii], in which Norman identifies a problem of researchers moving from research to development to a business practice, MiniBUG hopes to transition users from a prototype to pilot to production unit.

The process involved iteration from low-fidelity materials to begin defining a high-fidelity prototyping system. First, we used a web-enabled microcontroller, the Yellow Jacket 1.0 [ix], and cardboard models to study interactions and enclosures. User scenarios and wireframes were developed to explore the miniBUG user experience. We used a visible synthesis [x] of walkthrough sketches to portray user actions and processes. Through the visible synthesis we were able to quickly see how actions moved from one scenario to the next. We next integrated the hardware into Bug module form and compatibility.

The miniBUG platform is being developed using a low fidelity process, paralleling the way that existing hardware microcontrollers are used for conceptual prototyping. MiniBUG is not only a product but also a production process. The key to miniBUG's interaction is simplicity in its interface, but not its functions. The interface is browser-based, including an online IDE, web services and API interfaces. The ability to manage code on the device itself, through a browser and without need for an IDE, is a powerful concept. It provides implicit scalability and code sharing through cloud based systems, and direct migration to production systems.

MiniBUG will seek certifications that can extend to user products. MiniBUG products will leverage Bug Labs' supply chain and manufacturing relationships.

TANGIBLE USER INTERACTION OF MINIBUG

The miniBUG initiative has two main goals: to support an entire project life cycle from prototype to production, and to support the full learning curve of users who may vary from inventors to technicians. We have identified several critical moments through field research that miniBUG will address to achieve a successful user experience. Critical moments include: instant gratification style feedback, centralized services, web services, simple wireless protocols, and click-through prototype to pilot actions [xi]. Instant gratification includes instant feedback, for example when the device powered on the web site will display sensor data to confirm that the device is awake. Instant gratification also includes supporting early user success with example code. The services we identified as centralized are a dashboard, an online IDE, and a graphical interface displaying the device state. This combination of features will guide people through the production process and will ensure feedback and success throughout iterative development.

The enclosure service will recommend options for the material and enclosure production methods. The options will span DIY 3-D printing such as Makerbot [xii] to professional design services. The end user interface will be programmable and flexible. Because iterative process for designing objects is found to enhance creativity [xiii], we aim to develop a tool for faster iteration. MiniBUG products can evolve to become more innovative through this variety of open source and customizable attributes.

RELATED WORK

Related work extending to the 3-tier prototype, pilot, production model includes BUG from Bug Labs. BUGbase has been using the same business model to go from prototype to pilot to product. Bug Labs followed two case studies closely with this life cycle model —Accenture and DARPA [xiv]. These organizations followed the model of moving from prototype to pilot to production, iterating based on feedback, and receiving advisement and services for board redesign and enclosure modifications. Other modular hardware related work includes devices such as VoodooIO [xv], and Blades & Tiles [xvi], and Gumstix [xvii], which include capabilities similar to miniBUG. Like miniBUG, these devices have pieces that attach as various modules. However unlike other prototyping TUIs, miniBUG has an added initiative to see users through the production process.

FUTURE WORK

Future work will move miniBUG from the prototyping stage to a production unit. The current form factor may be changed, and we may fork other forms of the miniBUG, allowing it to be encased in smaller forms and different shapes. Other future work will entail bridging miniBUG to other platforms to increase its functionality and improve the flexibility of the system.

CONCLUSION

While many hardware prototyping platforms exist, including other toolkits and microcontrollers, there is no one-stop solution to tie system-based prototyping together with piloting and production. MiniBUG is being developed to solve this problem in an inexpensive device, one that includes a process for bringing new products to market.

ACKNOWLEDGMENTS

We would like to thank Bug Labs and the Test Kitchen at Bug Labs for supporting this endeavor.

REFERENCES

i Bug Labs. http://www.buglabs.net/.

ii Von Hippel, E. A., De Jong, J. and Flowers, S. Comparing Business and Household Sector Innovation. Consumer Products: Findings from a Representative Study in the UK (September 27, 2010). http://ssrn.com/abstract=1683503

iii MiniBUG. http://www.buglabs.net/testkitchen/projects/minibug

iv Ishii, H. Tangible Bits: Beyond Pixels. In *Proc. TEI 2008*, ACM Press (2008), xv-xxv.

v Bug Labs. Test Kitchen http://www.buglabs.net/testkitchen

vi Unpublished observations. 2010.

vii Productizing Panel. Open Hardware Summit. September 23, 2010. New York. http://www.isoc-ny.org/p2/?p=1237

viii Norman, D.A. The Research-Practice Gap: The Need for Translational Developers. *Interactions 17*, 4 (2010), 9-12.

ix Yellow Jacket 1.0. http://bit.ly/cIiJb1.

x Scott K. M., Visible Synthesis Interactions. *Interactions17*, 4 (2010), 13-17.

xi Bug Labs. Unpublished customer survey. 2008.

xii Makerbot. http://makerbot.com/.

xiii Dow, S. P., Heddleston, K., Klemmer, S.R. The efficacy of prototyping under time constraints. In Proc. C&C 2009, ACM Press (2009), 165-174.

xiv Bug Labs Government Case Study. 2010. http://www.buglabs.net/gov

xv Villar N., and Gellersen H. A Malleable Control Structure for Softwired User Interfaces. In *Proc. TEI 2007*, ACM Press (2007), 49-56.

xvi Sankaran, R., Ullmer, B., Ramanujam,J., et al. Decoupling interaction hardware design using libraries of reusable electronics. In *Proc. TEI 2009*, ACM Press (2009), 331-337.

xvii Gumstix. http://www.gumstix.com/

Pillow-Talk: Seamless Interface for Dream Priming Recalling and Playback

Edwina Portocarrero
edwina@media.mit.edu

David Cranor
cranor@mit.edu
MIT Media Lab
Cambridge, MA 02139

V.Michael Bove
vmb@media.mit.edu

ABSTRACT

Pillow-Talk is the first of a series of objects designed to aid creative endeavors through the unobtrusive acquisition of unconscious self-generated content to permit reflexive self-knowledge. Composed of a seamless recording device embedded in a pillow and a playback and visualization system in a jar, Pillow-Talk crystallizes that which we normally forget. This allows users to capture their dreams in a less mediated way, aiding recollection by priming the experience and providing no distraction for recall and capture through embodied interaction.

Author Keywords

Reflective Interaction, Creativity Support Tools, Emotion and Affective user Interface, Ubiquitous Computing/Smart Environments

ACM Classification Keywords

H5.2. Information Interfaces and Presentation

ACM General Terms

Design, Human Factors

INTRODUCTION

Either physiologically described as the response to neural processes, psychologically as reflections of the subconscious, religiously as messages from the divine, dreams have been a topic of speculation and interest throughout recorded history and yet, there is no universally agreed biological definition of dreaming. Whether dreams perform an emotional or cognitive function is still unclear and greatly debated, but even if the utility of dreams is unknown they still have meaning. Dreams have been sought for divination, determined dates for religious activities, been aids for healing and served as the source of artistic inspiration. Niels Bohr reports that he developed the model of the atom based on a dream of sitting on the sun with all the planets hissing around on tiny cords, while Remedios Varo and Dalí found inspiration in them for their paintings and Luis Buñuel, David Lynch and Maya Deren used dreams spatial and temporal qualities in their films [1]. Hippocrates developed the idea that the dream was a window on illness, reflecting the body's state, idea similar to the Huichol Indians from the north of Mexico who use dreams not only as insight on healing, but extend their use to political, spiritual, moral and artistic realms [2].

Recently, due to the sharp increase of PTSD (Post-Traumatic Stress Disorder) among soldiers returning from war zones, much attention has been paid to the treatment of nightmares by training patients to rewrite their troubling dreams and rehearsing more benign scenarios through I.R.T (Image Rehearsal Therapy) [3,4,5,6].

Remembering dreams does not come easy for most people. It requires conscious effort and practice. Most of the advise for recalling suggests the use of pen and paper and a flashlight by the bed to jolt notes down. Nonetheless, not only does lying still is crucial to facilitate recall, but even the slightest movement is enough for the dream to evaporate from our minds. Sitting up and writing demands an excessive physical and mental effort that is counterproductive to reminiscing.

Through the use of conductive textiles, Pillow-Talk provides little mediation between dreams, thoughts, musings and their recollection; so that they can later serve the user in whatever way she might see fit: either for inspiration, self knowledge, therapeutical use or pure pleasure.

It has been noted that people almost never have nightmares under scientific observation, while dreams are easier to remember when making a conscious effort. Pillow-Talk in and of itself serves as an inhibiting agent of nightmares and as a primer for recalling. Furthermore, by being a recording and playback system, it could aid treatment by becoming an altering agent of the narrative through its visual design and output.

By pressing a soft sensor stitched onto the Pillow, a recording mechanism is activated, capturing the users narration of their dream memory and transmitting it to the Jar, where it is stored for later playback.

TEI'11, January 22–26, 2011, Funchal, Portugal.

Almost any part of our self that is not conscious by day can come through in dreams. We can access thoughts that are wiser than our usual ideas, and behaviors that are more primitive.

The digitalization of information allowed by Pillow-Talk, unlike a dream diary, gives the user the potential to analyze dreams not only on a case by case basis, but provides a powerful tool to evaluate dreams over time, qualify and quantify themes, characters and emotions. Speech to text recognition could allow data analysis, revealing common themes not only presented in the particular user's dreams, but among different users.

Pillow-Talk could serve as a powerful tool to bring further insight into the fears and desires of a determined culture or generation as interpreted through their dreams. "Myths are public dreams, dreams are private myths... dreams talk about permanent conditions within your own psyche as they relate to the temporal conditions of your life right now" [7].

This could be of great importance, for it could help relieve any sense of alienation and create empathy, by illustrating that every individual problem should be seen in reference to the human situation as a whole [8].

RELATED WORK

Pillow-Talk invites users to bring to light the potential of their sleeping mind by providing a seamless interface where to capture their dreams without distraction. It also offers a tangible and evocative visualization of such as an inviting and intimate interface for playback.

Persuasive Technology and Reflective Design

Persuasive technology aims to change attitudes and habits through persuasion, but it is mostly used in sales and management, politics, religion and public health [9]. Nonetheless, we find it a compelling field, for it exposes the individual to otherwise unrevealed knowledge about themselves.

Unlike most Persuasive Technology, which gathers data usually used by a third party, the Persuasive Mirror gives the user access to her own behavioral data by providing continuous feedback [10].

Omo is a relational machine, making the user conscious of the emotional and visceral aspects of breathing through imitation [11].

Francois Pachet's "Reflexive Interactions" sprouted from the idea that the creation of content technologies can enhance individual realization and establish inner dialogs through which personal content can emerge. They intend to produce an interaction in which an object has to be constructed not directly nor intentionally, but as a bi-product of an interaction between the user and an image of herself, typically produced by a machine learning system. This is a compelling to our research, if we take the dream as an unconscious construction of an object and it's recalling an interaction with one's own image [12].

Figure1. Jar closed reminiscent of caught fireflies and open Jar with exposed speaker.

Pillows as Interface

There is a myriad of projects that make use of the intimate qualities of a pillow as an interface.

The Dreaming Pillow is a beautiful project exploring dream imagery taking the pillow as a canvas. Using capacitive sensing, it is reactive to touch: stroking the pillow enables the user to delve into the oniric landscape [13].

move.me uses pillows as an intimate input and output interface of adaptive ambient technology [14].

Pillowtalk is intended to connect remote lovers. The pillow emits a soft glow when the distance loved one has retired to bed; his heartbeat made audible in real time [15].

DESIGN

Technology

Pillow-Talk is composed of two separate but interrelated objects:

The Pillow, a seamless, robust, detachable, wireless interface, captures the users dreams and musings through embedded interaction. And the Jar: a tangible visualization and playback device

The Jar is a simple Mason jar with amber colored LED's dangling inside it, evocative of fireflies. The neck of the Jar encloses the Animator: a costume made platform designed to expedite the process of prototyping physical computing projects. It is Arduino powered, incorporates data storage, sound playback, 16-channel PWM LED control and wireless communication via an Xbee radio into a single small board. The Animator is powered with a Polymer Lithium Ion 1000mAh battery and a simple speaker is used for playback.

It was important to the design to make it visually evocative and have a seamless user interface that drew from the natural affordances of the object.

By adding a piece of conductive Velcro to the lid and two small pieces of copper tape to the mouth of the jar, playback is activated just by unscrewing the lid. No obvious switches are needed: voiced dreams start flowing from the mouth of the jar.

Both objects communicate through Xbee radios to a central computer which runs the software to capture, save and transmit the recordings.

Inspired by Leah Buechley's work on textile computing, the Pillow makes use soft sensors as the primary interface. Considerations such as handling and washing have been crucial to the design, thus the circuit has been specifically made to resist every day use while providing optimum comfort and performance [16].

Early Design

The first Pillow iteration made use of a Lilypad Arduino, an XBee radio module, a Lilypad Xbee breakout board, a Lilypad LiPower and a Bluetooth mini headset for recording sewn into a small pillow nested into the normal size pillow. All connections were stitched together using conductive thread. This comprised the main recording system, which was attached to the exposed switch with metal snaps. Flexible and Soft Velcro stitched across with conductive thread composed the soft switch and was the main user interface.

Interaction Design

It's impossible to learn from your dreams if you can't remember them. The proposed solutions for dream recollection usually require the dreamer to:

- Prime oneself onto remembering dreams. Pillow-Talk, by being a pillow specially designed for dream recollection, serves as an incentive. Its design invokes its purpose, providing a gentle reminder to the user.

- Keep a pen and paper by one's bed. A dream journal can encourage recall and, at the very least, help document any fragment you do remember upon awaking. It has been noted though, that to capture detail it is best to lie still. Pen and paper requires physical and mental effort, thus distracting the dream. By making a pillow the interface for recalling, we minimize the effort and hence optimize the chances for recall.

Pillow-Talk allows the user to record her dreams by simply bending the pillow's corner to start recording. This makes it hard to accidentally activate the switch while sleeping but easy enough to do upon awaking without requiring strenuous effort. Unbending the corner saves the recording onto a file on the user's computer and sends it to the Jar.

Transmission feedback is visually represented by dimming the otherwise glowing LED's and flickering one, acknowledging acquisition.

The user, whenever she sees convenient, can go back to listening the captured dreams by simply opening the Jar. A randomly picked dream is then streamed from the mouth of the Jar. Additionally, the audio files are stored onto the user's computer.

While Pillow-Talk is envisioned as a tool for remembering dreams, the use of voice as the input permits otherwise impossible detail and nuance expressed in the prosody of the dreamer to shed insight into the emotional impact of the dream content.

Changes Prompted by User Interactions

Most individuals reported holding the switch closed as they were recording, making no real use of the hook and loop advantages of Velcro. Furthermore, constant use showed significant wear and tear on the Soft and Flexible Velcro, making the only contact point the thread it had been sewn with; and while more robust Velcro would have proved more resistant, it would also have been harsh to the touch.

Having different elements sewn together implied a complicated stitching process. The tread frayed over time, changing its resistance.

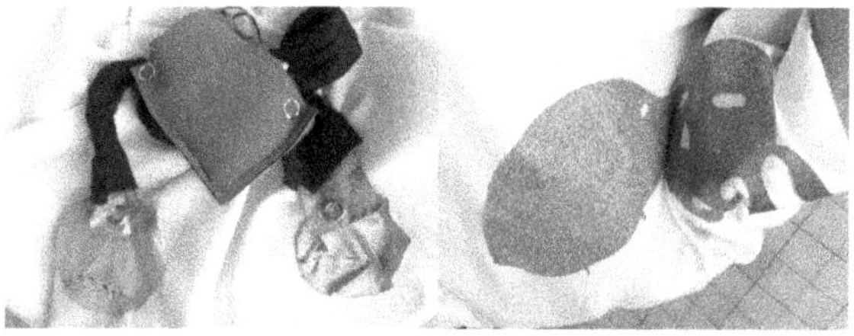

Figure2. The inside of Pillow: a neoprene pouch with electronic components and the exposed switch: two patches of conductive fabric personalized after the users renderings.

Our new design consists of a much simpler, smaller and safer system. We take advantage of the compact design of the Arduino Fio. It integrates the Xbee radio break-out board and the power supply, thus leaving almost no need for stitching. The Arduino Fio, a Polymer Lithium Ion 1000mAh battery and an Xbee radio module are encapsulated in a neoprene pouch. The pouch uses snaps for easy access, powering and removal of components. This minimizes stitching with conductive thread, only needed for the connection to the switch.

Taking in consideration the daily use of a pillow, two long pieces of isolated stretchy conductive fabric are sewn into the pins of the micro-controller on one end and onto metal snaps on the opposite end connecting to the exposed switch.

We also decided to model the exposed switch out from a user's renderings of her dream creatures. We scanned, vectorized and laser cut the hand drawn illustrations on conductive fabric. Personalization of the pillow proved to be a good iteration giving the Pillow further intimate appeal.

EVALUATION

We conducted a pilot study to identify the benefits of our idea and the implementation of the design.

Pilot Study

Our pilot study helped identify the benefits of using Pillow-Talk over a paper based dream diary. We considered three cases: a user who normally remembered his dreams but fails at writing them down, a user who rarely remembers a dream and a user who remembers his dreams periodically.

We asked each individual to be in possession of Pillow-Talk for 3 to 5 days. In all cases, having a pillow specifically designed to record dreams onto served as a primer for retrieval. While two users presented a more quiet sleep, one misplaced the pillow while sleeping and thus failed at accessing the switch and recording on multiple occasions. Another design issue was the need to turn on the device before retiring to sleep. While sometimes a conscious effort was made, on many others the need to sleep was stronger than the reminder. The Jar proved to be a delightful playback object, stimulating the use of the Pillow and adding value to the user's perceptions of their unconscious wonderings. The randomized playback was sometimes welcomed, while other times it proved frustrating when having the desire to listen to a specific dream. In no occasion was discomfort reported.

FUTURE WORK

Based on evaluation, future development will include having multiple switch locations so that the user need not to find the placement of a single one upon awaking.

Designing the Pillow onto a certain shape that would inhibit it's misplacement is also considered.

Visualizing a captured dream though the flickering light of the Jar is evocative and stimulating, but it fails at maintaining each dream's particular quality. We plan a new interface, in which each dream is coined onto a unique material representation. The Jar would then become a platform for playback.

Image Rehearsal Therapy (I.R.T) opens new possibilities in the design of Pillow-Talk, extending it from a capture and playback mechanism, to being a trigger for dream content through its visual appearance.

CONCLUSIONS

We presented Pillow-Talk, a tangible and seamless device for dream priming , recalling and playback.

Through our evaluation, we observed that Pillow-Talk encouraged dream recalling with its mere presence and bridged the gap between dream recalling and the excessive effort required by writing. The use of voice was successful at providing cues about the emotional state of the dreamer while recalling, which could serve as a powerful tool of auto analysis.

The work incited curiosity among peers offering different applications including the treatment of nightmares for people suffering from PTSD (Post-Traumatic Stress Disorder).

ACKNOWLEDGEMENTS

Many thanks to the Media Lab Community, specially to the High-Low Tech Group.

REFERENCES

1. Dieterle, Bernard and Engel, Manfred (eds.). The Dream and the Enlightenment / Le Rêve et les Lumières. Paris, Honoré Champion, 2003.
2. Cambero S., El Chamanismo y las Raíces de la Terapéutica en la Medicina Tradicional de los Huicholes. Guadalajara, Universidad de Guadalajara, 1990.
3. Grieger, T.,M.D., et al.,Posttraumatic Stress Disorder and Depression in Battle-Injured Soldiers *The American Journal of Psychiatry* October 2006.
4. Barry Krakow; Antonio Zadra, Clinical Management of Chronic Nightmares: Imagery Rehearsal. *Behavioral Sleep Medicine*, Volume 4, Issue 1 February 2006, pages 45 - 70.
5. Talbot M., Nightmare Scenario. The New Yorker, November, 2009.
6. Kershaw S., Following a Script to Escape a Nightmare. The New York Times, July 2010.
7. Campbell J.,and Moyers B.,, The Power Myth. Betty Sue Flowers (ed.). New York: Doubleday, 1988.
8. C. G. Jung, R. F. C. Hull, Two Essays on Analytical Psychology: The Meaning of Psychology for Modern Man. Princeton University Press, 1979.
9. Fogg, B. J. (2002). Persuasive Technology: Using Computers to Change What We Think and Do. Morgan Kaufmann.
10. Del Valle, A. and Opalach, A.. The persuasive mirror: Computerized persuasion for healthy living. *HCI International*, Las Vegas, NV (2005).
11. http://web.media.mit.edu/~monster/
12. Pachet, F., Sony CSL-Paris. The Future of Content is in Ourselves. *ACM Journal of Computers in Entertainment*, 6(3), (2008).
13. Leung, A. and Oswald, O. "The dreaming pillow (L'oreiller rêveur)". *ACM SIGGRAPH* (2008).
14. Nack, F., et al. "Pillows as Adaptive Interfaces in Ambient Environments." *International Workshop in Human Centered Multimedia* (2007).
15. http://imd.dundee.ac.uk/~jmontgomery/wp/
16. Buechley,L. and Eisenberg, M. (2007) Fabric PCBs, Electronic Sequins and Socket Buttons:Techniques for E-TextileCraft. *Journal of Personal and Ubiquitous Computing.*

Programmable Blobs : A Rheologic Interface for Organic Shape Design

Akira Wakita **Akito Nakano** **Nobuhiro Kobayashi**
Metamorphic Architecture Lab.
Graduate School of Media and Governance, Keio University
5322 Endo Fujisawa-shi Kanagawa, 252-0882, Japan
{wakita, akito, nobukoba}@sfc.keio.ac.jp

ABSTRACT
Programmable Blobs is an attempt of actuated shape display using fluid material. We have developed an environment where we can program the shape of gel geometrically and topologically using our unique magnetic fluid called *pBlob*. This enables us to experience organic shape changes in real space, like a metaball in the CG world. The control hardware is composed of electromagnets arranged in the honeycomb structure and their control circuits. On/off control and PWM control vary the blob shapes and realize animations. We describe the method of blob creation, details of the mechanism and the language for transformation control, and propose some applications we are developing at present.

Author Keywords
Blob, Metaball, Kinetic Interface, Programmable Matter

ACM Classification Keywords
H.5.1 Multimedia Information Systems: Artificial, augmented, and virtual realities; H.5.2 User Interfaces: Haptic I/O.

General Terms
Design, Human Factors, Languages, Theory.

INTRODUCTION

TUI has enabled us to program shapes and behavior of various materials. Some of them are paper [4, 16] and fabric [1, 5] with new interaction, and toolkits [14, 18] for assembling transformable structures. An attempt of kinetic surface can also actuate shapes of various scales on wall surfaces or tabletops [11, 15, 17]. As seen from these works, a lot of researches have so far been done for the materials that do not lose their shapes. Meanwhile, researches for programming fluid matters have not yet been done that much. We propose the method to control shapes and behavior of viscous fluid and its design principle, as the first step of rheologic user interface. The concept of our method is to expand a CG metaball [2] to a real space. As we create unique magnetic gel and combine it with the workbench that controls magnetic force, the metamorphic shape and behavior of the gel can be controlled both geometrically and topologically. We have named this magnetic gel *pBlob* (programmable blob), and developed a control environment. In this paper, we describe the hardware, method of material synthesis, design principles for programming blobby materials and applications.

TEI'11, January 22-26, 2011, Funchal, Portugal.

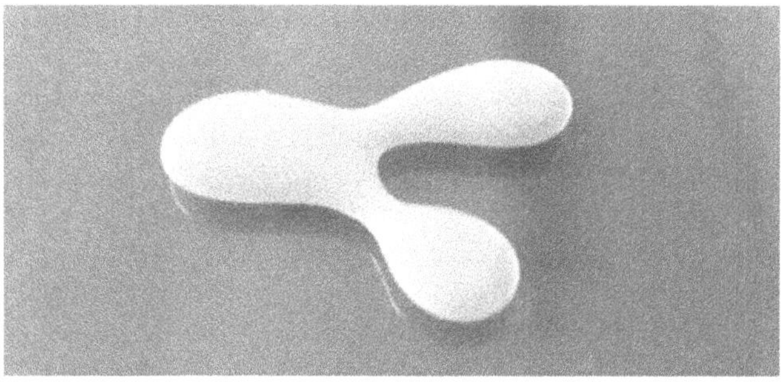

Figure 1. The organic-looking white object is the *pBlob*, gel magnetic fluid with flexible locomotion.

RELATED WORKS

In recent years, very soft programmable matter has been attracting much attention. Soft shape-shifting robot blob [8] can move and change its shape as the volume of air is controlled in itself. Claytronics [7] construct voxel shapes using small modular robots. There are also some attempts that use real clay [19], focusing on haptic interaction with materials. Magnetic thinking putty [12] is the magnetic clay that allows flexible change of its shape using strong neodymium magnet. As a case with more fluid material, media installation [6, 10] using magnetic fluid is well-known.

MECHANISM

The system consists of *pBlobs* (programmable blobs), magnetic units and electric circuits. The *pBlob* is gel magnetic fluid with the behavior similar to a metaball.

Since it is gel, it retains the properties of viscoelasticity between liquid and solid. If a strong magnetic force acts on the *pBlob* from a distant place, it moves from one place to another. Generating the underfloor magnetic force controls the shape and locomotion of the *pBlob*. The following sections describe the details of our prototype system.

Blobware

In order to create a blob that behaves like a metaball, we referenced the method to create slime. By mixing water, polyvinyl alcohol (PVA) and borax, we can easily create the slime similar to the store-bought one. With this material, we mixed the iron powder to magnetize it. With the operations up to here, we could obtain ferromagnetic gel, but the friction with the floor surface was too large to move the blob smoothly even though we used the strong magnet. In addition, we had another problem that the iron powder gradually rusted to deteriorate. As we tried some materials, we solved the problem of the rust by using ferrous ferric oxide (iron oxide black, Fe_3O_4). The problem of the friction was improved by putting the blob in a container filled with poppy oil. The poppy oil effectively works for the blob; i.e., it reduces the friction to move the blob smoothly and it keeps the blob wet. We also examined the materials of the container in order to reduce the friction. First, we examined a hard-glass container and an acrylic container, but the friction was so large that a large magnetic force was required to realize the smooth locomotion. If the magnetic force was raised, the blob moved although a part of the blob got stuck on the floor surface. As we examined various materials, using polystyrene realized the ideal blob locomotion.

The recipe of the *pBlob*, obtained after much trial and error, is shown below. Every material is inexpensive and anyone can easily create the *pBlob* through the procedure below.

The materials are: water, PVA, borax, magnetic powder (ferrous ferric oxide), watercolor, and poppy oil. These materials except poppy oil were mixed in the proportion of 50:50:1:2:1. step1: Mix the watercolor with water. step2: Mix ferrous ferric oxide with the colored water. step3: Mix PVA and stir the mixture well. step4: Mix borax. To mix it evenly, stretch the mixture as thinly as possible. step5: Put the created blob in the container filled with poppy oil.

Hardware

We referenced the structure of the actuated workbench [13], the tabletop UI using electromagnets, and devised our unique measures to prototype the hardware.

As Figure 2 shows, a magnetic unit is composed of an electromagnet, an iron core and an aluminum post. We utilized commonly-available electromagnets. A bobbin has a diameter of 18mm, a height of 30mm and a hole diameter of 7mm. A coil is wrapped with an enamel wire of a diameter of 0.4mm 400 times. Inserting an iron core to the electromagnet hole strengthens the magnetic force. This electromagnet is set in the circuit, to which electrical current of DC 25V and 2.4A is applied. Arduino and software created through processing are used to control on/off and PWM.

An aluminum post is a hexagonal cylinder whose long axis is 21mm. The electromagnet and the iron core are set in this post. The aluminum post has the following two roles: one is to let the heat the electromagnet generates out effectively using the property of aluminum's good thermal conductivity, and the other is to keep the distance between electromagnets constant. Since the unit is a hexagonal cylinder, it can be arranged in the honeycomb structure. If the unit is arranged in the grid structure, the horizontal and vertical distances between adjacent electromagnets differ from the diagonal one. In the honeycomb structure, different from the grid arrangement, the distance between the adjacent electromagnets is constant and the *pBlob* can be easily controlled. In our prototype hardware, seven electromagnet units are arranged in the honeycomb structure, set in the 15cm x 15cm acrylic container. Although the actuation range is limited in this container area, tiling more units allows to actuate the larger area. The container with the *pBlob* is set on this hardware and the shape and locomotion is controlled using magnetic force.

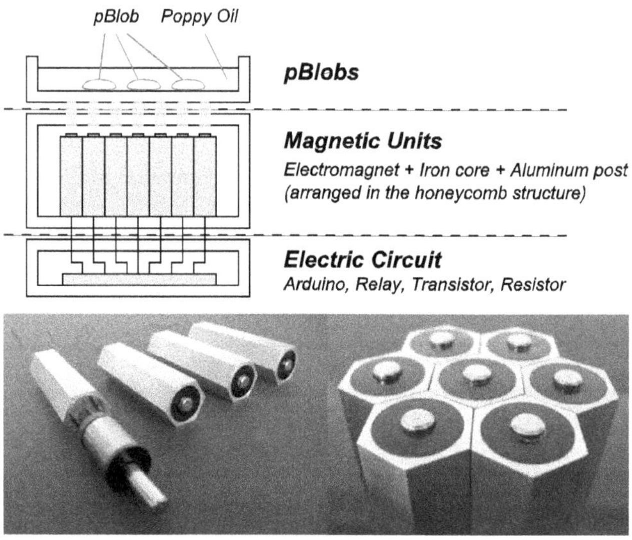

Figure 2. Top: The hardware composition. Bottom: Electromagnet unit and honeycomb arrangement.

METAMORPHIC DESIGN

Geometric Transformation

Translate is the operation to move the object from the current coordinate location to another. In the description below, the coordinate of the *pBlob* is referred to as p_i and the electromagnet below the *pBlob* is referred to as m_i. First, suppose that the *pBlob* is located at p_0 (Figure 3). At this moment, the electromagnet m_0 of p_0 is turned on. If the electromagnet m_1 of p_1, located adjacently to p_0, is turned on and m_0 is turned off, the *pBlob* is translated from p_0 to p_1. As translation finishes, the *pBlob* maintains to be circular since it is affected by the electromagnet m_1.

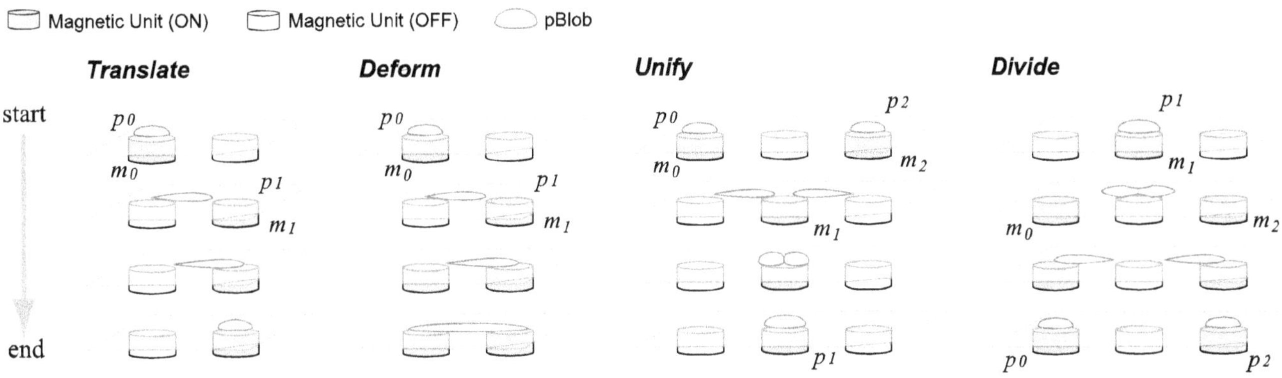

Figure 3. Deformation process. Four types of modification and their electromagnet control steps.

Deform is the operation to change the shape using resultant force vectors. As Figure 3 shows, a circular *pBlob* changes its shape to be long and thin. First, in the similar manner as *translate*, translate the *pBlob* from p_0 to p_1. During translation, when the *pBlob* is long and thin, turn m_0 on. Then, the *pBlob* is pulled to both p_1 and p_0, and its long and thin shape is maintained. Turning on multiple neighboring electromagnets allows to modify the blob shape variously.

Topological Transformation

Unify is the operation to combine two *pBlobs* to become a larger *pBlob* by giving them the vectors facing each other. Suppose one *pBlob* is located at p_0 and the other at p_2, and p_1 is located between the *pBlobs*. Turn the electromagnet m_1 on and turn m_0 and m_2 off. Then, the two *pBlobs* start moving toward p_1. As the two *pBlobs* contact at p_1, the oil between them are gradually removed and the *pBlobs* are pulled by each other to become one larger *pBlob* naturally (Figure 4). *Divide* is the operation opposite to *unify*, where one *pBlob* is stretched to be divided into two *pBlobs*.

Our hardware implements the fundamental four operations. Combining these operations allows to create various complex shapes. It is also possible to control the shape weight by giving different duty cycle to adjacent electromagnets or to translate the blob in an arbitrary direction using the resultant force vectors.

APPLICATIONS

Shape Design Tool

The design tool to which the principle of the metaball is applied can be a new creation environment. As represented by blobitecture or blobject [9], a lot of artifacts with organic shapes have been created in late years in architecture or product design fields. A shape design tool using *pBlobs* can be used as an organic shape modeler for these artifacts. This tool is not used only for modeling shapes, but for designing organic texture and behavior of blobjects. It is expected that this tool will also stimulate the creators' inspiration.

If the shapes created using *pBlobs* can be reconstructed in a PC, the tool can also be interlocked with the normal CAD/CG digital design processes. We succeeded in

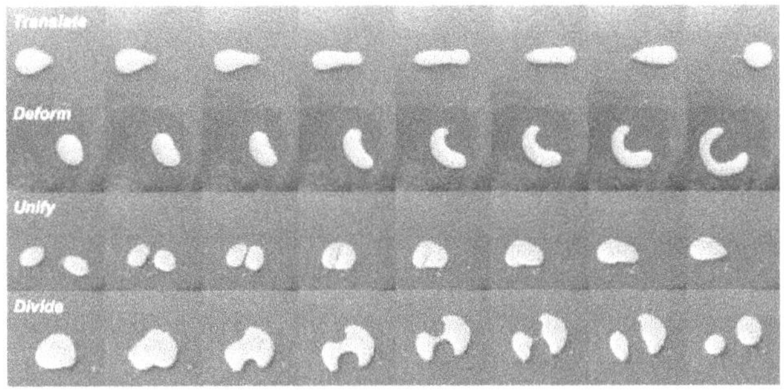

Figure 4. Snapshots of transformation (*translate, deform, unify* and *divide* from the top).

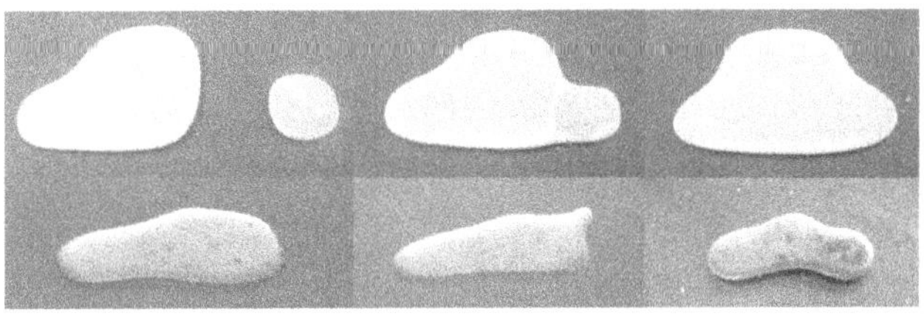

Figure 5. Blobjectical trial for automobile design. Top: *Unify* operation for shape creation, Bottom: Local transformation using resultant force vectors.

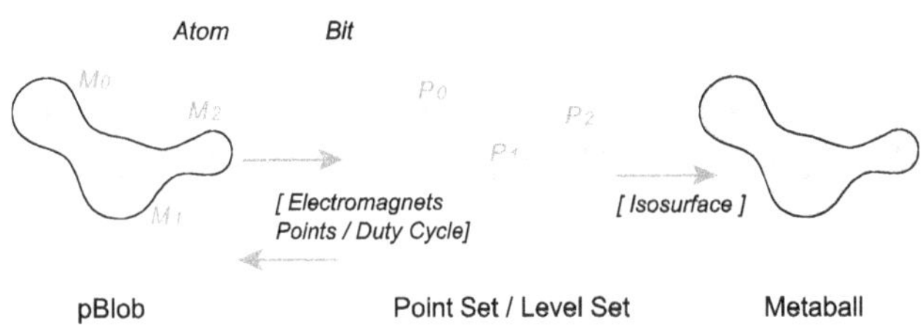

Figure 6. Reconstruction of a shape for CG

reconstruction of blob shapes in a PC with the following procedure. First, if a favorable *pBlob* shape is obtained, the coordinate values and the duty cycle of the electromagnets that are turned on at that moment are transmitted to the PC. The coordinate values are used as a point set of control particles for the metaball algorithm and the duty cycle is used as a level set. Then, create an isosurface [3] and divide it into a mesh. As shown in Figure 6, *pBlobs* and metaballs can be mutually reconstructed.

Media Arts and Entertainments

pBlob locomotion reminds us of primitive organisms. This might be applied to media arts and entertainments. The interaction that a *pBlob* follows human movements builds up the illusion of life, and the *pBlob* will be a virtual pet. If the *pBlob* is interlocked with artificial intelligence, a new agent might be created. In addition, if the *pBlob*'s movement is controlled using the joystick or other interfaces, games such as mazes or *Pac-Man* can be created.

Living Thing Simulation

Moving a lot of *pBlobs* in an autonomous decentralized way enables living thing simulation such as *Conway's Game of Life*. Different from the decentralized cells of *Game of Life*, the *pBlobs* are available for topological movements such as *unify* or *divide*, which may produce more organic patterns. In some situations, phenomena such as emergence might be simulated.

DISCUSSION

User Interface Strategy

From our experiences, we know it is difficult to grasp fluids in our hands. Although we do not directly touch *pBlobs*, it is necessary to feel that we naturally move *pBlobs* by our own will, which gives us embodied interactions. We introduce the concept of *Force* of *Star Wars* to the user interface. For example, if a *divide* operation is executed, we gesture as if we stretch and separate a virtual blob into two parts using our both hands. For a *translate* operation, we sweep the virtual blob in a desired direction.

Long Hours of Operation

The problems of thermal runaway had been assumed in long hours of operations, although such conditions were not observed. The iron cores and the hexagonal aluminum containers worked as heat sinks and they helped dissipate the heat effectively. Long hours of operation also affect the *pBlob* locomotion. The magnetic powder of the *pBlob* settles out by its own weight and the *pBlob* slows down. Stirring the *pBlob* using a fine stick regains smooth locomotion, but we need to improve the *pBlob* materials if long hours of automatic operation are required.

CONCLUSION AND FUTURE WORK

We have mentioned the method to program the shape and behavior of gel magnetic fluid using electromagnets. As a short-term prospect, we expect to remove media such as poppy oil to make blobs stand alone. Our long-term prospect is to construct the 3-dimensional system by building up the present 2-dimensional system in hierarchy.

REFERENCES

1. Berzowska, J. et al. Skorpions: Kinetic Electronic Garments, Ubicomp'07.
2. Blinn, J. F. A Generalization of Algebraic Surface Drawing. ACM Trans. Graph. 1, 3 (Jul. 1982), pp.235-256.
3. Bloomenthal, J. Introduction to Implicit Surfaces. Morgan Kaufmann, 1997.
4. Coelho, M. Hall, L. Berzowska, J. Maes, P. Pulp-based computing: a framework for building computers out of paper, In Proc. CHI'09, pp.3527-3528.
5. Coelho, M. and Maes, P. Shutters: a permeable surface for environmental control and communication, In Proc. TEI'09, pp.13-18.
6. Frey, M. SnOil - Ein plastisches Display basierend auf Ferrofluid, http://www.freymartin.de/de/projekte/snoil
7. Goldstein, Seth Copen and Campbell, Jason D. and Mowry, Todd C. Programmable Matter, IEEE Computer, vol.38, no.6, p.99-101, 2005.
8. iRobot, Shape-Shifting Blob 'Bot, http://spectrum.ieee.org/automaton/robotics/robotics-software/irobot-soft-morphing-blob-chembot
9. John K. Waters, Blobitecture: Waveform Architecture and Digital Design, Rockport Pub, 2003.
10. Kodama, S. Dynamic ferrofluid sculpture: organic shape-changing art forms. Commun. ACM vol.51, no.6 (Jun. 2008), 79-81.
11. Leithinger, D. and Ishii, H. Relief: a scalable actuated shape display. In Proc.TEI'10. pp.221-222.
12. Magnetic Thinking Putty, http://www.puttyworld.com/midnightcolors.html
13. Pangaro, G., Maynes-Aminzade, D., and Ishii, H. The actuated workbench: computer-controlled actuation in tabletop tangible interfaces. In Proc. UIST'02. pp.181-190.
14. Parkes, A. and Ishii, H. Kinetic sketchup: motion prototyping in the tangible design process. In Proc. TEI'09. pp.367-372.
15. Poupyrev, I., Nashida, T., and Okabe, M. Actuation and tangible user interfaces: the Vaucanson duck, robots, and shape displays. In Proc. TEI'07, pp.205-212.
16. Qi, J. and Buechley, L. Electronic popables: exploring paper-based computing through an interactive pop-up book In Proc TEI'10, pp.121-128.
17. Raffle, H., Joachim, M. W., and Tichenor, J. Super cilia skin: an interactive membrane. In Proc. CHI'03 Extended Abstracts, pp.808-809.
18. Raffle, H. S., Parkes, A. J., and Ishii, H. Topobo: a constructive assembly system with kinetic memory. In Proc. CHI'04. pp.647-654.
19. Reed, M. Prototyping digital clay as an active material. In Proc. TEI'09. pp.339-342.

ShakeOnIt: An Exploration Into Leveraging Social Rituals For Information Access

David Cranor, Amanda Peyton, Arlene Persaud, Rajiv Bhatia, Sinbae Kim, and V. M. Bove

MIT Media Lab	MIT Sloan	Harvard GSD	Harvard SEAS
20 Ames Street	50 Memorial Drive	48 Quincy Street	29 Oxford Street
Cambridge, MA 02142	Cambridge, MA 02142	Cambridge, MA 02138	Cambridge, MA 02138

{cranor, peyton, rajiv.bhatia, vmb}@mit.edu {apersaud, kim79}@harvard.edu

ABSTRACT

We have created a system which utilizes a pair of sensor-outfitted gloves to test for the performance of a series of multi-person gestures known as a "secret handshake." The fact that a new user of the system is required to rehearse the handshake performance with someone who is already experienced in performing it adds a novel layer of security to information access which is inherently social.

Author Keywords

Cooperative gestures, handshake, authentication, gestural interface, social interaction

ACM Classification Keywords

H5.m. Information interfaces and presentation: Miscellaneous.

General Terms

Human Factors, Security.

INTRODUCTION AND MOTIVATION

Members of many social groups use specialized interaction methods known as "secret handshakes" to greet and identify one another [3]. These handshakes can be simple or complex, ranging from a basic clasping of hands to an elaborate series of gestures [3]. Similarly, a user of a computer system may be required to identify themselves to the system in order to access certain information by providing credentials through the use of a password, biometric, or other access control system.

However, unlike the learning of a password or the adding of fingerprint data to a biometric database, the process of learning to perform an elaborate secret handshake includes non-transient periods of practice and interpersonal communication with one or more members of the "approved users" group. Additionally, because a secret handshake requires the presence of two performers in order to be performed causes it to be, by definition, a social activity.

TEI'11, January 22–26, 2011, Funchal, Portugal.

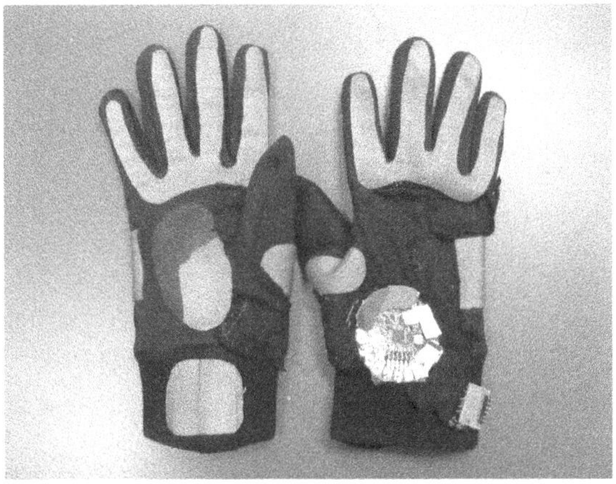

Figure 1. Secret handshake detecting gloves.

A computer system which tests for social integration would add a novel dimension to information access. As a result, we have created a pair of sensor-outfitted gloves which can demonstrate a test for the successful performance of an elaborate secret handshake between two users.

RELATED WORK

The iBand [2] is a device demonstrated by researchers from Media Lab Europe and the University of London's Institute of Education which facilitates information transfer between two users shaking hands. The device itself consists of a wristband outfitted with LEDs, an accelerometer, and an infrared transceiver which facilitate the automatic transfer of personal information when two people wearing iBands shake hands.

Patel et al. [5] have done work regarding using gesture as an authentication scheme. In their system, a single user authenticates to a public computer terminal by performing a series of gestures with a personal device that is known to the system to belong to the user. In this way, the user can prove their identity to the terminal without the use of a password.

There have also been papers published in the literature which detail the use of synchronous and cooperative gesturing as an interaction and information sharing framework [1,4]. Morris et al. discuss cooperative gesturing amongst a group of users in order to send a single, combined command to a system [4]. Hinckley describes methods by which a combination of users and displays can bump the displays together in different ways in order to share information amongst them [1].

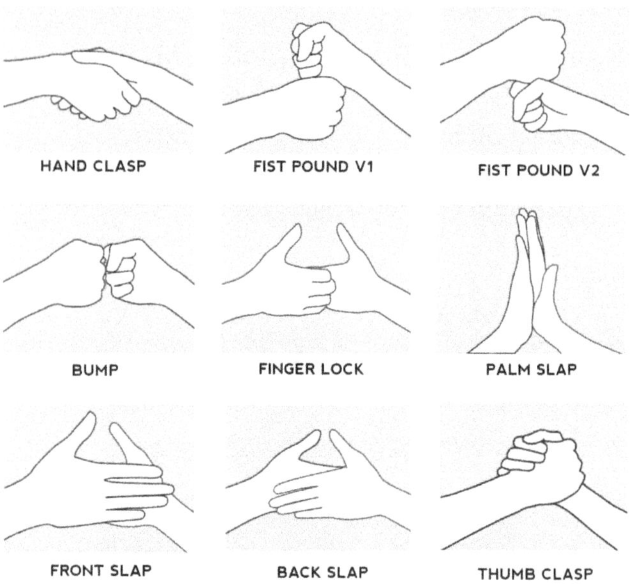

Figure 2. Gestures detected by the system.

The goal in creating ShakeOnIt was to combine elements from these projects in order to explore the possibilities of leveraging an already socially accepted cooperative gesturing system into a computer mediated authentication scheme.

SYSTEM OVERVIEW

The system itself consists of two form-fitting gloves outfitted with conductive patches as well as a Lilypad Arduino microcontroller development board allowing for the detection of nine different gestures. A host computer displays the gesture currently being performed, as well as information regarding the success of the secret handshake.

Soft Sensors

Each glove is outfitted with six patches of iron-on conductive fabric on the front of the fingers, the palm of the hand, the wrist, the back of the fingers, the bottom of the hand, and the top of the hand.

These patches are connected to the microcontroller by means of conductive thread sewn into the gloves as well as a ribbon cable which tethers the gloves together.

Microcontroller Firmware

The microcontroller determines the gesture currently being performed by setting all of the pins connected to the patches on one of the gloves as inputs, driving a single patch on the other glove to a logical high state, and checking which of the input patches (if any) are connected to this output. This process is repeated for the five remaining output patches, and a 6x6 array of current patch connections between the two gloves is recorded. If this array matches the pre-determined "fingerprint" of a known gesture, the corresponding gesture ID is transmitted to the host computer through a wired serial connection.

Gesture Visualization Program

The host computer is running a program written in Processing which receives the data from the microcontroller and displays a pictogram of the gesture currently being performed by the users of the system. If the users perform a predetermined series of gestures in the correct order, an "access granted" graphic is displayed.

FUTURE WORK

The current implementation of the system described in this paper does not lend itself to heavy use due to the wires connecting the gloves together and to the host computer. Plans are currently being developed to re-make the system to be wire-free in order to facilitate conducting a formal user study. Also, we plan to evaluate methods of sensing the motion of the users' hands when moving between the gestures as well as the cadence of the performance in order to obtain a more sensitive measure of the users' familiarity with one another. One idea which is currently being discussed to is to create a pair of rings, each outfitted with an accelerometer to sense motion and a wireless transceiver to transmit the motion data to the host computer.

CONCLUSION

This project demonstrates the electronic augmentation of a currently accepted social authentication system, the "secret handshake," in order to allow a computer to determine if several users are sufficiently integrated into a given social group. We look forward to building a prototype of this system suitable for a formal user study as well as further exploring the general idea of leveraging existing social rituals to create novel computer interfaces.

REFERENCES

1. Hinckley, K. Synchronous gestures for multiple persons and computers. In *Proc. UIST 2003*, ACM Press (2003), 149-158.
2. Kanis, M., Winters, N., Agamanolis, S., Gavin, A., and Cullinan, C. Toward wearable social networking with iBand. *Ext. Abstracts CHI 2005,* ACM Press (2005), 1521-1524.
3. Lundmark, T. *Tales of Hi and Bye: Greeting and Parting Rituals Around the World.* Cambridge University Press, Port Melbourne, VIC, Australia, 2009.
4. Morris, M. R., Huang, A., Paepcke, A., and Winograd, T. Cooperative gestures: multi-user gestural interactions for co-located groupware. In *Proc. CHI 2002,* ACM Press (2006), 1201-1210.
5. Patel, S. N., Pierce, J. S., and Abowd, G. D. A gesture-based authentication scheme for untrusted public terminals. In *Proc. UIST 2004*, ACM Press (2004), 157-160.

Designing Through Making: Exploring the Simple Haptic Design Space

Camille Moussette
Umeå Institute of Design
Umeå University, Umeå 90187, Sweden
camille.moussette@dh.umu.se

Richard Banks
Microsoft Research Cambridge
7 J J Thomson Ave, Cambridge CB3 0FB, UK
rbanks@microsoft.com

ABSTRACT
In this paper we describe the development and realization of basic haptic design tools. A series of devices or setups allow designers and other stakeholders to adopt a hands-on approach to haptics, and ultimately develop a greater sensitivity and understanding of haptic concepts. By offering tangible manifestations that are relatively abstract and modular, designers can relate to, explore and discuss haptic interfaces and possible variations with greater ease and confidence.

The five Simple Haptics devices that we built offer a basic platform to play and experiment with haptic interfaces. Each setup starts with a simple haptic idea and provides a graspable and experienceable unit to support discussion and variation related the haptic design activities.

Author Keywords
Haptics, Design Tools, Interaction Design, Tangible Interfaces.

ACM Classification Keywords
H5.m. Information interfaces and presentation (e.g., HCI): Miscellaneous.

INTRODUCTION
Designing haptic interfaces is absolutely not trivial. Despite an already established research field [1,6,10], designers are generally unfamiliar with the haptic domain. The challenges can be very daunting at first, as the current haptic systems are commonly very complex, expensive and/or highly technical. Our main hypothesis is that designers can refine their mastery and develop a heightened sensitivity to haptics only if their work with and through the material.

Hayward and McKlean [5,15] published an overview of the challenges and technical issues around building haptic interfaces. Their work, presented under the Do-It-Yourself (DIY) movement, directly aims at demystifying and democratizing haptics, opening the field and lowering the barrier to entry for non-experts. They note, like many others [3,9,12,13], the surprisingly limited body of knowledge around the activities and processes of designing haptics.

Designing for our touch sense remains unnatural to most of us. We, designers and users alike, usually experience these sensations and haptic stimulations directly, but we do not usually verbalize and communicate them explicitly in details. The lexicon and vocabulary around the subject is sure limited but nevertheless growing, [15, 19]. The reliance on prototypes, actuated artifacts and semi-working models is almost a necessity to develop a shared understanding and evolve haptic design ideas.

DESIGNING THROUGH MAKING
Transitioning from ideation to materialization is particularly difficult in the haptic realm. Haptic concepts or ideas presented visually or orally have limited reach and usefulness. To fully appreciate and evaluate haptics proposals, stimulations and forces need to be applied on our skin and body. Moving, actuating and influencing the world and its atoms require its load of energy and some level of control. Sketching haptics require a different set of constraints and skills than traditional design sketching activities (interfaces mockups, hand-written drawings, volumetric models, etc).

From the start, we decided to embrace our medium and rely on the process of making to experiment, understand, and critically explore the subject. Our hypothesis was that by building things, manifesting ideas quickly, testing alternatives and variations, making mistakes, truly feeling what works and what doesn't, we would develop a heightened sensitivity to haptics [2,3]. By sketching in hardware [7,16], designing through making [18], and by being fully engaged in the matter, important knowledge and understanding of haptics would be acquired.

SIMPLE HAPTICS
Our work intentionally explores simple actuated mechanisms that we started calling Simple Haptics. They are directly inspired by Hayward's self-contained non-programmable mechanical devices made to explore haptic illusions [4]. We purposely avoid the typical arm (or finger) force-feedback systems as they are highly technical and generally deliver low quality stimuli compared to real physical interaction with the world.

TEI'11, January 22–26, 2011, Funchal, Portugal.

Our Simple Haptics devices make use of natural qualities of the materials and of the assembly mechanisms, i.e. glued versus screwed. When inert and non-actuated, these devices have certain qualities and characteristics, from an industrial design perspective at least. Our goal with Simple Haptics was to leverage these qualities, and augment them with actuation or basic mechanism to produce simple haptic interfaces.

It is important to state that our devices are not final haptic proposals or interfaces per se. We view these devices as platforms and building blocks to sketch, understand, explore, experiment quickly, build variations and develop a design sensitivity of the subject. They were built as design tools or tangible work artifacts to engage and discuss while designing haptics.

We decided to arbitrarily limit our work to five setups or haptic concepts. For each of them, we explored and built numerous versions and variations. All the devices, with associated electronic controls and user interfaces, were built during a 12-week period using readily available workshop materials and simple electronics.

Slacker

The idea at the origin of the Slacker device is to have a device with a fixed shell or case, but the inside can *feel* different: being loose or solid, shaky or secure, reactive or inert.

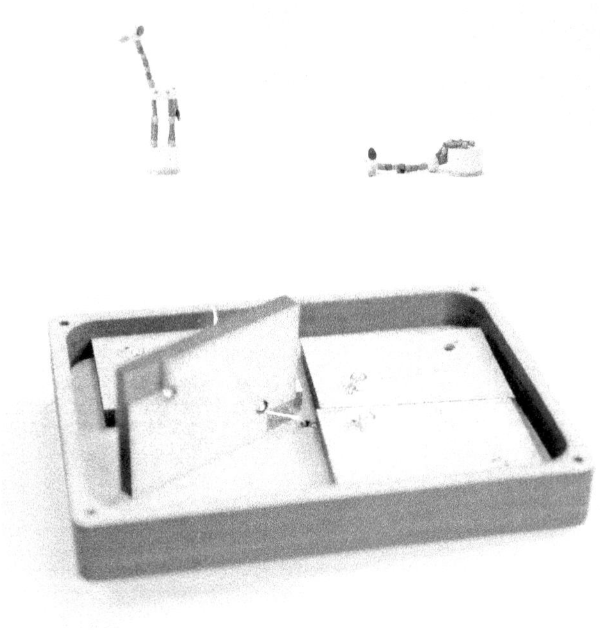

Figure 1. Inspiration and Slacker device. The internal parts can be "clutched" (loose or solid).

The first version had a simple button or responded to a mouse click on the computer to trigger/release the mechanism. The final iteration used an accelerometer to detect movement (shake) and activate/deactivate the clutch accordingly. The default configuration chosen for the device was the *Shake to Solidify* pattern, but other testers found the reverse *Shake to Release* more intuitive at first. There are no right or wrong configurations. It really depends on the designers' intention in building a more final and specific solution.

Springer

Springer evolves from today's visual interfaces that often spring back when dragging or scrolling an object out of bound. The simple proposal is to have the haptic perception that an internal physical object is really springing back as the user interface does so.

The main challenge was to create a setup that crank and release a dead-weight attached to elastic cords inside the device. The final solution has the springing user interface on an adjacent computer, but ideally this visual interface would sit on top of the device.

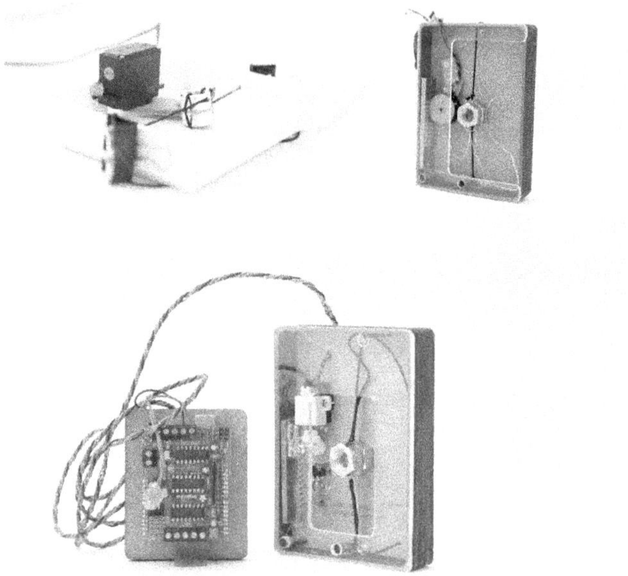

Figure 2. Evolution of the Springer device.

Winder

The Winder setup offers a mechanism to move weight along one axis of the device. This way, the center of mass of the whole unit can be moved. The load can be easily modulated by adding or removing steel nuts.

The prototypes use a common type of miniature geared-motor, available in different gear ratio configurations. Variations of speed and torque (thus working load) can be tested whilst keeping the same electronics and control program.

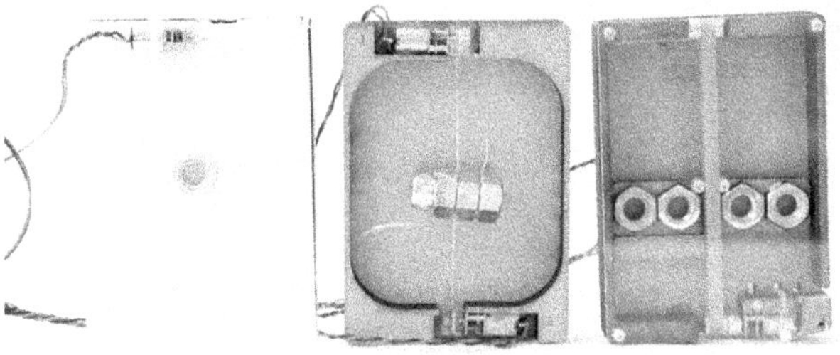

Figure 3. Three iterations of the Winder device.

Spinner

The principle of the Spinner is to simply have a rotating weight inside the device. If the weight spins fast, it feels similar to slow and cyclic vibration. If moved sequentially, the center-of-mass of the whole unit can be positioned around. Again, the speed, position and load can be varied at the designer' s will.

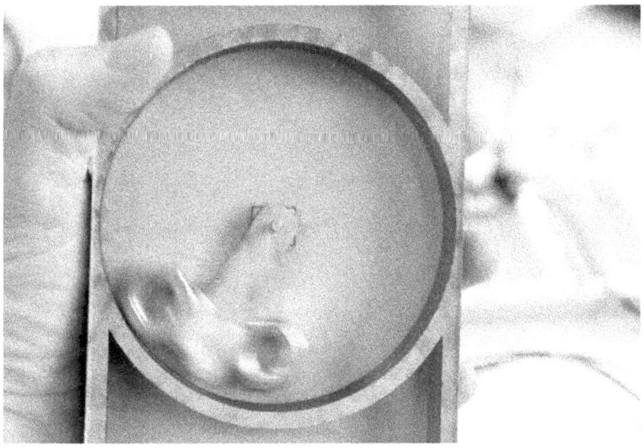

Figure 4. First version of the Spinner device.

Slider

The concept behind the Slider is to offer a moveable source of actuation and explore to what extent users can perceive the dynamic source compared to a static source. The device is built around a motorized slider, and offer two different sources of haptic stimulation: a vibrating one and a poking one (solenoid). The source position, speed, cycle time and actuation rhythm/power can be changed via an user interface on the computer.

One important characteristic of this setup is the ability to change material at the interface (back panel) between the dynamic source and the user's hand. The intention is to let the designers explore different materials and feel for themselves how the haptic qualities are changing in relation to the different variables.

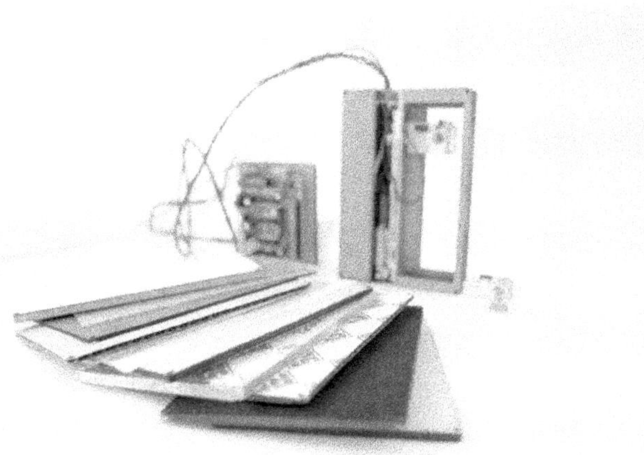

Figure 5. Slider device, with 2 dynamic sources, and the different materials for testing.

DISCUSSION

Our initial hypothesis of acquiring haptic knowledge and expertise through making and sketching in hardware seems to hold true, at least partially. As designers we truly feel that we now have a more acute sensitivity and understanding of haptics after the 12-week period. We also acknowledged the use of a new vocabulary to communicate haptic concepts in our day-to-day design activities. We adopted terms like clutching, winding, solidify to document and explain key characteristics in the devices we built.

By constantly manipulating and trying out various configurations, we found that material properties and assembly techniques matter very much while designing haptics. Our perception on the sense of touch is all about a collection of small and converging cues. Finding a haptically interesting stimulation in relation to both aesthetic and functional qualities is very demanding. While developing our series of devices, we found that relative change/modification was more easily recognized and felt, compared to static stimulation. For example with the Winder unit, it is quite difficult to recognize where the load is on the first grasp. Once the load starts moving, then it is felt instantly and we are quite good at extrapolating the internal position/configuration of the device.

Overall, using the Simple Haptics devices provided a valuable platform for discussing and developing a shared understanding of haptics beyond oral communication and visual static depictions. Being able to "feel" haptics is crucial in designing haptic systems, even though some of the stimulations are not perfect or in refined forms.

FUTURE WORK

In the near future, we plan to deploy the devices to designers and design students in order to evaluate their usefulness. We initially built only five setups and some of them were relatively crude. The possibilities to quickly exchange motors and actuators are limited. We would like to refine the modular aspect of the devices, to support quicker variations and a larger range of haptic explorations.

CONCLUSION

Our work initially set out to provide simple haptic design tools for designers to understand, play and expand their sensitivity to the haptic design activities. During 12 weeks, we decided to embrace our medium and rely on the process of making to experiment, understand, and critically explore the subject. Our hypothesis was that by building things, manifesting ideas quickly, testing alternatives and variations, we would develop a heightened sensitivity to haptics. Our preliminary results seem to support this assertion.

The resulting Simple Haptics devices that we built offer a platform to play and experiment with haptic interfaces. Each setup starts with a simple haptic idea and provides a graspable and experienceable unit to support discussion and variation related the haptic design activities. They were built as design tools or tangible work artifacts to engage and discuss while designing haptics.

ACKNOWLEDGMENTS

We would like to thank the Computer Mediated Living group at Microsoft Research Cambridge for their support and feedback for this work. The help of Nick Trim and the Social-Digital Systems group has been especially appreciated.

REFERENCES

1. Biggs, S.J. and Srinivasan, M.A. (2002), Haptic interfaces, in Stanney, K. (Ed.), Handbook of Virtual Environments, Lawrence Erlbaum, Inc., London.
2. Buchenau, M. and Suri, J. F. (2000) Experience prototyping. In Proceedings of the Conference on Designing interactive Systems: Processes, Practices, Methods, and Techniques (New York City, New York, United States,August 17 - 19, 2000). D. Boyarski and W. A. Kellogg, Eds. DIS '00. ACM Press, New York, NY, 424-433.
3. Buxton, Bill, (2007) Sketching User Experiences: Getting the Design Right and the Right Design, Morgan Kaufmann.
4. Hayward, V. (2008). A Brief Taxonomy of Tactile Illusions and Demonstrations That Can Be Done In a Hardware Store. Brain Research Bulletin (special issue on Robotics and Neuroscience), 75:742-752.
5. Hayward, V. and MacLean, K. E. (2007). Do It Yourself Haptics, Part-I. IEEE Robotics and Automation Magazine, Vol. 14, No. 4, pp. 88-104.
6. Hayward V, Astley OR, Cruz-Hernandez M, Grant D, Robles-De-La-Torre G. (2004) Haptic Interfaces and Devices. Sensor Review 24(1), pp. 16-29.
7. Holmquist, L. E. (2006) Sketching in hardware. interactions 13, 1 (Jan. 2006), 47-60.
8. Ivan Poupyrev , Shigeaki Maruyama , Jun Rekimoto, (2002) Ambient touch: designing tactile interfaces for handheld devices, Proceedings of the 15th annual ACM symposium on User interface software and technology, October 27-30, Paris, France.
9. Jones, M. and Marsden, G. (2006) Mobile Interaction Design, John Wiley & Sons Ltd, England.
10. Kortum, P., (2008) HCI Beyond the GUI: Design for Haptic, Speech, Olfactory, and Other Nontraditional Interfaces. Morgan Kaufmann.
11. Lim, Y.-K., Stolterman, E., and Tenenberg, J. (2008). The anatomy of prototypes: Prototypes as filters, prototypes as manifestations of design ideas. ACM Trans. Comput.-Hum. Interact. 15,2, Article 7 (July 2008), 27 pages.
12. Linjama, J.Hakkila, J. and Ronkainen, S. (2005) Gesture Interfaces for Mobile Devices – Minimalist Approach for Haptic Interaction. In Workshop Proc. for Hands on Haptics: Exploring Non-Visual Visualisation Using the Sense of Touch 2005. CHI 2005.
13. Luk, J., Pasquero, J., Little, S., MacLean, K., Levesque, V., Hayward, V. (2006) A Role for Haptics in Mobile Interaction: Initial Design Using a Handheld Tactile Display Prototype. Proc. of CHI 2006, Montreal, Canada, April 24-27, pp. 171-180.
14. MacLean, K. E. (2000). Application-Centered Haptic Interface Design, chapter in Human and Machine Haptics, M. Srinivasan and M. Cutkosky, Eds.: MIT Press.
15. MacLean, K. E. and Hayward, V. (2008). Do It Yourself Haptics, Part-II. IEEE Robotics and Automation Magazine, 15(1):104-119.
16. Moussette C. and Dore F., (2010). Sketching in Hardware and Building Interaction Design: Tools, Toolkits and an Attitude for Interaction Designers, Proc. of Design Research Society 2010, Montreal (Canada)
17. Saffer, Dan, (2008) Designing Gestural Interfaces, O'Reilly Media, Inc, Usa
18. Sheil, Bob, (2005), Design Through Making, Academy Press
19. Weber, E. H. , (1978) The sense of touch, (H. E. Ross and D. J. Murray, trans.), Academic Press.

Haptics for Tangible Interaction: A Vibro-Tactile Prototype

Andrea Bianchi
KAIST
Daejeon, Korea
andrea@kaist.ac.kr

Ian Oakley
MITI
Funchal, Portugal
ian@uma.pt

Jong Keun Lee
KAIST
Daejeon, Korea
mango@kaist.ac.kr

Dong Soo Kwon
KAIST
Daejeon, Korea
kwonds@kaist.ac.kr

Vassilis Kostakos
MITI
Funchal, Portugal
vk@uma.pt

ABSTRACT

Research on tangible interaction and digital haptics has rarely intertwined, despite the natural relationship between physicality and touch. This paper addresses this relatively unexplored domain by presenting the Haptic Wheel, a freestanding single-axis rotational controller incorporating vibro-tactile cues. In addition to describing the hardware and implementation, the paper discusses the potential application of the system for eyes-free interaction, password entry and as an active puck on a tabletop system. The paper suggests that systems with active haptic feedback have unexploited potential as tools for tangible interaction.

Author Keywords

Haptics, Tactons, Vibrotactile, Rotary controller

ACM Classification Keywords

H.5.2 User Interfaces: Haptic I/O

General Terms: Design, Security

INTRODUCTION

Tangible interaction, despite its focus on physical manipulation, has had limited engagement with work on digital haptics, or touch feedback. Notable exceptions include some of the most striking tangible systems, such as Brave et al's inTouch [2]. This point is reinforced by a recent survey of tangible interaction that identifies actuation as a challenging but underdeveloped aspect of the field [6]. This paper addresses this shortcoming by presenting the design and implementation of a haptic device suitable for use in a range of tangible systems.

The device is a standalone, light-weight and low-cost rotational haptic controller, the Haptic Wheel. It is capable of delivering various tactons [3], or structured vibrotactile cues. A wheel was selected for development as it supports a rich natural interaction (turning) that can perform selections (e.g. at specific angles), navigation or control an analog property. This paper describes the hardware design, interaction techniques and applications to which this device (and the feedback paradigm it embodies) can add value, both as a standalone system and as one element of a larger tangible interface.

TEI'11, January 22–26, 2011, Funchal, Portugal.

RELATED WORK

A number of authors have produced rotary haptic devices. Recent examples include the Haptic Dial [4] and SmartPuck [5]. Broadly similar in design, the former uses a DC motor to generate torque profiles (varying magnitude, direction, velocity and acceleration) for virtual prototyping of controls, while the latter uses smaller battery-powered stepper motors for a similar purpose. The Haptic dial is a fixed device, while the SmartPuck is standalone, mobile and intended for a tabletop UI. Commercial systems based on this concept also exist, such as the iDrive force-feedback dial co-developed by Immersion Corporation and BMW.

What is common to these systems is a distinctive feedback paradigm based on the use of single degree of freedom end-effectors generating active rotational force-feedback. While clearly useful, this approach suffers the disadvantage that it is only capable of presenting cues to users in response to their interaction (in terms of movement or applied force). Quite simply, without a user's active input, such a device has nothing to push against and is incapable of producing meaningful output. For example, such devices are not able to render passive cues indicating particular system states. The paper explores how vibro-tactile cues [3], implemented in the Haptic Wheel, could achieve this objective more readily in the context of a mobile rotary controller.

THE HAPTIC WHEEL

The Haptic Wheel (diameter 8 cm, height 7.3 cm) is an electromechanical dial capable of continuous revolutions both clockwise and anti-clockwise. Physically, it is a standalone handle resembling the rotary control of a safe which turns on a slim base. It integrates a rotary encoder to track its absolute orientation, a binary switch mounted on its top center (for selection input) and a low-cost eccentric vibration motor to generate haptic feedback in the form of vibro-tactile stimuli. The casing is composed of a physically separate housing and base both formed of Polyjet resin using a 3D printer. The housing and base are jointed together with a bearing to minimize the friction created as the former rotates on the latter. The result is a rugged-feeling device which rotates with a level, pleasant sensation of mild, smooth friction. There is no noticeable inertia.

The electronics of the wheel include an Arduino Mini micro-controller (which manages the wheel's input and output devices), a Bluetooth communication module, (which features an LED showing communication channel status), a lithium-ion battery and charging circuits. The micro-controller can be programmed by connecting the

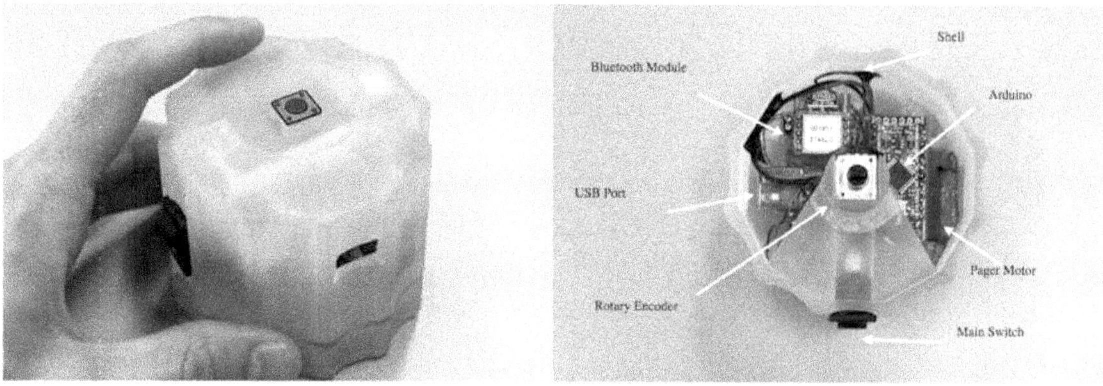

Figure 1. The Haptic Wheel in use (left) and plan view of internal mechanism (right)

wheel through a built in USB socket (which also serves to charge the battery). The wheel's software is written in the Arduino framework. Standalone programs can be uploaded or it can optionally be interfaced to a PC through its Bluetooth connection for more sophisticated applications. The cost for producing the prototype is approximately 150 USD, of which 100 USD is attributable to printing the casing and the remainder for the electronic components.

INTERACTIONS AND APPLICATIONS

Interaction with the Haptic Wheel is via rotational movements and button selections. All output takes the form of haptic sensations, either body-based proprioceptions derived from the actual act of turning the wheel or explicit tactile cues generated by the device and felt through its casing. Although its vibrotactile actuator is simple, it is capable of producing a range of discernible cues in the form of a set of tactons based on oscillating frequencies of motor activation: off, 2Hz, 4Hz, 16Hz and continuous. A short pilot study on these cues revealed that they can be perceived with an accuracy of 100% [1] and therefore can reliably indicate system states. The cues were also designed to possess a clear and discernible order from low to high frequency. Thus, ascent through the frequencies can be mapped to clockwise rotation of the wheel, while descent can be mapped to anti-clockwise movement. This mapping supports active and dynamic manipulation of the wheel.

The Haptic Wheel is aimed at a range of application areas. For example, it provides a rich mix of kinesthetic and tactile cues suitable for eyes-free interaction in visually demanding tasks such as driving. By providing dynamic physical cues in such tasks, it has the potential to reduce cognitive load and free up visual attention. A less safety critical eyes-free task is media control [e.g. 7]. However, the system is also suitable for tasks in which visually obfuscating or obscuring information is desirable. One such task is password entry [1]. In this system, users' passwords are encoded as sequences of tactons. By recognizing and selecting (via button click) each in turn, users are able to input a password eyes-free and with no possibility of visual observation (or shoulder surfing). Finally, as a hand-sized, wireless, standalone puck, the Haptic Wheel is also ideal for deployment as a tracked object or token on a tangible tabletop interface. In contrast to previous dial and wheel systems, it is low-power and mechanically simple, generating no directional forces (and thereby requiring no grounding to absorb the resultant inverse forces) while still able to present rich and digitally controlled haptic information that can complement the physical information inherent in a spatial arrangement of tokens on a tabletop.

CONCLUSIONS

This paper presented the Haptic Wheel and discussed the applications and interactions it supports. This simple, standalone and cost-effective system highlights the advantages of combining haptics with tangible interaction and suggests avenues for future research on this topic.

REFERENCES

1. Bianchi, A., Oakley, I., Lee, J., Kwon, D. The haptic wheel: design & evaluation of a tactile password system. In Ext. Abs. of CHI'10, pp. 3625-3630.
2. Brave, S., Ishii, H., and Dahley, A. 1998. Tangible interfaces for remote collaboration and communication. In CSCW '98. ACM, New York, NY, 169-178.
3. Brewster, S. A., Brown, L. M., Non-visual information display using tactons. Ext. Abs. of CHI '04, pp. 787-788.
4. Ha, S., Kim, L., Park, S., Jun, C., Rho, H., Virtual prototyping enhanced by a haptic interface. CIRP Annals - Manufacturing Tech., vol. 58, 2009.
5. Kim, L., Cho, H., Park, S., Han, M., A tangible user interface with multimodal feedback. LNCS, Springer, vol. 4552, pp. 94-103, 2007.
6. Shaer, O. Hornecker, E. Tangible User Interfaces. Foundations and Trends in HCI. Vol. 3 Nr. 1-2, 2010.
7. Snibbe, S. S., MacLean, K. E., Shaw, R., Roderick, J., Verplank, W. L., and Scheeff, M. Haptic techniques for media control. In Proc. of UIST '01, pp. 199-208.

Cloth Displays: Interacting with Drapable Textile Screens

Julian Lepinski
Human Media Lab
Queen's University
Kingston, Ontario, Canada
lepinski@gmail.com

Roel Vertegaal
Human Media Lab
Queen's University
Kingston, Ontario, Canada
roel@cs.queensu.ca

ABSTRACT
In this paper, we present a user interface for a textile computer display. It allows users to interact in ways that flow from the natural properties of cloth, with an interface that physically conforms to the shape of the object on which a task is performed. While recent work on flexible interfaces has shown promising results, physical properties such as the rigidity of the display remain a barrier to interaction scenarios that are truly physically flexible. We discuss interaction techniques for our cloth user interface, which include gestures such as pinching, draping, stretching and squeezing. Our interaction techniques employ the unique physical characteristics of cloth, including flexibility and shape-taking. We reflect on the system and examine potential directions for future work.

Author Keywords: Textile User Interface, Organic User Interface, Flexible Displays.

ACM Classification Keywords
H5.2 [Information interfaces and presentation]: User Interfaces. - Graphical user interfaces.

General Terms Human Factors

INTRODUCTION
Traditional user interfaces, such as graphical user interfaces (GUIs), are usually designed for surfaces that are rigid and inflexible. Recent work, such as Siftables [8], and commercial products like the Optimus OLED keyboard, design for the use of small and thin displays embedded into appliances. However, physical properties, such as the rigidity of the display, remain a barrier to flexible form factor scenarios. Interactive cloth presents a relatively recent direction in user interface design. In its flexibility and lightness, interactive cloth has the potential to fit organic form factors in ways that provide more flexible and lightweight interactions with objects of different shapes or forms.

TEI'11, January 22–26, 2011, Funchal, Portugal.

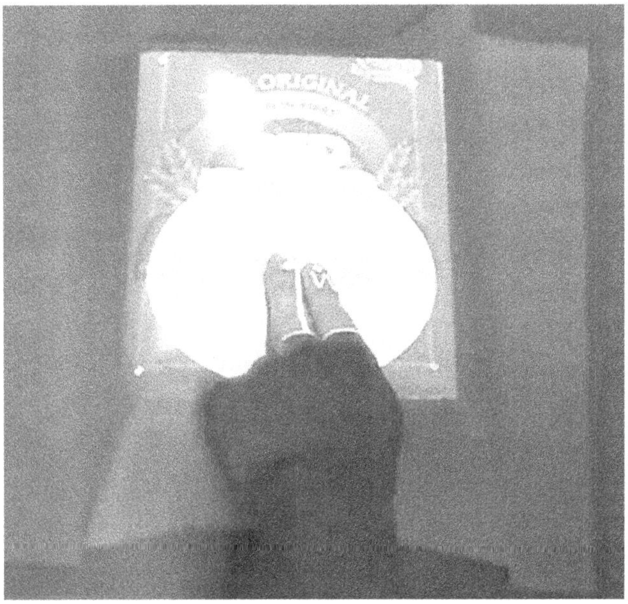

Figure 1. Cloth draped over a cereal box provides an interactive menu to its ingredients in a language of choice.

Rather than enforcing its own shape, cloth takes the shape of underlying objects, allowing it to assume a wide range of forms. Interaction with a piece of cloth draped over an object provides a tight coupling with the object itself. In this paper, we explore how textile displays could be draped over real objects that do not have a display, or that have a form that does not fit traditional displays. As cloth takes the form of an object, affordances provided by the object's shape become part of the available interaction vocabulary. These properties make cloth an ideal interface for interacting with live objects, such as humans.

Physical interactions with, and the properties of, cloth are natural and well understood by users; cloth may be folded, draped, stretched and touched. Interaction styles, such deformations, have logical effects that are easy to comprehend: a piece of cloth grows larger when stretched, and takes the shape of a rigid object when draped over it. This means that a users pre-existing knowledge of the interactive properties of cloth can be of use in developing a cloth interface.

RELATED WORK

Technological Developments

Current research on textile displays, such as Lumalive [12], and Flexible Organic LED displays (FOLED) may provide the back-bone for a future cloth computing device. FOLED displays are thin, light and flexible, and currently provide visual fidelity comparable to a computer display, while having many of the physical characteristics of a thick piece of paper. A review conducted by Sweatman [16] found rapid improvements in the performance of OLED technologies over the past two decades, with decreasing costs. Further work on e-ink, which has seen real commercial release, is another area from which the necessary interface technology may be drawn.

Textiles in Computing

Current research on interactions with physical textiles has largely focused on fabric coloured with thermochromic ink, and has often used the textiles in clothing. Wakita and Shibutani [18] describe a wearable ambient display created with a textile that uses thermochromic ink to change colours based on touch interactions. Berzowska describes her concept of memory rich clothing, by which she means clothing that exhibits its history; in this case, its touch history [2]. These systems evince the universality of textiles and their potential for interactivity in everyday scenarios.

Bergelin discusses using textiles as an interactive surface for a toy known as Spookies [1]. While the first iteration of the Spookies toy uses the textiles to simply cover physical LEDs and buttons, a later version uses woven thermochromic ink coupled with electronics to generate heat and change colours and shadings on the toy programmatically. Similar to Bergelins work, Nack et al. developed small interactive throw pillows [9].

Current textile interfaces largely seek to hide the computing elements of the device and allow users to interact directly with the cloth and objects they envelop. We extend this work by providing a general textile interface that may envelop numerous objects and shapes, rather than a single object.

Paper Interfaces

The Digital Desk system, described by Newman and Wellner [10] was one of the first systems to couple physical paper with graphics projections, blurring the line between virtual and physical, as users interacted with physical paper to perform regular computing tasks. Similar to Digital Desk, in PaperWindows, Holman et al. [7] use standard sheets of paper, augmented with motion-capture markers, to display projected data. This allows for a paper display that can be folded in all three dimensions. The sheets are interacted with using simple hand gestures, such as a rubbing motion used to transfer images from one sheet of paper to another.

Guimbretiere [4] developed systems that closed the loop between digital and physical documents, capturing physical input to annotate and modify associated digital versions of these documents.

Finally, work by Usuda [17] and Schwesig et al. [15] have discussed the use of tactile input, such as folding and bending, to interact with augmented physical paper and paper-like devices. Schwesig et al. describe their Gummi interface as a bendable computer. Made up of sandwiched flexible electronic components, users interact with Gummi by two-dimensional positioning and bending of the interface.

Gestured Interaction

Work on contact gestured interaction often focuses on gestured control of touch sensitive surfaces, such as the Smart-skin system described by Rekimoto [14]. Further work includes Han's on a low-cost multi-touch interface [5]. These systems demonstrate the power of coupling input and output, and use generalized gestures that may be broadly applied to numerous application scenarios.

In [13] Piper, Ratti and Ishii discuss the Illuminating Clay system. This system uses a laser scanner to track the topography of clay on a table and projects an interface directly on the clay. Users interact with the system by shaping and molding the clay, and view the system output on the same. The authors argue that their system provides an improved interface for tasks, such as creating and modifying the topography of a space; they operate directly on the topography through the clay, rather than indirectly through devices such as a mouse or keyboard and CAD software.

IMPLEMENTATION

Our system was implemented by optically tracking retro-reflective points on the cloth and on the users hands, and projecting imagery on the cloth from above, using off-the-shelf hardware and custom software.

Tracking

The hardware used for tracking both our cloth and the user's interaction and gestures consists of two eyebox2 cameras [19]. These provide a stereoscopic image of the interaction area from which three-dimensional tracking data is calculated. The eyebox2 is a 1.3 megapixel video camera fitted with an infrared filter over the lens. In the housing that surrounds the camera lens is a matrix of infrared emitting LEDs.

We developed a stereo vision algorithm for image capture and point recognition in the system. The vision algorithm detects bright clusters within the camera image, each of which is a single reflective square.

The individual points tracked on each camera are then used to calculate the height of each point in space. For the purposes of our work it was necessary that the height be sufficiently accurate to detect changes in the physical shape of the cloth, to differentiate between gestures above and physical contact with the cloth. Our height tracking is accurate to approximately 2cm within a range of 30cm above the work area (50cm by 50cm).

Figure 2: Our generalized set of gestures. Clockwise from upper left: Stretch, squeeze, drape, hover, touch, pinch, and peel.

Projection System and Physics Engine

While our system tracks numerous points on the surface of the cloth, the actual surface is continuous. For this reason, the physics engine models the surface of the cloth and interpolates to determine the position of points between the tracked points. The physics engine itself models the sur-face of the cloth as a series of weighted balls, connected by springs. By varying the mass and the spring constants of nodes, we obtained a model that closely approximated our actual cloth. This model deforms naturally, can fold over it-self, and can be stretched, returning to its original shape once released. This physics engine was also necessary for simulating virtual cloth responses to user actions, such as the pinch and peel gesture. The hardware used for the display system consists of a BENQ DLP projector, operating at a resolution of 1024x768, mounted above the workspace.

The Gesture Engine

The gesture engine operates on data received when a user interacts with the cloth. Since both the physical cloth and the users fingers are augmented with infrared markers, the 3D locations of all interaction elements are known to the system. Based on predefined gesture routines, the gesture engine monitors user interactions and changes the system state as the user interacts with the cloth. These routines are defined as a set of display states, with transitions between these states triggered by specific gestures.

DESIGN

We will now discuss guiding principles for our interaction design. The development of our interaction techniques drew heavily from the principles of Organic and Tangible Inter-faces [6]. Our design principles are as follows:

1. Interactions flow from the cloth metaphor: Users have preexisting ideas about how they interact with cloth, and these should be adhered to as much as possible.

2. Input equals output: Our system should avoid splitting user attention between input device and the display [6].

3. Form follows function: Shape provides valuable information to users as well as system on possible functionalities of the underlying object.

4. Physical or gestural interaction: There are cases where physical touch is not desired, for example, for reasons of hygiene or registration. We therefore included remote gestures, which can be executed while hovering above the cloth.

Gestures

We developed the following six interaction techniques to manipulate information presented on the cloth display:

Stretch: Cloth is stretched from opposing corners, or from two points on the cloth. As a stretch gesture physically in-creases the size of the cloth, this gesture is typically used to zoom or enlarge graphics on the cloth display. The user's region of interest may be defined by the points held by the users when they executed the gesture.

Squeeze: To perform a squeeze, cloth is pushed together from opposing corners, or from two points on the surface of the cloth. The natural counterpoint for the stretch gesture, squeezing the cloth reduces the visible surface area, often reversing the effect of the stretch gesture.

Drape: Here, the cloth is placed over an object, taking the object's shape. In the drape gesture, the cloth becomes aware of the underlying topography of the surface upon which it sits. The cloth display may adapt appropriately to this contextual information, whether by displaying information about the underlying object or adapting the display area in accordance with the available surfaces.

Hover: A finger or hand is held above the surface of the cloth. Such a virtual gesture allows interaction without disturbing the cloth itself, and may be used in situations where touch may not be appropriate or desired due to the situation of the cloth or underlying objects. The hover gesture often precedes a touch gesture, and indicates attention or interest. Hover gestures may elicit additional information about the area beneath the hover (with a fisheye lens for pictures, for example).

Touch: When touching the cloth, pressure is applied to one or more points on the cloth surface. It is detected by sensing the distance of the finger to the cloth. In simple implementations, touch (along with hover) may duplicate the functions of a standard GUI, and act as a mouse click. This allows a cloth interface to include all functionality presented by a standard GUI.

Pinch & Peel: Fingers are pinched together on or above the surface of the cloth. A pinch indicates that the user is grasping information or elements displayed on the surface of the cloth. A pinch may be focusing action, selection, or the physical grasping of graphical objects on the display. A peel gesture follows a pinch, and may be used to rearrange displayed information or elements, or to remove a layer.

APPLICATION SCENARIOS

Our system has been applied in a number of scenarios that are in the realm of in-situ augmented reality. In these scenarios, our cloth computer acts as a thin contextual display interface to interact with other objects.

Medical Imaging. Our first application is in operating rooms. Here, a surgical drape augmented with markers is projected on to display information, such as X-Rays, directly on the topography of the body. Surgeons can interact with scan data over the body by using the hover and peel gestures to navigate layers of imaging information.

Augmented Objects. Fig 1. demonstrates our cloth display as a reusable interactive display for augmenting everyday objects with high-resolution contextual information. After draping the cloth over the object, our camera determines the type of object through pattern matching its contours. The system then projects a graphical interface onto the object. In this example, users browse the contents and origin of the ingredients of a type of cereal directly via the product label.

Interactive Clothing. We also experimented with presenting data on clothing. This is useful for presenting, for example, data about the physiology of a patient, such as blood pressure and heart rate directly onto the body as the patient moves through a hospital setting. The tracking and projection equipment can be mounted on a bed, or, as long the patient stays within a range of up to 2m, be in a fixed location as well.

Textile Windows. Our final application is a low-cost textile version of PaperWindows [7]. Here, the drape is used to interact with otherwise non-interactive pieces of real paper. For example, after draping the cloth over a paper map of a city the map becomes fully searchable. Users can zoom the map by stretching and squeezing the cloth, and use route finding applications by touching locations on the map.

CONCLUSIONS

In this paper, we presented a prototype cloth computing interface. It allows for contextual interaction with a user's environment by draping a physically flexible cloth display over otherwise non-interactive objects. Future systems will require further developments into flexible, LED based display technologies such as Lumalive. We have presented some applications aimed at providing contextual interfaces to everyday objects that are otherwise not augmented with an electronic display, including surgical drapes, product labels and paper maps.

REFERENCES

1. L. Berglin. Spookies: combining smart materials and information technology in an interactive toy. In IDC '05, pp. 17–23, New York, NY, USA, 2005. ACM.
2. J. Berzowska and M. Coelho. Memory-rich clothing. In CHI '06, pp. 275–278, New York, NY, USA, 2006.
3. K. Cheng and K. Pulo. Direct interaction with large-scale display systems using infrared laser tracking devices. In AP Vis '03, pp. 67–74, Darlinghurst, Australia, 2003. Australian Computer Society.
4. F. Guimbretière. Paper augmented digital documents. In UIST '03, pp. 51–60, New York, NY, USA, 2003.
5. J.Y. Han. Low-cost multi-touch sensing through frus-trated total internal reflection. In UIST '05, pp. 115– 118. ACM: New York, NY, USA, 2005.
6. D. Holman and R. Vertegaal. Organic user interfaces: designing computers in any way, shape, or form. Comm. Of the ACM, 51(6):48–55, 2008.
7. D. Holman, R. Vertegaal, M. Altosaar, N. Troje, and D. Johns. Paper windows: interaction techniques for digital paper. In CHI '05, pp. 591–599, ACM: New York, NY, USA, 2005.
8. D. Merrill, J. Kalanithi, and P. Maes. Siftables: towards sensor network user interfaces. In TEI '07, pages 75– 78, ACM: New York, NY, USA, 2007.
9. F. Nack, et al. Pillows as adaptive interfaces in ambient environments. In HCM '07, pp. 3–12. ACM: New York, NY, USA, 2007.
10. W. Newman and P. Wellner. A desk supporting computer-based interaction with paper documents. In CHI '92, pp. 587–592, ACM: New York, NY, USA, 1992.
11. R.G. O'Hagan, A. Zelinsky, and S. Rougeaux. Visual gesture interfaces for virtual environments. Interacting with Computers, 14(3): pp. 231–250, 2002.
12. Philips. Lumalive. http://www.lumalive.com/.
13. B. Piper, C. Ratti, and H. Ishii. Illuminating clay: a 3-d tangible interface for landscape analysis. In CHI '02, pp. 355–362, ACM: New York, NY, USA, 2002.
14. J. Rekimoto. SmartSkin: an infrastructure for freehand manipulation on interactive surfaces. In CHI '02, pp. 113–120. ACM: New York, NY, USA, 2002.
15. C. Schwesig, I. Poupyrev, and E. Mori. Gummi: a bendable computer. In CHI '04, pp. 263–270, ACM: New York, NY, USA, 2004.
16. D. Sweatman. Organic Devices: A Review. In Micro-Electronic Engineering Research Conference, 2001.
17. H. Usuda. Ultra magic paper interface. In Proceedings of SIGGRAPH'97. ACM: New York, NY, USA, 1997.
18. A. Wakita and M. Shibutani. Mosaic textile: wearable ambient display with non-emissive color-changing modules. In ACE '06. ACM: New York, NY, USA, 2006.
19. Xuuk. eyebox2. http://www.xuuk.com/.

An Inflatable Hemispherical Multi-touch Display

Andrew Stevenson, Christopher Perez and Roel Vertegaal
Human Media Lab
Queen's University
Kingston, ON, Canada K7L 3N6
{andrews, perez, roel}@cs.queensu.ca

ABSTRACT
In this paper, we introduce a multi-touch display surface that can be dynamically deformed from a flat circular display to a convex or concave hemispherical display. A rubber latex material is used for the display surface allowing it to inflate or deflate as air is pumped into or out of an airtight container. The elasticity of the display surface also allows users to deform the surface by varying the pressure exerted on it. This deformation may be detected by the device and provides a z-axis input in addition to the typical x,y-axis inputs of flat-screen displays.

Author Keywords
Input devices, Multitouch, Haptic I/O, Organic User Interfaces.

ACM Classification Keywords
H5.2. Information interfaces and presentation (e.g., HCI): User Interfaces.

General Terms
Human Factors.

INTRODUCTION
When manipulating objects in a computer system it is desirable for the physical properties of the interface medium to resemble the virtual objects being manipulated [10, 19]. With the traditional flat screen display, users have to settle for a geometric projection of a three-dimensional virtual object onto a two-dimensional display surface.

This paper proposes a single display surface that can be flat or domed, and whose curvature can change dynamically and incrementally between those states. This flexibility allows the display surface to mimic a wider variety of objects, in particular spherical and hemispherical objects. More importantly, the user can interact with a surface shape appropriate to the context of the task at hand.

TEI'11, January 22–26, 2011, Funchal, Portugal.

The Applications section of this paper describes such an example using Google Earth [4], where the display is hemispherical when zoomed out and flat when zoomed in. Other applications include using the device as a musical instrument, especially a drum.

The tactile properties of the rubber latex surface offer a novel way to experience haptic feedback. The firmness of the display surface changes as the air density in the container changes, allowing the surface to mimic the density of different materials. Finally, the Applications section describes how an inflated display can be used to probe and navigate a 3-D brain scan.

BACKGROUND
Different characteristics of the inflatable display have been explored by existing research. Volumetric display interfaces have been considered [1] and built [5] using motion-captured gestures and 3-dimensional displays. Unlike a motion-capture approach, our inflatable display allows interaction with fingertip contact on a surface.

Globe4D [3] and ViBall [11] are examples of a half-sphere and spherical display, respectively. Globe4D excels as an interactive globe, but is not designed to manipulate general spherical objects. Though ViBall's uses can be more varied, it uses external projection causing occlusion when the user is close to the display. Internal projection in the inflatable display eliminates hand shadows and its actuated deformable display surface allows a wider variety of object shapes to be accurately represented.

CrystalDome [14] and DOME [20] have explored projection from underneath a half-sphere onto its interior. DOME additionally uses head tracking to present a customized view to users on opposite sites of the display and requires cooperation between its six projectors to correctly illuminate a point on the display. CrystalDome uses sensors mounted on the table near the display to track hand movements, and supports the translation, scaling, and rotation of images on the display.

Sphere [2] uses a single projector housed internally at the base of its spherical display [7] and has an internal infrared camera used to track hand movement on the surface of the sphere. Both the projector and IR camera share the same optical path, similar to our inflatable display.

In the past, the editing of 3-D objects by direct gestural interaction has been studied for regular planar interfaces [12, 16] and there has been work with motion-captured gestures to edit 3-D objects displayed on a separated flat surface [18] or on a 3-D volumetric Actuality Perspecta display [5]. Sheng et al. [18] examined the use of a physical object, such as a sponge, as a proxy for the user to hold and deform while gestures were detected via motion-capture. Again, the 3-D object being edited was displayed on a separate screen. Our approach is similar because the user deforms a physical object by applying pressure to it, but we detect the deformation of the display surface itself rather than the position of the users hands.

Harrison and Hudson [6] describe a tactile display surface with many similarities to ours. It is also a rear-projection multi-touch display device with a latex surface that can be deformed with pneumatics, but Harrison and Hudson emphasize display surface buttons that can be positively or negatively inflated for tactile feedback. Kim et al. present an inflatable mouse [13] that can sense pressure input from the user and also provide actuated inflation and deflation.

DESIGN CRITERIA

The design philosophy of this project was to unify input and output interfaces as much as possible. We attempted to implement this duality in each interaction property of the inflatable display to help create an organic user experience. We identified two main interaction properties of the inflatable display: the image on the display surface, and the shape of the display surface. For the display surface we chose to use rear projection to avoid hand shadows, requiring the projector to be mounted inside or underneath the flexible display surface. We also wanted the display surface to function as a multi-touch input device to allow the user to interact directly with the shaped data display. Multi-touch detection should occur in both the inflated and deflated states.

Haptics and Shape of the Display Surface

The inflation and deflation of the display surface should allow the display to automatically reshape itself according to the context of the user task, or for the user to easily customize the shape of the display surface to their liking. For example, if the device is being used as a drum the volume of air in the container and can be adjusted to give the surface a specific pitch when struck. Actuated inflation also provides haptic output in the form of the surface's firmness. As the air density behind the surface increases it feels firmer and offers more resistance to external pressure. When the user pushes on the surface, it is able to push back at varying strengths. The user should able to deform the shape of the display surface by applying pressure with their fingertips or hands. User input through pressure is typically asymmetrical, whereas actuated inflation will always result in a symmetrical deformation of the surface. The inputs and outputs described above should be intimately linked with each other and the user task so when an input is changed, it immediately updates one or more outputs for direct feedback. More concretely, as the user touches and pushes on the surface, the display image and surface shape should also change in a way that is intuitive, logical, and consistent with the application [17].

IMPLEMENTATION

This section describes the hardware used to create our prototype, depicted in Figure 1. Materials were chosen with our design criteria in mind.

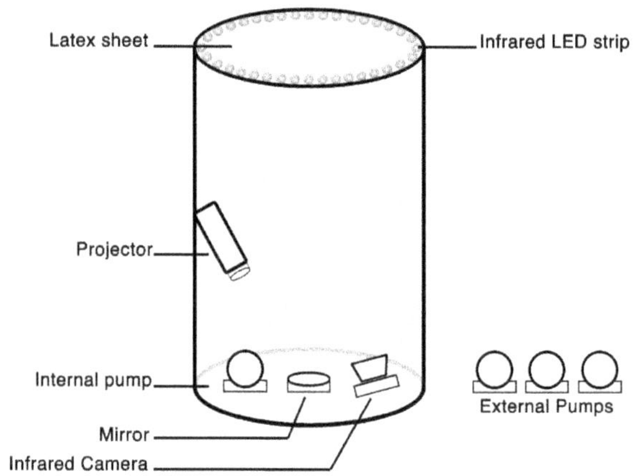

Figure 1. Schematic of the inflatable display canister.

The frame of our device is a plastic cylindrical canister with a height of 35 inches and a diameter of 14.5 inches. Holes were drilled in the side of the canister to run power and data cables for the internal electronic components and for air tubes. A sealant was used around the cables and air tubes to maintain an airtight container. A rubber latex sheet, cut from a 36 inch white balloon, was stretched over the canister's opening to form the display surface and held tightly in place with a metal brace.

An infrared camera placed at the bottom of the canister is used to track multi-touch input on the display surface. This tracking is aided by a strip of infrared emitting lights placed along the external circumference at the top of the canister and directed inward along the plane of the display surface. As a fingertip approaches and touches the surface, infrared light from the light strip reflects off the skin and down through the latex where it is picked up by the infrared camera. The areas of high infrared concentration represent fingertip contact and provide basic multi-touch tracking. As the user presses harder on the surface, the size of the tracked fingertip grows, providing a mechanism to measure z-axis deformation. This fingertip size information is not available in our current prototype's finger tracking software, but we plan to remedy this in the near future so z-axis values can be captured and used.

A pico projector is placed inside the canister, which projects an image onto the rear of the display surface. To enlarge the display, we positioned the projector along the wall of the canister and directed the projection down towards a mirror placed at the bottom of the canister, which then reflected the image up to the display surface. An alternate way to achieve this effect would be to use a projector with a short throw lens, but we were dissuaded from using one due to its relatively high cost and bulky size.

Four aquarium pumps (three external and one internal) were connected to the air tubes and used to move air into and out of the canister. The current flow rate of these pumps is moderate, and we discuss way to improve inflation speed in our Future Work section. An electronic relay was used to control the activation and deactivation of the individual pumps.

USER INTERACTIONS

The inflatable display has several characteristics that are not usually found in common display screens, and thus offers an opportunity to explore user interactions that are unique to it.

Haptic Experience

A latex rubber material is an uncommon choice for a multi-touch surface and has tactile properties that differ from traditional rigid flat screen displays. Fingertips glide across the rubber surface easily with light pressure, but become more difficult to drag across the surface as the amount of pressure and deformation increases.

Another interesting property of latex rubber is its elasticity, which causes it to return to its original shape immediately after finger pressure is removed. This results in user deformations that are temporary, and any output information that depends on such deformations is quickly lost unless explicitly remembered by the application. The latex rubber therefore lends itself well to tasks using probing actions of the surface where deformation retention is not a high requirement, such as navigating medical scans and other volumetric data [15]. This contrasts with other deformable displays such as Illuminating Clay [9], in which deformations are permanent and the material never returns to its original form.

Multi-touch Gestures and Z-axis Deformation

Multi-touch gestures for flat screen displays have coalesced around several basic and commonly used gestures for virtual object manipulation: one-touch gestures for object selection and translation; and two-touch gestures for object rotation and scaling (pinch zoom). The z-axis deformability of our rubber display material provides another dimension for meaningful gestures.

For example, when organizing a jumbled pile of images you could send the top image to the bottom of the pile with a gesture pressing it into the display surface. For even greater control, the degree of z-axis deformation could determine the depth of the object in the pile or stack.

Figure 2. A partially inflated display of the Earth.

Another possibility is using a pinch-and-lift gesture to remove a virtual object from the display surface. The rubber material allows the user to literally pinch the display surface, unlike with a flat screen display. The removed object could be "held" above the screen and when the user touches another part of the screen it could reappear there. This lift-and-drop operation could be used in unison with a drag-and-drop operation to intuitively move multiple objects around a workspace with ease.

Z-axis deformations used in conjunction with multi-touch lends itself well to artistic applications. Consider a multi-touch paint application, where the z-axis could be mapped to the lightness of a colour. Pressing harder on the surface could produce a darker paint tone. Multi-touch music applications could also be influenced, for instance, by mapping the z-axis to the pitch of a note.

APPLICATIONS

Current spherical displays do not allow for consistent interactions with earth data on different levels of zoom [2, 3, 6, 10]. We therefore used Google Earth as a proof-of-concept application to test the inflatable display, as shown in Figure 2. Since the Earth appears flat when close to its surface and round when far from its surface it is an ideal object to manipulate in our inflatable display.

When zoomed out, the display becomes fully inflated and the Earth can be viewed as a globe. Zooming in will incrementally deflate the display surface until it becomes flat and can be viewed as a two-dimensional map. This context switch is continuous and unobtrusive to the user's task, and allows different geographical viewpoints to be presented in the way most naturally suited for them.

Another application is a steel pan drum simulator, used to demonstrate negative inflation (a concave display surface). An image of a steel pan surface is displayed on the concave display screen, and striking the various notes with a finger will produce the correct sound. While this example does not use dynamic screen inflation or deflation, it does demonstrate the versatility of a deformable display surface.

McGuffin et al. describe the advantages of using deformations to browse volumetric data such as medical scans [13]. The inflatable display is well suited to this form of browsing, and in particular navigating 3-D brain scans.

The fully inflated display can represent the hemispherical surface of the brain, and pressing on the display can reveal the interior layers of the brain in that area of the scan. By pressing harder on the surface, the user can see deeper into the 3-D brain model.

FUTURE WORK

In the future we wish to improve our inflatable display prototype by augmenting its hardware and software, and exploring new interaction techniques. Z-axis information can be captured by using finger tracking software that provides the fingertip blob sizes in addition to the x,y screen coordinates. We also hope to make finger tracking more consistent during inflation. Currently, fingertips placed on the surface near the circumference appear different than those placed in the middle while the screen is inflated. A diffusion layer for the infrared light strip would help remedy this by providing a more uniform infrared light source. The airflow rate can be improved with a single more powerful pump or a pneumatic plunger that pushes a volume of air into the canister quickly. This provides a prompt inflation response to user input when necessary.

CONCLUSIONS

In this paper, we introduced a multi-touch display surface that can be dynamically deformed from a flat circular display to a convex or concave hemispherical display. We used a latex material for the display surface, which allows it to inflate or deflate as air is pumped into or out of an airtight container. The elasticity of the display surface also allows users to deform the surface by varying the pressure exerted on it. Applications include earth browsing with support for flat zooms as well as convex overview, and for medical or 3D image data manipulation.

ACKNOWLEDGEMENTS

This research was supported by grants from the Natural Sciences and Engineering Research Council of Canada, and by the Ontario Research Fund, with kind support by Autodesk Research and fuseproject.

REFERENCES

1. Balakrishnan, R., Fitzmaurice, G., and Kurtenbach, G. User interfaces for volumetric displays. *IEEE Computer*. (2001), 37-45.
2. Benko, H., Wilson, A. D., and Balakrishnan, R. Sphere: multi-touch interactions on a spherical display. In *Proc. UIST'08*, New York, NY, (2008), 77-86.
3. Companje, R., van Dijk, N., Hogenbirk, H., and Mast, D. Sphere4D, Time-Traveling with an Interactive Four-Dimensional Sphere. *Proc. ACM Multimedia'06*. ACM, New York, NY (2006), 959-960.
4. Google, Inc. *Google Earth* http://earth.google.com/ [accessed 14 Dec 2009]
5. Grossman, T., Wigdor, D., and Balakrishnan, R. Multi-finger gestural interaction with 3D volumetric displays. In *Proc. ACM UIST'04*, New York, NY (2004), 61-70.
6. Harrison, C. and Hudson, S. E. Providing dynamically changeable physical buttons on a visual display. In *Proc. CHI 2009*. ACM (2009), 299-308.
7. Holman, D. and Vertegaal, R. Organic user interfaces: designing computers in any way, shape, or form. *Commun. ACM*, 51, 6 (2008), 48-55.
8. Holman, D., Vertegaal, R., Altosaar, M., Troje, N., and Johns, D. PaperWindows: Interaction Techniques for Digital Paper. In *Proc. CHI'05*. ACM (2005), 591-599.
9. Ishii, H. The tangible user interface and its evolution. *Commun. ACM*, 51, 6 (2008), 32-36.
10. Ishii, H. and Ullmer, B. 1997. Tangible bits: towards seamless interfaces between people, bits and atoms. In *Proc. CHI'97*. ACM (1997), 234-241.
11. Kettner, S., Madden, C., and Ziegler, R. Direct Rotational Interaction With Spherical Projection, *In Interaction: Systems, Practice and Theory*, (2004).
12. Kim, H., Albuquerque, G., Havemann, S., and Fellner D.W. Tangible 3D: Immersive 3D Modeling through Hand Gesture Interaction. *IPT & EGVE Workshop*, (2005).
13. Kim, S., Kim, H., Lee, B., Nam, T., and Lee, W. Inflatable mouse: volume-adjustable mouse with air-pressure-sensitive input and haptic feedback. In *Proc. CHI 2008*. ACM (2008), 211-224.
14. Marchese, F.T., Borjesson, J., and Rose, J. *CrystalDome:* A Projected Hemispherical Display with a Gestural Interface. In *11th International Conference Information Visualization*, (2007).
15. McGuffin, M. J., Tancau, L., and Balakrishnan, R. Using Deformations for Browsing Volumetric Data. In *Proc. of the 14th IEEE Visualization'03*. IEEE Computing Society (2003), 53
16. Nishino, H., Utsumiya, K., and Korida, K. 3D Object Modeling Using Spatial and Pictographic Gestures. *ACM Symposium on Virtual Reality Software and Technology*. ACM (1998), 51-58.
17. Rekimoto, J. Organic interaction technologies: from stone to skin. *Commun.* ACM 51, 6 (2008), 38-44.
18. Sheng, J., Balakrishnan, R., and Singh, K. An Interface for Virtual 3D Sculpting via Physical Proxy *Graphite'06*, (2006).
19. Ullmer, B. and Ishii, H. Emerging frameworks for tangible user interfaces. *IBM Syst. J.* 39, 3-4 (2000), 915-931.
20. Webb, S. and Jaynes, C. The DOME: A portable multi-projector visualization system for digital artifacts, *IEEE Workshop on Emerging Display Technologies, Bonn, Germany*. (2005).

SurfaceMouse: Supplementing Multi-Touch Interaction with a Virtual Mouse

[1]Tom Bartindale [2]Chris Harrison [1]Patrick Olivier [2]Scott E. Hudson

[1]Newcastle University
CultureLab, Kings Walk
Newcastle Upon Tyne, NE1 7RU, UK
{t.l.bartindale,p.l.olivier}@ncl.ac.uk

[2]Human-Computer Interaction Institute
Carnegie Mellon University
5000 Forbes Ave., Pittsburgh, PA 15213
{chris.harrison, scott.hudson}@cs.cmu.edu

ABSTRACT

We present SurfaceMouse, a virtual mouse for multi-touch surface computing. Although moving away from the direct touch manipulation paradigm, our system brings many significant benefits seen in absolute clutched devices to surface computing. Features include high and variable control device gains, several degrees of freedom in a single hand gesture, ability to target small GUI items, and a familiar method for reaching far areas of large displays. Importantly, this benefit is realized by leveraging what users already know and have tremendous experience with - physical mice. Results from our proof-of-concept evaluation reflect this; users were able to use and recognize our system without training or prompts. Being entirely virtual, SurfaceMouse can be implemented in existing systems with little more than a software update.

ACM Classification: H.5.2 [User Interfaces]: Input devices and strategies; Graphical user interfaces.

General terms: Human Factors

Keywords: Table, surface, multi-user, scrolling, cursor.

INTRODUCTION

Recent developments in touch surface technologies have seen a proliferation of proposals for new interaction techniques. These include multi-touch actions for the direct manipulation of interface elements, as well as gestures for command invocation and multi-element selection. Indeed, multi-touch interaction affords many new and interesting avenues for expressive input and collaborative interaction. However, little attention has been paid to how mice could operate and supplement interaction in touch-driven systems. This is unfortunate given the well-established benefits of the mouse and its familiarity among users, with potentially thousands of hours of training.

In this paper, we describe SurfaceMouse, a virtual mouse implementation for multi-touch surfaces. A key design objective was to leverage as much pre-existing knowledge (and potentially muscle memory) regarding mice as possible, making interactions immediately familiar. To invoke SurfaceMouse, a user simply places their hand on an interactive surface as if there was a mouse present (Figure 1). The system recognizes this characteristic gesture and renders a virtual mouse under the hand, which can be used like a real mouse. In addition to two-dimensional movement (X and Y axes), our proof-of-concept implementation supports left and right clicking, as well as up/down scrolling. Importantly, SurfaceMouse does not preempt any existing touch interaction or multi-touch gestures. It simply acts as an additional gesture.

TEI'11, January 22–26, 2011, Funchal, Portugal.

MOTIVATION & BENEFITS

Although appearing at first glance to be a curious step back in surface computing, SurfaceMouse brings several significant benefits. Foremost, our approach provides an immediate, effective and intuitive means to provide high control-device (CD) gain on touch surfaces (vs. 1:1 of conventional direct finger input). The CD gain is easily controlled in software, and could be dynamically modified to aid different tasks or tailored to a user's motor ability. Additionally, because the cursor is decoupled from the finger/hand location, target occlusion can be dramatically reduced. It is well established that both of these attributes can improve pointing ease and accuracy.

Additionally, high targeting accuracy (plus left and right mouse buttons) could enable users to run existing desktop-class GUI applications. These tend to be unwieldy on touch surface due to their small interface elements (i.e., too small or dense for "big" fingers). Although not ideal, backwards

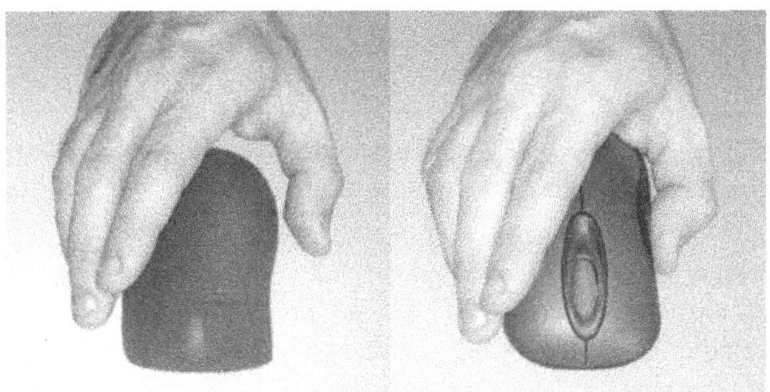

Figure 1. SurfaceMouse (left), Physical Mouse (right).

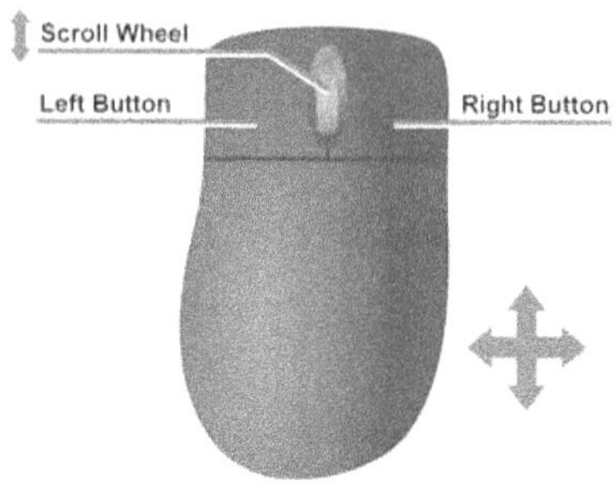

Figure 2. Actions available in our prototype implementation.

compatibility of software is a significant real-world issue given the huge volume of existing software. Moreover, an increasing number of computer systems are hybrid – running a conventional desktop operating system, but containing screens capable of multi-touch input (e.g., Windows 7 tablet computers). SurfaceMouse could help bring these two interface paradigms closer together and yield a more seamless user experience.

This ability to interact with smaller targets also means applications can make use of smaller GUI elements, allowing for more productive use of this screen space. This is especially important as screen real estate on many multi-touch platforms is at a premium. This issue is further compounded in multi-user environments. Conversely, large screen interaction can be troublesome due to the fact that users may not be able to reach all areas of the screen [1,21]. SurfaceMouse can be used within this scenario to enable in-direct interaction over larger physical distances.

As noted previously, SurfaceMouse immediately enables input with several degrees of freedom: continuous motion in two dimensions, two mouse buttons, and up/down scrolling (Figure 2). This level of expressivity is rare for a single-handed gesture. This success relies heavily on the years of training an average user has with physical mice. SurfaceMouse simply co-opts this knowledge and applies it to a new (albeit virtual) form. We suspect that if different movement/buttons binding were employed, interaction would prove less intuitive to users.

Finally, the lack of a physical device has several smaller benefits. First, SurfaceMouse can be deployed and updated entirely in software. Second, multiple users can invoke SurfaceMice for collaborative purposes, a central tenet of surface computing. When interaction is complete, SurfaceMice disappear, an important aspect when designing public displays, where physical objects can be removed or damaged easily. Third, the lack of physicality also allows SurfaceMouse to provide special button mappings to left- and right-handed users (handedness is automatically detected). Tabletop systems with physical mice are typically shaped for the right hand, which can be uncomfortable for left-handed users to manipulate.

RELATED WORK

As touch screens entered mainstream, pointing performance relative to conventional interaction became a popular research subject. The seminal paper by Sears and Shneiderman [20] showed correctly designed high precision capacitive touch screens could yield touch selection precision comparable to that of a mouse, for targets as small as 4 pixels. However, below four pixels, mice significantly outperformed touch selection. Vision-based multi-touch technologies have traditionally suffered from poorer accuracy due to factors such as limited camera resolution, illumination artifacts, and shadows.

For example, Forlines et al. [6] showed error rates for diffuse illumination-based [14] touch interaction were nearly twice that of mice, even when using relatively large targets (e.g., dimensions of 16 and 32 pixels). Wang and Ren [24] conducted a thorough exploration of contact point properties for FTIR surfaces [7]. This work found that different contact profiles occur as a consequence of varying degrees of arm extension. Similarly, Holz and Baudisch [9] found finger angle led to targeting variances on capacitive touch screens.

No matter what the sensing technique, the fact is that our fingers are simply larger than a digital cursor. This inherently reduces accuracy, both by having more contact area and often by introducing occlusion at the point of contact (see e.g., [4,9,23] for more discussion on the "fat finger problem"). Consequently, many techniques have been proposed for higher precision selection. These include visual enhancements [1,2,4,17,23], gesturing schemes [2,3] and bimanual manipulation [12,15]. There has also been work addressing issues regarding reach on large interactive surfaces [1,5,16].

The fluidity and precision of mice has been of interest to tabletop researchers previously. Hartmann et al. [8] experimented with placing physical mice and keyboards on tabletops to supplement interaction. Many compelling interactions were introduced, most of which are immediately applicable to this work. There has even been new work in extending the touch functionality of physical mouse [22].

Finally, closest to this work is SDMouse [13], which provides a partial, but powerful mouse implementation using cording gestures. For example, the index finger can be tracked on screen (the cursor rendered beneath it). To left click, the user presses their index and middle finger against the surface; to right click, the index and ring finger could be used. SurfaceMouse, although similar in appearance, has a significantly differently character of operation. In particular, we decouple cursor location from hand position in order to reduce occlusion and obtain a CD gain greater than 1:1, offering improved pointing accuracy. Secondly, rather than using cording gestures, we directly emulate conventional mouse controls (e.g., left click with a button). The graphic of a mouse provides a useful and omnipresent visual affordance. Moreover, users can use any fingers they like to operate these functions as per their preference. This further aided our objective of not requiring the user to learn anything new.

IMPLEMENTATION

Our initial prototype was written in C# (WPF) for use on a Microsoft Surface, which uses diffuse illumination tracking [14] (Figure 3). However, many other touch technologies are applicable, including FTIR [7], capacitive [18], IFSR [19], and optical fiber [10] technologies. In general, any interactive surface that allows for multiple points of interaction and a measurement of the area of contact should be sufficient.

When a new contact is detected, the system scans over all present blobs, finding the largest and makes the assumption it is a wrist contact. The system then checks that exactly five finger-sized blobs are present in a suitable configuration near the presumed wrist blob. If all criteria are met, SurfaceMouse is invoked. Figure 3 illustrates the high level process. To provide visual confirmation and ongoing feedback, a mouse image is rendered below the hand (appropriate for the user's handedness). This virtual mouse tracks with the hand. Simultaneously, mouse movement events are created using the relative motion of the wrist.

In addition to relative movement, SurfaceMouse also features two buttons and a scroll wheel, all of which function like their physical counterparts and track appropriately with the hand. We chose not to map button clicks to particular fingers (e.g., middle finger controls the scroll wheel). Anecdotally, there appear to be a wide variety of finger-to-function mappings. For example, some people use their index finger for left click and scrolling, and their middle finger for right click). To account for this, our system triggers a function when a blob appears in the active region of a particular function (e.g., the left button area), allowing for any digit to be used.

SurfaceMouse becomes inactive only after the wrist is lifted from the interactive surface. This allows fingers to be lifted for actions like clicking. When the user removes all contacts from the surface of the display, SurfaceMouse does not immediately disappear. Instead, a timeout is used to increase robustness when tracking is accidentally lost and also to allow for clutching, just like a real mouse.

FUNCTIONALITY

Hand Size

Our recognition algorithm requires discrimination between wrist, finger and non-SurfaceMouse contacts (e.g., tangibles, arms). To inform our size and shape constraints, we measured a variety of hands. As a result, our system is robust in its wrist and finger discrimination, and we can use the inferred hand size to create a virtual mouse appropriately sized to the user (e.g., for children).

Orientation

SurfaceMouse calculates orientation of the hand using the ovoid wrist blob. An orientation adjustment can be made on a personal basis to provide custom alignment with the fingers. This feature allows users to walk up to the surface and begin interaction with the interface regardless of their orientation relative to the surface. This is important in collaborative settings on horizontal surfaces, where people traditionally "sit around the table." Note that only the wrist blob is used for translation and rotation tracking. This allows for accurate use without fingers needing to be on the surface.

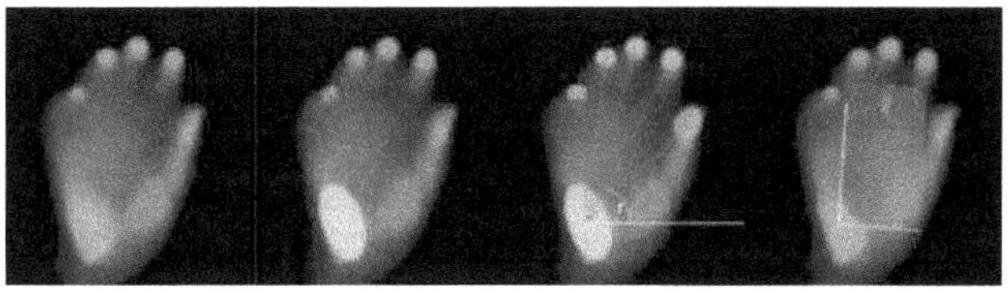

Figure 3. Left to right: 1) Infrared camera image of SurfaceMouse gesture; 2) Palm detection; 3) Finger tip detection; 4) Size, orientation, and handedness calculation.

Handedness

The system changes the horizontal orientation of the virtual mouse depending on whether a left or right hand is used. This hand feature is achieved by using the maximum and minimum angle of all finger blobs within the boundary area, compared with the center of the wrist. If this angle is above or below a certain value, handedness can be inferred. If the angle is ambiguous, our system defaults to right-handed mode (~80% of the population). Finally, handedness adaptation allows a single user to wield two mice, which is valuable in certain use contexts [11].

Scroll Wheel

In addition to virtual mouse buttons, we also include a virtual scroll wheel. This feature is accomplished by simply taking the relative movement of a finger blob when it appears in the scroll wheel area.

Microsoft Windows Driver

As a true test of our prototype's ability to perform as a mouse, we created a Microsoft Windows driver for our system. Since SurfaceMouse implements a standard array of mouse features, we simply send events through the standard mouse API to the OS. We chose to make a Windows driver, as our Microsoft Surface system is also able to run a conventional desktop version of Windows. In our proof-of-concept evaluation, described subsequently, this allowed users to interact with a standard desktop web browser using SurfaceMouse.

Multi-User

An additional advantage of using multi-touch technology is its innate ability to support multiple users. We capitalize on this ability, and allow each user to wield a SurfaceMouse. Although this feature was implemented, it was not possible to enable it outside of our simple sandbox as most operating systems only allow one mouse pointer.

EVALUATION

We evaluated our proof-of-concept SurfaceMouse for general usability compared to conventional touch selection on a Microsoft Surface. In order to get a preliminary understanding of the sensitivity and usability of our approach, we presented our prototype to nine beta testers (three female, average age 28) who had not seen or used the system, but were familiar with using a physical mouse.

First, they were presented with a standard desktop web browser, and asked to navigate through a variety of content using direct finger touches as the only interaction. Next, a short introduction was given outlining the gesture required to produce SurfaceMouse. Users then were presented with a simple sandbox environment in order to become familiar with the technique.

Then, using our SurfaceMouse mouse driver for Windows, testers were then asked to repeat the browsing task and freely navigate the web. The mouse driver displayed an image of SurfaceMouse on top of all windows (see Video Figure). The movement and acceleration profiles were set to the standard Windows values. During the session, users were encouraged to provide commentary on their impressions. Questions were also asked to elicit feedback, especially about how it compared to the earlier touch-driven browsing task.

Reactions were positive. People consistently used words like "natural" and "intuitive" to describe the experience. Participants immediately recognized what it was and how to use it without prompts. In regards to how it compared to touch-based interaction, at least half noted that they felt less frustrated when clicking on hyperlinks. This was because of the visual feedback afforded by the mouse pointer and the accuracy gained by indirectly controlling it. Scrolling without having to move the hand (i.e., retarget) was also seen as beneficial. Finally, the fact that SurfaceMouse disappeared when not needed was also liked. However, as expected, users missed the physicality afforded by a real mouse, and consequently, felt less in control of the pointer.

CONCLUSION

We presented SurfaceMouse, a virtual mouse implementation for multi-touch surface computing. It may seem odd to introduce a pointing device made for "desktop" computing into the new and exciting space of finger and touch manipulation. However, mice have well-established benefits that could be used to great effect in touch-driven environments and potentially solve several outstanding interaction problems, including reach and precision targeting. We discussed these and other benefits at length and also described unique interactions our approach enables. We concluded with a brief overview of qualitative feedback from our pilot testing.

REFERENCES

1. Abednego, M., Lee, J., Moon, W., and Park, J. I-Grabber: expanding physical reach a large-display tabletop environment through the use of a virtual grabber. *Proc. ITS '09*. 61-64.
2. Albinsson, P. and Zhai, S. High precision touch screen interaction. *Proc. CHI '03*. 105-112.
3. Baudisch, P., Cutrell, E., Robbins, D., Czerwinski, M., Tadler, P. Bederson, B., and Zierlinger. A. Drag-and- Pop and Drag-and-Pick: Techniques for Accessing Remote Screen Content on Touch and Pen-operated Systems. *Proc. Interact '03*. 57–64.
4. Benko, H., Wilson, A. D., and Baudisch, P. Precise Selection Techniques for Multi-Touch Screens. *Proc. CHI '06*. 1263–1272.
5. Echtler, F., Huber, M., and Klinker, G. Shadow tracking on multi-touch tables. *Proc. AVI '08*. 388-391.
6. Forlines, C., Wigdor, D., Shen, C., and Balakrishnan, R. Direct-touch vs. mouse input for tabletop displays. *Proc. CHI '07*. 647-656.
7. Han, J. Y. Low-cost multi-touch sensing through frustrated total internal reflection. *Proc. UIST '05*. 115-118.
8. Hartmann, B., Morris, M. R., Benko, H., and Wilson, A. D. Augmenting interactive tables with mice & keyboards. *Proc. UIST '09*. 149-152.
9. Holz, C. and Baudisch, P. The generalized perceived input point model and how to double touch accuracy by extracting finger-prints. *Proc. CHI '10*. 581-590.
10. Jackson, D., Bartindale, T., and Olivier, P. FiberBoard: compact multi-touch display using channeled light. *Proc. ITS '09*. 25-28.
11. Latulipe, C., Mann, S., Kaplan, C.S., & Clarke, C.L. symSpline: symmetric two-handed spline manipulation. *Proc. CHI '06*. 349-358.
12. Lepinski, J., Grossman, T., Fitzmaurice, G. The design and evaluation of multitouch marking menus. *Proc. CHI '10*. 2233-2242.
13. Matejka, J., Grossman, T., Lo, J., and Fitzmaurice, G. The design and evaluation of multi-finger mouse emulation techniques. *Proc. CHI '09*. 1073-1082.
14. Matsushita, N. and Rekimoto, J. HoloWall: designing a finger, hand, body, and object sensitive wall. *Proc. UIST '97*. 209-210.
15. Moscovich, T. and Hughes, J.F. Indirect mappings of multi-touch input using one and two hands. *Proc. CHI '08*. 1275-1284.
16. Nacenta, M. A., Sallam, S., Champoux, B., Subramanian, S., and Gutwin, C. Perspective cursor: perspective-based interaction for multi-display environments. *Proc. CHI '06*. 289-298.
17. Olwal, A., Feiner, S., and Heyman, S. Rubbing and tapping for precise and rapid selection on touch-screen displays. *Proc. CHI '08*. 295-304.
18. Rekimoto, J. SmartSkin: an infrastructure for freehand manipulation on interactive surfaces. *Proc. CHI '02*. 113-120.
19. Rosenberg, I. and Perlin, K. The UnMousePad: an interpolating multi-touch force-sensing input pad. *Proc. SIGGRAPH '09*. 1-9.
20. Sears, A., Shneiderman, B. High precision touchscreens: design strategies and comparisons with a mouse. *International Journal of Man-Machine Studies*, 34(4), April 1991, 593-613.
21. Shoemaker, G., Tang, A., and Booth, K. S. Shadow reaching: a new perspective on interaction for large displays. *Proc. UIST '07*. 53-56.
22. Villar, N., Izadi, S., Rosenfeld, D., Benko, H., Helmes, J., Wes-thues, J., Hodges, S., Ofek, E., Butler, A., Cao, X., and Chen, B. Mouse 2.0: multi-touch meets the mouse. *Proc. UIST '09*. 33-42.
23. Vogel, D. and Baudisch, P. Shift: a technique for operating pen-based interfaces using touch. *Proc. CHI '07*. 657-666.
24. Wang, F. and Ren, X. Empirical evaluation for finger input properties multi-touch interaction. *Proc. CHI '09*. 1063-1072.
25. Wu, M. and Balakrishnan, R. Multi-Finger and Whole Hand Gestural Interaction Techniques for Multi-User Tabletop Displays. *Proc. UIST '03*. 193-202.

Computational Clock Drawing Analysis for Cognitive Impairment Screening

Hyungsin Kim[1,2], Young Suk Cho[2], and Ellen Yi-Luen Do[1,2,3]
GVU Center[1], College of Computing[2] & College of Architecture[3]
Georgia Institute of Technology
Atlanta, Georgia, USA
{hyungsin, ycho47, ellendo}@gatech.edu

ABSTRACT
This paper presents computational support for the Clock Drawing Test (CDT), a simple cognitive dysfunction diagnosis tool. Despite its popularity of current use, the CDT has been administered the same way for the past three decades as a pencil-and-paper test. By making a computerized drawing test, we can understand the process of clock drawing construction rather than simply analyzing the final drawing. In this paper, we will first introduce our computerized Clock Drawing Test, the ClockReader. Then, we will describe two automated data-capturing methods with specific data examples. The automated data analysis can provide neuropsychologists with useful qualitative information, such as the process of drawing, as well as patients' planning strategies.

Author Keywords
Medical application, cognitive screening tool, pen-based computing, aging technologies, cognitive impairment.

ACM Classification Keywords
H5.m. Information interfaces and presentation (e.g., HCI): Miscellaneous.

General Terms
Human factors, experimentation, design.

INTRODUCTION
Sketch understanding is a topic of interest for diverse research areas [1]. In particular, sketches have been used as a fundamental source for neuropsychologists to understand their patients [8]. Drawings are one of the most critical data that can indicate patients' cognitive abilities and mental status. Lezak argues that drawing tasks have attained a central position in neuropsychological assessment [4]. Such drawing tasks are considered to be a rich source of information in understanding the presence (or absence) of cognitive and perceptual-motor abilities [4]. Despite the heavy use of drawing tasks in neuropsychological assessment, they are not fully utilized in supporting neuropsychologists' decision-making processes [7]. People argue that drawing tasks take a longer time to evaluate than other types of dementia-related tasks [9]. Not only is there the burden of administering the task; it also requires someone with the appropriate training and experience to conduct the tests. These drawings are predominantly analyzed at the end of the tests as a final product [7]. Neuropsychologists usually analyze drawings after the completion of a task, and rarely examine or analyze the process of how the drawings were constructed because of the difficulty in data collection. Considering that the clock drawing is a mental processing and reasoning task, the question is then, what information and insights can we obtain if we can capture the process of the drawing test? We believe that tracing the process can be a very useful approach in understanding patients' cognitive status.

In this paper, we present how computation can support an understanding of drawings from cognitive impairment screening tests. First, we will present a paradigm shift in neuropsychological assessment from a quantitative to a process-oriented approach. Second, we will describe the Clock Drawing Test (CDT); what it is and how it can be used in neuropsychological assessment. Then, we will introduce our sketch-based screening system called the ClockReader. By developing a computerized Clock Drawing Test, the ClockReader, we are able to capture the process of drawing. Furthermore, the data collected through this drawing process can be quantified in various ways to support the dementia diagnosis. Finally, we will conclude the paper with future directions.

PARADIGM SHIFT IN NEUROPSYCHOLOGICAL ASSESSMENT
Different theoretical paradigms have influenced the development of neuropsychological assessment [5]. Simply speaking, there have been long debates as to whether or not numerically represented quantitative data provide a better understanding of people's neuropsychological conditions, compared to descriptively written qualitative data [7].

In the early stages of neuropsychological testing development, many clinicians focused on using standardized achievement procedures, which employ the nomothetic interpretation of data [5]. This approach contributes to developing fixed and flexible test batteries emphasizing classical test theory. The main goal is to avoid

TEI'11, January 22–26, 2011, Funchal, Portugal.

using ideographic interpretations of test data that rely heavily on single case studies [5]. However, focusing on global achievement, such as taking test scores into consideration as the most important factor, could hinder a full understanding of our cognition. For example, Werner (1956) argued that every cognitive act involves "microgenesis." and "close observation and careful monitoring of behavior enroute to a solution (process) is more likely to provide more useful information than can be obtained from right or wrong scoring of final products (achievement)" [10].

As a leading researcher, Kaplan also argues that the process-oriented approach could best capture the quality of the patient's performance [3]. She emphasizes that the process approach gives neuropsychologists the advantages to (1) monitor the course of functioning, (2) make recommendations for therapeutic interventions, and (3) understand brain and behavior relations. Her approach became the "Boston Process Approach" [3]. Later, the proponents of the Boston Process Approach started to quantify the process as a natural evolutionary step [5]. Recently, Poreh stated this paradigm shift as a new term, called the Quantified Process Approach [5]. He proposed three different methodologies to conduct the Quantified Process Approach: the Satellite Testing Paradigm, the Composition Paradigm, and the Decomposition Paradigm.

The Clock Drawing Test is one of the exemplary tests, based on the composition paradigm. This composition paradigm involves the generation of new indices for existing tests using collected data that have not been previously analyzed [5]. In other words, the composition paradigm enables neuropsychologists to interpret patients' drawings from different perspectives that were previously overlooked. Tests under the composition paradigm do not lengthen the testing process and typically maintain a standardized administration. Poreh states that the composition paradigm could provide the fundamentals for the computerization of traditional tests [5]. For example, there are computer technologies, such as tablet-PC, to support handwriting tasks; voice recognition software to control the computer through the patients' voice; and online video cameras to capture patients' performance.

Our ClockReader System supports capturing various factors focused on a process-analysis and presents a new way to investigate the drawing data. In the next section, we will introduce the ClockReader System and its unique computational features implemented to capture a variety of processes during the clock-drawing construction.

CLOCK DRAWING TEST

The Clock Drawing Test (CDT) is one of the simplest, but most commonly used screening tools to detect cognitive impairment in the elderly [2]. By simply asking people to draw a clock, it easily identifies people with dementia [8]. Clock drawings from people with dementia frequently show missing or extra numbers, or misplaced clock hands [2]. The drawing clearly shows the degradation of the patient's cognition.

CLOCKREADER SYSTEM

The purpose of the ClockReader System is to enable patients to take the Clock Drawing Test without the presence of a human evaluator. The overarching goal of this system is to identify early dementia, delay or prevent the progression of the disease and increase the quality of life for aging people. The system consists of three main components: data collection, sketch recognition, and data analysis. First, the system would record and recognize a patient's freehand drawing and collect the data. Then, based on the scoring criteria, the system would automatically analyze the drawing and report the score.

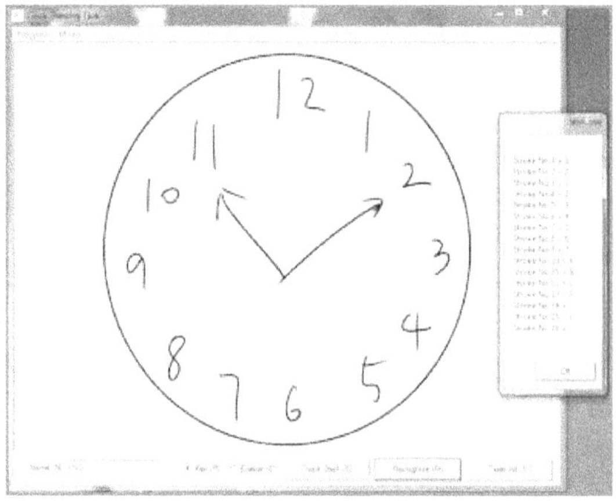

Figure 1. Screen shot of the ClockReader System

ClockReader is developed in C# programming language and is supported by "Microsoft Windows XP Tablet PC Edition Software Development Kit 1.7" and "Microsoft Visual Studio 2008." Figure 1 shows a screen shot of our ClockReader system. The small window on the right shows the results of the digit recognition. Figure 2 shows how a patient would draw a clock in the ClockReader system using a stylus on a tablet PC.

Figure 2. A picture that shows how a patient uses the ClockReader system

AUTOMATED DATA CAPTURING METHODS

The traditional paper-and-pencil based CDT has provided apparent visual references to identify aging people's dementia conditions. Here, we propose that the two novel automated data-capturing methods during the process of drawing could provide significant resources for understanding patients' drawings from a multifaceted perspective. In the following section, we describe the novel data-capturing methods enabled by computational supports from Pen-based Computing. As we mentioned in the previous section, the new methods are aligned with the Quantified Process Approach. The way we capture data is to collect a Bezier point from stroke-level character recognition during the clock-drawing process. Then we use the x- and y-coordinates of each Bezier point to reconstruct patients' clock drawings.

Automatic Process Capture

One of the advantages from automated data-capturing is that we can reconstruct the clock after the drawing is completed. First, the data provide us with information of how each stroke is drawn with a specific time stamp. This shows the process of how the clock is constructed from the tiny level, x- and y- coordinates of each Bezier point. It also tells the order of each character (digits and clock hands) from the drawing process. For example, one patient could draw a clock by starting to write anchoring numbers, such as 12, 6, 3, and 9. Then, later she might fill out the remaining numbers in a specific order. Another patient could draw a clock with a sequencing order starting from 1, 2, 3, and then filling out the numbers up to 12.

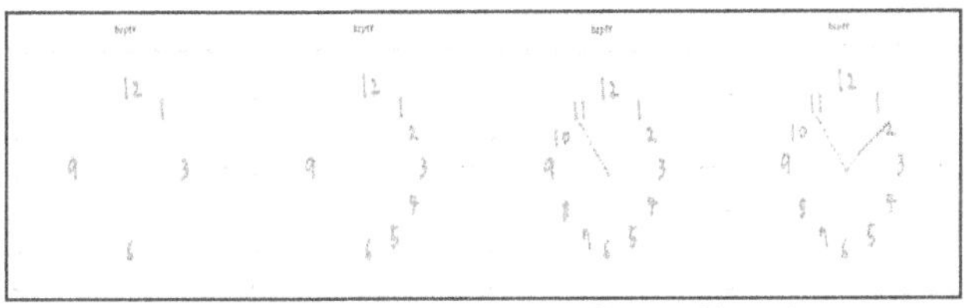

Figure 3: Reconstructed Clock Case 1

Second, the captured data not only provide a great deal of information about the drawing process; the data are also able to reconstruct drawings with the accumulated Bezier points. Figures 3 and Figures 4 show the process of two different drawing constructions. Figure 3 represents four steps as to how a clock is constructed. The patient first drew four anchoring numbers, such as 12, 3, 6, and 9, and then filled out the remaining numbers.

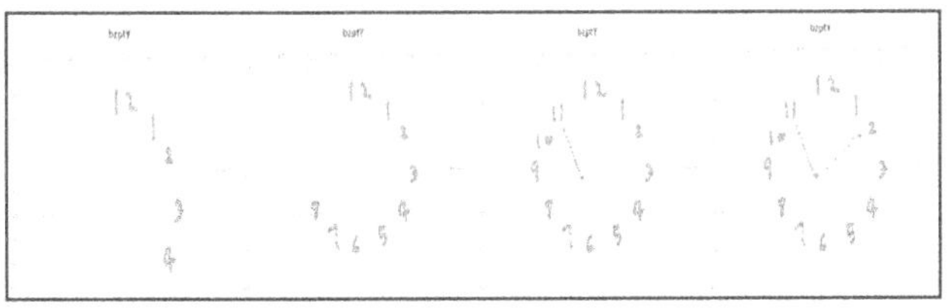

Figure 4: Reconstructed Clock Case 2

The visual drawn in Figure 4 shows that the clock is constructed first with the number 12, and then with the sequential order from 1, 2, 3, and up to 11. Then the patient drew the two clock hands. In addition to reconstructing a clock through automated captured data, the ClockReader System also includes a function to save the final output drawing as an Ink Serialized Format (ISF). Whenever a person completes the clock-drawing task by pressing the button "recognize," the ISF image is created and will be saved in the database. This would be a helpful resource included in the interface for clinicians. The drawings on the right side of Figure 5 show clock drawings in an ISF image format. Even though the final output indicated the same time, they are constructed from two different reconstruction processes. All of these data provide the spatial coordinate information of each digit and clock hand.

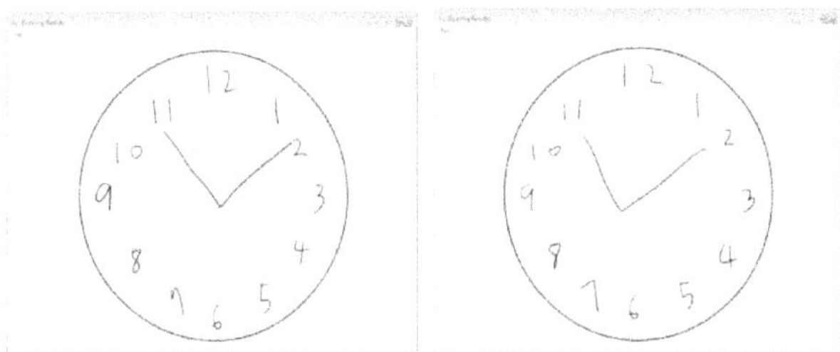

Figure 5: The ISF image of Clock Case 1 (left) and the ISF image of Clock Case 2 (right)

Automatic Time Capture

Automatically capturing time in the ClockReader System consists of two functions: total completion time and air time. The total completion time is always a good metric in neuropsychological assessments [9]. One of the characteristics of the Clock Drawing Test is that it only takes approximately 5 minutes. Given this short time, a person's visual-spatial, constructional and higher-order cognitive abilities can be examined [4]. In a busy clinical environment, neuropsychologists or neurologists do not record the completion time. If we compare multiple drawings from consecutive years, then we can see how a patient's clock representations change in dementia progression. The questions of concerns are: How is the patient's cognitive functioning? Is it getting better, worse, or staying the same? It would be meaningful to provide the total completion time for clinical specialists to understand disease progression over the years. For example, even though a patient may maintain the same scores within the past three years, the completion time may be different. They may take more time to finish drawing a clock. This could add another value in the CDT criteria. The ClockReader System automatically captures the total time, from the beginning of the drawing until its completion, and saves it in a separate database.

Measuring air time is the second advantage of capturing timing in the ClockReader System. Air time simply represents the time of non-writing. When a patient draws a clock, at a certain point, they may hesitate to draw, perhaps due to memory problems. Or perhaps they may experience difficulty in recalling a specific number on the clock face. None of the existing criteria for the Clock Drawing Test take this factor into consideration. However, air time could be a good index. For example, if a person has a hard time recalling all of the digits, the air time graphs would show vertical lines, without much fluctuation. Figure 5 shows an example of an airtime graph, which indicates some patterns of the drawing. The x-axis indicates a stroke order written when a patient draws a clock. The y-axis indicates the air time of each stroke drawn. The first stroke was written in 4.3 milliseconds. In this case, the 13th and 14th strokes pertain to clock hand drawings. The 13th stroke took 5 milliseconds to write down. This is the longest time for the patient to think before she actually wrote down something. This implies that the patient needed more time to draw a clock hand in order to set a time. Overall, patients have two critical moments in which they spend quiet time thinking before drawing something: initiation of drawing and setting a time.

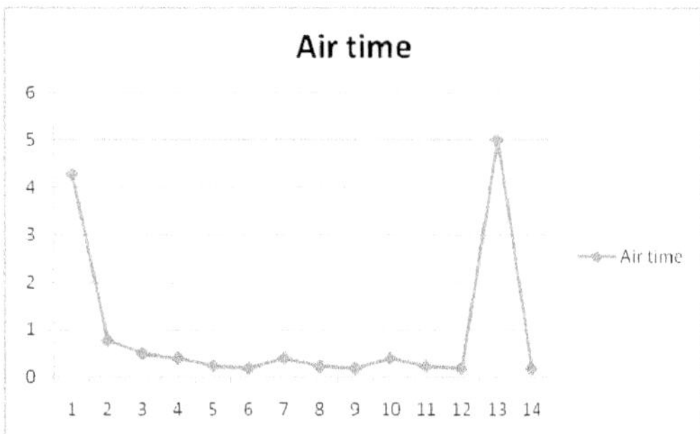

Figure 5: Air time during the Clock Drawing Test

In another example, once a person finishes filling out 12, 3, 6, and 9, the writing speed for the remaining digits can be faster. In the first quadrant, only the numbers 1 and 2 need to be filled out. As a result, the air time for 1 and 2 is typically faster if they are aging normally. Thus, air time can be an additional meaningful measurement.

Furthermore, studies on the handwriting process from Rosenblum and Werner demonstrate that a kinematic analysis of handwriting provides important information about the handwriting process among older people [6]. Their experimental results show that being a higher-age adult was consistently associated with longer on-paper and in-air time, as well as it was associated with lower speed and lower pressure [6].

CONCLUSION AND FUTURE DIRECTIONS

In this paper, we addressed how computation can help to understand drawings with respect to cognitive impairment screening tests. The Clock Drawing Test has been a significant influential screening tool over the past three decades. However, the way it is conducted has not changed until now. By making computerized testing, it can be beneficial to multiple stakeholders, such as clinical specialists (neuropsychologists and neurologists), people with dementia at all different stages, and their caregivers.

More importantly, in order to make a more powerful screening tool, we have proposed computational support to capture the process data during the Clock Drawing Test. The final result score only indicates the level of dementia, such as a mild cognitive stage of dementia. If we can quantify more information with computational power, utilization of the Clock Drawing Test can be maximized. Our two main automatic capturing approaches, such as process and timing, can provide useful information. With these new data collection methods, we believe that neuropsychologists will be able to investigate more qualitative features from the computerized Clock Drawing Test, the ClockReader. For future work, we plan to implement more advanced functions, such as an automatically replay of the clock-drawing process, like an animation, and capturing pressure during the drawing process. Once we meet our system development goal, we will move forward to design and develop rehabilitation systems, focusing on drawing tasks. We believe that this system can benefit the aging population and can help clinicians gain further insights in their analysis.

REFERENCES

1. Davis, R. Magic Paper: Sketch- Understanding Research. Computer, 40, 9 (2007), 34-41.
2. Freedman, M., Leach, L., E., K., E., W., Shulman, K. and Delis, D. Clock Drawing: A Neuropsychological Analysis. Oxford University Press, Oxford, 1994.
3. Kaplan, E. The process approach to neuropsychological assessment of psychiatric patients. Journal of Neuropsychiatry, 2 (1990), 72-87.
4. Lezak, M. D. Neuropsychological assessment. Oxford University Press, New York, 1995.
5. Poreh, A. The Quantified Process Approach to Neuropsychological Assesment. Psychology Press, New York, 2006.
6. Rosenblum, S. and Werner, P. Assessing the handwriting process in healthy elderly persons using a computerized system. Aging Clin Exp Res, 18, 5 (2006), 433-439.
7. Smith, A. D. On the Use of Drawing Tasks in Neuropsychological Assessment. Neuropsychology 23, 2 (2009), 231- 239.
8. Strauss, E., Sherman, E. M. S. and Spreen, O. A Compendium of Neuropsychological Tests: Administration, Norms, and Commentary. Oxford University Press, Oxford, 2006.
9. Rabins, P., Lyketsos, C. and Steele, C. Practical Dementia Care Oxford University Press, Oxford, 2006.
10. Werner, H. Microgenesis and aphasia. Journal of Abnormal Social Psychology, 52 (1956), 347-353.

Augmented Calligraphy: Experimental Feedback Design for Writing Skill Development

Takahiro Shichinohe   Tetsuo Yamabe   Takahiro Iwata   Tatsuo Nakajima
Dept. of Computer Science, Waseda University
{shichino777, yamabe, takahiroiwata, tatsuo}@dcl.info.waseda.ac.jp

ABSTRACT
In this demonstration, we introduce the augmented calligraphy system that aims at supporting a calligraphy learner's self-training process by giving feedback. In order to write characters well, body posture is a very important factor. However, it is difficult to keep proper posture without any assistance. Therefore, the system monitors the learner's posture by a web camera and notifies them if the posture moves into a bad shape. Several types of multimodal feedback were implemented, since we are particularly interested in how feedback design can decrease cognitive load.

Author Keywords
Calligraphy, augmented reality, entertainment computing, tangible interaction, design guideline.

ACM Classification Keywords
H.5.1 Information Interfaces and Presentation: Multimedia Information Systems—*Artificial, augmented, and virtual realities*

General Terms
Design, Human Factors

INTRODUCTION
Japanese calligraphy is an effective way to improve the literacy skill of Chinese and Japanese characters. Nowadays its artistic aspect is often focused, but as a practice a learner can also develop the sense of writing (e.g., the layout of letters) by copying again and again from a copybook. For example, in Japanese elementary schools, Japanese calligraphy is a compulsory subject, and it is also still one of the most popular lessons for adults. However, such repetition practice could easily get boring, since the process is not attractive and informative enough to keep interests. Particularly a copybook neither intuitively demonstrates writing process, nor gives feedback/incentives for writing skill development. On the other hand, the concept of mixed reality is getting realized today. For example, these days AR (augmented reality) toys are commercialized in the market. Users can interact with a virtual character by capturing a matrix code with a web camera. The character is superimposed on the code and animated as preliminary programmed. Real and virtual environments are united into a hybrid world. Then digitally augmented features provide new user experience to consumers and assist players in gaming. For example, pervasive game is one domain in the mixed reality games [2]. The rapid progress of pervasive computing technologies would seamlessly integrate games into our daily lives.

Therefore, in this paper, we applied the AR technology to enhance the interactivity of calligraphy. We introduce the augmented calligraphy system, which aims at giving feedback to assist a user to improve their writing skill. Conventional copybooks instruct, for example, how to control the strength of a brushstroke with markers and texts. However, it is not intuitive particularly for beginners to do self-training. Making invisible information visible improves bodily experience, since immediate feedback to the brushstroke would be given in real-time. Eventually it leads the user to better understanding of the training. In this work, we also addressed the importance of cognitive load, since calligraphy particularly requires concentration. Thus feedback should not interfere writing task, with providing proper amount of information to allow a user to recognize invisible information (e.g., how the user bends forward). Mixed reality technologies are expected to appear in future products. Thus we believe that our experiments and findings can be also utilized in a variety of AR application domains [1].

Figure 1. Calligraphy with augmentation

AUGMENTED CALLIGRAPHY SYSTEM
In order to keep the original look-and-feel of calligraphy, we applied *augmented traditional games* concept to the system design [1]. The system uses rather ordinary calligraphy tools than virtual simulation, and learners can naturally fol-

TEI'11, January 22–26, 2011, Funchal, Portugal.

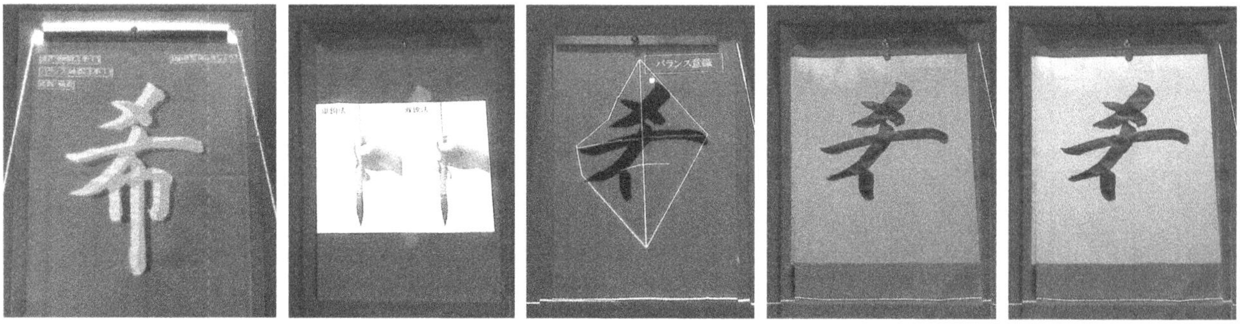

Figure 2. Examples of feedback and assistance information from the system

low its writing process without effortfully exposing themselves to the augmented environment (Figure 1). Users can also seamlessly turn on and off the augmentation support at any time. Figure 3 shows the augmented calligraphy system setup. The web camera on the top captures the image of characters written on paper, and their shape is recognized with OpenCV library. Another camera captures the shape of the user's posture from the side, and it detects how much the user bends forward while writing characters. Since a proper posture is important to do calligraphy well, the system gives warning feedback according to the calculated bending level.

Visual information such as feedback and guidance is given from the projector (Figure 2). For example, model characters are directly shown on the paper so that a learner can trace the line without switching their focus onto a copybook (Figure 2-(a)). Visual warning, such as "Keep a writing brush vertical to paper.", reminds a user of points and tips of the practice. For example, at the beginning of a practice, the system shows and emphasizes the correct pen holding style (Figure 2-(b)). Moreover it is also possible to visualize the balance of characters if necessary (Figure 2-(c)). This helps to recognize how the actual shape differs from the ideal one, since the balance of character is important point to perform good calligraphy. During the writing process, other advice remain on top of the paper, and lastly the user's score is shown (Figure 2-(a)). The score is calculated based on how the written character differs from the model ones.

Currently several feedbacks are supported with two modalities: visual and audio. The visual feedback supports both ambient and linguistic styles. The ambient style feedback changes the paper's color according to the user's posture. As shown in Figure 2-(d) and Figure 2-(e), the color changes from normal to yellow, and finally to red as the posture gets worse. In the linguistic feedback mode, a warning sentence is projected onto the paper and its size increases to draw more attention when the user's body bends forward. In the auditory feedback mode, a ring tone is played during writing process. Two parameters of the tone could be changed according to the posture: tempo and volume.

FUTURE WORK

In this project, we are particularly interested in feedback design, since it is tightly linked with the efficacy of self-

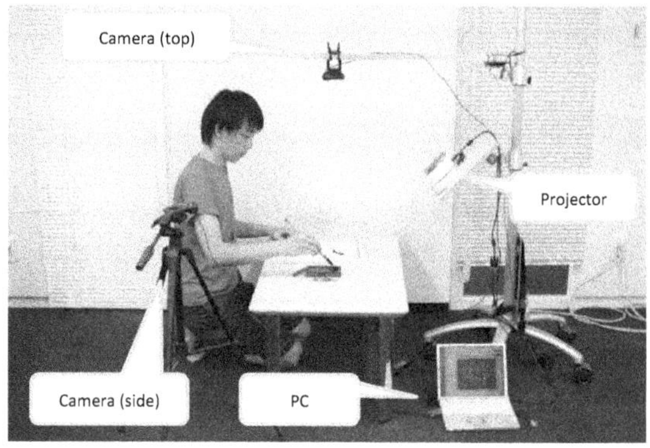

Figure 3. Augmented calligraphy system appearance

training process. In order to prevent from interfering learners' concentration, timing, modality and the complexity of information should be sufficiently considered in a design process. Immediate feedback could be frequently provided to the user in a short period, and thus cognitive load to recognize and process the information could increase accordingly. In order to support an elaborated training process, enough cognitive resource should be allocated to the main task. As we introduced with the augmented calligraphy system, increasing the variety of multimodality is one approach to avoid conflicts in a cognitive activity. Since most of activities require visual attention, other types of modalities will allow the user to interpret given messages with different cognitive resource. We believe that immediate feedback should be ambient (i.e., non linguistic) information, and verbal description should be used particularly in the case that a system needs to draw players' attention (e.g., report a system error). In future work, we will conduct a user study with the system on this perspective, in order to identify a feedback design guideline that is applicable to other AR applications.

REFERENCES

1. T. Iwata, T. Yamabe, M. Polojärvi, and T. Nakajima. Traditional games meet ict: a case study on go game augmentation. In *TEI '10*, 2010.

2. C. Magerkurth, A. D. Cheok, R. L. Mandryk, and T. Nilsen. Pervasive games: bringing computer entertainment back to the real world. *Computers in Entertainment*, 3(3):4–4, 2005.

Touch Trace Mirror: Asynchronous, Collaborative Messaging as a Concept for Creating a Relatedness Experience

Johanna Schmeer
University of the Arts Berlin
Rigaer Str. 15, 10247 Berlin, Germany
johanna.schmeer@designlab15.org
+49 151 21200200

Tom Baffi
Folkwang University of the Arts Essen
Rigaer Str. 15, 10247 Berlin, Germany
tom.baffi@designlab15.org
+49 151 11511000

ABSTRACT
In this paper we introduce the concept of volatile, asynchronous, collaborative messaging as a means of creating a relatedness experience, in this specific context for couples in a long-distance relationship.
Based upon the idea of message leaving in a romantic relationship, the "Touch Trace Mirror" is a mirror which enables leaving a message on a steamy bathroom mirror over a distance. It is a set of two bathroom mirrors, one to be placed in each partners apartment. Writing a message on one mirror will result in the message being sent to the partners mirror, where a light will emerge on the mirrors surface. If the partner places a finger on the light, it will move, letting the partner trace the message that his or her loved one wrote.
Initial user testing showed that the concept and the aesthetics of the interaction, which developed over two cycles of a user centered design process, seem promising for creating a joyful relatedness experience.

Author Keywords
affective technology, slow messaging, romantic, volatile, collaborative, asynchronous, non-verbal.

ACM Classification Keywords
H5.2 [Information interfaces and presentation]: User Interfaces - Input devices and strategies.

General Terms
Design, Human Factors.

CONTEXTUAL ANALYSIS
In a contextual analysis, we investigated the issues of communication in long-distance relationships with data from 100 participants of an online questionnaire, as well as four in-depth interviews with two couples (Ø 25,75 yrs). We then concentrated on four of several key findings:

1. It is hard to find a good time for communication, especially if the partner lives in a different time zone.
2. Couples miss each other especially in the morning and the evening, around the time of going to sleep or waking up alone.
3. Handwritten communication is wished for, but seldom achieved because it is time-intense.
4. Sometimes one partner wants to contact the other, but does not know what to talk about and has the feeling that there is "nothing special to say".

The requirements towards concepts for romantic communication, which have been explored and published by Howard, Vetere, Gibbs et al. (2004) [1], and King and Forlizzi (2007) [2], include allowing own forms of communication to develop, respecting privacy as a concern, and showing time and effort spent. We searched for a way to address both some of these requirements and our key findings in a concept.

TEI'11, January 22–26, 2011, Funchal, Portugal.

RELATED WORK
There are several existing concepts in the field of romantic communication involving collaborative messaging to create intimacy. The "MatchUs Board" by Bhandari and Bardzell (2008) [3] is a set of two connected boards using touch input and display technology. Drawings done by fingers on the board will synchronously appear on both boards, so that the partners can interact over a distance.
A similar, but more complex project from this area is the computer vision and projection system "Mutsogoto" by Hayashi, Agamanolis and Karau (2008) [4], which enables users to collaboratively draw on each others bodies and beds over a distance.
These concepts require synchronicity, which, as our contextual analysis showed, is often difficult to obtain when the long distance relationship has to bridge several time zones, or when the partners have different daily schedules. Our aim was to find a more "natural" form of asynchronous, collaborative messaging, which at the same time can be easily integrated into daily routines.

CONCEPT
The idea of leaving someone a message, as one couple in our research had mentioned hiding little handwritten or drawn notes in the partners apartment, for them later to discover, seemed suitable as an approach for developing a product that addresses the above mentioned issues. Thinking of which forms of leaving messages, or just traces, in the partners apartment already existed, we thought about how people leave a message on a steamy mirror, just after taking a shower. The idea came up to

connect two bathroom mirrors in the partners different apartments for sending and receiving handwritten messages. How this concept could be developed to create a relatedness experience, was to be tested in an initial user confrontation.

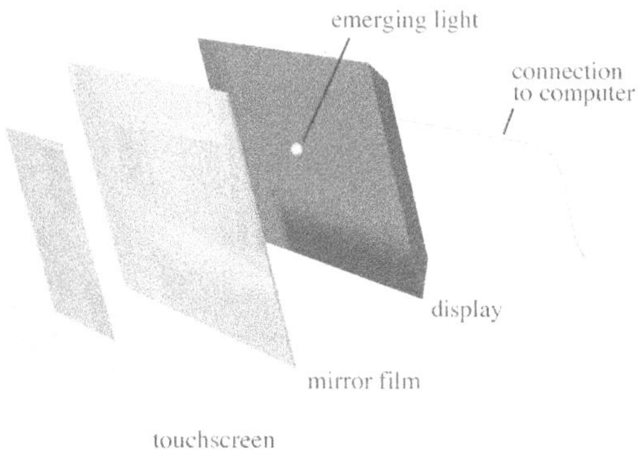

Figure 1. Prototype.

INITIAL USER CONFRONTATION

In an initial user confrontation, with three couples living in long distance relationships, we explored the ideas of either just letting a message, written by the partner, appear on the mirror through a technical device, or, not just letting it appear, but having the partner trace the received message onto the mirror, as a form of co-construction. Several forms of a technical guidance for the co-construction were evaluated, such as different mechanical constructions, as well as an emerging light on the surface, which is to be followed by the recipients finger.

Co-constructed message-writing was exposed to be the better way of communication fulfilling the need for creating a relatedness experience. The implementation with a light on the surface, which is to be traced by a finger, appeared the most natural and least technical to our users; creating an experience which comes closest to the finger being directly guided by the partners hand.

IMPLEMENTATION

The "Touch Trace Mirror" prototype [Fig. 1] consists of a touchscreen [5] with an integrated mirror film, a humidity sensor [6], two buttons, an Arduino Board [7], and a small computer with a wireless Internet connection.

Before the mirror is first used, a button on the back side of the mirror has to be pressed when the mirror is steamy, so that the humidity sensor is calibrated for detecting when that moment occurs. This should be done because the touchscreen will turn on, and show that a message is available, only when the mirror is steamy.

To send a message, one writes a message onto the steamy mirror after taking a shower. The touchscreen turns on automatically when the mirror is steamy and is ready for recording or displaying a message. There is no "send" button or confirmation for the message being delivered, which, as user testing confirmed, is not needed or expected, because it feels natural that a mirror does not have such a functionality. To receive a message, the partner places a finger on the emerging light on the mirrors surface [Fig. 2]. The light slowly blinks. When a finger is placed upon it, the light moves with a trace of light, at the same speed as the partner wrote the message. When the finger is lifted from the mirrors surface, although the message has not fully been received, the light will not continue moving. It will stay at the point until where it was constructed, and will blink again. This means that the message has to be written by the recipient entirely, otherwise it will not be received completely.

The aesthetics of the interaction, such as the fastness of the blinking, a trail of light behind the point when it moves, as well as important conceptual aspects, such as that the message is displayed in the same pace as is was written, because the pace is also an aspect of this communication, were evaluated in user tests and subsequently optimized.

Figure 2. Re-construction of a message.

CONCLUSION AND OUTLOOK

User confrontations with 6 users (3f, 3m Ø 27,2 yrs) in the first evaluation, and 4 users (2f, 2m Ø 35,5 yrs) in the second evaluation, showed that the concept has potential for creating a joyful relatedness experience. Reactions to the core concept were overall positive, as asynchronous and co-created messaging seem to be desirable and conceivable for couples living in a long-distance relationship. There is evidence from our user studies that the messages will also be valued more because of their volatile aspect. The thereby resulting thesis that inducing a volatile aspect into messaging makes the experience of receiving a message more significant, and that these messages are read with more attentiveness, needs more extensive user testing and should be further evaluated.

REFERENCES

1. Gibbs, Howard, Vetere et al. 2004. *Using cultural probes to explore mediated intimacy.*
2. Forlizzi, King 2007. *Slow messaging: intimate communication for couples living at a distance.*
3. Bardzell, Bhandari 2008. *Bridging Gaps: Affective Communication in Long Distance Relationships.*
4. Mutsugoto, http://www.mutsugoto.com/
5. EloTouchsystems Touchscreen ET1545L
6. Sensirion SHT-10 Humidity and Temperature Sensor
7. Arduino, http://www.arduino.cc

Touching the Void: Gestures for Auditory Interfaces

Katrin Wolf
T-Labs (Quality & Usability Lab), TU Berlin
E.-Reuther-Platz 7, 10587 Berlin
katrin.wolf@acm.org

Christina Dicke
HIT Lab NZ
University of Canterbury
Private Bag 4800, Christchurch
christina.dicke@hitlabnz.org

Raphael Grasset
HIT Lab NZ
University of Canterbury
Private Bag 4800, Christchurch
raphael.grasset@hitlabnz.org

ABSTRACT
Nowadays, mobile devices provide new possibilities for gesture interaction due to the large range of embedded sensors they have and their physical form factor. In addition, auditory interfaces can now be more easily supported through advanced mobile computing capabilities. Although different types of gesture techniques have been proposed for handheld devices, there is still little knowledge about the acceptability and use of some of these techniques, especially in the context of an auditory interface. In this paper, we propose a novel approach to the problem by studying the design space of gestures proposed by end-users for a mobile auditory interface. We discuss the results of this explorative study, in terms of the scope of the gestures proposed, the tangible aspects, and the users' preferences. This study delivers some initial gestures recommendations for eyes-free auditory interfaces.

Author Keywords
Gestures, tangible interface, embodied interaction, eyes-free, mobile, auditory display, participatory design.

ACM Classification Keywords
H.5.2 [User Interfaces]: *Haptic I/O*

General Terms
Design, Experimentation, Human Factors

INTRODUCTION
Current smartphones often come equipped with a wide range of advanced hardware and software features including those which can offer spatial sound rendering and even provide access to standard 3D sound APIs like OpenAL [5]. Beyond their potential usage for gaming or musical applications, these features can be exploited for the design of new user interfaces on mobile phones like spatial auditory interfaces. This paper is focused on mobile spatial auditory interfaces, specifically input control and interaction strategies that can be used in a mobile audio context.

TEI'11, January 22–26, 2011, Funchal, Portugal.

Lately, the manipulation of information on mobile devices has moved from keypad interaction to touch input. However, one of the drawbacks of this approach is that it requires a large part of the users' visual, cognitive, and motor attention, and could be harmful in some specific mobile situations (e.g. steering a car or walking in a busy urban environment). Speech recognition is alternative approach, but it is difficult to use in mobile situations due to the high signal-to-noise ratio caused by traffic, other conversations, and constantly changing environmental sound fields and levels.

Figure 1. Gesturing to interact with an auditory interface.

Gesture interaction techniques [3] exploiting inbuilt sensors (e.g. accelerometer, gyroscope, and/or digital compass) can overcome the previously described issues by providing an elegant, eyes-free solution for user input.

The large range of potential gestures that can be executed in a mobile context and the different input factors (DOF, user dexterity, mobile form factor, etc) need to be studied more thoroughly. The explorative study presented in this paper aims at shedding light on the type of gestures users will perform freely and intuitively when interacting with a spatial auditory interface.

For this purpose we asked participants in a qualitative user study to perform several tasks. Their actions and comments were recorded, analyzed, and are summarized in the results section of this paper. Discussions of the results, and suggestions and guidelines for gesture design are given in the discussion and conclusion sections.

RELATED WORK
Over the last few years we have seen an emergence of work on gesture techniques for spatial interaction design. One of the earliest mobile auditory interfaces presented was the

Nomadic Radio introduced by Sawhney et al. [8]. Gestures for mobile auditory interfaces have been explored in different projects and the validity of the approach has been shown in user studies like Pirhonen et al. [6]. In terms of techniques, Brewster et al. [2] presented one of the first spatialized audio systems combined with gestures. The Shoogle system [9] engaged the user to query information by shaking the device and delivered information by vibrotactile and sonified feedback. Similarly, Li et al. [4] presented a set of eyes-free gestures using a mobile keypad for an (non-spatial) auditory interface after surveying the most relevant tasks for end-users.

A recent study by Rico et al. [7] has observed the general social acceptability of some gesture techniques and demonstrated their impact in real use of some of the proposed metaphors. Similarly, Bhandari et al. [1] asked participants to match specific gestures to common tasks realized on mobile devices. Differently from our approach, the gestures were predefined by the authors and not designed by the participants.

In summary, gesture techniques have been well developed and explored for mobile devices. Yet there are only few studies exploring gestures as an input technique for spatial auditory interfaces, and none of these studies actively involves end-users in a participatory design process.

EXPERIMENT

Our motivation was to investigate how users would interact with basic elements of a spatial auditory interface without restricting them by pre-defined gestures or limited system capabilities. We were especially interested in which concepts and metaphors users would transfer from their everyday usage of computers and mobile phones to the entirely unknown domain of spatial auditory interfaces.

We solicited 10 participants, 4 male and 6 female, with a mean age of 30 (12-49) and a wide variety of professional backgrounds. All participants were familiar with desktop computers and were using them at least once a week for communication, accounting, or gaming. All participants owned a mobile phone but just one owned a smartphone.

Before the experiment began participants were familiarized with synthesized spatial sound by playback via headphones of sound scenes consisting of single and multiple sound sources. Finally, the participants were given a featureless phone dummy made of wood to perform the gesture they would envisage for each of the different task (see Fig 2.).

Users were allowed to perform any gestures with or on the device. The experiment was video recorded and we encouraged participants to verbalize their thoughts during each task (think-aloud method). We also interviewed the participants at the end of the session.

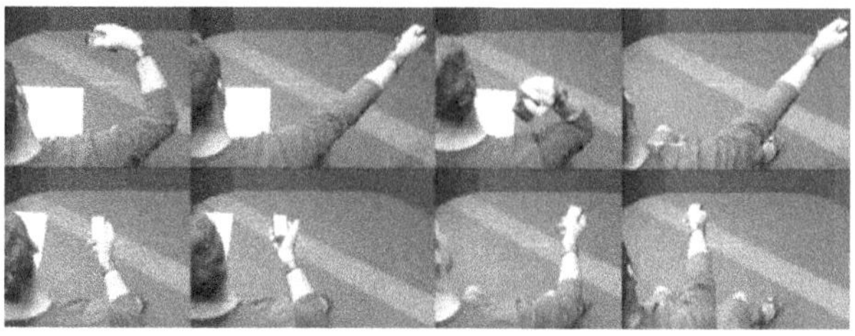

Figure 2. A gesture for moving a sound source (Task 14).

Tasks

The tasks for the user study were based on the concept of a traditional desktop interface (WIMP), using spatial sound to represent applications, menus, folders, and hierarchical file structures. Each of the tasks was explained symbolically and textually to the participant. A total of 20 tasks were structured in three main categories:

Item Selection

Task 1: Select a single sound source.
Task 2: Select a sound source from a list.
Task 3: Skip through sound sources in a list.
Task 4: Deselect a selected sound source.
Task 5: Select several disjointed items from a list.
Task 6: Select several contiguous items from a list.
Task 7: Select all items of a list.

Attention Prioritization

Task 8: Change the distance of a sound source.
Task 9: Maximize/focus attention on one sound source.
Task 10: Undo maximization of one specific sound source.
Task 11: Minimize one specific sound source.
Task 12: Undo minimization of several sound sources.
Task 13: Minimize all sound sources.

Item Manipulation

Task 14: Move a single sound source.
Task 15: Lock a single sound source.
Task 16: Unlock a single sound source.
Task 17: Pause a single sound source.
Task 18: Re-activate a paused sound source.
Task 19: Delete a single sound source.
Task 20: Activate/open a single sound source.

RESULTS

Participants used a total of 254 gestures, 98 of which were 3D movements with the device, 137 gestures were performed on the "touch screen", and 19 were combinations of both 3D and 2D gestures. An overview of the most frequently used gestures is presented in table 1. Essential gestures are illustrated and described in detail along with user comments and some notes on from which domains users transferred gestures to solve the tasks.

Touch-screen and embodied gestures

The pointing gesture (**Point**) was one of the most elemental 3D gestures to select an item (see Fig. 3, left). This gesture often preceded other gestures such as **TiltUp** (see Fig. 3, right) and **TiltDown**, **DoubleTouch**, **Arc**, etc.

Figure 3. Point (left) and TiltUp + Move (right) gestures.

Some gestures were similar to gestures already implemented on the iPhone or Android (**ScrollUp**, **ScrollDown**, **Drag&Drop**). More original gestures proposed by the participants were:

- **Arc**: The device is moved from point A to B in an arc shaped curve
- **Flick**: A flicking hand movement - like throwing a Frisbee disc
- **PageFlip**: Rotating the device around its vertical axis
- **Shoot**: pretend to shoot with the device

Disjointed item selections (like task 5) were usually realized by repeating the single-selection gestures from task 1 and 2. Most contiguous item selections (like task 6) were split into three different actions: Select 1st item + Browsing the list + Selecting last item using 2D as well as 3D or combinations of gestures. Regarding reversible commands (like undo/redo); participants preferred repeating the original commands (9 and 11) or inversing the gesture (e.g. "**Arc** towards user" and "**Arc** away from user").

Combinations of 2D and 3D gestures

Combined gestures were mostly found in tasks involving 2D object selection (**Hold**) combined with spatial object manipulations such as moving a sound source by 3D **PickUp&Drop**. Fig. 4 shows an example of a combination of a 3D gesture (**Point**) followed by a 2D gesture (**Drag&Drop**).

Figure 4: Selecting items with a combined gesture (Task 6).

Task	2D Gestures	3D Gestures
1	Scanning the screen with a finger + Hold for selection of a "touched" item (1)	Point + Touch (9)
2	Drag&Drop sidewards + Press (3) Drag&Drop sidwards + ScrollDown (3)	Point + TiltUp (2) Point + TiltDown (1) Point + TouchBelt (fig. 3) (1)
3	Drag&Drop sidwards (4) ScrollUp+ ScrollDown (2)	Shake left/right (3) PageFlip (1)
4	ScrollUp (3) Touch (2) Press (1)	Shake left/right (2) Flick (1)
5	n* Drag&Drop sidewards + ScrollDown (5) n* Drag&Drop sidewards + Press (1)	n* {Point + TiltUp}(2) n* {Point+TiltDown}(1) n* {Point + TouchBelly}(1)
6	Hold + n* {Drag&Drop + ScrollDown} (Fig. 4) (6) Touch + n* {Drag&Drop + Press&Hold} (2)	PageFlip (1) TiltUp + PageFlip + TiltDown (1)
7	DoubleTouch (3) Press&Hold (1) Draw a circle (O) (1) Drag&Drop+ScrollDown(1)	Draw a circle (O) (3) PointAll + TouchBelly (1)
8	ScrollUp + ScrollDown(6)	TiltUp + TiltDown (4)
9	DoubleTouch (4) Press&Hold (1)	Device to landscape format (3) Shake (1) Arc towards user (2)
10	DoubleTouch (4) Press&Hold (1)	Shake (4) Arc away from user (2)
11	Multitouch zoom out (1) Draw a dash (\) (1) Flip away (1)	Push away (2) Move downwards (2) Cross out (1)
12	DoubleTouch (2) ScrollDown (1)	Pull close (2) Move upwards (2) Shake (1)
13	Draw a circle (O) + ScrollDown (2) Draw a circle (O) + Draw a dash (\) (2)	Draw a circle (O) + TiltDown (2) PointUp + TiltDown (1)
14	Drag&Drop (3)	PickUp&Drop (8)
15	Press&Hold (3) Draw a circle (O) clockwise (2)	Lock (turn a key in a door) (2) TiltUp (2) DoubleTiltUp (1)
16	Press&Hold (3) Draw a circle (O) counterclockwise (2)	Unlock (turn a key in a door) (2) TiltUp (2) DoubleTiltUp (1)
17	Touch (4) DoubleTouch (2) Draw a dash (\) (2)	TiltDown (1) Move away (1)
18	Touch (4) DoubleTouch (2) Draw a dash (/) (2)	TiltUP (1) MoveCloser (1)
19	Cross out (X) (2) Flip away (1)	Cross out (X) (3) Flick (2) Shoot (1)
20	DoubleTouch (4) Touch (1)	Shake (2) TiltUp (2) TiltDown (1)

Table 1: Most frequently used 2D and 3D gestures by task. (Frequency is indicated by the number in brackets.)

Another example of a combined gesture is illustrated in Fig. 5: **TiltUp** (to select all sources) followed by the 2D **ScrollDown** gesture to mute all sound sources.

Gesture associations

We encouraged participants to think aloud during the experiment. Some of these comments offered insights into the participants' associations and intentions:

Windows 7: Shake gesture to quickly minimize every open window except the one shaken: participant shook the device to focus attention on a sound source. **Windows**: X-Button to close an application: participants

used the X-shape to delete a sound source.
🖐 **iPhone**: Slide finger across screen to scroll between different screens: participants used this to skip through sound sources in a list.
🖐 **Books**: Flipping pages: participant used this to skip through sound sources in a list.

Figure 5: Combined gesture to mute/minimize all sound sources (Task 13).

DISCUSSION

We distinguished three main categories of gestures used by participants: 2D gestures, 3D gestures, and combinations of both. With rising task complexity we noticed a preference of 2D and 3D gesture combinations. Participants often used 2D gestures (e.g. **Hold**) to address an object, and proceeded with a 3D gesture (**Tilt**, **Shake**, **Move**, etc.) to manipulate this object. Half of the users clearly preferred 2D gestures, few people were using solely 3D gestures, and almost all participants combined gestures for certain tasks.

From the think-aloud analysis we learned that feedback for successful (and unsuccessful) gestures is essential. Also participants wanted an overview of available commands executable on an object or container. The gestures were mostly created through associations with interaction techniques known from other devices and tool. Experiences from the real world were mainly used in case the person did not have an association with any technical context (e.g. "lock" a sound source). Although only one user owned a smartphone, several participants slid their fingers over the imaginary screen to skip through sound sources in a list or scroll up and down (iPhone or Android touchscreen gesture). Other noticeable analogies were based on the users' current usage of traditional desktop GUIs (e.g. x-icon to delete a sound source or the mouse shake to focus on a source). The **Touch**, **DoubleTouch**, and **Point** gestures show strong resemblance to using a remote control or computer mouse (DoubleClick = **DoubleTouch**). We also perceived that users favored reusing a set of basic gestures for different tasks (differentiate by a specific context) or using 'inverse' gestures over having a wide range of unique gestures. An alternative strategy to keep the gesture set small and simple is to use context menus, although this may slow down interaction and require more cognitive attention.

We also observed that participants generally preferred performing discreet gestures instead of very expressive gestures. Compared to the results gained in [1], where a preference of 2D gestures for public scenarios is advised, we identified the same tendency. In addition our participants also favored minimalistic 3D gestures.

CONCLUSION AND FUTURE WORK

Our study provides an overview of gestures users would perform to interact with basic elements of a spatial auditory interface. Users chose gestures based on pre-existing knowledge and the ability to translate experiences from other domains to the domain at hand. When the aim is to design an intuitive and user-centered interface for an auditory interface, we recommend using a small, context related gesture set, supporting gesture inversions for do-undo-commands and supporting gestural analogies from other domains. Clear and distinct feedback to actions and information about available commands is crucial to prevent frustration and to guarantee a successful interaction. Future work is required on good feedback strategies and how to create an easy to learn and memorizable gesture set.

REFERENCES

1. Bhandari, S. and Lim, Y. Exploring gestural mode of interaction with mobile phones. In *Proc. CHI 2008*, ACM Press (2008), 2979-2984.
2. Brewster, S., Lumsden, J., Bell, M., Hall, M., and Tasker, S. Multimodal 'eyes-free' interaction techniques for wearable devices. In *Proc. CHI 2003*, ACM Press (2003), 473-480.
3. Karam, M. and Schraefel, M. C. *A Taxonomy of Gestures in Human Computer Interactions*. Technical Report ECSTR-IAM05-009, Electronics and Computer Science, University of Southampton, 2005.
4. Li, K. A., Baudisch, P., and Hinckley, K. Blindsight: eyes-free access to mobile phones. In *Proc. CHI 2008*, ACM Press (2008), 1389-1398.
5. OpenAL API. www.openal.org.
6. Pirhonen, A., Brewster, S., and Holguin, C. Gestural and audio metaphors as a means of control for mobile devices. In *Proc. CHI 2002*, ACM Press (2002), 291-298.
7. Rico, J. and Brewster, S. 2010. Usable gestures for mobile interfaces: evaluating social acceptability. In *Proc. CHI 2010*, ACM Press (2010), 887-896.
8. Sawhney, N. and Schmandt, C. Nomadic radio: speech and audio interaction for contextual messaging in nomadic environments. In *Proc. ACM Transactions on Comput.-Hum. Interact. 2000*, ACM Press (2000), 353-383.
9. Williamson, J., Murray-Smith, R., and Hughes, S. Shoogle: excitatory multimodal interaction on mobile devices. In *Proc. CHI 2007*, ACM Press (2007), 121-124.

TOUCHtr4ck: Democratic Collaborative Music

Anna Xambó
Music Computing Lab
The Open University
Milton Keynes, UK
a.xambo@open.ac.uk

Robin Laney
Music Computing Lab
The Open University
Milton Keynes, UK
r.c.laney@open.ac.uk

Chris Dobbyn
Music Computing Lab
The Open University
Milton Keynes, UK
c.h.dobbyn@open.ac.uk

ABSTRACT
When electronic musicians compose collaboratively, they typically use their own single-user musical controllers. It may, therefore, be useful to develop novel controllers that support collaborative workflows and democratic principles. After describing the design principles for developing such controllers, we present *TOUCHtr4ck*, a prototype multi-touch system designed to facilitate such democratic relationships. Informal testing has revealed that this approach does facilitate democratic and collaborative music making, and can produce creative musical results.

Author Keywords
Collaboration, HCI, musical interface, tabletop groupware

ACM Classification Keywords
H.5.5 Information Interfaces and Presentation: Sound and Music Computing—*Systems*; H.5.3 Information Interfaces and Presentation: Group and Organization Interfaces—*Collaborative computing*

General Terms
Design, Experimentation

INTRODUCTION
The practice of composing electronic music tends to be an individual activity, even though musical composition and music making may also have a social dimension. Curiously, among the vast market of musical controllers available for musicians, few are designed for facilitating collaboration in the creative process. A study of the compositional processes of electronic musicians [5] found that this community would prefer a free and exploratory approach during the initial stages—when an idea can still change substantially—, which is not addressed by the traditional digital audio workstation (DAW) software they use. Within a spectrum from exploration to linearity in the creative process, interactive composition systems [2] become a trade-off between the two approaches, hence they offer an explorative approach under certain constraints. Using these real-time computer music systems, the process of composing and performing music happens simultaneously. With *Ableton Live*, for example, both processes can become one. But, even though collaborations can emerge from laptop ensembles using this software [7], musical dialogues in real time are more fully exploited by tangible user interfaces (TUI) such as the *reacTable* [11] or the *Squeezables* [20].

TEI'11, January 22–26, 2011, Funchal, Portugal.

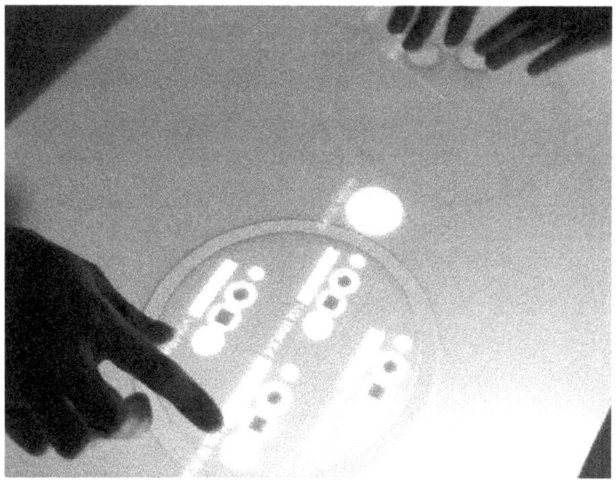

Figure 1. The TOUCHtr4ck prototype.

In our opinion, approaching the aspects that facilitate a musical controller to be more democratic is a key element for successful collaboration[1]. An early exploration of democratic collaborative electronic music making is *Mikrophonie I* (1963) by Stockhausen (reported by Blaine and Fels [18]). This piece is meant to be played by six musicians in three pairs: one pair of percussionists plays a tam-tam instrument; another pair records the resulting sounds with microphones; and the third pair applies filters to the output. Although the musicians follow an instructional score, and thus the performance requires musical expertise, it can be seen as a seminal example of a democratic piece because each performer's musical influence depends on the rest of the team.

We think there is a need to address more thoroughly the design of interfaces that enhance these democratic, collabora-

[1] The term *democratic collaborative music* is used to reference the process of creating music in collaboration, where all kinds of participants (experts and novices) can shape and dialogue their musical ideas under equal means.

tive musical creative processes. According to [13], interface design can support democratized performances by suggesting processes, environments and relationships. Furthermore, among the different genres, electronic music can be one of the most democratic in terms of the musical knowledge required: the extensive use of digital musical tools has contributed to a new aesthetic that also allows musicians with little technical knowledge to produce music easily, and to create music from novel and experimental processes [4, 1]. In consequence, we have developed *TOUCHtr4ck*—a multi-touch tabletop prototype intended for democratic collaborative music making—with the aim of allowing groups to perform music together in real time using both exploration and discovery (see Figure 1).

In the following section, some background on both computer-supported collaborative work and collaborative musical experiences is given. After that, an overview of some design principles for democratic collaborative music making are presented. Next, the design process for the prototype is introduced: concept, interface design, implementation and interaction mappings. Finally, an informal test of the approach is discussed and future work highlighted.

RELATED WORK

Computer-supported collaborative work

Interactive tabletops have been studied within the field of computer-supported collaborative work (CSCW). In the CSCW literature, facilitating the awareness of others [8] and enriching of existing work processes [6] are factors that have been considered when approaching co-located collaboration. Thus, our approach focuses on enhancing the workflow of collaborative music creation with special attention to facilitating communication among musicians by supporting the awareness of others.

Collaborative musical experiences

Collaborative musical experiences do not necessarily imply a democratic setting. In the *iltur* system, for example, expert musicians keep playing their own traditional instruments whereas novice musicians can record and manipulate these recordings in real time; this tends to mean that the collaboration is hierarchical [19]. Another example are *Sound Toys*, which are playful, explorative and collaborative musical objects designed specifically for novices [17]. The *reacTable* [11] or the *Squeezables* [20] propose to attract both novices and experts alike, although either its interface complexity or simplicity can bias. According to [14], attracting both experts and novices alike implies keeping a balance between ease of use and constraints more suitable to novices, with the presence of sufficient musical features to allow personal musical expressivity more suitable to experts. *TOUCHtr4ck* is intended to be a playful and exploratory musical controller that facilitates democratic relationships between performers. Thus, we are interested in providing both a highly engaging social experience, but also a satisfactory musical one.

DESIGN PRINCIPLES

In the literature on musical interfaces, design principles for musical controllers have been outlined with the aim of improving the experience of playing interactive composition systems [2], either individually or in collaboration. Jordà [9, 10] points out the relationship between new musical controllers and new music-making paradigms. According to Winkler [22], interactive music interfaces must provide feedback and interaction support. Cook [3] suggests some artistic principles such as "instant music, subtlety later" or "make a piece, not an instrument or a controller". Some of these are particularly relevant in collaborative interaction, e.g., the use of certain metaphors such as "catch and throw" facilitates the idea of a dialogue between several musicians, in which the musical material is received, modified and sent in real time [21]. In the context of democratic collaborative network music, new design principles related to engagement have also been recommended, such as facilitating the awareness of contributions, relationships between performers or dialogues mediated by technology [13]. Musical tabletops present an ideal setting for collaborative engagement because they make possible visual feedback, individual vs. shared spaces, and real-time multi-dimensional interaction [10, 14].

DESIGN PROCESS

Concept

The design of *TOUCHtr4ck* has been informed by our previous experience of designing and evaluating similar prototypes [14, 23]. The *tr4ck* prototype was designed for a PDA as an exploratory musical controller for recording and manipulating up to four sounds in sync. It provided positive results in terms of ease of use, productivity and satisfactory musical output, although it was limited to a single player [23]. In [14] we developed and evaluated a minimal tabletop interface for collaborative music making using multi-touch interaction. The prototype evaluated in this study proved to be useful for collaborative engagement, although more musical features, awareness and control features (e.g. individual vs. shared controls) were requested by users. Thus the question arose of whether a more democratic collaborative musical controller, combining the functionality of the former with the collaborative music making aspects of the latter, was possible.

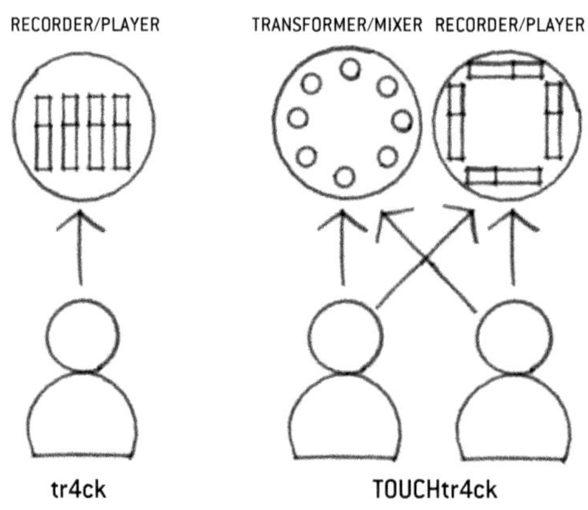

Figure 2. Design process for TOUCHtr4ck.

According to the previous experience reported above, and considering the design principles cited in the previous section, we established three main objectives for the design of a democratic collaborative musical controller, the *TOUCHtr4ck* prototype. Firstly, it should be exploratory, similar to the single-user *tr4ck*, by allowing instant and real-time shaping of unexpected musical ideas (in contrast to a more linear and sequential approach). Secondly, the interface design should invite democratic and interdependent collaboration, similar to *Mikrophonie I*, where there is a real-time division of labour, between producing, recording and transforming sounds (see Figure 2). Thirdly, the interface design should provide collaborative engagement, such as in our previous minimal tabletop interface. For that purpose, a similar setting of tabletop multi-touch interaction should be maintained. Accordingly, the interface design should be easy to use, but would incorporate both discrete and continuous actions in order to engage either experts or novices.

Consistent with these three objectives, the *TOUCHtr4ck* prototype allows musicians to record up to four samples and mix these collaboratively on a multi-touch tabletop surface. The prototype offers a plug and play approach, where sounds can be recorded and modified, and disruption of the workflow between editing and mixing is avoided by looping all tracks and showing changes in real time, which seems ideal for exploration. Democratic collaboration is supported by dividing these two main tasks into two modules which can be executed in parallel, and the possibility of modifying others' contributions. Additionally, the awareness of others is provided by real-time visual feedback. Finally, collaborative engagement seems to be associated to the personal motivation and the control level of the interface, hence using basic UI controllers (both discrete and continuous such as knobs, sliders or buttons) is intended to afford ease of learning and use at a general level.

Interface design
The interface design displays a number of circles with different UI controllers inside each (see Figure 3). Each circle represents a task such as recording/playing or transforming/mixing. The large circle on the right of Figure 3 shows four tracks. For each track it is possible to play, record or stop a sample, as well as to modify its volume. The large circle on the left allows participants to modify global controls such as the global volume and to manipulate a set of filters such as band-pass filter or reverb, among others. Filters affect only the tracks that are in play mode, and they are applied in sequence to the global output. Given that all the tracks are looping, and start at the same time, the circle in the middle indicates the start of the global loop with a bright yellow light pulse. This circle also permits changes in the global pitch shift.

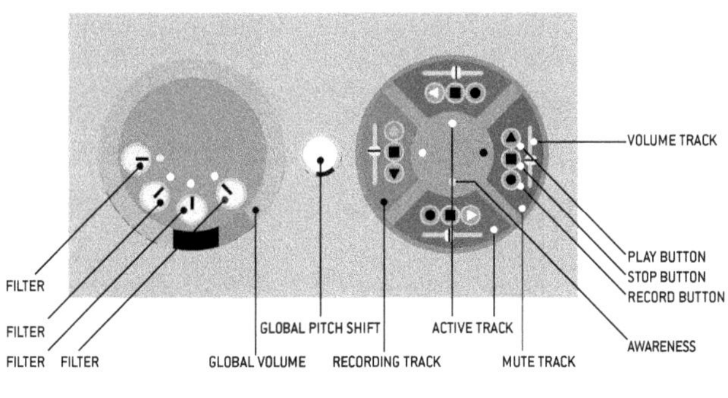

Figure 3. Interface design.

Implementation
The *TOUCHtr4ck* prototype was developed using open source tools. The computer vision framework reacTIVision [12] was used for the multi-touch finger tracking, and the table hardware (e.g. infrared illumination, camera and projector) was built according to the requirements of this framework. The audio software was built using the programming language for real-time audio synthesis SuperCollider 3 [15], and the graphics and control management with the programming language Processing [16]. Thus, the prototype is divided into model, view and control modules: the sound synthesis engine (e.g. playing, recording and transforming sound) is defined and managed in SuperCollider (the model), whilst the graphic interface and the interaction control of the TUIO messages sent by reacTIVision are managed in Processing (the view and the controller).

Interaction mappings
Three main interaction factors are identified for a democratic collaborative music making on multi-touch surfaces: awareness of others' actions; modifiability of others' actions; and the distinction of users' musical expertise.

Awareness
The awareness of others' actions is supported by the division of labour incorporated in the interface design. Each of the large circles is devoted to either editing or mixing, so its proximity to the subject indicates who is in charge of each task. Moreover, audiovisual feedback indicates the state of the tracks or filters, that is, whether they are mute, active or selected.

Modifiability
Modiability of others' actions is allowed through the use of the shared controls such as the global pitch shift. In addition, the division between the tasks implies that users can only have partial control of the musical result.

Expertise
Each user is able to add or reduce the number of tracks or filters in order to adapt to his or her expertise, within the limits of the interface design. This flexibility permits novices and experts alike to use the system, whilst maintaining, as much as possible, a democratic setting.

DISCUSSION AND FUTURE WORK
Informal testing was done with two expert musicians using the prototype as a proof-of-concept. The two participants formerly played in a band together, and currently they make electronic music using mainly DAW workstations, along

with individual musical controllers. Both interacted with the prototype for an interval of ten minutes. A playful attitude was observed during the whole session. Moreover, the musicians contributed similarly, using both shared and individual controls. After the session, an informal discussion was carried out, in which both described the prototype as an experimental tool not fully controllable, and which provided unexpected results that can be useful when composing music. They both agreed on the ease of use of the prototype, although commented about the need of more accuracy when recording.

In summary, we have provided a set of design principles for democratic collaborative music on interactive systems, and we have built a prototype upon these. After an informal evaluation, promising results have been obtained: Firstly, collaborative experience has been facilitated by awareness and modifiability of others' actions using a shareable interface; and secondly, experts found the musical controller playful and experimental, an approach which tends to be offered to novices only. Future work will involve, on the one hand, carrying out a formal testing with more users, in order to strengthen the design concept; and, on the other hand, to improve the prototype by providing more accuracy of control, more support for relationships between performers and more awareness of contributions. Furthermore, the benefits of a flexible design should be examined precisely. As a final remark, this approach specifically enhances the relationships between performers because collaborative work processes are facilitated which, in turn, affect the musical output.

ACKNOWLEDGEMENTS

We thank Gerard Roma, Josep Guasch, Andrew Milne and Adam Linson for their expert contributions; and the Open University for the opportunity to carry out this study.

REFERENCES

1. K. Cascone. The aesthetics of failure: "Post-digital" tendencies in contemporary computer music. *Computer Music Journal*, 24(4):12–18, 2000.
2. J. Chadabe. Interactive composing: An overview. *Computer Music Journal*, 8(1):22–28, 1984.
3. P. Cook. Principles for designing computer music controllers. In *Proc. NIME '01*, pages 1–4, 2001.
4. C. Cox and D. Warner. *Audio Culture: Readings in Modern Music*. Continuum, New York, 2004.
5. S. Gelineck and S. Serafin. From idea to realization - understanding the compositional processes of electronic musicians. In *Proc. Audio Mostly 2009*, 2009.
6. J. Halloran, Y. Rogers, T. Rodden, and I. Taylor. Creating new user experiences to enhance collaboration. In *Proc. INTERACT'03*, pages 479 – 486, 2003.
7. S. Heinz and S. O'Modhrain. Designing a shareable musical TUI. In *Proc. NIME '10*, pages 339–342, 2010.
8. E. Hornecker, P. Marshall, N. S. Dalton, and Y. Rogers. Collaboration and interference: Awareness with mice or touch input. In *Proc. CSCW '08*, pages 167–176. ACM, 2008.
9. S. Jordà. Fmol: Toward user-friendly, sophisticated new musical instruments. *Computer Music Journal*, 26(3):23–39, 2002.
10. S. Jordà. On stage: the reactable and other musical tangibles go real. *International Journal of Arts and Technology*, 1(3–4):268–287, 2008.
11. S. Jordà, G. Geiger, M. Alonso, and M. Kaltenbrunner. The reacTable: Exploring the synergy between live music performance and tabletop tangible interfaces. In *Proc. TEI'07*, 2007.
12. M. Kaltenbrunner and R. Bencina. reacTIVision: A computer-vision framework for table-based tangible interaction. In *Proc. TEI '07*, pages 69–74. ACM, 2007.
13. D. Kim-Boyle. Network musics - Play, engagement and the democratization of performance. In *Proc. NIME '08*, pages 3–8, 2008.
14. R. Laney, C. Dobbyn, A. Xambó, M. Schirosa, D. Miell, K. Littleton, and S. Dalton. Issues and techniques for collaborative music making on multi-touch surfaces. In *Proc. SMC'10*, pages 146–153, 2010.
15. J. McCartney. Rethinking the computer music language: SuperCollider. *Computer Music Journal*, 26(4):61–68, 2002.
16. C. Reas and B. Fry. *Processing: A Programming Handbook for Visual Designers and Artists*. MIT Press, 2007.
17. D. Robson. PLAY!: Sound toys for non-musicians. *Computer Music Journal.*, 26(3):50–61, 2002.
18. B. Tina and F. Sidney. Collaborative musical experiences for novices. *Journal of New Music Research*, 32(4):411 – 428(18), December 2003.
19. G. Weinberg and S. Driscoll. iltur: Connecting novices and experts through collaborative improvisation. In *Proc. NIME '05*, pages 17–22, 2005.
20. G. Weinberg and S.-L. Gan. The Squeezables: Toward an expressive and interdependent multi-player musical instrument. *Computer Music Journal*, 25(2):37–45, 2001.
21. D. Wessel and M. Wright. Problems and prospects for intimate musical control of computers. *Computer Music Journal*, 26(3):11–22, 2002.
22. T. Winkler. *Composing Interactive Music*. MIT Press, Cambridge, MA, USA, 1998.
23. A. Xambó. Interfaces for sketching musical compositions. Master's thesis, Universitat Pompeu Fabra, 2008.

New Technologies for Dynamic Tattoo Art

Breno Bitarello
Superior School of Industrial Design
State University of Rio de Janeiro
Rua Evaristo da Veiga 95, Rio de Janeiro, RJ 20031-040
brenobitarello@gmail.com

Hugo Fuks
Department of Informatics
Pontifical Catholic University of Rio de Janeiro
Marquês de São Vicente 225, Gávea. Rio de Janeiro, RJ 22453-900
hugo@inf.puc-rio.br

João Queiroz
Institute of Arts and Design / Graduate Program in Communication (Federal University of Juiz de Fora)
Campus Universitário S/N, Martelos. Juiz de Fora, MG 36036-900
queirozj@pq.cnpq.br

ABSTRACT
With the development of new technologies, new dynamic epithelial artifacts (*new tattoos*) are designed, enabling new types of situated and embodied multimodal communication. *New tattoos* (NTs) turn the skin into a source of dynamic and reversible inscription, possibly responsive to fine-grained organic variations, and dependent on oriented local perturbation. As new aesthetic-cognitive artifacts, NTs alter the operational and semiotic dimension of the skin, transforming it into a new frame of interactive interface. This paper aims at introducing some epithelial prostheses based on new biocompatible materials and technologies.

Author Keywords
Dynamic tattoo, design, biotechnology, cognitive extension.

ACM Classification Keywords
H5.m. Information interfaces and presentation (e.g., HCI): Miscellaneous.

General Terms
Design

INTRODUCTION
The design and application of new tattoo technologies has not changed dramatically since its origins. But things have altered recently. With the development of new technologies, new dynamic epithelial devices and artifacts are designed, enabling new types of multimodal situated and embodied communication. By "dynamic epithelial devices" we mean any dynamic (potentially changing in time) artifact intentionally inscribed or attached to the skin. There are projects associated with the use of new bio-technological devices, as well as with new synthesis of materials and new techno-scientific applications. These artifacts will convert the almost static aesthetic-technologic tattoo field into a new domain of experimental design of interfaces, improving on a new collection of non-verbal communication, and creating new forms of situated and embodied communication.

STATIC NATURE?
Any approach on the development of dynamic tattoos, based on new techno-scientific methods and models, should initiate on its own support -- the skin -- and the new available biologically compatible technologies. In a simplified form, tattoo is an invasive plastic inscription performed on the skin. The pigment is introduced in the dermis (second layer of the skin) (Figure 1), through micro-incisions made in different ways. Although the skin intensely renews itself because of the constant cells replacement, it does not absorb the pigments because they are in the dermis within the fibroblasts. Each fibroblast is surrounded by a conjunctive tissue prominent network that holds and immobilizes the cell. The elimination of the pigments particles is prevented due to the basal intact membrane restoration [3, 15]. (Many evidences indicate that in the very beginning, reverse attempts to the tattoo process were practiced. Even very old mummies have traces of attempts to remove the pigment inserted into the skin).

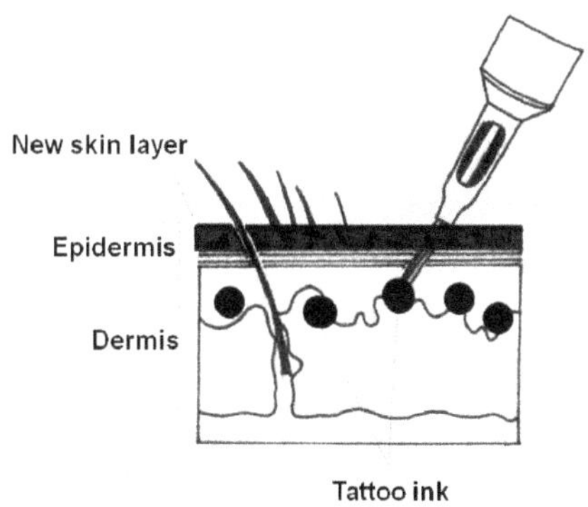

Figure 1. Tattoo Process.

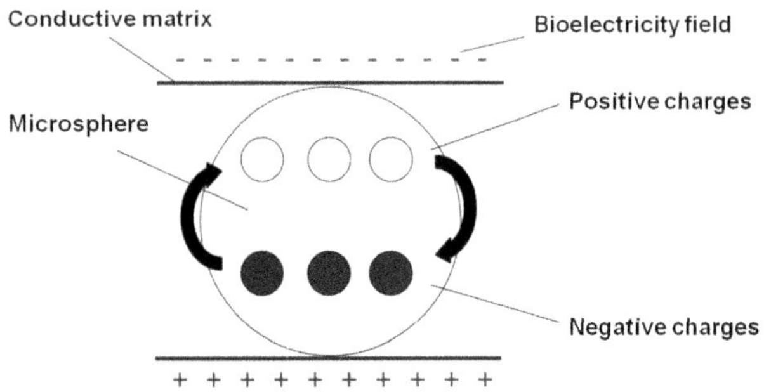

Figure 2. Electronic-ink, adapted from [13].

DIGITAL INK

E-ink, digital ink and electronic ink, are flexible matrix of pixels which are introduced in the skin. Through small surgery, encapsulated microspheres are embedded in the skin. The charge contained in these spheres is thrown in response to organic changes [5, 13]. As the body is both an electricity producer and a conductor, the charges can be attracted or repelled by the bioelectricity field, generating the images in the skin. The microspheres are between two conductive matrixes of bioelectricity; within them there are suspended charges in a translucent liquid [13, 22]. When the bioelectric field is generated and conducted to the matrixes through the body, it can attract or repel the spheres' charges and produce the images. The energy consumption of these inks is very low, and it should be possible to keep these artifacts in operation solely on the bioelectricity of the body [5] (Figure 2).

Companies are developing researches to design new tattoo forms based on digital inks. The pioneer was Philips Design, which included a new tattoo concept in its Design Probes [20]. The company develops a tattoo which is emotion and mechano-responsive (reagent to touch on the skin). The proposal is presented in the video "Electronic Tattoo" available on the company's website [20] (Figure 2). The video shows the dynamic displacement of a tattoo under the skin, based on positive feedback between two young people. When the girl's hand slips on the skin surface of her companion, images are produced. These tattoos should be able to respond not only to touch, but also by neural and endocrinal variations, perhaps even contextual-environmental.

LED TATTOOS

A recent paper at MIT Technology Review [10] describes a new type of ultrathin silicon transistor that can be incorporated into a soluble biomaterial film based in silk. The material has biocompatibility, elasticity and various resistance taxes. Researchers are developing ultrathin LEDs (light-emitting diodes) onto soluble water and biocompatible silk substrates that might act as photonic tattoos [10, 12]. These tattoos show blood-sugar readings, allowing the mapping of a great range of physiological functions. Medical applications of these transistors has been developed by researchers at Beckman Institute, at the University of Illinois and Tufts University [10].

The research has applications in controlling the Parkinson's symptoms. The applied electrodes allow deep neural stimuli due to the possibility of deep access to the nervous tissue layers. Experiments are successfully conducted with animal models (mice). Much like electronic tattoos, LED tattoos can be programmed with an external device enabling the design of complex visual patterns.

DATTOOS

The designer Hartmuth Esslinger created the "Dattoo" concept [7]. This is a tattoo that enables the host DNA reading to be activated. Dattoo's goal is to be performed both by minimally invasive methods as with recyclable materials. Only the sensors are inserted under the skin. The interface is printed as an interactive adhesive that enables both its easy application and removal. The display is prototyped (printed) on an adhesive surface that can be aggregated to the skin for a specified period of time, which allows the subject to have it removed or not.

OTHER TECHNOLOGIES

Researches focused on printing silicon transistors on flexible materials allow great advances in the design of new extremely thin and flexible displays. In the same way, researches of biocompatible devices for application in health and engineering, like biosensors and nanotransistors enables the development of technological artifacts (flexible displays, transistors and sensors based on biomaterials) that can be inserted and applied to the human body without harming the health.

Researchers at the Beckman Institute and Tufts University, have developed studies on ultrathin devices over flexible silk substrates [10]. The aim of these researches is the development of biodegradable circuits to enable better neural interfaces with transistors and LED tattoos to provide dynamic epithelial devices. Other possibilities to make these interactive displays are in progress. Several investigations have been developed, such as the production of extremely thin and flexible displays.

Researchers at HP Labs created, through silicon transistors printed on top of plastic, a flexible color display which could appear in future color e-readers and tablet computers [1]. HP is scaling up a process for making silicon electronics on rolls of plastic through silicon transistors, which can switch on and off pixels on the display [11]. In the same way, researchers at Samsung and Sungkyunkwan University develop flexible touch screens made with printed graphene (Figure 4) [2, 8]. This flexible graphene sheet with silver electrodes printed that can be used as a touch screen when connected to control software on a computer. This research can also results in sheets of atom-thick carbon made displays that are extremely fast.

Scientists from Empa and the Max Planck Institute for Polymer Research also developed researches with graphene transistors, corroborating the fact that graphene ribbons are considered to be strong candidates for future electronics applications [17].

Researchers at MIT are developing multifunctional fibers that act as sensors carrying light and sensing pressure to be used for medical imaging and structural monitoring [8]. Nicholas Kotov (University of Michigan) develops textiles coated with carbon nanotubes which form electronic sensors that look and feel like ordinary cotton [18]. Babak Parviz (University of Washington) develops piezoelectric materials, which produce an electric current when subjected to mechanical pressure [6]. Embedded technology promises not only to provide data wherever and whenever we need it but to transmit real-time data about ourselves [6]. The vast amount of research and development with promising initial results enables the future development of a new dynamic and interactive tattoo.

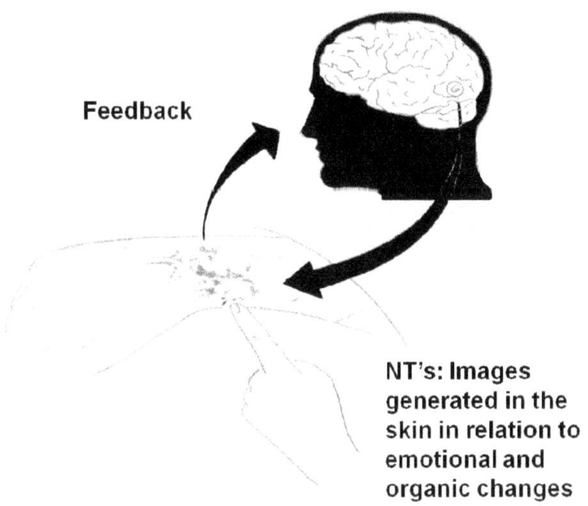

Figure 3. NT's: Image reacting to neural and endocrinal variations.

TECHNO TATTOOS

What we call here NTs (Figure 3) (dynamic and interactive images generated on the skin) can be developed from technological adhesives, (i.e., displays that can be aggregated to the skin without invasive procedures). These adhesives contain tiny sensors that allow the uptake of organic and environmental variations. The technology is already in development [1, 8, 9, 11]. Sensors detect organic variations and send data making use of wireless and body area network (BAN) for technological devices [4, 13, 19, 21]. Through skin bio-conductivity, organic variations patterns are established. A way to measure these values is through Galvanic Skin Response (GSR): small variations in the skin's bio-electricity caused by the sympathetic nervous system are captured between the electrodes inserted into the skin and are, thus, calculated; emotional changes can be identified [16] and translated into dynamic images generated on the skin.

The sensors in these devices capture changes such as temperature (bodily and environmental), pressure, brightness, movement variations, and so on. This data is captured as inputs and, in response, outputs are generated in the form of interactive images on the skin.

CONCLUSION

The skin is open to a new collection of interface design. It's a reasonable assumption that new forms of interpersonal relations will be established due to the creation of new patterns of communication associated with new ways of reading the organic states (neural, endocrinal systems) through interfaces based on quasi-automatic feedback. The development of a new collection of prostheses and aesthetic-cognitive artifacts should enable new interaction modes with the environment and its components. By aesthetic-cognitive prostheses and artifacts we mean any devices that extend some cognitive ability related to aesthetic fruition. The impact of developing technologies for the conception of "new" forms of organic interventions will have ramifications in unpublished areas, allowing the use of new interactive epithelial prostheses (*responsive dynamic tattoos*), and creating new paths for embodied communication. Such artifacts should not be analyzed separately, but in dense interaction with subject and complex environment. In subsequent works, we will analyze possible simulations of these technologies, developing alternatives and results for practical researches that have already begun exploring ethic considerations and its future context of use in terms of communication, design and arts. Our main purpose here is to present a preliminary approach of some of the materials and technologies to be used in the near future to design and produce new epithelial prostheses.

REFERENCES

1. A Flexible Color Display. http://www.technologyreview.com/computing/25138/page1/
2. Bigger, Stretchier Graphene. http://www.technologyreview.com/computing/21964/?a=f
3. Tatuagens, tinta e pele. http://www.drashirleydecampos.com.br/noticias/13072
4. Cherukuri, S., Venkatasubramanian, K. and Gupta, S.K.S. Biosec: A Biometric Based Approach for Securing Communication in Wireless Networks of Biosensors Implanted in the Human Body. *Proc. of the 2003 International Conference on Parallel Processing Workshops*.

5. Digital displays for your body. http://tinyurl.com/2dg2jab.
6. Embedded Technologies: Power From the People. http://tinyurl.com/2bc3sf2.
7. Esslinger, H. Dattoos. http://www.frogdesign.com/case-study/dattoos.html.
8. Fabricating a Multifunctional Fiber. http://www.technologyreview.com/computing/25780/?nlid=3226
9. Flexible Touch Screen Made with Printed Graphene. http://mobile.technologyreview.com/computing/25633/
10. Implantable Silicon-Silk Electronics. http://www.technologyreview.com/computing/23847/page1/.
11. Inexpensive, Unbreakable Displays http://www.technologyreview.com/computing/25561/
12. Kim, D., Kim, Y., Amsden, J., Panilaitis, B., Kaplan, D.L., Omenetto, F.G., Zakin, M.R. and Rogers, J.A. Silicon electronics on silk as a path to bioresorbable, implantable devices. APPLIED PHYSICS LETTERS, 95 (2009).
13. Levy, D. H.; Cherry, J. F. Changeable tattoos. C09D 11/00 (20060101). EUA, 09/280,496. 31 Mar. 2001, 30 Mar. 1999. USPTO Patent Full-Text and Image DatabasePatent, United States: United States Patent.
14. Liolios, C., Doukas, C., Fourlas, G. and Maglogiannis, I. An Overview of Body Sensor Networks in Enabling Pervasive Healthcare and Assistive Environments. *Proc. PETRA' 10 conf.*
15. Morsy, H., Mogensen, M., Thrane, L. and Jemec, G.B.E. Imaging of Intradermal Tattoos by Optical Coherence Tomography. Skin Research and Technology. 13, 444-448 (2007).
16. Madam, A.; Caneel, R. and Pentland, A. GroupMedia: Distributed Multi-modal Interfaces. State College: Pennsylvania, USA: 2004.
17. Nanoribbons for graphene transistors. www.eurekalert.org
18. Nanotubes Come into Fashion. http://www.technologyreview.com/energy/22448/
19. Pantelopoulos, A.; Bourbakis. A Survey on Wearable Sensor-Based Systems for Health Monitoring and Prognosis. IEEE *Trans. Syst., Man Cybern.-Part C: Appl. Rev., vol. 40, n. 1.*
20. Philips Design Probes. http://www.design.philips.com/probes/index.page.
21. Post, R., Reynolds, M., Gray, M., Paradiso, J. and Gershenfeld, N. Intrabody Buses for Data and Power. Phisics and Media. MIT Media Laboratory: Cambridge (1997).
22. Technology (E-INK). http://www.eink.com/technology/howitworks.html

Grocery Hunter: A Fun Mobile Game for Children to Combat Obesity

Hyungsin Kim [1,2], Anya Kogan[4], Chandan Dasgupta[5], Michael Misha Novitzky[2], and Ellen Yi-Luen Do[1,2,3]

GVU Center[1]
College of Computing[2] & College of Architecture[3]
Georgia Institute of Technology
Atlanta, GA, USA

HUGE[4]
New York, USA

Learning Sciences Research Institute[5]
University of Illinois at Chicago
Chicago, IL, USA

{hyungsin, misha}@gatech.edu, akogan@hugeinc.com, cdasgu2@uic.edu, ellendo@gatech.edu

ABSTRACT

This paper presents a handheld mobile game, Grocery Hunter that encourages children to take on healthy eating habits. Children can use a pocket PC to play the Grocery Hunter game to learn about food nutrition and healthy food choices. Childhood obesity in the United States has already reached epidemic proportions. The best way to help children attain and maintain healthy weight is through physical activity and nutritious eating. Our design addresses nutrition directly by teaching children healthy eating habits using an interactive game in the grocery store.

Author Keywords

Interactive design, mobile devices for children, health communications, just-in-time learning

ACM Classification Keywords

H.5.1 Multimedia Information Systems

General Terms

Human Factors, Experimentation, Design.

INTRODUCTION

The Grocery Hunter is a mobile system which teaches children to make smart choices at the grocery store while they are shopping with their parents. The prevalence of obesity in the United States has skyrocketed in the last 30 years [5]. In particular, childhood obesity in the United States has already reached epidemic proportions with 17% of children being classified as overweight [6]. Robinson and Killen [7] describe the major reasons for the increase in childhood obesity are the lack of exercise, consumption of poorer-quality food, excess television watching, and cultural values. Obese children are less likely to exercise and are more likely to have high blood pressures which in adulthood have shown to correlate with heart disease, stroke, and diabetes in middle adulthood [4]. Not only are the children who are overweight or obese affected but society is financially impacted with the health costs associated with the complications of these medical conditions. It is crucial to work on both prevention and treatment of child obesity. Thus, our design focuses on encouraging healthy eating habits in school age children.

TEI'11, January 22–26, 2011, Funchal, Portugal.

The target users for the system are children ages from 7 to 11. This period in child development is called middle childhood because it occurs in between early childhood and adolescence. It is also referred to as the school years because it is at this point in their development when they are attending elementary school. In general, children of this age group are capable of self-care such as dressing themselves, brushing their teeth, and washing themselves. This age group can entertain themselves. Their reading levels vary greatly from barely being able to read and write simple sentences to being able to read small novels. The children in this age range physically grow at a steady rate. A typical 10 year old will weigh 70 pounds and be 4 ½ feet tall. In general, a child will gain 5 to 7 pounds while increasing in height by 2 inches a year [2]. A child is considered overweight if they are up to twenty percent above what the ideal weight is for their age and height and are considered obese if they pass the twenty percent threshold. More specifically, a ten-year old child is more at risk for becoming an overweight adult if they are already obese than whether or not their parents were obese. This suggests that intervention in this age group will have everlasting effects.

DESIGN

The Grocery Hunter is a mobile gaming system which teaches children to make smart nutritional choices. There are several studies about using games to teach children how to eat the right food [1, 3]. The Grocery Hunter is used by kids when accompanying their parents on shopping trips. The system provides the child with a clue about a healthy grocery store item located in the vicinity of the unit, thus keeping the child near their parents and not interfering with the parents' shopping tasks. Once the child has found what they think is the appropriate item, they simply scan the item with the Grocery Hunter. If their choice was correct, the system confirms and provides nutritional information for that item. Otherwise, it indicates that the response was incorrect and provides them with an additional clue.

Advantages of the system design as well as the game flow diagram are described below.

- Directly addresses obesity: The Grocery Hunter directly addresses the objective of battling childhood obesity by encouraging healthy eating habits. While the children are searching for healthy items in the grocery store, they are either learning new information about healthy foods or are reinforcing prior knowledge. By encouraging children in this manner, they may increase the amount of nutritious food purchased and therefore consumed.
- Grow to be health conscious adults: Nutritionally educated children will grow into nutritionally conscious adults. In turn, they will be more likely to purchase and eat more nutritious food.
- Education through a game: The system educates the children about nutritious foods and their benefits by using gaming technology with which they become actively engaged. This type of system is a natural extension of a child's inclination for play.
- Only focus on healthy food: This system does not harp on the negative 'junk' food. Instead, it includes solely nutritious foods. This may help shift children's attention away from junk food and towards healthy food in a nonabrasive fashion.

USER SCENARIO

The following narrative describes a Grocery Hunter usage scenario in a grocery store.

Mrs. Marcy Gray has just picked up her daughter, Jane, from after-school care. She knows that her refrigerator is near empty at home and needs to stop by the grocery store before driving home. She usually tries to leave Jane with a babysitter during these trips, but could not do so today. She begrudgingly stops by the grocery store with Jane. Jane is already beginning to whine, as she hates sitting still in the cart while her mom looks through the aisles for Jane seems like an eternity. However, today is different. As Mrs. Gray enters the store, a grocery clerk politely offers a digital toy, called Grocery Hunter, for her daughter. Mrs. Gray accepts. She looks briefly at it, and then hands it to her daughter to figure out how it works. Accustomed to mobile toys, her daughter quickly takes the device and enters her age to begin. As Mrs. Gray is wheeling the cart through the vegetable aisle the device prompts Jane to look for an orange vegetable that is good for her eyes. Jane sees an apple and points the Grocery Hunter at it. The device responds, "Nice try, but this is an apple. It is great for your teeth. Would you like another hint about the orange vegetable?" Jane rejects the help and continues to point at other foods until she finally locates the carrots. The avatar congratulates her on the find and asks if she would like to play again. Jane agrees. As she plays round after round of this digital scavenger hunt, she barely notices the time pass. Soon, her mom is checking out and they are ready to go home. Mrs. Gray drops off the device at the checkout making a note to herself to be sure to use the device again next *time*.

PROTOTYPE IMPLEMENTATION

For prototyping purposes, a Pocket PC was used running an interactive program developed with Adobe Flash. The user interacts with the program through the touch screen. The system is geared towards children between 7 and 11 years old. Figure 1 left shows the startup screen of the Grocery Hunter game displayed in a handheld mobile device, and Figure 1 right shows one example quest that ask the children to "Go and find the orange vegetable that is good for your eyes" in the Grocery Hunter game.

Figure 1. Grocery Hunter Screenshot

SPECIFIC JUSTIFICATION FOR PROTOTYPING

There are several aspects of the prototype implementation that were chosen in order to appeal to the target audience (7-11 years of age) more effectively.

- Cartoon-like look and feel: The cartoons used in the design were meant to appeal to children within the target age range.
- Identifiable avatar: During consultation with members of the Cartoon Network, it was suggested that the main avatar in the Grocery Hunter be a popular cartoon character Bloo from their show 'Foster's Home for Imaginary Friends.' It was believed that this would allow children to quickly identify and thus enjoy using the Grocery Hunter.
- Adobe Flash: Adobe Flash was chosen for the development of the Grocery Hunter prototype for several reasons. Aesthetically, it was able to support the cartoon look and feel. Functionally, it supported the desired touch screen. Finally, the team members had previous experience using Flash, thus reducing overall implementation time.
- Pocket PC: The Pocket PC was the best touch screen hardware available for implementing our prototype at the time. The Pocket PC allows for a responsive system that is predictable given its onscreen mapping of buttons with overlapping text. Additionally, the Pocket PC has multiple methods of communication with other hardware devices such as USB, Bluetooth, and Wi-Fi which makes it ideal if a situation requires communication with a server unit.

USABILITY TESTING METHODS

Usability testing consisted of observation of the system usage as well as pre- and post- opinion surveys from both children and parents. Here, we describe our participants, environment, and procedure. For our preliminary user study, we recruited 6 children and their respective 6 parents for a total of 12 participants. All participation was voluntary. All child participants were between 7 and 11-years-old. Parents also participated by watching their children play, listening to our explanation of the final prototype, and then completing a questionnaire.

Grocery Hunter is designed for use in a real grocery store which has plenty of items children want to eat. However, usability testing in real grocery stores was impractical within the context of this project and at this preliminary stage. Thus, we created an artificial store outside of a local Jujutsu studio where kids took classes. We placed a set of groceries on a table. They included items for which the children had to search in the game, as well as other foods including healthy and non-healthy options to act as a distraction. The extra amount of food added realistic complexity to a task that was outside of its intended environment (grocery store). Having put the table outside in a public place, we also simulated the distractions that are found in an authentic grocery store. While running the test, one experimenter walked with the child, while another videotaped the screens and the third stayed with the parents. Figure 2 shows how a child used the game during the study.

PROCEDURE

The children received instructions from an experimenter on how to play with the Grocery Hunter. Parents were encouraged to observe their child, but were encouraged to abstain from aiding them. They were told that the intention was to study the child's individual interaction with the system. In a real scenario, some parents would help the child with the game, while others would not. Since we were testing only a small number of participants, we needed to minimize the number of independent variables in our system in order to obtain meaningful results. Therefore, we chose to control for parent intervention. We set up a video-recording of the experiment in order to capture each child's finger movements on the game screen as well as their overall body movement as they searched for the proper foods on the table.

Recording this behavior allowed us further analysis after the experiment itself, avoiding sole reliance on the behaviors that we were able to capture in our notes while on-site. Finger movements can be a good indicator of participant's mental perception of the system. For instance, if we saw them wavering between two buttons on the screen, we could hypothesize that the functionality of the two buttons was difficult to understand and predict. The body movements could also be an indicator of the difficulty of the clues.

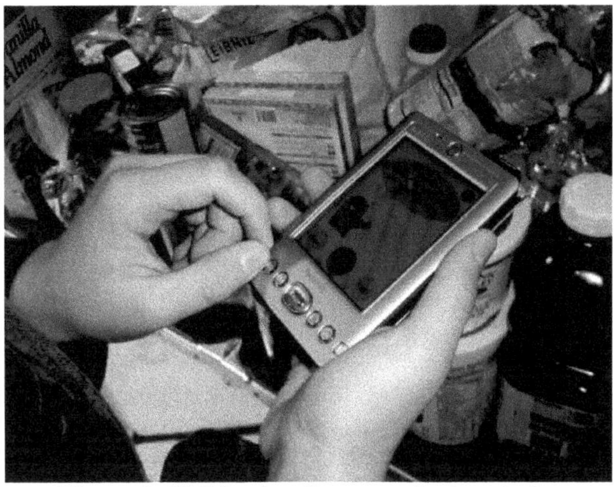

Figure 2. Child using the game during study

If the child walked back and forth along the table several times, it is likely that they did not know which food to choose. During the active portion of this experiment, we were observing, taking notes, and videotaping the participants at the same time. We did not have the child think aloud, as that may have been confusing for them due to their young age and lack of experience with such protocol. However, detailed observations were noted during each task. Children were encouraged to complete the tasks on their own without asking anyone for help. If questions arose, we encouraged them to think through the solution for themselves and we only intervened when absolutely necessary. Once intervention had begun, we gave them minimal hints to the solution to avoid giving out answers until no other alternative was possible. In a real scenario, the designers would not be present to explain their products to users. Therefore, we wanted to see how the child would use the device without us, so as to have the most generalizable test results possible. After each child completed the five clues available, they were given a verbal questionnaire by the same experimenter who followed them around the table. This way, the child was already comfortable with that person and more likely to be complete in their responses. They were given the questions verbally because children were assumed to be unfamiliar with questionnaires and could not be relied upon to answer fully and accurately on their own. By asking the questions aloud, the experimenter could judge the child's comprehension of the topic and elaborate if needed. While the children verbally answered their questions, their parents were given a written questionnaire. In the case of an adult, a written questionnaire was advisable so that the participants were more inclined to be honest when not being directly observed by an experimenter. The entire experiment, including the questionnaires, took each participant 30 minutes.

RESULTS AND DISCUSSION

A specific goal for the Grocery Hunter was to teach children healthier eating habits. The game was intended to be used in the context of a relevant task (i.e. shopping in a grocery store) so that it could be more engaging and meaningful for the children. Had the same information about nutrient content in various food items been given to the children while they were at home, it would not have been as relevant. Hence the key element here is the presence of an educational tool within a relevant environmental context. What this means is that the Grocery Hunter draws its power from its portable design and contextual implementation. All the children who used the Grocery Hunter prototype conveyed to us that they enjoyed using it and thought that it would benefit them by helping them make informed decisions while they were shopping with their parents. That the children enjoyed interacting with the Grocery Hunter is further strengthened by the fact that all the children indicated that they would like to play with it again. This enthusiasm also bears testimony to this design's ability to hold the user's attention. Even the adults who accompanied the children thought that the Grocery Hunter would help them while they were shopping. This kind of help actually happens at two levels – engagement and epistemology. At the level of engagement, the children are busy interacting with the Grocery Hunter and this alleviates the parents' concern of having to "run after" their kids. The game has been designed in such a way that the clues being given are both interesting and informative to the right extent. "Informative to the right extent" means that the correct information is presented in a succinct manner that does not overwhelm or bore the user. The effectiveness of the design is enhanced by the just-in-time manner in which the information is presented. The second level, epistemology, is perhaps more important. Our game teaches the user to "think healthy". As long as the user is inside the store, the game encourages them to think about food items around them from a nutritional perspective instead of the purely flavor-focused perspective. Inherently, we are all impulsive buyers and our decisions on what to buy are influenced a lot by the look-and-feel of the item. If something looks good and appealing, we are inclined to buy it. With kids, especially, various kinds of chocolates, candies, and chips are the hottest to-buy items. The game helps under such circumstances by keeping the user focused on the nutritional perspective of all the items in the store. Association of items with their nutritional advantages and disadvantages tends to carry over to situations outside the grocery store as well. Because of the level and duration of engagement with the game inside the store, the items become more closely associated with their nutritional characteristics. Thus, a carrot becomes more likely to evoke the thought of something orange and good for eyes. We feel that this sort of association will bear a strong influence on the kind of food choices the person makes as they grow up.

CONCLUSION

We learned about the many health hazards of obesity and that the best time to challenge this epidemic is in its infancy, specifically in children between seven and eleven-years-old. Fitness and nutrition are the two key solutions to obesity. Having developed several innovative ideas that focused on either fitness or nutrition, we finally chose a concept that tackled nutrition explicitly. Our solution, the Grocery Hunter, teaches children to make smart eating choices, while growing them into smart adult shoppers and easing the lives of their parents during a shopping trip. The Grocery Hunter exemplifies one of many potential new and interesting ways of placing nutritional facts in front of our users during key decision times. Since some children found the questions presented too hard, while others found them too easy, we think that creating an adaptive system would broaden the appeal of the game. We believe that once these and other findings are addressed, the Grocery Hunter has high market potential and would be capable of positively impacting the fight against childhood obesity. In future studies, we plan to develop more game modules that harness the knowledge of additional nutrition specialists. We also intend to explore the relationship between eating behavior changes and game play.

REFERENCES

1. Aoki, N., Ohta, S., Masuda, H., et al. Edutainment Tools for Initial Education of Type-1 Diabetes Mellitus: Initial Diabetes Education with Fun. *Studies in Health Technology and Informatics, 107(Pt 2)*, IOS Press (2004), 855-859.
2. Berger, K. S. *The Developing Person through Childhood and Adolescence*. Worth Publishers, 2003.
3. Engvall, J. and McCarthy, A.M. Innovative approaches for teaching children with chronic conditions. *Journal of Pediatric Health Care, 10,* 5 (1996), 239-242.
4. Freedman, D., Dietz, W., Srinivasan, S. and Berenson, F. The Relation of Overweight to Cardiovascular Risk Factors Among Children and Adolescents: The Bogalusa Heart Study. *Pediatrics, 103*, 6 (1999), 1175-1182.
5. How to avoid portion size pitfalls to help manage your weight, May 2007. http://www.cdc.gov/healthyweight/healthy_eating/portion_size.html
6. Huang, T.T. and Horlick M.N. Trends in Childhood Obesity Research: A Brief Analysis of NIH Supported Efforts. *The Journal of Law, Medicine & Ethics*, *35*, 1 (2007), 148-153.
7. Robinson, T. and Killen, J. Obesity Prevention for Children and Adolescents. In *Body Image, Eating Disorders, and Obesity in Youth*, United Book Press (2001), 261-292.

Interaction Mapping affects Spatial Memory and the Sense of Presence when navigating in a Virtual Environment

Hannu Järvinen
Department of Media Technology,
Aalto University School of Science and Technology
Espoo, Finland
hannu.jarvinen@hut.fi

Ulysses Bernardet
Laboratory for Synthetic Perceptive, Emotive and Cognitive Systems (SPECS)
Technology Department, Universitat Pompeu Fabra
Barcelona, Spain
ulysses.bernardet@upf.edu

Paul F.M.J. Verschure
Laboratory for Synthetic Perceptive, Emotive and Cognitive Systems (SPECS)
Technology Department, Universitat Pompeu Fabra
Barcelona, Spain
ICREA, Barcelona, Spain
paul.verschure@upf.edu

ABSTRACT
By their very nature, virtual reality worlds are spatial. Hence, one of the key requirements for virtual reality applications is the possibility to navigate within the virtual world. Previous studies have shown that the characteristics of the device used for navigation, both in terms of the physical properties, and the interaction logic, has effects on the user's experience. The question we address is how does different navigation modes with the same physical interface affect the user's experience. We selected two modes which differed in the way the user's actions were mapped to movements in the virtual environment. To quantify the difference between the two interaction mappings, spatial memory and the subjective sense of presence were compared. The results of our study showed that interaction mapping affects both, spatial memory and presence. Hence, not only the specific physical device but also the way it is used is important for the user's experience and recollection of it. Additionally, we found a correlation between spatial memory and subjective sense of presence, which indicates that the subjective sense of presence can be estimated from the performance in a spatial memory task.

Author Keywords
Navigation; Presence; Spatial Memory; Virtual Environment

ACM Classification Keywords
H.5.2 Information interfaces and presentation: User Interfaces

General Terms
Experimentation, Human Factors, Measurement, Performance.

INTRODUCTION
Virtual Reality (VR) technology, originally used in special applications for small interest groups, is becoming increasingly pervasive. The entertainment industry has embraced VR related technology, for instance in the form of 3D television that immerses the viewer and increases the sense of being part of the depicted scene. More sophisticated VR applications such as games, offer a possibility for active interaction. Here the user can, for example, move a character in a virtual world and interact with objects and other beings. Common to most interactive VR applications is the function to navigate through 3D space. Traditionally, mice, keyboards, and hand-held controllers specifically developed for game consoles, have been used for controlling the navigation. In research, more exotic devices, such as the "Cubic Mouse" [10] that allows the user to intuitively navigate in three-dimensional space have been developed. While the first navigation devices had limited functionality and digital control of the values, devices today have dozens of buttons and analog controls for smooth adjustment of the target values. State-of-the-art devices are not limited to hand-held joysticks and controllers, but comprise a variety of technologies, from pointing devices, gaze directed moving [6], walking-in-place and real walking mapped to virtual walking [19], to "infinite" floors [7]. Navigation by means of walking is frequently seen as the desired mode of interaction, and correspondingly a number of efforts were made to develop such technology [7, 12]. The goal is to offer an interaction system that mimics the way users walk in the real world.

A single user interface can implement a number of navigation modes, i.e. ways in which physical movements are mapped to movements in the virtual environment. Generally, the individual controls of the interaction device can be linked to any command parameters needed for controlling the movement in a virtual environment. Additional factors of the mapping include delay and gain. We will refer to these different modes in which the actions of the user are controlling movement in VR as *interaction mappings*.

Measuring spatial memory performance, and subjective sense of presence are widely used means to quantify the effects of different VR conditions on the user's experience. An example of using the performance in a spatial memory task to quantify navigation in a virtual environment is the study by Booth and colleagues, who showed that passive passengers remembered a route better than active drivers [5]. In another study, that compared different walking interaction techniques, the subjective sense of presence was used as a means of quantification [19]. This study showed that the subjective sense of presence was higher when real walking was mapped to the virtual walking, as compared to walking in place or pushing a button to induce virtual movements. Additionally, this study found that real walking is a more natural, easy and uncomplicated method than walking-in-place or push-button-fly. This suggests that the closer the match between the user actions and the induced visual stimuli the higher the reported subjective sense of presence. Yet, the details of how individual factors of the interaction mapping affect the experience are not known. For instance, difficulties in using a certain device might cause discomfort or frustration, and thus influence the experience [14].

The concept of "presence" has been defined in numerous ways, e.g. as the sense of "being there" in a scene depicted by a medium [1]. Naturally, measuring such a qualia is not a trivial task. While the standard approach for assessing the subjective sense of presence is to use questionnaires, they have been criticized for their lack of reliability, raising the issue of whether they are actually measuring presence at all [16, 17]. For these reasons, behavioral and physiological measures have been proposed and applied [17, 18, 9]. Unfortunately such measurements can only be used if the participants are expected to have behavioral or physiological responses to the stimulus. Moreover, measurement devices needed for recording the responses can set limitations for the user's movements. Thus, while in certain settings these measures might assess presence better, they are not suitable for general experiments. This is probably the main reason why, despite the criticism, questionnaires remain the most used technique for assessing the subjective sense of presence in a VE.

We hypothesize that, in addition to the physical properties of the interaction device, factors such as interaction mapping, gain and sensitivity of the movements, and the number of degrees of freedom affect the experience. With respect to the mapping between the physical movement of the user and the movement in the VE, we hypothesize that the more natural and intuitive the mapping is experienced, the better participants will remember what they have encountered, and the more immersed in the virtual world they will feel. Here, we investigated if the interaction mapping affects spatial memory and subjective sense of presence when navigating in a VE.

METHODS

The experiments were conducted in the mixed-reality space eXperience Induction Machine (XIM), an immersive room equipped with numerous sensors and actuators, and of a size of ~5.5x5.5m [2]. One of the key features of XIM is the marker-free, multi-person tracking system [13]. The virtual

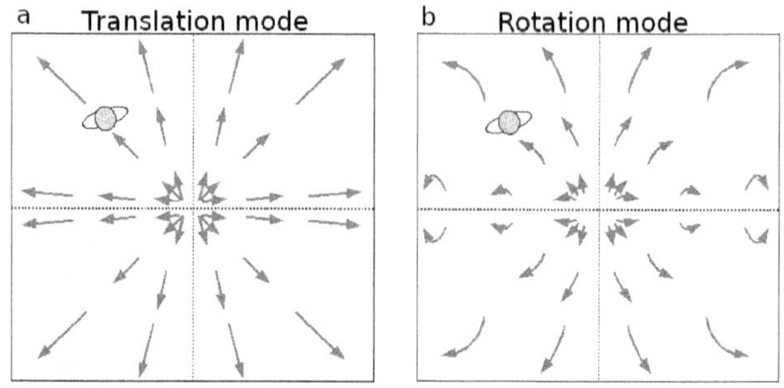

Figure 1. Vector-field illustration of the interaction mappings. (a) In the Translation mode, both axial components of the virtual vector from the center of the room were mapped to translational movements. (b) In the Rotation mode, other axis defined the magnitude of the rotational movement.

world was projected on the four sides of XIM, and implemented using the Game Engine Torque [11]. The top-level control of the interaction was implemented using the neuronal systems simulator `iqr` [4].

Navigation modes

The participant were navigating in the virtual world by physically moving in XIM. As opposed to using head-mounted displays, the interaction can be considered safe, since the participant will not inadvertently collide with a wall.

We tested two different conditions which differed in their interaction mapping. We implemented one mode that should be analog to walking (*Translation mode*), and one mode analog to driving a vehicle (*Rotation mode*). The two modes differed in the way participant's physical actions were translated to the movements in the VE. Location of the participant in XIM was used as an input (Figure 4). Difference between the conditions was the interaction mapping between the input and the navigation commands. In both modes the center of the room was the zero point, where no virtual movements occurred. In the *Translation mode*, the interaction induced a sensation of translational movement in the VE towards the direction defined by the virtual vector from the center of the room to the participant's location at the given time (Figure 1a). Contrary to this, in the *Rotation mode* only one axial component of the vector was mapped to the translational movement, and the other axis defined the magnitude of the rotation movement (Figure 1b). In both, translational and rotational mode, the speed was proportional to the length of the corresponding distance vector component. The gain of the virtual movements was adjusted to be suitable for pleasant navigation.

Assessment of spatial memory performance and subjective sense of presence

The spatial memory was assessed using a "map test": Participants were asked to place pictures of eight virtual objects in the corresponding positions on a 2D map of the VE. For measuring the subjective sense of presence, the participants filled in an Igroup Presence Questionnaire (IPQ), that comprises three factors of "presence": Spatial presence, involve-

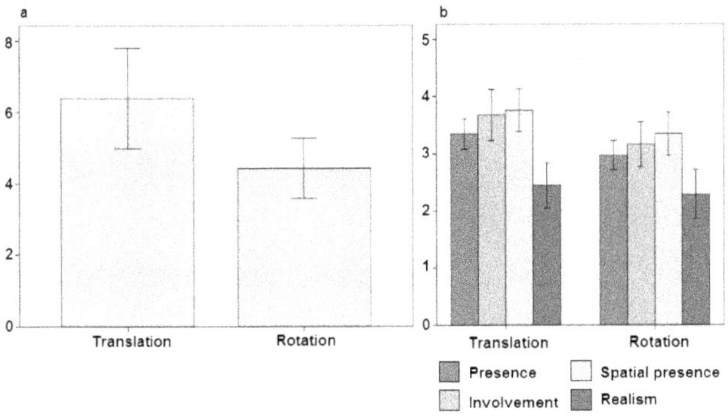

Figure 2. Differences between conditions found in (a) spatial memory, (b) subjective sense of presence, involvement, spatial presence, and realism. Error bars indicate 95% confidence intervals.

ment and realism [15]. The questionnaire was extended with two additional questions concerning the side-effects caused by the interaction, and one question asking if the participant felt disoriented. Data from the tracking system was recorded during the free exploration for subsequent analysis.

Experimental procedure

Each participant first underwent a short training, and then a six minute long free exploration period. No specific task was given, but the participants were asked to explore the environment as much as possible. The virtual world had a limited area for exploration, and a sound signal was played if participant crossed the outline of this area. Immediately after the VE experience, participant were asked to do the spatial memory test, and fill in the presence questionnaire.

Sample

The sample comprised 27 male participants of mean age 22.5 years (SD 3.5). Half (13) of the participants experienced the environment using the Translation mode and, the rest (14) of the group used the Rotation mode.

RESULTS

Performance in the spatial memory test

Participants using the Translation mode scored significantly higher in the spatial memory test than participants using the Rotation mode (Wilcoxon, $p < 0.05$) (Figure 2a). Note that for the Translation mode, there was a ceiling effect as many participants reached the maximum score.

Level of experienced immersion

The combined subjective sense of presence, as well as one of its underlying factors, involvement, were rated significantly higher in the Translation mode compared to the Rotation mode (Wilcoxon, $p < 0.05$, Figure 2b). The same trend was found in spatial presence and realism but the difference was not significant. Additionally, we found a moderate, but significant, correlation between the spatial memory score and subjective sense of presence (Pearson = 0.559; $p < 0.01$).

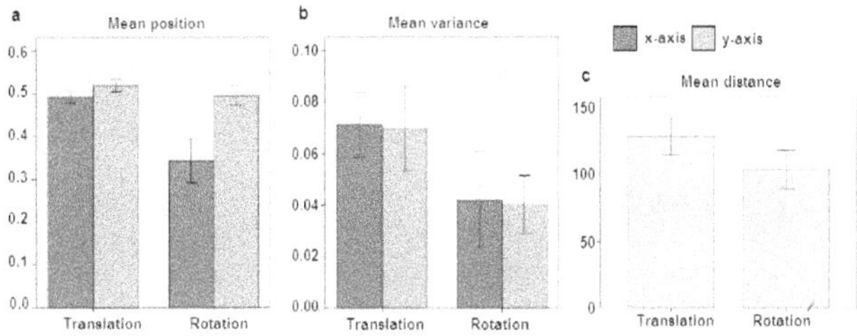

Figure 3. Differences in spatial behavior between conditions found in (a) mean positions, (b) mean variances, and (c) mean distances. Error bars indicate 95% confidence intervals.

Spatial behavior

Analysis of the tracking data showed differences for the behavior of the participants between the conditions. Variance of the positions was significantly different for both axes (Wilcoxon, x-axis $p < 0.005$, y-axis $p < 0.01$, Figure 3b), and mean position for x-axis (Wilcoxon, $p < 0.001$, Figure 3a). Recorded traces show that participants using the Rotation mode frequently combined the forward movement with rotational movements induced by stepping to either side (Figure 4). Participants using the Translation mode walked significantly further during the experiment (t-test, $p < 0.05$, Figure 3c), with a mean value of 128 meters, while participants using the Rotation mode average walked 104 meters.

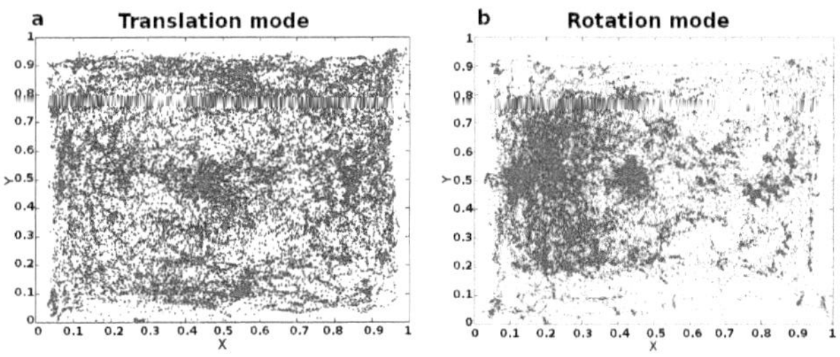

Figure 4. Traces of positions of all participants in (a) Translation mode (b) Rotation mode. The physical room size (5.5x5.5m) is scaled to a range from 0 to 1 for both axes.

Dizziness and disorientation

While some participants reported that they felt dizzy or had a headache, no correlations between these side-effects and the condition were found. Instead, participants using the Rotation mode reported feeling more disorientated than participants using the Translation mode. The difference was found to be significant (Wilcoxon, $p < 0.05$).

DISCUSSION AND CONCLUSION

Our study investigated two modes of navigation in a virtual environment using the same physical interface, and we found that the interaction mapping has an effect on both, spatial memory performance and subjective sense of presence. Moreover, the results of our study showed a relationship between the performance in the spatial memory task and the subjective sense of presence. It is in line with the earlier research reporting a correlation between the subjective sense of presence and performance in memory tasks [3, 8]. Our results support the notion that the subjective experience of presence can be quantified by measuring the performance in the spatial memory task and hence proposes an alternative method for assessing the subjective presence experienced by participants.

The analysis of the spatial behavior of the participants showed that the interaction mapping affects spatial behavior. Higher dispersion in the Translation mode indicates that participants were using a larger area compared to the Rotation mode. The eccentricity of the mean position in the Rotation mode indicates that participants were mainly inducing the forward movements combined with rotation movements equally to both sides. In the Translation mode instead, the mean value coinciding with the middle of the room and high dispersion indicates a homogeneous use of the entire room. This interpretation is supported by the finding that participants in the Translation mode walked more compared to the Rotation mode.

Better performance in the spatial memory test and higher subjective sense of presence might be caused by the closer analogy of the Translation mode to real walking. This interpretation supports results from earlier studies comparing different interaction devices. Further research is needed to come to a better understanding of the reasons for differences between the interaction mappings. Next to movement sensitivity and intensity, the level of sensori-motor contingency, but also required attention and working memory are candidate factors.

Acknowledgment
This work was carried out as part of the PRESENCCIA project, an EU funded Integrated Project under the IST programme (Project Number 27731).

REFERENCES

1. W. Barfield, D. Zeltzer, T. Sheridan, and M. Slater. Presence and performance within virtual environments. In *Virtual environments and advanced interface design*, pages 473–513. Oxford University Press, Inc., 1995.
2. U. Bernardet, S. Bermúdez i Badia, A. Duff, M. Inderbitzin, S. Groux, J. Manzolli, Z. Mathews, A. Mura, A. Väljamäe, and P. Verschure. The eXperience Induction Machine: A New Paradigm for Mixed-Reality Interaction Design and Psychological Experimentation. In *The Engineering of Mixed Reality Systems*, pages 357–379. Springer, 2010.
3. U. Bernardet, M. Inderbitzin, S. Wierenga, A. Väljamäe, A. Mura, and P. Verschure. Validating presence by relying on recollection: Human experience and performance in the mixed reality system XIM. In *11th Annual International Workshop on Presence, Padova, Italy*, 2008.
4. U. Bernardet and P. F. Verschure. iqr: A tool for the construction of multi-level simulations of brain and behaviour. *Neuroinformatics*, 8:113–134, 2010.
5. K. Booth, B. Fisher, S. Page, C. Ware, and S. Widen. Wayfinding in a virtual environment. In *Graphics Interface 2000*, 2000.
6. D. Bowman, D. Koller, and L. Hodges. Evaluation of Movement Control Techniques for Immersive Virtual Environments. 1996.
7. R. Darken, W. Cockayne, and D. Carmein. The omni-directional treadmill: a locomotion device for virtual worlds. In *Proc. of the UIST 1997*, pages 213–221. ACM, 1997.
8. H. Dinh, N. Walker, L. Hodges, C. Song, and A. Kobayashi. Evaluating the Importance of Multi-sensory Input on Memory and the Sense of Presence in Virtual Environments. In *Proc. IEEE Virtual Reality*, pages 222–228, 1999.
9. P. Emmelkamp, M. Krijn, A. Hulsbosch, S. De Vries, M. Schuemie, and C. Van der Mast. Virtual reality treatment versus exposure in vivo: a comparative evaluation in acrophobia. *Behaviour Research and Therapy*, 40(5):509–516, 2002.
10. B. Fröhlich and J. Plate. The cubic mouse: a new device for three-dimensional input. In *Proc. SIGCHI CHI*, pages 526–531. ACM, 2000.
11. Garage Games, Eugene, Oregon, USA. Torque game engine, 2008.
12. H. Iwata. Walking about virtual environments on an infinite floor. *Proc. IEEE Virtual Reality 1999*, pages 286–293, 1999.
13. Z. Mathews, S. B. i Badia, and P. F. M. J. Verschure. *Action-Planning and Execution from Multimodal Cues: An Integrated Model for Artificial Autonomous Systems*. Springer Verlag, 2010.
14. U. Rosebrock and P. Vamplew. The intent to move; generating spatial memory in Virtual Environments. In *Proc. VSMM 1999*, pages 407–416, 1999.
15. T. Schubert, F. Friedmann, and H. Regenbrecht. Embodied presence in virtual environments. *Visual representations and interpretations*, pages 268–278, 1999.
16. M. Slater. Measuring presence: A response to the Witmer and Singer presence questionnaire. *Presence*, 8(5):560–565, 1999.
17. M. Slater. How colorful was your day? Why questionnaires cannot assess presence in virtual environments. *Presence*, 13(4):484–493, 2004.
18. M. Slater, C. Guger, G. Edlinger, R. Leeb, G. Pfurtscheller, A. Antley, M. Garau, A. Brogni, and D. Friedman. Analysis of physiological responses to a social situation in an immersive virtual environment. *Presence*, 15(5):553–569, 2006.
19. M. Usoh, K. Arthur, M. Whitton, R. Bastos, A. Steed, M. Slater, and F. Brooks Jr. Walking > Walking-in-Place > Flying, in Virtual Environments. In *Proc. SIGGRAPH 1999*, pages 359–364. ACM Press/Addison-Wesley Publishing Co., 1999.

An Object-centric Interaction Framework for Tangible Interfaces in Virtual Environments

Johann Habakuk Israel[1], Oliver Belaifa[1], Adrienne Gispen[2], and Rainer Stark[1]
[1]Fraunhofer IPK, Pascalstr. 8-9, 10587 Berlin, Germany
[2]Stanford University, Stanford, CA 94305, USA
{johann.habakuk.israel, oliver.belaifa, rainer.stark}@ipk.fraunhofer.de, aegispen@stanford.edu

ABSTRACT

The spatial and semantic integration of tangible user interfaces (TUI) into virtual environments is a promising approach to enhance mixed reality-applications with dynamic three-dimensional graphics and graspable controls. Although various software frameworks for virtual reality periphery [e.g. 26, 31] and tangible interaction exist [cf. 7, 18, 22], a novel framework which provides a high-level TUI-object-centric interface (instead of device-centric interface) and duplex access to important physical properties of TUI-objects, e.g. three-dimensional position, sensor states, force actuators could foster the development of such mixed-reality applications.

This paper describes a TUI-VR-framework whose aim is to support the development of physically enriched VR-applications. It focuses on the spatial and manipulative properties of TUI-objects, leaving it to the application to implement interaction techniques, semantics and expressive physical/digital couplings [cf. 10, 27].

On the programming side, the primary goals of the framework are the integration of a device abstraction layer, a lightweight application programming interface and full duplex communication between the TUI-application and interaction devices. The framework allows for a distributed system configuration and is highly customizable. Various virtual reality tracking frameworks and devices (e.g. VRPN, Ascension MotionStar, force-feedback devices) and physical toolkits (e.g. Phidgets) are already integrated. Further adapters can also easily be integrated.

The capabilities and flexibility of the framework are illustrated at the end of the paper by means of two use cases.

Author Keywords

Tangible User Interfaces, Virtual Reality, Mixed Reality, Object Centric Interaction Framework, Device Abstraction Layer, Event-Driven Architecture, Client-Server Architecture.

ACM Classification Keywords

H.5.2. Information interfaces and presentation: User Interfaces: User interface management systems (UIMS), input devices and strategies; interaction styles; prototyping. D.2.2 Software: Software Engineering: User interfaces. C.2.4. Computer Systems Organization: Computer-Communication Networks: Distributed Systems; Client/server.

General Terms

Human Factors, Performance, Reliability.

TEI'11, January 22–26, 2011, Funchal, Portugal.

INTRODUCTION

Both concepts of virtual reality (VR [4, 30]) and tangible user interfaces (TUI [10, 12]) particularly emphasize spatial interaction, high interaction bandwidth between system and user, and a seamless integration of digital and physical system elements. But while tangible user interfaces are very strong in their physical and manipulative means, their computational power in terms of displaying highly dynamic contents is usually limited [10, 11]. On the other hand, virtual reality systems provide highly advanced means for displaying dynamic three-dimensional contents, but the possibilities for interaction are usually less advanced. They often rely on WIMP-like metaphors and employ a limited set of standard devices such as VR flight-sticks, force-feedback devices or basic props [cf. 4, 20].

This paper describes a software framework whose aim is to support the development of physically enriched VR-applications. It focuses on the spatial and manipulative properties of TUI-objects, leaving it to the application to implement interaction techniques, semantics and expressive physical/digital couplings [cf. 10]. It is an aim of this paper to raise attention for the field of virtual reality in the tangible interaction community in order to emphasize the great prospects of such a combination.

INTEGRATING VIRTUAL ENVIRONMENTS AND TANGIBLE USER INTERFACES

For certain domains, e.g. product design [17], engineering [19], architecture [35], and performing arts [15], environments which allow for real-time interaction with dynamic virtual contents and which provide direct, physical interaction have the potential to provide unique functionalities and address as yet unresolved issues in these domains.

The potential to enrich functional and interactive properties of interactive applications by integrating tangible interfaces into virtual environments has been impressively demonstrated by various authors. Hinckley [9] was among the first who integrated application specific physical objects (props) and three-dimensional visualizations in a medical application. In his application a puppet head and a pane controlled the visualization of a cutting pane in a volumetric medical data set, allowing for fast and direct interaction (even though control and visualization were dislocated). With these props, the user received more information about the problem domain than from a GUI alone.

Probably the most popular examples for integrating virtual and real objects are AR-Toolkit and its derivates [2, 3]. AR-toolkit allows spatial alignment of physical objects and digital three-dimensional graphics in live video streams, requires little hardware resources and provides an easy-to-use programming interface. Due to the novice-friendly programming-interface, AR-toolkit is one of the most widely used prototyping toolkits for creating physical/digital integrated applications. Another approach for integrating physical objects into immersive virtual environments was introduced by Lok [20], who created virtual hulls around physical objects in order to enhance their manipulability.

The integration of physical and virtual objects within an interactive environment raises both perceptual [6, 23] and implementation issues. The latter are discussed in the following section.

Implementation issues

Though there has been huge progress in past years, especially in the field of display resolution, current VR systems still face technological limitations, e.g. system update rate, restricted field of view, mismatches of resolution and image clarity, luminance and contrast, and viewpoint dependency [1, 6, 23]. This paper focuses on the implementation issues which are specific to tangible user interfaces.

For the seamless integration of tangible user interfaces (physical objects, props) into immersive virtual environments, the application needs to monitor the physical state of the TUIs, e.g. the spatial position and orientation (extrinsic) as well as the intrinsic states of the objects. Dumas et al. [7] pointed out that mixing tangible interaction with multimodal interfaces involves *time synchronization* of different modalities:

Fusion techniques handle the synchronization of co-referenced input events in multimodal systems. This consists of collecting and integrating data from multiple complementary input streams into an accurate interpretation of the user's intention. A simple example is Bolt's 'Put that there' [4] in which the vocal command 'put' must be linked to two pointing events in the correct order to achieve the desired representation. Fusion is one of the core properties of interaction in virtual environments, as all input events must be interpreted with reference to the location of the user, the interaction device, or both.

Fission techniques handle the selection of appropriate output channels for feedback and the construction and synchronization of output into a coherent message for the user. Fission techniques are essential to TUI-applications that output feedback to users via many different modalities, such as environments that employ ambient media [13] to display selected information to a user.

Bidirectional (duplex) interaction between the physical domain and the digital model is a key characteristic of tangible user interfaces [32]. Where other framework concepts often require collection of relevant data from different sources and transmission of feedback data to various actuators, TUI-frameworks should encapsulate input and output in a single software object in order to make it easy for the developer to implement a truly tangible behavior.

The proposed framework encapsulates all 'input' and 'output' channels of a TUI-object in a single API-class. Thus the software model of the framework corresponds on its API side to a great extend with the MCRpd interaction model of tangible user interfaces by Ullmer & Ishii [32]. It is expected that such a TUI-object centric programming interface will allow for faster development of TUI-applications and prototypes, freeing resources for the development of advanced interaction techniques and impressive physical/digital couplings.

Existing TUI-frameworks

Various authors emphasize the need for hardware abstraction and high-level interfaces in the field of TUI programming [cf. 7, 22, 27]. Shaer and Jacob [27] suggest a Tangible User Interface Modelling Language TUIML which is based on the TAC-paradigm [28]. It allows developers to specify interaction techniques, syntax and application behavior in a high-level manner. Klemmer et al. [18] introduced a vision-based toolkit which also allows for barcode tracking and RFID sensing. It targets rapid prototyping of table-based tangible interfaces in usually two-dimensional interaction spaces. The toolkit provides a high-level interface for physical objects (Phobs) and associated events (addition, updating, and removal). Identical event types are generated independently from the employed sensor hardware which allows for changing sensing technologies with minimal programming effort. Klemmer et al. regarded the API of their toolkit as a user interface for programmers. Accordingly they evaluated it in class studies among seven computer science students. Participants showed enthusiasm and reasonable learning effects, which affirmed the practicability of the authors' high-level event-based architecture.

Other solutions for tangible interaction on table surfaces include the TUIO protocol [16] and the Synlab API [22] which also implement event-based approaches and allow for distributed architectures. Both were employed in successful, portable installations e.g. for music composing or role-playing. Further toolkit architectures were introduced by Dumas et al. [7]. One architecture realized a bidirectional mapping of Java-based GUI elements and Phidgets controls. A second system uses a state machine to define the interaction flow in an abstract manner and provides uniform access to various external sensing systems, including Phidgets and speech recognition. The third system employs an agent-based approach and centralized message management. Dumas et al. conclude that '(...) choosing a type of architecture for a given tangible and multimodal application heavily depends on the type of application'. Furthermore simple WIMP-like interaction metaphors do "(...) not necessarily require a high-level architecture." [7, p. 53].

In addition to these frameworks for creating TUI applications, Marquardt et al. [21] introduce Visual Environment Explorer, a GUI application for visualizing and controlling event flow between distributed devices. The program connects with Phidgets devices using the Shared Phidgets toolkit, which controls the devices using a dMVC architecture. The application displays limited event history for each device and visualizes event flow and activity between devices and program. It allows developers to filter the type of events shown and examine data flow at reduced speed to aid in debugging. Marquardt et al. introduce an elegant visual language for displaying event flow of distributed systems, yet their application is limited by its device-centric view, as it links each device solely to an application program node. Adding an object abstraction layer could extend the program's practicability by allowing developers to associate semantically linked devices into TUI-objects and choose filter settings to display only those events relevant to a particular TUI-object.

Existing VR-Interaction-frameworks

VR-frameworks usually model the flow of interaction data as simplex (uni-directional) streams which route events from a source node (usually an interaction device or tracking system) to a sink note in the application. The OpenTracker framework [26] is capable of processing various tracking sources such as multiple AR-Toolkit markers [2, 3]. Each stream may be processed by various filters and sent across a network to one or more sinks. The framework allows for easy customization by means of xml files.

The Virtual Reality Peripheral Network VRPN [31] is a widely used framework which provides device abstraction and remote communication but is not intended for high-level VR programming. Vendor specific tracking-frameworks also exist, which usually allow for remote communication (e.g. DTrack, Ascension MotionStar).

Three-dimensional position and orientation data of tracked objects are mandatory in all VR-frameworks (6 DOF), yet no VR-framework provides a high-level object-centered interface.

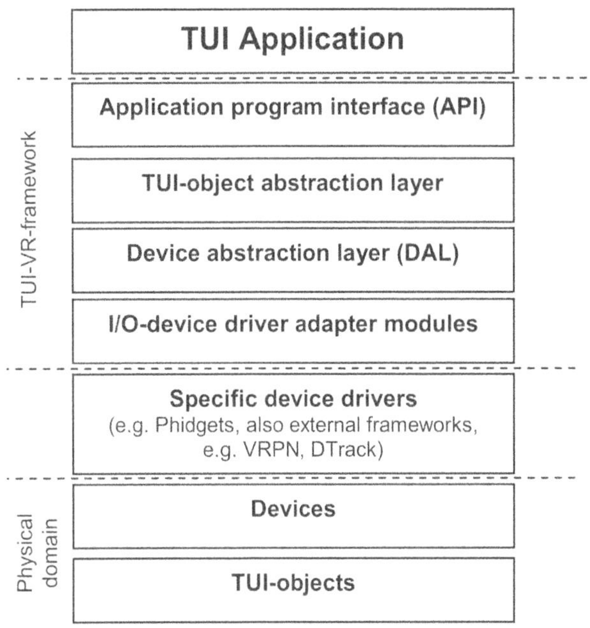

Figure 1. Principle architecture of the TUI-VR-framework.

THE TUI-VR-FRAMEWORK

The following section provides an overview of the TUI-VR-framework. Several design concepts are introduced. They implement the TUI-object-centric interaction paradigm and are intended to facilitate the development of VR- and TUI-applications. The framework targets two kinds of developers: *Application-developers* who develop mixed reality applications and *framework-developers* who intend to extend functionality by adding new devices, sensors or drivers to the framework.

Primary Goals

The primary goals and main contributions of this framework are the following:

1. The first goal of the framework is to integrate a *device abstraction layer* (*DAL*, figure 1, cf. [24]) to achieve code-independence from various specific device drivers and APIs. Present TUI-toolkits are usually limited to one technology, which often results in difficult or limited portability. Furthermore, devices which differ with respect to technology are controlled by different specialized drivers. This leads to high development efforts, especially if multiple devices must be integrated into one system. The framework

provides the integration of different devices as *plug-ins*. By using the DAL as part of the framework the developer has access to all registered devices.

2. The second goal of the framework is to provide a *lightweight application programming interface (API)* for TUI- or VR-application developers which implements a *TUI-object-centric* view and allows for rapid prototyping. This is achieved by decoupling the code from the I/O-device drivers with a new abstraction layer on top of the DAL: the TUI-object abstraction layer (figure 1). These TUI-objects function as controls for the environment, just as GUI-objects do in a graphical interface. In contrast, creating controls using a device-centric API would require additional development efforts for building one's own TUI-object representations.
3. The third goal of the framework is to enable *full duplex communication* between the TUI-application and the devices. TUI-objects usually consist of a set of sensors which generate data streams (e.g. three dimensional tracking data or analog button signals) and a set of physical properties which accept data streams (e.g. force feedback devices or LED arrays). In contrast, current tracking frameworks provide only simplex communication from the sensor to the application.
4. The fourth goal of the framework is to handle any necessary manipulation of data streams within the server-side configuration of TUI-objects. This is done by integrating *multi-stream processing* plug-in modules, or MSPs. Data streams can be configured to flow through MSPs to make fusion and fission of data streams (see fusion and fission techniques above) easier for the application developer.

Framework features

The framework was implemented in the programming language C++. The code of the framework can easily be ported to various platforms. Currently MS Windows, Linux and Mac OS versions are provided. The framework contains two parts: a client API and a customizable server (figure 2).

The server consists of a plug-in architecture for devices. Device driver adapter modules are dynamically loaded and are ready for use after a short registration process. Co-referenced data streams or those that require manipulation may flow through multi-stream processors (or MSPs), which are also implemented as plug-ins. The server is highly customizable by means of xml configuration files which are validated against xml schemas. This allows the application developer to use the server without programming. On the client side, he uses an object oriented API which provides him with the features mentioned above: a device abstraction layer, a lightweight programming interface, and full duplex communication.

The communication between the client and physical TUI-objects is realized across the network in full duplex mode. Applications may receive and send data from and to TUI-objects respectively. Two communication protocols are provided. In the default configuration, the reliable TCP/IP is used for control of the framework. Interaction data is transmitted by the fast but less reliable UDP.

Server Side Configuration

On the server side, the configuration will be done using xml (see figure 3), which is also validated against a schema. Each linked device driver adaptor has at least one entry in the device type table which describes its specification with respect to the device abstraction. Due to the fact that a device emits or receives data mostly as streams, it is reasonable to organize the data to flow through *ports*. The type of stream can be determined by the type of data and the flow direction. A source port gets data from the device; a sink port sends data to the device. In order to connect a certain device, it has to be instantiated and identified e.g. by its serial number, because multiple devices of the same type could be used. Xml definitions and instantiations of device types and devices may contain multiple ports, which are connected to those of different devices, e.g. a tracking port receives data from a magnetic tracking device (e.g.

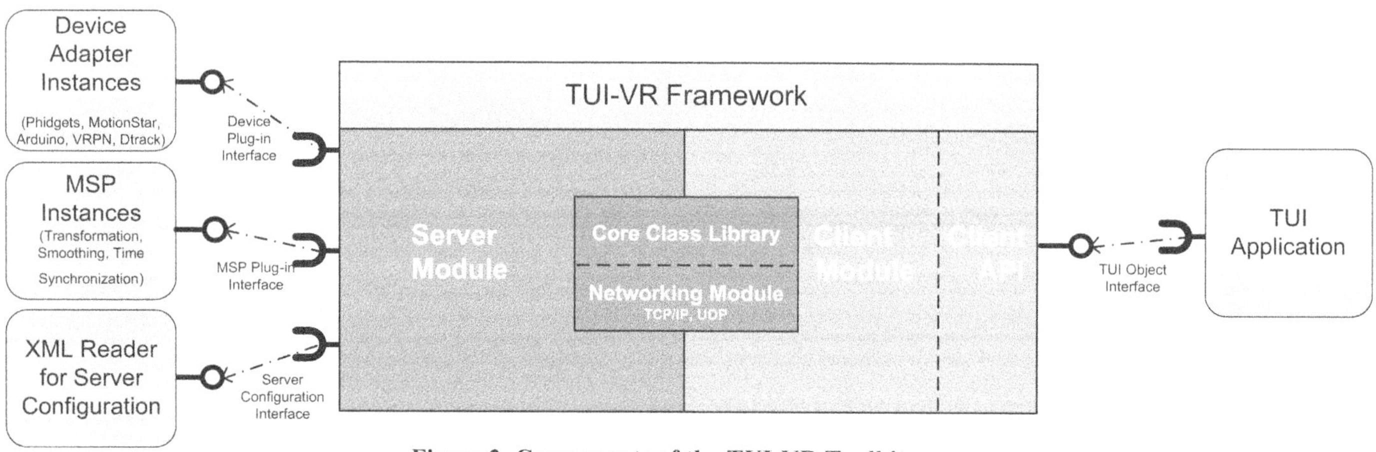

Figure 2. Components of the TUI-VR Toolkit.

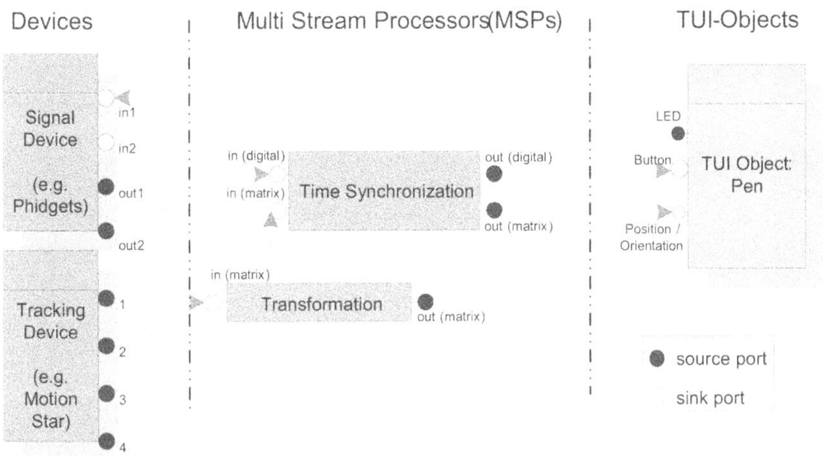

Figure 3. TUI-VR framework example configuration.

Ascension MotionStar) and a digital port from a physical button (e.g. Phidgets toolkit).

It can be helpful to process data before it reaches the client side; thus the framework provides the capability of routing data streams through *MSPs* on its way between devices and TUI-objects (figures 2, 3). For example, Kalman filtering of tracking data would be implemented using an MSP. Xml definitions and instantiation of MSP types may likewise include multiple ports, for example an MSP can allow for time synchronization of tracking data with digital data from a button. In this case the MSP must have input and output ports for both matrix data and digital data. Once written, an MSP can be plugged into any new client application that requires the same type of data processing. MSPs to perform smoothing of tracking data, transformation, and the time synchronization described above have already been implemented and are provided in the framework.

Like device types, *TUI-object types* also contain lists of source and sink ports. These ports need to be connected to specific device ports of instantiated devices as defined in the xml configuration. The TUI-object ports have to be compatible in data type and flow direction to their corresponding device and/or MSP ports. Usually a TUI-object encapsulates multiple ports, which are connected to different devices. For example a TUI-object might be connected to a position tracking port of a magnetic tracking device and a digital port from a sensor toolkit such as Phidgets [8] (figure 3). Fusion and fission can be performed by connecting device ports, MSP ports, and TUI-object ports such that co-referenced input streams are integrated into a single software object: a TUI-object definition available on the client side API. Once instantiated by the client, this object is ready to send and receive data to and from the incorporated devices.

Client API

For developing client applications, an object-oriented API is provided which allows for creating new software TUI-objects in a high-level programming environment (see figure 2). Each configured TUI-object instance is mapped to the client API, where it is represented as a *TUIObjectStub* class. Whenever a connection between a client and a server is established, these classes will be instantiated on the client side by receiving the necessary information from the server. Each data stream generated by a device is directed to the appropriate port of a TUI-object according to the configuration. The framework's client API implements both an event-driven architecture (described below) and the signals and slots programming pattern [5]. Thus the developer can choose to work with the stub classes or use signal and slots. The entire process of integrating TUI-objects into a TUI-VR application using the framework is outlined in figure 4.

Hardware Setup:

1. Build/prototype the TUI-object
2. Attach sensors and/or markers

Server Configuration in XML:

1. Create instances of the utilized devices (by referencing the specific device types)
2. Create instances of necessary MSPs
3. Choose a TUI-object type or create a new one
4. Create a TUI-object instance (by referencing the chosen type)
5. Define data flow by connecting device ports, TUI-object ports, and/or MSP ports.

Client Application:

1. Develop the application that utilizes the TUI-objects
2. Establish a connection to the TUI server
3. Connect the TUI-object source ports provided by the API to class methods using the signals and slots programming pattern.
4. Implement the class methods to realize the TUI-object behavior: to process incoming data streams, create TUI event handlers. To generate feedback, generate an IEvent and send it to the appropriate sink port of the selected TUI-object.

Figure 4. Steps required to implement a TUI-VR-application using the framework.

Event-driven architecture

The framework on both the client and the server side is based on an event-driven architecture (EDA, cf. [25]). In an EDA, loosely coupled components in a well distributed layered architecture process their data in an asynchronous manner. By installing conditional triggers, events are generated to signal certain state changes. All components associated with a certain trigger are notified by routing events through specific gateways based on their destination addresses. At the destination the asynchronous events are stored in a FIFO-queue.

If an event occurs in the TUI-VR framework for which at least one listener is registered, an event message will be created. Event messages contain information about the event, such as the intended recipient and the event type. Events are generated by a data stream and contain an *entityID* (device, MSP, or TUI-object instance id) and a *portID*, which represent the destination address at the client side. The framework provides an abstract class *IEvent*, which needs to be implemented by concrete event message classes. It can also be easily extended with new event types and corresponding data structures. Their contents (payload) are encapsulated in generic port events. This reduces the effort required for framework-developers to create new device adapters. The architecture of the framework uses event sources and sinks, which allows for flexible organization of the data flow.

Unfortunately, the flexibility of the event-driven architecture comes along with extra efforts when dealing with continuous input. Even though input, i.e. from tracking devices, is often regarded as continuous on a conceptual level, it must ultimately be quantized in order to pass it through a computer framework [14]. Current paradigms try to address this issue with a multi-tier approach or specifications based on conditions rather than events [cf. 27, 34]. In our framework the developer is still responsible for handling continuous input himself. To assist in this process, the framework developer is provided with an API (see next section) which allows for generation of parallel and discrete events based on continuous input, e.g. for the integration of haptic devices [29]. If the overhead resulting from the event-driven architecture leads to noticeable delays, it can be reduced by linking frequently used device-MSP-configurations into one module, reducing the number of involved instances and optimizing the data flow graph.

Device integration

In order to support the framework-developer in the integration of new devices, e.g. physical sensors or tracking systems, simple integration methods are provided: For each new device, an abstract *IDevice* class needs to be implemented. In addition, a DeviceDescriptor structure is needed, which contains information about the actual device instance, e.g. the device type with the source and sink channel specification.

USE CASES

While this framework certainly has the capacity to implement many of the more researched physical/digital couplings employed in TUI-applications, we have developed it with a view towards exploring the possibilities afforded by incorporating virtual reality into tangible interfaces. In the classic metaphor of tangible interaction, physical objects are data objects; that is, the digital is associated with or represented by the physical in order to allow direct manipulation of abstract data. In the following use cases, we describe a slightly different metaphor for interacting physically with digital information. By conceptualizing TUI-objects as physical *tools* that employ real-world interaction techniques to manipulate visually represented data (as opposed to objects as *representations* of digital data), it is possible to design TUI-VR applications that allow intuitive spatial interaction with dynamic digital data.

Use Case 1: Easy implementation of specialized modeling / interaction tools

The framework was integrated into an immersive sketching application for creative free-hand drawing and modelling by means of two tangible interfaces: a stylus and a two-handed tool for Bezier-curve extrusion (figure 5). The system underwent various studies among product designers and artists which showed its practicability and stimulating impact on creative design processes [13]. The system was set up in an immersive five-sided CAVE Environment, using a rendering cluster, a magnetic tracking system (Ascension MotionStar) and a Phidgets interface board. The stylus allows for drawing virtual ink directly into the virtual environment, following the movements of the stylus tip. The width of the stroke is scaled according to the force by which the user presses the frame of the stylus. The pressure is measured by means of a force sensor of the Phidgets toolkit. The framework associates the tracking input and force sensor input into one stylus software object.

The two-handed Bezier-tool allows for extruding a Bezier curve in 3d space by moving two handles which control the curves control points. If the user presses both handles which again contain Phidgets sensors, the curve is extruded along the path of the user's hands. The position and orientation (POSE) of the user's head, the stylus and both Bezier handles are measured by means of the magnetic tracking device.

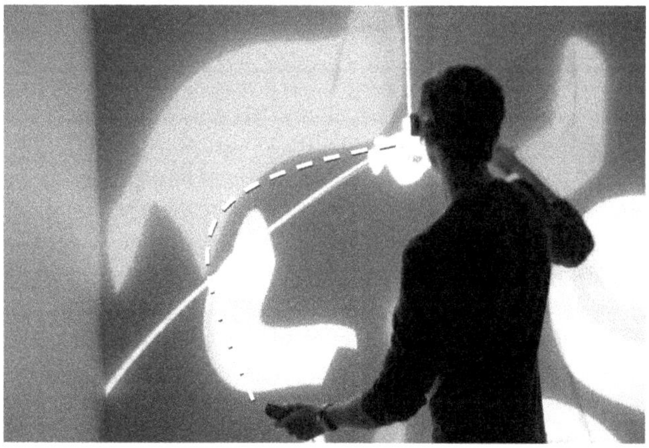

Figure 5: Bezier curves and physical handles. (The dashed line shows the curve from the user's perspective.)

The configuration of the TUI-objects with respect to the employed tracking and sensor devices as well as the routing of the device channels to properties of the TUI-object was implemented by means of the TUI-VR-framework. The strengths of the framework are noticeable when extending and reconfiguring the application: for example, we are currently working on implementing a gripper for modifying and stretching sketches, which provides vibro-tactile feedback when in use. To add this tool, we need only add a TUI-object type definition and a corresponding TUI-object instance, as the employed devices are already configured and the required device adapters are included in the framework.

Additional sensors could also easily be integrated into the stylus, allowing for different or more complex drawing modes. For example, undo/redo functionality could easily be mapped to an integrated scroll wheel. When the application-developer (or even a user) decides to employ new tracking and sensing technologies, e.g. optical tracking and wireless sensors, he/she only needs to add a new device instance (given the device type is already provided by the framework) and update the xml configurations of the affected TUI-object instance elements. Thus the application-developer has more resources to make actual use of the mixed reality, physical/digital infrastructure and needs to pay less attention to the technical realization.

Use Case 2: Duplex communication in Smart Hybrid Prototyping

An additional use case for the TUI-VR framework is in the area of Smart Hybrid Prototyping (SHP) [29]. Smart Hybrid Prototyping aids product development by creating interactive digital representations of products early in their development. This allows developers, decision makers, and customers to experience the functionality of a product early on, facilitating interdisciplinary collaboration and aiding in error detection. The TUI-VR framework's capacity to support duplex communication allows easy implementation of haptic interaction devices, which allow developers to experience product features that are difficult or impossible to simulate visually, such as weight, inertia, or absorption. This framework was used to implement a bidirectional force-feedback handle to simulate the kinematic behavior of the hatchback of an automobile (figure 6). The kinematic behavior was calculated based on the anchor points and characteristics of the pneumatic spring; these can be altered by the developer to compare the ergonomics of different configurations. Implementation of this tangible interface requires both an input sensor to calculate the angle of the physical handle and an electric motor to provide output in the form of resistance to the user. Using the TUI-VR framework, these devices were configured as a single bidirectional TUI-object. This application was set up in 1-to-1 scale in an immersive five-sided CAVE Environment.

Further existing applications of the framework include a semi-immersive system, which employs force-feedback devices for assembly/disassembly simulations in product development and modeling of flexible objects by means of tangible pliers [33].

CONCLUSION AND OUTLOOK

This framework is intended to easily integrate tangible interfaces and virtual environments in order to support both the TUI- and VR-community. Its main contributions are the implementation of a device abstraction layer, an object-centric lightweight API, full duplex communication between application and devices, and the processing of a data via multi-stream processors. The framework has the potential to enrich TUI-applications by incorporating dynamic graphical content; by the same token it can expand the possibilities for physical manipulation and interaction techniques in 3D-applications.

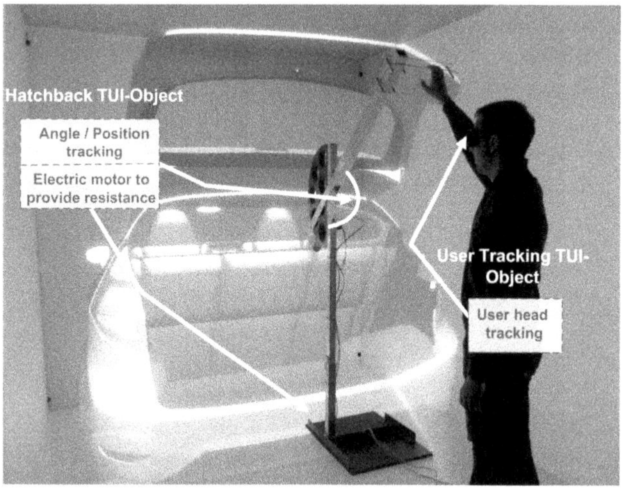

Figure 6: Smart Hybrid Prototyping Hatchback Simulation [29].

However, the possibilities for the application of this framework are by no means limited to the use cases described above. While we have focused mainly on using the framework to integrate TUI-objects into mixed reality environments, the framework's object abstraction layer would also be a powerful tool in many other types of tangible interfaces. For example, in spatially distributed systems, integrating semantically related sensors and actuators into software objects could considerably simplify the development and maintenance of such systems.

The flexible, pattern oriented design of the framework helps to minimize the development effort by means of several abstractions and allows for rapid prototyping. A primary aim of the toolkit was to provide an easy-to-use API for the *application-developer*. In addition the client side API allows developing TUI-based applications by easily mapping physical TUI-objects to the corresponding TUI software objects available in the client API. The integration of device specific code is not necessary. On the other hand, *framework-developers* who want to contribute new tracking and sensing technology or even TUI-prototypes to the tangible community could provide compatible device adapters (IDevice) and corresponding device type definitions, which could be easily integrated into existing mixed reality applications using the TUI-VR-framework. Thus, the integration effort involved in implementing specialized modeling or interaction tools is greatly reduced by the framework. This opens up the design space for TUI-

VR applications, leaving it to developers to implement tools whose functionality allows physical manipulation of virtual or hybrid objects. A sample set of TUI-objects is also currently under development, such as grippers, pens, force-feedback enabled levers etc.

As this framework primarily focuses on the spatial and manipulative properties of TUI-objects, it does not address the specification of application behavior and interaction syntax. For extending the practicability of the framework towards high-level TUI programming, we are currently considering providing interfaces for TUI specification languages, e.g. TUIML [27]. Further proposed extensions include support for continuous interaction on a conceptual level [cf. 27, 34], a GUI to aid developers in completing the xml configuration, the support of multiple TUI-servers, and logging and replay functionalities.

ACKNOWLEDGMENTS

This work has been funded by the BMBF project AVILUSplus (01IM08002).

REFERENCES

1. Azuma, R., Baillot, Y., Behringer, R., Feiner, S., Julier, S. and MacIntyre, B. Recent Advances in Augmented Reality *Computer Graphics*, *21*, 6 (2001), 34-47.
2. Billinghurst, M., Grasset, R. and Looser, J. Designing Augmented Reality Interfaces. *Copmuter Graphics*, *39*, 1 (2005), 17-22.
3. Billinghurst, M., Kato, H. and Poupyrev, I. MagicBook: Transitioning between Reality and Virtuality. *IEEE Computer Grapics and Applications*, May/June (2001), 1-4.
4. Bowman, D.A., Kruijff, E., LaViola Jr., J.J. and Poupyrev, I. *3D User Interfaces: Theory and Practice*. Addison-Wesley, Reading, Massachusetts, 2005.
5. Dalheimer, M.K. *Programming with QT: Writing portable GUI applications on Unix and Win32*. O'Reilly, Sebastopol, 2002.
6. Drascic, D. and Milgram, P. Perceptual issues in augmented reality. *SPIE Stereoscopic Displays and Applications VII, Virtual Reality Systems III*, *2653*, (1996), 123–134.
7. Dumas, B., Lalanne, D., Guinard, D., Koenig, R. and Ingold, R., Strengths and weaknesses of software architectures for the rapid creation of tangible and multimodal interfaces. In *Proc. TEI'08 Second International Conference on Tangible and Embedded Interaction*, Bonn (2008), 47-54.
8. Greenberg, S. and Fitchett, C., Phidgets: easy development of physical interfaces through physical widgets. In *Proc. UIST'01*, Orlando, Florida (2001), 209-218.
9. Hinckley, K., Pausch, R., Gobble, J. and Kassell, N., Passive real-world interface props for neurosurgical visualization. In *Proc. CHI'94*, (1994), 452–458.
10. Hornecker, E. and Buur, J., Getting a Grip on Tangible Interaction: A Framework on Physical Space and Social Interaction. In *Proc. CHI 2006*, (2006), 437–446.
11. Ishii, H., Tangible Bits: Beyond Pixels. In *Proc. Second International Conference on Tangible and Embedded Interaction (TEI'08)*, Bonn, Germany (2008), XV-XXV.
12. Ishii, H. and Ullmer, B., Tangible bits: towards seamless interfaces between people, bits, and atoms. In *Proc. CHI'97*, Atlanta, Georgia (1997), 234-241.
13. Israel, J.H., Wiese, E., Mateescu, M. and Stark, R. Investigating three-dimensional sketching for early conceptual design—Results from expert discussions and user studies. *Computers & Graphics*, *33*, 4 (2009), 462-473.
14. Jacob, R.J.K., Deligianndis, L. and Morrison, S. A Software Model and Specification Language for Non-WIMP User Interfaces. *ACM Transactions on Computer-Human Interaction*, *6*, 1 (1999), 1–46.
15. James, J., Ingalls, T., Qian, G., Olsen, L., Whiteley, D., Wong, S. and Rikakis, T., Movement-based interactive dance performance. In *Proc. 14th annual ACM international conference on Multimedia*, Santa Barbara, CA, USA (2006), 470-480.
16. Kaltenbrunner, M. and Bencina, R., reacTIVision: A Computer-Vision Framework for Table-Based Tangible Interaction. In *Proc. First international conference on Tangible and embedded interaction TEI'07*, Baton Rouge (2007), 69-74.
17. Keefe, D.F., Acevedo Feliz, D., Moscovich, T., Laidlaw, D.H. and LaViola, J., CavePainting: A Fully Immersive 3D Artistic Medium and Interactive Experience. In *Proc. ACM SI3D'01*, (2001), 85-93.
18. Klemmer, S.R., Li, J., Lin, J. and Landay, J.A., Papier-Mache: toolkit support for tangible input. In *Proc. CHI'04*, Vienna (2004), 399-406.
19. Krause, F.-L., Jansen, H., Kind, C. and Rothenburg, U. Virtual Product Development as an Engine for Innovation. In Krause, F.-L. (ed.) *The Future of Product Development. Proceedings of the 17th CIRP Design Conference*, Springer-Verlag, Berlin, Heidelberg, New York, 2007, 703-713.
20. Lok, B.C. Towards the merging of real and virtual spaces. *Communications of the ACM*, *47*, 8 (2004), 48-53.
21. Marquardt, N., Gross, T., Carpendale, S. and Greenberg, S., Revealing the invisible: visualizing the location and event flow of distributed physical devices. In *Proc. Fourth international conference on Tangible, embedded, and embodied interaction TEI'10*, Cambridge, Massachusetts, USA (2010), 41-48.
22. Mazalek, A., Tangible Toolkits: Integrating Application Development across Diverse Multi-User and Tangible Interaction Platforms. In *Proc. Let's Get Physical Workshop, DCC'06*, Eindhoven (2006).
23. Milgram, P. and Drascic, D., Perceptual Effects In Aligning Virtual And Real Objects In Augmented Reality Displays. In *Proc. 41st Annual Meeting of Human Factors & Ergonomics Society*, Albuquerque, NM, USA (1997), 1239-1243.
24. Ohlenburg, J., Broll, W. and Lindt, I. DEVAL – A Device Abstraction Layer for VR/AR. In *Universal Access in Human Computer Interaction. Coping with Diversity*, Springer, Berlin, Heidelberg, 2007, 497-506.
25. Philip, G.C. Software design guidelines for event-driven programming *Journal of Systems and Software*, *41*, 2 (1998), 79-91.
26. Reitmayr, G. and Schmalstieg, D., An open software architecture for virtual reality interaction. In *Proc. ACM VRST'01*, Baniff, Alberta, Canada (2001), 47-54.
27. Shaer, O. and Jacob, R.J.K. A specification paradigm for the design and implementation of tangible user interfaces. *ACM Transactions on Computer-Human Interaction (TOCHI)*, *16*, 4 (2009), 1-39.
28. Shaer, O., Leland, N., Calvillo-Gamez, E.H. and Jacob, R.J.K. The TAC paradigm: specifying tangible user interfaces. *Personal and Ubiquitous Computing*, *8*, 5 (2004), 359-369.
29. Stark, R. and Beckmann-Dobrev, B., Ein interdisziplinärer Ansatz zur multimodalen funktionalen Absicherung mechatronischer Systeme am Beispiel einer PKW-Heckklappe. In *Proc. 3. Grazer Symposium Virtuelles Fahrzeug* Graz (2010), 18-27.
30. Sutherland, I.E., The Ultimate Display. In *Proc. IFIP Congress*, (1965), 506-508.
31. Taylor, R.M., Hudson, T.C., Seeger, A., Weber, H., Juliano, J. and Helser, A.T., VRPN: a device-independent, network-transparent VR peripheral system. In *Proc. ACM VRST'01*, Baniff, Alberta, Canada (2001), 55-61.
32. Ullmer, B. and Ishii, H. Emerging frameworks for tangible user interfaces. In Carroll, J.M. (ed.) *Human-computer interaction in the new millennium*, Addison-Wesley, Reading, Massachusetts, USA, 2001, 579–601.
33. Völlinger, U., Wewetzer, M., Hausser, F. and Ley, A., An Adaptive Multiresolutional Approach for Interactive Simulation of Cloth. In *Proc. IASTED Technology Conferences 2010*, (2010).
34. Wingrave, C.A. and Bowman, D.A., Tiered Developer-Centric Representations for 3D Interfaces: Concept-Oriented Design in Chasm. In *Proc. IEEE Virtual Reality*, Reno, Nevada, USA (2008), 193-200.
35. Woksepp, S. and Olofsson, T. Credibility and applicability of virtual reality models in design and construction. *Advanced Engineering Informatics*, *22*, 4 (2008), 520-528.

SketchTop: Design Collaboration on a Multi-touch Tabletop

Paul Clifton[1], Ali Mazalek[1], Jon Sanford[2], Claudia Rébola[2], Seunghyun "Tina" Lee[2], Natasha Powell[2]
Digital Media Program[1], School of Industrial Design[2]
Georgia Institute of Technology
Atlanta, GA, USA
paulgclifton@gmail.com, mazalek@gatech.edu, jon.sanford@coa.gatech.edu, crw@gatech.edu, tinalee@gatech.edu, nanpowell@gmail.com

ABSTRACT
Computer mediated group collaboration, particularly in the design and engineering disciplines, is in need of better applications that suit the needs of effective exchange of information. Multi-touch surfaces offer the capabilities to augment and better enable face-to-face interaction with digital content and applications. This paper presents the design, development and testing of SketchTop, a multi-touch sketching application for collocated design collaboration.

Author Keywords
Multi-touch tabletop, Design, Collaboration

ACM Classification Keywords
H.5.3. [Information Interfaces and Presentation]: Group and Organization Interfaces---*Collaborative computing*

General Terms
Design, experimentation.

INTRODUCTION
Studies have shown that groups using interactive technologies to facilitate and enhance collaboration produce better results than individuals [6, 8, 15, 20]. However, few studies have examined the use of multi-user interactive surfaces for complex design activities in which interdisciplinary teams work by sharing visual information [11, 12, 13-14]. Despite its collaborative nature, design is typically a linear process where information is passed sequentially between team members who contribute their own unique expertise [11, 16]. The design process is often a series of design and redesign iterations that involve passing work between domains, which can be time-consuming and costly, and can result in poor final outcomes [9].

TEI'11, January 22–26, 2011, Funchal, Portugal.

On the other hand, interactive collaboration enables team members to share expertise synchronously during the design process. This reduces time and cost and results in better design outcomes [16]. Multi-touch tabletops can facilitate and enhance interactive collaboration by bringing collaborators together during the design process. Although interactive tables can enable real-time sharing of design information, usability issues such as the orientation of objects, definition of territories, and access to input devices can significantly affect the collaborative experience [18]. Our research explores when and how digital tabletops can be used in the collaborative design process. This paper reports on the design, development and testing of SketchTop, a multi-touch tabletop system that supports collaborative design through synchronous communication, and the creation and sharing of design sketches.

BACKGROUND
We synthesize research from the domains of collaborative design work and tabletop collaboration.

Collaborative Design
Based on our background research, we discovered that most collaborative design work occurs during the ideation phases of a project, and a primary tool used for communication and thinking during this type of work is sketching [1]. Detailed mockups are usually made individually after the initial ideation phases [2]. Therefore, digital tabletops are suited to facilitate and enhance the kind of interactions designers use to develop and communicate ideas at the beginning of a project. By bringing disciplines together for this phase of design, the process can be flattened and major design issues can be uncovered early.

Previous collaborative tabletop systems have focused on the combination of real and digital objects [5], the spaces and tools required for collaborative design [3], and the organizational aspects of collaborative work [7]. SketchTop focuses on the interaction design for a simple sketching interface to support interdisciplinary design teams during ideation and brainstorming by facilitating simultaneous editing of content and manipulation of interface objects.

Tabletop Collaboration

Previous research shows that factors such as orientation of objects on the table, definition of territories and access to input devices effect collaboration on tabletop systems.

Orientation of Objects

The problem of orientation is that objects can appear upside down depending on where people are located around a table. Kruger discusses different ways systems solve this problem: automatic orientation based on user location or screen position, or manual orientation either through direct manipulation or GUI-like tools. Based on user studies of these techniques, Kruger suggests several important factors in the orientation of objects on the table. Objects should be manually orientable to any angle. Rotation interactions should be lightweight so that they do not interfere with group communication, and users should be able to control the orientation of their own objects [10]. SketchTop uses a two-point, manual, rotate-translate-resize interaction as a flexible way to manipulate interface elements [4].

Definition of Territories

Studies have demonstrated that collaborators partition tabletop workspaces into three types of territories: personal, group, and storage [19]. Personal territories are primarily used for thinking. The group territory is for sharing information, and storage territories organize information or hold it to be recalled later. People are adept at partitioning workspaces; therefore lightweight and flexible mechanisms for moving and resizing objects can facilitate the definition of territories [19]. By giving users complete control over the location and orientation of all screen objects, SketchTop allows users to define territories as required by the state of the collaboration.

Access to Input Devices

In order to facilitate group-work, tabletops should provide the ability for multiple users to interact with the system simultaneously [18]. Marshall compared different combinations of interface devices: single mouse, multiple mice, single touch, and multi-touch, to determine the effects of equity of access with user participation [17]. The results show that multi-touch supports more equitable participation with respect to group members' contribution to the work. SketchTop combines true multi-touch with the use of light pens, ensuring that all users can work simultaneously.

CONCEPTUAL DESIGN

Based on our research, we developed an initial design for a tabletop application, Figure 1, that we implemented as a paper prototype and evaluated in a pilot study.

Design Criteria

In general, the design needs to support territoriality, provide mechanisms for reorienting content and tools for sketching, and allow simultaneous input from multiple users. The initial design provided four personal spaces, a group space and a mechanism for tagging sketches along a timeline,

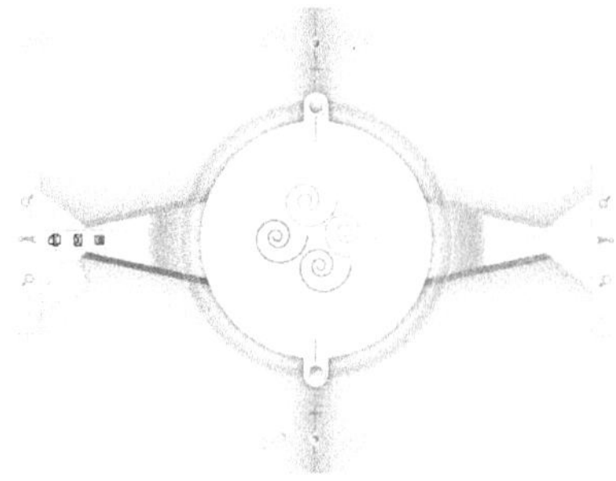

Figure 1: SketchTop's initial interface

which acts as a storage space. Users sketch inside their personal space then drag the sketches into the group space for sharing. Shared tools on the short sides of the table access features such as exporting sketches. Tagging and history tools are on the long sides of the table. The group space rotates using a set of handles, providing manual control of the orientation of shared objects. The entire group space rotates, giving users the ability to present sets of sketches to the rest of the team. The multi-touch capability of the table provides the ability for all users to sketch and share sketches simultaneously. The groups negotiate the use of shared resources as they would at a standard table. The ability to create and share sketches provides users the type of support for collaborative work afforded by pen and paper, whiteboards, and other sketching media with the added benefit of digital editing, storing and version tracking of their sketches.

Pilot Study

We produced and tested a paper mock-up of our design to study the usability of the interface and how well the application facilitated interdisciplinary design collaboration. Groups of two, three, and four people from design and engineering backgrounds came to the lab. We asked them to show us how they would perform certain actions using the interface; then, we gave them a tutorial on the interface and asked them to perform a design task as a group. Afterwards, they answered a questionnaire about their experiences and took part in a group interview.

RESULTS

The pilot study revealed three main issues with the design: the size and shape of group and personal spaces, the location and ownership of tools, and the clarity of the interface. The group and personal spaces needed to be similarly shaped and resizable to facilitate transitions between individual and group work. They also needed to be flexible to support movement around the table. Rotating the entire group space proved unintuitive, and users often rotated individual sketches instead. Users confused the functions of shared tools, and wanted personal sets of tools that they could place in a location near where they stood. The use of the tagging and history features was not clear, although users did consider them valuable.

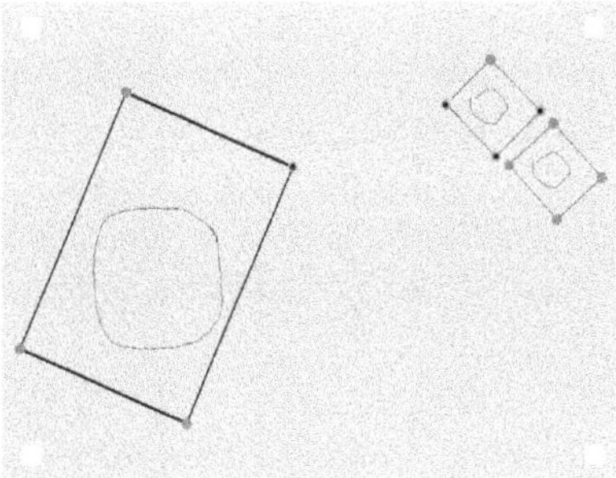

Figure 2: The fluid SketchTop interface

Figure 3: Copying a canvas

Based on these results, we refined our design to provide floating, resizable canvases, which allow users to create their own territories as needed, and simultaneous access to tools and canvases. We removed the history feature based on the focus of the user study and time constraints.

THE SKETCHTOP SYSTEM

The SketchTop application, shown in Figure 2, aims to be as flexible as possible to give users the ability to move around the table as they work and define territories as the design process progresses. SketchTop runs on a 50-inch, diffused illumination based tabletop running the reacTIVision engine for tracking touch input. The pens emit infrared light and are treated as touches by the system.

User Scenario

SketchTop is designed for groups of designers and engineers to brainstorm about a design. When a group approaches the table, each member creates a new canvas by touching one of the green new canvas buttons in the corner of the screen. One of the designers asks what features the device they are designing needs to have and begins writing a list on one of the canvases. During the discussion of features, another designer begins sketching an example of his idea about ergonomics. He then copies his sketch and passes it to one of the engineers to see if the form poses any problems for the hardware design. The engineer turns the sketch so it is facing him and resizes the canvas so he has room to sketch the hardware design. After hashing out some of the design issues, the group decides to make a more detailed large format sketch, so one of them creates a new canvas and resizes it so that it takes up the entire screen. They then draw on this canvas together, illustrating the shape of the device and the placement of the features. The final sketch is then exported and emailed around for review.

Features and Interactions

SketchTop provides a natural interface by eliminating standard GUI tools and replacing them with objects that mimic the behavior of pen and paper. Users sketch with a light pen on the page, within the frame of the canvas, and they manipulate the size, orientation, and location of the canvas using different combinations of the handles. Touching and dragging any combination of two handles simultaneously resizes and rotates the canvas. To delete a canvas one user touches two handles, and a second user touches and drags a third handle. The copy appears near the original as shown in Figure 3.

USER EVALUATION

We conducted a user study that compared using SketchTop with pen and paper for a collaborative design task.

Methodology

We assigned one group each of five, three, and one person to use either a standard table or SketchTop to design an electrically augmented toilet for people with disabilities. After an interface tutorial, the groups had 30 minutes to complete the task. We recorded their work and observed their collaborative actions. After the session, each group member filled out a questionnaire about the collaboration and the interface. Finally, as a group, the participants took part in an interview about their experiences.

Results

As a collaborative design tool, SketchTop succeeds in providing the ability to communicate ideas to a group. While pen and paper do result in higher-fidelity sketches, due to hardware limitations of our system, the nature of the collaboration remained the same across both systems. Groups used sketches to illustrate ideas, and document design progress the same regardless of the interface they used. They also used the same types of verbal and non-verbal communications across interfaces. For this task, groups collaborated the same way, spent the same amount of time collaborating, and produced equivalent results regardless of the interface.

Users found that creating new canvases, and moving, resizing and rotating them was clear, usable, and useful. Deleting the canvas was not clear, but it was useful once they understood the interaction. Copying canvases was not clear or easy, and therefore, was not used, even though users did consider it important. Furthermore, users would prefer to copy parts of sketches instead of entire canvases. Users also wanted to use the entire frame for manipulating canvases instead of discreet handles, and an active frame could make interactions easier and more obvious.

Discussion

The nature of collaboration changed very little between pen and paper and SketchTop. The desire for features like copy and paste that are not possible with pen and paper indicate how digital tabletops might improve the design process. Given that, the user study illustrates that digital tabletops have the potential to be effective tools for design collaboration and that they can augment collaborative work in ways that people do find useful, but there is still work to be done concerning the implementation of these systems. Towards that end, SketchTop illustrates an interface design that allows simultaneously editing the content of objects and manipulating them.

The study also pointed out another level of interactions that need to be designed and implemented. Users require the ability to interact with parts of sketches to erase and copy and paste single elements. The canvas and page metaphor does work for most people and provides a solid base for designing the interactions and implementing the features that could make SketchTop a viable tool.

CONCLUSION AND FUTURE WORK

SketchTop furthers the research in tabletop application design by showing that an appropriately designed tabletop application can support collocated collaborative design by providing users with the ability to communicate and iterate ideas generated during early phases of the design process. This understanding can lead to further work in how digital tabletops can augment the design process by making it more interactive across disciplines and eventually about how tabletops can play a role in remote collaboration. Furthermore, it develops and points to research that must be done on interaction levels within applications of this sort.

REFERENCES

1. Arvola, M. and Artman, H. Interaction walkthroughs and improvised role play. Design and semantics of form and movement, 42.
2. Do, E. The Right Tool at the Right Time--drawing as an interface to knowledge based design aids. 1996.
3. Haller, M., Brandl, P., Leithinger, D., Leitner, J., Seifried, T. and Billinghurst, M. Shared Design Space: Sketching ideas using digital pens and a large augmented tabletop setup. Advances in Artificial Reality and Tele-Existence. 185-196.
4. Hancock, M., Vernier, F., Wigdor, D., Carpendale, S. and Shen, C., Rotation and translation mechanisms for tabletop interaction. In *Proc. First IEEE International Workshop on Horizontal Interactive Human-Computer Systems*, TABLETOP'06, IEEE (2006), 79-86.
5. Hartmann, B., Morris, M.R., Benko, H. and Wilson, A.D. Pictionaire: supporting collaborative design work by integrating physical and digital artifacts *Proc. 2010 ACM* conference *on Computer supported cooperative work*, ACM (2010).
6. Hill, G. W. Group versus individual performance: Are TV+1 heads better than one? Psychological Bulletin, 91, 3 (1982), 517-539.
7. Hinrichs, U., Carpendale, S., Scott, S. and Pattison, E. Interface currents: Supporting fluent collaboration on tabletop displays. *Smart Graphics '05*, Springer-Verlag New York Inc, 2005, 185.
8. Kerr, N. L. and Tindale, R. S. Group Performance and Decision Making. Annual Review of Psychology, 55, 1 (2004), 623-655.
9. Klein, M. and Lu, S. C. Y. Conflict resolution in cooperative design. Artificial Intelligence in Engineering, 4, 4 (1989), 168-180.
10. Kruger, R., Carpendale, S., Scott, S. D. and Greenberg, S. Roles of Orientation in Tabletop Collaboration: Comprehension, Coordination and Communication. Computer Supported Cooperative Work (CSCW), 13, 5 (2004), 501-537.
11. Kvan, T. Collaborative design: what is it? Automation in Construction, 9, 4 (2000), 409-415.
12. Lahti, H., Seitamaa-Hakkarainen, P. and Hakkarainen, K. Collaboration patterns in computer supported collaborative designing. Design Studies, 25, 4 (2004), 351-371.
13. Lawson, B. How designers think: the design process demystified. Architectural Press, Oxford ; Boston, 1997.
14. Lawson, B. What designers know. Elsevier/Architectural Press, Oxford ; Burlington, MA, 2004.
15. Lorge, I., Fox, D., Davitz, J. and Brenner, M. A survey of studies contrasting the quality of group performance and individual performance, 1920-1957. Psychological Bulletin, 55, 6 (1958), 337-372.
16. Priest, J. W. and Sánchez, J. M. Product development and design for manufacturing : a collaborative approach to producibility and reliability. Marcel Dekker, New York, 2001.
17. Marshall, P., Hornecker, E., Morris, R., Sheep Dalton, N. and Rogers, Y. When the fingers do the talking: A study of group participation with varying constraints to a tabletop interface. City, 2008.
18. Scott, S. D., Grant, K. D. and Mandryk, R. L. System Guidelines for Co-located, Collaborative Work on a Tabletop Display. 2003.
19. Scott, S. D., Carpendale, M. S. T. and Inkpen, K. M. Territoriality in Collaborative Tabletop Workspaces. 2004.
20. Yetton, P. and Bottger, P. Individual versus group problem solving: An empirical test of a best-member strategy. Behavior & Human Decision Processes Academic Press Inc, 29, 3 (1982), 307-321.

Bizarro Game Controllers Studio Proposal

Amanda Williams
Wyld Collective Ltd
3421 Ave. de l'Hotel de Ville
Montréal, QC H2X 3B5

Concordia University
1515 Rue St-Catherine Ouest
Montréal, QC H3G 1M8
Canada
metamanda@gmail.com

Eric Kabisch
fluxt design
Laboratory for Ubiquitous
Computing and Interaction
University of California, Irvine
6210 Donald Bren Hall
Irvine, CA 92697-3425
USA
ekabisch@uci.edu

Abstract
Tangible interfaces are increasingly becoming commercially available products in the current generation of game controllers like the Nintendo Wii Remote, Microsoft's Kinect, and Sony's Eye. Tangible interaction researchers and designers can push the envelope of game controllers by thinking creatively about input device design. At the same time, the constraints of controlling a playable game can provide us with a fun, engaging, and useful design exercise.

Keywords
Hacking, Wii Remote, Wii Nunchuk, DIY.

ACM Classification Keywords
H5.m. Information interfaces and presentation (e.g., HCI): Miscellaneous.

General Terms
Design, Human Factors

Introduction
Tangible interfaces, though relatively young as a topic of research, are increasingly becoming commercially available in the current generation of game controllers: first the Nintendo Wii Remote and the iPhone/iPod Touch, and more recently Microsoft's Kinect and Sony's

Eye. In crossing over to commercial products, some aspects of tangible interaction have remained very similar – for example, the use of cameras and accelerometers for motion tracking, the emphasis on gestural and embodied interaction, and the increased availability of users' physical gestures to other collaborators. However, other aspects have shifted. While tangible interfaces are often designed specifically for, and in tandem with, a particular application, tangible game controllers are intended to support interaction with a wide variety of games and applications. For the most part, users' gestural interactions are still intended to manipulate action on a conventional, focal screen. At the same time the availability of affordable off-the-shelf components that support tangible and gestural interaction can support the quick production of research prototypes [1].

The "Bizarro Game Controllers" studio aims to explore how tangible interaction research(ers) can, on the one hand, push the envelope of game controller design beyond the current industry standard. On the other hand, we also hope to explore how we might learn from current game controller design and selectively use some of its tricks and conventions in our own work. We invite participants to bring a sensor or camera they've been dying to play with, and/or to consider how to harness a particular embodied motion, interaction, or gesture, and spend the afternoon in our studio turning those ideas into a bizarre game controller.

Studio Proposal

We expect three main learning phases for participants in this studio. First, using simple test programs we will try to understand sensor ranges and calibration so that participants can see what sort of input they might expect from their game controllers. This will include mapping these sensor inputs to simple interactive sketches in Processing, to get a "feel" for their interactional properties as well as an understanding of the number ranges to expect from the sensors. Second, we will spend some time tweaking and calibrating the hardware and/or software support for the game controllers in order to obtain ranges of data optimal for user control. Next, we will provide an open-source testing platform, written in Processing, that supplies version of several classic video games (such as Pong, Space Invaders, etc.) for testing purposes; a real game, even if it is very simple, provides a good test for whether a controller is allowing a user to actually feel in control. If time allows, we will also supply containers and fabric so that participants can create the packaging for their controllers (we invite participants to bring their own materials for this purpose as well).

Expected skills:

- Basic hardware skills: competence with prototyping simple circuits on a breadboard.

- Intermediate programming skills with Arduino and either Processing or Java.

Expected preparation:

- We will expect participants to bring a laptop computer with Arduino, Processing, and required libraries installed.

- Participants will be expected to have given some thought to the sort of controller they want to build. They should know what materials they will need on hand in order to build their game controller. While we may be able to supply basics such as perf-boards, resistors, capacitors, and LEDs, any special or particular sensors should be brought by participants. If this presents difficulties for people who want to participate, they may contact us to figure out how to procure what they need.

- Participants will be expected to bring their own Arduino. If they intend to make a wireless game controller, they should bring their own XBee as well. Bluetooth is not encouraged due to issues with pairing and interference when there are too many Bluetooth devices in close proximity.

Studio Topics to be covered

The topics to be covered will be:

- Wiring sensors to Arduino I/O pins and displaying data in the Serial Monitor and in graphical Processing sketches in order get a feel for sensor ranges and calibration.
- Refining the use of sensor data for the purposes of controlling game interaction.
- Testing controllers on a real game.
- Packaging the game controller.

We believe that mastering these basic arrangements will prepare participants to explore more elaborate prototypes on their own, and provide a springboard for them to proceed to design their own games to take advantage of their fancy new bizarro game controller.

Studio Learning Goals

The aim of the Bizarro Game Controller Studio is to bring together a dynamic and diverse group of artists, researchers, designers and hackers to explore the intersection between tangible interfaces and the current generation of video game controllers.

The goals of our studio include:

- To push the envelope of game controller design, where current commercially available controllers typically use blob tracking on cameras, accelerometers, gyroscopes, and conventional buttons, aiming to control action on a conventional screen. If constrained only by our imaginations, what other materials, data, and bodily interactions might we use to control gameplay?
- To understand some of the constraints and demands of game controller design, and grasp its similarities and differences with other tangible interaction research.
- To build connections amongst people from different cities and institutions, who share a love of design and hacking.

Studio Supporting Web Documents

We will base studio activities on the Arduino and Processing platforms. More information on Arduino and Processing is available at:
http://arduino.cc/
http://www.processing.org/

For inspiration, we encourage participants to investigate wiimote hacks (a substantial community of wiimote hacking has grown online since the Nintendo Wii was released) and game controllers for disabled gamers. These may provide some insight into creative ways to use the body to control games:
http://www.gimpgear.us/wiimote.htm
http://hackawii.com/

Acknowledgements

We thank TEI reviewers and participants, as well as those who have played a role in the authors' explorations into game controller design, including Cindy Poremba, Heather Kelley, Morgan Kennedy, Lynn Hughes, and Bart Simon.

Citations

[1] Schlömer, T., Poppinga, B., Henze, N., and Boll, S. 2008. Gesture recognition with a Wii controller. In *Proceedings of the 2nd international Conference on Tangible and Embedded interaction* (Bonn, Germany, February 18 - 20, 2008). TEI '08. ACM, New York, NY, 11-14.

Electronics as Material: littleBits

Ayah Bdeir
MS MIT Media Lab
540 West 21st street
New York, NY 10011
ayah@littleBits.cc

Ted Ullrich
MID Georgiatech
71 S 4th Street Apt. 2
Brooklyn, NY 11211
tullrich@gmail.com

TEI'11, January 22–26, 2011, Funchal, Portugal.

Abstract
Electronics are everywhere. We now produce, consume and throw out more electronic gadgets than ever before. Yet, creativity with electronics starts when they can be thought of as sketching materials like paper, screws, cardboard.

This Studio will allow participants to create prototypes of interactive gadgets using a diverse library of materials: littleBits (an opensource kit of pre-assembled electronics that snap together with tiny magnets), combined with traditional design materials (foam, fabric, paper, clay etc).

The Studio structure is in several phases. The participants start by conceptualizing an interactive object or small scale installation, break down the interaction, and build it using familiar and unfamiliar materials. Participants will then present their creation and discuss the process of expanding their materials library to include light, sound, sensing, and motion. Finally, the participants will come up with ideas for new littleBits modules to suggest or contribute to the open source kit and community.

Keywords
Studio, interaction design, industrial design, prototyping, electronics, littleBits, opensource.

ACM Classification Keywords
H.5.2 User Interfaces (D.2.2, H.1.2, I.3.6): Prototyping.

General Terms
Design, Experimentation.

Introduction

Electronics are everywhere. We now produce, consume and throw out more electronic gadgets than ever before. Yet, engineering is mysticized, electronic objects are black-boxed and creativity is limited by the tools and materials available to each discipline [1].

Well, disciplines are dead (we think), engineering is not that hard, and until creativity is less constrained, we will continue to see more of the same, and waste more of the same.

With the growing DIY community and open source movement, technology creation has been moving from the hands of large corporations and big development labs to those of small studios and individuals. With the democratization of technology gaining more momentum, creativity with electronics will explode when they can be used as, and combined with other traditional materials such as paper, cardboard and screws.

Studio Proposal

The Electronics as Materials Studio will offer the participants the opportunity to experiment with materials that were previously intimidating or prohibitive to them: electronics components and electric circuits. In the studio, the participants will create and build a prototype of an animated object, small-scale interactive installation or interactive product. The participants will use a diverse library of sketching materials, some of which are familiar to them, such as paper, cardboard, clay, crayons, paint, screws, tape, glue, LEGOs etc. Other materials available are more abstract, less accessible, and usually require expert skill set and platform: light, sound, motion, display, etc. This second set of materials will be represented by littleBits, a kit of pre-assembled electronics, that snap together with tiny magnets.

littleBits: A toolkit of tiny circuitboards

littleBits is a growing library of preassembled circuit boards, made easy by tiny magnets (figure 1). Just as LEGOs allow you to create complex structures with very little engineering knowledge, littleBits are simple, intuitive, space-sensitive blocks that make prototyping with sophisticated electronics a matter of snapping small magnets together (figure 2). With a growing number of available modules: switches, batteries, buttons, sensors, etc (figure 3), littleBits aims to move electronics from late stages of the design process to its earliest ones, and from the hands of experts, to those of artists, makers and designers. All logic and circuitry is pre-engineered, so you can play with electronics without knowing electronics. Tiny magnets act as connectors and enforce polarity, so you can't put things in the wrong way.

Agenda

The Studio structure is in several phases.

Phase 1: Brainstorming

The first step of the studio is a brainstorming phase. The participants start by conceptualizing an interactive object or small scale installation individually or in groups, and they come up with ideas for prototypes they want to build: a coffeemaker with a vibration-based menu, an electronically enhanced dollhouse, a speaking door. The participants then throw out their ideas to the group and we build on top of them to create 5 or 6 more feasible, solid, creative ideas.

Phase 2: littleBits demo

Phase 2 will be a short demo and presentation about littleBits. We present all the different modules, how they snap to each other, the color codes, their illustrations. And participants play with the modules to get comfortable with the toolkit. We also present the online littleBits community where people suggest new modules, share schematics, and create their own littleBits. In this phase we also demo the other craft and construction materials at hand to get the participants familiar with them (figure 4).

Phase 3: Interaction Design
In Phase 3 of the Studio, we take the 5 or 6 ideas the group came up with in Phase 1 and we break down the interaction. Where do we need motion, where do we need sound, what happens when this button is pushed, etc. We create a rough diagram of the interaction that acts like the brief for the prototypes

Phase 4: Prototyping in teams
In Phase 4 we break out in groups of 3 and the participants start to prototype their gadgets. They integrate the circuitboards with the other materials and spend time discussing and finetuning the interactive object and its interface (figure 5).

Phase 5: Presentation/Discussion
Here we go around the room and participant teams present their invention, how they interact with it, how they used littleBits, what other materials they used, what difficulties they had, and how the toolkit enhanced their process. Finally, the participants will come up with ideas for new littleBits modules to suggest or contribute to the open source kit and community.

Studio Learning Goals

At the end of the studio participants will be less intimidated by electronics, electronic components and circuitboards. In the Electronics as Material Studio, participants will learn to think of motion, sound, light, displays as materials and modes of expression. They will learn to be creative using these materials and prototype their creations with them. Participants will be able to push their creativity further by adopting interactivity in their process while working with physical animation, and iteration with electronics.

For more info

For more information, videos, pictures and press about littleBits, please visit: www.littleBits.cc.

Figure 1: the littleBits starter kit

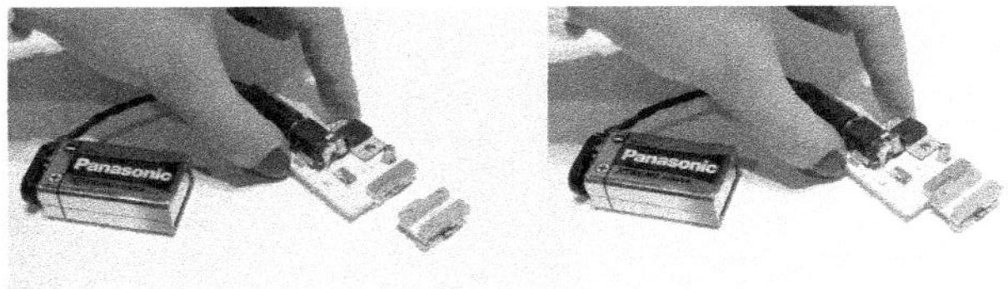

Figure 2: Playing with littleBits: Snapping modules to create light

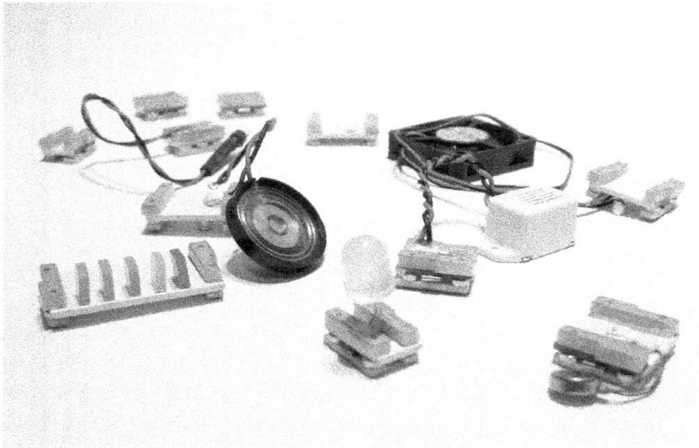

Figure 3: The littleBits toolkit contains LED modules, buzzer modules, motors, etc.

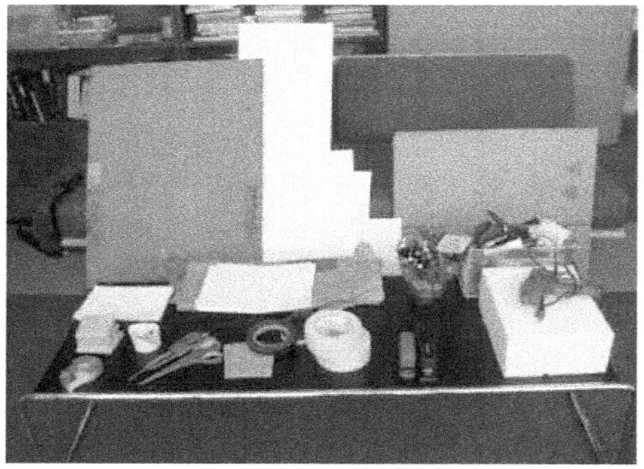

Figure 4: A small sample of the materials library

Figure 5: A designer using traditional contruction materials to integrate with electronics

Acknowledgements

We would like to thank Eyebeam, Creative Commons, Paul Rothman, Youngjin Chung, Jie Qi, Ted Ullrich

References

Electronics as Material: littleBits, *TEI 2009*, ACM Press (2009).

Fine Bookbinding Meets Electronics

Daniela K. Rosner
School of Information, UC Berkeley
102 South Hall
San Francisco, CA 94720-4600
daniela@ischool.berkeley.edu

Hannah Perner-Wilson
MIT Media Lab, High-Low Tech
77 Mass. Ave
Cambridge, MA 02139
plusea@media.mit.edu

Jie Qi
MIT Media Lab, High-Low Tech
77 Mass. Ave
Cambridge, MA 02139
jieqi@mit.edu

Leah Buechley
MIT Media Lab, High-Low Tech
77 Mass. Ave
Cambridge, MA 02139
leah@media.mit.edu

TEI'11, January 22–26, 2011, Funchal, Portugal.

Abstract

As technologies, finely bound books are compact, durable forms that get passed from one generation to the next. As handcrafted objects, they exemplify manual control and dexterity, patience and care, and continuity with the past. Paper-based electronic books, by contrast, are relatively new objects that enable novel interactions with material. Here we explore connections between centuries-old and contemporary building techniques by adding electronics to traditional binding. What kinds of details would be interesting to learn about the past? How could we use conductive fibers to talk to the future? What could gilded edges tell us about our interactions with books? In this studio, participants will build basic bookbinding and e-textiles skills to enable new material explorations.

Keywords

Bookbinding, e-textiles, handicraft, craft.

ACM Classification Keywords

H5.m. Information interfaces and presentation: Miscellaneous.

General Terms

Design.

Introduction

Fine bookbinding is an age-old handwork practice that requires detailed understanding of materials and techniques. Through a series of discrete, skilled activities — folding, sawing, sewing, pressing, gluing, chopping, rounding, backing, lining, pairing, staining, covering, and lettering— books develop from parts and pieces into encased archival objects. By contrast, e-textiles activities have recently developed from experiments combining fashion with electrical circuitry [1]. Novel interactive wearables, objects and surfaces push the boundaries of techniques (painting, sewing) and materials (conductive paints and fibers) by producing a variety of unusual forms, from handcrafted textile sensors [3] to computational sketchbooks [2] and painted electronic pop-up books [4]. Here we look at fine bookbinding as a site to explore the intersections of past and future handwork practices.

Studio Proposal

This studio will be structured in four parts. The first part of the studio will involve brief presentations of a personal book that participants bring to the workshop. In order to better understand how a book is structured, participants will spend the second part of the studio learning basic bookbinding techniques by creating a simple book using plain and decorative papers, boards and paste. In the third part of the studio, participants will get a feel for how to integrate a microcontroller and electronic circuitry with one of their books by testing and extending a simple prepared Arduino program. The forth part of the studio will involve material explorations using old books and materials. Techniques will be based on the first author's ongoing apprenticeship-based qualitative study of fine bookbinding in the UK and US.

Our studio is for participants with an intermediate level knowledge of electronics and programming. We expect participants to have the following skills:

- Basic hardware skills: competence with prototyping simple circuits on a breadboard, such as turning on an LED with a battery and resistor.

- Basic programming skills with Arduino and either Processing or Java.

- No prior knowledge of bookbinding is required.

Studio Topics to be covered

This studio will cover the following topics:

- Sewing to connect individual pages
- Setting and assembling a spine
- Pasting up end papers and covering boards
- Hand tooling with gold/silver foil, gold leaf
- Creating circuitry with copper tape, conductive fabric tape, conductive glue, conductive thread, velostat, conductive paint (copper and carbon), pencils (graphite),

Studio Learning Goals

We hope that participants will gain a better appreciation for fine binding practices as well as learn basic techniques for integrating electronics with paper and binding. By experimenting with materials, tooling and techniques, participants can extend their existing skills in electronics and computation into the developing paper-based domain.

Studio Supporting Web Documents

Recent painted paper circuit concepts include:

"Paper Computing" by Leah Buechley
http://www.youtube.com/watch?v=-LyKmaz_3uI

High-Low Tech Paper Circuits tutorial:
http://hlt.media.mit.edu/wiki/pmwiki.php?n=Main.PaperCircuits

"Touch to interact with brain" by Takashi Kondo
http://www.flickr.com/photos/t_kondo/4788541619/

"Rip to hear message"
http://www.flickr.com/photos/t_kondo/4788555023/in/photostream/

"Electronic Popables" by Jie Qi
http://vimeo.com/user1892233

Book of paintable electronics examples resulting from day-long workshop:
http://www.youtube.com/watch?v=n7IQhMCYru8

Arduino libraries:
http://www.arduino.cc/en/Reference/Libraries

The first workshop on paintable electronics took place at the Cambridge Science Festival. Each participant was given a pre-programmed micro-controller, a selection of components wherein the power supply travels through the pages. Participants were asked to make a page of a book.
Video:
http://www.youtube.com/watch?v=n7IQhMCYru8
Photos:
http://www.flickr.com/photos/plusea/sets/72157623998025530/

Acknowledgements

We thank the many TEI and e-textiles researchers, designers, and artists that inspired this studio, particularly Alex Taylor, Nicolas Villar, and Tim Regan.

Citations

[1] Buechley, L., Eisenberg, M. "The LilyPad Arduino: Toward Wearable Engineering for Everyone," *IEEE Pervasive Computing* 7, no. 2 (2008): 12-15.

[2] Buechley, L., Hendrix, S. and Eisenberg, M."Paints, paper, and programs: first steps toward the computational sketchbook," in *Proceedings of the 3rd International Conference on Tangible and Embedded* Interaction (Cambridge, United Kingdom: ACM, 2009), 9-12.

[3] Handcrafted textile sensors: www.howtogetwhatyouwant.at

[4] Qi, J., Buechley, L."Electronic popables: exploring paper-based computing through an interactive pop-up book," in *Proceedings of the fourth international conference on Tangible, embedded, and embodied interaction* (Cambridge, Massachusetts, USA: ACM, 2010), 121-128.

A Toolkit for Tinkering with Tangibles & Connecting Communities

Edward Baafi
High-low Tech Group
MIT Media Lab
Room E14-548U
77 Massachusetts Ave
Cambridge, MA 02139 USA
ed@modk.it

Amon Millner
Franklin W Olin College of Engineering
Computers and Cognition Lab
& MIT Media Lab
Lifelong Kindergarten Group
1 Olin Way, Needham, MA 02492
millner@media.mit.edu

TEI'11, January 22–26, 2011, Funchal, Portugal.

Abstract

In this hands-on Studio, you'll explore Modkit [1], a new toolkit for creating tangible interfaces (e.g., bike handlebars with interactive lights and sounds). Modkit makes it possible for novices and experienced programmers/designers to bring tangibles to life by offering graphical command blocks inspired by the Scratch programming environment [2]. Modkit tools work with the Arduino [3] platform's library of code (such as C/C++) to enable users to participate in a community rich with project ideas and sample files. Modkit supports multiple representations of code – graphical command blocks can become editable text-based code to offer additional avenues for learning and sharing. The Studio welcomes members of the research, industrial, academic, maker, and I-just-want-to-have fun communities of all experience levels to participate. Participants will have opportunities to use Modkit in personally-meaningful ways. Participants who wish to extend Modkit tools with new functionality will have opportunities to do so. The organizers will conclude the Studio with a discussion around activities, example projects, and approaches to adapting the toolkit to different settings. Participants will contribute to brainstorming about potential uses, future directions, and collaborations.

Keywords
Graphical programming, Modkit, construction kit, Arduino, Scratch, educational technology, sensors

ACM Classification Keywords
K.3.1 Computer Uses in Education. D.2.6 Programming Environments. H.5.2 User Interfaces (prototyping)

General Terms
Languages, Design.

Introduction
Developing tangible interfaces often involves creating or selecting an electronic circuit as well as writing code to run on a microcontroller. This Studio explores new ways to enable novices and experts to explore designing tangible interfaces using a new toolkit called Modkit that builds upon approachable yet extensible platforms. Modkit offers a graphical programming environment that features Scratch-like command blocks. The interface (shown in Figure 1) allows users to drag and drop commands – snapping the blocks together to create programs that are not susceptible to syntax errors. Blocks in Modkit's pallete are labeled to closely match text commands that control Arduino boards. Modkit blends the easy-to-understand blocks interface with connections to the C/C++ language aspects of Arduino programming to support both novices and experts in exploring programming of the physical world through making tangible interfaces.

This Studio will introduce Modkit as a means for designing systems that involve sensing, actuation, programming, embedded design, and crafting. Each participant will have varying experience in each design capacity. Participants with experience using tools (such as Mindstorms NXT [4], Fritzing [5], or Phidgets [6]) that also help people develop one or more of these design capacities are welcome to explore the merits of Modkit for prototyping.

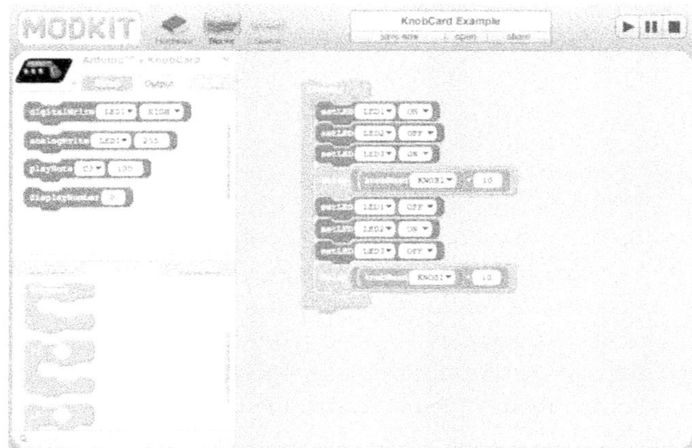

Figure 1 The Modkit graphical programming interface

Studio Overview
The Studio focuses on two main themes: Exploring and Extending. First, the organizers will invite participants to share what they would like to take away from the Studio. Participants will then explore Modkit programming by using Crimp Cards - easy-to-assemble kits of hardware components (shown in Figure 2). (No soldering will be necessary in this phase of the Studio.) After tinkering with connecting sensors and actuators to Arduino-based boards, participants will extend their initial explorations into mock-ups and prototypes - by combining components of different crimp card kits and/or soldering or breadboarding new circuits.

Studio organizers will lead a discussion about the range of projects participants created or attempted to create.

The discussion will offer ideas to participants about ways they could adapt Modkit to better meet the needs of the projects they envisioned. Participants will then have opportunities to add code or hardware components to Modkit – extending the experimental version of the toolkit to meet new needs. During a culminating discussion at the end of the Studio, the organizers will go over the approaches to introducing physical and computational toolkits to diverse communities. We will end the discussion by covering approaches to designing toolkits.

Figure 2 an Arduino board with a Crimp Card project attached

Studio Learning Goals

The organizers welcome both novices and experts to leverage their professional, hobbyist, and life skills as they collectively explore projects. Doing so will put participants in a position to leave with better understandings of how to:

- Use Modkit to create and program tangible interface sketches and prototypes.
- Incorporate found and manufactured materials into interactive projects – combining them in unexpected ways.
- Translate feedback from different types of sensors into light, motion, or sound.
- Apply knowledge of computing to personal and community/societal needs.
- Determine if Modkit meets a project's needs or when peer platforms are more appropriate.
- Develop Modkit activities for future designers from all backgrounds.
- Extend Modkit to better support certain applications or user groups.

Studio Supporting Web Documents

See http://modk.it/tei11.

Acknowledgements

We would like to thank the Scratch Team, the Arduino Team, the Modkit alpha testers and the Learn 2 Teach, Teach 2 Learn program.

References

[1] Modkit. http://www.modk.it

[2] Scratch. http://scratch.mit.edu

[3] Arduino. http://arduino.cc

[4] LEGO Mindstorms. http://mindstorms.lego.com

[5] Fritzing. http://fritzing.org

[6] Phidgets. http://www.phidgets.com

Modular Robotics Studio

Eric Schweikardt
Modular Robotics
2500 Pearl Street #310
Boulder, Colorado 80302 USA
eric@modrobotics.com

TEI'11, January 22–26, 2011, Funchal, Portugal.

Abstract
The Modular Robotics Studio will engage participants in a structured exploration (guided play) and reflective discussion of the principles and practice of building interactive experiences with a modular reconfigurable construction kit of robot components.

Keywords
Modular robots, constructionism, distributed computing

ACM Classification Keywords
H5.m. Information interfaces and presentation (e.g., HCI): Miscellaneous.

General Terms
Design, Human Factors

Introduction
Tangible Embedded Embodied Interaction often entails microcontrollers embedded in physical things and places. Most tangible interactive experiences today engage a single, or a small number of microcontrollers; however in the future tangible interaction experiences will be driven by systems of many connected and communicating microcontrollers. The behavior of these distributed systems will emerge from the bottom-up interactions of the component parts.

The Cubelets modular robotics construction kit toy is designed to introduce the ideas of tangible distributed computing. Cubelets consists of a kit of twenty small (40mm) plastic blocks that users snap together magnetically to build robots. The kit includes Sensor blocks that detect light, sound, physical proximity, and manual input; Action blocks that shine light, produce sound, and move; and Think blocks that compute arithmetic functions such as minimum, average, and sum.

Figure 1. A light-avoiding robot built from Cubelets.

The blocks communicate by passing simple number values across their faces, creating an ad-hoc network. Snapping these blocks together with a battery block results in a construction whose behavior depends on the physical configuration of the blocks. For example, a very simple light-avoiding robot consists of two light sensor blocks atop motor-driven tread action blocks. Each light sensor block produces a number proportional to the amount of light it senses; the motor-drive tread block actuates proportional to the number it receives from the nearer light sensor. The robot moves and turns away from the brightest nearby light.

The Studio

No prior experience with robotics or programming is required. Anyone who wants to play is welcome and will have a successful experience.

The Studio will consist of several phases. In the first phase, Schweikardt will provide an overview of the emergent principles that are inherent in Cubelets, drawing from literature of design,complexity, and constructionist learning. Particular emphasis will be given to Braitenberg's book, *Vehicles*[1], and the bottom-up worldview of local-to-global versus the top-down "omniscient" view that has dominated design thinking from the 17th century watchmakers to software and hardware designers of today.

In the second phase of the Studio, Schweikardt will introduce the functions of the Cubelets blocks and explain the basic algorithm that controls the blocks' operation. A detailed understanding of this algorithm is not necessary for a successful play experience, but those interested in distributed embedded interaction may find it relevant.

In the third phase of the Studio, in pairs or small groups, participants will play with the Cubelets and construct simple robots that perform tasks. For example, one group might try to construct a robot that follows the edge of a table; another might try to construct pair of robots that find one another and 'mate'.

In the fourth phase of the Studio, participants will present their robots and discuss the challenges they faced and how they overcame them. These individual reports will morph into a larger discussion of how these concepts can be realized in tangible embedded, embodied interaction.

Studio Topics

The modular robotics studio will cover the following topics:

- A world made of tiny robots
- Global complexity from simple local interactions
- Modular reconfigurable robots
- Design in a bottom-up world
- There is no god, god is everywhere.
- How Cubelets work

References

[1] Braitenberg, V. (1984). *Vehicles: Experiments in Synthetic Psychology*. Cambridge, MA: MIT Press.

[2] Schweikardt, E., & Gross, M. D. (2006). *roBlocks: A Robotic Construction Kit for Mathematics and Science*

Studio Learning Goals

Participants in the modular robotics studios will learn to think about tangible interaction not as a single centrally controlled process, but as the interaction of many simple and local processes.

Studio Supporting Web Documents

Schweikardt's start-up company, Modular Robotics, maintains a web site at www.modrobotics.com, and over the coming months plans to post details about the Cubelets kit and related topics on this site. Numerous technical papers have been published on the Cubelets (formerly roBlocks) kit, which was the topic of Schweikardt's PhD thesis at Carnegie Mellon University [2,3].

Education. Paper presented at the ACM International Conference on Multimedia Interaction. (ICMI) Banff, Canada.

[3] Schweikardt, E., & Gross, M. (2008). *The Robot is the program: interacting with roBlocks.* Tangible and Embedded Interaction, Bonn, Germany.

SketchChair Studio TEI 2011

Greg Saul
JST, ERATO, IGARASHI
Design UI Project, 1-28-1,
Koishikawa, Bunkyo-ku, Tokyo,
112-0002 Japan
GregSaul@gmail.com

Manfred Lau
JST, ERATO, IGARASHI
Design UI Project, 1-28-1,
Koishikawa, Bunkyo-ku, Tokyo,
112-0002 Japan
Manfred.lau@gmail.com

Jun Mitani
University of Tsukuba &
JST, ERATO, IGARASHI
Design UI Project, 1-28-1,
Koishikawa, Bunkyo-ku, Tokyo,
112-0002 Japan
mitani@cs.tsukuba.ac.jp

Takeo Igarashi
The University of Tokyo &
JST, ERATO, IGARASHI
Design UI Project, 1-28-1,
Koishikawa, Bunkyo-ku, Tokyo,
112-0002 Japan
takeo@acm.org

TEI'11, January 22–26, 2011, Funchal, Portugal.

Abstract

SketchChair is an application that allows novice users to take part in the entire process of designing and fabricating their own full-sized usable chairs from scratch. During the studio, participants will be able to design, build and take home their own scale model paper chair.

Participants will be introduced to *SketchChair* whilst learning how to use a paper cutting plotter to make slice form models. Furthermore we will discuss the considerations around designing tools for customization and CNC production.

Keywords

User-generated Design, Rapid Prototyping, User Interface, Sketch-based modeling, Fabrication, Customization.

ACM Classification Keywords

I.3.5 [Computer Graphics]: Computational Geometry and Object Modeling; H.1.2 User/Machine Systems; J.6 Computer-aided engineering (computer aided design).

General Terms

Design, Experimentation.

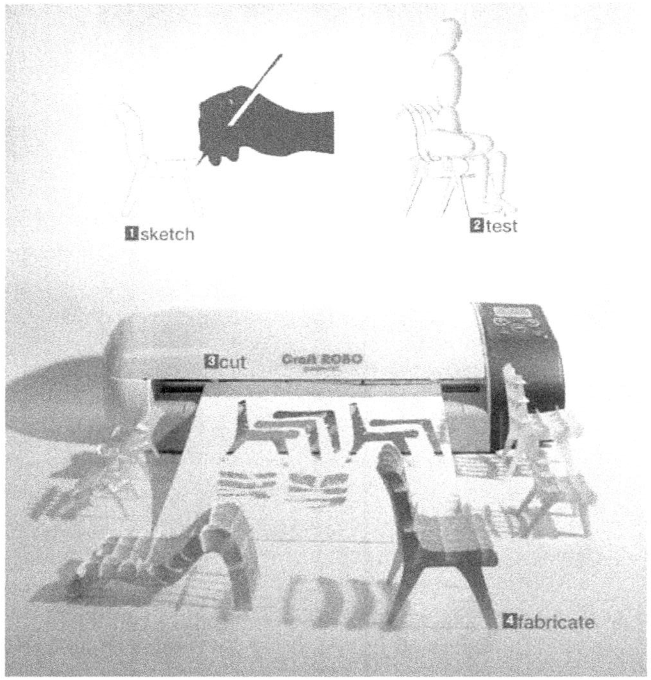

Figure 1. paper chairs designed using the *SketchChair*.

Introduction

Recently, there have been significant advances in digital manufacturing technologies. Tools, such as 3D printers, laser cutters, and computer-controlled milling machines, have become cheaper and more accessible to consumers. These 'desktop manufacturing' or 'personal fabrication' processes are providing the means for people who might normally be consumers to become creators[1,2]. However, CAD (computer aided design) systems that enable novice users to design their own products have lagged behind.

Designing tools for these new processes is an interesting field of research that delivers new possibilities in addition to new challenges. For example a user can design or customize a product before it's being manufactured by a company. This means products can be more relevant and meaningful to a user's needs than a mass produced equivalent.

We will engage in this area of research with other interested participants. To do this, participants will use the *SketchChair* design environment to design and construct their own chairs. Whilst using *SketchChair* participants will be introduced to the general idea of design tools for customized design. Furthermore we will be sharing insights we gained from the sessions that users designed and built chair with the help of this tool. And introducing participants to the process of using a paper cutting plotter to construct three dimensional products (slice forms).

The *SketchChair* System

We present a system that brings us one step closer towards the goal of personal fabrication. Our *SketchChair* software allows even novice users to take part in the entire pipeline of producing a real-world chair, or a paper scale prototype. This process includes concept development, refinement, testing, and fabrication of an actual chair. The system utilizes a simple 2D sketch interface that is easy for novice users to understand and use but also provides more powerful tools that can be used to refine a design by more experienced users. We provide tools for testing the ergonomics of the design, including a physics simulation of a human figure that can be scaled to match the intended user's height. Our system automatically generates the 2D profiles of the individual pieces of the chair. We use a laser cutter or CNC milling machine to produce the actual pieces from plywood and assemble them to create the real-world chair. Alternatively a paper cutting plotter is used to produce paper prototype chairs.

Studio Plan

The studio will be broken up into 3 areas;

First an introduction slideshow and video, participants are introduced to the activity of making Sketch Furniture. Then slides of other inspiring furniture will be presented, this is intended to give participants an idea of what they could design.

Participants will then design their own sketch furniture using the *SketchChair* software. We will then gather cut profiles from each person and cut these over the lunch hour using a paper plotter. After the lunch hour participants will construct their scale furniture.

Lastly, participants will share their designs with the group and there will be time for a discussion on the topics covered.

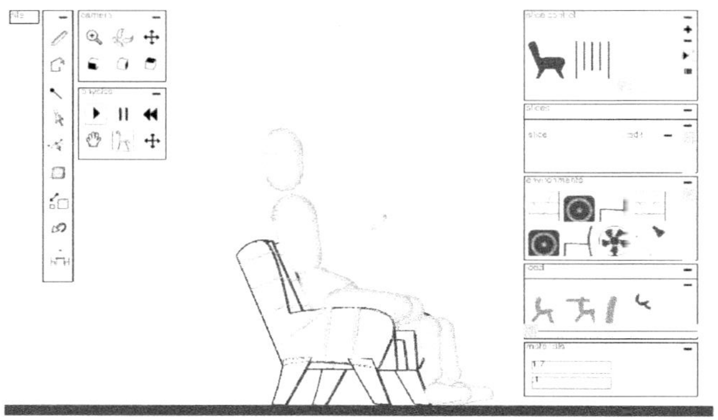

Figure 2. *SketchChair* interface.

Learning Objectives

By participating in this workshop we hope that people have fun and also can take away a small chair, but we also hope to provide some insights into the following;

-Gain a greater understanding of using laser cutter to make things.

-Learn how to make models using a paper cutting plotter from paper sliceforms.

-Understand the current trends in designing for CNC production and its implications for developers and consumers.

Experience Level

Participants should not need any prior experience to take part in this studio. We think that any person familiar with the use of basic computer operation will have the skills required to design and build a *SketchChair*. Construction of the chairs is reasonable easy and does not require the use of tools, pieces are simply slotted together.

Studio Supporting Web Documents

A demo of the current system can be found here: http://www.SketchChair.com

Citations

References

[1] Gross, M. 2007.Now More Than Ever: computational
thinking and a science of design, Japan Society for the Science of Design, 16(2): 50 – 54.
[2] Landay, J. 2009. Design Tools for the Rest of Us.

Do-it-Yourself Creation of Pervasive, Tangible Applications

Juan R. Velasco
University of Alcalá
ITEA2 DiYSE Dissemination Coordinator
juanramon.velasco@uah.es

Marc Roelands
Bell Labs, Alcatel-Lucent, Belgium
ITEA2 DiYSE Project Coordinator
marc.roelands@alcatel-lucent.com

Dries De Roeck
Centre for User Experience Research (CUO)
IBBT/K.U.Leuven, Belgium

Rob Moonen
Laurea, Finland

Lieven Trappeniers
Bell Labs, Alcatel-Lucent, Belgium
Ambient Media Department Head

Miguel A Lopez-Carmona
University of Alcala, Spain

Ivan Marsa-Maestre
University of Alcala, Spain

Emmanuel Marilly
Bell Labs, Alcatel-Lucent, France

Noël Crespi
Institut Telecom, Telecom SudParis, France

Yacine Ghamri-Doudane
ENSIIE, France

Abstract
As technology advances and becomes more pervasive, the DiY (Do-it-Yourself) paradigm that emerged on the furniture & home decoration market in the 70's is now experiencing a second birth in the digital realm. Continuing from the prosumer paradigm, where people are allowed not only to surf a network obtaining content and information, but also (co-)create such elements themselves, the user-centered participation is expected to further increase beyond the Web 2.0 as we know it.
In line with the supporting ITEA2 DiY Smart Experiences (DiYSE) project, this studio aims to offer participants the opportunity to create, design and share pervasive applications within the smart space ecosystem provided by the DiYSE framework and its development methodology.

Keywords
DiY, creation, smart objects, smart spaces, Arduino

ACM Classification Keywords
H5.m. Information interfaces and presentation: Miscellaneous. D.2.2 Software Engineering: Design Tools and Techniques. C.2.1. Computer-communication Networks: Network Architecture and Design

The ITEA2 DiYSE Project

The ITEA2 Do-it-Yourself Smart Experiences project (DiYSE) aims at enabling ordinary people to easily create, setup and control applications in their smart living environments as well as in the public Internet-of-Things space, allowing them to leverage aware services and smart objects for obtaining highly personalized, social, interactive, flowing experiences at home and in the city.

The main objectives of DiYSE are to:

- Allow people to control their smart environment at home and in the urban area as part of an open Internet-of- Things world. DiY tools, services and application templates together with an Internet-of-Things application-creation environment will lower the barrier to application creation and distribution for non-technical people;

- Create an interoperable cross-domain substrate on which these smart experiences can flourish and co-exist;

- Conceive a layer on the smart elements in the environment, so that interaction with these elements can be carried out on a semantically-meaningful level, with the urban area defined as an open platform for innovations – sharing data, mutualising resources and making resources interoperable;

- Create a sustainable marketplace for these user-created applications;

- Evolve from unconnected to networked and finally ambient service blocks – both hardware and software; and

- Integrate the project results into demonstrators of the DiY toolkit and user cases.

40 partners form 7 European countries contribute to this effort:

Detailed Studio Proposal

One of the goals of the ITEA2 project "Do-it-Yourself Smart Experiences" (DiYSE) is the creation of smart spaces where users can interact together and with their environment by using the applications they create on-the-fly, consisting in new or reused components that have been created by other users. Special emphasis is put in the use of context-aware wireless sensor and effector networks, applications demanding dynamic composition of services over advanced communication infrastructures and being accessed through multi-modal interfaces. The proposed one-day studio aims to give participants the opportunity to experience the possibilities of DiY creation of pervasive applications, first by understanding how some example demonstration scenarios work, and then by experiencing first-hand the design and creation of pervasive applications within the DiYSE framework.

Following the example of other successful TEI studios in the last years, our studio will take the form of five sessions, which will guide the participants throughout the DiYSE development methodology, reveal the internals of some demonstration scenarios, give the participants the opportunity to create, share, and re-use smart objects within a DiYSE ecosystem, and finally extract some collective conclusions.

- **Session 1: The DiYSE ecosystem and the development of smart objects (1 hour).** In this session, studio coordinators will introduce the DiYSE framework for smart environments, and the methodology for the development of smart objects (sensors, effectors, services...) within a DiYSE ecosystem.

- **Session 2: Possibilities of the prosumer paradigm (1 hour).** In this session, we will show participants some real applications of the DiY creation of pervasive and tangible applications within the DiYSE framework. In particular, we will explore the different possibilities of the ecosystem by means of three different scenarios: the creation of family applications within a shopping center, the aggregation of user-generated information for cooperation in outdoor environments, and the use of smart spaces to improve social interactions in elderly people. This session will also provide some insights on how the methodology is used to create the different applications from the user point of view.

- **Session 3: Creating DiYSE smart objects (1 hour).** This session will consist on a facilitated individual exercise. Each participant will be given a DiYSE developer kit, consisting of an Arduino-based board and a set of different sensors and effectors which can be plugged in to the board. A visual interface will be used to program information sensing / acting behaviors on the devices, turning them into DiYSE smart objects, which will be deployed into the DiYSE ecosystem.

- **Session 4: DiY creation of pervasive applications (1 hour).** This session will consist on a facilitated team exercise. Each team will be given a DiYSE prosumer kit, consisting of an Android-based mobile device with a visual DiYSE application development interface. The goal of this exercise is that every team design at least one tangible interactive application making use of the different DiYSE objects created by all participants in the previous session.

- **Session 5: Presentations and conclusions (1 hour).** In this session, every team will present their applications to the others, and a question/feedback round will be held for each proposal. Finally, the studio organizers will incentivize further discussion on all matters treated in the studio, allowing the participants to extract some concluding remarks from the experience.

Studio Topics to be covered

The studio will broadly cover the following topics: human centered design, service design, middleware, context management, service personalization and multimodal interaction. The studio will also cover other topics directly related to the DiYSE environment, such as the reference architecture, the development of smart objects and the use of such objects in the development of DiY pervasive applications.

Studio Target Audiences

Since the topic is focusing on a Do-it-Yourself creation environment, we aim to include people from a wide variety of backgrounds. This can be both technical as non-technical in order to evaluate and get feedback on as many aspects as possible.

Studio Learning Goals

The studio will offer the participants a general view of our smart environment ecosystem framework DiYSE, along with the required background on the development methodology to be able to use it. Participants will get a hands-on experience on the design and development of both smart objects and pervasive applications within the DiYSE ecosystem. By allowing people to create their own applications during the studio, we aim to get feedback on the tools being developed. This feedback can be both from a technical point of view as from a user point of view.

Studio Supporting Web Documents

More information about the DiYSE project can be found in the DiYSE ITEA2 project homepage (http://dyse.org). After the conference, all materials from the studio will be made available online for further reference.

Cardboard Modeling Studio: a Designerly Exploration Tool for Rich and Embodied Interaction

Joep Frens
Eindhoven University of Technology
Dept. of Industrial Design
P.O. Box 513, 5600 MB,
Eindhoven, the Netherlands
j.w.frens@tue.nl

TEI'11, January 22–26, 2011, Funchal, Portugal.

Abstract
Central to this studio is the question of *how to design* for rich and embodied (meaningful) interaction. We approach this question from a designerly perspective and find inspiration in the theory of ecological perception and in the domain of tangible and embodied interaction. As we aim for a meaningful interaction style that is firmly rooted in human experience and the diverse human skills, we present cardboard modeling as a designerly exploration tool that offers experiential insight into the solution domain of a given interaction design challenge. The studio has two distinct parts: part one aims at familiarizing the participants with the cardboard modeling technique and part two emphasizes the use of the cardboard modeling technique as an instrument to explore meaningful interaction. During the second part of the studio also the quality of the interaction solutions are discussed through presentations. The studio runs from 9.30h to approximately 17.00h.

Keywords
Cardboard modeling, design, experiential exploration tools, meaningful interaction, rich interaction

ACM Classification Keywords
A.m General literature: Miscellaneous.

General Terms
Design, Theory

Introduction
Central to this studio is the question of how to design for rich and embodied (meaningful) interaction. Before digging deeper into the setup of the studio a few words on what is meant with meaningful interaction.

Interactive products can be regarded as having three properties: form, interaction, and function [1]. In traditional non-interactive products these three properties are related. For form invites to interact and in this interaction functionality is reached. Yet in interactive products there is a division between form, interaction, and function; they are designed separately and as a result become unmeshed. Where traditional products offer a rich variation in meaningful action-possibilities, our state-of-the-art interactive products offer standardized controls with abstract labels; they are operated through menus on screens with navigation-buttons often regardless of form or function. Our state-of-the-art interactive products mainly address people's cognitive skills.

In this studio we investigate how to create meaningful and rich interaction (see figure 1) by re-meshing form, interaction, and function, by making information-for-use accessible for all of people's skills: their perceptual-motor, emotional, and cognitive skills [2]. We take inspiration from the theory of ecological perception [3] and the domain of tangible and embodied interaction. Key to this studio is the hands-on approach, for to design for rich interaction is to experientially explore the quality of these three properties and the relations between them. Taking cues from the design practice we present cardboard modeling as an appropriate tool for this, see figure 2.

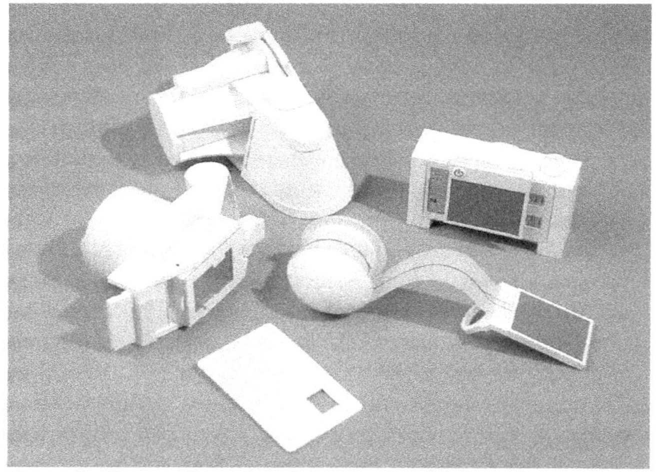

Figure 1, Five cardboard prototypes of rich interactive camera's

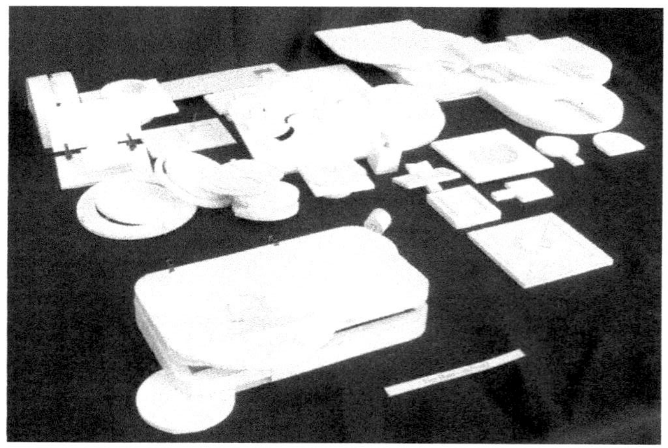

Figure 2, Exploration of meaningful interaction in cardboard (student work of Ties Bunt)

Detailed studio setup

The studio requires no previous skills or knowledge and consist of two parts:

Part one is focused at acquiring basic skills in cardboard modeling while learning to use the technique to explore the solution domain of interaction design problems:

- Introduction to cardboard modeling.
- Prototyping form: creating a set of basics forms.
- Prototyping action-possibilities: constructing simple mechanisms.

Part two is focused at the exploration of meaningful interaction possibilities using the newly acquired cardboard modeling techniques:

- Introduction to meaningful interaction.
- Exploring a given design challenge.
- Presentations.

Learning goals

1. Acquiring new cardboard modeling skills.
2. Acquiring new exploration skills.
3. Acquiring new insights into meaningful interaction possibilities.

References

[1] Frens, J.W. (2006). *Designing for Rich Interaction: Integrating Form, Interaction, and Function*. Unpublished Doctoral Dissertation, Eindhoven University of Technology, Eindhoven, the Netherlands. (retrievable from http://www.richinteraction.nl)

[2] Overbeeke, C.J., Djajadiningrat, J.P., Wensveen, S.A.G., and Hummels, C.C.M. (1999). Experiential and respectful. *Proceedings of Useful and Critical*, UIAH Helsinki.

[3] Gibson, J.J. (1986). *The Ecological Approach to Visual Perception.* Hillsdale, NJ, USA: Lawrence Erlbaum.

Building Interactive Systems Using Unconventional Electronics

John Sarik
Columbia University
500 W 120th St. Rm 1300
New York, NY 10027 USA
jcs2160@columbia.edu

Ioannis Kymissis
Columbia University
500 W 120th St. Rm 1300
New York, NY 10027 USA
johnkym@ee.columbia.edu

Abstract
Many interactive systems use "conventional" silicon-based sensors and electronics that limit their functionality and scalability. Organic, amorphous inorganic, and other "unconventional" electronics are ideal for applications that require mechanical flexibility or large-area sensing. In this studio participants will use simple control electronics and a range of unconventional materials to design and build a custom interactive system that combines organic light-emitting diodes and piezoelectric pressure sensors.

Keywords
fabrication, large-area, organic light-emitting diode, piezoelectric

ACM Classification Keywords
H.5.2 [Information Interfaces and Presentation (e.g., HCI)]: User Interfaces—Prototyping

General Terms
Design

Introduction

When developing prototype interactive systems, researchers and designers are often limited to using commercial off-the-shelf components. These components were not designed with these applications in mind and therefore may be less than ideal. Conventional silicon-based sensors and electronics are not suited to create systems that must be large, flexible, non-planar, or fabricated directly on materials that cannot tolerate high processing temperatures. The Columbia Laboratory for Unconventional Electronics (CLUE) is developing a collection of devices that can be easily integrated into complex systems on a variety of substrates and investigating new materials and fabrication techniques to enable the fabrication of these devices outside of a laboratory setting. Using these devices, materials, and fabrication techniques it is possible to create interactive systems that could not be created using conventional electronics.

Studio Proposal

In this studio participants will design and build an interactive system that combines two relatively simple elements: an organic light-emitting diode (OLED) [1] and a piezoelectric pressure sensor [2]. The studio will be divided into different phases that cover how to design, build, and test the system. By going through these steps to produce a working system, participants will gain a better understanding of the advantages and challenges of working with unconventional electronics. The skill level required is entry level to intermediate. No prior fabrication experience is required, but participants should have a basic understanding of electronics and be comfortable with soldering and simple programming.

Studio Topics

The studio will begin with a brief introduction to sensors. Participants will take measurements using familiar conventional pre-packaged sensors and unconventional custom-fabricated sensors. These measurements will demonstrate the need for techniques for processing sensor data and highlight important differences in sensitivity, resolution, and power consumption between conventional and unconventional sensors.

Next, participants will use simple fabrication techniques, such as screen-printing and spin coating, to build two devices, shown in Figure 1. The first device is an OLED based on a Tris(2,2'-bipyridine)ruthenium(II) complex. A layer of antimony tin oxide (ATO), a transparent conductor, is screened on a plastic square. The light emitting material is blanket deposited using spin coating. To finish the device, a layer of gallium indium (GaIn) eutectic is screened on top. This creates a red OLED with a turn-on voltage of less than 5 V. The second device is a pressure sensor based on the piezoelectric material Polyvinylidene fluoride (PVDF). A layer of silver is screen printed on the top and bottom of a poled PVDF film. When a pressure is applied a charge is generated across the two silver electrodes.

To interface with these devices, participants will assemble an Arduino-based control platform. A prototype platform for interfacing with OLEDs is shown in Figure 2. The OLEDs require a constant-current drive for ideal operation and the pressure sensor requires a charge amplifier. Larger OLEDs need a more powerful driver and smaller pressure sensors need a more sensitive amplifier. Participants will explore these limits by experimenting with devices of different sizes.

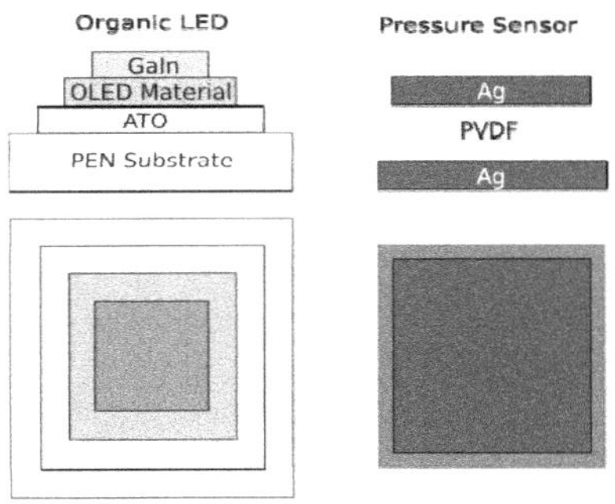

Figure 1: Single device architectures.

Figure 2: Prototype Arduino control platform.

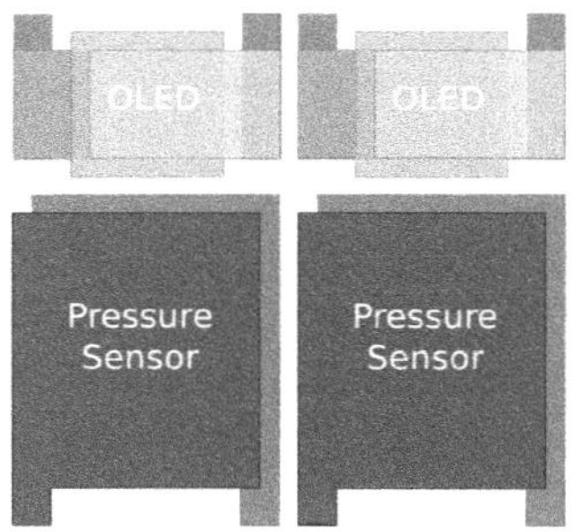

Figure 3: Interactive system using unconventional eletronics.

Now participants are ready to design and build their own interactive system. The OLEDs and pressure sensors can be fabricated on a single large-area, mechanically flexible PVDF substrate to create an integrated sensor system. One example system that combines two OLEDs and two pressure sensors is shown in Figure 3. The behavior of the system can be changed using the Arduino control platform. This system could be used to create a Simon-like memory game or a light-up drum kit. Additionally, participants are not limited to this one system. After a brief introduction to LayoutEditor, a computer aided design program for device fabrication, and a discussion of how to design devices, participants can design their own system. Custom screens can be quickly produced using the designs from LayoutEditor, a water-soluble knife-cut film, and a portable cutting plotter. This will allow participants to explore systems with unique form factors and device designs. The studio will conclude with a demonstration of the participants' networks.

Studio Learning Goals

At the end of the studio, participants will be able to fabricate unconventional electronic devices and integrate them into electronic systems. However, the devices presented here are only a small sample of what's possible. The studio aims to start a discussion on ways to use other unconventional electronics in interactive systems and encourage collaboration between researchers who develop novel sensors and researchers who need sensors for novel applications. After the studio, instead of searching for a sensor from a catalog, hopefully participants will consider fabricating an application-specific sensor.

Studio Supporting Web Documents

This studio is based on research conducted at the Columbia Laboratory for Unconventional Electronics www.kymissis.columbia.edu and fabrication exercises from the Columbia University course Modern Display Science and Technology http://sites.google.com/site/elen4193/

Acknowledgements

The studio organizers would like to thank the members of the Columbia Laboratory for Unconventional Electronics for their help developing and troubleshooting the studio activities.

References

[1] Gao, F.G. and Bard, A.J. Solid-State Organic Light-Emitting Diodes Based on Tris(2,2'-bipyridine)ruthenium(II) Complexes. Journal of the American Chemical Society, 122, 30 (2000), 7426-7427

[2] Hsu, Y-J., Z. Jia, and I. Kymissis, A Locally Amplified Organic Transistor Sensor Based on a Piezoelectric Polymer. Proc. 2009 MRS Spring Meeting, 2009.

Napkin Schematics Studio

Nathan Seidle
SparkFun Electronics
6175 Longbow Drive
Boulder, CO 80301
nathan@sparkfun.com

Abstract
In the *Napkin Schematics Studio*, tangible interaction designers who have basic experience with microcontrollers (for example, Arduino) will brainstorm about project design and development with the guidance of an experienced electronics designer. Then, working in small groups, the participants will build working prototypes of selected designs from the brainstorming session.

Keywords
Schematic design, microcontrollers, sensors, power, data, wireless, enabling, prototyping

ACM Classification Keywords
H5.m. Information interfaces and presentation (e.g., HCI): Miscellaneous.

General Terms
Design, Experimentation, Measurement, Theory

Introduction
It's not the technology, it's how you use it. You don't need to build a really complex robot to do something interesting. Many people have a great idea but lack specific technical know-how to realize it. The Napkin Schematics Studio shows people who have basic experience with microcontrollers how adding a few components on top can create amazing outcomes.

Napkin Schematics (scribbling on whiteboards) is designed to allow participants to come up with an idea and then have the surrounding group give immediate feedback.

In the first half of the session, guided by an experienced engineer as moderator, project ideas are brought up and then hashed out. Pitfalls such as power, heat, size, and 'gotchas' of a dreamed-up electronics device are discussed to help the individual projecteer. It's somewhat like 'tips and tricks' on steroids.

In the second half of the session, working in small groups, we build a few of the projects discussed. The groups would be 3-5 person teams building a widget to help them do a task or overcome a common everyday problem. The Studio will conclude with a demonstration of all the projects built and a discussion of lessons learned.

Problems

Here are some examples of projects and problems:

You want to build an automatic sprinkler system? OK, have you figured out how to control the solenoids? What voltage do they run at? Relays should work for that, transistors may not be able to handle the power. Have you figured out how to run the data from point A to point B?

You want to build a GPS system that tells you how to get home. GPS units use about 40mA per hour, how many hours do you need it to last? The battery needs to be XYZ big. You may not be able to use that GPS since it's 5V and your battery options are 3.3V.

You want to tell if grandpa has fallen? How might you detect that? An accelerometer? What type of characteristic (motion) are you looking for that says he's in trouble? Zero g or negative g would indicate he is not upright, but is that enough? How much data do you need to transmit? How far? How often? These all affect the battery size. We can't ask grandpa to carry a car battery with him...

Projects

The following is a sample of projects, ranging in complexity,to indicate what might be built in the Studio:

BlenderDefender is a motion activated blender that keeps cats off counters. (http://www.plasma2002.com/blenderdefender/)

Homehound is a device that simply points in the direction of home - whereever home may be. Homehound is based completely on Momobot – just without the sexy knit covering. (http://momobots.com/)

Pitcher notifier is a device that attaches underneath a pitcher of beer. Once the inclination of the pitcher surpasses 90 degrees from level, we assume the pitcher is empty and the waitstaff is notified to bring another. (http://courses.cit.cornell.edu/ee476/FinalProjects/s2004/mda24/BeverageMonitor.htm)

Avalanche glove uses an accelerometer and a vibration motor built into a glove, to indicate to the user the direction to dig toward (up) to escape.

RFID reader detector lets the user know when a electromagnetic field is present.

(http://www.instructables.com/id/RFID-Reader-Detector-and-Tilt-Sensitive-RFID-Tag/)

Follower uses a low-cost camera and a couple servos to motion track (follow) your movement.

Topics

We will cover any topic the audience wants to learn about. Napkin Schematics uses the moderator's knowledge of the various technologies available as well as the knowledge of the group. These include:

- Sensors: Accelerometers, sound, light, force, identification, infrared, GPS, heart rate, compass, proximity, pressure, flex, big red buttons
- Outputs: Motors, buzzers, sound/MP3, speech, LEDs, EL wire, matrices, segment displays, LCDs, vibration
- Wireless communication: Low-power, Bluetooth, WiFi, Cellular, long range
- Power: Batteries (lithium polymer, NiMH, alkaline, SLAs), solar, kinetic, thermal

Requirements

Napkin Schematics Studio works best for designers who have basic experience with microcontrollers—simple analog circuits and programming—but who lack more sophisticated technical knowledge to extend their repertoire beyond simple applications.

Studio Learning Goals

The goal of the Napkin Schematics Studio is to enable participants who have an idea about a tangible interaction project to get started with building a working prototype. Participants will learn about specific hardware and software technologies that may be relevant to their project. More importantly, by observing and participating in a brainstorming session guided by an expert engineering designer, participants will learn to think strategically about technological constraints and opportunities inherent in tangible interaction projects with microcontroller hardware and software.

Work Plan

The Napkin Schematics Studio takes place in three phases:

Phase I: Brainstorming and white board work: discussion of projects and methods to realize them.
Phase II: Build session: Hands-on construction in small groups of selected projects from Phase I.
Phase III: Finale—Present what you've got! 3 minutes per group.

Materials

Participants are encouraged to bring various sensors or apparatus that they would like to incorporate as well as basic materials for building microcontroller circuits (e.g., breadboard, jumpers, etc). The organizer will provide a *SparkFun Inventor's Kit* for each group (that they get to take home!). The organizer will also have available various sensors and parts to use on loan (e.g., special-purpose sensors, actuators). A work room with a whiteboard and work tables and electrical outlets are required. A soldering station or two would be convenient, if it can be arranged.

Prototyping with Microsoft .NET Gadgeteer

Nicolas Villar
Microsoft Research
7 JJ Thomson Avenue
Cambridge, CB3 0FB, UK
nvillar@microsoft.com

James Scott
Microsoft Research
7 JJ Thomson Avenue
Cambridge, CB3 0FB, UK
james.scott@microsoft.com

Steve Hodges
Microsoft Research
7 JJ Thomson Avenue
Cambridge, CB3 0FB, UK
steve.hodges@microsoft.com

Abstract
Microsoft .NET Gadgeteer is a new prototyping platform that makes it easier to construct, program and shape new kinds of computing objects. It is comprised of modular hardware, software libraries and 3D CAD support. Together, these elements support the key activities involved both in the rapid prototyping and the small-scale production of custom embedded, interactive and connected devices. We propose to organize and run a studio at TEI 2010 where participants are introduced to the platform and its capabilities. Participants will work in groups, assembling electronic modules, writing software and designing a case or enclosure for their device. The end-result will be that each group develops a fully functional device, which can be exhibited at the TEI demo session.

Keywords
Rapid prototyping, modular hardware, personal fabrication, 3D printing

ACM Classification Keywords
H5.m. Information interfaces and presentation (e.g., HCI): Miscellaneous.

General Terms
Design

Introduction

Microsoft .NET Gadgeteer is a rapid prototyping platform for small electronic devices built on Microsoft .NET Micro Framework and the Microsoft Visual Studio development environment. It combines the advantages of object-oriented programming, solderless assembly of electronics with a kit of peripherals, and support for quick physical form factor design using CAD. This powerful combination allows embedded and handheld devices to be iteratively prototyped in a matter of hours rather than days or weeks.

Figure 1. A .NET Gadgeteer mainboard, extended with a button, multicolor LED and USB modules. The USB module allows the mainboard to be temporarily connected to a PC for programming and debugging.

The kit currently includes over 30 different hardware modules, which can be used to extend an embedded computing mainboard (which includes an ARM processor) with communication, display, user input/output, sensing and actuation capabilities (e.g. Figure 1). Modules can be easily connected and disconnected from the mainboard via a system of connectors and fine-pitch ribbon cables. All components share standardized mounting features, which allows them to be flexibly positioned and affixed inside a custom enclosure. Figure 2 shows how the modules can be used in conjunction with simple prototyping materials to build a simple hardware prototype in less than an hour.

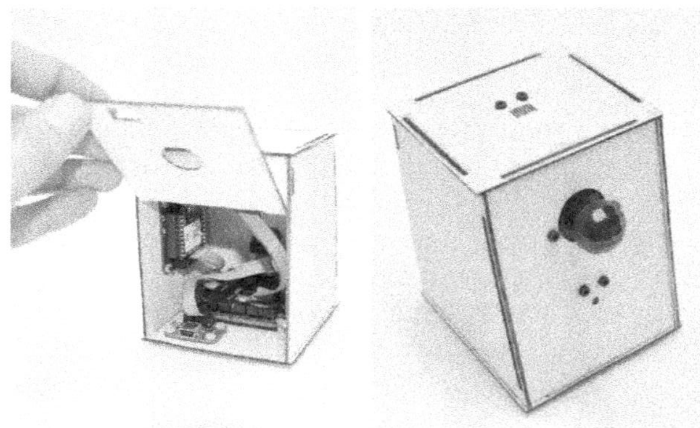

Figure 2. A simple prototype for a wireless sensor node to detect ambient light and movement in a room, built using .NET Gadgeteer modules and cardboard in less than an hour.

Microsoft Visual Studio, the C# programming language, the .NET Micro Framework and custom .NET Gadgeteer libraries provide the software development environment used to write and debug the code that runs on the mainboard. The .NET Gadgeteer libraries include software classes for each hardware module, making it easy to interface with the modules in an object-oriented and event-driven manner. One example .NET Gadgeteer project shows how to develop a simple MP3 player by writing less than 10 lines of code. The mainboard can be temporarily connected to a PC for programming and interactive debugging. When disconnected from the PC, the device operates autonomously.

In addition to the code libraries, .NET Gadgeteer includes a detailed CAD library with accurate 3D models of each hardware component. These models can be loaded into a 3D authoring environment – such as Solidworks or Rhino – and used as a basis and reference against which to design custom enclosures. In this way, the form-factor of the device can be highly customized. The resulting designs can be physically rendered using a 3D printer (e.g. Figure 3).

In our design and implementation of all aspects of .NET Gadgeteer our motivation has been to provide a prototyping experience that has a both low threshold for entry – allowing non expert developers and designers to quickly sketch and construct functional devices - together with a high ceiling that allows experienced users to create sophisticated and capable devices that can be used in practice. A simple-to-use yet versatile hardware platform, comprehensive software libraries coupled with a fully-featured programming environment and support for physical case designs that can be batch-produced using rapid manufacturing technologies, all contribute to this experience. Our goal was to build a platform that was broadly useful, including for hobbyist use, for educational scenarios, for small-scale production runs of prototype devices, and for industrial applications.

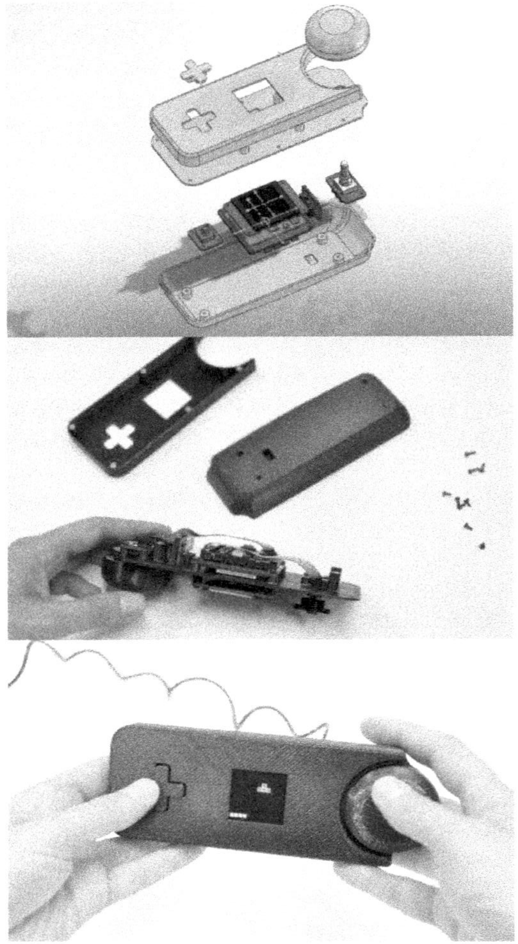

Figure 3. Design, assembly and testing of a custom enclosure for a handheld game developed with .NET Gadgeteer. The case was designed using the .NET Gadgeteer 3D CAD library as reference, in a few hours. It was physically rendered using a Dimension FDM machine, overnight.

Studio Proposal

The goal of a TEI studio based around Microsoft .NET Gadgeteer is to introduce the platform - its capabilities and associated workflow - to the researchers and expert practitioners that attend the conference.

The topics of rapid development for embedded devices and tangible computational objects, as well as the integration of electronic prototyping with rapid manufacturing methods, should be highly relevant to the TEI community. We believe that attendees would find the practical nature of the studio a valuable and rewarding activity. Feedback from attendees would be directly used for refinement of the platform. In addition, the experience should form the basis of interesting discussion and reflection on the future of rapid prototyping practices and possibilities of small-scale manufacturing of custom devices.

Studio Format and Topics Covered

We propose to organize a hands-on studio, where participants are guided through the process of designing, programming and assembling a fully-functional device using .NET Gadgeteer. We would aim to showcase the results of the studio during the main TEI conference, potentially during the demo session.

Attendance would be limited to 12 participants, grouped into 3 teams. In order to maximize the productivity of the studio, the ideal team configuration would include one person with some experience in programming, and a second person with some previous experience in industrial design or use of 3D CAD packages. The remaining team members would ideally come from a complementary background – such as usability, HCI theory, art or education.

To this end, we would ask interested participants to register their interest in participating via e-mail. Since this would need to be done well in advance of the conference, we would solicit the TEI organizers' help in advertising a registration deadline through the mailing lists. After this deadline, participants would be notified of acceptance and assigned a group. In case it is not possible to form groups in our ideal configuration, we would be able to support teams with additional assistance from our team members, and we would potentially ask the TEI organizers for help through expert student volunteers.

During the morning, the studio would follow a guided tutorial format, where participants are introduced to the principal concepts and tools. Participants would then be asked to spend a short time brainstorming a new device concept around a specific theme. The rest of the day would be spent with participants executing their design. Our goal is to allow participants both connect, program and design an enclosure for their device by the end of the day. We aim to have access to 3D printing facilities during the conference, allowing us to physically render the CAD designs overnight, in time to exhibit the completed and assembled devices at the TEI demo session. More details about these requirements, alternative and backup options, can be found in the supplementary logistics document.

Second International Workshop on Organic User Interfaces

Audrey Girouard
Human Media Lab
Queen's University
Kingston, Ontario, Canada
audrey@cs.queensu.ca

Roel Vertegaal
Human Media Lab
Queen's University
Kingston, Ontario, Canada
roel@cs.queensu.ca

Ivan Poupyrev
Disney Research
Pittsburgh, PA, USA
ivan.poupyrev@disneyresearch.com

TEI'11, January 22–26, 2011, Funchal, Portugal.

Abstract
Advances in display, sensor and actuator technology are changing the field of TEI, and opening new research areas. While modern interfaces have been designed for traditional planar and static display devices, next-generation UI allow digital objects to change their shape and embed displays anywhere. Fitting into the paradigm of Organic User Interfaces, these developments require us to re-examine and reevaluate some of the basic design principles and interaction styles currently used. This Second International Workshop on Organic User Interfaces will bring together experts to discuss, brainstorm and prototype next generation of user interfaces.

Keywords
Organic User Interfaces, Tangibles, Flexible displays

ACM Classification Keywords
H.5.2 User Interfaces: Input devices and strategies; B.4.2 Input/Output Devices: Channels and controllers;

General Terms
Design, Experimentation.

Motivation for the Workshop
In the last decade, tangible and embedded user interfaces have taken the computing power out of the standard desktop environment and into the real world [6], allowing interactions with the digital world to be done with everyday objects. However, until recently, these interactions were still limited to planar displays,

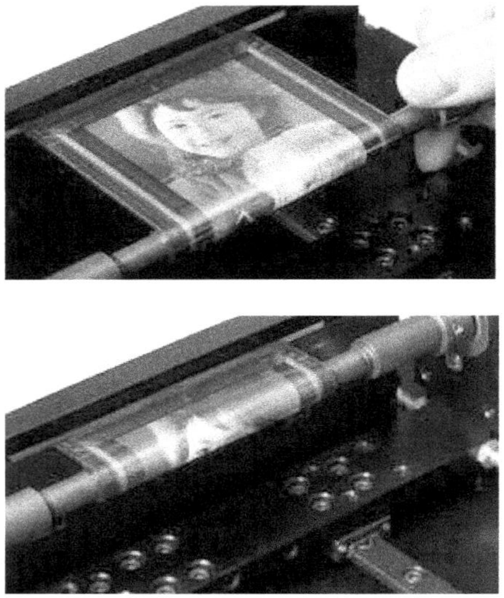

Fig 1. Rollable organic light-emitting diode (OLED) display [9].

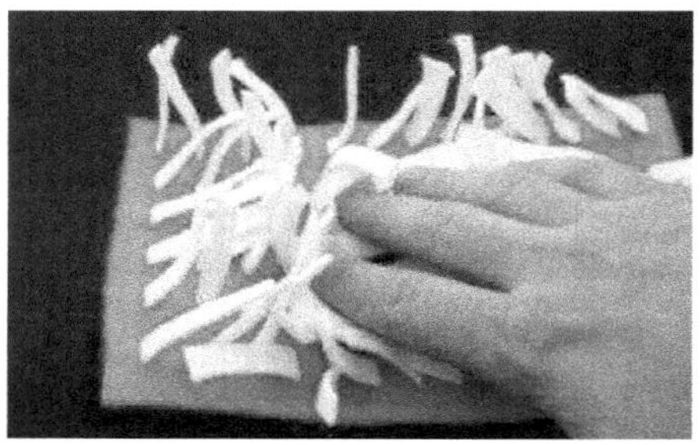

Fig 2. Sprout, a texturally rich surface for communication [2].

to objects with static shapes. We believe that the physical shape of displays and computing devices play key role in designing its user interface.

New advances in display, sensor and actuating technologies are changing the field of TEI. With e-ink electrochemical pixels and organic thin-film circuit boards, developments in manufacturing technology have produced displays so thin and flexible that they are beginning to resemble paper. Flexible organic light-emitting diode technology will let us to embed displays in any object, providing a rich environment to share information [9] (Fig 1). New actuating technologies allow for "claytronic"-type devices that can actively re-shape themselves on multiple scales, from hand-held gadgets to entire buildings (Fig 2). Combined with the advances in sensor technologies allowing us to track the position of multiple fingers, twists and pressure on surfaces of any shape, and the ability for flexible display to become the input device, any object will display information and allow user input, no matter how complex, dynamic or flexible its structure [10]. These developments are not only opening up new opportunities for user interface innovation, but also require us to re-examine some of the basic design principles of modern user interfaces, designed for traditional, planar and static display devices.

Organic User Interfaces

These advances fit into the new Human Computer Interaction (HCI) paradigm of Organic User Interfaces (OUI). *Organic User Interfaces* is an emerging vision for future user interfaces that attempts to map out a future where these technologies are a common place. It is based on an understanding *physical shape* of the displays and computing devices will become an important design variable for future interfaces. Indeed, not only will future displays be able to take any arbitrary shape, but the shape itself will by dynamic, either modified by the user, or self-actuated.

OUIs are flexible non-planar displays that act both as output and input devices. "When flexible, OUIs have the ability to become the data on display through deformation, either via manipulation or actuation. Their fluid physics-based graphics are shaped through multi-touch and bi-manual gestures." [5] OUI design principles include that they should be created so the function of the device equals its form, for an intuitive interaction. They should be made from transitive, shape shifting materials that allows the form of the display to follow its changing function and flow [11].

Following the significant interest resulted from the publication of the special issue of Communication of ACM on organic user interfaces [11] and the first workshop on OUIs and transitive materials at CHI 2009 [3], this workshop seeks to debate and develop further the concepts behind OUI vision and further stimulate research in related areas, such as in tangible, embedded and embodied interfaces.

Workshop themes and topics

The proposed topics for the workshop are centered on the main directions of OUI, and will include:

When displays can take on any form

What would happen when any object, from a credit card to a building, no matter how complex, dynamic or flexible will be wrapped with high resolution, full-color, interactive graphics?

- *Interaction with free-form displays devices*

  The emerging technologies will allow us to create display devices that can take any shape or form, i.e. a

Fig 3. Programmable matter by folding [4].

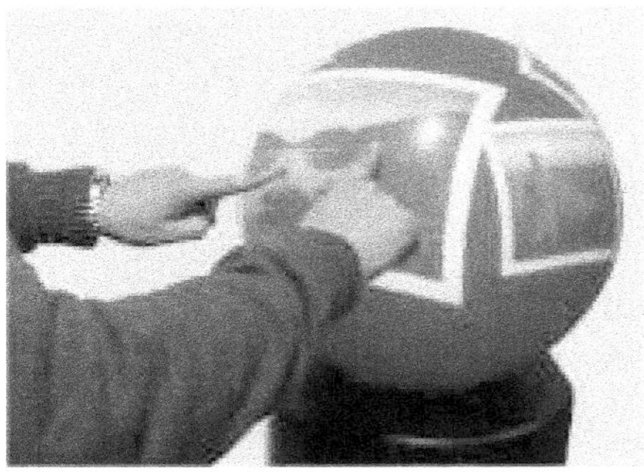

Fig 4. A spherical display surface [1].

circle, triangle, sphere. How we might develop user interfaces for such displays? What kind of new applications and interaction styles would be possible?

- *Emerging display technologies: flexible, textile, paper and printed displays for OUI*

  Recent advances in materials have resulted in thin flexible paper-like displays, textile-based, printable displays and others non-planar displays such as a sphere [1, 9] (Fig 1 & 4). We invite overviews and reports on emerging display technologies as well as their comparison. How will we interact with displays that come in any shape imaginable? What new interaction principles and visual designs become possible when curved computers are a reality?

When displays can change their shape

We no longer require the physical shape of computing to be static. We will be able to bend, twist, pull and fold digital devices just like origami [4] (Fig 3). We can also augment future computing devices with new actuating devices and materials, to dynamically alter their shape, as with the Sprout interface [2] (Fig 2).

- *Shape-shifting, actuator technologies, claytronics*

  How can we make objects that can dynamically change their shape? What novel actuators will allow creating such interfaces? How can properties of new materials, such as flexibility or shape, be used to create new interfaces and applications? For example, if devices become foldable or stretchable, how can that lead to new interaction paradigms?

- *Kinetic interactions*

  With the physical shape itself being a form of display, its physical kinetic motion will become an important design variable in future interfaces. How do we use physical motion for communicating information?

When the display is the input device

Current point-and-click interfaces designed for fixed planar coordinate systems, and controlled via separate input device will not be sufficient. Rather, multi-touch, full gesture, multimodal interactions will be required.

- *Input techniques for organic user interfaces and new sensor technologies*

  What kind of interaction techniques and modalities are possible? What are new sensor technologies that can be used for OUIs? What are the most important sensory modalities for OUIs: vision, haptic or other?

Other organic user interfaces topics of interest

- *Future applications and themes of OUI*

  What kind of new applications would be made possible by OUIs? Are specific themes more appropriate for OUIs, such as building interfaces for creativity, learning, or well-being? By embedding computation in objects that change form with function, can we promote the reuse of objects?

- *Tools for developing physical interfaces*

  OUI and TEI interfaces present an interesting design, engineering and reusability problem. Advances in such tools include software environments for rapid prototyping of hardware devices, e.g. Frizting [7], or hardware toolkits that allow flexibility and power [8], but they may not always be basic enough to allow non-programming expert to use them. How can we create better, reconfigurable and dynamic tools, while providing expressiveness and details? How can we combine computation and physical materials? How can we program all these devices and materials? Are we programming computers or programming these materials and devices directly?

Workshop Goals

This workshop will bring together interface designers, architects, engineers and scientists interested in the OUI vision; to stimulate exchange and debate between them; and to promote collaboration and brainstorming through prototyping sessions, with the following aims:

(1) To survey and discuss the current state of the field of user interface research in general and to survey trends that lead toward the organic user interface concept, identifying current and new directions of research as well as unsolved problems.

(2) To debate the scope and mission of Organic User Interface research and its connection to other fields, such as tangibles and embedded interfaces.

(3) To imagine where the underlying technological changes will take us in the next 10-20 years.

(4) To put together the collective knowledge and creativity of participants in a tangible form, through prototyping session that will illustrate key concepts of organic user interfaces.

(5) To create and maintain a broad community of researchers developing around this topic.

Workshop Supporting Web Documents

We will provide a website before the workshop at http://www.humanmedialab.org/. It will contain detailed information about the call for papers, and the list of accepted participants and proceedings with their workshop papers. The website will be maintained after the workshop.

References

[1] Benko, H. and Wilson, A.D., Design Challenges of Interactive Spherical User Interfaces. in ACM CHI 2009 Workshop on Programming Reality, (2009), 4p.

[2] Coelho, M. and Maes, P. Sprout I/O: a texturally rich interface. Proc. TEI'08, 2008.

[3] Coelho, M., Poupyrev, I., Sadi, S., Vertegaal, R., Berzowska, J., Buechley, L., Maes, P. and Oxman, N. Programming reality: from transitive materials to organic user interfaces. Proc. CHI'09 Extended Abstracts, 2009.

[4] Hawkes, E., An, B., Benbernou, N.M., Tanaka, H., Kim, S., Demaine, E.D., Rus, D. and Wood, R.J. Programmable matter by folding. Proceedings of the National Academy of Sciences. 2010, -.

[5] Holman, D. and Vertegaal, R. Organic user interfaces: designing computers in any way, shape, or form. Commun. ACM, 51 (6). 2008, 48-55.

[6] Jacob, R.J.K., Girouard, A., Hirshfield, L.M., Horn, M.S., Shaer, O., Solovey, E.T. and Zigelbaum, J., Reality-Based Interaction: A Framework for Post-WIMP Interfaces. in Proc. CHI'08, (2008), 201-210.

[7] Knörig, A., Wettach, R. and Cohen, J. Fritzing: a tool for advancing electronic prototyping for designers. Proc. TEI'09, ACM, 2009.

[8] Ngai, G., Chan, S.C.F., Ng, V.T.Y., Cheung, J.C.Y., Choy, S.S.S., Lau, W.W.Y. and Tse, J.T.P. i*CATch: a scalable plug-n-play wearable computing framework for novices and children. Proc. CHI'10, 2010.

[9] Ricker, T. Sony's rollable OLED display can wrap around a pencil, our hearts. Engadget, May 26, 2010.

[10] Schwesig, C., Poupyrev, I. and Mori, E. Gummi: a bendable computer. Proc. CHI'04, 2004.

[11] Vertegaal, R. and Poupyrev, I. Introduction. Commun. ACM, 51 (6). 2008, 26-30.

TEI Work-in-Progress Workshop

Ellen Yi-Luen Do
Georgia Institute of Technology
Atlanta, GA 30332 USA
ellendo@gatech.edu

Ian Oakley
Universidade da Madeira
Funchal, 9000-390 Portugal
ian@uma.pt

Mark D Gross
Carnegie Mellon University
Pittsburgh, PA 15213 USA
mdgross@cmu.edu

Abstract
The TEI Work-in-Progress workshop invited submissions about designing, making, studying, exploring and experiencing of projects on tangible, embedded and embodied interaction. The workshop aimed to provoke, intrigue, and inspire the TEI community by sharing work-in-progress practice, late breaking innovation, cutting-edge research, and controversial and compelling work. It provided a venue for eliciting feedback and fostering discussions and collaborations among TEI colleagues. The TEI Work-in-Progress workshop provided an opportunity for members of the TEI community with common and diverse interests to meet in the context of a focused and interactive discussion and a showcase for exciting new work that is still at an early stage.

Keywords
Tangible interaction, design, exploration, work-in-progress, gadget, widget

ACM Classification Keywords
H5.m. Information interfaces and presentation (e.g., HCI): Miscellaneous.

General Terms
Design, Documentation, Experimentation, Human Factors, Languages, Measurement, Performance, Theory, Verification.

Introduction

The TEI Work-in-Progress workshop provides an opportunity for both practitioners and researchers to present a concise report of new findings or other types of innovative or thought-provoking work relevant to the Tangible, Embedded and Embodied Interaction community.

With the TEI Work-in-Progress workshop, we provide a venue for new, exciting, late breaking, cutting edge, unusual, challenging and thought-provoking TEI work that might not otherwise be seen at the conference. If you are working in an emerging area in TEI, submit your paper to the TEI Work-in-Progress workshop. If you are interested in defining the field, addressing basic or applied research, reflecting on design practice, discussing new methodologies and emerging application ideas, presenting innovations in sensing and actuation technologies, issues in TEI design and pedagogical modules, or suggesting promising directions for future research, submit your paper to the TEI Work-in-Progress workshop.

TEI Work-in-Progress Workshop

The purpose of the TEI Work-in-Progress Workshop is to provide an intimate atmosphere, in the form of a mini-symposium environment, to facilitate a discussion between the participants of the workshop.

The difference between the TEI Work-in-Progress and the main conference venues (e.g., papers, demonstrations) is that the Work-in-Progress venue targets work that may not necessarily have been completed or remains at an early stage. However, all submissions should make some contribution to the body of TEI knowledge. This TEI Work-in-Progress workshop aims to attract participation from a broad range of disciplines covering a spectrum of topics and methodologies from all of TEI's constituent communities.

Topics of Interest

The TEI Work-in-Progress workshop invites accounts of the design (rationale, process, outcomes, and/or evaluation) of an innovative TEI application or system, controversial ideas (just want to be cool?), novel prototypes (don't look at the duct tape now), evaluations of systems, techniques, practices or other phenomena (fly on the wall, or Wizard of Oz) relevant to TEI, inconclusive but valuable user studies and experiments (won't do that again!), and anything else that can give a fresh perspective on TEI (twist and shout? paradigm shift? methods and toolkits?).

We invite submissions that explore technical or practical limitations in technologies or methodologies (cool hacks for vending machines?); that introduce promising, although currently non-viable techniques (hair and tongue interaction, or vapor ware); that describe new processes, techniques, or tools for use in interactive system design, development or deployment of TEI projects; and that explore topics outside of current discussion (human-soup bowl interfaces?).

Submissions of Work-in-Progress paper may also include reflections from practice (It's not a bug, it's a feature!), including lessons learned or principles derived from real-word experiences and backed by thought-provoking and well-substantiated analyses. We also welcome submissions that discuss the latest progress in engineering design (dancing in the rain with my solar activated boots?) or a new domain application (looks Ma, no hands! My apron is frying the eggs) in our everyday lives or outer space expedition (telemedicine and architectural robotics).

We invite work that would otherwise not have been presented at TEI 2011 for to the TEI Work-in-Progress workshop. In essence, any compelling paper that will provoke new ideas or stir up discussions within the TEI community is appropriate for the TEI Work-in-Progress workshop.

Submission Guideline

The TEI Work-in-Progress workshop paper submission should be a 6-page paper prepared in the ACM Extended Abstract Format, submitted anonymously by sending it to tei-2011-wip@googlegroups.com with the subject title <TEI Work-in-Progress Workshop Submission>.

Please find the Extended Abstract format template at http://www.sigchi.org/chi2010/authors/format.html#extendedformat.

Workshop papers are reviewed and selected for presentation at the TEI Work-in-Progress workshop on January 23rd, 2011. The TEI Work-in-Progress workshop proceedings will be made available on the TEI 2011 web site.

TEI Work-in-Progress is a refereed but non-archival publication venue. Your Work-in-Progress paper will have assigned page numbers in the workshop digital proceedings. This will not be considered as a formal publication and copyright will remain with authors. As such, inclusion of the paper in the digital workshop proceedings will not limit use of the material in future publications including submitting a paper based on this work to other conferences or journals.

Here be Monsters!

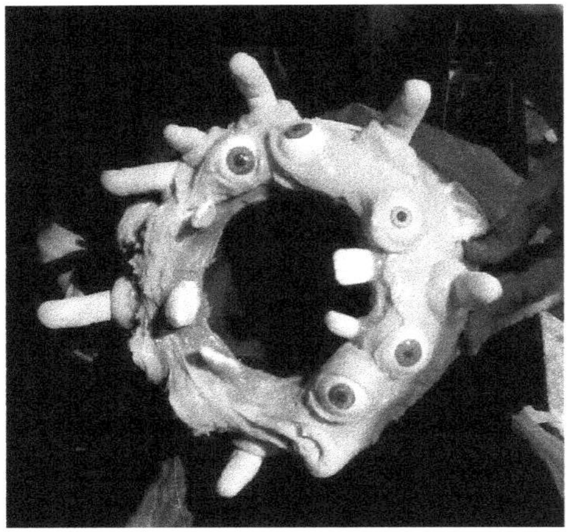

Figure 1. The monster eye prototype

Martin Jonsson
Södertörn University.
141 89 Huddinge, Sweden
martin.jonsson@sh.se

Magnus Mattsson
Independent artist
Ljusstöparbacken 5
117 65 Stockholm, Sweden
magnus@magnusmattsson.se

TEI'11, January 22–26, 2011, Funchal, Portugal.
ACM 978-1-4503-0478-8/11/01.

Abstract
In this work we present the monster eye installation, consisting of an artifact with which you can examine secrets that are hidden inside the walls.

Keywords
Tangible interaction, art exploration, augmented reality

ACM Classification Keywords
H.1.2,, H5, H5.m: Miscellaneous.

General Terms
Design

Introduction
The research field of human-computer interaction is increasingly coming to recognize the importance of the physical and material dimensions of interaction with computational artifacts. Related issues have been discussed extensively within the research area of tangible interaction [1, 2]. The highly design oriented and explorative nature of this domain also raises issues related to art and artistic expression, explored e.g. in a previously presented interactive installation [3].

The work presented here origins in a joint project between Södertörn University, Sweden and a center for children's culture in Stockholm where we wanted to explore how an old building could be fitted with interactive installations that allow for bodily engagement and that would interplay with the sense of

Figure 2. The monster eye in action.

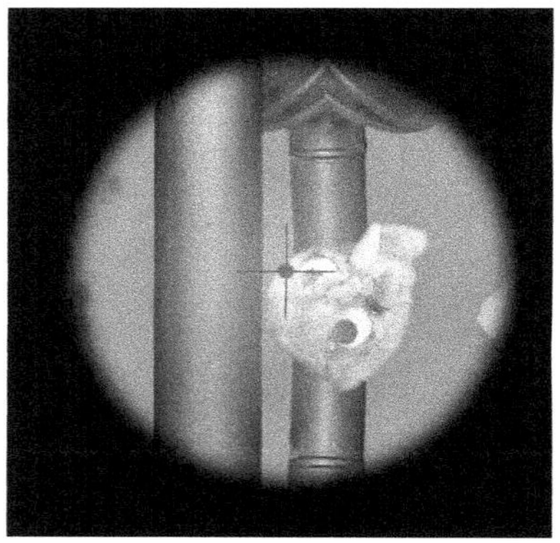

Figure 3. The projected image showing the inside of the walls

magic intrinsic to the building. A scope of the project was to examine how novel interactive technologies can create new means for children to engage in embodied exploration and interaction with various forms of cultural and artistic expressions.

The monster eye prototype

A series of prototypes was developed in close collaboration with a group of children who actively participated in the development process. The final concept is based on an idea of an augmented reality system using a portable projector, similar to the ideas behind the SixthSense project [4]. In this prototype the mini projector is combined with a Nintendo Wii remote control. By using the IR-camera on the Wii-remote, the projected image can move in accordance with the motion of the projector, to create an illusion that the projector shows what is *inside* the walls. Thus you could e.g. see pipes and cables hidden in the walls. A graphical application was also developed in collaboration with the kids tied to the project. In the application there are monsters running about among the pipes in the wall. You can catch the monsters by shaking the eye, causing the monster eye to sneeze, capturing the monster in a glob of snot.

The artistic expression

A professional artist was involved in the project, focusing on the expression and crafting of both the physical and digital manifestations of the prototype. In the work we wanted to create an item that could stem from a post-apocalyptic world, populated by mutants and monsters, inspired for example by the artworks of Salvador Dali and Dana Schutz. There is however also a playful dimension in the expression, a corny craziness like a Disney world beyond control.

Discussion

With this work we want to explore how the artistic expression of the physical manifestation affects the interactive experience. In general, the design of the interactive physical objects used within the TEI community is often slick and minimalistic, lacking a distinctive expression of its own. Expressive and carefully crafted objects however have a potential to stimulate imagination and make the experience richer. It is also interesting to explore aspects around materiality. In this case the tangible interactive object was crafted in silicon, adding a soft organic feeling to the interaction. Another interesting quality of the prototype is related to the *'weirdness'* of the expression. The fact that it is very different from the user's earlier experiences of interaction with technology makes it possible to create an interactive experience that to some extent is detached from preconceptions with respect to technology use.

References

[1] Fernaeus, Y., Tholander, J. and Jonsson, M. Beyond representations: towards an action-centric perspective on tangible interaction. *International Journal of Arts and Technology*, 1, 3 (2008), 249-267.

[2] Jonsson, M., Tholander, J. and Fernaeus, Y. Setting the stage – Embodied and spatial dimensions in emerging programming practices. *Interacting with Computers*, 21, 1-2 (January 2009 2009), 117-124.

[3] Jonsson, M. and Fernaeus, Y. *Erzulie's altar*. Dorkbot Sthlm, Ersta konsthall, Stockholm, 2006.

[4] Mistry, P. and Maes, P. SixthSense: a wearable gestural interface. In *Proceedings of the ACM SIGGRAPH ASIA 2009 Sketches* (Yokohama, Japan, 2009). ACM

Tardigotchi: Considerations on Pets and Digital Simulations

Douglas Easterly
Programme Director
Media Design
Victoria University of Wellington
139 Vivian Street
Wellington, 6011 New Zealand
douglas.easterly@vuw.ac.nz

Matthew Kenyon
Assistant Professor
School of Visual Arts
Pennsylvania State University
University Park, PA 16802 USA
mck16@psu.edu

Tiago Rorke
Diatom
23 Rivers House
Aitman Drive
London, TW8 0ES
tiago@diatom.cc

TEI'11, January 22–26, 2011, Funchal, Portugal.
ACM 978-1-4503-0478-8/11/01.

Abstract
Tardigotchi is a device art object that could be described as a game, toy, vivarium and digital pet. The authors of this paper, Tardigotchi's inventors, will describe its composition and interactive functions, precedents that led to this work, as well as some related scientific and philosophical themes.

Keywords
art, alife, pets, toy, game, interactive

ACM Classification Keywords
J.5. Computer Applications: Arts and Humanities.

General Terms
Design

Introduction
Over the past decade, Easterly and Kenyon have created a series of artworks that investigate a range of cultural phenomena. In 2004, they created a work called Spore; a cybernetic houseplant that was watered based on stock market calculations [1]. In addition to the common understanding that people seek easy pathways to fortune via the stock market [2], we also witness the disruptive effects that the stock market can radiate upon society. Spore brought these sentiments into light by pairing the vitality of a living organism to the capriciousness of this system. At the same time,

this artwork examined the nurturing relationships humans engage in with other organisms. We were elucidated by the fact that many viewers were quite concerned about the welfare of the plant.

Tardigotchi

Continuing such dialogues, the authors of this paper created Tardigotchi. The front of Tardigothchi's enclosure features a pixelated character, which is paired to an organism living just behind the miniature LED display. This organism is a Tardigrade - amazingly versatile creatures: they can survive in a wide array of environments, including the vacuum of deep space; they can also live without water for close to a decade.

Figure 1. Tardigotchi's enclosure.

Interactivity

Via Facebook or onboard interface, users can play-with and feed the virtual pet, which in turn stimulates playing and feeding of the tardigrade. The latter process is achieved through a syringe that injects a moss-water mixture into its silicone enclosure. Playing is symbolized through activating a miniature lamp. A microcontroller within the enclosure manages the animations and physical actuation of these exchanges.

Discussion

This project was inspired by the commercial success of Tamagotchi. How is it that humans can be so emotionally attached to a simulation? Concerning real pets, Psychologist Harold Herzog reasons that intricate memetic systems are at play – rapidly building demand for one breed of pet, while simultaneously reducing the popularity of others [3]. The eminent biologist E.O. Wilson offers a varying explanation through his *biophilia* hypothesis. His argument states humans have an innate love for other living organisms [4]. Perhaps these biological forces are mobilized by the design affordances in the Tamagotchi – and Tardigotchi.

References

[1] Easterly, D. and Kenyon, M. 2005. Spore 1.1. In *ACM SIGGRAPH 2005 Emerging Technologies* (Los Angeles, California, July 31 - August 04, 2005). D. Cox, Ed. SIGGRAPH '05. ACM, New York, NY, 18.

[2] Taleb, N.N. *Fooled by Randomness*. Random House, New York, NY, USA, 2005.

[3] Herzog, H. Darwinism and the Study of Human-Animal Interactions. *Society and Animals 10*, 4 (2002), 361-367.

[4] Wilson, E.O. *Biophilia*. Harvard University Press, Cambridge, MA, USA, 1984.

Zeugen: Seeing and Being Seen

Morgan Rauscher
(Artist)
Emily Carr University of Art and Design
1399 Johnston Street, Granville Island
Vancouver, BC V6H 3R9 CANADA
me@morganrauscher.com

Randy Glenn
(Engineering Consultant)
Surreality Labs
380 River Oaks Boulevard West
Oakville, ON L6H 5E7 CANADA
randy.glenn@gmail.com

TEI'11, January 22–26, 2011, Funchal, Portugal.
ACM 978-1-4503-0478-8/11/01.

Abstract
Electronic media technology provides artists with tools for exploring interactivity. New immersive media sensations can result from the interactions between viewers and electronic artwork. "Zeugen" is an interactive and immersive new media artwork that was developed as a part of a creative exploration into the sensations of seeing and being seen.

Keywords
Art, Interactive, Mechatronic, Immersive, New Media, Creative-electronics

ACM Classification Keywords
H5.m. Information interfaces and presentation (e.g., HCI): Miscellaneous. J5.2. Arts, fine and performing.

General Terms
Design

Introduction
"Zeugen" consists of thirty-two human-cast robotic faces and a face tracking system, which together follow the movements of viewers in a gallery space. When a viewer approaches the work, the artificial eye lids suddenly open to reveal a grid of thirty-two watching pairs of eyes. The viewer has access to the front (face side) of the work where the faces are installed, and the

back (tech side) of the work where the technology driving the robotic faces is exposed. The high-tech, kinetic tech side and the polished face side are both important visual elements.

Zeugen

At first glance, the faces appear uniform because of the use of a casting process that removes most recognizable features of race, age, and even gender. Upon closer inspection, the viewer may realize that the faces have unique features. Their individual characteristics give them different 'personalities'; these features include eye color, face shape, and animatronics motion gestures made by the robotic eyes.

Interactivity on the face side is driven by the tech side of the work, which consists of mechatronic elements. Thirty-two individual robotic contraptions, microcontrollers, and a computer are exposed. On the computer screen, the viewer can see a video stream taken from the front of the work, and a 'face tracking box' that frames the faces of viewers interacting on the face side of the work.

The role of the participant in "Zeugen" is twofold: the viewer is meant to look at the work, while also being 'seen' by the work. When the viewer is looking at the tech side of the work, their interactivity role is absent. The work is only responsive to people standing on the face side. On the tech side, the viewer becomes the 'examiner' without any expectations of interactivity.

A self-reflexive experience can be generated by a visual event using an 'Artwork Mirror'. Self-reflexivity, as exhibited by the mirror event, requires a combination of both seeing and being seen by oneself.

Relevant new media artworks that have influenced "Zeugen" include the "Wooden Mirror" [1], "Watch" [2], "Watched and Measured" [3], "Access" [4], and the Opto-Isolator" [5]

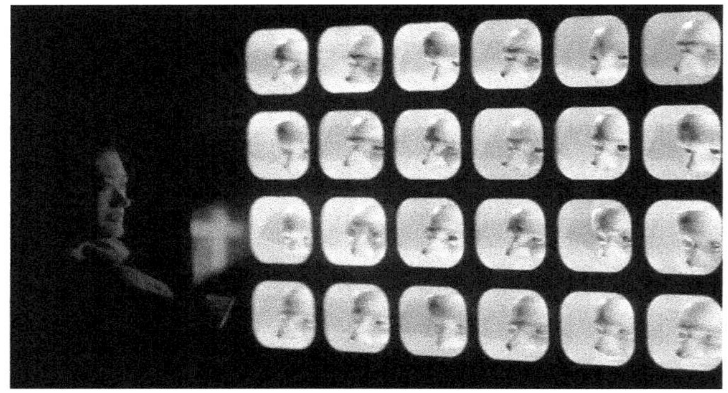

figure 1. Morgan Rauscher, "Zeugen", 2009 (Surrey Art Gallery [Interactive Futures '09])

Acknowledgements

We thank the Emily Carr University of Art + Design and the Social Sciences and Humanities Research Council of Canada for generously supporting our research.

Citations

[1] Rozin, D., The Wooden Mirror. 1999: New York.

[2] Rokeby, D., Watch. 1995: Kwangju, South Korea.

[3] Rokeby, D., Watched and Measured. 2000.

[4] Sester, M., Access. 2006.

[5] Levin, G. and G. Baltus, Opto-Isolator. 2007, Bitforms gallery: NYC.

Sidetrack

Jacek Barcikowski
ul. Gotowca 37/16
10-087 Olsztyn,
Poland
j.barcikowski@skylined.pl

Jennifer Kay
Minard Road 3.1 38
Glasgow g41 2hw
Scotland, United Kingdom
jeaniekay.cph@gmail.com

Martina Pagura
Via Zoppolana 44
33080 Castions di Zoppola (PN)
Italy
martina.pagura@gmail.com

TEI'11, January 22-26, 2011, Funchal, Portugal.
ACM 978-1-4503-0478-8/11/01.

Abstract
In this paper we describe the concept of Sidetrack, table, the motivation that lead to its creation and information about how does it work.

Keywords
Tangible user interface, peripheral interactions, physical computing, data visualisation.

ACM Classification Keywords
H5.m. Information interfaces and presentation: Miscellaneous.

General Terms
Design, Human Factor, Experimentation.

Introduction
The Sidetrack table allows you to reflect on your daily working routine by drawing a pattern of your behaviour. By placing sensors in areas you wish to observe, the marker moves as you move from space to space. Incorporating the mechanics of an old printer and a turntable, the handcrafted table becomes an omniscient narrator of the intangible pockets of time and energy you dedicate to working.

Concept

The Sidetrack table peripherally records you as you work in the home, tracing a pattern as you move from space to space. Markers plot this pattern as the table spins, oscillating in time with your movement between rooms. Sensors are placed in the areas you want to observe, for example the desk, or the kitchen.
By placing tags on the table, you purposefully work towards set tasks, with the patterns reflecting the journey towards these objectives. In this way, giving value to the intangible effort and pockets of time you devote whilst working from home.

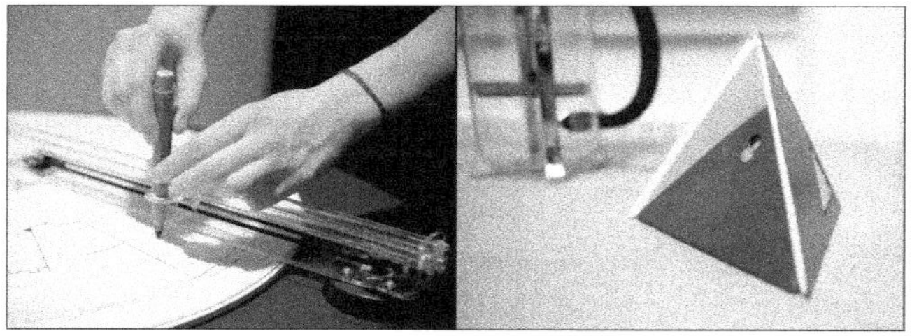

figure 1 Placing marker inside drawing arm (left) and Sidetrack presence sensor (right).

Motivation

The Sidetrack concept arose from the research around professionals, who completely engaged in their work, found it difficult to separate home life from work. In most cases, they were often stationary in front of their desk with little interaction with other areas around the home. They did not generally avoid their work, so the notion of being 'sidetracked' was a healthy way to alternate their somewhat static day.

How does it work?

The table mechanics were built with the motors from an old printer and turntable combined with custom components to sustain the operation of the arm. The movement of the arm itself is defined by the presence sensors placed around the home, recording where you are, whilst you work. Each day is then recorded on a paper disc for you to reflect and decipher your working pattern, creating a tangible culmination of your day.

figure 2. Sidetrack table drawing a pattern.

tendrils: Exploring the Poetics of Collective Touch in Wearable Art

Thecla Schiphorst
School of Interactive Arts and Technology,
102 Avenue, Surrey, British Columbia, V3T 0A3
Canada
thecla@sfu.ca

Jinsil Seo
School of Interactive Arts and Technology,
102 Avenue, Surrey, British Columbia, V3T 0A3
Canada
jinsils@sfu.ca

TEI'11, January 22–26, 2011, Funchal, Portugal.
ACM 978-1-4503-0478-8/11/01.

Abstract
This paper summarizes the artistic concepts underlying the design of *tendrils,* a responsive kinetic wearable art-work in the form of an interactive garment. The design process of *tendrils* is based in artistic exploration influenced by the *somatic turn:* an approach to designing for experience using embodied practice. Based on a somaesthetic framework for the design of expressive interaction [1], *tendrils* emphasizes four main concepts, 1) the *experience* of the sensory self, 2) design for *poetics* of interaction, 3) *materiality* based in soft-circuit design as well as the sensory materiality of the body, and 4) the computational *semantics* that supports sensory input and response through touch, both locally on the garment and collectively through iphone/ipod touch interaction. *tendrils* is described based on its artistic concept and execution.

Keywords
Art/Design installation, Embodiment, Somaesthetics, Wearable Interaction, Touch, Interaction Aesthetics, Materials Exploration, Kinaesthesia, Kinetic Response

ACM Classification Keywords
H5.2. [User Interfaces] Interaction Styles, Theory and Methods, User-centered Design.

General Terms
Design

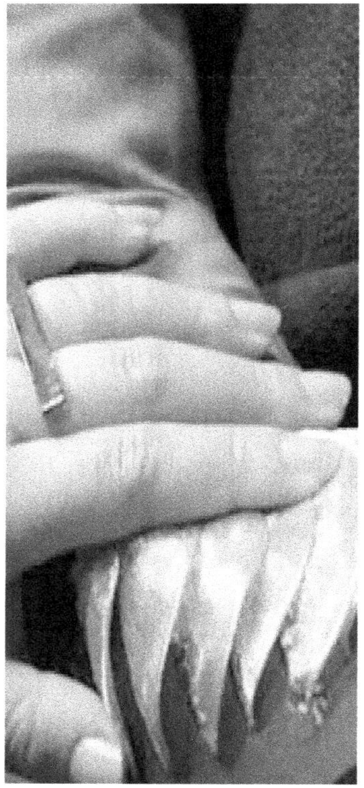

Figure 3. *tendrils* stroke-sensor is hand-sewn using conductive silk organza and a row of resistors to enable positional tactile data to be sensed directly on the garment

Introduction

tendrils is based in artistic exploration that highlights the concept of *somaesthetics* as an approach to the design of expressive interaction. Somaesthetics is a term coined by Richard Shusterman [2], a pragmatist philosopher interested in the critical study of bodily experience as a focus of sensory-aesthetic appreciation and agency. Somaesthetics offers a bridging strategy between embodied practices based in somatics, and the design of an aesthetics of interaction for technology.

Figure 2: kinetic interaction responds to collective touch

This design framework has been explored by Schiphorst [1] in prior tangible and wearable networked art. This framework highlights four constructs: experience, poetics of interaction, materiality and semantics (how the system constructs meaningful behaviors from the quality of the tactile input). This *research through art* methodology integrates multisensory interaction with soft circuits and garment design, developing new communication metaphors for wearable technologies as a sensory site of experience that highlight embodied communication.

Concept: *tendrils* and Touch

tendrils in an interactive kinetic garment constructed from vibrant raw silks, soft-circuits, hand crafted tactile stroke-sensors, LEDs and motors that responds to collective touch, both locally on the garment surface, and through a remote iPhone-iPod Touch App served through a networked link. *tendrils* is a metaphor for the particles, filaments and networks that combine to create our collective selves, the interstitial signals that flow within our bodies, enacting Merleaux-Ponty's notion of the "flesh of the world". Like a tidal-pool, *tendrils* reflects movement and visual patterns as an eco-system of tiny sensory-motor responses, in which we touch 'something of the self' within an elemental architecture. The *tendrils* garment is reminiscent of an active and intelligent skin that poetically responds by shivering, quivering, sighing, and 'alighting'. These skin-like responses are actuated by a series of small, interconnected motors and lights that reflect the inner energy and nervous system of the garment. Based on biological cellular structures that alter their structural form as a response to touch, *tendrils'* subtle movements reflect its ecological connection to our larger movements as a whole. The *tendrils* garment is constructed from soft circuits using conductive fabric and thread. The aesthetic and material properties are shaped equally by the needs of the electronic elements, material characteristics of the textiles and qualities of the wearer's physical movement.

References

[1] Schiphorst, T. 2009. Soft(n): Towards a Somaesthetics of Tactile Interaction. CHI '09. ACM, New York, NY, 2427-2438.

[2] Shusterman, R. 2008. *Body Consciousness: A Philosophy of Mindfulness and Somaesthetics*. Cambridge University Press, Cambridge, MA.

LightBox - Exploring Interaction Modalities with Colored Light

Figure 1. An animated lighting sequence visualized on the hi-power LEDs of *LightBox*

Alexander Wiethoff
University of Munich
Amalienstrasse 17
Munich, 80639, Germany
alexander.wiethoff@ifi.lmu.de

Magdalena Blöckner
University of Munich
Amalienstrasse 17
Munich, 80639, Germany
bloeckner@cip.ifi.lmu.de

Abstract
In this paper we describe a prototype for the simple and playful exploration of various interaction modalities with colored light.

Keywords
Interactive Lighting Design, Prototyping.

ACM Classification Keywords
H5.2. Information interfaces and presentation (e.g., HCI): Prototyping.

General Terms
Design.

TEI'11, January 22–26, 2011, Funchal, Portugal.
ACM 978-1-4503-0478-8/11/01.

Introduction
In lighting design, more than in many other design disciplines, it is mandatory to approach a new concept by iterative trying and testing. As light is an intangible and very transient medium, which is influenced by a wide variety of factors, new design concepts need to be applied and tried on an experimental basis in order to arrive at an aesthetically appealing result. Thus applying good lighting design concepts is a challenging task which demands careful consideration. Things are even more complex when adding a layer of interactivity to the project. To investigate this type of setups, we have crated *LightBox,* a tool for exploring interaction with colored light and for testing concepts for responsive environments [1]. The ultra-bright multi-colored light-emitting diodes (LEDs) of our system can generate any visible lighting color. They can be addressed and controlled individually, thus simulating effects ranging from a solid beam of light to very subtle animations, transitions and dimmed lighting effects.

Implementation
LightBox is housed in an aluminum suitcase measuring 48x38x25cm. The lid of the suitcase contains a panel of 12x12 LEDs, assembled from 12 hi-power single, 24 volt/10 watt *Colormix* red, green and blue (RGB) LED strips. These LED strips respond to digital multiplex (DMX) signals, a common data standard in industry for

controlling lights. The suitcase contains a PC running a custom software, as well as a 24- and a 9-volt supply to power and control the LED panel and additional experimental setups, e.g., for gathering input via sensors. In addition, we built in four simple circuits (consisting of one sensor element each) using suitable resistors and a micro-controller that reads out sensor values and transmits them to the computer. There, the data is interpreted and processed. Each sensor can be plugged into the aluminum suitcase from the outside, using 3.5mm stereo jacks and sockets. In addition to the sensorial equipment, we have developed a custom software application that lets users interact with *LightBox* using a graphical user interface (GUI).

Interaction Modalities

LightBox can display predefined content and turn it into a visual color experience. With a custom-built *Screen Capturing software*, the user can capture any area of the computer screen, for example a video from *YouTube*® or similar content. The software translates the captured area into DMX signals that in turn control the RGB LEDs in the prototype. By using this software, even novice users unfamiliar with DMX signals can easily define their own lighting animations. As an example, we displayed an animated, rotating globe. The texture of the globe contained lighter and darker regions, which created an intensive and rapid interplay of a colors when transferred to the (relatively low resolution) LED panel. In another modality, users can interact with the sensorial equipment. We built four types of sensor circuits: heat, motion, light and sound sensors that influence different animations in terms of size or luminance, depending on environmental changes. For example, an animated red circle would grow in size while changing in intensity and color from white to red when the heat sensor measured an increased temperature. This equipment is meant to inspire the designers' imagination for opportunistic interaction possibilities. In a playful interaction approach, they can use the sensorial equipment as a possible starting point for brainstorming and reflecting about reactive input and output methods in interactive lighting design.

Conclusion

In this paper we presented *LightBox*, a miniature lighting lab that allows designers to explore interaction modalities for interactive lighting design. Considering the fact that permanent interactive lighting installations are highly work- and cost-intensive, we believe in an approach, in which early concepts can be tried and explored on a small scale beforehand. The benefit of our system is that new concepts can be tried and tested before implementing them in the real world. Explorative prototypes such as *LightBox* might spark the inspiration of artists and designers in the design process while making a complex intangible relationship between interactivity and lighting design more graspable.

Acknowledgements

We would like to thank the company Feno for their generous support along the project.

References

[1] Bullivant, L.: 4dspace: Interactive Architecture. John Wiley & Sons (Publisher) 2005.

The Presence Table: A Reactive Surface for Ambient Connection

Matthew Canton
California College of the Arts
1111 Eighth Street
San Francisco, CA 94107 USA
matthew.canton@gmail.com
www.matthewcanton.com

Abstract
The Presence Table is a prototype that connects two households through an ambient, expressive interaction. The surface of the table illuminates and creates a reactive trace of human gestures and everyday objects. This trace is shared through a network connection to a linked surface at another location.

Keywords
Presence, domestic technology, intimacy, family

ACM Classification Keywords
H.5.m. Information interfaces and presentation (e.g., HCI): Miscellaneous.

General Terms
Design, Experimentation, Human Factors

TEI'11, January 22–26, 2011, Funchal, Portugal.
ACM 978-1-4503-0478-8/11/01.

Introduction
The Presence Table is an exploration of the possibilities of ubiquitous computing in the domestic space. It developed from design research with family members who lived apart but maintained a close sense of emotional connection. The research and design studies were published and publicly presented as part of my MFA Thesis in Design at California College of the Arts.

Initial research was conducted with people aged 20-35 who lived in San Francisco. The research expanded to include their parents and other family members. Home studies, interviews, and structured activities were used to gain insights into how families relied on technology to keep in touch. One key finding in the research phase was that adults and their parents had conflicting feelings about how often they communicated. The young adults sought to reassure their parents with messages and updates, but also expressed a desire for emotional distance and a sense of independence.

The Presence Table
The Presence Table was one of several prototypes developed following the research phase. It was created to explore how an ambiguous, expressive and non-invasive interaction might enhance the feeling of presence and connection between distant family members. Work from Kaye et. al. exploring intimacy through minimal connections [1] was a key influence.

The Presence Table was designed to resemble a traditional piece of furniture.

The prototype was tested with two family members who lived apart.

I chose to engage interaction through a table surface because it is an area of daily activity in people's homes. A table may be used for eating and socializing. It may be used for working, reading, and corresponding. When not in use, it may display familiar objects. Gaver et. al. explored the flow of objects and activity on a surface with the History Tablecloth [2]. The Presence Table extends this approach by allowing one surface to reflect and respond to activity at a distant location. Because it would be deployed in people's homes, the first prototype was designed to resemble a traditional piece of furniture with a wooden surface. A second prototype with a glass and acrylic surface was developed as an aesthetic counterpoint.

Technology Development

The table had to sense gestures and give feedback without using a projector or external display. To accomplish this, the surface was embedded with fiber optic wires. The system uses a camera inside the table, tracking data from a Community Core Vision[1] application, and custom software created with Processing[2]. The software controls an LCD that sends light up to the fiber optic wires at the surface of the table. The software also records signals and transmit them across the internet to a paired table in another location. An RFID (radio-frequency identification) reader is placed below the surface. Objects tagged with RFID chips can be placed on the table to change the illuminated colors. The system allows people to create their own interpretations through variations in movement and color. Extended activity at the table also triggers a chime sound at both locations.

Testing

The tables were tested with a young woman who lived in San Francisco and her mother who lived in Menlo Park, CA. The prototypes were set up to have a persistent connection for four days. Mother and daughter reported using the tables at various times of day to signal their presence to each other. Both felt that the tables imparted a sense of "calm" in their interactions. The mother reported that it gave her comfort to know her daughter was at home, without having to call or send a message. But the ambiguity of the signals brought conflicting feelings about the shared connection: "I thought about her more than I normally would, because every time I passed the table I would check to see if she was 'there' or not." Both participants reflected on the tension between intimacy and privacy in their relationship. Ultimately, the project highlighted the particular resonance of these issues for family members living apart.

Acknowledgements

I would like to thank my thesis committee: Brenda Laurel, Wendy Ju and Paul Montgomery at California College of the Arts, and Jofish Kaye at the Nokia Research Center, Palo Alto.

Citations

[1] Kaye, J. and Goulding, L. 2004. Intimate objects. In *Proceedings of the 5th conference on Designing Interactive Systems (DIS '04)*. ACM, New York, NY, USA, 341-344.

[2] Gaver, W., Bowers, J., Boucher, A., Law, A., Pennington, S. and Villar, N. 2006. The history tablecloth: illuminating domestic activity. In *Proceedings of the 6th Conference on Designing Interactive systems (DIS '06)*. ACM, New York, NY, USA, 199-208.

[1] http://ccv.nuigroup.com/

[2] http://www.processing.org

Skintimacy: Exploring Interpersonal Boundaries through Musical Interactions

Alexander Müller
TU Berlin
Deutsche Telekom Laboratories
Design Research Lab
Ernst-Reuter-Platz 7, Berlin
a.mueller@telekom.de

Jochen Fuchs
FH Potsdam
Deutsche Telekom Laboratories
Design Research Lab
Ernst-Reuter-Platz 7, Berlin
Jochen.fuchs@fh-potsdam.de

Konrad Röpke
HS Magdeburg-Stendal
Industrial Design Institute
Breitscheidstr. 2, Magdeburg
konradroepke@gmail.com

TEI'11, January 22–26, 2011, Funchal, Portugal.
ACM 978-1-4503-0478-8/11/01.

Abstract
With 'Skintimacy' we present a skin-based interface for a collaborative musical performance. The experimental setup is intended to be both an evocative tool for interpersonal interaction and touch, as well as an alternative digital musical instrument. By integrating the human skin and touch into the musician-computer interface, we propose a bodily-close haptic and emotional experience. Our intention, our research question, the system design, and first observations of this phenomenological experience are outlined below.

Keywords
Skin-based interfaces, Musical interface, Intimacy, Interaction design

ACM Classification Keywords
H5.m. Information interfaces and presentation: Miscellaneous.

General Terms
Exploration

Introduction – The Role of Human Body
After HCI research advanced the interest in and the relevance of embodied interactions [1], which is predominantly predicated on phenomenological

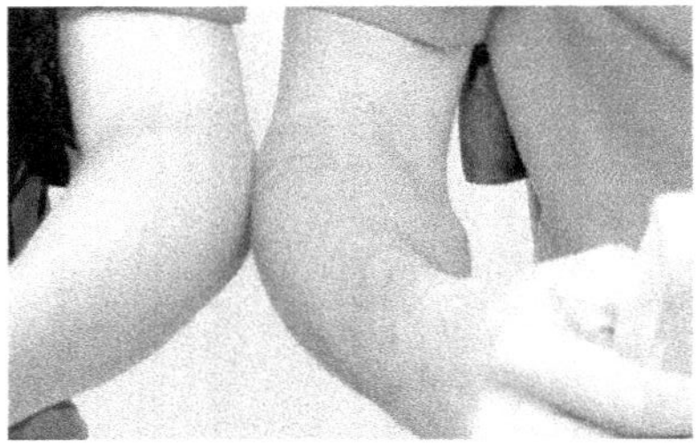

Is this an unintended touch?

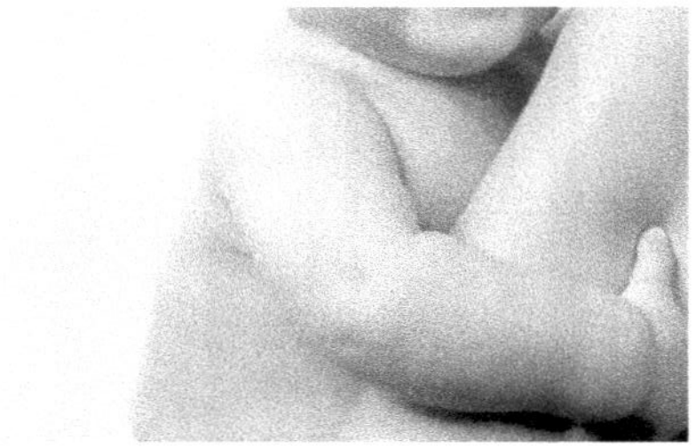

Intended touch

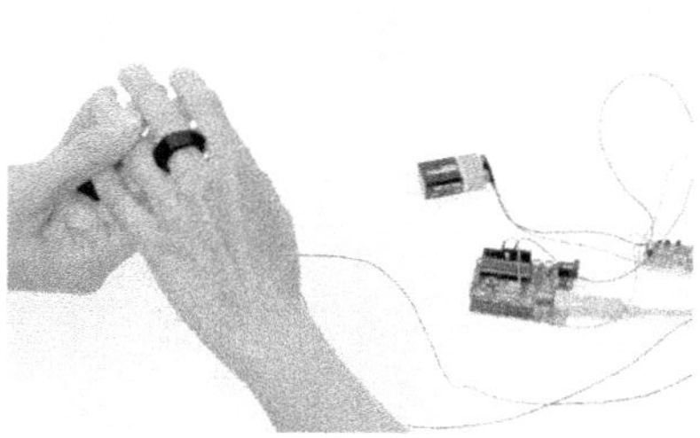

Skintimacy Prototype

philosophies (e.g. by Heidegger, Merleau-Ponty and lately Thompson), traditional physical borders between the human body and technical devices have been disappearing. Consequently, these transformative phenomena - the new spectra of 'inbetweenness' - occur. New interaction scenarios will not only emerge between instruments and humans, but also between humans among themselves. The performance artist Stelarc has radically emphasized his claim for a new role of the human body within a digitalized world [7]. Referring to the skin as a central computer input, research projects like *Skinput* [3] and *Sixth Sense* [4] adduced technological evidence of its practicability. Our work was also inspired by new interfaces for musical expression e.g. the Freqtric Drums [5] and Daniel Brinkmann's installation *Skinstruments* [6].

Experiencing Intimacy

The question of intimacy is brought to the foreground with the upcoming trend in HCI to use skin (and the precision of the sense of touch) as an interface. Benthien states that *"historically [...] tactus was understood early on in the sense of intimacy, since [...] it essentially precludes a collective experience"* [2].
As an experimental collaborative instrument, *Skintimacy* is designed to give an auditively perceivable answer to the question: How can intimacy be experienced through sound when humans interact through mutual touch and perform with each other? Furthermore, since the instrument evokes interpersonal interaction, we want to employ *Skintimacy* as a playful tool that allows for the observation of intimate behaviour. We have discovered that personal and intimate borders are shifting significantly in a performative context where a computational (musical) process is linked to interpersonal touch.

Setup and Interaction Design of Skintimacy

The system consists of an open electric circuit that is connected to two different persons, an arduino board and sound synthesis software. By closing the open electric circuit through touch, and also by involving more persons, the sound is triggered. The pitch and 'colour' of sound do not only depend on the strength of the touch but also on the velocity as soon as one changes the physical contact. Galvanic Skin Response provides values for the sound mapping.

Further Steps

In order to continue our observations of use scenarios, we want to enable a broader access to *Skintimacy* through collaborative performances in an exhibition. Furthermore, we are about to develop more prototypes with a mapping refinement and an improvement of the current system referring the measurability of touch.

References

[1] Dourish, P., *Where the Action is: The Foundations of Embodied Interaction*, MIT Press, 2001.

[2] Benthien, C., *Skin – on the cultural border between self and the world*, Columbia University Press, 2002.

[3] Harrison, C., Tan, D., Morris, D., Skinput: Appropriating the Body as an Input Surface, in *Proceedings of CHI 2010*, Atlanta, USA, 2010.

[4] P. Mistry, P. Maes, L. Chang. WUW - Wear Ur World - A Wearable Gestural Interface, in *Proceedings of CHI 2009*, Boston, USA, 2009.

[5] Tetsuaki, B. et. Al., Freqtric drums: a musical instrument that uses skin contact as an interface, in *Proceedings of NIME 2007*, New York, USA, 2007.

[6] http://www.daanbrinkmann.com/

[7] Hauser, J. (ed.), *sk-interfaces*, Liverpool University Press, 2008

SoLu - Hyperinstrument

André Rangel Macedo
Researcher at Research Center for Science and Technology of the Arts, Portuguese Catholic University - School of the Arts.
Art Director - 3KTA.NET
Rua Soeiro Pereira Gomes
54 rc dto, 4100-470 Porto,
Portugal
ar@andrerangel.pt

Anne-Kathrin Siegel
Master Student at Engineering Faculty of Porto University
Creative Director - 3kta net
Rua de Sande, 2 rc, hab1
4100-446 Porto, Portugal
me@a-ks.eu

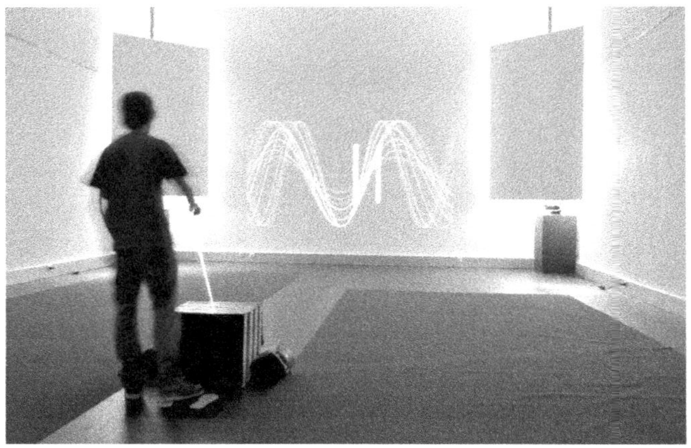

TEI'11, January 22–26, 2011, Funchal, Portugal.
ACM 978-1-4503-0478-8/11/01.

Abstract
Demonstration of a proposal of correspondence between Light and Sound. This proposal is materially exemplified by means of a new hyperinstrument, which gives its users the control over a multi-sensorial algorithmic composition generated in real-time. The employed methodology and mathematical model were presented with some detail in a previous, insofar as they pretend to be matter and reference for future developments in the field of multi-sensorial composition. Audiovisual documentation of the demonstration and previous paper available at: http://3kta.net/solu

Keywords
Sound, light, interaction, synesthesia, hyperinstrument, meta-conception, generative design, algorithmic composition.

ACM Classification Keywords
H.5 Information Interfaces and Presentation; J.5 Arts and Humanities.

General Terms
Design, Experimentation, Performance, Theory

Introduction
There is in contemporary art a growing interest in interactive and multi-modular works (Campos, Traldi, Oliveira & Manzoli, 2007). The power of modern computers and its processing ability offer new

possibilities to musical, visual, multi-sensorial interactive composition. The Art of today is real- time Art, live Art where what counts is its instantaneity (Virilio, 2005): the hyperinstrument created to this demonstration is therefore part of that present Art trend, for it calculates audio-visual composition in real-time. As a hyperinstrument, the main goal of its meta-conception was its easy and intuitive utilization by human beings.

The hyperinstrument prototype that we present allow people with few or very few skills, while users and creators of audiovisual, to participate in a process of generative algorithmic composition.

Sound and Light

Sound and light occurrences are phenomena of energy transport studied simultaneously by physics. They both propagate through waves and they both need a time interval between their emission and their reception. In spite of big differences in greatness and speed, both sound waves and electromagnetic waves are represented by the wavelength and frequency. Along the times there have been several models and devices that aimed the real-time performance of visual and sound events. Of all the possible correspondences between sound and light, the mapping of musical notes or heights to color tonalities was the most common proposal in the last 300 years. Considering that the piano is the most commonly used instrument in the process of composition, and is besides that, from all the elements of the classical orchestra, the one that produces the largest spectrum of musical heights, we have decided to take it as a reference in our demonstration. The correspondence between light and sound that we propose was obtained by applying the mathematical model [1] that was better adjusted to convert the exponential spacing of the intervals between the fundamental frequencies of the notes comprised in a piano's texture into linear spacing from the wavelengths of the visible electromagnetic spectrum.

Conclusion

The implemented algorithm, which allows the correspondence between sound frequency and color light frequency, will certainly integrate future multi-sensorial compositions, seen that we consider its reutilization and betterment. We conclude that the correspondence between color light frequency and sound frequency associated to the conception of interactive multi-sensorial systems is fertile ground to future researches.

Notes

[1] Mathematical model developed to convert fundamental frequencies values of the piano notes to the color wavelengths of the visible spectrum: $n = 700 - (12*(\log(f/220)/\log(2))+36)*3.44827586207$

References

[1]CAMPOS, Cleber; TRALDI, Cesar; de OLIVEIRA, Luis Felipe; MANZOLLI , Jônatas; (2008), *Anticipation, Improvisation and Multimodality: Musical Meaning on Interactive Performance.* Music Department, Arts Institute, University of Campinas [Online]: http://recherche.ircam.fr/ equipes/analyse-synthese/EMUS/AGORA/ abstract_poster/manzolli_poster_EMUS_ AGORA_abstract.pdf

[2] VIRILIO, Paul; Lotringer, Sylvère (2005), *The Accident of Art*. Semiotext(e) Ed.

[3] www.3kta.net/solu

iLand: A Tangible Location Aware Narrative Experience

Mara Dionisio
Madeira-ITI
Universidade da Madeira
Campus da Penteada
Funchal.Portugal
maradionisio@hotmail.com

Valentina Nisi
Madeira-ITI Universidade da
Madeira Campus da Penteada,
Funchal, Portugal
valentina.nisi@gmail.com

Jos P.van Leeuwen
Madeira-ITI Universidade da
Madeira Campus da Penteada,
Funchal, Portugal
jospvl@gmail.com

TEI'11, January 22–26, 2011, Funchal, Portugal.
ACM 978-1-4503-0478-8/11/01.

Abstract
iLand is a technology enhanced location aware narrative experience that captures and exposes the rich oral culture and traditions in the Island of Madeira for a wide variety of audience in particular foreigners and tourists. Using the Madeira main city, Funchal, as a setting to bring a new level of engagement of the audience with the old part of the city and its traditional stories. With this aim in mind we designed an immersive experience in the old part of the city were the local settings and its tangible details merge with the story world and events. As the experience unfolds the audience is taken deeper into the local traditions as well as into the old part of the city. In order to achieve this we designed and produced a series of short stories carefully distributed in the real space. The experience is mediated through the Placeware location aware mobile story platform [1] to functions as a tangible interface between the local stories and architectural setting and its audience.

Keywords
Interactive narrative, Locative media, Mobile Devices, Narrative experience design

ACM Classification Keywords
J.5. Arts and Humanities, H5.2. User Interfaces.

General Terms
Design

Introduction

Stories are all around us but sometimes it's hard to access to them. Often the people who have them do not find the right opportunity or setting to share. Through the iLand project we designed an opportunity to uncover and share this stories.

iLand: the narrative experience

We started by connecting with local people part of our social network like friends and relatives asking them for stories. The stories collected in this way were colored by personal shades of drama, personal details and warmth that could not be found in formally written accounts. We selected eight stories for production, based on the potential drama and the thematic connection to religious and spiritual matters. We wanted our audience to learn about the folklore of the island and to remain open regarding the truth and the value of these folkloristic tales.

While developing the stories' plot and characters we designed the iLand LAMS experience as a whole. We targeted foreigners as well as madeiran users, as long as they not familiar with Funchal old part of town. The location chosen was Rua Santa Maria in Funchal, since it is has a mysterious as well as traditional atmosphere that fits the type of experience that we want our audience to have.

Fig. 1. Video Frames from the iLand stories.

The tangible delivery platform

As our story delivery platform we used Placeware [1], the second iteration of the system used for the MPL experience. Placeware runs on a Window Mobile, GPS enabled smart phone. It has wide touch screen that allows an easy use of a map based interface and the presentation of multimedia videos. As the application starts, a map of the place is displayed and the system obtains the GPS coordinates for the user's position, represented as a circle on the map. The circle moves as the user walks. Small dots represent the stories on the map. When the user position overlaps with the dots the phone vibrates and the dot enlarges. The user has then the option of clicking on the dot to watch the story video fragment. After watching the story the application returns to the map and the user continues the tour.

Fig. 2. Placeware interface

References

[1] Nisi, Valentina, Ian Oakley, Martine Posthuma de Boer (2010) "Locative Narratives as Experience: A New Perspective on Location Aware Multimedia Stories" in *ARTECH 2010 Proceedings of the 5th International Conference on Digital Arts*, Guimarães, Portugal, 59-64.

Acknowledgments

Thanks to Madeira Life Project and its team under which framework the project was funded.

NUVE: In Between the Analog and Virtual Body

João Martinho Moura
engageLab / Dep. Inf. Sys.
University of Minho
4800-058 Guimarães, Portugal
jm@jmartinho.net

Né Barros
Balleteatro
Institute of Philosophy-Aesthetics, Politics and Art Research Group
University of Porto
4150-564 Porto, Portugal
nebarros@gmail.com

Pedro Branco
engageLab / Dep. Inf. Sys.
University of Minho
4800-058 Guimarães, Portugal
pbranco@dsi.uminho.pt

Adérito Fernandes Marcos
engageLab / Laboratory of Distance Education (LEaD), Universidade Aberta, Lisbon, Portugal
marcos@univ-ab.pt

TEI'11, January 22–26, 2011, Funchal, Portugal.
ACM 978-1-4503-0478-8/11/01.

Abstract
NUVE is an artistic project that aims to explore the artistic possibilities offered by the digital dance performances in the interaction between the individual and his virtual double. In NUVE we conceptualized, developed and implemented a digital artifact, resulting in a fluid digital performance based on the theme of the analog body versus the digital virtual body.

Keywords
Dance, performance, virtual double, generative.

ACM Classification Keywords
H5.2. User Interfaces. J.5. Arts and Humanities.

General Terms
Design, Experimentation, Human Factors.

Introduction
Contemporary art sets the scenery for a body exploration based on movements, actions and behaviors. Among the different crossings, the digital art is still under expansion on the dance domain. Despite the art of dance has appropriated a variety of new technologies, it is still a domain to explore with the potential at an aesthetic and at an artistic level.

NUVE emerges from a line of work being developed by the first author [1] that explores full body interaction

Photos: balleteatro@LuisFerraz

Performances videos at http://nuve.jmartinho.net/tei2011

and expressive gestures to compose immersive audio and visual flows supporting artistic expressiveness. In the author's previous work physical expressive gestures are rendered in digital compositions formed by musical and visual movements, composing an enriched audio-visual experience [2].

Concept

In NUVE the body is the first engine of action, but the choreographic body evolves into a relation with its own "virtual double" in a way to create a dialog challenging the choreographic boundaries and adding new dimensions to the gesture. Throughout the choreography a tension is built between the performer's silhouette and the "virtual double". At some stage in the narrative, the "virtual body" detaches itself from the performer and the choreography evolves, the "virtual double" is no longer shadowing the performer but in a way seems to gain life from him/her and both perform together.

NUVE follows the line of generative digital art, composing in real-time ever evolving visual scenarios that flow with the performer movement and gesture contrasting light and darkness, body and gestures, real and digital. The audio and visual sequences of the narrative are pre-established to follow the created choreography.

Implementation

NUVE is developed with the openFrameworks [3] platform, an open source C++ programming language toolkit. It relies on an infrared firewire camera to capture the image of the stage 30 frames per second. Appropriately infrared lights are employed to obtain the best possible image of the dancer. A combination of standard image processing techniques is then used to capture the silhouette and the movement of the performer. At some points during the choreography the performer interacts with a particle based system that flows in the scene. This seamless interaction between the full body of the dancer and the virtual particles is possible by computing the different speed of the different areas of the body and feeding it those to the particles physics system.

The sound composition was created with the software SuperCollider, a system to program generative sound [4]. In opposition to previous work [1] in this project the audio is not generated in real-time, instead the sound aesthetics was carefully crafted specifically for NUVE.

Conclusion

NUVE project is an example of the synergies among the various facades of creativity, being it the performance, the visual, the audio and the technological, brought together in a coherent and complementary fashion and seeking the poetics that can result when the languages of arts and the technology mutually comprehend.

References

[1] Moura, J. M., Sousa, J., Branco, P., Marcos, A. F. You Move You Interact: a full-body dance in-between reality and virtuality. Proc. ARTECH 2008, Porto, Portugal. Pages 49- 54.

[2] Moura, J. M. You Move You Interact. www.ymyi.org

[3] openFrameworks. http://www.openframeworks.cc/

[4] SuperCollider. http://www.audiosynth.com

Osciloscopiando

Daniela Steinsapir
Learning, design and technology
School of Education, Stanford University
United States
danielast@gmail.com

Paulo Blikstein
Assistant Professor
Learning Technologies Lab, Stanford University
United States
paulob@stanford.edu

Author Keywords
art, experimental, hacking, interactive

ACM Classification Keywords
B.4.2 Hardware, INPUT/OUTPUT AND DATA COMMUNICATIONS, Input/Output Devices: Image display

General Terms
Experimentation, Performance

Rationale
Osciloscopiando, an interactive video sculpture composed by a found and hacked oscilloscope from the 70's, utilizes multimedia and experimental art as a means of questioning the relationship between mass production, technology, and our society's attribution to value objects. This piece "re-employs" seemingly outmoded forms of mass production in novel and different ways. We are especially interested in the remaking of those old mass produced objects that seem no longer relevant to our society and transform them into new objects, changing our memories and our perceptions of them. By transforming the function of these objects both physically and conceptually, and anthropomorphizing the machine, the piece calls attention to one's own ideas about the old and the new, the useful and the disposable, evoking the discomfort of the unexpected, forcing the viewer to question his perceptual experience, and reflect on the nature and value of mass produced objects. Being interactive, it gives the viewer an active role on the decision whether to be removed or not from a reality to which they have become accustomed. The interactivity, thus, becomes an open invitation for the viewer to be part of the artists' own creative process. The inspiration for Osciloscopiando, as part of Steinsapir's "Recycling Junk" series, was based on the idea of constant change, within the fast replacement cycle of home appliances and technology in general.

The fact that everything becomes quickly disposable is the source of inspiration to recycle them and repurpose both their physicality and application. In addition, the artist's own process is made visible for the audience. Commonly those circuits are hidden inside technological objects, they are covered, disguised, hidden by the main objects – this work rescues those circuits as the main and prime material to create her pieces. Furthermore, the user interaction with the piece, using a metallic camera to inspect the oscilloscope's interior, resembles the act to taking a patient's heartbeat with a stethoscope

TEI'11, January 22–26, 2011, Funchal, Portugal.
ACM 978-1-4503-0478-8/11/01.

– further bringing into light issues of life and death objects in a consumer society.

References

Steinsapir's work takes a variety of different forms, each of which incorporates different found objects and technologies. Her work includes: interactive video installations, electro-mechanical sculptures, digital murals and electronic paintings. By functioning interactively, the success and, to some degree, the very existence of each work depends on both the hardware and software of her works in such a way that physical acts are interpreted visually. Literally translating the physical human gesture into a digital language, she draws a conceptual link between mass culture, technological mediation and psychological processes.[1]

Osciloscopiando, is part of the series of works, "*Recycling Junk*", a body of work that shows the beauty, harmony, and symmetry of discarded electronics. The recycling junk series was exhibited at Steinsapir's solo show, *Electrocicando*, 2009, at the Galeria Ana Maria Mathei[2], In Santiago, Chile. One of the pieces that was part of the show as well, was *Cable a Tierra*. It is a video piece that shows the interior of an old oscilloscope. Daniela intensified its elements by means of monochromatic lighting and shadow effects. Continuing the *Recycling Junk series,* Daniela created, *Osciloscopiando*, an interactive video-mechanical sculpture.

Concept

Part of the oscilloscope's interior was hacked by the addition of a new LCD screen, a desk lamp transformed into a webcam handle and by various of the scope's knobs that were hacked to give them new functionalities. The created mechanical handle (from a desk lamp) is mounted on a cart attached to a webcam which records video. When activated, it makes a real-time abstract video based on the oscilloscope's interior. The real time video is being processed by software to enhance its circuitry through lighting, contrast and color effects.

The piece is user-activated by the turning on a switch. That action turns on the interior lights of the oscilloscope. When the oscilloscope is on, a video image appears on the LCD screen. By moving the mechanical handle, which contains the webcam that records the scope's interior, users are invited to make their own video. Thus, by interacting with various hacked switches of the oscilloscope the user can start modifying the video being created. One of its knobs controls the hue of the video, others control the line thickness or apply different filters to the image being processed.

As described by Anjee Hestrup Alvarez in the 2007, at the Chicana/o Biennal at Macla, Galeria, movimiento de Arte y Cultura Latina[3], in San Jose California, "Looking at the impact of mass production, Daniela Steinsapir, created the interactive video piece sculpture Osciloscopiando, (Recycling Junk series). By recycling mass-produced objects that have since lost their relevance, such as an oscilloscope, Daniela transforms the objects into an experimental, interactive art pieces. The placement of a real time video camera on the side of the obsolete machine is an open invitation for the viewer to interact with the piece by moving the camera's arm to create various images on the screen. The interaction with the Osciloscopiando allows the viewer to mediate on the complex relationship between material and culture.

[1] www.danielast.com
[2] http://www.galeriamatthei.cl/

[3] 2007 Anjee Helstrup-Alvarez, "Introduction," The Chicana/o Biennial. San Jose: Movimiento de Arte y Cultura Latino Americana, 2007. (Exhibition Catalogue)

Sensor Poetics

Kjen Wilkens
UK/Germany
http://kjenwilkens.com
kjen.wilkens@network.rca.ac.uk

TEI'11, January 22–26, 2011, Funchal, Portugal.
ACM 978-1-4503-0478-8/11/01.

Abstract
Sensor Poetics proposes the idea of a fictional gadget called the 'weather camera' and uses this as a scenario to pose questions about story telling, data narratives, our relation to weather and the possibility of a digital product long-tail.

Keywords
Data narratives, story telling, product long-tail, internet of things, weather

ACM Classification Keywords
Computer Applications

General Terms
Design

Introduction
Considering both the massive rise in public and private data, as well as the recent popularity of data driven research methods, my work tries to critically reflect on the personal impact of this data leaping into all aspects of our lives. I seek to uncover uncanny and playful implications of a data obese future.

What if we would use a weather 'camera' instead of a photo camera to capture special moments? As a sensor device it could record wind, light, temperature, humidity and air quality for the current time and location. How would we use this sensor data to tell the stories of these moments? How would we share these stories with our family and friends? Would we engage in 'casual storm chasing'?

Figure 1: Scenario picture of the "weather camera"

Story Telling for a Data Obese Future

Starting from the assumption that more and more objects will produce sensor data and eventually form what is being called The Internet of Things, this project explores the narrative power of such data streams. It explores ways in which telling stories about the everyday might change if new methods of recording exist and the emotional value of data that is connected to personal memories.

A Special Relation to the Weather

The example used for this project is the subculture of weather enthusiasts since they already exhibit a strong relation to data and measuring and their main medium of exchange is the Internet. A psychological study[1] of an online community of weather enthusiasts has shown that weather often plays a significant role in organizing autobiographical memory. The project proposes a portable weather 'camera' device that is operated like a snapshot camera to sample a specific moment of weather and a web-community to tell the corresponding stories of these moments. The weather camera is equipped with sensors to record wind, light, temperature, humidity and air quality as well as a GPS sensor delivering temporal and spatial context. The software for annotating, browsing and sharing the sensor data then enables a new way of browsing personal memory through exploring relationships between different situations and their sensor readings.

The Digital Product Long-Tail

The project also explores the possibility of a digital product long-tail. Based in the idea that new ways of production such as rapid prototyping and rapid manufacturing might enable a whole new range of products which wouldn't usually exist in today's market place due to needed economies of scale. What if becomes possible to create your own weird, niche, hyper-local, hyper-specialized digital gadgets? Will subcultures create theire own Internet connected devices? How will these devices be made, distributed, updated and disposed?

Acknowledgements

Story writing: Alex Burrett, Product Design: Molly Anderson, Programming: Steffen Fiedler, Outdoor Photography: Ludwig Zeller; Thanks to: Kevin Grennan, Veronica Ranner, J. Paul Neeley

Citations

[1] Strauss, S., Orlove, B.S..Weather, climate, culture. Berg Publishers (2003), P. 103ff

Hug@ree | A RTiVISS Experience

figure 1: Sketches of the interactions at the two installation spaces.

Mónica Mendes
CIEAM and Departamento de Artes Multimédia, Universidade de Lisboa
Lisbon, Portugal
monica.mendes@fba.ul.pt

Pedro Ângelo
LCD – Laboratório de Criação Digital, AZ Audiência Zero
Porto, Portugal
pedroangelo@audienciazero.org

Nuno Correia
CITI and Departamento de Informática, Universidade Nova de Lisboa
Lisbon, Portugal
nmc@di.fct.unl.pt

TEI'11, January 22–26, 2011, Funchal, Portugal.
ACM 978-1-4503-0478-8/11/01.

Abstract
Hug@ree is an interactive installation that provides a bond between urban beings and the forest. Participants hug a real tree, triggering their registration in the virtual world for further interaction.

Keywords
Environmental Art, Experimental Design, Real-time Video, Interactive Installation, Tangible interfaces, Sustainability, Social Responsibility.

ACM Classification Keywords
H.5.0[Information Interfaces and Presentation]:General
H.5.1[Information Interfaces and Presentation]: Multimedia Information Systems - Video

General Terms
Design, Experimentation, Human Factors.

Introduction
Hug@ree and engage into a playful symbiotic relationship with nature, for everyone should hug a real tree every now and then [2].

Hug@ree is part of Real-Time Interactive Video Systems for Sustainability (RTiVISS), an experimental investigation actively reflecting on the questions: how can we propose constructive approaches to the destructive dynamics that aggravate climate change? Can art foster awareness and respect for nature? [4]

figures 2 and 3: *Hug@ree Sprint* collaborative work.

figure 4: *Hug@ree* interaction at Pop Up City Lisbon 2010 exhibition.

figure 5: *Hug@ree* "10/10/10 Global Work Party" participants.

This immersive experience provides the interaction with trees and videos of trees in real-time, raising environmental issues in urban culture. Its implementation aims to express new values regarding sustainability in the present and future.

Implementation and Interaction Design

The *Hug@ree* experience is composed of two distinct moments. In an outdoor space, a real tree is instrumented with several conductive wires ergonomically distributed around its trunk. These wires form capacitive sensors that are used to detect the proximity of participants' body. A microcontroller attached to the wires triggers a hug when most of the sensors detect proximity, contact and pressure, sending a signal through a wireless radio transmitter to the indoor installation space. While a camera continually records the tree outside, custom software captures and keeps in memory the last few seconds of video.
When a hug trigger reaches the wireless radio receiver, the software saves the video and sends it to an interactive tangible projection. Then, participants may access and place the video loop of their own hug on the displayed tree-like structure, becoming leaves of a collective experience.
Multiple *Hug@ree* installations around the world will upload their leaves to the online platform, creating a global shared nature embrace. The online platform also enables participants to upload a photo of themselves, their hug being part of the world when an installation participant hugs the tree for real.

Conclusions and Future Work

Hug@ree addresses networking practices and actions that contribute to change the current behavior regarding environmental protection.
The aim is to promote new activities to move society towards more inclusive modes of production and sharing knowledge for the design of a better world.
The interactive installation recently premiered at *Pop Up City* [3]. The venue for this international exhibition is Santa Catarina Palace, one of Lisbon's sightseeing highlights. Meanwhile, upgrading the online platform that links together all *Hug@ree* installations was the challenge tackled at the *Codebits* hackathon [5].
The project has also crowdsourced photos and videos of people hugging real trees as part of the *350.org* and *Greenpeace* "10/10/10 Global Work Party" [1].
So far, these resources have been used for testing and the contributors were the first to populate the world of *Hug@ree*.
Additionally, we propose to setup a new node for *Hug@ree* at TEI'11 to foster locals' awareness of the rich natural beauty of Madeira island's Laurissilva forest endangered by recent forest fires.

Acknowledgements

This research is done in the framework of the PhD in Digital Media of the UT Austin-Portugal Program funded by FCT (ref. SFRH/BD/42555/2007). We thank AZ Labs members, who collaborated in the *sprint & hackathon*.

References

[1] *Hug@ree project at "10/10/10 Global Work Party", 350.org/Greenpeace* http://www.350.org/en/hugree

[2] *Hug@ree* concept and research outcomes http://www.monicamendes.info/rtiviss/hugatree

[3] *Pop Up City Lisbon*, Nov4-Dec11 2010 http://www.popup-city.com/lisbon-2010/en/

[4] *RTiVISS blog on research iterations* http://www.rtiviss.com

[5] *Sapo Codebits*, Nov11-13 2010 http://codebits.eu

SolaColor: Space Coloration with Solar Light

Tomoko Hashida
IML,The University of Tokyo
7-3-1 Hongo, Bunkyo-ku
Tokyo 113-8656
hashida@nae-lab.org

Takeshi Naemura
Dept.Inform.&Commun.Eng.,
The University of Tokyo
7-3-1 Hongo, Bunkyo-ku
Tokyo 113-8656
naemura@nae-lab.org

Yasuaki Kakehi
KEIO University
5322 Endo, Fujisawa-shi
Kanagawa 252-8520
ykakehi@sfc.keio.jp

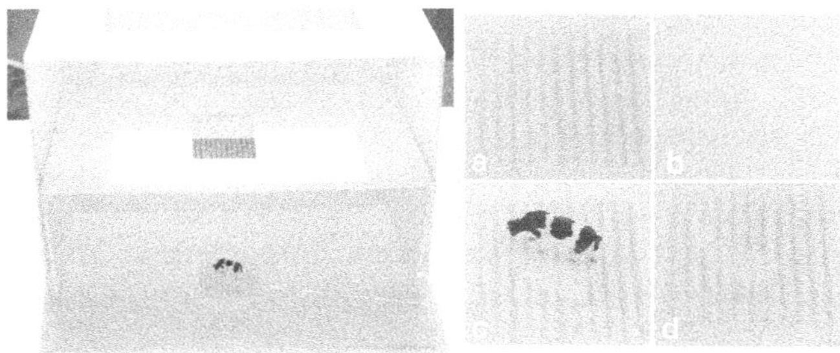

Figure 1: Overview of a miniature SolaColor and the color pattern it forms. a: appearance of color; b: disappearance of color; c: white shadow with cow; d: remaining shadow

TEI'11, January 22–26, 2011, Funchal, Portugal.
ACM 978-1-4503-0478-8/11/01.

Abstract
SolaColor is a scheme for creating a place (namely, a floor space) whose color is varied in response to sunlight. The aim of this work is to create sustainable spatial rendition by utilizing sunlight. A feature of this spatial-rendition scheme is rendering places by color—rather than contrast—of lighting. By means of SolaColor, areas in sunlight are colored in pink, while shaded areas are colored white. When this scheme is practically applied, time-varying patterns appear in synchronization with the movement of the sun. When a person or object enters a space created by SolaColor, white shadows oriented according to the position of the sun are formed in the manner of a sundial. The scheme can be implemented by utilizing photochromic material and optical design, and it can be introduced in any location under sunlight without the need for an electrical-power supply.

Keywords
solar light, photochromic material, sustainable spatial rendition

ACM Classification Keywords
H5.m. Information interfaces and presentation: Miscellaneous

General Terms Design, Experimentation

Introduction
Attempts regarding environmentally conscious and sustainable information-display schemes and open-space renditions that utilize sunlight are being actively made. For example, "Sun_D" is a daylight display scheme that works without any electro-luminous means and utilizes existing light sources such as the sun [1]. Another example that utilizes the movement of the sun across the sky is the "One-day Poem Pavillion"—which projects verses of a poem one by one periodically in accordance with the time of day [2]. Both the above-described rendition schemes, however, are restricted to expression by exploiting contrast of light. In the present report, a scheme—

called "SolaColor"—for rendering a floor space in color in coordination with the movement of the sun is proposed (Fig. 1).

SolaColor

Aiming to practically implement the above-mentioned scheme, the authors focused on optically designing a photochromic material that can control coloring and color elimination by light. As the photochromic material, diarylethene (DAE-BT, Yamada Chemical Co., Ltd.) was applied [3]. Basically, SolaColor is configured from white paper with DAE-BT, a UV cutoff filter, a UV bandpass filter, and sunlight. An overview of its optical design is shown in Figure 2. In the case that sunlight including both ultraviolet (UV) light and visible light (VL) is used as the light source, the white paper with DAE-BT becomes lightly colored in pink (see Fig. 2(i)). When a UV bandpass filter is placed in the light path, only UV light is transmitted, so it appears to be colored dark pink (see Fig. 2(ii)). And when a UV cutoff filter is placed in the light path, it becomes transparent and appears as white paper (see Fig. 2(iii)).

Examples of renditions using these basic configurations are shown in Figure 3. For example, in the case that a real object is placed in front of the UV bandpass filter, the UV light is blocked off by the object, and a white silhouette in the shape of the object appears on the DAE-BT paper in the place where the pink coloring was eliminated by the blocking (Fig. 3(i)). In addition, when a two-layer slit screen formed with UV cutoff filters is combined with the UV bandpass filter, two alternative renditions can be produced in accordance with the sun's elevation and orientation change: UV light is transmitted when the slits placed on the light path are overlapping (Fig. 3(ii -a)) or UV light is blocked when the slits placed on light path the are staggered (Fig. 3(ii -b)). In this manner, patterns and information can be periodically rendered on, and erased from, a floor surface in accordance with the configuration of the slit screen. We suppose that SolaColor will ultimately be embedded into architectural structures. In the manner described above, spatial designs with patterns that change according to the time variation of shadows of people and objects in a building, as well as the sun, can be created.

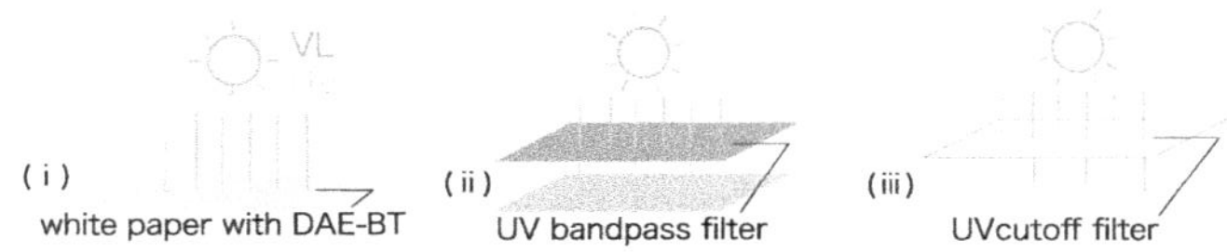

Figure 2: Basic optical designs: (i) faded coloring under sunlight; (ii) coloring using UV bandpass filter; (iii) eliminating color by UV cut-off filter.

Figure 3: Optical design for renditions: (i) generation of white shadow by object; (ii) generation of time-varying patterns by two-layer slit screen

A prototype of SolaColor was constructed in miniature. An overview of the prototype is shown in Figure1. An experiment using the prototype aimed at spatial rendering periodically on a floor space between 10 am and 2 pm, namely, rendering a striped pattern for approximately four minutes and, in a similar manner, erasing the color for another four minutes. To perform this experiment, a spatial model incorporating the optical design shown in Fig. 3(ii) was designed and produced. The rendering results produced by the model set up outdoors are shown in Figure 1. Patterns formed when the striped pattern is rendered by coloring and then eliminated are, respectively, shown in Fig. 1(a) and (b). Furthermore, it was confirmed that when the striped pattern is formed, a white shadow appears when an object is placed in the light path (see Fig. 1(c)), and the shadow remains (for several tens of seconds) on that spot when the object is taken away (Fig. 1(d)).

Citations

[1] http://www.sun-d.ch/
[2] http://people.artcenter.edu/~jsong5/thesis/
[3] http://www.ymdchem.co.jp/products/opt2.html#photo1

Immersive Data Grasping Using the e^{X}plore Table

Marius Brade
Chair of Media Design
Technische Universität Dresden
Dresden, Germany
marius.brade@tu-dresden.de

Mandy Keck
Chair of Media Design
Technische Universität Dresden
Dresden, Germany
mandy.keck@tu-dresden.de

Dietrich Kammer
Chair of Media Design
Technische Universität Dresden
Dresden, Germany
dietrich.kammer@tu-dresden.de

Rainer Groh
Chair of Media Design
Technische Universität Dresden
Dresden, Germany
rainer.groh@tu-dresden.de

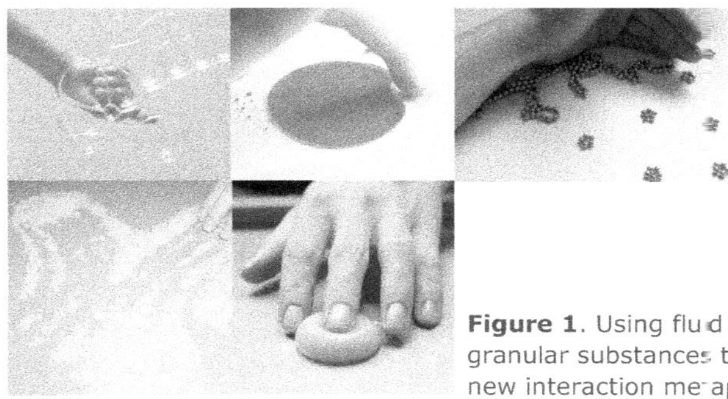

Figure 1. Using fluid and granular substances to inspire new interaction metaphors

TEI'11, January 22–26, 2011, Funchal, Portugal.
ACM 978-1-4503-0478-8/11/01.

Abstract
Accustomed to traditional user experiences with mouse and keyboard, designers are challenged to break free and find new and compelling approaches to interaction design for natural user interfaces. Tangible and embodied interaction works in parallel, is quick, and allows cooperative work. This exploration serves to inspire and provoke critical reflection on interaction design for natural user interfaces based on physical substances that are used in everyday life – like eggs, soap bubbles, and magnets.

Keywords
Inspiration, interface design, tangible user interface, physical materials

ACM Classification Keywords
H5.m. Information interfaces and presentation (e.g., HCI): Miscellaneous.

General Terms
Design, Experimentation, Performance

Introduction
Natural user interfaces aim to exploit interaction from everyday life that is commonplace and easily learned. However, it is not immediately apparent which interaction paradigms from the physical realm can be adopted for virtuality. We conceived and created the *e^{x}plore Table* to capture and explore natural interaction with the intention of eliciting appropriate interface

Figure 3. The bubbles framework

metaphors for natural user interfaces. It allows experiments with different kinds of substances and enables the observation and recording of the flow of events during interaction with these substances. The basic task used in the experiments is valid both for the real world and virtual interaction: gathering and structuring of items and data, respectively.

Setup

Figure 2 shows the setup of the e^xplore Table. Its structure is made up of a wooden base frame with an acryl glass panel on top. Liquid substances are kept from flowing over by a special boundary. Two video cameras capture user interaction from underneath and above the glass (cp. Figure 1). The results are instantly displayed with a projector and recorded for later review.

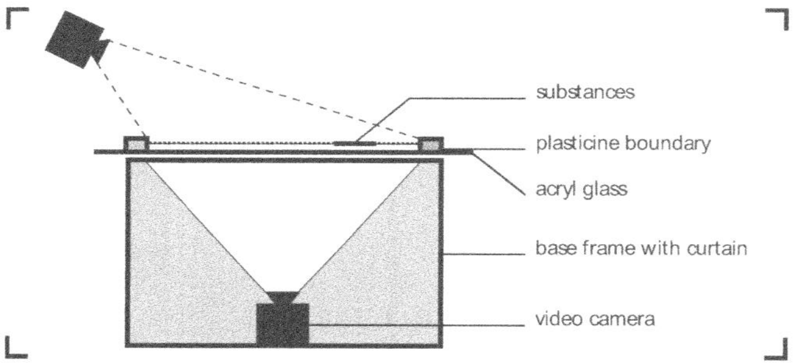

Figure 2. Schematic setup of the e^xplore Table

Engineering Interface Metaphors

The observed flow of interaction with physical substances needs to be adapted, modified, and translated into algorithms as shown by the bubbles framework in Figure 3. For this prototype, ActionScript 3, FlashBuilder, Adobe Flex Framework as well as AS3 Delaunay Library were used by our students. The visual algorithms are based on Voronoi diagrams and mimic natural behavior of soap bubbles as explored in Figure 1. Bubbles representing data objects can be created, combined, moved and deleted similar to experiences in the real world.

Conclusions and Future Work

This art exploration provokes thought concerning the interaction design for natural user interfaces. It is important to observe natural behavior of substances to exploit the potentials of new technologies like multi-touch [1] and tracking of whole body movements. As a result, exciting new interfaces can be designed. This meets the demand expressed by Johnny Chung Lee: "Natural interaction is achieved through clever designs that constrain the problem in ways that are transparent to the user" [2].

Acknowledgements

We thank T. Heinig, I. Reiche, D. Schmidt, H. Leitner, B. Eschrich, D. Menzel, T. Reinsch, F. Angelova and A. Kürbis for performing and conducting the experiments.

On behalf of Marius Brade this research (contract no. 080951799) has been funded by the European Social Fond and the Free State of Saxony as well as SAP Research. On behalf of Dietrich Kammer and Mandy Keck this work has been supported by the European Union and the Free State Saxony through the European Regional Development Fund.

References

[1] North C., Dwyer T., Lee B., Fisher D., Isenberg P., Robertson G. and Inkpen K. *Understanding Multi-touch Manipulation for Surface Computing*. In Human-Computer Interaction – INTERACT 2009. Lecture Notes in Computer Science, 2009, Volume 5727/2009, 236-249.

[2] Lee, J. C. 2010. *In search of a natural gesture.* XRDS 16, 4 (Jun. 2010), 9-12

ReplayMyPlay: Model Energy Playground

Sibel Deren Guler
ReplayMyPlay
5530 Penn Ave Unit 7.
Pittsburgh, PA 15206 USA
deren@replaymyplay.com

TEI '11, January 22–26, 2011, Funchal, Portugal.
ACM 978-1-4503-0478-8/11/01.

Abstract
The proposed exploration exhibits a prototype structure of ReplayMyPlay, an energy-harvesting play structure that converts the mechanical energy from the motion of children's play into electric power.

Keywords
Play, energy conservation, education, electricity generation

ACM Classification Keywords
Design, Experimentation, Human Factors

General Terms
Play, energy, education, conservation

Background
ReplayMyPlay is an energy-harvesting play structure that converts the mechanical energy from the motion children's play into electric power. The moving parts of the playground structures are retrofitted with a drive system that turns the shaft of generator. The energy is stored in a rechargeable battery and is used as needed while a visual interface installed next to the structure displays how much energy is created through play. The mission of ReplayMyPlay is to engage the community in a collaborative effort to make an impact for a more sustainable future while empowering youth. Though the project's primary target is children, a diverse audience of all ages is easily reached. The structures are designed in accordance with playground safety codes. ReplayMyPlay is based in Pittsburgh, PA where it has

grown out of a Micro Spark award granted in late 2009 by The Sprout Fund's Spark Program, with support of the Grable Foundation [2].

Inspiration

ReplayMyPlay addresses the issue of energy conservation and human power generation.
There are several related projects that have influenced the design of ReplayMyPlay [1].

- Empower Playgrounds makes energy-harvesting merry-go-round structures in rural areas of Ghana to power the lights in schools.
- Playpumps International builds merry-go-round structures that power water pumps in African villages.
- Dr. Raj Pandian has designed an air compression system to make seesaw structures that generate enough electricity for low-power appliances [3].

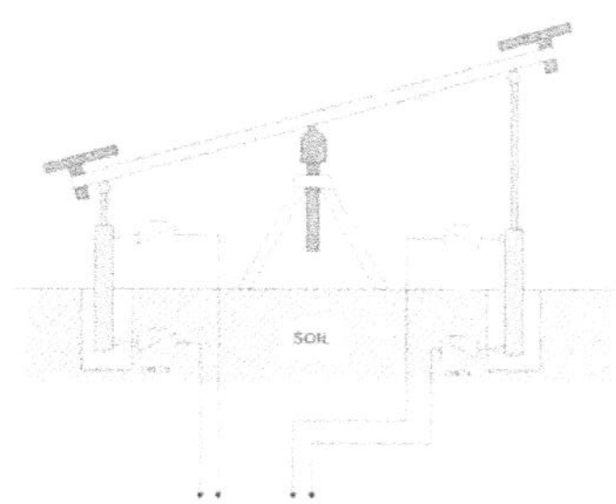

Figure 1: Compressed air seesaw [3].

Concept of exploration

The demonstration of ReplayMyPlay includes a scale model of a merry-go-round. Viewers may spin this smaller structure and see how electricity is generated through mechanical motion. A visual interface installed next to the structure displays a multi-meter and markers of how much energy is needed for everyday activities. Interaction with the small merry-go-round activates a video illustrating various activities that could be powered. As the user turns the merry-go-round the amount of energy available increases and the video continues to play for as long as the structure is in motion. This analogy shows the capability of a life-size structure through a scaled user-controlled game.

Figure 2. A ReplayMyPlay exhibit [2].

Acknowledgements

Thanks to The Sprout Fund, The Grable Foundation intuVision Inc. and Sloan Valve Co for their support; and to Laura Miller for her assistance and dedication.

References

[1] Dean, Tamara. *Human-powered Home*. New Society publishers, B.C., Canada, 2008.

[2] Guler, Sibel Deren. Proposal For a ReplayMyPlay Merry-go-round, 2010.

[3] Pandian, S.R., A human power conversion system based on children's play, *Proc. IEEE Int. Symp. Technology and Society,* Worcester, MA, 2004

Social Bits: Toward Artistic Expression Powered by Small Information Generated by Daily Lives of People

Hideaki Ogawa
h.o
www.howeb.org
ogawa@howeb.org

Jayme Cochrane
University of Art & Design Linz
Linz, Austria
Jayme.Cochrane@gmail.com

Mahir M. Yavuz
University of Art & Design Linz
Linz, Austria
mmyavuz@gmail.com

Emiko Ogawa
h.o
www.howeb.org
emiko@howeb.org

Junichi Yura
h.o
www.howeb.org
yurayura@howeb.org

Taizo Zushi
h.o
www.howeb.org
zushi@howeb.org

TEI'11, January 22–26, 2011, Funchal, Portugal.
ACM 978-1-4503-0478-8/11/01.

Abstract
In this paper we describe the basic concept of Social Bits and we introduce two art pieces named Kazamidori and Monster created under the concept of Social Bits.

Keywords
Social Bits, Tangible Bits, Media Architecture

ACM Classification Keywords
H5.m. Information interfaces and presentation (e.g., HCI): Miscellaneous.

General Terms
Conference publication.

Social Bits
Social Bits is trace of small information generated by daily lives of people. We are generating bits as a piece of our presence through social media and sensor information. By giving this metaphor to bit, this Social Bits enables us to imagine the new expression and experience architecture activated by social energy.

Social Bits is a study focusing on the artistic output of social interactions in real world locations. This research studies and analyzes the collective information cloud created by humans worldwide, as well as introducing new mediums, materials and platforms to present the artistic results. In this study, we realized 2 permanent installations for expressing social meaning of Ars Electronica.

Works: Kazamidori and Monster

Kazamidori is a weathervane in the Internet age. Kaza (wind) mi (watch) dori (bird) is Japanese expressing the weathervane. People of former days had noticed the natural behavior of bird that it had a habit to watch at the direction of wind, and they adapted it to the design of weathervane. Kazamidori is a device to indicate social wind of interests on the Internet. It works by using the social energy of web accesses to Ars Electronica. When somebody comes to the web site of Ars Electronica, Kazamidori will point at the direction of the place of the visiting person. Kazamidori will be showing the virtual visitors continuously coming from all over the world to Ars Electronica, at the gate of physical Ars Electronic Center.

Monster is look of Kazamidori at night. The monster appearing on a façade of Ars Electronica Center tries to eat visitors to enter the entrance of the AEC. When there are virtual visitors to Ars Electronica, he will gaze at the direction, and he will pace back and forth for both real and virtual visitors. Despite the function is the same as the Kazamidori, It just gives us the creeps a little bit. "Scaring "will lead to speculation, and it is triggering a rumor. There are possibilities that the same fact is conveyed as totally different content, depending on the medium and information design.

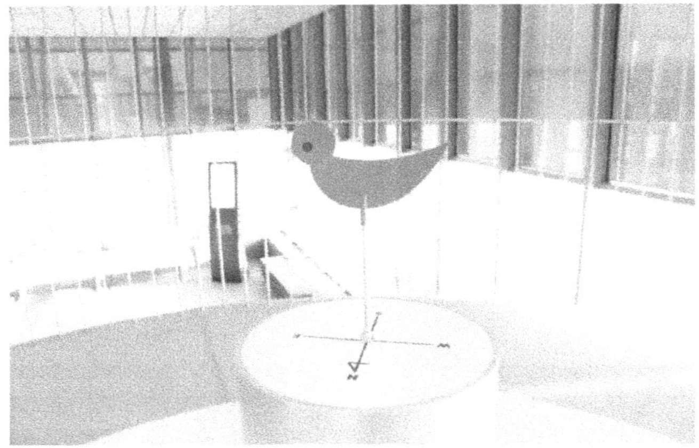

figure 1. Kazamidori at the entrance of Ars Electronica Center

figure 2. Monster on the façade of Ars Electronica Center

References

[1] Social Bits Project: http://www.socialbits.org/

Espanta Espíritos – A User-driven, Multisensorial Sculpture

Yago de Quay
FEUP
R. de Mouzinho da Silveira 317 2º
4050-421 Porto, Portugal
+351 966 089 603
yagostucky@gmail.com

Figure 1. Espanta Espíritos during the Future Place festival

Abstract

Who never whispered a secret to a wind chime, or saw it scare off evil spirits will have the opportunity to do so on a massive scale. The Espanta Espíritos is an interactive sculpture that embodies the spiritual and physical features of a wind chime. This piece presents itself as a giant wind chime made out of recyclable material, the size of a person, ready for outdoors or indoors. People can whisper secrets to the Espanta Espíritos, and through a microphone and a camera, it will register these secrets forever. Natural wind, or a specially designed reactive fan, will cause the Espanta Espíritos to move, and then play these recordings through different audio effects, recreating the secret as if said by spirits. To enhance the illusion, phantasmagoric videos of those who whispered will be projected on the sculpture.

TEI'11, January 22–26, 2011, Funchal, Portugal.
ACM 978-1-4503-0478-8/11/01.

Keywords

user-generated content, haptic, video, audio, sculpture, installation

ACM Classification Keywords

H5.1. Information interfaces and presentation: Multimedia Information Systems

General Terms

Design, Human Factors, Performance

Introduction

Built during the summer of 2010, Espanta Espíritos blends haptic, visual and auditory senses with the real, the spiritual and the virtual in one space. in its simplicity the art work favors users input – secrets and faces – and replays them, old and new, in a morphed and sensory rich way. Although this piece uses advanced technology, it preserves the ancient function held by the wind chime of attracting kind spirits, the secrets, and frightening away lurking evil spirits, the morphed sounds. It makes the private become public, yet unrecognizable. Constructs rich narratives from people's secrets. Becomes wiser with time.

In its core, the goal behind Espanta Espíritos is to: 1) seamlessly unify old symbols with new media; 2) encourage community involvement in an artistic project; and 3) Promote sustainable design.

figure 2. User recording a new spirit in the Espanta Espíritos

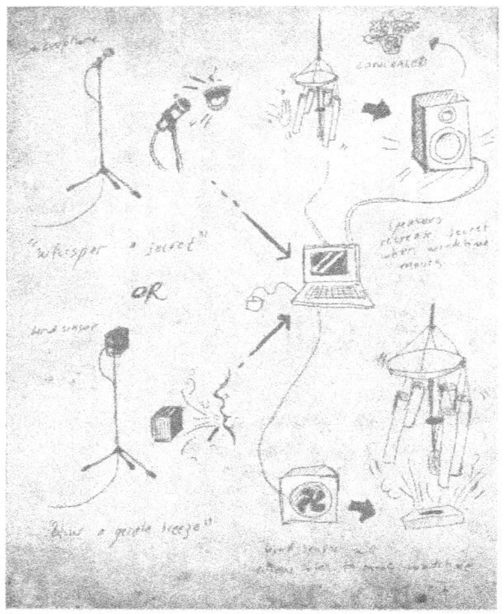

figure 3. Careful thought was put into the interaction design

Sculpture

The sculpture consists of carefully selected and painted materials. The symbols illustrate spiritual traditions of various cultures from all over the world.

Interaction

From the design of the podium to the instructions on paper, the focus was always to make something that was intuitive. This was achieved by matching the spiritual connotations that symbolize wind chime with physical metaphors, for example the contact between the chimes and the striker. While at the Future Places festival, the installation collected more than 500 recordings that portray a wide range of emotions.

Video

Video recording of whisperers are replayed through a projector and coupled with effect to add a "ghost" appearance.

Sound

Sound is at the core of this piece and it provides most of the experience. Recordings (secrets) from users are replayed through six different modulation effects, representing each one of the chimes. An audio recording will never sound the same twice, and the way random selection is coupled with user-generated content, the reproductions are unlimited.

Technology

Powerful software and hardware ensure that the installation is robust. Continuous information from the podium and the wind chime travels through Phidgets to a Max/MSP patch. Video and audio is processed in Jitter and Ableton Live 8, respectively.

Espanta Espíritos was first debuted in front of Porto's Faculty of Engineering's (FEUP) library where it was exhibited for one week. On October 2010 it was selected along 7 others, from over 120 international submissions, to be exhibited for three days in the Future Places festival.

Acknowledgements

Many thanks to my colleagues at FEUP, as well as the owners of Maus Hábitos Bar, my mother Isabel, for the paintings and my supervisor Carlos Guedes.

References

Video description: http://wp.me/pRnGK-5Y

Talking Tangibles: Design for Peripheral Interaction

Saskia Bakker
Department of Industrial Design, Eindhoven University of Technology
Eindhoven, the Netherlands
s.bakker@tue.nl

ABSTRACT
This paper describes ongoing research in a 4 year PhD project that started in June 2009. With the computer becoming pervasive in everyday life, a need for new interaction styles has emerged. In the realm of the vision of calm technology [6], we see potential in interaction shifting to the periphery of the attention. The aim of this research is to study interactive systems designed for peripheral interaction by combining physical artifacts and audio.

Author Keywords
Tangible interaction, sound design, calm technology, attention, periphery, user centered design.

ACM Classification Keywords
H5.2. Information interfaces and presentation: Auditory (non-speech) feedback, Interaction styles, Theory and methods, User-centered design.

General Terms
Design.

INTRODUCTION

With the upcoming of pervasive technologies, the computer is becoming ubiquitous in everyday life. As a result, intelligence and thus information can be everywhere nowadays. However, most traditional methods of human computer interaction require the user's focused attention to be effective; we need to consciously look at a screen to perceive information from the computer and we need to consciously use the keyboard, mouse or touch screen to interact with these kinds of technologies.

When we look at the physical world, a lot of information is present there too: the weather, the time of the day, the activity of people around us, etc. However, we do not have to specifically attend to this information to perceive it. Furthermore, many physical actions are performed without directly paying attention to them. Tying your shoelaces, moving a cup to your mouth to drink, looking at your watch, all these activities can be done without focused attention. Perceiving information as well as interacting with the physical world frequently takes place in the *periphery* of the attention. However, these human skills are not often leveraged in interaction with technology. Weiser and Brown [6] introduced the term *calm technology*, "technology that engages both the center and the periphery of our attention and in fact moves back and forth between the two" [6, p. 8]. Given the potential of the before mentioned human attention skills, we see this as a valuable approach to fitting new technologies into our lives.

Although peripheral perception and action could involve all our senses, we are particularly interested in combining tangible interaction [5] and audio. As becomes clear from previously mentioned examples of peripheral actions, they are mostly performed on small or wearable objects (e.g. shoe-laces, a cup, a watch). Furthermore, as sound can be perceived without having to look at the source, this modality is naturally used for monitoring ongoing information streams. The aim of the research laid out in this paper therefore is to study the potential of interactive systems designed for peripheral interaction by combining physical artifacts and audio. The research is conducted through the design and evaluation of such systems, which we call 'Talking Tangibles'. Design research challenges include: how to leverage human attention skills in interaction design? What kinds of tangibles are suitable? What kinds of sounds are suitable? In which application areas could this be used? At which moments would this type of interaction be possible and relevant?

In this paper, we present the current status of the research, which we think lays a solid basis of theory and experiential data for design research in this area.

EXPLORING THE DESIGN SPACE

To gain initial insights regarding the approach to design for peripheral interactions, we created three simple interactive demonstrators that provide audible information, designed to be perceived in the periphery of the attention. The AudioResponse made users aware of environmental sounds through a soundscape of piano tones. EntranceSounds informed office workers of the activity in the office when someone entered. RainForecasts played sound samples indicating the short term rain forecasts. These systems were each implemented in an office for three weeks [1]. Although these demonstrators did not involve tangible interaction, their evaluation revealed interesting insights for further design and evaluation of Talking Tangibles. Open interviews showed that participants did perceive some of the sounds in the periphery of their attention, after having gotten used to the systems. Furthermore, we saw that the

TEI'11, January 22–26, 2011, Funchal, Portugal.
ACM 978-1-4503-0478-8/11/01.

information users picked up from the systems differed from our expectation in several cases, depending on the context, experience, interest and knowledge of the user. From these explorations, we learned that an iterative approach, in which systems are experimented with for a period of time, seems suitable when designing Talking Tangibles systems.

THEORETICAL BACKGROUND

This research is grounded in theory on the human attention process, which describes attention as the division of mental resources over different potential activities [4]. When certain activities do not require many resources, such as tying your shoe-laces, one is able to perform multiple such activities at the same time; mental resources are allocated to both activities. To support the design of peripheral interactions, we have created an illustration that captures our current understanding of the center and periphery of the attention, see Figure 1. As seen in this overview, we understand the center of the attention as the one activity to which most mental resources are allocated, and the periphery as all other remaining potential activities, regardless of whether resources are allocated to them or not. This is more elaborately explained in [2].

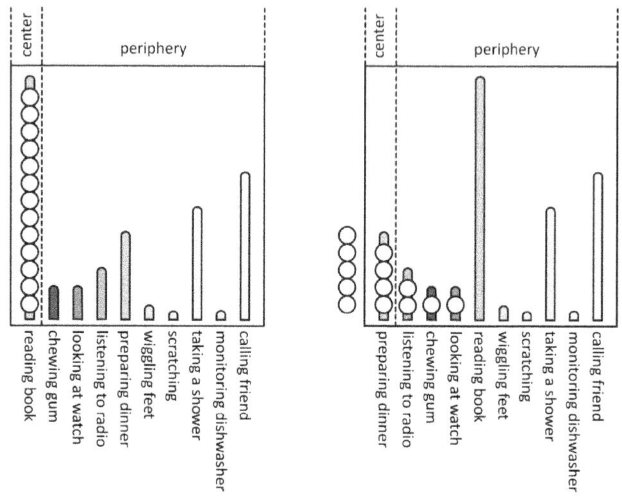

Figure 1. Two examples of the center and periphery of the attention; division of mental resources during a high attentional task (left) and during a combination of low attentional tasks (right). Vertical bars represent potential tasks with varying resource demand (height) and likelihood of being performed (color intensity). Mental resources are represented by white circles.

QUALITATIVE EXPERIMENT ON ATTENTION

Apart from a theoretical understanding of the human attention process, we were also interested in gaining experiential information, to facilitate a link to the everyday context, as well as to gain inspiration for the design process. We therefore conducted a user study on attention and particularly the periphery of the attention in everyday life. In this study, we gathered qualitative data from 13 participants of diverse ages and backgrounds. Since people are usually not aware of their actions and perceptions that take place in the periphery of the attention, the study started with a sensitizing week [3], in which the participants performed several exercises such as video observation and creating a short diary, to reflect on the way they utilize their periphery in everyday life. After this week of sensitizing, the participants took part in an extensive group interview on their experience of the periphery of their attention.

The data gathered through this study is currently being analyzed, but the preliminary results indicate that audio is currently often used to monitor ongoing events in the periphery of the attention. Furthermore, most peripheral actions are performed with the hands, on small or wearable objects, which supports our choice for tangible interaction.

CONCLUSIONS AND FUTURE WORK

This paper presents ongoing research on designing for peripheral interaction, by combining tangible artifacts and audio. We have gained an extensive understanding of human attention abilities, both from literature and experiential data. As a result, we have seen that both tangible interaction and audio seem suitable for our purpose. The next step in our research is to iteratively explore potential applications of Talking Tangibles. This will include designing and prototyping Talking Tangibles systems, which could be static, mobile or wearable artifacts. Moreover, we will thoroughly evaluate these systems to assess user experience over a period of time. We have focused our initial explorations on the office context, but intent to explore other contexts in the next iteration.

ACKNOWLEDGEMENTS

I thank my supervisors Dr. Elise van den Hoven, Prof. Berry Eggen and Prof. Kees Overbeeke, as well as my colleagues and the participants, without whom our studies would not have been possible.

REFERENCES

1. Bakker, S., Hoven, E. van den, and Eggen, B. Exploring Interactive Systems Using Peripheral Sounds. In *Proc. HAID 2010*, Springer-Verlag (2010), 55-64.
2. Bakker, S., Hoven, E. van den, and Eggen, B. Design for the Periphery. In *Proc. EuroHaptics 2010 Special Symposium*, (2010), 71-80.
3. Sleeswijk Visser, F., Stappers, J.P., Lugt, R. van der, and Sanders, E.B.N. Contextmapping: Experiences from practice. *CoDesign 1*, 2 (2005), 119-149.
4. Sternberg, R.J. *Cognitive Psychology*. Harcourt College Publishers, Orlando, FL, 1999.
5. Ullmer, B., and Ishii, H. Emerging frameworks for tangible user interfaces. *IBM Systems Journal 39*, 3-4 (2000), 915-931.
6. Weiser, M. en Brown, J.S. The Coming Age of Calm Technology. *Beyond Calculation: the next fifty years of computing*. Springer-Verlag (1997), 75-85.

Authentication on Public Terminals with Private Devices

Andrea Bianchi
Korea Advanced Institute of Science and Technology
Daejeon, Korea
andrea@kaist.ac.kr

ABSTRACT
Authentication in public spaces, such as ATM PIN entry, is inherently susceptible to security attacks based on observation in person or via cameras. This paper briefly introduces the idea of decoupling the authentication process in two separate sub-tasks (the interaction needed for PIN input and its transmission to the terminal), each with different usability and security goals. In order to support this idea, we present two research projects based on multimodal feedback and physical proximity and explain how they fit into this model.

Author Keywords
PIN entry, password, security, usability, observation.

ACM Classification Keywords
H5.2. User Interfaces: Input devices and strategies.

General Terms
Design, Security

INTRODUCTION
Authentication by means of passwords or numerical PINs to public terminals, such as ATMs and credit card kiosks, is commonplace. Although such systems have long been the object of studies and systematic improvements, public terminals are still prone to a wide range of security threats [8]. Paradoxically, the most effective attacks simply rely on the hazardous behavior of users who unintentionally expose themselves to attackers: a typical example is the observation attack, in which passwords are stolen by means of camera or shoulder-surfing [4].

Recently researchers in usability and security have devoted substantial efforts towards finding methods to resist observation attacks during authentications on public terminals. These methods include systems that use non-visual modalities such as haptics to obfuscate displayed cues [2], the use of eye-trackers as an input technology [5] and a range of techniques to indirectly type PINs [e.g. 3].

These methods are clearly effective, but they also introduce higher complexity for users, which is often mitigated by compromising security for improved usability. It is furthermore clear that most methods proposed to counter observation attacks, despite the approach chosen, operate under the same underlying assumption: public terminals are intrinsically vulnerable to observation attacks because they take the form of physical installations situated in public spaces (e.g., public kiosks).

In this paper we argue that, by simply shifting the authentication process from a public terminal to a safer user-owned private device (e.g. [7]), such as a mobile phone, we can achieve better security without compromising usability. In fact, by decoupling the authentication process into two modular and independent sub-tasks - the input-interaction and the PIN-transmission - we can achieve a highly usable front-end PIN entry interface backed up by a secure system for transmitting it to the terminal. A running theme through this work is an emphasis on physical and multi-sensory input which relies on techniques such as haptic feedback and physical proximity to ensure security. We believe that this approach makes the interfaces described in this work particular salient to the research area of tangible interaction.

OUR APPROACH IN PRACTICE
By subdividing the authentication process into two modular and independent components, the input method and the transmission of the PIN to the terminal, we can simultaneously improve usability of the input interface and achieve a secure transmission channel between the private device and the terminal. We present briefly two prototypes, the Phone Lock [1] and LuxPass: the former shows an example of how users can choose different PIN modalities (haptics or audio) according to their preferences and security levels; the latter shows an example of how we can transmit a PIN from the phone to the terminal, without need of pairing the two and avoiding eavesdropping by third parties (known as the Man-In-The-Middle (MITM) attack).

Phone Lock
The Phone Lock is a PIN entry system for mobile phones resistant to visual observation because is based on locating and identifying auditory or tactile cues rather than visual ones. Phone Lock provides users an interaction technique in two modalities (audio and haptic) and leaves the choice of which to select to the users themselves.

In general, the Phone Lock interaction is based on a paradigm of randomization of cue location prior to user search and selection for a password item. The user directly manipulates a dial drawn on the display of a touch screen phone. Different segments of the dial are associated with different cues, each of which is played in response to a

TEI'11, January 22–26, 2011, Funchal, Portugal.
ACM 978-1-4503-0478-8/11/01.

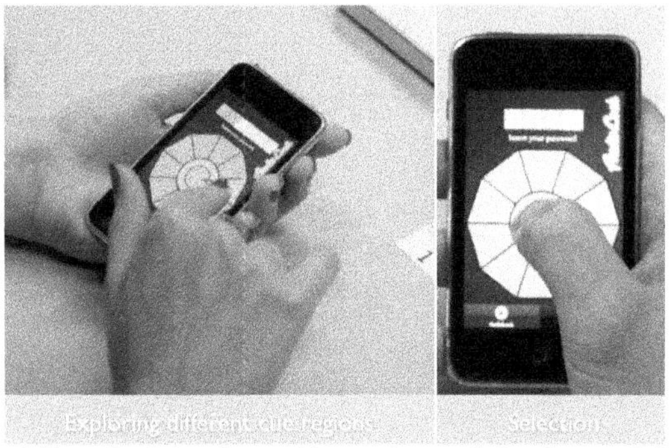

Figure 1 Phone Lock interface and interaction: exploring the cues (left) and selection of a cue (right).

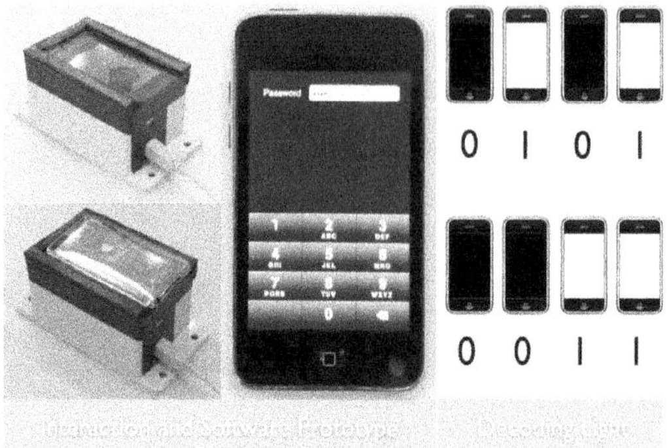

Figure 2 LuxPass receiver unit prototypes (left) and software GUI. Simplified example of light encoding (right).

user's touch. The Phone Lock wheel is simple to configure with differently sized cue sets and segment sizes, but in our implementations we used a maximum of either 10 iconic audio cues (i.e., spoken numbers from zero to nine) or 10 distinguishable tactile patterns (i.e., vibration patterns). Audio cues are delivered via headphones to ensure they remain private, while tactile cues are rendered using a pager motor mounted on the phone.

We developed a prototype for the Apple iPhone (Figure 1) and run a user study [1], whose preliminary results suggests that, with the use of appropriate cues sets, the system maintains or improves upon the performance, usability and security of previous observation resistant PIN systems [2].

LuxPass

LuxPass (Figure 2) is a novel interaction method that allows users to authenticate to a public terminal using a mobile phone without requiring explicit pairing. The goal in this case is to shift in time and space the authentication procedure, enabling the user to authenticate on their mobile phone at a convenient time, and then to complete their transaction by transmitting the authentication data from the phone to the public terminal.

Although previous work in this direction has focused on either ensuring a direct communication channel with a pre-agreed third-party infrastructure, or by using out-of-band (OOB) side channels to establish a paired connection [6] between the phone and the terminal (e.g., using accelerometer data to establish a connection), LuxPass adopts a different approach in which physical proximity is sufficient to achieve a secure transaction.

LuxPass works by displaying messages through modulated patterns of light on a mobile phone screen that are then sensed by a device and decoded back into a PIN. LuxPass relies on close physical contact with a sensor terminal to ensure this channel is private. A key advantage of this approach is that it is based on standard component of a mobile device (the screen) making it economical and easy to deploy. Although further explorations are needed, results from in-progress studies seemed encouraging: users expressed positive consensus toward LuxPass. Moreover, a security user study in a lab setting demonstrated the strength of LuxPass against observation and MITM attacks.

CONCLUSIONS

In this paper we have briefly introduced a method to decouple the authentication process into two independent subtasks - the input interaction and the PIN transmission to the terminal - and we have presented our previous work to support this framework. Further research is needed for improving both the components of the system and in finding better ways to integrate them. Regardless, we believe that decoupling authentication into sub-tasks will become common practice in the design of secure public terminals.

ACKNOWLEDGMENTS

We thank Ian Oakley and Dong Soo Kwon for their valuable advice and contributions to this work.

REFERENCES

1. Bianchi, A., Oakley, I., Kostakos, V., Kwon, D., The Phone Lock: Audio and Haptic shoulder-surfing resistant PIN entry methods. In Proc of TEI'11.
2. Bianchi, A., Oakley, I., Kwon, D., The secure haptic keypad: a tactile password system. In Proc. of CHI'10, pp.1089-1092.
3. De Luca, A., Hertzschuch, K., Hussmann, H., ColorPIN: securing PIN entry through indirect input. In Proc. of CHI'10, pp.1103-1106.
4. De Luca, A., Langheinrich, M., and Hussmann, H., Towards understanding ATM security: a field study of real world ATM use. In Proc. of SOUPS'10, pp. 1-10.
5. Forget, A., Chiasson, S., Biddle, R., Shoulder-surfing resistance with eye-gaze entry in cued-recall graphical passwords. In Proc. of CHI'10, pp.1107-1110.
6. Kobsa, A., Sonawalla, R., Tsudik, G., Uzun, E., Wang, Y., Serial hook-ups: a comparative usability study of secure device pairing methods. In Proc. of SOUPS '09.
7. Mccune, J.M., Perrig, A., Reiter, M.K., Seeing-is-believing. In Proc. of IEEE Symposium on Security and Privacy, pp. 110–124, 2005.
8. Rogers, J. Please enter your 4-digit PIN. Financial Services Technology, U.S. Edition, Issue 4, Mar. 2007.

Ambient Persuasive Guidance

Gerrit Boehm
Middlesex University, London
g.boehm@mdx.ac.uk

ABSTRACT
This study presents solutions for particular problems commuters encounter during the walking phase of their journey in public transport facilities, e.g. the London Underground. Commuters get obstructed or have collisions at bottleneck situations, making their walking inefficient and stressful. The notion presented here is to reinforce existing infrastructures with embedded *ambient persuasive technologies* (APT) acting as *psychological guiding measures* (PGM) to enhance pedestrians' situational awareness. The aim is to provide enhanced feedback to change commuters' behaviour to improve the flow and quality of walking. A set of novel analog and digital design interventions has been developed for various bottleneck situations. This study will yield insight into new forms of interactive, dynamic information to support commuters during the walking parts of their journey using PGM, rather than physical components.

Author Keywords
Ambient Persuasive Technologies, Psychological Guiding Measures, Situational Awareness, Dynamic guidance.

ACM Classification Keywords
H5.m. Information interfaces and presentation: Miscellaneous.

General Terms
Design, Experimentation

INTRODUCTION
London has an estimated population of 7.6 million (2008) [6], and is projected to increase to 8.8 million by 2029 [11]. This number of people imposes a great impact on the operational system of the London Underground.

An insufficient pedestrian flow, as people cause obstructions or evoke collisions, due to architectural or informational reasons, can have an impact on commuters flow and stress level. These areas are called bottlenecks, which together with other delays in the overall journey are trigger points for causing stress and frustration. It makes infrastructure and information design in transport facilities become more important, not just to improve the efficiency, but also the quality of travelling through the setting, i.e. with less stress and more comfort.

TEI'11, January 22–26, 2011, Funchal, Portugal.
ACM 978-1-4503-0478-8/11/01.

THE STUDY
The following study aims to develop *ambient persuasive technologies* [1, 7, 9], i.e. *"interactive computing systems designed to change people's attitudes and behaviors"* [3] embedded into the environment, which act *as psychological guiding measures* [5] for a more effective *self-organisation* by enhancing *situational awareness* [2], to improve the pedestrian flow and the quality of walking.

Psychological Guiding Measures
Helbing argues that, self-organisation means that pedestrian motion forms emergent patterns, which may not lead to optimal flow. Hence, the optimisation of new or modification of existing pedestrian facilities may often be required [5]. For example at a pedestrian crossroad, a roundabout traffic flow behaviour can emerge, which can be improved by placing an object in it's middle – suppressing the more straightforward, but ultimately more collision inducing walking route. Furthermore, in order to prevent unwanted direction changes, and to keep an efficient pedestrian flow *"psychological guiding measures"* (which Helbing only refers to as, an interesting poster to draw people towards it) or railings can be used to initiate the roundabout traffic flow (Figure 1), which according to Helbing can increase the efficiency up to 13% [5].

Rather than modifying the infrastructure, by using railings and other sort of physical objects, this research will focus on the notion of PGM, extending Helbing's vision further. In Helbing's example, an interesting poster is used to induce people to move towards the right side, altering their walking behaviour accordingly. It is assumed that dynamic, interactive cues, designed with the intention to nudge [10] pedestrian's walking behaviour in a subtle way, may produce more *psychological engagement* (i.e. attract attention and affect pedestrian behaviour), than merely using a static, non-interactive 'poster' or signage.

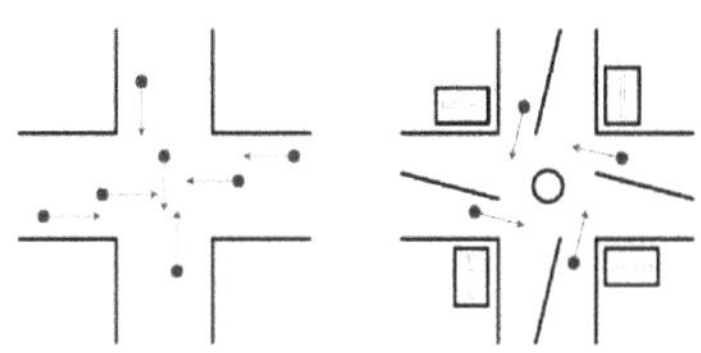

Figure 1. Psychological Guiding Measures illustrated by '!' to initiate roundabout traffic flow.

Intervention 1: Perspective guidance graphics
This is the notion of using perspective or anamorphic graphics, as PGM to assist pedestrians to organise themselves more efficiently at bottlenecks by strategically

placing illusions of physical barriers to change their walking behaviour.

These perspective graphics, although actually flat and static, appear to be dynamic as they morph into different 3D shapes, depending on the viewing angle (Figure 2). They are designed to morph into the intended form right at the moment and place the graphic is needed most. For example, an illusion of 3 triangular divider protruding from the wall, aiming to change commuters' behaviour to walk as close as possible around corners from one side – based on the notion of *cutting corners* [4] – to minimise collision avoidances.

Figure 2. Perspective guidance graphic

Intervention 2: Platform distribution

This APT is concerned with the distribution of commuters on a platform. Data about how many passengers are in the individual train carriages is collected, using video detection and sensors to estimate the capacity of each carriage of the in-coming train. This information will be displayed on the LED screens, currently used on the London Underground to indicate the time of the next arriving train, allowing commuters to distribute themselves on the platform accordingly to where the least crowed carriage will stop.

Intervention 3: Augmented self-organisation

This PGM is concerned with the potential of 'responsive', dynamic information at train doors, for faster boarding and alighting. The notion of responsive graphic is based on the principle of the zoetrope. This is a rotating cylinder with vertical slits and a series of images on its inside, which produce the illusion of motion, when viewed in quick succession through the slits. However, in this study the animation can be seen on a linear display, generated through body movement, rather than a rotating device. The hypothesis is that (H_1) motion displays, which are self-generated through body movement, draw more attention than static graphics. Also, due to its self-generated graphics, (H_2) it provides a certain kind of personal control, i.e. interactivity, which makes it more likely to be accepted and followed as guidance instructions, than static graphics.

Intervention 4: Enhanced Perception

This APT is concerned with the enhanced perception for collision avoidance around narrow corners or walls. It is based on the notion of a hagioscope, which is an architectural wall opening, mainly found in churches, allowing a direct view of the altar, if for example obstructed by a wall. The concept is, that instead of constructing an opening into the structure of a corner, which might affect the stability, two screens with cameras are applied showing the view of the opposite side, giving an illusion of transparency at the edge of the corner.

The aim is to provide people with an enhanced perception of their environment, allowing them to make trajectory changes earlier to avoid potential collisions, which is likely to occur around corners, due to the inherent phenomenon of cutting corners [4].

All experiments are designed to investigate how interactants perceive, comprehend and react on non-verbal signals. All studies will be conducted at the Pedestrian Accessibility and Movement Environment Laboratory (PAMELA), in collaboration with University College London (UCL) [8].

CONCLUSION

The initial study will investigate *Intervention 1,* providing data about the perception, reaction and effects of (analogue) PGM on pedestrian behaviour, which will provide viable data for the subsequent empirical studies of the remaining interventions. This paper yield an initial insight into the development of APT acting as PGM, exploring novel ways to support commuters during the walking stages of their journeys to improve the flow and quality of travelling in public transport facilities without coercion.

ACKNOWLEDGMENTS

I would like to thank UCL for providing PAMELA. As well as Magnus Moar, who provided helpful feedback and comments on previous drafts of this document.

REFERENCES

1. Davis, J. Towards Participatory Design of Ambient Persuasive (2008).
2. Endsley, M.R. Design and evaluation for situation awareness enhancement. Human Factors Society (1988).
3. Fogg, B.J. Persuasive Technology: Using Computers to Change What We Think and Do. Morgan Kaufmann (2003).
4. Gehl, J. Life Between Buildings: Using Public Space. Arkitektens Forlag (1996).
5. Helbing, D., Molnar, P., Farkas I.J. and Bolay, K. Self-organizing pedestrian movement. In *Environment and Planning B: Planning and Design* (2001), 361-383.
6. Key Figures for People and Society: Population and Migration. http://neighbourhood.statistics.gov.uk/
7. Matthew, A.P. Using the Environment as an Interactive Interface to Motivate Positive Behavior Change in a Subway Station. In *CHI '05* (2005), 1637-1640.
8. PAMELA. http://www2.cege.ucl.ac.uk/cts/arg/pamela2/laboratory/
9. Rogers, Y., Hazlewood, W.R., Marshall, P., Dalton, N. and Hertrich, S. Ambient Influence: Can Twinkly Lights Lure and Abstract Representations Trigger Behavioral Change? UbiComp'10 (2010).
10. Thaler, R.H. and Sunstein, C.R. Nudge: improving decisions about health, wealth and happiness. Penguin (2009).
11. The Independent. London leads the way in UK population increase. http://www.independent.co.uk

Spatial Relationships: A Framework for Understanding the Relationships Between Real and Virtual Spaces

Paul Clifton
Digital Media Program
Georgia Institute of Technology
Atlanta, GA, USA
paulgclifton@gmail.com

ABSTRACT
In this paper, I describe how representation, mapping, and interaction create the basis of a framework for discussing the relationships between real and virtual spaces and describe the design of an installation to illustrate these concepts.

Author Keywords
Virtual spaces, Frameworks, Installations.

ACM Classification Keywords
H5.m. Information interfaces and presentation (e.g., HCI): Miscellaneous.

General Terms
Design, Theory

INTRODUCTION
Systems that combine real and virtual spaces create different relationships between the two depending on their purposes and the technologies they implement. These relationships can be described in terms of the way the virtual space is represented, how it maps on to the real space, and the way that users interact with it. The ways different fields describe space, from its uses to its geometry, provide a basis for discussing how virtual space represents real space. The attributes of the real space that a virtual space takes on provide the elements of its mapping. The ways that interactors access virtual spaces influence how they understand and use them. These elements, which I will illustrate in the form of an installation piece, provide the beginnings of a framework that I will develop as my research progresses, which will catalogue and analyze different types of spatial relationships and their strengths and weaknesses for accomplishing their goals. My research questions include what are the ways real and virtual spaces relate to one another, and how do interfaces create or change these relationships.

TYPES OF SPACES
Descriptions of types of space come from all types of fields, from engineering and mathematics to architecture and media studies. In some cases, a division is made between real and virtual space, and often, the two are broken down further. Normal spaces, like parks and houses, contrast with non-spaces, described by Marc Augé as spaces void of culture meant for passing through [1]. Virtual spaces are often described using the same language, usually from architecture, as real spaces. Navigable virtual space provides a 3D environment through which avatars move and interact as people do in real space [2]. Even Novak's Liquid Architectures, while reactive, behave spatially like buildings [3].

Another way to distinguish between types of spaces is the geometry that describes them. Euclidean geometry describes the world of our daily experience with rules stating that lines extend forever on an infinite plane, and that parallel lines never intersect. Non-Euclidean geometries change these rules in order to describe spaces that do not behave like we expect. One example of a non-Euclidean space is the surface of a Klein bottle. Klein bottles are non-orientable, closed surfaces with no inside or outside. On a Klein bottle, if a person were to walk in one direction, he would end up at the point at which he started; however, the top of his head would be pointing in the opposite direction. Figure 1 shows a two dimensional projection of a Klein bottle. The two vertical edges connect, and the two horizontal edges connect with a half twist, so the two x's actually touch each other. While Klein bottles cannot exist physically in three-dimensional space, by creating a relationship between real and virtual space using embodied interaction, people can experience existing on the surface of one.

Representation and Mapping
The relationships between real and virtual space are created through two attributes of the virtual space, representation and mapping. Representation refers to the way the designer chooses to portray the space to its viewers. Just as maps represent real spaces as projections of points on to a two-dimensional plane, virtual representations of space illustrate data spatially. The data can be designed to create a virtual space analogous to a real space, as seen in video games like Second Life, or the data can be collections of data points, like weather data, that has been represented spatially for the sake of illustration. In the case of the installation that I

TEI'11, January 22–26, 2011, Funchal, Portugal.
ACM 978-1-4503-0478-8/11/01.

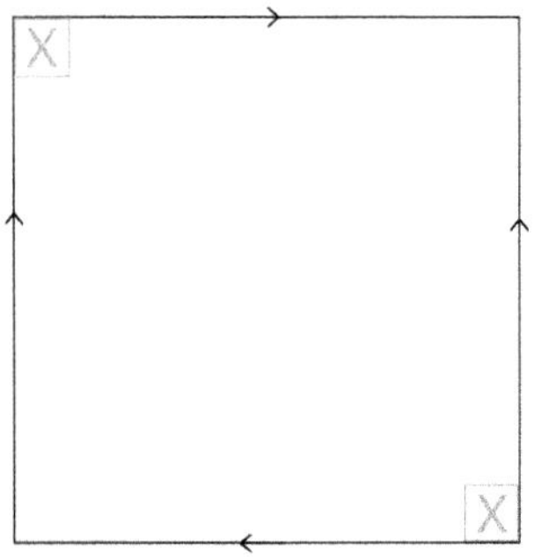

Figure 1: 2D Projection of a Klein bottle showing congruent edges

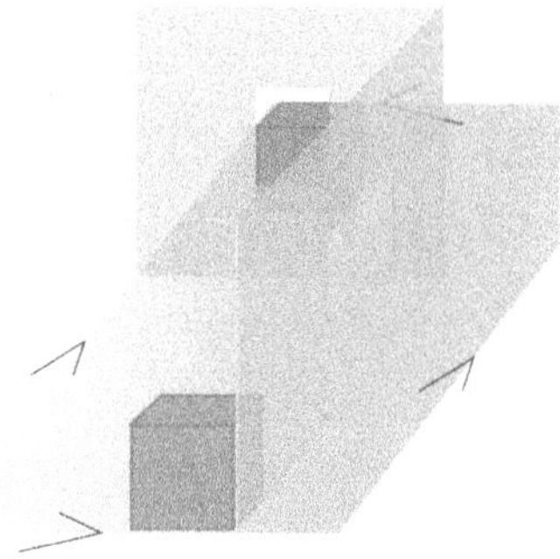

Figure 2: The design of the installation

describe later, the space acts like a real space with respect to movement and interaction, but the space represented is not analogous to any real space. It is meant to be understood as a space that is not physically accessible but is physically comparable to the real space to which it relates.

Mapping refers to the relationship between the real space and the virtual space. Virtual spaces can have a one-to-one relationship with real space in which everything in the virtual space has an exact analogue to the real space. One example of this is the inSpace project, which reflects movements of real objects in analogous virtual objects [4]. Virtual spaces can be extensions of real space like in flight simulators, where the real space is a airplane cockpit and the virtual space is seen through the cockpit's windshield as if it were actually the outside of a plane. Other mappings abstract different aspects of the real world and map them to a virtual world. One example of this is the Nintendo Wii, which maps movement in the real world to movement in a virtual world. In my installation, the virtual world is viewed as an extension of the real world, as in a simulator, although the space represented does not map to an actual real space.

Installation Design

The installation I proposed to build places the real space on the surface of a virtual Klein bottle. The virtual space extends outward from the gallery space in all directions and is viewable through framed windows on two sides of the gallery as shown in Figure 2. This situates the real space as a small part of a much larger virtual space. Objects in the physical room are also visible in the virtual space, as if the viewer can see around the entire surface. Moving physical objects changes the position of the virtual objects. Lights shined on the walls of the gallery at the correct place glare in the windows to the virtual world. These interactions allow the viewer to create a mental map of the larger space of which the gallery is a small part.

The installation will use a combination of projectors and computer vision to create these effects. By projecting the virtual space to look like it is outside of a window, the sense of perspective can create the illusion that the virtual space exists in the same world as the real space but is not directly accessible from it. The objects will be designed to be easily tracked by computer vision and their location will translate to a position in the virtual world. The virtual space will most likely be designed in a game engine like Unity, which will take input from the computer vision system and keep track of the locations of the virtual objects. Over the course of the next semester, I will research and test tools and techniques for creating the desired effect.

Conclusion

Different ways of representing space virtually, mapping it to real space, and interacting with it, lead to many possibilities for enhancing the display of and connection to data, whether for entertainment or instruction. By looking at existing examples of systems that combine real and virtual space and designing new systems that show novel applications of these relationships, I can begin to explore which types of relationships are appropriate for different applications and enhance the way people understand their relationship to the world around them. The design of this installation is a first step towards those goals.

REFERENCES

1. Augé, M. Non-places: introduction to an anthropology of supermodernity. Verso, 1995.
2. Manovich, L. *The Language of New Media*. Cambridge: The MIT Press, 2001. Print.
3. Novak, M. 1991. Liquid architectures in cyberspace. In *Cyberspace: First Steps*, M. Benedikt, Ed. MIT Press, Cambridge, MA, 225-254.
4. Reilly, D., et al. "Space Matters: Physical-Digital and Physical-Virtual Co-Design in the inSpace Project." IEEE Pervasive Computing, Volume 9, Number 3 (July-September 2010). IEEE Computer Society, pp. 54-63.

Art, Engineering, and Invention

Jill Coffin
Department of Digital Media, Georgia Institute of Technology
Atlanta, Georgia USA
jill@gatech.edu

ABSTRACT
In this paper I describe my dissertation-in-progress, *Art, Engineering, and Invention*. This research draws upon a triad of practice, evidence, and theory to discuss how art and engineering can resolve into an interdisciplinary practice of creating innovative technological art as well as technologies.

Author Keywords
Technological art, engineering, interdisciplinary practice.

ACM Classification Keywords
H5.m. Information interfaces and presentation (e.g., HCI): Miscellaneous.

General Terms
Theory.

INTRODUCTION
The research goal of my dissertation, titled *Art, Engineering, and Invention*, is to contribute to the understandings of how art and engineering can resolve into an interdisciplinary practice of creating innovative technological art as well as technologies. This work joins the inquiry and dialogs of the *Leonardo* community, Linda Candy and Ernest A. Edmonds, Dieter Daniels, Cornelius Borck, Sylvie Lacerte, Edward Shanken, Billy Klüver and Robert Rauchenberg, Jill Scott, Steven Wilson, Mark Tribe, Ken Goldberg, Simon Penny, Pamela Jennings, the NSF CreativeIT program, STEM to STEAM (STEM + arts) initiatives, and the growing critical mass of arts/technology/science practice. Understanding the dynamics and articulating the vocabulary of hybrid and collaborative interdisciplinary art and engineering practice can contribute to its teaching, practice, and survival through trends in funding cycles. My contribution draws upon a triad of practice, evidence, and theory.

I. PRACTICE
My own practice of creating technological art serves as an illustration and starting point. After an undergraduate degree in mathematics and a decade as a practicing fine artist, I joined the Digital Media program at Georgia Institute of Technology. Here I completed graduate minors in computer science and polymer, textile, and fiber engineering. The first project I describe, *Robotany*, originated as a way to engineer shape memory alloys into textiles. This was engineering work I was doing under a visiting fellowship at the Department of Electrical Engineering, Swiss Federal Institute of Technology in Zürich (ETHZ). At the same time, I was daydreaming of a bare, leafless tree alone in the desert. The tree communicates with people through gestures and a sixth sense. As it happened, I discovered that I needed a flexible yet rigid armature to support the motion of the shape memory alloy (s.m.a.) wires I was working with in the lab. I went to the lobby of the lab building and used the branches from live trees in planters to support the s.m.a. wires. As the wires contracted and moved the branches, my tree came alive. This project evolved into *Breeze*, a roboticized live Japanese maple that senses and responds to human movement. *Breeze* appeared at the Belluard Bollwerk International Art Festival in Fribourg, Switzerland in 2006 where it won the Concours de création. Video documentation is available at dm.gatech.edu/~jill/robotany. Through watching visitors interact with *Breeze*, I realized the totemic nature of the original daydream.

Figure 1. Visitors interacting with *Breeze*

In the process of building *Breeze,* I ended up created a novel robotic mechanism (see Figure 2). Its novelty lies in its radial use of s.m.a.'s to actuate. This radial pattern came from the morphology of the tree. I have moved forward from the experience of building *Breeze* to begin a series of steel, kinetic wall sculptures combining these radial, robotic, s.m.a. mechanisms in different configurations.

TEI'11, January 22–26, 2011, Funchal, Portugal.
ACM 978-1-4503-0478-8/11/01.

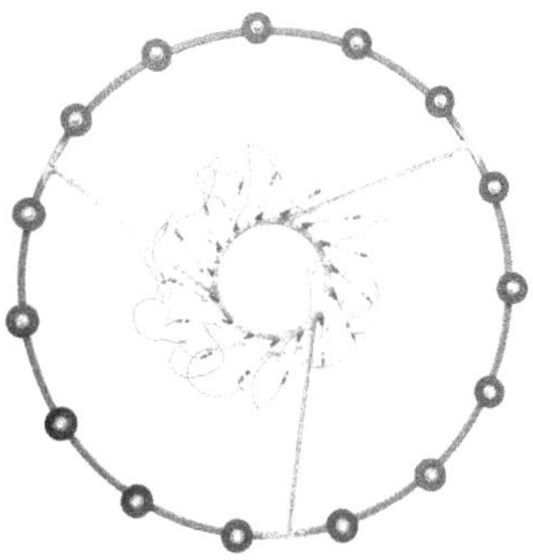

Figure 2. *Robotany* mechanism used in *Breeze*

The second project, called *Jade* (in progress, depicted in Figure 3), builds upon a large, live jade plant. Some of the round, rubbery leaves will be pruned and replaced with similarly shaped components made from an elastomer. These artificial leaves hold heartbeat. Visitors can pluck a leaf from the tree, hold it to their chest and record their heartbeat into it before placing the leaf back on the tree. Inaudible sound waves produced within the leaf will make the elastomer pulse with the rhythm of the recorded heartbeat. Visitors touching the leaves can feel the heartbeats left by other visitors.

In a parallel phase of this project, I am engineering a textile that pulses according to a recorded heartbeat signal. It is the intention that this textile could serve as an infant soothing blanket or a swaddler to induce low-level rhythmic tactile stimulation in infants to avoid apnea/SIDS as medical evidence suggests. In order to do this, I created small pods that translate sound signals into inaudible, soft pulses (see *Designing from Everyday Experience*, paper and demo to appear at TEI 2011). When incorporated into touch screens, computer mice and video game controllers, these pods provide advantages over current haptic technologies including vibromotors, magnetic coils with rigid armatures, rollers, and electro-active polymers. This experience has led me to develop a research program of haptics through sound.

Figures 3 and 4. *Jade* concept and a touchscreen with haptic sound pods embedded underneath. The pods can be miniaturized.

II. EVIDENCE

Artists are entering the technological academy through the Digital Media program at Georgia Institute of Technology and programs like it. Due to degree requirements and project work, these artists often become fluent in technology development. Some of these artists, perhaps responding to local technological agendas, have begun developing technologies independently from, but in parallel with, computer science and engineering labs at Georgia Tech. These parallel projects provide an opportunity to conduct a comparative case study of work processes among artists, engineers, and computer scientists working with similar technologies and similar goals. I wrote this observation into a proposal for the NSF CreativeIT program under the auspices of my advisor, Dr. Jay David Bolter. The project, awarded as NSF #1002820, is a qualitative study of three dyads of artists and engineers working separately on similar technologies. The study is guided by the question, "What are the similarities and differences between the mindsets (ontologies and epistemologies) and work practices (methodologies and techniques) of these artists, computer scientists, and engineers?" This research is intended to yield practical knowledge to help inter-disciplinary researchers, educators, practitioners, and team leaders maximize the possibilities of interdisciplinary creative work along similar disciplinary trajectories and minimize setbacks by mediating disciplinary differences. We will address questions like "What common ground may be found between an artist's and an information technologist's prototyping methods?" and "How might artists and engineers understand and learn from each other's disciplinary training (and thus synthesize true inter-disciplinary partnerships)?" There will be immediate and direct application of this knowledge to the undergraduate Computational Media curriculum at Georgia Tech.

III. THEORY

Results from the projects described above are combined with theoretical considerations that arise from reflections on the literature and phenomenology of art and engineering. For example, I describe a phenomenology of art that reveals destabilization to be a fundamental characteristic. This destabilization operates within the context of social and cultural practices. On the other hand, engineering practice prioritizes stabilization. It stabilizes natural forces and materials so that devices can act reliably. This stabilization incorporates social and cultural practices so that in the moments of acting with an engineered object, such as a bridge or an iPhone, we can act within a reliable threshold of activity with the technology. Thus engineered technologies fundamentally aim to stabilize reality. How then are the destabilizing practices of art and stabilizing practices of engineering resolved into a practice of technological art? This guiding question forces an articulation of the dynamics of art and engineering within the interdisciplinary practice of creating novel art and technological artifacts.

Material-Centered Design and Evaluation of Tangible User Interfaces

Tanja Doering
Pervasive Computing and User Interface Engineering
University of Duisburg-Essen, Germany
tanja.doering@uni-due.de

ABSTRACT
This paper presents an overview of an ongoing doctoral research project on materiality and tangible user interfaces (TUIs). The aim of the thesis is to address materiality as an important design element of tangible user interfaces and develop a material-based design knowledge for TUIs, e.g., in the form of material-based design patterns and evaluation methods. This is done iteratively in three steps: (1) compilation of interdisciplinary material theories and their application to tangible user interfaces, (2) exploratory prototyping of material-based interaction, and (3) validation of developed design knowledge and evaluation techniques in evaluations of TUI prototypes in different application domains.

Author Keywords
Tangible user interface, material, material-centered interaction, material iconography, material culture, analysis.

ACM Classification Keywords
H5.2 Information interfaces and presentation (e.g., HCI): User Interfaces – *theory and methods*.

General Terms
Design, Human Factors, Theory.

INTRODUCTION
An important quality of tangible user interfaces is the materiality of the objects used for the interaction. However, the meaning of material qualities for tangible user interfaces has yet not been explored and investigated sufficiently. Since the technical realization of TUI prototypes still is challenging, and there is no guide on how to choose appropriate low-tech materials for interaction, the material selection –especially within engineering disciplines– often is based on easy availability and technical aspects rather than anticipated user experience. However, a big potential of tangible user interfaces is that they take advantage of materials and form for interaction. From a design perspective, form factors have been discussed as important features of TUIs [2]. Discussions on using material properties for designing tangible user interfaces have just started (e.g., [4]). Yet, there do not exist structured approaches for designers and engineers how to use material properties and cultural material knowledge to construct meaningful, intuitive, and appropriate tangible user interfaces. This doctoral research work in progress addresses this issue and investigates how TUI-relevant design knowledge on material properties and material semantics can be derived and then guided into material-centered methods for design and evaluation of tangible user interfaces.

TEI'11, January 22–26, 2011, Funchal, Portugal.
ACM 978-1-4503-0478-8/11/01.

INTERDISCIPLINARY MATERIAL THEORIES
Currently, debates on the importance and the value of materials take place in many trans- and interdisciplinary contexts. From the potentials of novel and smart materials developed in engineering and material sciences to an "associative material mind" [6] applied in architecture and design to the relatively young significance of material usage in art [7] or the claim of a "material turn" as part of the cultural turn in cultural studies [4] materiality is an ongoing and vivid topic. Tangible user interfaces constitute a further field of research that stresses the importance and potentials of materiality for interactions between humans and computers. Thus, tangible interaction should be examined and discussed in the context of results from material discussions in other disciplines. Based on literature review and expert interviews, this doctoral research project collects material knowledge from art history, architecture, ethnography and material sciences and puts it in relation to existing frameworks and methods from product design (e.g., [1]) and computer science.

In a first literature study, methods from material culture (e.g., [3]) and art history (e.g., [7]) were examined. In order to better understand meaningful material usage for tangible user interfaces the following questions were addressed:

- *Material Mind:* How can we integrate a collective "material mind" into design knowledge for tangible user interfaces?
- *Material Properties:* How can we better understand material properties for meaningful and context adequate interaction?
- *Material Mapping:* How does the used material relate to the linked digital data and what mappings are useful?

The analysis led to a first structured approach to guide material-centered analysis of tangible interaction (see figure 1) and future work will include developing this further into a generative framework.

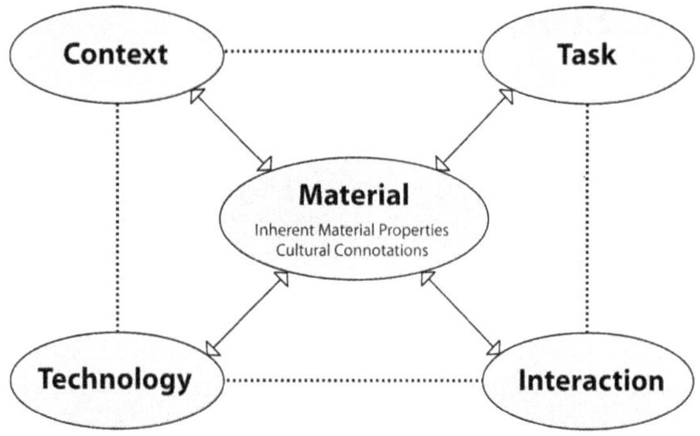

Figure 1: A structural approach for a material-centered analysis of TUIs derived from material culture and material iconography. Inherent material properties and cultural connotations are interpreted regarding (a) the context of use, (b) task, (c) interaction, and (d) technology.

TOWARDS MATERIAL-CENTERED METHODS FOR TANGIBLE COMPUTING

After "taking a step back" and examining the landscape of material theories and methods, the derived criteria are applied in a structured analysis of existing tangible user interfaces regarding used material qualities and designed interaction techniques. This is currently being done by applying the developed approach (see figure 1) to a collected comprehensive catalogue of TUI prototypes, presented in exhibitions or published at scientific conferences. This is expected to lead into deeper design knowledge on how to use materials for tangible interaction, e.g., in the form of material-centered interaction patterns that support designers and engineers in material selection.

VALIDATION: PROTOTYPING AND IN-SITU EVALUATIONS

Based on solid theory work, practical parts of this thesis will include material-focused prototyping of TUIs, and furthermore, in order to validate the developed design concepts, their application and material-centered evaluation in concrete application domains (e.g., therapy/play, work context, home context). This could, for example, be achieved by comparative studies, but furthermore, will need specific refinements of existing evaluation methods, e.g. regarding the measurement of user experiences with different materials. Among first exploratory prototypes is the soap bubble user interface [5], a TUI that uses soap bubbles for human-computer interaction and, in this case, employs an extreme and unusual material with specific material properties to define and constrain interaction techniques, which include gently touching, blowing, or waving hands to move a soap bubble (see figure 2). The material-focused approach led to a concept for ephemeral user interfaces: UIs that can be created when needed, but only last for a short time.

SUMMARY

The central question of this thesis is: *What can interaction design and engineering learn from interdisciplinary material theories and methods for the design and evaluation of tangible user interfaces?* And, in more detail: *how can we integrate knowledge about a material mind, material properties, and material mappings into design knowledge for tangible user interfaces?* Results are derived from three iterative steps (1) theory compilation through literature review and expert interviews, (2) explorative material-focused prototyping, and (3) validation of derived design guidelines and methods in in-situ evaluations in different application contexts.

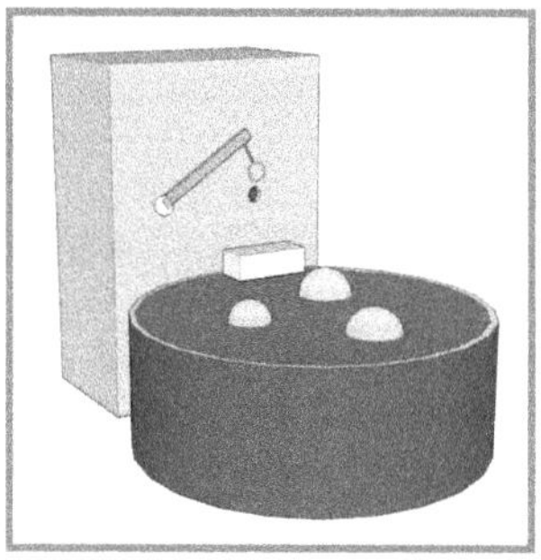

Figure 2: The soap bubble user interface: an ephemeral user interface. Setup (left) and one of the realized material specific interaction techniques (right).

ACKNOWLEDGEMENTS

I would like to thank Albrecht Schmidt for PhD supervision and generous support and Axel Sylvester for co-developing the soap bubble user interface.

REFERENCES

1. Ashby, M. & Johnson, K. (2002). Materials and design: The art and science of material selection in product design. Oxford: Butterworth-Heinemann.
2. Baskinger, M. and Gross, M. 2010. Cover Story: Tangible interaction = form + computing. *interactions* 17, 1 (Jan. 2010), 6-11.
3. Prown, J. D. Mind in Matter: An Introduction to Material Culture Theory and Method. In Winterthur Portfolio, Vol. 17, No. 1, 1982, 1-19.
4. Robles, E. and Wiberg, M. 2010. Texturing the "material turn" in interaction design. In Proceedings of TEI '10. ACM, New York, NY, 137-144.
5. Sylvester, A., Doering, T., and Schmidt, A. 2010. Liquids, smoke, and soap bubbles: reflections on materials for ephemeral user interfaces. In Proceedings of TEI '10. ACM, New York, NY, 269-270.
6. Wachs, M. E. Material Mind. Neue Materialien in Kunst und Architektur. Kovac, 2008.
7. Wagner, M. Lexikon des künstlerischen Materials. Werkstoffe der modernen Kunst von Abfall bis Zinn. C.H. Beck. 2002.

TouchSound: Making Sounds with Everyday Objects

Huaishu Peng
Carnegie Mellon University
5000 Forbes Avenue, Pittsburgh, PA, USA
huaishup@andrew.cmu.edu

ABSTRACT
In this paper I am presenting TouchSound, a wearable device that generates sounds and music by interacting with everyday objects by hand. By mixing tactile and auditory sensations, TouchSound promotes enjoyable musical experiences. It could be used by musicians to explore new ways to perform music, for educators to teach music to kids, and provide an opportunity for people to play music by touching everyday objects.

Author Keywords
Tangible interfaces, musical instrument, ubiquitous.

ACM Classification Keywords
H5.2. Haptic I/O.

General Terms
Design

INTRODUCTION
Auditory and tactile sensations are two of the five basic sensations of human beings. With auditory sensation, people perceive sounds from the environment, and with tactile sensation, people feel the shape and texture of objects, as well as interact with them physically. The two senses are often experienced together. For instance, pianos and drums generate sounds when people press or beat them. Some researchers are trying to explore this combination in a further way. Hiroshi Ishii et.al [2] exploited glass bottles as an interface to control music and sounds. Smus et.al [1] from Carnegie Mellon University demonstrated jeans that people can drum on by tapping.

One of the limitations shared by these projects is that the music is confined to a group of certain objects. It would be impossible for people to play sounds or music without them. Is it possible for us to find a way to generate sounds or music by hand whenever and whatever we want without the presence of traditional musical instruments or certain music devices?

In this paper, I present TouchSound, a wearable device in progress which allows people to make sounds by touching the surface of various everyday objects. Wearing this bracelet-like device on one's wrist, the user can play with sounds or even create music when they are at home, at the office, or on the street. No traditional instruments or specific "music objects" are needed. Music becomes ubiquitous with TouchSound. The richness of interaction of TouchSound could be used by musicians to perform music in new ways, or early music education for kids. It provides a novel music experience.

CONCEPT
A traditional way to store sounds is to embed sound signals in given materials like magnetic strips or compact discs. To play music, a corresponding device is needed to decode the information into a sound wave. We can interpret TouchSound as one of music players, that instead of reading information from certain materials, it extracts the information from everyday objects and translates the information to sounds. Such information could be the color of the surface of an object, the temperature, the conductivity, magnetism ability, etc. By carefully mapping such information into elements of sounds, we can play sounds with everyday things.

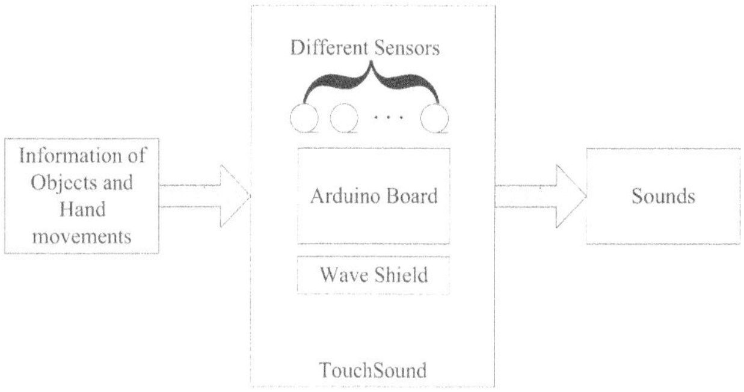

Figure 1. System Architecture.

The main part of the TouchSound system is an Arduino board with a wave shield to store sound effects. Several different sensors are connected to Arduino as system input and a speaker as sound output. Firgure 1 shows the structure of the system.

Input
TouchSound acquires information with different sensors as the system input. The information is classified into two categories: object information and hand interaction information.

Information	Color	Temperature	Magnetism	Conductivity	Hands Movement	Hands Pressure
Sensors	Color Sensor	Temperature	Magnetometer	Resistor	Accelerometer	Pressure Sensor
Music Elements	Pitch	Timbre			Tempo	Loudness

Table 1. The sensors and mapping of information.

Object information refers to the information of an object's own properties. I use different sensors to recognize the color, temperature, magnetism and conductivity ability of the surface of an object.

Hand interaction information is generated when people interact with the object, including the movement of one's hand across the surface and the pressure generated against it.

Mapping

I use four basic elements to create music, pitch, timbre, loudness and tempo. The information acquired from sensors is mapped to these four elements. To be more specific, I mapped red, orange, yellow, green, blue, indigo and violet, the color of rainbow, to the seven music notes C, D, E, F, G, A, B. The color depth will influence the octave. To change the timbre, I mapped conductivity, magnetism, and temperature. Similarly, the speed of the hands movement and the pressure of touching are mapped to tempo and loudness, respectively. Table 1 demostrates the system input and mapping of TouchSound.

Output

Following the mapping rules, Arudino will pick a corresponding sample from the wave shield, which will be played with certain time, loudness, through the speaker.

Appearance Design

TouchSound device is designed to be worn on user's wrist like bracelet. Arduino board will be replaced by Lilypad Arduino[3] and all the sensors will be sewed into the bracelet. Three 3 Volts Watch Batteries will provide the power for driving the device. See Figure 2.

Figure 2. Picture of Current Prototype Hardware.

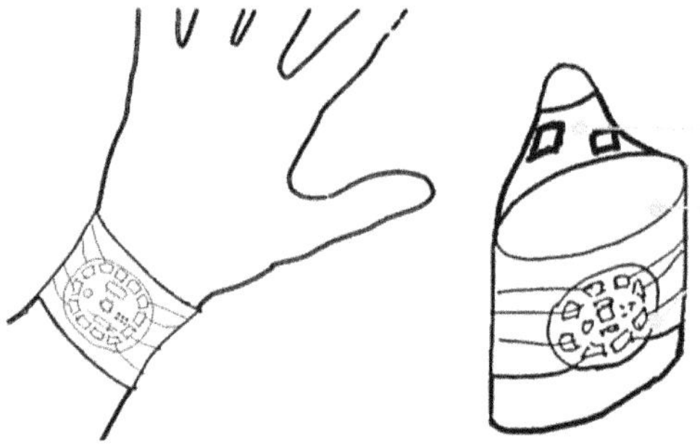

Figure 3. Appearance Design of TouchSound.

INTERACTION

Wearing TouchSound, people can touch objects like a wall, desk, clothes, or whatever they want to generate sounds. By touching surfaces with different colors, people can change the pitch of the sound, and by pressing their hands with different force, the sound will come with different volume accordingly. With one's hands movement at a different speed, the tempo of the sounds will also change. And if one's hand slides across a surface with different conductivity, temperature or magnetism, sound can be generated in different timbre. The diversity of generating sound with TouchSound makes the interaction have different possibilities.

CONCLUSION AND FUTURE WORK

In this paper, I describe TouchSound, a wearable device in progress for people to generate music by touching everyday objects. TouchSound can recognize information of normal objects and map them to basic music elements, so that one can perform music ubiquitously. In the future, I will keep working on construction TouchSound and make it appropriate to wear on one's hand.

REFERENCES

1. Boris Smus, Mark D. Gross, Ubiquitous Drums: a Tangible, Wearable Musical Interface, *in Proceedings of CHI 2010*, ACM Press
2. Hiroshi Ishii, Ali Mazalek, and Jay Lee, Bottles as a Minimal Interface to Access Digital Information, *in Proceedings of CHI 2001*, ACM Press
3. LilyPad Arduino, http://www.arduino.cc/en/Main/ArduinoBoardLilyPad

Feedback Fridge: Tangible Visualization of Nutritional Data with Preventive Effect

Philipp Schoessler
University of the Arts Berlin
Berlin, Germany
pschoessler@ymail.com

ABSTRACT
The Feedback Fridge is a system that makes the visualization of nutritional data tangible and thereby more understandable to the user. Using RFID (radio-frequency identification) technology and one inflatable airbag inside every compartment of a refrigerator the fridge reacts on the kind of food that is put into it. Is the food healthy or unhealthy? Low in fat or high in fat? By inflating or deflating the airbags correspondingly the user is shown how nutritious or healthy his food is. This visualization also has a certain preventive effect by pushing food out of the fridge if the airbags get too big. The Feedback Fridge can thereby help enhance people's health and lead them to a balanced and nutritious diet.

Author Keywords
RFID, Food, nutritional values, healthy food, feedback, healthy eating, refrigerator, visualization, preventive action.

ACM Classification Keywords
H5.m. Information interfaces and presentation (e.g., HCI): Miscellaneous.

General Terms
Design, Experimentation

INTRODUCTION
RFID technology is becoming more and more ubiquitous and affordable. So far RFID is applied to food packages for supply chain control [1]. Sooner or later RFID tags will be put on food packaging to give the consumer additional information about what he is buying for instance nutritional facts of food, minimum shelf-life or place of origin. The METRO Group Future Store Initiative is already testing the deployment of RFID on sales floors [2] as well as retail stores such as Wal-Mart and Home Depot [3]. This information can make it easier for the consumer to decide on what to buy. I developed a concept and prototype for a refrigerator that can visualize the nutritional information by inflating airbags that are built into the fridge [Fig1]. At the same time the airbags function as "preventers" as they push food out of the fridge if the nutritional data inside the fridge exceeds a certain amount or if the nutritional value of the food inside is too low.

TEI'11, January 22–26, 2011, Funchal, Portugal.
ACM 978-1-4503-0478-8/11/01.

MOTIVATION
In most countries nutritional facts are listed on food packages but so far only the minority of consumers can properly interpret these facts. Furthermore it is relatively easy too just ignore the facts on food packaging. Therefore a lot of people unintentionally buy and eat unhealthy food. This can lead among other things to obesity and artery and cardiovascular diseases. This let me to my concept of developing a system that can show people the effects of their eating habits and at the same time help them to a balanced diet that can enhance their health. The refrigerator seemed to be the perfect medium for displaying nutritional data since almost every household has at least one refrigerator and most of our food is being stored there. Another point is that we usually use the refrigerator several times a day which means that the data is also being perceived several times a day.

Figure 1. Feedback Fridge in action

THE SYSTEM
The Feedback Fridge system consists of a midrange RFID reader attached to the fridge door [Fig1] that can read tags for up to 50cm. For this system to work the food has to be tagged with RFID responders.

As soon as the user puts tagged food into the fridge and passes the fridge door the tag is being read by the RFID reader and the corresponding nutritional facts are being pulled from a database. These values are then being translated by a simple algorithm into a certain volume. With the help of an Arduino micro-controller, a compressor and two solenoid valves [Fig2] the airbags are then inflated according to this value [Fig1]. Nutritional values that affect the amount of air that is being pumped into the airbags are fat, sugar, calories and sodium. The higher these values the more the airbags are being inflated. If healthy food that is low on these values is put into the fridge the airbags will either inflate less or even deflate. If food that has already been put into the fridge is taken out and passes the RFID reader within its reading range the airbag's volume is being adjusted. The airbags always represent the food that is currently inside the fridge.

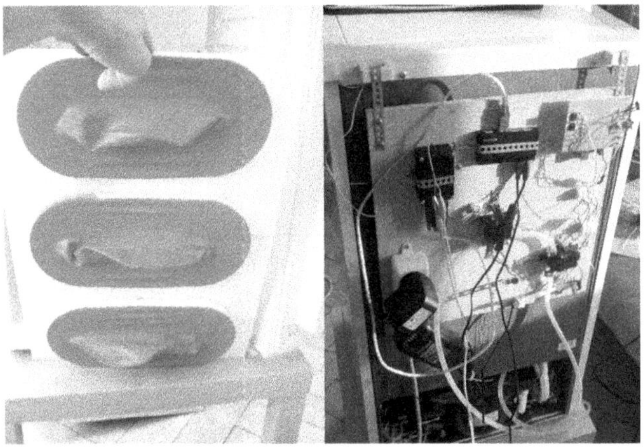

Figure 2. Technical setup of the Feedback Fridge

Preventive Effect

With the inflating and deflating of the airbags the space inside the fridge has become variable. If too much unhealthy food is in the fridge the space to put in more food is thereby being reduced. That way it becomes impossible for the user to put more food into the fridge. The user is being forced to either take food out or put healthy food in. If the user still tries to put in more unhealthy food the airbags start to push the food out [Fig3]. That way the Feedback Fridge forces the user to adjust to a balanced diet.

Tangible Visualization

By inflating the airbags according to the nutritional value that is in the Feedback Fridge this system helps users to understand and interpret the data. The user can directly interact with the airbags by putting food in or taking food out of the fridge. I believe that this tangible representation of information is being more easily understood by the user than a mere 2D- display of the nutritional facts (i.e. LCD-screen on the fridge door). The Feedback Fridge functions as a test object. It is being fed first and the user can read from it and react accordingly.

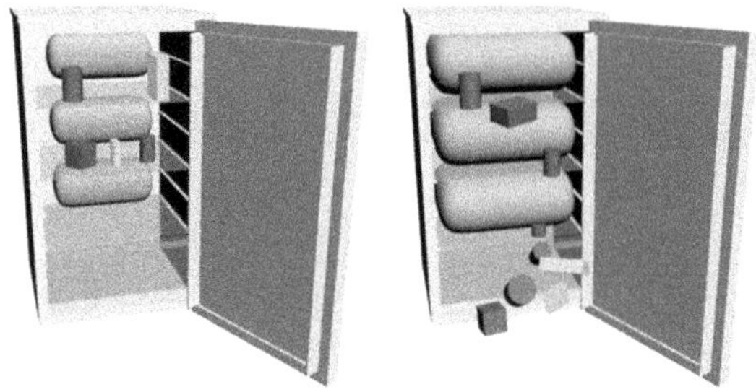

Figure 3. (left) balanced diet (right) unbalanced diet

Another advantage of the tangible representation in this system is that the information can't be ignored. The user is always directly confronted with the data as soon as the fridge's door is opened.

The fridge has become aware of its content and reacts accordingly by either getting "fatter" or "thinner" just as the human body would react to food. This anthropomorphizing of the fridge encourages people to reflect on their diets.

CONCLUSION AND ETHICAL ISSUES

At this point it has to be said that the Feedback Fridge at the current stage of development is not aiming to be a real product but to be thought-provoking. It is doubtful that people would want a product in their households that forces them to a certain behavior and basically denies its proper usage. Even though it might be desirable to have technology shape people's decisions and the effects their actions have, as Latour claims [4], humans have proven more than once that they can and will find ways to circumvent technology that tries to constrain their actions. In conclusion, Feedback Fridge shows that combining existing RFID technology and tangible visualization of nutritional data can help Individuals understand the relevance it has for their personal health. By bringing the representation of data into the physical world the visualization itself can interact with its environment and is able to trigger events that can underline a certain statement or purpose.

ACKNOWLEDGMENTS

Thank goes to Professor Joachim Sauter, Assistant Professor Jussi Ängeslevä and Technical Advisor Matt Karau.

REFERENCES

1. Wikipedia *http://en.wikipedia.org/wiki/Food_packaging#RFID*
2. METRO Group Future Store Initiative *http://www.future-store.org/fsi-internet/html/en/1613/index.html*
3. Tarver T.(2008). *Food Technology Magazine*, p. 55.
4. Latour, B. (1992). *Where Are the Missing Masses? The Sociology of a Few Mundane Artifacts*. In: W.E. Bijker and J. Laws. *Studies in Sociotechnical Change*. Cambridge, Mass.: MIT Press), pp. 225–258.

Bouncing Glow: Methods of Creating Content Elements for One-Pixel-Displays

Daniel Wessolek
Interaction Design
Faculty of Art & Design
Bauhaus University Weimar
daniel.wessolek@uni-weimar.de

ABSTRACT
This paper describes novel methods of generating patterns as content for One-Pixel-Displays. These patterns of varying light intensity are created as content elements for One-Pixel-Displays or computer controllable light sources in general. The elements are intended as the language foundations for storytelling within a new medium. We argue that content creation in this field is running behind the hardware developments and therefore needs to be explored. One example presented is the time-based mapping of the vertical position of a simulated bouncing ball to light intensity variations of a light source, in this case a TFT and a DMX-controlled incandescent light bulb. The other example is the mapping of different sound recordings to light. These methods show promising first results for creating content elements.

Author Keywords
Design, Light, Mapping, One-Pixel-Display, Light Intensity Patterns, Simulation of Physics, Sound Recordings

ACM Classification Keywords
H.5.m Information Interfaces and Presentation: Miscellaneous

General Terms
Design, Experimentation

INTRODUCTION
With *Bouncing Glow* we describe our efforts to generate content for One-Pixel-Displays. The hardware of these One-Pixel-Displays might be based on incandescent, LED, electroluminescent, or OLED technologies coupled with control circuitry. The medium of film, for example, has been explored widely as narrative by filmmakers, artists and designers.

TEI'11, January 22–26, 2011, Funchal, Portugal.
ACM 978-1-4503-0478-8/11/01.

Little research and art creation has yet been done to animate these single glowing entities as novel media. How can we create meaningful content for these displays despite the obvious limitations?

BACKGROUND AND RELATED WORK
Controllable light sources have become very common e.g. as LED displays in the urban context. Recently there have been some attempts to focus on freely configurable displays. *Liberated Pixels* as Seitinger coins them in the title of her PhD Thesis Defense are represented in her research as the examples *Urban Pixels* [5] and *Light Bodies* [6]. In *Urban Pixels* the focus lays on freely reconfigurable, independent and wirelessly controllable light sources (resembling bigger display structures). In *Light Bodies* the responsive interaction in a performative context is highlighted. Pintus in her paper *Tangible Lightscapes* [2] calls attention to the aspects of product communication through light. A well known commercial and patented example is Apples *Breathing Status LED Indicator* that mimicks the rhythm of breathing [1]. Here we build on our own research completed under the title *Semiotic Foundations of Illuminants as Time-Based Medium in Space: Experiments and Artifacts* [8].

Figure 1: Processing sketch mapping vertical position of a bouncing ball to light intensity

APPROACHES FOR ANIMATING ONE-PIXEL-DISPLAYS
Via this process, fundamentals research on how to animate One-Pixel-Displays, we discovered two main approaches of mapping sensor or simulation data on light intensity values. One is the mapping of natural forces e.g. gravity, the other the transformation of sound data to light intensity variations over time. Both directions showed promising first results and might be coupled with direct user interaction.

Physical Simulation and Motion Sensory Data Mapping

In order to see the results of mapping physical simulations to a light source, we mapped the vertical position of a simulated bouncing ball to light intensity (Figure 1). The relative height of the ball is discreetly mapped to the light intensity, where the ground line is either represented by full light or complete blackness. The luminance intensity changes incrementally from light to dark as the ball begins its fall to finally bouncing on the ground line repeatedly (ie. loosing kinetic energy). The experimental set up in physical space resulted in what we perceive and describe as *Bouncing Glow*. As the only light source, the controlled light in the dark room seemed to suggest the space itself to be bouncing. This was a similar effect to that on screen and is an effect to be evaluated further with other observants.

Mapping of Sound Recordings

The other approach was the direct mapping of amplitude data of several audio recordings, e.g. human heart beat, human breathing, sea shore, bird sounds to light. This showed that the synesthetic experience is somewhat transported through light too.

Reality based Simulation vs. Cartoon based Animation

An unanswered question is that of the user acceptance of *realistic* and *exaggerated cartoon like* animations on One-Pixel-Displays. We assume that the most realistic data mapping does not lead to the best user experience. Examples of this are rotoscoped video or film shots, which can create the feeling of odd motion, although based on real movements. An aspect to look into further is the relevance of the initial mental models the observer creates while exposed to the situation. This, so we assume, strongly influences the observers future perception.

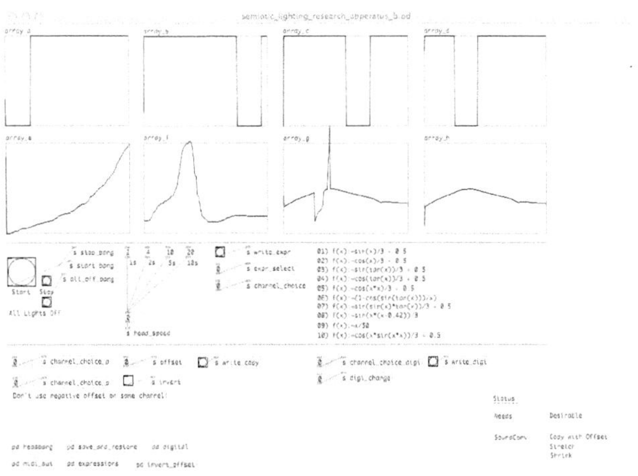

Figure 2: Pure Data patch to map sound recordings to light intensity variations over time

HARDWARE AND SOFTWARE

For our experiments we built hardware and software prototypes. The *Bouncing Glow* experiment consists of a Processing [3] sketch combining a simulated bouncing ball with an on screen output of different tones of gray.

Additionally the vertical positions of the ball have been mapped to a DMX dimmer controlled incandescent light bulb diffused by a yellow bucket. The processing patch hereby communicates through Pure Data over an DMX interface to the dimmer. For the sound to light conversion we built a patch (Figure 2) in Pure Data [4] allowing us to import sound samples and convert them to DMX signals. Another approach taken was the use of wav2c [7] in order to generate data arrays from sound files. Real-time based programming languages for sound and video processing have shown to be the more reliable choice.

CONCLUSION

This paper describes two paths for developing content elements for One-Pixel-Displays by mapping data directly to light intensity values. Initial experimental settings have been created and demonstrated. These also require further evaluation in the form of user studies. These experimental approaches also create space for further research in the field of content creation for One-Pixel-Displays to interact with each other and/or the user. Concurrently, artistic explorations of One-Pixel-Displays will be carried out, based on aesthetic intuition.

ACKNOWLEDGMENTS

I would like to thank my Ph.D. Advisors Prof. Dr. Ute Holl and Prof. Wolfgang Sattler, as well as my former mentor Prof. Ursula Damm. I also want to thank Jamie L. Ferguson for our ongoing dialogue on this matter, and the Bauhaus University Weimar Kreativfonds 2009 for financial support.

REFERENCES

1. B. Q. Huppi, C. J. Stringer, J. Bell, and C. L. Capener. United States Patent 6658577: Breathing status LED indicator, 2003.
2. A. V. Pintus. Tangible lightscapes. *Proceedings of the fourth international conference on Tangible, embedded, and embodied interaction - TEI '10*, page 379, 2010.
3. Processing, an open source programming language and environment initiated by Ben Fry and Casey Reas. `http://processing.org`.
4. Software by Miller Puckette. `http://www-crca.ucsd.edu/~msp/software.html`.
5. S. Seitinger, D. S. Perry, and W. J. Mitchell. Urban Pixels : Painting the City with Light. *Image (Rochester, N.Y.)*, pages 839–848, 2009.
6. S. Seitinger, D. M. Taub, A. S. Taylor, and J. J. T. Ave. Light Bodies : Exploring Interactions with Responsive Lights. *Histoire*, pages 113–120, 2010.
7. Wav2c makes arrays out of sounds... `http://github.com/olleolleolle/wav2c`.
8. D. Wessolek. Semiotic Foundations of Illuminants as Time-Based Medium in Space: Experiments and Artifacts, 2008. Unpublished MFA Thesis, Bauhaus University Weimar, accessible through the author.

Character Interaction with Handheld Projectors

Karl D.D. Willis

Computational Design Lab
Carnegie Mellon University
5000 Forbes Avenue, Pittsburgh, PA 15213

Disney Research, Pittsburgh
4615 Forbes Avenue, Pittsburgh, PA 15213
karl@disneyresearch.com

ABSTRACT

I present a summary of my research dealing with character interaction using handheld projectors. My work draws from the tradition of pre-cinema handheld projectors that use direct physical manipulation to control projected imagery. I build upon this work with a system allowing users to interactively control characters by moving and gesturing with the handheld projector itself. This creates a unified interaction style where input and output are tied together within a single device. I present a prototype handheld platform, several games, and augmented reality application scenarios to illustrate the approach.

Author Keywords

Interaction techniques, handheld projector, pico projector, character, gesture, movement, augmented reality.

ACM Classification Keywords

H5.m. Information interfaces and presentation (e.g., HCI): Miscellaneous.

General Terms

Design, Experimentation, Human Factors, Theory.

INTRODUCTION

Handheld projectors have the ability to situate projected imagery side by side with physical objects in almost any space. The affordances created by their size allow users to grasp them in a single hand, attach them to their bodies, or move them from space to space. Market research predicts as many as 39 million devices with embedded projectors on the market by 2014 [4]. Despite these projections only a relatively small amount of research has focused on developing new applications and interaction techniques for handheld projectors [e.g. 1,2,5,7].

One of the major challenges when dealing with handheld projectors is to develop interaction techniques that accommodate movement. Projected imagery moves, shakes, and distorts with the users every move. My approach utilizes gestural movement of the projector to control and interact with projected characters (Figure 1). I label this the *MotionBeam* metaphor [6], as the projected character behaves as if it is attached to the end of a metaphorical beam. The approach draws from the tradition of pre-cinema handheld projectors, such as the Japanese *Utushi-e* performance [3], that use direct physical manipulation to control projected imagery. This creates a unified interaction style where input and output are tied together within a single device. To outline the use of the *MotionBeam* metaphor, I have developed a handheld projection device, several prototype games, and augmented reality (AR) application scenarios.

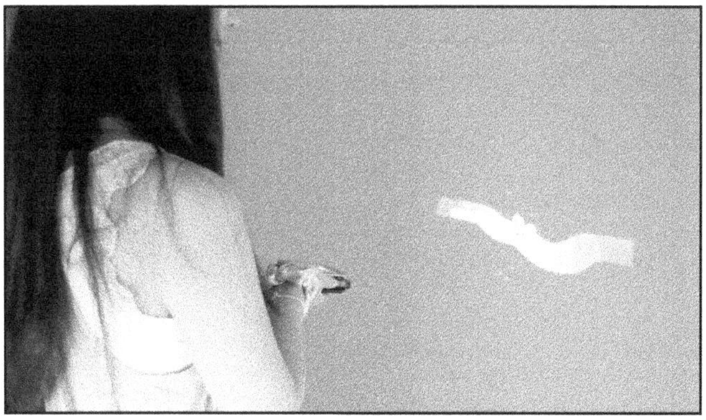

Figure 1. Character interaction with a handheld projector and a prototype racing game.

The *MotionBeam* metaphor is a powerful tool to blend virtual characters into the physical world. Character interaction has applicability to a range of important domains such as games, educational software, virtual worlds, storytelling, and numerous other applications where an avatar is used to represent a user. Characters will not only perceive and react to physical objects in the environment, but will increasingly be able to 'push back' on the world to actuate and control physical objects. Although these future technologies will no doubt empower new forms of interaction, we can build the foundations for richer interaction with virtual content in the physical world today.

PROTOTYPE

The character interaction prototype is implemented using an iPod Touch, a laser projector, and a sensor unit (Figure 2). Attached sensors include an ultrasonic distance sensor, a 9DOF accelerometer/gyroscope/magnetometer, and an infrared receiver.

TEI'11, January 22–26, 2011, Funchal, Portugal.
ACM 978-1-4503-0478-8/11/01.

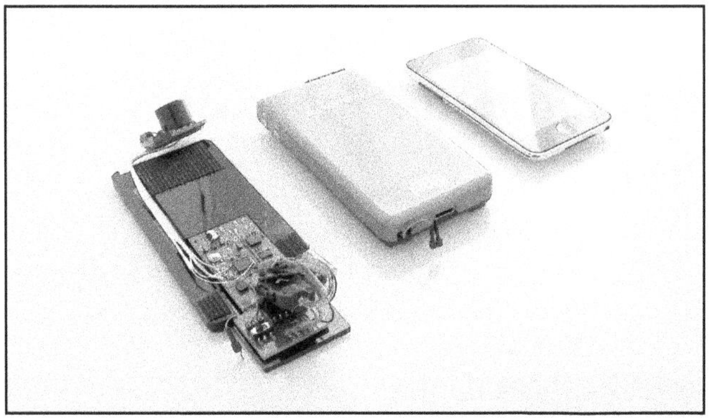

Figure 2. The components used in our prototype. From left to right, a sensor unit, a handheld projector, an iPod Touch.

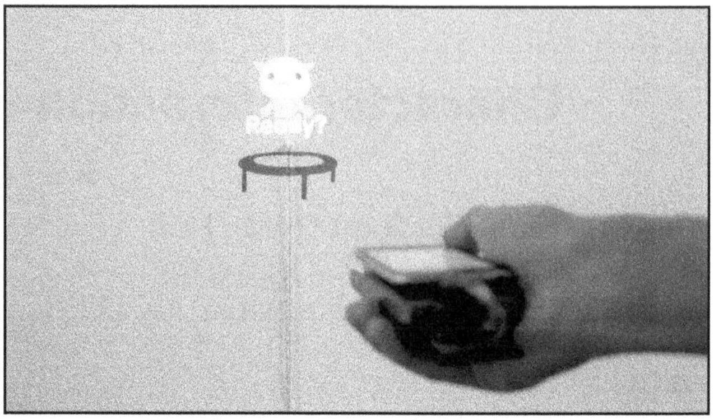

Figure 3. A projected character starts bouncing when it encounters a trampoline in the environment.

Character Game

The character game interaction is based on guiding a character through the game space by pointing the projection device up, down, left, and right. The goal is to search for the character's missing car by following a trail of 'bread-crumbs'. The position of the character stays fixed to the middle of the projection frame, and the background scrolls based on the direction of movement. Along the way the user encounters objects to be collected such as stars, and objects to be avoided such as 'bad-guy' characters.

Racing Game

The aim of the racing game is to guide a character along a racetrack without falling off. The user controls the direction of the vehicle by tilting the projection device from side to side (Figure 1). As the game progresses the speed of the vehicle increases and the track becomes gradually more difficult. The perspective of the game can be changed by tilting the device downward; this allows the user to navigate their way through tunnels and around other obstacles not visible from the top down view.

Augmented Reality Interaction

In addition to the character and racing games I have explored several interaction scenarios that link character interaction to the physical world. An IR receiver attached to the device is used to detect the presence of IR 'tags' –small LEDs that emit IR light at timed intervals much like a conventional TV remote control. These interactions were developed as an interactive standby screen for each of the two games. In each scenario a character is projected from the device and its behavior changes when moved over an IR tagged sticker. For example, a character starts bouncing when it finds the trampoline sticker (Figure 3), or a character's vehicle starts spinning when it drives over a puddle sticker.

I developed a preliminary example demonstrating how the *MotionBeam* metaphor can be used to affect objects in the physical environment. In this interaction scenario the user 'drives' a character along the top of several picture frames. When the character jumps from one picture frame to the next, it jolts the picture frame out of place and causes the car to fall from the screen. The ability to perceive and respond to the immediate physical environment is a key component of augmented reality systems. Characters that respond by actuating the physical world further enhance the illusion of virtual content existing side by side in the 'real world'.

SUMMARY

Handheld projectors have the potential to seamlessly merge virtual content into the physical world. The ability to situate virtual content with physical objects *in any location* opens up numerous avenues for exploration. We are now on the verge of being able to design our environments and interact with them like never before. The challenge remains to imagine just how we want the world to be.

ACKNOWLEDGMENTS

This work was carried out in collaboration with Ivan Poupyrev and Takaaki Shiratori.

REFERENCES

1. Blaskó, G., Coriand, F. and Feiner, S., Exploring Interaction with a Simulated Wrist-Worn Projection Display. In Proc. *ISWC 2005*, IEEE (2005), 2-9.
2. Cao, X. and Balakrishnan, R., Interacting with Dynamically Defined Information Spaces using a Handheld Projector and a Pen. In Proc. *UIST '06*, ACM (2006), 225-234.
3. Kobayashi, G. *Utsushi-e*. Chuo University Press, Tokyo, 1987.
4. Markets And Markets Global Pico Projector Market. 2010, http://www.marketsandmarkets.com/Market-Reports/pico-projector-market-196.html.
5. Raskar, R., van Baar, J., Beardsley, P., Willwacher, T., Rao, S. and Forlines, C. iLamps: Geometrically Aware and Self-Configuring Projectors. *ACM Transactions on Graphics 22*, 3 (2003), 809-818.
6. Willis, K.D.D. and Poupyrev, I., MotionBeam: Designing for Movement with Handheld Projectors. In Proc. *Ext. Abstracts CHI '10*, ACM (2010), 3253-3258.
7. Yoshida, T., Hirobe, Y., Nii, H., Kawakami, N. and Tachi, S., Twinkle: Interacting with Physical Surfaces using Handheld Projector. In Proc. *VR '10*, IEEE (2010), 87-90.

Microinteractions beside Ongoing Manual Tasks

Katrin Wolf
T-Labs (Quality & Usability Lab)
Technical University Berlin
Ernst-Reuther-Platz 7, 10587 Berlin
katrin.wolf@acm.org
+49 30 835354265

ABSTRACT

This paper explores how microinteractions as finger gestures allow executing a secondary task without interrupting the manual primary tasks such as driving a car or using a smart stylus. An analyses of Bock's Grip Taxonomy helps to identify manual primary tasks that have a huge benefit of not being interrupted by secondary tasks to control mobile applications and devices. This vision could offer the possibility to use the mobile phone safely while holding a steering wheel of the car as well as augment the functionality of a smart stylus such as change the stroke width without stopping to write or to draw.

After discussing some in this research field used tracking technologies, such as EMG or depth camera, we explore the benefits and device hardware of our prototype, which uses accelerometers to track finger gestures without disable any hand-skills, like its flexibility or tactile sense.

Author Keywords

Wearable, mobile, spatial, gestures, microinteractions.

ACM Classification Keywords

H5.2. [User Interfaces]: Interaction styles.

General Terms

Design, Human Factors, Experimentation.

INTRODUCTION

Bock et al [1] developed a grip taxonomy that compared 14 grip taxonomies of 92 years human hand's research. Bock identified 33 different manual grasps and classified them as 3 main types: palm, pad, and side. For investigating microinteractions that are executable beside manual tasks; we have chosen 3 tasks: each one is using one grip of each main group of Bock's taxonomy (see Table 1). Therefore, we ensure research results that are scalable to preferably a wide range of manual activities.

Primary tasks such as driving a car, using a smart stylus, focusing a camera, turning a key in a lock, or insert a cash card into a bank automat does not need our complete cognitive effort nether all of our fingers are strictly involved into these processes. This offers the possibility to perform tasks in parallel. These can be completely separated like answering a phone.

Grasp type (Bock [5])	Description (Bock [5])	Involved hand-parts (Bock [5])	Potentially still movable hand-parts
Palm (i.e. Steering a car)	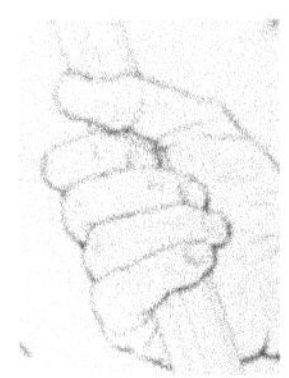 Encompass grasp	Low power grasp performed by 2-directional force between palm (finger 2-5) and abandoned thumb	Particular fingers and thumb
Pad (i.e. Inserting a cash card into an ATM)	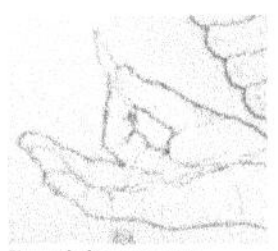 Precision grasp	2-directional force between abandoned thumb and index finger	Finger 1-3: middle, ring, and little finger
Side (i.e. Drawing with a stylus on a graphic tablet)	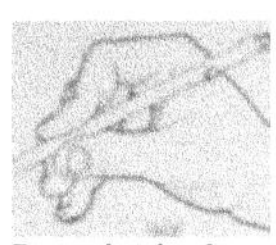 Dynamic tripod	2-directional force between : a) added thumb and middle finger while index finger stabilizes or b) thumb and index finger while middle finger stabilization	Ring, little finger Stabilizer: index finger or middle finger

Table 1. Microgesture options while ongoing manual tasks: Analysis of Otto Bock's grasp types: Palm, Pad, and Side. Graphics by Kapandji [4]. Fingers are counted starting from the thumb

But there is also the possibility of redesigning the primary tasks by augmenting them. For instance, micro-finger-gestures could control automotive functions while driving a car, but without releasing the steering wheel. Also tiny movements with the little finger could select the color or the stroke with a smart stylus during drawing with it.

TEI'11, January 22–26, 2011, Funchal, Portugal.
ACM 978-1-4503-0478-8/11/01.

Each primary task is different, but there are a few common requirements guiding the interaction design for the secondary task:

The secondary task has to be realizable with fingers that are not in particular involved in the primary task (see Fig.1).

The system that tracks the microinteractions shall not bug the primary task at all. Therefore we aim to keep the complete flexibility of the fingers as well as not disable the tactile sense of the finger tips by covering them with e.g. data gloves.

RELATED WORK

The presented approach in this paper is related to microinteractions that are performed by finger gestures. That focuses on gesture-based interaction styles as well as on wearable but hands-free gesture tracking systems.

Computer vision based gesture tracking for identifying pinch gestures is investigated by Loclair [5]. Vardy [8] tracks finger flexion with a camera integrated in a wrist band. Howard [3] is using optical detectors (that are also integrated in a wrist band) for measuring LED light that is reflected by the fingers.

Harrison [2], Saponas [7], and Rekimoto [7] are measuring natural finger gestures by body transmitted signals, such as acoustic signals, EMG, and electrodes that display forearm movements.

We aim to investigate which interaction design (namely microgestures) might be best suited to apply secondary tasks for a wide range of primary tasks. Therefore we are designing hardware to track the input gestures for these secondary tasks. Our design is meant to reflect the benefits and challenges of wearable input devices regarding primary task compatibility, wearing comfort, and quality of measurements.

INTERACTION DESIGN

Many manual tasks are often performed without using actively all fingers. In example while driving a car the steering wheel is almost at any time just lightly touched by a palm grip and not grasped with power. The fingers are mostly floating above the wheel and can easily be moved without risking to loose control of the car, as it is shown in Figure 1 graphic (1)-(3). Our gesture set is build of touches, tabs, and spatial movements. One big challenge is to define gestures which can be recognized clearly as input gestures and not mixed up with natural ones. A second problem is the definition of the gesture starting event. To avoid misinterpreted gestures, we build up our set from dynamically performed gestures. Moreover, we have chosen gestures that are usually not being performed while the primary task AND that are designed as unique and distinguishable as possible.

Our guideline is resulting into synchronous and inverse gestures (Fig.1, (4)-(6), (10): Touch or Tab, (7): Flip, (5), (8), (11), (12): Touch&Drag, (9): Ream, and (13): Surround. The touch and tap gestures can also be augmented by touching or tabbing a specific rhythm to be identified clearly as an input gesture.

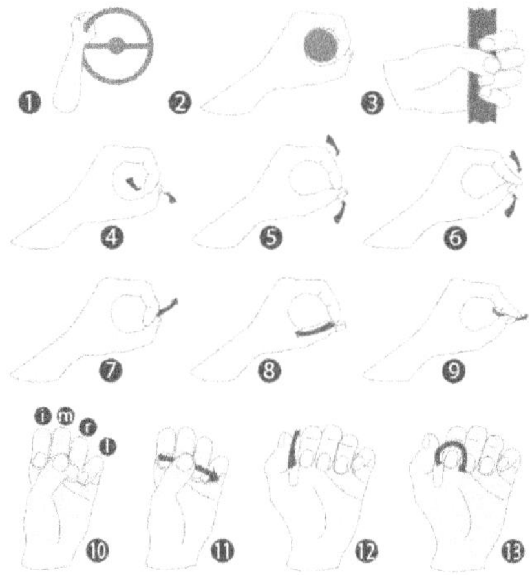

Figure 1. Microgestures for palm grip that show finger interactions which are performable while steering a car.

DEVICE HARDWARE

We are using the accelerometer ADXL335 and integrated it into a finger ring to measure the microgestures. A second similar sensor will necessarily be fixated on the backhand. This is important to generate unique data for identifying the finger gestures rightly and not mixing them with data that come from arm or whole body movements.

REFERENCES

1. Bock, O., Feix, T.: Grasp Taxonomy Comparison Sheet, DOI = http://web.student.tuwien.ac.at/~e0227312/documents / taxonomy_comparison.pdf.
2. Harrison, C. et. al.: Skinput: Appropriating the Body as an Input Surface, In Proc. CHI 2010.
3. Howard, B, Howard, S.: Lightglove: Wrist-Worn Virtual Typing and Pointing, In Proc. ISWC 2001.
4. Kapandji, I. A. The Physiology of the Joints, Vol. 1, Upper Limb. Edinburgh: Churchill Livingstone, 1982.
5. Loclair, C., Gustafson, S., Baudisch, P.: PinchWatch: A Wearable Device for One-Handed Microinteractions, In Proc. MobileHCI 2010.
6. Rekimoto, J. et al.: GestureWrist and GesturePad: Unobtrusive Wearable Interaction Devices, In Proc. ISWC 2001, pp. 21-27.
7. Saponas, T. et. al.: Enabling Always-Available Input with Muscle-Computer Interfaces, In Proc. UIST 2009.
8. Vardy, A. et al.: The WristCam as Input Device, In ISWC, pp. 199–202, 1999.

Designing for an Everyday UbiComp with Tangible and Embodied Materials

Jim Wood
Goldsmiths, University of London
New Cross, London, UK
jim.wood@gold.ac.uk

ABSTRACT
This paper describes research from the author's PhD studies that explore the use and development of digital tools and methods to enable prototyping and fabrication of digital artefacts that may belong in the next generation of ubiquitous or pervasive computing. By expanding from the current interest in physical computing, digital making and the DIY culture grown from the Internet, the research aims to show a new direction by an open source approach to the field. It is the author's thesis that whilst those envisaging the near-future technologies of ubiquitous computing, place much effort on networking protocols and embedded technologies, it is necessary to examine how these technical and mediated connections will be held on a more practical level. In such there is a role for design and creative approaches to act as an interlocutor, both in methods and materials. How in everyday life will we understand our networked watch, pen or broach, how could it embody our knowledge or emotions, and could it in turn have its own agency and knowing? This research has focused on three areas of study, *methods, tools and communities*. In each of these areas, projects have been or are being carried out; case studies, design proposals, participatory tools and the creation of exemplar artefacts. This paper will introduce some of the findings to date.

Author Keywords
Ubiquitous Computing, Digital Artefact, Design Research

ACM Classification Keywords
H5.m. Information interfaces and presentation: Miscellaneous.

General Terms
Design, Theory

INTRODUCTION
The original vision of Ubiquitous computing [9] has inspired much further research and discourse since the 1990s. However that proposal for a "Calm Technology" has sometimes been superseded by an over-interpretation of ubiquitous as meaning disappearing and invisible. Recent revisions have restated the importance of engaging and social experiences, [8] as exemplified by Interaction Design [7] and Tangible Media. [5] The integration of computing into everyday spaces and objects has created ever smaller and more ingenious use of embedded technologies. But where are the methods to bring this new era of HCI into everyday life and play? How can we enable engagement with ubiquitous computing platforms and networks in a participatory way, such as in play or creative expression?

TEI'11, January 22–26, 2011, Funchal, Portugal.
ACM 978-1-4503-0478-8/11/01.

DESIGN METHODS: CASE STUDY
This research in designing within a ubicomp paradigm has lead to a first case study concerning the use of tangible design methods in participatory and creative scenarios. A prototype for a design methods tool was devised to enable the conceptualization of uses for "the internet of things" - that is to say the contemporary interest in connecting everyday objects together in networks, for the home, in social settings or over the internet. This is related to the use of RFID (Radio Frequency Identification) tags and the possibilities for peer-to-peer communication between devices in the Near Field Communication (NFC) standard.

Using Participatory Design Methods
The conceptual approach for this project is based on the idea of design methods cards. These are commonly used for teaching or facilitating workshops, brainstorming or role-playing, and would be used as cues or instructions for starting activities or describing the ideation process. *Paper prototyping* is another well known and documented method from HCI research used for prototyping user interfaces, especially displays [7]. Though the author's interest is sketching and describing actions rather than outputs. In that light, the discipline of Participatory Design provides a more useful framework for engaging users in designing or co-designing by enacting with props or games that represent scenarios. These types of cards, as discussed are best designed for group activities, or what Johansson & Linde call "exploratory design games" [5].

Graphical Languages and Symbolic Notation
In developing a graphic and symbolic method for describing interactions between technological artefacts inspiration was taken from UML (Unified Modelling Language) the graphical notation system that is used to model software processes, particularly in object-oriented programming. Another initial reference was a design study into RFID interactions by Timo Arnall and Schulze & Webb, [2], designers working with a view towards how technology is mediated through design and communication.

Prototype and findings
A case study was defined based on the *Touchatag* service, a web-based authentication system using a Mifare reader and stickers, and the concept was to device a kit for the end user on the client side, rather than the server side. The project was given the working title 't2t' in reference to p2p mode

of NFC, and the cards were designed after a number of iterations. Experiments were made with different materials, plastics, cards, and paper laser-cut into the card shapes. The findings were that what the plastic objects whilst having a pleasing aesthetic, were too expensive to produce and over specified, and thus the latest revision was made with paper and card, with the addition of a game board to make more explicit the surface for play.

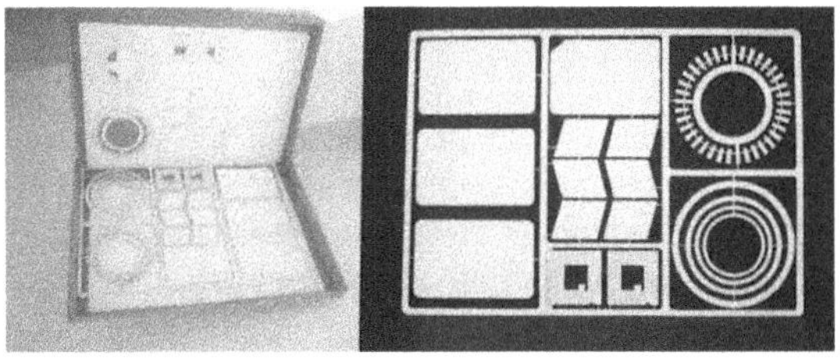

Figure 1. t2t 2nd version, box and detail.

TOOLS: TANGIBLE, EMBODIED OBJECTS

This practical work on *tools* represents the exploration of the PhD thesis into the idea of digital tools that are used tangibly, may have embedded technologies, but importantly are an embodiment to everyday objects. This follows on from the first case study's aim to map out interactions of NFC technologies, and to depict the transparent transactions in a common language. In simplest design terms, we can see it as moving from a 2d sketch from, as used by t2t cards, and moving into a 3d form of models and objects. When observing and participating in workshops using interactive prototyping methods and open-source hardware such as Arduino [1], I noticed the participant's difficulty in attaching sensors or actuators to an object that might be used in a hack or as a prop. This inspired the idea that it might be fitting for some components to be stick-able and to improve opportunities for interaction or sensing. Imagine it being as simple as adding a thumb-tack to a wall, slapping on a sticker. Thinking of recent interpretations of wearable computing in embroidery and textiles [3], and a newer discussion about material computing, based on a craft approach to embedded interfaces and substrates [4] it seems evident the possibilities for experimentation with a material-led approach.

Embodying sensor devices

A first set of tools proposed is based on the idea of ubiquitous computing artefacts as stick-ons – devices as items which are attached to another object – and have the possibility to enhance or change the hosts use, or translate it. For instance a piezo sensor to pick up vibrations; a light dependent resistor to pick up luminosity; an accelerometer to pick up movement, the action that each embodies. Experimentation with these electrical components could benefit from being available in a stick-on format that could be easily attached to the surface or object. In this project the device is inspired by organisms that attach themselves to another, and thus the concept name is LIM-pet, a device in the form of a seashell with a stick on surface.

COMMUNITIES: CREATIVE ARTEFACTS & NETWORKS

As well as the projects above the author has been engaged with experimental arts and media practice, both during and before the PhD study. Many have been *community* focused. In 2007 the author took part in the Mediamatic Hackers workshop that generated projects for the Picnic festival of the same year. The project created was 'Badger' that used the festivals social network tool to create a physical artefact -a pin badge, based on social groupings and preferences. In 2009 as *Punch and Hole* the project Tag-Pet was created to promote the Takeaway Festival at Kinetica, London as part of a brief for projects based on RFID tickets. The TagPet project created around 400 pet icons generated from festival visitor's smartcards, and was realized as stickers and taken as keepsakes. The project was later re-made at the first UK Maker Faire, Newcastle.

CONCLUSIONS

The explorations with materials and the conception of methods and processes for considering design in ubicomp scenarios have helped the author to open a dialog about everyday ubicomp with a wider range of audience.

ACKNOWLEDGMENTS

Thanks to supervisors Mike Waller and Terry Rosenberg and staff and colleagues at Design Department, Goldsmiths.

REFERENCES

1. Arduino, http://www.arduino.cc (accessed 8.8.10)
2. Arnall, T. (2005) A Graphic Language for Touch
3. Buechley, L. and Eisenberg, M. (2007) Fabric PCBs, electronic sequins, and socket buttons: Techniques for e-textile craft. Personal and Ubiquitous Computing.
4. Coelho, M., Poupyrev, I., Sadi, S. and Vertegal, R. (2009) Programming Reality: From Transitive Materials to Organic User Interfaces, in the Extended Abstracts of Conference on Human Factors in Computing Systems (CHI '09). Boston, USA. ACM, New York, USA.
5. Ishii, H. (2004) Bottles: A Transparent Interface as a Tribute to Mark Weiser, IEICE Transactions on Information and Systems, vol. E87-D, no. 6.
6. Johansson, M. Linde,P. (2005) Playful Collaborative Exploration: New Research Practice in Participatory Design Journal of Research Practice, Vol.1,Issue.1.
7. Preece, J., Rogers, Y. & Sharp, H., (2002) Interaction Design: Beyond Human-computer Interaction, New York, NY: J. Wiley & Sons.
8. Rogers, Y. (2006) "Moving on from Weiser's Vision of Calm Computing: Engaging UbiComp Experiences" Ubiquitous Computing: 8th International Conference, UbiComp 2006, Orange County, CA, USA, September 17-21, 2006, Proceedings. 1st ed. Springer.
9. Weiser, M. (1991) The Computer for the 21st century, Scientific American, vol.265, no.3, p.94-10

Author Index

NOTES

www.ingramcontent.com/pod-product-compliance
Ingram Content Group UK Ltd.
Pitfield, Milton Keynes, MK11 3LW, UK
UKHW051413290926
15471UKWH00009B/1583

9 781450 306287